1990 Tax Rate Schedules

Schedule X—Single

If line 5 is: Over—	But not over—	The tax is:	of the amount over—
$0	$19,450	. . . . 15%	$0
19,450	47,050	$2,917.50 + 28%	19,450
47,050	97,620	10,645.50 + 33%	47,050
97,620	. . . .	Use **Worksheet** below to figure your tax.	

Schedule Z— Head of household

If line 5 is: Over—	But not over—	The tax is:	of the amount over—
$0	$26,050	. . . . 15%	$0
26,050	67,200	$3,907.50+ 28%	26,050
67,200	134,930	15,429.50 + 33%	67,200
134,930	. . . .	Use **Worksheet** below to figure your tax.	

Schedule Y-1—Married filing jointly or Qualifying widow(er)

If line 5 is: Over—	But not over—	The tax is:	of the amount over—
$0	$32,450	. . . . 15%	$0
32,450	78,400	$4,867.50 + 28%	32,450
78,400	162,770	17,733.50 + 33%	78,400
162,770	. . . .	Use **Worksheet** below to figure your tax.	

Schedule Y-2— Married filing separately

If line 5 is: Over—	But not over—	The tax is:	of the amount over—
$0	$16,225	. . . . 15%	$0
16,225	39,200	$2,433.75 + 28%	16,225
39,200	123,570	8,866.75 + 33%	39,200
123,570	. . . .	Use **Worksheet** below to figure your tax.	

Worksheet (Keep for your records)

1. If your filing status is:
   - Single, enter $27,333.60
   - Head of household, enter $37,780.40
   - Married filing jointly or Qualifying widow(er), enter $45,575.60
   - Married filing separately, enter $36,708.85 . . . . 1. _____

2. Enter your taxable income from line 5 of the Form 1040-ES worksheet . . . . . . 2. _____

3. If your filing status is:
   - Single, enter $97,620
   - Head of household, enter $134,930
   - Married filing jointly or Qualifying widow(er), enter $162,770
   - Married filing separately, enter $123,570 . . . . 3. _____

4. Subtract line 3 from line 2. Enter the result. (If the result is zero or less, use the schedule above for your filing status to figure your tax. DO NOT use this worksheet.) . . . . . . 4. _____

5. Multiply the amount on line 4 by 28% (.28). Enter the result . . . . 5. _____

6. Multiply the amount on line 4 by 5% (.05). Enter the result . . . . 6. _____

7. Multiply $574 by the number of exemptions claimed. (If married filing separately, see **Note** below.) Enter the result . . . . 7. _____

8. Compare the amounts on lines 6 and 7. Enter the **smaller** of the two amounts here . . . . . . 8. _____

9. **Tax.** Add lines 1, 5, and 8. . . . . 9. _____

Note: *If married filing separately and you did **not** claim an exemption for your spouse, multiply $574 by the number of exemptions claimed. Add $574 to the result and enter the total on line 7 above.*

1991 ANNUAL EDITION

WEST'S FEDERAL TAXATION:

COMPREHENSIVE VOLUME

1991 ANNUAL EDITION

WEST'S FEDERAL TAXATION:

COMPREHENSIVE VOLUME

GENERAL EDITORS

Eugene Willis, Ph.D., C.P.A.

James E. Smith, Ph.D., C.P.A.

William H. Hoffman, Jr., J.D., Ph.D., C.P.A.

William A. Raabe, Ph.D., C.P.A.

CONTRIBUTING AUTHORS

D. Larry Crumbley, Ph.D., C.P.A.
Texas A & M University

Steven C. Dilley, J.D., Ph.D., C.P.A.
Michigan State University

Patrica C. Elliott, D.B.A., C.P.A.
University of New Mexico

Mary Sue Gately, Ph.D., C.P.A.
Texas Tech University

William H. Hoffman, Jr., J.D., Ph.D., C.P.A.
University of Houston

Jerome S. Horvitz, J.D., LL.M. in Taxation
University of Houston

Marilyn Phelan, J.D., Ph.D., C.P.A.
Texas Tech University

William A. Raabe, Ph.D., C.P.A.
University of Wisconsin-Milwaukee

Boyd C. Randall, J.D., Ph.D.
Brigham Young University

W. Eugene Seago, J.D., Ph.D., C.P.A.
Virginia Polytechnic Institute and State University

James E. Smith, Ph.D., C.P.A.
College of William and Mary

Willis C. Stevenson, Ph.D., C.P.A.
University of Wisconsin-Madison

Eugene Willis, Ph.D., C.P.A.
University of Illinois at Urbana

WEST PUBLISHING COMPANY

St. Paul   New York   Los Angeles   San Francisco

Composition: Carlisle Communications, Ltd.

Interior design: Dave Corona

Copyediting: Patricia Lewis

Cover design: Peter Thiel

Indexing: Linda Buskus, Northwind Editorial Services

COPYRIGHT © 1990 by WEST PUBLISHING CO.
COPYRIGHT © 1983, 1984, 1985, 1986, 1987,
1988, 1989
By **West Publishing Co.**
  50 West Kellogg Boulevard
  P.O. Box 64526
  St. Paul, MN 55164–1003

Library of Congress Cataloging in Publication
Data
Main entry under title:
West's Federal Taxation.
Includes index.
1. Income tax—United States—Law
I. Hoffman, William H.   II.   Willis, Eugene

ISBN 0–314–74172–0 KF6369.W47 343'.73'052

ISSN 0741–5184

1990 ANNUAL EDITION

PREFACE

Simply stated, *West's Federal Taxation: Comprehensive Volume* is an abridged version of *West's Federal Taxation: Individual Income Taxes* and *West's Federal Taxation: Corporations, Partnerships, Estates, and Trusts*. In condensing all of this material to a manageable form, it was necessary to utilize our editorial license to pick and choose. Thus, a great deal of useful, but not essential, information had to be pruned in order to arrive at the final product. What to cover or not to cover in any abridgement process is, understandably so, a judgment call. We can only hope that we acted correctly in making most of our decisions.

The *Comprehensive Volume* is designed primarily to serve the needs of those who offer only one course in Federal taxation, although our surveys indicate that many of our adopters use it successfully for a two course sequence. In cases where the *Comprehensive Volume* is used for only one course, a broad scope of coverage could be the ultimate objective. Although the income taxation of individuals should be stressed, it is conceivable that some may wish to devote significant classroom time to other areas of Federal taxation. For example, the allocation of course coverage might be structured as follows: 60 percent to the individual income tax (chapters 1–15) and 40 percent to the tax treatment of corporations, partnerships, etc. (chapters 16–27).

For those who encounter time constraints and/or want to emphasize some areas and not others, the last segment of the text (chapters 16–27) possesses potential for selectivity. Thus, an instructor who wants to cover corporations (chapters 16–20) and tax practice (chapter 24) and not the other subjects (chapters 21–23, and 25–27), can proceed accordingly without disrupting the flow of the material. In this regard, there exists flexibility for a number of different combinations for partial coverage of the last segment of the text (e.g., for a "light" coverage of corporations select chapters 16 and 17 but for a "heavy" concentration assign chapters 16–20).

Special Features

If the *Comprehensive Volume* is to be used in whole (or in part) for a one-course tax offering, the pace of coverage of the subject matter may have to be accelerated. In recognition of this fact, we have followed certain guidelines.

- Although not eliminated entirely, the research orientation has been kept to a minimum. By restricting judicial analysis and controlling the number of footnotes, the reader is spared some measure of distraction. The result is a quicker coverage of the textual material.

- In an accelerated setting, there is a decided constraint placed on the amount of problem solving that can be expected from the reader. We have, therefore, made every effort to limit the quantity of the problem materials. In this connection, we strive to maintain the integrity of the quality of such materials.

- For those users who feel the need for some material on research methodology, the last chapter in the text, "Working with the Tax Law," is available. Along with the usual problem materials, this chapter also includes numerous research projects, arranged by chapter numbers, dealing with the subject matter treated in the text.

- Once knowledge of the tax law has been acquired, it needs to be used. The tax minimization process, however, normally requires careful planning. Because we recognize the importance of planning procedures, most chapters include a separate section (designated *Tax Planning Considerations*) illustrating the applications of such procedures to specific areas.

- Most chapters contain one or more *Concept Summaries* that synthesize important concepts in chart or tabular form.

- There is a great deal of useful material contained in the appendixes to the text. In addition to the usual Subject Index, the following items are included: Tax Rates and Tables (Appendix A); Tax Forms (Appendix B); Glossary of Tax Terms (Appendix C); Table of Code Sections Cited (Appendix D); and Comprehensive Tax Return Problems for 1989 (Appendix E).

Supplements

Other products in our 1991 instructional package include the following:

- A *Solutions Manual* that has been carefully checked to ensure that it is error-free. All problems are labeled by topical coverage and a matrix has been added indicating which problems are new, modified or unchanged in the new edition. The solutions are referenced to pages in the text.

- The 1991 *Instructor's Guide* contains expanded Instructor's Summaries that can be used as lecture outlines and provide the instructor with teaching aids and information not contained in the text. It also includes solutions to the research problems (chapter 27 in the text), and the comprehensive tax return problems (Appendix E in the text).

- New with the 1991 Edition is a separate *Test Bank* with a greatly expanded set of examination questions and solutions.

- *Westest*, a microcomputer test generation program for IBM PC's and compatibles and the Apple II family of computers.

- A Major New Addition: *West's CD-ROM Federal Tax Library* (Compact Disk with Read-Only Memory) provides a complete tax research library on a desktop. The *Federal Tax Library* is a set of seven compact disks with a software package that reads the disks through a PC. Each of these disks has a remarkable storage capacity—roughly 1,000 times more than a single-sided floppy disk. A brief list of the library contents includes: complete IRS Code and Regulations, 1986 Tax Reform Act with Amendments and Legislative History, Federal Court Cases on Tax, Tax Court Cases, Revenue Rulings, and Revenue Procedures. This is available to qualified adopters.

- A *Student Study Guide* prepared by David M. Maloney, University of Virginia and William A. Raabe, University of Wisconsin (Milwaukee). This *Study Guide*

includes a chapter review of key concepts and self-evaluation tests with solutions.

- *Transparency Masters* for selected complex problems, with a larger typeface for greater readability.

- *Transparency Acetates* for selected cumulative problems.

- *WFT Practice Sets*, 1990–91 Edition, prepared by John B. Barrack, University of Georgia. This year we have two separate expanded *Practice Sets*, one for Individuals, and one for Corporations and Partnerships. They are designed to cover all the common forms that would be used by a tax practitioner for the average client.

- Limited free use to qualified adopters of WESTLAW, a computer-assisted tax and legal research service that provides access to hundreds of valuable information sources.

- *West's Internal Revenue Code of 1986 and Treasury Regulations: Annotated and Selected: 1991 Edition* by James E. Smith, College of William and Mary. This provides the opportunity for the student to be exposed to the Code and the Regulations in a single volume book, which also contains useful annotations.

- *West's Federal Taxation Newsletter Update* will be mailed to adopters twice a year. It will focus on new tax legislation and updated information.

Software

The trend toward increased use of the computer as an essential tool in tax practice has accelerated. To insure that the West's Federal Taxation instructional package continues to set the pace in this important area, the following products are available to be used with the 1991 edition:

- *BNA Income Tax Spreadsheet* (Educational Version): A comprehensive, menu-driven individual tax computation and planning package.

- *TurboTax:* A program for use in preparing and printing Federal income tax returns for individuals.

- *West's Federal Taxation: Tax Planning with Spreadsheets:* Prepared by Sam A. Hicks, Jr., Virginia Polytechnic Institute and State University, contains Lotus-based tax computation and planning templates for individual and corporate taxpayers and is available free to adopters. An educational version of VP Planner Plus, a spreadsheet program that is completely compatible with Lotus 1–2–3 (Release 2) and can be used to run *West's Federal Taxation: Tax Planning with Spreadsheets*, and a brief guide, can be purchased by students.

The outstanding features of all of these software products are that they are powerful, easy to learn, and easy to use. We believe that tax education can be raised to a higher level through the use of computers and well-designed software. These new software packages take the drudgery out of performing the complex computations involved in solving difficult tax problems. This allows students to concentrate on applying concepts and interpreting results.

To enable students to take advantage of these software products, the 1991 Edition contains numerous tax return and tax planning problems. The tax planning problems allow students to evaluate alternative tax planning strategies and calculate the effects of various alternatives on the taxpayer's liability. Problems that lend themselves to solutions using the software packages described above are identified by a computer symbol to the left of the problem number. The instruc-

tions for each of these problems identify which software packages are appropriate for solving the problems.

Tax Forms

- Although it is not our purpose to approach the presentation and discussion of taxation from the standpoint of preparation of tax returns, some orientation to forms is necessary. Because 1990 forms will not be available until later in the year, most tax return problems in this edition are written for tax year 1989. The 1989 problems may be solved manually, or many may be solved using the tax return preparation software (*TurboTax*) that may be purchased by students who use this text.

- Appendix E contains comprehensive tax return problems written for tax year 1989. Each of these problems lends itself for use as a term project because of the sophistication required for satisfactory completion. Solutions to the problems in Appendix E are contained in the Instructor's Guide.

- For the reader's convenience, Appendix B contains a full reproduction of most of the 1989 tax forms frequently encountered in actual practice.

- Most tax textbooks are published in the spring, long before tax forms for the year of publication are available from the government. We believe that students should be exposed to the most current tax forms. As a result, we write several new forms problems and provide adopters with reproducible copies of these problems, along with blank tax forms and solutions on the new forms. Shortly after the beginning of 1991, adopters will receive selected tax return problems, updated and solved on 1990 forms.

Tax Law Updates

Since the original edition was issued in 1983, we have followed a policy of annually revising the text material to reflect statutory, judicial, and administrative changes in the Federal tax law and to correct any errors or other shortcomings. The 1991 edition has been thoroughly revised to reflect the Revenue Reconciliation Act of 1989 and related developments.

In the event of further *significant* tax law changes, a separate supplement will be written for each of the three texts in the West's series. Our aim is to provide a timely, complete, and easy to use supplement for each text.

Acknowledgements

As is the case with any literary undertaking, we will welcome user comments. Please rest assured that any such comments will not be taken lightly and, we hope, will lead to improvements in later editions of *West's Federal Taxation: Comprehensive Volume*.

We are most appreciative of the many suggestions that we have received for revising the text, many of which have been incorporated in past editions and in the 1991 edition. In particular, we would like to thank the following people for reviewing the text:

Martin E. Batross, Franklin University
John J. Connors, University of Wisconsin–Milwaukee
Edmund D. Fenton, Jr., Eastern Kentucky University
Leslie C. Grow, Central Missouri State University

Joseph M. Hagan, Louisiana State University
Joseph D. Kaderabeck, Balwin-Wallace College
Cecyl Stott, Southwest Texas State University
James P. Trebby, Marquette University
John Wilguess, Oklahoma State University

Finally, this 1991 Edition would not have been possible without the technical assistance of and the manuscript review by Bonnie Hoffman, CPA, and Freda Mulhall, CPA. We are indebted to them for their efforts.

Eugene Willis
William H. Hoffman, Jr.
James E. Smith
William A. Raabe

May, 1990

Contents in Brief

Contents in Brief

TABLE OF CONTENTS

3 GROSS INCOME: CONCEPTS AND INCLUSIONS

4 GROSS INCOME: EXCLUSIONS

9   Deductions: Employee Expenses   9–1

10 DEDUCTIONS AND LOSSES: CERTAIN ITEMIZED DEDUCTIONS 10–1

11 TAX CREDITS 11–1

14 ALTERNATIVE MINIMUM TAX   14–1

15 ACCOUNTING PERIODS AND METHODS   15–1

16 CORPORATIONS: OPERATING RULES, ORGANIZATION, AND CAPITAL STRUCTURE   **16–1**

17 CORPORATIONS: DISTRIBUTIONS NOT IN COMPLETE LIQUIDATION · 17–1

18 CORPORATIONS: DISTRIBUTIONS IN COMPLETE LIQUIDATION AND AN OVERVIEW OF REORGANIZATIONS · 18–1

19 CORPORATE ACCUMULATIONS   19–1

20 S CORPORATIONS   20–1

22 Tax-Exempt Entities — 22–1

23 Taxation of International Transactions — 23–1

24   Tax Administration and Practice   24–1

25 THE FEDERAL GIFT AND ESTATE TAXES

26 INCOME TAXATION OF TRUSTS AND ESTATES

27   WORKING WITH THE TAX LAW   27–1

APPENDIXES

1991 ANNUAL EDITION

WEST'S FEDERAL TAXATION:

COMPREHENSIVE VOLUME

1

AN INTRODUCTION TO TAXATION AND UNDERSTANDING THE FEDERAL TAX LAW

OBJECTIVES

Provide a brief history, including trends, of the Federal income tax.

Describe some of the criteria for selecting a tax base.

Explain the different types of taxes existing in the United States at the Federal, state, and local levels.

Furnish an introduction to the Federal income tax on individuals and corporations.

Introduce the major employment taxes such as the Federal Insurance Contributions Act (FICA) and the Federal Unemployment Tax Act (FUTA).

Briefly review the audit process in connection with tax administration.

Explain the causal factors that have led to our present income tax system.

Describe the economic, social, equity, and political considerations that justify various aspects of the tax law.

Review the role played by the IRS and the courts in the evolution of the Federal tax system.

The primary objective of this chapter is to provide an overview of the Federal tax system. Some of the topics covered include the following:

- A brief review of the historical aspects of the Federal income tax.
- A summary of the different types of taxes existing at the Federal, state, and local levels.
- Some highlights illustrating how the tax laws are administered.
- A discussion of tax concepts that help in understanding the reasons for various tax provisions.
- Illustrations of the influence that the IRS and the courts have had in the evolution of current tax law.

HISTORY OF U.S. TAXATION

Early Periods

The concept of an income tax can hardly be regarded as a newcomer to the Western Hemisphere. Although an income tax was first enacted in 1634 by the English colonists in the Massachusetts Bay Colony, this form of taxation was not adopted by the Federal government until 1861. In fact, both the Federal Union and the Confederate States of America used the income tax to provide funds to finance the Civil War. Although modest in its reach and characterized by broad exemptions and low rates, the income tax generated $376 million of revenue for the Federal government during the Civil War.

When the Civil War ended, the need for additional revenue disappeared and the income tax was repealed. As was true before the war, the Federal government was able to finance its operations almost exclusively from customs duties (tariffs). It is interesting that challenges to the constitutionality of the Civil War income tax were not upheld by the courts.

When a new Federal income tax on individuals was enacted in 1894, its opponents were prepared to and did again challenge its constitutionality. The U.S. Constitution provided that " . . . No Capitation, or other direct, Tax shall be laid, unless in Proportion to the Census or Enumeration herein before directed to be taken." In *Pollock v. Farmers' Loan and Trust Co.*,[1] the U.S. Supreme Court found that the income tax was a direct tax that was unconstitutional because it was not apportioned among the states in proportion to their populations.

A Federal corporate income tax, enacted by Congress in 1909, fared better in the judicial system. The U.S. Supreme Court found this tax to be constitutional because it was treated as an excise tax.[2] In essence, it was a tax on the right to do business in the corporate form. As such, it was likened to a form of the franchise tax. It should be noted that the corporate form of doing business was developed in the late nineteenth century and was an unfamiliar concept to the framers of the U.S. Constitution. Since a corporation is an entity created under law, jurisdictions possess the right to tax its creation and operation. Using this rationale, many states still impose franchise taxes on corporations.

The ratification of the Sixteenth Amendment to the U.S. Constitution in 1913 sanctioned both the Federal individual and corporate income taxes and, as a consequence, neutralized the continuing effect of the *Pollock* decision.

---

1. 3 AFTR 2602, 15 S.Ct. 912 (USSC, 1895). See chapter 27 for an explanation as to how judicial decisions are cited.

2. *Flint v. Stone Tracy Co.*, 3 AFTR 2834, 31 S.Ct. 342 (USSC, 1911).

Revenue Acts

Following ratification of the Sixteenth Amendment, Congress enacted the Revenue Act of 1913. Under this Act, a flat 1 percent tax was levied upon the income of corporations. Individuals paid a normal tax rate of 1 percent on taxable income after deducting a personal exemption of $3,000 for a single individual and $4,000 for a married taxpayer. Surtax rates of 1 to 6 percent were applied to high-income taxpayers.

Various revenue acts were passed during the period from 1913 to 1939. In 1939, all of these revenue laws were codified into the Internal Revenue Code of 1939. In 1954, a similar codification of the revenue law took place. The current law consists of the Internal Revenue Code of 1986, which largely carries over the provisions of the 1954 Code. The Code has been amended several times since 1986. This matter is discussed further in chapter 27 under Origin of the Internal Revenue Code.

Historical Trends

The income tax has proved to be a major source of revenue for the Federal government. Figure 1–1 contains a breakdown of the major revenue sources.[3] The importance of the income tax is demonstrated by the fact that estimated income tax collections from individuals and corporations amount to 51 percent of the total receipts.

The need for revenues to finance the war effort during World War II converted the income tax into a "mass tax." For example, in 1939, less than 6 percent of the U.S. population was subject to the Federal income tax. In 1945, over 74 percent of the population was subject to the Federal income tax.[4]

Certain changes in the income tax law are of particular significance in understanding the Federal income tax. In 1943, Congress passed the Current Tax Payment Act, which provided for the first pay-as-you-go tax system. The pay-as-you-go feature of the U.S. income tax system compels employers to withhold for taxes a specified portion of an employee's wages. Persons with income from other than wages must make periodic (e.g., quarterly) payments to the taxing authority (the Internal Revenue Service) for estimated taxes due for the year.

One trend that has caused considerable concern among many persons and groups has been the increased complexity of the Federal income tax laws. Often,

---

FIGURE 1–1 Federal Budget Receipts—1990

Individual income taxes	41%
Corporation income taxes	10
Social insurance taxes and contributions	34
Excise taxes	3
Borrowing	8
Other	4
	100%

---

3. *United States Budget in Brief, 1990*, Office of Management and Budget (Washington, D.C.: U.S. Government Printing Office, 1989).

4. Richard Goode, *The Individual Income Tax* (Washington, D.C.: The Brookings Institution, 1964), pp. 2–4.

under the name of tax reform, Congress has added to this complexity through frequent changes in the tax laws. Increasingly, this has forced many taxpayers to seek the assistance of tax professionals. At this time, therefore, substantial support exists for tax law simplification.

CRITERIA USED IN THE SELECTION OF A TAX STRUCTURE

Adam Smith first identified certain "canons of taxation" that are still considered when evaluating a particular tax structure. These canons of taxation are as follows:[5]

- *Equality.* Each taxpayer enjoys fair or equitable treatment by paying taxes in proportion to his or her income level. Ability to pay a tax is the measure of how equitably a tax is distributed among taxpayers.

- *Convenience.* Administrative simplicity has long been valued in formulating tax policy. If a tax is easily assessed and collected and the costs of its administration are low, it should be favored. The withholding (pay-as-you-go) system has been advocated because of its convenience for taxpayers.

- *Certainty.* A "good" tax structure exists if the taxpayer can readily predict when, where, and how a tax will be levied. Individuals and businesses need to know the likely tax consequences of a particular type of transaction.

- *Economy.* A "good" tax system involves only nominal collection costs by the government and minimal compliance costs on the part of the taxpayer. Although the government's cost of collecting Federal taxes amounts to less than one-half of 1 percent of the revenue collected, the complexity of our existing tax structure imposes substantial taxpayer compliance costs.

By these canons, the Federal income tax is a contentious product. *Equality* is present as long as one accepts ability to pay as an ingredient of this component. *Convenience* exists due to a heavy reliance on pay-as-you-go procedures. *Certainty* probably generates the greatest controversy. Certainty is present in the sense that a mass of administrative and judicial guidelines are available to aid in interpreting the tax law. In another sense, however, certainty does not exist since many questions remain unanswered, and frequent changes in the tax law by Congress lessen stability. *Economy* is present if one considers only the effort of the IRS in its collection procedure. Economy is not present, however, if taxpayer compliance efforts are the central focus.

THE TAX STRUCTURE

Tax Base

A tax base is the figure to which the tax rate is applied. In the case of the Federal income tax, the tax base is *taxable income*. As noted later in the chapter (Figure 1–2), taxable income is gross income reduced by certain deductions (both business and personal).

---

5. *The Wealth of Nations*, Book V, Chapter II, Part II (New York: Dutton, 1910).

Tax Rates

Tax rates are applied to the tax base to determine a taxpayer's liability. The tax rates may be proportional or progressive. A tax is *proportional* if the rate of tax remains constant for any given income level.

EXAMPLE 1   T has $10,000 of taxable income and pays a tax of $3,000, or 30%. Y's taxable income is $50,000 and the tax on this amount is $15,000, or 30%. If this constant rate is applied throughout the rate structure, the tax is proportional. □

A tax is *progressive* if a higher rate of tax applies as the tax base increases. The Federal income tax, Federal gift and estate taxes, and most state income tax rate structures are progressive.

EXAMPLE 2   If T, a married individual filing jointly, has taxable income of $10,000, the tax for 1990 is $1,500 for an average tax rate of 15%. If, however, T's taxable income was $50,000, the tax would be $9,781.50 for an average tax rate of 19.563%. The tax is progressive, since higher rates are applied to greater amounts of taxable income. □

Incidence of Taxation

The degree to which the total tax burden is shared by various segments of society is difficult to assess. Assumptions must be made concerning who absorbs the burden for payment of the tax. For example, since dividend payments to shareholders are not deductible by a corporation and such amounts are generally taxable to shareholders, a form of double taxation on the same income is being levied. Concern over double taxation is valid to the extent that corporations are *not* able to shift the corporate tax to the consumer through higher commodity prices. Many research studies have shown a high degree of shifting of the corporate income tax. Thus, when the corporate tax can be shifted, it becomes merely a consumption tax that is borne by the ultimate purchasers of goods.

The U.S. Federal income tax rate structure for individuals is becoming less progressive. For example, for 1986 there were 15 rates, ranging from 0 to 50 percent. Subsequently, these rates have been reduced to 15 percent and 28 percent. Because many deductions and other tax savings procedures have been eliminated, Congress expects the lower rates to reach a larger base of taxable income.

MAJOR TYPES OF TAXES

Property Taxes

Normally referred to as *ad valorem* taxes because they are based on value, property taxes are a tax on wealth, or capital. In this regard, they have much in common with death taxes and gift taxes discussed later in the chapter. Although property taxes do not tax income, the income actually derived (or the potential for any such income) may be relevant insofar as it affects the value of the property being taxed.

Property taxes fall into two categories: those imposed on realty and those imposed on personalty. Both have added importance, since they usually generate a deduction for Federal income tax purposes (see chapter 10).

Ad Valorem Taxes on Realty.   Property taxes on realty are exclusively within the province of the states and their local political subdivisions (e.g., cities, counties, school districts). They represent a major source of revenue for local governments, but their importance at the state level has waned over the past few years. The trend has been for the states to look to other types of taxes (e.g., sales, income, severance) to meet their fiscal needs. Most of the revenue derived from property taxes on realty is used to provide essential governmental services (e.g., police and fire protection, public education, waste disposal, utility sources).

Particularly in those jurisdictions that do not impose ad valorem taxes on personalty, what is included in the definition of realty could have an important bearing on which assets are or are not subject to tax. Primarily a question of state property law, *realty* generally includes real estate and any capital improvements thereto that comprise fixtures. Simply stated, a fixture is something so permanently attached to the real estate that its removal will cause irreparable damage. A built-in bookcase might well be a fixture, whereas a movable bookcase would not. Certain items such as electrical wiring and plumbing when installed in a building cease to be personalty and become realty.

Some of the characteristics of ad valorem taxes on realty can be summarized as follows:

- Property owned by the Federal government is exempt from tax. Similar immunity usually is extended to property owned by state and local governments and by certain charitable organizations.

- Some states provide for lower valuations on property dedicated to agricultural use or other special uses (e.g., wildlife sanctuaries).

- Some states partially exempt the homestead portion of property from taxation. Modern homestead laws normally operate to protect some or all of a personal residence (including a farm or ranch) from the actions of creditors pursuing claims against the owner.

- Lower taxes may apply to a residence owned by an elderly taxpayer (e.g., age 65 and older).

- When non-income-producing property (e.g., a personal residence) is converted to income-producing property (e.g., a rental house), typically the appraised value increases.

- Some jurisdictions extend immunity from tax for a specified period of time (a *tax holiday*) to new or relocated businesses.

Unlike the ad valorem tax on personalty (see page 1–7), the tax on realty is difficult to avoid. Since real estate is impossible to hide, a high degree of taxpayer compliance is not surprising. The only avoidance possibility that is generally available lies with the assessed value of the property. For this reason, both the assessed value of the property and, particularly, a reassessed value upward are not without their share of controversy and litigation. For these purposes, at least, everyone is convinced that his or her property is worth less than that belonging to neighbors or near-neighbors.

The four methods currently in use for assessing the value of real estate are as follows:

1. Actual purchase or construction price.

2. Contemporaneous sales prices or construction costs of comparable properties.

3. Cost of reproducing a building, less allowance for depreciation and obsolescence from the time of actual construction.

4. Capitalization of income from rental property.

Because all of these methods suffer faults and lead to inequities, a combination of one or more is not uncommon. For example, because of rising real estate values and construction costs, the use of actual purchase or construction price (method 1) places the purchaser of a new home at a definite disadvantage compared with the owner who acquired similar property years before. As another illustration, if the capitalization of income (method 4) deals with property subject to rent controls, the property may be undervalued.

Ad Valorem Taxes on Personalty.   *Personalty* can be defined as all assets that are not realty. At the outset, it may be helpful to distinguish between the *classification* of an asset (realty or personalty) and the *use* to which it is placed. Both realty and personalty can be either business use or personal use property. Examples of this distinction include a residence (realty that is personal use), an office building (realty that is business use), surgical instruments (personalty that is business use), and regular wearing apparel (personalty that is personal use). The distinction, important for ad valorem and for Federal income tax purposes, becomes confused when personalty is often referred to as *personal* property to distinguish it from *real* property. Such designation does not give a complete picture of what is involved. The description personal residence, however, is clearer since one can identify a residence as being realty. What is meant, in this case, is realty that is personal use property.

Personalty can be also classified as tangible property or intangible property. For ad valorem tax purposes, intangible personalty includes stocks, bonds, and various other securities (e.g., bank shares).

Generalizations concerning the ad valorem taxes on personalty are as follows:

• Particularly with personalty devoted to personal use (e.g., jewelry, household furnishings), taxpayer compliance ranges from poor to zero. In some jurisdictions, enforcement of the tax on these items is not even attempted. For automobiles devoted to personal use, many jurisdictions have converted from value as the tax base to arbitrary license fees based on the weight of the vehicle. Recently, some jurisdictions are taking into consideration the age factor (e.g., automobiles six years or older are not subject to the ad valorem tax as they are presumed to have little, if any, value).

• For personalty devoted to business use (e.g., inventories, trucks, machinery, equipment), taxpayer compliance and enforcement procedures are measurably better.

• Which jurisdiction possesses the authority to tax movable personalty (e.g., railroad rolling stock) always has been and continues to be a troublesome issue.

• The ad valorem tax on intangibles, although it still exists in some jurisdictions, largely has fallen into disfavor. Undoubtedly the lack of effective enforcement capability on the part of the taxing authorities has contributed to this decline in use.

Transaction Taxes

Characteristically imposed at the manufacturer's, wholesaler's, or retailer's level, transaction taxes cover a wide range of transfers. Like many other types of taxes

(e.g., income taxes, death taxes, and gift taxes), transaction taxes usually are not peculiarly within the exclusive province of any level of taxing authority (Federal, state, or local government). As the description implies, these levies place a tax on transfers of property and normally are determined by a percentage rate multiplied by the value involved.

Federal Excise Taxes.   Long one of the mainstays of the Federal tax system, Federal excise taxes had declined in relative importance until recently. In late 1982, Congress substantially increased the Federal excise taxes on such items as tobacco products, fuel and gasoline sales, telephone usage, and air travel passenger tickets. Other Federal excise taxes include the following:

- Manufacturers' excise taxes on trucks, trailers, tires, firearms, sporting equipment, coal, and the gas guzzler tax on automobiles.

- Alcohol taxes.

- Miscellaneous taxes (e.g., the tax on wagering).

The list of transactions covered, although seemingly impressive, has diminished over the years. At one time, for example, there was a Federal excise tax on admission to amusement facilities (e.g., theaters) and on the sale of such *luxury* items as leather goods, furs, jewelry, and cosmetics.

When reviewing the list of both Federal and state excise taxes, one should recognize the possibility that the tax laws may be trying to influence social behavior. For example, the gas guzzler tax is intended as an incentive for the automobile companies to build cars that are fuel efficient. It is imposed on the manufacturers of automobiles and progresses in amount as the mileage ratings per gallon of gas decrease.

Since alcohol and tobacco are considered by many to be harmful to a person's health, why not increase their cost with the imposition of excise taxes and thereby discourage their use? Unfortunately, mixed evidence exists to support a high level of correlation between the imposition of an excise tax and consumer behavior.

State Excise Taxes.   Many state and local excise taxes parallel the Federal version. Thus, all states tax the sale of gasoline, liquor, and tobacco products; however, the rates vary significantly. For gasoline products, for example, compare the 22 cents per gallon imposed by the state of Nebraska with the 9 cents per gallon levied by the state of Wyoming. For tobacco sales, contrast the 2 cents per pack of cigarettes in effect in North Carolina with the 40 cents per pack applicable in Connecticut. In the latter situation, is it surprising that the smuggling of cigarettes from North Carolina for resale elsewhere is so widespread? Here might be a situation where an excise tax encourages criminal conduct more than it discourages consumer use.

Other excise taxes found at some state and local levels include those on admission to amusement facilities; hotel occupancy and the rental of various other facilities; and the sale of playing cards, oleomargarine products, and prepared foods. Most states impose a transaction tax on the transfer of property that requires the recording of documents (e.g., real estate sales). Some extend the tax to the transfer of stocks and other securities.

General Sales Taxes.   The distinction between an excise tax and a general sales tax is easy to make. One is restricted to a particular transaction (e.g., the 9.1 cents per gallon Federal excise tax on the sale of gasoline), while the other covers a multitude of transactions (e.g., a 5 percent tax on *all* retail sales). In actual practice,

however, the distinction is not always that clear. Some state statutes might exempt certain transactions from the application of the general sales taxes (e.g., sales of food to be consumed off the premises, sales of certain medicines and drugs). Also, it is not uncommon to find that rates vary depending on the commodity involved. In many states, for example, preferential rates are allowed for the sale of agricultural equipment, or different rates (either higher or lower than the general rate) apply to the sale of automobiles. With many of these special exceptions and classifications of rates, a general sales tax can take on the appearance of a collection of individual excise taxes.

A *use tax* is an ad valorem tax, usually at the same rate as the sales tax, on the use, consumption, or storage of tangible property. The purpose of a use tax is to prevent the avoidance of a sales tax. Every state that imposes a general sales tax levied on the consumer also has a use tax. The states without either tax are Alaska, Delaware, Montana, New Hampshire, and Oregon.

EXAMPLE 3	T resides in a jurisdiction that imposes a 5% general sales tax but lives near a state that has no tax at all. T purchases an automobile for $10,000 from a dealer located in the neighboring state. Has T saved $500 in sales taxes? The state use tax is designed to pick up the difference between the tax paid in another jurisdiction and what would have been paid in the state where T resides. □

Because the use tax is difficult to enforce for many purchases, it is often avoided. In some cases, for example, it may be worthwhile to make purchases through an out-of-state mail-order business. In spite of shipping costs, the avoidance of the local sales tax that otherwise might be incurred could make the price of such products as computer components cheaper. Some states are taking steps to curtail this loss of revenue. For items such as automobiles (refer to Example 3), the use tax probably will be collected when the purchaser registers the item in his or her home state.

Local general sales taxes, over and above those levied by the state, are common. It is not unusual to find taxpayers living in the same state who pay different general sales taxes due to the location of their residence.

Severance Taxes.   Severance taxes are an important source of revenue for many states. These transaction taxes are based on the notion that the state has an interest in its natural resources (e.g., oil, gas, iron ore, coal); therefore, their extraction is an occasion for the imposition of a tax.

Death Taxes

A *death tax* is a tax on the right to transfer property or to receive property upon the death of the owner. Consequently, a death tax falls into the category of an excise tax. If the death tax is imposed on the right to pass property at death, it is classified as an *estate tax*. If it taxes the right to receive property from a decedent, it is termed an *inheritance tax*. As is typical of other types of excise taxes, the value of the property transferred measures the base for determining the amount of the death tax.

Of the two, inheritance tax and estate tax, the Federal government imposes only an estate tax. State governments, however, levy inheritance taxes, estate taxes, or both.

EXAMPLE 4

At the time of her death, D lived in a state that imposes an inheritance tax but not an estate tax. S, one of D's heirs, lives in the same state. D's estate would be subject to the Federal estate tax, and S would be subject to the state inheritance tax. □

The Federal Estate Tax.   The Revenue Act of 1916 incorporated the estate tax into the tax law. Although never designed to generate a large source of revenue, its original purpose was to prevent large concentrations of wealth from being kept within the family for many generations. Whether this objective has been accomplished is debatable. Like the income tax, estate taxes can be reduced through various planning procedures.

The gross estate includes property the decedent owned at the time of death. It also includes life insurance proceeds when paid to the estate or when paid to a beneficiary other than the estate if the deceased-insured had any ownership rights in the policy. Quite simply, the gross estate represents property interests subject to Federal estate taxation. All property included in the gross estate is valued as of the date of death or, if the alternate valuation date is elected, six months later.

Deductions from the gross estate in arriving at the taxable estate include funeral and administration expenses, certain taxes, debts of the decedent, casualty losses incurred during the administration of the estate, transfers to charitable organizations, and, in some cases, the marital deduction. The marital deduction is available for amounts actually passing to a surviving spouse (a widow or widower).

Once the taxable estate has been determined and certain taxable gifts have been added to it, the estate tax can be computed. From the amount derived from the appropriate tax rate schedules, various credits are subtracted to arrive at the tax, if any, that is due. It is important to recognize the difference between a deduction and a credit. A credit is a dollar-for-dollar reduction of tax liability. A deduction, however, only benefits the taxpayer to the extent of his or her tax bracket. An estate in the 50% tax bracket, for example, would need $2 of deductions to prevent $1 of tax liability from developing. In contrast, $1 of credit neutralizes $1 of tax liability.

Although many other credits also are available, probably the most significant one is the unified transfer tax credit. The main reason for this credit is to eliminate or reduce the estate tax liability for modest estates. For deaths after 1986, the amount of the credit is $192,800. Based on the estate tax rates, the amount of the credit covers a tax base of $600,000.

EXAMPLE 5

D had never made any taxable gifts before his death in 1990. If D died with a taxable estate of $600,000 or less, no Federal estate tax will be due because of the application of the unified transfer tax credit of $192,800. Under the tax law, the estate tax on a taxable estate of $600,000 is $192,800. □

State Death Taxes.   As noted earlier, states usually levy an inheritance tax, an estate tax, or both. The two forms of death taxes differ according to whether the tax is imposed on the heir or on the estate.

Characteristically, an inheritance tax divides the heirs into classes based on their relationship to the decedent. The more closely related the heir, the lower the rates imposed and the greater the exemption allowed. Some states completely exempt from taxation amounts passing to a surviving spouse.

Gift Taxes

Like a death tax, a *gift tax* is an excise tax levied on the right to transfer property. In this case, however, the tax is directed to transfers made during the owner's life and not at death. Also, a gift tax applies only to transfers that are not supported by full and adequate consideration.

EXAMPLE 6   D sells to his daughter property worth $20,000 for $1,000. Although property worth $20,000 has been transferred, only $19,000 represents a gift, since this is the portion not supported by full and adequate consideration.   □

The Federal Gift Tax.   First enacted in 1932, the Federal gift tax was intended to complement the estate tax. Without any tax applicable to lifetime transfers by gift, it would be possible to avoid the estate tax and escape taxation entirely.

Only taxable gifts are subject to the gift tax. For this purpose, a taxable gift is measured by the fair market value of the property on the date of transfer less the annual exclusion of $10,000 per donee and, in some cases, less the marital deduction, which allows tax-free transfers between spouses. Each donor is allowed an annual exclusion of $10,000 for each donee. The purpose of the annual exclusion is to avoid the need to report and pay a tax on "modest" gifts. Without the exclusion, the Internal Revenue Service could face a real problem of taxpayer noncompliance.

EXAMPLE 7   On December 31, 1989, D (a widow) gives $10,000 to each of her four married children, their spouses, and her eight grandchildren. On January 3, 1990, she repeats the same procedure. Although D transferred $160,000 [$10,000 × 16 (number of donees)] in 1989 and $160,000 [$10,000 × 16 (number of donees)] in 1990 for a total of $320,000 ($160,000 + $160,000), she has not made a taxable gift as a result of the annual exclusion.   □

A special election applicable to married persons allows one-half of the gift made by the donor-spouse to be treated as being made by the nondonor-spouse. The effect of this election to split the gifts of property made to third persons is to increase the number of annual exclusions available. Also, it allows the use of the nondonor-spouse's unified transfer tax credit and may lower the tax brackets that will apply.

For taxable gifts made after 1976, the gift tax rate schedule is the same as that applicable to the estate tax. The schedule is commonly referred to as the *unified transfer tax schedule*.

The Federal gift tax is cumulative in effect. What this means is that the tax base for current *taxable* gifts includes past *taxable* gifts. Although a credit is allowed for prior gift taxes, the result of adding past taxable gifts to current taxable gifts is to push the donor into a higher tax bracket. Like the Federal estate tax rates, the Federal gift tax rates are progressive.

The unified transfer tax credit is available for all taxable gifts made after 1976. As was true with the Federal estate tax, the amount of this credit is $192,800. There is, however, only one unified transfer tax credit, and it applies both to taxable gifts and to the Federal estate tax. In a manner of speaking, therefore, once the unified transfer tax credit has been exhausted for Federal gift tax purposes, it is no longer

available to insulate a decedent from the Federal estate tax. For further information on the Federal gift tax, see chapter 25.

In summary, transfers by gift and transfers by death made after 1976 will be subject to the unified transfer tax. The same rates and credits apply. Further, taxable gifts made after 1976 will have to be added to the taxable estate in arriving at the tax base for applying the unified transfer tax at death.

State Gift Taxes.   The states currently imposing a state gift tax are Delaware, Louisiana, New York, North Carolina, South Carolina, Tennessee, and Wisconsin. Most of the laws provide for lifetime exemptions and annual exclusions. Like the Federal gift tax, the state taxes are cumulative in effect. But unlike the Federal version, the amount of tax depends on the relationship between the donor and the donee. Like state inheritance taxes, larger exemptions and lower rates apply when the donor and donee are closely related to each other.

Income Taxes

Income taxes are levied by the Federal government, most states, and some local governments. The trend in recent years has been to place greater reliance on this method of taxation. This trend is not consistent with what is happening in other countries, and in this sense, our system of taxation is somewhat different.

Income taxes generally are imposed on individuals, corporations, and certain fiduciaries (estates and trusts). Most jurisdictions attempt to assure their collection by requiring certain pay-as-you-go procedures (e.g., withholding requirements as to employees and estimated tax prepayments for other taxpayers).

Federal Income Taxes.   Chapters 2 through 15 deal primarily with the application of the Federal income tax to individuals. The procedure for determining the Federal income tax applicable to individuals is summarized in Figure 1−2.

FIGURE 1−2 Formula for Federal Income Tax on Individuals

Income (broadly conceived)	$xx,xxx
Less: Exclusions (income that is not subject to tax)	(x,xxx)
Gross income (income that is subject to tax)	$xx,xxx
Less: Certain business deductions (usually referred to as deductions *for* adjusted gross income)	(x,xxx)
Adjusted gross income	$xx,xxx
Less: The greater of certain personal and employee deductions (usually referred to as *itemized deductions* or as deductions *from* adjusted gross income) *or* The standard deduction (including any additional standard deduction) *and*	(x,xxx)
Less: Personal and dependency exemptions	(x,xxx)
Taxable income	$xx,xxx
Tax on taxable income (see Tax Rate Schedules in Appendix A)	$ x,xxx
Less: Tax credits (including Federal income tax withheld and other prepayments of Federal income taxes)	(xxx)
Tax due (or refund)	$ xxx

The standard deduction and personal and dependency exemptions are explained in chapter 2.

The rules for the application of the Federal corporate income tax do not require the computation of adjusted gross income and do not provide for the standard deduction and personal and dependency exemptions. All allowable deductions of a corporation fall into the business-expense category. In effect, therefore, the taxable income of a corporation is the difference between gross income (net of exclusions) and deductions.

Chapter 16 summarizes the rules relating to the tax formula for corporations.

State Income Taxes.   All but the following states impose an income tax on individuals: Alaska, Florida, Nevada, South Dakota, Texas, Washington, and Wyoming. New Hampshire and Tennessee have an income tax, but its application is limited to dividend and interest income.

Nearly all states have an income tax applicable to corporations. It is difficult to determine those that do not, because a state franchise tax sometimes is based in part on the income earned by the corporation.

Local Income Taxes.   Cities imposing an income tax include, but are not limited to, Baltimore, Cincinnati, Cleveland, Detroit, Kansas City (Mo.), New York, Philadelphia, and St. Louis.

Employment Taxes

Classification as an employee usually leads to the imposition of employment taxes and to the requirement that the employer withhold specified amounts for income taxes. The material that follows concentrates on the two major employment taxes: FICA (Federal Insurance Contributions Act—commonly referred to as the Social Security tax) and FUTA (Federal Unemployment Tax Act). Both taxes can be justified by social and public welfare considerations: FICA offers some measure of retirement security, and FUTA provides a modest source of income in the event of loss of employment.

FICA Taxes.   The tax rates and wage base under FICA are not constant, and as Figure 1–3 indicates, the increases over the years have been quite substantial. There appears to be every reason to predict that the rate and base amount will continue to rise in the future. Also note that Figure 1–3 represents the employee's share of the tax. Since the employer must match the employee's portion, the *total* cost of FICA becomes 15.3 percent (7.65% × 2) for 1990.

A spouse employed by another spouse is subject to FICA. Exempted, however, are children under the age of 18 who are employed in a parent's trade or business.

FUTA Taxes.   The purpose of FUTA is to provide funds that the states can use to provide unemployment benefits. This leads to the somewhat unusual situation of one tax being handled by both Federal and state governments. The end product of such joint administration is to compel the employer to observe a double set of rules. Thus, state and Federal returns must be filed and payments made to both governmental units.

FUTA applies at a rate of 6.2 percent in 1990 on the first $7,000 of covered wages paid during the year to each employee. The Federal government allows a credit for FUTA paid (or allowed under a merit rating system) to the state. The credit cannot exceed 5.4 percent of the covered wages. Thus, the amount required to be paid to the IRS could be as low as 0.8 percent (6.2 percent − 5.4 percent).

FIGURE 1–3   FICA Rates and Base

Year	Percent	Base Amount	Maximum Tax
1978	6.05%	$17,700	$1,070.85
1979	6.13%	22,900	1,403.77
1980	6.13%	25,900	1,587.67
1981	6.65%	29,700	1,975.05
1982	6.70%	32,400	2,170.80
1983	6.70%	35,700	2,391.90
1984	6.70%	37,800	2,532.60
1985	7.05%	39,600	2,791.80
1986	7.15%	42,000	3,003.00
1987	7.15%	43,800	3,131.70
1988	7.51%	45,000	3,379.50
1989	7.51%	48,000	3,604.80
1990	7.65%	51,300	3,924.45
1991 on	7.65%	—*	—**

*Not yet determined by Congress.
**Cannot be computed until the wage base is set by Congress.

States follow a policy of reducing the unemployment tax on employers who experience stability in employment. Thus, an employer with little or no turnover among employees might find that the state rate could drop to as low as 0.1 percent or, in some states, even to zero. The reason for the merit rating credit is obvious. Steady employment means the state will have lower unemployment benefits to pay.

FUTA is to be distinguished from FICA in the sense that the incidence of taxation falls entirely upon the employer. A few states, however, levy a special tax on employees either to provide disability benefits or supplemental unemployment compensation, or both.

Other Taxes

To complete the overview of the U.S. tax system, some missing links need to be covered that do not fit into the classifications discussed elsewhere in this chapter.

Federal Customs Duties.   One tax that has not yet been mentioned is the tariff on certain imported goods. Generally referred to as a customs duty or levy, this tax, together with selective excise taxes, provided most of the revenues needed by the Federal government during the nineteenth century. Considering present times, it is remarkable to note that tariffs and excise taxes alone paid off the national debt in 1835 and enabled the U.S. Treasury to pay a surplus of $28 million to the states.

In recent years, tariffs have served the nation more as an instrument for carrying out protectionist policies than as a means of generating revenue. Thus, a particular U.S. industry might be saved from economic disaster, so the argument goes, by placing customs duties on the importation of foreign goods that can be sold at lower prices. The protectionist would contend that the tariff therefore neutralizes the competitive edge held by the producer of the foreign goods.

Protectionist policies seem more appropriate for less-developed countries whose industrial capacity has not yet matured. In a world where a developed

country should have everything to gain from the encouragement of international free trade, such policies may be of dubious value. History proves that tariffs often lead to retaliatory action on the part of the nation or nations affected.

Miscellaneous State and Local Taxes.   Most states impose a franchise tax on corporations. Basically, a *franchise tax* is one levied on the right to do business in the state. The base used for the determination of the tax varies from state to state. Although corporate income considerations may come into play, this tax most often is based on the capitalization of the corporation (either with or without certain long-term indebtedness).

Closely akin to the franchise tax are *occupational taxes* applicable to various trades or businesses, such as a liquor store license, a taxicab permit, or a fee to practice a profession such as law, medicine, or accounting. Most of these are not significant revenue producers and fall more into the category of licenses than taxes. The revenue derived is used to defray the cost incurred by the jurisdiction in regulating the business or profession in the interest of the public good.

Value Added Taxes

At least in the Common Market countries of Western Europe, the *value added tax* (VAT) has gained acceptance as a major source of revenue. Although variously classified, a VAT resembles a national sales tax since it taxes the increment in value as goods move through production and manufacturing stages to the marketplace. A VAT has its proponents in the United States as a partial solution to high Federal budget deficits and increases in employment taxes. Its incorporation as part of our tax system in the near future is problematical, however.

TAX ADMINISTRATION

Internal Revenue Service

The responsibility for administering the Federal tax laws rests with the Treasury Department. Administratively, the IRS is part of the Department of the Treasury and is responsible for enforcing the tax laws.

The Commissioner of Internal Revenue is appointed by the President. His responsibilities are to establish policy and to supervise the activities of the entire IRS organization. The National Office organization of the IRS includes a Senior Deputy Commissioner and several Deputy Commissioners and Assistant Commissioners who have supervisory responsibility over field operations.

The Audit Process

Selection of Returns for Audit.   The IRS utilizes mathematical formulas and statistical sampling techniques to select tax returns that are most likely to contain errors and to yield substantial amounts of additional tax revenues upon audit.

Though the IRS does not openly disclose all of its audit selection techniques, the following observations may be made relative to the probability of selection for audit:

* Certain groups of taxpayers are subject to audit much more frequently than others. These groups include individuals with gross income in excess of $50,000, self-employed individuals with substantial business income and deductions, and taxpayers with prior tax deficiencies. Also vulnerable are cash businesses (e.g., cafes and small service businesses) where the potential for tax avoidance is high.

EXAMPLE 8   T owns and operates a liquor store on a cash-and-carry basis. Since all of T's sales are for cash, T might well be a prime candidate for an audit by the IRS. Cash transactions are easier to conceal than those made on credit.   □

- If information returns (e.g., Form 1099, Form W–2) are not in substantial agreement with reported income, an audit can be anticipated.

- If an individual's itemized deductions are in excess of norms established for various income levels, the probability of an audit is increased.

- Filing of a refund claim by the taxpayer may prompt an audit of the return.

- Certain returns are selected on a random sampling basis under the Taxpayer Compliance Measurement Program (TCMP). TCMP is used to develop, update, and improve the mathematical formulas and statistical sampling techniques used by the IRS.

- Information obtained from other sources (e.g., informants, news items). The tax law permits the IRS to pay rewards to persons who provide information that leads to the detection and punishment of those who violate the tax laws. Such rewards may not exceed 10 percent of the taxes, fines, and penalties recovered as a result of such information.

EXAMPLE 9   After 15 years of service, F is discharged by her employer, Dr. T. Shortly thereafter, the IRS receives an anonymous letter informing it that Dr. T keeps two separate sets of books, one of which substantially understates his cash receipts.   □

EXAMPLE 10   During a divorce proceeding it is revealed that T, a public official, kept large amounts of cash in a shoe box at home. Such information is widely disseminated by the news media and comes to the attention of the IRS. Needless to say, the IRS would be interested in knowing whether such amounts originated from a taxable source and, if so, whether they were reported on T's income tax returns.   □

UNDERSTANDING THE FEDERAL TAX LAW

The Federal tax law is a mosaic of statutory provisions, administrative pronouncements, and court decisions. Anyone who has attempted to work with this body of knowledge would have to admit to its complexity. For the person who has to trudge through a mass of rules to find the solution to a tax problem, it may be of some consolation to know that the law's complexity can generally be explained. Whether sound or not, there is a reason for the formulation of every rule. Knowing these reasons, therefore, is a considerable step toward understanding the Federal tax law.

At the outset one should recognize that the Federal tax law has as its *major objective* the raising of revenue. But although the fiscal needs of the government are important, other considerations exist that explain certain portions of the law. Economic, social, equity, and political factors also play a significant role. Added to these factors is the marked impact the Internal Revenue Service and the courts have had and will continue to have on the evolution of Federal tax law. These

matters are treated in the remainder of the chapter, and wherever appropriate, the discussion is tied to subjects covered later in the text.

Revenue Needs

The foundation of any tax system has to be the raising of revenue to cover the cost of government operations. Ideally, annual outlays should not be expected to exceed anticipated revenues, thereby leading to a balanced budget with no resulting deficit. Many states have achieved this objective by passing laws or constitutional amendments precluding deficit spending. Unfortunately, the Federal government has no such conclusive prohibition, and mounting annual deficits have become an increasing concern for many.

When finalizing the Tax Reform Act (TRA) of 1986, a deficit-conscious Congress was guided by the concept of *revenue neutrality*. The concept means that the changes made in the tax law will neither increase nor decrease the net result previously reached under the prior rules. Revenue neutrality does not mean that any one taxpayer's tax liability will remain the same, as this will depend upon the circumstances involved. Thus, one taxpayer's increased tax liability could be another's tax savings. Although revenue neutral tax reform does not reduce deficits, at least it does not aggravate the problem.

One can expect budget deficit considerations to play an ever-increasing role in shaping future tax policy. The Technical and Miscellaneous Revenue Act of 1988 and the Revenue Reconciliation Act of 1989 are good examples of the application of the concept of revenue neutrality. While extending some expiring tax benefits, Congress was careful not to add to the existing deficit. This was accomplished by curtailing or eliminating some tax benefits.

Economic Considerations

The use of the tax system in an effort to accomplish economic objectives has become increasingly popular in recent years. Generally, it involves utilization of tax legislation to amend the Internal Revenue Code and looks toward measures designed to help control the economy or to encourage certain activities and businesses.

Control of the Economy.   Congress has made use of depreciation write-offs as a means of controlling the economy. Theoretically, shorter asset lives and accelerated methods should encourage additional investment in depreciable property acquired for business use. Conversely, longer asset lives and the required use of the straight-line method of depreciation dampen the tax incentive for capital outlays.

Compared with past law, TRA of 1986 generally cut back on faster write-offs for property acquired after 1986. Particularly hard hit was most depreciable real estate, where class lives were extended from 19 years to as long as 31½ years and the straight-line method was made mandatory. These changes were made in the interest of revenue neutrality and in the belief that the current economy is stable.

Of more immediate impact on the economy is a change in the tax rate structure. With lower tax rates, taxpayers are able to retain additional spendable funds. Although TRA of 1986 lowered tax rates for most taxpayers, with the reduction or elimination of many deductions and credits, lower rates may not lead to lower tax liabilities. Thus, only time will tell what effect the tax rate changes made by TRA of 1986 will have on the economy.

Encouragement of Certain Activities.   Without passing judgment on the wisdom of any such choices, it is quite clear that the tax law does encourage certain types of economic activity or segments of the economy. If, for example, one

assumes that technological progress should be fostered, the favorable treatment allowed research and development expenditures can be explained. Under the tax law, such expenditures can be either deducted in the year incurred or capitalized and amortized over a period of 60 months or more. In terms of timing the tax savings, such options usually are preferable to a capitalization of the cost with a write-off over the estimated useful life of the asset created. If the asset developed has an indefinite useful life, no write-off would be available without the two options allowed by the tax law.

Recent legislation further recognized the need to stimulate technological progress through the use of the tax laws. In addition to the favorable write-off treatment just noted, certain research and development costs qualify for a 20 percent tax credit (see chapter 11).

Is it desirable to encourage the conservation of energy resources? Considering the world energy situation and our own reliance on foreign oil, the answer to this question has to be yes. The concern over energy usage was a prime consideration that led to the enactment of legislation to make various tax savings for energy conservation expenditures available to taxpayers.

Are ecological considerations a desirable objective? If they are, it explains why the tax law permits a 60-month amortization period for costs incurred in the installation of pollution control facilities.

Is saving desirable for the economy? Saving leads to capital formation and thereby makes funds available to finance home construction and industrial expansion. The tax law provides incentives to encourage saving through preferential treatment accorded to private retirement plans. Not only are contributions to Keogh (H.R. 10) plans and certain Individual Retirement Accounts (IRAs) deductible, but income from such contributions accumulates free of tax. As noted below, the encouragement of private sector pension plans can also be justified under social considerations.

Encouragement of Certain Industries.   No one can question the proposition that a sound agricultural base is necessary for a well-balanced national economy. Undoubtedly this can explain why farmers are accorded special treatment under the Federal tax system. Among these benefits are the election to expense rather than capitalize certain soil and water conservation expenditures and fertilizers and the election to defer the recognition of gain on the receipt of crop insurance proceeds.

Encouragement of Small Business.   At least in the United States, a consensus exists that what is good for small business is good for the economy as a whole. Whether valid or not, this assumption has led to a definite bias in the tax law favoring small business.

In the corporate tax area, several provisions can be explained by the motivation to benefit small business. One provision permits the shareholders of a small business corporation to make a special election that generally will avoid the imposition of the corporate income tax. Furthermore, such an election enables the corporation to pass through to its shareholders any of its operating losses. Known as the S election, it is discussed in chapter 18.

Social Considerations

Some of the Federal tax law can be explained by looking to social considerations. This is particularly the case when dealing with the Federal income tax on individuals. Notable examples and the rationale behind each are summarized as follows:

- Certain benefits provided to employees through accident and health plans financed by employers are nontaxable to employees. It would appear socially desirable to encourage such plans since they provide medical benefits in the event of an employee's illness or injury.

- Most premiums paid by an employer for group term insurance covering the life of the employee are nontaxable to the employee. These arrangements can be justified on social grounds in that they provide funds for the family unit to help it adjust following the loss of wages caused by the employee's death.

- A contribution made by an employer to a qualified pension or profit sharing plan for an employee receives special treatment. The contribution and any income it generates will not be taxed to the employee until the funds are distributed. Such an arrangement also benefits the employer by allowing a tax deduction when the contribution is made to the qualified plan. Private retirement plans should be encouraged since they supplement the subsistence income level the employee otherwise would have under the Social Security system.

- A deduction is allowed for contributions to qualified charitable organizations. The deduction attempts to shift some of the financial and administrative burden of socially desirable programs from the public (the government) to the private (the citizens) sector.

- A tax credit is allowed for amounts spent to furnish care for certain minor or disabled dependents to enable the taxpayer to seek or maintain gainful employment (see chapter 11). Who could deny the social desirability of encouraging taxpayers to provide care for their children while they work?

- A tax deduction is not allowed for certain expenditures deemed to be contrary to public policy. This disallowance extends to such items as fines, penalties, illegal kickbacks, bribes to government officials, and gambling losses in excess of gains. Social considerations dictate that these activities should not be encouraged by the tax law. Permitting the deduction would supposedly encourage such activities.

Many other examples could be included, but the conclusion would be unchanged. Social considerations do explain a significant part of the Federal tax law.

Equity Considerations

The concept of equity is relative. Reasonable persons can, and often do, disagree about what is fair or unfair. In the tax area, moreover, equity is most often tied to a particular taxpayer's personal situation. To illustrate, compare the tax positions of those who rent their personal residences with those who own their homes. Renters receive no Federal income tax benefit from the rent they pay. For homeowners, however, a large portion of the house payments they make may qualify for the Federal interest and property tax deductions. Although it may be difficult for renters to understand this difference in tax treatment, the encouragement of home ownership can be justified on both economic and social grounds.

In the same vein, compare the tax treatment of a corporation with that of a partnership. Although the two businesses may be of equal size, similarly situated, and competitors in production of goods or services, they are not treated comparably under the tax law. The corporation is subject to a separate Federal income

tax; the partnership is not. Whether the differences in tax treatment can be justified logically in terms of equity is beside the point. The point is that the tax law can and does make a distinction between these business forms.

Equity, then, is not what appears fair or unfair to any one taxpayer or group of taxpayers. It is, instead, what the tax law recognizes. Some recognition of equity does exist, however, and offers an explanation of part of the law. The concept of equity appears in tax provisions that alleviate the effect of multiple taxation and postpone the recognition of gain when the taxpayer lacks the ability or wherewithal to pay the tax. Equity considerations also mitigate the effect of the application of the annual accounting period concept and cope with the eroding results of inflation.

Alleviating the Effect of Multiple Taxation.   The income earned by a taxpayer may be subject to taxes imposed by different taxing authorities. If, for example, the taxpayer is a resident of New York City, income might generate Federal, state of New York, and city of New York income taxes. To compensate for this apparent inequity, the Federal tax law allows a taxpayer to claim a deduction for state and local income taxes. The deduction does not, however, neutralize the effect of multiple taxation since the benefit derived depends on the taxpayer's Federal income tax rate. Only a tax credit, rather than a deduction, would eliminate the effects of multiple taxation on the same income.

Equity considerations can explain the Federal tax treatment of certain income from foreign sources. Since double taxation results when the same income is subject to both foreign and U.S. income taxes, the tax law permits the taxpayer to choose between a credit and a deduction for the foreign taxes paid.

The Wherewithal to Pay Concept.   The *wherewithal to pay* concept recognizes the inequity of taxing a transaction when the taxpayer lacks the means with which to pay the tax. It is particularly suited to situations in which the taxpayer's economic position has not changed significantly as a result of the transaction.

An illustration of the wherewithal to pay concept is the provision of the tax law dealing with the treatment of gain resulting from the sale of a personal residence. If the proceeds are rolled over (reinvested) in another personal residence within a specified time period, the gain will not be taxed (see chapter 12).

EXAMPLE 11   T sold his personal residence (cost of $60,000) for $100,000 and moved to another city. Shortly thereafter, T purchased a new personal residence for $100,000. □

In Example 11, T had an economic gain of $40,000 [$100,000 (selling price) – $60,000 (cost of residence)]. It would be inequitable to force T to pay a tax on this gain for two reasons. First, without disposing of the property acquired (the new residence), T would be hard-pressed to pay the tax. Second, T's economic position has not changed significantly.

Mitigating the Effect of the Annual Accounting Period Concept.   For purposes of effective administration of the tax law, all taxpayers must report to and settle with the Federal government at periodic intervals. Otherwise, taxpayers would remain uncertain as to their tax liabilities, and the government would have difficulty judging revenues and budgeting expenditures. The period selected for final settlement of most tax liabilities, in any event an arbitrary determination, is one year. At the close of each year, therefore, a taxpayer's position becomes

complete for that particular year. Referred to as the annual accounting period concept, its effect is to divide each taxpayer's life, for tax purposes, into equal annual intervals.

The finality of the annual accounting period concept could lead to dissimilarity in tax treatment for taxpayers who are, from a long-range standpoint, in the same economic position.

EXAMPLE 12   R and S are two sole proprietors and have experienced the following results during the past four years:

	Profit (or Loss)	
Year	R	S
1987	$50,000	$150,000
1988	60,000	60,000
1989	70,000	70,000
1990	50,000	(50,000)

Although R and S have the same profit of $230,000 over the period from1987–1990, the finality of the annual accounting period concept places S at a definite disadvantage for tax purposes. The net operating loss procedure offers S some relief by allowing him to apply some or all of his 1990 loss to the earliest profitable years (in this case, 1987). Thus, he would be in a position with a net operating loss carryback to obtain a refund for some of the taxes he paid on the $150,000 profit reported for 1987. □

The same reasoning used to support the deduction of net operating losses can be applied to explain the special treatment accorded by the tax law to excess capital losses and excess charitable contributions. Carryback and carryover procedures help mitigate the effect of limiting a loss or a deduction to the accounting period in which it was realized. With such procedures, a taxpayer might be able to salvage a loss or a deduction that might otherwise be wasted.

Coping with Inflation.   Because of the progressive nature of the income tax, a wage adjustment to compensate for inflation can increase the income tax bracket of the recipient. Known as *bracket creep*, the overall impact is an erosion of purchasing power. Congress recognized this problem and began to adjust various income tax components in 1985 through an indexation procedure. Indexation is based upon the rise in the consumer price index over the prior year.

Because TRA of 1986 significantly raised the amount of each exemption and the standard deduction and lowered the tax rates, the indexation procedure was temporarily suspended. However, indexation has resumed as follows: beginning in 1989 as to dollar amounts of the tax brackets and the standard deduction and beginning in 1990 as to personal and dependency exemptions.

Political Considerations

A large segment of the Federal tax law is made up of statutory provisions. Since these statutes are enacted by Congress, is it any surprise that political considerations influence tax law? For purposes of discussion, the effect of political

considerations on the tax law is divided into the following topics: special interest legislation, political expediency situations, and state and local government influences.

Special Interest Legislation.   There is no doubt that certain provisions of the tax law can largely be explained by looking to the political influence some pressure groups have had on Congress. Is there any other realistic reason, for example, that prepaid subscription and dues income are not taxed until earned while prepaid rents are taxed to the landlord in the year received?

Special interest legislation is not necessarily to be condemned if it can be justified on economic, social, or some other utilitarian grounds. At any rate, it is an inevitable product of our political system.

Political Expediency Situations.   Various tax reform proposals rise and fall in favor depending upon the shifting moods of the American public. That Congress is sensitive to popular feeling is an accepted fact. Therefore, certain provisions of the tax law can be explained on the basis of political expediency existing at the time of enactment.

Measures that deter more affluent taxpayers from obtaining so-called preferential tax treatment have always had popular appeal and, consequently, the support of Congress. Provisions such as the alternative minimum tax, the imputed interest rules, and the limitation on the deductibility of interest on investment indebtedness can be explained on this basis (see chapters 10 and 11).

Other changes partially founded on the basis of political expediency include the lowering of individual income tax rates, raising the amount of the dependency exemption, and increasing the amount of the earned income credit.

State and Local Influences.   Political considerations have played a major role in the nontaxability of interest received on state and local obligations. In view of the furor that has been raised by state and local political figures every time any kind of modification of this tax provision has been proposed, one might well regard it as next to sacred.

Somewhat less apparent has been the influence state law has had in shaping our present Federal tax law. Of prime import in this regard has been the effect of the community property system employed in some states.[6] At one time, the tax position of the residents of these states was so advantageous that many common law states actually adopted community property systems. Needless to say, the political pressure placed on Congress to correct the disparity in tax treatment was considerable. To a large extent this was accomplished in the Revenue Act of 1948, which extended many of the community property tax advantages to residents of common law jurisdictions. The major advantage extended was the provision allowing married taxpayers to file joint returns and compute the tax liability as if the

---

6. The nine states with community property systems are Louisiana, Texas, New Mexico, Arizona, California, Washington, Idaho, Nevada, and Wisconsin. The rest of the states are classified as common law jurisdictions. The difference between common law and community property systems centers around the property rights possessed by married persons. In a common law system, each spouse owns whatever he or she earns. Under a community property system, one-half of the earnings of each spouse is considered owned by the other spouse. Assume, for example, H and W are husband and wife and their only income is the $40,000 annual salary H receives. If they live in New York (a common law state), the $40,000 salary belongs to H. If, however, they live in Texas (a community property state), the $40,000 salary is divided equally, in terms of ownership, between H and W.

income had been earned one-half by each spouse. This result is automatic in a community property state since half of the income earned by one spouse belongs to the other spouse. The income-splitting benefits of a joint return are now incorporated as part of the tax rates applicable to married taxpayers. See chapter 2.

Influence of the Internal Revenue Service

The influence of the IRS is recognized in many areas beyond its role in the issuance of the administrative pronouncements that make up a considerable portion of our tax law. In its capacity as the protector of the national revenue, the IRS has been instrumental in securing the passage of much legislation designed to curtail the most flagrant tax avoidance practices (to close tax loopholes). In its capacity as the administrator of the tax laws, the IRS has sought and obtained legislation to make its job easier (to attain administrative feasibility).

The IRS as Protector of the Revenue.   Innumerable examples can be given of provisions in the tax law that stemmed from the direct influence of the IRS. Usually, such provisions are intended to preclude the use of a loophole as a means of avoiding the tax consequences intended by Congress. Working within the letter of existing law, ingenious taxpayers and their advisers devise techniques that accomplish indirectly what cannot be accomplished directly. As a consequence, legislation is enacted to close the loopholes that taxpayers have located and exploited. Some tax law can be explained in this fashion and is discussed in the chapters to follow.

In addition, the IRS has secured from Congress legislation of a more general nature that enables it to make adjustments based on the substance, rather than the formal construction, of what a taxpayer has done. One such provision permits the IRS to make adjustments to a taxpayer's method of accounting when the method used by the taxpayer does not clearly reflect income (see chapter 15).

EXAMPLE 13   T, an individual cash basis taxpayer, owns and operates a pharmacy. All drugs and other items acquired for resale (e.g., cosmetics) are charged to the purchases account and written off (expensed) for tax purposes in the year of acquisition. As this procedure does not clearly reflect income, it would be appropriate for the IRS to require that T establish and maintain an ending inventory account.   □

Administrative Feasibility.   Some of the tax law is justified on the grounds that it simplifies the task of the IRS in collecting the revenue and administering the law. With regard to collecting the revenue, the IRS long ago realized the importance of placing taxpayers on a pay-as-you-go basis. Elaborate withholding procedures apply to wages, while the tax on other types of income may be paid at periodic intervals throughout the year. The IRS has been instrumental in convincing the courts that accrual basis taxpayers should pay taxes on prepaid income in the year received and not when earned. The approach may be contrary to generally accepted accounting principles, but it is consistent with the wherewithal to pay concept.

Of considerable aid to the IRS in collecting revenue are the numerous provisions that impose interest and penalties on taxpayers for noncompliance with

the tax law. Provisions such as the penalties for failure to pay a tax or to file a return that is due, the negligence penalty for intentional disregard of rules and regulations, and various penalties for civil and criminal fraud serve as deterrents to taxpayer noncompliance.

One of the keys to an effective administration of our tax system is the audit process conducted by the IRS. To carry out this function, the IRS is aided by provisions that reduce the chance of taxpayer error or manipulation and therefore simplify the audit effort that is necessary. An increase in the amount of the standard deduction, for example, reduces the number of individual taxpayers who will choose the alternative of itemizing their personal deductions. With fewer deductions to check, the audit function is thus simplified.

Influence of the Courts

In addition to interpreting statutory provisions and the administrative pronouncements issued by the IRS, the Federal courts have influenced tax law in two other respects. First, the courts have formulated certain judicial concepts that serve as guides in the application of various tax provisions. Second, certain key decisions have led to changes in the Internal Revenue Code. Understanding this influence helps to explain some of our tax law.

Judicial Concepts Relating to Tax.   A leading tax concept developed by the courts deals with the interpretation of statutory tax provisions that operate to benefit taxpayers. The courts have established the rule that these relief provisions are to be narrowly construed against taxpayers if there is any doubt about their application.

EXAMPLE 14   When a taxpayer has a gain on the sale of a personal residence, the gain is not subject to Federal income tax if the proceeds from the sale are reinvested in another principal residence. The tax law specifies a period of time in which the reinvestment must take place. The courts have held that the nontaxability of gain is a relief provision to be narrowly construed. Thus, failure to meet the replacement period requirements, even if beyond the control of the taxpayer, will cause the gain to be taxed. □

Important in this area is the *arm's length* concept. Particularly in dealings between related parties, transactions may be tested by looking to whether the taxpayers acted in an "arm's length" manner. The question to be asked is: Would unrelated parties have handled the transaction in the same way?

EXAMPLE 15   T, the sole shareholder of X Corporation, leases property to X for a yearly rental of $6,000. To test whether the corporation should be allowed a rent deduction for this amount, the IRS and the courts will apply the arm's length concept. Would X Corporation have paid $6,000 a year in rent if the same property had been leased from an unrelated party (rather than from the sole shareholder)? Suppose it is determined that an unrelated third party would have paid an annual rental for the property of only $5,000. Under these circumstances, X Corporation will be allowed a deduction of only $5,000. The other $1,000 it paid for the use of the property represents a nondeductible

dividend. Accordingly, T will be treated as having received rent income of $5,000 and dividend income of $1,000. ☐

Judicial Influence on Statutory Provisions.   Some court decisions have been of such consequence that Congress has incorporated them into statutory tax law. For example, many years ago the courts held that stock dividends distributed to the shareholders of a corporation were not taxable as income. This result was largely accepted by Congress, and a provision in the tax statutes now covers the issue.

On occasion, however, Congress has reacted in a negative manner with respect to judicial interpretations of the tax law.

EXAMPLE 16   L leases unimproved real estate to T for 40 years. At a cost of $200,000, T erects a building on the land. The building is worth $100,000 when the lease terminates and L takes possession of the property. Does L have any income either when the improvements are made or when the lease terminates? In a landmark decision, a court held that L must recognize income of $100,000 upon the termination of the lease. ☐

Congress felt that the result reached in Example 16 was inequitable in that it was not consistent with the wherewithal to pay concept. Consequently, the tax law was amended to provide that a landlord does not recognize any income either when the improvements are made (unless made in lieu of rent) or when the lease terminates.

Summary

In addition to its necessary revenue-raising objective, the Federal tax law has developed in response to several other factors:

- *Economic considerations*. The emphasis here is on tax provisions that help regulate the economy and encourage certain activities and types of businesses.

- *Social considerations*. Some tax provisions are designed to encourage (or discourage) certain socially desirable (or undesirable) practices.

- *Equity considerations*. Of principal concern in this area are tax provisions that alleviate the effect of multiple taxation, recognize the wherewithal to pay concept, mitigate the effect of the annual accounting period concept, and recognize the eroding effect of inflation.

- *Political considerations*. Of significance in this regard are tax provisions that represent special interest legislation, reflect political expediency situations, and exhibit the effect of state and local law.

- *Influence of the IRS*. Many tax provisions are intended to aid the IRS in the collection of the revenue and in the administration of the tax law.

- *Influence of the courts*. Court decisions have established a body of judicial concepts relating to tax law and have, on occasion, led Congress to enact statutory provisions to either clarify or negate their effect.

These factors explain various tax provisions and thereby help in understanding why the tax law developed to its present state.

PROBLEM MATERIALS

Discussion Questions

1. A tax protester refuses to pay the Federal income tax on the grounds that the tax is unconstitutional. Any comment?

2. Before the ratification of the Sixteenth Amendment to the U.S. Constitution, the Federal income tax on corporations was held to be constitutional, whereas the Federal income tax on individuals was not. Why?

3. Analyze the Federal income tax in light of Adam Smith's canons of taxation.

4. Is FICA a proportional or progressive tax? Explain.

5. T's personal residence is subject to three separate ad valorem property taxes. How could this be possible?

6. After T converts her personal residence into a rental house, she finds that the ad valorem taxes on the property increase. Why might this happen?

7. T buys a new home for $150,000, its cost of construction plus the usual profit margin for the builder. The new home is located in a neighborhood largely developed 10 years ago when the homes sold for approximately $50,000 each. Assuming the homes of his neighbors are worth (in current values) in the vicinity of $150,000, could T be at a disadvantage with regard to the ad valorem tax on realty?

8. T's personal residence is appraised at the same amount as is his next-door neighbor's residence. The neighbor is retired. T is somewhat surprised to learn that his neighbor pays less real estate property tax to the city than T does. Could there be a logical explanation for the apparent inequity?

9. While out of town on business, U stays at a motel with an advertised room rate of $30 per night. When checking out, U is charged $33. What would be a plausible reason for the extra $3 U had to pay?

10. On a recent trip to a nearby supermarket, T spent $42.00, of which $2.00 was for general sales tax. If T lives in a jurisdiction that imposes a 6% general sales tax on foodstuffs, why was the bill not $42.40?

11. T, a resident of Wyoming (which imposes a general sales tax), goes to Montana (which does not impose a general sales tax) to purchase her automobile. Will T successfully avoid the Wyoming sales tax? Explain.

12. States that generate a large amount of revenue from severance taxes on oil and gas (e.g., Alaska, Oklahoma, and Texas) are very vulnerable to OPEC pricing and production policies. Explain.

13. The retail purchase price of cigarettes in North Carolina is lower than in other states. Why?

14. Why might a person who purchases a product from an establishment located in jurisdiction X wish to take delivery in jurisdiction Y? Would it matter whether or not the person resided in jurisdiction X? Explain.

15. "There is no Federal inheritance tax." Do you agree or disagree with this statement?

16. During his life, T has accumulated considerable wealth as a result of personal service income. T is quite distressed when he learns that upon his death the wealth will be subject to death taxes. He feels this is unfair since the wealth accumulated has already been subject to taxation (the income tax). Please comment.

17. A decedent who leaves all of his property to his surviving spouse and to qualified charitable organizations will not be subject to a Federal estate tax. Explain.

18. How much property can D, a widow, give to her three married children, their spouses, and five grandchildren over a period of 12 years without making a taxable gift?

19. A married person might be able to give twice as much property to a donee without incurring a Federal gift tax. Explain this statement.

20. At a social function you attended in early March of 1990, you overheard a guest, the CEO of a corporation, remark, "Thank goodness this is the end of FICA for a while!" Interpret this remark.

21. T, a sole proprietor, owns and operates a grocery store. T's wife and his 17-year-old son work in the business and are paid wages. Will the wife and son be subjected to FICA? Explain.

22. T, the owner and operator of a construction company that builds outdoor swimming pools, releases most of his construction personnel during the winter months. Should this hurt T's FUTA situation? Why or why not?

23. Compare FICA and FUTA in connection with each of the following:
    a. Incidence of taxation.
    b. Justification for taxation.
    c. Reporting and filing requirements.
    d. Rates and base involved.

24. T is an ardent member of a religion that advocates tithing (contributing 10% of annual income to the church). Presuming T complies with this guideline, could it increase the chance that T's individual Federal income tax return will be selected for audit by the IRS? Why or why not?

25. T, the owner and operator of a cash-and-carry military surplus retail outlet, has been audited many times by the IRS. When T mentions this fact to his next-door neighbor, an employee with Ford Motor Company, he is somewhat surprised to learn that the neighbor has never been audited by the IRS. Is there any explanation for this apparent disparity in treatment?

26. While Dr. T and his family are out of town on vacation, their home is burglarized. Among the items stolen and reported to the police are $35,000 in cash and gold coins worth $80,000. Shortly after the incident, Dr. T is audited by the IRS. Could there be any causal connection between the burglary and the audit? Explain.

27. What is meant by revenue neutral tax reform?

28. In what manner does the tax law encourage technological progress?

29. What purpose is served by provisions in the tax law that encourage private sector pension plans?

30. Discuss the probable justification for the following provisions of the tax law:
    a. The election permitted certain corporations to avoid the corporate income tax.
    b. A provision that excludes from income certain benefits furnished to employees through accident and health plans financed by employers.
    c. Nontaxable treatment for an employee as to premiums paid by an employer for group term insurance covering the life of the employee.
    d. The tax treatment to the employee of contributions made by an employer to qualified pension or profit sharing plans.
    e. The deduction allowed for contributions to qualified charitable organizations.

31. What purpose is served by the credit allowed for certain child or disabled dependent care expenses?

32. What purpose is served by allowing a deduction for home mortgage interest and property taxes?

33. T owns and operates a trucking firm. During the year, his employees incur a substantial number of fines for violating the highway speed limit. T considers these fines a necessary expense of running the business as he knows his firm cannot make a profit by observing the posted speed limit. Are these fines deductible for income tax purposes? Why or why not?

34. Give an example of how the community property system has affected the Federal tax law.

35. Forcing accrual basis taxpayers to recognize prepaid income when received (as opposed to when earned) accomplishes what objective?

36. Under current tax law, a donor generally can make a gift of up to $10,000 per year to a donee without having to file a Federal gift tax return and pay a Federal gift tax. How does this provision simplify the administrative responsibility of the IRS for enforcement of the tax laws?

37. T leases a building from L for 20 years. During the term of the lease, T makes significant capital improvements to the property that revert to L on the termination of the lease. Several years after the lease has terminated, L sells the building for a profit, a portion of which is attributable to the value of the improvements made by T.

    a. Should the improvements made by T be taxed to L?

    b. If so, when (at the time when made, on the termination of the lease, or on the sale of the property)?

2

TAX DETERMINATION; PERSONAL AND DEPENDENCY EXEMPTIONS; AN OVERVIEW OF PROPERTY TRANSACTIONS

OBJECTIVES   Explain how an individual's tax liability is determined.

Develop greater understanding of the standard deduction and other components of the tax formula for individuals.

Apply the rules for determining dependency exemptions and filing status.

Introduce the basic concepts of property transactions and their effect on taxable income.

Discuss several basic tax planning ideas for individual taxpayers.

Individuals are subject to Federal income tax based on taxable income. This chapter explains how taxable income and the income tax of an individual taxpayer are determined.

To compute taxable income, it is necessary to understand the tax formula in Figure 2–1. Although the tax formula is rather simple, determination of an individual's taxable income can be quite complex. This complexity stems from the numerous provisions that govern the determination of gross income and allowable deductions.

After computing taxable income, the appropriate rates must be applied. This requires a determination of the individual's filing status, since different rates apply for single taxpayers, married taxpayers, and heads of household. The basic tax rate structure is progressive, with a rate of 15 percent on taxable income up to specified amounts and 28 percent on additional taxable income.[1] In certain circumstances, a rate as high as 33 percent applies.

Once the individual's tax has been computed, prepayments and credits are subtracted to determine whether the taxpayer owes additional tax or is entitled to a refund.

When property is sold or otherwise disposed of, the result could affect the determination of taxable income. Although property transactions are covered in detail in chapters 12 and 13, an understanding of certain basic concepts is helpful in working with some of the materials to follow. The concluding portion of this chapter furnishes an overview of the area, including the distinction between realized and recognized gain or loss, the classification of such gain or loss (ordinary or capital), and treatment for income tax purposes.

TAX FORMULA

Most individuals compute taxable income using the tax formula shown in Figure 2–1. Special provisions govern the computation of taxable income and the tax liability for certain minor children who have unearned income in excess of specified

---

FIGURE 2–1 Tax Formula

Income (broadly conceived)	$xx,xxx
Less: Exclusions	(x,xxx)
Gross income	$xx,xxx
Less: Deductions *for* adjusted gross income	(x,xxx)
Adjusted gross income	$xx,xxx
Less: The greater of— Total itemized deductions *or* standard deduction	(x,xxx)
Personal and dependency exemptions	(x,xxx)
Taxable income	$xx,xxx

---

1. The 1990 Tax Table was not available from the IRS at the date of publication of this text. The Tax Table for 1989 and the Tax Rate Schedules for 1989 and 1990 are reproduced in Appendix A.

amounts. These provisions are discussed under Tax Determination—Unearned Income of Certain Minor Children Taxed at Parents' Rate later in the chapter.

Before illustrating the application of the tax formula, a brief discussion of the components of the formula is necessary.

Components of the Tax Formula

Income (Broadly Conceived).   This includes all income, both taxable and nontaxable, of the taxpayer. Although it is essentially equivalent to gross receipts, it does not include a return of capital or receipt of borrowed funds.

EXAMPLE 1   T needed money to purchase a house. He sold 5,000 shares of stock for $100,000. He had paid $40,000 for the stock. In addition, he borrowed $75,000 from a bank. T has taxable income of $60,000 from the sale of the stock ($100,000 selling price − $40,000 return of capital). He has no income from the $75,000 he borrowed from the bank because he has an obligation to repay that amount.   □

Exclusions.   For various reasons, Congress has chosen to exclude certain types of income from the income tax base. The principal income exclusions are discussed in chapter 4. A partial list of these exclusions is shown in Figure 2-2.

Gross Income.   Gross income is defined broadly in the Internal Revenue Code as "all income from whatever source derived."[2] It includes, but is not limited to, the items shown in the partial list in Figure 2-3. It does not include unrealized gains. Gross income is discussed in chapters 3 and 4.

FIGURE 2-2 Partial List of Exclusions from Gross Income

Accident insurance proceeds	Life insurance paid on death
Annuities (to a limited extent)	Meals and lodging (furnished for employer's convenience)
Bequests	
Child support payments	Military allowances
Cost-of-living allowance (for military)	Minister's dwelling rental value allowance
Damages for personal injury or sickness	Railroad retirement benefits (to a limited extent)
Death benefits (up to $5,000)	Scholarship grants (to a limited extent)
Disability benefits	Social Security benefits (to a limited extent)
Gifts	Veterans's benefits
Group term life insurance, premium paid by employer (coverage not over $50,000)	Welfare payments
Inheritances	Workers' compensation benefits

---

2. § 61(a).

FIGURE 2—3   Partial List of Gross Income Items

Alimony	Group term life insurance, premium paid by employer (coverage over $50,000)
Annuities	
Awards	Hobby income
Back pay	Interest
Bargain purchase from employer	Jury duty fees
Bonuses	Living quarters, meals (unless furnished for employer's convenience)
Breach of contract damages	
Business income	Mileage allowance
Clergy fees	Military pay (unless combat pay)
Commissions	Notary fees
Compensation for services	Partnership income
Death benefits in excess of $5,000	Pensions
Debts forgiven	Prizes
Director's fees	Professional fees
Dividends	Punitive damages
Embezzled funds	Reimbursement for moving expenses
Employee awards (in certain cases)	Rents
Employee benefits (except certain fringe benefits)	Rewards
Employee bonuses	Royalties
Estate and trust income	Salaries
Farm income	Severance pay
Fees	Strike and lockout benefits
Gains from illegal activities	Supplemental unemployment benefits
Gains from sale of property	Tips and gratuities
Gambling winnings	Travel allowance
	Wages

EXAMPLE 2   L received the following amounts in 1990:

Salary	$30,000
Interest on savings account	900
Gift from her aunt	10,000
Prize won in state lottery	1,000
Alimony from ex-husband	12,000
Child support from ex-husband	6,000
Damages for injury in auto accident	25,000

Review Figures 2−2 and 2−3 to determine the amount L must include in the computation of taxable income and the amount she may exclude. After you have determined these amounts, check the answer in footnote 3.[3] □

Deductions for Adjusted Gross Income.   Individual taxpayers have two categories of deductions: (1) deductions *for* adjusted gross income (deductions to arrive at adjusted gross income) and (2) deductions *from* adjusted gross income.

Deductions *for* adjusted gross income include ordinary and necessary expenses incurred in a trade or business, employee business expenses if such expenses are reimbursed by the employer, alimony paid, certain payments to an Individual Retirement Account, forfeited interest penalty for premature withdrawal of time deposits, the capital loss deduction, and others.[4] The principal deductions *for* adjusted gross income are discussed in chapters 5, 6, 7, 8, and 9.

Adjusted Gross Income.   This is an important subtotal that serves as the basis for computing percentage limitations on certain itemized deductions, such as medical expenses and charitable contributions. For example, medical expenses are deductible only to the extent they exceed 7.5 percent of adjusted gross income.

EXAMPLE 3   T earned a salary of $23,000 in 1990. He contributed $2,000 to his Individual Retirement Account (IRA) and sustained a $1,000 capital loss on the sale of XYZ Corporation stock. His adjusted gross income (AGI) is computed as follows:

Gross income		
Salary		$23,000
Less: Deductions *for* AGI		
IRA contribution	$2,000	
Capital loss	1,000	3,000
AGI		$20,000

□

EXAMPLE 4   Assume the same facts as in Example 3, except that T also had medical expenses of $1,800 in 1990. Medical expenses may be included in itemized deductions to the extent they exceed 7.5% of AGI. In computing his itemized deductions, T may include medical expenses of $300 [$1,800 medical expenses − $1,500 (7.5% × $20,000 AGI)]. □

Itemized Deductions.   As a general rule, personal expenditures are disallowed as deductions in arriving at taxable income. However, Congress has chosen to allow

---

3. L must include $43,900 in computing taxable income ($30,000 salary + $900 interest + $1,000 lottery prize + $12,000 alimony). She can exclude $41,000 ($10,000 gift from aunt + $6,000 child support + $25,000 damages).

4. § 62. See chapter 5 for details.

certain specified expenses as itemized deductions, Personal expenditures allowed as itemized deductions include medical expenses, certain taxes and interest, and charitable contributions.

In addition to the personal expenses discussed above, taxpayers are allowed itemized deductions for expenses related to (1) the production or collection of income and (2) the management of property held for the production of income.[5] These expenses, sometimes referred to as *nonbusiness expenses*, differ from trade or business expenses (discussed previously). Trade or business expenses, which are deductions *for* AGI, must be incurred in connection with a trade or business. Nonbusiness expenses, on the other hand, are expenses incurred in connection with an income-producing activity that does not qualify as a trade or business. Such expenses are itemized deductions.

EXAMPLE 5   H is the owner and operator of a video game arcade. All allowable expenses he incurs in connection with the arcade business are deductions *for* AGI. In addition, H has an extensive portfolio of stocks and bonds. H's investment activity is not treated as a trade or business. All allowable expenses that H incurs in connection with these investments are itemized deductions.   □

Itemized deductions include, but are not limited to, the expenses listed in Figure 2–4. See chapter 10 for a detailed discussion of itemized deductions.

Standard Deduction.   The standard deduction is a specified amount set by Congress and is dependent on the filing status of the taxpayer. The effect of the

---

FIGURE 2–4   Partial List of Itemized Deductions

Medical expenses in excess of 7.5% of AGI

State and local income taxes

Real estate taxes

Personal property taxes

Interest on home mortgage

Investment interest (to a limited extent)

Charitable contributions

Casualty and theft losses in excess of 10% of AGI

Moving expenses

Miscellaneous expenses (to the extent such expenses exceed 2% of AGI)

   Union dues

   Professional dues and subscriptions

   Certain educational expenses

   Tax return preparation fee

   Investment counsel fees

   Unreimbursed employee business expenses (after 20% reduction for meals and entertainment)

---

5.   § 212.

standard deduction is to exempt a taxpayer's income, up to the specified amount, from Federal income tax liability. In the past, Congress has attempted to set the tax-free amount represented by the standard deduction approximately equal to an estimated poverty level,[6] but it has not always been consistent in doing so.

The standard deduction is the sum of two components: the basic standard deduction and the additional standard deduction.[7] Figure 2—5 lists the basic standard deduction allowed for taxpayers in each filing status. All taxpayers who are allowed a *full* standard deduction will be entitled to the applicable amount listed in Figure 2—5. The standard deduction amounts are subject to adjustment for inflation each year.

Certain taxpayers are not allowed to claim *any* standard deduction, and the standard deduction is *limited* for others. These provisions are discussed later in the chapter.

A taxpayer who is age 65 or over *or* blind qualifies for an additional standard deduction. Two additional standard deductions are allowed for a taxpayer who is age 65 or over *and* blind. The additional standard deduction provisions also apply to a qualifying spouse who is age 65 or over or blind, but not to dependents. The additional standard deduction amounts are listed in Figure 2—6.

The total standard deduction (the sum of the basic standard deduction and any additional standard deductions) is compared to total itemized deductions to determine whether the taxpayer will itemize. Taxpayers are allowed to deduct the greater of itemized deductions or the standard deduction. Taxpayers whose itemized deductions are less than the standard deduction will compute their taxable income using the standard deduction rather than itemizing.

EXAMPLE 6   T, who is single, is 66 years old. She had total itemized deductions of $3,600 during 1990. Her total standard deduction is $4,050 ($3,250 basic standard deduction plus $800 additional standard deduction). T will compute her taxable income for 1990 using the standard deduction ($4,050), since it exceeds her itemized deductions ($3,600). □

FIGURE 2—5   Basic Standard Deduction Amounts

Filing Status	Standard Deduction Amount	
	1989	1990
Single	$3,100	$3,250
Married, filing jointly	5,200	5,450
Surviving spouse	5,200	5,450
Head of household	4,550	4,750
Married, filing separately	2,600	2,725

6. S.Rep. No. 92—437, 92nd Cong., 1st Sess., 1971, p. 54. Another purpose of the standard deduction was discussed in chapter 1 under Influence of the Internal Revenue Service—Administrative Feasibility. The size of the standard deduction has a direct bearing on the number of taxpayers who are in a position to itemize deductions. A reduction of such taxpayers, in turn, requires less audit effort on the part of the IRS.

7. § 63(c)(1).

FIGURE 2–6   Amount of Each Additional Standard Deduction

Filing Status	1989	1990
Single	$750	$800
Married, filing jointly	600	650
Surviving spouse	600	650
Head of household	750	800
Married, filing separately	600	650

Exemptions.   Exemptions are allowed for the taxpayer, the taxpayer's spouse (generally), and for each dependent of the taxpayer. The exemption amount is $2,000 in 1989 and $2,050 in 1990.

Application of the Tax Formula

The tax formula shown in Figure 2–1 is illustrated in Example 7.

EXAMPLE 7   J, age 25, is single and has no dependents. She is a high school teacher and earned a $20,000 salary in 1990. Her other income consisted of a $1,000 prize won in a sweepstakes contest she had entered and $500 interest on municipal bonds received as a graduation gift in 1987. During 1990, she sustained a deductible capital loss of $1,000. Her itemized deductions were $3,800. J's taxable income for the year is computed as follows:

Income (broadly conceived)		
Salary		$20,000
Prize		1,000
Interest on municipal bonds		500
		$21,500
Less: Exclusion—		
Interest on municipal bonds		(500)
Gross income		$21,000
Less: Deduction *for* adjusted gross income—		
Capital loss		(1,000)
Adjusted gross income		$20,000
Less: The greater of—		
Total itemized deductions	$3,800	
or standard deduction	$3,250	(3,800)
Personal and dependency exemptions		
(1 × $2,050)		(2,050)
Taxable income		$14,150

The structure of the individual income tax return (Form 1040, 1040A, or 1040EZ) differs somewhat from the tax formula in Figure 2–1. On the tax return, gross income generally is the starting point in computing taxable income. With few exceptions, exclusions are not reported on the tax return.

Individuals Not Eligible for the Standard Deduction

The following individual taxpayers are ineligible to use the standard deduction and must therefore itemize:[8]

- A married individual filing a separate return where either spouse itemizes deductions.

- A nonresident alien.

- An individual making a return for a period of less than 12 months because of a change in annual accounting period.

Special Limitations for Individuals Who Can Be Claimed as Dependents

Special rules apply to the standard deduction and personal exemption of an individual who can be claimed as a dependent on another person's tax return.

A dependent's basic standard deduction is limited to the greater of $500 or the individual's earned income for the year.[9] However, if the individual's earned income exceeds the normal standard deduction, the standard deduction is limited to the appropriate standard deduction amount shown in Figure 2–5. These limitations apply only to the basic standard deduction. A dependent who is 65 or over or blind or both is also allowed the additional standard deduction amount on his or her own return (refer to Figure 2–6). These provisions are illustrated in Examples 8 through 14.

EXAMPLE 8   M, who is 17 years old and single, is claimed as a dependent on her parents' tax return. During 1990, she received $1,000 interest (unearned income) on a savings account. She also earned $400 from a part-time job. When M files her own tax return, her standard deduction is $500 (the greater of $500 or earned income of $400). ☐

EXAMPLE 9   Assume the same facts as in Example 8, except that M is 67 years old and is claimed as a dependent on her son's tax return. In this case when M files her own tax return, her standard deduction is $1,300 [$500 (the greater of $500 or earned income of $400) + $800 (the additional standard deduction allowed because M is 65 or over)]. ☐

EXAMPLE 10   K, who is 18 years old and single, is claimed as a dependent on his parents' tax return. During 1990, he received interest (unearned income) of $1,400 on a savings account. Since he did not work during 1990, he had no earned income. K's standard deduction is $500 (the greater of $500 or earned income). ☐

EXAMPLE 11   Assume the same facts as in Example 10, except that K is blind. On his own tax return, K's standard deduction is $1,300 [$500 (the greater of $500 or earned income) + $800 (the additional standard deduction allowed because K is blind)]. ☐

---

8. § 63(c)(6).
9. § 63(c)(5). Although the $500 amount is subject to adjustment for inflation each year, the amount was not adjusted for 1990 because of the "rounding down" provisions of § 1(f)(6).

EXAMPLE 12   P, who is 16 years old and single, earned $1,000 from a summer job and had no unearned income during 1990. She is claimed as a dependent on her parents' tax return. Her standard deduction for 1990 is $1,000 (the greater of $500 or earned income). □

EXAMPLE 13   J, who is a 20-year-old, single, full-time college student, is claimed as a dependent on his parents' tax return. During 1990, he received interest (unearned income) of $1,000 on a savings account. He worked during the summer as a musician, earning $3,600. J's standard deduction is $3,250 (the greater of $500 or $3,600 earned income, but limited to the $3,250 standard deduction for a single taxpayer). □

EXAMPLE 14   Assume the same facts as in Example 13, except that J is blind. On his own tax return, J's standard deduction is $4,050 [$3,250 (the greater of $500 or $3,600 earned income, but limited to the $3,250 standard deduction for a single taxpayer) + $800 (the additional standard deduction allowed because J is blind)]. □

The taxpayer who claims an individual as a dependent is allowed to claim an exemption for the dependent. The dependent cannot claim a personal exemption on his or her own return.

PERSONAL AND DEPENDENCY EXEMPTIONS

The use of exemptions in the tax system is based in part on the concept that a taxpayer with a small amount of income should be exempt from income taxation. An exemption frees a specified amount of income from tax ($2,000 in 1989 and $2,050 in 1990). For years after 1989, the exemption amount is to be indexed (adjusted) annually for inflation. An individual who is not claimed as a dependent by another taxpayer is allowed to claim his or her own personal exemption. In addition, a taxpayer may claim an exemption for each dependent.

EXAMPLE 15   B, who is single, supports her mother and father, who have no income of their own, and claims them as dependents on her tax return. B may claim a personal exemption for herself plus an exemption for each dependent. On her 1990 tax return, B may deduct $6,150 for exemptions ($2,050 per exemption × 3 exemptions). □

Personal Exemptions

The Code provides a personal exemption for the taxpayer and an additional exemption for the spouse if a joint return is filed. However, when separate returns are filed, a married taxpayer cannot claim an exemption for his or her spouse unless the spouse has no gross income and is not claimed as the dependent of another taxpayer.

The determination of marital status generally is made at the end of the taxable year, except when a spouse dies during the year. Spouses who enter into a legal separation under a decree of divorce or separate maintenance before the end of the

year are considered to be unmarried at the end of the taxable year. The effect of death or divorce upon marital status is illustrated as follows:

	Marital Status for 1990
1. W is the widow of H who dies on January 3, 1990.	W and H are considered to be married for purposes of filing the 1990 return.
2. W and H entered into a divorce decree that is effective on December 31, 1990.	W and H are considered to be unmarried for purposes of filing the 1990 return.

Dependency Exemptions

As indicated in Example 15, the Code allows a taxpayer to claim a dependency exemption for each eligible individual. A dependency exemption may be claimed for each individual for whom the following five tests are met:

- Support.
- Relationship or member of the household.
- Gross income.
- Joint return.
- Citizenship or residency.

Support Test.   Over one-half of the support of the individual must be furnished by the taxpayer. Support includes food, shelter, clothing, medical and dental care, education, etc. However, a scholarship received by a student is not included for purposes of computing whether the taxpayer furnished more than one-half of the child's support.[10]

EXAMPLE 16   H contributed $2,500 (consisting of food, clothing, and medical care) toward the support of his son, S, who earned $1,500 from a part-time job and received a $2,000 scholarship to attend a local university. Assuming that the other dependency tests are met, H may claim S as a dependent since he has contributed more than one-half of S's support. The $2,000 scholarship is not included as support for purposes of this test. □

If the individual does not spend funds that have been received from any source, such unexpended amounts are not counted for purposes of the support test. For example, Social Security benefits received by the individual are not considered in applying the support test if such amounts are not spent on items considered *support*.

EXAMPLE 17   S contributed $2,000 toward his father's support during the year. His father received $1,800 in Social Security benefits and $300 of dividend income. All of these amounts were used for his support during the year. Since the Social

10.   Reg. § 1.152–1(c).

Security payments expended for support are considered in the determination of whether the support test has been met, S cannot claim his father as a dependent because he has not contributed more than one-half of the total support. □

EXAMPLE 18   S contributed $3,000 toward her father's support during the year. In addition, her father received $2,400 in Social Security benefits, $200 of interest, and wages of $600. The Social Security benefits, interest, and wages were deposited in the father's savings account and were not used for his support. Thus, the Social Security benefits, interest, and wages are not considered as support provided by S's father, and S may claim her father as a dependent if the other tests are met. □

Capital expenditures for items such as furniture, appliances, and automobiles are included in total support if the item does, in fact, constitute support.[11]

EXAMPLE 19   F purchased a television set costing $150 and gave it to his minor daughter. The television set was placed in the child's bedroom and was used exclusively by her. F should include the cost of the television set in determining the support of his daughter. □

EXAMPLE 20   F paid $6,000 for an automobile that was titled and registered in his name. F's minor son is permitted to use the automobile equally with F. Since F did not give the automobile to his son, the $6,000 cost is not includible as a support item. However, the out-of-pocket operating expenses for the benefit of the child are includible as support. □

One exception to the support test is based on the existence of a *multiple support agreement*. A multiple support agreement permits one of a group of taxpayers who furnish more than one-half of the support of an individual to claim a dependency exemption for that individual even if no one person provides more than 50 percent of the support.[12] Any person who contributed more than 10 percent of the support is entitled to claim the exemption if each person in the group who contributed more than 10 percent files a written consent. This provision frequently enables one of the children of aged dependent parents to claim an exemption when none of the children meets the 50 percent support test. Each person who is a party to the multiple support agreement must meet all other requirements (except the support requirement) for claiming the exemption. A person who does not meet the relationship or member of household requirement, for instance, cannot claim the dependency exemption under a multiple support agreement, even though he or she contributes more than 10 percent of the individual's support.

EXAMPLE 21   M, who resides with her son, received $6,000 from various sources during 1990. This constituted her entire support for the year. The support was received from the following:

---

11. Rev.Rul. 57–344, 1957–2 C.B. 112; Rev.Rul.   12. § 152(c).
     58–419, 1958–2 C.B. 57.

	Amount	Percentage of Total
A, a son	$2,880	48
B, a son	600	10
C, a daughter	1,800	30
D, a friend	720	12
	$6,000	100

If they file a multiple support agreement, either A or C may claim the dependency exemption for M. B may not claim M because he did not contribute more than 10% of her support, nor would B's consent be required in order for A and C to file a multiple support agreement. D does not meet the relationship or member of household test and therefore cannot be a party to the multiple support agreement. The decision as to who claims M will rest with A and C. It is possible for C to claim M, even though A furnished more of M's support. ☐

A second exception to the 50 percent support requirement can occur for a child of parents who are divorced or separated under a decree of separate maintenance. Under decrees executed after 1984, the custodial parent is allowed to claim the exemption unless that parent agrees in writing not to claim a dependency exemption for the child.[13] Thus, claiming the exemption is dependent on whether or not a written agreement exists, not on meeting the support test.

EXAMPLE 22   H and W obtain a divorce decree in 1989. In 1990, their two children are in the custody of W. H contributed over half of the support for each child. Absent any written agreement relative to the dependency exemptions, W (the custodial parent) is entitled to the exemptions in 1990. However, H may claim the exemptions if W agrees in writing that he may do so. ☐

For the noncustodial parent to claim the exemption, the custodial parent must complete Form 8332 (Release of Claim to Exemption for Child of Divorced or Separated Parents). The release can apply to a single year, a number of specified years, or all future years. The noncustodial parent must attach a copy of Form 8332 to his or her return. Form 8332 is not required, however, if there is a pre-1985 agreement that allows the noncustodial parent to claim the exemption and the noncustodial parent provides at least $600 of support for each child.

Relationship or Member of the Household Test.   To be a dependent, the individual must be either a relative of the taxpayer or a member of the taxpayer's household. The Code contains a detailed listing of the various blood and marriage relationships that qualify. Note, however, that the relationship test is met if the individual is a relative of either spouse and a relationship, once established by marriage, continues regardless of subsequent changes in marital status.

---

13. § 152(e).

The following individuals may be claimed as dependents of the taxpayer if the other tests for dependency are met:[14]

1. A son or daughter of the taxpayer, or a descendant of either (grandchild).

2. A stepson or stepdaughter of the taxpayer.

3. A brother, sister, stepbrother, or stepsister of the taxpayer.

4. The father or mother of the taxpayer, or an ancestor of either (grandparent).

5. A stepfather or stepmother of the taxpayer.

6. A son or daughter of a brother or sister (nephew or niece) of the taxpayer.

7. A brother or sister of the father or mother (uncle or aunt) of the taxpayer.

8. A son-in-law, daughter-in-law, father-in-law, mother-in-law, brother-in-law, or sister-in-law of the taxpayer.

9. An individual (other than an individual who at any time during the entire taxable year was the spouse of the taxpayer) who, for the entire taxable year of the taxpayer, has as his or her principal place of abode the home of the taxpayer and is a member of the taxpayer's household.

The following rules are also prescribed in the Code:[15]

-   A legally adopted child is treated as a natural child.

-   A foster child qualifies if the child has his or her principal place of abode in the taxpayer's household.

Gross Income Test.   The dependent's gross income must be less than the exemption amount ($2,050 in 1990) unless the dependent is a child of the taxpayer and is under 19 or a full-time student under the age of 24.[16] A parent who provides over half of the support of a child who, at the end of the year, is under 19 or is a full-time student under 24 may claim a dependency exemption for such child. However, the dependent child may not claim a personal exemption on his or her own income tax return if claimed by the parents.

A child is defined as a son, stepson, daughter, stepdaughter, adopted son, or adopted daughter and may include a foster child.[17] For the child to qualify as a student for purposes of the dependency exemption, he or she must be a full-time student at an educational institution during some part of five calendar months of the year.[18] This exception to the gross income test for dependent children who are under 19 or full-time students under 24 permits a child or college student to earn money from part-time or summer jobs without penalizing the parent with the loss of the dependency exemption.

Joint Return Test.   If a dependent is married, the supporting taxpayer (e.g., the parent of a married child) is not permitted a dependency exemption if the married

---

14. § 152(a). However, under § 152(b)(5), a taxpayer may not claim someone who is a member of his or her household as a dependent if their relationship is in violation of local law. For example, the dependency exemption was denied because the taxpayer's relationship to the person claimed as a dependent constituted *cohabitation*, a crime under applicable state law. *Cassius L. Peacock, III*, 37 TCM 177, T.C. Memo. 1978–30.

15. § 152(b)(2).

16. § 151(c)(1).

17. Reg. § 1.151–3(a).

18. Reg. §§ 1.151–3(b) and (c).

individual files a joint return with his or her spouse.[19] However, if neither the dependent nor the dependent's spouse is required to file a return but they file a joint return solely to claim a refund of all tax withheld and no tax liability would exist for either spouse on separate returns, the join return rule does not apply. See Figure 2-9 and the related discussion concerning income level requirements for filing a return.

EXAMPLE 23   P provides over half of the support of his son J. He also provides over half of the support of M, who is J's wife. In 1990, J had wages of $1,500, and M earned $1,800. J and M file a joint return for the year. Neither J nor M was required to file a return because each had income below the level required for filing. P is allowed to claim both as dependents.   □

Citizenship or Residency Test.   To be a dependent, the individual must be either a U.S. citizen, resident, or national or a resident of Canada or Mexico for some part of the calendar year in which the tax year of the taxpayer claiming the exemption begins.

TAX DETERMINATION

Tax Table Method

Most taxpayers compute their tax using the Tax Table. Taxpayers who are eligible to use the Tax Table compute taxable income (as shown in Figure 2-1) and determine their tax by reference to the Tax Table. The following taxpayers, however, may not use this method:

- An individual who files a short period return (see chapter 15).
- Individuals whose taxable income exceeds the maximum (ceiling) amount in the Tax Table. The 1989 Tax Table applies to taxable income below $50,000.
- An estate or trust.

The 1990 Tax Table was not available at the date of publication of this text. Therefore, the 1989 Tax Table will be used to illustrate the tax computation using the Tax Table method.

EXAMPLE 24   B, a single taxpayer, is eligible to use the Tax Table. For 1989, B had taxable income of $25,025. To determine B's tax using the Tax Table (see Appendix A), find the $25,000 to $25,050 income line. The first column to the right of the taxable income column is for single taxpayers. B's tax for 1989 is $4,596.   □

Tax Rate Schedule Method

There are only two brackets for each filing status (15 percent and 28 percent). The 28 percent rate applies to taxable income above the following levels:

---

19. § 151(c)(2).

Filing Status	28% Rate Applies to Taxable Income Over
Single	$19,450
Head of household	26,050
Married, filing jointly	32,450
Married, filing separately	16,225

The 15 percent rate applies to taxable income less than or equal to these amounts. The 1990 Tax Rate Schedules are reproduced in Appendix A.

Use of the 1990 Tax Rate Schedule for a married couple filing jointly is illustrated in the following example.

EXAMPLE 25   B and D, who are married, file a joint return for 1990. They had taxable income of $37,450. Their tax is computed as follows:

Tax on $32,450 at 15%	$4,867.50
28% tax on $5,000 ($37,450 − $32,450)	1,400.00
Total tax liability	$6,267.50

The *marginal rate* (the highest rate applied in computing the tax) for B and D is 28%. Their *average rate* (the tax liability divided by taxable income) is 16.74% ($6,267.50 ÷ $37,450). □

The basic rate structure, as shown in the 1990 Tax Rate Schedule (reproduced inside the front cover of this text), applies rates of 15, 28, and 33 percent. The 15 percent rate applies to taxable income up to a specified amount, then the 28 percent rate applies (as illustrated in Example 25). A 33 percent rate applies to a limited range of income, then the rate drops back to 28 percent. Computation of the income tax for single taxpayers using Tax Rate Schedule X is illustrated in Examples 26 through 30.

EXAMPLE 26   T, who is single, had taxable income of $19,450. The 15% rate applies to all of T's taxable income, and the tax is $2,917.50 ($19,450 × 15%). T's marginal rate (the highest rate applied in computing the tax) is 15%, and the average rate is 15% ($2,917.50 tax liability divided by $19,450 taxable income). □

Note in Example 26 that the tax on $19,450 (the maximum amount subject to the 15 percent rate) is $2,917.50. Example 27 illustrates the graduated rate structure of the Tax Rate Schedules; that is, the 28 percent rate applies to taxable income above $19,450.

EXAMPLE 27   V, who is single, had taxable income of $29,450. V's tax liability is computed as follows:

Tax on $19,450 at 15%	$2,917.50
Tax on ($29,450 − $19,450) at 28%	2,800.00
Total tax	$5,717.50

V's marginal rate is 28%, and the average rate is 19.41% ($5,717.50 tax liability divided by $29,450 taxable income). ☐

Bracket Phase-Out.   As illustrated in Examples 26 and 27, the basic rate structure consists of two rates, 15 percent and 28 percent. However, Congress has chosen to deny the benefit of using the 15 percent rate to taxpayers whose taxable income exceeds specified levels. The Tax Rate Schedules are designed to phase out the benefit of using the 15 percent rate. When taxable income exceeds specified levels, a marginal rate of 33 percent is used to phase out the savings from using the 15 percent rate. The 33 percent rate used in the *bracket phase-out* computation can be thought of as the regular 28 percent rate plus a 5 percent *surtax*. The additional 5 percent is applied to income within the third bracket (see Figure 2–7) in order to recapture part or all of the tax savings from applying the 15 percent rate to income in the first bracket.

EXAMPLE 28   G, who is single, had taxable income of $67,050. G's tax liability is computed as follows:

Tax on $19,450 at 15%	$ 2,917.50
Tax on ($47,050 − $19,450) at 28%	$ 7,728.00
Tax on ($67,050 − $47,050) at 33%	6,600.00
Total tax	$17,245.50

G's marginal rate is 33% and the average rate is 25.72% ($17,245.50 tax liability divided by $67,050 taxable income). ☐

The maximum savings that a single taxpayer could derive from using the 15 percent rate is 13 percent (28 percent − 15 percent) of the first $19,450 of taxable income, or $2,528.50. In order to fully phase out a single taxpayer's savings from using the 15 percent bracket, the additional 5 percent surtax must be applied to $50,570 (5% of $50,570 = $2,528.50). Examination of Rate Schedule X shows that the 33 percent rate applies to $50,570 ($97,620 − $47,050). The full bracket phase-out is illustrated in Example 29.

FIGURE 2–7   1990 Phase-Out Ranges for 15% Bracket

	Filing Status			
	Single	Head of Household	Married, Joint*	Married, Separate
5% of taxable income from–to	$47,050– 97,620	$ 67,200– 134,930	$ 78,400– 162,770	$ 39,200– 123,570

* Also applies to surviving spouse.

EXAMPLE 29   K had taxable income of $97,620, which places her at the top of the phase-out range for single taxpayers. Her tax is computed as follows:

Tax on $19,450 at 15%	$ 2,917.50
Tax on ($47,050 − $19,450) at 28%	$ 7,728.00
Tax on ($97,620 − $47,050) at 33%	16,688.10
Total tax	$27,333.60

K's marginal rate is 33% and the average rate is 28% ($27,333.60 tax liability divided by $97,620 taxable income). This 28% average rate on all taxable income illustrates the complete phase-out of the savings from the use of the 15% rate. □

Exemption Phase-Out.   An additional layer of complexity arises once the bracket phase-out has been accomplished. Taxpayers whose taxable income exceeds the top of the phase-out range (the top of the third bracket) are subject to an exemption phase-out computation.

The exemption phase-out is similar in concept to the bracket phase-out. That is, an additional 5 percent rate is applied in order to recapture the tax savings resulting from the deduction for exemptions. The exemption phase-out only applies *after* the bracket phase-out has been completed.

A taxpayer who has completed the bracket phase-out in 1990 has saved $574 for each exemption (28% of $2,050). To fully recapture this savings, the additonal 5 percent rate must be applied to $11,480 ($11,480 × 5% = $574).

EXAMPLE 30   M, who is single with no dependents, had taxable income of $109,100. The tax on the first $97,620 can be computed as follows:

Tax on $19,450 at 15%	$ 2,917.50
Tax on ($47,050 − $19,450) at 28%	$ 7,728.00
Tax on ($97,620 − $47,050) at 33%	16,688.10
Tax on first $97,620	$27,333.60

In addition to the $27,333.60 tax on $97,620 computed above, it is necessary to compute tax on $11,480 ($109,100 taxable income − $97,620) at a 33% rate. This results in additional tax of $3,788.40, for total tax of $31,122. Analysis of the total tax of $31,122 shows that all $109,100 has been taxed at the 28% rate, and the additional 5% rate has been applied to $11,480.

$109,100 × 28%	$30,548
$11,480 × 5%	574
Total tax	$31,122

M's marginal rate is 33% and the average rate is 28.53% ($31,122 tax divided by $109,100 taxable income). The bracket and exemption benefits have been phased out completely. If M had any income in excess of $109,100, that excess would be taxed at the 28% rate. □

If M in Example 30 had taxable income of $103,620, the additional 5 percent rate would apply to $6,000 ($103,620 − $97,620), and only part of the savings from the exemption deduction would be recaptured. On the other hand, if M had taxable income in excess of $109,100, the additional 5 percent rate would apply only to $11,480 because that is all that is necessary to recapture the $574 savings from the exemption deduction, as illustrated in Example 30.

The exemption phase-out is so complex that the IRS provides a worksheet to be used in the computation. A filled-in worksheet for 1989 is reproduced in Figure 2-8 (the 1990 worksheet was not available at the date of publication of this text). The computations reflected on the worksheet are for a single taxpayer with taxable income of $110,000.

In the case of married taxpayers filing separate returns, the additional tax liability because of the exemption phase-out is determined as if the taxpayer were allowed a personal exemption for his or her spouse.[20] This prevents married taxpayers from avoiding the full effect of the phase-out of personal exemptions by filing separate returns.

Computation of Net Taxes Payable or Refund Due

The pay-as-you-go feature of the Federal income tax system requires payment of all or part of the taxpayer's income tax liability during the year. These payments take the form of Federal income tax withheld by employers or estimated tax paid by the taxpayer or both. These amounts are applied against the tax from the Tax Table or Tax Rate Schedules to determine whether the taxpayer will get a refund or pay additional tax.

Employers are required to withhold income tax on compensation paid to their employees and to pay this tax over to the government. The employer notifies the

FIGURE 2-8 Exemption Phase-Out Worksheet

1. If your filing status is: Single, enter $26,076.40 / Head of household, enter $36,066.80 / Married filing jointly or Qualifying widow(er), enter $43,489.60 / Married filing separately, enter $35,022.35	**1.** 26,076.40
2. Enter your taxable income from line 5 of the Form 1040-ES worksheet	**2.** 110,000.00
3. If your filing status is: Single, enter $93,130 / Head of household, enter $128,810 / Married filing jointly or Qualifying widow(er), enter $155,320 / Married filing separately, enter $117,895	**3.** 93,130.00
4. Subtract line 3 from line 2. Enter the result. (If the result is zero or less, use the schedule above for your filing status to figure your tax. DON'T use this worksheet.)	**4.** 16,870.00
5. Multiply the amount on line 4 by 28% (.28). Enter the result	**5.** 4,723.60
6. Multiply the amount on line 4 by 5% (.05). Enter the result	**6.** 843.50
7. Multiply $560 by the number of exemptions claimed. (If married filing separately, see Note below.) Enter the result	**7.** 560.00
8. Compare the amounts on lines 6 and 7. Enter the **smaller** of the two amounts	**8.** 560.00
9. **Tax.** Add lines 1, 5, and 8. Enter the total here and on line 6 of the Form 1040-ES worksheet	**9.** 31,360.00

Note: *If married filing separately and you did not claim an exemption for your spouse, multiply $560 by the number of exemptions claimed. Add $560 to the result and enter the total on line 7 above.*

20. § 1(g).

employee of the amount of income tax withheld on Form W–2 (Wage and Tax Statement). The employee should receive this form by January 31 after the year in which the income tax is withheld.

Estimated tax must be paid by taxpayers who receive income that is not subject to withholding or income from which not enough tax is being withheld. These individuals must file Form 1040–ES (Estimated Tax for Individuals) and pay in quarterly installments the income tax and self-employment tax estimated to be due (see chapter 12 for a thorough discussion).

The income tax from the Tax Table or the Tax Rate Schedules is reduced first by the individual's tax credits. There is an important distinction between tax credits and tax deductions. Tax credits reduce the tax liability dollar-for-dollar. Tax deductions reduce taxable income on which the tax liability is based.

EXAMPLE 31

L is a taxpayer in the 28% tax bracket. As a result of incurring $1,000 in child care expenses (see chapter 11 for details), she is entitled to a $200 child care credit ($1,000 child care expenses × 20% credit rate). L also contributed $1,000 to the American Cancer Society and included this amount in her itemized deductions. The child care credit results in a $200 reduction of L's tax liability for the year. The contribution to the American Cancer Society reduces taxable income by $1,000 and results in a $280 reduction in L's tax liability ($1,000 reduction in taxable income × 28% tax rate). □

Tax credits are discussed in chapter 11. Several of the more common credits are as follows:

- Earned income credit.
- Credit for child and dependent care expenses.
- Credit for the elderly.
- Foreign tax credit.

Computation of an individual's net tax payable or refund due is illustrated in Examples 32 and 33.

EXAMPLE 32

Y, age 30, is a head of household taxpayer with two dependents. During 1990, Y had the following: taxable income, $30,000; income tax withheld, $3,950; estimated tax payments, $800; and credit for child care expenses, $200. Y's net tax payable is computed as follows:

Income tax (from 1990 Tax Rate Schedule, Appendix A)		$ 5,013.50
Less: Tax credits and prepayments—		
Credit for child care expenses	$ 200	
Income tax withheld	3,950	
Estimated tax payments	800	(4,950.00)
Net taxes payable or (refund due)		$ 63.50

□

EXAMPLE 33

EXAMPLE 33 Assume the same facts as in Example 32, except that income tax withheld was $4,150. Y's refund due is computed as follows:

Income tax		$ 5,013.50
Less: Tax credits and prepayments—		
Credit for child care expenses	$ 200	
Income tax withheld	4,150	
Estimated tax payments	800	(5,150.00)
Net taxes payable or (refund due)		$ (136.50)

☐

Unearned Income of Certain Minor Children Taxed at Parents' Rate

Before the Tax Reform Act (TRA) of 1986, a dependent child could claim an exemption on his or her own return even if claimed as a dependent by the parents.

EXAMPLE 34 In 1986, H and W established a savings account for their dependent child K, age 9. K, who had no other income, earned interest of $1,050 on the account during 1986. K's taxable income for 1986 was zero because the interest of $1,050 was offset by K's exemption of $1,080 (the exemption amount applicable to 1986). ☐

Example 34 illustrates the pre-1987 use of a child's exemption to shelter unearned income from taxation. For pre-1987 years, an additional tax motivation existed for shifting income from parents to children. Although a child's unearned income in excess of the exemption amount was subject to tax, it was subject to tax at the child's rate.

EXAMPLE 35 Assume the same facts as in Example 34, except that K's interest income for 1986 was $5,000. Assume further that K's parents were in the 50% tax bracket (the top rate applicable to 1986). K's tax on the interest would have been $495. Had his parents kept the funds in their account, their tax would have been $2,500 ($5,000 interest × 50% tax rate). The income shifting procedure would have resulted in tax savings for the family of $2,005 ($2,500 tax at parents' rate minus $495 tax at child's rate). ☐

To reduce the tax savings that can result from shifting income from parents to children, the net unearned income (commonly called investment income) of certain minor children is taxed as if it were the parents' income.[21] Unearned income includes such income as taxable interest, dividends, capital gains, rents, royalties, pension and annuity income, and income (other than earned income) received as the beneficiary of a trust. This provision, commonly referred to as the

---

21. § 1(i).

kiddie tax, applies to any child for any taxable year if the child has not reached age 14 by the close of the taxable year, has at least one living parent, and has unearned income of more than $1,000. The *kiddie tax* provision does not apply to a child 14 or older. However, the limitation on the use of the standard deduction and the unavailability of the personal exemption do apply to such child as long as the child is eligible to be claimed as a dependent by a parent.

The term *parent* is defined in the Senate Finance Committee Report as a parent or stepparent of the child. No statutory definition exists for the term.

Net Unearned Income.   Net unearned income of a dependent child is computed on the following page.

Unearned income
Less: $500
Less: The greater of
- $500 of the standard deduction *or*
- The amount of allowable itemized deductions directly connected with the production of the unearned income
Equals: Net unearned income

If net unearned income is zero (or negative), the child's tax is computed without using the parents' rate. If the amount of net unearned income (regardless of source) is positive, the net unearned income will be taxed at the parents' rate. The $500 amounts in the preceding formula are subject to adjustment for inflation each year (refer to footnote 9).

Election to Claim Certain Unearned Income on Parents' Return.   If all of the following requirements are met concerning a child under 14, the parents may elect to report the child's unearned income on the parents' own tax return. The child, then, is treated as having no gross income and is not required to file a tax return.

- Gross income is from interest and dividends only.
- Gross income is more than $500 and less than $5,000.
- No estimated tax has been paid in the name and Social Security number of the child.
- No amount of tax has been deducted and withheld under the backup withholding rules.

If any of the interest is from certain private activity bonds, that amount is a tax preference to the parents for purposes of the parents' alternative minimum tax (see chapter 14).

Tax Determination.   If a child under age 14 has net unearned income and the parental election either is not or cannot be made, the tax on the net unearned income (defined as "allocable parental tax") must be computed as though included in the parents' return and allocated to the child. Form 8615 (see Appendix B) is used to compute the tax. The steps required in this computation are illustrated in the following example.

EXAMPLE 36   H and W have a child, S (age 10). In 1990, S received $2,500 of interest and dividend income. Investment-related fees paid by S were $200. H and W had $69,450 of taxable income, not including their child's investment income. H and W do not make the parental election.

1.	**Determine S's net unearned income.**	
	Gross income	$ 2,500
	Less: $500	(500)
	Less: The greater of	
	• $500 or	
	• Investment expense	(500)
	Equals: Net unearned income	$ 1,500
2.	**Determine allocable parental tax.**	
	Parents' taxable income	$69,450
	Plus: S's net unearned income	1,500
	Equals: Revised taxable income	$70,950
	Tax (rounded)	$15,648
	Less: Tax on parents' taxable income	15,228
	Allocable parental tax	$ 420
3.	**Determine S's nonparental source tax.**	
	Adjusted gross income	$ 2,500
	Less: Standard deduction	(500)
	Less: Personal exemption	(–0–)
	Equals: Taxable income	$ 2,000
	Less: Net unearned income	(1,500)
	Nonparental source taxable income	$ 500
	Equals: Tax ($500 × .15 rate)	$ 75
4.	**Determine S's total tax liability.**	
	Nonparental source tax (step 3)	$ 75
	Allocated parental tax (step 2)	420
	Total tax	$ 495

□

EXAMPLE 37   Assume the same facts as in Example 36, except that the parents elect to claim on their own tax return the unearned income of S. The gross income in excess of $1,000 for S amounts to $1,500 ($2,500 − $1,000). The parents include this amount in gross income. Assume further that the parents taxable income increases from $69,450 to $70,950, resulting in a tax liability of $420 more than would result on the parents' taxable income alone. This amount is the same as that in Step 2 of Example 36. To their tax liability the parents must add for S the lesser of $75 or 15% of gross income between $500 and $1,000. Thus, they must include $75 [the smaller of $75 or 15% of $2,000 ($2,500 − $500)] for S. The following total tax for the family unit results:

	Without Election	With Election
H and W	$15,228	$15,723*
S	495	–0–
	$15,723	$ 15,723

* $15,648 + $75.

Although in this case there is no tax saving, the family enjoys the convenience of filing one tax return rather than two. □

Do not assume, though, that filing the parental election is wise in every case. Parents who have substantial itemized deductions based on adjusted gross income (see chapter 10) may find that total taxes for the family unit are increased by making the parental election. Calculations must be made both with the parental election and without the election to determine the appropriate choice.

Other Provisions.   If parents have more than one child subject to the tax on net unearned income, the tax for the children is computed as shown in Example 36 and then allocated to the children based on their relative amounts of income. For children of divorced parents, the taxable income of the custodial parent is used to determine the allocable parental tax, and this parent is the one who may elect to report the child's unearned income. For married individuals filing separate returns, the individual with the greater taxable income is the applicable parent.

FILING CONSIDERATIONS

Under the category of filing considerations, the following questions need to be resolved:

- Is the taxpayer required to file an income tax return?
- If so, which form should be used?
- When and how should the return be filed?
- In computing the tax liability, which column of the Tax Table or which Tax Rate Schedule should be used?

The first three of these questions are discussed under Filing Considerations—Filing Requirements. The last question is treated under Filing Considerations—Filing Status.

Filing Requirements

General Rules.   An individual must file a tax return if certain minimum amounts of gross income have been received. The general rule is that a tax return is required for every individual who has taxable income that equals or exceeds the sum of the exemption amount plus the applicable standard deduction.[22] For

---

22. The gross income amounts for determining whether a tax return must be filed will be adjusted for inflation each year.

FIGURE 2–9   Filing Levels

Filing Status	1989 Gross Income	1990 Gross Income
Under 65 and not blind	$ 5,100	$ 5,300
Under 65 and blind	5,100	5,300
65 or older	5,850	6,100
Married filing joint return		
Both spouses under 65 and neither blind	$ 9,200	$ 9,550
Both spouses under 65 and one or both spouses blind	9,200	9,550
One spouse 65 or older	9,800	10,200
Both spouses 65 or older	10,400	10,850
Married filing separate return		
All—whether 65 or older or blind	$ 2,000	$ 2,050
Head of household		
Under 65 and not blind	$ 6,550	$ 6,800
Under 65 and blind	6,550	6,800
65 or older	7,300	7,600
Qualifying widow(er)		
Under 65 and not blind	$ 7,200	$ 7,500
Under 65 and blind	7,200	7,500
65 or older	7,800	8,150

example, a single taxpayer under age 65 must file a tax return in 1990 if gross income equals or exceeds $5,300 ($2,050 exemption plus $3,250 standard deduction).

Figure 2–9 lists the income levels[23] that require tax returns under the general rule, and also lists amounts that require tax returns under certain special rules.

The additional standard deduction for being 65 or older is taken into consideration in determining the gross income filing requirements. For example, note in Figure 2–9 that the 1990 filing requirement for a single taxpayer 65 or older is $6,100 ($3,250 basic standard deduction + $800 additional standard deduction + $2,050 exemption). However, the additional standard deduction for blindness is not taken into account. The 1990 filing requirement for a single taxpayer under 65 and blind is $5,300 ($3,250 basic standard deduction + $2,050 exemption).

Filing Requirements for Dependents.   Computation of the gross income filing requirement for an individual who can be claimed as a dependent on another person's tax return is subject to more complex rules. Such an individual must file a return if he or she has any of the following:

• Earned income only and gross income that is more than the total standard deduction (including any additional standard deduction) that the individual is allowed for the year.

---

23.   § 6012(a)(1).

- Unearned income only and gross income of more than $500, plus any additional standard deduction that the individual is allowed for the year.

- Both earned income and unearned income and gross income of more than the larger of earned income (but limited to the applicable basic standard deduction) or $500, plus any additional standard deduction that the individual is allowed for the year.

Thus, the filing requirement for a dependent who has no unearned income is the total of the basic standard deduction plus *any* additional standard deduction, which includes the additional deduction for blindness. For example, the 1990 filing requirement for a single dependent who is under 65 and not blind is $3,250, the amount of the basic standard deduction for 1990. The filing requirement for a single dependent under 65 and blind is $4,050 ($3,250 basic standard deduction + $800 additional standard deduction).

A self-employed individual with net earnings from a business or profession of $400 or more must file a tax return regardless of the amount of gross income.

Even though an individual's gross income is below the filing level amounts and he or she does not therefore owe any tax, the individual will have to file a return to obtain a tax refund of amounts that have been withheld. A return is also necessary to obtain the benefits of the earned income credit allowed to taxpayers with little or no tax liability. Chapter 11 discusses the earned income credit.

Selecting the Proper Form.   The 1990 tax forms had not been released at the date of publication of this text. The following comments apply to 1989 forms. It is possible that some provisions will change with respect to the 1990 forms.

Individual taxpayers file a return on either Form 1040 (the long form), Form 1040A (the short form), or Form 1040EZ (see Appendix B). Form 1040A is a short form that is used by many taxpayers who have uncomplicated tax situations. In 1989, an individual was required to use Form 1040 (the most complex form) rather than Form 1040A for any of the following reasons:

- Taxable income was $50,000 or more.

- The taxpayer had income other than wages, salaries, tips, unemployment compensation, dividends, or interest.

- The taxpayer claimed credits other than credits for child or dependent care or the earned income credit.

- The taxpayer was required to use the Tax Rate Schedules.

- The taxpayer claimed any deductions other than the deduction for payments to an IRA.

Form 1040EZ is also a form for taxpayers with uncomplicated tax situations. In 1989, this form could be used by single taxpayers with no dependents who satisfied all of the following requirements:

- Was not 65 or over or blind.

- Had taxable income of less than $50,000.

- Had only wages, salaries, tips, and taxable scholarships and had interest income of $400 or less.

- Did not itemize deductions, claim any adjustments to income, or claim any tax credits.

Taxpayers who could not use Form 1040EZ used either Form 1040 or Form 1040A.

When and Where to File. Tax returns of individuals are due on or before the fifteenth day of the fourth month following the close of the tax year. For the calendar year taxpayer, therefore, the usual filing date is on or before April 15 of the following year.[24] When the due date falls on a Saturday, Sunday, or legal holiday, the last day for filing falls on the next business day. If the return is mailed to the proper address with sufficient postage and is postmarked on or before the due date, it is deemed to be timely filed.

If a taxpayer is unable to file his or her return by the specified due date, a four-month extension of time can be obtained by filing Form 4868 (Application for Automatic Extension of Time to File U.S. Individual Income Tax Return).[25] Further extensions may be granted by the IRS upon a showing by the taxpayer of good cause. For this purpose, Form 2688 (Application for Extension of Time to File U.S. Individual Income Tax Return) should be used. An extension of more than six months will not be granted if the taxpayer is in the United States.

Although obtaining an extension excuses a taxpayer from a penalty for failure to file, it does not insulate against the penalty for failure to pay.[26] If more tax is owed, the filing of Form 4868 should be accompanied by an additional remittance to cover the balance due.

The return should be sent or delivered to the Regional Service Center of the IRS for the area where the taxpayer lives.[27]

If it is necessary to file an amended return (e.g., because of a failure to report income or to claim a deduction or tax credit), Form 1040X is filed by individual taxpayers. The form is generally filed within three years of the filing date of the original return or within two years from the time the tax was paid, whichever is later.

Filing Status

The amount of tax will vary considerably depending on which Tax Rate Schedule is used. This is illustrated in the following example.

EXAMPLE 38 The following amounts of tax are computed using the 1990 Tax Rate Schedules for a taxpayer (or taxpayers in the case of a joint return) with $40,000 of taxable income (see Appendix A).

Filing Status	Amount of Tax (rounded)
Single	$8,672
Married, filing joint return	6,982
Married, filing separate return	9,131
Head of household	7,814

24. § 6072(a).
25. Reg. § 1.6081–4.
26. For an explanation of these penalties, refer to chapter 1.
27. The Regional Service Centers and the geographical area each covers can be found on the back cover of *Your Federal Income Tax*, IRS Publication 17 (for 1989).

Rates for Single Taxpayers.   A taxpayer who is unmarried or separated from his or her spouse by a decree of divorce or separate maintenance and does not qualify for another filing status must use the rates for single taxpayers. Marital status is determined as of the last day of the tax year, except when a spouse dies during the year. In such a case, marital status is determined as of the date of death. State law governs whether a taxpayer is considered married, divorced, or legally separated.

Under a special relief provision, however, it is possible for married persons who live apart to qualify as single. Married taxpayers who are considered single under the *abandoned spouse rules* are allowed to use the head of household rates. See the discussion of this filing status under Abandoned Spouse Rules.

Rates for Married Individuals.   The joint return [Tax Rate Schedule Y, Code § 1(a)] was originally enacted in 1948 to establish equity between married taxpayers in common law states and those in community property states. Before enactment of the joint return rates, taxpayers in community property states were in an advantageous position relative to taxpayers in common law states.

EXAMPLE 39   A and B are husband and wife. A earns a salary of $40,000. B is not employed. Before enactment of the joint return provisions, their income tax would vary significantly depending on whether they lived in a common law state or a community property state. If they lived in a common law state, A would report $40,000 of income on his tax return. However, if they lived in a community property state, A and B would each report $20,000 of income. Because the rate structure is progressive (the higher the income, the higher the tax rate), the tax paid by A and B would be higher in a common law state than in a community property state. □

Under the joint return Tax Rate Schedule, the progressive rates are constructed based on the assumption that income is earned equally by the two spouses.

If married individuals elect to file separate returns, each reports only his or her own income, exemptions, deductions, and credits, and each must use the Tax Rate Schedule applicable to married taxpayers filing separately. It is generally advantageous for married individuals to file a joint return since the combined amount of tax is lower. However, special circumstances (e.g., significant medical expenses incurred by one spouse subject to the 7.5 percent limitation) may warrant the election to file separate returns.

The Code places some limitations on deductions, credits, etc., when married individuals file separately. If either spouse itemizes deductions, the other spouse must also itemize. Married taxpayers who file separately cannot take either of the following:

• The credit for child and dependent care expenses (in most instances).

• The earned income credit.

The joint return rates also apply for two years following the death of one spouse, providing the surviving spouse maintains a household for a dependent child.[28] This filing status is commonly referred to as surviving spouse status.

---

28. § 2(a).

EXAMPLE 40   H dies in 1989 leaving W with a dependent child. For the year of H's death (1989), W files a joint return with H (presuming the consent of H's executor is obtained). For the next two years (1990 and 1991), W, as a surviving spouse, may use the joint return rates. In subsequent years, W may use the head-of-household rates if she maintains a household as her home that is the domicile of the child.   □

Rates for Heads of Household.   Unmarried individuals who maintain a household for a dependent (or dependents) are entitled to use the head-of-household rates.[29] The tax liability using the head-of-household rates falls between the liability using the joint return Tax Rate Schedule and the liability using the Tax Rate Schedule for single taxpayers.

To qualify for head-of-household rates, a taxpayer must pay more than half the cost of maintaining a household as his or her home. The household must also be the principal home of a dependent relative as defined in § 152(a).[30] As a general rule, the dependent must live in the taxpayer's household for over half the year.

The general rule has two exceptions. One exception is that an unmarried child (child also means grandchild, stepchild, or adopted child) need not be a dependent in order for the taxpayer to qualify as a head of household. This exception also applies to a married child if the child is claimed by the noncustodial parent as a result of a written agreement between the custodial parent and the noncustodial parent (refer to Example 22).

EXAMPLE 41   M maintains a household in which S, her nondependent unmarried son and she reside. Since S is not married, M qualifies for the head-of-household rates.   □

Another exception to the general rule is that head-of-household status may be claimed if the taxpayer maintains a separate home for his or her parent or parents if at least one parent qualifies as a dependent of the taxpayer.[31]

EXAMPLE 42   S, an unmarried individual, lives in New York City and maintains a household in Detroit for his dependent parents. S may use the favorable head-of-household rates even though his parents do not reside in his New York home.   □

Abandoned Spouse Rules.   When married persons file separate returns, several unfavorable tax consequences result. For example, the taxpayer must use the Tax Rate Schedule for married taxpayers filing separately. To mitigate such harsh treatment, Congress enacted provisions commonly referred to as the *abandoned spouse rules*. These rules allow a married taxpayer to file as a head of household if all of the following conditions are satisfied:

• The taxpayer does not file a joint return.

• The taxpayer paid more than one-half the cost of maintaining his or her home for the tax year.

---

29. § 2(b).
30. § 2(b)(1)(A)(i).

31. § 2(b)(1)(B).

- The taxpayer's spouse did not live in the home during the last six months of the tax year.

- The home was the principal residence of the taxpayer's child, stepchild, or adopted child for more than half the year.

- The taxpayer could claim the child, stepchild, or adopted child as a dependent.[32]

GAINS AND LOSSES FROM PROPERTY TRANSACTIONS—IN GENERAL

Gains and losses from property transactions are discussed in detail in chapters 12 and 13. Because of their importance in the tax system, however, they are introduced briefly at this point.

On the sale or other disposition of property, gain or loss may result. Such gain or loss has an effect on the income tax position of the party making the sale or other disposition when the *realized* gain or loss is *recognized* for tax purposes. Without realized gain or loss, generally, there can be no recognized gain or loss. The concept of realized gain or loss can be expressed as follows:

$$\text{Amount realized from the sale} - \text{Adjusted basis of the property} = \text{Realized gain (or loss)}$$

The amount realized is the selling price of the property less any costs of disposition (e.g., brokerage commissions) incurred by the seller. Simply stated, adjusted basis of the property is determined as follows:

Cost (or other original basis) at date of acquisition[33]

Add:	Capital additions
Subtract:	Depreciation (if appropriate) and other capital recoveries (see chapter 8)
Equals:	Adjusted basis at date of sale or other disposition

All realized gains are recognizable (taxable) unless some specific provision of the tax law provides otherwise (see chapter 12 dealing with certain nontaxable exchanges). Realized losses may or may not be recognizable (deductible) for tax purposes, depending on the circumstances involved. Generally, losses realized from the disposition of personal use property (property neither held for investment nor used in a trade or business) are not recognizable.

EXAMPLE 43   During the current year, T sells his sailboat (adjusted basis of $4,000) for $5,500. T also sells one of his personal automobiles (adjusted basis of $8,000) for $5,000. T's realized gain of $1,500 from the sale of the sailboat is recognizable. On the other hand, the $3,000 realized loss on the sale of the automobile is not recognized and will not provide T with any deductible tax benefit. □

---

32. The dependency requirement does not apply, however, if the taxpayer could have claimed a dependency exemption except for the fact that the exemption was claimed by the noncustodial parent under a written agreement. Refer to Example 22 and related discussion.

33. Cost usually means purchase price plus expenses incident to the acquisition of the property and incurred by the purchaser (e.g., brokerage commissions). For the basis of property acquired by gift or inheritance and other basis rules, see chapter 12.

Once it has been determined that the disposition of property results in a recognizable gain or loss, the next step is to classify such gain or loss as capital or ordinary. Although ordinary gain is fully taxable and ordinary loss is fully deductible, the same may not hold true for capital losses.

GAINS AND LOSSES FROM PROPERTY TRANSACTIONS—CAPITAL GAINS AND LOSSES

Before 1987, preferential long-term capital gain treatment was accorded to the sale or exchange of capital assets that had been held for the appropriate long-term holding period. Recognized gains and losses on capital assets are classified as long term if the property is held for *more than one year.*

The favorable long-term capital gain rules applicable before 1987 provided for a deduction equal to 60 percent of net capital gain. The provisions were intended to encourage the formation of private capital investment. After 1987, net capital gain is taxed as ordinary income.

Definition of a Capital Asset

Capital assets are defined in the Code as any property held by the taxpayer *other than* property listed in § 1221. The list in § 1221 includes inventory, accounts receivable, and depreciable property or real estate used in a business. Thus, the sale or exchange of assets in these categories usually results in ordinary income or loss treatment (see chapter 13).

EXAMPLE 44

C owns a pizza parlor. During the current year, C sells two automobiles. The first automobile, which had been used as a pizza delivery car for three years, was sold at a loss of $1,000. Because this automobile is an asset used in his business (a § 1231 asset), C has an ordinary loss deduction of $1,000, rather than a capital loss deduction. The second automobile, which C had owned for two years, was C's personal car. It was sold for a gain of $800. The personal car is a capital asset. Therefore, C has a capital gain of $800. □

The principal capital assets held by an individual taxpayer include assets held for personal (rather than business) use, such as a personal residence or an automobile, and assets held for investment purposes (e.g., corporate securities and land).

Computation of Net Capital Gains and Losses

Short-term capital gains and losses (those on assets held for one year or less) are offset initially, and long-term capital losses are used to offset long-term capital gains. Any net short-term capital losses are used then to offset net long-term capital gains. The same offsetting process is used if a taxpayer has net long-term capital losses and net short-term capital gains.

EXAMPLE 45

In the current year, T has the following capital gains and losses: short-term losses of $4,000, short-term gains of $3,000, long-term gains of $6,000, and long-term losses of $2,000. T has net short-term capital losses of $1,000

($4,000 − $3,000) and net long-term capital gains of $4,000 ($6,000 − $2,000). The $1,000 net short-term capital loss is used to offset the $4,000 net long-term capital gain, resulting in an excess of net long-term capital gain over net short-term capital loss of $3,000. ☐

Capital Loss Limitation

Capital losses are first offset against capital gains. If an individual taxpayer has net capital losses, such losses are deductible as a deduction *for* adjusted gross income to a maximum of $3,000 per year. Any unused amounts are carried over for an indefinite period.

EXAMPLE 46   In 1990, T has $1,000 of net long-term capital losses and $2,000 of net short-term capital losses. T's other income is $100,000. T's capital loss deduction for 1990 is $3,000, which consists of $2,000 short-term capital loss and $1,000 long-term capital loss. ☐

When a taxpayer has both short-term and long-term capital losses, and the losses together exceed $3,000, the short-term losses must be used first in absorbing the $3,000 limitation.

EXAMPLE 47   R has short-term capital losses of $2,500 and long-term capital losses of $5,000 in 1990. R's other income is $50,000. R uses the losses as follows:

Short-term loss	$2,500
Long-term loss	500
Maximum 1990 capital loss deduction	$3,000

The remaining long-term capital loss of $4,500 ($5,000 loss minus $500 used in 1990) may be carried over for an indefinite period. See chapter 13 for a detailed discussion of capital loss carryovers. ☐

Corporate Capital Losses.   Corporate taxpayers may offset capital losses only against capital gains. Capital losses in excess of capital gains may not be used to reduce ordinary income of a corporation. A corporation's unused capital losses are subject to a carryback and carryover. Capital losses are initially carried back three years and then carried forward five years to offset capital gains that arise in those years. See chapter 13 for a discussion of capital losses of individual and corporate taxpayers.

TAX PLANNING CONSIDERATIONS

Income of Minor Children

Taxpayers can use several strategies to avoid or minimize the effect of the new rules that tax the unearned income of certain minor children at the parents' rate. The *kiddie tax* rules do not apply once a child reaches age 14. Parents should consider

giving a younger child assets that defer taxable income until the child reaches age 14. For example, U.S. Government Series EE Savings Bonds can be used to defer income until the bonds are cashed in.

Growth stocks typically pay little in the way of dividends. However, the profit on an astute investment may more than offset the lack of dividends. The child can hold the stock until he reaches age 14. If he sells it at a profit, the profit will be taxed at his low rates.

Taxpayers in a position to do so should employ their children in their business and pay them a reasonable wage for the work they actually perform (e.g., light office help, such as filing). The child's earned income will be sheltered by the standard deduction, and the parent's business is allowed a deduction for the wages. The kiddie tax rules have no effect on *earned* income, even if earned from the parents' business.

Alternating between Itemized Deductions and the Standard Deduction

When total itemized deductions are approximately equal to the standard deduction from year to year, it is possible for cash basis taxpayers to save taxes by proper timing of payments. To obtain a deduction for itemized deductions in one year and make use of the standard deduction in the next year, taxpayers should shift deductions from one year to the other. This will result in a larger benefit over the two-year period than otherwise would be available.

EXAMPLE 48

T, who is single, is a cash basis and calendar year taxpayer. For tax years 1989 and 1990, T's itemized deductions are as follows:

	1989	1990
Charitable contribution	$1,300	$1,300
Other itemized deductions (e.g., interest, taxes)	1,100	1,100
Total itemized deductions	$2,400	$2,400

As presently structured, in neither year will T be able to benefit from these itemized deductions, since they do not exceed the standard deduction applicable to a taxpayer claiming single status ($3,100 in 1989 and $3,250 in 1990). Thus, T's benefit for both years totals $6,350 ($3,250 + $3,100), all based on the standard deduction. □

EXAMPLE 49

Assume the same facts as in Example 48, except that in late 1989 T prepays the charitable contribution for 1990. With this change, T's position for both years becomes:

	1989	1990
Charitable contribution	$2,600	$ –0–
Other itemized deductions	1,100	1,100
Total itemized deductions	3,700	$1,100

Under these circumstances, T would claim itemized deductions of $3,700 for 1989 and the standard deduction of $3,250 for 1990. A comparison of the total benefit of $6,950 ($3,700 + $3,250) with the result reached in Example 48 of $6,350 ($3,100 + $3,250) clearly shows the advantage of this type of planning.   □

Deduction for Medical Expenses

Generally, medical expenses are deductible only if they are paid on behalf of the taxpayer, his or her spouse, and their dependents. Since deductibility may rest on dependency status, planning becomes important in arranging multiple support agreements.

EXAMPLE 50   During 1990, M will be supported by her two sons (S_1 and S_2) and her daughter (D), each to furnish approximately one-third of the required support. If the parties decide that the dependency exemption should be claimed by the daughter under a multiple support agreement, any medical expenses incurred by M should be paid by D.   □

In planning the decision under a multiple support agreement, one should take into account which of the parties is most likely to exceed the 7.5 percent limitation (see chapter 10). In Example 50, for instance, D might be a poor choice if she and her family do not expect to incur many medical and drug expenses of their own.

One exception exists to permit the deduction of medical expenses paid on behalf of someone who is not a spouse or a dependent. If the person could be claimed as a dependent *except* for the gross income or joint return test, the medical expenses are, nevertheless, deductible.

EXAMPLE 51   In 1990, T pays for all of the medical expenses of her uncle (U) and her married son (S). U otherwise qualifies as T's dependent, except that he had gross income of $2,500. Also, S otherwise qualifies as a dependent, except that he filed a joint return with his wife. Even though T may not claim dependency exemptions for U and S, she can claim the medical and drug expenses she paid on behalf of each.   □

PROBLEM MATERIALS

Discussion Questions

1. Rearrange the following components to show the formula for arriving at the amount of Federal taxable income:
    a. Deductions *for* adjusted gross income.
    b. The greater of the standard deduction or itemized deductions.
    c. Income (broadly conceived).
    d. Adjusted gross income.
    e. Exclusions.
    f. Personal and dependency exemptions.
    g. Gross income.

2. P earned a salary of $45,000 in 1990. To obtain money for a down payment on a house, she sold 100 shares of XYZ Corporation stock for $34,000. She had paid $22,000 for the stock five years ago. What is P's gross income for 1990?

3. H earned a salary of $50,000 and incurred a $5,000 capital loss in 1990. He incurred medical expenses of $5,000. He had other itemized deductions of $6,000. Compute H's total itemized deductions for 1990.

4. T, age 20 and a full-time student at Midwestern State University, is claimed as a dependent on his parents' tax return. During the summer of 1990, T earned $2,500 from a part-time job. T's only other income consisted of $1,200 in interest on a savings account. Compute T's tax liability for 1990.

5. Assume the same facts as in Question 4, except that T is not claimed as a dependent on his parents' return. Compute T's tax liability for 1990.

6. Discuss the special limitations that apply to the personal exemption and standard deduction of an individual who can be claimed as a dependent of another taxpayer.

7. What tests must be met to qualify as a dependent of another person? Do any of these tests have exceptions? Explain.

8. If an individual who may qualify as a dependent does not spend funds that he or she has received (e.g., wages or Social Security benefits), are such unexpended amounts considered in applying the support test? Are such amounts included in applying the gross income test?

9. F contributed $2,100 toward the support of his son, S, who is 18 years old and a full-time college student. S earned $1,100 interest on a savings account and $900 working at a supermarket during the summer. S used all his earnings for his support. He also received a $1,000 scholarship from the college he attended. Can F claim S as a dependent? Explain.

10. M's only income was $2,200 in Social Security benefits she received during the year. She spent $1,700 of this amount toward her own support. M lives with her daughter D, who contributed $1,500 toward M's support. Can D claim M as a dependent? Explain.

11. M purchased a stereo system for her son G, age 16. The stereo was placed in G's room and used exclusively by G. M also purchased a new sports car, titled and registered in her own name, that was used 90% of the time by G. Should the cost of these items be considered as support in determining whether M may claim G as a dependent?

12. Z, who is a dependent of his parents, is a full-time student at Central City College. During 1990, Z, age 20, earned $1,500 from a part-time job. Because he is claimed as a dependent by his parents, Z will not be allowed to claim an exemption for himself when filing his own tax return. True or false? Explain.

13. D, age 18, was a full-time university student during 1990. D earned $2,800 from a part-time job during 1990. D lives with his grandparents, who provided 80% of his support in 1990. D's grandparents can claim him as a dependent in 1990. True or false? Explain.

14. J's support is provided by her daughter (30%), her son (30%), and an unrelated friend (40%). Can J be claimed as a dependent by any of the individuals who contributed to her support? Explain.

15. H and W, who are the parents of C, a minor child, were divorced during 1986. W was awarded custody of C. H provided 70% of C's support in 1990, and W provided 30%. Who may claim the dependency exemption for C in 1990? Explain.

16. B, who is married, must use either (a) the rates for married taxpayers filing jointly or (b) the rates for married taxpayers filing separately. True or false? Explain.

17. B, who is unmarried, expects to have adjusted gross income of $22,000 in 1990. B does not itemize deductions. How much income tax can B save if N, his 10-year-old nephew, moves in with him and qualifies as his dependent in 1990?

18. A single individual age 65 or over and blind is required to file a Federal income tax return in 1990 if he or she has gross income of $6,100 or more (refer to Figure 2–9).

    a. Explain how the $6,100 filing requirement was computed.

    b. In general, explain the effect of the additional standard deduction on the determination of gross income requirements for filing.

19. T and S are engaged to be married. Each has gross income of $20,000 for 1990. Assume that they plan to make use of the standard deduction and have no dependency exemptions or tax credits. What is the overall effect on the total Federal income taxes that would be paid if they marry before the end of 1990?

20. K, age 67 and blind, earned $4,500 of interest and received Social Security benefits of $7,200 in 1990. Is K required to file a tax return?

21. H, age 67, is married to W, who is age 62 and blind. H and W file a joint return. How much gross income can they earn before they are required to file an income tax return for 1990?

22. V, a high school student, earned $1,000 from a summer job in 1990. V is aware that this amount is below the income level that would require her to file a return and therefore does not plan to file. Do you have any advice for V?

23. What remedy is available to an individual who failed to claim a deduction or tax credit on a tax return that has been filed with the IRS?

24. During 1990, T had a $5,000 long-term capital loss on the sale of common stock he had held as an investment. In addition, he had a $2,000 loss on the sale of his personal automobile, which he had owned for a year. How do these transactions affect T's taxable income for 1990?

25. Ten years ago, T purchased a personal residence for $140,000. In the current year, she sells the residence for $105,000. T's friend tells her she has a recognizable loss of $35,000 from the sale. Do you agree with the friend's comment? Elaborate.

26. List some assets that are not capital assets.

27. Why is it important to determine whether an asset is an ordinary asset or capital asset?

28. If an individual has a salary of $30,000 and net long-term capital losses of $4,500, what amount is deductible?

29. If a corporation has net short-term capital losses of $20,000 and net long-term capital gains of $6,000, what amounts are deductible by the corporation? How are any unused losses treated?

Problems

30. Compute the taxpayer's taxable income for 1990 in each of the following cases:

    a. H is married and files a joint return with his wife W. H and W have two dependent children. They have adjusted gross income of $30,000 and $3,300 of itemized deductions.

    b. S is unmarried and has no dependents. He has adjusted gross income of $25,000 and itemized deductions of $4,200.

c. G is a full-time college student who is claimed as a dependent by her parents. She earned $2,500 from a part-time job and had interest income of $1,200. Her itemized deductions were $400.

d. M is a full-time college student who is claimed as a dependent by his parents. He earned $1,500 from a part-time job and had interest income of $1,100. His itemized deductions were $700.

31. Determine the standard deduction and exemption amount as instructed for the following taxpayers:

a. S, age 35, is a single taxpayer with no dependents. What was the total of his standard deduction and exemption amount for 1989? What is it for 1990?

b. G, age 66, is a single taxpayer with no dependents. What was the total of his standard deduction and exemption amount for 1989? What is it for 1990?

c. M is a college student who is claimed as a dependent on her parents' Federal income tax return in 1990. She earned interest of $400 in 1990. What is the total of M's standard deduction and exemption amount for 1990?

d. Assume the same facts as in (c), except that M also earned $3,000 from a summer job in 1990. What is the total of her standard deduction and exemption amount in 1990?

e. B, age 21, is a full-time college student who was claimed as a dependent by her parents during 1990. She earned $400 interest plus $3,000 from a part-time job during 1990. What is the total of B's standard deduction and exemption amount for the year?

32. X, age 30, is single, and has no dependents. In 1990, X earned $22,000 and had itemized deductions of $2,100. Compute X's taxable income and tax before prepayments or credits for 1990.

33. T, who is single, earned $77,000 in 1990. He incurred a short-term capital loss of $5,000 and had total itemized deductions of $9,800. Compute T's taxable income and tax before prepayments and credits for 1990.

34. Determine the Federal income tax liability for the following taxpayers for 1990:

a. D, who is single and has no dependents, earned $35,640. She had total itemized deductions of $2,990.

b. H and W are married and file a joint return. They earned $36,680 and had total itemized deductions of $3,140.

c. B is a widow who qualifies as a head of household. She has a son, age 10, who qualifies as her dependent. She earned $36,680 and had total itemized deductions of $2,990.

d. H is married, files a separate return, and has no dependents. He earned $35,640 and had total itemized deductions of $2,370.

35. B, age 13, is a full-time student supported by his parents who claim him on their tax return for 1990. B's parents present you with the following information and ask that you prepare B's 1990 Federal income tax return:

Wages from summer job	$1,400
Interest on savings account at First National Bank	500
Interest on XYZ Corporation bonds B received as a gift from his grandfather two years ago	900
Dividend from Z Corporation	500

a. What is B's taxable income for 1990?

b. B's parents file a joint return for 1990 on which they report taxable income of $64,250. Compute B's 1990 tax liability.

36. Assume the same facts as in Problem 35, except that B earned no dividends and no interest from First National Bank. What is B's taxable income for 1990?

37. R is a wealthy executive who had taxable income of $200,000 in 1990. He is considering transferring title in a duplex he owns to his son S, age 6. S has no other income and is claimed as a dependent by R. Net rental income from the duplex is $4,000 a year, which S will be encouraged to place in a savings account. Will the family save income taxes in 1990 if R transfers title in the duplex to S? Explain.

38. Compute the 1990 tax liability for each of the following taxpayers:
    a. E, age 24, is single and has no dependents. During 1990, he earned a salary of $36,000, had deductions *for* AGI of $2,000, and had itemized deductions of $3,100.
    b. L, age 66, is single and has no dependents. She earned a salary of $28,000 in 1990 and had itemized deductions of $3,500.

39. H and J, both 40 years of age, are married and have no children. They file separate returns for 1990. H claims itemized deductions of $6,600, and J's itemized deductions total $1,700. Because her itemized deductions are less than the standard deduction, J intends to use the standard deduction for computing her taxable income. What is the amount of the standard deduction J may claim in 1990? Explain.

40. L, age 22, is single and lives with her parents, who provide 70% of her support. L, a part-time student at Parkland Community College, earned a salary of $8,000 in 1990 and had itemized deductions of $2,500. What is L's taxable income for 1990?

41. Compute the 1990 tax liability for each of the following taxpayers:
    a. H and M, both age 46, are married, have two dependent children, and file a joint return. In 1990, their combined salaries totaled $110,000. They had deductions *for* AGI of $4,000 and total itemized deductions of $6,000.
    b. D, age 45, is single and has no dependents. In 1990, he had a salary of $140,000, deductions *for* AGI of $3,000, and total itemized deductions of $12,000.
    c. B and C, both age 65, are married, have no dependents, and file a joint return in 1990. Their combined salaries for 1990 were $220,000. They had deductions *for* AGI of $6,000 and itemized deductions of $20,000.

42. Compute the 1990 tax liability for each of the following taxpayers:
    a. F, age 65, is single and has no dependents. In 1990, he earned $104,260, had deductions *for* AGI of $4,000, and had itemized deductions of $3,700.
    b. J, who is single and has no dependents, has taxable income of $85,000 in 1990.
    c. X, who is single and has no dependents, has taxable income of $95,000 in 1990.
    d. N and P, both age 34, have one dependent child, L, age 10. In 1990, N and P have taxable income of $100,000. L receives interest income of $3,000 during the year. Compute L's 1990 tax liability.

43. T, age 12 and a full-time student, is claimed as a dependent on his parents' 1990 Federal income tax return, on which they reported taxable income of $175,000. During the summer of 1990, T earned $1,800 from a job as a model. His only other income consisted of $1,200 in interest on a savings account. Compute T's taxable income and tax liability for 1990.

44. R, age 14 and a full-time student, is claimed as a dependent on her parents' 1990 Federal income tax return, on which they reported $220,000 of taxable income. During 1990, R earned $3,000 of interest on a savings account. Compute R's taxable income and tax liability for 1990.

45. L, who is 12 years old, is claimed as a dependent on her parents' tax return. During 1990, she received $12,200 in dividends and interest and incurred itemized deductions of $800 related to the management of her portfolio assets. She also earned $700 wages from a part-time job. Compute the amount of income that is taxed at her parents' rate.

46. M, who is 12 years old, is claimed as a dependent on her parents' tax return. During 1990, she received $12,000 in dividends and interest and incurred itemized deductions of $800 related to the management of her portfolio assets. She also earned $1,700 wages from a part-time job. Compute the amount of income that is taxed at her own rate.

47. J, who is 16 years old, is claimed as a dependent on her parents' tax return. During 1990, she received $10,000 in dividends and interest and incurred itemized deductions of $1,000 related to the management of her portfolio assets. She also earned $3,500 wages from a part-time job. Compute her income tax for the year.

48. W, age 67 and single, is claimed as a dependent by his daughter. He earned $900 interest and $1,050 wages from a part-time job. Compute W's taxable income for 1990.

49. G, age 67 and single, is claimed as a dependent by her son. She earned $300 interest and $1,650 wages from a part-time job. Compute G's income tax for 1990.

50. K, age 65 and single, had gross income of $133,000 in 1990. He paid alimony of $30,000, had a capital loss of $5,000, medical expenses of $8,000, and other itemized deductions of $3,000. Compute his income tax.

51. B, age 65 and single, had gross income of $123,000 in 1990. She had a capital loss of $5,000, medical expenses of $8,000, and other itemized deductions of $3,000. Compute her income tax.

52. C had the following gains and losses from the sale of capital assets during 1990: $5,000 STCG, $7,000 STCL, $1,000 LTCG, and $5,500 LTCL. What is the amount and character of C's capital loss carryover to 1991?

53. In each of the following independent cases, determine the number of personal and dependency exemptions T may claim for 1990. Assume any dependency test not mentioned has been met. Unless otherwise specified, T is unmarried.

Case 1. T provides 80% of the support of his nephew (age 17), who lives with him. During the year, the nephew has gross income of $2,000 and is a full-time student.

Case 2. Assume the same facts as in Case 1, except that the $2,000 was paid to the nephew as a scholarship to cover tuition at State University.

Case 3. T provides over 50% of the support of his son S and his son's wife D. S (age 22) is a full-time student at a university. During 1990, D earned $3,500 on which income taxes were withheld. On January 31, 1991, D filed a separate return for tax year 1990. All parties reside in New York.

Case 4. Assume the same facts as in Case 3, except that all parties reside in California.

Case 5. During 1990, T gave his father, F (age 68), cash of $1,000 and a used automobile (cost of $2,000). F's total expenditures for food, lodging, and clothing for 1990 amount to $3,000 ($1,000 received from T and $2,000 withdrawn from F's savings account). F dies on June 3, 1990.

Case 6. T and his two brothers each provide 15% of the support of their mother. The mother derives the remainder of her support from Social Security benefits.

54. Determine the correct number of personal and dependency exemptions in each of the following situations:

a. T, age 66 and disabled, is a widower who maintains a home for his unmarried daughter who is 24 years old. The daughter earned $3,000 and attends college on a part-time basis. T provides more than 50% of her support.

b. T, a bachelor age 45, provides more than 50% of the support of his father, age 70. T's father had gross income of $900 from a part-time job.

c. T, age 45, is married and has two dependent foster children who live with him and are totally supported by T. One of the foster children, age 14, had $2,100 of gross income. T and his spouse file a joint return.

d. T, age 67, is married and has a married daughter, age 22. T's daughter attended college on a full-time basis and was supported by T. The daughter filed a joint return with her spouse. T filed a joint return with his spouse, age 62.

55. Compute the number of personal and dependency exemptions in the following independent situations:

a. T, a single individual, provides 60% of the support of his mother, age 69. T's mother received dividend income of $800 and $1,500 in Social Security benefits.

b. T, a married individual filing a joint return, provides 100% of the support of his son, age 21, who is a part-time student. T's son earned $2,000 during the year from part-time employment.

c. T is divorced and provides $2,000 of child support for his child who is living with her mother, who provides support of $2,500. An agreement executed in 1986 between T and his former wife provides that the noncustodial parent is to receive the dependency exemption. T's former wife provides him with a completed Form 8332.

56. Has T provided more than 50% support in the following situations?

a. T paid $6,000 for an automobile that was titled in his name. His 19-year-old son, S, uses the automobile approximately 50% of the time while attending a local college on a full-time basis. S earned $4,000 from a part-time job that was used to pay his college and living expenses. The value of S's room and board provided by T amounted to $1,200.

b. T contributed $4,000 to his mother's support during the year. His mother received $5,000 in Social Security benefits that she placed in her savings account for future use.

c. Assume the same facts as in (b), except that T's mother used the funds for her support during the year.

57. F contributed the following items toward the support of his son S:

Food, clothing, shelter	$2,300
Television set given to S as a Christmas present	300
Books for college	250

S, age 23, is a full-time student at the University of Georgia College of Law. In June, he married J, who is supported by her parents. S earned $3,300 during the summer and contributed the following items toward his own support:

Clothing	$ 600
Used car purchased for transportation to college	1,000
Insurance, maintenance, and operating expenses for car	800
Entertainment	420

S received a $2,000 scholarship from the University of Georgia. Which of the following statements is correct?

a. F provided over half of S's support but cannot claim S as a dependent because S's gross income exceeds the maximum amount allowable for a dependent.

b. S's income will not prevent F from claiming S as a dependent. However, F cannot claim S as a dependent because he provided less than half of S's support.

c. F cannot claim S as a dependent for two reasons: F did not provide over half of S's support, and S's income exceeds the maximum amount allowable for a dependent.

d. Based on the facts given, there is nothing that would prevent F from claiming S as a dependent. However, if S and J file a joint return, F will not be allowed to claim S as a dependent.

e. None of the above.

58. A, B, and C contribute to the support of their mother, M, age 67. M lives with each of the children for approximately four months during the year. Her total living costs amounted to $6,000 and were paid as follows:

From M's Social Security benefits	$1,700
By A	500
By B	1,300
By C	1,300
By T, M's unrelated friend	1,200
	$6,000

a. Which, if any, of these individuals may claim M as a dependent (assume no multiple support agreement is filed)?

b. If a multiple support agreement is filed, who must be a party to it, and who may claim the exemption for M under the agreement?

59. Which of the following individuals are required to file a tax return for 1990? Should any of these individuals file a return even if such filing is not required? Why?

a. T is married and files a joint return with his spouse, B. Both T and B are 47 years old. Their combined gross income was $9,000.

b. T is a dependent child under age 19 who received $1,000 in wages from a part-time job and $1,900 of dividend income.

c. T is single and is 67 years old. His gross income from wages was $5,800.

d. T is a self-employed single individual with gross income of $4,400 from an unincorporated business. Business expenses amounted to $3,900.

60. Can T use Tax Rate Schedule Z (head of household) in 1990?

a. T's wife died in 1989. T maintained a household for his two dependent children during 1990 and provided over one-half of the cost of the household.

b. T is unmarried and lives in an apartment. He supported his aged parents, who live in a separate home. T provides over one-half of the funds used to maintain his parents' home. T also claimed his parents as dependents since he provided more than one-half of their support during the year.

c. T is unmarried and maintains a household (over one-half of the cost) for his 18-year-old married daughter and her husband. His daughter filed a joint return with her husband solely for the purpose of obtaining a refund of income taxes that were withheld. Neither T's daughter nor her husband was required to file a return.

61. Indicate in each of the following situations which of the Tax Rate Schedules T should use for calendar year 1990:

a. T, the mother and sole support of her three minor children, was abandoned by her husband in late 1989.

b. T is a widower whose wife died in 1989. T furnishes all of the support of his household, which includes two dependent children.

    c. T furnishes all of the support of his parents, who live in their own home in a different city. T's parents qualify as his dependents. T is not married.

    d. T's household includes an unmarried stepchild, age 18, who has gross income of $6,000 during the year. T furnishes all of the cost of maintaining the household. T is not married.

62. M, age 66, is a widow. Her husband died in 1988. M maintains a home in which she and her 28-year-old son reside. Her son G, who is blind, is a piano player at a local nightclub, where he earned $12,000 during 1990. G contributed $3,000 of his income toward household expenses and put the remainder in a savings account that he used to return to college full-time to pursue a master's degree in music starting in August 1990. M contributed $12,000 toward household expenses. What is the most favorable filing status available to M for 1990, and how many exemptions may M claim?

63. You are to solve this puzzle using your skills as a tax expert. Sam and Sally were contemplating marriage in December 1989. Sam's salary for 1989 was $12,000, and Sally's was $40,000. Sam had total itemized deductions of $1,900; Sally's itemized deductions totaled $2,800. Sam, who earned interest of $2,000 on a savings account, made a deductible $2,000 contribution to his IRA. Sally made a deductible $1,000 contribution to her IRA. Sam and Sally planned to marry in December 1989 if marriage would save them any Federal income tax. Otherwise, they planned to marry in January 1990. Which of the following statements is correct?

    a. Sam and Sally married in December 1989.

    b. Sam and Sally married in January 1990.

64. B, who is single and age 35, has adjusted gross income of $40,000 in 1989. He does not itemize deductions. N, his recently orphaned 10-year-old cousin, moved in with him in April, and B provided all of N's support during the remainder of 1989.

    a. Compute B's taxable income and tax liability for 1989.

    b. Assume that B has the same amount of adjusted gross income in 1990 and that N continues to reside with him through the end of the year. Compute B's taxable income and tax liability for 1990.

65. H, age 65 and single, earned a salary of $42,000 and made a deductible $2,000 contribution to his Individual Retirement Account in 1990. He incurred medical expenses of $3,500 and had other itemized deductions of $3,000. Compute H's taxable income for 1990.

66. In 1990, D earned a salary of $30,000 and had a long-term loss of $4,000 on the sale of stock. She also had a $2,500 short-term loss on the sale of land held as an investment and a $1,500 gain on the sale of her personal automobile. She had owned the automobile for two years. Compute D's adjusted gross income and capital loss carryover based on this information.

67. K, age 39, is single. She maintains a household that is the residence of her two children, B, age 8, and G, age 11. The children are claimed as dependents by their father, who provides $2,000 child support for each of them. During 1990, K earned a salary of $48,000. Other items that affected her taxable income are as follows:

Total itemized deductions	$4,500
Capital gains	
Short-term	300
Long-term	3,500
Capital losses	
Short-term	(900)
Long-term	(700)
Interest income	650

K provides all the support for her mother, M, who lives in a nursing home. M qualifies as K's dependent.

    a. Compute K's adjusted gross income and taxable income for 1990.

    b. What is K's filing status for 1990?

68. H, single with no dependents, had a short-term capital loss of $2,600 in 1990. He earned a salary of $15,000 and had itemized deductions of $2,100.

    a. Compute H's taxable income for 1990.

    b. Assume the same facts as in (a), except that H also had a $1,400 long-term capital loss in 1990. Compute H's taxable income and capital loss carryforward to 1991.

69. N, age 67, is married to H, age 65. N and H file a joint return for 1990. During 1990, N's salary was $92,000. N has an extensive portfolio of stock investments. During 1990, he engaged in several stock transactions, with the following results:

Capital gains	
Short-term	$ 3,700
Long-term	9,000
Capital losses	
Short-term	(2,500)
Long-term	(1,200)

N and H had total itemized deductions of $9,400 during 1990. N received interest of $4,800 on City of Phoenix bonds.

    a. Compute taxable income for N and H for 1990.

    b. Assume the same facts as in (a), except that N's long-term capital gain was only $900.

70. T is a single, cash basis calendar year taxpayer. For the years 1989 and 1990, he expects adjusted gross income of $20,000 and the following itemized deductions:

Church pledge	$1,200
Interest on home mortgage	1,500
Property taxes	700

Discuss the tax consequences of the following alternatives:

    a. In 1989, T pays his church pledge for 1989 and 1990 ($1,200 for each year).

    b. T does nothing different.

Cumulative Problems

71. John and Karen Sanders, both age 25, are married and file a joint return in 1989. They have one child, Linda, who was born on June 30, 1989. John's Social Security number is 266–77–2345, and Karen's is 467–33–1289. They live at 105 Bradley, Columbus, OH 43211.

John, a computer programmer, earned $31,000, and his employer withheld $4,500. Karen, a medical student at Ohio State University, received $15,000 of income from a trust her father had established to pay for her education. This amount must be included in computing taxable income. In addition, Karen was awarded a $3,000 nontaxable scholarship by the medical school in 1989.

In examining their records, you find that John and Karen are entitled to the following itemized deductions:

State and local income taxes	$1,150
Real estate taxes	1,570
Home mortgage interest	3,840
Charitable contributions	620
Total	$7,180

John and Karen made estimated Federal tax payments of $1,200 in 1989.

Part 1—Tax Computation

Compute (a) adjusted gross income, (b) taxable income, and (c) net tax payable or refund due for John and Karen. Suggested software (if available): *TurboTax* for tax return solutions or *WEST–TAX Planner* if tax return solutions are not desired.

Part 2—Tax Planning

Assume that all amounts from 1989 will be approximately the same in 1990 except for the following:

  a. John's salary will increase by 10%.

  b. John's employer will withhold $5,000 of Federal income tax.

How much additional estimated tax should the Sanders pay in 1990 so they will neither owe any tax nor receive any refund for 1990? Suggested software (if available): *TurboTax* (planning mode) or *WEST–TAX Planner*.

72. Henry and Wanda Black, 4030 Beachside Drive, Longboat Key, FL 33548, file a joint Federal income tax return for 1989. Henry, age 66, is a restaurant manager for Gourmet Tacos. His Social Security number is 344–99–7642. Wanda, who is 54, is a manager at Timothy's Beauty Salon. Her Social Security number is 654–33–7890. The Blacks come to you in early December 1989 seeking tax advice.

The Blacks have received or will receive the following amounts during 1989:

  a. Henry's salary, $38,000.

  b. Wanda's salary, $40,000.

  c. Proceeds from October 9, 1989, sale of XYZ Corporation stock (cost of $12,000) acquired on April 6, 1981, $26,000.

  d. Interest on bonds issued by the City of Sarasota, $900.

  e. Life insurance proceeds received on the death of Henry's mother, $75,000.

  f. Value of property inherited from Henry's mother, $130,000.

In examining the Blacks' records, you find the following items of possible tax consequence (all applicable to 1989):

  g. The Blacks had other itemized deductions as follows:

Real estate taxes	$3,200
Home mortgage interest	4,500
Charitable contributions (cash)	2,600

  h. Henry's employer withheld $6,800 of Federal income tax, and Wanda's employer withheld $7,000. In addition, they made estimated tax payments of $6,400.

Henry and Wanda's son Steven lived with the Blacks during 1989 except for nine months during which he was away at college. Steven, age 23, is a law student and plans to graduate in 1991. During the summer, Steven earned $2,100 and used the money he earned to pay for his college expenses. His parents contributed $3,000 toward his support.

Part 1—Tax Computation

Compute the following amounts for the Blacks if they file a joint return for 1989: gross income, adjusted gross income, taxable income, and net tax payable or refund due. Suggested software (if available): *TurboTax* for tax return solutions or *WEST-TAX Planner* if tax return solutions are not desired.

Part 2—Tax Planning

The Blacks are contemplating a divorce and would prefer not filing jointly. They have asked you to compute their tax liabilities if they file separately rather than jointly. If they file separately, they will split itemized deductions and estimated tax payments equally, and each spouse will report one-half of the capital gain since they owned the XYZ Corporation stock jointly (refer to item c). Wanda will claim an exemption for Steven (assume he qualifies as her dependent). Will the Blacks have to pay more tax if they file separately? Explain. Suggested software (if available): *TurboTax* for tax return solutions or *WEST–TAX Planner* if tax return solutions are not desired.

3

GROSS INCOME: CONCEPTS AND INCLUSIONS

OBJECTIVES Explain the all-inclusive concept of gross income and the underlying realization requirement.

Describe the cash and accrual methods of accounting for gross income.

Explain the principles applied to determine who is subject to tax on a particular item of income.

Analyze the sections of the Internal Revenue Code that describe the determination of gross income from the following specific sources: alimony, below-market interest rate loans, annuities, prizes and awards, group term life insurance, unemployment compensation, and Social Security benefits.

Computation of the income tax liability of an individual or a corporation begins with the determination of gross income. Section 61 provides an all-inclusive definition of gross income and supplements it with a list of items (not all-inclusive) that are includible in gross income (e.g., compensation for services, rents, interest, dividends, alimony). Other Code sections contain specific rules for particular types of income, and still other sections provide guidance for determining the tax period in which the income should be reported. Supreme Court decisions establish the framework for deciding who must pay the tax on the income.

Congress has provided that certain items are excluded from taxation (e.g., interest on certain state and municipal bonds). The *exclusions* appear in §§ 101– 150 of the Code and are discussed in chapter 4.

Gross Income—What Is It?

Definition

Section 61(a) of the Internal Revenue Code defines the term *gross income* as follows:

> Except as otherwise provided in this subtitle, gross income means all income from whatever source derived.

Since the sweeping scope of the definition is apparent, the Supreme Court has stated:

> The starting point in all cases dealing with the question of the scope of what is included in "gross income" begins with the basic premise that the purpose of Congress was to use the full measure of its taxing power.[1]

The clause, "Except as otherwise provided in this subtitle," refers to sections of the Code in which Congress has exempted certain types of income from the tax base. Such exclusions are discussed in chapter 4.

Economic and Accounting Concepts

The term *income* is used in the Code but is not separately defined. Thus, early in the history of our tax laws, the courts were required to interpret "the commonly understood meaning of the term which must have been in the minds of the people when they adopted the Sixteenth Amendment to the Constitution."[2] In determining the definition of income, the Supreme Court rejected the economist's concept of income.

For the *economist*, economic income is measured by first determining the fair market value of the taxpayer's net assets at the beginning and end of the year. After this determination is made, economic income is defined as the sum of the taxpayer's change in net worth plus actual consumption of goods and services for the tax period. Economic income also includes imputed values for such items as the rental value of an owner-occupied home and the value of food a taxpayer might grow for personal consumption.

1. *James v. U.S.*, 61–1 USTC ¶9449, 7 AFTR2d 1361, 81 S.Ct. 1052 (USSC, 1961).

2. *Merchants Loan and Trust Co. v. Smietanka*, 1 USTC ¶42, 3 AFTR 3102, 41 S.Ct. 386 (USSC, 1921).

EXAMPLE 1   T's economic income is calculated as follows:

Fair market value of T's assets on December 31, 1990	$220,000	
Less liabilities on December 31, 1990	(40,000)	
Net worth on December 31, 1990		$180,000
Fair market value of T's assets on January 1, 1990	$200,000	
Less liabilities on January 1, 1990	(80,000)	
Net worth on January 1, 1990		120,000
Increase in net worth		$ 60,000
Consumption		
Food, clothing, and other personal expenditures		25,000
Imputed rental value of T's home she owns and occupies		12,000
Economic income		$ 97,000

☐

The need to value assets annually would make compliance with the law burdensome and would cause numerous controversies between the taxpayer and the IRS over valuation. In addition, using market values to determine income for tax purposes could result in liquidity problems. That is, the taxpayer's assets may increase in value even though they are not readily convertible into the cash needed to pay the tax (e.g., commercial real estate). Thus, the IRS, Congress, and the courts have rejected the economist's concept of income as impractical.

In contrast, the *accountant's concept of income* is founded on the realization principle. According to this principle, income is not recognized until it is realized. Realization entails (1) an exchange of goods or services between the accounting entity and some independent, external group and (2) assets received in the exchange that are capable of being objectively valued. The mere appreciation in the market value of assets before a sale or other disposition is not sufficient to warrant income recognition. Also, imputed savings arising from the self-construction of assets to be used in one's own operations are not income because there is no exchange.

The Supreme Court in *Eisner v. Macomber*[3] added the realization requirement to a judicial definition of income that had been formulated in early cases:

> Income may be defined as the gain derived from capital, from labor, or from both combined, provided it is understood to include profit gained through a sale or conversion of capital assets. . . . Here we have the essential matter: not a gain accruing to capital; not a *growth* or *increment* of value *in* investment; but a gain, a profit, something of exchangeable value, *proceeding from* the property, *severed from* the capital however invested or employed, and *coming in*, being *"derived"*—that is, *received* or *drawn by* the recipient for his separate use, benefit and disposal—that is, income derived from the property.

Thus, the early Supreme Court definition of income can be simply restated as the gain realized from capital, from labor, or from a combination of the two.

---

3. 1 USTC ¶32, 3 AFTR 3020, 40 S.Ct. 189 (USSC, 1920).

Comparison of Accounting and Taxable Income

Although income tax rules frequently parallel financial accounting measurement concepts, differences do exist. Of major significance, for example, is the fact that unearned (prepaid) income received by an accrual basis taxpayer often is taxed in the year of receipt. For financial accounting purposes, such prepayments are not treated as income until earned. Because of this and other differences, many corporations report financial accounting income that is substantially different from the amounts reported for tax purposes (see chapter 16, Reconciliation of Taxable Income and Accounting Income).

An explanation for some of the variations between accounting and taxable income was given in a Supreme Court decision involving inventory and bad debt adjustments.[4] The relevant portion of the opinion follows:

> The primary goal of financial accounting is to provide useful information to management, shareholders, creditors, and others properly interested; the major responsibility of the accountant is to protect these parties from being misled. The primary goal of the income tax system, in contrast, is the equitable collection of revenue. . . . Consistently with its goals and responsibilities, financial accounting has as its foundation the principle of conservatism, with its corollary that 'possible errors in measurement [should] be in the direction of understatement rather than overstatement of net income and net assets.' In view of the Treasury's markedly different goals and responsibilities, understatement of income is not destined to be its guiding light.
>
> . . . Financial accounting, in short, is hospitable to estimates, probabilities, and reasonable certainties; the tax law, with its mandate to preserve the revenue, can give no quarter to uncertainty.

In some instances, the tax law specifically permits rapid write-offs (e.g., limited expensing under § 179) and deferrals of income that are not available in financial accounting. The student should note specific differences between tax accounting and financial accounting mentioned in the text.

Form of Receipt

Gross income is not limited to cash received. "It includes income realized in any form, whether in money, property, or services. Income may be realized [and recognized], therefore, in the form of services, meals, accommodations, stock or other property, as well as in cash."[5]

EXAMPLE 2 | ABC Corporation allowed T, an employee, to use a company car for his vacation. T realized income equal to the rental value of the car for the time and mileage. □

EXAMPLE 3 | M, an XYZ Corporation shareholder, bought real estate from the company for $10,000 when the property was worth $15,000. M realized income (a constructive dividend) of $5,000, the difference between the fair market value of the property and the price M paid. □

---

4. *Thor Power Tool Co. v. Comm.*, 79–1 USTC ¶9139, 43 AFTR2d 79–362, 99 S.Ct. 773 (USSC, 1979).

5. Reg. § 1.61–1(a).

EXAMPLE 4   T owed $10,000 on a mortgage. The creditor accepted $8,000 in full satisfaction of the debt. T realized income of $2,000 from retiring the debt.   □

Recovery of Capital Doctrine

The Constitution grants Congress the power to tax income but does not define the term. Because the Constitution does not define income, it would seem that Congress could simply tax gross receipts. Although Congress does allow certain deductions, none are constitutionally required. However, the Supreme Court has held that there can be no income subject to tax until the taxpayer has recovered the capital invested.[6]

> . . . We must withdraw from the gross proceeds an amount sufficient to restore the capital value that existed at the commencement of the period under consideration.

In its simplest application, the *recovery of capital doctrine* means a seller can reduce the gross receipts (selling price) by the adjusted basis in the property sold. This net amount, in the language of the Code, is gross income. But the recovery of capital doctrine also has subtle implications.

EXAMPLE 5   T sold common stock for $15,000. He had purchased the stock for $12,000. T's gross receipts are $15,000. This amount consists of a $12,000 recovery of capital and $3,000 of gross income.   □

YEAR OF INCLUSION

Taxable Year

The annual accounting period or taxable year is a basic component of our tax system. Generally, a taxable entity may use a *calendar year* to report income. Those entities who keep adequate books and records generally may use a *fiscal year* (a period of 12 months ending on the last day of any month other than December) or a 52–53 week year that ends on the same day of the week nearest the last day of the same month each year. A retailer considering a 52–53 week year might choose a year ending in January so that he or she can properly account for Christmas returns, and on a Saturday so that inventory can be taken on Sunday. Automobile dealers often select a fiscal year ending in September so that the taxable year corresponds with their natural business year (i.e., the change in car models).

The lifetime earnings of a taxable entity must be divided into these 12-month intervals and a progressive tax rate schedule must be applied to the taxable income for each interval. Therefore, determining the period into which a particular item of income is allocated is often of more than just academic interest. Determining this period is important because (1) Congress may change the tax rate schedule, (2) the entity's income may rise or fall between years so that placing the income in a particular year may mean that the income is taxed at a different marginal rate, or (3) the entity may undergo a change in its status and a different tax rate schedule may apply (e.g., an individual might marry or a proprietorship might incorporate).

---

6. *Doyle v. Mitchell Bros. Co.*, 1 USTC ¶17, 1 AFTR
    235, 38 S.Ct. 467 (USSC, 1916).

Several provisions in the Code contain limitations based on gross income or derivatives of gross income. For example, as discussed in chapter 2, generally a dependent's gross income cannot exceed the exemption amount. Also, medical expenses are deductible (as an itemized deduction) only to the extent the expenses exceed 7.5 percent of the taxpayer's adjusted gross income, and only miscellaneous expenses in excess of 2 percent of adjusted gross income are allowed as an itemized deduction. Thus, it is important to determine *when* the item of income is subject to taxation.

Accounting Methods

The year an item of income is subject to tax often depends upon which acceptable accounting method the taxpayer regularly employs. The three primary methods of accounting are (1) the cash receipts and disbursements method, (2) the accrual method, and (3) the hybrid method. Most individuals use the cash receipts and disbursements method of accounting, whereas most corporations use the accrual method. The Regulations require the accrual method for determining purchases and sales when inventory is an income-producing factor.[7] Some businesses employ a hybrid method that is a combination of the cash and accrual methods of accounting. Generally, when a hybrid method is used, inventory is accounted for under the accrual method, and the cash method is used for all other income and expense items.

In addition to these *overall accounting methods*, a taxpayer may choose to spread the gain from the sale of property over the collection periods by electing the *installment method* of income recognition. Contractors may either spread profits from contracts over the periods in which the work is done (the *percentage of completion method*) or defer all profit until the year in which the project is completed (the *completed contract method*).

The Commissioner has the power to prescribe the accounting method to be used by the taxpayer. Section 446(b) grants the IRS broad powers to determine if the accounting method used *clearly reflects income*:

> Exceptions—If no method of accounting has been regularly used by the taxpayer, or *if the method used does not clearly reflect income, the computation of taxable income shall be made under such method as, in the opinion of the Secretary or his delegate, does clearly reflect income.*

A change in the method of accounting requires the consent of the IRS.

Cash Receipts Method.   Under the *cash receipts method*, property or services received are included in the taxpayer's gross income in the year of *actual* or *constructive* receipt by the taxpayer or agent, regardless of whether the income was earned in that year. The receipt of income need not be reduced to cash in the same year. All that is necessary for income recognition is that property or services received have a fair market value—a cash equivalent. Thus, if a cash basis taxpayer receives a note in payment for services, he or she has income in the year of receipt equal to the fair market value of the note. However, a creditor's mere promise to pay (e.g., an account receivable), with no supporting note, is not usually considered to have a fair market value. Thus, the cash basis taxpayer defers income recognition until the account receivable is collected.

---

7. Reg. § 1.446–1(c)(2)(i). See the Glossary of Tax Terms in Appendix C for a discussion of the terms "accrual method," "accounting method," and "accounting period." Other circumstances for which the accrual method must be used are presented in chapter 15.

EXAMPLE 6   D, an accountant, reports his income by the cash method. In 1990, he performed an audit for X and billed the client for $5,000, which was collected in 1991. In 1990, D also performed an audit for Y. Because of Y's precarious financial position, D required Y to issue an $8,000 secured negotiable note in payment of the fee. The note had a fair market value of $6,000. D collected $8,000 on the note in 1991. D's gross income for the two years is as follows:

	1990	1991
Fair market value of note received from Y	$6,000	
Cash received		
From X on account receivable		$ 5,000
From Y on note receivable		8,000
Less: Recovery of capital		(6,000)
Total gross income	$6,000	$ 7,000

□

Accrual Method.   Under *accrual accounting*, an item is generally included in the gross income of the year in which it is earned, regardless of when the income is collected. The income is earned when (1) all the events have occurred that fix the right to receive such income and (2) the amount thereof can be determined with reasonable accuracy.

Generally, the taxpayer's rights to the income accrue when title to property passes to the buyer or the services are performed for the customer or client. If the rights to the income have accrued but are subject to a potential refund claim (e.g., under a product warranty), the income is reported in the year of sale, and a deduction is allowed in subsequent years when actual claims accrue.

Where the taxpayer's rights to the income are being contested (e.g., a contractor who fails to meet specifications), the year in which the income is subject to tax depends upon whether payment has been received. If payment has not been received, no income is recognized until the claim has been settled. Only then is the right to the income established. However, if the payment is received before the dispute is settled, the court-made *claim of right doctrine* requires the taxpayer to recognize the income in the year of receipt.[8]

EXAMPLE 7   A contractor completed a building in 1990 and presented a bill to the customer. The customer refused to pay the bill and claimed that the contractor had not met specifications. A settlement with the customer was not reached until 1991. Assuming the customer had a valid claim, no income would accrue to the contractor until 1991. If the customer paid for the work and then filed suit for damages, the contractor could not defer the income (the income would be taxable in 1990).   □

The measure of accrual basis income is generally the amount the taxpayer has a right to receive. Unlike the cash basis, the fair market value of the customer's obligation is irrelevant in measuring accrual basis income.

---

8. *North American Oil Consolidated Co. v. Burnet*, 3 USTC ¶943, 11 AFTR 16, 52 S.Ct. 613 (USSC, 1932). See the Glossary of Tax Terms in Appen-   dix C for a discussion of the term "claim of right doctrine."

EXAMPLE 8 | Assume the same facts as in Example 6, except D is an accrual basis taxpayer. D must recognize $13,000 ($8,000 + $5,000) income in 1990, the year his rights to the income accrued. □

Exceptions Applicable to Cash Basis Taxpayers

Constructive Receipt.   Income that has not actually been received by the taxpayer is taxed as though it had been received—the income is *constructively received*—under the following conditions:

- The amount is made readily available to the taxpayer.

- The taxpayer's actual receipt is not subject to substantial limitations or restrictions.

The rationale for the constructive receipt doctrine is that if the income is available, the taxpayer should not be allowed to postpone the income recognition. For instance, a taxpayer is not permitted to defer income for December services by refusing to accept payment until January. However, determining whether the income is *readily available* and whether *substantial limitations or restrictions exist* necessitates a factual inquiry that sometimes leads to a judgment call. Some examples of the application of the constructive receipt doctrine follow:

EXAMPLE 9 | P received a salary check on December 31 but after banking hours. P must recognize income on December 31 because the funds were made available to him on that date. □

EXAMPLE 10 | T is a member of a barter club. In 1990, T performed services for other club members and earned 1,000 points. Each point entitles him to $1 in goods and services sold by other members of the club, and the points can be used at any time. In 1991, T exchanged his points for a new color TV. T must recognize $1,000 income in 1990 when the 1,000 points were credited to his account.

□

EXAMPLE 11 | On December 31, an employer issued a bonus check to an employee but asked him to hold it for a few days until the company could make deposits to cover the check. The income was not constructively received on December 31 since the issuer did not have sufficient funds in its account to pay the debt. □

EXAMPLE 12 | R owned interest coupons that matured on December 31. The coupons could be converted to cash at any bank at maturity. Thus, the income is *constructively received* on December 31. □

EXAMPLE 13 | GM Company mails dividend checks on December 31, 1990. The checks will not be received by shareholders until January. The shareholders do not realize income until 1991. □

The constructive receipt doctrine does not reach income that the taxpayer is not yet entitled to receive, even though he or she could have contracted to receive the income at an earlier date.

EXAMPLE 14

X offered to pay Y $100,000 for land in December 1990. Y refused but offered to sell the land to X on January 1, 1991, when Y would be in a lower tax bracket. If X accepted Y's offer, the gain would be taxed in 1991 when the sale was completed. □

EXAMPLE 15

T is a professional athlete who reports his income by the cash method. In negotiating a contract, the club owner made two alternative offers to T:

1. $1,000,000 cash upon signing in 1991.
2. $100,000 per year plus 10% interest for 10 years.

T accepted the second offer. The income is taxed according to the amount he actually receives ($100,000 per year plus interest). The $1,000,000 T could have contracted to receive in 1991 is not constructively received in that year because he accepted the alternative offer. If the final contract had provided that T could receive either the lump sum or installment payments, the $1,000,000 would have been constructively received in 1991. □

Original Issue Discount. Lenders frequently make loans that require a payment at maturity of more than the amount of the original loan. The difference between the amount due at maturity and the amount of the original loan is actually interest but is referred to as *original issue discount.* Under the general rules of tax accounting, the cash basis lender would not report the original issue discount as interest income until the year the amount is collected, although an accrual basis borrower would deduct the interest as it accrues. However, the Code puts the lender and borrower on parity by requiring that the original issue discount be reported when it accrues, regardless of the taxpayer's accounting method.[9]

EXAMPLE 16

On July 1, 1990, T, a cash basis taxpayer, paid $84,232 for an 18-month certificate of deposit with a maturity value of $100,000. The effective interest rate on the certificate was 12%. T must report $5,054 interest income for 1990:

$$(.12 \times \$84,232)(\tfrac{1}{2} \text{ year}) = \underline{\underline{\$5,054}}$$ □

The original issue discount rules do not apply to U.S. savings bonds (discussed in the following paragraphs) or to obligations with a maturity date of one year or less from the date of issue.

Series E and Series EE Bonds. Certain U.S. government savings bonds (Series E before 1980 and Series EE after 1979) are issued at a discount and are redeemable for fixed amounts that increase at stated intervals. No interest

9. §§ 1272(a)(3) and 1273(a).

payments are actually made. The difference between the purchase price and the amount received on redemption is the bondholder's interest income from the investment.

The income from these savings bonds is generally deferred until the bonds are redeemed or mature. Furthermore, Series E bonds can be exchanged within one year of their maturity date for Series HH bonds, and the interest on the Series E bonds can be further deferred until maturity of the Series HH bonds. Thus, U.S. savings bonds have attractive income deferral features not available with corporate bonds and certificates of deposit issued by financial institutions.

Of course, the deferral feature of government bonds issued at a discount is not an advantage if the investor has insufficient income to be subject to tax as the income accrues. In fact, the deferral may work to the investor's disadvantage if he or she has other income in the year the bonds mature or the bunching of the bond interest into one tax year creates a tax liability. Fortunately, U.S. government bonds have a provision for these investors. A cash basis taxpayer can elect to include in gross income the annual increment in redemption value.

When the election is made to report the income from the bonds on an annual basis, it applies to all such obligations the taxpayer owns at the time of the election and all such securities acquired subsequent to the election. A change in the method of reporting the income from the bonds requires permission from the IRS.

Amounts Received under an Obligation to Repay.   The receipt of funds with an obligation to make repayment in the future is the essence of borrowing. Because the taxpayer's assets and liabilities increase by the same amount, no income is realized when the borrowed funds are received. Because amounts paid to the taxpayer by mistake and customer deposits are often classified as borrowed funds, receipt of the funds is not a taxable event.

EXAMPLE 17   A customer erroneously paid a utility bill twice. The utility company does not recognize income from the second payment because it has a liability to the customer. ☐

EXAMPLE 18   A lessor received a damage deposit from a tenant. No income is recognized by the lessor before forfeiture of the deposit because the lessor has an obligation to repay the deposit if no damage occurs. However, if the deposit is in fact a prepayment of rent, it is taxed in the year of receipt. ☐

Exceptions Applicable to Accrual Basis Taxpayers

Prepaid Income.   For financial reporting purposes, advance payments received from customers are reflected as prepaid income and as a liability of the seller. However, for tax purposes, the prepaid income often is taxed in the year of receipt.

EXAMPLE 19   In December 1990, a tenant paid his January 1991 rent of $1,000. The accrual basis landlord must include the $1,000 in his 1990 income for tax purposes, although the unearned rent income is reported as a liability on the landlord's December 31, 1990, balance sheet. ☐

Taxpayers have repeatedly argued that deferral of income until it is actually earned properly matches revenues and expenses. Moreover, a proper matching of income with the expenses of earning the income is necessary to clearly reflect income, as required by the Code. The IRS responds that § 446(b) grants it broad powers to determine whether an accounting method clearly reflects income. The IRS further argues that generally accepted financial accounting principles should not dictate tax accounting for prepaid income because of the practical problems of collecting Federal revenues. Collection of the tax is simplest in the year the taxpayer receives the cash from the customer or client.

Over a 40-year period of litigation, the IRS has been only partially successful in the courts. In cases involving prepaid income from services to be performed at the demand of customers (e.g., dance lessons to be taken at any time in a 24-month period), the IRS's position has been upheld.[10] In such cases, the taxpayer's argument that deferral of the income was necessary to match the income with expenses was not persuasive because the taxpayer did not know precisely when each customer would demand services and, thus, when the expenses would be incurred. However, taxpayers have had some success in the courts when the services were performed on a fixed schedule (e.g., a baseball team's season-ticket sales).[11] In some cases involving the sale of goods, taxpayers have successfully argued that the prepayments were mere deposits or in the nature of loans.

Against this background of mixed results in the courts, Congressional intervention, and taxpayers' strong resentment of the IRS's position, in 1971 the IRS modified its prepaid income rules, as explained in the following paragraphs.

Deferral of Advance Payments for Goods.   Generally, a taxpayer can elect to defer recognition of income from *advance payments for goods* if the taxpayer's method of accounting for the sale is the same for tax and financial reporting purposes.[12]

EXAMPLE 20   B Company will ship goods only after payment for the goods has been received. In December 1990, B received $10,000 for goods that were not shipped until January 1991. The company can elect to report the income for tax purposes in 1991, assuming the company reports the income in 1991 for financial reporting purposes. □

Deferral of Advance Payments for Services.   Revenue Procedure 71–21[13] permits an accrual basis taxpayer to defer recognition of income for *advance payments for services* to be performed by the end of the tax year following the year of receipt. No deferral is allowed if the taxpayer might be required to perform any services, under the agreement, after the tax year following the year of receipt of the advance payment.

---

10. *Automobile Club of Michigan v. U.S.*, 57–1 USTC ¶9593, 50 AFTR 1967, 77 S.Ct. 707 (USSC, 1957); *American Automobile Association v. U.S.*, 61–2 USTC ¶9517, 7 AFTR2d 1618, 81 S.Ct. 1727 (USSC, 1961); *Schlude v. Comm.*, 63–1 USTC ¶9284, 11 AFTR2d 751, 83 S.Ct. 601 (USSC, 1963).

11. *Artnell Company v. Comm.*, 68–2 USTC ¶959, 22 AFTR2d 5590, 400 F.2d 981 (CA–7, 1968). See also *Boise Cascade Corp. v. U.S.*, 76–1 USTC ¶9286, 37 AFTR2d 76–696, 530 F.2d 1367 (Ct. Cls., 1976).

12. Reg. § 1.451–5(b). See Reg. § 1.451–5(c) for exceptions to this deferral opportunity. The financial accounting conformity requirement is not applicable to contractors who use the completed contract method.

13. 1971–2 C.B. 549.

EXAMPLE 21   X Corporation, an accrual basis taxpayer, sells its services under 12-month, 18-month, and 24-month contracts. The corporation provides services to each customer every month. In 1990, X Corporation sold the following customer contracts with service periods beginning April 1:

Length of Contract	Total Proceeds
12 months	$6,000
18 months	3,600
24 months	2,400

Fifteen hundred dollars of the $6,000 may be deferred (3/12 × $6,000) and $1,800 of the $3,600 may be deferred (9/18 × $3,600) because those amounts will not be earned until 1991. However, the entire $2,400 received on the 24-month contracts is taxable in the year of receipt (1990), since a part of the income will still be unearned by the end of the tax year following the year of receipt. □

Revenue Procedure 71–21 does *not apply* to prepaid rent, prepaid interest, or amounts received under guarantee or warranty contracts. Thus, the income will still be taxed in the year of receipt if collected before the income is actually earned. However, there is a special condition on the definition of the term *rent*:

> "Rent" does not include payments for the use or occupancy of rooms or other space where significant services are also rendered to the occupant. . . .

The effect of the definition is to allow hotels, motels, tourist homes, and convalescent homes to defer the recognition of income under the rules discussed above.

In summary, Revenue Procedure 71–21 will result in conformity of tax and financial accounting in a very limited number of prepaid income cases. It is not apparent why prepaid rents and interest may not be deferred, why revenues under some service contracts may be spread over two years, and why revenues under longer service contracts must be reported in one year. Although Revenue Procedure 71–21 has reduced the number of controversies involving prepaid income, a consistent policy has not yet evolved.

INCOME SOURCES

Personal Services

It is a well-established principle of taxation that income from personal services must be included in the gross income of the person who performs the services. This principle was first established in a Supreme Court decision, *Lucas v. Earl.*[14] Mr. Earl entered into a binding agreement with his wife under which Mrs. Earl was to receive one-half of Mr. Earl's salary. Justice Holmes used the celebrated *fruit* and *tree* metaphor to explain that the fruit (income) must be attributed to the tree from

---

14. 2 USTC ¶496, 8 AFTR 10287, 50 S.Ct. 241
     (USSC, 1930).

which it came (Mr. Earl's services). A mere *assignment of income* does not shift the liability for the tax.

In the case of a child, the Code specifically provides that amounts earned from personal services must be included in the child's gross income. This result applies even though the income is paid to other persons (e.g., the parents).

Income from Property

Income from property (interest, dividends, rent) must be included in the gross income of the *owner* of the property. If a father clips interest coupons from bonds shortly before the interest payment date and gives the coupons to his son, the interest will still be taxed to the father. A parent who assigns rents from rental property to a child will be taxed on the rent since the parent retains ownership of the property.

Who is to pay the tax on income accrued at the time of the transfer of income-producing property, and when does the income accrue? The position of the IRS is that in the case of a gift, interest accrues on a daily basis. However, the cash basis donor does not recognize the income until it is collected by the donee.[15]

EXAMPLE 22 | F, a cash basis taxpayer, gave S bonds with a face amount of $10,000 and an 8% stated rate of interest. The gift was made on November 30, and the interest is payable each January 1. When S collects the interest in January, F must recognize $732 in interest income (8% × $10,000 × 334/365). S will recognize $68 in interest income ($800 − $732). □

When property that has accrued interest is sold, a portion of the selling price is treated as interest and is taxed to the seller in the year of sale.

EXAMPLE 23 | Assume the same facts as in Example 22, except that F sold the bonds on November 30 to an unrelated party for $10,000 plus accrued interest of $732. F must recognize $732 in interest income when the bonds are sold. □

Dividends, unlike interest, do not accrue on a daily basis because the declaration of the dividend is at the discretion of the board of directors of the corporation. Generally, dividends are taxed to the person who is entitled to receive them—the shareholder of record as of the corporation's record date. However, the Tax Court has held that a donor does not shift dividend income to the donee if a gift of stock is made after the date of declaration but before the date of record.[16] The *fruit* has sufficiently ripened as of the declaration date to tax the dividend to the donor of the stock.

EXAMPLE 24 | On June 20, the board of directors of Z Corporation declares a $10 per share dividend. The dividend is payable on June 30, to shareholders of record on June 25. As of June 20, M owned 200 shares of Z Corporation's stock. On June 21, M sold 100 of the shares to N for their fair market value and gave 100 of the

---

15. Rev.Rul. 72–312, 1972–1 C.B. 22.   16.   *M. G. Anton*, 34 T.C. 842 (1960).

shares to S. Assume both N and S are shareholders of record as of June 25. N (the purchaser) will be taxed on $1,000, since he is entitled to receive the dividend. However, M (the donor) will be taxed on the $1,000 received by S (the donee) because the gift was made after the declaration date of the dividend. □

Income from Partnerships, S Corporations, Trusts, and Estates

A *partnership* is not a separate taxable entity. Rather, the partnership merely files an information return (Form 1065), which serves to provide the data necessary for determining the character and amount of each partner's distributive share of the partnership's income and expenses. Each partner must then report his or her distributive share of the partnership's income and deductions for the partnership's tax year ending within or with his or her own tax year. The income must be reported by each partner as if earned, even if such amounts are not actually distributed. Because a partner pays tax on income as the partnership earns it, a distribution by the partnership to the partner is treated under the recovery of capital rules.

EXAMPLE 25   T owned a one-half interest in the capital and profits of T & S Company (a partnership). For tax year 1990, the partnership earned revenue of $150,000 and had operating expenses of $80,000. During the year, T withdrew from his capital account $2,500 per month (for a total of $30,000). For 1990, T must report $35,000 as his share of the partnership's profits [½ × ($150,000 − $80,000)] even though he received a distribution of only $30,000. □

A *small business corporation* may elect to be taxed similarly to a partnership. Thus, the shareholders pay the tax on the corporation's income. The electing corporation is referred to as an *S corporation*. Generally, the shareholder reports his or her proportionate share of the corporation's income and deductions for the year, whether or not any distributions are actually made by the corporation.

EXAMPLE 26   Assume the same facts as in Example 25, except that T & S Company is an S corporation. T's income for the year is his share of the taxable income earned by the corporation ($35,000) rather than the amount actually distributed to him. □

The *beneficiaries* of *estates and trusts* generally are taxed on the income earned by the estates or trusts that is actually distributed or required to be distributed to them. Any income not taxed to the beneficiaries is taxable to the estate or trust.

Income in Community Property States

General Rules.   State law in Louisiana, Texas, New Mexico, Arizona, California, Washington, Idaho, Nevada, and Wisconsin is based upon a community property system. All other states have a common law property system. The basic difference between common law and community property systems centers around the property rights of married persons.

Under a *community property* system, all property is deemed to be either separately owned by the spouse or belonging to the marital community. Property may be held separately by a spouse if it was acquired before marriage or received by gift or inheritance following marriage. Otherwise, any property is deemed to be community property. For Federal tax purposes, each spouse is taxed on one-half of the income from property belonging to the community.

The laws of Texas, Louisiana, and Idaho distinguish between separate property and the income it produces. In these states, the income from separate property belongs to the community. Accordingly, for Federal income tax purposes, each spouse is taxed on one-half of the income. In the remaining community property states, separate property produces separate income that the owner-spouse must report on his or her Federal income tax return.

What appears to be income, however, may really represent a recovery of capital. A recovery of capital and gain realized on separate property retains its identity as separate property. Items such as nontaxable stock dividends, royalties from mineral interests, and gains and losses from the sale of property take on the same classification as the assets to which they relate.

Income from personal services (salaries, wages, income from a professional partnership) is generally treated as one-half earned by each spouse in all community property states.

Items Specifically Included in Gross Income

The general principles of gross income determination (discussed in the previous sections) as applied by the IRS and the courts have on occasion yielded results Congress found unacceptable. Consequently, Congress has set forth more specific rules for determining the gross income from certain sources. Some of these special rules appear in §§ 71–90 of the Code.

Alimony and Separate Maintenance Payments

When a married couple divorce or become legally separated, state law generally requires a division of the property accumulated during the marriage. In addition, one spouse may have a legal obligation to support the other spouse. The Code distinguishes between the support payments (alimony or separate maintenance) and the property division in terms of the tax consequences.

Alimony and separate maintenance payments are *deductible* by the party making the payments and are *includible* in the gross income of the party receiving the payments. Thus, income is shifted from the income earner to the income beneficiary, who is required to pay the tax on the amount received.

EXAMPLE 27   H and W were divorced, and H was required to pay W $15,000 of alimony each year. H earns $61,000 a year. The tax law presumes that because W received the $15,000, she is more able than H to pay the tax on that amount. Therefore, W must include the $15,000 in her gross income, and H is allowed to deduct $15,000 from his gross income.   □

A transfer of property other than cash to a former spouse under a divorce decree or agreement is not a taxable event. The transferor is not entitled to a deduction and does not recognize gain or loss on the transfer. The transferee does not recognize income and has a basis equal to the transferor's basis.

EXAMPLE 28

H transfers stock to W as part of a 1990 divorce settlement. The basis of the stock to H is $12,000, and the stock's value at the time of the transfer is $15,000. W later sells the stock for $16,000. H is not required to recognize gain from the transfer of the stock to W, and W has a realized and recognized gain of $4,000 ($16,000–$12,000) when she sells the stock. □

In the case of cash payments, however, it is often difficult to distinguish payments under a support obligation (alimony) and payments for the other spouse's property (property settlement). In 1984 Congress developed objective rules to classify the payments.

Post-1984 Agreements and Decrees.   Payments made under post-1984 agreements and decrees are classified as alimony only if the following conditions are satisfied:

1. The payments are in cash.

2. The agreement or decree does not specify that the cash payments are not alimony.

3. The payor and payee are not members of the same household at the time the payments are made.

4. There is no liability to make the payments for any period after the death of the payee.

Requirement 1 simplifies the law by clearly distinguising alimony from a property division; that is, if the payment is not in cash, it must be a property division.

Requirement 2 allows the parties to determine by agreement whether or not the payments will be alimony. The prohibition on cohabitation—requirement 3—is aimed at assuring the alimony payments are associated with duplicative living expenses (maintaining two households). Requirement 4 is an attempt to prevent alimony treatment from being applied to what is, in fact, a payment for property rather than a support obligation. That is, a seller's estate generally will receive payments for property due after the seller's death. Such payments after the death of the payee could not be for the payee's support.

Front-Loading.   As a further safeguard against a property settlement being disguised as alimony, special rules apply to post-1986 agreements if payments in the first or second year exceed $15,000. If the change in the amount of the payments exceeds statutory limits, *alimony recapture* results to the extent of the excess alimony payments. In the *third* year, the payor must include the excess alimony payments for the first and second years in gross income, and the payee is allowed a deduction for these excess alimony payments.

The recapture computation provides an objective technique for determining alimony recapture. Thus, at the time of divorce, the taxpayers can ascertain the tax consequences of the alimony arrangement. The general concept is that if the alimony payments decrease by over $15,000 between years, there will be alimony recapture with respect to the *decrease* in excess of $15,000 each year.

EXAMPLE 29

H and W enter into a post-1986 divorce agreement under which W is to receive alimony payments of $30,000 in Year 1, $20,000 in Year 2, and $15,000 in Year 3. There is no alimony recapture because payments did not decrease by more than $15,000 per year. □

Step 1 in the alimony recapture computation is to determine the decrease from Year 2 to Year 3. Year 2 alimony is recaptured to the extent this decrease exceeds $15,000. Step 2 requires that the *average* payments for Years 2 and 3 be compared with the Year 1 payment. For this computation, *revised* alimony for Year 2 is used. Revised alimony is equal to the amount of alimony deducted by the payor in Year 2 minus the amount of Year 2 alimony that is recaptured in step 1. The excess of Year 1 alimony over average alimony for Years 2 and 3 is recaptured to the extent that it exceeds $15,000.

EXAMPLE 30 H and W enter into a post-1986 divorce decree under which W is to receive alimony payments of $60,000 in Year 1, $40,000 in Year 2, and $20,000 in Year 3.

Step 1: Year 2 alimony recapture:	
Year 2 alimony	$40,000
Minus: Year 3 alimony	20,000
Decrease	$20,000
Minus: Allowable decrease	15,000
Year 2 alimony recapture	$ 5,000
Step 2: Year 1 alimony recapture:	
Year 1 alimony	$60,000
Minus: Average of Year 2 and Year 3 alimony*	27,500
Decrease	$32,500
Minus: Allowable decrease	15,000
Year 1 alimony recapture	$17,500

*[($40,000 Year 2 alimony − $5,000 recaptured) + $20,000 Year 3 alimony] divided by 2.

The total amount of alimony recaptured is $22,500 ($5,000 of Year 2 payments + $17,500 of Year 1 payments). ☐

For 1985 and 1986 agreements and decrees, alimony recapture is required during the second and third years if payments decrease by more than $10,000. A special formula is applied to compute the recapture amounts.

Post-1984 agreements are not subject to alimony recapture if the decrease in payments is due to death of either spouse or remarriage of the payee because these are events that typically terminate alimony under state law. In addition, the recapture rules do not apply to payments that are contingent in amount (e.g., a percentage of income from certain property or a percentage of the payor spouse's compensation), are to be made over a period of three years or longer (unless death, remarriage, or other contingency occurs), and involve contingencies beyond the payor's control.

EXAMPLE 31 Under a 1990 divorce agreement, H was to receive an amount equal to one-half of W's income from certain rental properties for 1990–1993. Payments were to cease upon the death of H or W or upon the remarriage of H. H received $50,000 in 1990 and $50,000 in 1991; however in 1992, the property was vacant, and H received nothing. W, who deducted alimony in 1990 and 1991, is not required to recapture any alimony in 1991 because the payments were contingent. ☐

Pre-1985 Agreements and Decrees.   Because payments will continue to be made under pre-1985 agreements for many years, these provisions are briefly reviewed here. The requirements for alimony treatment under pre-1985 agreements are as follows:

1. The payments must be made pursuant to either (a) a court order (a decree of divorce, separate maintenance decree, or decree of support) or (b) a written separation agreement (in short, the payments cannot be voluntary).

2. The payments must be either (a) for a period of more than 10 years or (b) subject to a contingency (e.g., the death of either spouse, remarriage of the recipient, or change in the economic status of either spouse).

3. The payments must be in "discharge of a legal obligation arising from the marital or family obligations."[17]

The third requirement presents numerous problems because the *legal obligation* is determined under state law. Many states require that a spouse be paid for his or her *fair share* of the property that has been accumulated during the marriage but retained by the other spouse. Additionally, a state may impose a support obligation on the spouse. Only payments under the support obligation satisfy the marital obligation requirement (requirement 3). Thus, a cash payment may be (1) solely for support, (2) solely for property, or (3) in part for support and in part for property. Moreover, the labels the spouses attach to the payments (by pre-1985 agreement) do not control.

Child Support.   A taxpayer does not realize income from the receipt of child support payments made by his or her former spouse. This is true because the money is received subject to the duty to use the money for the child's benefit.

In many cases, it is difficult to determine whether an amount received is alimony or child support. Under pre-1985 decrees and agreements, according to the Supreme Court, if the decree or agreement does not specifically provide for child support, none of the payments will be treated as such.[18]

EXAMPLE 32   A pre-1985 divorce agreement provides that H is required to make periodic alimony payments of $500 per month to W. However, when H and W's child reaches age 21, marries, or dies (whichever occurs first), the payments will be reduced to $300 per month. W has custody of the child. Although it is reasonable to infer that $200 ($500 − $300) is for child support, the entire $500 is alimony because no payments are specified as child support.   □

In 1984, Congress changed the results in Example 32 but only as to post-1984 agreements and decrees. Under the revision, if the amount of the payments would be reduced upon the happening of a contingency related to a child (e.g., the child attains age 21 or dies), the amount of the future reduction in the payment will be deemed child support.[19]

---

17. §§ 71(a) and (b) prior to amendment by § 422 of the Deficit Reduction Act of 1984.

18. *Comm. v. Lester,* 61–1 USTC ¶9463, 7 AFTR2d 1445, 81 S.Ct. 1343 (USSC, 1961).

19. § 71(c)(2). Pre-1985 agreements can be amended so that the revision will apply [§ 422(e) of the Deficit Reduction Act of 1984].

CONCEPT SUMMARY 3–1

Tax Treatment of Payments and Transfers Pursuant to Post–1984 Divorce Agreements and Decrees

	Payor	Recipient
Alimony	Deduction from gross income.	Included in gross income.
Alimony recapture	Included in gross income of the third year.	Deducted from gross income of the third year.
Child support	Not deductible.	Not includible in income.
Property settlement	No income or deduction.	No income or deduction; basis for the property received is the same as the transferor's basis.

EXAMPLE 33   The facts are the same as in Example 32 except that the agreement is a post-1984 agreement. Child support payments are $200 each month and alimony is $300 each month. ☐

Imputed Interest on Below-Market Loans

As discussed earlier in the chapter, generally no income is recognized unless it is realized. Realization generally occurs when the taxpayer performs services or sells goods and thus becomes entitled to a payment from the other party. It follows that no income is realized if the goods or services are provided at no charge. Under this interpretation of the realization requirement, before 1984, interest-free loans were used to shift income between taxpayers.

EXAMPLE 34   D (daughter) is in the 20% tax bracket and has no investment income. F (father) is in the 50% tax bracket and has $200,000 in a money market account earning 10% interest. F would like D to receive and pay tax on the income earned on the $200,000. Because F would also like to have access to the $200,000 should he need the money, he does not want to make an outright gift of the money, nor does he want to commit the money to a trust.

Before 1984, F could achieve his goals as follows. F could transfer the money market account to D in exchange for D's $200,000 non-interest-bearing note, payable on F's demand. As a result, D would receive the income, and the family's taxes would be decreased by $6,000.

Decrease in F's tax—	
(.10 × $200,000) .50 =	($10,000)
Increase in D's tax—	
(.10 × $200,000) .20 =	4,000
Decrease in the family's taxes	($ 6,000)

☐

Under the 1984 amendments to the Code, F in Example 34 is required to recognize imputed interest income. Also, D is deemed to have incurred interest

expense equal to F's imputed interest income. D's interest may be deductible on her return as portfolio interest if she itemizes deductions (see chapter 10). To complete the fictitious series of transactions, F is then deemed to have given D the amount of the imputed interest D did not pay. The gift received by D is not subject to income tax (see chapter 4), although F may be subject to the unified transfer tax on the amount deemed given to D (refer to chapter 1).

Imputed interest is calculated using the rate the Federal government pays on new borrowings and is compounded semiannually. This Federal rate is adjusted monthly and is published by the IRS. Actually, there are three Federal rates: short-term (not over three years and including demand loans), mid-term (over three years but not over nine years), and long-term (over nine years).

EXAMPLE 35

Assume the Federal rate applicable to the loan in Example 34 is 12% through June 30 and 13% from July 1 through December 31. F made the loan on January 1, and the loan is still outstanding on December 31. F must recognize interest income of $25,780, and D has interest expense of $25,780. F is deemed to have made a gift of $25,780 to D.

Interest calculations	
January 1–June 30—	
.12 ($200,000) (½ year)	$12,000
July 1–December 31—	
.13 ($200,000 + $12,000)(½year)	13,780
	$25,780

☐

If interest is charged on the loan but is less than the Federal rate, the imputed interest is the difference between the amount that would have been charged at the Federal rate and the amount actually charged.

EXAMPLE 36

Assume the same facts as in Example 35, except that F charged 6% interest, compounded annually.

Interest at the Federal rate	$ 25,780
Less interest charged (.06 × $200,000)	(12,000)
Imputed interest	$ 13,780

☐

The imputed interest rules apply to the following *types* of below-market loans:

1. Gift loans (made out of love, affection, or generosity, as in Example 34).
2. Compensation-related loans (employer loans to employees).
3. Corporation-shareholder loans (a corporation's loans to its shareholders).
4. Tax avoidance loans and other loans that significantly affect the borrower's or lender's Federal tax liability (discussed in the following paragraphs).

The effects of the first three types of loans on the borrower and lender are summarized in Concept Summary 3–2.

Concept Summary 3—2

Effect of Certain Below-Market Loans on the Lender and Borrower

Gift	Step 1	Interest income	Interest expense
	Step 2	Gift made	Gift received
Compensa-	Step 1	Interest income	Interest expense
tion-related	Step 2	Compensation expense	Compensation income
Corporation to	Step 1	Interest income	Interest expense
shareholder	Step 2	Dividend paid	Dividend income

Tax Avoidance and Other Below-Market Loans.   In addition to the three specific types of loans that are subject to the imputed interest rules, the Code provides a catchall provision for *tax avoidance loans* and other arrangements that have a significant effect on the tax liability of the borrower or lender. The contours of this vague provision are to be established in Regulations. The Conference Report provides an example (see Example 37, page 3—22) of an arrangement that might be subject to the imputed interest rules.[20]

EXAMPLE 37   Annual dues for the XY Health Club are $400. In lieu of paying dues, a member can make a $4,000 deposit, refundable at the end of one year. The club can earn $400 interest on the deposit.

If interest were not imputed, an individual with $4,000 could, in effect, earn tax-exempt income on the deposit. That is, rather than invest the $4,000, earn $400 in interest, pay tax on the interest, and then pay $400 in dues, the individual could avoid tax on the interest by making the deposit. Thus, income and expenses are imputed as follows: interest income and nondeductible health club fees for the club member; income from fees and interest expense for the club. □

Many commercially motivated transactions could be swept into this other below-market loans category. However, the temporary Regulations have carved out a frequently encountered exception for customer prepayments. If the prepayments are included in the recipient's income under the recipient's method of accounting, the payments are not considered loans and, thus, are not subject to the imputed interest rules.[21]

EXAMPLE 38   Landlord, a cash basis taxpayer, charges tenants a damage deposit equal to one month's rent on residential apartments. When the tenant enters into the lease, the landlord also collects rent for the last month of the lease.

The prepaid rent for the last month of the lease is taxed in the year received and thus is not considered a loan. The security deposit is not taxed when

---

20. H. Rep. No. 98–861, 98th Cong., 2d Sess., 1984, p. 1023.   21. Temp. Reg. § 1.7872–2(b)(l)(i).

received and is therefore a candidate for imputed interest. However, neither the landlord nor the tenant derives an apparent tax benefit, and thus the security deposit should not be subject to the imputed interest provisions. But if making the deposit would reduce the rent paid by the tenant, the tenant could derive a tax benefit, much the same as the club member in Example 37.

□

Exceptions and Limitations.   No interest is imputed on total outstanding gift loans of $10,000 or less between individuals, unless the loan proceeds are used to purchase income-producing property. This exemption eliminates from these complex provisions immaterial amounts that do not result in apparent shifts of income.

On loans of $100,000 or less between individuals, the imputed interest cannot exceed the borrower's net investment income for the year. The rationale for this limitation is that the loan cannot cause a shift of more income (from lender to borrower) than was earned by the borrower. As a further limitation, or exemption, if the borrower's net investment income for the year does not exceed $1,000, no interest is imputed on loans of $100,000 or less. However, these limitations for loans of $100,000 or less do not apply if a principal purpose of a loan is tax avoidance. According to the Senate Report, if a principal purpose of a loan is to shift income to a taxpayer in a lower tax bracket (as illustrated in Example 34), the purpose is a proscribed one. Therefore, in such a case interest is imputed, and the imputed interest is not limited to the borrower's net investment income.

EXAMPLE 39   F made interest-free gift loans as follows:

Borrower	Amount	Borrower's Net Investment Income	Purpose
S	$ 8,000	$ 1,000	Education
D	9,000	500	Purchase of stock
B	25,000	–0–	Purchase of a business
M	60,000	15,000	Purchase of a residence
O	120,000	–0–	Purchase of a residence

Assume that tax avoidance is not a principal purpose of any of the loans. The S loan is not subject to the imputed interest rules because the $10,000 exception applies. The $10,000 exception does not apply to the D loan because the proceeds were used to purchase income-producing assets. However, under the $100,000 exception, the imputed interest is limited to D's investment income ($500). Since the $1,000 exception also applies to this loan, no interest will be imputed.

No interest is imputed on the B loan because the $100,000 exception applies. Interest will be imputed on the M loan based on the lesser of (1) the lender's $15,000 net investment income or (2) the interest as calculated by applying the Federal rate to the outstanding loan. None of the exceptions apply to the O loan.   □

As with gift loans, there is a $10,000 exemption for compensation-related loans and corporation-shareholder loans. However, the $10,000 exception does not apply if tax avoidance is one of the principal purposes of a loan. This vague tax avoidance standard makes practically all compensation-related and corporation-shareholder loans suspect. Nevertheless, the $10,000 exception should apply when an employee's borrowing was necessitated by personal needs (e.g., to meet unexpected expenses) rather than tax considerations.

Measuring Income.   The measurement of the gift, compensation, or dividend resulting from a loan depends upon whether the loan is (1) a *demand loan* payable at the demand of the lender or (2) a *term loan* due as of a specific date. In the case of a demand loan, the interest is calculated using the short-term rate, and the forgone interest is the measure of the gift, compensation, or dividend. In the case of a term loan, the difference between the face amount of the loan and its present value at the date of the loan is the measure of the gift, compensation, or dividend. The interest income is computed by applying the imputed interest rate to the balance of the loan. For both the demand loan and the term loan, semiannual compounding is required.

EXAMPLE 40	R, the employer, loaned $100,000 interest-free to E, an employee, on January 1 of the current tax year. The loan was due in five years, and the Federal *mid-term* rate was 10.7% compounded semiannually (the equivalent of 11% with annual compounding).

R's compensation expense and E's compensation income for the current tax year are computed as follows:

Face amount	$100,000
Less present value of $100,000 due in 5 years, i = 11%	(59,345)
Original issue discount	$ 40,655

R's interest income and E's interest expense are computed as follows:

Year	Beginning Balance	Applicable Interest @ 11%	Ending Balance
1990	$ 59,345*	$ 6,528	$ 65,873
1991	65,873	7,246	73,119
1992	73,119	8,043	81,162
1993	81,162	8,928	90,090
1994	90,090	9,910	100,000
		$40,655	

*Beginning loan balance equals $100,000 face amount minus $40,655 original issue discount.

☐

For income tax purposes (but not for gift tax purposes), term gift loans are treated as demand loans.

EXAMPLE 41   Assume the same facts as in Example 40, except that the $100,000 was received by E as a gift loan. Further assume that the Federal *short-term* rate was 9.76% compounded semiannually (the equivalent of 10% with annual compounding). The amount of the gift is $40,655 (calculated using the *mid-term* rate), but R's interest income and E's interest expense are equal to the Federal *short-term* rate times the amount of the loan (.10 × $100,000 = $10,000). □

The apparent rationale for treating all gift loans as demand loans is that as a practical matter, the lender could receive his or her principal at any time at his or her demand.

Income from Annuities

Annuity contracts generally require the purchaser (the annuitant) to pay a fixed amount for the right to receive a future stream of payments. Typically, the issuer of the contract is an insurance company and will pay the annuitant a cash value if the annuitant cancels the contract. The insurance company invests the amounts received from the annuitant, and the income earned serves to increase the cash value of the policy. No income is recognized at the time the cash value of the annuity increases because the taxpayer has not actually received any income. The income is not constructively received because, generally, the taxpayer must cancel the policy to receive the increase in value (the increase in value is subject to substantial restrictions).

EXAMPLE 42   T, age 50, paid $30,000 for an annuity contract that is to pay him $500 per month beginning when he reaches age 65 and continuing until his death. If T should cancel the policy after one year, he would receive $30,200. The $200 increase in value is not includible in the gross income of T, as long as T does not actually receive the $200. □

The tax accounting problem associated with receiving payments under an annuity contract is one of apportioning the amounts received between recovery of capital and income.

EXAMPLE 43   In 1990, T purchased for $15,000 an annuity intended to be a source of retirement income. In 1992, when the cash value of the annuity was $17,000, T collected $1,000 on the contract. Is the $1,000 gross income, recovery of capital, or a combination of recovery of capital and income? □

The statutory solution to this problem depends upon whether the payments began before or after the annuity starting date and upon when the policy was acquired.

Collections before the Annuity Starting Date.   Generally, an annuity contract specifies a date on which monthly or annual payments will begin—the annuity starting date. Often the contract will also allow the annuitant to collect a limited amount before the starting date. The amount collected may be characterized as either an actual withdrawal of the increase in cash value or a loan on the policy. In 1982, Congress changed the rules applicable to these withdrawals and loans.

Collections (including loans) equal to or less than the post–August 13, 1982, increases in cash value must be included in gross income. Amounts received in excess of post–August 13, 1982, increases in cash value are treated as a recovery of capital until the taxpayer's cost has been entirely recovered. Additional amounts are included in gross income. The taxpayer may also be subject to a penalty on early distributions of 10 percent of the income recognized. The penalty generally applies if the amount is received before the taxpayer reaches age 59½ or is disabled.

EXAMPLE 44

T, age 50, purchased an annuity policy for $30,000 in 1989. In 1991, when the cash value of the policy has increased to $33,000, T withdraws $4,000. T must recognize $3,000 of income ($33,000 cash value − $30,000 cost) and must pay a penalty of $300 ($3,000 × 10%). ☐

The 1982 rules were enacted because Congress perceived abuse of the recovery of capital rule. Previously, individuals could purchase annuity contracts that guaranteed an annual increase in cash value and withdraw the equivalent of interest on the contract but recognize no income. This is no longer possible. In addition, the individual must recognize income from borrowing on the contract (e.g., pledging the contract as security for a loan) as well as from an actual distribution.

Collections on and after the Annuity Starting Date.   The annuitant can exclude from income (as a recovery of capital) the proportion of each payment that the investment in the contract bears to the expected return under the contract. The *exclusion amount* is calculated as follows:

$$\frac{\text{Investment}}{\text{Expected return}} \quad \times \quad \text{Annuity payment} \quad = \quad \text{Exclusion amount}$$

The *expected return* is the annual amount to be paid to the annuitant multiplied by the number of years the payments will be received. The payment period may be fixed (a *term certain*) or for the life of one or more individuals. When payments are for life, the taxpayer must use the annuity table published by the IRS to determine the expected return (see Figure 3–1). This is an actuarial table that contains life expectancies.[22] The expected return is calculated by multiplying the appropriate multiple (life expectancy) by the annual payment.

EXAMPLE 45

The taxpayer, age 54, purchased an annuity from an insurance company for $90,000. He was to receive $500 per month for life. His life expectancy (from Figure 3–1) is 29.5 years from the annuity starting date. Thus, his expected return is $500 × 12 × 29.5 = $177,000, and the exclusion amount is $3,051 [($90,000 investment/$177,000 expected return) × $6,000 annual payment]. The $3,051 is a nontaxable return of capital, and $2,949 is included in gross income. ☐

22. The life expectancies in Figure 3–1 apply for annuity investments made on or after July 1, 1986. See *Pension and Annuity Income*, IRS Pub-

lication 575 (Rev. Nov. 87), pp. 22–24 for the IRS table to use for investments made before July 1, 1986.

FIGURE 3-1   Ordinary Life Annuities: One Life–Expected Return Multiples

Age	Multiple	Age	Multiple	Age	Multiple
5	76.6	42	40.6	79	10.0
6	75.6	43	39.6	80	9.5
7	74.7	44	38.7	81	8.9
8	73.7	45	37.7	82	8.4
9	72.7	46	36.8	83	7.9
10	71.7	47	35.9	84	7.4
11	70.7	48	34.9	85	6.9
12	69.7	49	34.0	86	6.5
13	68.8	50	33.1	87	6.1
14	67.8	51	32.2	88	5.7
15	66.8	52	31.3	89	5.3
16	65.8	53	30.4	90	5.0
17	64.8	54	29.5	91	4.7
18	63.9	55	28.6	92	4.4
19	62.9	56	27.7	93	4.1
20	61.9	57	26.8	94	3.9
21	60.9	58	25.9	95	3.7
22	59.9	59	25.0	96	3.4
23	59.0	60	24.2	97	3.2
24	58.0	61	23.3	98	3.0
25	57.0	62	22.5	99	2.8
26	56.0	63	21.6	100	2.7
27	55.1	64	20.8	101	2.5
28	54.1	65	20.0	102	2.3
29	53.1	66	19.2	103	2.1
30	52.2	67	18.4	104	1.9
31	51.2	68	17.6	105	1.8
32	50.2	69	16.8	106	1.6
33	49.3	70	16.0	107	1.4
34	48.3	71	15.3	108	1.3
35	47.3	72	14.6	109	1.1
36	46.4	73	13.9	110	1.0
37	45.4	74	13.2	111	.9
38	44.4	75	12.5	112	.8
39	43.5	76	11.9	113	.7
40	42.5	77	11.2	114	.6
41	41.5	78	10.6	115	.5

The exclusion ratio (investment ÷ expected return) applies until the annuitant has recovered his or her investment in the contract. Once the investment is recovered, the entire amount of subsequent payments is taxable. If the annuitant dies before recovering his or her investment, the unrecovered cost is deductible in the year the payments cease (usually the year of death).

EXAMPLE 46   Assume the taxpayer in Example 45 received annuity payments for 30.5 years (366 months). For the last 12 months [366 − (12 × 29.5) = 12], the taxpayer would include $500 each month in gross income. If instead the taxpayer died after 36 months, he is eligible for a deduction of $80,847 on his final tax return.

Cost of the contract	$90,000
Cost previously recovered $90,000/$177,000 × 36 ($500) =	(9,153)
Deduction	$80,847

Prizes and Awards

Before 1954, there was uncertainty relative to the taxability of prizes and awards. Taxpayers often sought to treat prizes and awards as nontaxable gifts. In many situations, it was difficult to determine whether the prize or award was in the nature of a gift. In 1954, Congress added § 74 to eliminate this uncertainty.

The fair market value of prizes and awards (other than scholarships exempted under § 117, to be discussed subsequently) must be included in income. Therefore, TV giveaway prizes, door prizes, and awards from an employer to an employee in recognition of performance are fully taxable to the recipient.

An exception is provided if the award is received in recognition of religious, charitable, scientific, educational, artistic, literary, or civic achievement and the recipient transfers the award to a qualified governmental unit or nonprofit organization. In such cases, the recipient must be selected without any action on his or her part to enter a contest or proceeding, and the recipient must not be required to render substantial future services as a condition for receiving the prize or award. Thus, the benefit of the exclusion appears to be to allow the recipient to avoid any annual limitation on the charitable contributions deduction (see chapter 10).

Another exception is provided for certain employee achievement awards in the form of tangible personal property (e.g., a gold watch). The awards must be made in recognition of length of service or safety achievement. Generally, the ceiling on the excludible amount is $400. However, if the award is a qualified plan award, the ceiling on the exclusion is $1,600.

Group Term Life Insurance

Before 1964, the IRS did not attempt to tax the value of life insurance protection provided to an employee by the employer. Some companies took undue advantage of the exclusion by providing large amounts of insurance protection for executives. Therefore, Congress enacted § 79, which created a limited exclusion. Current law allows an exclusion for premiums on the first $50,000 of group term life insurance protection.

The benefits of this exclusion are available only to employees. Proprietors and partners are not considered employees. Moreover, the Regulations generally require broad-scale coverage of employees to satisfy the *group* requirement (e.g., shareholder-employees would not constitute a qualified group). The exclusion applies only to term insurance (protection for a period of time but with no cash surrender value) and not to ordinary life insurance (lifetime protection plus a cash surrender value that can be drawn upon before death).

As mentioned, the exclusion applies to the first $50,000 of group term life insurance protection. For each $1,000 coverage in excess of $50,000, the employee must include the following amounts in gross income.

Uniform Premiums for $1,000 of Group Term Life Insurance Protection	
Attained Age Last Day of the Employee's Tax Year	Cost per $1,000 of Protection for One-Month Period
Under 30	8 cents
30–34	9 cents
35–39	11 cents
40–44	17 cents
45–49	29 cents
50–54	48 cents
55–59	75 cents
60–64	$1.17

EXAMPLE 47

XYZ Corporation has a group term life insurance policy with coverage equal to the employee's annual salary. T, age 52, is president of the corporation and receives an annual salary of $75,000. T must include $144 in gross income from the insurance protection for the year.

$$\left(\frac{\$75,000 - \$50,000}{\$1,000} \right) \times (.48) \times (12 \text{ months}) = \$144 \qquad \square$$

Generally, the amount that must be included in income, computed from the above table, is much less than the price an individual would pay for the same amount of protection. Thus, even the excess coverage provides some tax-favored income for employees when group term life insurance coverage in excess of $50,000 is desirable. However, if the plan discriminates in favor of certain key employees (e.g., officers), the key employees are not eligible for the exclusion. In such a case, the key employees must include in gross income the greater of actual premiums paid by the employer or the amount calculated from the Uniform Premiums table. The other employees are still eligible for the $50,000 exclusion and continue to use the Uniform Premiums table to compute the income from excess insurance protection.

Unemployment Compensation

In a series of rulings over a period of 40 years, the IRS exempted unemployment benefits from tax. These payments were considered social benefit programs for the promotion of the general welfare. As previously discussed, the scope of § 61, gross income, is probably broad enough to include unemployment benefits (since an increase in wealth is realized when the payments are received). Nevertheless, the IRS had chosen to exclude such benefits.

In 1978, Congress addressed the unemployment compensation issue and provided that unemployment benefits are taxable only if the recipient's adjusted gross income exceeds certain levels. In 1986, Congress readdressed the issue by providing that all unemployment compensation benefits are includible in gross income.

Social Security Benefits

If a taxpayer's income exceeds a specified base amount, as much as one-half of Social Security retirement benefits must be included in gross income. The taxable amount of Social Security benefits is the *lesser* of the following:

- .50 (Social Security benefits)
- .50 [modified adjusted gross income + .50 (Social Security benefits) – base amount]

Modified adjusted gross income is, generally, the taxpayer's adjusted gross income from all sources (other than Social Security), plus the foreign earned income exclusion and any tax-exempt interest received. The *base amount* is as follows:

- $32,000 for married taxpayers who file a joint return.
- $0 for married taxpayers who do not live apart for the entire year but file separate returns.
- $25,000 for all other taxpayers.

EXAMPLE 48	A married couple with adjusted gross income of $40,000, no tax-exempt interest, and $11,000 of Social Security benefits who file jointly must include one-half of the benefits in gross income. This works out as the lesser of the following:

1. .50 ($11,000) = $5,500
2. .50 [$40,000 + .50 ($11,000) − $32,000] = .50 ($13,500) = $6,750

  If the couple's adjusted gross income were $15,000 and Social Security benefits totaled $5,000, none of the benefits would be taxable since .50 [$15,000 + .50 ($5,000) − $32,000] = $0. □

TAX PLANNING CONSIDERATIONS

The materials in this chapter focused on the all-inclusive concept of gross income. Not much was discussed concerning ways to minimize taxable income. However, a few observations can be made with regard to timing the recognition of income, shifting income to relatives, accounting for community property, and the treatment of alimony.

Tax Deferral

General. Since deferred taxes are tantamount to interest-free loans from the government, the deferral of taxes is a worthy goal of the tax planner. However, the tax planner must also consider the tax rates for the years the income is shifted from and to. For example, a one-year deferral of income from a year in which the taxpayer's tax rate was 15 percent to a year in which the tax rate will be 28 percent would not be advisable if the taxpayer expects to earn less than a 13 percent after-tax return on the deferred tax dollars.

  The taxpayer can often defer the recognition of income from appreciated property by postponing the event triggering realization (the final closing on a sale

or exchange of property). If the taxpayer needs cash, obtaining a loan by using the appreciated property as collateral may be the least costly alternative. When the taxpayer anticipates reinvesting the proceeds, a sale may be inadvisable.

EXAMPLE 49

T owns 100 shares of XYZ Company common stock with a cost of $10,000 and a fair market value of $50,000. Although the stock's value has increased substantially in the past three years, T thinks the growth days are over. If he sells the XYZ stock, T will invest the proceeds from the sale in other common stock. Assuming T is in the 28% marginal tax bracket, he will have only $38,800 [$50,000 − .28 ($50,000 − $10,000)] to reinvest. The alternative investment must substantially outperform XYZ in the future in order for the sale to be beneficial. □

Selection of Investments.   Because no tax is due until a gain has been recognized, the law favors investments that yield appreciation rather than annual income.

EXAMPLE 50

S can buy a corporate bond or an acre of land for $10,000. The bond pays $1,000 of interest (10%) each year, and S expects the land to increase in value 10% each year for the next 10 years. She is in the 40% (combined Federal and state) tax bracket. Assuming the bond would mature or the land would be sold in 10 years and S would reinvest the interest at a 10% before-tax return, she would accumulate the following amount at the end of 10 years.

		Bonds	Land
Original investment		$10,000	$10,000
Annual income	$ 1,000		
Less tax	(400)		
	$ 600		
Compound amount reinvested for 10 years at 6% after-tax	× 13.18	7,908	
		$17,908	
Compound amount, 10 years at 10%			× 2.59
			$25,900
Less tax on sale: 40%($25,900 − $10,000)			(6,360)
			$19,540

Therefore, the value of the deferral that results from investing in the land rather than in the bond is $1,632 ($19,540 − $17,908). □

Series E and EE bonds can also be purchased for long-term deferrals of income. As discussed in the chapter, Series E bonds can be exchanged for new Series HH bonds to further postpone the tax. In situations where the taxpayer's goal is merely to shift income one year into the future, bank certificates of deposit are useful tools. If the maturity period is one year or less, all interest is reported in the year of maturity. Time certificates are especially useful for a taxpayer who realizes an unusually large gain from the sale of property in one year (and thus is in a high tax bracket) but expects his or her income to be less the following year.

Cash Basis.   The timing of income from services can often be controlled through the use of the cash method of accounting. Although taxpayers are somewhat constrained by the constructive receipt doctrine (they cannot turn their backs on income), seldom will customers and clients offer to pay before they are asked. The usual lag between billings and collections (e.g., December's billings collected in January) will result in a continuous deferring of some income until the last year of operations. A salaried individual approaching retirement may contract with his or her employer before the services are rendered to receive a portion of the compensation in the lower tax bracket retirement years.

Prepaid Income.   For the accrual basis taxpayer who receives advance payments from customers, the transactions should be structured to avoid payment of tax on income before the time the income is actually earned. Revenue Procedure 71–21 provides the guidelines for deferring the tax on prepayments for services, and Reg. § 1.451–5 provides the guidelines for deferrals on sales of goods. In addition, with respect to both the cash and accrual basis taxpayer, income can sometimes be deferred by stipulating that the payments are deposits rather than prepaid income. For example, a landlord should require an equivalent damage deposit rather than require prepayment of the last month's rent under the lease.

Shifting Income to Relatives

The tax liability of a family can be minimized by shifting income from higher- to lower-bracket family members. This can be accomplished through gifts of income-producing property. Furthermore, in many cases, the shifting of income can be accomplished with no negative effect on the family's investment plans.

EXAMPLE 51	B, who is in the 28% tax bracket, would like to save for his children's education. All of the children are under 14 years of age. Mr. B could transfer income-producing properties to the children, and the children could each receive income of up to $500 each year with no tax liability. The next $500 would be taxed at the child's tax rate. After a child has more than $1,000 income, there is no tax advantage to shifting more income to the child (because the income will be taxed at the parents' rate) until the child is 14 years old (when all income will be taxed at the child's tax rate). ☐

The Uniform Gifts to Minors Act, a model law adopted by all states (but with some variations among the states), facilitates income shifting. Under the Act, a gift of intangibles (e.g., bank accounts, stocks, bonds, life insurance contracts) can be made to a minor but with an adult serving as custodian. Usually, a parent who makes the gift is also named as custodian. The state laws allow the custodian to sell or redeem and reinvest the principal and to accumulate or distribute the income, practically at the custodian's discretion provided there is no commingling of the child's income with the parent's property. Thus, the parent can give appreciated securities to the child, and the donor custodian can then sell the securities and reinvest the proceeds, thereby shifting both the gain and annual income to the child. Such planning is limited by the tax liability calculation provision for a child under the age of 14 (refer to chapter 2).

U.S. government bonds (Series E and EE) can be purchased by the parent for his or her children. When this is done, the children generally should file a return and elect to report the income on the accrual basis.

EXAMPLE 52   F (father) pays $7,500 for Series EE bonds in 1990 and immediately gives them to S (son), who will enter college the year of original maturity of the bonds. The bonds have a maturity value of $10,000. S elects to report the annual increment in redemption value as income for each year the bonds are held. The first year the increase is $250, and S includes that amount in his gross income. If S has no other income, no tax will be due on the $250 bond interest since such an amount will be more than offset by S's available standard deduction. The following year, the increment is $260, and S includes this amount in income. Thus, over the life of the bonds, S will include $2,500 in income ($10,000 − $7,500), none of which will result in a tax liability, assuming S has no other income. However, if the election had not been made, S would be required to include $2,500 in income on the bonds in the year of original maturity, if redeemed as planned. This amount of income might result in a tax liability. □

In some cases, it may be advantageous for the child not to make the accrual election. For example, a child under age 14 with investment income of more than $1,000 each year and parents in the 28 percent tax bracket would probably benefit from deferring the tax on the savings bond interest. The child would also benefit from the use of the usually lower tax rate (rather than subjecting the income to his or her parents' tax rate) if the bonds mature after the child is age 14 or older.

Alimony

The person making alimony payments favors a divorce settlement that includes a provision for deductible alimony payments. On the other hand, the recipient prefers that the payments do not qualify as alimony. If the payor is in a higher tax bracket than the recipient, both parties may benefit by increasing the payments and structuring them so that they qualify as alimony.

EXAMPLE 53   H and W are negotiating a divorce settlement. H has offered to pay W $10,000 each year for 10 years, but payments would cease upon W's death. W is willing to accept the offer, if the agreement will specify that the cash payments are not alimony. H is in the 33 percent tax bracket, and W's marginal rate is 15 percent.
    If H and W agree that H would pay W $12,000 of alimony each year, W as well as H would have improved after-tax cash flows.

	Annual Cash Flows	
	H	W
Non-alimony payments	$(10,000)	$10,000
Alimony payments	$(12,000)	$12,000
Tax effects		
.33 ($12,000)	3,960	
.15 ($12,000)		(1,800)
After-tax cash flows	$ (8,040)	$10,200
Benefit of alimony option	$ 1,960	$ 200

Both parties benefit at the government's expense if the $12,000 alimony option is used. □

PROBLEM MATERIALS

Discussion Questions

1. What are some of the differences between accounting, tax, and economic concepts of income?

2. Which of the following would be considered "income" for the current year by an economist but would not be gross income for tax purposes? Explain.
   a. Securities acquired two years ago for $10,000 had a value at the beginning of the current year of $12,000 and a value at the end of the year of $13,000.
   b. An individual lives in the home he owns.
   c. A corporation obtained a loan from a bank.
   d. A shareholder paid a corporation $3,000 for property worth $5,000.
   e. An individual owned property that was stolen. The cost of the property three years ago was $2,000, and an insurance company paid the owner $6,000 (the value of the property on the date of theft).
   f. At the end of the current year a shareholder sold stock for 200% of all dividends to be paid on the stock from the date of sale until the shareholder's death.
   g. An individual found a box of seventeenth-century Spanish coins while diving off the Virginia coast.
   h. An individual received a $200 rebate from the manufacturer upon the purchase of a new car.

3. According to economists, because our tax system does not impute income to homeowners for the rental value of their homes, the non-homeowner who invests in securities (rather than a home) is taxed more heavily than the homeowner. This leads to overinvesting in homes. Why do you suppose the laws are not changed to tax homeowners on the rental value of their homes?

4. Evaluate the arguments in favor of deferring the recognition of income until a sale or exchange occurs in the following cases:
   a. A farmer owns appreciated land.
   b. A corporation owns appreciated inventory.
   c. An investor owns appreciated stock listed on the New York Stock Exchange.

5. T had owned a tract of land for several years when the local government decided to build an airport near the property. T's cost of the property was $50,000. The local government paid T $10,000 for invasion of his airspace. What is T's gross income from the receipt of the $10,000?

6. T is in the 28% tax bracket. He has the following alternative uses of his time: (1) T can work and earn $600 (before tax), or (2) T can stay at home and paint his house. If T selects (1), he must pay $500 to have his house painted. Which alternative would our tax laws encourage T to select?

7. Comment on the following: "Our tax laws encourage the taxpayer to hold appreciated investment assets and to sell investment assets that have declined in value."

8. A corporation pays all of its monthly salaried employees on the last Friday in each month. What would be the tax consequences to the employees if the date of payment were changed to the first Monday of the following month?

9. T believes that his tax rates will be lower in 1991 than in 1990. To take advantage of the lower rates, T instructs his employer to wait until January 1991 to give him

his salary check for December 1990. In the past, T has always received his December check on or before December 31. Evaluate T's tax planning strategy.

10. T is a cash basis attorney. On December 31, 1990, a client was on the way to T's office to pay T a $5,000 fee. T met the client on the elevator, and the client offered T $5,000 cash. As T reached for the cash, the elevator came to an abrupt halt, causing T to fall against a railing, bump his head, and lose consciousness. On January 1, 1991, T awoke in the hospital to the sound of the persistent client stuffing $5,000 into T's pajama pocket. When should T report the $5,000 as income?

11. Is a cash basis taxpayer ever taxed on income before cash or its equivalent is actually or constructively received?

12. M, an accrual basis taxpayer, performed services for a client in 1990. The charge for the service was $450, but the customer paid only $200 in 1990 because he claimed that M did not adequately perform the service. M and the client negotiated a settlement in 1991, and the client paid an additional $150. What is M's 1990 income from the contract?

13. In 1990, T, an accrual basis taxpayer, rendered services for a customer with a poor credit rating. T's charge for the service was $1,000. T sent a bill to the customer for $1,000 but reported only $500 of income. He justified reporting only $500 as follows: "I'm being generous reporting $500. I'll be lucky if I collect anything." How much should T include as gross income from the contract in 1990.

14. In January 1990, T, a cash basis taxpayer, purchased for $2,000 a five-year Series EE U.S. government bond with a maturity value of $3,000. He also purchased for $2,000 a three-year bank certificate of deposit with a maturity value of $2,500. Is T required to recognize any interest income in 1990?

15. M is in the wholesale hardware business. His customers pay for the goods at the time they place the order. Often, M is out of stock on particular items and must back order the goods. When this occurs, he usually retains the customer's payment, orders the goods from the manufacturer, and ships the goods to the customer within a month. At the end of the year there were several unfilled orders. Is it possible for M to defer the recognition of income from the receipt of advance payments on the unfilled orders?

16. F (father) paid $200 for an automobile that needed repairs. He worked nights and weekends to restore the car. Several individuals offered to purchase the car for $2,800. F gave the car and a list of potential buyers to S (son), whose college tuition was due in a few days. S sold the car for $2,800 and paid his tuition. Does F have any taxable income from the transaction?

17. F, a cash basis taxpayer, sold a bond with accrued interest of $750, for $10,250. F's basis in the bond was $9,000. Compute F's income from this transaction.

18. Father gave Son 100 shares of X Corporation stock on June 20. X Corporation had declared a $1 per share dividend on the stock on June 15, payable on June 30 to holders of record as of June 25. Who must report the dividend income, Father or Son?

19. P transferred rental properties to a corporation. P's objective was to minimize his liability for injuries that may occur on the property. The tenants continued to pay rents to P. Who must include the rents in gross income?

20. Who pays the tax on undistributed income of (a) an S corporation and (b) an estate?

21. What is the purpose of the front-loading rules?

22. A post-1984 divorce agreement between H and W provides that H is to pay W $500 per month for 13 years. H and W have a child who is 8 years old. Termination of the monthly payments will coincide with the child's attaining age 21. Can the monthly payments qualify as alimony?

23. H and W were divorced. Under the terms of the divorce agreement, H was to pay W $10,000 each year for five years. If W died before the end of five years, H was no longer obligated to make the payments. W remarried after receiving payments for two years. Under the laws of the particular state, alimony ceases upon remarriage of the payee. H continued to make the payments in accordance with the original agreement. Is W required to include in gross income the payments received in the third year and thereafter?

24. H and W were divorced. They jointly owned a home in the mountains with a basis of $50,000 and a fair market value of $80,000. According to the terms of the divorce, W gave H $40,000 for his one-half interest in the mountain home. W later sold the house for $85,000. What is W's gain from the sale?

25. T received an interest-free loan from his employer. He received $24,200 on January 1, 1990, and signed a note for that amount due on December 31, 1991. At the time of the loan, the applicable Federal rate was 10% (compounded annually). What are the effects of the loan on T's 1990 taxable income?

26. T is an employee and the sole shareholder of T Corporation. The corporation loaned T $50,000 and did not charge T interest. The IRS agent imputed interest on the loan, which the agent characterizes as a corporation-shareholder loan. T insists that the loan is an employer-employee loan. What difference does it make?

27. Suppose the annuity tables used by the IRS were outdated and that people lived longer than the tables indicated. How would this affect Federal revenues?

28. R's employer provided him with group term life insurance protection equal to his wages for the previous year, $30,000. The employer's cost of the coverage was $300, and the Uniform Premium amount was $270. The plan was declared discriminatory because officers received insurance equal to three times their annual salaries. What is R's gross income from the insurance protection?

29. When a taxpayer is receiving Social Security benefits, could a $1,000 increase in income from services cause the taxpayer's adjusted gross income to increase by more than $1,000?

30. Why do you suppose that no more than one-half of a recipient's Social Security benefits are taxable?

Problems

31. Does the taxpayer realize gross income from the following events?
    a. T bought a used piano for $50. When he started repairing the piano, he discovered it was stuffed with Confederate notes with a face amount of $10,000. T knows that collectors will pay him $30 for the Confederate notes.
    b. Same as (a), except the notes have a value of $500.
    c. T also discovered oil on his property during the year, and the value of the land increased from $10,000 to $5,000,000.

32. Determine the taxpayer's income for tax purposes in each of the following cases:
    a. In the current year, RST Corporation purchased $1,000,000 par value of its own bonds and paid the bondholders $980,000 plus $50,000 of accrued interest. The bonds had been issued 10 years ago at par and were to mature 25 years from the date of issue. Does the corporation recognize income from the purchase of the bonds?
    b. A shareholder of a corporation sold property to the corporation for $60,000 (the shareholder's cost). The value of the property on the date of sale was $50,000. Does the taxpayer have any taxable income from the sale?

c. T was a football coach at a state university. Because of his disappointing record, he was asked to resign and accept one-half of his pay for the remaining three years of his contract. The coach resigned, accepting $75,000.

33. Which of the following investments will yield the greater after-tax value assuming the taxpayer is in the 40% tax bracket (combined Federal and state) in all years and the investments will be liquidated at the end of five years?

a. Land that will increase in value by 10% each year.

b. A taxable bond yielding 10% before tax, and the interest can be reinvested at 10% before tax.

c. Common stock that will increase in value at the rate of 5% (compounded) each year and pays dividends equal to 5% of the year-end value of the stock. The dividends can be reinvested at 10% before tax.

d. A tax-exempt state government bond yielding 8%. The interest can be reinvested at a before-tax rate of 10%, and the bond matures in 10 years.

Given: Compound amount of $1 at the end of five years:

Interest Rate	Factor
6%	1.33
8%	1.47
10%	1.61

Compound value of annuity payments at the end of five years:

Interest Rate	Factor
6%	5.64
8%	5.87
10%	6.11

34. Determine the taxpayer's income for tax purposes in each of the following cases:

a. R borrowed $30,000 from the First National Bank. R was required to deliver to the bank stocks with a value of $30,000 and a cost of $10,000. The stocks were to serve as collateral for the loan.

b. P owned a lot on Sycamore Street that measured 100 feet by 100 feet. His cost of the lot is $10,000. The city condemned a 10-foot strip of the land so that it could widen the street. P received a $2,000 condemnation award.

c. M owned land zoned for residential use only. The land cost $5,000 and had a market value of $7,000. M spent $500 and several hundred hours petitioning the county supervisors to change the zoning to A–1 commercial. The value of the property immediately increased to $20,000 when the county approved the zoning change.

35. X, Inc., is a dance studio that sells dance lessons for cash, on open account, and for notes receivable. The company also collects interest on bonds held as an investment. The company's cash receipts for 1990 totaled $219,000:

Cash sales	$ 60,000
Collections on accounts receivable	120,000
Collections on notes receivable	30,000
Interest on bonds	9,000
	$219,000

The balances in accounts receivable, notes receivable, and accrued interest on bonds at the beginning and end of the year were as follows:

	1-1-90	**12-31-90**
Accounts receivable	$25,000	$22,000
Notes receivable	12,000	11,000
Accrued interest on bonds	3,000	4,000
	$40,000	$37,000

The fair market value of the notes is equal to 75% of their face amount. There were no bad debts for the year, and all notes were for services performed during the year. Compute the corporation's gross income:

a. Using the cash basis of accounting.

b. Using the accrual basis of accounting.

c. Using a hybrid method—accrual basis for lessons and cash basis for interest income.

36. M owns a life insurance policy. The cash surrender value of the policy increased $1,500 during the year. He purchased a certificate of deposit on June 30 of the current year for $37,600. The certificate matures in three years when its value will be $50,000 (interest rate of 10%). However, if M redeems the certificate before the end of the first year, he receives no interest. M also purchased a Series EE U.S. government savings bond for $6,000. The maturity value of the bond is $10,000 in six years (yield of 9%), and the redemption price of the bond increased by $400 during the year. M has owned no other savings bonds. What is M's current year gross income from the above items?

37. R is an accrual basis taxpayer. Determine his 1990 gross income from the following transactions:

a. In December 1990, R sold goods under terms that specified that the customer owned the product but could return it within 30 days of purchase if not completely satisfied. In January 1991, goods sold in December for $20,000 (cost of $12,000) were returned by dissatisfied customers.

b. R performed services in 1990 and sent his customer a bill for $5,000. The customer placed a $5,000 check in the mail on December 31, 1990, but R did not receive the check until January 3, 1991.

c. In 1990, R collected $4,000 from the sale of a product that cost R $2,800. The customer claimed the product was defective and filed a suit in 1990 for refund. In 1991 (before R filed his 1990 return), the court awarded the customer damages of $2,000.

d. R sold goods that cost $3,500 for $5,000. The customer gave R a note for $5,000. However, the customer was a poor credit risk, and the fair market value of the note was only $2,000.

38. P is a cash basis taxpayer. Determine her 1990 gross income from the following transactions:

a. In 1988, P negotiated her 1989 salary. The employer offered to pay P $200,000 in 1989. P countered that she wanted $10,000 each month in 1989 and the remaining $80,000 in January 1990. P wanted the $80,000 income shifted to 1990 because she expected her 1990 tax rates to be lower. The employer agreed to P's terms.

b. In 1989, P was running short of cash and needed money for Christmas. Her employer loaned her $20,000 in November 1989. P signed a note for $20,000 plus 10% interest, the applicable Federal rate. In January 1990, the employer subtracted the $20,000 and $333 interest from the $80,000 due P and paid P $59,667.

c. On December 31, 1990, Z offered to buy land from P for $30,000 (P's basis was $8,000). P refused to sell in 1990, but at that time, P contracted to sell the land to Z in 1991 for $30,000.

39. Discuss the tax effects of the following transactions on an accrual basis taxpayer:

a. On December 15, 1989, B signed a contract to purchase land from T. Payment for the land was to be made on closing, January 15, 1990. During the interval between the contract and the closing dates, B's attorney was to verify that T had good title to the land. The closing was completed on January 15, 1990.

b. M collected $1,500 for services rendered the client in 1989. Late in 1989, the client complained that the work was not done in accordance with contract specifications. Also in 1989, the parties agreed to allow an arbitrator to settle the dispute. In January 1990, the arbitrator ordered M to refund $500 to the client.

40. The Z Apartments requires its new tenants to pay the rent for the first and last months of the annual lease and a $300 damage deposit, all at the time the lease is signed. In December 1990, a tenant paid $600 for January 1991 rent, $600 for December 1991 rent, and $300 for the damage deposit. In January 1992, Z refunded the tenant's damage deposit. What are the effects of these payments on Z's taxable income for 1990, 1991, and 1992?

a. Assume Z is a cash basis taxpayer.

b. Assume Z is an accrual basis taxpayer.

41. M has asked you to review portions of her tax return. She provides you with the following information:

Gain on redemption of a 2-year 10% certificate of deposit		
Proceeds received, June 30, 1990	$10,000	
Purchase price, July 1, 1988	(8,200)	
Gain		$1,800
Gain on redemption of a 6-month 9% certificate of deposit		
Proceeds received, March 31, 1990	$ 5,000	
Purchase price, October 1, 1989	(4,580)	
Gain		420
Gain from 8% Series E savings bond		
Proceeds received, September 30, 1990	$ 2,500	
Purchase price, June 30, 1977	(780)	
Gain		1,720
Distributions from a family partnership		1,500

M's share of the partnership's earnings were $1,400. Determine M's 1990 gross income from the preceding items.

42. a. T is a cash basis taxpayer. On December 1, 1990, T gave a corporate bond to his son, S. The bond had a face amount of $10,000 and paid $900 each January 31. Also on December 1, 1990, T gave common stocks to his daughter, D. Dividends totaling $720 had been declared on the stocks on November 30, 1990, and were payable on January 15, 1991. D became the shareholder of record in time to collect the dividends. What is T's 1991 gross income from the bond and stocks?

b. In 1990, T's mother was unable to pay her bills as they came due. T, his employer, and his mother's creditors entered into an arrangement whereby T's employer would withhold $500 per month from T's salary and the employer would pay the $500 to the creditors. In 1990, $3,000 was withheld from T's salary and paid to the creditors. Is T required to pay tax on the $3,000?

c. F is considering purchasing a zero coupon (no interest is paid until maturity) corporate bond for himself and for his minor son, S (age 4). The bonds have an issue price of $300 and pay $1,000 at the end of 10 years. F is in the 28% tax bracket, and S has no other taxable income. Would the zero coupon bond be an equally suitable investment for F and S?

43. a. An automobile dealer has several new cars in inventory but often does not have the right combination of body style, color, and accessories. In some cases, the dealer makes an offer to sell a car at a certain price, accepts a deposit, and then orders the car from the manufacturer. When the car is received from the manufacturer, the sale is closed, and the dealer receives the balance of the sales price. At the end of the current year, the dealer has deposits totaling $8,200 for cars that have not been received from the manufacturer. When is the $8,200 subject to tax?

b. T Corporation, an exterminating company, is a calendar year taxpayer. It contracts to service homeowners once a month under a one-year or a two-year contract. On April 1 of the current year, the company sold a customer a one-year contract for $60. How much of the $60 is taxable in the current year if the company is an accrual basis taxpayer? If the $60 is payment on a two-year contract, how much is taxed in the year the contract is sold?

c. X, an accrual basis taxpayer, owns an amusement park whose fiscal year ends September 30. To increase business during the fall and winter months, X sold passes that would allow the holder to ride free during the months of October through March. During the month of September, $6,000 was collected from the sale of passes for the upcoming fall and winter. When will the $6,000 be taxable to X?

d. The taxpayer is in the office equipment rental business and uses the accrual basis of accounting. In December, he collected $5,000 in rents for the following January. When is the $5,000 taxable?

44. T owns 100% of the stock of T, Inc., an S corporation. For 1990, the corporation earned $90,000 taxable income but paid only $25,000 in dividends to T. T is also a beneficiary of a trust. The trustee can distribute or withhold income according to the needs of the beneficiary. In 1990, the trust earned $20,000 but distributed only $8,000 to T because T had adequate income from other sources. What is T's taxable income from the S corporation and trust for 1990?

45. Mr. and Mrs. X are in the process of negotiating their divorce agreement. What would be the tax consequences to Mr. X and Mrs. X if the following, considered individually, become part of the agreement?

a. Mrs. X is to receive $1,000 per month until she dies or remarries. She also is to receive $500 per month for 12 years for her one-half interest in their personal residence. She paid for her one-half interest in the house out of her earnings.

b. Mrs. X is to receive a principal sum of $100,000. Of this amount, $50,000 is to be paid in the year of the divorce and $5,000 per year will be paid to her in each of the following 10 years or until her death.

c. Mrs. X is to receive the family residence (value of $120,000 and basis of $75,000). The home was jointly owned by Mr. and Mrs. X. In exchange for the residence, Mrs. X relinquished all of her rights to property accumulated during the marriage. She also is to receive $1,000 per month until her death or remarriage but for a period of not longer than 10 years.

46. Under the terms of a post-1986 divorce agreement, W is to receive payments from H as follows: $50,000 in Year 1, $40,000 in Year 2, and $20,000 each year for Years 3 through 10. W is also to receive custody of their minor son. The payments will decrease by $5,000 per year if the son dies or when he attains age 21 and will cease upon W's death.

    a. What will be W's taxable alimony in Year 1?

    b. What will be the effect of the Years 2 and 3 payments on W's taxable income?

47. Under the terms of their divorce agreement, H is to transfer common stocks (cost of $25,000, market value of $60,000) to W in satisfaction of W's property rights. W is also to receive $15,000 per year until her death or remarriage. W originally asked for $9,000 alimony and $5,000 child support. It was the understanding between H and W that W would use $5,000 of the amount received for the support of the children. How will the terms of the agreement affect H's taxable income?

48. a. M (mother) is in the 28% tax bracket, and S (son) is in the 15% tax bracket. M loans S $50,000, and S invests the money in a bond that yields a 10% return. If M had not made the loan, she would have purchased the bond. The relevant Federal rate is 13%. There are no other loans between the family members. What is the effect of the preceding transactions on M's and S's combined tax for the year?

    b. T, an individual, had outstanding interest-free loans receivable as follows:

Borrower	Amount of Loan	Use of the Loan Proceeds
S, T's son	$ 15,000	Medical school tuition
D, T's daughter	25,000	Start of an unincorporated business
R, T's employee	2,000	Payment of medical bills
B, T's brother	110,000	Payment of attorney fees

S had $1,500 net investment income for the year. D's income was $5,000 earned by the business and $1,500 of dividends. R's only income was his $12,000 salary. B is in prison serving 145 years to life and has no income.

All loans were outstanding for the entire year, and the Federal rate is 12% compounded semiannually (12.36% effective annual rate).

Compute T's imputed interest income.

49. On June 30, 1990, T borrowed $50,000 from his employer. On July 1, 1990, T used the money as follows:

Interest-free loan to T's controlled corporation (operated by T on a part-time basis)	$21,000
Interest-free loan to S (T's son)	9,000
National Bank of Grundy 9% certificate of deposit ($15,260 due at maturity, June 30, 1991)	14,000
National Bank of Grundy 10% certificate of deposit ($7,260 due at maturity, June 30, 1992)	6,000
	$50,000

T's employer did not charge him interest. The applicable Federal rate was 12% throughout the relevant period. S had investment income of $800 for the year, and he used the loan proceeds to pay medical school tuition. There were no other outstanding loans between T and S. What are the effects of the preceding transactions on T's taxable income for 1990?

50. Indicate whether the imputed interest rules should apply in the following situations:

    a. T is a cash basis attorney who charges his clients based on the number of hours it takes to do the job. The bill is due upon completion of the work. However, for clients who make an initial payment when the work begins, T grants a discount on the final bill. The discount is equal to 10% interest on the deposit.

b. L Telephone Company requires that customers make a security deposit. The deposit is refunded after the customer has established a good record for paying the telephone bill. The company pays 6% interest on the deposits.

c. D asked F for a $125,000 loan to purchase a new home. F made the loan and did not charge interest. F never intended to collect the loan, and at the end of the year F told D that the debt was forgiven

51. Mr. Z is the sole shareholder of Z, Inc. He is also employed by the corporation. On June 30, 1989, Z borrowed $8,000 from Z, Inc., and on July 1, 1990, he borrowed an additional $3,000. Both loans were due on demand. No interest was charged on the loans and the Federal rate was 10% for all relevant dates. Z used the money to purchase stock, and he had no investment income. Determine the tax consequences to Z and Z, Inc., in each of the following situations.

a. The loans are considered employer-employee loans.

b. The loans are considered corporation-shareholder loans.

52. T purchased an annuity from an insurance company for $12,000 on January 1, 1990. The annuity was to pay him $1,500 per year for life. At the time he purchased the contract, his life expectancy was 10 years.

a. Determine T's taxable income from the annuity in the first year.

b. Assume T lives 20 years after purchasing the contract. What would be T's taxable income in the nineteenth year?

c. Assume T died in 1993, after collecting a total of $6,000. What will be the effect of the annuity on his 1993 gross income?

53. In 1990, R purchased an annuity for $50,000. He was 59 at the time he purchased the contract. Payments were to begin when R attained age 62. In 1990, when the cash surrender value had increased to $51,000, R exercised a right to receive $1,500 and accept reduced payments after age 62. In 1992, when he had a life expectancy of 22.5 years, R received his first annual $3,000 payment under the contract.

a. What is R's income from the contract in 1990?

b. Compute R's taxable collections under the annuity contract in 1992.

54. Indicate whether the following items result in taxable income to the recipient. If the item is not taxable, explain why.

a. S won the Miss Centerville beauty contest and received a $1,000 cash prize.

b. L won the master's mile run. As the winner, L received a $1,000 cash prize paid by a philanthropist who sponsored the race to encourage running.

c. Mr. and Mrs. D are married and file a joint return. They had adjusted gross income of $19,000 before considering unemployment benefits of $1,800.

55. T does not think she has an income tax problem but would like to discuss her situation with you just to make sure she will not get hit with an unexpected tax liability. Base your suggestions on the following relevant financial information:

a. T's share of the SAT Partnership income is $40,000, but none of the income can be distributed because the partnership needs the cash for operations.

b. T's Social Security benefits totaled $8,400, but T loaned the cash received to her nephew.

c. T assigned to a creditor the right to collect $1,200 interest on some bonds she owned.

d. T and her husband lived together in California until September, when they separated. T has heard rumors that her husband had substantial gambling winnings since they separated.

56. M and W are married and file a joint return. In 1990, they received $9,000 in Social Security benefits and $28,000 taxable pension benefits, interest, and dividends.

a. Compute the couple's adjusted gross income on a joint return.

b. If M works part-time and earns $6,000, how much would M and W's adjusted gross income increase?

c. Assume W cashed certificates of deposit that had paid $8,000 in interest each year and purchases State of Virginia bonds that pay $6,000 in interest each year. How much would M and W's adjusted gross income decrease? (Assume W had no gain or loss from cashing the certificates.)

57. In the following problems, assume the unmarried taxpayer has no tax-exempt interest income and receives $6,000 per year in Social Security benefits:

a. Compute the maximum adjusted gross income from other sources the taxpayer can receive without including any of the Social Security benefits in adjusted gross income.

b. How much adjusted gross income from other sources must the taxpayer receive before $3,000 in Social Security benefits are included in adjusted gross income?

58. The LMN Partnership has a group term life insurance plan. Each partner has $100,000 protection, and each employee has protection equal to twice his or her annual salary. Employee V (age 34) had $80,000 insurance under the plan, and partner N (age 46) had $100,000 coverage. The cost of V's coverage for the year was $110, and the cost of N's protection was $380.

a. Assuming the plan was nondiscriminatory, how much must V and N include in gross income from the insurance?

b. Assuming the plan is discriminatory, how much must N include in his gross income from the insurance?

Cumulative Problems

59. Thomas R. Rucker, age 42, is single and is employed as a plumber for Ajax Plumbing Company. Tom's Social Security number is 262–06–3814. Tom lives at 252 Mason Place, Grand View, WV 22801. His salary was $38,000, and his employer withheld Federal income tax of $7,600.

Tom's mother, Sue Rucker, age 68, lives in a small house Tom bought for her in Florida. She has no income of her own and is totally dependent on Tom for her support. To provide his mother with some spending money, Tom assigned to her the income from some XYZ Corporation bonds he owns. The interest received by Tom's mother was $1,050. Tom retained ownership of the bonds but surrendered all rights to the interest on the bonds.

Over the years, Tom and his physician, Joe Zorn, have become good friends. During 1990, Tom incurred doctor bills of $350. Instead of paying Zorn in cash, Tom did the plumbing work for a new bar Zorn had installed in his basement in September 1990. Tom and Zorn agreed that the value of Tom's services was equal to the $350 in medical bills.

On September 5, 1990, Tom sold 100 shares of ABC Corporation stock for $3,100. He had acquired the stock on May 2, 1981, for $1,600.

Tom's itemized deductions for 1990 were as follows:

State income tax withheld	$ 900
Real estate taxes paid	600
Home mortgage interest (paid to Grand View Savings and Loan)	2,800
Cash contributions to First Church	800

Part 1—Tax Computation

Compute Tom's 1990 Federal income tax payable (or refund due). Suggested software (if available): *WEST–TAX Planner* or *BNA Individual Income Tax Spreadsheet.*

Part 2—Tax Planning

For 1991, assume that all items of income and expense will be approximately the same as in 1990, except for the following:

> Tom expects a 10% increase in salary and taxes withheld beginning January 1, 1991.
>
> He does not expect to incur any medical expenses.
>
> His real estate taxes will increase to $800.
>
> He expects to contribute $1,200 to First Church.
>
> He does not expect to have any capital gains or losses in 1991.

Tom plans to marry in June 1991. His fiancée, Sarah, plans to quit her job in Pittsburgh and move to Grand View to be with Tom. She does not plan to seek employment after the move. Sarah earned $18,000 through May 1991. Her employer withheld Federal income tax of $3,600, state income tax of $900, and FICA of $1,377.

Compute the estimated total tax liability for the Ruckers for 1991. Should Tom ask his employer to withhold more or less than the amount withheld last year? How much? Suggested software (if available): *WEST–TAX Planner.*

 60. Dan and Freida Butler, husband and wife, file a joint return. The Butlers live at 625 Oak Street, Corbin, KY 27521. Dan's Social Security number is 482–61–1231, and Freida's is 162–79–1245.

During 1990, Dan and Freida furnished over half of the total support of each of the following individuals:

a. Gina, their daughter, age 22, who was married on December 21, 1990, has no income of her own, and for 1990 files a joint return with her husband, who earned $8,000 during 1990.

b. Sam, their son, age 17, who had gross income of $2,500 and who dropped out of high school in February 1990.

c. Ben Brow, Freida's brother, age 21, who is a full-time college student with gross income of $2,500.

Dan, a radio announcer for WJJJ, earned a salary of $36,000 in 1990. Freida was employed part-time as a real estate salesperson by Corbin Realty and was paid commissions of $18,000 in 1990. Freida sold a house on December 30, 1990, and will be paid a commission of $1,500 (not included in the $18,000) on the January 10, 1991, closing date.

Dan and Freida own 500 shares of stock in Q Corporation. Q declared a dividend of $3 per share on the stock on December 15, 1990, and mailed dividend checks on December 31. Dan and Freida received their dividend check on January 4, 1991.

Dan and Freida had itemized deductions as follows:

State income tax withheld	$1,900
Real estate taxes paid	900
Interest on home mortgage (paid to Corbin Savings and Loan)	5,600
Cash contributions to the Boy Scouts	420

Their employers withheld Federal income tax of $9,400 (Dan $5,900, Freida $3,500), and the Butlers paid estimated tax of $800.

Part 1—Tax Computation

Compute Dan and Freida's 1990 Federal income tax payable (or refund due). Suggested software (if available): *WEST-TAX Planner.*

Part 2—Tax Planning

Dan plans to reduce his work schedule and work only halftime for WJJJ in 1991. He has been writing songs for several years and wants to devote more time to developing a career as a songwriter. Because of the uncertainty in the music business, however, he would like you to make all computations assuming he will have no income from songwriting in 1991. To make up for the loss of income, Freida plans to increase the amount of time she spends selling real estate. She estimates she will be able to earn $33,000 in 1991. Assume all other income and expense items will be approximately the same as they were in 1990. Will the Butlers have more or less disposable income (after Federal income tax) in 1991? Suggested software (if available): *WEST–TAX Planner.*

61. Sam T. Seymour would like to forget 1989 (and almost did as a result of his drinking problem). Although he received a salary of $65,800 and $380 of interest income, a divorce nearly brought him to financial ruin. The divorce was final on February 28, 1989. Under the agreement, Sam was required to do the following:

   • Pay his minor daughter Pam's private school tuition of $10,800.

   • Pay his ex-wife, Patricia Ann Seymour, a $40,000 lump-sum payment on March 1, 1989, and $2,000 each month thereafter through February 1995. The payments are to cease upon Patricia's death.

   • Transfer to Patricia stock acquired in 1984 for $40,000 that now has a market value of $82,000.

   Patricia retained custody of Pam but spent only $4,000 for Pam's support in 1989. The divorce agreement was silent as to whether Sam could claim Pam as a dependent and as to whether the cash payments to Patricia would constitute alimony.

   Sam paid the tuition and made the $40,000 lump-sum payment but, because he was dismissed from his job in August 1989, was able to make only seven of the monthly payments to Patricia.

   On November 1, 1989, when the applicable Federal rate was 10%, Sam was compelled to borrow $35,000 from his mother (Mollie Seymour). He gave her a non-interest-bearing second mortgage on his residence. There were no other loans outstanding between Sam and his mother.

   Other information relevant to Sam's 1989 return is as follows:

   a. Sam's disabled brother, Fred Seymour, lived with Sam from April through December 1989. Fred's only income was $3,600 of Social Security disability payments, and Sam contributed $4,000 towards Fred's support. No one else contributed to Fred's support. Fred's Social Security number is 245–99–4444.

   b. Sam's only deductible items were home mortgage interest, $2,080; state income tax, $2,380; county property taxes, $3,000; charitable contributions, $200.

   c. Sam's employer withheld $16,337 of Federal income tax.

   d. Sam is 47 years old, his Social Security number is 215–71–1041, and he lives at 170 Ford Street, Gretna, TN 37929.

   e. Patricia Ann Seymour's Social Security number is 712–15–9701.

   Compute Sam's 1989 Federal income tax payable (or refund due). If you use tax forms for your computations, you will need Form 1040 and Schedule A. Suggested software (if available): *TurboTax* for tax return solutions, *WEST–TAX Planner* or *BNA Individual Income Tax Spreadsheet* if tax return solutions are not desired.

4

GROSS INCOME: EXCLUSIONS

ITEMS SPECIFICALLY EXCLUDED FROM GROSS INCOME

Chapter 3 discussed the concepts and judicial doctrines that affect the determination of gross income. If an income item is within the all-inclusive definition of gross income, the item can be excluded only if the taxpayer can locate specific authority for doing so. Chapter 4 focuses on the exclusions Congress has authorized.

STATUTORY AUTHORITY

Sections 101 through 150 provide the authority for excluding specific items from gross income. In addition, other exclusions are scattered throughout the Code. Each exclusion has its own legislative history and reason for enactment. Certain exclusions are intended as a form of indirect welfare payments. Other exclusions prevent double taxation of income or provide incentives for socially desirable activities (e.g., nontaxable interest on certain U.S. government bonds where the owner uses the funds for educational expenses).

In some cases, exclusions have been enacted by Congress to rectify the effects of judicially imposed decisions. For example, § 109 was enacted to exclude the value of improvements made by a lessee from the lessor's income upon termination of the lease. Previously, the Supreme Court held that such amounts were includible in gross income.[1] In this court decision, the lessor was required to include the fair market value of the improvements in gross income upon the termination of the lease despite the fact that there had been no sale or disposition of the property. Congress provided relief in this situation by enacting § 109, which defers taxing the value of the improvements until the property is sold.[2]

Section 123 was enacted to counter a District Court's decision in *Arnold v. U.S.*[3] In *Arnold*, the court included in gross income the insurance proceeds paid to the taxpayer as reimbursement for temporary housing expenses incurred as a result of a fire in the taxpayer's home. Similar payments made by a government agency to families displaced by urban renewal projects had been held nontaxable in a previous Revenue Ruling. Dissatisfied with the results in *Arnold*, Congress exercised its authority by exempting from tax the insurance proceeds received in circumstances similar to that case.

GIFTS AND INHERITANCES

Beginning with the Income Tax Act of 1913 and continuing to the present, Congress has allowed the recipient of a gift to exclude the value of the property from gross income. The exclusion applies to gifts made during the life of the donor (*inter vivos* gifts) and transfers that take effect upon the death of the donor (bequests and inheritances). However, as discussed in chapter 3, the recipient of a gift of income-producing property is subject to tax on the income subsequently earned from the property. Also, as discussed in chapter 1, the donor or the decedent's estate may be subject to gift or estate taxes on the transfer.

In numerous cases, gifts are made in a business setting. For example, a salesperson gives a purchasing agent free samples; an employee receives cash from his or her employer on retirement; a corporation makes payments to employees who were victims of a natural disaster; a corporation makes a cash payment to a former

---

1. *Helvering v. Bruun*, 40–1 USTC ¶9337, 24 AFTR 652, 60 S.Ct. 631 (USSC, 1940).

2. If the improvements were made by the tenant in lieu of rent, the value of the improvements is not eligible for exclusion.

3. 68–2 USTC ¶9590, 22 AFTR2d 5661, 289 F.Supp. 206 (D.Ct.N.Y., 1968).

employee's widow. In these and similar instances, it is frequently unclear whether a gift was made or the payments represent compensation for past, present, or future services.

The courts have defined a *gift* as "a voluntary transfer of property by one to another without adequate [valuable] consideration or compensation therefrom."[4] If the payment is intended to be for services rendered, it is not a gift, even though the payment is made without legal or moral obligation and the payor receives no economic benefit from the transfer. To qualify as a gift, the payment must be made "out of affection, respect, admiration, charity or like impulses."[5] Thus, the cases on this issue have been decided on the basis of the donor's intent.

CONCEPT SUMMARY 4—1

Summary of Principal Exclusions from Gross Income

1. Donative items
    Gifts, bequests, inheritances, and employee death benefits [§§ 102 and 101(b)]
    Life insurance proceeds paid by reason of death (§ 101)
    Scholarships (§ 117)

2. Personal and welfare items
    Injury or sickness payments (§ 104)
    Public assistance payments (Rev.Rul. 71—425, 1971—2 C.B. 76)
    Amounts received under insurance contracts for certain living expenses (§ 123)
    Reimbursement for the costs of caring for a foster child (§ 131)

3. Wage and salary supplements
    a. Fringe benefits
        Accident and health benefits (§§ 105 and 106)
        Lodging and meals furnished for the convenience of the employer (§ 119)
        Rental value of parsonages (§ 107)
        Employee achievement awards [§ 74(c)]
        Employer contributions to employee group term life insurance (§ 79)
        Group legal service plan benefits (§ 120)*
        Cafeteria plans (§ 125)
        Educational assistance payments (§ 127)*
        Child or dependent care (§ 129)
        Services provided to employees at no additional cost to the employer (§ 132)
        Employee discounts (§ 132)
        Working condition and *de minimis* fringes (§ 132)
        Athletic facilities provided to employees (§ 132)
        Tuition reductions granted to employees of educational institutions (§ 117)
    b. Military benefits
        Combat pay (§ 112)
        Mustering-out pay (§ 113)
        Housing, uniforms, and other benefits (§ 134)
    c. Foreign earned income (§ 911)

4. Investor items
    Interest on state and local government obligations (§ 103)
    Improvements by lessee to lessor's property (§ 109)

5. Benefits for the elderly
    Social Security benefits (except in the case of certain higher income taxpayers)
    Gain from the sale of personal residence by elderly taxpayers (§ 121)

6. Other benefits
    Income from discharge of indebtedness (§ 108)
    Recovery of a prior year's deduction that yielded no tax benefit (§ 111)
    Educational savings bonds (§ 135)

* Exclusion treatment applies to payments made before October 1, 1990.

---

4. *Estate of D. R. Daly*, 3 B.T.A. 1042 (1926).

5. *Robertson v. U.S.*, 52—1 USTC ¶9343, 41 AFTR

1053, 72 S.Ct. 994 (USSC, 1952).

In a landmark case, *Comm. v. Duberstein*,[6] the taxpayer (Duberstein) received a Cadillac from a business acquaintance. Duberstein had supplied the businessman with the names of potential customers with no expectation of compensation. The Supreme Court concluded:

> . . . despite the characterization of the transfer of the Cadillac by the parties [as a gift] and the absence of any obligation, even of a moral nature, to make it, it was at the bottom a recompense for Duberstein's past service, or an inducement for him to be of further service in the future.

Duberstein was therefore required to include the fair market value of the automobile in gross income.

Similarly, a bequest may be taxable if it represents a disguised form of compensation for services.

EXAMPLE 1   T agreed to perform services for D. In exchange for the services, D promised to bequeath specific securities to T. The value of the securities on the date of D's death must be included in T's gross income.   □

LIFE INSURANCE PROCEEDS

Generally, insurance proceeds paid to the beneficiary by reason of the death of the insured are exempt from income tax. Congress chose to exempt life insurance proceeds for the following reasons:

- For family members, life insurance proceeds serve much the same purpose as a nontaxable inheritance.

- In a business context (as well as in a family situation), life insurance proceeds replace an economic loss suffered by the beneficiary.

EXAMPLE 2   X Corporation purchased a life insurance policy to cover its key employee. If the proceeds were taxable, the corporation would require more insurance coverage to pay the tax as well as to cover the economic loss of the employee.   □

Thus, in general, Congress concluded that making life insurance proceeds exempt from income tax was a good policy. It should be noted, however, that life insurance proceeds are subject to the Federal estate tax.

The income tax exclusion applies only when the insurance proceeds are received by reason of the death of the insured. If the owner cancels the policy and receives the cash surrender value, the owner of the policy must recognize gain to the extent of the excess of the amount received over the cost of the policy (but a loss is not deductible). Also, if the beneficiary receives the insurance proceeds in payment of an amount due from the decedent, the amount is paid by reason of the liability rather than by reason of death. Thus, the insurance proceeds are taxable.

---

6. 60–2 USTC ¶9515, 5 AFTR2d 1626, 80 S.Ct. 1190 (USSC, 1960).

EXAMPLE 3   T sold property to D, who agreed to pay the purchase price in installments. T reported his gain by the installment method (gain is prorated on the basis of collections). D pledged his life insurance as security for the debt. T collected on the insurance policy when D died. The insurance proceeds are taxed to T the same as if D had paid his liability. ☐

Another exception to exclusion treatment applies if the insurance contract has been *transferred for valuable consideration*. The insurance proceeds are includible in the gross income of the transferee to the extent the insurance proceeds received exceed the amount paid for the policy by the transferee plus any subsequent premiums paid.

EXAMPLE 4   A pays premiums of $500 for an insurance policy in the face amount of $1,000 upon the life of B and subsequently transfers the policy to C for $600. C receives the proceeds of $1,000 on the death of B. The amount that C can exclude from gross income is limited to $600 plus any premiums paid by C subsequent to the transfer. ☐

The Code, however, provides exceptions to the rule illustrated in the preceding example. The four exceptions include transfers to the following:

1. A partner of the insured.
2. A partnership in which the insured is a partner.
3. A corporation in which the insured is an officer or shareholder.
4. A transferee whose basis in the policy is determined by reference to the transferor's basis.

The first three exceptions facilitate the use of insurance contracts to fund buy-sell agreements.

EXAMPLE 5   R and S are equal partners who have an agreement that allows either partner to purchase the interest of a deceased partner for $50,000. Neither partner has sufficient cash to actually buy the other partner's interest, but each has a life insurance policy on his own life in the amount of $50,000. R and S could exchange their policies (usually at little or no taxable gain), and upon the death of either partner, the surviving partner could collect tax-free insurance proceeds. The proceeds could then be used to purchase the decedent's interest in the partnership. ☐

The fourth exception applies to policies that were transferred pursuant to a tax-free exchange (e.g., a transfer of insurance policies to a corporation by its controlling shareholders in exchange for the corporation's stock).

Interest on Life Insurance Proceeds

Investment earnings arising from the reinvestment of life insurance proceeds are generally subject to income tax. Often the beneficiary will elect to collect the insurance proceeds in installments. The annuity rules (discussed in chapter 3) are

used to apportion the installment payment between the principal element (excludible) and the interest element (includible).

EXAMPLE 6

H was the beneficiary of a $100,000 life insurance policy on his wife. Under the terms of the policy, H elected to collect the proceeds as an annuity of $15,000 each year. His life expectancy was 10 years. Thus, H's cost is $100,000, his expected return is $150,000 (10 × $15,000), and his exclusion ratio is 100/150. Each payment received by H during the initial 10-year period will be a recovery of capital of $10,000 [$15,000 × (100/150)] and $5,000 of interest income. ☐

EMPLOYEE DEATH BENEFITS

Frequently, an employer makes payments to a deceased employee's surviving spouse, children, or other beneficiaries. If the payments are made out of a legal obligation (e.g., the decedent's accrued salaries), the amounts are generally taxable to the recipient just the same as if the employee had lived and collected on the obligation. But where the employer makes voluntary payments, the gift issue arises. Generally, the IRS considers such payments to be compensation for prior services rendered by the deceased employee.[7] However, some courts have held that payments to an employee's surviving spouse or other beneficiaries are gifts if the following are true:[8]

- The payments were made to the surviving spouse and children rather than to the employee's estate.

- The employer was not obligated to pay any additional compensation to the deceased.

- The employer derived no benefit from the payments.

- The surviving spouse and children performed no services for the employer.

- The decedent had been fully compensated for services rendered.

- Compensation payments were made pursuant to a board of directors' resolution that followed a general company policy of providing such payments for families of deceased employees (but not exclusively for families of shareholder-employees).

These factors, together, indicate whether the payment was made as an *act of affection or charity*. A widow's case for exclusion is greatly strengthened if the payment is made in *light of her financial needs*.

Section 101(b) attempts to eliminate or reduce controversy in this area by providing an automatic exclusion of the first $5,000 paid by the employer to the employee's beneficiaries by reason of the death of the employee. The $5,000 exclusion must be apportioned among the beneficiaries on the basis of each beneficiary's percentage of the total death benefits received. When the employer's payments exceed $5,000, the beneficiaries may still be able to exclude the entire amount received as a gift if they are able to show gratuitous intent on the part of the employer.

02, 1962–2 C.B. 37.
ey J. Carter v. Comm., 72–1 USTC

¶9129, 29 AFTR2d 332, 453 F.2d 61 (CA–2, 1972), and cases cited therein.

EXAMPLE 7   When H died, his employer paid his accrued salary of $3,000 to W, H's widow. The employer's board of directors also authorized payments to W ($4,000), H's daughter ($2,000), and H's son ($2,000) "in recognition of H's many years of service to the company."

The $3,000 accrued salary is compensation for past services and was owed to H at the time of his death. Therefore, the $3,000 is includible in gross income. The additional payments to the widow and children were not owed to H. However, because the payments were made in recognition of H's past service, under the *Duberstein* decision, the payments are not gifts. The employee death benefit exclusion enables the widow and children to exclude the following amounts:

$$\text{Widow} \quad \frac{\$4,000}{\$8,000} \times \$5,000 = \$2,500$$

$$\text{Daughter} \frac{\$2,000}{\$8,000} \times \$5,000 = \quad 1,250$$

$$\text{Son} \quad \frac{\$2,000}{\$8,000} \times \$5,000 = \quad \underline{1,250}$$

$$\underline{\underline{\$\,5,000}}$$

Besides avoiding the gift issue in many cases, the employee death benefit exclusion is intended to allow a substitute for tax-exempt life insurance proceeds.

SCHOLARSHIPS

Payments or benefits received by a student at an educational institution may be (1) compensation for services, (2) a gift, or (3) a scholarship. If the payments or benefits are received as compensation for services (past or present), the fact that the recipient is a student generally does not render the amounts received nontaxable.

EXAMPLE 8   State University waives tuition for all graduate teaching assistants. The tuition waived is intended as compensation for services and is therefore included in the graduate assistant's gross income. □

As discussed earlier, gifts are not includible in gross income.

The scholarship rules are intended to provide exclusion treatment for education-related benefits that cannot qualify as gifts but are not compensation for services. According to the Regulations, "a scholarship is an amount paid or allowed to, or for the benefit of, an individual to aid such individual in the pursuit of study or research."[9] The recipient must be a candidate for a degree at an educational institution.

EXAMPLE 9   T entered a contest sponsored by a local newspaper. Under the contest rules, each contestant would submit an essay on local environmental issues. The

---

9. Prop.Reg. § 1.117–6(a)(3)(i).

contest prize was one year's tuition at State University. T won the contest. The newspaper had a legal obligation to T (as contest winner). Thus, the benefits are not a gift. However, since the tuition payment aided the individual in pursuing his studies, the payment is a scholarship. □

A scholarship recipient may exclude from gross income the amount used for tuition and related expenses (fees, books, supplies, and equipment required for courses), provided the conditions of the grant do not require that the funds be used for other purposes. Amounts received for room and board are not excludible and are treated as earned income for purposes of calculating the standard deduction.

EXAMPLE 10   T received a scholarship from State University of $9,500 to be used to pursue a bachelor's degree. T spent $4,000 on tuition, $3,000 on books and supplies, and $2,500 for room and board. T may exclude $7,000 ($4,000 + $3,000) from gross income. The $2,500 spent for room and board is includible in T's gross income.

The scholarship was T's only source of income. Her parents provided more than 50% of T's support and claimed T as a dependent. T's standard deduction will equal her $2,500 gross income. Thus, she has no taxable income. □

Timing Issues

Frequently, the scholarship recipient is a cash basis taxpayer who receives the money in one tax year but pays the educational expenses in a subsequent year. The amount eligible for exclusion may not be known at the time the money is received. In that case, the transaction is held *open* until the educational expenses are paid.

EXAMPLE 11   In August 1990, T received $10,000 as a scholarship for the academic year 1990–1991. T's expenditures for tuition, books, and supplies were as follows:

August–December 1990	$3,000
January–May 1991	4,500
	$7,500

T's gross income for 1991 would include $2,500 ($10,000 − $7,500) that is not excludible as a scholarship. □

Disguised Compensation

Some employers make scholarships available solely to the children of key employees. The tax objective of these plans is to provide a nontaxable fringe benefit to the executives by making the payment to the child in the form of an excludible scholarship. However, the IRS has ruled that the payments are generally includible ⸻ the gross income of the parent-employee.[10]

48, 1975–2 C.B. 55. *Richard T. Ar-*
r.C. 996 (1977).

COMPENSATION FOR INJURIES AND SICKNESS

Damages

A person who suffers harm caused by another is often entitled to compensatory damages. The tax consequences of the receipt of damages depend on the type of harm the taxpayer has experienced. The taxpayer may seek recovery for a loss of income, expenses incurred, property destroyed, or personal injury.

Generally, reimbursement for a loss of income is taxed the same as the income replaced. A recovery of expenses is generally taxable under the broad concept of gross income (but the expenses paid may be deductible, as discussed in subsequent chapters). A payment for damaged or destroyed property is treated as an amount received in a sale or exchange of the property. Thus, the taxpayer has a realized gain if the damage payments received exceed the property's basis. Damages for personal injuries receive special treatment under the Code.

Personal Injury. The legal theory of personal injury damages is that the amount received is intended "to make the plaintiff [the injured party] whole as before the injury."[11] It follows that if the damage payments received were subject to tax, the after-tax amount received would be less than the actual damages incurred and the injured party would not be "whole as before the injury."

Congress has specifically excluded from gross income the amount of any damage payments received (whether by suit or agreement) on account of personal injuries or sickness. The courts have applied the exclusion to any personal wrong committed against the taxpayer (e.g., breach of promise to marry, invasion of privacy, libel, slander, assault, battery). The exclusion also applies to compensation for loss of income (ordinarily taxable, as previously discussed) and recovery of expenses (except medical expenses deducted by the taxpayer) resulting from the personal injury.

In libel and slander cases, a single event can cause both a personal injury and damage to a business reputation. The measurement of damages to the business reputation is based on the estimated loss of income. Taxpayers argue that the amounts received for loss of income in these cases is no different from other personal injury cases and thus should be excluded. According to the IRS, however, the business reputation damages are separate from the personal injury and are taxable.[12]

EXAMPLE 12

P, a television announcer, was dissatisfied with the manner in which R, an attorney, was defending the television station in a libel case. P stated on television that R was botching the case. R sued P for slander. The damages R claimed were for loss of income from clients and potential clients who heard P's statement. R's claim is for damages to his business reputation, and the amounts received are taxable.

R collected on the suit against P and was on his way to a party to celebrate his victory when a negligent driver, N, drove his truck into R's automobile, injuring R. R filed suit for the personal injuries and claimed as damages the

---

11. *C. A. Hawkins*, 6 B.T.A. 1023 (1928).

12. Rev.Rul. 85–143, 1985–2 C.B. 55, in which the IRS announced it would not follow the Ninth Court of Appeals decision in *Roemer v. Comm.*, 83–2 USTC ¶9600, 52 AFTR2d 83–5954, 716 F.2d 693 (CA–9, 1983). See also *Wade E. Church*, 80 T.C. 1104 (1983).

loss of income for the period he was unable to work as a result of the injury. All amounts received by R from N, including the reimbursement for lost income, are nontaxable because the claims are based on a personal injury.   □

Punitive Damages.   In addition to seeking *compensatory* damages, the injured party may seek *punitive* damages, which are often awarded to punish the defendant for gross negligence or the intentional infliction of harm. While some courts have held that punitive damages are taxable under the broad concept of gross income, other courts have permitted exclusion treatment. The Revenue Reconciliation Act of 1989 clarifies congressional intent on this issue by providing that punitive damages are includible in gross income *unless* the claim arises out of physical injury or physical sickness. Thus, punitive damages received for loss of reputation are taxable, although the compensatory damages are excludible. Punitive damages arising out of a physical injury claim are excludible.

Workers' Compensation

State workers' compensation laws require the employer to pay fixed amounts for specific job-related injuries. The state laws were enacted so that the employee will not have to go through the ordeal of a lawsuit to recover the damages (and possibly not collect damages because of some defense available to the employer). Although the payments are intended, in part, to compensate for a loss of future income, Congress has specifically exempted workers' compensation benefits from inclusion in gross income.

Accident and Health Insurance Benefits

The income tax treatment of accident and health insurance benefits depends on whether the policy providing the benefits was purchased by the taxpayer or the taxpayer's employer. Benefits collected under an accident and health insurance policy *purchased by the taxpayer* are excludible. In this case, benefits collected under the taxpayer's insurance policy are excluded even though the payments are a substitute for income.

EXAMPLE 13   B purchased a medical and disability insurance policy. The insurance company paid B $200 per week to replace wages he lost while in the hospital. Although the payments serve as a substitute for income, the amounts received are tax-exempt benefits collected under B's insurance policy.   □

EXAMPLE 14   J's injury resulted in a partial paralysis of his left foot. He received $5,000 from his accident insurance company, under a policy he had purchased, for the injury. The $5,000 accident insurance proceeds are tax-exempt.   □

A different set of rules applies if the accident and health insurance protection was *purchased by the individual's employer*, as discussed in the following section.

EMPLOYER-SPONSORED ACCIDENT AND HEALTH PLANS

Congress encourages employers to provide employees, retired former employees, and their dependents with accident and health and disability insurance plans. The

premiums are deductible by the employer and excluded from the employee's income. Although § 105(a) provides the general rule that the employee has includible income when he or she collects the insurance *benefits,* two exceptions are provided.

Section 105(b) excludes payments received for medical care of the employee, spouse, and dependents except to the extent such amounts relate to medical expenses that were deducted by the taxpayer in a prior year.

EXAMPLE 15

D incurred $3,000 of medical expenses in 1990. D claimed the medical expenses as an itemized deduction on his 1990 return. D's adjusted gross income for 1990 was $30,000, and he had no other medical expenses. Because only medical expenses in excess of 7.5% of adjusted gross income may be claimed as an itemized deduction on D's 1990 return, the expense reduced taxable income by only $750 [$3,000 − .075($30,000) = $750]. In 1991, D received a $2,000 reimbursement from his employer-sponsored health insurance plan. The general rule of § 105(b) excludes the $2,000 from D's income. However, because D deducted the medical expenses on his return, the exception in § 105(b) applies. D is required to include in 1991 gross income the $750 deducted on his 1990 return. □

Section 105(c) excludes payments for the permanent loss or the loss of the use of a member or function of the body or the permanent disfigurement of the employee, spouse, or a dependent. Payments that are a substitute for salary (e.g., related to the period of time absent) are includible.

EXAMPLE 16

E lost an eye in an automobile accident unrelated to his work. As a result of the accident, E incurred $2,000 of medical expenses, which he deducted on his return. He collected $10,000 from an accident insurance policy carried by his employer. The benefits were paid according to a schedule of amounts that varied with the part of the body injured (e.g., $10,000 for loss of an eye, $20,000 for loss of a hand). Because the payment was for loss of a *member or function of the body,* § 105(c) applies and the $10,000 is excluded from income. E was absent from work for a week as a result of the accident. His employer provided him with insurance for the loss of income due to illness or injury. E collected $500, which is includible in gross income. □

Medical Reimbursement Plans

In lieu of, and in some cases in addition to, providing the employee with insurance coverage for hospital and medical expenses, the employer may agree to reimburse the employee for these expenses. The amounts received through the insurance coverage (insured plan benefits) are excluded from income under § 105 (as previously discussed). Unfortunately in terms of cost considerations, the insurance companies that issue this type of policy usually require a broad coverage of employees. An alternative is to have a plan that is not funded with insurance (a self-insured arrangement). The benefits received under a self-insured plan can be excluded from the employee's income, if the plan does not discriminate in favor of highly compensated employees.

MEALS AND LODGING

Furnished for the Convenience of the Employer

As discussed in chapter 3, income can take any form, including meals and lodging. However, § 119 excludes from income the value of meals and lodging provided to the employee and the employee's spouse and dependents under the following conditions:

- The meals and/or lodging are *furnished* by the employer, on the employer's *business premises*, for the *convenience of the employer*.

- In addition to the above requirements, in the case of lodging the employee is *required* to accept the lodging as a condition of employment.

Each of these requirements has been strictly construed by the courts.

At least two questions have been raised with regard to the *furnished by the employer* requirement:

- Who is considered an *employee*?

- What is meant by *furnished*?

The IRS and some courts have reasoned that because a partner is not an employee, the exclusion does not apply to a partner. However, the Tax Court and the Fifth Court of Appeals have ruled in favor of the taxpayer on this issue.[13]

The Supreme Court held that a cash meal allowance was ineligible for the exclusion because the employer did not actually furnish the meals.[14] Similarly, one court denied the exclusion where the employer paid for the food and supplied the cooking facilities but the employee prepared the meal.[15]

The *on the employer's business premises* requirement, applicable to both meals and lodging, has resulted in much litigation. The Regulations define business premises as simply "the place of employment of the employee."[16] Thus, the Sixth Court of Appeals held that a residence, owned by the employer and occupied by an employee, two blocks from the motel that the employee managed was not part of the business premises.[17] However, the Tax Court considered an employer-owned house across the street from the hotel that was managed by the taxpayer to be on the business premises of the employer.[18] Perhaps these two cases can be reconciled by comparing the distance from the lodging facilities to the place where the employer's business was conducted. The closer the lodging to the business operations, the more likely the convenience of the employer is served.

The *convenience of the employer* test is intended to focus on the employer's motivation for furnishing the meals and lodging rather than on the benefits received by the employee. If the employer furnishes the meals and lodging

---

13. Rev.Rul. 80, 1953–1 C.B. 62; *Comm. v. Doak*, 56–2 USTC ¶9708, 49 AFTR 1491, 234 F.2d 704 (CA–4, 1956); *Comm. v. Moran*, 56–2 USTC ¶9789, 50 AFTR 64, 236 F.2d 595 (CA–8, 1956); *Robinson v. U.S.*, 60–1 USTC ¶9152, 5 AFTR2d 315, 273 F.2d 503 (CA–3, 1960); *Briggs v. U.S.*, 56–2 USTC ¶10020, 50 AFTR 667, 238 F.2d 53 (CA–10, 1956), but see *G. A. Papineau*, 16 T.C. 130 (1956); *Armstrong v. Phinney*, 68–1 USTC ¶9355, 21 AFTR2d 1260, 394 F.2d 661 (CA–5, 1968).

14. *Comm. v. Kowalski*, 77–2 USTC ¶9748, 40 AFTR2d 6128, 98 S.Ct. 315 (USSC, 1977).

15. *Tougher v. Comm.*, 71–1 USTC ¶9398, 27 AFTR2d 1301, 441 F.2d 1148 (CA–9, 1971).

16. Reg. § 1.119–1(c)(1).

17. *Comm. v. Anderson*, 67–1 USTC ¶9136, 19 AFTR2d 318, 371 F.2d 59 (CA–6, 1966).

18. *J.B. Lindeman*, 60 T.C. 609 (1973).

primarily to enable the employee to perform his or her duties properly, it does not matter that the employee considers these benefits to be a part of his or her compensation.

The Regulations give the following examples in which the tests for excluding meals are satisfied:[19]

- A waitress is required to eat her meals on the premises during the busy lunch and breakfast hours.

- A bank furnishes a teller meals on the premises to limit the time the employee is away from his or her booth during the busy hours.

- A worker is employed at a construction site in a remote part of Alaska. The employer must furnish meals and lodging due to the inaccessibility of other facilities.

The *employee required* test applies only to lodging. If the employee's use of the housing would serve the convenience of the employer, but the employee is not required to use the housing, the exclusion is not available.

EXAMPLE 17   U, a utilities company, has all of its service personnel on 24-hour call for emergencies. The company encourages its employees to live near the plant so that the employees can respond quickly to emergency calls. Company-owned housing is available rent-free. Only 10 of the employees live in the company housing because it is not suitable for families.

Although the company-provided housing serves the convenience of the employer, it is not required. Therefore, the employees who live in the company housing cannot exclude its value from gross income. ☐

In addition, if the employee has the *option* of cash or lodging, the *required* test is not satisfied.

EXAMPLE 18   T is the manager of a large apartment complex. The employer gives T the option of rent-free housing (value of $6,000 per year) or an additional $5,000 per year. T selects the housing option. Therefore, he must include $6,000 in gross income. ☐

Other Housing Exclusions

An *employee of an educational institution* may be able to exclude the value of campus housing provided by the employer. Generally, the employee does not recognize income if he or she pays annual rents equal to or greater than 5 percent of the appraised value of the facility. If the rent payments are less than 5 percent of the value of the facility, the excess must be included in gross income.

EXAMPLE 19   X University provides on-campus housing for its full-time faculty during the first three years of employment. The housing is not provided for the convenience of the employer. Professor B pays $3,000 annual rent for the use of a

---

19. Reg. § 1.119–1(f).

residence with an appraised value of $100,000 and an annual rental value of $12,000. Professor B must recognize $2,000 gross income [.05($100,000) − $3,000 = $2,000] for the value of the housing provided to him. □

Ministers of the gospel can exclude (1) the rental value of a home furnished as compensation or (2) a rental allowance paid to them as compensation, to the extent the allowance is used to rent or provide a home. The housing or housing allowance must be provided as compensation for the conduct of religious worship, the administration and maintenance of religious organizations, or the performance of teaching and administrative duties at theological seminaries.

EXAMPLE 20   Pastor B is allowed to live rent-free in a house owned by the congregation. The annual rental value of the house is $6,000 and is provided as part of the pastor's compensation for ministerial services. Assistant Pastor C is paid a $4,500 cash housing allowance. He uses the $4,500 to pay rent and utilities on a home he and his family occupy. Neither Pastor B nor Assistant Pastor C is required to recognize gross income associated with the housing or housing allowance. □

Military personnel are allowed housing exclusions under various circumstances. Authority for these exclusions is found in Federal laws that are not part of the Internal Revenue Code.

OTHER EMPLOYEE FRINGE BENEFITS

Specific Benefits

In recent years, Congress has enacted exclusions to encourage employers to (1) finance and make available child care facilities, (2) provide the means for employees to obtain legal services, (3) provide athletic facilities for employees, and (4) finance certain employees' basic education. These provisions are summarized as follows:

- The employee does not have to include in gross income the value of child and dependent care services paid for by the employer and incurred to enable the employee to work. The exclusion cannot exceed $5,000 per year ($2,500 if married and filing separately). For a married couple, the annual exclusion cannot exceed the earned income of the spouse who has the lesser amount of earned income. For an unmarried taxpayer, the exclusion cannot exceed the taxpayer's earned income.

- Any benefit received by the employees from coverage under qualified group legal service plans provided by the employer is excluded. The exclusion is limited to an annual premium value of $70 per employee.

- The value of the use of a gymnasium or other athletic facilities by employees, their spouses, and their dependent children may be excluded from an employee's gross income. The facilities must be on the employer's premises, and substantially all of the use of the facilities must be by employees and their family members.

- Qualified employer-provided educational assistance (tuition, fees, books, and supplies) at the undergraduate level is excludible from gross income. The exclusion is subject to an annual employee statutory ceiling of $5,250.

- An employee (including retired and disabled former employees) of a nonprofit educational institution can exclude undergraduate tuition reductions granted to the employee and his or her spouse and dependents. The exclusion extends to undergraduate tuition reductions granted by any nonprofit educational institution to employees (and their families) of any other nonprofit educational institution. The exclusion also applies to graduate tuition reductions if the recipient is a teaching or research assistant. Thus, the graduate assistant whose tuition is waived can exclude the tuition reduction from income, if other university employees are granted the same benefit.

EXAMPLE 21 University Y allows the dependent children of University X employees to attend University Y with no tuition charged. University X grants reciprocal benefits to the children of University Y employees. Also, the dependent children can attend tuition-free the university where their parents are employed. Employees who take advantage of these benefits are not required to recognize gross income. □

Until recently, if an employee was granted a choice between cash and a nontaxable fringe benefit, the better view was that having the option of cash made the fringe benefit taxable. However, in 1981, Congress enacted the *cafeteria plan rules*, which allow the employee to choose nontaxable benefits (e.g., group term life insurance, health and accident protection, and child care) rather than cash compensation. The rules also provide for such noncash benefits to remain nontaxable. Cafeteria plans provide tremendous flexibility in tailoring the employee-pay package to fit individual needs. Some employees (usually the younger group) prefer cash, while others (usually the older group) will opt for the fringe benefit program.

EXAMPLE 22 Y Corporation offers its employees (on a nondiscriminatory basis) a choice of any one or all of the following benefits:

	Cost
Group term life insurance	$ 200
Hospitalization insurance for family members	2,400
Child care payments	1,800
	$4,400

If a benefit is not selected, the employee receives cash equal to the cost of the benefit. T, an employee, has a spouse who works for another employer that provides hospitalization insurance but no child care payments. T elects to receive the group term life insurance, the child care payments, and $2,400 of cash. Only the $2,400 must be included in T's gross income. □

General Classes of Excluded Benefits

An employer can confer numerous forms and types of economic benefits on employees. Under the all-inclusive concept of income, the benefits are taxable unless one of the provisions previously discussed specifically excludes the item

from gross income. The income is the fair market value of the benefit. This reasoning can lead to results that Congress considers unacceptable, as illustrated in the following example.

EXAMPLE 23   T is employed in New York as a ticket clerk for Trans National Airlines. His mother in Miami, Florida is ill. T has no money. Trans National has daily flights from New York to Miami that often leave with empty seats. The cost of a ticket is $400, and T is in the 28% tax bracket. If Trans National allows T to fly without charge to Miami, under the general gross income rules, T has income equal to the value of a ticket. Therefore, T must pay $112 tax (.28 × $400) on a trip to Miami. Because T does not have $112, he cannot visit his mother, and the airplane flies with another empty seat. □

If Trans National in Example 23 will allow employees to use resources that would otherwise be wasted, why should the tax laws interfere with the employee's decision to take advantage of the available benefit? Thus, to avoid the undesirable results that occur in Example 23 and in similar situations as well as to create uniform rules for fringe benefits, Congress established four broad classes of nontaxable employee benefits:[20]

- No-additional-cost services.
- Qualified employee discounts.
- Working condition fringes.
- *De minimis* fringes.

No-Additional-Cost Services.   Example 23 illustrates *the no-additional cost* type of fringe benefit. To qualify as nontaxable, the service must be offered to customers in the ordinary course of the business in which the employee works and the employer must not incur substantial additional costs (including forgone revenues) in providing the service to the employee. Therefore, T in Example 23 would not be required to recognize income from the flight on the company plane.

Note that if T were employed in a hotel owned by Trans National, the receipt of the airline ticket would be taxable because T did not work in that line of business. However, the Code allows the exclusion for reciprocal benefits offered by employers in the same line of business.

EXAMPLE 24   T is employed as a desk clerk for Plush Hotels, Inc. The company and Chain Hotels, Inc., have an agreement that allows any of their employees to stay without charge in either company's resort hotels during the off-season. T would not be required to recognize income from taking advantage of the plan by staying in a Chain Hotel. □

The no-additional-cost exclusion extends to the employee's spouse and dependent children and to retired and disabled former employees. In Temporary Regulations, the IRS has conceded that partners who perform services for the

---

20. See, generally, § 132.

partnership are employees for purposes of the exclusion.[21] (As discussed earlier in the chapter, the IRS's position is that partners are not employees for purposes of the § 119 meals and lodging exclusion.) However, the exclusion is not allowed to highly compensated employees unless the availability of the benefit is not discriminatory.

Qualified Employee Discounts.   When the employer sells goods or services (other than no-additional-cost benefits just discussed) to the employee for a price that is less than the price charged regular customers, the employee realizes income equal to the discount. However, the discount can be excluded from the gross income of the employee, subject to the following conditions and limitations:

- The exclusion is not available for real property (e.g., a house) or for personal property of the type commonly held for investment (e.g., common stocks).

- The property or services must be from the same line of business in which the employee works.

- In the case of *property*, the exclusion is limited to the *gross profit component* of the price to customers.

- In the case of *services*, the exclusion is limited to 20 percent of the customer price.

EXAMPLE 25   X Corporation, which operates a department store, sold a television set to a store employee for $300. The regular customer price is $500, and the gross profit rate is 25%. The corporation also sold the employee a service contract for $120. The regular customer price on the contract is $150. The employee must recognize $75 income.

Customer price for property	$ 500
Less: Gross profit (25%)	(125)
	$ 375
Employee price	300
Income	$ 75
Customer price for service	$ 150
Less: 20 percent	(30)
	$ 120
Employee price	120
Income	$–0–

□

EXAMPLE 26   Assume the same facts as in Example 25, except the employee is a clerk in a hotel operated by X Corporation. Because the line of business requirement is not met, the employee must recognize $200 income ($500 − $300) from the purchase of the television and $30 income ($150 − $120) from the service contract.   □

---

21. Temp.Reg. § 1.132–1T(b).

As in the case of no-additional-cost benefits, the exclusion applies to employees (including service partners), employees' spouses and dependent children, and retired and disabled former employees. However, the exclusion does not apply to highly compensated individuals unless the availability of the discount is not discriminatory.

Working Condition Fringes.   Generally, an employee is not required to include in gross income the cost of property or services provided by the employer if the employee could deduct the cost of those items if he or she had actually paid for them.

EXAMPLE 27   T is a certified public accountant employed by an accounting firm. The employer pays T's annual dues to professional organizations. T is not required to include the payment of the dues in gross income because if he had paid the dues, he would have been allowed to deduct the amount as an employee business expense (as discussed in chapter 9).   ☐

In many cases, this exclusion merely avoids reporting income and an offsetting deduction. However, in three specific situations, the working condition fringe benefit rules allow an exclusion where the expense would not be deductible if paid by the employee:

- The value of parking space provided to an employee may be excluded even though parking is ordinarily a nondeductible commuting expense (see chapter 9).

- Automobile salespeople are allowed to exclude the value of certain personal use of company demonstrators (e.g., commuting to and from work).

- The employee business expense would be eliminated by the 2 percent floor on miscellaneous deductions under § 67 (see chapter 10).

Unlike the other fringe benefits discussed previously, working condition fringes can be made available on a discriminatory basis and still qualify for the exclusion.

EXAMPLE 28   R Corporation's offices are located in the center of a large city. The company pays for parking spaces to be used only by the company's officers. The parking space rental qualifies as a working condition fringe and may be excluded from gross income even though the plan is discriminatory.   ☐

De Minimis **Fringes.**   As the term suggests, *de minimis* fringe benefits are so small that accounting for them is impractical. The House Report contains the following examples of *de minimis* fringes:

- The typing of a personal letter by a company secretary, occasional personal use of a company copying machine, monthly transit passes provided at a discount not exceeding $15, occasional company cocktail parties or picnics for employees, occasional supper money or taxi fare for employees because of overtime work, and certain holiday gifts of property with a low fair market value are excluded.

- Subsidized eating facilities operated by the employer are excluded if located on or near the employer's business premises, if revenue equals or exceeds direct operating costs, and if nondiscrimination requirements are met.

When taxpayers venture beyond the specific examples contained in the House Report, there is obviously much room for disagreement as to what is *de minimis*. However, note that except in the case of subsidized eating facilities, the *de minimis* fringe benefits can be granted in a manner that favors highly compensated employees.

EXAMPLE 29

R Corporation's officers are allowed to have personal letters typed by company secretaries. On the average, a secretary will spend one hour each month on the letters. The benefit is *de minimis*, which means accounting for the cost is impractical in view of the small amount of money involved. If the costs are too small to be of concern, whether the benefits are discriminatory is also immaterial. □

Taxable Fringe Benefits

If the fringe benefits cannot qualify for any of the specific exclusions or do not fit into any of the general classes of excluded benefits, the taxpayer must recognize gross income equal to the fair market value of the benefits. Obviously, problems are frequently encountered in determining values. The IRS has issued extensive Regulations addressing the valuation of personal use of an employer's automobiles and meals provided at an employer-operated eating facility.[22]

If a fringe benefit plan discriminates in favor of highly compensated employees, generally, the highly compensated employees are not allowed to exclude the benefits they receive that other employees do not enjoy. However, the highly compensated employees, as well as the other employees, are generally allowed to exclude the nondiscriminatory benefits.

EXAMPLE 30

T Company has a medical reimbursement plan that reimburses officers for 100% of their medical expenses, but reimburses all other employees for only 80% of their medical expenses. Mr. T, the president of the company, was reimbursed $1,000 during the year for medical expenses. Mr. T must include $200 in gross income [(1 − .80) × $1,000 = $200]. Mr. Z, an employee who is not an officer, received $800 (80% of his actual medical expenses) under the medical reimbursement plan. None of the $800 is includible in his gross income. □

Exceptions to this general nondiscrimination requirement occur for *de minimis* and working condition fringe benefits discussed above. The *de minimis* benefits are not subject to tax because the accounting problems that would be created are out of proportion to the amount of the additional tax that would result. A nondiscrimination test would simply add to the compliance problems. In the

---

22. Reg. § 1.61–2 T(j). Generally, the income from the personal use of the employer's automobile is based on the lease value of the automobile (what it would have cost the employee to lease the au- tomobile). Meals are valued at 150% of the employer's direct costs (e.g., food and labor) of preparing the meals.

case of working condition fringes, the types of services required vary with the job. Therefore, a nondiscrimination test probably could not be satisfied, although usually there is no deliberate plan to benefit a chosen few.

FOREIGN EARNED INCOME

A U.S. citizen is generally subject to U.S. tax on his or her income regardless of the income's geographic origin. The income may also be subject to tax in the foreign country, and thus the taxpayer must carry a double tax burden. Out of a sense of fairness and to encourage U.S. citizens to work abroad (so that exports might be increased), Congress has provided alternative forms of relief from taxes on foreign earned income. The taxpayer can elect *either* (1) to include the foreign income in his or her taxable income and then claim a credit for foreign taxes paid or (2) to exclude the foreign earnings from his or her U.S. gross income. The foreign tax credit option is discussed in chapter 11, but as is apparent from the following discussion, most taxpayers will choose the exclusion.

Foreign earned income consists of the earnings from the individual's personal services rendered in a foreign country (other than as an employee of the U.S. government). To qualify for the exclusion, the taxpayer must be either

- a bona fide resident of the foreign country (or countries), or
- present in a foreign country (or countries) for at least 330 days during any 12 consecutive months.

EXAMPLE 31   T's trips to and from a foreign country in connection with his work were as follows:

	Arrived in Foreign Country	Arrived in United States
	March 10, 1989	February 1, 1990
	March 7, 1990	June 1, 1990

During the 12 consecutive months ending on March 10, 1990, T was present in the foreign country for at least 330 days (365 days less 28 days in February and 7 days in March 1990). Therefore, all income earned in the foreign country through March 10, 1990, is eligible for the exclusion. The income earned from March 11, 1990, through May 31, 1990, is also eligible for the exclusion because T was present in the foreign country for 330 days during the 12 consecutive months ending on May 31, 1990. □

The exclusion is *limited* to $70,000 per year. For married persons, both of whom have foreign earned income, the exclusion is computed separately for each spouse. Community property rules do not apply (the community property spouse is not deemed to have earned one-half of the other spouse's foreign earned income). A taxpayer who is present in the country for less than the entire year must compute the maximum exclusion on a daily basis ($70,000 divided by the number of days in the entire year and multiplied by the number of days present in the foreign country during the year).

In addition to the exclusion for foreign earnings, the *reasonable housing costs* incurred by the taxpayer and the taxpayer's family in a foreign country in excess of a base amount may be excluded from gross income. The base amount is 16 percent of the U.S. government pay scale for a GS–14 (Step 1) employee, which varies from year to year.

As previously mentioned, the taxpayer may elect to include the foreign earned income in Federal adjusted gross income and claim a credit (an offset against U.S. tax) for the foreign tax paid. The credit alternative may be advantageous if the individual's foreign earned income far exceeds the excludible amount so that the foreign taxes paid exceed the U.S. tax on the amount excluded. However, once an election is made, it applies to all subsequent years, unless affirmatively revoked. A revocation is effective for the year of the change and the four subsequent years.

INTEREST ON CERTAIN STATE AND LOCAL GOVERNMENT OBLIGATIONS

At the time the Sixteenth Amendment was ratified by the states, there was some question as to whether the Federal government possessed the constitutional authority to tax interest on state and local government obligations. Taxing the interest on these obligations was thought to violate the doctrine of intergovernmental immunity in that the tax would impair the state and local governments' ability to finance their operations.[23] Thus, interest on state and local government obligations was specifically exempted from Federal income taxation. However, the Supreme Court recently concluded that there is no constitutional prohibition against levying a nondiscriminatory Federal income tax on state and local government obligations. Nevertheless, currently the statutory exclusion still exists.

Obviously, the exclusion of the interest reduces the cost of borrowing for state and local governments. A taxpayer in the 28 percent tax bracket requires only a 5.76 percent yield on a tax-exempt bond to obtain the same after-tax income as a taxable bond paying 8 percent interest [$5.76\% \div (1 - .28) = 8\%$].

The lower cost for the state and local governments is more than offset by the revenue loss of the Federal government. Also, tax-exempt interest is considered to be a substantial loophole for the very wealthy. For this reason, bills have been proposed to Congress calling for Federal government subsidies to those state and local governments that voluntarily choose to issue taxable bonds. Under the proposals, the tax-exempt status of existing bonds would not be eliminated.

The current exempt status applies solely to state and local government bonds. Thus, income received from the accrual of interest on a condemnation award or an overpayment of state income tax is fully taxable. Nor does the exemption apply to gains on the sale of tax-exempt securities.

During recent years, state and local governments have developed sophisticated financial schemes to attract new industry. For example, local municipalities have issued bonds to finance the construction of plants to be leased to private enterprise. Because the financing could be arranged with low interest rate municipal obligations, the plants could be leased at a lower cost than the private business could otherwise obtain. However, Congress has placed limitations on the use of tax-exempt securities to finance private business.[24]

---

23. *Pollock v. Farmer's Loan & Trust Co.*, 3 AFTR 2557, 15 S.Ct. 912 (USSC, 1895).

24. See § 103(b).

DIVIDENDS

General Information

A *dividend* is a payment to a shareholder with respect to his or her stock. Dividends to shareholders are taxable only to the extent the payments are made from *either* the corporation's *current earnings and profits* (in many cases the same as net income per books) or its *accumulated earnings and profits* (somewhat similar to retained earnings per books). Distributions that exceed earnings and profits are treated as a nontaxable recovery of capital and reduce the shareholder's basis in the stock. Once the shareholder's basis is reduced to zero, any subsequent distributions are taxed as capital gains (see chapter 13).

Some payments are frequently referred to as dividends but are not considered dividends for tax purposes.

- Dividends received on deposits with savings and loan associations, credit unions, and banks are actually interest (a contractual rate paid for the use of money).

- Patronage dividends paid by cooperatives (e.g., for farmers) are rebates made to the users and are considered reductions in the cost of items purchased from the association. The rebates are usually made after year-end (after the cooperative has determined whether it has met its expenses) and are apportioned among members on the basis of their purchases.

- Mutual insurance companies pay dividends on unmatured life insurance policies that are considered rebates of premiums.

- Shareholders in a mutual investment fund are allowed to report as capital gains their proportionate share of the fund's gains realized and distributed. The capital gain and ordinary income portions are reported on the Form 1099 that the fund supplies its shareholders each year.

Stock Dividends

When a corporation issues a simple stock dividend (e.g., common stock issued to common shareholders), the shareholder has merely received additional shares to represent the same total investment. Thus, the shareholder does not realize income.[25] However, if the shareholder has the *option* of receiving either cash or stock in the corporation, the individual realizes gross income whether he or she receives stock or cash. A taxpayer who elects to receive the stock could be deemed to be in constructive receipt of the cash he or she has rejected. However, the amount of the income in this case is the value of the stock received, rather than the cash the shareholder has rejected. See chapter 13 for a detailed discussion of stock dividends.

TAX BENEFIT RULE

Generally, if a taxpayer obtains a deduction for an item in one year and later recovers a portion of the prior deduction, the recovery is included in gross income in the year received.

---

25. *Eisner v. Macomber*, 1 USTC ¶32, 3 AFTR 3020, 40 S.Ct. 189 (USSC, 1920); § 305(a).

EXAMPLE 32   A taxpayer deducted as a loss a $1,000 receivable from a customer when it appeared the amount would never be collected. The following year, the customer paid $800 on the receivable. The taxpayer must report the $800 as income in the year it is received. □

However, § 111 provides that no income is recognized upon the recovery of a deduction, or the portion of a deduction, that did not yield a tax benefit in the year it was taken. If the taxpayer in Example 32 had no tax liability in the year of the deduction (e.g., the itemized deductions and personal exemptions exceeded adjusted gross income), the recovery would be partially or totally excluded from income in the year of the recovery.

EXAMPLE 33   Before deducting a $1,000 loss from an uncollectible receivable in 1989, T had adjusted gross income of $5,300. Because T's standard deduction and personal exemption for the year totaled $5,100, the $1,000 loss yielded only $200 in tax benefits ($5,300 − $5,100 = $200). If the customer makes payments on the debt in a subsequent year, the first $200 collected will be taxable as a recovery of a prior deduction, and any additional amounts collected would be nontaxable because only $200 of the loss yielded a reduction in taxable income. □

INCOME FROM DISCHARGE OF INDEBTEDNESS

A transfer of appreciated property in satisfaction of a debt is an event that triggers the realization of income. The transaction is treated as a sale of the appreciated property followed by payment of the debt. Foreclosure by a creditor is also treated as a sale or exchange of the property.

EXAMPLE 34   T owed the State Bank $100,000 on an unsecured note. The note was satisfied by T when he transferred to the bank common stock with a basis of $60,000 and a fair market value of $100,000. T must recognize $40,000 gain on the transfer. T also owed the bank $50,000 on a note secured by land. When T's basis in the land was $20,000 and the land's fair market value was $50,000, the bank foreclosed on the loan and took title to the land. T must recognize a $30,000 gain on the foreclosure. □

In some cases, a creditor will not exercise his or her right of foreclosure and will even forgive a portion of the debt to assure the vitality of the debtor. In such cases, the debtor realizes income from discharge of indebtedness.

EXAMPLE 35   X Corporation is unable to meet the mortgage payments on its factory building. Both the corporation and the mortgage holder are aware of the depressed market for industrial property in the area. Foreclosure would only result in the creditor's obtaining unsalable property. To improve X Corporation's financial position and thus improve X's chances of obtaining the additional credit from other lenders necessary for survival, the creditor agrees to forgive all amounts past due and to reduce the principal amount of the mortgage. □

Generally, the income realized by the debtor from the forgiveness of a debt is taxable.[26] A similar debt discharge (produced by a different creditor motivation) associated with personal use property is illustrated in Example 36.

EXAMPLE 36

In 1985, T borrowed $60,000 from National Bank to purchase her personal residence. T agreed to make monthly principal and interest payments for 15 years. The interest rate on the note was 8%. In 1990, when the balance on the note had been reduced through monthly payments to $48,000, the bank offered to accept $45,000 in full settlement of the note. The bank made the offer because interest rates had increased to 12%. T accepted the bank's offer. As a result, T must recognize $3,000 ($48,000 − $45,000) income. □

The following discharge of indebtedness situations are subject to special treatment:[27]

1. Creditors' gifts.

2. Discharges under Federal bankruptcy law.

3. Discharges that occur when the debtor is insolvent.

4. Discharge of the farm debt of a solvent farmers.

5. A seller's cancellation of the buyer's indebtedness.

6. A shareholder's cancellation of the corporation's indebtedness.

7. Forgiveness of loans to students.

If the creditor reduces the debt as an act of *love, affection or generosity,* the debtor has simply received a nontaxable gift (situation 1). Rarely will a gift be found to have occurred in a business context. A businessperson may settle a debt for less than the amount due, but as a matter of business expediency (e.g., high collection costs or disputes as to contract terms) rather than generosity.

In situations 2, 3, and 4, the Code allows the debtor to reduce his or her basis in assets by the realized gain from the discharge.[28] Thus, the realized gain is merely deferred until the assets are sold (or depreciated). Similarly, in situation 5 (a price reduction), the debtor reduces the basis in the specific assets financed by the seller.

A shareholder's cancellation of the corporation's indebtedness to him or her (situation 6) usually is considered a contribution of capital to the corporation. Thus, the corporation's paid-in capital is increased and its liabilities are decreased by the same amount.

Many states make loans to students on the condition that the loan will be forgiven if upon completion of study the student will practice a profession in the state. The amount of the loan that is forgiven (situation 7) is excluded from gross income.

---

26. *U.S. v. Kirby Lumber Co.,* 2 USTC ¶814, 10 AFTR 458, 52 S.Ct. 4 (USSC, 1931), codified in § 61(a)(12).

27. §§ 108 and 1017.

28. §§ 108(a), (e), and (g). Note that § 108(b) pro- vides that other tax attributes (e.g., net operating loss) will be reduced by the realized gain from the debt discharge prior to the basis adjustment unless the taxpayer elects to apply the basis adjustment first.

EDUCATIONAL SAVINGS BONDS

The Technical and Miscellaneous Revenue Act of 1988 created an exclusion associated with the funding of higher education.[29] The effective date of this provision is for taxable years beginning after December 31, 1989.

The provision allows the taxpayer to exclude from gross income the interest earned on certain Series EE U.S. government savings bonds that are redeemed to pay qualified higher education expenses. The exclusion applies only if both of the following requirements are satisfied:

- The savings bonds are issued after December 31, 1989.

- The savings bonds are issued to an individual who is at least 24 years old at the time of issuance.

The exclusion is not available for a married couple who file separate returns.

The redemption proceeds must be used to pay qualified higher education expenses. *Qualified higher education expenses* consist of tuition and fees paid to an eligible education institution for the taxpayer, spouse, or dependents. If the redemption proceeds (both principal and interest) exceed the qualified higher education expenses, only a pro rata portion of the interest will qualify for exclusion treatment.

EXAMPLE 37   T's redemption proceeds from qualified savings bonds during the taxable year were $6,000 (principal of $4,000 and interest of $2,000). T's qualified higher education expenses were $5,000. Since the redemption proceeds exceed the qualified higher education expenses, only $1,667 ($5,000/$6,000 × $2,000) of the interest is excludible. □

The exclusion is limited by the application of the wherewithal to pay concept. That is, once the modified adjusted gross income exceeds $40,000 ($60,000 on a joint return), the phase-out of the exclusion commences. The exclusion is completely phased out once the modified adjusted gross income reaches $55,000 ($90,000 on a joint return). The otherwise excludible interest is reduced by the amount calculated as follows:

$$\frac{\text{Modified AGI} - \$40,000}{\$15,000} \times \frac{\text{Excludible interest}}{\text{before phase-out}} = \frac{\text{Reduction in}}{\text{excludible interest}}$$

On a joint return, $60,000 is substituted for the $40,000 and $30,000 is substituted for the $15,000. The phase-out amounts are to be indexed for inflation.

EXAMPLE 38   Assume the same facts as in Example 37, except that T's modified adjusted gross income is $50,000. The phase-out provision will result in T's interest exclusion being reduced by $1,111 [($50,000 − $40,000)/$15,000 × $1,667)]. Therefore, T's exclusion is $556 ($1,667 − $1,111). □

Modified adjusted gross income is adjusted gross income prior to the § 911 foreign earned income exclusion and the educational savings bond exclusion.

---

29. § 135.

TAX PLANNING CONSIDERATIONS

The present law excludes certain types of economic gains from taxation. Therefore, tax planning techniques may be useful to assist taxpayers in obtaining the maximum benefits from the exclusion of such gains. Following are some of the tax planning opportunities made available by the exclusions described in this chapter.

Life Insurance

Life insurance offers several favorable tax attributes. As discussed in chapter 3, the annual increase in the cash surrender value of the policy is not taxable (because no income has been actually or constructively received). By borrowing on the policy's cash surrender value, the owner can actually receive in cash the increase in value of the policy but without recognition of income.

Employee Benefits

Generally, employees view accident and health insurance, as well as life insurance, as necessities. Employees can obtain group coverage at much lower rates than individuals would have to pay for the same protection. Premiums paid by the employer can be excluded from the employees' gross income. Because of the exclusion, employees will have a greater after-tax and after-insurance income if the employer pays a lower salary but also pays the insurance premiums.

EXAMPLE 39

Individual A receives a salary of $30,000. The company has group insurance benefits, but A was required to pay his own premiums as follows:

Hospitalization and medical insurance	$1,400
Term life insurance ($30,000)	200
Disability insurance	400
	$2,000

To simplify the analysis, assume A's tax rate on income is 28%. After paying taxes of $8,400 (.28 × $30,000) and $2,000 for insurance, A has $19,600 ($30,000 − $8,400 − $2,000) for his other living needs.

If A's employer reduced A's salary by $2,000 (to $28,000) but paid A's insurance premiums, A's tax liability would be only $7,840 ($28,000 × .28). Thus, A would have $20,160 ($28,000 − $7,840) to meet his other living needs. The change in the compensation plan would save $560 ($20,160 − $19,600).

□

Similarly, employees must often incur expenses for child care and parking. The employee can have more income for other uses if the employer pays these costs for the employee but reduces the employee's salary by the cost of the benefits.

The use of cafeteria plans has increased dramatically in recent years. These plans allow the employees to tailor their benefits to meet their individual situations. Thus, where a married couple are both working, duplications of

benefits can be avoided and other needed benefits can often be added. If less than all of the employee's allowance is spent, then the employee can receive cash.

The meals and lodging exclusion enables the employee to receive from his or her employer what he or she ordinarily must purchase with after-tax dollars. Although the requirements that the employee live and take his or her meals on the employer's premises limit the tax planning opportunities, in certain situations, the exclusion is an important factor in the employee's compensation (e.g., hotels, motels, restaurants, farms, and ranches).

The employees' discount provision is especially important for manufacturers and wholesalers. Employees of manufacturers can avoid tax on the manufacturer's, wholesaler's, and retailer's markups. The wholesaler's employees can avoid tax on an amount equal to the wholesale and retail markups.

It should be recognized that the exclusion of benefits is generally available only to employees. Proprietors and partners must pay tax on the same benefits their employees receive tax-free. By incorporating and becoming an employee of the corporation, the former proprietor or partner can also receive these tax-exempt benefits. Thus, the availability of employee benefits is a consideration in the decision to incorporate.

Investment Income

Tax-exempt state and local government bonds are almost irresistible investments for many high-income taxpayers. To realize the maximum benefit from the exemption, the investor can purchase zero coupon bonds. These investments pay interest only at maturity, just as a Series EE U.S. government savings bond does. The advantage of the zero coupon feature is that the investor can earn tax-exempt interest on the accumulated principal and interest. If the investor purchases a bond that pays the interest each year, the interest received may be such a small amount that an additional tax-exempt investment cannot be made. In addition, there may be transaction costs (broker's fees) associated with reinvesting the interest. The zero coupon feature avoids these problems.

Series EE U.S. government savings bonds can earn tax-exempt interest if the bond proceeds are used for "qualified higher education expenses." Many taxpayers can foresee these expenditures being made for their childrens' educations. However, in deciding whether to invest in the bonds, the investor must take into account the income limitations for excluding the interest from gross income.

PROBLEM MATERIALS

Discussion Questions

1. T owned land that she leased to a corporation. The corporation constructed a building on the land. When the lease expired, the building would belong to T. The building had a fair market value of $40,000 when the lease expired. Why should T be allowed to exclude from gross income the fair market value of the building she received?

2. Who pays the income tax on a gift of the income from a certain piece of property—the donee or the donor?

3. a. A served as chairman of the local school board. Upon completion of his term in office, the organization awarded him a silver serving tray in recognition of

his outstanding service to the organization. The value of the tray is $200. Is A required to include the value of the tray in his income?

b. Assume the employees took up a collection and purchased the tray for A.

4. T was driving down a road when he saw that B was having trouble changing a tire. T stopped and helped B. As B was leaving, he gave T $20 and thanked him. Is T required to include the $20 in gross income?

5. Friends In Need is an unincorporated organization of individuals who have pledged to help one another. The Friends have a burial fund whereby a participant contributes $1 each month. If a member or a member's spouse or child dies during the month, the member or his or her estate will receive $300 to help with burial expenses. T's wife died during the year, and T collected $300 from the burial fund to which he had contributed $48. Is T required to include the $300 in gross income?

6. What are the two principal tax benefits of buying life insurance that has a cash surrender value?

7. M Corporation purchased a $1,000,000 insurance policy on the life of the company's president. The company paid $100,000 of premiums, the president died, and the company collected the face amount of the policy. How much must M Corporation include in gross income?

8. Company A provides its employees with $10,000 group term life insurance. Company B does not provide insurance but generally gives the family of a deceased employee $10,000. Compare the tax consequences of the insured and uninsured plans.

9. T received an academic scholarship to State University. Under the scholarship agreement, he received tuition ($1,500), books ($400), and room and board ($5,000). What is T's gross income from the scholarship?

10. X Company has a scholarship program for children of its employees. Employees with more than four years of service can receive up to $1,000 as reimbursement of college tuition paid by the employee. Are the payments excludible as scholarships?

11. V was injured in an accident unrelated to his employment. While V was away from work, he collected his regular salary of $4,500 and $3,600 on his accident and health income continuation insurance he had purchased for $900. What is V's income from the payments?

12. R and T were traveling together in a defectively manufactured automobile. As a result of the defects, the automobile ran off the road and crashed into a tree. R and T each broke an arm in the accident. R was a baseball pitcher and was unable to pitch for one year as a result of the accident. He received a $400,000 damage award in a suit against the automobile manufacturer. T was a 65-year-old retiree and received $25,000 as an award for damages. The difference in the damage awards was largely due to R's greater loss of earnings. Is R taxed on any of the $400,000 received?

13. What nontaxable benefits can a company provide its retired former employees?

14. What nontaxable fringe benefits are available to employees that are not available to partners and proprietors?

15. How does one determine if the meals and lodging supplied by the employer are to serve a valid business purpose? Is the tax treatment of meals and lodging affected if the employer advertises that the meals and lodging provided are one of the employees' fringe benefits?

16. P, a full-time employee of State University, is allowed to use the university's tennis courts when they are not being used by the tennis team and physical education classes. Does P derive gross income from the use of the tennis courts?

17. The management of X Life Insurance Company believes it is good business to encourage employees to exercise and stay healthy. Therefore, the company built a gymnasium in the basement of the main office building and made the facility available to all of the company's 1,200 employees. Z Life Insurance Company has only 30 employees. It is not feasible for Z Company to maintain its own gymnasium, but the company would like to encourage employees to exercise. Therefore, Z Company has offered to pay membership fees for any employee who wishes to join the health club located in the adjoining building. Compare the tax treatment of the health facility benefits provided the employees of the two companies.

18. T is employed by X, Inc., an automobile manufacturing company. X sold T a new automobile at company cost of $8,400. The price charged a dealer would have been $10,000, and the retail price of the automobile was $11,500. What is T's gross income from the purchase of the automobile?

19. Z Corporation is opening a branch in Kazonbi, an African country that does not levy an income tax on citizens of foreign countries. T, a U.S. citizen, is considering two offers from his employer, Z Corporation. He can work for 6 months in Kazonbi and 6 months in the United States and receive a salary of $4,000 per month, or he can work in Kazonbi for 12 months at the same monthly salary. T would prefer to spend as much time in the United States as possible and prefers the first alternative. However, he asks your advice as to how income taxes might affect his decision.

20. T owns 100 shares of stock in XYZ Corporation. The corporation declares a dividend that gives T the option of receiving 10 additional shares of XYZ stock or $200 cash. T elects to receive 10 additional shares of stock. What are the tax consequences to T?

21. R received a $100,000 condemnation award when the state took his real estate for a new school. R used the money to purchase State of Virginia bonds, which paid him $7,500 interest in 1990. The state condemned other property owned by R. However, R contested the amount the state was willing to pay for this second piece of property. At the end of 1990, the court awarded R $100,000 for the land and $7,500 interest on the condemnation award. How much of the interest is R required to include in grosss income?

22. X, a cash basis taxpayer, was in a contract dispute with Y. In 1990 X performed services for Y, but Y would not pay. X had no gross income and $6,000 of itemized deductions and personal exemptions in 1990. In 1991 the dispute was settled, and X received $10,000. Can X exclude any of the $10,000 under the tax benefit rule?

23. In 1990, F received a $400 factory rebate on supplies purchased and deducted as a business expense in 1989. In 1990, S received a $400 factory rebate on a personal-use automobile purchased in December 1989. Both F and S had over $10,000 of taxable income in 1989 and 1990. Is the receipt of $400 taxable to F or S?

24. How does the tax treatment of a corporation's income generated by the retirement of bonds for less than book value (issue price plus amortized discount or less amortized premium) differ from the income derived from a shareholder's forgiveness of the corporation's indebtedness?

25. In 1981, R purchased real estate for $50,000. By 1988, the property had appreciated to $150,000. In 1988, R borrowed $120,000 and gave a mortgage on the property as security for the debt. In 1990, when the value of the property equaled the balance on the mortgage ($120,000), R transferred the property to the mortgagee in satisfaction of the debt. Did R realize income from discharge of indebtedness?

26. H and W are married, file a joint return, and are in the 33% marginal tax bracket. They would like to save for their child's education. What would be the advantage of buying State of Virginia bonds as compared to buying Series EE U.S. government bonds?

Problems

27. Determine whether the following may be excluded from gross income as gifts, bequests, scholarships, prizes, or life insurance proceeds:

    a. Uncle told Nephew, "Come live with me and take care of me in my old age and you can have all my property after my death." Nephew complied with Uncle's request. Uncle's will made Nephew sole beneficiary of the estate.

    b. Uncle told Nephew, "If you study hard and make the dean's list this year, I will pay your tuition for the following year." Nephew made the dean's list, and Uncle paid the tuition.

    c. Uncle told Nephew, "If you make the dean's list this year, I will pay you $500." Nephew made the dean's list, and Uncle paid the $500.

    d. D cashed in her life insurance contract and collected $10,000. She had paid premiums totaling $7,000.

28. Determine the taxable life insurance proceeds in the following cases:

    a. B purchased a sports franchise and player contracts from S. As part of the transaction, B purchased a life insurance contract on a key player from S for $50,000. One month later, the player was killed in an automobile accident, and B collected $500,000 on the life insurance contract.

    b. P and R formed a partnership and agreed that upon the death of either partner, the surviving partner would purchase the decedent's partnership interest. P purchased a life insurance policy on R's life and paid $5,000 in premiums. Upon R's death, P collected $100,000 on the life insurance policy and used the proceeds to purchase R's interest in the partnership.

    c. Same as (b), except the partnership was incorporated and P and R owned all the stock. Upon incorporation, P and R transferred their life insurance policies to the corporation in exchange for stock. When R died, the corporation redeemed (purchased) R's stock, using the $100,000 life insurance proceeds.

29. Determine the effect on Z's gross income of the following:

    a. Z Company sells furniture to customers on credit. Customers are required to purchase credit life insurance, with the proceeds payable to Z. The company collected $3,000 when a customer died.

    b. A, a major shareholder in Z Company, transferred his life insurance policy to the corporation in exchange for additional stock. A had paid $6,000 in premiums. When A died, the company collected the face amount of the policy of $25,000. During the time it held the policy, Z Company paid additional premiums of $1,000.

    c. Z Company also purchased an insurance policy on the life of the company president, B. The company had paid $10,000 in premiums, and the cash surrender value of the policy was $10,500 when B died. The company collected $25,000, which was the face amount of the policy.

30. T died at age 35. He was married and had five minor children. His employer, XYZ Plumbing Company, made payments to Mrs. T as follows:

T's accrued salary at date of death	$1,200
Family death benefits under long-standing company policy ($4,000 is paid to the spouse and $1,000 is paid to each child of a deceased employee)	4,000
A payment authorized by the board of directors to help Mrs. T pay debts accumulated by T	1,500

T and Mrs. T filed a joint return in the year of T's death. Determine the amounts from above that must be included in their gross income.

31. F was awarded an academic scholarship to State University. He received $6,000 in August and $6,000 in December 1990. F had enough personal savings to pay all expenses as they came due. F's expenditures for the relevant period were as follows:

Tuition, August 1990	$2,900
Tuition, December 1990	3,200
Room and board	
August–December 1990	3,000
January–May 1991	2,400
Books and educational supplies	
August–December 1990	700
January–May 1991	850

Determine the effect on F's gross income for 1990 and 1991.

32. Which of the following payments for damages would be taxable?
    a. A corporation received $100,000 from a competitor for infringement of its patent rights.
    b. A woman is paid $60,000 because her personal files were incorporated in a biography without her consent.
    c. A client is paid $12,000 by an investment counselor as reimbursement for a loss resulting from the counselor's poor advice.

33. R was injured in an accident that was not related to his employment. He incurred $12,000 in medical expenses and collected $4,000 on a medical insurance policy he purchased. He also collected $9,000 in medical benefits under his employer's group plan. Originally, the doctor diagnosed R's injury as requiring no more than 3 months of disability. Because of subsequent complications, R was unable to return to work until 14 months after the accident. While away from the job, R collected $200 per week on his employer's wage continuation plan. R also owned an insurance policy that paid him $100 per week while he was disabled. What are the tax consequences to R of the receipt of the following?
    a. $13,000 medical benefits.
    b. $300 per week to replace R's wages.

34. T, age 45, is an officer of XYZ Company, which provided T with the following nondiscriminatory fringe benefits in 1990:
    a. Hospitalization insurance for T and his dependents. The cost of coverage for T was $450, and the additional cost for T's dependents was $400.
    b. Reimbursement of $700 from an uninsured medical reimbursement plan available to all employees.
    c. Group term life insurance protection of $120,000. (Each employee received coverage equal to twice his or her annual salary.)
    d. Salary continuation payments of $2,600 while T was hospitalized for an illness.

In addition, T was covered by his employer's workers' compensation insurance policy. Premiums on the policy were $2 per $1000 salary ($120 for T's coverage). While T was ill, he collected $1,600 on a salary continuation insurance policy he had purchased.

Determine the amounts T must include in gross income.

35. T served as the manager of an orphanage in 1990. In this connection, he had the following transactions:
    a. He received no salary from his job but was given room and board (valued at $3,600) on the premises. No other person was employed by the orphanage, which is a tax-exempt organization.
    b. The orphanage paid $300 in tuition for a night course T took at a local university. The course was in the field of philosophy and dealt with the meaning of life. The payment was authorized by the orphanage's trustees in a written resolution.
    c. The orphanage paid $500 of the premiums on T's life insurance policy and all of his medical expenses of $1,800. Again, the payment was made pursuant to a resolution approved by the trustees.

    Determine the effect of these transactions on T's gross income.

36. A, age 40, is an officer of the XYZ Company, which provided the following nondiscriminatory fringe benefits for the year:
    a. Group term life insurance protection of $80,000.
    b. Group hospitalization insurance, $1,080.
    c. Reimbursement of $2,800 from an uninsured medical reimbursement plan maintained exclusively for highly compensated employees.
    d. Salary continuation payments for $3,000 while A was hospitalized for an illness.

    In addition, A collected $1,800 from a wage continuation policy he had purchased. Which items are includible in gross income?

37. The UW Union and I Corporation are negotiating contract terms. What would be the tax consequences of the following options? (Assume the union members are in the 28% marginal tax bracket and all benefits would be provided on a nondiscriminatory basis.)
    a. The company would eliminate the $100 deductible on health insurance benefits, and the employees would take a $100 reduction in pay. Most employees incur more than $100 each year for medical expenses.
    b. The employees would get an additional paid holiday with the same annual income (the same pay but less work) or an increase in pay equal to the holiday pay but no additional paid holiday (more pay and the same work).
    c. An employee who did not need health insurance (because the employee's spouse works and receives family coverage) would be allowed to receive the cash value of the coverage.

38. Determine the taxpayer's gross income for each of the following:
    a. T is the manager of a plant. The company owns a house one mile from the plant (rental value of $6,000) that T is allowed to occupy.
    b. M works for an insurance company that allows employees to eat in the cafeteria for $.50 a meal. Generally, the cost to the insurance company of producing a meal is $5.00, and a comparable meal could be purchased for $4.00. M ate 150 meals in the cafeteria during the year.
    c. Z is a Methodist minister and receives a housing allowance of $600 per month from his church. Z is buying his home and uses the $600 to make house payments ($450) and to pay utilities ($150).
    d. P is a college professor and lives in campus housing. He is not charged rent. The value of the house is $100,000, and the annual rental value is $7,200.

39. Does the taxpayer recognize gross income in the following situations?

a. A is a registered nurse working in a community hospital. She is not required to have her lunch on the hospital premises, but she can eat in the cafeteria at no charge. The hospital adopted this policy to encourage employees to stay on the premises and be available in case of emergencies. During the year, A ate most of her meals on the premises. The total value of those meals was $750.

b. J is the manager of a hotel. His employer will allow him to live in one of the rooms rent free or to receive a $200 per month cash allowance for rent. J elected to live in the hotel.

c. S is a forest ranger and lives in his employer's cabin in the forest. He is required to live there, and because there are no restaurants nearby, the employer supplies S with groceries that he cooks and eats on the premises.

d. T is a partner in the ABC Ranch (a partnership). He is the full-time manager of the ranch. ABC has a business purpose for T's living on the ranch.

40. T is employed by F Bowling Lanes, Inc. Determine T's gross income in each of the following situations:

a. T's children are allowed to use the lanes without charge. Each child can also bring a friend without charge. This benefit is available to all employees. During the year, the children bowled 200 games, and the usual charge was $1.50 per game. Friends of T's children bowled 150 games.

b. The company has a lunch counter. T is allowed to take home the leftover donuts each night. The company's cost was $400, and the value of the donuts T took home was $150.

c. The company pays T's subscription to *Bowling Lanes Management,* a monthly journal.

41. X Corporation would like you to review its employee fringe benefits program with regard to the effects of the plan on the company's president (P), who is also the majority shareholder:

a. All employees receive free tickets to State University football games. P is seldom able to attend the games and usually gives his tickets to his nephew. The cost of P's tickets for the year was $75.

b. The company pays all parking fees for its officers but not for other employees. The company paid $1,200 for P's parking for the year.

c. Employees are allowed to use the copy machine for personal purposes as long as the privilege is not abused. P is president of a trade association and made extensive use of the copy machine to prepare mailings to members of the association. The cost of the copies was $900.

d. The company is in the household moving business. Employees are allowed to ship goods without charge whenever there is excess space on a truck. P purchased a dining room suite for his daughter. Company trucks delivered the furniture to the daughter. Normal freight charges would have been $600.

e. The company has a storage facility for household goods. Officers are allowed a 20% discount on charges for storing their goods. All other employees are allowed a 10% discount. P's discounts for the year totaled $400.

42. Which of the following benefits are excludible from an employee's gross income even though provided on a discriminatory basis (they favor higher paid employees)?

a. Occasional use of the employer's typewriter to type a personal letter.

b. A 10% discount on merchandise.

c. Parking.

d. Meals provided in a subsidized eating facility.

43. R is a U.S. citizen and a production manager for XYZ Company. On May 1, 1989, he was temporarily assigned to the Monterrey, Mexico, plant. On August 6, 1989, he returned to the United States for medical treatment. On September 1, 1989, he returned to his duties in Monterrey. Except for a two-week period in the United States (December 16–31, 1989), he worked in Monterrey until December 1, 1990, when he was transferred to Boston, Massachusetts. R's salary was $4,000 per month in 1989 and $5,000 per month in 1990. His housing expense did not exceed the base amount. Compute R's foreign earned income exclusion in 1989 and 1990.

44. Determine M's taxable income from the items below.
    a. M owns 100 shares of BE Company common stock. The company has a dividend reinvestment plan. Under the plan, M can receive an $18 cash dividend or an additional share of stock with a fair market value of $18. M elected to take the stock.
    b. M owns 100 shares of NB Corporation. The company declared a dividend, and M was to receive an additional share of the company's stock with a fair market value of $18. M did not have the option to receive cash. However, a management group announced a plan to repurchase all available shares for $18 each. The offer was part of a takeover defense.
    c. M collected $125 on a corporate debenture. The corporation had been in bankruptcy for several years. M had correctly deducted the cost of the bond in a prior year because the bankruptcy judge had informed the bondholders they would not receive anything in the final liquidation. Later the company collected on an unanticipated claim and had the funds to make partial payment on the bonds.

45. Determine T's gross income from the following receipts for the year:

Interest on U.S. government savings bonds	$ 500
Sale of State of Virginia bonds (basis of $9,000)	10,000
Interest on Virginia tax refund	1,500
Interest on Pulaski County school bonds	800
Sale of Augusta County bonds (basis of $4,000)	3,500
Patronage dividend from the Good Life Food Co-operative (a health food store)	200

46. How does the tax benefit rule apply in the following cases?
    a. In 1989, T paid X $5,000 for locating a potential client. The deal fell through, and in 1990, X refunded the $5,000 to T.
    b. In 1989, T paid an attorney $300 for services in connection with a title search. Because the attorney was negligent, T incurred some additional costs in acquiring the land. In 1990, the attorney refunded his $300 fee to T.
    c. In 1990, T received a $90 dividend with respect to 1990 premiums on her life insurance policy.
    d. In 1990, a cash basis farmer received a $400 patronage dividend with respect to 1989 purchases of cattle feed.

47. T, who is in the 28% tax bracket, recently collected $100,000 on a life insurance policy she carried on her father. She currently owes $120,000 on her personal residence and $120,000 on business property. National Bank holds the mortgage on both pieces of property and has agreed to accept $100,000 in complete satisfaction of either mortgage. The interest rate on the mortgages is 8%, and both mortgages are payable over 10 years. T can also purchase Montgomery County school bonds yielding 8%. What would be the tax consequences of each of the following alternatives, assuming T currently deducts the mortgage interest on her tax return?

a. Retire the mortgage on the residence.

b. Retire the mortgage on the business property.

c. Purchase tax-exempt bonds but not pay off either mortgage.

Which alternative should T select?

48. T had total assets of $100,000 and liabilities of $150,000; it was apparent that T could not meet his liabilities as they came due. Determine the consequences of the following agreements T reached with his creditors.

a. The State Bank agreed to extend the due date for an additional year on a $30,000 note due in exchange for an increase in the interest rate.

b. T's older brother, Z, forgave T's $10,000 debt. When asked about why he did it, Z responded, "T's my brother."

c. An equipment supplier agreed to reduce the amount T owed for equipment by $5,000 "to help a good customer stay in business."

Cumulative Problems

49. Oliver W. Hand was divorced from Sandra D. Hand on May 12, 1989. On September 6, 1990, Oliver married Beulah Crane. Oliver and Beulah will file a joint return for 1990. Oliver's Social Security number is 262–60–3814. Beulah's number is 259–68–4184, and she will adopt "Hand" as her married name. The Hands live at 210 Mason Drive, Atlanta, GA 30304. Sandra's Social Security number is 219–74–1361.

Oliver is 49 and is employed by Atom, Inc., as an electrical engineer. His salary for 1990 was $56,000. Beulah is 30 and earned $29,000 as a marriage counselor in 1990. She was employed by Family Counselors, Inc.

The decree of divorce required Oliver to pay Sandra $1,000 per month for 132 months. Oliver was also required to pay $200 a month in support of Daisy Hand, his 11-year-old daughter. Sandra was granted custody of Daisy and can document that she provided $2,000 of support for Daisy. Oliver made 12 payments in 1990. Oliver's employer provided him with group term life insurance coverage in the amount of $90,000 in 1990.

Beulah's employer provided Beulah with free parking in a parking garage adjacent to the office building where Beulah works. The monthly charge to the general public is $50.

Oliver received dividends of $40 on Z Corporation stock he owned before marriage, and Beulah received dividends of $50 on her separately owned M Corporation stock. They received dividends of $100 on jointly owned B Corporation stock, which they acquired after marriage. Oliver and Beulah live in a common law state.

Combined itemized deductions for Oliver and Beulah in 1990 were as follows:

State income taxes withheld		
Oliver	$2,600	
Beulah	800	$3,400
Real estate taxes on residence		820
Home mortgage interest (paid to Atlanta Federal Savings and Loan)		4,020
Cash contributions to church		900

In 1990, Beulah received a refund of 1989 state income taxes of $450. She had deducted state income taxes withheld as an itemized deduction on her 1989 return. Oliver received a $300 refund on his 1989 state income taxes. He had used the standard deduction in 1989.

Additional information:

- Oliver's employer withheld Federal income tax of $7,650 and $3,924 of FICA (Social Security) tax. Beulah's employer withheld $2,900 of Federal income tax and $2,219 of FICA tax.

Part 1—Tax Computation

Compute the Hands' net tax payable (or refund due) for 1990. Suggested software (if available): *WEST–TAX Planner* or *TurboTax* (planning mode).

Part 2—Tax Planning

Assume the Hands came to you in early December of 1990 seeking tax planning advice for 1990 and 1991. They provide you with the following information:

a. All the facts previously presented will be essentially the same in 1991 except for the items described in (b), (c), (d), and (e) below.

b. Oliver inherited $100,000 from his mother on December 1. He will use part of his inheritance to pay off the mortgage on the Hands' residence on January 3, 1991. Consequently, there will be no mortgage interest expense in 1991.

c. Oliver expects a 6% salary increase in 1991, and Beulah expects a 10% increase.

d. The Hands have pledged to contribute $2,400 to their church in 1991 (as opposed to $900 contributed in 1990). However, they could use Oliver's inherited funds to pay the pledge before the end of 1990 if you advise them to do so to achieve an overall tax savings.

e. The Hands acquired 100 shares of ABC Corporation stock on July 5, 1990, at a total cost of $2,000. The value of the stock has increased rapidly, and it is now worth $5,000. The Hands plan to sell the stock and ask whether they should sell it in 1990 or wait until 1991.

Advise the Hands as to the appropriate tax planning strategy for 1990 and 1991. Support your recommendations by computing their tax liabilities for 1990 and 1991 considering the various available alternatives. Suggested software (if available): *WEST–TAX Planner*.

 50. Archie S. Monroe (Social Security number 363–33–1411) is married to Annie B. Monroe (Social Security number 259–68–4284). The Monroes live at 215 Adams Dr., Thor, VA 24317. They file a joint return and have two dependent children (Barry and Betty). In 1990, Archie and Annie had the following transactions:

a. Salary received by Archie from Allen Steel Company (Archie is vice president). $65,000

b. Interest received on jointly owned State of Nebraska bonds. 8,000

c. Group term life insurance premiums paid by Archie's employer (coverage of $40,000). 80

d. Annual increment in the value of Series E government savings bonds (the Monroes have not previously included the accrued amounts in gross income). 400

e. Taxable dividends received from Allen Steel Company, a U.S. corporation (the stock was jointly owned). Of the $5,900 in dividends, $1,000 was mailed on December 31, 1990, and received by Archie and Annie on January 4, 1991. 5,900

f. Alimony payments to Archie's former wife (Rosa T. Monroe, Social Security number 800–60–2580) under a divorce decree.   9,000

g. Itemized deductions.

State income tax   1,600

Real estate tax on residence   600

Interest on personal residence (paid to Thor Federal Savings)   3,000

Cash contribution to church   700

h. Federal income tax withheld.   11,976

Part 1—Tax Computation

Compute the Monroes' net tax payable (or refund due) for 1990. Suggested software (if available): *WEST–TAX Planner.*

Part 2—Tax Planning

The Monroes plan to sell 200 shares of stock they purchased on July 12, 1980, at a cost of $18,000. The stock is worth $10,000 in December 1990, and the Monroes' broker predicts a continued decline in value. Annie plans to resume her career as a model in 1991, and her earnings will move the Monroes into the top tax bracket. How much Federal income tax will the Monroes save for 1990 if they sell the stock in 1990? Should they sell the stock in 1990 or 1991? Suggested software (if available): *WEST–TAX Planner.*

5

DEDUCTIONS AND LOSSES: IN GENERAL

OBJECTIVES   Explain the importance of deductions *for* and *from* adjusted gross income.

Classify the deductions *for* and *from* adjusted gross income.

Define the meaning of "ordinary," "necessary," and "reasonable" in relation to deductible business expenses.

Explain the differences between cash basis and accrual basis.

Discuss the following disallowance possibilities: public policy limitations, political activities, investigation of business opportunities, hobby losses, vacation home rentals, payment of expenses of others, personal expenditures, unrealized losses, capital expenditures, and transactions between related parties.

Explain the substantiation requirements that must be met to take a deduction.

Examine the nondeductibility of expenses and interest related to tax-exempt income.

Describe various tax planning techniques concerning the time value of deductions, unreasonable compensation, shifting deductions, hobby losses, and substantiation requirements.

CLASSIFICATION OF DEDUCTIBLE EXPENSES

As discussed in chapters 3 and 4, § 61 provides an all-inclusive definition of gross income. Deductions, however, must be specifically provided for by law. The courts have established the doctrine that an item is not deductible unless a specific provision in the tax law allows its deduction. Whether and to what extent deductions shall be allowed depends on legislative grace.[1]

It is important to classify deductible expenses as deductions *for* adjusted gross income (deductions subtracted from gross income in calculating adjusted gross income) or deductions *from* adjusted gross income (AGI). Deductions *for* AGI can be taken whether or not the taxpayer itemizes. Deductions *from* AGI result in a tax benefit only if they exceed the taxpayer's standard deduction. If itemized deductions (*from* AGI) are less than the standard deduction, they are of no tax benefit.

Deductions *for* AGI are also important in determining the *amount* of itemized deductions because many itemized deductions (e.g., medical expenses and personal casualty losses) are limited to amounts in excess of specified percentages of AGI. Itemized deductions that are deductible only to the extent that they exceed a specified percentage of AGI are increased when AGI is decreased. Likewise, when AGI is increased, such itemized deductions are decreased.

EXAMPLE 1   T, who earns a salary of $20,000 and has no other income, itemizes deductions in 1990. His medical expenses for the year were $1,800. Since medical expenses are deductible only to the extent they exceed 7.5% of AGI, T's medical expense deduction is $300 [$1,800 − (7.5% × $20,000)]. If T had a $2,000 deduction *for* AGI, his medical expense deduction would be $450 [$1,800 − (7.5% × $18,000)]. If the $2,000 deduction was *from* AGI, his medical expense deduction would remain $300 since AGI would be unchanged.   □

The preceding example illustrates the effect on adjusted gross income of a deduction *for* AGI. Changes in income recognition (an increase or decrease) have a like impact on AGI and, consequently, on itemized deductions.

A deduction *for* adjusted gross income is also more valuable to the taxpayer who lives in a state that begins its tax computation with Federal AGI rather than with Federal taxable income. A lower base of Federal AGI will result in lower state income taxes.

Deductions for Adjusted Gross Income

To understand how deductions of individual taxpayers are classified, it is necessary to understand the role of § 62. Section 62 merely classifies various deductions as deductions *for* adjusted gross income. It does not provide the authority for taking the deduction. For example, § 212 allows individuals to deduct expenses attributable to income-producing property. Section 62(a)(4) classifies § 212 expenses that are attributable to rents or royalties as deductions *for* AGI. Likewise, a deduction for trade or business expenses is allowed by § 162; such expenses are classified as deductions *for* AGI by § 62(a)(1).

---

1. *New Colonial Ice Co. v. Helvering*, 4 USTC ¶1292,
    13 AFTR 1180, 54 S.Ct. 788 (USSC, 1934).

If a deduction is not listed in § 62, it is *not* a deduction for AGI; it is an itemized deduction. Following is a list of the items classified as deductions *for* AGI by § 62.

1. Expenses attributable to a trade or business carried on by the taxpayer, if such trade or business does not consist of the performance of services by the taxpayer as an employee.

2. Expenses incurred by a taxpayer in connection with the performance of services as an employee if such expenses are reimbursed, an adequate accounting is made to the employer, and the employee is not allowed to keep any excess reimbursements.

3. Deductions that result from losses on the sale or exchange of property by the taxpayer.

4. Deductions attributable to property held for the production of rents and royalties.

5. The deduction for payment of alimony allowed by § 215.

6. Certain contributions to pension, profit sharing, and annuity plans of self-employed individuals.

7. The deduction for certain retirement savings allowed by § 219.

8. A certain portion of lump-sum distributions from pension plans taxed under § 402(e).

9. Penalties forfeited because of premature withdrawal of funds from time savings accounts or deposits.

10. Trade or business expenses of a *qualified performing artist* incurred in connection with the performance of services as an employee in the performing arts.

11. The deduction for certain required repayments of supplemental unemployment compensation benefits.

12. Depreciation and depletion deductions allowed to a life tenant of property; an income beneficiary of property held in trust; or an heir, legatee, or devisee of an estate.

13. The deduction for reforestation expenses allowed by § 194.

Items 1 through 8 are covered in detail in various chapters throughout the text. Although items 9 through 13 are not covered in detail in the text, they are included here to provide a complete list of deductions covered by § 62.

Itemized Deductions

Section 63(d) defines itemized deductions as the deductions allowed other than "the deductions allowable in arriving at adjusted gross income"; that is, deductions that are not deductions *for* adjusted gross income are itemized deductions.

Section 212 allows deductions for ordinary and necessary expenses paid or incurred for the following:

- The production or collection of income.

- The management, conservation, or maintenance of property held for the production of income.

- Expenses paid in connection with the determination (including tax return preparation), collection, or refund of any tax.

Section 62(a)(4) classifies § 212 expenses that are related to rent and royalty income as deductions *for* AGI. All other § 212 expenses are itemized deductions (deductions *from* AGI).

Investment-related expenses (e.g., safe deposit box rentals) are deductible as itemized deductions attributable to the production of investment income.

Taxpayers are also allowed to deduct certain expenses that are primarily personal in nature. These expenses, which are not generally related to the production of income, are deductions *from* AGI (itemized deductions). Some of the more frequently encountered deductions in this category include the following:

- Contributions to qualified charitable organizations (not to exceed 50 percent of AGI).

- Medical expenses (in excess of 7.5 percent of AGI).

- State and local taxes (e.g., real estate taxes and state and local income taxes).

- Personal casualty losses (in excess of an aggregate floor of 10 percent of AGI and a $100 floor per casualty).

- Certain personal interest (e.g., mortgage interest on a personal residence).

Certain miscellaneous itemized deductions are deductible only to the extent that in the aggregate they exceed 2 percent of adjusted gross income. Other miscellaneous itemized deductions are fully deductible. Itemized deductions are discussed in detail in chapter 10.

Trade or Business Expenses

Section 162(a) permits a deduction for all ordinary and necessary expenses paid or incurred in carrying on a trade or business, including reasonable salaries paid for services and expenses for the use of business property. Such expenses are deducted *for* AGI.

It is sometimes difficult to determine whether an expenditure is deductible as a trade or business expense. The term "trade or business" is not defined in the Code or Regulations, and the courts have not provided a satisfactory definition. Therefore, it is usually necessary to ask one or more of the following questions to determine whether an item qualifies as a trade or business expense:

- Was the use of the particular item related to a business activity? For example, if funds are borrowed for use in a business, the interest is deductible as a business expense (as a deduction *for* AGI).

- Was the expenditure incurred with the intent to realize a profit or to produce income? For example, expenses in excess of the income from raising horses would not be deductible if the activity were classified as a personal hobby rather than a trade or business.

- Were the taxpayer's operation and management activities extensive enough to indicate the carrying on of a trade or business?

Section 162 excludes the following items from classification as trade or business expenses:

- Charitable contributions or gifts.

- Illegal bribes and kickbacks and certain treble damage payments.

- Fines and penalties.

A bribe paid to a domestic official is not deductible if it is illegal under the laws of the United States. Foreign bribes (sometimes referred to as grease payments) are deductible unless they are unlawful under the Foreign Corrupt Practices Act of 1977.

Ordinary and Necessary Requirement. The terms "ordinary" and "necessary" are found in both §§ 162 and 212. Section 162 governs the deductibility of trade or business expenses, and § 62(a)(1) classifies trade or business expenses of individuals as deductions *for* AGI. To be deductible under § 162, any trade or business expense must be ordinary and necessary. In addition, compensation for services must be "reasonable" in amount.

Many expenses that are necessary are *not* ordinary. The words "ordinary and necessary" are not defined in the Code or Regulations. However, the courts have held that an expense is necessary if a prudent businessperson would incur the same expense and the expense is expected to be appropriate and helpful in the taxpayer's business.[2]

EXAMPLE 2   T purchased a manufacturing concern that had just been adjudged bankrupt. Because the business had a poor financial rating, T satisfies some of the obligations to employees and outside salespeople incurred by its former owners. Although there was no legal obligation to pay these debts, T felt this was the only way to keep salespeople and employees. The Second Court of Appeals found that such payments were necessary in that they were both appropriate and helpful.[3] However, the Court held that such payments were *not* ordinary but were in the nature of capital expenditures to build a reputation. Therefore, no deduction was allowed. □

An expense is ordinary if it is normal, usual, or customary in the type of business conducted by the taxpayer and is not capital in nature. However, an expense need not be recurring to be deductible as ordinary.

EXAMPLE 3   T engaged in a mail-order business. The post office judged that his advertisements were false and misleading. Under a fraud order, the post office stamped "fraudulent" on all letters addressed to T's business and returned them to the senders. T spent $30,000 on legal fees in an unsuccessful attempt to force the post office to stop. The legal fees (though not recurring) were ordinary business expenses because such fees were normal, usual, or customary in the circumstances. □

The Regulations under § 212 require that expenses bear a reasonable and proximate relationship to the production or collection of income or to the management, conservation, or maintenance of property held for the production of income.[4]

EXAMPLE 4   W owns a small portfolio of investments, including 10 shares of T, Inc., common stock worth $1,000. W incurred $350 in travel expenses to attend the

---

2. *Welch v. Helvering*, 3 USTC ¶1164, 12 AFTR 1456, 54 S.Ct. 8 (USSC, 1933).

3. *Dunn and McCarthy, Inc. v. Comm.*, 43–2 USTC

¶9688, 31 AFTR 1043, 139 F.2d 242 (CA–2, 1943).

4. Reg. § 1.212–1(d).

annual shareholders' meeting at which she voted her 10 shares against the current management group. No deduction is permitted, because a 10-share investment is insignificant in value in relation to the travel expenses incurred.

□

Reasonableness Requirement.   Code § 162(a)(1) refers to reasonableness solely with respect to salaries and other compensation for services. The courts, however, have held that for any business expense to be ordinary and necessary it must also be reasonable in amount.[5]

What constitutes reasonableness is a question of fact. If an expense is unreasonable, the excess amount is not allowed as a deduction. The question of reasonableness generally arises with respect to closely held corporations where there is no separation of ownership and management. In such cases, transactions between the shareholders and the company may result in the disallowance of deductions for excessive salaries and rent expense paid by the corporation. However, an unusually large salary will be viewed by the courts in light of all relevant circumstances, and such a salary may be found reasonable despite its size.[6] If excessive payments for salaries and rents bear a close relationship to the percentage of stock ownership of the recipients, such amounts are generally treated as dividends to the shareholders and are not deductible by the corporation. However, deductions for reasonable salaries will not be disallowed solely because the corporation has paid insubstantial portions of its earnings as dividends to its shareholders.

EXAMPLE 5

XYZ Corporation is closely held in equal ownership interests by X, Y, and Z. The company has been highly profitable for several years and has not paid dividends. X, Y, and Z are key officers of the company, and each receives a salary of $200,000. Salaries for similar positions in comparable companies average only $100,000. Amounts paid to X, Y, and Z in excess of $100,000 may be deemed unreasonable, and a total of $300,000 in salary deductions may be disallowed. The excess amounts may be treated as dividends rather than salary income to X, Y, and Z because such amounts are proportional to stock ownership. Salaries are deductible by the corporation but dividends are not.

□

Business and Nonbusiness Losses

Section 165 provides for a deduction for losses not compensated for by insurance. As a general rule, deductible losses of individual taxpayers are limited to those incurred in a trade or business or in a transaction entered into for profit. However, individuals are also allowed to deduct losses that are the result of a casualty. Casualty losses include, but are not limited to, fire, storm, shipwreck, and theft (see chapter 7 for a further discussion of this topic). Deductible personal casualty losses are reduced by $100 per casualty, and the aggregate of all casualty losses is reduced by 10 percent of adjusted gross income. A personal casualty loss is an itemized deduction.

---

5. *Comm. v. Lincoln Electric Co.*, 49–2 USTC ¶9388, 38 AFTR 411, 176 F.2d 815 (CA–6, 1949).

6. *Kennedy, Jr. v. Comm.*, 82–1 USTC ¶9186, 49 AFTR2d 82–628, 671 F.2d 167 (CA–6, 1982), *rev'g* 72 T.C. 793 (1979).

DEDUCTIONS AND LOSSES—TIMING OF EXPENSE RECOGNITION

Importance of Taxpayer's Method of Accounting

A taxpayer's method of accounting is a major factor in determining taxable income. The method used determines when an item is includible in income and when an item is deductible on the tax return. Usually, the taxpayer's regular method of recordkeeping is used for income tax purposes. The taxing authorities do not require uniformity among all taxpayers, but they do require that the method used clearly reflect income and that items be handled consistently. The most common methods of accounting are the cash method and the accrual method.

Throughout the portions of the Code dealing with deductions, the phrase "paid or incurred" is used. "Paid" has reference to the cash basis taxpayer who gets a deduction only in the year of payment. "Incurred" concerns the accrual basis taxpayer who obtains the deduction in the year in which the liability for the expense becomes certain (refer to chapter 4).

Cash Method Requirements

The expenses of cash basis taxpayers are deductible only when they are actually paid with cash or other property. Promising to pay or issuing a note does not satisfy the "actually paid" requirement. However, the payment can be made with borrowed funds. Thus, at the time taxpayers charge expenses on their bank credit cards, they are allowed to claim the deduction because they are deemed to have simultaneously borrowed money from the credit card issuer and constructively paid the expenses.

Although the cash basis taxpayer must have actually or constructively paid the amount, payment does not assure a current deduction. Cash basis as well as accrual basis taxpayers cannot take a current deduction for capital expenditures, except through amortization or depreciation over the life of the asset. The Regulations set forth the general rule that an expenditure that creates an asset having a useful life that extends substantially beyond the end of the tax year must be capitalized.[7]

EXAMPLE 6   T, a cash basis taxpayer, rents property from L. On July 1, 1990, T paid $2,400 rent for the 24 months ending June 30, 1992. The prepaid rent extends 18 months—substantially beyond the year of payment. Therefore, T must capitalize the prepaid rent and amortize the expense on a monthly basis. His deduction for 1990 is $600. ☐

The Tax Court and the IRS took the position that an asset that would expire or would be consumed by the end of the tax year following the year of payment had a life that extended substantially beyond the year of payment and had to be prorated. However, the Ninth Circuit Court held that such expenditures are currently deductible, and the Supreme Court apparently concurs.[8]

---

7. Reg. § 1.461–1(a).

8. *Zaninovich v. Comm.*, 80–1 USTC ¶9342, 45 AFTR2d 80–1442, 616 F.2d 429 (CA–9, 1980), *rev'g* 69 T.C. 605 (1978). Cited by the Supreme Court in *Hillsboro National Bank v. Comm.*, 83–1 USTC ¶9229, 51 AFTR2d 83–874, 103 S.Ct. 1134 (USSC, 1983).

EXAMPLE 7   Assume the same facts as in Example 6, except that T was required to pay only 12 months rent in 1990. T paid $1,200 on July 1, 1990. The entire $1,200 would be deductible in 1990. □

The payment, however, must be required (and not a voluntary prepayment) to obtain the current deduction under the one-year rule.

To obtain a current deduction for an asset, the taxpayer also must demonstrate that an allowance of the current deduction will not result in a material distortion of income. Generally, the deduction will be allowed if the item is recurring (e.g., rent) or was made for a business purpose (rather than to manipulate income). Deduction of prepaid interest is disallowed by § 461(g).

Limitations on Who Can Use the Cash Method.   In the cash method of accounting, possibilities exist for the manipulation of taxable income between years. Code § 448 lessens these possibilities by prohibiting the use of the cash method by the following taxpayers:

- Corporations (other than S corporations).

- Partnerships where one of the partners is a corporation (other than an S corporation), except in certain specified cases.

- Trusts subject to tax under § 511(b) with respect to activities of the trust constituting an unrelated trade or business.

- Tax shelters, regardless of income level.

Exceptions are provided for small businesses, certain farms, certain personal service corporations, and entities not fitting into one of the four classifications just listed. Small businesses whose average annual gross income for the preceding three years does not exceed $5 million are allowed to use the cash method.

Accrual Method Requirements

The period in which an accrual basis taxpayer can deduct an expense is determined by applying the economic performance test. The economic performance test is met only when the service, property, or use of property giving rise to the liability is actually performed for, provided to, or used by the taxpayer.

EXAMPLE 8   On December 15, 1990, a rusted water main broke and flooded the business premises of T, an accrual basis calendar year taxpayer. An outside firm surveyed the damage and estimated the cleanup fee at $6,000. T signed a contract (paying 20% down) on December 20, 1990. Because of the holidays, the cleanup crew did not start work until January 2, 1991. T cannot deduct the $1,200 until 1991, when the services are performed. □

An exception to the economic performance requirements provides that certain recurring items may be deducted if the following conditions are met:

- Such items are treated consistently.

- Either they are not material in amount or such accrual results in better matching of income and expenses.

- The all-events test is met.

- Economic performance occurs within a reasonable period but not more than 8½ months after year-end. The all-events test is met when all the events have

occurred that determine the fact of the liability and the amount of the liability can be determined with reasonable accuracy.

EXAMPLE 9   T, an accrual basis calendar year taxpayer, entered into a monthly maintenance contract during the year. T makes a monthly accrual at the end of every month for this service and pays the fee some time between the first and fifteenth of the following month when services are performed. The amount involved is immaterial, and all other tests are met. The December 1990 accrual is deductible even though the service is performed on January 12, 1991.   □

EXAMPLE 10   T, an accrual basis calendar year taxpayer, shipped merchandise sold on December 30, 1990, via Greyhound Van Lines on January 2, 1991, and paid the freight charges at that time. Since she reported the sale of the merchandise in 1990, the shipping charge should also be deductible in 1990 since that results in a better matching of income and expenses.   □

Reserves for estimated expenses that are frequently employed for financial accounting purposes generally are not allowed for tax purposes because the economic performance test cannot be satisfied.

EXAMPLE 11   T Airlines is required by Federal law to conduct tests of its engines after 3,000 flying hours. Aircraft cannot return to flight until the tests have been conducted. An unrelated garage does all of the company's tests for $1,500 per engine. For financial reporting purposes, the company accrues an expense based upon $.50 per hour of flight and credits an allowance account. The actual amounts paid to the garage are offset against the allowance account. However, for tax purposes, the economic performance test is not satisfied until the work has been done.   □

DISALLOWANCE POSSIBILITIES

The tax law provides for the disallowance of certain types of expenses. Without specific restrictions in the tax law, taxpayers might attempt to deduct certain items that in reality are personal, nondeductible expenditures. For example, specific tax rules are provided to determine whether an expenditure is for trade or business purposes and therefore deductible, or related to a personal hobby and therefore nondeductible.

Certain disallowance provisions represent a codification or extension of prior court decisions. For example, the courts had denied deductions for payments deemed to be in violation of public policy. Thus, the tax law was changed to provide specific authority for the disallowance of such deductions. Detailed discussions of specific disallowance provisions in the tax law follow.

Public Policy Limitation

Justification for Denying Deductions.   The courts developed the principle that a payment that is in violation of public policy is not a necessary expense and therefore is not deductible.[9]

---

9. *Tank Truck Rentals, Inc. v. Comm.*, 58–1 USTC ¶9366, 1 AFTR2d 1154, 78 S.Ct. 507 (USSC, 1958).

A bribe or fine, for example, may be appropriate, helpful, and even contribute to the profitability of an activity. The courts have held that to allow such expenses would frustrate sharply defined public policy. A deduction would dilute the effect of the penalty since the government would be indirectly subsidizing a taxpayer's wrongdoing.

The IRS and the courts were always free to restrict deductions if, in their view, the expenses were contrary to public policy. It was often necessary for taxpayers to go to court to determine if their expense violated public policy.

Recognizing that the public policy doctrine could be arbitrarily applied in cases where no governmental body had clearly defined such a policy, Congress enacted legislation in an attempt to limit the use of the doctrine. The legislation identifies and limits disallowance of deductions to certain types of expenditures that are considered contrary to public policy. Deductions are disallowed for the following expenses:

- Bribes and kickbacks (in the case of foreign bribes and kickbacks, only if the payments violate the U.S. Foreign Corrupt Practices Act of 1977).

- Fines and penalties paid to a government for violation of law.

EXAMPLE 12   Y Corporation, a moving company, consistently loads its trucks with weights in excess of the limits allowed by state law because the additional revenue more than offsets the fines levied. Because the fines are for violation of public policy, they are not deductible. □

- Two-thirds of the treble damage payments made to claimants resulting from violation of the antitrust law.

No deduction is permitted for a kickback that is illegal under state law (if such state law is generally enforced) and that subjects the payor to a criminal penalty or the loss of license or privilege to engage in a trade or business.

Legal Expenses Incurred in Defense of Civil or Criminal Penalties.   Generally, legal expenses are deductible *for* adjusted gross income as ordinary and necessary business expenses if incurred in connection with a trade or business activity. Legal expenses may also be deductible *for* adjusted gross income as expenses incurred in conjunction with rental property held for the production of income. Legal expenses are deductible *from* adjusted gross income if they are for fees for tax advice relative to the preparation of the taxpayer's income tax returns. These tax-related legal fees are itemized deductions (discussed more fully in chapter 10) that are deductible only to the extent that they exceed 2 percent of adjusted gross income.

Personal legal expenses are not deductible. Legal fees incurred in connection with a criminal defense are deductible if the crime is associated with the taxpayer's trade or business activity.[10] To deduct legal expenses, the taxpayer must be able to show that the origin and character of the claim are directly related to a trade or business or an income-producing activity. Otherwise, the legal expenses are personal and nondeductible.

---

10. *Comm. v. Tellier* 66–1 USTC ¶9319, 17 AFTR2d 633, 86 S.Ct. 1118 (USSC, 1966).

EXAMPLE 13   T, a financial officer of X Corporation, incurred legal expenses in connection with the defense in a criminal indictment for evasion of X Corporation's income taxes. T may deduct her legal expenses because she is deemed to be in the trade or business of being an executive, and such legal action impairs her ability to conduct this business activity.   □

Expenses Relating to an Illegal Business.   The usual expenses of operating an illegal business (e.g., a numbers racket) are deductible. However, § 162 disallows a deduction for fines, bribes to public officials, illegal kickbacks, and other illegal payments.

An exception applies to expenses incurred with regard to illegal trafficking in drugs. Drug dealers are not allowed a deduction for ordinary and necessary business expenses incurred in such a business. However, a deduction for cost of goods sold is allowed.

Political Contributions and Lobbying Activities

Political Contributions.   Generally, no business deduction is permitted for direct or indirect payments for political purposes. Historically, the government has been reluctant to grant favorable tax treatment to business expenditures for political purposes because of the possible abuses and the need to prevent undue influence upon the political process.

Lobbying Expenditures.   A deduction is allowed for certain expenses incurred to influence legislation, provided that the proposed legislation is of direct interest to the taxpayer. A direct interest exists if the legislation is of such a nature that it will, or may reasonably be expected to, affect the trade or business of the taxpayer. Dues and expenses paid to an organization that consists of individuals with a common direct interest in proposed legislation are deductible in proportion to the organization's legislative activity. A common direct interest exists where an organization consists of persons with the same direct interests in legislation or proposed legislation. However, no deduction is allowed for any expenses incurred to influence the public on legislative matters or for any political campaign.

EXAMPLE 14   T, a contractor, drove to his state capitol to testify against proposed legislation that would affect building codes. T believes that the proposed legislation is unnecessary and not in the best interest of his company. The expenses are deductible because the legislation is of direct interest to T's company. If T later journeyed to another city to make a speech concerning the legislation at a Lion's Club meeting, his travel expenses would not be deductible because the expenses were incurred to influence the public on legislative matters.   □

Investigation of a Business

Investigation expenses are those expenses paid or incurred to determine the feasibility of entering a new business or expanding an existing business. They include such costs as travel, engineering and architectural surveys, marketing reports, and various legal and accounting services. How such expenses are treated for tax purposes depends on a number of variables, including the following:

- The current business, if any, of the taxpayer.
- The nature of the business being investigated.
- The extent to which the investigation has proceeded.
- Whether or not the acquisition actually takes place.

If the taxpayer is in a business the same as or similar to that being investigated, all expenses in connection therewith are deductible in the year paid or incurred. The tax result would be the same whether or not the taxpayer acquired the business being investigated.

EXAMPLE 15   T, an accrual basis sole proprietor, owns and operates three motels in Georgia. In 1990, T incurs expenses of $8,500 in investigating the possibility of acquiring several additional motels located in South Carolina. The $8,500 is deductible in 1990 whether or not T acquires the motels in South Carolina. □

When the taxpayer is not in a business that is the same as or similar to the one being investigated, the tax result usually depends on whether the new business is acquired. If the business is not acquired, all investigation expenses generally become nondeductible.

If a taxpayer is in a business that is not the same as or similar to the business being investigated, and the investigation effort actually leads to the acquisition of a new business, the expenses must be capitalized. At the election of the taxpayer, such expenses may be amortized over a period of 60 months or more.

Hobby Losses

Deductions for business or investment expenses are permitted only if the taxpayer can show that the business or investment activity was entered into for the purpose of making a profit. Certain activities may have profit-seeking or personal attributes, depending upon individual circumstances (e.g., raising horses and operating a farm used as a weekend residence). Personal losses are not deductible, although losses attributable to profit-seeking activities may be deducted and used to offset a taxpayer's other income. For this reason, provisions that limit the deductibility of hobby losses are necessary.

General Rules.   If a taxpayer (an individual or an S corporation) can show that an activity has been conducted with the intent to earn a profit, any losses from the activity are fully deductible and § 183 is not applicable. The hobby loss rules apply only if the activity is not engaged in for profit. Hobby expenses are deductible only to the extent of hobby income.

The Regulations stipulate the following relevant factors to be considered in determining whether an activity is profit-seeking or a hobby:[11]

- Whether the activity is conducted in a businesslike manner.
- The expertise of the taxpayers or their advisers.
- The time and effort expended.

---

11. Reg. §§ 1.183–2(b)(1) through (9).

- The expectation that the assets of the activity will appreciate in value.
- The previous success of the taxpayer in the conduct of similar activities.
- The history of income or losses from the activity.
- The relationship of profits earned to losses incurred.
- The financial status of the taxpayer (e.g., if the taxpayer does not have substantial amounts of other income, this fact may indicate that the activity is engaged in for profit).
- Elements of personal pleasure or recreation in the activity.

Presumptive Rule of § 183.   The Code provides a rebuttable presumption that an activity is profit-seeking if it shows a profit in at least three of any five consecutive years (two of seven years for activities involving horses) ending with the taxable year in question. If these profitability tests are met, the activity is presumed to be a trade or business rather than a personal hobby. In effect, the IRS bears the burden of proving that the activity is personal rather than trade or business related.

EXAMPLE 16   N, an executive for a large corporation, is paid a salary of $200,000. His wife is a collector of antiques. Several years ago she opened an antique shop in a local shopping center and spends most of her time buying and selling antiques. She occasionally earns a small profit from this activity but more frequently incurs substantial losses. If such losses are business related, they are fully deductible against N's salary income if a joint return is filed.

- As a tax adviser you should initially determine if the antique "business" has met the three-out-of-five years profit test.
- If the presumption is not met, the activity may nevertheless qualify as a business if the taxpayer can show that the intent is to engage in a profit-seeking activity. It is not necessary to show actual profits.
- Attempts should be made to fit the operation within the nine criteria prescribed in the Regulations and previously listed. These criteria are the factors considered in trying to rebut the § 183 presumption. □

If an activity is deemed to be a hobby, the expenses are deductible only to the extent of the income from the hobby. These expenses must be deducted in the following order:

- Amounts deductible under other Code sections without regard to the nature of the activity, such as property taxes.
- Amounts deductible under other Code sections had the activity been engaged in for profit, but only if those amounts do not affect adjusted basis (e.g., maintenance).
- Amounts deductible under other Code sections had the activity been engaged in for profit, which affects adjusted basis (e.g., depreciation).

These deductions are deductible (*from* adjusted gross income) as itemized deductions to the extent they exceed 2 percent of adjusted gross income.

EXAMPLE 17   T, the vice president of an oil company, has AGI of $80,000. He decides to pursue painting in his spare time. He used a home studio, comprising 10% of the home's square footage. During the current year, T incurs the following expenses:

Correspondence study course	$ 350
Art supplies	300
Fees paid to models	1,000
Home studio expenses:	
Total property taxes	900
Total home mortgage interest	10,000
Depreciation on studio furnishings	900
Depreciation on 10% of home	500
Total home maintenance and utilities	3,600

During the year, T sold paintings for a total of $3,200. If the activity is held to be a hobby, T is allowed deductions as follows:

Gross income		$3,200
Deduct: Taxes and interest (10% of $10,900)		1,090
Remainder		$2,110
Deduct: Study Course	$ 350	
Art Supplies	300	
Models' fees	1,000	
Maintenance and utilities (10%)	360	2,010
Remainder		100
Depreciation ($500, but limited to $100)		100
Net income		$ -0-

T includes the $3,200 of income in AGI, making his AGI $83,200. The taxes and interest are itemized deductions, deductible in full. The remaining $2,110 of expenses are reduced by 2% of T's AGI ($1,664) so the net deduction is $446. Since the property taxes and home mortgage interest are deductible anyway, the net effect is a $2,754 ($3,200 less $446) increase in taxable income.   □

EXAMPLE 18   If T's activity in Example 17 is held to be a business, he could have deducted expenses totalling $2,510 ($2,010 plus $500 of depreciation) *for* AGI, in addition to the $1,090 of taxes and interest. All expenses would be trade or business expenses deductible *for* AGI. His reduction in AGI would be as follows:

Gross income		$3,200
Less: Taxes and interest	$1,090	
Other business expenses	2,010	
Depreciation	500	3,600
Reduction in AGI		$ (400)

□

Rental of Vacation Homes

Restrictions on the deductions allowed for part-year rentals of personal residences (including vacation homes) were written into the law to prevent taxpayers from deducting essentially personal expenses as rental losses. Before these restrictions were added, many taxpayers who had vacation homes tried to treat the homes as rental property and generate rental losses as deductions *for* adjusted gross income. For example, a summer cabin would be rented (or held out for rent) for 2 months per year, used for vacationing for 1 month, and left vacant the rest of the year. The taxpayer would then deduct 11 months' depreciation, maintenance, etc., as rental expenses, resulting in a rental loss. Section 280A eliminates this treatment by allowing deductions on residences used primarily for personal purposes only to the extent of income generated. Thus, only a break-even situation is allowed; no losses can be deducted.

There are three possible tax treatments for residences used for both personal and rental purposes. The treatment is dependent upon the relative time the residence is used for personal purposes versus rental use.

Primarily Personal Use.   If the residence is rented for less than 15 days per year, it is treated as a personal residence. The rental income is excluded from income, and mortgage interest and real estate taxes are allowed as itemized deductions, as with any personal residence. No other expenses (e.g., depreciation, utilities, maintenance) are deductible.

EXAMPLE 19   T owns a vacation cottage on the lake. During the current year, she rented it for $1,600 for two weeks, lived in it two months, and left it vacant the remainder of the year. The year's expenses amounted to $6,000 interest expense, $500 property taxes, $1,500 utilities and maintenance, and $2,400 depreciation. Since the property was not rented for at least 15 days, the income is excluded, the interest and property tax expenses are itemized deductions, and the remaining expenses are nondeductible personal expenses. □

Primarily Rental Use.   If the residence is not used for personal use for the greater of more than 14 days or more than 10 percent of the total days rented, the residence is treated as rental property. The expenses must be allocated between personal and rental days if there are any personal use days during the year. In such a case, the deduction of the expenses allocated to rental days can exceed rental income and result in a rental loss, which may be deductible under the passive loss rules (discussed in chapter 6).

EXAMPLE 20   Assume T in Example 19 had rented the cottage for 120 days. The cottage would be primarily rental if she did not use it for personal purposes for more than 14 days. □

EXAMPLE 21   Assume T in Example 19 had rented the cottage for 200 days. She could use it for personal use for no more than 20 days (10% of the rental days) for it to be primarily rental. □

EXAMPLE 22

Assume that T in Example 19 used the cottage for 12 days and rented it for 48 days for $4,800. Since she did not use the cottage for more than 14 days, the expenses must be allocated between personal and rental days, and the cottage is treated as rental property.

Percentage of Use	Rental 80%	Personal 20%
Income	$4,800	$ -0-
Expenses		
Interest ($6,000)	$4,800	$1,200
Property taxes ($500)	400	100
Utilities and maintenance ($1,500)	1,200	300
Depreciation ($2,400)	1,920	480
Total expenses	$8,320	$2,080
Rental loss	($3,520)	$ -0-

T deducts the $3,520 rental loss *for* AGI (assuming she meets the passive loss rules, discussed in chapter 6). She also has itemized interest of $1,200 and taxes of $100. The portion of utilities and maintenance and depreciation attributable to personal use is not deductible. ☐

Personal/Rental Use.   If the residence is rented for 15 or more days *and* is used for personal purposes for the greater of (1) more than 14 days or (2) more than 10 percent of the rental days, it is treated as a personal/rental residence and expenses are allowed only to the extent of income.

EXAMPLE 23

Assume that T in Example 19 had rented the property for 30 days and lived in it for 30 days. The residence is classified as personal/rental property since T used it more than 14 days and rented it for more than 14 days. The expenses must be allocated, and the rental expenses are allowed only to the extent of rental income. ☐

If a residence is classified as personal/rental property, the expenses that are deductible anyway (e.g., real estate taxes) must be deducted first. If a positive net income results, otherwise nondeductible expenses (e.g., maintenance, utilities, insurance) are allowed next. Finally, depreciation is allowed if any positive balance remains.

Expenses must be allocated between personal and rental days before the limits are applied. The courts have held that taxes and interest, which accrue ratably over the year, are allocated on the basis of 365 days.[12] The IRS, however, disagrees and allocates taxes and interest on the basis of total days of use.[13] Other expenses (utilities, maintenance, depreciation, etc.) are allocated on the basis of total days used.

---

12. *Bolton v. Comm.*, 82–2 USTC ¶9699, 51 AFTR2d   13.   Prop.Reg. § 1.280A–3(d)(4).
    83–305, 694 F.2d 556 (CA–9, 1982).

EXAMPLE 24   S rents her vacation home for 60 days and lives in the home for 30 days. The limitations applicable to personal/rental residences apply. S's gross rental income is $10,000. For the entire year, the real estate taxes are $2,190; S's mortgage interest expense is $10,220; utilities and maintenance expense equals $2,400; and depreciation is $9,000. Using the IRS approach, these amounts are deductible in this specific order:

Gross income	$10,000
Deduct: Taxes and interest (60/90 × $12,410)	8,273
Remainder to apply to rental operating expenses and depreciation	1,727
Deduct: Utilities and maintenance (60/90 × $2,400)	1,600
Balance	$ 127
Deduct: Depreciation (60/90 × $9,000 = $6,000 but limited to above balance)	127
Net income	$ -0-

The nonrental use portion of taxes and interest ($4,137 in this case) is deductible if the taxpayer elects to itemize (see chapter 10). The personal use portion of utilities, maintenance, and depreciation is not deductible in any case. Also note that the basis of the property is not reduced by the $5,873 depreciation not allowed ($6,000 – $127) because of the above limitation. (See chapter 12 for discussion of the reduction in basis for depreciation allowed or allowable.) □

EXAMPLE 25   Using the court's approach in allocating property taxes and interest, S, in Example 24, would have this result:

Gross income	$10,000
Deduct: Taxes and interest (60/365 × $12,410)	2,040
Remainder to apply to rental operating expenses and depreciation	$ 7,960
Deduct: Utilities and maintenance (60/90 × $2,400)	1,600
Balance	$ 6,360
Deduct: Depreciation (60/90 × $9,000, but limited to $6,360)	6,000
Net rental income	$ 360

S can deduct $10,370 ($12,410 paid – $2,040 deducted as expense in computing rental income) of personal use interest and taxes. □

Note the contrasting results in Examples 24 and 25. Using the IRS's approach (Example 24) results in no rental gain or loss and an itemized deduction for taxes and interest of $4,137. In Example 25, S has net rental income of $360 and $10,370 of itemized deductions. The court's approach decreases her taxable income by $10,010 ($10,370 itemized deductions less $360 net rental income). The IRS's approach reduces her taxable income by only $4,137.

EXAMPLE 26   Assume that S in Example 24 had not lived in the home at all during the year. The property is a rental property. The rental loss is calculated as follows:

Gross income	$10,000
Expenses	
Taxes and interest	$12,410
Utilities and maintenance	2,400
Depreciation	9,000
Total expenses	$23,810
Rental loss	($13,810)

Whether any of the rental loss would be deductible would depend upon whether S actively participated in the rental activity and met the other requirements for passive losses (discussed in chapter 6).   □

Expenditures Incurred for Taxpayer's Benefit or Taxpayer's Obligation

Generally, an expense must be incurred for the taxpayer's benefit or arise from the taxpayer's obligation. An individual cannot claim a tax deduction for the payment of the expenses of another individual.

EXAMPLE 27   During the current year, F pays the interest on his son, T's, home mortgage. Neither F nor T can take a deduction for the interest paid because the obligation is not F's and F's son did not pay the interest. The tax result would have been more favorable had F made a cash gift to T and let him pay the interest. The interest then could have been deducted by the son, and (depending upon other gifts and the amount involved) F might not have been liable for any gift taxes. A deduction would have been created with no cash difference to the family.   □

One exception to this rule is the payment of medical expenses for a dependent. Such expenses are deductible by the payor.

Disallowance of Personal Expenditures

Section 262 states that "except as otherwise expressly provided in this chapter, no deduction shall be allowed for personal, living, or family expenses." Thus, to justify a deduction an individual must be able to identify a particular Section of the Code that sanctions the deductibility of an otherwise nondeductible personal expenditure (e.g., charitable contributions, § 170; medical expenses, § 213; moving expenses, § 217). Sometimes the character of a particular expenditure is not easily determined.

EXAMPLE 28   During the current year, H pays $1,500 in legal fees and court costs to obtain a divorce from his wife, W. Involved in the divorce action is a property settlement that concerns the disposition of income-producing property owned

CONCEPT SUMMARY 5–1

Vacation/Rental Home

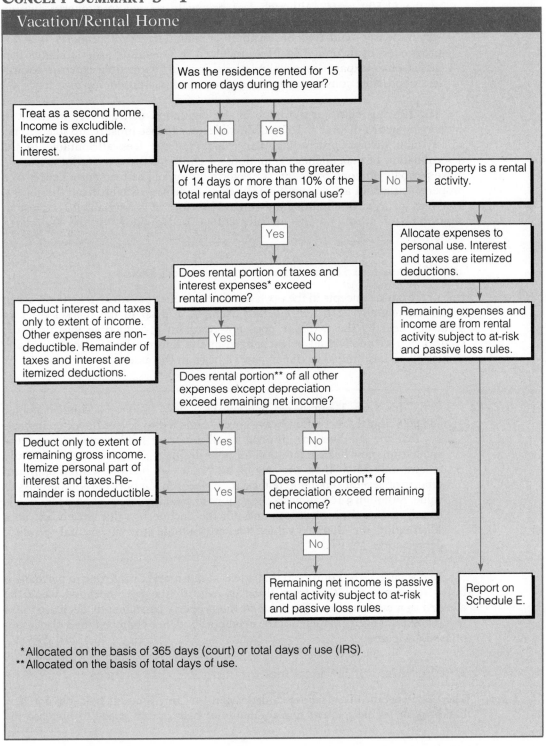

Was the residence rented for 15 or more days during the year?

No → Treat as a second home. Income is excludible. Itemize taxes and interest.

Yes ↓

Were there more than the greater of 14 days or more than 10% of the total rental days of personal use?

No → Property is a rental activity.

↓ Allocate expenses to personal use. Interest and taxes are itemized deductions.

↓ Remaining expenses and income are from rental activity subject to at-risk and passive loss rules.

Yes ↓

Does rental portion of taxes and interest expenses* exceed rental income?

Yes → Deduct interest and taxes only to extent of income. Other expenses are non-deductible. Remainder of taxes and interest are itemized deductions.

No ↓

Does rental portion** of all other expenses except depreciation exceed remaining net income?

Yes → Deduct only to extent of remaining gross income. Itemize personal part of interest and taxes. Remainder is nondeductible.

No ↓

Does rental portion** of depreciation exceed remaining net income?

Yes → Deduct only to extent of remaining gross income. Itemize personal part of interest and taxes. Remainder is nondeductible.

No ↓

Remaining net income is passive rental activity subject to at-risk and passive loss rules.

Report on Schedule E.

*Allocated on the basis of 365 days (court) or total days of use (IRS).
**Allocated on the basis of total days of use.

by H. In a similar situation, the Tax Court[14] held that H could not deduct any of the $1,500 costs. "Although fees primarily related to property division concerning his income-producing property, they weren't ordinary and necessary expenses paid for conservation or maintenance of property held for production of income. Legal fees incurred in defending against claims that arise from a taxpayer's marital relationship aren't deductible expenses regardless of possible consequences on taxpayer's income-producing property." □

The IRS has clarified the issue of the deduction of legal fees incurred in connection with a divorce.[15] To be deductible, an expense must relate solely to tax advice in a divorce proceeding. For example, legal fees attributable to the determination of dependency exemptions of children, the creation of a trust to make periodic alimony payments, or determination of the tax consequences of a property settlement are deductible if the fees are distinguishable from the general legal fees incurred in obtaining a divorce. Therefore, it is advisable to request an itemization of attorney's fees to substantiate a deduction for the tax-related amounts.

Disallowance of Deductions for Unrealized Losses

One of the basic concepts in the tax law is that a deduction can be taken only when a loss has actually been realized. For example, a drop in the market price of securities held by the taxpayer does not result in a deductible loss until the securities are actually sold or exchanged at the lower price. Furthermore, any deductible loss is limited to the taxpayer's basis in the asset.

EXAMPLE 29

Early this year, T purchased a home in a new residential subdivision for $80,000. Shortly thereafter, heavy spring rains led to severe flooding, indicating that the subdivision's drainage facilities were inadequate. Because the subdivision now has a reputation for poor drainage, T estimates that he could receive only $50,000 on the sale of his home. He has the written appraisal reports of several reputable real estate brokers to support the $30,000 loss in value. Although § 165 allows a deduction for casualty losses, such deduction is based on actual physical loss and not the decline in value that might be a "fluctuation in market value not attributable to any actual physical depreciation."[16] □

In one case,[17] the court held that a loss in fair market value due to permanent buyer resistance resulting from flood damage to the neighborhood would be allowed as a casualty loss. The value of the property permanently decreased as a result of the changed character of the neighborhood. See chapter 7 for a discussion of casualty losses.

Disallowance of Deductions for Capital Expenditures

The Code specifically disallows a deduction for "any amount paid out for new buildings or for permanent improvements or betterments made to increase the

14. *Harry H. Goldberg*, 29 TCM 74, T.C.Memo., 1970–27.
15. Rev.Rul. 72–545, 1972–2 C.B. 179.
16. *Joe B. Thornton*, 47 T.C. 1 (1966).
17. *Finkbohner, Jr. v. U.S.*, 86–1 USTC ¶9393, 57 AFTR2d 86–1400, 788 F.2d 723 (CA–11, 1986).

value of any property or estate."[18] The Regulations further define capital expenditures to include those expenditures that add to the value or prolong the life of property or adapt the property to a new or different use.[19] Incidental repairs and maintenance of the property are not capital expenditures and can be deducted as ordinary and necessary business expenses. Repairing a roof is a deductible expense, but replacing a roof is a capital expenditure subject to depreciation deductions over its useful life. The tune-up of a delivery truck is an expense; a complete overhaul is probably a capital expenditure.

Exceptions.   There are several exceptions to the general rule regarding capitalization of expenditures. Taxpayers can elect to expense certain mineral developmental costs and intangible drilling costs. Certain farm capital expenditures (such as soil and water conservation) and certain research and experimental expenditures may be immediately expensed.

In addition, § 179 permits an immediate write-off of certain amounts of depreciable property. These provisions are discussed more fully in chapter 8.

Capitalization versus Expense.   When an expenditure is capitalized rather than expensed, the deduction is at best deferred and at worst lost forever. Although an immediate tax benefit for a large cash expenditure is lost, the cost can be deducted in increments over a longer period of time. If the expenditure is for some improvement that has an ascertainable life, it can be capitalized and depreciated or amortized over that life. Costs that can be amortized include copyrights and patents. However, there are many other expenditures, such as land and payments made for goodwill, that cannot be amortized or depreciated. Goodwill has an indeterminate life, and land is not a depreciable asset since its value generally does not decline.

EXAMPLE 30   T purchased a prime piece of land located in an apartment-zoned area. T paid $500,000 for the property, which had an old but usable apartment building on it. T immediately had the building demolished at a cost of $100,000. The $500,000 purchase price and the $100,000 demolition costs must be capitalized, and the basis of the land is $600,000. Since land is a nondepreciable asset, no deduction is allowed. More favorable tax treatment might result if T rented the apartments in the old building for a period of time to attempt to establish that there was no intent to demolish the building. If T's attempt is successful, it might be possible to allocate a substantial portion of the original purchase price of the property to the building (a depreciable asset). When the building is later demolished, any remaining adjusted basis can be deducted as an ordinary (§ 1231) loss. (See chapter 13 for a discussion of the treatment of § 1231 assets.) □

In some cases, a taxpayer might prefer to capitalize rather than expense a particular item if the property is depreciable. An immediate deduction could create a net operating loss that expires in 15 years (unless utilized). No tax benefit (or a smaller tax benefit) would be derived from an immediate deduction. The same expenditure, if capitalized and depreciated over a longer future period, could be offset against taxable income later (or against higher tax bracket income in future years) resulting in a greater tax benefit.

---

18. § 263(a)(1).   19. Reg. § 1.263(a)–1(b).

Capitalization Elections.   Because of the tax avoidance possibilities inherent in allowing elective "capitalize or expense" decisions, the treatment of most expenditures, by law, is not elective. However, in certain cases, it is permissible to elect to capitalize *or* to expense immediately a particular item. For example, § 266 allows some taxpayers (but not individuals, S corporations, or personal holding companies) an opportunity to capitalize certain "taxes and carrying charges." This election applies to carrying charges, interest on indebtedness, and certain taxes (such as property and employer-paid payroll taxes) paid during the construction period on realty or personalty. It does not matter whether the property is business or nonbusiness in nature. A taxpayer may elect to capitalize some expenditures and not others. For example, one could elect to capitalize property taxes and expense interest on the construction indebtedness. A new election may be made for each project. One could elect to capitalize expenditures on a factory being constructed and expense the same type of items on a constructed machine. On unimproved and unproductive real estate (land held for later sale, for example), a new election must be made for each year.

Section 189 requires individuals, S corporations, and personal holding companies to capitalize construction period interest and taxes, subject to specific rules for amortizing such amounts (see chapter 8). This Code Section was intended both to match expenses with income in accordance with the traditional accounting principle and to restrict tax shelter opportunities for individuals.

Transactions between Related Parties

The Code places restrictions on the recognition of gains and losses between related parties. Because of relationships created by birth, marriage, and business, there would be endless possibilities for engaging in various types of financial transactions that would produce tax savings with no real economic substance or change. For example, a wife could sell property to her husband at a loss and deduct the loss on their joint return, and her husband could hold the asset indefinitely. This illustrates the creation of an artificial loss. Such "sham" transactions have resulted in a complex set of laws designed to eliminate these abuses.

Losses.   Section 267 provides for the disallowance of any "losses from sales or exchanges of property . . . directly or indirectly" between related parties. Upon the subsequent sale of such property to a nonrelated party, any gain recognized is reduced by the loss that was previously disallowed.

EXAMPLE 31   F sells common stock with a basis of $1,000 to his son, T, for $800. T sells the stock several years later for $1,100. F's $200 loss is disallowed upon the sale to T, and only $100 of gain is taxable to T upon the subsequent sale.   ☐

EXAMPLE 32   F sells common stock with a basis of $1,000 to his son, T, for $800. T sells the stock to an unrelated party for $900. T's gain of $100 is not recognized because of F's previously disallowed loss of $200. Note that the offset may result in only partial tax benefit upon the subsequent sale. If the property had not been transferred to T, F could have recognized a $100 loss upon the subsequent sale to the unrelated party ($1,000 basis – $900 selling price).   ☐

EXAMPLE 33   F sells common stock with a basis of $1,000 to an unrelated third party for $800. F's son repurchased the same stock in the market on the same day for $800. The $200 loss is not allowed because the transaction is an indirect sale between related parties.   □

Unpaid Expenses and Interest.   Section 267 also prevents related taxpayers from engaging in tax avoidance schemes in which one related taxpayer uses the accrual method of accounting and the other is on the cash basis. For example, an accrual basis closely held corporation could borrow funds from a cash basis individual shareholder. At the end of the year, the corporation would accrue and deduct the interest, but the cash basis lender would not recognize interest income since no interest had been paid. Section 267 specifically defers the deduction of the accruing taxpayer until the recipient taxpayer must include it in income (when actually paid to the cash basis taxpayer). This rule applies to interest as well as other expenses, such as salaries and bonuses.

Relationships and Constructive Ownership.   Section 267 operates to disallow losses and defer deductions only between related parties. Losses or deductions generated by similar transactions with an unrelated party are allowed. Related parties include the following:

- Brothers and sisters (whether by the whole or half blood), spouses, ancestors (parents, grandparents) and lineal descendants (children, grandchildren) of the taxpayer.

- A corporation owned more than 50 percent (directly or indirectly) by the taxpayer.

- Two corporations that are members of a controlled group.

- A series of other complex relationships between trusts, corporations, and individual taxpayers.

The law provides that constructive ownership rules are applied to determine whether the taxpayers are related. Constructive ownership rules state that stock owned by certain relatives or related entities is deemed to be owned by the taxpayer for purposes of applying the loss and expense deduction disallowance rules. For example, a taxpayer is deemed to own not only his or her stock but the stock owned by his or her lineal descendants, ancestors, brothers and sisters or half-brothers and half-sisters, and spouse. The taxpayer is also deemed to own his or her proportionate share of stock owned by any partnership, corporation, estate, or trust of which he or she is a member. Additionally, an individual is deemed to own any stock owned, directly or indirectly, by his or her partner. However, constructive ownership by an individual of the partnership's and the other partner's shares does not extend to the individual's spouse or other relatives.

EXAMPLE 34   The stock of V Corporation is owned 20% by T, 30% by T's father, 30% by T's mother, and 20% by T's sister. On July 1 of the current year, T loaned $10,000 to V Corporation at 11% annual interest, principal and interest payable on demand. For tax purposes, V Corporation uses the accrual basis and T uses the cash basis. Both are on a calendar year. Since T is deemed to own the 80%

owned by her parents and sister, she constructively owns 100% of V Corporation. If the corporation accrues but does not pay the interest within the taxable year, no deduction can be taken until payment is made to T.   □

Substantiation Requirements

The tax law is built on a voluntary system. Taxpayers file their tax returns, report income and take deductions to which they are entitled, and pay their taxes through withholding or estimated tax payments during the year. The taxpayer carries the burden of proof for substantiating expenses deducted on his or her return and thus must retain adequate records for such substantiation. Upon audit, the function of the Internal Revenue Service is to disallow any undocumented or unsubstantiated deductions. As can be imagined, this relationship has resulted in numerous conflicts between taxpayers and the IRS.

Some events throughout the year should be documented as they occur. For example, it is generally advisable to receive a pledge payment statement from one's church, in addition to a canceled check, for proper documentation of a charitable contribution. Other types of deductible expenditures may require receipts or some other type of support.

Some types of deductible expenditures, such as business entertainment, gifts, and travel, have been subject to abuse. To prevent such abuse, the law provides that no deduction will be allowed for any travel, entertainment, or business gift expenditure unless properly substantiated by adequate records. Such records should contain the following information:

- The amount of the expense.
- The time and place of travel or entertainment (or date of gift).
- The business purpose of such expense.
- The business relationship of the taxpayer to the person entertained (or receiving the gift).

This means that taxpayers must maintain an account book or diary in which the above information is recorded at the time of the expenditure. Documentary evidence, such as itemized receipts, is required to support all expenditures for lodging while traveling away from home and for any other expenditure of $25 or more. If a taxpayer fails to keep adequate records, each expense must be established by a written or oral statement of the exact details of the expense and by other corroborating evidence.

EXAMPLE 35   B had travel expenses substantiated only by canceled checks. The checks established the date, place, and amount of the expenditure. Because neither the business relationship nor the business purpose was established, the deduction will be disallowed.   □

EXAMPLE 36   D had travel and entertainment expenses substantiated by a diary showing the time, place, and amount of the expenditure. His oral testimony provided the business relationship and business purpose. However, since he had no receipts, any expenditures of $25 or more would be disallowed.   □

Specific rules for deducting travel, entertainment, and gift expenses are discussed in chapter 9. Certain mixed-use (both personal and business) and listed property is also subject to the adequate records requirement (discussed in chapter 8).

Expenses and Interest Relating to Tax-Exempt Income

Certain income, such as interest on municipal bonds, is tax-exempt, and § 212 allows the taxpayer to deduct expenses incurred for the production of income. If it were not for the disallowance provisions of § 265, it might be possible to make money at the expense of the government by excluding interest income and deducting interest expense.

EXAMPLE 37

P, a taxpayer in the 28% bracket, purchased $100,000 of 6% municipal bonds. At the same time, she used the bonds as collateral on a bank loan of $100,000 at 8% interest. A positive cash flow would result from the tax benefit as follows:

Cash paid out on loan	($8,000)
Cash received from bonds	6,000
Tax savings from deducting interest expense (28% of $8,000 interest expense)	2,240
Net positive cash flow	$ 240

□

To eliminate the possibility illustrated in Example 37, § 265 specifically disallows as a deduction the expenses of producing tax-exempt income. Interest on any indebtedness incurred or continued to purchase or carry tax-exempt obligations is disallowed under § 265. There are special rules for nonbanking financial institutions.

Judicial Interpretations. It is often difficult to show a direct relationship between borrowings and investment in tax-exempt securities. Suppose, for example, that a taxpayer borrows money, adds it to existing funds, buys inventory and stocks, then later sells the inventory and buys municipal bonds. A series of transactions such as these can completely obscure any relationship between the loan and the tax-exempt investment. One solution would be to disallow interest on any debt to the extent that the taxpayer held any tax-exempt securities. This approach would preclude individuals from deducting part of their home mortgage interest if they owned any municipal bonds. However, the law was not intended to go to such extremes. As a result, judicial interpretations have tried to show reasonableness in the disallowance of interest deductions under § 265.

In one case,[20] a company used municipal bonds as collateral on short-term loans to meet seasonal liquidity needs. The Court disallowed the interest deduction

---

20. *The Wisconsin Cheeseman, Inc. v. U.S.*, 68–1 USTC ¶9145, 21 AFTR2d 383, F.2d 420 (CA–7, 1968).

CONCEPT SUMMARY 5–2

Classification of Expenses

Expense Item	Deductible For AGI	Deductible From AGI	Not Deductible	Applicable Code §
Investment expenses				
Rent and royalty	X			§ 62(a)(4)
All other investments		X[4]		§ 212
Employee expenses				
Commuting expenses			X	§ 262
Travel and transportation[1]		X[4, 5]		§ 162(a)(2)
Reimbursed expenses	X			§ 62(a)(2)(A)
Moving expenses		X		§ 217
Entertainment[1]		X[4, 5]		§ 212
All other employee expenses[1]		X[4, 5]		§ 212
Certain expenses of performing artists	X			§ 62(a)(2)(B)
Trade or business expenses	X			§ 162
Casualty losses				
Business	X			§ 165(c)(1)
Personal		X[6]		§ 165(c)(3)
Tax determination, Collection, or Refund expenses		X[4]		§ 212
Bad debts	X			§ 166
Medical expenses		X[7]		§ 213
Charitable contributions		X		§ 170
Taxes				
Trade or business	X			§ 162
Personal taxes				
Real property		X		§ 164(a)(1)
Personal property		X		§ 164(a)(2)
State and local income		X		§ 164(a)(3)
Investigation of a business[2]	X			§ 162
Interest				
Business	X			§ 162
Personal[3]		X		§ 163(a)
All other personal expenses			X	§ 262

1. Deduction *for* AGI if reimbursed, an adequate accounting is made, and employee is required to repay excess reimbursements.
2. Provided certain criteria are met.
3. Subject to the excess investment interest provisions and consumer interest phase-out.
4. Subject (in the aggregate) to a 2%-of-AGI floor imposed by § 67.
5. Only 80% of meals and entertainment are deductible.
6. Subject to a 10%-of-AGI floor and a $100 floor.
7. Subject to a 7.5%-of-AGI floor.

on the grounds that the company could predict its seasonal liquidity needs and therefore knew it would have to borrow the money to continue to carry the tax-exempt securities. The same company *was* allowed an interest deduction on a building mortgage, even though tax-exempt securities it owned could have been sold to pay off the mortgage. The Court reasoned that short-term liquidity position would have been impaired if the tax-exempt securities were sold. Furthermore, the Court ruled that carrying the tax-exempt securities bore no relationship to the long-term financing of a construction project.

In another case,[21] the Court disallowed an interest deduction to a company that refused to sell tax-exempt securities it had received from the sale of a major asset. The company's refusal to sell the tax-exempt securities necessitated large borrowings to finance company operations. The Court found that the primary reason that the company would not sell its bonds to reduce its bank debt was the tax savings, even though other business reasons existed for holding the municipal bonds. Moreover, there was a direct relationship between the bonds and the debt because they both arose from the same transaction.

EXAMPLE 38   In January of the current year, T borrowed $100,000 at 8% interest. She used the loan proceeds to purchase 5,000 shares of stock in P Corporation. In July, she sold the stock for $120,000 and reinvested the proceeds in City of Denver bonds, the income from which is tax-exempt. Assuming the $100,000 loan remained outstanding throughout the entire year, the interest attributable to the period in which the bonds were held cannot be deducted. □

TAX PLANNING CONSIDERATIONS

Time Value of Tax Deductions

Cash basis taxpayers often have the ability to make early payments for their expenses at the end of the tax year. This permits such payments to be deducted currently instead of in the following tax year. Because of the time value of money, a tax deduction this year may be worth more than the same deduction next year. Before employing this strategy, the taxpayer must consider next year's expected income and tax rates and whether a cash flow problem may develop from early payments.

The time value of money as well as tax rate changes must be taken into consideration when an expense can be paid and deducted in either of two years.

EXAMPLE 39   T pledged $5,000 to her church's special building fund. She can make the contribution in December 1990 or January 1991. T is in the 33% tax bracket in 1990 because of the 15% bracket phase-out, and in the 28% bracket in 1991. She itemizes in both years. If she takes the deduction in 1990, she saves $354 ($1,650 − $1,296), due to the decrease in the tax rates and the time value of money.

---

21. *Illinois Terminal Railroad Co. v. U.S.*, 67–1 USTC ¶9374, 19 AFTR2d 1219, 375 F.2d 1016 (Ct.Cls., 1967).

	1990	1991
Contribution	5,000	5,000
Tax bracket	.33	.28
Tax savings	$1,650	$1,400
Discounted @ 8%	1.0	.926
Savings in present value	$1,650	$1,296

☐

EXAMPLE 40   Assume the same facts as in Example 39, except that T is in the 28% bracket in both 1990 and 1991. T's savings by taking the deduction in 1990 is $104 ($1,400 − $1,296), due to the time value of money.

	1990	1991
Contribution	$5,000	$5,000
Tax bracket	.28	.28
Tax savings	$1,400	$1,400
Discounted @ 8%	1.0	.926
Savings in present value	$1,400	1,296

☐

Unreasonable Compensation

In substantiating the reasonableness of a shareholder-employee's compensation, an internal comparison test is sometimes useful. If it can be shown that employees who are nonshareholders receive the same (or more) compensation as shareholder-employees in comparable positions, it is evident that compensation is not unreasonable.

Another possibility is to demonstrate that the shareholder-employee has been underpaid in prior years. For example, the shareholder-employee may have agreed to take a less-than-adequate salary during the unprofitable formative years of the business, provided this "postponed" compensation will be paid in later, more profitable years. This agreement should be documented, if possible, in the corporate minutes.

It is important to keep in mind that in testing for reasonableness, it is the *total* pay package that must be taken into account. One must look at all fringe benefits or perquisites, such as contributions by the corporation to a qualified pension plan (even though those amounts are not immediately available to the covered employee-shareholder).

Shifting Deductions

Taxpayers should manage their obligations to avoid the loss of a deduction. Deductions can be shifted among family members, depending upon who makes the payment. For example, a father buys a condo for his daughter and puts the title in both names. The taxpayer who makes the payment gets the deduction for the property taxes. If the condo is owned by the daughter only and her father makes the payment, neither is entitled to a deduction.

Hobby Losses

To demonstrate that an activity has been entered into for the purpose of making a profit (it is not a hobby), a taxpayer should treat the activity as a business. The business should engage in advertising, use business letterhead stationery, and maintain a business phone.

If a taxpayer's activity earns a profit in three out of five consecutive years, the presumption is that the activity is engaged in for profit. It may be possible for a cash basis taxpayer to meet these requirements by timing the payment of expenses or the receipt of revenues. The payment of certain expenses incurred before the end of the year might be made in the following year, or the billing of year-end sales might be delayed so that collections are received in the following year.

It should be kept in mind that the three-out-of-five-years rule under § 183 is not absolute. All it does is shift the presumption. If a profit is not made in three out of five years, the losses may still be allowed if the taxpayer can show that such losses are due to the nature of the business. For example, success in artistic or literary endeavors can take a long time. Also, due to the present state of the economy, full-time farmers and ranchers are often unable to show a profit; how can one expect a part-time farmer or rancher to do so?

Merely satisfying the three-out-of-five-years rule does not guarantee that one is automatically home free. If the three years of profits are insignificant relative to the losses of other years, or if the profits are not from the ordinary operation of the business, the Internal Revenue Service may still be able to establish that the taxpayer is not engaged in an activity for profit. If a taxpayer in such a situation can show conformity with the factors enumerated in the Regulations[22] or can show evidence of business hardships (e.g., injury, death, or illness), the government cannot override the presumptive rule of § 183.[23]

Substantiation Requirements

One relatively painless method of meeting the substantiation requirements for business meals or entertainment would be to pay the bill by credit card. The time, place, and amount of the expenditure are substantiated. At the same time, the taxpayer should write on the back of the receipt the name and relationship of the person entertained and a notation of what business was discussed. This would meet the rest of the requirements specified by § 274(d).

PROBLEM MATERIALS

Discussion Questions

1. T, who had adjusted gross income of $30,000, had deductions of $5,000. Would it matter to T whether they were *for* or *from* AGI? Why or why not?

2. If a taxpayer is audited and $1,000 of income is added to his adjusted gross income, will his tax increase (ignoring penalties and interest) be equal to $1,000 multiplied by his tax bracket? Discuss.

---

22. Reg. §§ 1.183-2(b)(1) through (9).
23. *Faulconer, Sr. v. Comm.*, 84-2 USTC ¶9955, 55   AFTR2d 85-302, 748 F.2d 890 (CA-4, 1984), rev'g 45 TCM 1084, T.C.Memo. 1983-165.

3. Are the following items deductible *for* AGI, deductible *from* AGI, or nondeductible personal items?
   a. Unreimbursed travel expenses of an employee.
   b. Alimony payments.
   c. Charitable contributions.
   d. Medical expenses.
   e. Safe deposit box rentals in which stocks and bonds are kept.
   f. Repairs made on a personal residence.
   g. Expenses related to tax-exempt municipal bonds.

4. Are the following expenditures deductible *for* AGI, deductible *from* AGI, nondeductible personal items, or capital expenditures?
   a. Repairs made to a rental property.
   b. State income taxes.
   c. Investment advice subscriptions.
   d. Child support payments.
   e. New roof on rental property.
   f. New roof on personal residence.
   g. Mortgage interest on personal residence.

5. Define and contrast the "ordinary" and "necessary" tests for business expenses.

6. T, a cash basis taxpayer, decides to reduce his taxable income for 1990 by buying $10,000 worth of supplies on December 28, 1990. The supplies will be used up in 1991 and 1992. Can T deduct this expenditure in 1990? Would your answer differ if T bought the supplies because a supplier was going out of business and had given T a significant discount on the supplies?

7. T, a cash basis taxpayer, borrowed $20,000 on December 18, 1990, for two years at 12% interest. As a condition of the loan, the lender wanted T to prepay the two years' interest. T, who had heard that he could deduct no more than one year's interest, convinced the lender to accept prepayment of only one year's interest in December and the rest in January 1991 so that he could deduct the rest of the interest in 1991. T then deducted $2,400 interest in 1990 and in 1991. Can he do this?

8. Which of the following businesses must use the accrual method of accounting?
   a. A corporation with annual gross receipts of $12 million from equipment rentals.
   b. A partnership (not a tax shelter) engaged in farming that has annual gross receipts of $8 million.
   c. A corporation that acts as an insurance agent. Annual gross receipts are $1 million.
   d. A manufacturer with annual gross receipts of $600,000.
   e. A retailer with annual gross receipts of $250,000.

9. T operates a drug-running operation. Which of the following expenses incurred by T are deductible?
   a. Bribes paid to border guards.
   b. Salaries to employees.
   c. Price paid for drugs purchased for resale.
   d. Kickbacks to police.
   e. Rent on an office.

10. When J died, he left equal shares of stock to his four children, although he made it clear that he wanted Jill and John (the two children who were interested in his

business) to run the business. This was quite all right with the other two children, who were to receive $100,000 each per year from the company and were free to pursue their own interests. Jill and John each received reasonable salaries of $250,000 and $210,000, respectively. They paid the other two children salaries of $100,000 each. What were they trying to accomplish from a tax standpoint? Will it work? If not, what are the tax consequences to the corporation and to the other two children?

11. T is an executive in X Corporation. She used insider information to buy X Corporation stock just before public announcement of the discovery of huge oil reserves on company-owned property. She was caught and incurred legal expenses and treble damage payments. Can she deduct either expense?

12. How are expenses (e.g., travel, meals, and lodging) incurred in connection with the investigation of a new business opportunity treated if the new business is acquired? If the new business is *not* acquired?

13. If a taxpayer is unable to meet the requirements of § 183 relative to earning a profit in at least three of five consecutive years, is it possible to qualify the activity as a business? Why or why not?

14. If a taxpayer meets the requirements of § 183 relative to earning a profit in at least three of five consecutive years, is it still possible for the IRS to treat the activity as a hobby of the taxpayer? Why or why not?

15. Contrast the differing results obtained in a personal/rental situation by allocating property taxes and interest on the IRS's basis and the court's basis. Which method would the taxpayer prefer?

16. Discuss the tax treatment of the rental of a vacation home if it is:
    a. Rented 10 days during the year.
    b. Rented 130 days during the year; used personally for 12 days.
    c. Rented for 250 days; used personally for 40 days.

17. T repaired the roof on his factory at a cost of $1,500 in the current year. During the same year, S replaced the roof on her small rental house for $1,500. Both taxpayers are on the cash basis. Are their expenditures treated the same on their tax returns? Why or why not?

18. T owns 20% of X Corporation; 20% of X's stock is owned by S, T's mother; 15% is owned by R, T's brother; the remaining 45% is owned by unrelated parties. T is on the cash basis, and X Corporation is on the accrual basis. On December 31, 1990, X accrued T's salary of $5,000 and paid it on April 4, 1991. Both are on a calendar year. What is the tax effect to T and X?

19. Discuss the reasons for the disallowance of losses between related parties. Would it make any difference if a parent sold stock to an unrelated third party and the child repurchased the same number of shares of the stock in the market the same day?

20. T sold 100 shares of XYZ Company stock to F, her brother, for $8,000. She had originally paid $7,100 for the stock. F later sold the stock for $6,000 on the open market. What are the tax consequences to T and F?

21. Would your answer to Question 20 differ if T had sold the stock to F for $6,500?

22. The Acme Corporation is owned as follows:

T	20%
P, T's wife	20%
S, T's mother	15%
R, T's father	25%
Q, an unrelated party	20%

T and P each loaned the Acme Corporation $10,000 out of their separate funds. On December 31, 1990, Acme accrued interest at 12% on both loans. The interest was paid on February 4, 1991. Acme is on the accrual basis, and T and P are on the cash basis. What is the tax treatment of this interest expense/income to T, P, and Acme?

23. Would a record of the past year's travel expenses meet the substantiation requirements if the record were compiled at the time the tax return for that year was prepared? Explain.

24. Discuss the tracing problems encountered in the enforcement of the restrictions of § 265 that disallow a deduction for the expenses of producing tax-exempt income.

Problems

25. R has adjusted gross income of $20,000 and itemized deductions as follows:

Medical expenses (before 7.5% of AGI reduction)	$1,600
Charitable contributions	1,900
Deductible interest	5,300
Deductible taxes	900
Miscellaneous itemized deductions (before 2% of AGI reduction)	600

If R contributed $2,000 to his deductible Individual Retirement Account (IRA), by how much would his taxable income be reduced?

26. P, who is single, has a sole proprietorship and keeps her books on the cash basis. Following is a summary of her receipts, disbursements, and other items related to her business account for 1990:

Receipts	
Sales	$28,000
Dividend received from AT&T	300
Interest on savings account	450
Long-term capital gain on sale of stock	1,200
Disbursements	
Rent on building used 75% for business and 25% for living quarters	6,000
Salary paid to part-time secretary	3,000
Taxes	
Sales tax on personal purchases	280
Gross receipts tax on sales	840
State income taxes	750
Estimated Federal income tax payments	2,500
Charitable contributions	1,400
Purchase of delivery truck on December 31, 1990, received and placed in service on January 8, 1991	9,200
Insurance on business property (policy runs from October 1, 1990, to September 30, 1991)	1,200
Depreciation on business equipment	1,000
Business supplies	980

Calculate P's adjusted gross income for 1990.

27. T, a cash basis taxpayer, rented a building from J on October 1, 1990, paying $12,000 (one full year's rent) in advance and a $10,000 deposit. The lease is for 15 years with no option to renew. T adds improvements costing $40,000 that have a 20-year life and that will revert to J upon termination of the lease.

    a. How much rent can T deduct in 1990?

    b. How much does J include in income if he is an accrual basis taxpayer? A cash basis taxpayer?

    c. How is the deposit of $10,000 treated by both?

    d. How are the improvements treated by both T and J?

28. D runs an illegal numbers racket. His gross income was $500,000. He incurred the following expenses:

Illegal kickbacks	$20,000
Salaries	80,000
Rent	24,000
Utilities and telephone	9,000
Bribes to police	25,000
Interest	6,000
Depreciation on equipment	12,000

    What is his net income from this business that is includible in taxable income? If the business was an illegal drug operation, would your answer differ?

29. T traveled to a neighboring state to investigate the purchase of two restaurants. His expenses included travel, legal, accounting, and miscellaneous expenses. The total was $12,000. He incurred the expenses in March and April 1990.

    a. What can he deduct in 1990 if he was in the restaurant business and did not acquire the two restaurants?

    b. What can he deduct in 1990 if he was in the restaurant business and acquired the two restaurants and began operating them on July 1, 1990?

    c. What can he deduct in 1990 if he did not acquire the two restaurants and was not in the restaurant business?

    d. What can he deduct in 1990 if he acquired the two restaurants but was not in the restaurant business when he acquired them?

30. L is a housewife who makes pottery items at home for sale to others. She had the following income and expenses for the year:

Sales	$1,000
Expenses	
Materials	400
Advertising	250
Travel	350
Classes in ceramics	500
	$1,500
Net loss	$ (500)

    How much must L include in income? What can she deduct, assuming AGI of $30,000?

31. T, an executive with an adjusted gross income of $100,000 before consideration of income or loss from his miniature-horse business, also raises miniature horses. His income comes from winning horse shows, stud fees, and sales of yearlings. His home is on 20 acres, 18 of which he uses to pasture the horses and upon which he has erected stables, paddocks, fences, tack houses, and so forth. He uses an

office in his home that is 10% of the square footage of the home.

He uses the office exclusively for keeping records of breeding lines, histories, and show and veterinary records. His records show the following income and expenses for 1990:

Income from fees, prizes, and sales	$22,000
Expenses:	
Entry fees	1,000
Feed and veterinary bills	4,000
Supplies	900
Publications and dues	500
Travel to horse shows	2,300
Salaries and wages of employees	8,000
Depreciation on horse equipment	3,000
Depreciation on horse farm improvements	7,000
Depreciation on 10% of home	1,000
Total home mortgage interest	24,000
Total property taxes on home	2,200
Total property taxes on horse farm improvements	800

The mortgage interest is only on his home. The horse farm improvements are not mortgaged.

How must T treat the income and expenses of the operation if the minature horse activity is held to be a hobby?

32. How would your answer in Problem 31 differ if the horse operation was held to be a business?

33. J is a promoter, real estate developer, and investor. Because he has inherited wealth, he can afford to be somewhat of a wheeler-dealer. He is single, age 41. During 1990, J incurred expenses in traveling to the state capitol to testify against proposed legislation for a green belt around the city because it interfered with some of his development plans. The expenses amounted to $900. He also spent $300 traveling to various locations to speak to civic groups against the proposed legislation.

J also incurred $1,600 of expense investigating the purchase of a computer franchising operation. He did not purchase the operation because he felt that his lack of expertise in that type of business was too big an obstacle to overcome.

J was involved in a promoting scheme with a legislator and took as his fee a parcel of land worth $18,000. The scheme resulted in the newspaper's making defamatory remarks about J, who sued and was awarded $50,000 for slander and damage to his business reputation.

J's other income and expenses for the year were as follows:

Income	
Interest	$ 80,000
Dividends	160,000
Short-term capital loss	(50,000)
Long-term capital gains	175,000
Other fees	24,000
Expenses	
Office expenses	17,000
Expenses incurred on land held for resale	6,000
Tax advice	5,000
All other itemized deductions	34,000

Calculate J's taxable income for 1990.

34. During 1990, P's vacation home was used as follows: 30 days of occupancy by P, 120 days of rental to unrelated parties, and 215 days of vacancy. Further information concerning the property is summarized as follows:

Rental income	$4,500
Expenses	
Real estate taxes	$1,095
Interest on mortgage	2,555
Utilities and maintenance	1,200
Repairs	400
Landscaping	1,700
Depreciation	3,000

Compute P's net rental income or loss and the amounts that P can itemize on her income tax return.

35. Would your answer differ in Problem 34 if P had used the home for 5 days instead of 30? Explain, showing computations if needed.

36. Would your answer to Problem 34 differ if P had rented the home for 10 days instead of 120? Explain, showing computations if needed.

37. T, single, age 40, had the following income and expenses in 1990:

Income	
Salary	$43,000
Rental of vacation home (rented 60 days, used personally 60 days, vacant 245 days)	4,000
Municipal interest	2,000
Dividend from General Motors	400
Expenses	
Interest	
On home mortgage	8,400
On vacation home	4,745
On loan used to buy municipal bonds	3,100
On various credit cards	600
Taxes	
State and local sales tax	700
Property tax on home	2,200
Property tax on vacation home	1,095
State income tax	3,300
Charitable contributions	1,100
Tax return preparation fee	300
Utilities and maintenance on vacation home	2,600
Depreciation related to rental of vacation home	3,500

Calculate T's taxable income for 1990.

38. J sold stock (basis of $20,000) to her brother, B, for $16,000.
    a. What are the tax consequences to J?
    b. What are the tax consequences to B if he later sells the stock for $21,000? For $14,000? For $18,000?

39. What is R's constructive ownership of X Corporation, given the following information?

Shares owned by R	900
Shares owned by S, R's uncle	600
Shares owned by T, R's partner	30
Shares owned by U, a partnership owned by R and T equally	300
Shares owned by V, R's granddaughter	570
Shares owned by unrelated parties	600

40. T was divorced on November 1, 1990, after separating from her husband H, on June 1, 1990. Her 21-year-old daughter, D, who is a full-time student, lives with her. T provides over one-half of D's support. T is 43 years of age. T, H, and D all live in Texas.

    During the year, the following income items were noted by T:

T's salary	$12,000
H's salary	36,000
D's salary	2,500
Municipal bond interest earned in December	300
General Motors dividend received during the marriage	180
Alimony received	1,000
FMV of land received in divorce settlement	18,000
Original cost of land received in divorce settlement	10,000

    The following expenses were paid by T:

Cost of leveling the land received in the divorce settlement	1,500
Interest paid	
On loan incurred to invest in municipal bonds	320
On T's share of home mortgage	3,100
On D's auto loan	1,600
All other itemized deductions	2,000

    a. Calculate T's taxable income for 1990.
    b. What is T's filing status?

41. J has a brokerage account and buys on the margin, which resulted in interest expense of $6,000 during the year. The brokerage account generated income as follows:

Municipal interest	$30,000
Taxable dividends, interest, and capital gains	60,000

    How much investment interest can J deduct?

Cumulative Problems

42. Thomas J. Smith, age 36, is single and lives at 1648 South Mill Road, Chicago, Illinois, 60609. His Social Security number is 623–33–9281. He does not want to designate $1 to the Presidential Election Campaign.

    Thomas, who is employed as an executive, earned $60,000 during the year. His employer withheld $8,500 in Federal income tax, $1,100 in state income tax and the appropriate amount of FICA (Social Security) tax.

    Thomas was divorced in 1985 and is entitled to a dependency exemption for Susan, his 8-year-old daughter who lives with her mother. Susan's Social Security number is 623–84–6144. Her mother, Joan, is 31, and her Social Security number

is 666–44–8888. Thomas paid $5,000 for Susan's support and $6,000 in alimony to Joan. He sold 100 shares of General Co. stock on April 18, 1989, for $5,000. He had purchased them on September 4, 1986, for $3,000. He sold 300 shares of U.S. United Co. stock on July 8, 1989, for $6,000. He had acquired them on April 17, 1989, for $10,000. Thomas had the following interest and dividend items in 1989:

Interest credited to his savings account at State Street Savings	$400
Dividends from General Co. stock	300
Dividends from U.S. United Co. stock	200
Dividends from AT&T stock	400
Interest on City of Denver general obligation bonds	300

Other items that may have tax consequences are:

a. Thomas paid $600 for tax return preparation, $50 for a safe deposit box, and $320 for investment advice.

b. He made charitable contributions of $2,600 during the year, $500 of which was charged on his MasterCard.

c. Thomas paid the following expenses for Susan, in addition to child support:

Dental and medical bills	$1,400
Piano lessons	300
Private school fees	1,200

d. He incurred unreimbursed medical expenses (doctor and hospital) of $800, personal property taxes of $200, $460 additional state income taxes paid in 1989 upon filing his 1988 state income tax return, and $300 in credit card interest.

e. His home expenses included home mortgage interest of $8,400 (he bought the home in 1984 and the interest is on the original mortgage), real property taxes of $450, and utilities and maintenance of $2,400.

Calculate the net tax payable (or refund due) for 1989. If you use tax forms in your solution, you will need Form 1040 and Schedules A, B, and D. Suggested software (if available): *TurboTax* for tax return solutions, *WEST–TAX Planner* or *BNA Individual Income Tax Spreadsheet* if tax return solutions are not desired.

43. John and Mary Jane are married, filing jointly. They are both under age 65 and are expecting their first child in early 1991. John's salary in 1990 was $60,000, from which $12,000 of Federal income tax and $3,200 of state income tax were withheld. Mary Jane made $30,000 and had $5,000 of Federal income tax withheld and $2,000 of state income tax withheld.

They had $400 of savings account interest and $800 of dividends during the year. They made charitable contributions of $2,000 during the year and paid an additional $200 in state income taxes in 1990 upon filing their 1989 state income tax return. Their deductible home mortgage interest was $8,200, and their property taxes came to $1,600. They had no other deductible expenses.

a. Calculate their tax (or refund) due for 1990. Suggested software (if available): *WEST–TAX Planner*.

b. Assume that they had come to you for advice in December 1990. John had learned that he was to receive a $20,000 bonus. He wants to know if he should take it in December 1990 or in January 1991 Mary Jane will quit work in January to stay home with the baby. Their itemized deductions will decrease by $2,000 because Mary Jane will not have state income taxes withheld. Suggested software (if available): *TurboTax* for tax return solutions or *WEST–TAX Planner* if tax return solutions are not desired.

6

PASSIVE ACTIVITY LOSSES

OBJECTIVES

Discuss tax shelters and the reasons for at-risk and passive loss limitations.

Explain the at-risk limitation.

Examine the rationale for the passive loss limitations.

Identify taxpayers who are subject to the passive loss rules.

Describe how the passive loss rules limit deductions for losses.

Examine the definition of passive activities.

Analyze and apply the tests for material participation.

Consider special rules related to rental activities.

Evaluate the rules for identifying passive activities.

Apply the passive loss limitations in determining the amount of a passive loss deduction.

Highlight exceptions to the passive loss rules.

Determine the proper tax treatment upon the disposition of a passive activity.

Suggest tax planning strategies to minimize the effect of the passive loss limitations.

THE TAX SHELTER PROBLEM

Before Congress enacted legislation to reduce or eliminate their effectiveness, *tax shelters* were popular investments for tax avoidance purposes. The ability of taxpayers to avoid or reduce the tax bite through tax shelter investments has been limited greatly by the *at-risk limitations* and the *passive loss rules.*

The first major provision aimed at the tax shelter strategy was the at-risk limitation enacted in 1976. The objective of the at-risk rules was to limit a taxpayer's tax shelter deductions to the amount *at risk*, that is, the amount the taxpayer stood to lose if the investment turned out to be a financial disaster. Before the at-risk rules were enacted, tax shelter promoters sold tax shelters with the promise of write-offs equal to some multiple of the taxpayer's investment. These multiple write-offs were generally made possible through the use of *nonrecourse debt* to acquire assets for the tax shelter. Nonrecourse debt is an obligation for which the endorser is not personally liable. An example of nonrecourse debt is a mortgage on real estate acquired by a partnership without the assumption of any liability for the mortgage by the partnership or any of the partners. The acquired property generally is pledged as collateral for the loan.

| EXAMPLE 1 | T invested $20,000 for a 10% interest in a tax shelter. Through the use of $800,000 of nonrecourse financing, the partnership acquired assets worth $1,000,000. Depreciation, interest, and other deductions related to the activity resulted in a loss of $400,000, of which T's share was $40,000. Because T has only $20,000 at risk, he cannot deduct more than $20,000 of the loss. If the activity is passive, the deduction will be limited further by the passive loss rules. □ |

The passive loss rules, enacted in the Tax Reform Act of 1986, have nearly made the term *tax shelter* obsolete. Now such investments are generally referred to as passive investments, or *passive activities,* rather than tax shelters.

Passive activities include certain rental activities and any trade or business in which the investor does not *materially participate.* Losses from such investments are referred to as passive losses. The passive loss rules require that income and deductions be classified as *active, portfolio,* or *passive.* Taxpayers other than closely held corporations (see Example 9) cannot offset passive losses against active income or portfolio income. Such losses can only be offset against passive income.

| EXAMPLE 2 | K, a physician, earned $150,000 from his practice in 1985 (before the passive loss rules were enacted). He also received $10,000 in dividends and interest on various portfolio investments. During the year, he acquired a 20% interest in a tax shelter investment that produced a $300,000 loss not subject to the at-risk limitation. In 1985, K would have been allowed to deduct his $60,000 share of the tax shelter loss, resulting in adjusted gross income of $100,000 ($150,000 salary + $10,000 dividends and interest − $60,000 tax shelter loss). □ |

| EXAMPLE 3 | Assume the same facts as in Example 2, except that the year is 1990 and that K does not materially participate in the operations of the activity. K's $60,000 share of the loss is a *passive loss* and is not deductible in 1990. It is treated as a *suspended loss,* which is carried over to the future. If K has passive income from this investment, or other passive investments, in the future, the sus- |

pended loss can be offset against that passive income. If K does not have passive income against which he can offset the suspended loss in the future, he will be allowed to offset the loss against other types of income upon eventual disposition of the passive activity. K's adjusted gross income in 1990 is $160,000 ($150,000 salary + $10,000 portfolio income), compared to $100,000 based on the same set of facts in 1985. □

AT-RISK RULES

The at-risk provisions limit the deductibility of losses from business and income-producing activities. These provisions, which apply to individuals and closely held corporations, are designed to prevent a taxpayer from deducting losses in excess of the actual economic investment in an activity.

Under the at-risk rules, a taxpayer's deductible losses from an activity for any taxable year are limited to the amount the taxpayer has at risk at the end of the taxable year (the amount the taxpayer could actually lose in the activity). The initial amount considered at risk is generally the sum of the following:[1]

- The adjusted basis of property (including cash) contributed to the activity.

- Amounts borrowed for use in the activity for which the taxpayer has personal liability or has pledged as security property not used in the activity.

This amount generally is increased each year by the taxpayer's share of income and is decreased by the taxpayer's share of losses and withdrawals from the activity.

A taxpayer generally is not considered at risk with respect to borrowed amounts if either of the following is true:

- The taxpayer is not personally liable for repayment of the debt (nonrecourse loans).

- The lender has an interest (other than as a creditor) in the activity (except to the extent provided in Treasury Regulations).

Although taxpayers are generally not considered at risk with regard to nonrecourse loans, there is an important exception. This exception provides that, in the case of an activity involving the holding of real property, a taxpayer is considered at risk for his or her share of any qualified nonrecourse financing that is secured by real property used in the activity.

The taxpayer also is not considered at risk with respect to amounts for which he or she is protected against loss by guarantees, stop-loss arrangements, insurance (other than casualty insurance), or a similar arrangement.

Any losses disallowed for any given taxable year by the at-risk rules may be deducted in the first succeeding year in which the rules do not prevent the deduction. However, if such losses are incurred in a passive activity, they will be subject to the passive loss limitations.

EXAMPLE 4   In 1990, T invests $40,000 in an oil partnership (not a passive activity) that, by the use of nonrecourse loans, spends $60,000 on intangible drilling costs applicable to T's interest. Since T has only $40,000 of capital at risk, he cannot deduct more than $40,000 against his other income. The nondeductible loss of $20,000 can be carried over to 1991. □

---

1. § 465(b)(1).

EXAMPLE 5   Assume that in 1991, T has taxable income from oil of $20,000. He can deduct the carried-over loss against the $20,000 of income.   ☐

EXAMPLE 6   Assume that in 1991, T has an additional loss from the oil venture of $5,000 but he has increased his at-risk capital by $20,000. He can deduct the $5,000 plus $15,000 of the loss carried over from 1990.   ☐

Recapture of previously allowed losses occurs to the extent the at-risk amount is reduced below zero.[2] This rule applies if the amount at risk is reduced below zero by distributions to the taxpayer, by changes in the status of indebtedness from recourse to nonrecourse, or by the commencement of a guarantee or other similar arrangement that affects the taxpayer's risk of loss.

Generally, a taxpayer's amount at risk is separately determined with respect to separate activities. Nevertheless, activities are treated as one activity (aggregated) if the activities constitute a trade or business and either of the following is true:

- The taxpayer actively participates in the management of that trade or business.

- In the case of a trade or business carried on by a partnership or an S corporation, 65 percent or more of the entity's losses is allocable to persons who actively participate in the management of the trade or business.

PASSIVE LOSS RULES

Before the enactment of the passive loss rules, taxpayers were able, by investing in activities in which they did not participate (passive activities), to create tax losses that did not cause actual (or potential) economic losses.

The classic example of a tax shelter that created noneconomic tax losses was a limited partnership owning rental property, because the at-risk limitation did not apply to real estate before 1987. An individual could buy an interest in a limited partnership, which in turn would buy rental property with a large nonrecourse mortgage. Since the entire cost (including the mortgage) attributable to the building could be depreciated and the interest paid on the mortgage could be expensed, tax losses were generated. There was no real *economic loss*, however, since the rental income generated was sufficient to make the mortgage payments and the real estate in most cases, was appreciating on the open market. Furthermore, the individual limited partners were not personally liable for the mortgage.

EXAMPLE 7   T invested $20,000 for a 10% interest in a limited partnership. The partnership paid $200,000 down and negotiated a 10-year nonrecourse mortgage of $800,000 at 9% interest to acquire a $1,000,000 building to be used for rental purposes. The building was placed in service in January 1984, and the 15-year depreciation schedule applicable to 1984 was used (see Table 8-4 in chapter 8). The depreciation deduction was 12% in 1984, 10% in 1985, and 9% in 1986. Total depreciation for the 3-year period was $310,000 ($1,000,000 × 31%). Interest was $72,000 in 1984 ($800,000 × 9%), $64,800 in 1985 [($800,000 − $80,000 payment on principal) × 9%], and $57,600 in 1986 [($800,000 −

---

2.   § 465(e).

$80,000 - $80,000) × 9%]. Total interest was $194,400 ($72,000 + $64,800 + $57,600). The partnership's rental income was $390,000 during the 3-year period, and taxes, insurance, and other expenses totaled $120,000. The partnership's loss for the 3-year period is computed as follows:

Rental income		$390,000
Expenses		
Interest	$194,400	
Taxes, insurance, other	120,000	
Depreciation	310,000	624,400
Partnership's loss		$234,400
T's 10% share of loss		$ 23,440

At the end of three years, T would have deducted $23,440, or $3,440 more than he invested. From an economic perspective, however, T probably did not lose $23,440. The value of his partnership interest could have increased because of appreciation of the building (on which $310,000 of depreciation was taken), increased rents, or other factors. ☐

Some tax shelters offered write-offs in the first year of two or more times the amount of the initial investment. These write-offs were deducted against the investor's other income, such as salary and interest. To eliminate these tax shelter losses, the passive loss rules were added to the law, effective in 1987.

Overview of the Passive Loss Rules

The passive loss rules require classification of income and losses into three categories: (1) active (e.g., salaries), (2) passive (e.g., income or loss from limited partnership interests), and (3) portfolio (e.g., interest and dividends). For taxpayers other than closely held corporations, losses generated by passive activities cannot offset active or portfolio income.[3] Closely held corporations (see Example 9) can offset passive losses against active income, but not against portfolio income. Tax *credits* from passive activities can be offset only against the tax attributable to passive income.[4] The unused losses and credits are carried over and may be used to offset future passive income or deducted when a taxpayer disposes of his or her entire interest in the passive activity in a fully taxable transaction. Credits can be lost forever if a taxable disposition does not result in sufficient tax to offset the credits.

Special rules apply in the case of (1) a passive activity that is converted to an active activity, (2) the death of a taxpayer owning an interest in a passive activity, (3) the installment sale of such an interest, and (4) the gift of a passive activity. Transfers of passive activities at death and by gift are covered later in the chapter under Dispositions of Passive Interests.

Taxpayers Subject to the Passive Loss Rules

The passive loss rules apply to individuals, estates, trusts, closely held C corporations, and personal service corporations.[5] Passive income or loss from investments

---

3. § 469(a)(1)(A).

4. § 469(a)(1)(B).

5. § 469(a).

in S corporations or partnerships flows through to the owners, and the passive loss rules are applied at the owner level.

Application of the passive loss limitation to personal service corporations is intended to prevent taxpayers from sheltering personal service income by creating personal service corporations and acquiring passive activities at the corporate level.

EXAMPLE 8   Five attorneys, who earn a total of $1,000,000 a year in their individual practices, form a personal service corporation. Shortly after its formation, the corporation invests in a passive activity that produces a $200,000 loss during the year. Because the passive loss rules apply to personal service corporations, the $200,000 loss is not deductible by the corporation. □

Determination of whether a corporation is a *personal service corporation* is based on rather broad definitions. A personal service corporation is a corporation that meets *both* of the following conditions:

- The principal activity is the performance of personal services.
- Such services are substantially performed by owner-employees.

Personal service corporations include those in the fields of health, law, engineering, architecture, accounting, actuarial science, performing arts, and consulting.[6] A corporation is treated as a personal service corporation if more than 10 percent of the stock (by value) is held by owner-employees.[7] A shareholder is treated as an owner-employee if he or she is an employee or shareholder on *any day* during the testing period.[8] For these purposes, shareholder status and employee status do not even have to occur on the same day.

Application of the passive loss rules to closely held (non-personal service) corporations also is intended to prevent individuals from incorporating to avoid the passive loss limitation. A corporation is classified as a closely held corporation if, at any time during the taxable year, more than 50 percent of the value of its outstanding stock is owned, directly or indirectly, by or for not more than five individuals. Closely held corporations (other than personal service corporations) may offset passive losses against *active* income, but not against portfolio income.

EXAMPLE 9   Y Corporation, a closely held corporation, has $500,000 of passive losses from a rental activity, $400,000 of active business income, and $100,000 of portfolio income. The corporation may offset $400,000 of the $500,000 passive loss against the $400,000 of active business income, but may not offset the remainder against the $100,000 of portfolio income. □

Individual taxpayers are not allowed to offset passive losses against *either* active or portfolio income. Application of the passive loss limitation as illustrated in Example 9 prevents individuals from transferring their portfolio investments to closely held corporations for the purpose of offsetting passive losses against portfolio income.

---

6. § 448(d).

7. § 469(j)(2).

8. § 269A(b)(2).

Disallowed Passive Losses

The passive loss rules disallow 100 percent of losses on passive activities acquired after October 22, 1986. However, under transition rules the disallowance provisions for losses on passive activities acquired before October 23, 1986, are phased in over five years. If a taxpayer has a loss on a passive activity acquired before October 23, 1986 (the date of enactment of TRA of 1986), a percentage of the loss may be deducted under the transition rules. Congress enacted the phase-in schedule to provide some relief to taxpayers who had committed their investment funds to passive activities prior to enactment of the passive loss limitations. The applicable percentages are shown in the following table.

Taxable Years Beginning in	Losses and Credits Allowed	Losses and Credits Disallowed
1987	65%	35%
1988	40%	60%
1989	20%	80%
1990	10%	90%
1991	0%	100%

EXAMPLE 10   T acquired a passive activity in 1984. In 1990, a loss of $10,000 was realized on this activity. Under the transition rules, $1,000 (10% of $10,000) is deductible in 1990. That is, $1,000 can be deducted against active and/or portfolio income in 1990. The $9,000 disallowed loss is suspended. A suspended loss can be carried forward and deducted against passive income in later years. If T has no passive income in later years, the suspended loss is deducted when the passive activity is disposed of in a fully taxable transaction (see Example 62). If the passive activity had been acquired after October 22, 1986, no deduction would be allowed in 1990, and the entire $10,000 would be suspended. □

A suspended loss on a pre-enactment passive activity is not added to a following year's loss in calculating that year's disallowed loss.

EXAMPLE 11   Assume the taxpayer in Example 10 had another loss of $20,000 on the pre-enactment passive activity in 1991. Pre-enactment passive activity losses are not deductible in 1991. The entire $20,000 loss is suspended. □

If a taxpayer has both pre-enactment and post-enactment activities, the transition percentage is applied to the lesser of (1) the pre-enactment passive activity loss or (2) the net passive loss from pre-enactment and post-enactment activities.

EXAMPLE 12   T has two passive activity investments. Investment A was purchased in 1985 and Investment B was purchased in 1987. In 1990, Investment A generated a $10,000 loss and Investment B generated an $8,000 gain. The net passive loss is $2,000. The allowable deduction is $200 (10% of $2,000). The remaining $1,800 is suspended and carried over. □

EXAMPLE 13	In Example 12, if Investment A had generated income of $10,000 and Investment B had generated an $8,000 loss, the net passive gain of $2,000 would be included in income. □

EXAMPLE 14	In Example 12, assume Investment A (the pre-enactment activity) had generated a loss of $10,000 and Investment B had generated a loss of $8,000. The net passive loss is $18,000. Only $1,000 (10% of $10,000) could be deducted in 1990. The remaining $17,000 ($8,000 post-enactment loss plus 90% of $10,000 pre-enactment loss) would be suspended and carried over to 1991. □

Passive Activities Defined

Code § 469(c) provides a broad definition of the term *passive activity*, but it is necessary to examine the Temporary Regulations[9] to understand how the definition is to be applied. According to the Code, the following activities are to be treated as passive activities:

- Any *trade or business* in which the taxpayer does not *materially participate*.

- Any *rental activity*, whether or not the taxpayer materially participates.

This definition is contained in § 469, which was enacted in TRA of 1986. Application of the definition raised some difficult questions:

- What constitutes material participation?

- Are all kinds of rental businesses to be treated as rental activities?

Section 469 of the Code requires that a taxpayer participate on a *regular, continuous,* and *substantial* basis in order to be a material participant. There were many situations in which it was difficult or impossible to determine whether the taxpayer had met these material participation standards. Section 469 also states that, except as provided in the Regulations, a limited partner shall not be treated as a material participant. The first set of Temporary Regulations, issued in February 1988, helps taxpayers cope with these material participation issues.

The original Code definition of passive activities is illustrated in Examples 15 through 18. The Temporary Regulations are discussed immediately thereafter.

EXAMPLE 15	T invested in a *limited partnership* that engaged in cattle-feeding operations. The investment is a passive activity. T cannot deduct losses from this passive activity against his active and portfolio income unless he materially participates in the activity. □

EXAMPLE 16	T invested in a *general partnership* that engaged in cattle-feeding operations and materially participates in the activity. The operation is not a passive activity. Any losses generated by the cattle-feeding operations can be deducted against T's active or portfolio income. □

---

9. The Temporary Regulations are also Proposed Regulations. Temporary Regulations have the same effect as Final Regulations. Refer to chapter 25 for a discussion of the different categories of regulations.

Example 17   T in Example 16 is a college professor who did not materially participate in the cattle-feeding operation. Although the activity is not a limited partnership, it is still a passive activity to T because he did not materially participate. T cannot deduct losses against his salary and portfolio income. □

Example 18   T owns a triplex. He lives in one unit and rents the other two. The two rented units constitute a passive activity. T may be able to deduct losses from the two units, subject to specified limits, if he qualifies for the real estate rental exception (discussed later in the chapter). □

Material Participation

If an individual taxpayer materially participates in a nonrental trade or business activity, any loss from that activity will be treated as an active loss that can be offset against active income. On the other hand, if a taxpayer does not materially participate, the loss will be treated as a passive loss, which can only be offset against passive income. Therefore, controlling whether a particular activity is treated as active or passive is an important part of the tax strategy of a taxpayer who owns an interest in one or more businesses. Consider the following examples.

Example 19   T, a corporate executive, earns a salary of $200,000 per year. In addition, T owns a separate business, acquired in 1988, in which he participates. The business produces a loss of $100,000 in 1990. If T materially participates in the business, the $100,000 loss is an active loss that may be offset against his active income from his corporate employer. If he does not materially participate, the loss is passive and is suspended. T may use the suspended loss in the future only if he has passive income or disposes of the activity. □

Example 20   K, an attorney, earns $250,000 a year in her law practice. In 1988, she acquired interests in two activities, A and B, in which she participates in 1990. Activity A, in which she does *not* materially participate, produces a loss of $50,000. K has not yet met the material participation standard for Activity B, which produces income of $80,000. However, K can meet the material participation standard if she spends an additional 50 hours in Activity B during the year. Should K attempt to meet the material participation standard for Activity B? If she continues working in Activity B and becomes a material participant, the $80,000 income from the activity is *active,* and the $50,000 passive loss from Activity A must be suspended. A more favorable tax strategy would be for K to *not meet* the material participation standard for Activity B, thus making the income from that activity passive. This would enable her to offset the $50,000 passive loss from Activity A against the passive income from Activity B. □

It would be possible to devise numerous scenarios in which the taxpayer could control the tax outcome by increasing or decreasing his or her participation in different activities. Examples 19 and 20 demonstrate some of the possibilities. The conclusion reached in most analyses of this type will be that taxpayers will benefit by having profitable activities classified as passive, so that any passive losses can

be used to offset passive income. On the other hand, if the activity produces a loss, the taxpayer will benefit if it is classified as active so the loss will not be subject to the passive loss limitations.

As discussed above, a nonrental trade or business in which a taxpayer owns an interest must be treated as a passive activity unless the taxpayer materially participates. The Staff of the Joint Committee on Taxation explained the importance of the material participation standard as follows:[10]

> Congress believed that there were several reasons why it was appropriate to examine the materiality of a taxpayer's participation in an activity in determining the extent to which such taxpayer should be permitted to use tax benefits from the activity. A taxpayer who materially participated in an activity was viewed as more likely than a passive investor to approach the activity with a significant nontax economic profit motive, and to form a sound judgment as to whether the activity had genuine economic significance and value. A material participation standard identified an important distinction between different types of taxpayer activities. It was thought that, in general, the more passive investor seeks a return on capital invested, including returns in the form of reductions in the taxes owed on unrelated income, rather than an ongoing source of livelihood. A material participation standard reduced the importance, for such investors, of the tax-reduction features of an investment, and thus increased the importance of the economic features in an investor's decision about where to invest his funds.

The Code provides that material participation requires the taxpayer to be involved in the operations of the activity on a *regular, continuous,* and *substantial* basis.[11] The Temporary Regulations provide more specific tests for determining whether a taxpayer is a material participant.

Code § 469(c)(2) provides that rental activities are treated as passive activities. Under the Temporary Regulations, however, some rental activities are treated as passive activities and some are not. The Temporary Regulations provide guidelines for identifying rental activities that are not automatically treated as passive activities. These rules are discussed later in the chapter under Rental Activities. If a rental activity is not automatically treated as a passive activity, it is treated as a trade or business, subject to the seven material participation rules discussed below.

A special exception exists under which a taxpayer might be allowed to deduct a limited amount of a loss on rental real estate, even though the activity is classified as passive. This provision is covered under Exceptions to the Passive Loss Rules.

Tests Based on Current Participation.   Material participation is achieved by meeting any one of seven tests provided in the Regulations. The first four tests are quantitative tests that require measurement, in hours, of the taxpayer's participation in the activity during the year.

Rule 1.   The individual participates in the activity for more than 500 hours during the year.

---

10. *General Explanation of the Tax Reform Act of 1986 ("Blue Book"),* prepared by The Staff of the Joint Committee on Taxation, May 4, 1987, H.R. 3838, 99th Cong., p. 212.

11. § 469(h)(1).

The purpose of the 500-hour requirement is to restrict deductions from the types of trade or business activities Congress intended to treat as passive activities. The 500-hour standard for material participation was adopted for the following reasons:[12]

- Few investors in traditional tax shelters devote more than 500 hours a year to such an investment.

- The IRS believes that income from an activity in which the taxpayer participates for more than 500 hours a year should not be treated as passive.

Rule 2.   The individual's participation in the activity for the taxable year constitutes substantially all of the participation in the activity of all individuals (including non-owner employees) for the year.

EXAMPLE 21   T, a physician, operates a separate business in which he participates for 80 hours during the year. He is the only participant and has no employees in the separate business. T meets the material participation standards of Rule 2. If T had employees, it would be difficult to apply Rule 2 because the Temporary Regulations do not define the term *substantially all.*   □

Rule 3.   The individual participates in the activity for more than 100 hours during the year, and the individual's participation in the activity for the year is not less than the participation of any other individual (including non-owner employees) for the year.

EXAMPLE 22   J, a college professor, owns a separate business in which she participates 110 hours during the year. She has an employee who works 90 hours during the year. J meets the material participation standard under Rule 3, but probably would not meet it under Rule 2 because her participation is only 55 percent of the total participation. It is not likely that 55 percent would meet the *substantially all* requirement of Rule 2.   □

Rules 2 and 3 are included because the IRS recognizes that the operation of some activities does not require more than 500 hours of participation during the year.

Rule 4.   The activity is a significant participation activity for the taxable year, and the individual's aggregate participation in all significant participation activities during the year exceeds 500 hours. A significant participation activity is one in which the individual's participation exceeds 100 hours during the year.

The *significant participation* rule treats taxpayers whose aggregate participation in several significant participation activities exceeds 500 hours as material participants. Rule 4 thus accords the same treatment to an individual who devotes an aggregate of more than 500 hours to several significant participation activities as to an individual who devotes more than 500 hours to a single activity.

---

12. T.D. 8175, 1988–1 C.B. 191.

EXAMPLE 23   T owns five different businesses. His participation in each activity during the year was as follows:

Activity	Hours of Participation
A	110
B	140
C	120
D	150
E	100

Activities A, B, C, and D are significant participation activities, and T's aggregate participation in those activities is 520 hours. Therefore, Activities A, B, C, and D are not treated as passive activities. Activity E is not a significant participation activity (not more than 100 hours), so it is not included in applying the 500-hour test. Activity E will be treated as a passive activity, unless T meets one of the other material participation tests with respect to Activity E. □

EXAMPLE 24   Assume the same facts as in the previous example, except that Activity A does not exist. All of the activities would be treated as passive. Activity E is not counted in applying the more than 500-hour test, so T's aggregate participation in significant participation activities is 410 hours (140 in Activity B + 120 in Activity C + 150 in Activity D). T could meet the significant participation test for Activity E by participating for one more hour in the activity. This would cause Activities B, C, D, and E to be treated as nonpassive activities. Before deciding whether to participate for at least one more hour in Activity E, T should assess the overall effect such participation would have on his tax liability. □

Tests Based on Prior Participation.   The tests in Rules 5 and 6 are based on material participation in prior years. Under these rules, a taxpayer who is no longer a material participant in an activity can continue to be *classified* as a material participant. The IRS takes the position that material participation in a trade or business for a long period of time is likely to indicate that the activity represents the individual's principal livelihood, rather than a passive investment.[13] Consequently, withdrawal from the activity, or reduction of participation to the point where it is not material, does not change the classification of the activity from active to passive.

Rule 5.   *The individual materially participated in the activity for any five taxable years (whether consecutive or not) during the ten taxable years that immediately precede the taxable year.*

Rule 1 (the 500-hour rule) is the only test that can be used in determining whether a taxpayer was a material participant in an activity for any taxable year beginning before 1987. Rules 2 through 7 are irrelevant for this purpose.[14]

---

13. Ibid., p. 60.

14. Temp. and Prop.Regs. § 1.469–5T(j).

EXAMPLE 25   D, who owns a 50% interest in a restaurant, was a material participant in the operations of the restaurant from 1985 through 1989. He retired at the end of 1989 and is no longer involved in the restaurant except as an investor. D will be treated as a material participant in the restaurant in 1990. Even if he does not become involved in the restaurant as a material participant again, he will continue to be treated as a material participant in 1991, 1992, 1993, and 1994. In 1995 and later years, D's share of income or loss from the restaurant will be classified as passive. □

> *Rule 6.   The activity is a personal service activity, and the individual materially participated in the activity for any three preceding taxable years (whether consecutive or not).*

As indicated above, the material participation standards differ for personal service activities and other businesses. An individual who was a material participant in a personal service activity for *any three years* prior to the taxable year continues to be treated as a material participant after withdrawal from the activity.

EXAMPLE 26   E, a CPA, retires from the EFG partnership after working full-time in the partnership for 30 years. As a retired partner, he will continue to receive a share of the profits of the firm for the next 10 years, even though he will not participate in the firm's operations. E also owns an interest in a passive activity that produces a loss for the year. E continues to be treated as a material participant in the EFG partnership, and his income from the partnership is active income. He will not be allowed to offset the loss from his passive investment against the income from the EFG partnership. □

Facts and Circumstances Test.   Rule 7 provides a facts and circumstances test to determine whether the taxpayer has materially participated. The Code criteria of regular, continuous, and substantial participation are used in applying the test.

> *Rule 7.   Based on all the facts and circumstances, the individual participates in the activity on a regular, continuous, and substantial basis during the year.*

The Temporary Regulations do not define what constitutes regular, continuous, and substantial participation. However, a part of the Temporary Regulations has been reserved for further development of this test. Presumably, additional guidelines will be issued in the future. For the time being, taxpayers should rely on Rules 1 through 6 in making the determination as to the nature of an activity.

Participation Defined.   Participation generally includes any work done by an individual in an activity that he or she owns. Participation does not include work if it is of a type not customarily done by owners *and* if one of the principal purposes of such work is to avoid the disallowance of passive losses or credits. Also, work done in an individual's capacity as an investor (e.g., reviewing financial reports in a non-managerial capacity) is not counted in applying the material participation tests. Participation by an owner's spouse counts as participation by the owner.[15]

---

15.   Temp. and Prop.Regs. § 1.469–5T(f)(3).

EXAMPLE 27   T, who is a partner in a CPA firm, owns a computer store that has operated at a loss during the year. In order to offset this loss against the income from his CPA practice, T would like to avoid having the computer business classified as a passive activity. Through December 15, he has worked 400 hours in the business in management and selling activities. During the last two weeks of December, he works 80 hours in management and selling activities and 30 hours doing janitorial chores. Also during the last two weeks in December, T's wife participates 40 hours as a salesperson. She has worked as a salesperson in the computer store in prior years, but has not done so during the current year. If any of T's work is of a type not customarily done by owners *and* if one of the principal purposes of such work is to avoid the disallowance of passive losses or credits, it is not counted in applying the material participation tests. It is likely that T's 480 hours of participation in management and selling activities would count as participation, but the 30 hours spent doing janitorial chores would not. However, the 40 hours of participation by T's wife would count, and T would qualify as a material participant under the more than 500 hour rule (480 + 40 = 520). □

Limited Partners.   Generally, a *limited partner* is not deemed to participate materially unless the partner qualifies under Rule 1, 5, or 6 in the above list. However, a *general partner* may qualify as a material participant by meeting any of the seven material participation tests. If an unlimited, or general, partner also owns a limited interest in the same limited partnership, all interests are treated as a general interest.[16]

Rental Activities

According to the Code, any rental activity is to be treated as a *passive activity.*[17] A *rental activity* is defined as any activity where payments are received principally for the use of tangible property.[18] The Temporary Regulations hold that an activity *generally* is a rental activity if

- tangible property held in connection with the activity is used by customers or held for use by customers, *and*

- the expected gross income from the activity represents payments principally for the use of such property.[19]

However, the Temporary Regulations provide six exceptions to the general definition of rental activity. An activity that is treated as a *nonrental activity* under any of the six exceptions will not automatically be classified as passive. Instead, the activity will be treated as an activity that is subject to the *material participation standards.* If the taxpayer materially participates in the activity, any income or loss from the activity will be active. Otherwise, the income or loss will be passive. The six exceptions are discussed below.

1. The average period of customer use for such property is seven days or less.

Under this exception, activities involving the short-term use of tangible property such as automobiles, videocassettes, tuxedos, tools, and other such

---

16. Temp. and Prop.Regs. § 1.469–5T(e)(3)(iii).
17. § 469(b)(2).
18. § 469(j)(8).
19. Temp. and Prop.Regs. § 1.469–1T(e)(3)(i).

property will not be treated as rental activities. The provision also applies to short-term rentals of hotel or motel rooms.

This exception is based on the presumption that a person who rents property for seven days or less is generally required to provide *significant services* to the customer. Providing such services supports a conclusion that the person is engaged in a service business rather than a rental business.

2. *The average period of customer use for such property is 30 days or less, and significant personal services are provided by the owner of the property.*

For longer term rentals, the presumption that significant services are provided is not automatic, as it is in the case of the seven-day exception. Instead, the taxpayer must be able to *prove* that significant personal services are rendered in connection with the activity. Therefore, an understanding of what constitutes significant personal services is necessary in order to apply this rule.

Significant personal services include only services provided by *individuals*. This provision excludes such items as telephone and cable television services. Four additional categories of *excluded services* are not considered significant personal services:[20]

- Services necessary to permit the lawful use of the property.

- Services performed in connection with the construction of improvements to property.

- Services performed in connection with the performance of repairs that extend the property's useful life for a period substantially longer than the average period for which such property is used by customers.

- Services similar to those commonly provided in connection with long-term rentals of high-grade commercial or residential real property (including cleaning and maintenance of common areas, routine repairs, trash collection, elevator service, and security at entrances or perimeters).

3. *Extraordinary personal services are provided by the owner of the property without regard to the average period of customer use.*

Extraordinary personal services are services provided by individuals where the use by customers of the property is incidental to their receipt of such services. For example, a patient's use of a hospital bed is incidental to his use of medical services. Another example would be the use of a boarding school's dormitory, which is incidental to the scholastic services received.

4. *The rental of such property is treated as incidental to a nonrental activity of the taxpayer.*

Rentals of real property incidental to a nonrental activity are not considered a passive activity. The Temporary Regulations provide that the following rentals are not passive activities:[21]

- *Property held primarily for investment.* This occurs where the principal purpose for holding the property is the expectation of gain from the appreciation of the

---

20. Temp. and Prop.Regs. § 1.469–1T(e)(3)(iv).

21. Temp. and Prop.Regs. §§ 1.469–1T(e)(3)(vi)(B) and (E).

property and the gross rental income is less than 2 percent of the lesser of (1) the unadjusted basis or (2) the fair market value of the property.

EXAMPLE 28   A taxpayer invests in vacant land for the purpose of realizing a profit on its appreciation. He leases the land during the period he holds it. The unadjusted basis is $250,000 and its fair market value is $350,000. The lease payments are $4,000 per year. Because gross rental income is less than 2% of $250,000, the activity is not a rental activity. □

• *Property used in a trade or business.* This occurs where the property is owned by a taxpayer who is an owner of the trade or business using the rental property. Also, it is required that the property was used in the trade or business during the year or during at least two of the five preceding taxable years. The 2 percent test above is also applied.

EXAMPLE 29   A farmer owns land with an unadjusted basis of $250,000 and a fair market value of $350,000. He used it for farming purposes in 1988 and 1989. In 1990 he leased the land to another farmer for $4,000. The activity is not a rental activity. □

• *Property held for sale to customers.* If property is held for sale to customers and rented during the year, the rental of the property is not a rental activity.

EXAMPLE 30   An automobile dealer rents automobiles held for sale to customers to persons who are having their own cars repaired. The activity is not a rental activity. □

EXAMPLE 31   A taxpayer acquires land upon which to construct a shopping center. Before beginning construction, he rents it to a business for use as a parking lot. Since the land was not acquired as an investment, nor used in his trade or business, nor held for sale to customers, the rental is a rental activity. □

• *Lodging rented for the convenience of an employer.* If an employer provides lodging for an employee incidental to the employee's performance of services in the employer's trade or business, no rental activity exists.

EXAMPLE 32   J has a farming business. He rents houses on his property to migrant workers during the harvest season. J does not have a rental activity. □

• A partner who rents property to a partnership that is used in the partnership's trade or business does not have a rental activity.

EXAMPLE 33   B, the owner of a business, incorporates the business, retaining the land and building as his separate property. He then rents the property to the business. B does not have a rental activity. □

The rules above were written to prevent taxpayers from converting active or portfolio income into a passive activity for the purpose of offsetting other passive losses.

In other cases, passive activity income is reclassified as nonpassive activity income. Such cases include significant participation activities, rentals of nondepreciable property, net investment income from passive equity-financed lending activities, net income from certain property rented incidental to development activities, and property rented to a nonpassive activity.[22]

5. *The taxpayer customarily makes the property available during defined business hours for nonexclusive use by various customers.*

EXAMPLE 34   P is the owner-operator of a public golf course. Some customers pay daily greens fees each time they use the course, while others purchase weekly, monthly, or annual passes. The golf course is open every day from sunrise to sunset, except on certain holidays and on days when the course is closed due to weather conditions. P is not engaged in a rental activity, regardless of the average period of use of the course by customers. □

6. *The property is provided for use in an activity conducted by a partnership, S corporation, or joint venture in which the taxpayer owns an interest.*

EXAMPLE 35   B, a partner in the ABC Partnership, contributes the use of a building to the partnership. The partnership has net income of $30,000 during the year, of which B's share is $10,000. Unless the partnership is engaged in a rental activity, none of B's income from the partnership is income from a rental activity. □

Calculation of Passive Losses

A passive activity loss is defined in the Code as the amount (if any) by which aggregate losses from all passive activities exceed the aggregate income from all passive activities for the year.[23] The Temporary Regulations, on the other hand, define passive loss as the amount (if any) by which passive activity deductions for the taxable year exceed the passive activity gross income for the taxable year.[24]

While the passive loss definitions in the Code and Temporary Regulations appear very similar, there is an important difference. The Code definition implies that there are two steps in determining the amount of a passive loss:

- Compute the passive loss or passive income for each separate passive activity.

- Offset net passive income from profitable activities against net passive losses from unprofitable activities.

The approach specified in the Temporary Regulations requires subtracting the *expenses* from all passive activities from the *income* from all passive activities. If expenses exceed income, the net result is a passive loss.

---

22. Temp. and Prop.Regs. §§ 1.469–2T(f)(2) through (7).

23. § 469(d)(1).

24. Temp. and Prop.Regs. § 1.469–2T(a).

Until the disparity between the Code and Temporary Regulations is resolved, taxpayers should follow the Code since it is a higher ranking source of authority. In addition, the Code requires any suspended passive losses to be allocated among different activities of the taxpayer (see Example 52). This cannot be done unless the Code approach to computing passive losses is followed. The Code definition of passive loss is illustrated in Example 36.

EXAMPLE 36   In the current year, a taxpayer participates in two activities deemed to be passive activities. Both activities were acquired in 1987. Activity A has generated passive income of $5,500. Activity B has generated a passive loss of $8,500. The $5,500 of passive income is sheltered by $5,500 of the passive loss. However, the net passive loss of $3,000 ($8,500 less $5,500) may not be applied against other nonpassive income. The loss may be carried forward to the succeeding year and applied against any passive income of that year. Such losses are called *suspended losses*. □

Identification of Passive Activity

Identifying what constitutes an *activity* is an important step in applying the passive loss limitations. Taxpayers who are involved in complex business operations need to be able to determine whether a given segment of their overall business operations constitutes a separate activity or is to be treated as part of a single activity. Proper treatment is necessary in order to determine whether income or loss from an activity is active or passive.

EXAMPLE 37   T owns a business with two separate departments. Department A produces $120,000 of income, and Department B produces a $95,000 loss. T participates for 700 hours in the operations of Department A. He participates for 100 hours in Department B. If T is allowed to treat both departments as a single activity, he is a material participant in the activity because his participation (700 + 100) exceeds 500 hours. Therefore, T can offset the $95,000 loss from Department B against the $120,000 of income from Department A. □

EXAMPLE 38   Assume the same facts as in Example 37. If T is required to treat each department as a separate activity, he is a material participant with respect to Department A (700 hours), and the $120,000 profit is active income. However, he is not a material participant with respect to Department B (100 hours), and the $95,000 loss is a passive loss. T cannot offset the $95,000 passive loss from Department B against the $120,000 of active income from Department A. □

Upon disposition of a passive activity, a taxpayer is allowed to offset suspended losses from the activity against other types of income. Therefore, identifying what constitutes an activity is of critical importance.

EXAMPLE 39   P owns a business with two departments. She participates for 200 hours in Department A, which had a loss of $125,000 in the current year. P participates for 250 hours in Department B, which had a $70,000 loss. P disposes of Department B during the year. She is allowed to treat the two departments as

separate activities. P will be allowed to offset the passive loss from Department B against other types of income in the following order: gain from disposition of the passive activity, other passive income, and nonpassive income. She will have a suspended loss of $125,000 from Department A.   □

EXAMPLE 40   Assume the same facts as in Example 39, except that P is required to treat the two departments as a *single activity.* Because she has not disposed of the entire activity (Departments A and B combined), P will not be allowed to utilize the $70,000 loss from Department B. She will have a suspended loss of $195,000 ($125,000 from Department A and $70,000 from Department B).   □

In May 1989, the Treasury Department issued Temporary Regulations to provide guidance as to what constitutes an activity.[25] As these Temporary Regulations are long (196 pages) and complex, only the general rules will be discussed here. Refer to the Regulations for the numerous special rules and exceptions.

The first step in determining what constitutes an activity is to identify a taxpayer's *undertakings.* An undertaking is the smallest unit that can constitute an activity. An undertaking may include diverse business and rental operations. The primary factors considered in identifying an undertaking are *location* and *ownership.* Generally, under the *undertaking rule,* business and rental operations that are conducted at the same location and are owned by the same person are treated as part of the same undertaking. Business and rental operations that are conducted at different locations or not owned by the same person constitute separate undertakings. These rules are illustrated in Examples 41 through 43.[26]

EXAMPLE 41   J is the owner of a department store and a restaurant. He conducts both businesses in the same building. J participates 450 hours in the operations of the department store, which produces income of $100,000 during the year. He participates for 100 hours in the operations of the restaurant, which produces a $45,000 loss. The department store and the restaurant are treated as a single activity because they are owned by the same person and business is conducted at the same location. J is a material participant in the activity (450 hours + 100 hours exceeds 500 hours). Therefore, the $45,000 loss from the restaurant can be offset against the $100,000 of income from the department store.   □

EXAMPLE 42   Assume the same facts as in Example 41 and that J also operates an automotive center in a mall near the department store/restaurant building. The department store, restaurant, and automotive center are all part of a single activity because all three undertakings are operated in close proximity.   □

EXAMPLE 43   Assume the same facts as in Example 42, except that the automotive center is located several blocks from the department store/restaurant building. The department store/restaurant operations constitute an activity, and the automotive center constitutes a separate activity.   □

---

25. Temp. and Prop.Regs. § 1.469–4T.
26. Temp. and Prop.Regs. § 1.469–4T(c)(4), Examples 1, 2, and 3.

The basic undertaking rule is modified if the undertaking includes both rental and nonrental operations. In these circumstances, the rental and nonrental operations generally must be treated as separate activities.[27] This rule is necessary because rental operations are always treated as passive, whereas nonrental operations are treated as passive only if the owner is not a material participant.

EXAMPLE 44   B owns a building in which she rents apartments to tenants and operates a restaurant. Sixty percent of B's gross income is attributable to the apartments, and 40% is attributable to the restaurant. The apartment undertaking and the restaurant operation are treated as two separate activities. The apartment undertaking is a passive activity. The classification of the restaurant undertaking will depend on whether B is a material participant.[28]   □

Under a special exception, rental and nonrental operations may be treated as a single operation, rather than as separate operations, when either the rental or nonrental operations are a predominant part of the undertaking. This exception applies when less than 20 percent of the gross income from the undertaking is attributable to either rental or nonrental operations.[29]

EXAMPLE 45   Assume the same facts as in Example 44, except that 85% of B's gross income from the undertaking is attributable to apartment rentals and 15% is attributable to the restaurant. Because less than 20% of the gross income is attributable to nonrental operations (the restaurant), the rental operation and the restaurant operation will be considered a single activity.   □

In Example 45, the rental operation is the predominant part of the undertaking (85 percent rental vs. 15 percent nonrental). Therefore, the entire undertaking will be treated as a single activity that is a rental activity. If, on the other hand, the restaurant produced 85 percent of the gross income and the apartment rentals produced 15 percent, the restaurant would be the predominant part of the undertaking. The entire undertaking would be treated as a single activity that is a nonrental activity. The material participation tests would be applied to determine whether the activity was active or passive.

The exception illustrated in Example 45 is intended to reduce the accounting burdens on taxpayers in circumstances where one part of the undertaking is predominant. When the exception applies, taxpayers are not required to separate their rental and nonrental operations into separate activities.

In addition to the basic rules discussed above, the new activity regulations address many other complex issues. For example, taxpayers with rental real estate operations at different locations are covered by rather flexible rules. These rules permit taxpayers to treat their real estate operations at different locations as separate activities or to combine operations or portions of operations at different locations into larger activities.

Flexibility is also provided when a taxpayer sells part of an integrated, interrelated economic unit. Under certain circumstances, taxpayers may elect to

---

27. Temp. and Prop.Regs. § 1.469–4T(d)(4).

28. Temp. and Prop.Regs. § 1.469–4T(d)(4), Example 2.

29. Temp. and Prop.Regs. § 1.469–4T(d)(2).

treat such parts as separate activities in order to trigger the deduction of losses upon disposition.

Income Not Treated as Passive.   Certain items of income and expense are not taken into account in computing passive activity losses.[30] Some of these income items are discussed in this section. Others are beyond the scope of this text. Deductions that are not treated as passive are covered in the following section.

Portfolio income of an activity is not included in computing the passive income or loss from the activity. This provision negates any tax benefit taxpayers would otherwise achieve by transferring assets that produce portfolio income to an activity that produces a passive loss. Thus, it is possible that an activity might produce a passive loss *and* portfolio income in the same year.

EXAMPLE 46

K owns an activity that produces a passive loss of $15,000 during the year. He transfers to the activity corporate stock that produces portfolio income of $15,000. The passive loss cannot be offset against the portfolio income. K must report a passive loss of $15,000 and portfolio income of $15,000 from the activity. □

Portfolio income includes interest, annuities, royalties, dividends, and other items. However, such income is excluded from the passive loss computation if it is *not derived* in the ordinary course of business.[31] For example, interest earned on loans made in the ordinary course of a trade or business of lending money would not be treated as portfolio income. In addition, interest on accounts receivable arising from the performance of services or the sale of property would not be treated as portfolio income if credit is customarily offered to customers by the business.

Gains on dispositions of portfolio assets are also treated as portfolio income. The rules for determining whether other gain is to be treated as portfolio income are very complex and are beyond the scope of this text. Refer to the Temporary and Proposed Regulations for additional information.[32]

Compensation paid to or on behalf of an individual for services performed or to be performed is not treated as passive activity gross income.[33]

EXAMPLE 47

T owns 50% of the stock of X, Inc., an S corporation that owns rental real estate. X pays T a $10,000 salary for services he performs for the corporation in connection with management of the rental real estate. The corporation has a $30,000 passive loss on the property during the year. T must report compensation income of $10,000 and a passive loss of $15,000 ($30,000 × .50). □

Some of the other income items that are specifically excluded from the passive loss computation are listed below:[34]

---

30. Temp. and Prop.Regs. § 1.469–2T(a)(2).
31. Temp. and Prop.Regs. § 1.469–2T(c)(3).
32. Temp. and Prop.Regs. § 1.469–2T(c)(2).

33. Temp. and Prop.Regs. § 1.469–2T(c)(4).
34. Temp. and Prop.Regs. § 1.469–2T(c)(7).

- Gross income of an individual from intangible property (such as a patent, copyright, or literary, musical, or artistic composition) if the taxpayer's personal efforts significantly contributed to the creation of the property.

- Gross income attributable to a refund of any state, local, or foreign income, war profits, or excess profits tax.

- Gross income of an individual for a covenant not to compete.

Deductions Not Treated as Passive.   The general rule is that a deduction is treated as a passive activity deduction if and only if the deduction arises in connection with the conduct of an activity that is a passive activity. The Temporary Regulations list several items that are not to be treated as passive activity deductions:[35]

- Any deduction for an expense that is clearly and directly allocable to portfolio income.

- Any deduction for a loss from the disposition of property of a type that produces portfolio income.

- Any deduction with respect to a dividend if the dividend is not included in passive activity gross income.

- Any deduction for qualified residence interest or interest that is capitalized pursuant to a capitalization provision.

- Any miscellaneous itemized deduction that is disallowed by operation of the 2 percent floor.

- Any deduction allowed under § 170 for a charitable contribution.

- Any net operating loss carryforward allowed under § 172.

- Any capital loss carryforward allowed under § 1212(b).

Suspended Losses

The determination of whether a loss is suspended under the passive loss rule is made after the application of the at-risk rules as well as other provisions relating to the measurement of taxable income. A loss that would not be allowed for the year because the taxpayer is not at risk with respect to it is suspended under the at-risk provision and not under the passive loss rule.

A taxpayer's basis is reduced by deductions (e.g., depreciation) even if the deductions are not currently usable because of the passive loss rule.

EXAMPLE 48   T's adjusted basis in a passive activity is $10,000 at the beginning of 1991. His loss from the activity in 1991 is $4,000. Since T had no passive activity income, the $4,000 cannot be deducted. At year-end, T has an adjusted basis of $6,000 in the activity and a suspended loss of $4,000. □

EXAMPLE 49   T in Example 48 had a loss in the activity in 1992 of $9,000. Since the $9,000 exceeds T's at-risk amount ($6,000) by $3,000, that $3,000 loss is disallowed by the at-risk rules. If T has no passive activity income, the remaining $6,000

---

35. Temp. and Prop.Regs. § 1.469–2T(d).

cannot be deducted. At year-end, T has a $3,000 unused loss under the at-risk rules, $10,000 ($4,000 for 1991 plus $6,000 for 1992) of suspended passive losses, and an adjusted basis in the activity of zero. ☐

EXAMPLE 50

T in Example 49 realized a $1,000 gain in 1993. Because the $1,000 increases his at-risk amount, $1,000 of the $3,000 unused loss can be reclassified as a passive loss. If T has no other passive income, the $1,000 income is offset against $1,000 of suspended passive losses. At the end of 1993, T has no taxable passive income, $2,000 ($3,000 − $1,000) of unused losses under the at-risk rules, $10,000 ($10,000 + $1,000 of reclassified unused at-risk losses − $1,000 of passive losses offset against passive gains), and an adjusted basis in the activity of zero. ☐

EXAMPLE 51

In 1994, T had no gain or loss from the activity in Example 50. He contributed $5,000 more to the passive activity. Because the $5,000 increases his at-risk amount, the $2,000 of unused losses under the at-risk rules is reclassified as a passive loss. T gets no passive loss deduction in 1994. At year-end, he has no unused losses under the at-risk rules, $12,000 of suspended passive losses ($10,000 + $2,000 of reclassified unused at-risk losses), and an adjusted basis of $3,000 ($5,000 additional investment − $2,000 of reclassified losses). ☐

Interest deductions attributable to passive activities are treated as passive activity deductions but are not treated as investment interest. (See chapter 10 for a detailed discussion of investment interest.) As a result, these interest deductions are subject to limitation under the passive loss rule and not under the investment interest limitation.

Carryovers of Suspended Losses. To determine the suspended loss for an activity, passive activity losses must be allocated among all activities in which the taxpayer has an interest. The allocation is made to the activity by multiplying the disallowed passive activity loss from all activities by a fraction, the numerator of which is the loss from the activity and the denominator of which is the sum of the losses for the taxable year from all activities having losses.

EXAMPLE 52

T has investments in three passive activities (acquired in 1990) with the following income and losses for that year:

Activity A		($ 30,000)
Activity B		(20,000)
Activity C		25,000
Net passive loss		($ 25,000)
Allocated to:		
	A ($25,000 × $30,000/$50,000)	$ 15,000
	B ($25,000 × $20,000/$50,000)	10,000
Total suspended losses		($ 25,000)

☐

Suspended losses are carried over indefinitely and are deducted from the activities to which they relate in the immediately succeeding taxable year.[36]

EXAMPLE 53   Assume the same facts as in Example 52. In 1991, the disallowed loss from 1990 of $15,000 for Activity A is treated as a deduction from Activity A. Likewise, the disallowed loss of $10,000 from Activity B is treated as a deduction from Activity B.   □

Upon the taxable disposition of a passive activity, the suspended passive losses from that activity can be offset against the taxpayer's nonpassive and portfolio income. See Dispositions of Passive Interests later in the chapter.

Calculation of Passive Credits.   Credits arising from passive activities are limited much like passive losses. They can be utilized only against regular tax attributable to passive income,[37] which is calculated by comparing the tax on all income (including passive income) with the tax on income excluding passive income.

EXAMPLE 54   A taxpayer owes $50,000 of tax, disregarding net passive income, and $80,000 of tax, considering both net passive and other taxable income (disregarding the credits in both cases). The amount of tax attributable to the passive income is $30,000.

Tax due (before credits) including net passive income	$ 80,000
Less: Tax due (before credits) without including net passive income	(50,000)
Tax attributable to passive income	$ 30,000

□

In the preceding example, a maximum of $30,000 of passive activity credits can be claimed; the excess credits are carried over. These passive activity credits (such as the jobs credit, low-income housing credit, research activities credit, and rehabilitation credit) can be used against the *regular* tax attributable to passive income only. If a taxpayer has a net loss from passive activities during a given year, no credits can be used. Likewise, if a taxpayer has net passive income but the alternative minimum tax applies to that year, no passive activity credits can be used. (The alternative minimum tax is discussed in chapter 14.) In addition, the unused passive losses are carried over.

When the passive activity that generates tax credits fits under the exception for rental real estate activities (discussed subsequently under Exceptions to the Passive Loss Rules), such credits must be converted into deduction equivalents.

---

36. § 469(b).   37. § 469(d)(2).

The deduction equivalent is the deduction necessary to reduce one's tax liability by an amount equal to the credit. A taxpayer with $5,000 of credits and a tax bracket of 28 percent would have a deduction equivalent of $17,857 ($5,000 divided by 28 percent). See the subsequent discussion under the rental real estate exception for examples calculating deduction equivalents.

Carryovers of Passive Credits.   Tax credits attributable to passive activities can be carried forward indefinitely much like suspended passive losses. Unlike passive losses, however, passive credits can be lost forever when the activity is disposed of in a taxable transaction.

EXAMPLE 55   T sold a passive activity for a gain of $10,000. The activity had suspended losses of $40,000 and suspended credits of $15,000. The $10,000 gain is offset by $10,000 of the suspended losses, and the remaining $30,000 of suspended losses is deductible against T's active and portfolio income. The suspended credits are lost forever because no tax was generated by the sale of the activity. This is true even if T has a positive taxable income or is subject to the alternative minimum tax. □

EXAMPLE 56   If T in Example 55 had realized a $100,000 gain on the sale of the passive activity, the $15,000 of suspended credits could have been used to the extent of regular tax attributable to the net passive income.

Gain on sale	$100,000
Less: Suspended losses	40,000
Net gain	$ 60,000

If the tax attributable to the net gain of $60,000 is $15,000 or more, the entire $15,000 of suspended credits can be used. If the tax attributable to the gain is less than $15,000, the excess of the suspended credit over the tax attributable to the gain is lost forever. □

When there is adequate regular tax liability from passive activities to trigger the use of suspended credits, such credits lose their character as passive credits. They are reclassified as regular tax credits and made subject to the same limits as other credits (discussed in chapter 11).

This reclassification of passive credits can occur when they cannot be used in the year of reclassification because the taxpayer is subject to the alternative minimum tax (discussed in chapter 14). Tax credits cannot reduce the tax calculated under the alternative minimum tax rules; the credits are carried over under the general rules for tax credits. Form 8582–CR (Passive Activity Credit Limitations) is used to report passive activity credits.

EXAMPLE 57   During the year, T had the following regular tax, alternative minimum tax, and credits:

Activity	Regular Tax	Alternative Minimum Tax	Tax Credits	Carried Over As Passive	Carried Over As Regular
Passive	$ 50	$150	$150	$100	$ 50
Active	500	450	150	—	150
	$550	$600	$300	$100	$200

Even though T has to pay the alternative minimum tax of $600 because it exceeds the regular tax of $550, he can reclassify $50 of the suspended passive credits as regular credits because of the $50 of regular tax generated by passive income. He has suspended passive credits of $100 left over for use against future passive income tax. The $50 of reclassified credits can be used in a future year (together with the $150 of active credits) against tax attributable to active and portfolio income. The entire $200 of regular tax credit carryovers is subject to the general rules governing credits. (See chapter 11.) □

Exceptions to the Passive Loss Rules.   The passive loss rules do not apply to working interests in any oil or gas property. In addition, a transitional exception exists for investors in low-income housing. The most significant exception, however, is for rental real estate activities. Generally, up to $25,000 of losses on rental real estate activities of an individual may be deducted against nonpassive or portfolio income.[38] The annual $25,000 deduction is reduced by 50 percent of the taxpayer's AGI in excess of $100,000. Thus, the entire deduction is phased out at $150,000. If married individuals file separately, the $25,000 deduction is reduced to zero unless they lived apart for the entire year. If they lived apart for the entire year, the loss amount is $12,500 each, and the phase-out begins at $50,000. AGI for purposes of the phase-out is calculated without regard to IRA deductions, Social Security benefits, and net losses from passive activities.

To qualify for the $25,000 exception, a taxpayer must meet the following requirements:[39]

- Actively participate in the rental real estate activity.

- Own 10 percent or more (in value) of all interests in the activity during the entire taxable year (or shorter period during which the taxpayer held an interest in the activity).

The difference between active participation and material participation is that the former can be satisfied without regular, continuous, and substantial involvement in operations as long as the taxpayer participates in the making of management decisions in a significant and bona fide sense. Management decisions that are relevant in this context include such decisions as approving new tenants, deciding on rental terms, and approving capital or repair expenditures.

The $25,000 allowance is available after all active participation rental losses and gains are netted and applied to other passive income.

EXAMPLE 58   K, who has $90,000 of AGI before considering rental activities, has $85,000 of losses from a rental real estate activity in which she actively participates. She

38. § 469(i).   39. § 469(i)(6).

also actively participates in another rental real estate activity from which she has $25,000 of income. She has other passive income of $36,000. The net rental loss of $60,000 is offset by the $36,000 of passive income, leaving $24,000 that can be deducted against other income. ☐

The $25,000 offset allowance is an aggregate of both deductions and credits in deduction equivalents. The deduction equivalent of a passive activity credit is the amount of deductions that would reduce the tax liability for the taxable year by an amount equal to the credit.[40] If the total deduction and deduction equivalent exceed $25,000, the taxpayer must allocate on a pro rata basis, first among the losses (including real estate rental activity losses suspended in prior years) and then to credits in the following order: (1) credits other than rehabilitation credits, (2) rehabilitation credits, and (3) low-income housing credits.

EXAMPLE 59

T is an active participant in a real estate rental activity that produces $8,000 of income, $26,000 of deductions, and $1,500 of credits. T, who is in the 28% tax bracket, may deduct the net passive loss of $18,000 ($8,000 less $26,000). After deducting the loss, he has an available deduction equivalent of $7,000 ($25,000 less $18,000 passive loss). Therefore, the maximum amount of credits that may be claimed by T is $1,960 ($7,000 × 28%). Since the actual credits are less than this amount, the entire $1,500 credit may be claimed. ☐

EXAMPLE 60

B who is in the 28% tax bracket is an active participant in three separate rental real estate activities. She has $20,000 of losses from Activity A, $10,000 of losses from Activity B, and $4,200 of passive credits from Activity C. B's deduction equivalent from the credits is $15,000 ($4,200 ÷ .28). Total passive deductions and deduction equivalents are $45,000 ($20,000 + $10,000 + $15,000) and therefore exceed the maximum allowable amount of $25,000. The taxpayer must allocate pro rata first from among losses and then from among credits. Deductions from Activity A are limited to $16,667 ($25,000 × [$20,000 ÷ ($20,000 + $10,000)], and deductions from Activity B are limited to $8,333 ($25,000 × [$10,000 ÷ ($20,000 + $10,000)]).

Since the amount of passive deductions exceeds the $25,000 maximum, the deduction balance of $5,000 and passive credit of $4,200 must be carried forward. The suspended losses and credits by activity are as follows:

		Activity		
	Total	A	B	C
Allocated losses	$30,000	$ 20,000	$10,000	$ –0–
Allocated credits	4,200	–0–	–0–	4,200
Utilized losses	25,000	(16,667)	(8,333)	–0–
Suspended losses	5,000	3,333	1,667	–0–
Suspended credits	4,200	–0–	–0–	4,200

☐

---

40. § 469(j)(5).

Further complications arise when both losses and credits are generated by passive rental activities. Recall that the phase-out of rental losses begins when the taxpayer's AGI reaches $100,000. For each two dollars by which AGI exceeds $100,000, one dollar of the $25,000 loss is disallowed. When the taxpayer's AGI reaches $150,000, no real estate rental loss is allowed.

Where real estate rental activities generate rehabilitation credits and low-income housing credits on property placed in service before 1990, the phase-out range is between $200,000 and $250,000 of AGI.

EXAMPLE 61

T has a net passive activity loss attributable to a low-income housing activity placed in service before 1990. If her AGI is $175,000, she cannot deduct a loss on the activity, because her AGI exceeds the upper limit of the loss phase-out range of $150,000. She could use up to $25,000 of deduction equivalents ($7,000 of credits) of a low-income housing credit because that phase-out does not begin until AGI reaches $200,000. □

For tax years ending after 1989, low-income housing credits on property placed in service after 1989 are not subject to the $25,000 deduction equivalent phaseout rules.

Dispositions of Passive Interests

When a taxpayer disposes of his or her entire interest in a passive activity, the actual economic gain or loss on the investment finally can be determined. As a result, under the passive loss rules, upon a fully taxable disposition, any overall loss from the activity realized by the taxpayer is recognized and allowed against any income. Special rules apply to dispositions of certain property that disallow their classification as passive income. Included in these rules are dispositions of partnership interests and S corporation stock, partial interests in property, property used in more than one activity, and substantially appreciated property formerly used in a nonpassive activity.[41]

Since the purpose of the disposition rule is to allow the taxpayer's real economic losses to be deducted, credits (which are not related to the measurement of such loss) are not allowable just by reason of a disposition. Credits will be allowed *only* when there is sufficient tax on passive income to absorb such credits.

A fully taxable disposition generally includes a sale of the property to a third party at arm's length and thus, presumably, for a price equal to the property's fair market value. Gain recognized upon a transfer of an interest in a passive activity generally is treated as passive and is first offset by the suspended losses from that activity.

EXAMPLE 62

T sold an apartment house with an adjusted basis of $100,000 for $180,000. In addition, T has suspended losses associated with that specific apartment house of $60,000. The total gain, $80,000, and the taxable gain, $20,000, are calculated as follows:

---

41. Temp. and Prop.Regs. §§ 1.469–2T(c)(2)(i) and (ii).

Net sales price	$ 180,000
Less: Adjusted basis	(100,000)
Total gain	$ 80,000
Less: Suspended losses	(60,000)
Taxable gain (passive)	$ 20,000

☐

If current and suspended losses of the passive activity exceed the gain realized or if the sale results in a realized loss, the sum of

- any loss from the activity for the tax year (including losses suspended in the activity disposed of), plus

- any loss realized on the disposition

in excess of

- net income or gain for the tax year from all passive activities (without regard to the activity disposed of)

is treated as a loss that is not from a passive activity.

EXAMPLE 63

T sold an apartment house with an adjusted basis of $100,000 for $150,000. In addition, T has current and suspended losses associated with that specific apartment house of $60,000 and has no other passive activities. The total gain, $50,000, and the deductible loss, $10,000, are calculated as follows:

Net sales price	$ 150,000
Less: Adjusted basis	(100,000)
Total gain	$ 50,000
Less: Suspended losses	(60,000)
Deductible loss	$ (10,000)

The $10,000 deductible loss is offset against the taxpayer's ordinary income and portfolio income. ☐

Disposition of a Passive Activity at Death.   A transfer of a taxpayer's interest in an activity by reason of the taxpayer's death results in suspended losses being allowed (to the decedent) to the extent they exceed the amount, if any, of the step-up in basis allowed.[42] Suspended losses are lost to the extent of the amount of the basis increase. The losses allowed generally would be reported on the final return of the deceased taxpayer.

EXAMPLE 64

A taxpayer dies with passive activity property having an adjusted basis of $40,000, suspended losses of $10,000, and a fair market value at the date of the decedent's death of $75,000. The heir's basis for the property is $75,000, which

---

42. § 469(g)(2).

is fair market value at the date of death (see chapter 12). The step-up in basis would be $35,000 (fair market value at date of death in excess of adjusted basis). None of the $10,000 suspended loss would be deductible by either the decedent or the beneficiary. The total of adjusted basis ($40,000) and the suspended losses ($10,000) did not exceed the fair market value of the property ($75,000). □

EXAMPLE 65   A taxpayer dies with passive activity property having an adjusted basis of $40,000, suspended losses of $10,000, and a fair market value at the date of the decedent's death of $45,000. Since the basis increase under § 1014 would be only $5,000 ($45,000 − $40,000), the suspended losses allowed are limited to $5,000 ($10,000 suspended loss at time of death − $5,000 increase in basis). The $5,000 loss available to the decedent would be reported on the decedent's final income tax return. □

Disposition of a Passive Activity by Gift.   In a disposition of a taxpayer's interest in a passive activity by a gift, the suspended losses are added to the basis of the property.[43]

EXAMPLE 66   A taxpayer makes a gift of passive activity property having an adjusted basis of $40,000, suspended losses of $10,000, and a fair market value at the date of the gift of $100,000. The taxpayer cannot deduct the suspended losses in the year of the disposition. The suspended losses transfer with the property and are added to the adjusted basis of the property. □

Installment Sale of a Passive Activity.   An installment sale of a taxpayer's entire interest in a passive activity triggers the recognition of the suspended losses.[44] The losses are allowed in each year of the installment obligation in the ratio that the gain recognized in each year bears to the total gain on the sale.

EXAMPLE 67   T sold his entire interest in a passive activity for $100,000. His adjusted basis in the property was $60,000. If T uses the installment method, his gross profit ratio is 40% ($40,000/$100,000). If T received a $20,000 down payment, he would recognize a gain of $8,000 (40% of $20,000). If the activity had a suspended loss of $25,000, T would deduct $5,000 [($8,000 ÷ $40,000) × $25,000] of the suspended loss in the first year. □

Passive Activity Changes to Active.   If a formerly passive activity becomes an active one, suspended losses are allowed against income from the now active business.[45] The activity must continue to be the same activity.

Nontaxable Exchange of a Passive Activity.   In a nontaxable exchange of a passive investment, the taxpayer keeps the suspended losses, which generally become deductible when the acquired property is sold. If the activity of the old and new property are the same, suspended losses can be used.

---

43. § 469(j)(6).   45. § 469(f).
44. § 469(g)(3).

EXAMPLE 68

A taxpayer exchanged a duplex for a limited partnership interest in a § 721 nonrecognition transaction. The suspended losses from the duplex will not be deductible until the limited partnership interest is sold. Two separate activities exist: a rental real estate activity and a limited partnership activity. If the taxpayer had continued to own the duplex and the duplex had future taxable income, the suspended losses would have become deductible before the time of disposition. ☐

EXAMPLE 69

In a § 1031 nontaxable exchange (see chapter 12 for details), a taxpayer exchanged a duplex (rental activity) for an apartment house. The suspended losses from the duplex will be deductible against future taxable income of the apartment house. The same rental activity exists for the apartment house. ☐

TAX PLANNING CONSIDERATIONS

Utilizing Passive Losses

Taxpayers who have passive activity losses should adopt a strategy of generating passive activity income that can be sheltered by existing passive losses. One approach is to buy an interest in any passive activity that is generating income.

Losses from passive activities acquired after October 22, 1986, are not covered by the phase-in rules. From a tax perspective, it would be foolish to buy a loss-generating passive activity after that date unless one has other passive income to shelter or the activity is rental real estate that can qualify for the $25,000 exception.

A taxpayer with existing passive losses might consider buying rental property. If a large down payment is made and the straight-line method of ACRS (discussed in chapter 8) is elected, a positive net income could be realized. The income would be sheltered by other passive losses, depreciation expense would be spread out evenly and preserved for future years, and depreciation recapture (discussed in chapter 13) is avoided upon the sale of the property. Future gain realized upon the sale of the rental property could be sheltered by existing suspended passive losses.

Taxpayers with passive losses should consider all other trades or businesses in which they have an interest. If they show that they do not materially participate in the activity, the activity becomes a passive activity. Any income generated could be sheltered by existing passive losses and suspended losses. Family partnerships in which certain members do not materially participate would qualify. The silent partner in any general partnership engaged in a trade or business would also qualify.

PROBLEM MATERIALS

Discussion Questions

1. Discuss tax shelters and how taxpayers used such investments to reduce, defer, or eliminate income taxes.

2. What does "at risk" mean? What is its significance?

3. Explain how the at-risk limitation and the passive loss rules have reduced the effectiveness of tax shelter investments.

4. What is nonrecourse debt? How was it used to generate large tax shelter deductions?

5. What constitutes a taxpayer's initial at-risk amount, and what causes increases and decreases in the amount at risk?

6. T invested $10,000 in a cattle-feeding operation that used nonrecourse notes to purchase $100,000 in feed, which was fed to the cattle and expensed. T's share of the expense was $18,000. How much can he deduct?

7. What is a passive activity?

8. Under the passive loss rules, taxpayers must classify income and losses into three categories. Name these three categories and discuss each category briefly.

9. Describe the limitations that apply to passive activity losses and passive activity credits.

10. Passive losses and credits for any particular year may be suspended. When can suspended losses and credits be used?

11. Distinguish between the passive loss limitations that apply to pre-enactment activities and those that apply to post-enactment activities.

12. In 1990, T incurred a $100,000 loss on a passive activity that he acquired in 1985 and a $40,000 loss on a passive activity he acquired in 1988. How much may he deduct?

13. In 1990, T incurred a $100,000 loss on a passive activity that he acquired in 1985 and had $40,000 of income on a passive activity he acquired in 1988. How much may he deduct?

14. Discuss whether the passive loss rules apply to the following: individuals, closely held C corporations, S corporations, partnerships, and personal service corporations.

15. Define *passive activity*, and discuss the difficult questions raised by the Code definition of the term.

16. What is the significance of the term *material participation?* Why is the extent of a taxpayer's participation in an activity important in determining whether a loss from the activity is deductible or nondeductible?

17. T owns an interest in an activity that produces a $100,000 loss during the year. Would T generally prefer to have the activity classified as active or passive? Discuss.

18. T owns an interest in an activity that produces $100,000 of income during the year. Would T generally prefer to have the activity classified as active or passive? Discuss.

19. Why did the IRS adopt the more-than-500-hour standard for material participation?

20. K, a physician, operates a separate business that he acquired in 1985. He participated for 90 hours in the business in 1990, and the business incurred a loss of $20,000. Under what circumstances would the loss be deductible as an ordinary loss?

21. J, an attorney, operates a separate business that he acquired in 1985. He has one part-time employee in the business. J participated for 130 hours in the business in 1990, and the business incurred a loss of $20,000. Under what circumstances would the loss be deductible as an ordinary loss?

22. Z, a professor, operates three separate businesses, all acquired in 1985. She participates for less than 500 hours in each business. Each business incurs a loss during the year. Are there any circumstances under which Z may treat the losses as active?

23. In 1989, P retired as a partner in a CPA firm he founded 30 years ago. He continues to share in the profits, although he no longer participates in the activities of the firm. P also owns an interest in a passive activity that he acquired in 1984. The passive activity produced a loss of $50,000 in 1990. Can P offset the passive loss against his income from the CPA firm?

24. Some types of work are counted in applying the material participation standards, and some types are not counted. Discuss and give examples of each type.

25. Some rental operations automatically are treated as passive activities, and others are treated as passive only if the owner does not meet the material participation standards. How can one differentiate between the two categories?

26. What are *significant personal services*, and what is the importance of such services in determining whether a rental activity is treated as a passive activity?

27. What are *extraordinary personal services*, and what is the importance of such services in determining whether a rental activity is treated as a passive activity?

28. Discuss which types of services are treated as significant personal services. Which types are not treated as significant personal services?

29. Discuss the following issues in connection with the calculation of passive losses:
    a. What constitutes a passive activity?
    b. What types of income are not treated as passive income?
    c. What types of deductions are not treated as passive deductions?

30. What is a suspended loss? Why is it important to allocate suspended losses in cases where a taxpayer has interests in more than one passive activity?

31. Suspended credits may be lost upon the disposition of a passive activity, whereas suspended losses are generally usable. Explain.

32. In connection with passive activities, what is a *deduction equivalent*? How is a deduction equivalent computed?

33. What is the difference between material participation and active participation with regard to the passive loss rules?

34. Upon the taxable disposition of a passive activity, what happens to the suspended losses? The suspended credits?

35. Is a hobby loss ever treated as a passive loss? Why or why not?

Problems

36. In 1988, T invested $100,000 in a limited partnership that has a working interest in an oil well. In 1988, his share of the losses of the partnership was $45,000. In 1989, his share of the losses was $95,000. In 1990, his share of partnership income was $10,000, and he invested an additional $15,000 in the venture. How much can T deduct in 1988? In 1989? In 1990?

37. In 1989, T invested $50,000 in a limited partnership that has a working interest in an oil well. In 1989, his share of the partnership loss was $35,000. In 1990, his share of the partnership loss was $25,000. Which of the following statements is correct?
    a. T can deduct $35,000 in 1989 and $25,000 in 1990.
    b. T can deduct $14,000 in 1989 and $3,000 in 1990.
    c. T can deduct $35,000 in 1989, and, if he invests an additional $10,000 in the partnership in 1990, he can deduct $25,000 in 1990.
    d. T can deduct $14,000 in 1989 and $5,000 in 1990.
    e. None of the above.

38. Taxpayer has an investment in a passive limited partnership purchased in 1985 and incurred losses from it of $100,000 in both 1989 and 1990. Assuming he has enough at risk to deduct the losses, how much can he deduct in 1989 and 1990?

39. Xenoz, Inc., a closely held, personal service corporation has $100,000 of passive losses in 1990. In addition, Xenoz had $80,000 of active business income and $20,000 of portfolio income. How much of the passive loss may Xenoz use to offset other types of income in 1990?

40. In 1985, C acquired an interest in a partnership in which she is not a material participant. The partnership was profitable until 1989. C's basis in her partnership interest at the beginning of 1989 was $50,000. In 1989, C's share of the partnership loss was $35,000. In 1990, her share of the partnership loss was $25,000. Which of the following statements is incorrect?

    a. C can deduct $7,000 in 1989 and $2,500 in 1990.
    b. C can deduct $7,000 in 1989 and $1,500 in 1990.
    c. If C invests an additional $10,000 in the partnership in 1990, she can deduct $7,000 in 1989 and $2,500 in 1990.
    d. None of the above.

41. F acquired a 20% interest in the ABC Partnership for $100,000 in 1985. The partnership was profitable until 1990, and F's basis in the partnership interest was $120,000 at the end of 1989. ABC incurred a loss of $400,000 in 1990 and reported income of $200,000 in 1991. Assuming F is not a material participant in ABC, how much of F's loss from ABC Partnership is deductible in 1990 and 1991, respectively?

42. K has two investments in nonrental passive activities. Activity A was acquired in 1985, and Activity B was acquired in 1990. Her share of the loss from Activity A was $10,000 in 1990, and her share of the income from Activity B was $6,000. How will K's 1990 taxable income be affected by these passive investments?

43. H has two investments in nonrental passive activities. Activity A, which was acquired in 1985, was profitable until 1990. Activity B was acquired in 1990. H's share of the loss from Activity A was $10,000 in 1990, and his share of the loss from Activity B was $6,000. What is the total of H's suspended losses from these activities as of the end of 1990?

44. S acquired an activity in 1985. The loss from the activity was $50,000 in 1990. S had adjusted gross income of $140,000 before considering the loss from the activity. The activity is an apartment building, and S is an active participant. What is her adjusted gross income after the loss is considered?

45. B acquired an activity in 1985. The loss from the activity was $50,000 in 1990. B had adjusted gross income of $140,000 before considering the loss from the activity. The activity is an apartment building, and B is not an active participant. What is B's AGI after considering the activity?

46. N acquired an activity in 1985. The loss from the activity was $50,000 in 1990. N had adjusted gross income of $140,000 before considering the loss from the activity. The activity is a bakery, and N is not a material participant. What is N's AGI after considering this activity?

47. R acquired an activity in 1985. The loss from the activity was $50,000 in 1990. R had adjusted gross income of $140,000 before considering the loss from the activity. The activity is a service station, and R is a material participant. What is R's AGI after considering this activity?

48. J acquired an activity in 1988. The loss from the activity was $50,000 in 1990. J had adjusted gross income of $140,000 before considering the loss from the

activity. The activity is a grocery store, and J is not a material participant. What is J's AGI after considering the activity?

49. D acquired an activity in 1988. The loss from the activity was $50,000 in 1990. D had adjusted gross income of $140,000 before considering the loss from the activity. The activity is a grocery store, and D is a material participant. What is D's AGI after considering the activity?

50. Taxpayer has investments in four passive activity partnerships purchased in 1984. In 1989, the income and losses were as follows:

Partnership	Income (Loss)
A	$ 60,000
B	(60,000)
C	(30,000)
D	(10,000)

In 1990, he sold all four interests as follows:

Partnership	Gain (Loss) on Sale*	1990 Income (Loss)
A	$ 80,000	$20,000
B	(20,000)	4,000
C	(17,000)	(9,000)
D	20,000	(3,000)

* Before suspended losses. (None before 1989).

a. Calculate taxpayer's deductible loss, if any, in 1989.

b. Calculate taxpayer's gain or loss on the sale of each of the partnerships and explain how the gains or losses are treated.

51. H and W are married with no dependents and live together in Ohio, which is not a community property state. Since W has large medical expenses, H and W seek your advice about filing separately to save taxes. Their income and expenses for 1990 are as follows:

H's salary	$ 60,000
W's salary	20,000
Dividends and interest (joint)	1,500
Rental loss from actively managed units (joint)	(22,000)
W's medical expenses	5,800
All other itemized deductions:*	
H	8,000
W	2,000

* None subject to limitations.

Would H and W pay less in taxes if they filed jointly or separately for 1990?

52. T, who has AGI of $80,000 before considering rental activities, is active in three separate rental real estate activities and is in the 28% tax bracket. She had $12,000 of losses from Activity A, $18,000 of losses from Activity B, and income of $10,000 from Activity C. She also had $2,100 of tax credits from Activity A. Calculate her deductions and credits allowed and the suspended losses and credits.

53. T died owning an interest in a passive activity property with an adjusted basis of $80,000, suspended losses of $8,000, and a fair market value of $85,000. What can be deducted on her final income tax return?

54. In 1989, T gave her son a passive activity with an adjusted basis of $100,000. Fair market value of the activity was $180,000, and the activity had suspended losses of $25,000. In 1990, the son realized income from the passive activity of $12,000. What is the effect on T and T's son in 1989 and 1990?

55. T invested $150,000 in a passive activity in 1982. On January 1, 1989, his adjusted basis in the activity was $30,000. His share of the losses in the activity were as follows:

Year	Gain (Loss)
1989	($40,000)
1990	(30,000)
1991	50,000

How much can T deduct in 1989 and 1990? What is T's taxable income from the activity in 1991? Keep in mind the at-risk rules as well as the passive loss rules.

56. Would your answer to Problem 55 differ if T had purchased the activity in 1987?

57. T acquired a passive activity in 1989 that generated tax credits of $2,000 and income of $4,000. The regular tax attributable to the income was $1,120. However, T paid taxes of $80,000 under the alternative minimum tax provisions. In 1990, the activity generated $1,000 of income upon which $280 of regular tax was due. T paid regular taxes that year of $40,000. When and how can he use the $2,000 of credits?

58. T sold a passive activity in 1990 for $150,000. His adjusted basis was $50,000. T used the installment method of reporting the gain. The activity had suspended losses of $12,000. T received $60,000 in the year of sale. What is his gain? How much of the suspended losses can T deduct?

59. If T in Problem 58 had no suspended losses, was in the 28% tax bracket, and had $10,000 of tax credits attributable to the activity, how much of the credits could he use in 1990?

7

DEDUCTIONS AND LOSSES: CERTAIN BUSINESS EXPENSES AND LOSSES

OBJECTIVES

Determine the amount of the bad debt deduction.

Distinguish between business and nonbusiness bad debts and recognize the tax consequences of the distinction.

Examine the tax treatment for worthless securities and § 1244 stock.

Calculate the amount of loss for business use property.

Define the term "casualty" and compute the amount of casualty and theft losses.

Recognize the alternative tax treatments for research and experimental expenditures.

Discuss the rationale for the net operating loss deduction.

Recognize the impact of the carryover of a net operating loss.

Working with the tax formula for individuals requires the proper classification of items that are deductible *for* adjusted gross income (AGI) and items that are deductions *from* AGI (itemized deductions). Business expenses and losses, discussed in this chapter, are reductions of gross income to arrive at the taxpayer's adjusted gross income. Expenses and losses incurred in connection with a transaction entered into for profit and expenses attributable to rents and royalties are deducted for AGI. All other expenses and losses incurred in connection with a transaction entered into for profit are deducted from AGI. Deductible losses on personal use property are deducted as itemized deductions. Itemized deductions are deductions from AGI.

Bad Debts

If a taxpayer sells goods or provides services on credit and the account receivable subsequently becomes worthless, a bad debt deduction is permitted only if income arising from the creation of the account receivable was previously included in income. No deduction is allowed, for example, for a bad debt arising from the sale of a product or service when the taxpayer is on the cash basis because no income is reported until the cash has been collected. Permitting a bad debt deduction for a cash basis taxpayer would amount to a double deduction because the expenses of the product or service rendered are deducted when payments are made to suppliers and to employees, or at the time of the sale.

EXAMPLE 1   T, an individual engaged in the practice of accounting, performed accounting services for X for which he charged $8,000 ($7,700 for services and $300 for materials). X never paid the bill, and his whereabouts are unknown.

If T is an accrual basis taxpayer, the $8,000 would be included in income when the services were performed. The $300 would be a business expense when the costs were incurred. When it is determined that X's account will not be collected, the $8,000 will be expensed as a bad debt.

If T is a cash basis taxpayer, the $8,000 would not be included in income until payment is received. However, the $300 would be a business expense at the time the expense was incurred. When it is determined that X's account will not be collected, the $8,000 will not be a bad debt expense since it was never recognized as income.   ☐

Specific Charge-Off Method

For tax years beginning after 1986, taxpayers (other than certain financial institutions) may use only the *specific charge-off* method in accounting for bad debts. The *reserve* method for computing deductions for bad debts is allowed only for certain financial institutions.

A taxpayer using the specific charge-off method may claim a deduction when a specific business debt becomes either partially or wholly worthless or when a specific nonbusiness debt becomes wholly worthless. The taxpayer must satisfy the IRS that a debt is partially worthless and must demonstrate the amount of worthlessness.

If a business debt previously deducted as partially worthless becomes totally worthless in a future year, only the remainder not previously deducted can be deducted in the future year.

In the case of total worthlessness, a deduction is allowed for the entire amount in the year the debt becomes worthless. The amount of the deduction depends on

the taxpayer's basis in the bad debt. If the debt arose from the sale of services or products and the face amount was previously included in income, that amount is deductible. If the taxpayer purchased the debt, the deduction is equal to the amount the taxpayer paid for the debt instrument.

One of the more difficult tasks is determining if and when a bad debt is worthless. The loss is deductible only in the year of partial or total worthlessness for business debts and only in the year of total worthlessness for nonbusiness debts. Legal proceedings need not be initiated against the debtor when the surrounding facts indicate that such action will not result in collection.

EXAMPLE 2
In 1988, J loaned $1,000 to K, who agreed to repay the loan in two years. In 1990, K disappeared after the note became delinquent. If a reasonable investigation by J indicates that he cannot find K or that a suit against K would not result in collection, J can deduct the $1,000 in 1990. □

Bankruptcy is generally an indication of at least partial worthlessness of a debt. Bankruptcy may create worthlessness before the settlement date. If this is the case, the deduction must be taken in the year of worthlessness, not in the later year upon settlement.

EXAMPLE 3
In Example 2, assume K filed for personal bankruptcy in 1989 and that the debt is a business debt. At that time, J learned that unsecured creditors (including J) were expected to receive ultimately 20¢ on the dollar. In 1990, settlement is made and J receives only $150. He should deduct $800 ($1,000 loan less $200 expected settlement) in 1989 and $50 in 1990 ($200 balance less $150 proceeds). J is not permitted to wait until 1990 to deduct the entire $850. □

Reserve Method.   As a result of the repeal of the reserve method, the balance in any reserve for bad debts is includible in income ratably over a period of four years. This inclusion begins with the first tax year beginning after December 31, 1986.

Business versus Nonbusiness Bad Debts

A *nonbusiness* bad debt is a debt unrelated to the taxpayer's trade or business either when it was created or when it became worthless. The nature of a debt

---

CONCEPT SUMMARY 7−1

Specific Charge-Off Method

Expense deduction and account write-off	The expense arises and the write-off takes place when a specific business account becomes either partially or wholly worthless or when a specific nonbusiness account becomes wholly worthless.
Recovery of accounts previously written off	If the account recovered was written off during the current taxable year, the write-off entry is reversed. If the account recovered was written off during a previous taxable year, income is recognized subject to the tax benefit rule.

depends on whether the lender was engaged in the business of lending money or if there is a proximate relationship between the creation of the debt and the lender's trade or business. The use to which the borrowed funds are put by the debtor is of no consequence. Loans to relatives or friends are the most common type of nonbusiness bad debt.

EXAMPLE 4   J loaned his friend, S, $1,500. S used the money to start a business, which subsequently failed. Even though proceeds of the loan were used in a business, the loan is a nonbusiness bad debt because the business was S's, not J's. □

The distinction between a business bad debt and a nonbusiness bad debt is important. A business bad debt is deductible as an ordinary loss in the year incurred, whereas a nonbusiness bad debt is always treated as a short-term capital loss. Thus, regardless of the age of a nonbusiness bad debt, the deduction may be of limited benefit due to the capital loss limitations on deductibility in any one year. The maximum amount of a net short-term capital loss that an individual can deduct against ordinary income in any one year is $3,000 (see chapter 13 for a detailed discussion). Although no deduction is allowed when a nonbusiness bad debt is partially worthless, the taxpayer is entitled to deduct the net amount of the loss upon final settlement.

The following examples are illustrations of business bad debts adapted from the Regulations.[1]

EXAMPLE 5   In 1989, L sold his business but retained a claim (note or account receivable) against B. The claim became worthless in 1990. L's loss is treated as a business bad debt because the debt was created in the conduct of L's former trade or business. Business bad debt treatment is accorded to L despite the fact that he was holding the note as an investor and was no longer in a trade or business when the claim became worthless. □

EXAMPLE 6   In 1988, L died and left his business assets to his son, S. One of the business assets inherited by S was a claim against B that became worthless in S's hands in 1990. S's loss is a business bad debt since the loss is sustained as a proximate incident to the conduct of the trade or business in which S is engaged at the time the debt becomes worthless. □

The nonbusiness bad debt provisions are not applicable to corporations. It is assumed that any loans made by a corporation are related to its trade or business. Therefore, any bad debts of a corporation are business bad debts.

Loss of Deposits in Insolvent Financial Institutions

Qualified individuals can *elect* to deduct losses on deposits in qualified financial institutions as personal casualty losses in the year in which the amount of the loss can be reasonably estimated. If the election is made to treat a loss on a deposit as

---

1. Reg. § 1.166–5(d).

a personal casualty loss, no bad debt deduction for the loss will be allowed. As a personal casualty loss, the loss would be subject to the $100 per event floor and the 10 percent of AGI aggregate floor. Both floors limiting casualty losses are explained later in the chapter. The amount of loss to be recognized under the election is the difference between (1) the taxpayer's basis in the deposit and (2) a reasonable estimate of the amount to be received.

If the individual does not elect to deduct the loss as a casualty loss, it will be treated as a nonbusiness bad debt and, hence, as a short-term capital loss. As a short-term capital loss, it will be subject to the capital loss limitation rules (refer to the discussion in chapter 13).

Loans between Related Parties

Loans between related parties (especially family members) raise the issue of whether the loan was *bona fide* or was a gift. The Regulations state that a bona fide debt arises from a debtor-creditor relationship based on a valid and enforceable obligation to pay a fixed or determinable sum of money. Thus, individual circumstances must be examined to determine whether transfers between related parties are gifts or loans. Some considerations are these:

- Was a note properly executed?
- Was there a reasonable rate of interest?
- Is there collateral?
- What collection efforts were made?
- What was the intent of the parties?

EXAMPLE 7	L loans $2,000 to his widowed mother for an operation. L's mother owns no property and is not employed, and her only income consists of Social Security benefits. No note is issued for the loan, no provision for interest is made, and no repayment date is mentioned. In the current year, L's mother dies leaving no estate. Assuming the loan is not repaid, L cannot take a deduction for a nonbusiness bad debt because the facts indicate that no debtor-creditor relationship existed. □

WORTHLESS SECURITIES

A loss is allowed under § 165 for a security that becomes completely worthless during the year. Such securities are shares of stock, bonds, notes, or other evidence of indebtedness issued by a corporation or government. The losses generated are usually treated as capital losses deemed to have occurred on the *last day* of the taxable year. By treating the loss as having occurred on the last day of the taxable year, a loss that otherwise would have been classified as short term (if the date of worthlessness was used) may be classified as a long-term capital loss. Capital losses may be of limited benefit due to the $3,000 capital loss limitation.

EXAMPLE 8	T, a calendar year taxpayer, owns stock in X Corporation (a publicly held company). The stock was acquired as an investment on November 30, 1989, at a cost of $5,000. On April 1, 1990, the stock became worthless. Since the stock

CONCEPT SUMMARY 7–2

Bad Debt Deductions

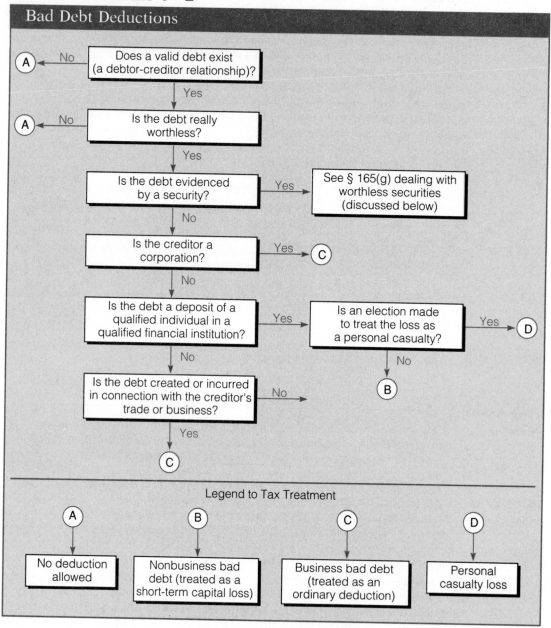

is deemed to have become worthless as of December 31 of 1990, T has a capital loss from an asset held for 13 months (a long-term capital loss). □

Securities in Affiliated Corporations

If securities of an affiliated corporation become worthless during the taxable year, the corporate taxpayer's loss will be treated as an *ordinary loss* rather than a capital loss. A corporation is treated as an affiliated corporation to the parent if two requirements are satisfied. First, the corporate shareholder must own at least 80

percent of the voting power of all classes of stock and at least 80 percent of each class of nonvoting stock of the affiliated company. Second, more than 90 percent of the gross receipts of the affiliate must be from sources other than royalties, rents, dividends, interest, annuities, and gains from sales or exchanges of stocks and securities.

Small Business Stock

The general rule is that shareholders receive capital gain or loss treatment upon the sale or exchange of stock. However, it is possible to receive an ordinary loss deduction if the loss is sustained on small business stock—§ 1244 stock. This loss could arise from a sale of the stock or from the stock becoming worthless. Only *individuals*[2] who acquired the stock from the corporation are eligible to receive ordinary loss treatment under § 1244, and the ordinary loss treatment is limited to $50,000 ($100,000 for married individuals filing jointly) per year. The corporation must meet certain qualifications for the worthlessness of § 1244 stock to be treated as an *ordinary*—rather than a capital—loss. The major qualification is that the total amount of money and other property received by the corporation for stock as a contribution to capital (or paid-in surplus) does not exceed $1,000,000. The $1,000,000 test is made at the time of the issuance of the stock. Section 1244 stock can be common or preferred stock. Section 1244 applies only to losses. If § 1244 stock is sold at a gain, the Section has no application, and the gain will be capital gain.

EXAMPLE 9   On July 1, 1988, T, a single individual, purchased 100 shares of X Corporation common stock for $100,000. The X stock qualified as § 1244 stock. On June 20, 1990, T sold all of the X stock for $20,000. Because the X stock is § 1244 stock, T would have $50,000 of ordinary loss and $30,000 of long-term capital loss.

□

LOSSES OF INDIVIDUALS

An individual may deduct the following losses under § 165(c):

- Losses incurred in a trade or business.

- Losses incurred in a transaction entered into for profit.

- Losses caused by fire, storm, shipwreck, or other casualty or by theft.

A taxpayer suffering losses from damage to nonbusiness property can deduct only those losses attributable to fire, storm, shipwreck, or other casualty or theft. Although the meaning of the terms "fire, storm, shipwreck, and theft" is relatively free from dispute, the term "other casualty" needs further clarification. It means casualties analogous to fire, storm, or shipwreck. The term also includes accidental loss of property provided the loss qualifies under the same rules as any other casualty. These rules are that the loss must result from an event that is (1) identifiable; (2) damaging to property; and (3) sudden, unexpected, and unusual in nature. A *sudden event* is one that is swift and precipitous and not gradual or progressive. An *unexpected event* is an event that is ordinarily unanticipated and

---

2. The term "individuals" includes a partnership but not a trust or an estate.

occurs without the intent of the one who suffers the loss. An *unusual event* is one that is extraordinary and nonrecurring, that does not commonly occur during the activity in which the taxpayer was engaged when the destruction occurred. Examples include hurricanes, tornadoes, floods, storms, shipwrecks, fires, auto accidents, mine cave-ins, sonic booms, and vandalism. Weather that causes damages (drought, for example) must be unusual and severe for the particular region. Damage must be to the taxpayer's property to qualify as a casualty loss.

The deduction for a casualty loss from an automobile accident can be taken only if the damage was not caused by the taxpayer's willful act or willful negligence.

EXAMPLE 10   T parks her car on a hill and fails to set the brake properly and to curb the wheels. As a result of T's negligence, the car rolls down the hill and is damaged. The repairs to T's car should qualify for casualty loss treatment since T's act of negligence appears to be simple rather than willful. □

Events That Are Not Casualties

Not all "acts of God" are treated as casualty losses for income tax purposes. Because a casualty must be sudden, unexpected, and unusual, progressive deterioration (such as erosion due to wind or rain) is not a casualty because it does not meet the suddenness test.

Examples of nonsudden events that do not qualify as casualties include disease and insect damages. In the past, some courts have held that termite damage over periods of up to 15 months after infestation constituted a sudden event and was, therefore, deductible as a casualty loss.[3] On the other hand, when the damage was caused by termites over periods of several years, some courts have disallowed a casualty loss deduction.[4] Despite the existence of some judicial support for the deductibility of termite damage as a casualty loss, the current position of the IRS is that termite damage is not deductible.[5]

Other examples of events that are not casualties are losses resulting from a decline in value rather than an actual loss of the property. No loss was allowed where the taxpayer's home declined in value as a result of a landslide that destroyed neighboring homes but did no actual damage to the taxpayer's home.[6] Similarly, a taxpayer was allowed a loss for the actual flood damage to his property but not for the decline in market value due to the property's being flood-prone.[7]

The Eleventh Court of Appeals has stated that loss of present value generated by a fear of future damage cannot be factored into the fair market value of the property. However, the Court has held that permanent buyer resistance, as evidenced by changes made to the neighborhood surrounding the taxpayer's home following a flood, does affect the fair market value and may be included in a determination as to what the fair market value is after the disaster.[8]

3. *Rosenberg v. Comm.*, 52–2, USTC ¶9377, 42 AFTR 303, 198 F.2d 46 (CA–8, 1952); *Shopmaker v. U.S.*, 54–1 USTC ¶9195, 45 AFTR 758, 119 F.Supp. 705 (D.Ct.Mo., 1953).

4. *Fay v. Helvering*, 41–2 USTC ¶9494, 27 AFTR 432, 120 F.2d 253 (CA–2, 1941); *U.S. v. Rogers*, 41–1 USTC ¶9442, 27 AFTR 423, 120 F.2d 244 (CA–9, 1941).

5. Rev.Rul. 63–232, 1963–2 C.B. 97.

6. *H. Pulvers v. Comm.*, 69–1 USTC ¶9222, 23 AFTR2d 69–678, 407 F.2d 838 (CA–9, 1969).

7. *S. L. Solomon*, 39 TCM 1282, T.C.Memo 1980–87.

8. *Finkbohner, Jr. v. U.S.*, 86–1 USTC ¶9393, 57 AFTR2d 86–1400, 788 F.2d 723 (CA–11, 1986).

Theft Losses

Theft includes, but is not necessarily limited to, larceny, embezzlement, and robbery. Theft does not include misplaced items.

Theft losses are computed like other casualty losses (discussed in the following section), but the *timing* for recognition of the loss differs. A theft loss is deducted in the year of discovery, not the year of the theft (unless, of course, the discovery occurs in the same year as the theft). If, in the year of the discovery, a claim exists (e.g., against an insurance company) and there is a reasonable expectation of recovering the fair market value of the asset from the insurance company, no deduction is permitted. If, in the year of settlement, the recovery is less than the asset's fair market value, a partial deduction may be available.

EXAMPLE 11   J's new sailboat was stolen from the storage marina in December 1988. He discovered the loss on June 3, 1989, and filed a claim with his insurance company that was settled on January 30, 1990. Assuming there is a reasonable expectation of full recovery, no deduction is allowed in 1989. A partial deduction may be available in 1990 if the actual insurance proceeds are less than the lower of the adjusted basis or decline in fair market value of the asset. (Loss measurement rules are discussed later in this chapter.) □

When to Deduct Casualty Losses

General Rule.   Generally, a casualty loss is deducted in the year the loss occurs. However, no casualty loss is permitted if a reimbursement claim with a *reasonable prospect of full recovery* exists.[9] If the taxpayer has a partial claim, only part of the loss can be claimed in the year of the casualty, and the remainder is deducted in the year the claim is settled.

EXAMPLE 12   G's new sailboat was completely destroyed by fire in 1990. Its cost and fair market value were $10,000. G's only claim against the insurance company was on a $7,000 policy that was not settled by year-end. The following year, 1991, G settled with the insurance company for $6,000. G is entitled to a $3,000 deduction in 1990 and a $1,000 deduction in 1991. If the sailboat were held for personal use, the $3,000 deduction in 1990 would be reduced first by $100 and then by 10% of G's 1990 adjusted gross income. The $1,000 deduction in 1991 would be reduced by 10% of G's 1991 adjusted gross income (see the following discussion). □

If a taxpayer receives reimbursement for a casualty loss sustained and deducted in a previous year, an amended return is not filed for that year. Instead, the taxpayer must include the reimbursement in gross income on the return for the year in which it is received to the extent that the previous deduction resulted in a tax benefit.

Disaster Area Losses.   An exception to the general rule for the time of deduction is allowed for casualties sustained in an area designated as a disaster

---

9. Reg § 1.165-1(d)(2)(i).

area by the President of the United States. In such cases, the taxpayer may *elect* to treat the loss as having occurred in the taxable year immediately preceding the taxable year in which the disaster actually occurred. The rationale for this exception is to provide immediate relief to disaster victims in the form of accelerated tax benefits.

If the due date, plus extensions, for the prior year's return has not passed, a taxpayer makes the election to claim the disaster area loss on the prior year's tax return. If the disaster occurs after the prior year's return has been filed, it is necessary to file either an amended return or a refund claim. In any case, the taxpayer must show clearly that such an election is being made.

Disaster loss treatment also applies in the case of a personal residence that has been rendered unsafe for use as a residence because of a disaster. This provision applies when, within 120 days after the President designates the area as a disaster area, the state or local government where the residence is located orders the taxpayer to demolish or relocate the residence.

Measuring the Amount of Loss

Amount of Loss.   The rules for determining the amount of a loss depend in part on whether business use or personal use property was involved. Another factor that must be considered is whether the property was partially or completely destroyed.

If business property or property held for the production of income (e.g., rental property) is *completely destroyed*, the loss is always equal to the adjusted basis of the property at the time of destruction.

EXAMPLE 13   T's automobile, which was used only for business, was destroyed by fire. T had unintentionally allowed his insurance coverage to expire. The fair market value of the automobile was $9,000 at the time of the fire, and its adjusted basis was $10,000. T is allowed a loss deduction of $10,000 (the basis of the automobile). The $10,000 loss is a deduction *for* AGI.   □

A different measurement rule applies for *partial destruction* of business property and property held for the production of income, and for *partial* or *complete destruction* of personal use property. In these situations, the loss is the *lesser* of the following:

1. The adjusted basis of the property.

2. The difference between the fair market value of the property before the event and the fair market value immediately after the event.

EXAMPLE 14   K's automobile, which is used only for business purposes, was damaged in a wreck. At the date of the wreck, the fair market value of the automobile was $12,000, and its adjusted basis was $9,000. After the wreck, the value of the automobile was appraised at $4,000. K's loss deduction is $8,000 (the lesser of adjusted basis or the decrease in fair market value). The $8,000 loss is a deduction *for* AGI.   □

The deduction for the loss of property that is part business and part personal must be computed separately for the business portion and the personal portion.

Any insurance recovery reduces the loss for business, production of income, and personal use losses. In fact, a taxpayer may realize a gain if the insurance proceeds exceed the amount of the loss. Chapter 13 discusses the treatment of net gains and losses on business property and property held for the production of income.

A taxpayer will not be permitted to deduct a casualty loss for damage to insured personal use property unless he or she files a timely insurance claim with respect to the damage to the property. This rule applies to the extent that any insurance policy provides for full or partial reimbursement for the loss.

Generally, an appraisal before and after the casualty is needed to measure the amount of the loss. However, the cost of repairs to the damaged property is acceptable as a method of establishing the loss in value provided the following criteria are met:

- The repairs are necessary to restore the property to its condition immediately before the casualty.

- The amount spent for such repairs is not excessive.

- The repairs do not extend beyond the damage suffered.

- The value of the property after the repairs does not, as a result of the repairs, exceed the value of the property immediately before the casualty.[10]

Reduction for $100 and 10 Percent of AGI.   The amount of the loss for personal use property must be reduced by a $100 per event floor and a 10 percent of AGI aggregate floor. The $100 floor applies separately to each casualty and applies to the entire loss from each casualty. For example, if a storm damages both a taxpayer's residence and automobile, only $100 is subtracted from the total amount of the loss. The losses are then added together, and the total is reduced by 10 percent of the taxpayer's adjusted gross income. The resulting loss is the taxpayer's itemized deduction for casualty and theft losses.

EXAMPLE 15   G, who had AGI of $30,000, was involved in a motorcycle accident. His motorcycle, which had a fair market value of $12,000 and an adjusted basis of $9,000, was completely destroyed. He received $5,000 from his insurance company. G's casualty loss deduction is $900 [$9,000 basis − $5,000 insurance − $100 floor − $3,000 (.10 × $30,000 AGI)]. The $900 casualty loss is an itemized deduction (*from* AGI). □

When a nonbusiness casualty loss is spread between two taxable years because of the *reasonable prospect of recovery* doctrine, the loss in the second year is not reduced by the $100 floor. This result occurs because this floor is imposed per event and has already reduced the amount of the loss in the first year. However, the loss in the second year is still subject to the 10 percent floor based on the taxpayer's second year adjusted gross income (refer to Example 12).

Taxpayers who suffer qualified disaster area losses can elect to deduct such losses in the year preceding the year of occurrence. The disaster loss will be treated as having occurred in the preceding taxable year, and hence, the 10 percent of AGI floor will be determined by using the adjusted gross income of the year for which the deduction is claimed.

---

10. Reg. § 1.165–7(a)(2)(ii).

Multiple Losses.   The rules for computing loss deductions where there are multiple losses are explained in Examples 16 and 17.

EXAMPLE 16   During the year, T had the following losses:

Asset	Adjusted Basis	Fair Market Value of Asset		Insurance Recovery
		Before the Casualty	After the Casualty	
A	$900	$600	$–0–	$400
B	300	800	250	100

Assets A and B were used in T's business at the time of the casualty. The following losses are allowed:

Asset A: $500. The complete destruction of a business asset results in a deduction of the adjusted basis of the property (reduced by any insurance recovery) regardless of the asset's fair market value.

Asset B: $200. The partial destruction of a business (or personal) asset results in a deduction equal to the lesser of the adjusted basis ($300) or the decline in value ($550), reduced by any insurance recovery ($100). Both Asset A and Asset B losses are deductions *for* adjusted gross income. The $100 floor and the 10% of AGI floor do not apply because the assets are business assets.   □

EXAMPLE 17   During the year, T had adjusted gross income of $20,000 and the following separate casualty losses:

Asset	Adjusted Basis	Fair Market Value of Asset		Insurance Recovery
		Before the Casualty	After the Casualty	
A	$ 900	$ 600	$ –0–	$ 200
B	2,500	4,000	1,000	–0–
C	800	400	100	250

Assets A, B, and C were held for personal use, and the losses to these three assets are from three different casualties. The computation of the loss for each asset is as follows:

Asset A: $300. The lesser of the adjusted basis of $900 or the $600 decline in value, reduced by the insurance recovery of $200, minus the $100 floor.

Asset B: $2,400. The lesser of the adjusted basis of $2,500 or the $3,000 decline in value, minus the $100 floor.

Asset C: $0. The lesser of the adjusted basis of $800 or the $300 decline in value, reduced by the insurance recovery of $250, minus the $100 floor.

T's itemized casualty loss deduction for the year is $700:

Asset A loss	$ 300
Asset B loss	2,400
Asset C loss	–0–
Total loss	$ 2,700
Less: 10% of AGI (10% × $20,000)	(2,000)
Itemized casualty loss deduction	$ 700

☐

Statutory Framework for Deducting Losses of Individuals

Casualty and theft losses incurred by an individual in connection with a trade or business are deductible *for* adjusted gross income. These losses are not subject to the $100 per event and the 10 percent of AGI limitations.

Losses incurred by an individual in a transaction entered into for profit are not subject to the $100 per event and the 10 percent of AGI limitations. If these losses are attributable to rents or royalties, the deduction is *for* AGI. However, if these losses are not connected with property held for the production of rents and royalties, they are deductions *from* AGI. More specifically, these losses are classified as other miscellaneous itemized deductions. An example of this type of loss would be a theft of a security. The aggregate of certain miscellaneous itemized deductions is subject to a 2 percent of AGI floor (explained in chapter 10).

Casualty and theft losses attributable to personal use property are subject to the $100 per event and the 10 percent of AGI limitations. These losses are itemized deductions, but they are not subject to the 2 percent of AGI floor. The treatment of casualty gains and losses is summarized in Concept Summary 7–3.

Personal Casualty Gains and Losses

If a taxpayer has personal casualty and theft gains as well as losses, a special set of rules applies for determining the tax consequences. The term *personal casualty gain* means the recognized gain from a casualty or theft. A *personal casualty loss* for this purpose is a casualty or theft loss after the application of the $100 floor. A taxpayer who has both gains and losses for the taxable year must first net (offset) the personal casualty gains and personal casualty losses. If the gains exceed the losses, the gains and losses will be treated as gains and losses from the sale of capital assets. The capital gains and losses will be short term or long term, depending on the period the taxpayer held each of the assets. In the netting process, personal casualty and theft gains and losses are not netted with the gains and losses on business and production of income property.

EXAMPLE 18   During the year, T had the following personal casualty gains and losses (after deducting the $100 floor):

Asset	Holding Period	Gain or (Loss)
A	Three months	($ 300)
B	Three years	(2,400)
C	Two years	3,200

T would compute the tax consequences as follows:

Personal casualty gain	$ 3,200
Personal casualty loss ($300 + $2,400)	(2,700)
Net personal casualty gain	$ 500

T would treat all of the gains and losses as capital gains and losses and would have the following:

Short-term capital loss (Asset A)	$ 300
Long-term capital loss (Asset B)	2,400
Long-term capital gain (Asset C)	3,200

□

If personal casualty losses exceed personal casualty gains, all gains and losses are treated as ordinary items. The gains—and the losses to the extent of gains—will

CONCEPT SUMMARY 7−3

Casualty Gains and Losses

	Business Use or Production of Income Property	Personal Use Property
Event creating the loss	Any loss sustained.	Casualty or theft loss.
Amount	The lesser of the decline in fair market value or the adjusted basis, but always the adjusted basis if the property is totally destroyed.	The lesser of the decline in fair market value or the adjusted basis.
Insurance	Insurance proceeds received reduce the amount of the loss.	Insurance proceeds received (or for which there is an unfiled claim) reduce the amount of the loss.
$100 floor	Not applicable.	Applicable per event.
Gains and losses	Gains and losses are netted (see detailed discussion in chapter 13).	Personal casualty and theft gains and losses are netted.
Gains exceeding losses		The gains and losses are treated as gains and losses from the sale of capital assets.

(Continued)	**Business Use or Production of Income Property**	**Personal Use Property**
Losses exceeding gains		The gains—and the losses to the extent of gains—are treated as ordinary items in computing adjusted gross income. The losses in excess of gains, to the extent they exceed 10% of adjusted gross income, are itemized deductions.

be treated as ordinary income and ordinary loss in computing adjusted gross income. Losses in excess of gains are deducted as itemized deductions to the extent such losses exceed 10 percent of adjusted gross income.

EXAMPLE 19

During the year, T had adjusted gross income of $20,000 and the following personal casualty gain and loss (after deducting the $100 floor):

Asset	Holding Period	Gain or (Loss)
A	Three years	($2,700)
B	Four months	200

T would compute the tax consequences as follows:

Personal casualty loss	($2,700)
Personal casualty gain	200
Net personal casualty loss	($2,500)

T would treat the gain and the loss as ordinary items. The $200 gain and $200 of the loss would be included in computing adjusted gross income. T's itemized deduction for casualty losses would be computed as follows:

Casualty loss in excess of gain ($2,700 − $200)	$ 2,500
Less: 10% of AGI (10% × $20,000)	(2,000)
Itemized deduction	$ 500

☐

RESEARCH AND EXPERIMENTAL EXPENDITURES

Section 174 covers the treatment of *research and experimental expenditures*. The Regulations define research and experimental expenditures as follows:

. . . all such costs incident to the development of an experimental or pilot model, a plant process, a product, a formula, an invention, or similar property, and the

improvement of already existing property of the type mentioned. The term does not include expenditures such as those for the ordinary testing or inspection of materials or products for quality control or those for efficiency surveys, management studies, consumer surveys, advertising, or promotions.[11]

Expenses in connection with the acquisition or improvement of land or depreciable property are not research and experimental expenditures. Rather, they increase the basis of the land or depreciable property. However, depreciation on a building used for research may be a research and experimental expense. Only the depreciation that is a research and experimental expense (not the cost of the asset) is subject to the three alternatives discussed below.

The law permits the following three alternatives for the handling of research and experimental expenditures.

- Expensing in the year paid or incurred.
- Deferral and amortization.
- Capitalization.

If the costs are capitalized, a deduction may not be available until the research project is abandoned or is deemed worthless. Since many products resulting from research projects do not have a definite and limited useful life, a taxpayer should ordinarily elect to write off the expenditures immediately or to defer and amortize them. It is generally preferable to elect an immediate write-off of the research expenditures because of the time value of the tax deduction.

The law also provides for a research activities credit. The credit amounts to 20 percent of certain research and experimental expenditures. (The credit is discussed more fully in chapter 11.)

Expense Method

A taxpayer can elect to expense all of the research and experimental expenditures incurred in the current year and all subsequent years. The consent of the IRS is not required if the method is adopted for the first taxable year in which such expenditures were paid or incurred. Once such an election is made, the taxpayer must continue to expense all qualifying expenditures unless a request for a change is made to the IRS. In certain instances, a taxpayer may incur research and experimental expenditures before actually engaging in any trade or business activity. In such instances, the Supreme Court has applied a liberal standard of deductibility and permitted a deduction in the year of incurrence.[12]

Deferral and Amortization Method

The deferral and amortization method is allowed for the treatment of research and experimental expenditures if the taxpayer makes an election. Under the election, research and experimental expenditures are amortized ratably over a period of not less than 60 months. A deduction is allowed beginning with the month in which the taxpayer first realizes benefits from the experimental expenditure. The election is binding, and a change requires permission from the IRS.

The option to treat research and experimental expenditures as deferred expense is usually employed when a company does not have sufficient income to

---

11. Reg. § 1.174–2(a)(1).

12. *Snow v. Comm.*, 74–1 USTC ¶9432, 33 AFTR2d   74–1251, 94 S.Ct. 1876 (USSC, 1974).

offset the research and experimental expenses. Rather than create net operating loss carryovers that might not be utilized because of the 15-year limitation on such carryovers, the deferral and amortization method may be used. The deferral of research and experimental expenditures should also be considered if the taxpayer expects higher tax rates in the future.

NET OPERATING LOSSES

The requirement that every taxpayer file an annual income tax return (whether on a calendar year or a fiscal year) may result in certain inequities for taxpayers who experience cyclical patterns of income or expense. Inequities result from the application of a progressive rate structure to amounts of taxable income determined on an annual basis. A net operating loss in a particular tax year would produce no tax benefit if the Code did not include provisions for the carryback and carryforward of such losses to profitable years.

EXAMPLE 20

J has a business that realizes the following taxable income or loss over a five-year period: Year 1, $50,000; Year 2, ($30,000); Year 3, $100,000; Year 4, ($200,000); and Year 5, $380,000. She is married and files a joint return. P, on the other hand, has a taxable income pattern of $60,000 every year. He, too, is married and files a joint return. Note that both J and P have total taxable income of $300,000 over the five-year period. Assume there is no provision for carrybacks or carryover of net operating losses. A comparison of their five-year tax bills follows:

Year	J's Tax	P's Tax
1	$ 9,782	$12,582
2	–0–	12,582
3	24,862	12,582
4	–0–	12,582
5	107,548	12,582
	$142,192	$62,910

The computation of tax is made without regard to any net operating loss benefit. Rates from the 1990 Tax Rate Schedule are used to compute the tax.

Even though J and P realized the same total income ($300,000) over the five-year period, J had to pay taxes of $142,192, while P paid taxes of $62,910. □

To provide partial relief from this inequitable tax treatment, a deduction is allowed for net operating losses. This provision permits the offset of net operating losses for any one year against taxable income of other years. A net operating loss is intended as a relief provision for business income and losses. Thus, only losses from the operation of a trade or business (or profession), casualty and theft losses, or losses from the confiscation of a business by a foreign government can create a net operating loss. In other words, a salaried individual with itemized deductions and personal exemptions in excess of gross income is not permitted to deduct such excess amounts as a net operating loss. On the other hand, a personal casualty loss is treated as a business loss and can therefore create (or increase) a net operating loss for a salaried individual.

Carryback and Carryover Periods

General Rules.   A net operating loss must be applied initially to the three taxable years preceding the year of the loss, unless an election is made not to carry the loss back at all. It is carried first to the third prior year, then to the second prior year, then to the immediately preceding tax year (or until used up). If the loss is not fully used in the carryback period, it must be carried forward to the first year after the loss year, and then forward to the second, third, etc., year after the loss year. The carryover period is 15 years. If a loss is sustained in 1990, it is used in this order: 1987, 1988, 1989, 1991 through 2005.

If the loss is being carried to a preceding year, an amended return is filed on Form 1040X or a quick refund claim is filed on Form 1045. In any case, a refund of taxes previously paid is requested. When the loss is carried forward, the current return shows a net operating loss deduction for the prior year's loss.

Sequence of Use of NOLs.   Where there are net operating losses in two or more years, the rule is always to use the earliest year's loss first until it is completely absorbed. The later years' losses can then be used until they also are absorbed or lost. Thus, one year's return could show net operating loss carryovers from two or more years. Each loss is computed and applied separately.

Election to Forgo Carryback.   A taxpayer can *irrevocably elect* not to carry back a net operating loss to any of the three prior years. In such case, the loss is available as a carryover for 15 years. A taxpayer would make the election if it is to his or her tax advantage. For example, a taxpayer might be in a low marginal tax bracket in the carryback years but expect to be in a high marginal tax bracket in future years. Therefore, it would be to the taxpayer's advantage to use the net operating loss to offset income in years when the tax rate is high rather than use it when the tax rate is relatively low.

Computation of the Net Operating Loss

Since the net operating loss provisions apply solely to business-related losses, certain adjustments must be made to reflect a taxpayer's *economic* loss. The required adjustments for corporate taxpayers are usually insignificant because a corporation's tax loss is generally similar to its economic loss. However, in computing taxable income, individual taxpayers are allowed deductions for such items as personal and dependency exemptions and itemized deductions that do not reflect actual business-related economic losses. Detailed coverage of the net operating loss computation is beyond the scope of this text.

TAX PLANNING CONSIDERATIONS

Documentation of Related-Taxpayer Loans, Casualty Losses, and Theft Losses

Since non-bona fide loans between related taxpayers may be treated as gifts, adequate documentation is needed to substantiate a bad debt deduction if the loan subsequently becomes worthless. Documentation should include proper execution of the note (legal form) and the establishment of a bona fide purpose for the loan. In addition, it is desirable to stipulate a reasonable rate of interest and a fixed maturity date.

Since a theft loss is not permitted for misplaced items, a loss should be documented by a police report and evidence of the value of the property (e.g., appraisals, pictures of the property, newspaper clippings). Similar documentation of the value of property should be provided to support a casualty loss deduction because the amount of loss is measured by the decline in fair market value of the property.

Casualty loss deductions must be reported on Form 4684.

Small Business Stock

Because § 1244 limits the amount of loss classified as ordinary loss on a yearly basis, a taxpayer might maximize the benefits of § 1244 by selling the stock in more than one taxable year. The result could be that the losses in any one taxable year would not exceed the § 1244 limits on ordinary loss.

Casualty Losses

A special election is available for taxpayers who sustain casualty losses in an area designated by the President as a disaster area. This election affects only the timing, not the calculation, of the deduction. The deduction can be taken in the year before the year in which the loss occurred. Thus, an individual can take the deduction on the 1989 return for a loss occurring between January 1 and December 31, 1990. The benefit, of course, is a faster refund (or reduction in tax). It will also be advantageous to carry the loss back if the taxpayer's tax rate in the carryback year is higher than the tax rate in the year of the loss.

To find out if an event qualifies as a disaster area loss, one can look in any of the major tax services or in the Weekly Compilation of Presidential Documents or the Internal Revenue Bulletin.

PROBLEM MATERIALS

Discussion Questions

1. Dr. T, an individual, cash basis taxpayer, is engaged in the general practice of dentistry. Dr. T performed extensive bridge and crown work on Mr. S, for which he charged $3,500 ($2,500 for services and $1,000 for materials and lab work). Since Mr. S never paid the bill and has left for parts unknown, Dr. T feels that he is entitled to a bad debt deduction of $3,500. Comment on Dr. T's tax position on this matter.

2. B made a loan to a friend three years ago to help the friend purchase an automobile. B's friend has notified him that the car has been sold and the most he will be able to repay is 50% of the loan. Discuss the possibility of B taking a bad debt deduction for half of the loan.

3. Discuss the difference between business and nonbusiness bad debts. How is the distinction determined? How is each treated on the return?

4. What factors are to be considered in determining whether a bad debt arising from a loan between related parties is, in fact, a bad debt?

5. Discuss a taxpayer's options for the tax treatment of a loss incurred on a deposit in a qualified financial institution. Also note the consequences of each option.

6. Discuss the tax treatment of any remaining balance in a reserve for bad debts account.

7. Discuss whether a bond that is worthless is a worthless security or a bad debt.

8. Compare the tax treatment of losses on § 1244 stock with the usual treatment of losses on capital stock.

9. Suspecting that inventory has been taken from his business, D takes a count of the merchandise. The count verifies that D has indeed lost inventory. Given the fact that D cannot prove theft of the merchandise, discuss whether D, an individual, may take a deduction for the loss of the merchandise.

10. What "acts of God" give rise to a casualty loss? Which ones do not? Discuss.

11. When casualty losses exceed casualty gains, the amount of the casualty loss subject to the 10% of AGI floor is only the casualty loss in excess of casualty gains. Discuss the significance of netting losses against gains in this manner rather than having the entire casualty loss subject to the 10% of AGI floor.

12. What is a disaster area loss? Why might a taxpayer benefit from making the disaster area loss election?

13. Discuss the tax consequences of not making an insurance claim when insured personal use property is subject to a casualty or theft loss.

14. Is it generally advantageous for a taxpayer to spread a casualty loss between two years under the reasonable prospect of recovery doctrine?

15. M's 10-year-old automobile was extensively damaged in a collision in which he was not at fault. The original cost of the automobile was $10,000, and the cost of repairing it was $5,000. Discuss any problems with using the $5,000 as the measurement of the loss.

16. Discuss whether a loss in connection with a transaction entered into for profit is a deduction *for* adjusted gross income or *from* adjusted gross income.

17. May C, an individual farmer, take a loss on a crop that is damaged by a severe hail storm?

18. Why do most taxpayers elect to write off research and experimental expenditures rather than capitalize and amortize such amounts? Are there some situations in which the capitalization and amortization approach would be preferable?

19. What is the rationale behind the net operating loss deduction? Who benefits from this provision?

Problems

20. M loaned T $10,000 on April 1, 1989. In 1990 T filed for bankruptcy. At that time, it was revealed that T's creditors could expect to receive 60¢ on the dollar. In February 1991, final settlement was made and M received $3,000. How much loss can M deduct and in which year? How is it treated on M's return?

21. X Company had employed the allowance method for computing its bad debts for tax purposes through the year 1986. At the beginning of 1990, the credit balance in the allowance account was $50,000. During 1990, X identified $80,000 of accounts as worthless. Determine the tax consequences to X associated with the allowance for bad debts and the bad debt expense for 1990.

22. In 1989, W deposited $20,000 with a commercial bank. On July 1, 1990, W was notified that the bank was insolvent, and he subsequently received only 30% of the deposit. W also has a salary of $40,000, long-term capital gain of $9,000, and itemized deductions (other than casualty and theft) of $7,000. Determine W's possible deductions with respect to the deposit.

23. X, a married taxpayer filing a joint return, had the following items for the year 1990:

   - Salary of $150,000.
   - Gain of $30,000 on the sale of § 1244 stock X acquired three years ago.
   - Loss of $120,000 on the sale of § 1244 stock X acquired two years ago.
   - Stock acquired on December 15, 1989, for $5,000 became worthless on March 28, 1990.

   Determine X's adjusted gross income for 1990.

24. When J returned from a vacation in Hawaii on November 8, 1990, she discovered that a burglar had stolen her silver, stereo, and color television. In the process of removing these items, the burglar damaged some furniture that originally cost $1,400. J's silver cost $3,640 and was valued at $6,500; the stereo system cost $8,400 and was valued at $6,200; the television cost $840 and was worth $560. J filed a claim with her insurance company and was reimbursed in the following amounts on December 20, 1990:

Silver	$2,800
Stereo	5,600
Television	490

   The insurance company disputed the reimbursement claimed by J for the damaged furniture, but she protested and was finally paid $280 on January 30, 1991. The repairs to the furniture totaled $448. J's adjusted gross income for 1990 was $12,000, and it was $15,000 for 1991. How much can J claim as a casualty loss? In which year?

25. K owned three acres of land in Kansas upon which he had his home, two rental houses, an apartment building, and his construction company. A tornado hit the area and destroyed one of the rental houses, damaged the apartment building, and destroyed some of K's construction equipment. The tenant of K's other rental house moved out for fear of another tornado, and K lost $450 in rent. Other losses were as follows:

Item	Adjusted Basis	FMV Before	FMV After	Insurance Proceeds
Rental house #1	$ 34,500	$ 43,500	$ –0–	$30,000
Apartment building	100,000	225,000	180,000	31,500
Equipment	90,000	112,500	–0–	75,000

   a. How much is K's casualty loss before applying any limitation?

   b. Assuming the loss occurred on March 3, 1991, and that the area was designated by the President as a disaster area, what options are open to K with respect to the timing of the loss deduction?

26. On June 15, 1990, T was involved in an accident with his personal automobile. T had purchased the car new two years ago for $14,000. At the time of the accident, the car was worth $10,000. After the accident, the car was appraised at $3,000. T had an insurance policy that had a 20% deductible clause. Because T was afraid that the policy would be cancelled, he made no claim against the insurance policy for the damages to the car.

   On September 17, 1990, T was involved in an accident with his business automobile. The automobile had a fair market value of $12,000 before the accident, and it was worthless after the accident. T had a basis in the car of

$15,000 at the time of the accident. The car was covered by an insurance policy that insured the car for fair market value. T made a claim and collected against the policy. T earned a salary of $50,000 and had other itemized deductions of $8,000 for the year. Determine taxable income for T and his wife, who file a joint return for 1990.

27. W, single and age 38, had the following income and expense items in 1990:

Nonbusiness bad debt	$ 6,000
Business bad debt	2,000
Nonbusiness long-term capital gain	4,000
Nonbusiness short-term capital loss	3,000
Salary	40,000
Interest income	1,000

Determine W's adjusted gross income for 1990.

28. Assume that in addition to the information in Problem 27, W had the following items in 1990:

Personal casualty gain on an asset held for four months	$10,000
Personal casualty loss on an asset held for two years	1,000

Determine W's adjusted gross income for 1990.

29. Assume that in addition to the information in Problems 27 and 28, W had the following items in 1990:

Personal casualty loss on an asset held for five years	$50,000
Interest expense on home mortgage	3,000

Determine W's taxable income and net operating loss for 1990.

30. X Corporation, a manufacturing company, decided to develop a new line of fireworks. Because of the danger involved, X purchased an isolated parcel of land for $200,000 and constructed a building for $400,000. The building was to be used for research and experimentation in creating the new fireworks. The project was begun in 1990. X had the following expenses in 1990 in connection with the project:

Salaries	$50,000
Utilities	4,000
Materials	12,000
Insurance	6,000
Cost of market survey to determine profit potential for new fireworks line	5,000
Depreciation on the building	8,000

X had the following expenses in 1991 in connection with the project:

Salaries	$70,000
Utilities	8,000
Materials	15,000
Insurance	10,000
Depreciation on the building	11,000

The benefits from the project will be realized starting in August of 1992.

a. If X Corporation elects to expense research and experimental expenditures, determine the amount of the deduction for 1990, 1991, and 1992.

b. If X Corporation elects a 60-month deferral and amortization period, determine the amount of the deduction for 1990, 1991, and 1992.

Cumulative Problems

31. Ned Wilson, age 60, single, and retired, has no dependents. Ned lives at 231 Wander Lane, Salt Lake City, UT 84201. Ned's Social Security number is 985–12–3774. During 1990, Ned had the following income and expense items:

    a. On January 27, 1989, Ned deposited $8,000 in a savings account at the ABC Financial Company. The savings account bore interest at 15%, compounded semiannually. Ned received a $600 interest payment on July 27, 1989, but received no interest payments thereafter. The finance company filed for bankruptcy on January 12, 1990. Ned received a $710 check in final settlement of his account from the bankruptcy trustee on December 20, 1990.

    b. On January 1, 1990, a fire severely damaged a two-story building owned by Ned, who occupied the second story of the building as a residence and had recently opened a hardware store on the ground level. The following information is available with respect to the incident:

	Adjusted Basis	Fair Market Value	
		Before	After
Building	$64,000	$130,000	$50,000
Inventory	35,000	55,000	None
Store equipment	3,000	1,800	None
Home furnishings	12,600	6,000	800
Personal auto	8,900	7,800	7,600

    Ned's fire insurance policy paid the following amounts for damages:

Building	$50,000 (policy maximum)
Inventory	33,000
Store equipment	None
Home furnishings	1,000 (policy maximum)
Personal auto	None

    Assume all of the destroyed property was acquired on December 15, 1989.

    c. On March 1, 1985, Ned loaned a neighboring businessman $15,000. The debtor died of a heart attack on June 21, 1990. Ned had no security and was unable to collect anything from the man's estate.

    d. Ned received $72,000 of interest income from Salt Lake City Bank.

    e. On March 2, 1990, Ned sold a piece of real estate he had been holding for speculation for $90,000. Ned had bought the land July 18, 1975, for $52,800.

    f. Ned made a charitable contribution of $3,000.

    g. Ned made four quarterly estimated tax payments of $5,000 each.

    Part 1—Tax Computation
    Compute Ned's 1990 Federal income tax payable (or refund due), assuming he deducts the lost deposit as a bad debt. Suggested software (if available): *WEST–TAX Planner* or *BNA Individual Income Tax Spreadsheet*.

    Part 2—Tax Planning
    Determine whether Ned should elect to treat the deposit in ABC Financial Company as a casualty loss rather than as a bad debt. Suggested software (if available): *WEST–TAX Planner* or *BNA Individual Income Tax Spreadsheet*.

32. Jane Smith, age 40, is single and has no dependents. She is employed part-time as a legal secretary by Legal Services, Inc. She owns and operates Typing Services

located near the campus of San Jose State University at 1986 Campus Drive. She is a cash basis taxpayer. Jane lives at 2020 Oakcrest Road, San Jose, CA 95134. Jane's Social Security number is 123–89–6666. Jane indicates that she wishes to designate $1 to the Presidential Election Campaign Fund. During 1989, Jane had the following income and expense items:

a. $10,000 salary from Legal Services, Inc.

b. $32,000 gross receipts from her typing services business.

c. $300 cash dividend from Buffalo Mining Company, a Canadian corporation.

d. $1,000 Christmas bonus from Legal Services, Inc.

e. $10,000 life insurance proceeds on the death of her sister.

f. $5,000 check given to her by her wealthy aunt.

g. $100 won in a bingo game.

h.   Expenses connected with the typing service:

Office rent	$5,000
Supplies	2,400
Utilities and telephone	3,680
Wages to part-time typists	4,000
Payroll taxes	600
Equipment rentals	3,000

i. $4,000 interest expense on a home mortgage (paid to San Jose Savings and Loan).

j. $5,000 fair market value of silverware stolen from her home by a burglar on October 12, 1989. Jane had paid $4,000 for the silverware on July 1, 1979. She was reimbursed $1,500 by her insurance company.

k.   Jane had loaned $2,100 to a friend, Joan Jensen, on June 3, 1986. Joan declared bankruptcy on August 14, 1989, and was unable to repay the loan.

l.   Legal Services, Inc., withheld Federal income tax of $400 and FICA tax of $826.

m.   Jane made four quarterly estimated tax payments of $1,250 each.

Part 1—Tax Computation

Compute Jane Smith's 1989 Federal income tax payable (or refund due). If you use tax forms for your computations, you will need Forms 1040 and 4684 and Schedules A, C, D, and SE. Suggested software (if available): *TurboTax* for tax return solutions, *WEST–TAX Planner* or *BNA Individual Income Tax Spreadsheet* if tax return solutions are not desired.

Part 2—Tax Planning

In 1990, Jane plans to quit her part-time job with Legal Services, Inc. Therefore, items a, d, and l will not recur in 1990. Jane plans to work full-time in her typing services business (refer to item b) and expects gross receipts of $50,000. She projects that all business expenses (refer to item h) will increase by 10%, except for office rent, which, under the terms of her lease, will remain the same as in 1989. Items e, f, g, j, and k will not recur in 1990. Items c and i will be approximately the same as in 1989.

Jane would like you to compute the minimum amount of estimated tax (refer to item m) she will have to pay for 1990 so that she will not have to pay any additional tax upon filing her 1990 Federal income tax return. Suggested software (if available): *TurboTax* (planning mode), *WEST–TAX Planner* or *BNA Individual Income Tax Spreadsheet.*

8

DEPRECIATION, COST RECOVERY, AMORTIZATION, AND DEPLETION

OBJECTIVES

Determine the amount of depreciation and amortization under pre-ACRS rules.

Determine the amount of cost recovery under ACRS rules.

Explain the operation of the rules governing listed property.

Explain the alternative tax treatments for intangible drilling and development costs.

Determine the amount of depletion expense.

Explain the reporting procedures for depreciation and cost recovery.

The Internal Revenue Code provides for a deduction for the consumption of the cost of an asset through depreciation, cost recovery, amortization, or depletion. These deductions are applications of the recovery of capital doctrine (discussed in chapter 3). Before discussing each cost consumption method, however, it is beneficial to review the difference between the classification of an asset (realty or personalty) and the use to which it is placed (business or personal). Personalty can be defined as all assets that are not realty. Both realty and personalty can be either business use (which includes both property used in a trade or business and property held for the production of income) or personal use property. Examples of this distinction include a residence (realty that is personal use), an office building (realty that is business use), a dump truck (personalty that is business use), and regular wearing apparel (personalty that is personal use).

A further distinction is made between tangible and intangible property. Tangible property is any property with physical substance (e.g., equipment, buildings), while intangible property lacks such substance (e.g., goodwill, patents).

A write-off of the cost (or other adjusted basis) of an asset is known as depreciation, cost recovery, depletion, or amortization. Depreciation and cost recovery relate to tangible property, depletion involves certain natural resources (e.g., oil, coal, gravel), and amortization concerns intangible property. As noted later, a write-off for income tax purposes is not allowed when an asset lacks a determinable useful life (e.g., land, goodwill) or when it is not business use property.

The depreciation rules were completely overhauled by the Economic Recovery Tax Act of 1981 (ERTA). Hence, *most* property placed in service after December 31, 1980, is subject to the accelerated cost recovery system (ACRS). However, property acquired before January 1, 1981, that is still in use, as well as *certain* property acquired after December 31, 1980, is subject to the pre-ERTA depreciation rules. The Tax Reform Act (TRA) of 1986 completely revised the ACRS rules for property placed in service after December 31, 1986. Therefore, a knowledge of all of the depreciation and cost recovery rules may be needed as Example 1 illustrates.

EXAMPLE 1   ABC owns equipment purchased in 1980. The equipment has a 10-year useful life. The business also owns several trucks purchased in 1986. In 1988, the business purchased a computer. To compute the depreciation and cost recovery for 1990, ABC will use the pre-ERTA depreciation rules for the equipment, the pre-TRA of 1986 cost recovery rules for the trucks, and the post-TRA of 1986 cost recovery rules for the computer.   □

This chapter first discusses the pre-ERTA depreciation rules, including the amortization rules not changed by ERTA, and then discusses the pre-TRA and post-TRA of 1986 ACRS rules.[1]

DEPRECIATION AND AMORTIZATION

Section 167 permits a depreciation deduction in the form of a reasonable allowance for the exhaustion, wear and tear, and obsolescence of business property and property held for the production of income (e.g., rental property held by an investor). Obsolescence refers to normal technological change due to

---

1. Depreciation is covered in § 167, and ACRS appears in § 168.

reasonably foreseeable economic conditions. If rapid or abnormal obsolescence occurs, a taxpayer may change to a shorter estimated useful life if there is a "clear and convincing basis for the redetermination."

The taxpayer must adopt a reasonable and consistent plan for depreciating the cost or other basis of assets over the estimated useful life of the property (e.g., the taxpayer cannot arbitrarily defer or accelerate the amount of depreciation from one year to another). The basis of the depreciable property must be reduced by the depreciation allowed and by not less than the allowable amount. The *allowed* depreciation is the depreciation actually taken, whereas the *allowable* depreciation is the amount that could have been taken under the applicable depreciation method. For example, if the taxpayer does not claim any depreciation on property during a particular year, the basis of the property still must be reduced by the amount of depreciation that should have been deducted. See Concept Summary 8–1.

EXAMPLE 2

On January 1, T paid $6,000 for a truck to be used in his business. He chose a four-year estimated useful life, no salvage value, and straight-line depreciation. Thus, the allowable depreciation deduction was $1,500 per year. However, depreciation actually taken (allowed) was as follows:

Year 1	$1,500
Year 2	–0–
Year 3	–0–
Year 4	1,500

The adjusted basis of the truck must be reduced by the amount of allowable depreciation of $6,000 ($1,500 × 4 years) despite the fact that T claimed only $3,000 depreciation during the four-year period. Therefore, if T sold the truck at the end of Year 4 for $1,000, a $1,000 gain would be recognized since the adjusted cost basis of the truck is zero. □

Qualifying Property

As mentioned earlier, the use rather than the character of property determines whether a depreciation deduction is permitted. Property must be used in a trade or business or held for the production of income to qualify as depreciable.

CONCEPT SUMMARY 8–1

Depreciation and Cost Recovery: Relevant Time Periods

System	Date Property Is Placed in Service
§ 167 depreciation	Before January 1, 1981, and *certain* property placed in service after December 31, 1980.
Pre-TRA of 1986 ACRS	After December 31, 1980, and before January 1, 1987.
Post-TRA of 1986 ACRS	After December 31, 1986.

EXAMPLE 3   T is a self-employed CPA who uses her automobile for both personal and business purposes. A depreciation deduction is permitted only for the business use part. Assume the automobile was acquired at a cost of $12,000 and T's mileage during the year was 10,000 miles, of which 3,000 miles were for business. Only 30% of the cost, or $3,600, would be subject to depreciation.   □

The basis for depreciation generally is the adjusted cost basis used to determine gain if the property is sold or disposed of. However, if personal use assets are converted to business or income-producing use, the basis for depreciation and for loss is the *lower* of the adjusted basis or fair market value when the property is converted.

EXAMPLE 4   T acquires a personal residence for $30,000. Four years later, he converts the property to rental use when the fair market value is only $25,000. The basis for depreciation is $25,000 since the fair market value is less than the adjusted basis. The $5,000 decline in value is deemed to be personal (since it occurred while the property was held for personal use) and therefore nondeductible.   □

The Regulations provide that tangible property is depreciable only to the extent that the property is subject to wear and tear, decay or decline from natural causes, exhaustion, and obsolescence.[2] Thus, land and inventory are not depreciable, but land improvements are depreciable (e.g., paved surfaces, fences, landscaping).

Amortization of intangible property is not permitted unless the property has a definite and limited useful life. For example, patents and copyrights have a definite and limited legal life and are therefore eligible for amortization. Goodwill is not amortizable since its life extends for an unlimited period.

Other Depreciation Considerations

For property subject to depreciation under § 167, taxpayers generally must take into account the *salvage value* (assuming there is a salvage value) of an asset in calculating depreciation. An asset cannot be depreciated below its salvage value. However, the Code permits a taxpayer to disregard salvage value for amounts up to 10 percent of the basis in the property. This rule applies to tangible personal property (other than livestock) with an estimated useful life of three years or more.

EXAMPLE 5   The XYZ Company acquired a machine for $10,000 in 1980 with an estimated salvage value of $3,000 after 10 years. The company may disregard salvage value to the extent of $1,000 and compute the machine's depreciation based upon a cost of $10,000 less $2,000 salvage. The adjusted basis may be reduced to $2,000 (depreciation of $8,000 may be taken) despite the fact that the actual salvage value is $3,000.   □

This rule was incorporated into the law to reduce the number of IRS and taxpayer disputes relative to the salvage value that should be used.

---

2. Reg. § 1.167(a).

Another consideration is the *choice of depreciation methods* from among the several allowed. Section 167 provides for the following alternative depreciation methods for property placed into service before January 1, 1981, and for *certain* property placed in service after December 31, 1980:

- The straight-line method (cost basis less salvage ÷ estimated useful life).

- The declining-balance method (DB) using a rate not to exceed twice the straight-line rate. Common methods included 200 percent DB (double-declining balance), 150 percent DB, and 125 percent DB. Salvage value is not taken into account under any of the declining-balance methods. However, no further depreciation can be claimed once net book value (cost minus depreciation) and salvage value are the same.

- The sum-of-the-years' digits method (SYD).

- Any other consistent method that does not result in greater total depreciation being claimed during the first two-thirds of the useful life than would have been allowable under the double-declining balance method. Permissible methods include machine hours and the units-of-production method.

EXAMPLE 6

On January 1, 1980, T acquired a new automobile to be used in his business. The asset cost $10,000 with an estimated salvage value of $2,000 and a four-year estimated useful life. The following amounts of depreciation could be deducted, depending on the method of depreciation used (note that pre-ERTA rules [depreciation calculated under § 167] continue to apply for the entire useful life of assets acquired before 1981):

	1980	1981	1982	1983
1. Straight-line				
$10,000 cost less ($2,000 salvage value reduced by 10% of cost) ÷ 4 years	$2,250	$2,250	$2,250	$2,250
2. Double-declining balance				
a. $10,000 × 50% (twice the straight-line rate)	5,000			
b. ($10,000 − $5,000) × 50%		2,500		
c. ($10,000 − $5,000 − $2,500) × 50%			1,250	
d. ($10,000 − $5,000 − $2,500 − $1,250) × 50%				250*
3. Sum-of-the-years' digits**: $10,000 cost less ($2,000 salvage value reduced by 10% of cost) or $9,000				
a. $9,000 × 4/10	3,600			
b. $9,000 × 3/10		2,700		
c. $9,000 × 2/10			1,800	
d. $9,000 × 1/10				900

*Total depreciation taken cannot exceed cost minus estimated salvage value ($1,000 in this example).

**The sum-of-the-years' digits (SYD) method formula is

$$\text{Cost minus salvage value} \times \frac{\text{Remaining life at the beginning of the year}}{\text{Sum-of-the-years' digits of the estimated life}}$$

In this example, the denominator for SYD is 1 + 2 + 3 + 4, or 10. The numerator is 4 for Year 1 (the number of years left at the beginning of Year 1), 3 for Year 2, etc. The denominator can be calculated by the following formula:

$$S = \frac{Y(Y + 1)}{2} \text{ where Y = estimated useful life}$$

$$\text{e.g., } S = \frac{4(4 + 1)}{2} = 10$$

□

EXAMPLE 7   Using the depreciation calculations in Example 6, the depreciation reserve (accumulated depreciation) and net book value at the end of 1983 are as follows:

	Cost	**−**	**Depreciation**	**=**	**Net Book Value***
Straight-line	$10,000		$9,000		$1,000
Double-declining balance	10,000		9,000		1,000
Sum-of-the-years' digits	10,000		9,000		1,000

*Note that an asset may not be depreciated below its salvage value even when a declining-balance method is used.

□

In 1969, Congress placed certain restrictions on the use of accelerated methods for new and used realty subject to the depreciation rules under § 167. These restrictions were imposed to reduce the opportunities for using real estate investments as tax shelters. The use of accelerated depreciation frequently resulted in the recognition of ordinary tax losses on economically profitable real estate ventures.

The following methods were permitted for residential and nonresidential real property:[3]

	Nonresidential Real Property (commercial and industrial buildings, etc.)	**Residential Real Property (apartment buildings, etc.)**
New property acquired after July 24, 1969, and generally before January 1, 1981	150% DB, SL	200% DB, SYD, 150% DB, or SL
Used property acquired after July 24, 1969, and generally before January 1, 1981	SL	125% DB if estimated useful life is 20 years or greater, or SL

Restrictions on the use of accelerated methods were not imposed on new tangible personalty (e.g., machinery, equipment, and automobiles). However, the

---

3.   § 167(j). See the Glossary of Tax Terms in Appendix C for the definition of residential rental property.

200 percent declining-balance and sum-of-the-years' digits methods were not permitted for used tangible personal property. The 150 percent declining-balance method was permitted for used tangible personalty that had a useful life of at least three years. Since the acquisition of used property did not result in any net addition to gross private investment in our economy, Congress chose not to provide as rapid accelerated depreciation for used property. It should be noted that accelerated methods (200 percent declining-balance and sum-of-the-years' digits) were permitted for new residential rental property. Presumably, the desire to stimulate construction of new housing units justified the need for such accelerated methods.

The determination of a *useful life* for a depreciable asset often led to disagreement between taxpayers and the IRS. One source of information was the company's previous experience and policy with respect to asset maintenance and utilization. Another source was the guideline lives issued by the IRS.[4] In 1971, the IRS guideline life system was modified and liberalized by the enactment of the Asset Depreciation Range (ADR) system.[5]

Accelerated Cost Recovery System (ACRS)

General Considerations

The depreciation rules before ERTA were designed to allocate depreciation deductions over the period the asset was used in business so that the deductions for the cost of an asset were matched with the income produced by the asset (the so-called matching concept). Often this led to controversies between taxpayers and the IRS concerning the estimated useful life of an asset, and it delayed the tax benefit to be derived from the recoupment of a capital investment in the form of a deduction for depreciation.

One way to resolve the estimated useful life problem was to utilize the Asset Depreciation Range (ADR) system, which specified ranges for particular assets. Taxpayers could select a useful life for an asset within the specified range for that particular asset. However, many assets were not eligible for ADR, or taxpayers saw fit not to elect the system. In such cases, useful lives were determined according to the facts and circumstances pertaining to each asset or by agreement between the taxpayer and the IRS.

For property placed in service after December 31, 1980, the ADR system and depreciation calculated under § 167 have generally been replaced by the § 168 accelerated cost recovery system (ACRS). Under ACRS, the cost of an asset is recovered over a predetermined period that is generally shorter than the useful life of the asset or the period the asset is used to produce income. The change was designed to encourage investment, improve productivity, and simplify the law and its administration. However, the pre-ACRS depreciation rules will continue to apply in the following situations:

- Property placed in service after 1980 whose life is not based on years (e.g., units-of-production method).

- The remaining depreciation on property placed in service by the taxpayer before 1981.

---

4. Rev.Proc. 72–10, 1972–1 C.B. 721, superseded by Rev.Proc. 83–35, 1983–1 C.B. 745.

5. Reg. § 1.167(a)–11.

- Personal property acquired after 1980 if the property was owned or used during 1980 by the taxpayer or a related person (antichurning rule).

- Property that is amortized (e.g., leasehold improvements).

For property placed in service after December 31, 1986, ACRS has been revised by TRA of 1986. However, the pre-TRA of 1986 ACRS rules still apply to property placed in service after December 31, 1980 and before January 1, 1987.

Eligible Property under ACRS

Assets used in a trade or business or for the production of income are depreciable if they are subject to wear and tear, decay or decline from natural causes, or obsolescence. Assets that do not decline in value on a predictable basis or that do not have a determinable useful life (e.g., land, goodwill, stock, antiques) are not depreciable.

New or used tangible depreciable property (real or personal) placed in service after December 31, 1980 (except for the four exceptions noted above), is subject to the ACRS rules. Property placed in service before January 1, 1987, is subject to pre-TRA of 1986 ACRS rules, and property placed in service after December 31, 1986, is subject to post-TRA of 1986 ACRS rules.

Personalty: Recovery Periods and Methods

Classification of Property: Pre-TRA of 1986.   Pre-TRA of 1986 ACRS provides that the cost of eligible personalty (and certain realty) is recovered over 3, 5, 10, or 15 years. The classification of property by recovery period is as follows:

---

3 years .... Autos, light-duty trucks, R & D equipment, racehorses over 2 years old and other horses over 12 years old, and personalty with an ADR midpoint life of 4 years or less.[6]

5 years .... Most other equipment except long-lived public utility property. Also includes single-purpose agricultural structures and petroleum storage facilities, which are designated as § 1245 property under the law.

10 years .... Public utility property with an ADR midpoint life greater than 18 but not greater than 25 years, burners and boilers using coal as a primary fuel if used in a public utility power plant and if replacing or converting oil- or gas-fired burners or boilers, railroad tank cars, mobile homes, and realty with an ADR midpoint life of 12.5 years or less (e.g., theme park structures).

15 years .... Public utility property with an ADR midpoint life exceeding 25 years (except certain burners and boilers using coal as a primary fuel).

Taxpayers have the choice of using (1) the straight-line method over the regular or optional (see below) recovery period or (2) a prescribed accelerated method over the regular recovery period. These two methods are both part of the ACRS system. However, a convenient name is not provided for either of the two methods. Hereafter, the straight-line method will be referred to as the *optional (or elective) straight-line method.* The method using percentages prescribed in the Code will be referred to as the *statutory percentage method.*

---

6. Rev.Proc. 83–35, 1983–1 C.B. 745 is the source for the ADR midpoint lives.

The rates to be used in computing the deduction under the statutory percentage method are shown in Table 8–1 (all tables are located at the end of the chapter prior to the Problem Materials) and are based on the 150 percent declining-balance method, using the half-year convention and an assumption of zero salvage value. The half-year convention assumes all property is placed in service at mid-year and thus provides for a half-year's cost recovery.

EXAMPLE 8

In December 1982, T buys the following business assets: $34,000 of machinery, $6,000 of office furniture, and $16,000 of light-duty trucks. The machinery and office furniture are five-year properties, and the trucks are three-year properties. T's depreciation deductions using the statutory percentage method are as follows:

1982	
25% of $16,000 (trucks)	$ 4,000
15% of $40,000 (machinery and furniture)	6,000
	$10,000
1983	
38% of $16,000	$ 6,080
22% of $40,000	8,800
	$14,880
1984	
37% of $16,000	$ 5,920
21% of $40,000	8,400
	$14,320
1985	
21% of $40,000	$ 8,400
1986	
21% of $40,000	$ 8,400

☐

Note that in 1982, T got a half-year's cost recovery deduction (since the half-year convention is reflected in the percentages in Table 8–1) although she held the property only one month.

In the year that personal property is disposed of, no cost recovery is allowed.

EXAMPLE 9

Assume the same facts as in Example 8. If T sold the trucks on December 1, 1983, T would only have cost recovery of $8,800 for the machinery and furniture. T would have no cost recovery for the trucks even though they were held for 11 months.   ☐

Reduction of Basis for Investment Tax Credit.   For personalty placed in service after 1982 and before January 1, 1986, the basis of the property for the ACRS write-off must be reduced by one-half the amount of the investment tax credit taken on the property. Investment tax credit was not allowed on realty. (See chapter 11 for details.)

EXAMPLE 10   On January 1, 1985, T purchases a machine, which is five-year ACRS property, for $10,000. T takes a $1,000 investment tax credit on the property (10% of $10,000). The basis of the property must be reduced by $500 (½ of the $1,000 investment tax credit). Thus, T's cost recovery allowance will be based on $9,500 [$10,000 (cost) − $500 (reduction for investment tax credit)]. T's cost recovery deduction for 1985 will be $1,425 (15% of $9,500). □

As an alternative to reducing the basis of the property, a taxpayer may elect to take a reduced investment tax credit. Under this election, the investment tax credit is 8 percent (rather than 10 percent) for recovery property that is not three-year property and 4 percent (instead of 6 percent) for three-year property. In Example 10, if the reduced investment tax credit election were made, T's cost recovery deduction for 1985 would be $1,500 (15% of $10,000).

TRA of 1986 repealed the investment tax credit for property placed in service after December 31, 1985. Therefore, the reduction of basis for the investment tax credit is not a concern for such property.

Classification of Property: Post-TRA of 1986.   The general effect of TRA of 1986 is to lengthen asset lives. Post-TRA of 1986 ACRS provides that the depreciation basis of eligible personalty (and certain realty) is recovered over 3, 5, 7, 10, 15, or 20 years. The classification of property by recovery period is as follows:

3-year 200% class	ADR midpoints of 4 years and less.[7] Excludes automobiles and light trucks. Includes racehorses more than 2 years old and other horses more than 12 years old.
5-year 200% class	ADR midpoints of more than 4 years and less than 10 years, including automobiles, light trucks, qualified technological equipment, renewable energy and biomass properties that are small power production facilities, research and experimentation property, semiconductor manufacturing equipment, and computer-based central office switching equipment.
7-year 200% class	ADR midpoints of 10 years and more and less than 16 years, including single-purpose agricultural or horticultural structures and property with no ADR midpoint not classified elsewhere. Includes railroad track and office furniture, fixtures, and equipment.
10-year 200% class	ADR midpoints of 16 years and more and less than 20 years.
15-year 150% class	ADR midpoints of 20 years and more and less than 25 years, including sewage treatment plants, and telephone distribution plants and comparable equipment used for the two-way exchange of voice and data communications.
20-year 150% class	ADR midpoints of 25 years and more, other than real property with an ADR midpoint of 27.5 years and more, and including sewer pipes.

Accelerated depreciation is allowed for these six ACRS classes of property. Two hundred percent declining-balance is used for the 3-, 5-, 7-, and 10-year

---

7. Rev.Proc. 87–56, 1987–2 C.B. 674 is the source for the ADR midpoint lives.

classes, with a switchover to straight-line depreciation when it yields a larger amount. One hundred and fifty percent declining-balance is allowed for the 15- and 20-year classes, with an appropriate straight-line switchover.

The property in each of these classes may be depreciated using straight-line depreciation if an election is made. Certain property is not eligible for accelerated depreciation and must be depreciated under an alternative depreciation system (ADS). Both the straight-line election and ADS are discussed later in the chapter.

The original ACRS system gave the taxpayer a half-year of depreciation for the tax year he or she placed an asset in service but allowed the taxpayer to recover the balance of the depreciable basis over the years remaining in the property's recovery period. No recovery allowance existed for the year of disposition or retirement. Thus, conceptually, the taxpayer was considered to have placed property in service at the beginning of the recovery period but was allowed only a half-year's worth of depreciation for the placed-in-service year. By contrast, the new system views property as placed in service in the middle of the first year. Thus, for example, the statutory recovery period for three-year property begins in the middle of the year an asset is placed in service and ends three years later. In practical terms, the new rule means that taxpayers must wait an extra year to recover the total cost of depreciable assets. That is, the actual write-off periods are 4, 6, 8, 11, 16, and 21 years. The new system also allows for a half-year of cost recovery in the year of disposition or retirement.

The methodology for computing the cost recovery is the same as under the original ACRS method. The depreciation basis is multiplied by the percentages that reflect the applicable depreciation method and the applicable convention. The percentages are shown in Table 8–2.

EXAMPLE 11 | T acquires a five-year class asset on April 10, 1990, for $30,000. T's cost recovery deduction for 1990 is $6,000 [$30,000 × .20 (Table 8–2)]. □

EXAMPLE 12 | Assume the same facts as in Example 11, except that T disposes of the asset on March 5, 1992. T's cost recovery deduction for 1992 is $2,880 [$30,000 × ½ × .192 (Table 8–2)]. □

Under the original ACRS rules for personal property, the half-year convention was used no matter what the pattern of acquisitions was during the year. Thus, if a substantial dollar amount of assets was acquired late in the tax year, the half-year convention still applied. The law now contains a provision to curtail the benefits of such tax planning. If more than 40 percent of the value of property other than eligible real estate (see Realty: Recovery Periods and Methods: Post-TRA of 1986, for a discussion of eligible real estate) is placed in service during the last quarter of the year, a *mid-quarter convention* applies. Property acquisitions are then grouped by the quarter they were acquired and depreciated accordingly. Acquisitions during the first quarter would receive 10.5 months of depreciation; the second quarter, 7.5 months; the third quarter, 4.5 months; and the fourth quarter, 1.5 months. The percentages are shown in Table 8–3.

CONCEPT SUMMARY 8–2

Cost Recovery Periods: Post-TRA of 1986

Class of Property	Examples
3-year	Tractor units for use over-the-road. Any horse that is not a racehorse and is more than 12 years old at the time it is placed in service. Any racehorse that is more than 2 years old at the time it is placed in service. Breeding hogs. Special tools used in the manufacturing of motor vehicles such as dies, fixtures, molds, and patterns.
5-year	Automobiles and taxis. Light and heavy general-purpose trucks. Buses. Trailers and trailer-mounted containers. Typewriters, calculators, and copiers. Computers and peripheral equipment. Breeding and dairy cattle.
7-year	Office furniture, fixtures, and equipment. Breeding and work horses. Agricultural machinery and equipment. Single-purpose agricultural or horticultural structures.
10-year	Vessels, barges, tugs, and similar water transportation equipment. Assets used for petroleum refining, manufacture of grain and grain mill products, manufacture of sugar and sugar products, and manufacture of vegetable oils and vegetable oil products.
15-year	Land improvements. Assets used for industrial steam and electric generation and/or distribution systems. Assets used in the manufacture of cement. Railroad track. Assets used in pipeline transportation. Electric utility nuclear production plant. Municipal wastewater treatment plant.
20-year	Farm buildings except single-purpose agricultural and horticultural structures. Gas utility distribution facilities. Water utilities. Municipal sewer.

EXAMPLE 13   X Corporation acquires the following five-year class property:

Property Acquisition Dates	Cost
February 15	$ 200,000
July 10	400,000
December 5	600,000
Total	$1,200,000

If X Corporation uses statutory percentage ACRS, the cost recovery for the first two years would be computed as indicated below. Since 50% ($600,000/$1,200,000) of the acquisitions are in the last quarter, the mid-quarter convention applies.

Year 1		
February 15	[$200,000 × .35 (Table 8-3)]	$ 70,000
July 10	($400,000 × .15)	60,000
December 5	($600,000 × .05)	30,000
Total		$160,000
Year 2		
February 15	[$200,000 × .26 (Table 8-3)]	$ 52,000
July 10	($400,000 × .34)	136,000
December 5	($600,000 × .38)	228,000
Total		$416,000

□

Realty: Recovery Periods and Methods

Pre-TRA of 1986.   Under the original version of ACRS, realty is assigned a 15-year recovery period. Component depreciation generally is no longer allowed.[8]

Real property other than low-income housing can be depreciated using the 175 percent declining-balance method with a switchover to straight-line depreciation when it yields a larger amount. Low-income housing is depreciated using the 200 percent declining-balance method with an appropriate straight-line switchover. In either case, an assumption of zero salvage value is made. Statutory percentages for real property are shown in Table 8-4, which contains rates for low-income housing as well as for other 15-year real estate.

Since the half-year convention does not apply to 15-year real property, Table 8-4 is structured differently from Tables 8-1 and 8-2. The cost recovery deduction for 15-year real property is based on the month the asset is placed in service rather than on the half-year convention.

EXAMPLE 14

T purchased a warehouse for $100,000 on January 1, 1984. The first year's cost recovery allowance using the statutory percentage method is $12,000 (12% of $100,000). Cost recovery deductions for 1985, 1986, and 1987 are, respectively, $10,000, $9,000, and $8,000. (Refer to Table 8-4 for percentages.)   □

EXAMPLE 15

Assume the same facts as in Example 14, except the property is low-income housing. Cost recovery deductions for 1984 through 1987 are $13,000, $12,000, $10,000, and $9,000.   □

---

8. See the Glossary of Tax Terms in Appendix C for
a definition of component depreciation.

The Deficit Reduction Act of 1984 changed the recovery period for real property to 18 years. This applies generally to property placed in service after March 15, 1984. However, the 15-year recovery period is retained for low-income housing as well as for real property placed in service before March 16, 1984.

Eighteen-year real property placed in service after June 22, 1984, is subject to a mid-month convention.[9] This means that real property placed in service at any time during a particular month is treated as if it were placed in service in the middle of such month. This allows for one-half month's cost recovery for the month the property is placed in service. If the property is disposed of before the end of the recovery period, one-half month's cost recovery is permitted for the month of disposition regardless of the specific date of disposition. Statutory percentages for 18-year real property with a mid-month convention are shown in Table 8–5.

EXAMPLE 16

T purchased a building for $300,000 and placed it in service on August 21, 1984. The first year's cost recovery using the statutory percentage method is $12,000 (4% × $300,000). (See Table 8–5 for percentages.) □

EXAMPLE 17

Assume the same facts as in Example 16 and that T disposes of the building on May 3, 1990. The cost recovery in the year of disposition is $6,750 ($300,000 × 6% × 4.5/12). □

Public Law 99–121 extended the minimum recovery period for real property (except low-income housing) from 18 years to 19 years. This applies to property placed in service after May 8, 1985. Statutory percentages for 19-year real property are shown in Table 8–6. Because the percentages are determined using a mid-month convention, the computation of cost recovery is mechanically the same as illustrated with respect to 18-year property with the mid-month convention.

Post-TRA of 1986.   Residential rental real estate is given a recovery period of 27.5 years and is depreciated using the straight-line method. *Residential rental real estate* includes property for which 80 percent or more of the gross rental revenues are from nontransient dwelling units (e.g., an apartment building). Hotels, motels, and similar establishments are not residential rental property. Low-income housing is classified as residential rental real estate. Nonresidential real estate has a recovery period of 31.5 years and is depreciated using the straight-line method.

Note that some items of real property are not real estate for purposes of the revised ACRS. Single-purpose agricultural structures are in the seven-year ACRS class. Land improvements are in the 15-year ACRS class.

All eligible real estate is depreciated using the mid-month convention. Regardless of when during the month the property is placed in service, it is deemed to have been placed in service at the middle of the month. In the year of disposition, a mid-month convention is also used.

Depreciation is computed by multiplying the applicable rate (Table 8–7) by the depreciation basis.

---

9. A transitional rule, which provides for a full-month convention, is effective for property placed in service after March 15, 1984, and before June 23, 1984.

EXAMPLE 18

T acquired a building on April 1, 1990, for $800,000. If the building is classified as residential rental real estate, the cost recovery for 1990 is $20,608 (.02576 × $800,000). If the building is classified as nonresidential real estate, the 1990 cost recovery is $17,992 (.02249 × $800,000). □

Straight-Line Election under ACRS

Pre-TRA of 1986.   Taxpayers may *elect* to write off an asset using the straight-line method rather than the statutory percentage method. The straight-line recovery period may be equal to the prescribed recovery period under the statutory percentage method, or it may be a longer period. Allowable straight-line recovery periods for each class of property are summarized as follows:

3-year property............................	3, 5, or 12 years
5-year property............................	5, 12, or 25 years
10-year property..........................	10, 25, or 35 years
15-year property..........................	15, 35, or 45 years
18-year real property and low-income housing (placed in service after March 15, 1984)	18, 35, or 45 years
19-year real property and low-income housing (placed in service after May 8, 1985)..........	19, 35, or 45 years

If the straight-line option is elected, the half-year convention is applied in computing the cost recovery deduction for property other than 15-year, 18-year, or 19-year real property. The effect of electing the straight-line method for personal property is to extend the stated statutory recovery period by one year (e.g., three to four and five to six years). There is no cost recovery deduction in the year of disposition of property other than 15-year, 18-year, or 19-year real property. This rule is applicable to both the statutory percentage method and the optional straight-line method.

EXAMPLE 19

J acquired a light-duty truck (three-year property) on March 1, 1986, at a cost of $10,000. J elects to write off the cost of the truck using the optional straight-line method with a recovery period of five years. Because the half-year convention applies, J can deduct only $1,000 [($10,000 ÷ 5) × ½] in 1986. □

EXAMPLE 20

Assume the same facts as in Example 19. If J disposes of the truck at any time during 1987, no cost recovery deduction is allowed for 1987, the year of disposition. □

The half-year convention does not apply for 15-year, 18-year, or 19-year real property for which the straight-line option is elected. Nor is the cost recovery deduction disallowed in the year of disposition. The first year's deduction and the

deduction for the year of disposition are computed on the basis of the number of months the property was in service during the year. Examples 21 and 22 illustrate the calculations for 15-year real property.

EXAMPLE 21

K acquired a store building on October 1, 1983, at a cost of $150,000. K elects the straight-line method using a recovery period of 15 years. K's cost recovery deduction for 1983 is $2,500 [($150,000 ÷ 15) × 3/12]. ☐

EXAMPLE 22

Assume the same facts as in Example 21 and that K disposes of the asset on September 30, 1985. K's cost recovery deduction for 1985 would be $7,500 [($150,000 ÷ 15) × 9/12]. ☐

If the straight-line option is elected for 18-year or 19-year real property, the cost recovery allowances in the year the property is placed in service and in the year of disposition are computed the same (except for the use of different rates) as under statutory percentage cost recovery. Table 8–8 contains the applicable percentages to be used if the straight-line option is elected for 19-year real property. (The tables that contain the percentages for 18-year real property using the straight-line method over 18, 35, and 45 years and 19-year real property using the straight-line method over 35 and 45 years are not reproduced in this text.)

For each class of property other than 15-year, 18-year, or 19-year real estate, the straight-line election applies to *all* assets in a *particular class* that are placed in service during the year for which the election is made and later to the entire recovery period for those vintage assets. The election may be changed for property of the same class placed in service in other taxable years. By contrast, the straight-line election for 15-year, 18-year, or 19-year real property may be made on a *property-by-property* basis within the same year.

Post-TRA of 1986. Although straight-line depreciation is required for all eligible real estate as previously discussed, the taxpayer may elect to use the straight-line method for personal property. The property is depreciated using the class life (recovery period) of the asset with a half-year convention or a mid-quarter convention, whichever is applicable. The election is available on a class-by-class and year-by-year basis. The percentages for the straight-line election with a half-year convention appear in Table 8–9.

EXAMPLE 23

T acquired a 10-year class asset on August 4, 1990, for $100,000. T's cost recovery deduction for 1990 is $5,000 ($100,000 × .050). T's cost recovery deduction for 1991 is $10,000 ($100,000 × .100). ☐

Election to Expense Assets

Section 179 (Election to Expense Certain Depreciable Business Assets) permits an election to write off up to $10,000 of the acquisition cost of tangible personal property used in a trade or business.[10] Such amounts that are expensed may not be

---

10. From 1982 through 1986, the write-off amount was limited to $5,000.

capitalized and depreciated. The election is an annual election and applies to the acquisition cost of property placed in service that year. The amount shown is per taxpayer, per year. On a joint return, the statutory amounts apply to the couple. If the taxpayers are married and file separate returns, each spouse is eligible for 50% of the statutory amount.

EXAMPLE 24

T acquires machinery (five-year class) on February 1, 1990, at a cost of $40,000 and elects to expense $10,000 under § 179. T's statutory percentage cost recovery deduction for 1990 is $6,000 [($40,000 cost − $10,000 expensed) × .200]. T's total deduction for 1990 is $16,000 ($10,000 + $6,000). □

Section 179 has two additional limitations. First, the ceiling amount on the deduction is reduced dollar-for-dollar when property (other than eligible real estate) placed in service during the taxable year exceeds $200,000. Second, the amount expensed under § 179 cannot exceed the aggregate amount of taxable income derived from the conduct of any trade or business by the taxpayer. Taxable income of a trade or business is computed without regard to the amount expensed under § 179. Any expensed amount in excess of taxable income is carried forward to future taxable years and added to other amounts eligible for expensing (it is subject to the ceiling rules for the future years). These two limitations apply to property placed in service after December 31, 1986.

EXAMPLE 25

T owns a computer service and operates it as a sole proprietorship. In 1990, she will net $5,000 before considering any § 179 deduction. If T spends $204,000 on new equipment, her § 179 expense deduction would be computed as follows:

§ 179 deduction before adjustment	$10,000
Less: Dollar limitation reduction ($204,000 − $200,000)	(4,000)
Remaining § 179 deduction	$ 6,000
Business income limitation	$ 5,000
§ 179 deduction allowed	$ 5,000
§ 179 deduction carryforward ($6,000 − $5,000)	$ 1,000

□

The basis of the property for purposes of cost recovery is reduced by the § 179 amount after it is adjusted for property in excess of $200,000. This adjusted amount does not reflect any business income limitation. This is illustrated in Example 26.

EXAMPLE 26

Assume the same facts as in Example 25 and that the new equipment is five-year class property. T's statutory percentage cost recovery deduction for 1990 is $39,600 [($204,000 − $6,000) × .200]. □

Conversion of the expensed property to personal use at any time results in recapture income (see chapter 13). A property is converted to personal use if it is

not used predominantly in a trade or business. Regulations provide for the mechanics of the recapture.[11]

ACRS Antichurning Rules

Pre-TRA of 1986.   Generally, the ACRS deduction was larger than the depreciation deduction under pre-1981 rules. Thus, there was concern that some taxpayers might engage in transactions that did not result in an actual ownership change in an attempt to change pre-1981 property into post-1980 recovery property. To prevent this, the original ACRS provisions contain antichurning rules that prevent the use of ACRS on personal property acquired after 1980 if the property was owned or used during 1980 by the taxpayer or a related person (it is *churned* property). Therefore, the taxpayer must use pre-1981 depreciation rules on churned property.

EXAMPLE 27   T began renting a tractor to use in his farming business in 1979. T used the tractor until 1982, at which time he purchased it. T is not entitled to use ACRS because he used the tractor in 1980. Instead, he must use the pre-1981 depreciation rules.   □

In addition, ACRS does not apply to real property if *any* of the following is true:

- The property was owned by the taxpayer or a related person at any time during 1980.

- The taxpayer leases the property to a person or anyone related to such person who owned the property at any time during 1980.

- The property is acquired in nonrecognition transactions, such as certain like-kind exchanges or involuntary conversions (see chapter 12). However, this applies only to the extent that the basis of the property includes an amount representing the adjusted basis of other property owned by the taxpayer or a related person during 1980.

EXAMPLE 28   In 1986, J made a nontaxable like-kind exchange. He gave an apartment building, held since 1978, with an adjusted basis of $300,000 and a fair market value of $400,000. He also gave $200,000 in cash. In exchange, J received an apartment building worth $600,000. The basis of the new building is $500,000 [$300,000 (basis of old building) + $200,000 (cash paid)], but only $200,000 of the basis is subject to the ACRS rules. The $300,000 carryover basis is subject to the pre-ACRS rules.   □

A person is considered related to a previous user or owner if a family or fiduciary relationship exists or if ownership of 10 percent of a corporation or partnership exists.

Post-TRA of 1986.   TRA of 1986 contains antichurning rules similar to those just discussed in connection with the original ACRS provisions. Hence, taxpayers

---

11. Reg. § 1.179–1(e).

are prevented from depreciating personal property placed in service by the taxpayer or a related person before 1987 under the revised ACRS rules.

Business and Personal Use of Automobiles and Other Listed Property

Generally effective for property placed in service after June 18, 1984, limits exist on ACRS deductions and investment tax credits with respect to business and personal use of automobiles and other listed property. If the listed property *is predominantly used* for business, the taxpayer is allowed to take the investment tax credit and use statutory percentage ACRS to recover cost. In cases where the property is *not predominantly used* for business, cost is recovered using a straight-line recovery, and no investment tax credit can be taken.

TRA of 1986 repealed the investment tax credit for property placed in service after December 31, 1985. Therefore, the issue of whether investment tax credit can be taken is relevant only through 1985. (Because of the repeal of the investment tax credit, the credit is not discussed further in this section.)

Listed property includes the following:

* Any passenger automobile.

* Any other property used as a means of transportation.

* Any property of a type generally used for purposes of entertainment, recreation, or amusement.

* Any computer or peripheral equipment, with the exception of equipment used exclusively at a regular business establishment, including a qualifying home office.

* Any cellular telephone or other similar telecommunications equipment.

* Any other property specified in the Regulations.

Automobiles and Other Listed Property Used Predominantly in Business.   For listed property to be considered as predominantly used in business, the percentage of use for business must exceed 50 percent. The use of listed property for production of income does not qualify as business use for purposes of the more-than-50 percent test. However, if the more-than-50 percent test is met, production of income and business use percentages are used to compute the ACRS deduction.

EXAMPLE 29   On September 1, 1990, T places in service listed five-year recovery property. The property cost $10,000. If T uses the property 40% for business and 25% for the production of income, the property will not be considered as predominantly used for business. The cost would be recovered using straight-line cost recovery. If, however, T uses the property 60% for business and 25% for the production of income, the property will be considered as used predominantly for business. T's cost recovery for the year would be $1,700 ($10,000 × .200 × 85%). □

The base for determining the percentage of business usage for listed property is determined under the Regulations. The Regulations provide that for automobiles a mileage-based percentage is to be used. Other listed property is to use the

most appropriate unit of time (e.g., hours) the property is actually used (rather than available for use).[12]

The law places special limitations on statutory percentage ACRS recovery for passenger automobiles. These statutory dollar limits were imposed on passenger automobiles because of the belief that the tax system was being used to underwrite automobiles whose cost and luxury far exceeded what was needed for their business use.

A *passenger automobile* is any four-wheeled vehicle manufactured for use on public streets, roads, and highways with an unloaded gross vehicle weight rating of 6,000 pounds or less. This definition specifically excludes vehicles used directly in the business of transporting people or property for compensation such as taxicabs, ambulances, hearses, and trucks and vans as prescribed by the Regulations.

The limits placed on the amounts of ACRS statutory percentage recovery for passenger automobiles are as follows:

Year	Recovery Limitation
1	$ 2,660
2	4,200
3	2,550
Succeeding years until the cost is recovered	1,475

However, these limits are imposed before any percentage reduction for personal use. In addition, the limitation in the first year includes any amount the taxpayer elects to expense under § 179. If the passenger automobile is used partly for personal use, the personal use percentage is ignored for the purpose of determining the unrecovered cost available for deduction in later years.

EXAMPLE 30   On July 1, 1990, T places in service an automobile that cost $14,000. The car is always used 80% for business and 20% for personal use. The cost recovery for the automobile would be as follows:

1990—$2,128	[$14,000 × 20% (limited to $2,660) × 80%]
1991—$3,360	[$14,000 × 32% (limited to $4,200) × 80%]
1992—$2,040	[$14,000 × 19.2% (limited to $2,550) × 80%]
1993—$1,180	[$14,000 × 11.52% (limited to $1,475) × 80%]
1994—$1,180	[$14,000 × 11.52% (limited to $1,475) × 80%]
1995—$1,180	[$1,640 unrecovered cost ($14,000 − $12,360*) (limited to $1,475) × 80%]
1996—$ 132	[$165 unrecovered cost ($14,000 − $13,835 × 80%)]

*($2,660 + $4,200 + $2,550 + $1,475 + $1,475). While the statutory percentage method appears to restrict the deduction to $645 [$14,000 × 5.76% (limited to $1,475) × 80%], the unrecovered cost of $1,640 (limited to $1,475) multiplied by the business usage percentage is deductible. At the start of 1993 (Year 4), there is an automatic switch to the straight-line depreciation method. Under this method, the unrecovered

---

12.   Reg. § 1.280F–6T(e).

cost up to the maximum allowable limit ($1,475) is deductible in the last year of the recovery period (1995 or Year 6). Because the limit restricts the deduction, the remaining unrecovered cost is deductible in the next or succeeding year(s), subject to the maximum allowable yearly limit ($1,475), multiplied by the business usage percentage.

The total cost recovery for the years 1990–1996 is $11,200 (80% business usage × $14,000). □

The cost recovery limitations are maximum amounts. If the ACRS percentages produce a lesser amount of cost recovery, the lesser amount is used.

EXAMPLE 31   On April 2, 1990, T places in service an automobile that cost $10,000. The car is always used 70% for business and 30% for personal use. The cost recovery for 1990 would be $1,400 ($10,000 × 20% × 70%). □

Note that the cost recovery limitations apply *only* to passenger automobiles and not to other listed property.

Automobiles and Other Listed Property Not Used Predominantly in Business. The cost of listed property that does not pass the more-than-50 percent business usage test in the year the property is placed in service must be recovered using the straight-line method. Under TRA of 1986, the straight-line method to be used is that required under the alternative depreciation system (ADS) (explained later in the chapter). This system requires a straight-line recovery period of five years for automobiles. However, even though the straight-line method is used, the cost recovery allowance for passenger automobiles cannot exceed the limitations.

EXAMPLE 32   On July 27, 1990, T places in service an automobile that cost $20,000. The auto is used 40% for business and 60% for personal use. The cost recovery allowance for 1990 is $800 [$20,000 × 10% (Table 8–11) × 40%]. □

EXAMPLE 33   Assume the same facts as in Example 32, except that the auto cost $50,000. The cost recovery allowance for 1990 is $1,064 [$50,000 × 10% = $5,000 (limited to $2,660) × 40%]. □

If the listed property fails the more-than-50 percent business usage test, the straight-line method must be used for the remainder of the property's life. This applies even if at some later date the business usage of the property increases to more than 50 percent. However, even though the straight-line method must continue to be used, the amount of cost recovery will reflect the increase in business usage.

EXAMPLE 34   Assume the same facts as in Example 32, except that in 1991, T uses the auto 70% for business and 30% for personal use. T's cost recovery allowance for 1991 is $2,800 [$20,000 × 20% (Table 8–11) × 70%]. □

Change from Predominantly Business Use.   If the business use percentage of listed property falls to 50 percent or lower after the year the property is placed in

service, the property is subject to *cost recovery recapture*. The amount required to be recaptured and included in the taxpayer's return as ordinary income is the excess depreciation.

Excess depreciation is the excess of the ACRS percentage deduction taken in prior years over the amount that would have been allowed if the straight-line method had been used since the property was placed in service.

EXAMPLE 35   T purchased a car on January 22, 1990, at a cost of $20,000. Business usage was 80% in 1990, 70% in 1991, 40% in 1992, and 60% in 1993. ACRS deductions in 1990 and 1991 are $2,128 (80% × $2,660) and $2,940 (70% × $4,200), respectively. T's excess depreciation to be recaptured as ordinary income in 1992 is $668, calculated as follows:

1990	
ACRS allowance	$ 2,128
Straight-line ($20,000 × 10% × 80%)	(1,600)
Excess	$ 528
1991	
ACRS allowance	$ 2,940
Straight-line ($20,000 × 20% × 70%)	(2,800)
1991 excess	$ 140
1990 excess	528
Total excess	$ 668

After the business usage of the listed property drops below the more-than-50 percent level, the straight-line method must be used for the remaining life of the property.

EXAMPLE 36   Assume the same facts as in Example 35. T's cost recovery allowance for the years 1992 and 1993 would be $1,020 and $885, computed as follows:

1992—$1,020	[($20,000 × 20%) limited to $2,550 × 40%]
1993—$885	[($20,000 × 20%) limited to $1,475 × 60%]

Substantiation Requirements.   Listed property is now subject to the substantiation requirements of § 274. This means that business usage must be proven as to the amount of expense or use, the time and place of use, the business purpose for the use, and the business relationship to the taxpayer of persons using the property. Substantiation will require adequate records or sufficient evidence corroborating the taxpayer's statement. However, these substantiation requirements do not apply to vehicles that, by reason of their nature, are not likely to be used more than a *de minimis* amount for personal purposes.

CONCEPT SUMMARY 8—3

Listed Property Cost Recovery

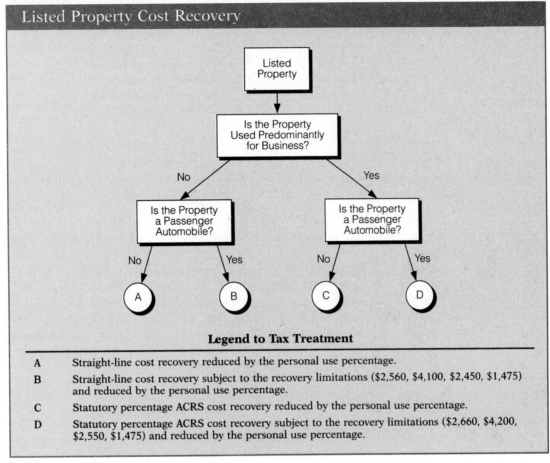

Legend to Tax Treatment

A	Straight-line cost recovery reduced by the personal use percentage.
B	Straight-line cost recovery subject to the recovery limitations ($2,560, $4,100, $2,450, $1,475) and reduced by the personal use percentage.
C	Statutory percentage ACRS cost recovery reduced by the personal use percentage.
D	Statutory percentage ACRS cost recovery subject to the recovery limitations ($2,660, $4,200, $2,550, $1,475) and reduced by the personal use percentage.

Alternative Depreciation System (ADS)

TRA of 1986 provides for an *alternative depreciation system (ADS)*, which must be used for the following:

- To calculate the portion of depreciation treated as a tax preference item for purposes of the corporate and individual alternative minimum tax (see chapter 14).

- To compute depreciation allowances for property for which any of the following is true:
  - Used predominantly outside the United States.
  - Leased or otherwise used by a tax-exempt entity.
  - Financed with the proceeds of tax-exempt bonds.
  - Imported from foreign countries that maintain discriminatory trade practices or otherwise engage in discriminatory acts.

- To compute depreciation allowances for earnings and profits purposes (see chapter 17).

In general, depreciation is computed using straight-line recovery without regard to salvage value. However, for purposes of the alternative minimum tax, depreciation of personal property is computed using the 150 percent declining-balance method with an appropriate switch to the straight-line method.

The taxpayer must use the half-year or the mid-quarter convention, whichever is applicable, for all property other than eligible real estate. The mid-month convention is used for eligible real estate. The applicable depreciation rates are found in Tables 8–10, 8–11, and 8–12.

The recovery periods under the alternative depreciation system are as follows:[13]

- The ADR midpoint life for property that does not fall into any of the following listed categories.

- Five years for qualified technological equipment, automobiles, and light-duty trucks.

- Twelve years for personal property with no class life.

- Forty years for all residential rental property and all nonresidential real property.

The Technical and Miscellaneous Revenue Act of 1988 allows taxpayers to *elect* to use the 150 percent declining-balance method to compute the regular tax rather than the 200 percent declining-balance method that is available for personal property. Hence, there will be no difference between the cost recovery for computing the regular tax and the alternative minimum tax. However, taxpayers that make this election must use the ADS recovery periods in computing the cost recovery for the regular tax, and the ADS recovery periods generally are longer than the regular recovery periods under ACRS.

Examples of the classification of property by class life for the ADS recovery periods are as follows:[14]

3-year .... Special tools used in the manufacture of motor vehicles, breeding hogs.

5-year .... Automobiles, light general-purpose trucks.

7-year .... Breeding and dairy cattle.

9.5-year .... Computer-based telephone central office switching equipment.

10-year .... Office furniture, fixtures, and equipment; railroad track.

12-year .... Racehorses more than 2 years old at the time they are placed in service.

EXAMPLE 37   On March 1, 1990. T purchases computer-based telephone central office switching equipment for $80,000. If T uses statutory percentage ACRS cost recovery (assuming no § 179 election), the cost recovery for 1990 is $16,000 [$80,000 × 20% (Table 8–2, 5-year class property)]. If T elects to use ADS 150% declining-balance cost recovery (assuming no § 179 election), the cost recovery for 1990 is $6,312 [$80,000 × 7.89% (Table 8–10, 9.5-year class property)]. □

---

13. The class life for certain properties described in §168(e)(3) are specially determined under §168(g)(3)(B).

14. Rev.Proc. 87–56, 1987–2 C.B. 674 is the source for the recovery periods.

In lieu of depreciation under the regular ACRS method, taxpayers may *elect* straight-line under ADS for property that qualifies for the regular ACRS method. The election is available on a class-by-class and year-by-year basis for property other than eligible real estate. The election for eligible real estate is on a property-by-property basis. One reason for making this election is to avoid a difference between deductible depreciation and earnings and profits depreciation.

EXAMPLE 38

T acquires an apartment building on March 17, 1990, for $700,000. T takes the maximum cost recovery for determining taxable income. T's cost recovery for computing 1990 taxable income would be $20,153 [$700,000 × .02879 (Table 8–7)]. However, T's cost recovery for computing T's earnings and profits would be only $13,853 [$700,000 × .01979 (Table 8–12)].   □

DEPLETION

In developing an oil or gas well, four types of expenditures must be made by the producer. The first type is the payment for the natural resource (the oil under the ground). Because natural resources are physically limited, these costs are recovered through depletion. The second type occurs when the property is made ready for drilling: the cost of labor in clearing the property, erecting derricks, and drilling the hole. These costs, called intangible drilling and development costs, generally have no salvage value and are a lost cost if the well is dry. The third type of cost is for tangible assets such as tools, pipes, and engines. Such costs are capital in nature and must be capitalized and recovered through depreciation. Finally, there are costs that are incurred after the well is producing, including such items as labor, fuel, and supplies. They are clearly operating expenses that are deductible currently when incurred (on the accrual basis) or when paid (on the cash basis).

The expenditures for depreciable assets and operating expenses pose no unusual problems for producers of natural resources. The tax treatment of depletable costs and intangible drilling and development costs is quite a different matter.

Intangible Drilling and Development Costs (IDC)

Intangible drilling and development costs can be handled in one of two ways at the option of the taxpayer. They can be *either* charged off as an expense in the year in which they are incurred or capitalized and written off through depletion. The election is made in the first year that such expenditures are incurred either by taking a deduction on the return or by adding them to the depletable basis. No formal statement of intent is required. Once made, the election is binding on both the taxpayer and the Internal Revenue Service for all such expenditures in the future. If the taxpayer fails to make the election to expense such costs on the original timely filed return the first year such expenditures are incurred, an automatic election to capitalize them has been made and is irrevocable.

As a general rule, it is more advantageous to expense intangible drilling and development costs. The obvious benefit of an immediate write-off (as opposed to a deferred write-off through depletion) is not the only advantage. Since a taxpayer can use percentage depletion, which is calculated without reference to basis (see Example 42), the intangible drilling and development costs may be completely lost as a deduction if they are capitalized.

Depletion Methods

Wasting assets (e.g., oil, gas, coal, gravel) are subject to depletion, which simply is a form of depreciation applicable to natural resources. Land generally cannot be depleted.

The owner of an interest in the wasting asset is entitled to deduct depletion. An owner is one who has an economic interest in the property. An economic interest requires the acquisition of an interest in the minerals in place and the receipt of income from the extraction or severance of such minerals. Like depreciation, depletion is a deduction *for* adjusted gross income.

There are two methods of calculating depletion: cost and percentage. Cost depletion can be used on any wasting asset (and is the only method allowed for timber). Percentage depletion is subject to a number of limitations, particularly as to oil and gas deposits. Depletion should be calculated both ways, and generally the method that results in the *largest* deduction is used. The choice between cost and percentage depletion is an annual election.

Cost Depletion.   *Cost depletion* is determined by using the adjusted basis of the asset. Such basis is divided by the estimated recoverable units of the asset (e.g., barrels, tons) to arrive at the depletion per unit. The depletion per unit then is multiplied by the number of units sold (*not* the units produced) during the year to arrive at the cost depletion allowed. Cost depletion, therefore, resembles the units-of-production method of calculating depreciation.

EXAMPLE 39   On January 1, 1990, T purchased the rights to a mineral interest for $1,000,000. At that time, the remaining recoverable units in the mineral interest were estimated to be 200,000. Under these circumstances, the depletion per unit becomes $5 [$1,000,000 (adjusted basis) ÷ 200,000 (estimated recoverable units)]. If during the year 60,000 units were mined and 25,000 were sold, the cost depletion would be $125,000 [$5 (depletion per unit) × 25,000 (units sold)]. □

If later it is discovered that the original estimate was incorrect, the depletion per unit for future calculations must be redetermined based on the revised estimate.

Percentage Depletion.   *Percentage depletion* (also referred to as statutory depletion) is a specified percentage provided for in the Code. The percentage varies according to the type of mineral interest involved. A sample of these percentages is shown in Figure 8–1. The rate is applied to the gross income from the property, but in no event may percentage depletion exceed 50 percent of the taxable income from the property before the allowance for depletion.

EXAMPLE 40   Assuming gross income of $100,000, a depletion rate of 22%, and other expenses relating to the property of $60,000, the depletion allowance is determined as follows:

Gross income	$100,000
Less: Other expenses	(60,000)
Taxable income before depletion	$ 40,000
Depletion allowance [the lesser of $22,000 (22% × $100,000) or $20,000 (50% × $40,000)]	(20,000)
Taxable income after depletion	$ 20,000

FIGURE 8−1   Sample of Percentage Depletion Rates

22% Depletion

Cobalt	Sulfur
Lead	Tin
Nickel	Uranium
Platinum	Zinc

15% Depletion

Copper	Oil and gas
Gold	Oil shale
Iron	Silver

14% Depletion

Borax	Magnesium carbonates
Calcium carbonates	Marble
Granite	Potash
Limestone	Slate

10% Depletion

Coal	Perlite
Lignite	Sodium chloride

5% Depletion

Gravel	Pumice
Peat	Sand

The adjusted basis of the property would be reduced by $20,000, the depletion allowed. If the other expenses had been only $55,000, the full $22,000 could have been deducted, and the adjusted basis would have been reduced by $22,000. □

Note that percentage depletion is based on a percentage of the gross income from the property and makes no reference to cost. When percentage depletion is used, it is therefore possible to deduct more than the original cost of the property. If percentage depletion is used, however, the adjusted basis of the property (for computing cost depletion) must be reduced by the amount of percentage depletion taken until basis reaches zero.

TAX PLANNING CONSIDERATIONS

Depreciation and ACRS

Depreciation schedules should be reviewed annually for possible retirements, abandonments, obsolescence, and changes in estimated useful lives.

EXAMPLE 41

An examination of the depreciation schedule of X Company reveals the following:

- Asset A was abandoned when it was discovered that the cost of repairs would be in excess of the cost of replacement. Asset A had an adjusted basis of $3,000.

- Asset D was being depreciated over a period of 10 years, but a revised estimate showed that its estimated remaining life is only 2 years. Its original cost was $60,000, and it had been depreciated under the straight-line method for 3 years. It was a pre-ERTA asset and was not subject to ACRS provisions.

- Asset J had become obsolete this year, at which point, its adjusted basis was $8,000.

The depreciation expense on Asset D should be $21,000 [$60,000 (cost) − $18,000 (accumulated depreciation) = $42,000 ÷ 2 (remaining estimated useful life)]. Assets A and J should be written off for an additional expense of $11,000 ($3,000 + $8,000). □

Because of the deductions for depreciation, interest, and ad valorem property taxes, investments in real estate can be highly attractive. In figuring the economics of such investments, one should be sure to take into account any tax savings that result.

EXAMPLE 42

In early January 1990, T (an individual in the 28% tax bracket) purchased residential rental property for $170,000 (of which $20,000 was allocated to the land and $150,000 to the building). T made a down payment of $25,000 and assumed the seller's mortgage for the balance. Under the mortgage agreement, monthly payments of $1,000 are required and are applied toward interest, taxes, insurance, and principal. Since the property was already occupied, T continued to receive from the tenant rent of $1,200 per month. T actively participates in this activity and hence comes under the special rule for a rental real estate activity with respect to the limitation on passive activity losses (refer to chapter 6).

During the first year of ownership, T's expenses were as follows:

Interest	$10,000
Taxes	800
Insurance	1,000
Repairs and maintenance	2,200
Depreciation ($150,000 × .03485)	5,228
Total	$19,228

The deductible loss from the rental property is computed as follows:

Rental income ($1,200 × 12 months)	$ 14,400
Less expenses (see above)	(19,228)
Net loss	$ (4,828)

But what is T's overall position for the year when the tax benefit of the loss is taken into account? Considering just the cash intake and outlay, it is summarized as follows:

Intake—		
Rental income	$14,400	
Tax savings [28% (income tax bracket) × $4,828 (loss from the property)]	1,352	$ 15,752
Outlay—		
Mortgage payments ($1,000 × 12 months)	$12,000	
Repairs and maintenance	2,200	(14,200)
Net cash benefit		$ 1,552

It should be noted, however, that should T cease being an active participant in the rental activity, the passive loss rules would apply, and T could lose the current period benefit of the loss.

Depletion

Since the election to use the cost or percentage depletion method is an annual election, a taxpayer can use cost depletion (if higher) until the basis is exhausted and then switch to percentage depletion in the following years.

EXAMPLE 43   Assume the following facts for T:

Remaining depletable basis	$ 11,000
Gross income (10,000 units)	100,000
Expenses (other than depletion)	30,000

Since cost depletion is limited to the basis of $11,000 and if the percentage depletion is $22,000 (assume a 22% rate), T would choose the latter. His basis is then reduced to zero. In future years, however, he can continue to take percentage depletion since percentage depletion is taken without reference to the remaining basis. ☐

TABLES

TABLE 8-1   ACRS Statutory Percentages for Property Other Than 15-Year Real Property, 18-Year Real Property, or 19-Year Real Property

For Property Placed in Service after December 31, 1980, and before January 1, 1987

The applicable percentage for the class of property is:

Recovery Year	3-Year	5-Year	10-Year	15-Year Public Utility
1	25	15	8	5
2	38	22	14	10
3	37	21	12	9
4		21	10	8
5		21	10	7
6			10	7
7			9	6
8			9	6
9			9	6
10			9	6
11				6
12				6
13				6
14				6
15				6

TABLE 8-2   Accelerated Depreciation for Personal Property Assuming Half-Year Convention

For Property Placed in Service after December 31, 1986

Recovery Year	3-Year (200% DB)	5-Year (200% DB)	7-Year (200% DB)	10-Year (200% DB)	15-Year (150% DB)	20-Year (150% DB)
1	33.33	20.00	14.29	10.00	5.00	3.750
2	44.45	32.00	24.49	18.00	9.50	7.219
3	14.81*	19.20	17.49	14.40	8.55	6.677
4	7.41	11.52*	12.49	11.52	7.70	6.177
5		11.52	8.93*	9.22	6.93	5.713
6		5.76	8.92	7.37	6.23	5.285

TABLE 8−2   (*Continued*)

For Property Placed in Service after December 31, 1986

Recovery Year	3-Year (200% DB)	5-Year (200% DB)	7-Year (200% DB)	10-Year (200% DB)	15-Year (150% DB)	20-Year (150% DB)
7			8.93	6.55*	5.90*	4.888
8			4.46	6.55	5.90	4.522
9				6.56	5.91	4.462*
10				6.55	5.90	4.461
11				3.28	5.91	4.462
12					5.90	4.461
13					5.91	4.462
14					5.90	4.461
15					5.91	4.462
16					2.95	4.461
17						4.462
18						4.461
19						4.462
20						4.461
21						2.231

*Switchover to straight-line depreciation.

TABLE 8−3   Accelerated Depreciation for Personal Property Assuming Mid-Quarter Convention

For Property Placed in Service after December 31, 1986 (Partial Table*)

		3-Year		
Recovery Year	First Quarter	Second Quarter	Third Quarter	Fourth Quarter
1	58.33	41.67	25.00	8.33
2	27.78	38.89	50.00	61.11
		5-Year		
Recovery Year	First Quarter	Second Quarter	Third Quarter	Fourth Quarter
1	35.00	25.00	15.00	5.00
2	26.00	30.00	34.00	38.00

*The figures in this table are taken from the official tables that appear in Rev.Proc. 87−57, 1987−2 C.B. 687. Because of their length, the complete tables are not presented.

TABLE 8–4   ACRS Statutory Percentages for 15-Year Real Property

**For Property Placed in Service after December 31, 1980,
and before January 1, 1987
15-Year Real Property: Low-Income Housing**

If the recovery year is:	And the month in the first recovery year the property is placed in service is:											
	1	2	3	4	5	6	7	8	9	10	11	12
	The applicable percentage is (use the column for the month in the first year the property is placed in service):											
1	13	12	11	10	9	8	7	6	4	3	2	1
2	12	12	12	12	12	12	12	13	13	13	13	13
3	10	10	10	10	11	11	11	11	11	11	11	11
4	9	9	9	9	9	9	9	9	10	10	10	10
5	8	8	8	8	8	8	8	8	8	8	8	9
6	7	7	7	7	7	7	7	7	7	7	7	7
7	6	6	6	6	6	6	6	6	6	6	6	6
8	5	5	5	5	5	5	5	5	5	5	6	6
9	5	5	5	5	5	5	5	5	5	5	5	5
10	5	5	5	5	5	5	5	5	5	5	5	5
11	4	5	5	5	5	5	5	5	5	5	5	5
12	4	4	4	5	4	5	5	5	5	5	5	5
13	4	4	4	4	4	4	5	4	5	5	5	5
14	4	4	4	4	4	4	4	4	4	5	4	4
15	4	4	4	4	4	4	4	4	4	4	4	4
16	–	–	1	1	2	2	2	3	3	3	4	4

TABLE 8—4   (*Continued*)

**For Property Placed in Service after December 31, 1980,
and before March 16, 1984
15-Year Real Property (other than low-income housing)**

If the recovery year is:	And the month in the first recovery year the property is placed in service is:											
	1	2	3	4	5	6	7	8	9	10	11	12
	The applicable percentage is (use the column for the month in the first year the property is placed in service):											
1	12	11	10	9	8	7	6	5	4	3	2	1
2	10	10	11	11	11	11	11	11	11	11	11	12
3	9	9	9	9	10	10	10	10	10	10	10	10
4	8	8	8	8	8	8	9	9	9	9	9	9
5	7	7	7	7	7	7	8	8	8	8	8	8
6	6	6	6	6	7	7	7	7	7	7	7	7
7	6	6	6	6	6	6	6	6	6	6	6	6
8	6	6	6	6	6	6	6	6	6	6	6	6
9	6	6	6	6	5	6	5	5	5	6	6	6
10	5	6	5	6	5	5	5	5	5	5	6	5
11	5	5	5	5	5	5	5	5	5	5	5	5
12	5	5	5	5	5	5	5	5	5	5	5	5
13	5	5	5	5	5	5	5	5	5	5	5	5
14	5	5	5	5	5	5	5	5	5	5	5	5
15	5	5	5	5	5	5	5	5	5	5	5	5
16	—	—	1	1	2	2	3	3	4	4	4	5

TABLE 8–5   ACRS Cost Recovery Table for 18-Year Real Property

For Property Placed in Service after June 22, 1984, and before May 9, 1985
18-Year Real Property (18-Year 175% Declining Balance)
(Assuming Mid-Month Convention)

If the recovery year is:	And the month in the first recovery year the property is placed in service is:											
	1	2	3	4	5	6	7	8	9	10	11	12
	The applicable percentage is (use the column for the month in the first year the property is placed in service):											
1	9	9	8	7	6	5	4	4	3	2	1	0.4
2	9	9	9	9	9	9	9	9	9	10	10	10.0
3	8	8	8	8	8	8	8	8	9	9	9	9.0
4	7	7	7	7	7	8	8	8	8	8	8	8.0
5	7	7	7	7	7	7	7	7	7	7	7	7.0
6	6	6	6	6	6	6	6	6	6	6	6	6.0
7	5	5	5	5	6	6	6	6	6	6	6	6.0
8	5	5	5	5	5	5	5	5	5	5	5	5.0
9	5	5	5	5	5	5	5	5	5	5	5	5.0
10	5	5	5	5	5	5	5	5	5	5	5	5.0
11	5	5	5	5	5	5	5	5	5	5	5	5.0
12	5	5	5	5	5	5	5	5	5	5	5	5.0
13	4	4	4	5	4	4	5	4	4	4	5	5.0
14	4	4	4	4	4	4	4	4	4	4	4	4.0
15	4	4	4	4	4	4	4	4	4	4	4	4.0
16	4	4	4	4	4	4	4	4	4	4	4	4.0
17	4	4	4	4	4	4	4	4	4	4	4	4.0
18	4	3	4	4	4	4	4	4	4	4	4	4.0
19		1	1	1	2	2	2	3	3	3	3	3.6

TABLE 8—6   ACRS Cost Recovery Table for 19-Year Real Property

For Property Placed in Service after May 8, 1985, and before January 1, 1987
19-Year Real Property (19-Year 175% Declining Balance)
(Assuming Mid-Month Convention)

If the recovery year is:	And the month in the first recovery year the property is placed in service is:											
	1	2	3	4	5	6	7	8	9	10	11	12
	The applicable percentage is (use the column for the month in the first year the property is placed in service):											
1	8.8	8.1	7.3	6.5	5.8	5.0	4.2	3.5	2.7	1.9	1.1	0.4
2	8.4	8.5	8.5	8.6	8.7	8.8	8.8	8.9	9.0	9.0	9.1	9.2
3	7.6	7.7	7.7	7.8	7.9	7.9	8.0	8.1	8.1	8.2	8.3	8.3
4	6.9	7.0	7.0	7.1	7.1	7.2	7.3	7.3	7.4	7.4	7.5	7.6
5	6.3	6.3	6.4	6.4	6.5	6.5	6.6	6.6	6.7	6.8	6.8	6.9
6	5.7	5.7	5.8	5.9	5.9	5.9	6.0	6.0	6.1	6.1	6.2	6.2
7	5.2	5.2	5.3	5.3	5.3	5.4	5.4	5.5	5.5	5.6	5.6	5.6
8	4.7	4.7	4.8	4.8	4.8	4.9	4.9	5.0	5.0	5.1	5.1	5.1
9	4.2	4.3	4.3	4.4	4.4	4.5	4.5	4.5	4.5	4.6	4.6	4.7
10	4.2	4.2	4.2	4.2	4.2	4.2	4.2	4.2	4.2	4.2	4.2	4.2
11	4.2	4.2	4.2	4.2	4.2	4.2	4.2	4.2	4.2	4.2	4.2	4.2
12	4.2	4.2	4.2	4.2	4.2	4.2	4.2	4.2	4.2	4.2	4.2	4.2
13	4.2	4.2	4.2	4.2	4.2	4.2	4.2	4.2	4.2	4.2	4.2	4.2
14	4.2	4.2	4.2	4.2	4.2	4.2	4.2	4.2	4.2	4.2	4.2	4.2
15	4.2	4.2	4.2	4.2	4.2	4.2	4.2	4.2	4.2	4.2	4.2	4.2
16	4.2	4.2	4.2	4.2	4.2	4.2	4.2	4.2	4.2	4.2	4.2	4.2
17	4.2	4.2	4.2	4.2	4.2	4.2	4.2	4.2	4.2	4.2	4.2	4.2
18	4.2	4.2	4.2	4.2	4.2	4.2	4.2	4.2	4.2	4.2	4.2	4.2
19	4.2	4.2	4.2	4.2	4.2	4.2	4.2	4.2	4.2	4.2	4.2	4.2
20	0.2	0.5	0.9	1.2	1.6	1.9	2.3	2.6	3.0	3.3	3.7	4.0

TABLE 8–7   Straight-Line Depreciation for Real Property Assuming Mid-Month Convention*

For Property Placed in Service after December 31, 1986
27.5-Year Residential Real Property

The applicable percentage is (use the column for the
month in the first year the property is placed in service):

Recovery Year(s)	1	2	3	4	5	6	7	8	9	10	11	12
1	3.485	3.182	2.879	2.576	2.273	1.970	1.667	1.364	1.061	0.758	0.455	0.152
2–18	3.636	3.636	3.636	3.636	3.636	3.636	3.636	3.636	3.636	3.636	3.636	3.636
19–27	3.637	3.637	3.637	3.637	3.637	3.637	3.637	3.637	3.637	3.637	3.637	3.637
28	1.970	2.273	2.576	2.879	3.182	3.485	3.636	3.636	3.636	3.636	3.636	3.636
29	0.000	0.000	0.000	0.000	0.000	0.000	0.152	0.455	0.758	1.061	1.364	1.667

31.5-Year Nonresidential Real Property

The applicable percentage is (use the column for
the month in the first year the property is placed in service):

Recovery Year(s)	1	2	3	4	5	6	7	8	9	10	11	12
1	3.042	2.778	2.513	2.249	1.984	1.720	1.455	1.190	0.926	0.661	0.397	0.132
2–19	3.175	3.175	3.175	3.175	3.175	3.175	3.175	3.175	3.175	3.175	3.175	3.175
20–31	3.174	3.174	3.174	3.174	3.174	3.174	3.174	3.174	3.174	3.174	3.174	3.174
32	1.720	1.984	2.249	2.513	2.778	3.042	3.175	3.175	3.175	3.175	3.175	3.175
33	0.000	0.000	0.000	0.000	0.000	0.000	0.132	0.397	0.661	0.926	1.190	1.455

*The official tables contain a separate row for each year. For ease of presentation, certain years are grouped in these two tables. In some instances, this will produce a difference of .001 for the last digit when compared with the official tables.

TABLE 8—8   ACRS Cost Recovery Table for 19-Year Real Property: Optional Straight-Line

For Property Placed in Service after May 8, 1985, and before January 1, 1987
19-Year Real Property for Which an Optional 19-Year Straight-Line Method Is
Elected (Assuming Mid-Month Convention)

If the recovery year is:	And the month in the first recovery year the property is placed in service is:											
	1	2	3	4	5	6	7	8	9	10	11	12
	The applicable percentage is (use the column for the month in the first year the property is placed in service):											
1	5.0	4.6	4.2	3.7	3.3	2.9	2.4	2.0	1.5	1.1	.7	.2
2	5.3	5.3	5.3	5.3	5.3	5.3	5.3	5.3	5.3	5.3	5.3	5.3
3	5.3	5.3	5.3	5.3	5.3	5.3	5.3	5.3	5.3	5.3	5.3	5.3
4	5.3	5.3	5.3	5.3	5.3	5.3	5.3	5.3	5.3	5.3	5.3	5.3
5	5.3	5.3	5.3	5.3	5.3	5.3	5.3	5.3	5.3	5.3	5.3	5.3
6	5.3	5.3	5.3	5.3	5.3	5.3	5.3	5.3	5.3	5.3	5.3	5.3
7	5.3	5.3	5.3	5.3	5.3	5.3	5.3	5.3	5.3	5.3	5.3	5.3
8	5.3	5.3	5.3	5.3	5.3	5.3	5.3	5.3	5.3	5.3	5.3	5.3
9	5.3	5.3	5.3	5.3	5.3	5.3	5.3	5.3	5.3	5.3	5.3	5.3
10	5.3	5.3	5.3	5.3	5.3	5.3	5.3	5.3	5.3	5.3	5.3	5.3
11	5.3	5.3	5.3	5.3	5.3	5.3	5.3	5.3	5.3	5.3	5.3	5.3
12	5.3	5.3	5.3	5.3	5.3	5.3	5.3	5.3	5.3	5.3	5.3	5.3
13	5.3	5.3	5.3	5.3	5.3	5.3	5.3	5.3	5.3	5.3	5.3	5.3
14	5.2	5.2	5.2	5.2	5.2	5.2	5.2	5.2	5.2	5.2	5.2	5.2
15	5.2	5.2	5.2	5.2	5.2	5.2	5.2	5.2	5.2	5.2	5.2	5.2
16	5.2	5.2	5.2	5.2	5.2	5.2	5.2	5.2	5.2	5.2	5.2	5.2
17	5.2	5.2	5.2	5.2	5.2	5.2	5.2	5.2	5.2	5.2	5.2	5.2
18	5.2	5.2	5.2	5.2	5.2	5.2	5.2	5.2	5.2	5.2	5.2	5.2
19	5.2	5.2	5.2	5.2	5.2	5.2	5.2	5.2	5.2	5.2	5.2	5.2
20	.2	.6	1.0	1.5	1.9	2.3	2.8	3.2	3.7	4.1	4.5	5.0

TABLE 8-9 Straight-Line Depreciation for Personal Property Assuming Half-Year Convention*

For Property Placed in Service after December 31, 1986

ACRS Class	% First Recovery Year	Other Recovery Years		Last Recovery Year	
		Years	%	Year	%
3-Year	16.67	2–3	33.33	4	16.67
5-Year	10.00	2–5	20.00	6	10.00
7-Year	7.14	2–7	14.29	8	7.14
10-Year	5.00	2–10	10.00	11	5.00
15-Year	3.33	2–15	6.67	16	3.33
20-Year	2.50	2–20	5.00	21	2.50

*The official table contains a separate row for each year. For ease of presentation, certain years are grouped in this table. In some instances, this will produce a difference of .01 for the last digit when compared with the official table.

TABLE 8-10 Alternative Minimum Tax: 150% Declining-Balance Assuming Half-Year Convention

For Property Placed in Service after December 31, 1986 (Partial Table*)

Recovery Year	3-Year 150%	5-Year 150%	9.5-Year 150%	10-Year 150%
1	25.00	15.00	7.89	7.50
2	37.50	25.50	14.54	13.88
3	25.00**	17.85	12.25	11.79
4	12.50	16.66**	10.31	10.02
5		16.66	9.17**	8.74**
6		8.33	9.17	8.74
7			9.17	8.74
8			9.17	8.74
9			9.17	8.74
10			9.16	8.74
11				4.37

*The figures in this table are taken from the official table that appears in Rev.Proc. 87–57, 1987–2 C.B. 687. Because of its length, the complete table is not presented.

**Switchover to straight-line depreciation.

TABLE 8–11 ADS Straight-Line for Personal Property Assuming Half-Year Convention

**For Property Placed in Service after
December 31, 1986
(Partial Table*)**

Recovery Year	5-Year Class	9.5-Year Class	12-Year Class
1	10.00	5.26	4.17
2	20.00	10.53	8.33
3	20.00	10.53	8.33
4	20.00	10.53	8.33
5	20.00	10.52	8.33
6	10.00	10.53	8.33
7		10.52	8.34
8		10.53	8.33
9		10.52	8.34
10		10.53	8.33
11			8.34
12			8.33
13			4.17

*The figures in this table are taken from the official table that appears in Rev.Proc. 87–57, 1987–2 C.B. 678. Because of its length, the complete table is not presented. The tables for the mid-quarter convention also appear in Rev.Proc. 87–57.

TABLE 8–12 ADS Straight-Line for Real Property Assuming Mid-Month Convention

For Property Placed in Service after December 31, 1986

Recovery Year	Month Placed in Service											
	1	2	3	4	5	6	7	8	9	10	11	12
1	2.396	2.188	1.979	1.771	1.563	1.354	1.146	0.938	0.729	0.521	0.313	0.104
2–40	2.500	2.500	2.500	2.500	2.500	2.500	2.500	2.500	2.500	2.500	2.500	2.500
41	0.104	0.312	0.521	0.729	0.937	1.146	1.354	1.562	1.771	1.979	2.187	2.396

PROBLEM MATERIALS

Discussion Questions

1. Discuss whether a taxpayer can depreciate personal property (personalty).

2. If a taxpayer does not claim depreciation in one year, can an excess amount be claimed during a subsequent year? How is the basis for depreciable property affected by the failure to claim depreciation during any one year?

3. If a personal use asset is converted to business use, why is it necessary to compute depreciation on the lower of fair market value or adjusted basis at the date of conversion?

4. Discuss whether a parking lot that is used in a business can be depreciated.

5. What depreciation methods can be used for the following assets that were acquired after 1969 and before January 1, 1981?
    a. Used machinery and equipment used in the business.
    b. New apartment building held for investment.
    c. Land held for business use.
    d. Used apartment building held for investment.
    e. New factory used for business.
    f. New automobile used in the business.

6. Can a taxpayer disregard salvage value on property acquired and placed in service after December 31, 1980?

7. Discuss the different ACRS recovery periods for ACRS real property depending on when the property is placed in service.

8. Why would a taxpayer elect the optional straight-line method for an asset acquired after 1986?

9. Discuss the applicable conventions if a taxpayer elects to use straight-line cost recovery for property placed in service after December 31, 1986.

10. Why is the basis of an asset reduced by the § 179 amount before the amount of the cost recovery allowance is computed?

11. Discuss the limitation on the § 179 amount that can be expensed and its impact on the basis of the property.

12. Discuss the tax consequences of listed property passing or failing the more-than-50% business usage test.

13. Discuss whether the statutory dollar limitations apply to the cost recovery of a computer that meets the more-than-50% business use test.

14. If a taxpayer does not pass the more-than-50% business use test on an automobile, discuss whether the statutory dollar limitations on cost recovery are applicable.

15. Discuss the tax consequences that result when a passenger automobile, which satisfied the more-than-50% business usage test during the first two years, fails the test for the third year.

16. Discuss the extent to which the 150% declining-balance method can be used under the alternative depreciation system.

17. Briefly discuss the differences between cost depletion and percentage depletion.

Problems

18. On January 1, 1979, X Company acquired an automobile for use in its business for $9,000. No depreciation was taken in 1979 or 1980 since the company had net operating losses and wanted to "save" the deductions for later years. In 1981, the company claimed a three-year life for the automobile (and no salvage value) and deducted $3,000 of depreciation using a straight-line rate. On January 1, 1982, the automobile was sold for $4,500. Calculate the gain or loss on the sale of the automobile in 1982.

19. X acquired a personal residence in 1978 for $60,000. In January 1980, he converted the residence to rental property when the fair market value was $64,000.

   a. Calculate the amount of depreciation that can be taken in 1980, assuming that the straight-line rate is used, there is no salvage value, and the residence has a 30-year estimated useful life.

   b. What would your answer be if the property were worth only $40,000 in 1980?

20. T, who is single, acquired a new machine for $42,000 on January 1, 1979. Calculate the total depreciation deduction allowed in the first year if the estimated useful life is 10 years (salvage value of $5,200) under each of the following methods:

   a. 200% declining-balance.

   b. Sum-of-the-years' digits.

   c. 150% declining-balance.

   d. Straight-line.

21. Taxpayer acquired a building for $250,000 (exclusive of land) on January 1, 1984. Calculate the cost recovery using the statutory percentage method for 1984 and 1985 if:

   a. The real property is low-income housing.

   b. The real property is a factory building.

22. On December 2, 1984, W purchased and placed in service a warehouse. The warehouse cost $800,000. W used the ACRS statutory percentage cost recovery method. On July 7, 1989, W sold the warehouse.

   a. Determine W's cost recovery for 1984.

   b. Determine W's cost recovery for 1989.

23. T, who is single, acquired a new copier (five-year class property) on March 2, 1990, for $28,000. What is the maximum amount that T can deduct in 1990 assuming the following:

   a. The taxable income derived from T's trade or business (without regard to the amount expensed under § 179) is $100,000.

   b. The taxable income derived from T's trade or business (without regard to the amount expensed under § 179) is $3,000.

24. H owns a small business that he operates as a sole proprietor. In 1990, H will net $9,000 of business income before consideration of any § 179 deduction. H spends $205,000 on new equipment in 1989. If H also has $3,000 of § 179 deduction carryforwards from 1989, determine his § 179 expense deduction for 1990 and the amount of any carryforward.

25. K acquired a machine on June 5, 1989, for $50,000. The machine is a five-year class asset. Calculate K's deduction for 1990 assuming the following:

   a. K elects the straight-line method over the five-year recovery period and does not elect immediate expensing under § 179.

   b. K elects immediate expensing under § 179 and does not elect the straight-line method.

26. Q is the proprietor of a small business. In 1990, his business income, before consideration of any § 179 deduction, is $5,000. Q spends $203,000 on new equipment and furniture for 1990. If Q elects to take the § 179 deduction on a desk that cost $15,000 (included in the $203,000), determine Q's total cost recovery for 1990 with respect to the desk.

27. During May 1990, T bought the following business assets:

Factory machinery (seven-year class property)	$80,000
Light-duty truck (five-year class property)	30,000

    Calculate T's cost recovery allowances for 1990 using the statutory percentage method, assuming T does not make the § 179 election.

28. On March 10, 1990, T purchased three-year class property for $20,000. On December 15, 1990, T purchased five-year class property for $50,000.
    a. Calculate T's cost recovery for 1990, assuming T does not make the § 179 election or use straight-line depreciation.
    b. Calculate T's cost recovery for 1990, assuming T does elect to use § 179 and does not elect to use straight-line depreciation.

29. T acquired a building for $250,000 (exclusive of land) on January 1, 1990. Calculate the cost recovery for 1990 and 1991 if the real property is residential rental property. Nonresidential real property.

30. U acquires a warehouse on March 1, 1990, at a cost of $2,500,000. On September 30, 1997, U sells the warehouse. Calculate U's cost recovery for 1990. For 1997.

31. On July 1, 1990, A places in service a computer (five-year class property). The computer cost $20,000. A used the computer 65% for business. The remainder of the time, A used the computer for personal purposes. If A does not elect § 179, determine her cost recovery deduction for the computer for 1990.

32. On February 16, 1990, T purchased and placed into service a new car. The purchase price was $18,000. T drove the car 12,000 miles during the remainder of the year, 9,000 miles for business and 3,000 miles for personal use. T used the statutory percentage method of cost recovery. Calculate the total deduction T may take for 1990 with respect to the car.

33. On June 5, 1990, R purchased and placed in service a $15,000 car. The business use percentage for the car is always 100%. Compute R's cost recovery deduction in 1996.

34. On May 7, 1990, S purchased and placed in service a $30,000 car. The business use percentage for the car is always 40%. Compute S's cost recovery deduction in 1990.

35. On March 10, 1990, T purchased an automobile for $12,000. During the year, the car was used 90% for business use and 10% for personal use. Compute the cost recovery deduction on the automobile for 1990.

36. On June 20, 1990, T purchased and placed in service a new car. The purchase price was $30,000. The car was used 30% for business, 30% for the production of income, and 40% for personal use. Determine the total deduction T may take for 1990 with respect to the car.

37. On June 14, 1990, T purchased and placed in service a new car. The purchase price was $16,000. The car was used 75% for business and 25% for personal use in both 1990 and 1991. In 1992, the car was used 40% for business and 60% for personal use. Compute the cost recovery allowance for the car in 1992 and the cost recovery recapture.

38. In 1990 R purchased a computer (five-year property) for $120,000. The computer was used 60% for business, 20% for income production, and 20% for personal use. In 1991 the usage changed to 40% for business, 30% for income production, and 30% for personal use. Compute the cost recovery for 1991 and any cost recovery recapture. Assume R did not make a § 179 election on the computer in 1990.

39. On March 5, 1990, T purchased office furniture and fixtures for $40,000. The assets are seven-year class property and have an ADS midpoint of 9.5 years. Determine T's cost recovery deduction for computing 1990 taxable income, using the alternative depreciation system and assuming T does not make a § 179 election.

40. In 1990 L purchased a light-duty truck for $12,000. The truck is used 100% for business. L did not make a § 179 election with respect to the truck. If L uses statutory percentage ACRS, determine L's cost recovery for 1990 for computing taxable income and for computing L's alternative minimum tax.

41. In June 1990, T purchased and placed in service railroad track costing $600,000.
    a. Calculate T's cost recovery deduction for 1990 for computing taxable income, assuming T does not make the § 179 election or use straight-line cost recovery.
    b. Calculate T's cost recovery deduction for 1990 for computing taxable income, assuming T does not make the § 179 election but does elect to use ADS 150% declining-balance cost recovery.

42. T acquired a mineral interest during the year for $5,000,000. A geological survey estimated that 250,000 tons of the mineral remained in the deposit. During the year, 70,000 tons were mined and 45,000 tons were sold for $6,000,000. Other expenses amounted to $4,000,000. Assuming the mineral depletion rate is 22%, calculate T's lowest taxable income.

43. T purchased an oil interest for $2,000,000. Recoverable barrels were estimated to be 500,000. During the year, 120,000 barrels were sold for $3,840,000, regular expenses (including depreciation) were $1,240,000, and IDC were $1,000,000. Calculate the taxable income under the expensing and capitalization methods of handling IDC.

Cumulative Problems

44. John Smith, age 31, is single and has no dependents. At the beginning of 1990, John started his own excavation business and named it Earth Movers. John lives at 1045 Center Street, Lindon, UT, and his business is located at 381 State Street, Lindon, UT. The zip code for both addresses is 84059. John's Social Security number is 321–09–6456, and the business identification number is 98–1234567. John is a cash basis taxpayer. During 1990, John had the following items in connection with his business:

Fees for services	$120,000
Building rental expense	12,000
Office furniture and equipment rental expense	2,400
Office supplies	500
Utilities	1,000
Salary for secretary	15,000
Salary for equipment operators	55,000
Payroll taxes	7,000
Fuel and oil for the equipment	10,000
Purchase of a front-end loader on January 15, 1990, for $50,000. John made the election under § 179.	50,000
Purchase of a new dump truck on January 18, 1990	30,000
During 1990, John had the following additional items:	
Interest income from First National Bank	8,000
Dividends from Exxon	500
Quarterly estimated tax payments	1,000

Assuming John does not itemize his deductions, compute his Federal income tax payable (or refund due). Suggested software (if available): *WEST–TAX Planner* or *BNA Individual Income Tax Spreadsheet*.

45. Bob Brown, age 30, is single and has no dependents. He was employed as a barber until May 1989 by Hair Cuts, Inc. In June 1989, Bob opened his own styling salon, the Style Shop, located at 465 Willow Drive, St. Paul, MN 55455. Bob is a cash basis taxpayer. He lives at 1021 Snelling Avenue, St. Paul, MN 55455. His Social Security number is 821–56–7102. Bob does not wish to designate $1 to the Presidential Election Campaign Fund. During 1989, Bob had the following income and expense items:

   a. $10,800 salary from Hair Cuts, Inc.

   b. $920 Federal income tax withheld by Hair Cuts, Inc.

   c. $350 cash dividend from General Motors.

   d. $5,000 gross receipts from his own hair styling business.

   e. Expenses connected with Bob's hair styling business:
      - $100 laundry and cleaning
      - $2,400 rent
      - $700 supplies
      - $500 utilities and telephone

   f. Bob purchased and installed a fancy barber chair on June 3, 1989. The chair cost $6,400. Bob did not make the § 179 election.

   g. Bob purchased and installed furniture and fixtures on June 5, 1989. These items cost $7,000. Bob did not make the § 179 election.

   h. Bob had no itemized deductions.

   Compute Bob Brown's 1989 Federal income tax payable (or refund due). If you use tax forms for your computations, you will need Forms 1040 and 4562 and Schedules C and SE. Suggested software (if available): *TurboTax* for tax return solutions, *WEST–TAX Planner* or *BNA Individual Income Tax Spreadsheet* if tax return solutions are not desired.

9

Deductions: Employee Expenses

Employees frequently incur expenses in connection with employment activities. Some of these expenses are deductible and some are not. Certain deductible expenses are subject to specific reductions and limitations. After determining which expenses are deductible and applying any limitations, the expenses must be classified as deductions *for* or deductions *from* AGI.

The rules for computing and classifying expenses incurred by self-employed individuals sometimes differ from those applicable to employees. Therefore, it is important to determine whether an individual is an employee or is self-employed. Guidelines for making this determination are discussed in the following section. This discussion is followed by coverage of the rules for computing and classifying employee business expenses.

CLASSIFICATION OF EMPLOYMENT-RELATED EXPENSES

Self-Employed versus Employee Status

In many instances it is difficult to distinguish between an individual who is self-employed and one who is performing services as an employee. Expenses of self-employed individuals are deductible as trade or business expenses (*for* adjusted gross income).

EXAMPLE 1   N, a self-employed CPA, incurred transportation expenses of $1,000 in connection with his business. The transportation expenses are deductions *for* AGI because they are expenses incurred by a self-employed individual.   ☐

Expenses incurred by an employee in an employment relationship are subject to limitations. Only reimbursed employee expenses are deductible *for* adjusted gross income. All other deductible employee expenses are deducted *from* adjusted gross income.

EXAMPLE 2   K, a CPA employed by N, incurred unreimbursed transportation expenses of $1,000 in connection with his employment activities. Because K is an employee, the transportation expenses are deductions *from* adjusted gross income (subject to a 2% floor discussed in Example 7).   ☐

EXAMPLE 3   G, a CPA employed by N, incurred entertainment expenses of $1,000 in connection with his employment activities. N reimbursed G for these entertainment expenses. G must include the $1,000 reimbursement in gross income, and he may take a $1,000 deduction *for* AGI.   ☐

As the preceding examples illustrate, because of the differences in the treatment of expenses, it is important to determine when an employer-employee relationship exists.

Generally, an employer-employee relationship exists when the employer has the right to specify the end result and the ways and means by which the end result is to be attained. Thus, an employee is subject to the will and control of the employer with respect not only to what shall be done but also to how it shall be done. If the individual is subject to the direction or control of another only to the

extent of the end result (e.g., the preparation of a taxpayer's return by an independent CPA) and not as to the means of accomplishment, an employer-employee relationship does not exist.

Certain factors may indicate an employer-employee relationship. They include the right to discharge without legal liability the person performing the service, the furnishing of tools or a place to work, and payment based on time spent rather than the task performed. However, each case is tested on its own merits, and the right to control the means and methods of accomplishment is the definitive test. Generally, physicians, lawyers, dentists, contractors, subcontractors, and others who offer services to the public are not classified as employees.

EXAMPLE 4

D is a lawyer whose major client accounts for 60% of her billings. She does the routine legal work and income tax returns at the client's request. She is paid a monthly retainer in addition to amounts charged for extra work. D is a self-employed individual. Even though most of her income is from one client, she still has the right to determine how the end result of her work is attained. □

EXAMPLE 5

E is a lawyer hired by D to assist D in the performance of services for the client mentioned in Example 4. E is under D's supervision; D reviews E's work and D pays E an hourly fee. E is an employee of D. □

EXAMPLE 6

F is a practical nurse who works as a live-in nurse. She is under the supervision of the patient's doctor and is paid by the patient. F is not an employee of either the patient (who pays her) or the doctor (who supervises her). The ways and means of attaining the end result (care of the patient) are under her control. □

Real estate agents and direct sellers are classified as self-employed persons if two conditions are met. The first condition is that substantially all of their income for services must be directly related to sales or other output. The second condition is that their services must be performed under a written contract that specifies that they are not to be treated as employees for tax purposes. The Internal Revenue Service may not issue any rulings or regulations dealing with classification as employees or independent contractors until Congress enacts legislation clarifying the issue.

A self-employed individual is required to file Schedule C of Form 1040, and all related allowable expenses are deductions *for* adjusted gross income.

Deductions for or from AGI

The Code specifies that reimbursed employee expenses are deductible *for* adjusted gross income. All unreimbursed employee expenses are deductions *from* adjusted gross income (AGI) and can be deducted only if the employee-taxpayer itemizes deductions. Partially reimbursed expenses require an apportionment between these two categories (*for* and *from* AGI).

The distinction between deductions *for* and deductions *from* AGI is important. No benefit is received for an item that is deductible *from* AGI if a taxpayer's

itemized deductions are less than the standard deduction. Refer to chapter 5 for a detailed discussion of deductions *for* versus deductions *from* AGI.

Limitations on Itemized Deductions

Many itemized deductions, such as medical expenses and charitable contributions, are subject to limitations expressed as a percentage of AGI. These limitations may be expressed as floors or ceilings. For example, medical expenses are deductible only to the extent they exceed 7.5 percent of AGI (there is a 7.5 percent floor). Charitable contributions in excess of 50 percent of AGI are not deductible in the year of the contribution. In other words, there is a 50 percent ceiling on the deductibility of charitable contributions. These limitations are discussed more fully in chapter 10.

Miscellaneous Itemized Deductions Subject to the 2 Percent Floor.   Certain miscellaneous itemized deductions, including unreimbursed employee business expenses, must be aggregated and then reduced by 2 percent of AGI. Expenses subject to the 2 percent floor include the following:

- All § 212 expenses, except expenses of producing rent and royalty income (refer to chapter 5).

- All unreimbursed employee expenses (after 20 percent reduction, if applicable).

- Professional dues and subscriptions.

- Union dues and work uniforms.

- Employment-related education expenses.

- Malpractice insurance premiums.

- Expenses of job hunting (including employment agency fees and resumé-writing expenses).

- Home office expenses of an employee or outside salesperson.

- Legal, accounting, and tax return preparation fees.

- Hobby expenses (up to hobby income).

- Investment expenses, including investment counsel fees, subscriptions, and safe deposit box rental.

- Custodial fees relating to income-producing property or an IRA or a Keogh plan.

- Any fees paid to collect interest or dividends.

- Appraisal fees establishing a casualty loss or charitable contribution.

All miscellaneous itemized deductions subject to the 2 percent floor are added together and reduced by 2 percent of AGI. Only the excess is deductible.

Miscellaneous Itemized Deductions Not Subject to the 2 Percent Floor. Certain miscellaneous itemized deductions, including the following, are not subject to the 2 percent floor:

- Impairment-related work expenses of handicapped individuals.

- Federal estate tax on income in respect of a decedent.

- Certain adjustments when a taxpayer restores amounts held under a claim of right.
- Amortizable bond premium.
- Gambling losses to the extent of gambling winnings.
- Deductions allowable in connection with personal property used in a short sale.
- Certain terminated annuity payments.
- Certain costs of cooperative housing corporations.

EXAMPLE 7

T, who has AGI of $20,000, has the following miscellaneous itemized deductions:

Gambling losses (to extent of gains)	$1,200
Tax return preparation fees	300
Unreimbursed employee transportation	200
Professional dues and subscriptions	260
Safe deposit box rental	30

T's itemized deductions are as follows:

Deduction not subject to 2% floor (gambling losses)		$1,200
Deductions subject to 2% floor ($300 + $200 + $260 + $30)	$ 790	
Less 2% of AGI	(400)	390
Total miscellaneous itemized deductions		$1,590

If T's AGI were $40,000, the floor would be $800 (2% of $40,000), and T could not deduct any expenses subject to the 2% floor. □

Percentage Reduction for Meals and Entertainment Expenses

Deductions for meals and entertainment (including entertainment facilities) are limited to 80 percent of allowable expenditures.

EXAMPLE 8

T spends $100 for deductible business entertainment. He is not reimbursed by his employer. Only $80 is allowed as a deduction. This $80 is combined with other miscellaneous itemized deductions subject to the 2% floor, and the total is reduced by 2% of AGI. □

The 80 percent limit applies to the following items:

- Any expense for food or beverages.
- Any expense that constitutes entertainment, amusement, or recreation (or expense related to a facility used in connection with these activities).

Transportation expenses are not affected by this provision—only meals and entertainment.

EXAMPLE 9   T pays a $20 cab fare to meet her client for dinner at The Ritz. The meal costs $90, and T leaves a $15 tip. T's deduction is $104 [($90 + $15) 80% + $20 cabfare]. ☐

The 80 percent rule applies to taxes and tips relating to meals and entertainment. Cover charges, parking fees at an entertainment location, and room rental fees for a meal or cocktail party are also subject to the 80 percent rule.

EXAMPLE 10   S incurs the following expenses for a business meal:

Cost of meal	$50
Tax on meal	2
Tip	8
Total	$60

S's deduction is limited to $48 (80% of $60). ☐

The 80 percent rule is applied after determining the allowable amount of the expenditure. "Lavish or extravagant" expenses are excluded before the application of the 80 percent rule.

EXAMPLE 11   T consumed a meal while in travel status. Of his $100 expenditure, $30 is disallowed as lavish or extravagant. His deduction is limited to $56 (80% of $70). ☐

EXAMPLE 12   S, who is self-employed, purchased two tickets to an entertainment event from a scalper and used the tickets to entertain a client. She paid $200 and the face value of the tickets was $100. S's deduction cannot exceed $80 (80% of $100). ☐

The 80 percent rule is applied before application of the 2 percent floor previously discussed.

EXAMPLE 13   T incurs unreimbursed meal and entertainment expenses of $1,000 in the course of his job as a salesman. His AGI is $20,000, and he has no other expenses subject to the 2% floor. If T itemizes, his deduction is limited to $400, as follows:

Expenses	$1,000
Less: 20%	(200)
Amount subject to 2% of AGI floor	$ 800
Less 2% of AGI	(400)
Deductible	$ 400

☐

It does not matter where or how meal and entertainment expenses are incurred. Only 80 percent of meals incurred in the course of travel away from home, in connection with moving expenses, or in connection with education expenses are deductible. In addition, the cost of meals furnished by an employer to employees on the employer's premises may be subject to the 80 percent rule in computing the employer's deduction.

Exceptions for Luxury Water Travel.   If meals and entertainment incurred in the course of luxury water travel are not separately stated, the 80 percent rule does not apply. If meals and entertainment are separately stated or are clearly identifiable, the 80 percent rule is applied before the limitation on luxury water travel expenses (discussed later in the chapter).

Exceptions to the 80 Percent Rule.   The 80 percent rule has eight exceptions. Exceptions one and two apply where the full value of meals or entertainment is included in the compensation of employees or the income of independent contractors.

EXAMPLE 14   T won an all-expense-paid pleasure trip to Europe for selling the most insurance in her company during the year. X, T's employer, included the fair market value of the trip on T's W–2 (Wage and Tax Statement). X need not allocate any of the cost to meals or entertainment. X deducts the entire amount, and T receives no deduction.   □

The third exception applies to meals and entertainment in a subsidized eating facility or where the *de minimis* fringe benefit rule is met (refer to chapter 4).

EXAMPLE 15   General Hospital has an employee cafeteria on the premises for doctors, nurses, and other employees. Such employees need to be available during meal breaks for emergencies. The cafeteria operates at a loss and is subsidized by the hospital. The 80% rule does not apply to such subsidy.   □

EXAMPLE 16   Y Company gives a ham, a fruitcake, and a bottle of wine to each employee at year-end. Y's costs for these items are not subject to the percentage reduction rule. The *de minimis* fringe benefit exclusion applies to business gifts of packaged foods and beverages.   □

Exception four applies to fully reimbursed employee business meals and entertainment expenses. The 80 percent rule applies to the taxpayer making the reimbursement.

EXAMPLE 17   T is a salesman who paid for lunch with a customer. He made an adequate accounting to his employer, Y, who reimbursed T. T omits both the reimbursement and the expense on his return. Y (the employer) can deduct only 80% of the expenditure on his return.   □

Exception five relates to traditional employer-paid recreation expenses for employees.

EXAMPLE 18   X Company provides a yearly Christmas party and an annual spring picnic for its employees and their families. X's reasonable costs for these events are fully deductible. □

The sixth exception is applicable to items such as samples and promotional activities made available to the general public.

EXAMPLE 19   The owner of a hardware store advertises that tickets to a baseball game will be provided to the first 50 people who purchase a lawn mower from the store during a sale. The full amount of the face value of the tickets is deductible by the owner. □

EXAMPLE 20   A wine merchant permits potential customers to sample wine that he is offering for sale. The merchant can deduct in full the cost of wine used as a sample, along with reasonable costs associated with the wine tasting. For example, food that is provided with the wine to demonstrate the suitability of the wine for particular types of meals is deductible in full. □

The seventh exception applies to expenses for attendance at a sports event meeting certain charitable fund-raising requirements. This is discussed later in the chapter under Entertainment Expenses.

Exception number eight is a rather obvious one. The cost of providing meals or entertainment is fully deductible if the meals or entertainment are sold by the taxpayer in a bona fide transaction. A restaurant, for example, may deduct the full amount of its ordinary and necessary expenses in providing meals to paying customers.

EMPLOYEE BUSINESS EXPENSES

The tax treatment of employee business expenses depends on whether the expenses are reimbursed or unreimbursed and, if reimbursed, whether the employee renders an adequate accounting and returns amounts in excess of substantiated expenses. When meals and entertainment expenses are reimbursed, the 80 percent limit applies to the employer's deduction.

EXAMPLE 21   T, who is employed by M Corporation, incurred meal and entertainment expenses of $1,000 during the year. If M Corporation reimburses T for these expenses, the corporation is subject to the 80% limit and may deduct only $800 ($1,000 × 80%). □

If the meals and entertainment expenses are not reimbursed, the 80 percent limit applies at the employee level, as shown in Example 22.

EXAMPLE 22   B, who works for XYZ Corporation, incurred meal and entertainment expenses of $2,000 during the year. XYZ Corporation does not reimburse B for

these expenses. B is subject to the 80% limit and may include $1,600 ($2,000 × 80%) as a miscellaneous itemized deduction. The total of miscellaneous itemized deductions is reduced by 2% of AGI (see Example 23). □

Reporting Unreimbursed Employee Expenses

An employee's reporting requirements for unreimbursed expenses are rather straightforward. Unreimbursed meal and entertainment expenses are subject to the 80 percent limit (refer to Example 22). Furthermore, unreimbursed employee business expenses are treated as miscellaneous itemized deductions subject to the 2 percent floor.

EXAMPLE 23

K, who is employed by X Corporation, had adjusted gross income of $50,000 in 1990. During the year, she incurred $1,500 of transportation and lodging expense and $1,000 of meals and entertainment expense. K was not reimbursed for these expenses. Her miscellaneous itemized deduction is computed as follows:

Transportation and lodging	$1,500
Meals and entertainment ($1,000 × 80%)	800
Total	$2,300
Less: 2% of $50,000 AGI	1,000
Deduction	$1,300

K must report the $2,500 of expenses and apply the 80% limit on Form 2106 (Employee Business Expenses). The $2,300 amount is then transferred to Schedule A, where the 2% floor is applied. □

Reporting Reimbursed Employee Expenses

Determining how to report reimbursed employee business expenses can be more difficult. The reporting requirements depend on the answers to the following questions:

- Did the employee render an adequate accounting?
- If the reimbursement was more than the expenses, was the employee allowed to keep the excess?

The reporting treatment for reimbursed employee business expenses depends on whether the employee renders an *adequate accounting* to the employer. An employee can render an adequate accounting by submitting a record, with receipts and other substantiation, to the employer. The following pertinent facts are required: amount, place, date, and business purpose of the expenditure and the business relationship of the parties involved.

   Many companies reduce their paperwork by adopting a policy of reimbursing employees a flat dollar amount per day of business travel (a *per diem allowance*). The amount of expenses that is deemed substantiated is equal to the lesser of the per diem allowance or the amount of the Federal per diem rate. The position of the IRS is that a per diem allowance not exceeding $122 [$88 (lodging) + $34 (meals

and incidental expenses)] per day in high-cost localities or $85 [$59 (lodging) + $26 (meals and incidental expenses)] in all other areas within the continental United States is deemed substantiated. If the employee actually substantiates the elements of time, place, and business purpose of the expenses, the adequate accounting requirements are satisfied.

With regard to transportation expenses, an employee who receives a reimbursement of not more than the standard mileage rate allowed for tax purposes will be treated as rendering an adequate accounting. The mileage rate for 1989 is 25.5 cents, and the rate for 1990 is 26 cents. The rate is adjusted annually by the IRS as warranted.

Employee Does Not Render an Adequate Accounting.   If the reimbursement is *equal* to the expenses or if the employee substantiates the expenses *and* returns any excess, the reimbursements are excluded from gross income and are not reported on Form W-2. Thus, there are no further reporting requirements for the employee. However, if the employee is not required to or does not submit an adequate accounting or is not required to or does not return any portion of a per diem allowance not used for business expenses, the full amount of the reimbursement is reported as wages on Form W-2. The employee, then, may claim the related expenses on Form 2106, resulting in an itemized miscellaneous deduction subject to the 80 percent limitation and the 2 percent of AGI floor, in the same manner as unreimbursed expenses are reported.

Both substantiation and the requirement that excess reimbursements be returned must be satisfied within a reasonable period of time. Although this timeliness requirement depends on the facts and circumstances, two safe harbor methods are set forth in the Regulations. The first safe harbor is the *fixed date* method. In any of the following situations, the "reasonable period of time" requirement will be met.

- An advance is made within 30 days of when the expense is paid or incurred.

- An expense is substantiated within 60 days after it is paid or incurred.

- The excess amount is returned within 120 days after the expense is paid or incurred.

The second safe harbor is the *periodic statement* method. Here, the employer provides the employee with a statement (no less frequently than quarterly) stating the amount paid in excess of the expenses that have been substantiated and requesting the employee to substantiate any additional business expenses and/or to return any remaining unsubstantiated amounts within 120 days of the statement. Any expenses substantiated or returned within that period will be treated as being substantiated or returned within a reasonable period of time.

Further, the requirement to return amounts of reimbursement in excess of expenses is fulfilled if the employee returns any portion of a per diem allowance that relates to days of travel not substantiated even though he or she need not return the portion that exceeds the amount allowed for the substantiated days. Consider the following example.

EXAMPLE 24   E received from his employer an advance per diem allowance for meals of $200 based on an anticipated 5 days of business travel at $40 per day to a locality for which the Federal meals and incidental expenses rate is $34 and E substantiates 3 full days of business travel. E meets the requirement to return

amounts in excess of expenses if he returns $80 ($40 × 2 days), the portion of the allowance attributable to the 2 unsubstantiated days of travel. This is so even though E is not required to return the $18 portion of the allowance that exceeds the amount deemed substantiated for the 3 substantiated days of travel.

Actual per diem ($40 × 3 days)	$120
Deemed substantiated at Federal rate ($34 × 3 days)	102
Excess portion of per diem	$ 18

The $18 excess per diem is taxable to E and is reported as wages on E's Form W-2. □

An employee's reimbursement may be *less than* the business expenses incurred. If the reimbursement is reported as wages on Form W-2, the expenses are reported in the same manner as unreimbursed expenses. If the reimbursement is reported as a separate item [as "EBE" (employee business expenses)], the amount offsets a portion of the business expenses on Form 2106 and will result in a miscellaneous itemized deduction on Schedule A.

EXAMPLE 25   J, who is employed by T Company, had adjusted gross income of $40,000. During the year, she incurred $2,000 of transportation and lodging expense and $1,000 of meals and entertainment expense, all fully substantiated. J received $2,100 reimbursement, not reported as wages, for these expenses. Thus, the reimbursement rate is 70% ($2,100 reimbursement/$3,000 expenses). J must offset her deductions on Form 2106 with the $2,100 reimbursement. Because J was reimbursed for 70% of her expenses, the other 30% will be treated as unreimbursed expenses. Her itemized deduction will consist of the $600 ($2,000 × 30%) of unreimbursed transportation and lodging expenses and $300 ($1,000 × 30%) of unreimbursed meal and entertainment expenses as follows:

Transportation and lodging	$600
Meals and entertainment ($300 × 80%)	240
Total	$840
Less: 2% of $40,000 AGI	(800)
Deduction	$ 40

In summary, J must report $3,000 of expenses and the $2,100 reimbursement on Form 2106 and $40 as a miscellaneous itemized deduction on Schedule A. □

When the reimbursement *exceeds* the expenses incurred by the employee, the reporting requirement will depend on whether the employee is allowed to keep the excess reimbursement. If the employee must repay any excess, the same rules that apply when reimbursements equal expenses must be used. However, if the

employee is allowed to keep the excess reimbursement, the expenses will be treated as if they *had not been* reimbursed. The reimbursement will be reported as wages on Form W-2, and the expenses will be reported on Form 2106 first and then on Schedule A as a miscellaneous itemized deduction.

TRANSPORTATION EXPENSES

An employee may deduct unreimbursed employment-related transportation expenses as miscellaneous itemized deductions (*from* AGI, subject to the 2 percent floor). Transportation expense includes only the cost of transporting the employee from one place to another when the employee is not away from home *in travel status*. Such costs include taxi fares, automobile expenses, tolls, and parking.

Commuting from home to one's place of employment is a personal, nondeductible expense. The fact that one employee drives 30 miles to work and another employee walks six blocks is of no significance.[1]

EXAMPLE 26   G is employed by X Corporation. He drives 22 miles each way to work. One day G drove to a customer's office from his place of work. The drive was a 14-mile round trip to the customer's office. G can take a deduction for 14 miles of business transportation. The remaining 44 miles are a nondeductible commuting expense. □

Exceptions to Disallowance of Commuting Expenses.   The general rule that disallows a deduction for commuting expenses has several exceptions. An employee who uses an automobile to transport heavy tools to work and who otherwise would not drive to work will be allowed a deduction. However, the deduction is allowed only for the additional costs incurred to transport work implements. Additional costs are those exceeding the cost of commuting by the same mode of transportation without the tools. For example, the rental of a trailer for transporting tools is deductible, but the expenses of operating the automobile are not deductible.[2] The Supreme Court has held that a deduction is permitted only if the taxpayer can show that he or she would not have used the automobile were it not necessary to transport tools or equipment.[3]

Another exception is provided for an employee who has a second job. The expenses of getting from one job to another are deductible. If the employee goes home between jobs, the deduction is based on the distance between jobs.

EXAMPLE 27   In the current year, T holds two jobs, a full-time job with B Corporation and a part-time job with C Corporation. During the 250 days that she works (adjusted for weekends, vacation, and holidays), T customarily leaves home at 7:30 A.M. and drives 30 miles to the B Corporation plant, where she works until 5:00 P.M. After dinner at a nearby cafe, T drives 20 miles to C Corporation and works from 7:00 to 11:00 P.M. The distance from the second job to T's home is 40 miles. Her deduction is based on 20 miles (the distance between jobs). □

---

1. *Tauferner v. U.S.,* 69–1 USTC ¶9241, 23 AFTR2d 69–1025, 407 F.2d 243 (CA–10, 1969).

2. Rev.Rul. 75–380, 1975–2 C.B. 59.

3. *Fausner v. Comm.,* 73–2 USTC ¶9515, 32 AFTR2d 73–5202, 93 S.Ct. 2820 (USSC, 1973).

It is sometimes difficult to distinguish between a nondeductible commuting expense and a deductible transportation expense necessary to the taxpayer's business. If the taxpayer is required to incur a transportation expense to travel between work stations, that expense is deductible. However, the commuting costs from home to the first work station and from the last work station to home are not deductible.

EXAMPLE 28

V works for a firm in downtown Denver and commutes to work. V occasionally works in a customer's office. On one such occasion, he drove directly to the customer's office, a round-trip distance from his home of 40 miles. He did not go into his office, which is a 52-mile round-trip. None of his mileage is deductible. □

EXAMPLE 29

T, a general contractor, drove from his home to his office, then drove to three building sites to perform his required inspections, and finally drove home. The costs of driving to his office and driving home from the last inspection site are nondeductible commuting expenses. The other transportation costs are deductible. □

Also deductible is the reasonable travel cost between the general working area and a temporary work station outside that area. What constitutes the general working area depends on the facts and circumstances of each situation. For example, a bank manager who must spend an occasional day at a remote branch office in the suburbs can deduct transportation expenses (or mileage) as an employee expense. If an employee is permanently reassigned to a new location, however, the assignment is deemed to be for an indefinite period, and the expenses are nondeductible commuting expenses. Furthermore, if an employee customarily works on several temporary assignments in a localized area, that localized area becomes the regular place of employment. Transportation from home to these locations becomes a personal, nondeductible commuting expense.

EXAMPLE 30

S, a building inspector in Minneapolis, regularly inspects buildings for building code violations for his employer, a general contractor. During one busy season, the St. Paul inspector became ill, and S was required to inspect several buildings in St. Paul. The expenses for transportation for the trips within Minneapolis and St. Paul are deductible. □

Computation of Automobile Expenses

A taxpayer has two choices in computing automobile expenses. The actual operating cost, which includes depreciation, gas, oil, repairs, licenses, and insurance, may be used. Records must be kept that detail the automobile's personal and business use. Only the percentage (based upon the ratio of business miles to total miles) allocable to business transportation and travel is allowed as a deduction. Complex rules for the computation of depreciation (discussed in chapter 8) apply if the actual expense method is used.

Use of the automatic mileage method is the second alternative. For 1990, the deduction is based on 26 cents per mile for all business miles. For 1989 the

deduction was based upon 25.5 cents per mile for the first 15,000 business miles driven. Eleven cents per mile was allowed for any miles in excess of 15,000.[4] Parking fees and tolls are allowed in addition to expenses computed using the automatic mileage method.

Generally, a taxpayer may elect either method for any particular year. However, the following restrictions apply:

- If two or more vehicles are in use (for business purposes) at the *same* time (not alternately), a taxpayer may not use the automatic mileage method.

- A basis adjustment is required if the taxpayer changes from the automatic mileage method to the actual operating cost method. Depreciation is considered allowed for the first 15,000 business miles in accordance with the following schedule for the most recent five years:

Year	Rate per Mile
1990	11 cents
1989	11 cents
1988	10.5 cents
1987	10 cents
1986	9 cents

EXAMPLE 31   T purchased his automobile in 1987 for $9,000. It is used 90% for business purposes. T drove the automobile for 10,000 business miles in 1989; 8,500 miles in 1988; and 6,000 miles in 1987. At the beginning of 1990, the basis of the business portion is $5,455.

Cost ($9,000 × 90%)	$8,100
Less depreciation:	
1989 (10,000 miles × 11 cents)	(1,100)
1988 (9,000 miles × 10.5 cents)	(945)
1987 (6,000 × 10 cents)	(600)
Adjusted business basis 1/1/90	$5,455

- Use of the standard mileage rate in the first year the auto is placed in service is considered an election to exclude the auto from the ACRS method of depreciation (discussed in chapter 8).

- A taxpayer may not switch to the automatic mileage method if the ACRS statutory percentage method or expensing under § 179 has been used.

Any reimbursement for auto expenses is subject to the same rules relating to substantiation and return of excess amounts as are other employee business expenses: If the reimbursement is reported as wages on Form W-2, the deduction

---

4.   Rev. Proc. 89–66, I.R.B.52, 13.

is figured in the same manner as if the automobile expenses are unreimbursed. If the reimbursement is reported as a separate item on Form W-2, the amount is reported on Form 2106 as an offset from the automobile expenses, thereby reducing the itemized miscellaneous deduction allowed, subject to the 2% of AGI floor. Frequently, taxpayers discover that actual automobile expenses, such as for depreciation, gas, oil, and repairs, exceed the amount of expense calculated under the standard mileage rate prescribed by the IRS.

TRAVEL EXPENSES

Definition of Travel Expenses

An itemized deduction is allowed for unreimbursed travel expenses related to a taxpayer's employment, subject to the 2 percent floor. Travel expenses are more broadly defined in the Code than are transportation expenses. Travel expenses include transportation expenses and meals and lodging while away from home in the pursuit of a trade or business. Meals cannot be lavish or extravagant under the circumstances. Transportation expenses are deductible even though the taxpayer is not away from home. A deduction for travel expenses is available only if the taxpayer is away from his or her tax home. Travel expenses also include reasonable laundry and incidental expenses. To the extent that travel expenses are reimbursed, they are reported in the same manner discussed previously for employee expenses. The unreimbursed part is a miscellaneous itemized deduction subject to the 2 percent floor. Unreimbursed meals and entertainment expenses are subject to the 80 percent rule.

Away-from-Home Requirement

The crucial test for the deductibility of travel expenses is whether the employee is away from home overnight. "Overnight" need not be a 24-hour period, but it must be a period substantially longer than an ordinary day's work and must require rest, sleep, or a relief-from-work period.[5] A one-day or intracity business trip is not travel, and meals and lodging for such a trip are not deductible.

The employee must be away from home for a temporary period. If the taxpayer-employee is reassigned to a new post for an indefinite period of time, that new post becomes his or her tax home. *Temporary* indicates that the assignment's termination is expected within a reasonably short period of time. The position of the IRS is that the tax home is the business location, post, or station of the taxpayer. Thus, travel expenses are not deductible if a taxpayer is reassigned for an indefinite period and does not move his or her place of residence to the new location.

EXAMPLE 32   T's employer opened a branch office in San Diego. T was assigned to the new office for three months to train a new manager and to assist in setting up the new office. T tried commuting from his home in Los Angeles for a week and decided that he could not continue driving several hours a day. He rented an apartment in San Diego, where he lived during the week. He spent weekends with his wife and children at their home in Los Angeles. T's rent, meals,

---

5. *U.S. v. Correll*, 68–1 USTC ¶9101, 20 AFTR2d
   5845, 88 S.Ct. 445 (USSC, 1967); Rev.Rul. 75–
   168, 1975–1 C.B. 58.

laundry, incidentals, and automobile expenses in San Diego are deductible. The transportation expense related to his weekend trips home is personal and is limited to what the cost of meals and lodging in San Diego would have been. □

EXAMPLE 33

Assume that T in Example 33 was transferred to the new location to become the new manager permanently. T's wife and children continued to live in Los Angeles until the end of the school year. T is no longer "away from home" because the assignment is not temporary. T's travel expenses are not deductible. □

Determining the Tax Home.   Under ordinary circumstances, there is no problem in determining the location of a taxpayer's tax home and whether or not the taxpayer is on a temporary work assignment away from that tax home. Under other circumstances, however, this is a controversial problem that has found the IRS and various courts in conflict.[6]An example of this problem is the situation in which a construction worker cannot find work in the immediate area and takes work several hundred miles away, with the duration of that work uncertain. The IRS has published criteria for determining whether a work assignment is temporary rather than permanent or indefinite.[7]

In general, the IRS regards a work assignment of less than a year as temporary. A work assignment of more than two years is regarded as indefinite or permanent, regardless of the facts and circumstances. The nature of a work assignment expected to last between one and two years will be determined on the basis of the facts and circumstances of the specific case.

The following objective factors are to be used in determining whether the home that the taxpayer claims to be away from is the taxpayer's actual tax home:

• Whether the taxpayer has used the claimed home for lodging purposes while performing work in the vicinity thereof immediately before the current job.

• Whether the taxpayer continues to maintain bona fide work contacts (such as job seeking, leave of absence, ongoing business) in the area during the alleged temporary employment.

• Whether the taxpayer's living expenses at the claimed home are duplicated because work requires the taxpayer to be away from home.

• Whether the taxpayer has a family member or members (marital or lineal only) currently residing at the claimed home or currently continues to use the claimed home frequently for the purposes of his or her own lodging.

Travel expenses are disallowed unless the taxpayer clearly demonstrates a realistic expectation as to the temporary nature of the job and satisfies all four of the above requirements. If the taxpayer clearly demonstrates the expectation that the job is of a temporary nature and satisfies two of the above requirements, the deductibility question will be decided on the basis of all the facts and circumstances of the case. If it is determined that the assignment is indefinite rather than temporary, no deduction will be allowed for the traveling expenses.

If an employee establishes a new home as the result of a work assignment or if there is no established tax home, living expenses are of a personal nature and are therefore nondeductible.

---

6.   Rev.Rul. 73–529, 1973–2 C.B. 37.

7.   Rev.Rul. 83–82, 1983–1 C.B. 45.

EXAMPLE 34   H is employed as a long-haul truck driver. He stores his clothes and other belongings at his parents' home and stops there for periodic visits. The rest of the time, H is on the road, sleeping in his truck and in motels. His meals, lodging, laundry, and incidental expenses are not deductible because he has no tax home from which he can be absent.[8] □

Disallowed and Limited Travel Expenses

The possibility always exists that taxpayers will attempt to treat vacation or pleasure travel as deductible business travel. To prevent such abuses, the law contains limitations for certain travel expenses.

Nonbusiness Conventions.   One tactic taxpayers used in an attempt to deduct the cost of vacations was to attend a tax or financial seminar at a vacation resort. They then took the travel expenses as a deduction under § 212, which allows deductions related to the production of income or determination of taxes.

A further refinement was that the seminar or convention promoters would videotape the lectures and supply a copy to the participants. Many participants did not attend any lectures but would take the videotapes home and view them later. In the meantime, the taxpayer would enjoy several days of vacation at the resort and deduct the expenses.

In an attempt to prevent such abuses, the law disallows all deductions related to attending a convention, seminar, or similar meeting unless the expenses are related to a trade or business of the taxpayer. The restriction does not apply to trade or business conventions and seminars. For example, a CPA who is an employee of an accounting firm can deduct the expenses of attending a tax seminar. A stockbroker can deduct the cost of attending a convention regarding investments. A physician attending either the tax or the investment meeting can deduct nothing. If the lectures are videotaped, both the CPA and the stockbroker must attend convention sessions to view the videotaped materials along with other participants. This requirement does not disallow deductions for costs (other than travel, meals, and entertainment) of renting or using videotaped materials related to business.

EXAMPLE 35   A CPA is unable to attend a convention at which current developments in taxation are discussed. She paid $200 for videotapes of the lectures that she viewed at home later. The $200 is a miscellaneous itemized deduction (subject to the 2% floor) if the CPA is an employee. If she is self-employed, the $200 is a deduction *for* AGI. □

Luxury Water Travel.   Limits are placed on the deductibility of travel by water. The deduction is limited to twice the highest amount generally allowable for a day of travel for Federal employees serving in the United States.

EXAMPLE 36   During the taxable year, the highest Federal per diem rate is $136. T took a six-day trip from New York to London on the *Queen Mary II* to meet with customers. The maximum deduction related to the water travel is $1,632 [($136 × 2) × 6 days]. □

---

8. *Moses Mitnick*, 13 T.C. 1 (1949).

If the expenses of luxury water travel include separately stated amounts for meals or entertainment, those amounts must be reduced by 20 percent before the application of this per diem limitation. If the meals and entertainment are not separately stated (or otherwise clearly identifiable), the 20 percent reduction does not apply.

The per diem rule does not apply to any expense allocable to a convention, seminar, or other meeting held on any cruise ship. The deduction for such a meeting is limited to $2,000 per individual per year. This deduction is restricted to ships registered in the United States and sailing to ports of call located within the United States or its possessions (e.g., Puerto Rico). Thus, a cruise on a ship of U.S. registry sailing to Bermuda would not qualify. A cruise on the same ship from Florida to Puerto Rico would qualify.

Educational Travel.   No deduction is allowed for travel that by itself is deemed by the taxpayer to be educational. This does not apply to a deduction claimed for travel that is necessary to engage in an activity that gives rise to a business deduction relating to education.

EXAMPLE 37   M, a German teacher, travels to Germany to maintain general familiarity with the language and culture. No travel expense deduction is allowed. ☐

EXAMPLE 38   J, a scholar of French literature, travels to Paris to do specific library research that cannot be done elsewhere and to take courses that are offered only at the Sorbonne. The travel costs are deductible, assuming that the other requirements for deducting education expenses (discussed later in the chapter) are met. ☐

Combined Business and Pleasure Travel

To be deductible, travel expenses need not be incurred in the performance of specific job functions. Travel expenses incurred in attending a professional convention are deductible by an employee if attendance is connected with services as an employee. For example, an employee of a CPA firm could deduct travel expenses incurred in attending a meeting of the American Institute of Certified Public Accountants.

Travel deductions have been abused in the past by persons who claimed a tax deduction for what was essentially a personal vacation. As a result, several provisions have been enacted to govern deductions associated with combined business and pleasure trips. If the business/pleasure trip is from one point in the United States to another point in the United States, the transportation expenses are deductible only if the trip is *primarily for business*. If the trip is primarily for pleasure, no transportation expenses can be taken as a deduction. However, even though a trip is primarily for pleasure (or other personal reasons), any expenses incurred at the destination that are properly allocable to business are deductible.

EXAMPLE 39   J traveled from Seattle to New York on a combined business and pleasure trip. She spent five days conducting business and three days sightseeing and attending shows. Her plane and taxi fare amounted to $560. Her meals

amounted to $100 per day, and lodging and incidental expenses were $150 per day. She can deduct the transportation charges of $560 since the trip was primarily for business (five days of business versus three days of sightseeing). Meals are limited to $400 [5 days × ($100 × 80%)], and other expenses are limited to $750 (5 days × $150). All the travel expenses are miscellaneous itemized deductions subject to the 2% floor. ☐

EXAMPLE **40**

Assume the same facts as in the previous example, except that J conducted business for two days and vacationed the remaining six days. Since the trip is then primarily personal, no transportation expenses are deductible. Lodging and incidental expenses for two days ($300) and 80% of the meals for two days ($160) are deductible as miscellaneous itemized deductions subject to the 2% floor. ☐

The incremental costs paid for travel of a taxpayer's relative cannot be deducted unless that person's presence has a bona fide business purpose. Incidental services performed by family members do not constitute a bona fide business purpose.

When the trip is outside the United States, special rules apply. If the taxpayer is away from home for seven days or less or if less than 25 percent of the time was for personal purposes, no allocation of transportation expenses need be made. No allocation is required if the taxpayer has no substantial control over arrangements for the trip or the desire for a vacation is not a major factor in taking the trip. If the trip is primarily for pleasure, no transportation charges are deductible. In all other cases, all travel expenses must be allocated between business and personal expenses. Days devoted to travel are considered as business days. Weekends, legal holidays, and intervening days are considered business days, provided that both preceding and succeeding days were business days.

EXAMPLE **41**

K took a trip from New York to Japan primarily for business purposes. He was away from home from June 10 through June 19. He spent three days vacationing and seven days conducting business (including two travel days). K's air fare was $2,500, his meals amounted to $100 per day, and lodging and incidental expenses were $160 per day. Since K was away from home for more than seven days and more than 25% of his time was devoted to personal purposes, only 70% (7 days business/10 days total) of the travel is deductible. His deductions are as follows:

Transportation (70% × $2,500)		$1,750
Lodging ($160 × 7)		1,120
Meals ($100 × 7)	$ 700	
Less: 20%	(140)	560
Total		$3,430

Note that the $3,430 is a miscellaneous itemized deduction subject to the 2% floor. ☐

EXAMPLE 42

L, a fashion buyer for a large department store, travels to London primarily to view the spring collections. She is gone 10 days (including 2 days of travel). She spends 8 days (including travel time) engaged in business and 2 days sightseeing. Since less than 25% of the total time is spent vacationing, all her transportation expenses and all but 2 days of meals and lodging are deductible. The meals are reduced by 20%, and all the expenses are miscellaneous itemized deductions subject to the 2% floor. □

EXAMPLE 43

Assume L in Example 43 had spent six days vacationing, two days traveling, and two days conducting business. The trip probably would be primarily for pleasure, and none of the transportation expenses would be deductible. Two days of meals and lodging expenses would be deductible, subject to the same limitations. □

Foreign Convention Expenses

Certain restrictions are imposed on the deductibility of expenses paid or incurred to attend conventions located outside the North American area. For this purpose, the North American area includes the United States, its possessions (including the Trust Territory of the Pacific Islands), Canada, and Mexico. The expenses will be disallowed unless it is established that the meeting is directly related to a trade or business of the taxpayer. Disallowance will also occur unless the taxpayer shows that it is as reasonable for the meeting to be held in a foreign location as within the North American area.

The foreign convention rules will not operate to bar a deduction to an employer if the expense is compensatory in nature. For example, a trip to Paris won by a top salesperson is included in the gross income of the employee and is fully deductible by the employer.

MOVING EXPENSES

Moving expenses are deductible for moves in connection with the commencement of work (either as an employee or as a self-employed individual) at a new principal place of work. Reimbursement from employers must be included in gross income. Moving expenses are itemized deductions but are *not* subject to the 2 percent floor. Meals included as moving expenses are subject to the 80 percent rule. To be eligible for a moving expense deduction, a taxpayer must meet two basic tests: distance and time.

Distance Test

The distance test requires that the taxpayer's new job location must be at least 35 miles farther from the taxpayer's old residence than the old residence was from the former place of employment. In this regard, the location of the new residence is not relevant. This eliminates a moving deduction for taxpayers who purchase a new home in the same general area without changing their place of employment. Those who accept a new job in the same general area as the old job location are also eliminated. If a new job does not necessitate moving or if the move is for personal reasons (e.g., a better neighborhood), the taxpayer is not permitted a tax deduction.

EXAMPLE 44   J was permanently transferred to a new job location. The distance from J's former home to his new job (80 miles) exceeds the distance from his former home to his old job (30 miles) by more than 35 miles. J has met the distance requirements for a moving expense deduction. (See the following diagram.)

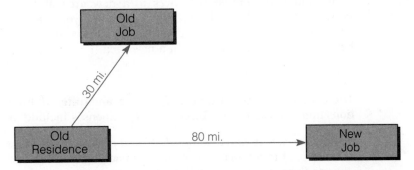

If J was not employed before the move, his new job must be at least 35 miles from his former residence. In this instance, the distance requirements would be met if J had not been previously employed. □

Time Requirements

To be eligible for a moving expense deduction, an employee must be employed on a full-time basis at the new location for 39 weeks in the 12-month period following the move. If the taxpayer is a self-employed individual, he or she must work in the new location for 78 weeks during the next two years. The first 39 weeks must be in the first 12 months. The taxpayer can work either as a self-employed individual or as an employee. The time requirement is suspended if the taxpayer dies, becomes disabled, or is discharged or transferred by the new employer through no fault of the employee.

It is obvious that an employee might not be able to meet the 39-week requirement by the end of the tax year. For this reason, two alternatives are allowed. The taxpayer can take the deduction in the year the expenses were incurred, even though the 39-week test has not been met. If the taxpayer later fails to meet the test, the income of the following year must be increased by an amount equal to the deduction previously claimed for moving expenses. The second alternative is to wait until the test is met and then file an amended tax return for the prior year.

When Deductible

The general rule is that expenses of a cash basis taxpayer are deductible only in the year of payment. However, if reimbursement is received from the employer, an election may be made to deduct the moving expenses in the year subsequent to the move in the following circumstances:

• The moving expenses are incurred and paid in 1990, and the reimbursement is received in 1991.

• The moving expenses are incurred in 1990 and are paid by the employee in 1991 (on or before the due date including extensions for filing the 1990 return), and the reimbursement from the employer is received in 1991.

The election to deduct moving expenses in the year the reimbursement is received is made by claiming the deduction on the return or filing an amended return or claim for refund for the taxable year the reimbursement is received.

The moving expense deduction is allowed regardless of whether the employee is transferred by the existing employer or is employed by a new employer. Also, it is allowed if the employee moves to a new area and obtains employment or switches from self-employed status to employee status (and vice versa). In addition, the moving expense deduction is allowed if an individual is unemployed before obtaining employment in a new area.

Classification of Moving Expenses

There are five classes of moving expenses, and different limitations and qualifications apply to each class. Direct moving expenses include the following:

1. *The expense of moving household and personal belongings.* This class includes fees paid to a moving company for packing, storing, and moving possessions and the rental of a truck if the taxpayer moves his or her own belongings. Also included is the cost of moving household pets. Reasonableness is the only limit on these direct expenses. Such expenses as refitting rugs or draperies and losses on the disposal of club memberships are not deductible as moving expenses.

2. *Travel to the new residence.* This includes the cost of transportation, meals, and lodging of the taxpayer and the members of the taxpayer's household en route. It does not include the cost of moving servants or others who are not members of the household. The taxpayer can elect to take actual auto expenses (no depreciation is allowed) or the automatic mileage method. In this case, moving expense mileage is limited to nine cents per mile for each car. These expenses are also limited by the reasonableness standard. For example, if one moves from Texas to Florida via Maine and takes six weeks to do so, the transportation, meals, and lodging must be allocated between personal and moving expenses.

Indirect moving expenses include the following:

3. *House-hunting trips.* Expenses of traveling (including meals and lodging) to the new place of employment to look for a home are deductible only if the job has been secured in advance of the house-hunting trip. The dollar limitation is explained below.

4. *Temporary living expenses.* Meals and lodging expenses incurred while living in temporary quarters in the general area of the new job while waiting to move into a new residence are deductible. (The dollar limits are discussed below.) These living expenses are limited to any consecutive 30-day period beginning after employment is secured.

5. *Certain residential buying and selling expenses.* Buying and selling expenses include those that would normally be offset against the selling price of a home and those expenses incurred in buying a new home. Examples are commissions, escrow fees, legal expenses, points paid to secure a mortgage, transfer taxes, and advertising. Also deductible are costs involved in settling an old lease or acquiring a new lease or both. Fixing-up expenses, damage deposits, prepaid rent, and the like are not deductible.

Buying and selling expenses of any asset normally increase the basis or reduce the selling price of that asset. Such expenses on the sale or purchase of a personal residence can be considered in computing basis or selling price or as a moving expense

under class 5. Any buying or selling expenses claimed as a moving expense deduction cannot be added to the basis of a new home or subtracted from the amount realized on the sale of an old home. This restriction eliminates any possible double benefit of deducting the costs at both points. Generally, since the taxpayer can defer the gain on the sale of a personal residence, the election to take the maximum amount as a moving expense deduction will be preferable. (The dollar limits are discussed below.)

EXAMPLE 45   T, an executive in the 28% tax bracket, incurred commission expenses of $5,000 on the sale of his personal residence when he was transferred to another state. He can deduct $3,000 (the dollar limitation on class 5 moving expenses) of the commission as a moving expense, which will save him $840 in taxes. The remaining $2,000 will reduce the realized gain on the sale of his home. If T buys a new home, the gain on the sale of the old one will be deferred if certain requirements are met resulting in no current tax (see chapter 12). □

Indirect moving expenses are limited to a total of $3,000. Furthermore, house-hunting and temporary living expenses may not exceed $1,500 in the aggregate. Direct moving expenses, as discussed previously, are unlimited.

Moving Expense Limits

Classes $1^9 + 2$	= No limit
Classes $3 + 4$	= $1,500 limit
Classes $3 + 4 + 5$	= $3,000 limit

Generally, the above dollar limitations apply regardless of filing status. If both spouses change jobs and file separate returns, the limitations are $750 (instead of $1,500) and $1,500 (instead of $3,000). If only one spouse makes a job change, the spouse who makes the change is allowed the full amount. If both change jobs, do not live together, and work at job sites at least 35 miles apart, each spouse applies the $1,500 and the $3,000 limits. It does not matter whether they file jointly or separately.

EXAMPLE 46   T, an employee of X Corporation, is hired by Y Corporation at a substantial increase in salary. T is hired in February 1990 and is to report for work in March 1990. The new job requires a move from Los Angeles to New York City. In connection with the move, T incurs the following expenses:

February 1990 house-hunting trip (no meals)	$ 650
Temporary living expenses in New York City incurred by T and family from March 10–30, 1990, while awaiting the renovation of their new apartment (including $400 of meals)	1,000
Penalty for breaking lease on Los Angeles apartment	2,400
Charge for packing and moving household goods	4,200
Transportation and lodging expenses during move (March 5–10)	700
Meal expense during move	300

9. The numbers refer to the types of moving expenses outlined previously.

T can deduct the following amount:

Moving household goods		$4,200
Transportation and lodging		700
Meals ($300 less 20%)		240
House-hunting trip	$ 650	
Temporary living expenses [$600 plus ($400 cost of meals × 80%)]	920	
	$1,570	
Limited to	$1,500	
Lease penalty	2,400	
	$3,900	
Limited to		3,000
Total itemized moving expense deduction		$8,140

□

Form 3903 is used to report the detailed calculations of the ceiling limitations, reimbursements, and change in job locations. If the employee is reimbursed for the move, such reimbursement is included in salary income on Form 1040. If the reimbursement is less than the moving expenses, the excess expenses are an itemized deduction. The meal expenses are reduced by 20 percent, but the moving expenses are not subject to the 2 percent floor. An over-reimbursement will result in a net increase in taxable income.

EDUCATION EXPENSES

General Requirements

An employee may deduct expenses incurred for education as ordinary and necessary business expenses provided such items were incurred for either of two reasons:

1. To maintain or improve existing skills required in the present job.

2. To meet the express requirements of the employer or the requirements imposed by law to retain his or her employment status.

Education expenses are not deductible if the education is for either of the following purposes:

1. To meet the minimum educational standards for qualification in the taxpayer's existing job.

2. To qualify the taxpayer for a new trade or business.

Thus, fees incurred for professional qualification exams (the bar exam, for example) and fees for review courses (such as a CPA review course) are not deductible.[10] A partial deduction may be allowed for non-accounting courses that

---

10. Reg. § 1.212–1(f) and Rev.Rul. 69–292, 1969–1 C.B. 84.

also maintain and improve an accountant's existing skills in a present job.[11] If the education incidentally results in a promotion or raise, the deduction can still be taken as long as the education maintained and improved existing skills and did not qualify a person for a new trade or business. A change in duties is not always fatal to the deduction if the new duties involve the same general work. For example, the IRS has ruled that a practicing dentist's education expenses incurred to become an orthodontist are deductible.[12]

Requirements Imposed by Law or by the Employer for Retention of Employment

Teachers qualify under the provision that permits the deduction of education expenses if additional courses are required by the employer or are imposed by law. Many states require a minimum of a bachelor's degree and a specified number of additional courses to retain a teaching job. In addition, some public school systems have imposed a master's degree requirement and have required teachers to make satisfactory progress toward a master's degree in order to keep their positions.

If the required education is the minimum degree required for the job, no deduction is allowed.

A taxpayer classified as an Accountant I who went back to school to obtain a bachelor's degree was not allowed to deduct the expenses. Although some courses tended to maintain and improve his existing skills in his entry-level position, the degree was the minimum requirement for his job.[13]

Maintaining or Improving Existing Skills

The "maintaining or improving existing skills" requirement in the Code has been difficult for both taxpayers and the courts to interpret. For example, a business executive may be permitted to deduct the costs of obtaining an M.B.A. on the grounds that the advanced management education is undertaken to maintain and improve existing management skills. The executive would be eligible to deduct the costs of specialized, nondegree management courses that were taken for continuing education or to maintain or improve existing skills. If the business executive incurred the expenses to obtain a law degree, the expenses would not be deductible, because they constitute training for a new trade or business. The Regulations deny the deduction by a self-employed accountant of expenses relating to law school.[14] In addition, several courts have disallowed deductions to IRS agents for the cost of obtaining a law degree, since the degree was not required to retain employment and the education qualified the agent for a new profession.[15]

Deductions for law school expenses were also denied for a supervisor[16] and a policeman[17] because the courses were part of a program that would qualify the taxpayers for new professions. It was irrelevant that the courses also maintained and improved existing skills and that neither practiced law.

---

11. *Howard Sherman Cooper,* 38 TCM 955, T.C. Memo. 1979–241.

12. Rev.Rul. 74–78, 1974–1 C.B. 44.

13. Reg. § 1.162–5(b)(2)(iii) Example (2); *Collin J. Davidson,* 43 TCM 743, T.C. Memo. 1982–119.

14. Reg. § 1.162–5(b)(3)(ii) Example (1).

15. *Joel A. Sharon,* 66 T.C. 515 (1976); *aff'd.* 78–2

USTC ¶9834; 43 AFTR2d 79–335; 591 F.2d 1273 (CA–9, 1978; *cert. denied,* 99 S.Ct. 2883 (USSC, 1979).

16. *James Burton,* 51 TCM 353, T.C. Memo 1986–38.

17. *Robert L. Edwards,* 46 TCM 768, T.C. Memo. 1983–413.

Classification of Specific Items

Education expenses include books, tuition, typing, and transportation (e.g., from the office to night school) and travel (e.g., meals and lodging while away from home at summer school).

EXAMPLE 47   T, who holds a bachelor of education degree, is a secondary education teacher in the Los Angeles, California, school system. The school board recently changed its minimum education requirement for new teachers by prescribing five years of college training instead of four. Under a grandfather clause, teachers who have only four years of college would continue to qualify if they show satisfactory progress toward a graduate degree. T enrolls at the University of Southern California and takes three graduate courses. T's unreimbursed expenses for this purpose are as follows:

Books and tuition	$ 250
Lodging while in travel status (June–August)	1,150
Meals while in travel status	800
Laundry while in travel status	220
Transportation	600

T has a miscellaneous itemized deduction subject to the 2% floor as follows:

Books and tuition	$ 250
Lodging	1,150
Meals (80% of $800)	640
Laundry	220
Transportation	600
	$2,860

□

ENTERTAINMENT EXPENSES

Many taxpayers attempt to deduct personal entertainment expenses as business expenses. In response to these abuses by taxpayers, Code § 274 restricts the deductibility of entertainment expenses. The law contains strict recordkeeping requirements and provides restrictive tests for the deduction of certain types of entertainment expenses.

Classification of Expenses

Entertainment expenses can be categorized as follows: those *directly related* to business and those *associated with* business. Directly related expenses are related to an actual business meeting or discussion. These expenses can be contrasted with entertainment expenses that are incurred to promote goodwill. To obtain a

deduction for directly related entertainment, it is not necessary to show that actual benefit resulted from the expenditure as long as there was a reasonable expectation of benefit. To qualify as directly related, the expense should be incurred in a clear business setting. If there is little possibility of engaging in the active conduct of a trade or business due to the nature of the social facility, it may be difficult to qualify the expenditure as directly related to business.

Expenses associated with, rather than directly related to, business entertainment must serve a specific business purpose, such as obtaining new business or continuing existing business. These expenditures qualify only if the expenses directly precede or follow a bona fide business discussion. Entertainment occurring on the same day as the business discussion meets the test.

Restrictions upon Deductibility

Business Meals.   Any business meal is deductible only if the following are true:

- The meal is directly related to or associated with the active conduct of a trade or business.

- The expense is not lavish or extravagant under the circumstances.

- The taxpayer (or an employee) is present at the meal.

A business meal with a business associate or customer is not deductible unless business is discussed. This requirement is not intended to disallow the deduction for a meal consumed while away from home on business.

EXAMPLE 48   T travels to San Francisco for a business convention. She pays for dinner with three colleagues and is not reimbursed by her employer. They do not discuss business. She can deduct 80% of the cost of her meal. However, she cannot deduct the cost of her colleagues' meals.   □

The *clear business purpose* test requires that meals be directly related to or associated with the active conduct of a business. A meal is not deductible if it serves no business purpose.

EXAMPLE 49   T decides what stocks to add to or remove from his portfolio on the basis of advice from his stockbroker. If T takes his stockbroker to lunch to discuss his portfolio, he cannot deduct the meal's cost because his investment activities are not considered a business. Similarly, there's no deduction if he has dinner with his tax adviser to discuss ways to reduce his income tax liability.   □

The taxpayer or an employee must be present at the business meal for the meal to be deductible.

EXAMPLE 50   T reserved a table (and picked up the tab) for a business meal. Although business was discussed, neither T nor an employee attended. A deduction for the meal expense is disallowed. T can take a deduction for a business gift, but such gifts are limited to $25 per person per year.   □

EXAMPLE 51   T, a party to a contract negotiation, buys dinner for other parties to the negotiation but does not attend the dinner. No deduction is allowed.   ☐

An independent contractor who renders significant services to the taxpayer is treated as an employee.

EXAMPLE 52   In Example 52, if T's attorney (who negotiates contracts for T) had attended the meal, T would be allowed a deduction.   ☐

The attendance requirement does not apply where there is a transfer for business purposes, such as a holiday gift of a ham or a bottle of wine.

Entertainment Facilities.   Deducting the cost of maintaining an entertainment facility (e.g., a hunting lodge, fishing camp, yacht, country club) lends itself to taxpayer abuse since such a facility could be used for personal vacations and entertainment. For this reason, the law allows deductions only for "dues or fees to any social, athletic, or sporting club or organization"[18] and imposes stringent recordkeeping requirements.

To obtain a deduction for the dues paid or incurred to maintain a club membership, a primary use test is imposed. Unless it can be shown that over 50 percent of the use of the facility was for business purposes, no deduction is permitted. In meeting the primary use test, the following rules govern:

- Consider only the days the facility is used. Thus, days of nonuse do not enter into the determination.

- A day of both business and personal use counts as a day of business use.

- Business use includes entertainment that is associated with or directly related to business.

Even if the primary use test is satisfied, only the portion of the dues attributable to the directly related entertainment qualifies for the deduction.

EXAMPLE 53   T, the sales manager of an insurance agency, is expected to incur entertainment expenses in connection with the sale of insurance. None of these expenses are reimbursed by his employer. During the year, T paid the following amounts to the Leesville Country Club:

Membership fee (refundable upon termination of membership)	$2,000
Annual dues	1,200
Meals relating to business use	900
Meals and other charges relating to personal use	400
Other charges relating to business use	200

---

18. §§ 274(a)(2)(A) and (C).

The club was used 120 days for purposes directly related to business and 80 days for personal use. The club was not used at all during the remaining days of the year. Since the facility was used for business more than 50% of the time (120 days out of 200 days), the primary use test is satisfied. The portion of the annual dues that can be deducted is $720 (120/200 = 60% × $1,200). None of the membership fee is deductible because it is refundable. The total deduction allowed is as follows:

Annual dues	$ 720
Business meals	900
Other business charges	200
Total	$1,820
Less 20%	(364)
Deductible	$1,456

Note that the $1,456 is a miscellaneous itemized deduction subject to the 2% floor. ☐

Ticket Purchases for Entertainment.   A deduction for the cost of a ticket for an entertainment activity is limited to the face value of the ticket. This limitation is applied before the 80 percent rule. The face value of a ticket includes any tax. Under this rule, the excess payment to a scalper for a ticket is not deductible. Similarly, the fee to a ticket agency for the purchase of a ticket is not deductible.

An exception exists for expenses of a sports event meeting certain charitable fund-raising requirements. The exception applies to the entire ticket package (e.g., parking, meals, seating). The full amount is deductible if the event:

- Is organized for the primary purpose of benefiting a tax-exempt charitable organization [described in § 501(c)(3)].

- Contributes 100 percent of the net proceeds to the charity.

- Uses volunteers for substantially all work performed in carrying out the event.

Expenditures for the rental or use of a luxury skybox at a sports arena in excess of the face value of regular tickets are disallowed as deductions. If a luxury skybox is used for entertainment that is directly related to or associated with business, the deduction is limited to the face value of nonluxury box seats. All seats in the luxury skybox are counted, even when some seats are unoccupied.

The taxpayer may also deduct stated charges for food and beverages under the general rules for business entertainment. The deduction for skybox seats, food, and beverages is limited to 80 percent of cost.

EXAMPLE 54   In 1990, AW, Inc., pays $6,000 to rent a 10-seat skybox at City Stadium for three football games. Nonluxury box seats at each event range in cost from $25 to $35 a seat. In March, an AW representative and five clients of AW use the skybox for the first game. The entertainment follows a bona fide business discussion, and AW spends $85 for food and beverages during the game. AW computes its deduction for the first sports event as follows:

Food and beverages	$ 85
Deduction for seats ($35 × 10 seats)	350
Total entertainment expense	$ 435
80% limitation	×.80
Deduction	$ 348

☐

Recordkeeping Requirements.   Section 274(d) provides that no deduction is permitted unless the taxpayer substantiates, by adequate records or by sufficient evidence corroborating the taxpayer's statements, the following:

- The amount of the expense.

- The time and place of the expense.

- The business purpose.

- The business relationship.

If reimbursements equal expenses and the employee makes an adequate accounting to the employer and returns any excess, both the reimbursements and the expenses are omitted from the tax return. In all other cases, the employee must submit a statement with the return. Where an employee owns more than 10 percent of the employer corporation's stock, the deemed substantiation method of Rev. Proc. 89–67 does not apply.

Business Gifts.   Business gifts are deductible to the extent of $25 per donee per year. An exception is made for gifts costing $4 or less (e.g., pens with the employee's or company's name on them) or promotional materials. Such items are not treated as business gifts subject to the $25 limitation. In addition, incidental costs such as engraving of jewelry and nominal charges for giftwrapping, mailing, and delivery are not included in the cost of the gift in applying the limitation. The $25 limitation applies to both direct and indirect gifts. A gift is indirect if it is made to a person's spouse or other family member or to a corporation or partnership on behalf of the individual. All such gifts must be aggregated in applying the $25 limit. Excluded from the $25 limit are gifts or awards to employees, such as for length of service, that are under $400.[19]Gifts to superiors and employers are not deductible.

It is necessary to maintain records substantiating the gifts. These substantiation requirements are similar to the rules applying to entertainment expenses previously discussed.

Business gifts made by employees are deductible *for* AGI if they are reimbursed. If unreimbursed, they are miscellaneous itemized deductions subject to the 2 percent floor.

OTHER EMPLOYEE EXPENSES

Office in the Home

Employees and self-employed individuals are not allowed a deduction for expenses of an office in the home unless a portion of the residence is used exclusively on a regular basis as either:

---

19.   § 274(b)(1)(C). § 274(b)(3)(C) allows a deduction for gifts to employees of up to $1,600 under a *qualified plan* as long as the average cost of all awards under the qualified plan does not exceed $400. Qualified plans are described in § 274(b)(3).

- The principal place of business for any trade or business of the taxpayer.

- A place of business used by clients, patients, or customers.

Employees must meet an additional test: the use must be for the convenience of the employer rather than merely being "appropriate and helpful."[20]

The exclusive use requirement means that a specific part of the home must be used solely for business purposes. A deduction, if permitted, will require an allocation of total expenses of operating the home between business and personal use based on floor space or number of rooms.

Even if the taxpayer meets the above requirements, the allowable home office expenses may not exceed the gross income from the business less all other business expenses attributable to the activity. Furthermore, the home office expenses that must be deducted first are those that would be allowable as itemized deductions anyway (e.g., mortgage interest and real estate taxes). All home office expenses of an employee are miscellaneous itemized deductions subject to the 2 percent floor, except those (such as interest) that qualify as other personal itemized deductions. Home office expenses of a self-employed individual are trade or business expenses and are deductible *for* AGI.

Any disallowed home office expenses can be carried forward and used in future years subject to the same limitations.

EXAMPLE 55

T is a certified public accountant employed by a regional CPA firm as a tax manager. He operates a separate business in which he refinishes furniture in his home. For this business, he uses two rooms in the basement of his home exclusively and regularly. The floor space of the two rooms constitutes 10% of the floor space of his residence. Gross income from the business totals $8,000. Expenses of the business (other than home office expenses) are $6,500. The following home office expenses are incurred:

Real property taxes on residence	$4,000
Interest expense on residence	7,500
Operating expenses of residence	2,000
Depreciation on residence (based on 10% business use)	250

T's deductions are determined as follows:

Business income		$ 8,000
Less: Other business expenses		(6,500)
		$ 1,500
Less: Allocable taxes ($4,000 × 10%)	$400	
Allocable interest ($7,500 × 10%)	750	(1,150)
		$ 350
Allocable operating expenses of the residence ($2,000 × 10%)		(200)
		$ 150
Allocable depreciation ($250, limited to remaining income)		(150)
		$ –0–

---

20. § 280 (A) (c)(1).

T has a carryover of $100 (the unused excess depreciation). Because T is self-employed, the allocable taxes and interest ($1,150), the other deductible office expenses ($200 + $150), and $6,500 of other business expenses are deductible *for* AGI. □

EXAMPLE 56

T, an accountant for the XYZ Corporation, maintains an office in her home. She uses the office primarily for reading professional journals, and her family uses the office for personal reasons. T occasionally brings home work relating to XYZ Corporation and uses the office at home on weekends and during the evenings. Her outside consulting activities are limited to the preparation of a few tax returns from which she received $1,000 gross income during the current year. Mortgage interest and real estate taxes allocable to the office amounted to $1,500. An allocable portion of other household expenses, including utilities and depreciation, was $1,000. The $1,500 mortgage interest and real estate taxes are deductible *from* adjusted gross income as itemized deductions. None of the other expenses are deductible because the office in T's home is not used exclusively and on a regular basis by T as a place of business. In addition, an employee must show that the office is used for the convenience of the employer. It appears that T's office is merely appropriate and helpful in the performance of her duties as an employee. This situation does not permit a deduction. □

The home office limitation cannot be circumvented by leasing part of one's home to an employer, using it as a home office, and deducting the expenses as a rental expense under § 212.

Miscellaneous Employee Expenses

Some miscellaneous employee expenses that are deductible are special clothing and its upkeep, union dues, and professional expenses. Others are professional dues, professional meetings, and employment agency fees for seeking employment in the same trade or business, whether or not a new job is secured. These expenses are reported by the employee in the same manner as other employee business expenses discussed previously in the chapter.

To be deductible, special clothing must be both specifically required as a condition of employment and not generally adaptable for regular wear. For example, a police officer's uniform is not suitable for off-duty activities. An exception is clothing used to the extent that the clothing takes the place of regular clothing (e.g., military uniforms).

The current position of the IRS is that expenses incurred in seeking employment are deductible if the taxpayer is seeking employment in the same trade or business. The deduction is allowed whether or not the attempts to secure employment are successful. An unemployed taxpayer can take a deduction providing there has been no substantial lack of continuity between the last job and the search for a new one. No deduction is allowed for persons seeking their first job or seeking employment in a new trade or business (whether successful or not).

The basic cost of one telephone in one's home is not deductible, even if the telephone is used for business. Any long-distance or toll charges relating to business are deductible. Other employee expenses that are not deductible are commuting expenses and any other expenditures of a personal nature.

Expenses of Employees Working Outside the United States

The U.S. income tax applies to the worldwide income of its citizens and residents. Since most other countries also have an income tax, expatriates (Americans working abroad) were at the distinct disadvantage of having to pay two income taxes on foreign earned income. The increased cost of living in some foreign countries plus the scarcity of adequate housing in less-developed countries made working abroad even more disadvantageous to Americans. To induce U.S. citizens and residents to accept employment or relocation overseas, U.S. companies were compelled to offer various cost differentials and tax equalization assurances. This increased their labor costs and placed U.S. concerns at an economic disadvantage with their foreign competitors. To mitigate the problem, Congress passed favorable legislation for foreign earned income.

The expatriate has the option of a flat-dollar exclusion (discussed in chapter 4), a considerably simplified excess housing allowance, or both. The provisions are summarized as follows:

- To qualify, the taxpayer must satisfy either the bona fide residence test or the physical presence test—330 full days of foreign residency out of 12 consecutive months. An exception to the 330-day rule is provided for expatriates who are forced to leave a country because of civil unrest or similar conditions, such as the widespread civil disorder in Lebanon.

- In addition to electing the foreign earned income exclusion, an expatriate may elect to exclude an amount determined on the basis of housing costs incurred. For this purpose, the housing cost amount consists of reasonable housing costs, including rent, insurance, and utilities. Housing costs do not include interest and taxes that are independently deductible. The amount to be excluded is the excess of these costs over 16 percent of the salary of a government employee holding grade GS–14. For those expatriates who are not reimbursed for housing costs, a special rule substitutes a deduction for the exclusion.

- Deductions or credits for foreign taxes attributable to the excluded income are not allowable. Consequently, the expatriate is placed in a position of having to forgo the foreign tax credit in order to obtain the exclusion.

- The exclusions are elective. Taxpayers are able to elect the income and housing-reimbursement exclusions separately, together, or not at all. Once elected, however, the exclusions are binding upon subsequent years unless affirmatively revoked. Revocation places the taxpayer in a five-year holding period during which the exclusions cannot be reelected.

The exclusion rule for expatriates is generally advantageous for those working in countries with low, if any, income taxes. If, on the other hand, the country imposes a high income tax, it may be preferable not to elect the exclusions and to use the foreign tax credit route to reduce or eliminate U.S. income taxes.

Contributions to Individual Retirement Accounts

An important and popular deduction *for* adjusted gross income is the amount contributed to an Individual Retirement Account (IRA). This amount may be as great as $2,000 per year for an individual.

CONCEPT SUMMARY 9–1

Determining the Deductibility of Employee Business Expenses

If the Expense Is	The 20% Reduction Applies to	And Is Deductible	And Is
1. Any allowable employee business expense (fully reimbursed and adequate accounting made and excess returned).	None.	*for* AGI	Omitted from the return, as are all reimbursements.[1,2]
2. Any allowable employee business expense (fully reimbursed and no adequate accounting made).	Meals and entertainment.	*from* AGI	A miscellaneous deduction subject to the 2% floor.
3. Any allowable business expense (partially reimbursed and adequate accounting made).	Unreimbursed part of meals and entertainment only.	Reimbursed portion is *for* AGI and unreimbursed is *from* AGI.	Unreimbursed part is a miscellaneous deduction subject to the 2% floor.[3]
Unreimbursed Expenses			
4. Transportation expenses.	None.	*from* AGI	A miscellaneous deduction subject to the 2% floor.[3]
5. Travel expenses.			
a. meals.	All.	*from* AGI	A miscellaneous deduction subject to the 2% floor.[3]
b. lodging.	None.	*from* AGI	A miscellaneous deduction subject to the 2% floor.[3]
c. incidentals.	None.	*from* AGI	A miscellaneous deduction subject to the 2% floor.[3]
6. Education expenses.	Only meal expenses.	*from* AGI	A miscellaneous deduction subject to the 2% floor.[3]
7. Moving expenses.	Only meal expenses.	*from* AGI	A miscellaneous deduction not subject to the 2% floor.[4]
8. A deductible IRA.	None.	*for* AGI	N/A
9. Home office expenses.	None.	*from* AGI	Interest and property taxes are not subject to the 2% floor, all others are.[3]
10. Professional or union dues.	None.	*from* AGI	A miscellaneous deduction subject to the 2% floor.[3]
11. Uniforms.	None.	*from* AGI	A miscellaneous deduction subject to the 2% floor.[3]
12. Job-hunting expenses (if in same field).	Only meal and entertainment expenses.	*from* AGI	A miscellaneous deduction subject to the 2% floor.[3]

If the Expense Is	The 20% Reduction Applies to	And Is Deductible	And Is
13. Entertainment expenses.	All.	*from* AGI	A miscellaneous deduction subject to the 2% floor.[3]
14. An outside salesperson's expenses.	Only meals and entertainment expenses.	*from* AGI	A miscellaneous deduction subject to the 2% floor.[3]

1. If reimbursements exceed expenses, the reimbursements are included in income; expenses are itemized, subject to the 2% floor.
2. Employer can deduct only 80% of meals and entertainment.
3. Miscellaneous deductions are added together and reduced by 2% of AGI.
4. Moving expenses are itemized, whether or not reimbursed.

TAX PLANNING CONSIDERATIONS

Self-Employed Individuals

Some taxpayers have the flexibility to be classified as either employees or self-employed individuals (e.g., real estate agents or direct sellers). Such taxpayers should not automatically assume that the latter is better until all factors are considered.

It is advantageous to deduct one's business expenses *for* adjusted gross income and avoid the 2 percent floor. However, a self-employed individual may have higher expenses, such as local gross receipts taxes, license fees, franchise fees, personal property taxes, and occupation taxes. The recordkeeping and filing requirements can be quite burdensome.

One of the most expensive considerations is the Social Security tax versus the self-employment tax. In 1990, for example, the Social Security tax rate for an employee is 7.65 percent, while a self-employed individual is subject to a self-employment tax rate of 15.3 percent. Both are levied on the first $51,300.

After analyzing all these factors, a taxpayer may decide that employee status is preferable to self-employed status.

Shifting Deductions between Employer and Employee

An employee can avoid the 2 percent floor for employee business expenses. Typically, an employee incurs travel and entertainment expenses in the course of employment. The corporation gets the deduction if it reimburses the employee, and the employee gets the deduction *for* AGI. An adequate accounting must be made, and excess reimbursements cannot be kept.

Transportation and Travel Expenses

Adequate detailed records should be kept of all transportation and travel expenses. Since the regular mileage allowance is 26 cents per mile (25.5 cents in 1989), a

new, expensive automobile used primarily for business may generate a higher expense based on actual cost. The election to expense part of the cost of the automobile under § 179, ACRS depreciation, insurance, repairs and maintenance, automobile club dues, and interest on the auto loan may result in automobile expenses greater than the automatic mileage allowance.

If a taxpayer wishes to sightsee or vacation on a business trip, it would be beneficial to schedule business on both a Friday and a Monday to turn the weekend into business days for allocation purposes. It is especially crucial to schedule appropriate business days when foreign travel is involved.

Unreimbursed Employee Business Expenses

The 2 percent floor for unreimbursed employee business expenses offers a tax planning opportunity for married couples. If one spouse has high miscellaneous expenses subject to the floor, it may be beneficial for the couple to file separate returns. If they file jointly, the 2 percent floor will be based on the incomes of both. Filing separately will lower the reduction to 2 percent of only one spouse's income.

Other provisions of the law should be considered, however. For example, filing separately could cost a couple losses of up to $25,000 from self-managed rental units under the passive loss rules (discussed in chapter 6).

Another possibility is to negotiate a salary reduction with one's employer in exchange for the 100 percent reimbursement of employee expenses. The employee would be better off because the 2 percent floor would not apply. The employer would be better off because expense reimbursements are not subject to Social Security and other payroll taxes.

Moving Expenses

Reimbursements of moving expenses must be included in gross income, and certain moving expenses may not be deductible because of the ceiling limitations. As a result, an employee may be required to pay additional income tax because of an employment-related move. Some employers reimburse their employees for these additional taxes, which are estimated and included in the employee's reimbursement.

Persons who retire and move to a new location incur personal nondeductible moving expenses. However, if the retired person accepts a full-time job in the new location before moving, the moving expenses become deductible.

Education Expenses

Education expenses are treated as nondeductible personal items unless the individual is employed or is engaged in a trade or business. A temporary leave of absence for further education is one way to reasonably assure that the taxpayer is still qualified, even if a full-time student. It has been held that an individual could deduct education expenses even though he resigned from his job, returned to school full-time for two years, and accepted another job in the same field upon graduation. The Court held that the student had merely suspended active participation in his field.[21] If the time period out of the field is too long, educational expense deductions will be disallowed. For example, a teacher who left the field for four years to raise her child and curtailed her employment searches and writing

---

21. *Stephen G. Sherman,* 36 TCM 1191, T.C.Memo. 1977–301

activities was denied a deduction. She was not actively engaged in the trade or business of being an educator.[22] To secure the deduction, an individual should be advised to arrange his or her work situation to preserve employee or business status.

Entertainment Expenses

Proper documentation of expenditures is essential because of the strict record-keeping requirements and the restrictive tests that must be met. For example, credit card receipts and cancelled checks as the sole source of documentation may be inadequate to substantiate the business purpose and business relationship.[23] Taxpayers should be advised to maintain detailed records of amounts, time, place, business purpose, and business relationships. A credit card receipt details the place, date, and amount of the expense. A notation made on the receipt of the names of the person(s) attending, the business relationship, and the topic of discussion should constitute proper documentation.

Associated with or goodwill entertainment is not deductible unless a business discussion is conducted immediately before or after the entertainment. Furthermore, a business purpose must exist for such entertainment. Taxpayers should be advised to arrange for a business discussion before or after such entertainment. They must provide documentation of the business purpose (e.g., to obtain new business from a prospective customer).

Since a 50 percent test is imposed for the deductibility of country club dues, it may be necessary to accelerate business use or reduce personal use of a club facility. The 50 percent test is made on a daily use basis, and detailed records should therefore be maintained to substantiate business versus personal use.

EXAMPLE 57

T confers with his CPA on December 5 and finds that he has used the country club 30 days for business and 33 days for personal use. On the advice of his CPA, T schedules four business lunches between December 5 and December 31 and refrains from using the club for personal purposes until January of the following year. Because of this action, T will meet the 50% test and will be permitted a deduction for a portion of the club dues.   □

Unreimbursed meals and entertainment are subject to the 80 percent rule in addition to the 2 percent floor. Negotiating a salary reduction, as previously discussed under Unreimbursed Employee Business Expenses, is even more valuable to the taxpayer.

PROBLEM MATERIALS

Discussion Questions

1. What difference does it make if an individual's expenses are classified as employment-related expenses or as expenses from self-employment?

2. Discuss the factors that may indicate an employer-employee relationship. What is the definitive test?

---

22. *Brian C. Mulherin*, 42 TCM 834, T.C. Memo. 1984–454; *George A. Baist*, 56 TCM 778, T.C. Memo. 1988–554.

23. *Kenneth W. Guenther*, 54 TCM 382, T.C. Memo. 1987–440.

3. How does the tax treatment of meals and entertainment differ from the treatment of other employee business expenses? Does the treatment differ if the expenses are reimbursed?

4. What is a reasonable period of time for purposes of returning excess reimbursements?

5. What constitutes an adequate accounting to an employer?

6. What tax return reporting procedures must be followed by an employee under the following circumstances?

    a. Expenses and reimbursements are equal, and an adequate accounting is made to the employer and any excess is returned.

    b. Reimbursements exceed expenses, and an adequate accounting is made to the employer.

    c. Expenses exceed reimbursements, and no accounting is made to the employer.

7. T received a reasonable per diem allowance while out of town on business for his employer. Because he stayed at the YMCA and ate at fast-food restaurants, his actual expenses were less than his per diem allowance. What are the tax consequences to T?

8. A taxpayer has two jobs. He drives 40 miles to his first job. The distance from the first job to the second is 32 miles. During the year he worked 200 days at both jobs. On 150 days, he drove from his first job to the second job. On the remaining 50 days, he drove home (40 miles) and then to the second job (42 miles). How much can he deduct?

9. J incurred travel expenses while away from home on company business. These expenses were not reimbursed by his employer. Can J deduct the travel expenses? If so, where and how are they deducted?

10. T accepts a three-year work assignment in another city. Are the rental payments and meal expenses incurred because of that work assignment deductible as travel expenses?

11. J takes a combined business and pleasure trip to Hawaii. What portion of the expenses is deductible?

12. G took a combined business and pleasure trip to Europe. She traveled to London from New York on Friday, vacationed on Saturday and Sunday, conducted business on Monday got snowed in at the airport on Tuesday, traveled to Paris on Wednesday, relaxed on Thursday (a legal holiday), conducted business on Friday, went sightseeing on Saturday and Sunday, picked up business samples and papers on Monday, and flew back to New York on Tuesday. What portion of her air fare can she deduct?

13. What are a taxpayer's two alternatives if she moves in November and cannot meet the 39-week test by December 31? Which alternative is financially preferable if she meets the test in the following year? If she does not meet the test?

14. Distinguish between direct moving expenses and indirect moving expenses. Why is it important to classify such items properly?

15. What limits are imposed on the deduction of expenses for tickets purchased for business entertainment? How are such expenses treated on an employee's return if they are reimbursed? Not reimbursed?

16. What difference does it make for the purpose of the education deduction if a taxpayer is improving existing skills or acquiring new ones? Under what general tax principle does the justification for this rule lie?

17. Discuss the difference between entertainment that is *directly related to* business and entertainment that is *associated with* business.

18. J, a stockbroker, buys his CPA's lunch, over which they discuss J's tax problems. Can J deduct the cost of the meal? Could the CPA get the deduction if he pays for the meal?

19. F asks your advice on December 1 regarding the tax deductibility of his country club dues. To date, the club has been used 40 days for purposes directly related to business use, 42 days for purposes associated with business use, and 84 days for personal use. During December, members of F's family have planned to use the facility 4 more days for personal parties. No business use is planned in December. What would you advise F to do?

20. To what extent may a taxpayer take a deduction for business gifts to a business associate? To an employee? To a superior?

21. How are deductible home office expenses treated for tax purposes? Is the deduction *for* or *from* AGI?

22. P took a cruise in the Hawaiian Islands on a ship of U.S. registry to attend a business-related seminar. The cost was $3,000. What, if anything, can she deduct?

Problems

23. In addition to air fare of $2,164 (first class), E incurred the following expenses on a trip. The trip was solely for business, and E was away from home overnight.

Meals	$150
Room	210
Taxi	60
Entertainment	80
Laundry	50

   If the expenses are *not* reimbursed by E's employer, how much can E deduct? Is the deduction *for* or *from* AGI?

24. T is a professor who consults on the side. She uses one-fifth of her home exclusively for her consulting business, and clients regularly meet her there. T is single and under 65. Her AGI (before considering consulting income) is $40,000. Other relevant data follows:

Income from consulting business	$3,600
Consulting expenses other than home office	1,100
Total costs relating to home	
Interest and taxes	8,000
Utilities	1,400
Maintenance and repairs	900
Depreciation (based on ⅕ business use)	1,200

   Calculate T's AGI for 1990.

25. D, a professor of French history, went to France during the year to research documents available only in France. His time on the trip was spent entirely on business. No vacation days were involved, and D kept adequate records. D received no reimbursements for the following carefully documented expenses:

Airfare and other transportation	$1,600
Hotels	1,200
Meals	900

    a. What can D deduct in 1990 if he has AGI of $30,000 and no other miscellaneous itemized deductions? Are the deductions *for* or *from* AGI?

    b. Would your answer differ if D had gone to France to soak up the culture and brush up on his French?

26. J, an executive, traveled to England to confer with branch office officials of his company. Because an inner-ear birth defect prevents him from flying, he traveled to England on the *Queen Elizabeth II*. The journey, which took six days and cost $1,800, was sold as a package deal with no breakdown of costs. How much can J deduct in 1990, assuming the U.S. government per diem amount is $100? Would your answer differ if the cost were broken down between transportation ($800) and meals and entertainment ($1,000)?

27. F, an executive of the ABC Corporation, owns 30% of the company's common stock. F incurred the following business expenses during the year:

Lodging	$2,100
Meals	1,200
Entertainment	980
Transportation	3,100

How should F treat these expenses on his 1990 income tax return, assuming that he made an adequate accounting to his firm and was fully reimbursed? How should he treat them if he did *not* make an adequate accounting?

28. T incurred the following employee expenses:

Travel while away from home (including meals of $500)	$2,000
Transportation	1,000
Entertainment of customers	900
Professional dues	600
Telephone for business use	500

T's employer paid T a $3,500 allowance to cover all of these expenses. T made an adequate accounting and the allowance was not reported on T's Form W-2. Calculate T's deductions *for* and *from* adjusted gross income. His AGI was $25,000.

29. P incurred the following expenses related to her employment as a chief executive officer:

Lodging while away from home	$2,800
Meals while away from home	1,200
Entertainment while away from home	2,000
Dues, subscriptions, and books	1,000
Transportation expenses	4,000

P's AGI was $100,000, and she received $6,600 after adequately accounting to her employer. What are P's deductions *for* and *from* AGI?

30. K received $4,400 in reimbursements under an accountable plan after she had made an adequate accounting to her employer. Her expenses were as follows:

Transportation expenses	$3,200
Meals while away from home	1,400
Lodging and incidentals	2,300
Dues, phone, and subscriptions	100
Entertainment	1,000

How much can K deduct *for* and *from* AGI? Assume K had AGI of $50,000 and no other miscellaneous itemized deductions.

31. P, an executive with X Corporation, incurred the following employee business expenses:

Lodging	$2,000
Meals	1,600
Transportation	2,400
Entertainment	1,500
Phone	500

P received $5,600 to cover the above expenses. He made an adequate accounting. In addition to incurring the above expenses, P incurred expenses in attending a seminar on communications for executives. He paid $500 in transportation, $100 in meals, and $300 in fees and books. He was not reimbursed.

P's salary was $50,000. He made a deductible contribution of $2,000 to his IRA. His only other income was interest of $800. He is 47 and single.

Calculate P's AGI and itemized employee expenses.

32. N took a business trip of 10 days. Seven days were spent on business (including travel time) and 3 days were personal. His unreimbursed expenses were as follows:

Airfare	$1,500
Lodging (per day)	200
Meals (per day)	100
Entertainment of clients	300

a. How much can N deduct if the trip is within the United States?

b. How much can N deduct if the trip is outside the United States?

33. S traveled from New York to Helsinki primarily on business for his employer. He spent 16 days (including travel) on business and 4 days sightseeing. S's expenses were as follows:

Airfare	$3,600
Meals	2,250
Lodging	2,850
Incidental expenses	300

S was not reimbursed. How are these expenses reported assuming an AGI of $100,000?

34. M took a business trip from Seattle to Chicago. He spent two days in travel, conducted business for four days, and visited friends for four days. He incurred the following expenses:

Airfare	$ 700
Lodging	2,000
Meals	1,600
Entertainment of clients	500

M received no reimbursements. What amount can M deduct?

35. T, who is age 42 and single, earned a salary of $60,000. She had other income consisting of interest of $2,000, dividends of $1,600, and long-term capital gains of $4,000.

T loaned a friend $5,000 two years ago. In the current year the friend died, leaving no assets. T will not receive any repayments on the loan.

T adequately accounted to her employer and received a reimbursement of $3,000.

She incurred the following expenses during the year:

Transportation	$2,300
Meals	1,600
Dues and subscriptions	800
Entertainment of clients	300
Total	$5,000

Calculate J's AGI and itemized employee business expenses.

36. H, an investment counselor, attended a conference on the impact of the new tax law on investment choices. His unreimbursed expenses were as follows:

Airfare	$250
Lodging	500
Meals	300
Tuition and fees	400

   a. How much can H deduct on his return? Are the expenses *for* or *from* AGI?

   b. Would your answer differ if H were a self-employed physician?

37. T incurred the following expenses when she was transferred from San Francisco to Dallas:

Loss on the sale of old residence	$7,000
Moving company's charges	2,100
House-hunting trip	1,200
Temporary living expenses for 60 days (including meals of $1,000)	3,000
Broker's fees on residence sold	5,000
Charges for fitting drapes in new residence	800

   a. How much can T deduct? Is the deduction *for* or *from* AGI?

   b. What would be T's tax consequences if the employer reimbursed her for all of the expenses?

38. Upon his graduation from college in Texas, T was hired by a Los Angeles brokerage firm. His moving expenses were not reimbursed. How much can T deduct of the following expenses? Are the expenses *for* or *from* his AGI of $20,000?

Loss of apartment deposit because of damage done by cat	$ 300
Apartment-hunting trip to Los Angeles (including meals of $300)	$1,400
Cost of shipping cat to Los Angeles	135
Payment to apartment-locating service	100
Expense of renting and driving a truck to Los Angeles to move household goods	2,200
Lodging in Los Angeles for two weeks after arrival (apartment was not ready)	800
Meals for two weeks after arrival	415

39. D belongs to a country club that she uses for entertaining clients of her employer as well as for personal use. She incurred charges as follows:

Initiation fee (nonrefundable)	$5,000
Annual dues	3,600
Business meals	4,000
Other business charges	800
Personal meals and charges	3,100

D kept careful records, which revealed the following use:

Days *associated with* business	60
Days *directly related* to business	50
Days for personal use	80

Forty of the personal use days occurred on the same days that the club was used for entertainment directly related to business.

a. How much can D deduct if she received no reimbursements?

b. Would your answer differ if she made an adequate accounting and received a $3,000 reimbursement?

40. T belongs to a country club that he uses for both business and personal purposes. Assuming none of his expenses are reimbursed, how much can he deduct on his tax return in the following two cases:

Annual dues		$5,000
Meals *directly related* to business		400
Meals *associated with* business		300
"Quiet business meals" (business was not discussed)		350
Personal meals and charges		2,000
Case (a) Days directly related to business	110	
Days associated with business	30	
Days for personal use	150	
Case (b) Days directly related to business	70	
Days associated with business	80	
Days for personal use	75	

41. M is an executive with a large manufacturing firm. He is 54 and married and has two children. His compensation was $126,000. His wife is not employed. M took a trip from New York to London primarily for business. He was away from home 12 days, spending 8 days conducting business and 4 days vacationing. He incurred transportation expenses of $3,000, lodging expenses of $200 per day, meals of $60 per day, and expenses of $500 while entertaining clients. M belonged to a country club that he used for both personal and business entertainment. His records reveal that he used the facility 57 days for purposes directly related to business, 14 days for purposes associated with business, and 93 days for personal use during the year. Expenses were as follows:

Annual dues	$6,000
Business meals	1,800
Business entertainment	965
Personal meals and charges	3,100

M received $8,600 in dividends and $3,400 in interest during the year. He paid $18,000 in alimony to his former wife.

Calculate M's adjusted gross income.

42. J is an accountant with XYZ Company. He is also a self-employed tax consultant with several clients and earns $12,000 per year from his outside consulting. He has an office in his home that he uses exclusively for meeting with his consulting clients and for work he performs for his clients. Based on square footage, he estimates that total expenses amount to $3,500, including $1,500 of taxes and interest on his home mortgage.

a. Can J take a deduction for an office in the home? If so, how does he report it and how much can he deduct?

b.   If the office was also used for work J brought home from his regular job, how would your answer to (a) differ? Assume J used the office 80% for his consulting business and 20% for his regular job.

43.   C is a self-employed wholesale jobber who had sales of $80,000 in 1990. He keeps meticulous business income and expense records.

His business expenses included an office in his home, used exclusively for his business. Expenses allocated to the home office on the basis of square footage were as follows:

Taxes and interest	$1,300
Utilities and maintenance	620
Office depreciation	1,200
Office supplies	380
Office furniture depreciation	700

C incurred the following business expenses:

Transportation	$6,000
Business meals	1,400
Business entertainment	900
Telephone, dues, and books	1,500
Other business expenses	2,000

C paid $20,000 to his former wife, of which $8,000 was child support and $12,000 was alimony. He made a $2,000 deductible contribution to his IRA. C received interest of $2,000 and dividends of $1,000 during the year. Calculate his AGI for 1990.

44.   T is a single, 37-year-old executive who earned $60,000 in 1990. He also earned $2,000 in dividends and had interest of $1,800 credited to his savings account. A former friend skipped town, owing T $1,500 and leaving him with no possibility of collecting this bona fide personal loan. An examination of T's records revealed the following:

*   T paid $5,000 in alimony and $3,000 in child support to his former wife.
*   T incurred education expenses to maintain and improve his existing skills. Tuition and books cost $580, transportation expenses amounted to $960, and parking fines totaled $80.
*   T paid $1,200 in country club dues and $920 for meals for clients. The club was used 200 days for business and 50 days for personal use.
*   T took a business trip to London. He flew there on a Thursday, conducted business on Friday, went sightseeing on Saturday and Sunday, conducted business on Monday and Tuesday, and flew home on Wednesday. His unreimbursed expenses amounted to $2,100 for airfare, $500 for meals, and $1,400 for lodging.

Calculate T's adjusted gross income and his itemized employee deductions.

45.   T and S are married and file a joint return. T is a manager and earned a salary and bonus of $31,000 in 1990. He incurred employee business expenses of $800 for transportation and $400 for meals and entertainment. He made an adequate accounting to his employer and was fully reimbursed. He took a combined business and pleasure trip to New York. He spent five days conducting business and three days sightseeing. His airfare and taxi expense amounted to $1,200, meals averaged $60 per day, and lodging was $80 per day. He was not reimbursed. He made a $2,000 contribution to his IRA.

S is a self-employed court reporter who works out of the home. One room is used regularly and exclusively for her business. She had receipts of $12,000 and incurred office expenses of $1,000 for depreciation, $300 for utilities, $150 for her home phone, and $500 for repairs and maintenance. She earned $200 in interest on her savings account and incurred other business expenses of $2,300. She made a payment of $2,000 to her IRA.

Calculate taxable income for T and S on a joint return, assuming all other itemized deductions totaled $4,100.

46. T is a single saleswoman who earned $38,000 in 1990. Her employer gave her a $5,000 expense account intended to cover all her employee expenses. She incurred expenses of $3,000 for transportation; $2,000 for meals and entertainment; and $2,200 for dues, subscriptions, phone, and gifts (none of which exceeded $25).

   She sold some stocks, realizing a $6,000 long-term capital gain. She had dividend income of $650 and earned interest of $900, of which $250 was on municipal bonds. During the year, she was awarded $10,000 from a competitor for defamation of character.

   In November, she spent her vacation cruising the Hawaiian Islands on a ship of U.S. registry. Daily lectures and seminars on improving selling techniques were conducted. She can prove that the cruise, which cost her $3,500, was directly related to her job.

   Calculate T's adjusted gross income and deductible itemized employee expenses.

Cumulative Problems

47. Sam Diamond is 38 and single with no dependents. His salary was $34,000, from which $3,800 was withheld for Federal income tax. The proper amount of FICA (Social Security) taxes and state income taxes of $1,400 were also withheld. Examination of his 1990 records revealed the following:

   a. Sam had other receipts as follows:

Dividends on AT&T stock	$370
Interest credited to savings account	92
State income tax refund (he itemized in 1989)	268

   b. Sam's other deductions were as follows:

Home mortgage interest	$7,900
Property taxes	620
Charitable contributions	580

   c. Sam paid his former wife $2,200 for support of their child, Mary, who lives with her mother.

   d. Sam received $5,000 in settlement of a damage claim resulting from a personal automobile accident.

   e. He took a business trip during 1990 and was reimbursed $1,500 by his employer. His expenses were as follows:

Transportation	$ 850
Meals	160
Lodging and incidentals	340
	$1,350

f. He drove a total of 8,000 business miles and uses the standard mileage rate to compute his automobile expense.

g. Sam incurred the following unreimbursed employee business expenses:

Business meals	$500
Publications and dues	250
Phone and miscellaneous	60
Business entertainment	290
Tuition and books for course at local college	612

Compute Sam's Federal income tax payable (or refund due) for 1990. Suggested software (if available): *WEST–TAX Planner* or *BNA Individual Income Tax Spreadsheet.*

48. Robert T. Washington is 40 years old and divorced. He is a wholesale broker for General Suppliers, Inc. His commissions and salary amounted to $104,000 in 1990. His employer withheld $21,000 in Federal income taxes. Robert lives in a state that has no state income tax. Examination of Robert's 1990 records revealed the following:

a. Robert paid his former wife Jean $12,000, of which $7,000 was alimony and $5,000 support for their daughter, Brenda, age 6. His ex-wife, who has custody of Brenda, can document that she spent $2,000 on her daughter's support. She has signed an agreeement that Robert gets the exemption.

b. Robert received dividends from Acme Company of $1,000 and interest on his money market account at Citizen's Federal of $3,200. His favorite uncle gave him $10,000 as a Christmas gift, which he invested in municipal bonds that earned $75 interest in 1990.

c. Since General Suppliers, Inc., has no offices (only a warehouse), Robert works out of a home office that constitutes 20% of his home's floor space. His expenses in connection with his home were as follows:

Depreciation (on office space only)	$ 600
Property taxes	1,800
Interest on home mortgage	12,000
Cleaning, repairs, and maintenance	1,300
Utilities	2,600

His local telephone service cost $300, of which 50% was business. His long-distance business calls totaled $800. His office furniture has been fully depreciated.

d. Robert belongs to a country club that he uses for business purposes. He used the club 80 days for purposes directly related to business and 120 days for personal use. His carefully kept records reveal that his dues amounted to $2,400, business-related meals were $1,560, and personal charges were $2,300.

e. Robert also had the following well-documented business expenses:

Magazines and dues	$160
Gifts to customers: (5 @ $50)	250
(10 @ $20)	200
Entertainment of customers	800
Cleaning and maintenance of business suits and silk ties	400

f. Business mileage on Robert's fully depreciated auto was 5,000 miles. Total mileage for the year on the car, which was placed in service on 1–1–85, was 30,000 miles.

g. Robert took a combined business and pleasure trip to San Francisco in June. He spent eight days conducting business and four days visiting museums. His airfare and taxi expense was $500; meals cost $50 per day; and lodging and incidentals amounted to $200 per day.

h. Other expenses included the following:

Contribution to United Negro College Fund	$1,000
Contribution to Methodist Church	1,200
Expenses of traveling to Olympia to speak to the Elks Club against proposed legislation regarding wholesalers	300
Personal doctor and dentist bills	2,600
Dentist bills for daughter	3,000
Tax preparation fee	350
Investment periodicals	50
Other itemized deductions	6,900

Compute Robert Washington's Federal income tax payable or refund due for 1990. Suggested software (if available): *WEST–TAX Planner* or *BNA Individual Income Tax Spreadsheet*.

49. George M. and Martha J. Jordan have no dependents and are both under age 65. George is an outside salesman for Consolidated Jobbers, and his Social Security number is 682–99–444. Martha is an executive with General Corporation, and her Social Security number is 741–88–6642. The Jordans live at 321 Oak Street, Lincoln, NE 68024. They both want to contribute to the Presidential Election Campaign Fund.

In 1989, George earned $32,000 in commissions. His employer withholds FICA but not Federal income taxes. George paid $6,000 in estimated taxes. Martha earned $62,000, from which $10,508 was withheld for Federal income taxes. Neither George nor Martha received any expense reimbursements.

George uses his two-year-old car on sales calls and keeps a log of all miles driven. In 1989, he drove 36,000 miles, 25,000 of them for business. He made several out-of-state sales trips, incurring air fare of $1,600, meals of $800, and lodging costs of $750. He also spent $1,400 during the year taking customers to lunch.

Martha incurred the following expenses related to her work: taxi fares of $125, business lunches of $615, and a yearly commuter train ticket of $800. During the year, Martha received $1,200 in interest from the employees' credit union, $100,000 life insurance proceeds upon the death of her mother in December, and $500 in dividends from General Motors. She contributed $2,000 to her Individual Retirement Account. Neither George nor Martha is covered by an employee retirement plan. Martha gave a gift valued at $500 to the president of her firm upon his promotion to that position.

The Jordans had additional expenditures as follows:

Charitable contributions (cash)	$ 800
Medical and dental expenses	1,400
Real property taxes	1,200
Home mortgage interest	9,381
Charge account interest	193
Tax return preparation fee	150

Part 1—Tax Computation

Compute the Jordans' Federal income tax payable or refund due, assuming they file a joint income tax return for 1989. You will need Form 1040, two copies of Form 2106, and Schedules A and B. Suggested software (if available): *TurboTax* for tax return solutions or *WEST–TAX Planner* if tax return solutions are not desired.

Part 2—Tax Planning

Martha and George ask your help in deciding what to do with the $100,000 Martha inherited in 1989. They are considering three conservative investment alternatives: Suggested software (if available): *WEST–TAX Planner* or *TurboTax* (planning mode).

- Invest in 8% long-term U.S. bonds.
- Invest in 7% Series EE bonds and elect to defer the interest earned.
- Invest in 6% municipal bonds.
a.   Calculate the best alternative for next year. Assume that Martha and George will have the same income and deductions in 1990, except for the income from the investment they choose.
b.   What other factors should the Jordans take into account?

10

DEDUCTIONS AND LOSSES: CERTAIN ITEMIZED DEDUCTIONS

OBJECTIVES

Distinguish between deductible and nondeductible personal expenses.

Define medical expenses and compute the medical expense deduction.

Contrast deductible taxes and nondeductible fees, licenses, etc.

Discuss rules relating to the Federal tax treatment of state income taxes.

Determine whether various types of interest are deductible.

Define charitable contributions and discuss related measurement problems and percentage limitations.

Enumerate the business and personal expenditures that are deductible either as miscellaneous itemized deductions or as other itemized deductions.

GENERAL CLASSIFICATION OF EXPENSES

Personal expenditures are specifically disallowed as deductions by § 262. Personal expenses can be contrasted with business expenses that are incurred in the production or expectation of profit. Business expenditures are deductions from gross income in arriving at adjusted gross income and are reported on Schedule C of Form 1040. Certain nonbusiness expenses are also deductible in arriving at adjusted gross income (e.g., expenses attributable to rents and royalties and forfeited interest on a time savings deposit).

This chapter is principally concerned with expenses that are essentially personal in nature but are deductible because of legislative grace (e.g., charitable contributions, medical expenses, and certain state and local taxes). If the Code does not specifically state that a personal type of expense is deductible, no deduction is permitted. Allowable personal expenses are deductible *from* adjusted gross income in arriving at taxable income if the taxpayer elects to itemize them. A taxpayer would so elect if the total of the itemized deductions exceeds the standard deduction based on the taxpayer's filing status. The total standard deduction is the sum of the basic standard deduction and the additional standard deduction. Chapter 2 described the situations in which a taxpayer is not eligible for the standard deduction. At this point, it may be helpful to review the computation in the tax formula for individuals that appears in chapter 2.

MEDICAL EXPENSES

General Requirements

Medical expenses paid for the care of the taxpayer, spouse, and dependents are allowed as an itemized deduction to the extent the expenses are not reimbursed. The medical expense deduction is limited to the amount by which such expenses *exceed* 7.5 percent of the taxpayer's adjusted gross income.

EXAMPLE 1   During 1990, T had medical expenses of $3,800. If T's AGI for the year is $40,000, the itemized deduction for medical expenses is limited to $800 [$3,800 − (7.5% × $40,000)]. □

Medical Expenses Defined

The term *medical care* includes expenditures incurred for the "diagnosis, cure, mitigation, treatment, or prevention of disease, or for the purpose of affecting any structure or function of the body."[1] A partial list of deductible and nondeductible medical items is shown in Figure 10–1 (see page 10–3).

A medical expense does not have to relate to a particular ailment to be deductible. Since the definition of medical care is broad enough to cover preventive measures, the cost of periodic physical and dental exams would qualify even for a taxpayer in good health.

The deductibility of *nursing home expenses* depends on the medical condition of the patient and the nature of the services rendered. If an individual enters a home for the aged for personal or family considerations and not because he or she requires medical or nursing attention, deductions are allowed only for the costs attributable to the medical and nursing care.

---

1. § 213(d)(1)(A).

FIGURE 10-1   Deductible and Nondeductible Medical Expenses

Deductible	Nondeductible
Medical (including dental, mental, and hospital) care	Funeral, burial, or cremation expenses
Prescription drugs	Nonprescription drugs (except insulin)
Special equipment	Bottled water

Wheelchairs
   Crutches
   Artificial limbs
   Eyeglasses (including contact lenses)
   Hearing aids
	Toiletries, cosmetics
	Diaper service, maternity clothes
	Programs for the *general* improvement of health

Transportation for medical care	Weight reduction
	   Health spas
	   Stop-smoking clinics
	   Social activities (e.g., dancing and
	   swimming lessons)

Medical and hospital insurance premiums	

EXAMPLE 2   T has a chronic heart ailment. His family has decided to place T in a nursing home equipped to provide medical and nursing care facilities. Total nursing home expenses amount to $15,000 per year. Of this amount, $4,500 is directly attributable to medical and nursing care. Since T is in need of significant medical and nursing care and is placed in the facility primarily for this purpose, all $15,000 of the nursing home costs are deductible (subject to the 7.5% floor). □

EXAMPLE 3   Assume the same facts as in the previous example, except that T does not have a chronic heart ailment. T enters the nursing home because he and his family feel that all of them would be more comfortable with this arrangement. Under these circumstances, only $4,500 of the expenses would be deductible because the move was primarily for personal considerations. □

Tuition expenses of a dependent at a special school may be deductible as a medical expense. The cost of medical care could include the expenses of a special school for a mentally or physically handicapped individual. The deduction will be allowed if the individual's condition is such that the resources of the school for alleviating such infirmities are a principal reason for the individual's presence there. If this is the case, the cost of meals and lodging, in addition to the tuition, is a proper medical expense deduction.

EXAMPLE 4   T's daughter D attended public school through the seventh grade. Because D was a poor student, she was examined by a psychiatrist who diagnosed an organic problem that created a learning disability. Upon the recommendation of the psychiatrist, D is enrolled in a private school so that she can receive individual attention. If the school has no special program for students with learning disabilities and does not provide special medical treatment, the expenses related to D's attendance would not be deductible as medical expenses. The cost of any psychiatric care, however, would qualify as a medical expense. □

Example 4 shows that the recommendation of a physician does not make the expenditure automatically deductible.

Capital Expenditures for Medical Purposes

Capital expenditures normally are adjustments to basis and are not deductible. However, both a capital expenditure for a permanent improvement and expenditures made for the operation or maintenance of the improvement may qualify as medical expenses. If a capital expenditure qualifies as a medical expense, the allowable cost is deductible in the year incurred. The tax law makes no provision for depreciating medical expenses as it does for other capital expenditures.

Some examples of capital expenditures for medical purposes are swimming pools if the taxpayer does not have access to a neighborhood pool, and air conditioners if they do not become permanent improvements (e.g., window units). Other examples include dust elimination systems, elevators, and a room built to house an iron lung. These expenditures are medical in nature if they are incurred as a medical necessity upon the advice of a physician, the facility is used primarily by the patient alone, and the expense is reasonable.

A capital improvement that ordinarily would not have a medical purpose qualifies as a medical expense if it is directly related to prescribed medical care and is deductible to the extent that the expenditure *exceeds* the increase in value of the related property. Appraisal costs related to capital improvements would also be deductible, but not as medical expenses. Such amounts are expenses incurred in the determination of the taxpayer's tax liability.

EXAMPLE 5

T is advised by his physician to install an elevator in his residence so that T's wife, who is afflicted with heart disease, will not be required to climb the stairs. The cost of installing the elevator is $3,000, and the increase in the value of the residence is determined to be only $1,700. Therefore, $1,300 ($3,000 − $1,700) is deductible as a medical expense. Additional utility costs to operate the elevator and maintenance costs are deductible as medical expenses as long as the medical reason for the capital expenditure continues to exist. ☐

To enable a physically handicapped individual to live independently and productively, the full cost of certain home-related capital expenditures incurred qualifies as a medical expense. These expenditures are subject to the 7.5 percent floor only, and the increase in the home's value is deemed be zero. Qualifying costs include expenditures for constructing entrance and exit ramps to the residence, widening hallways and doorways to accommodate wheelchairs, installing support bars and railings in bathrooms and other rooms, and adjusting electrical outlets and fixtures.[2]

Transportation and Lodging Expenses for Medical Treatment

Payments for transportation to and from a point of treatment for medical care are deductible as medical expenses (subject to the 7.5 percent floor). Transportation expenses for medical care include bus, taxi, train, or plane fare, charges for ambulance service, and out-of-pocket expenses for the use of an automobile. A

---

2. For a complete listing of the items that qualify, see Rev.Rul. 87–106, 1987–2 C.B. 67.

mileage allowance of nine cents per mile may be used instead of actual out-of-pocket automobile expenses. Whether the taxpayer chooses to claim out-of-pocket automobile expenses or the nine cents per mile automatic mileage option, related parking fees and tolls can also be deducted.

A deduction is also allowed for the transportation expenses of a parent who must accompany a child who is receiving medical care or for a nurse or other person giving medical assistance to a person who is traveling to get medical care and cannot travel alone.

A deduction is allowed for lodging while away from home for medical expenses if the following requirements are met:

- The lodging is primarily for and essential to medical care.
- Medical care is provided by a doctor in a licensed hospital or a similar medical facility (e.g., a clinic).
- The lodging is not lavish or extravagant under the circumstances.
- There is no significant element of personal pleasure, recreation, or vacation in the travel away from home.

Lodging expenses included as medical expenses cannot exceed $50 *per* night for *each* person. The deduction is allowed not only for the patient but also for a person who must travel with the patient (e.g., a parent traveling with a child who is receiving medical care).

EXAMPLE 6

T, a resident of Winchester, Kentucky, is advised by his family physician that M, T's dependent and disabled mother, needs specialized treatment for her heart condition. Consequently, T and M fly to Cleveland, Ohio, where M receives the therapy at a heart clinic on an outpatient basis. Expenses in connection with the trip are as follows:

Round trip air fare ($250 each)	$500
Lodging in Cleveland for two nights ($60 each per night)	240

T's medical expense deduction is $500 for transportation and $200 ($50 per night per person) for lodging. Because M is disabled, it is assumed that T's accompaniment of her is justified. □

No deduction is allowed for the cost of meals unless they are part of the medical care and are furnished at a medical facility.

Amounts Paid for Medical Insurance Premiums

Medical insurance premiums are included with other medical expenses subject to the 7.5 percent floor. If amounts are paid under an insurance contract to cover loss of life, limb, sight, etc., no amount can be deducted unless the coverage for medical care is separately stated in the contract.

Medical insurance premiums paid by the taxpayer under a group plan or an individual plan are included as medical expenses. If an employer pays all or part of the taxpayer's medical insurance premiums, the amount paid by the employer is not included in gross income by the employee and is not included in the employee's medical expenses.

If a taxpayer is self-employed, special rules apply regarding medical insurance premiums. For tax years beginning in 1990, up to 25 percent of the premiums paid for medical insurance coverage for periods before October 1, 1990 are deductible as a business expense (*for* AGI). Any excess can be claimed as a medical expense. For this special treatment to apply, the following conditions must be satisfied:

• The taxpayer must not be covered under a medical plan of an employer or of a spouse's employer.

• The plan must meet certain nondiscrimination rules.

The business deduction cannot exceed the net profit from the self-employment activity. For this purpose, net profit is determined on a pro rata basis for the portion of the 1990 tax year that ends before October 1, 1990.

EXAMPLE 7   During 1990, T was a self-employed real estate broker with no employees. For the calendar year, he had $45,000 net profit from real estate transactions and paid $4,000 in medical insurance premiums, of which $2,800 was for coverage for periods before October 1, 1990. T may deduct $700 (25% × $2,800) of the premiums as a business expense. The balance of $3,300 ($4,000 − $700) qualifies as a medical expense. The net profit limitation does not apply in this case because the business deduction for medical insurance premiums ($700) does not exceed the pro rata portion of T's net profit (9/12 × $45,000 = $33,750) for the tax year. □

Whether Congress will extend this provision beyond September 30, 1990, is impossible to predict.

Medical Expenses Incurred for Spouse and Dependents

In computing the medical expense deduction, a taxpayer may include medical expenses for a spouse, or for a person who was a dependent at the time the expenses were paid or incurred. In determining dependency status for medical expense deduction purposes, neither the gross income nor the joint return tests (see chapter 2) apply.

EXAMPLE 8   T (age 22) is married and a full-time student at a university. During 1990, T incurred medical expenses that were paid by M (T's mother). M provided more than half of T's support for the year. Even if T files a joint return with his wife, M may claim those medical expenses she paid. M would combine such expenses with her own in applying the 7.5% floor. □

Medical expenses paid on behalf of a former spouse are deductible if the parties were married when the expenditures were incurred. Also, medical expenses can be incorporated in the divorce decree and consequently may be deductible as alimony payments (*for* AGI).

For divorced persons with children, a special rule applies to the noncustodial parent. The noncustodial parent may claim any medical expenses he or she pays even though the custodial parent claims the children as dependents. This rule applies if the dependency exemptions could have been shifted to the noncustodial parent by the custodial parent's waiver (refer to chapter 2).

EXAMPLE 9   F and M are divorced in 1989, and M is awarded custody of their child C. During 1990, F makes the following payments to M: $3,600 for child support and $2,500 for C's medical bills. Together, F and M provide more than one-half of C's support. Even though M claims C as a dependent, F can combine C's medical expenses that he pays with his own. □

Year of Deduction

Regardless of a taxpayer's method of accounting, medical expenses are deductible only in the year *paid*. In effect, therefore, this places all individual taxpayers on a cash basis as far as the medical expense deduction is concerned. One exception, however, is allowed for deceased taxpayers. If the medical expenses are paid within one year from the day following the day of death, they can be treated as being paid at the time they were *incurred*. Thus, such expenses may be reported on the final income tax return of the decedent or on earlier returns if incurred before the year of death.

No current deduction will be allowed for payment of medical care to be rendered in the future unless the taxpayer is under an obligation to make the payment. Whether an obligation to make the payment exists depends upon the policy of the physician or the institution furnishing the medical care.

EXAMPLE 10   Upon the recommendation of his regular dentist, in late December 1990, T consults Dr. D, a prosthodontist who specializes in crown and bridge work. Dr. D tells T that he can do the restorative work for $12,000. To cover his lab bill, however, Dr. D requires that 40% of this amount be prepaid. Accordingly, T pays Dr. D $4,800 in December 1990. The balance of $7,200 is paid when the work is completed in July of 1991. Under these circumstances, the qualifying medical expenses are $4,800 for 1990 and $7,200 in 1991. The result would be the same even if T prepaid the full $12,000 in 1990. □

The IRS does allow a deduction for the portion of a lump-sum prepayment allocable to medical care made to a retirement home under a life care plan.[3]

Reimbursements

If medical expenses are reimbursed in the same year as paid, no problem arises. The reimbursement merely reduces the amount that would otherwise qualify for the medical expense deduction. But what happens if the reimbursement is received in a later year than the expenditure? Unlike casualty losses where reasonable prospect of recovery must be considered (refer to chapter 7), the expected reimbursement is disregarded in measuring the amount of the deduction. Instead, the reimbursement is accounted for separately in the year in which it occurs.

As a general rule, when a taxpayer receives an insurance reimbursement for medical expenses deducted in a previous year, the reimbursement must be included in gross income in the year of receipt. However, taxpayers are not required to report more than the amount previously deducted as medical expenses. Thus, a taxpayer who did not itemize deductions in the year the expenses were incurred is not required to include a reimbursement in gross income.

---

3. Rev.Rul. 75–302, 1975–2 C.B. 86.

The tax benefit rule applies to reimbursements if the taxpayer itemized deductions in the previous year. In this case, the taxpayer may be required to report some or all of the medical expense reimbursement in income in the year the reimbursement is received. Under the tax benefit rule, the taxpayer must include the reimbursement in income up to the amount of the deductions that decreased taxable income in the earlier year.

EXAMPLE 11   T has adjusted gross income of $20,000 for 1989. He was injured in a car accident and paid $1,300 for hospital expenses and $700 for doctor bills. T also incurred medical expenses of $600 for his dependent child. In 1990, T was reimbursed $650 by his insurance company for his car accident. His deduction for medical expenses in 1989 is computed as follows:

Hospitalization	$ 1,300
Bills for doctor's services	700
Medical expenses for dependent	600
Total	$ 2,600
Less: 7.5% of $20,000	(1,500)
Medical expense deduction (assuming T itemizes his deductions)	$ 1,100

Assume that T would have elected to itemize his deductions even if he had no medical expenses in 1989. If the reimbursement for medical care had occurred in 1989, the medical expense deduction would have been only $450 [($2,600 total medical expenses − $650 reimbursement) − $1,500 floor], and T would have paid more income tax.

Since the reimbursement was made in a subsequent year, T would include $650 in gross income for 1990. If T had not itemized in 1989, he would not include the $650 reimbursement in 1990 gross income because he would have received no tax benefit in 1989. □

TAXES

The deduction of certain state and local taxes paid or accrued by a taxpayer is permitted by § 164. The deduction was created to relieve the burden of multiple taxes upon the same source of revenue.

Deductibility as a Tax

One must make a distinction between a tax and a fee since fees are not deductible unless incurred as an ordinary and necessary business expense or as an expense in the production of income.

The IRS has defined a tax as follows:

A tax is an enforced contribution exacted pursuant to legislative authority in the exercise of taxing power, and imposed and collected for the purpose of raising revenue to be used for public or governmental purposes, and not as payment for some special privilege granted or service rendered. Taxes are, therefore, distinguished from various other contributions and charges imposed for particular purposes under particular powers or functions of the government. In view of such

distinctions, the question whether a particular contribution or charge is to be regarded as a tax depends upon its real nature.[4]

Thus, in accordance with the above definition, fees for dog licenses, automobile inspection, automobile titles and registration, hunting and fishing licenses, bridge and highway tolls, drivers' licenses, parking meter deposits, postage, etc., are not considered to be deductible. These items, however, could be deductible if incurred as a business expense or for the production of income. Deductible and nondeductible taxes are summarized in Figure 10–2.

Property Taxes, Assessments, and Apportionment of Taxes

Property Taxes.   State, local, and foreign taxes on real property are generally deductible only by the person against whom the tax is imposed. Cash basis taxpayers may deduct these taxes in the year of actual payment, and accrual basis taxpayers may deduct them in the year that fixes the right to deductibility.

Deductible personal property taxes must be *ad valorem* (assessed in relation to the value of the property). Therefore, a motor vehicle tax based on weight, model, year, and horsepower is not an ad valorem tax. However, a tax based on value and other criteria may qualify in part.

EXAMPLE 12   State X imposes a motor vehicle registration tax on 4% of the value of the vehicle plus 40 cents per hundredweight. B, a resident of the state, owns a car having a value of $4,000 and weighing 3,000 pounds. B pays an annual registration fee of $172. Of this amount, $160 (4% of $4,000) would be deductible as a personal property tax. The remaining $12, based on the weight of the car, would not be deductible.   □

Assessments for Local Benefits.   As a general rule, real property taxes do not include taxes assessed for local benefits since such assessments tend to increase

---

FIGURE 10–2   Deductible and Nondeductible Taxes

Deductible	Nondeductible
State, local, and foreign real property taxes	Federal income taxes
State and local personal property taxes	FICA taxes imposed on employees
State, local, and foreign income taxes	Employer FICA taxes paid on domestic household workers
The environmental tax	Estate, inheritance, and gift taxes
	General sales taxes
	Federal, state, and local excise taxes (e.g., gasoline, tobacco, spirits)
	Foreign income taxes if the taxpayer chooses the foreign tax credit option
	Taxes on real property to the extent such taxes are to be apportioned and treated as imposed on another taxpayer

---

4. Rev.Rul. 57–345, 1957–2 C.B. 132, and Rev.Rul. 70–622, 1970–2 C.B. 41.

the value of the property (e.g., special assessments for streets, sidewalks, curbing, and other like improvements). A taxpayer cannot deduct the cost of a new sidewalk (relative to a personal residence), even though the construction was required by the city and the sidewalk may have provided an incidental benefit to the public welfare. Such assessments are added to the adjusted basis of the taxpayer's property.

Assessments for local benefits are deductible as a tax if they are made for maintenance or repair or for meeting interest charges with respect to such benefits. In such cases, the burden is on the taxpayer to show the allocation of the amounts assessed for the different purposes. If the allocation cannot be made, none of the amount paid is deductible.

Apportionment of Real Property Taxes between Seller and Purchaser.   Real estate taxes for the entire year are apportioned between the buyer and seller on the basis of the number of days the property was held by each during the real property tax year. This apportionment is required without regard to whether the tax is paid by the buyer or the seller or is prorated pursuant to the purchase agreement. The rationale for apportioning the taxes between the buyer and seller is based on the administrative convenience of the IRS in determining who is entitled to deduct the real estate taxes in the year of sale. In making the apportionment, the assessment date and the lien date are disregarded.

EXAMPLE 13   The real property tax year in County R is April 1 to March 31. S, the owner on April 1, 1990, of real property located in County R, sells the real property to B on June 30, 1990. B owns the real property from June 30, 1990, through March 31, 1991. The tax for the real property tax year April 1, 1990, through March 31, 1991, is $730. The portion of the real property tax treated as imposed upon S, the seller, is $180 ($90/365 \times \$730$, April 1 through June 29, 1990), and $550 ($275/365 \times \$730$, June 30, 1990 through March 31, 1991) of the tax is treated as imposed upon B, the purchaser. Note that the allocable part of the real estate tax year applicable to the seller ends on the day before the sale, and the date of sale is included in the part of such year applicable to the purchaser. □

If the actual real estate taxes are not prorated between the buyer and seller as part of the purchase agreement, adjustments are required. The adjustments are necessary in order to determine the amount realized by the seller and the adjusted cost basis of the property to the buyer. If the buyer pays the entire amount of the tax, he or she has, in effect, paid the seller's portion of the real estate tax and has therefore paid more for the property than the actual purchase price. Thus, the amount of real estate tax that is apportioned to the seller (for Federal income tax purposes) and paid by the buyer is added to the buyer's cost basis. The seller must increase the amount realized on the sale by the same amount.

EXAMPLE 14   S sells real estate on October 3, 1990, for $50,000. The buyer, B, pays the real estate taxes of $1,095 for the calendar year, which is the real estate property tax year. Of the real estate taxes, $825 ($1,095 $\times$ $^{275}/_{365}$) is apportioned to and is deductible by the seller, S, and $270 ($1,095 $\times$ $^{90}/_{365}$) of the taxes is deductible by B. The buyer has, in effect, paid S's real estate taxes of $825 and has therefore paid $50,825 for the property. B's basis is increased to $50,825, and the amount realized by S from the sale is increased to $50,825. □

The opposite result occurs if the seller (rather than the buyer) pays the real estate taxes. In this case, the seller reduces the amount realized from the sale by the amount that has been apportioned to the buyer. The buyer is required to reduce his or her adjusted basis by a corresponding amount.

EXAMPLE 15

S sells real estate to B for $50,000 on October 3, 1990. While S held the property, he paid the real estate taxes for the calendar year, which is the real estate property tax year, in the amount of $1,095. Although S paid the entire $1,095 of real estate taxes, $270 of that amount is apportioned to B and is therefore deductible by B. The effect is that the buyer, B, has paid only $49,730 for the property. The amount realized by S, the seller, is reduced by $270, and B reduces his cost basis in the property to $49,730. □

Income Taxes

It is the position of the IRS that state and local income taxes imposed upon an individual are deductible only as itemized deductions (deductions *from* AGI) even if the taxpayer's sole source of income is from a business, rents, or royalties.

Cash basis taxpayers are entitled to deduct state income taxes withheld by the employer in the year such amounts are withheld. In addition, estimated state income tax payments are deductible in the year the payment is made by cash basis taxpayers even if the payments relate to a prior or subsequent year. If the taxpayer overpays state income taxes because of excessive withholdings or estimated tax payments, the refund that is received must be included in gross income of the following year to the extent that the deduction reduced the tax liability in the prior year.

EXAMPLE 16

T is a cash basis unmarried taxpayer who had $800 of state income tax withheld during 1990. Additionally in 1990, T paid $100 that was due when she filed her 1989 state income tax return and made estimated payments of $300 on her 1990 state income tax. When T filed her 1990 Federal income tax return in April 1991, she elected to itemize deductions, which amounted to $5,500, including the $1,200 of state income tax payments and withholdings, all of which reduced her tax liability.

As a result of overpaying her 1990 state income tax, T received a refund of $200 early in 1991. This would be included in T's 1991 gross income in computing her Federal income tax. It would not matter whether T received a check from the state for $200 or applied the $200 toward her 1991 state income tax. □

INTEREST

A deduction for interest has been allowed since enactment of the income tax law in 1913. Despite its long history of Congressional acceptance, the interest deduction continues to be one of the most controversial areas in the tax law.

The controversy has centered around the propriety of allowing the deduction of interest charges for the purchase of consumer goods and services and interest on borrowings used to acquire investments (investment interest). TRA of 1986 effectively put an end to this controversy by phasing out the deduction for personal interest and further limiting the deduction for investment interest after 1990. Even

when interest is allowed as a deduction, limits are imposed on the deductibility of prepaid interest. In addition, no deduction is permitted for interest on debt incurred to purchase or carry tax-exempt securities.

Disallowed and Allowed Items

Interest has been defined by the Supreme Court as compensation for the use or forbearance of money.[5] The general rule permits a deduction for all interest paid or accrued within the taxable year on indebtedness. This general rule is modified by other Code provisions that disallow or restrict certain interest deductions.

Personal (Consumer) Interest.   *Personal interest* is any interest allowable as a deduction, with some exceptions as follows:

- Trade or business interest.
- Investment interest.
- Interest on passive activities.
- Home mortgage interest to a limited extent if it is qualified residence interest.

For this purpose, trade or business interest does not include interest on indebtedness to finance employee business expenses; such interest is personal interest. Personal, or consumer, interest also includes finance charges on department store and bank credit card purchases and on gasoline credit cards. The term also includes late payment charges on utility bills as well as interest on income tax deficiencies and assessments.

Personal interest is no longer fully deductible. The phase-out of the deduction takes place over a five-year period as shown in Figure 10–3. The deduction is the percentage allowed times the total personal interest expense. Thus, for the tax years 1987–1990, some deduction may be allowed for personal interest.

Investment Interest.   Taxpayers frequently borrow funds that they then use to acquire investment assets. When the interest expense is large relative to the income from the investments, substantial tax benefits could result. Congress has therefore placed limitations on the deductibility of interest when funds are borrowed for the purpose of purchasing or continuing to hold investment property.

Prior to 1987, investment interest expense was deductible to the extent of $10,000 plus net investment income. Under TRA of 1986, investment interest ex-

FIGURE 10–3 Personal Interest Phase-out Percentages

Taxable Year Beginning in	Percentage Disallowed	Percentage Allowed
1987	35%	65%
1988	60%	40%
1989	80%	20%
1990	90%	10%
1991 and after	100%	–0–

5. *Old Colony Railroad Co. v. Comm.*, 3 USTC ¶ 880, 10 AFTR 786, 52 S.Ct. 211 (USSC, 1936).

pense is limited to net investment income for the year. This rule will be fully in effect in 1991. For the four years 1987–1990, investment interest expense in excess of net investment income is allowed based on the prior-law amount of $10,000, using the percentages in Figure 10–3. The computation is illustrated in Example 18.

Investment income is gross income from interest, dividends, annuities, and royalties not derived in the ordinary course of a trade or business. It also includes net gain attributable to the disposition of property producing the types of income just enumerated or held for investment. Income from a passive activity and income from a real estate activity in which the taxpayer actively participates are not included in investment income.

Net investment income is the excess of investment income over investment expenses. Investment expenses are those deductible expenses directly connected with the production of investment income. Investment expenses *do not* include interest expense. Some investment expenses may fall into the category of other miscellaneous deductions and be subject to the 2 percent floor (discussed later in the chapter).

EXAMPLE 17	T has AGI of $80,000, which includes dividends and interest income of $18,000. Besides investment interest expense, she had the following investment expenses in connection with her portfolio of stocks and bonds and had other pertinent itemized deductions as follows:

Safe deposit box rental (to hold investment securities)	$ 120
Investment counsel fee	1,200
City ad valorem property tax on stocks and bonds	3,000
Unreimbursed business travel	850
Uniforms	600

Before T can determine her investment expenses for purposes of calculating net investment income, those miscellaneous expenses that are not investment expenses are disallowed before any investment expenses are disallowed under the 2% of AGI floor:

Total disallowed (2% of AGI)	$1,600
Less: Unreimbursed business travel	(850)
Uniforms	(600)
Balance of disallowance represents disallowed investment expense	$ 150

T's investment expenses are calculated as follows:

Miscellaneous deductions investment expense ($120 + $1,200)	$1,320
Less: Disallowed portion (see above)	150
Deductible miscellaneous deductions investment expense	$1,170
Plus: Ad valorem tax on investment property	3,000
Total investment expenses	$4,170

T's net investment income is $13,830 ($18,000 investment income – $4,170 investment expenses).   ☐

After net investment income is determined, deductible investment interest expense can be calculated. Investment interest expense does not include qualified residence interest (see below) or interest taken into account in computing income or loss from a passive activity (see chapter 6). Also, it does not include interest that is otherwise nondeductible (e.g., interest on amounts borrowed to purchase or carry tax-exempt securities).

EXAMPLE 18

For 1990, T is a single person employed by a law firm. His investment activities for the year are as follows:

Net investment income	$30,000
Investment interest expense	44,000

T's investment interest deduction for 1990 is $31,000 as determined below:

Investment interest expense to the extent of net investment income	$30,000
Allowable excess as per Figure 10–3 (10% × $10,000)	1,000
Total interest allowed	$31,000

□

The amount of investment interest disallowed is carried over to future years. In Example 18, therefore, the amount that is carried over to 1991 is $13,000 ($44,000 investment interest expense − $31,000 allowed). No limit is placed on the carryover period.

The investment interest expense deduction is determined by completing Form 4952.

Qualified Residence Interest.   As previously stated, personal interest does not include qualified residence interest (interest on a home mortgage). *Qualified residence interest* is interest paid or accrued during the taxable year on indebtedness (subject to limitations) *secured* by any property that is a qualified residence of the taxpayer. Qualified residence interest falls into two categories: interest on acquisition indebtedness and interest on home equity loans. Before discussing each of these categories, however, the term qualified residence must be defined.

A *qualified residence* means the taxpayer's principal residence and one other residence of the taxpayer or spouse. The *principal residence* is one that meets the requirement for nonrecognition of gain upon sale under § 1034 (see chapter 13). The *one other residence,* or second residence, refers to one that is used as a residence if not rented or, if rented, meets the requirements for a personal residence under the rental of vacation home rules (refer to chapter 5). A taxpayer who has more than one second residence can make the selection each year as to which one is the qualified second residence. A residence includes, in addition to a house in the ordinary sense, cooperative apartments, condominiums, and mobile homes and boats that have living quarters (sleeping accommodations and toilet and cooking facilities).

Although in most cases, interest paid on a home mortgage would be fully deductible, there are limitations. If the indebtedness is acquisition indebtedness, interest paid or accrued during the tax year on aggregate indebtedness of $1,000,000 ($500,000 for married persons filing separate returns) or less is qualified residence interest. *Acquisition indebtedness* refers to amounts incurred in acquiring, constructing, or substantially improving a qualified residence of the taxpayer.

Any indebtedness incurred on or before October 13, 1987, and secured by a qualified residence at all times thereafter is treated as acquisition indebtedness and is not subject to the $1,000,000 limitation (but does reduce the $1,000,000 limitation).

Qualified residence interest also includes interest on home equity loans. These loans utilize the personal residence of the taxpayer as security. Since tracing rules do not apply to home equity loans, the funds from these loans can be used for personal purposes (e.g., auto purchases, medical expenses). By making use of home equity loans, therefore, what would have been nondeductible consumer interest becomes deductible qualified residence interest. However, interest is deductible only on home equity loans that do not exceed the *lesser of*

- the fair market value of the residence, reduced by the acquisition indebtedness, *or*

- $100,000 ($50,000 for married persons filing separate returns).

EXAMPLE 19

T owns a personal residence with a fair market value of $150,000 and an outstanding first mortgage of $120,000. T issues a lien on the residence and in return borrows $15,000 to purchase a new family automobile. All interest on the $135,000 of debt is treated as qualified residence interest. □

EXAMPLE 20

H and W, married taxpayers, took out a mortgage on their home for $200,000 in 1982. In March 1990, when the home had a fair market value of $400,000 and they owed $195,000 on the mortgage, H and W took out a home equity loan for $120,000. They used $90,000 of the home equity proceeds for home improvements and $30,000 for other purposes. In 1990 on a joint return, H and W can deduct all of the interest on both mortgages. The first mortgage qualifies because it is acquisition indebtedness. Of the $120,000 home equity loan, the full amount is deductible: The part of the home equity loan used for home improvements ($90,000) plus the first mortgage ($195,000) totals less than the $1,000,000 limitation on acquisition indebtedness. The part of the home equity loan used for other purposes ($30,000) is less than the $100,000 statutory ceiling. □

Any interest paid on a mortgage secured by a third or more residences or paid on indebtedness that exceeds the allowable amounts is deductible according to the use of the proceeds. If the proceeds are used for personal purposes, the interest is nondeductible, subject to the disallowance phase-in rules; if used for business, the interest is fully deductible. Interest on such proceeds used for investment purposes or in passive activities is subject to the limitations applicable to those activities.

Interest Paid for Services. It is common practice in the mortgage loan business to charge a fee for finding, placing, or processing a mortgage loan. Such

fees are often called *points* and are expressed as a percentage of the loan amount. In periods of tight money, it may be necessary to pay points to obtain the necessary financing. To qualify as deductible interest, the points must be considered compensation to a lender solely for the use or forbearance of money. The points cannot be a form of service charge or payment for specific services if they are to qualify as deductible interest.

Points are required to be capitalized and are amortized and deductible ratably over the life of the loan. A special exception permits the purchaser of a personal residence to deduct qualifying points in the year of payment. The exception also covers points paid to obtain funds for home improvements. However, points paid to refinance an existing home mortgage cannot be immediately expensed but must be capitalized and amortized as interest expense over the life of the new loan.

Points paid by the seller are not deductible because the debt on which they are paid is not the debt of the seller. Points paid by the seller are treated as a reduction of the selling price of the property.

Prepayment Penalty.   When a mortgage or loan is paid off in full in a lump sum before its term (early), the lending institution may require an additional payment of a certain percentage applied to the unpaid amount at the time of prepayment. This is known as a prepayment penalty and is considered to be interest (e.g., personal, qualified residence, investment) in the year it is paid.

Related Parties.   Nothing prevents the deduction of interest paid to a related party as long as the payment actually took place and the interest meets the requirements for deductibility as previously stated. Recall from chapter 5 that a special rule for related taxpayers applies when the debtor uses the accrual basis and the related creditor is on the cash basis. If this rule is applicable, interest that has been accrued but not paid at the end of the debtor's tax year is not deductible until payment is made and the income is reportable by the cash basis recipient.

Tax-Exempt Securities.   Section 265 provides that no deduction is allowed for interest on debt incurred to purchase or carry tax-exempt securities. A major problem has been for the courts to determine what is meant by the words *to purchase or carry.* Refer to chapter 5 for a detailed discussion of these issues.

Restrictions on Deductibility and Timing Considerations

Taxpayer's Obligation.   Allowed interest is deductible if the related debt represents a bona fide obligation for which the taxpayer is liable. Thus, a taxpayer may not deduct interest paid on behalf of another individual. For interest to be deductible, both debtor and creditor must intend that the loan be repaid. Intent of the parties can be especially crucial between related parties such as a shareholder and a closely held corporation. A shareholder may not deduct interest paid by the corporation on his or her behalf. Likewise, a husband may not deduct interest paid on his wife's property if he files a separate return, except in the case of qualified residence interest. If both husband and wife consent in writing, either the husband or the wife may deduct the allowed interest on the principal residence and one other residence.

Time of Deduction.   Generally, interest must be paid to secure a deduction unless the taxpayer uses the accrual method of accounting. Under the accrual method, interest is deductible ratably over the life of the loan.

EXAMPLE 21

In November 1990, T borrows $1,000 to purchase appliances for a rental house. The loan is payable in 90 days at 12% interest. On the due date in February 1991, T pays the $1,000 note and interest amounting to $30. T can deduct the accrued portion ($2/3 \times \$30 = \$20$) of the interest in 1990 only if he is an accrual basis taxpayer. Otherwise, the entire amount of interest ($30) is deductible in 1991. □

Prepaid Interest.   Accrual method reporting is imposed on cash basis taxpayers relative to interest prepayments that extend beyond the end of the taxable year. Such payments must be allocated to the tax years to which the interest payments relate. These provisions are intended to prevent cash basis taxpayers from *manufacturing* tax deductions before the end of the year by entering into prepayment of interest agreements. As previously noted, an exception allows immediate expensing of points paid to obtain funds to purchase or improve a personal residence.

Classification of Interest Expense

Whether interest is deductible *for* adjusted gross income or as an itemized deduction (*from* AGI) depends on whether the indebtedness has a business, investment, or personal purpose. If the indebtedness is incurred in relation to a business (other than performing services as an employee) or for the production of rent or royalty income, the interest is deductible *for* adjusted gross income. However, if the indebtedness is incurred for personal use, such as consumer interest or qualified residence interest, any deduction allowed is reported on Schedule A of Form 1040 if the taxpayer elects to itemize. If the taxpayer is an employee who incurs debt in relation to his or her employment, the interest is considered to be personal, or consumer, interest. Business expenses appear on Schedule C of Form 1040, and expenses related to rents or royalties are reported on Schedule E.

For classification purposes, the IRS has issued complex tracing rules[6] to establish the use to which borrowed funds are put.

Interest on amounts borrowed in excess of $50,000 in total on life insurance policies covering the life of a self-employed taxpayer or an officer or employee of a corporation is nondeductible. This result occurs even if the borrowed funds are used in a trade or business.

CHARITABLE CONTRIBUTIONS

Section 170 permits the deduction of contributions made to qualified domestic organizations by individuals and corporations. Contributions to qualified charitable organizations serve certain social welfare needs and therefore relieve the government of the cost of providing these needed services to the community.

The charitable contribution provisions are among the most complex in the tax law. To determine the amount deductible as a charitable contribution, several important questions must be answered:

- What constitutes a charitable contribution?

- Was the contribution made to a qualified organization?

---

6. T.D. 8145, 1987–2 C.B. 47, which contains Reg.
§ 1.163–8T.

- When is the contribution deductible?
- What special rules apply to contributions of property that has increased in value?
- What percentage limitations apply to the charitable contribution deduction?
- What recordkeeping and reporting requirements apply to charitable contributions?
- How is the value of donated property determined?

These questions are addressed in the sections that follow.

Criteria for a Gift

Section 170(c) defines a *charitable contribution* as a gift made to a qualified organization. The major elements needed to qualify a contribution as a gift are a donative intent, the absence of consideration, and acceptance by the donee. Consequently, the taxpayer has the burden of establishing that the transfer was made from motives of *disinterested generosity* as established by the courts.[7] As one can imagine, this test is quite subjective and has led to problems of interpretation.

Benefit Received Rule.   To the extent a tangible benefit is derived from a contribution, the value of such benefit cannot be deducted.

EXAMPLE 22   R purchases a ticket at $100 for a special performance of the local symphony (a qualified charity). If the price of a ticket to a symphony concert is normally $15, R is allowed only $85 as a charitable contribution. □

An exception to this benefit received rule provides for an automatic percentage as to how much can be deducted for the right to purchase athletic tickets from colleges and universities. Under this exception, 80 percent of the amount paid to or for the benefit of the institution qualifies as a charitable contribution deduction.

EXAMPLE 23   T donates $500 to State University's athletic department. The payment guarantees that T will have preferred seating on the 50-yard line. Subsequently, T buys four $35 game tickets. Under the exception to the benefit rule, however, T is allowed a $400 (80% of $500) charitable contribution deduction for the taxable year.

   If, however, T's $500 donation includes four $35 tickets, that portion [$140 ($35 × 4)] and the remaining portion of $360 ($500 − $140) are treated as separate amounts. Thus, T is allowed a charitable contribution deduction of $288 (80% of $360). □

Contribution of Services.   No deduction is allowed for a contribution of one's services to a qualified charitable organization. However, unreimbursed expenses related to the services rendered may be deductible. For example, the cost of a uniform (without general utility) that is required to be worn while performing services may be deductible, as are certain out-of-pocket transportation costs

---

7. *Comm. v. Duberstein,* 60–2 USTC ¶ 9515, 5 AFTR2d 1626, 80 S.Ct. 1190 (USSC, 1960).

incurred for the benefit of the charity. In lieu of these out-of-pocket costs for an automobile, a standard mileage rate of 12 cents per mile is allowed.[8] Deductions are permitted for transportation, reasonable expenses for lodging, and 80 percent of the cost of meals while away from home incurred in performance of the donated services. Also, there must be no significant element of personal pleasure, recreation, or vacation in such travel.

EXAMPLE 24   M, a delegate representing her church in Miami, Florida, travels to a two-day national meeting in Denver, Colorado, in February. After the meeting, M spends two weeks at a nearby ski resort. Under these circumstances, none of the transportation, meals, or lodging would be deductible since there is a significant element of personal pleasure, recreation, or vacation. □

Nondeductible Items.   In addition to the benefit received rule and the restrictions placed on contribution of services, the following items may not be deducted as charitable contributions:

- Dues, fees, or bills paid to country clubs, lodges, fraternal orders, or similar groups.
- Cost of raffle, bingo, or lottery tickets.
- Cost of tuition.
- Value of blood given to a blood bank.
- Donations to homeowners associations.
- Gifts to individuals.
- Rental value of property used by a qualified charity.

Qualified Organizations

To be deductible, a contribution must be made to one of the following organizations:

- A state or possession of the United States or any subdivisions thereof.
- A corporation, trust, or community chest, fund, or foundation that is situated in the United States and is organized and operated exclusively for religious, charitable, scientific, literary, or educational purposes or for the prevention of cruelty to children or animals.
- A veterans' organization.
- A fraternal organization operating under the lodge system.
- A cemetery company.

The IRS publishes a list of organizations that have applied for and received tax-exempt status under § 501 of the Code.[9] This publication is updated frequently

8. § 170(j).
9. Although this *Cumulative List of Organizations*, IRS Publication 78 (available by purchase from the Superintendent of Documents, U.S. Government Printing Office, Washington, DC 20402),

may be helpful, a qualified organization is not required to be listed. Not all organizations that qualify are listed in this publication (e.g., American Red Cross, University of Cleveland).

and may be helpful to determine if a gift has been made to a qualifying charitable organization.

Because gifts made to needy individuals are not deductible, a deduction will not be permitted if a gift is received by a donee in an individual capacity rather than as a representative of a qualifying organization.

Time of Payment

A charitable contribution generally is deducted in the year the payment is made. This rule applies to both cash and accrual basis individuals. An accrual basis corporation, however, is permitted a deduction in the year of accrual if the board of directors authorizes such payment during the taxable year and the contribution is made within two and one-half months after the close of the taxable year. The special exception for accrual basis corporations is illustrated in chapter 16.

A contribution is ordinarily deemed to have been made on the delivery of the property to the donee. For example, if a gift of securities (properly endorsed) is made to a qualified charitable organization, the gift is considered complete on the day of delivery or mailing. However, if the donor delivers the certificate to his or her bank or broker or to the issuing corporation, the gift is considered complete on the date the stock is transferred on the books of the corporation.

A contribution made by check is considered delivered on the date of mailing. Thus, a check mailed on December 31, 1990, is deductible on the taxpayer's 1990 tax return. If the contribution is charged on a bank credit card, the date the charge is made determines the year of deduction. For a pay-by-phone account, the date shown on the statement issued by the financial institution is the date of payment.

Recordkeeping and Valuation Requirements

Recordkeeping Requirements.   Cash contributions must be substantiated by one of the following:

- A cancelled check.
- A receipt, letter, or other written communication from the charitable organization (showing the name of the organization, the date, and the amount of the contribution).
- Other reliable written records (contemporaneous records or other evidence, such as buttons and tokens, given to contributors by the donee organization).

If a cash contribution of $3,000 or more is given to any one organization, the name of the organization and the amount of the contribution must be reported on the taxpayer's return.

The records required for noncash contributions vary depending on the amount of the contribution. If the value of the contribution is $500 or less, it must be evidenced by a receipt from the charitable organization. The receipt must show the following:

- The name of the charitable organization.
- The date and location of the charitable contribution.
- A reasonably detailed description of the contributed property.

Generally, charitable organizations do not attest to the fair market value of the donated property. Nevertheless, the taxpayer must maintain reliable written evidence of the following information concerning the donation:

- The fair market value of the property and how that value was determined.

- The amount of the reduction in the value of the property (if required) for certain appreciated property and how that reduction was determined.

- Terms of any agreement with the charitable organization dealing with the use of the property and potential sale or other disposition of the property by the organization.

- A signed copy of the appraisal if the value of the property was determined by appraisal. Only for a contribution of art with an aggregate value of $20,000 or more must the appraisal be attached to the taxpayer's return.

Additional information is required if the value of the donated property is over $500 but not over $5,000. Also, the taxpayer must file Section A of Form 8283 (Noncash Charitable Contributions) for such contributions.

For noncash contributions with a claimed value in excess of $5,000 ($10,000 in the case of nonpublicly traded stock), the taxpayer must obtain a qualified appraisal and file Section B of Form 8283. This schedule must show a summary of the appraisal and must be attached to the taxpayer's return. Failure to comply with these reporting rules may result in disallowance of the charitable contribution deduction. Additionally, significant overvaluation exposes the taxpayer to rather stringent penalties.

Valuation Requirements.   Property donated to a charity is generally valued at fair market value at the time the gift is made. The Code and Regulations give very little guidance on the measurement of the fair market value except to say, "The fair market value is the price at which the property would change hands between a willing buyer and a willing seller, neither being under any compulsion to buy or sell and both having reasonable knowledge of relevant facts."

Limitations on Charitable Contribution Deductions

In General.   The potential charitable contribution deduction is the total of all donations, both money and property, that qualify for the deduction. After this determination is made, the actual amount of the charitable contribution deduction that is allowed for individuals for the tax year is limited as follows:

- If the qualifying contributions for the year total 20 percent or less of adjusted gross income, they are fully deductible.

- If the qualifying contributions are more than 20 percent of adjusted gross income, the deductible amount may be limited to either 20 percent, 30 percent, or 50 percent of adjusted gross income, depending on the type of property given and the type of organization to which the donation is made.

- In any case, the maximum charitable contribution deduction may not exceed 50 percent of adjusted gross income for the tax year.

To understand the complex rules for computing the amount of a charitable contribution, it is necessary to understand the distinction between capital gain property and ordinary income property. In addition, it is necessary to understand when the 50 percent, 30 percent, and 20 percent limitations apply. If a taxpayer's contributions for the year exceed the applicable percentage limitations, the excess contributions may be carried forward and deducted during a five-year carryover period. These topics are discussed in the sections that follow.

Corporations are subject to an overall limitation of 10 percent of taxable income computed without regard to the contributions made and certain other adjustments. The rules applicable to contributions by corporations are discussed in detail in chapter 16.

Ordinary Income Property.   *Ordinary income property* is any property that, if sold, will result in the recognition of ordinary income. The term includes inventory for sale in the taxpayer's trade or business, a work of art created by the donor, and a manuscript prepared by the donor. It also includes a capital asset held by the donor for less than the required holding period for long-term capital gain treatment. Property that results in the recognition of ordinary income due to the recapture of depreciation is ordinary income property. If ordinary income property is contributed, the deduction is equal to the fair market value of the property less the amount of ordinary income that would have been reported if the property were sold. In most instances, the deduction is limited to the adjusted basis of the property to the donor.

EXAMPLE 25   T owned stock in EC Corporation that he donated to a local university on May 1, 1990. T had purchased the stock for $2,500 on March 3, 1990, and the stock had a value of $3,600 when he made the donation. Since the property had not been held for a sufficient period to meet the long-term capital gain requirements, a short-term capital gain of $1,100 would have been recognized had the property been sold. Because short-term capital gain property is treated as ordinary income property, T's charitable contribution deduction is limited to the property's adjusted basis of $2,500.   □

In Example 25, suppose the stock had a fair market value of $2,300 (rather than $3,600) when it was donated to charity. Because the fair market value now is less than the adjusted basis, the charitable contribution deduction becomes $2,300.

Capital Gain Property.   *Capital gain property* is any property that would have resulted in the recognition of long-term capital gain or § 1231 gain if the property had been sold by the donor. As a general rule, the deduction for a contribution of capital gain property is equal to the fair market value of the property.

Two major exceptions preclude the deductibility of the appreciation on long-term capital gain property. One exception concerns donations to certain private foundations. Private foundations are organizations that traditionally do not receive their funding from the general public (e.g., the Ford Foundation). Generally, foundations fall into two categories: operating and nonoperating. A private *operating* foundation is one that spends substantially all of its income in the active conduct of the charitable undertaking for which it was established. Other private foundations are *nonoperating* foundations. However, if a private nonoperating foundation distributes the contributions it receives according to special rules within two and one-half months following the year of the contribution, the organization is treated the same as public charities and private operating foundations. Often, only the private foundation knows its status (operating or nonoperating) for sure, and such status can change from year to year.

If capital gain property is contributed to a private nonoperating foundation (that is not treated the same as a private operating foundation), the taxpayer must reduce the contribution by the long-term capital gain that would have been recognized if the property had been sold at its fair market value. The effect of this provision is to limit the deduction to the property's adjusted basis.

EXAMPLE 26   T purchases stock for $800 on January 1, 1975, and donates it to a private nonoperating foundation on June 21, 1990, when it is worth $2,000. T's charitable contribution is $800, the stock's basis.   □

EXAMPLE 27   Assume the same facts as in the previous example, except that the donation is to either a private operating foundation or a public charity. Now, T's charitable contribution is $2,000.   □

A second exception applying to capital gain property relates to *tangible personalty*. Tangible personalty is all property that is not realty (land and buildings) and does not include intangible property such as stock or securities. If tangible personalty is contributed to a public charity such as a museum, church, or university, the charitable deduction may have to be reduced. The amount of the reduction is the long-term capital gain that would have been recognized if the property had been sold for its fair market value. The reduction occurs if the property is put to an unrelated use. The term *unrelated use* means a use that is unrelated to the exempt purpose or function of the charitable organization.

A taxpayer in this instance must establish that the property is not in fact being put to an unrelated use by the donee. The taxpayer must also establish that at the time of the contribution it was reasonable to anticipate that the property would not be put to an unrelated use. For a contribution of personalty to a museum, if the work of art is the kind of art normally retained by the museum, it will be reasonable for a donor to anticipate that the work of art will not be put to an unrelated use. This will be the case even if the object is later sold or exchanged by the museum.

EXAMPLE 28   T contributes a Picasso painting, for which he paid $20,000, to a local museum. It had a value of $30,000 at the time of the donation. The painting was displayed by the museum for a period of two years and subsequently sold for $50,000. The charitable contribution is not reduced by the unrealized appreciation. This is because the painting was put to a related use even though it was later sold by the museum.   □

As noted in chapter 14, for purposes of the alternative minimum tax, the net untaxed appreciation on charitable contributions is a tax preference item.

Fifty Percent Ceiling.   Contributions made to public charities may not exceed 50 percent of an individual's adjusted gross income for the year. Excess contributions may be carried over to the next five years. The 50 percent ceiling on contributions applies to the following types of public charities:

- A church or a convention or association of churches.
- An educational organization that maintains a regular faculty and curriculum.
- A hospital or medical school.
- An organization supported by the government that holds property or investments for the benefit of a college or university.
- A governmental unit that is Federal, state, or local.
- An organization normally receiving a substantial part of its support from the public or a governmental unit.

The 50 percent ceiling also applies to contributions to the following organizations:

- All private operating foundations.

- Certain private nonoperating foundations that distribute the contributions they receive to public charities and private operating foundations within two and one-half months following the year they receive the contribution.

- Certain private nonoperating foundations in which the contributions are pooled in a common fund and the income and principal sum are paid to public charities.

Thirty Percent Ceiling.   A 30 percent ceiling applies to contributions of cash and ordinary income property to private nonoperating foundations. The 30 percent ceiling also applies to contributions of appreciated capital gain property to 50 percent organizations unless the taxpayer makes a special election (see below).

In the event the contributions for any one tax year involve both 50 percent and 30 percent property, the allowable deduction first comes from the 50 percent property.

EXAMPLE 29   During 1990, T made the following donations to her church: cash of $2,000 and unimproved land worth $30,000. The land had been purchased by T four years ago for $22,000 and was held as an investment. T's adjusted gross income for 1990 is $50,000. Disregarding percentage limitations, T's potential deduction for 1990 is $32,000 [$2,000 (cash) + $30,000 (fair market value of land)]. Note that no reduction for the appreciation on the land is necessary since, if sold, it would have yielded a long-term capital gain.

In applying the percentage limitations, however, the *current* deduction for the land is limited to $15,000 [30% (limitation applicable to long-term capital gain property) × $50,000 (adjusted gross income)]. Thus, the total deduction for 1990 is $17,000 ($2,000 cash + $15,000 land). Note that the total deduction does not exceed $25,000, which is 50% of T's adjusted gross income.   □

Under a special election, a taxpayer may choose to forgo a deduction of the appreciation on capital gain property. Referred to as the *reduced deduction election,* this enables the taxpayer to move from the 30 percent limitation to the 50 percent limitation.

EXAMPLE 30   Assume the same facts as in Example 29, except that T makes the reduced deduction election. Now the deduction for 1990 becomes $24,000 [$2,000 (cash) + $22,000 (basis in land)] because both donations fall under the 50% limitation. Thus, by making the election, T has increased her charitable contribution deduction for 1990 by $7,000 [$24,000 (Example 30) − $17,000 (Example 29)].   □

Although the reduced deduction election appears attractive, it should be carefully considered. The election sacrifices a deduction for the appreciation on long-term capital gain property that might eventually be allowed. Note that in Example 29, the potential deduction was $32,000, yet in Example 30 only $24,000 is allowed. The reason for the decrease of $8,000 ($32,000 − $24,000) of potential deduction is that no carryover is allowed for the amount sacrificed by the election.

Twenty Percent Ceiling.   A 20 percent ceiling applies to contributions of appreciated long-term capital gain property to certain private nonoperating foundations.

Contribution Carryovers.   Contributions that exceed the percentage limitations for the current year can be carried over for five years. In the carryover process, such contributions do not lose their identity for limitation purposes. Thus, if the contribution originally involved 30 percent property, the carryover will continue to be classified as 30 percent property in the carryover year.

EXAMPLE 31   Assume the same facts as in Example 29. Because only $15,000 of the $30,000 value of the land was deducted in 1990, the balance of $15,000 may be carried over to 1991. But the carryover will still be treated as long-term capital gain property and will, therefore, be subject to the 30% of adjusted gross income limitation.   □

In applying the percentage limitations, current charitable contributions must be claimed first before any carryovers can be considered. If carryovers involve more than one year, they are utilized in a first-in, first-out order.

MISCELLANEOUS ITEMIZED DEDUCTIONS

According to § 262, no deduction is allowed for personal, living, or family expenses. However, there are a number of expenditures that one may incur that are related to employment. If an employee or outside salesperson incurs unreimbursed business expenses, including travel and transportation, the expenses are deductible as miscellaneous deductions. Beyond unreimbursed employee expenses and those of an outside salesperson, certain other expenses fall into the special category of miscellaneous itemized deductions. Some are deductible only if, in total, they exceed 2 percent of the taxpayer's adjusted gross income. These miscellaneous itemized deductions include (but are not limited to) the following:

- Professional dues to membership organizations.
- Uniforms or other clothing that cannot be used for normal wear.
- Fees incurred for the preparation of one's tax return or fees incurred for tax litigation before the IRS or the courts.
- Job-hunting costs.
- Fee paid for a safe deposit box used to store papers and documents relating to taxable income-producing investments.
- Investment expenses that are deductible under § 212 as discussed in chapter 5.
- Appraisal fees to determine the amount of a casualty loss or the fair market value of donated property.
- Hobby losses up to the amount of hobby income (see chapter 5).

Employee business expenses that are reimbursed generally are not itemized deductions but are deducted *for* adjusted gross income. Employee business expenses are discussed in depth in chapter 9.

OTHER MISCELLANEOUS DEDUCTIONS

Certain expenses and losses do not fall into any category of itemized deductions already discussed (medical, taxes, interest, charitable, and miscellaneous) but are nonetheless deductible.

- Moving expenses that meet the requirements for deductibility, discussed in chapter 9.

- Casualty and theft losses, discussed in chapter 7.

- Gambling losses up to the amount of gambling winnings.

- Impairment-related work expenses of a handicapped person.

- The unrecovered investment in an annuity contract when the annuity ceases by reason of death, discussed in chapter 3.

The amount of each expense that is allowable as a deduction may be limited by the rules within a particular category (casualty and theft losses, moving expenses, gambling losses).

Moving expenses and casualty and theft losses are separate line items on Schedule A (Form 1040). The remaining expenses and losses are deductible as "Other Miscellaneous Deductions."

Comprehensive Example of Schedule A

Harry and Jean Brown, married filing jointly, had the following transactions for the current year:

• Medicines that required a prescription	$ 430
• Doctor and dentist bills paid and not reimbursed	2,120
• Medical insurance premium payments	1,200
• Contact lenses	175
• Transportation for medical purposes (425 miles × 9 cents/mile + $4.75 parking)	43
• State income tax withheld	620
• Real estate taxes	1,580
• Interest paid on qualified residence mortgage	2,840
• Finance charges paid on credit cards	34
• Interest on loan to purchase personal auto	265
• Charitable contributions in cash	860
• Transportation in performing charitable services (860 miles × 12 cents/mile + $15.80 parking and tolls)	119
• Unreimbursed employee expenses (from a Form 2106)	870
• Tax return preparation	150
• Professional expenses (dues and publications)	135
• Safe deposit box (used for keeping investment documents and tax records)	35

The Browns' adjusted gross income is $40,000. The completed Schedule A (on page 10–27) for 1989 reports itemized deductions totaling $7,437.

SCHEDULES A&B
(Form 1040)
Department of the Treasury
Internal Revenue Service

Schedule A—Itemized Deductions
(Schedule B is on back)

▶ Attach to Form 1040. ▶ See Instructions for Schedules A and B (Form 1040).

OMB No. 1545-0074

19 89

Attachment
Sequence No. **07**

Name(s) shown on Form 1040

Harry and Jean Brown

Your social security number

371 30 3987

Medical and Dental Expenses (Do not include expenses reimbursed or paid by others.) (See Instructions on page 23.)	**1a**	Prescription medicines and drugs, insulin, doctors, dentists, nurses, hospitals, medical insurance premiums you paid, etc . .	**1a**	3,750	
	b	Other. (List—include hearing aids, dentures, eyeglasses, transportation and lodging, etc.) ▶ .... Contact lenses 175 Transportation 43	**1b**	218	
	2	Add the amounts on lines 1a and 1b. Enter the total here . . .	**2**	3,968	
	3	Multiply the amount on Form 1040, line 32, by 7.5% (.075) . .	**3**	3,000	
	4	Subtract line 3 from line 2. If zero or less, enter -0-. **Total** medical and dental . . ▶	**4**		968
Taxes You Paid (See Instructions on page 24.)	**5**	State and local income taxes	**5**	620	
	6	Real estate taxes	**6**	1,580	
	7	Other taxes. (List—include personal property taxes.) ▶	**7**		
	8	Add the amounts on lines 5 through 7. Enter the total here. **Total** taxes . . ▶	**8**		2,200
Interest You Paid (See Instructions on page 24.)	**9a**	Deductible home mortgage interest (from Form 1098) that you paid to financial institutions. Report deductible points on line 10.	**9a**	2,840	
	b	Other deductible home mortgage interest. (If paid to an individual, show that person's name and address.) ▶	**9b**		
	10	Deductible points. (See Instructions for special rules.)	**10**		
	11	Deductible investment interest. (See page 25.)	**11**		
	12a	Personal interest you paid. (See page 25.) . |12a| 299			
	b	Multiply the amount on line 12a by 20% (.20). Enter the result . .	**12b**	60	
	13	Add the amounts on lines 9a through 11, and 12b. Enter the total here. **Total** interest ▶	**13**		2,900
Gifts to Charity (See Instructions on page 25.)	**14**	Contributions by cash or check. (If you gave $3,000 or more to any one organization, show to whom you gave and how much you gave.) ▶	**14**	979	
	15	Other than cash or check. (You must attach Form 8283 if over $500.)	**15**		
	16	Carryover from prior year	**16**		
	17	Add the amounts on lines 14 through 16. Enter the total here. **Total** contributions . ▶	**17**		979
Casualty and Theft Losses	**18**	Casualty or theft loss(es) (attach Form 4684). (See page 26 of the Instructions.) . . . . ▶	**18**		
Moving Expenses	**19**	Moving expenses (attach Form 3903 or 3903F). (See page 26 of the Instructions.) . . . . ▶	**19**		
Job Expenses and Most Other Miscellaneous Deductions (See page 26 for expenses to deduct here.)	**20**	Unreimbursed employee expenses—job travel, union dues, job education, etc. (You MUST attach Form 2106 in some cases. See Instructions.) ▶	**20**	870	
	21	Other expenses (investment, tax preparation, safe deposit box, etc.). List type and amount ▶ ... Tax Prep. 150 ...... Professional Dues 135 Safety Deposit Box 35	**21**	320	
	22	Add the amounts on lines 20 and 21. Enter the total.	**22**	1,190	
	23	Multiply the amount on Form 1040, line 32, by 2% (.02). Enter the result here	**23**	800	
	24	Subtract line 23 from line 22. Enter the result. If zero or less, enter -0-. . . . . . ▶	**24**		390
Other Miscellaneous Deductions	**25**	Other (from list on page 26 of Instructions). List type and amount ▶ .... ▶	**25**		7,437
Total Itemized Deductions	**26**	Add the amounts on lines 4, 8, 13, 17, 18, 19, 24, and 25. Enter the total here. Then enter on Form 1040, line 34, the LARGER of this total or your standard deduction from page 17 of the Instructions . . . . ▶	**26**		

For Paperwork Reduction Act Notice, see Form 1040 Instructions.

Schedule A (Form 1040) 1989

TAX PLANNING CONSIDERATIONS

Effective Utilization of Itemized Deductions

Since an individual may use the standard deduction in one year and itemize deductions in another year, it is frequently possible to obtain maximum benefit by shifting itemized deductions from one year to another. For example, if a taxpayer's

itemized deductions and the standard deduction are approximately the same for each year of a two-year period, the taxpayer should use the standard deduction in one year and shift itemized deductions (to the extent permitted by law) to the other year. The individual could, for example, prepay a church pledge for a particular year or avoid paying end-of-the-year medical expenses to shift the deduction to the following year.

Utilization of Medical Deductions

When a taxpayer anticipates that his or her medical expenses will approximate the percentage floor, much might be done to generate a deductible excess. Any of the following procedures can help build a deduction by the end of the year:

- Incur the obligation for or have carried out needed dental work. Orthodontic treatment, for example, may have been recommended for a member of the taxpayer's family.

- Have elective remedial surgery that may have been postponed from prior years (e.g., tonsillectomies, vasectomies, correction of hernias, hysterectomies).

- Incur the obligation for capital improvements to taxpayer's personal residence recommended by a physician (e.g., an air filtration system to alleviate a respiratory disorder).

    As an aid to taxpayers who might experience temporary cash-flow problems at the end of the year, the use of bank credit cards is deemed to be payment for purposes of timing the deductibility of charitable and medical expenses.

Example 32   On December 12, 1990, T (a calendar year taxpayer) purchases two pairs of prescription contact lenses and one pair of prescribed orthopedic shoes for a total of $305. These purchases are separately charged to T's credit card. On January 6, 1991, T receives his statement containing these charges and makes payment shortly thereafter. The purchases are deductible as medical expenses in the year charged (1990) and not in the year the account is settled (1991). □

Recognizing which expenditures qualify for the medical deduction also may be crucial to exceeding the percentage limitations.

Example 33   T employs E (an unrelated party) to care for her incapacitated and dependent mother. E is not a trained nurse but spends approximately one-half of the time performing nursing duties (e.g., administering injections and providing physical therapy) and the rest of the time doing household chores. An allocable portion of E's wages that T pays (including the employer's portion of FICA taxes) qualifies as a medical expense. □

To assure a deduction for the entire cost of nursing home care for an aged dependent, it is helpful if the transfer of the individual to the home is for medical reasons and recommended by a doctor. In addition, the nursing home facilities should be adequate to provide the necessary medical and nursing care. To assure

a deduction for all of the nursing care expenses, it is necessary to show that the individual was placed in the home for required medical care rather than for personal or family considerations.

Proper documentation is required to substantiate medical expenses. The taxpayer should keep all receipts for credit card or other charge purchases of medical services and deductible drugs as well as all cash register receipts. In addition, medical transportation mileage should be recorded.

If a taxpayer or a dependent of the taxpayer must be institutionalized in order to receive adequate medical care, it may be good tax planning to make a lump-sum payment that would cover medical treatment for future periods. It is advised that a contract be negotiated with the institution so that the expense is fixed and the payment is not a mere deposit.

Protecting the Interest Deduction

Although the deductibility of prepaid interest by a cash basis taxpayer has been severely restricted, a notable exception allows a deduction for points paid to obtain financing for the purchase or improvement of a principal residence in the year of payment. However, such points must actually be paid by the taxpayer obtaining the loan and must represent a charge for the use of money. It has been held that points paid from the mortgage proceeds do not satisfy the payment requirement.[10] Also, the portion of the points attributable to service charges does not represent deductible interest.[11] For taxpayers financing home purchases or improvements, planning usually should be directed toward avoiding these two hurdles to immediate deductibility.

In rare instances, a taxpayer may find it desirable to forgo the immediate expensing of points in the year paid. Instead, it could prove beneficial to capitalize such points and write them off as interest expense over the life of the mortgage.

EXAMPLE 34 | X purchases a home on December 15, 1990, for $95,000 with $30,000 cash and a 15-year mortgage of $65,000 financed by the Greater Metropolis National Bank. X pays two points in addition to interest allocated to the period from December 15 until December 31, 1990, at an annual rate of 10%. Since X does not have enough itemized deductions to exceed the standard deduction for 1990, she should elect to capitalize the interest expense by amortizing the points over 15 years. In this instance, X would deduct $86.67 for 1991, as part of her qualified residence interest expense [$1,300 (two points) divided by 15 years], if she elects to itemize that year. □

Because the deduction for personal (consumer) interest will disappear after 1990 (see Figure 10–3 earlier in the chapter), taxpayers should consider making use of home equity loans. Recall that these loans utilize the personal residence of the taxpayer as security. Since the tracing rules do not apply to home equity loans, the funds from these loans can be used for personal purposes (e.g., auto loans, education). By making use of home equity loans, therefore, what would have been nondeductible consumer interest becomes deductible qualified residence interest.

---

10. *Alan A. Rubnitz,* 67 T.C. 621 (1977).   11. *Donald L. Wilkerson,* 70 T.C. 240 (1978).

Assuring the Charitable Contribution Deduction

For a charitable contribution deduction to be available, the recipient must be a qualified charitable organization. Sometimes the mechanics of how the contribution is carried out can determine whether or not a deduction results.

EXAMPLE 35   T wants to donate $5,000 to her church's mission in Seoul, Korea. In this regard, she considers three alternatives:

1. Send the money directly to the mission.

2. Give the money to her church with the understanding that it is to be passed on to the mission.

3. Give the money directly to the missionary in charge of the mission who is currently in the United States on a fund-raising trip.

If T wants to obtain a deduction for the contribution, she would be well advised to choose alternative 2. A direct donation to the mission (alternative 1) would not be deductible because the mission is a foreign charity. A direct gift to the missionary (alternative 3) does not comply since an individual cannot be a qualified charity for income tax purposes. □

When making donations of other than cash, the type of property chosen can have decided implications in measuring the amount, if any, of the deduction.

EXAMPLE 36   T wants to give $60,000 in value to her church in some form other than cash. In this connection, she considers four alternatives:

1. Stock held as an investment with a cost basis of $100,000 and a fair market value of $60,000.

2. Stock held for five years as an investment with a cost basis of $10,000 and a fair market value of $60,000.

3. The rent-free use for a year of a building that normally leases for $5,000 a month.

4. A valuable stamp collection held as an investment and owned for ten years with a cost basis of $10,000 and a fair market value of $60,000. The church plans to sell the collection if and when it is donated.

Alternative 1 is ill-advised as the subject of the gift. Even though T would obtain a deduction of $60,000, she would forgo the potential loss of $40,000 that would be recognized if the property were sold. Alternative 2 makes good sense since the deduction still is $60,000 and none of the $50,000 of appreciation that has occurred must be recognized as income. Alternative 3 yields no deduction at all and would not, therefore, appear to be a wise choice. Alternative 4 involves tangible personalty that the recipient does not plan to use. As a result, the amount of the deduction would be limited to $10,000, the stamp collection's basis. □

For property transfers (particularly real estate), the ceiling limitations on the amount of the deduction allowed in any one year (50 percent, 30 percent, or 20 percent of adjusted gross income, as the case may be) could be a factor to take into account. With proper planning, donations can be controlled to stay within the limitations and therefore avoid the need for a carryover of unused charitable contributions.

EXAMPLE 37   T wants to donate a tract of unimproved land held as an investment to the University of Maryland (a qualified charitable organization). The land has been held for six years and has a current fair market value of $300,000 and a basis to T of $50,000. T's adjusted gross income for the current year is estimated to be $200,000, and he expects much the same for the next few years. In the current year he deeds (transfers) an undivided one-fifth interest in the real estate to the university. □

What has T in Example 37 accomplished for income tax purposes? In the current year, he will be allowed a charitable contribution deduction of $60,000 (⅕ × $300,000), which will be within the applicable limitation of adjusted gross income (30% × $200,000). Presuming no other charitable contributions for the year, T has avoided the possibility of a carryover. In future years, T can arrange donations of undivided interests in the real estate to stay within the bounds of the percentage limitations. The only difficulty with this approach is the necessity of having to revalue the real estate each year before the donation since the amount of the deduction is based on the fair market value of the interest contributed at the time of the contribution.

It may be wise to avoid a carryover of unused charitable contributions, if possible, because that approach may be dangerous in several respects. First, the carryover period is limited to five years. Depending on the taxpayer's projected adjusted gross income rather than actual adjusted gross income, some of the amount carried over may expire without tax benefit after the five-year period has ended. Second, unused charitable contribution carryovers do not survive the death of the party making the donation and as a consequence are lost.

EXAMPLE 38   D dies in October of 1990. In completing her final income tax return for 1990, D's executor determines the following information: adjusted gross income of $104,000 and a donation of stock worth $60,000 by D to her church. The stock had been held by D as an investment and was purchased two years ago for $50,000. D's executor makes the reduced deduction election and, as a consequence, claims a charitable contribution deduction of $50,000. With the election, the potential charitable contribution deduction of $50,000 ($60,000 − $10,000) is less than the 50% ceiling of $52,000 ($104,000 × 50%). If the executor had not made the election, the potential charitable contribution deduction of $60,000 would have been reduced by the 30% ceiling to $31,200 ($104,000 × 30%). No carryover of the $28,800 ($60,000 − $31,200) would have been available. □

PROBLEM MATERIALS

Discussion Questions

1. X has a history of heart disease. Upon the advice of his doctor, he installs an elevator in his residence so he does not have to climb stairs. Is this a valid medical expense? If it is, how much of the expense is deductible?

2. T, a self-employed individual taxpayer, prepared his own income tax return for the past year and asked you to check it over for accuracy. Your review indicates that T failed to claim certain business entertainment expenses.

    a. Would the correction of this omission affect the amount of medical expenses T can deduct? Explain.

    b. Would it matter if T were employed rather than self-employed?

3. If T's medical expense deduction was $500 in 1990 and the amount reduced T's tax liability, how would a $300 insurance reimbursement be treated if received in 1991? Received in 1990? What if T had not itemized deductions in 1990 and received the $300 reimbursement in 1991?

4. T, a single individual, employs D as a housekeeper. T's household includes her infirm mother. Under what circumstances might some of D's wages qualify for the medical expense deduction claimed by T?

5. T is employed as an accountant in New Orleans, Louisiana. One of T's friends, Dr. D, practices general dentistry in Hot Springs, Arkansas. Once a year during the deer hunting season, T travels to Hot Springs for his annual dental checkup. While there, T makes use of Dr. D's deer lodge for hunting purposes. Do any of T's travel expenses for the trip to Arkansas qualify for the medical expense deduction? Why or why not?

6. T's son is performing poorly in public school. Not only is he failing most subjects but he responds negatively to constructive criticism from his teachers. Upon the recommendation of a child psychiatrist, T enrolls his son in X Academy, a private school that has a better teacher-to-student ratio and more personalized instruction. Is the tuition T pays to X Academy deductible as a medical expense? Explain.

7. T lives in a state that imposes no income tax but a sizable sales tax. U lives in a state that imposes an income tax but no sales tax. Are T and U similarly situated for Federal income tax purposes? Explain.

8. If a taxpayer overpays his or her state income tax due to excessive withholdings or estimated tax payments, how is the refund check treated when received in the subsequent year? Are the excess amounts paid deductible in the current year?

9. The city of Galveston, Texas, assessed beachfront property owners for the construction of jetties to protect shorelines from the destructive effects of the ocean. Is this assessment deductible?

10. How can home equity loans be used to avoid the nondeductibility of interest on amounts borrowed to finance the purchase of consumer goods?

11. Discuss the special problems that arise with respect to the deductibility of interest on a debt between related parties. How does § 267 of the Code relate to this problem?

12. If a taxpayer pays interest on behalf of another, is the payment deductible?

13. Why has Congress imposed limitations on the deductibility of interest when funds are borrowed for the purpose of purchasing or continuing to hold investment property?

14. What is ordinary income property? If inventory with an adjusted cost basis of $60 and fair market value of $100 is contributed to a public charity, how much is deductible?

15. What is capital gain property? What tax treatment is required if capital gain property is contributed to a private nonoperating foundation? To a public charity? What difference does it make if the contribution is tangible personalty and it is put to a use unrelated to the donee's business?

16. An accountant normally charges $100 an hour when preparing financial statements for clients. If the accountant performs accounting services for a church without charge, can the value of the donated services be deducted on his or her tax return?

17. What purpose does the reduced deduction election serve for charitable contribution purposes?

18. During 1990, T donated five dresses to the Salvation Army. The dresses were purchased three years ago at a cost of $1,200 and had been worn by T as personal

attire. Because the dresses are long-term capital assets, T plans to deduct $1,200 on her 1990 income tax return. Comment on T's understanding of the tax law governing charitable contributions.

19. In 1989, V had an excess charitable contribution that he could not deduct because of the percentage limitations. In 1990, V made further charitable contributions. In applying the percentage limitations for 1990, how are these transactions handled?

Problems

20. H and W are married and together have adjusted gross income of $24,000. They have no dependents, and they filed a joint return in 1990. Each pays $450 for hospitalization insurance. During the year, they paid the following amounts for medical care: $1,900 in doctor and dentist bills and hospital expenses and $310 for prescribed medicine and drugs. An insurance reimbursement for hospitalization was received in December 1990 for $700. Determine the deduction allowable for medical expenses paid in 1990.

21. X lives in Arkansas and discovers that he has a rare disease that can be treated only with surgery by a surgeon in France. X incurs $1,500 in air fare, $200 in meals taken at the medical facility, and $800 in lodging expenses for eight nights of lodging related to his medical care in France. What amount, if any, of these expenses is deductible?

22. During 1990, T paid the following medical expenses:

On behalf of S (T's son by a former marriage)	$8,000
On behalf of U (T's uncle)	4,000
Hospital bill for an operation performed on T in 1989	3,500

Of the $8,000 spent on S, $1,500 was for orthodontia services to be performed in 1991. The dentist required this amount as a deposit for the braces to be applied to S's teeth. T could claim S as a dependent, but S's mother refuses to sign the custodial parent's waiver. U could be claimed as T's dependent except for the gross income test. For these items, what amount qualifies as T's medical expenses for 1990?

23. Upon the advice of his physician, R, a heart patient, installs an elevator in his personal residence at a cost of $6,000. The elevator has a cost recovery period of five years. A neighbor who is in the real estate business charges R $40 for an appraisal that places the value of the residence at $50,000 before the improvement and $54,000 after. The value increases because R lives in a region where many older people retire and therefore would find the elevator an attractive feature in a home. As a result of the operation of the elevator, R noticed an increase of $55 in his utility bills for the current year. Disregarding percentage limitations, which of the above expenditures qualify as a medical expense deduction?

24. K, who had adjusted gross income of $21,000, incurred the following medical expenses during 1990: $3,000 for doctor and hospital bills, $1,100 for medical insurance premiums, and $400 for drugs and medicines that require a prescription. He was reimbursed for $1,600 of the doctor and hospital bills by his insurance company. Also, K is physically handicapped and spent $3,500 constructing entrance and exit ramps to his personal residence. The value of the home increased by $1,500 as a result of these expenditures. Compute K's medical expense deduction for 1990.

25. The city of Houston adopted a zoning ordinance that requires a minimum number of off-street parking spaces for each building. To finance the parking lots,

the city levied an assessment of $1,000 against each commercial property in each district. These funds were used to construct off-street parking for the commercial property. Is the $1,000 assessment deductible?

26. V uses the cash method of accounting and lives in a state that imposes an income tax (including withholding from wages). On April 14, 1990, he files his state return for 1989, paying an additional $700 in income taxes. During 1990, his withholdings for state income tax purposes amount to $2,950. On April 13, 1991, V files his state return for 1990 claiming a refund of $225. The refund is received by V on August 3, 1991.

    a. If V itemizes his deductions, how much may he claim as a deduction for state income taxes on his Federal return for calendar year 1990 (filed in April 1991)?

    b. How will the refund of $225 received in 1991 be treated for Federal income tax purposes?

27. In County Z the real property tax year is the calendar year. The real property tax becomes a personal liability of the owner of real property on January 1 in the current real property tax year, 1990. The tax is payable on July 1, 1990. On May 1, 1990, A sells his house to B, who uses the cash method of accounting, but B reports his income on the basis of a fiscal year ending July 31. On July 1, 1990, B pays the entire real estate tax for the year ending December 31, 1990. How much of the real estate tax for 1990 is considered to be imposed on B?

28. In 1990, M has $8,000 of investment income and the following miscellaneous deductions:

Unreimbursed employee business expenses (meals included at 80%)	$1,000
Tax return preparation fee	150
Investment expenses	600

    For purposes of the investment interest expense limitation, what is the total of M's net investment income in each of the following independent situations?

    a. AGI of $30,000.

    b. AGI of $70,000.

    c. AGI of $100,000.

29. X is married and files a joint tax return for 1990. X has investment interest expense of $95,000 for a loan made to him in 1990 to purchase a parcel of unimproved land. His income from investments (dividends and interest) totaled $15,000. After reducing his miscellaneous deductions by the applicable 2% floor, the deductible portion of investment expenses amounted to $2,500. X also has $3,000 as a net long-term capital gain from the sale of another parcel of unimproved land. Calculate X's investment interest deduction for 1990.

30. E borrowed $200,000 to acquire a parcel of land to be held for investment purposes. During 1990, she paid interest of $20,000 on the loan. She had adjusted gross income of $50,000 in 1990. Other 1990 items related to E's investments include the following:

Investment income	$10,200
Long-term gain on sale of stock	4,000
Investment counsel fees	1,500

E is unmarried and elected to itemize her deductions. She had no miscellaneous deductions other than the investment counsel fees. Determine E's investment interest deduction for 1990.

31. H and W, married taxpayers filing a joint return, incurred the following items of interest expense during 1990:

Interest on personal residence	$8,200
Interest on bank loan used to acquire an automobile	1,800
Interest on credit cards	900

    They acquired the residence in 1989 at a cost of $100,000 ($20,000 cash + $80,000 mortgage). The residence is worth $120,000. Compute the deduction for interest expense for H and W for 1990.

32. T and his wife W own a personal residence in the city. For many years, they have owned a beach house 50 miles away. They do not rent out the beach house because they spend every weekend there. Last year, they purchased a condominium in Boulder, Colorado, for their son to live in while he attends college. During 1990, they paid the following mortgage interest (each mortgage is secured by the respective property): $7,800 on their personal residence, $5,500 on the beach house, and $9,000 on the condominium. How much can T and W deduct for the year as qualified residence interest?

33. A, B, and C are equal owners in the X Corporation. All three shareholders make loans to X Corporation in 1989 and receive interest-bearing notes. A and B are brothers, and C is their uncle. All three owners are on the cash method of accounting, while X Corporation is on the accrual method. A, B, C, and X Corporation use a calendar year for tax purposes. Can X Corporation deduct for 1990 the interest payments made to A, B, and C on April 1, 1991?

34. Dr. X, a famous heart surgeon practicing in Chicago, performs heart surgery in charitable hospitals around the state during one day of each week. He incurs $250 per week in travel and related expenses pursuant to the rendition of these services. He receives no compensation for the services, nor is he reimbursed for the travel expenses. Assume his professional fees average $3,000 per operation and that he normally performs two operations each day. Based on these facts, what is Dr. X's charitable contribution deduction for the year?

35. Taxpayer's child attends a parochial school operated by the church the family attends. Taxpayer made a donation of $300 to the church in lieu of the normal registration fee of $100 for children of nonmembers. In addition, the regular tuition of $75 per week is paid to the school. Based on this information, what is the taxpayer's charitable contribution deduction?

36. Determine the amount of the charitable deduction allowed in each of the following situations:

    a. Donation of X Corporation stock (a publicly traded corporation) to taxpayer's church. The stock cost the taxpayer $2,000 four months ago and has a fair market value of $3,000 on the date of the donation.

    b. Donation of a painting to the Salvation Army. The painting cost the taxpayer $2,000 five years ago and has a fair market value of $3,500 on the date of the donation.

    c. The local branch of the American Red Cross uses a building rent-free for half of the current year. The building normally rents for $500 a month.

    d. Donation by a cash basis farmer to a church of a quantity of grain worth $900. The grain was raised by the farmer in the preceding year at a cost of $650, all of which was deducted for income tax purposes.

37. During 1990, T an individual, made the following contributions to his church:

Cash	$20,000
Stock in Y Corporation (a publicly traded corporation)	30,000

The stock in Y Corporation was acquired as an investment three years ago at a cost of $10,000. T's adjusted gross income for 1990 is $70,000.

a.   What is T's charitable contribution deduction for 1990?

b.   How are excess amounts, if any, treated?

38.   D died in 1990. Before she died, D made a gift of stock in Z Corporation (a publicly traded corporation) to her church. The stock was worth $35,000 and had been acquired as an investment two years ago at a cost of $30,000. In the year of her death, D had adjusted gross income of $60,000. In completing her final income tax return, how should D's executor handle the charitable contribution?

39.   On December 30, 1990, R purchased four tickets to a charity ball sponsored by the city of San Diego for the benefit of underprivileged children. Each ticket cost $200 and had a fair market value of $35. On the same day of the purchase, R gave the tickets to the minister of her church for personal use by his family. At the time of the gift of the tickets, R pledged $4,000 to the building fund of her church. The pledge was satisfied by check dated December 31, 1990, but not mailed until January 3, 1991.

a.   Presuming R is a cash basis and calendar year taxpayer, how much can be deducted as a charitable contribution for 1990?

b.   Would the amount of the deduction be any different if R is an accrual basis taxpayer? Explain.

40.   In 1990 T pays $500 to become a charter member of State University's Athletic Council. The membership ensures that T will receive choice seating at all of State's home football games. Also in 1990, T pays $120 (the regular retail price) for season tickets for himself and his wife. For these items, how much qualifies as a charitable contribution?

41.   Classify each of the following independent expenditures as nondeductible (ND) items, business (*dfor*) deductions, or itemized (*dfrom*) deductions. (*Note:* In many cases it may be necessary to refer to the materials from earlier chapters of the text.)

a.   Interest allowed on home mortgage accrued by a cash basis taxpayer.

b.   State income taxes paid by a sole proprietor of a business.

c.   Subscription to the *Wall Street Journal* paid by a vice president of a bank and not reimbursed by her employer.

d.   Automobile mileage for attendance at weekly church services.

e.   Street-paving assessment paid to the county by a homeowner.

f.   Speeding ticket paid by the owner-operator of a taxicab.

g.   Interest and taxes paid by the owner of residential rental property.

h.   Business entertainment expenses (properly substantiated) paid by a self-employed taxpayer.

i.   State and Federal excise taxes on tobacco paid by a self-employed taxpayer who gave his clients cigars as Christmas presents. The business gifts were properly substantiated and under $25 each.

j.   State and Federal excise taxes on cigarettes purchased by a heavy smoker for personal consumption.

k.   Federal excise taxes (9.1 cents per gallon) on the purchase of gasoline for use in the taxpayer's personal automobile.

l.   Theft loss of personal jewelry worth $300 but which originally cost $75.

m.   Maternity clothing purchased by a taxpayer who is pregnant.

n.   Medical expenses paid by an employer on behalf of an employee.

o. Qualified residence interest paid by a taxpayer on a loan obtained to build an artist studio in his personal residence. Assume that taxpayer's art activities are classified as a hobby.

p. Assume the same facts as in (o) except that the art activities are classified as a trade or business.

42. V had adjusted gross income of $30,000 in 1990. V's itemized deductions totaled $8,000, including $1,000 of miscellaneous itemized deductions (determined before considering the 2% floor). Determine V's allowable itemized deductions for 1990.

Cumulative Problems

43. Jane and Bill Smith are married taxpayers, age 44 and 42, respectively, who file a joint return. In 1989, Bill was employed as an assistant manager for a Ramada Inn at a salary of $28,000. Jane is a high school teacher and earned $20,000. Jane has two children, Joe and Sue, ages 13 and 15, from a previous marriage. The children reside with Jane and Bill throughout the school year and reside with Bob, Jane's former husband, during the summer. Pursuant to the divorce decree (which was executed in 1983), Bob pays $150 per month per child for each of the nine months during which Jane has custody of the children, but the decree is silent as to which parent may claim the exemptions. Bob claims that he spends $200 a month supporting each child during the three summer months when the children live with him. Jane can document that she and Bill provided support of $1,800 for each child in 1989.

In August, Bill and Jane decided to add a suite to their home to provide more comfortable accommodations for Mary, Jane's mother who had moved in with them the preceding February after the death of Jane's father. Not wanting to borrow the money for this addition Bill and Jane sold 400 shares of Amalgamated Corporation stock for $30 per share on May 9, 1989, and used the $12,000 to cover construction costs. They had purchased the stock on August 7, 1986, for $15 a share. They received dividends of $300 on the jointly owned stock before the sale.

Mary is 66 years old and received $3,600 in Social Security benefits during the year, of which she gave Bill and Jane $1,200 to use toward household expenses and deposited $2,400 in her personal savings account. Bill and Jane determine that they spent $1,500 of their own money for food, clothing, medical expenses, and other items for Mary, not counting the rental value of the portion of the house she occupies.

Bill and Jane received $1,600 interest on City of Akron bonds they had bought in 1989. Bill had heard from a friend that municipal bonds were paying good rates and that municipal bond interest was not taxable. To finance the purchase of the bonds, he borrowed $20,000 from the bank at 10% interest, figuring the deduction for interest would save him enough income tax to make the investment worthwhile. He paid the bank $2,000 interest during 1989. Other interest paid during the year included $4,530 on their home mortgage (paid to a Federal savings & loan) and $406 on various charge accounts.

Jane's favorite uncle died in February and willed Jane 50 shares of IBM stock worth $100 per share. Jane received dividends of $242 on the stock during the year.

In December 1989, Bill was riding a motorcycle he had just acquired for $8,200. In his eagerness to try it out, he neglected two things. First, he had forgotten to insure it. Second, he had not taken time to read the operating instructions. As a

result of his lack of familiarity with the motorcycle, he lost control of it as he was headed toward a large, concrete barn. Fortunately, Bill was able to jump off before the crash and escaped injury. The barn was not damaged. The motorcycle, however, was demolished. Bill sold it back to the dealer for parts for $600.

Bill and Jane paid doctor and hospital bills of $3,800 and were reimbursed by their insurance company for $1,400. Prescription medicines and drugs cost them $900, and premiums on their health insurance policy were $650. Included in the amounts paid for hospital bills was $800 for Mary, and of the $900 spent for medicines and drugs, $300 was for Mary.

Taxes paid during the year included $2,120 property taxes on their home and state income taxes (withheld) of $950. In March 1989, Bill and Jane received a refund on their 1988 state income taxes of $940. They had itemized deductions on their 1988 return and had received a tax benefit for the full amount of state income taxes reported.

Bill and Jane contribute $40 a week to the First United Church and have cancelled checks for these contributions totaling $2,080. In addition, Bill's employer withheld $360 from his check, per his instructions, as a contribution to United Way. Bill and Jane also have a receipt from the Salvation Army for some used clothing the family had contributed. Bill and Jane estimated the value of the clothes at $300.

Bill and Jane had $5,019 ($2,832 for Bill, $2,187 for Jane) of Federal income tax withheld in 1989 and paid no estimated Federal income tax.

Compute net tax payable or refund due for Bill and Jane Smith for 1989. If you use tax forms for your solutions, you will need Form 1040 and Schedules A, B, and D. Suggested software (if available): *TurboTax* for tax return solutions or *WEST–TAX Planner* if tax return solutions are not desired.

 44. Sam Worthing, age 45, is married and has two dependent children. In 1990, he incurred the following:

Salary received from his employer, Geophysics, Inc.	$60,000
Cost of art supplies. Sam took up painting as a hobby and plans to sell the paintings to friends and art galleries but had no willing purchasers during 1990.	1,000
Contribution of shares of Xerox stock to his church (fair market value of $1,000, cost of $400, and acquired in 1976).	1,000
Sam's wife, Irene, had a diamond ring that was stolen in April 1990. A police report was filed, but her ring was not recovered. It was not covered by insurance. The ring had recently been appraised at $2,000, which was also its original cost.	2,000
Travel (meals included at 80%) and auto expenses incurred in connection with Sam's employment (none of which was reimbursed).	2,500

Sam and his family moved from Nashville to Boston during the year and incurred the following unreimbursed expenses:

Moving van	$2,500	
House-hunting expenses (meals included at 80%)	1,800	
Sales commissions on the former house	3,500	7,800

Sam incurred and paid the following personal expenses:

Medical and dental bills for the family	1,500
State and local income and property taxes	4,500

Determine the Worthings' adjusted gross income and taxable income for 1990, assuming that a joint return is filed and that there are no other items of income or expense. Suggested software (if available): *WEST–TAX Planner* or *TurboTax* (planning mode).

11

TAX CREDITS

Tax credits are an important factor in determining the final amount of tax that must be paid or the amount of refund a taxpayer receives. This chapter examines the tax credits that enter into the calculation of one's tax liability.

Some tax credits are refundable if they exceed the taxpayer's tax liability. The amount of the credit is paid to the taxpayer even if he or she has no tax liability. Others are nonrefundable. In some cases, even though the allowed nonrefundable credit is not paid directly to the taxpayer, the portion not used up in the current year may reduce the tax liability for other years. In other situations, the credit is wasted if it exceeds the tax liability. The refundable or nonrefundable nature of tax credits is covered later in the chapter under Priority of Credits.

TAX POLICY CONSIDERATIONS

Congress has generally used tax credits to achieve social or economic objectives or to provide equity for different types of taxpayers. For example, the investment tax credit was introduced in 1962. It was expected to encourage growth in the economy, improve the competitive position of American industry at home and abroad, and help alleviate the nation's balance of payments problem.[1] However, the investment tax credit has been repealed for property placed in service after December 31, 1985. This is in line with Congress's new objective of removing or reducing the effect of taxes as a factor in business decisions.

A tax credit should not be confused with an income tax deduction. Certain expenditures of individuals are permitted as deductions from gross income in arriving at adjusted gross income (e.g., business expenses). Additionally, individuals are allowed to deduct certain nonbusiness personal and investment-related expenses *from* adjusted gross income. Whereas the tax benefit received from a tax deduction is dependent on the tax rate, a tax credit is not affected by the tax rate of the taxpayer.

EXAMPLE 1

Assume Congress wishes to encourage a certain type of expenditure. One way to accomplish this objective would be to allow a tax credit of 25% for such expenditures. Another way to accomplish this objective would be to allow an itemized deduction for the expenditures. Assume taxpayer A's tax rate is 15%, while taxpayer B's tax rate is 28%. The tax benefits available to each taxpayer, for a $1,000 expenditure, are summarized as follows:

	Taxpayer A	Taxpayer B
Tax benefit if a 25% credit is allowed	$250	$250
Tax benefit if an itemized deduction is allowed	150	280

These results make it clear that tax credits provide benefits on a more equitable basis than do tax deductions. This is even more apparent considering the fact that the deduction approach will benefit only those taxpayers who itemize deductions, while the credit approach benefits all taxpayers who make the specified expenditure. □

---

1. Summary of remarks of the Secretary of the Treasury, quoted in S.Rept. 1881, 87th Cong., 2nd Sess., reported in 1962–3 C.B. 707.

For many years, Congress made liberal use of the tax credit provisions of the Code in implementing tax policy. Although existing tax credits still carry out this objective, budget constraints and economic considerations have dictated the repeal of some credits (e.g., investment tax credit, political contributions credit). Nevertheless, such credits as those applicable to jobs for certain disadvantaged persons, child and dependent care, and expenses related to qualified low-income housing still reflect social policy considerations. Other credits, such as those applicable to research activities, have been retained based on economic considerations.

SPECIFIC BUSINESS-RELATED TAX CREDIT PROVISIONS

The business-related tax credits that form a single general business credit include the investment tax credit, jobs credit, research activities credit, and low-income housing credit. Each is determined separately under its own set of rules and is explained here in the order listed.

Investment Tax Credit

Since its original enactment in 1962, the investment tax credit (ITC) has been suspended, reinstated, repealed, and reenacted in response to varying economic conditions and political pressures. These changes in the tax laws have created a nightmare for tax practitioners. This phenomenon continued with the TRA of 1986 provisions related to the ITC. Although this act repealed the regular credit for most property placed in service after 1985, the ITC is still allowed for certain types of property under transitional rules (discussed below). In addition, practitioners will have to deal with carryover and recapture provisions related to the ITC for many years in the future. Because of all of these provisions, a basic understanding of the pre-1986 ITC is necessary.

The ITC has three components: the regular ITC, the credit for rehabilitation expenditures, and the business energy credit. The regular ITC was allowed before 1986 for most tangible personal property and is still allowed for transition property (discussed under Transition Property). The rehabilitation credit is allowed for expenditures to rehabilitate (1) industrial and commercial buildings originally placed in service before 1936 and (2) certified historic structures. The third component of the ITC, the business energy credit, is allowed to a limited extent for expenditures by businesses for certain energy conservation equipment. The latter two components of the ITC are discussed later in the chapter under Tax Credit for Rehabilitation Expenditures and Business Energy Credits.

Qualifying Property.   The ITC was allowed for most tangible personal property (e.g., automobiles, machinery, and furniture) and was not allowed for most real property (e.g., land and buildings). Both categories had exceptions. It was sometimes difficult to determine whether an item was tangible personal property that was eligible for the ITC or whether such property was a structural component of a building that was not eligible for the ITC. An item is generally considered to be tangible personal property if it can be removed without causing structural damage to the building.

Upon premature disposition of property on which the ITC has been taken, all or part of the credit that was taken is subject to recapture. Therefore, upon the disposition of property, it will continue to be necessary to determine whether the ITC was taken on the property if the recapture provisions apply.

Transition Property.   The ITC is still allowed for certain property placed in service after 1985 if the property qualifies as transition property.[2] An asset qualifies as *transition property* only if the taxpayer had, on December 31, 1985, a written, binding contract to acquire, construct, or reconstruct the asset. If this provision is satisfied, an additional requirement provides that the property must be placed in service by a specified date. The specified dates for *acquired* property are based on the asset depreciation range (ADR) midpoint lives of the assets. The following table shows the specified dates:

ADR Midpoint Life	Must Be Placed in Service Before
Less than 5 years	7/1/86
At least 5 but less than 7 years	1/1/87
At least 7 but less than 20 years	1/1/89
20 or more years	1/1/91

In addition to the preceding rules for acquired property, a complex set of rules for constructed or reconstructed property exists.

Computation of Qualified Investment.   Because of the recapture provisions and the carryover provisions applicable to the ITC, it is necessary to understand how the credit was computed. The ITC was based on the aggregate amount, without limit, of qualifying new property that was placed in service during the year. In addition, although used ITC property was included in the calculation of the ITC, the maximum includible cost for used property was $125,000 per year. For transition property in years after 1987, the maximum includible cost of used property was $150,000.

EXAMPLE 2   In 1985, T acquired used machinery (which was five-year recovery property) for use in his business. The cost of such property was $200,000. Only $125,000 of the machinery qualified for the ITC because of the limitation on used property. □

Any part of the cost of property that was deducted under the § 179 election to expense certain depreciable business assets could not be used for the credit computation.

Amount of the Credit.   The credit was based on the recovery period under ACRS (refer to chapter 8 for details). To avoid a basis reduction, the taxpayer could elect a reduced ITC rate. Rates for the full credit and the reduced credit were as follows:

Recovery Period (in years)	Full Credit Rate	Reduced Credit Rate
3	6%	4%
5, 10, or 15	10%	8%

---

2. § 49(e).

EXAMPLE 3

In 1985, T acquired and placed in service the following new assets: automobile, $9,000; light-duty truck, $12,000; office furniture, $2,500; and airplane, $120,000. T's tentative ITC (using the full credit rates) was computed as follows:

Qualifying Property	Cost	Recovery Period	Rate of Credit	Investment Tax Credit
Automobile	$ 9,000	3 years	6%	$ 540
Light-duty truck	12,000	3 years	6%	720
Office furniture	2,500	5 years	10%	250
Airplane	120,000	5 years	10%	12,000
Tentative investment tax credit				$13,510

☐

The amount computed in Example 3 is described as the tentative investment tax credit because the allowable credit for any year was subject to a ceiling limitation based on tax liability. Any ITC unused under this rule could first be carried back, then carried forward, as explained later in the chapter under Priority of Credits.

Taxpayers could compute the ITC using the full credit rate or a reduced credit rate. Taxpayers who used the full ITC rate were required to reduce the basis of the property (for property placed in service after 1982) by one-half of the ITC taken. No basis reduction was required if the ITC was computed using the reduced rate. The basis of transition property must be reduced by the *full* amount of any credit taken on the property.

EXAMPLE 4

In 1985, T purchased a machine, which was five-year ACRS property, for $10,000. T took a $1,000 ITC on the property (10% of $10,000). The basis of the property had to be reduced by $500 [½ of $1,000 (ITC)]. Thus, T's cost recovery allowance was based on $9,500 [$10,000 (cost) – $500 (reduction for ITC)]. If the property was transition property placed in service in 1986, the basis would have to be reduced by $1,000, the full amount of the 10% ITC. ☐

For purposes of this rule requiring a reduction in basis, the full rate for transition property placed in service in 1988 and later is 6½ percent. For 1987, the 10 percent rate was adjusted based on the number of months in the tax year remaining after June 1987. See Example 6.

Recapture of Investment Tax Credit. The amount of the ITC is based on the recovery period of the qualifying property (refer to Example 3). However, if property is disposed of (or ceases to be qualified ITC property) before the end of the recovery period, the taxpayer must recapture all or a portion of the ITC originally taken.[3] The amount of the ITC that is recaptured in the year of premature disposition (or disqualification as ITC property) is added to the taxpayer's regular tax liability for the recapture year (except for purposes of computing the alternative minimum tax).

---

3. § 47 (a)(5).

The portion of the credit recaptured is a specified percentage of the credit that was taken by the taxpayer. This percentage is based on the period the ITC property was held by the taxpayer, as shown in Figure 11–1.

EXAMPLE 5   T acquired office furniture (five-year recovery property) on October 3, 1985, at a cost of $5,000. T's ITC on the office furniture was $500 (10% of $5,000). T sold the furniture in June 1990. Since T held the furniture more than four years but less than five, he is required to recapture ITC of $100 (20% of $500). The effect of the recapture is to increase T's 1990 tax liability by the $100 of ITC recaptured. □

Recapture of the ITC generally is triggered by the following:

- Disposition of property through sale, exchange, or sale-and-leaseback transactions.
- Retirement or abandonment of property or conversion to personal use.
- Gifts of ITC property.
- Transfers to partnerships and corporations unless certain conditions are met.
- Like-kind exchanges (certain exceptions are provided).

Exceptions are provided for in the Code to prevent inequities. The following transactions illustrate some situations to which the recapture provisions are not applicable:

- A transfer of property to an estate by reason of death.
- A transfer pursuant to certain tax-free reorganizations.
- A liquidation of a subsidiary corporation where the assets are transferred to the parent without receiving a change in basis.
- A transfer of property between spouses or incident to divorce.

Reduction of Investment Tax Credit.   In general, a 35 percent reduction of the ITC is required for ITC earned on transition property *and* for carryovers of the ITC from pre-1986 years. The full 35 percent reduction applies for taxable years beginning on or after July 1, 1987.

FIGURE 11–1 ITC Recapture

If the Property Is Held for	The Recapture Percentage Is	
	For 15-Year, 10-Year, and 5-Year Property	For 3-Year Property
Less than 1 year	100	100
One year or more but less than 2 years	80	66
Two years or more but less than 3 years	60	33
Three years or more but less than 4 years	40	0
Four years or more but less than 5 years	20	0
Five years or more	0	0

EXAMPLE 6

In 1990, T placed in service qualified transition property that cost $54,000. The ITC of $5,400 (10% of $54,000) must be reduced by 35%. This reduction amount of $1,890 (35% of $5,400) is not allowed as a credit for any other year. The 35 percent reduction results in an effective rate of 6½ percent [10% − (35% of 10%)]. T is allowed a reduced regular ITC in the amount of $3,510 [$5,400 − $1,890 (reduction amount)] or 6½% × $54,000. □

A partial reduction applied to taxpayers having a taxable year that straddled July 1, 1987 (e.g., 1987 calendar year). For any year straddling July 1, 1987, the 35 percent reduction was prorated based on the number of months in the taxable year after June 30, 1987.

The 35 percent reduction also applies to *carryforwards* of the regular ITC, regardless of when the property was placed in service. Based on tax liability (specially defined later in the chapter under Priority of Credits) one of three situations develops:

1. If the taxpayer is able to use all of the reduced amount of carryforwards in the tax year, that is the end of the matter. None of the 35 percent reduction amount can be carried to any other year.

2. If only a portion of the reduced ITC carryforwards can be used, the unused portion *and* a corresponding portion of the reduction amount are carried forward to the next year. Assume that the taxpayer is able to use 20 percent of the reduced carryforwards. The other 80 percent *and* 80 percent of the reduction amount are carried forward.

3. If the taxpayer is not able to use any of the allowed ITC carryforward, the entire amount (both the reduced amount and the reduction amount) is carried forward to the next year.

Sooner or later, either in the current tax year or in a carryforward year, the entire reduction amount is lost permanently.

Tax Credit for Rehabilitation Expenditures

Taxpayers are allowed a tax credit for expenditures to rehabilitate industrial and commercial buildings and certified historic structures. This credit was introduced in 1978, as an extension of the ITC, to discourage the relocation of businesses from older, economically distressed areas (e.g., inner city) to newer locations and to preserve historic structures. Thus, no credit is allowed for the rehabilitation of personal use property.

The rates of credit and the structures to which the credit applies have been changed by Congress from time to time to ensure that the credit accomplishes its intended purpose. The operating features of this credit are summarized as follows:

Rate of the Credit for Rehabilitation Expenses	Nature of the Property
10%	Nonresidential buildings, other than certified historic structures, originally placed in service before 1936
20%	Residential and nonresidential certified historic structures

To qualify for the credit, a taxpayer is required to depreciate the costs of the rehabilitation using the straight-line method (refer to chapter 8 for details on depreciation provisions). The basis of a rehabilitated building must be reduced by the full rehabilitation credit that is allowed.

EXAMPLE 7   T spent $60,000 to rehabilitate a building that had originally been placed in service in 1932. T is allowed a credit of $6,000 (10% of $60,000) for rehabilitation expenditures. T then increases the basis of the building by $54,000 [$60,000 (rehabilitation expenditures) − $6,000 (credit allowed)] and must depreciate these capitalized expenditures using the straight-line method. □

To qualify for the credit, buildings must be substantially rehabilitated. A building has been *substantially rehabilitated* if qualified rehabilitation expenditures exceed the greater of (1) the adjusted basis of the property before the rehabilitation or (2) $5,000. Qualified rehabilitation expenditures do not include the cost of acquiring a building, the cost of facilities related to a building (such as a parking lot), and the cost of enlarging an existing building. Stringent rules apply concerning the retention of internal and external walls.

The rehabilitation credit must be recaptured if the rehabilitated property is disposed of prematurely or if it ceases to be qualifying property. The amount recaptured is based on a holding period requirement of five years.

EXAMPLE 8   On March 15, 1987, M placed in service $30,000 of rehabilitation expenditures on a building qualifying for a 10% credit. A credit of $3,000 ($30,000 × 10%) was allowed, and the basis of the building was increased by $27,000 ($30,000 − $3,000). The building was sold on December 15, 1990. M must recapture a portion of the rehabilitation credit based on the schedule in Figure 11–1. Because M held the rehabilitated property for more than three years but less than four, 40% of the credit, or $1,200, must be added to T's 1990 tax liability. Also, the adjusted basis of the rehabilitation expenditures is increased by the $1,200 recaptured amount. □

The passive activity rules as they apply to the rehabilitation credit are more liberal than for rental activities in general. Refer to chapter 6.

Business Energy Credits

Since 1978, a business energy credit has been allowed in order to encourage the conservation of natural resources and to develop alternative energy sources (to oil and natural gas). Most of these credits have now expired. Three remain through September 30, 1990: the credit for solar energy property (at a 10% rate), geothermal property (10%), and ocean thermal property (15%). Except that only new property is eligible for the credit, the rules regarding the regular ITC apply to these credits as well. In the case of recapture, however, if the property ceases to be energy property but still qualifies for the regular ITC, only the energy credit portion is affected. This is so because the business energy credit was allowed in addition to the regular ITC.

Reporting the ITC involves one or all of several forms:

- Form 3468, Computation of Investment Credit, is used for determining the amount of current year credit for all three components. Schedule B of the form is used for calculating the business energy credit.

- Form 4255, Recapture of Investment Credit (Including Energy Investment Credit), is used to determine the increase in tax from recapture.

- If the taxpayer also has any of the other business credits (e.g., jobs credit, research credit), Form 3800, General Business Credit, consolidates these for purposes of determining the current year amount allowed. This form is also used when the taxpayer has carrybacks or carryforwards of general business credits from other years.

Jobs Credit

The jobs credit (also referred to as the targeted jobs credit) was enacted to encourage employers to hire individuals from one or more of the following target groups traditionally subject to high rates of unemployment:

- Vocational rehabilitation referrals.
- Economically disadvantaged youths (age 18 to 22).
- Economically disadvantaged Vietnam-era veterans.
- Recipients of certain Social Security supplemental income benefits.
- General assistance recipients.
- Youths (age 16 to 19) participating in cooperative education programs.
- Economically disadvantaged ex-convicts.
- Eligible work incentive employees.
- Qualified summer youth employees (age 16 and 17).

The jobs credit is not available for wages paid to certain related parties. The credit is available for first-year wages paid to employees who started work on or before September 30, 1990.

Computation of the regular jobs credit differs from the computation of the credit for qualified summer youth employees only in the amount of wages eligible for the credit.

Computation of the Regular Jobs Credit. The regular jobs credit is equal to 40 percent of the first $6,000 of wages (per eligible employee) for the first year of employment. If the jobs credit is elected, the employer's tax deduction for wages is reduced by the amount of the credit. For an employer to qualify for the credit, an unemployed individual must be certified by a local jobs service office of a state employment security agency.

Wages will be taken into account in computing the regular jobs credit only if paid to an individual who is employed for at least 90 days or has completed 120 hours of work. The equivalent thresholds for qualified summer youth employees are 14 days or 20 hours.

EXAMPLE 9   In May 1990, T Company hires four handicapped individuals (certified to be eligible employees for the jobs credit). Each of these employees is paid wages of $7,000 during 1990. T Company's jobs credit is $9,600 [($6,000 × 40%) × 4 employees]. If the tax credit is taken, T Company must reduce its deduction for wages paid by $9,600. No credit is available for wages paid to these employees after their first year of employment. ☐

EXAMPLE 10   On August 1, 1990, M, a calendar year taxpayer, hired a member of a targeted group and obtained the required certification. During the last five months of 1990, this employee is paid $3,500. M is allowed a jobs credit of $1,400 ($3,500 × 40%). The employee continues to work for M in 1991 and is paid $7,000 through July 31. Because up to $6,000 of first-year wages are eligible for the credit, M is also allowed a 40% credit on $2,500 [$6,000 − $3,500 (wages paid in 1990)] of wages paid in 1991, or $1,000 ($2,500 × 40%). None of this employee's wages paid after July 31, 1991, the end of the first year of employment, are eligible for the jobs credit. Likewise, no credit is allowed for wages paid to persons newly hired after September 30, 1990. □

Computation of the Jobs Credit for Qualified Summer Youth Employees. The credit for qualified summer youth employees is allowed on wages for services during any 90-day period between May 1 and September 15. A qualified summer youth employee generally must be age 16 or 17 on the hiring date. The maximum wages eligible for the credit are $3,000 per summer youth employee. Thus, the maximum credit per employee for 1990 is $1,200 ($3,000 × .40). If the employee continues employment after the 90-day period as a member of another targeted group, the amount of wages subject to the regular jobs credit must be reduced by the wages paid to the employee as a qualified summer youth employee.

EXAMPLE 11   X Corporation employs T as a qualified summer youth employee beginning May 1, 1990. After 90 days, T continues his employment as a member of a second targeted group. T was paid $2,000 as a qualified summer youth employee. As a member of the second targeted group, T is paid another $5,000 in 1990. Of the $7,000 total paid to T, only $6,000 qualifies for the jobs credit. This amount consists of the $2,000 wages paid under the qualified summer youth employee program plus $4,000 ($6,000 − $2,000) paid to T as a member of the other targeted group. X Corporation's jobs credit for 1990 will be 40% of $6,000 ($2,000 + $4,000), or $2,400. □

Research Activities Credit

To encourage research and experimentation, usually described as research and development (R & D), a credit is allowed for certain qualifying expenditures paid or incurred through 1990. The research activities credit is the sum of two components: an incremental research credit and a basic research credit.

Incremental Research Activities Credit.   The incremental research activities credit applies at a 20 percent rate to the excess of qualified research expenses for the current taxable year (the credit year) over the base amount. These components of the credit are explained in order.

For expenses to be treated as *qualified research expenditures*, the research must meet the following tests:

- The expenditures must qualify for treatment as expenses under § 174 of the Code.

- The research must be for the purpose of discovering information technological in nature.

- Application of the research must be intended to be useful in the development of a new or improved business component of the taxpayer.

A business component is any product, process, computer software, technique, formula, or invention that is to be held for sale, lease, or license or used by the taxpayer in an existing trade or business of the taxpayer. For a start-up company (defined later), the trade or business requirement is satisfied if the results of the research are used in the active conduct of a future trade or business.

In general, research expenditures qualify if the research relates to a new or improved function, performance, reliability, or quality. Such expenses are not subject to a percentage limitation if the research is performed in-house (by the taxpayer or employees). If, however, the research is conducted by persons outside the taxpayer's business (under contract), only 65 percent of the amount paid qualifies for the credit.

EXAMPLE 12

M incurs the following research expenditures for the tax year.

| In-house wages, supplies, computer time | $50,000 |
| Paid to XY Scientific Foundation for research | 30,000 |

M's qualified research expenditures amount to $69,500 [$50,000 + ($30,000 × 65%)]. □

Beyond giving the general guidelines discussed above, the Code does not give specific examples of qualifying research. However, the credit is *not* allowed for research that falls into any of the following categories:

- Research conducted after the beginning of commercial production of the business component.

- Research related to the adaptation of an existing business component to a particular customer's requirement or need.

- Research related to the reproduction of an existing business component (in whole or in part) from a physical examination of the business component itself or from plans, blueprints, detailed specifications, or publicly available information with respect to such business component.

- Surveys and studies such as market research, testing, and routine data collection.

- Research on computer software developed by or for the benefit of the taxpayer primarily for internal use by the taxpayer (unless the software relates to a research activity that is qualified).

- Research conducted *outside* the United States.

- Research in the social sciences, arts, or humanities.

- Research to the extent funded by any grant or contract or otherwise by another person or government entity.

The *base amount* for the credit year is determined by multiplying the taxpayer's fixed base percentage by the average gross receipts for the four preceding taxable years. The fixed base percentage depends on whether the taxpayer is an existing firm or a start-up company. For purposes of the incremental research activities credit, an *existing firm* is one that both incurred qualified research expenditures *and* had gross receipts during each of at least three years

from 1984 to 1988. A *start-up company* is one that did not have both of the above during each of at least three years in the same 1984–1988 period.

For existing firms, the fixed base percentage is the ratio of total qualified research expenses for the 1984–1988 period to total gross receipts for this same period. Gross receipts are net of sales returns and allowances. The fixed base percentage cannot exceed a maximum ratio of .16, or 16 percent. Start-up companies are *assigned* a fixed base percentage ratio of .03, or 3 percent.

Further, for tax years that begin before October 1, 1990, and end after September 30, 1990, the current year qualified research expenses *and* the base amount must be apportioned in the same ratio that the number of days before October 1, 1990, bears to the total days in the tax year before January 1, 1991. For the calendar year 1990, this ratio is 273/365.

In working with these rules, the following steps are helpful:

1. Calculate the fixed base percentage.

2. Determine the base amount.

3. Apportion current year qualified research expenses and base amount.

The incremental research activities credit, then, is 20 percent of the amount of qualified research expenses that exceed the base amount.

This three step procedure is applied in the following example.

EXAMPLE 13

Y, a calendar year taxpayer, has both gross receipts (net of sales returns and allowances) and qualified research expenses as follows:

	Gross Receipts	Qualified Research Expenses
1984	$150,000	$25,000
1985	300,000	45,000
1986	400,000	30,000
1987	350,000	35,000
1988	450,000	50,000
1989	500,000	55,000
1990	650,000	73,000

Step 1. Aggregate qualified research expenses for the period 1984–1988 equal $185,000 ($25,000 + $45,000 + $30,000 + $35,000 + $50,000). Aggregate gross receipts for the same period total $1,650,000. Y's fixed base percentage is

$$\frac{\$185,000}{\$1,650,000} = .1121, \text{ or } 11.21\%$$

Step 2. Average gross receipts for the four preceding tax years are $425,000 [($400,000 for 1986 + $350,000 for 1987 + $450,000 for 1988 + $500,000 for 1989) ÷ 4]. Thus, Y's base amount is $47,643 ($425,000 × 11.21%).

Step 3. Qualified research expenses $= \$73,000 \times \dfrac{273}{365} = \$54,600.$

Base amount $= \$47,643 \times \dfrac{273}{365} = \$35,634$

Y's incremental research activities credit is $3,793:

Qualified research expenses for 1990	$54,600
Less: Base amount	35,634
Excess	$18,966
Rate	× 20%
Incremental research activities credit	$ 3,793

☐

A special rule limits the credit available for taxpayers who have incurred small amounts of research and experimentation costs during the base period. The rule provides that in no event shall the amount be less than 50 percent of qualified research expenses for the credit year.

EXAMPLE 14

Assume the same facts as in Example 13, except that qualified research and experimentation expenses in 1990 were $100,000 after apportionment. Incremental research and experimentation expenditures eligible for the credit are computed as follows:

Qualified expenses in 1990	$100,000
Minus: Base amount (50% of $100,000, because actual base amount of $35,634 is less than 50% of the 1990 expenses)	50,000
Incremental expenses	$ 50,000

☐

Qualified research and experimentation expenditures not only are eligible for the 20 percent credit but also can be expensed in the year incurred.[4] In this regard, the taxpayer has two choices:

1. Use the full credit and reduce the expense deduction for research expenses by 100 percent of the credit.

2. Retain the full expense deduction and reduce the credit by the product of 50 percent times the maximum corporate tax rate.

---

4. § 174. Also refer to discussion of rules for deduction of research and development expenditures in chapter 7.

As an alternative to the expense deduction, the taxpayer may capitalize the research expenses and amortize them over 60 months or more.

Basic Research Credit.   Corporations (but not S corporations or personal service corporations) are allowed an additional 20 percent credit for basic research payments through December 31, 1990, in excess of a base amount. *Basic research payments* are defined as amounts paid in cash (property transfers do not qualify) to a qualified basic research organization. However, two requirements must be met for the payments to qualify. First, such payments must be made pursuant to a written agreement between the corporation and the qualified organization. Second, basic research is to be performed by the qualified organization. These requirements exist because Congress wanted to provide increased tax incentives for corporate cash expenditures for university basic research but did not want the expenditures to represent a switching of donations from general university giving.

Basic research is defined generally as any original investigation for the advancement of scientific knowledge not having a specific commercial objective. However, the definition excludes basic research conducted outside the United States and basic research in the social sciences, arts, or humanities. This reflects the intent of Congress to encourage high-tech research in the United States.

The calculation of this additional credit for basic research expenditures is complex and is based on the amount of such expenditures in excess of a limited specially defined base amount. This amount in turn may be subject to cost of living adjustments.

Furthermore, the amount of these basic research expenditures that is eligible for this additional credit does not enter into the calculation of the incremental research expenditures credit. Thus, the portion of these basic research expenditures that does not exceed the base amount is not eligible for this additional credit, but does become a component of the regular credit for increasing research activities.

EXAMPLE 15   Y Corporation, a qualifying corporation, pays $75,000 to a university for basic research. Assume that Y Corporation's specially calculated base amount is $50,000. The basic research activities credit allowed is $5,000 [($75,000 − $50,000) × 20%]. The $50,000 of current year basic research expenditures that are not eligible for the credit because they do not exceed the base amount are treated as contract research expenses for purposes of the regular incremental research activities credit.   □

Low-Income Housing Credit

A credit is available to owners of qualified low-income housing projects. The purpose of this low-income housing credit is to encourage building owners to make affordable housing available for low-income individuals. Generally, the credit applies only if the rehabilitation expenses within a 24-month period exceed (1) not less than 10 percent of the building's adjusted basis or (2) $3,000 or more per low-income unit, but special exceptions abound.

This particular credit, more than any other, is influenced by many nontax factors. First, certification of the property by the appropriate state or local agency authorized to provide low-income housing credits is required. These credits are issued based on a nationwide allocation. Once issued, however, they remain in

effect for the entire credit period. Additional units require new certification based on allocations in effect at that subsequent time.

The amount of credit is based on the qualified basis of the property. The qualified basis depends on the number of units rented to low-income tenants. Low-income tenants are those whose income is a percentage of the area median gross income. Area median gross income is determined under the United States Housing Act of 1937. These special rules are seemingly endless.

Once declared eligible, the property must meet the required conditions continuously throughout a 30-year compliance period, although the credit itself is allowed over a 10-year period. After an initial 15-year compliance period, a 15-year *extended low-income commitment period* can be terminated in certain cases.

The credit rate is set monthly by the IRS so that the annualized credit amounts have a present value of 70 percent or 30 percent of the basis attributable to qualifying low-income units. Once determined, though, the percentage remains constant for that property.

The *qualified basis* is that portion of the basis of the entire property (eligible basis) that is rented to qualifying low-income tenants. The amount of credit is determined by multiplying the qualified basis by the applicable percentage.

EXAMPLE 16   C spends $100,000 to build a qualified low-income housing project completed January 1, 1990. The entire project is rented to low-income families. The credit rate for this 70% present credit value property for January 1990, is 8.89%. C may claim a credit of $8,890 ($100,000 × 8.89%) in 1990 and in each of the following nine years. Generally, first-year credits are prorated based on the date the project is placed in service. A full year's credit is taken in each of the next nine years, and any remaining first-year credit is claimed in the eleventh year.   □

Recapture of a portion of the credit may be required if the number of units set aside for low-income tenants falls below a minimum threshold, if the taxpayer disposes of the property or the interest in it, or if the taxpayer's amount at risk decreases. The low-income housing credit is scheduled to expire after December 31, 1990.

Finally, the passive activity rules (see chapter 6) as applied to low-income housing are more generous than for rental property in general.

OTHER TAX CREDITS

Earned Income Credit

Taxpayers whose income is below a specified level may be eligible for an earned income credit. In 1990, if an individual's adjusted gross income is $10,730 or less, the earned income credit is 14 percent of earned income not exceeding $6,810, for a maximum credit of $953.40. If an individual's adjusted gross income is greater than $10,730, the maximum earned income credit of $953.40 (14% times $6,810) is reduced by 10 percent of the amount of adjusted gross income (or, if greater, earned income) that exceeds $10,730. The credit is reduced to zero when either earned income or adjusted gross income reaches $20,264.

EXAMPLE 17   In 1990, T who otherwise qualifies for the earned income credit, receives wages of $11,220 and has no other income. T's earned income credit is $953.40 (14% × $6,810 of earned income) reduced by $49 [($11,220 − $10,730) × 10%]. Thus, T's earned income credit is $904.40 ($953.40 − $49) for 1990.   □

The phase-out levels of $10,730 and $20,264, along with the income base eligible for the credit, are adjusted annually for inflation.

It is not necessary to compute the credit as was done in Example 17. As part of the tax simplification process, the IRS issues an Earned Income Credit Table for the determination of the appropriate amount of the earned income credit. This table, along with a worksheet, is included in the instructions to both Form 1040 and Form 1040A.

To be *eligible* for the credit, the taxpayer must meet one of the following filing statuses:

- Married and entitled to a dependency exemption for a child.

- Surviving spouse with a child who qualifies as a dependent.

- Head of household with an unmarried (need not be a dependent) child, stepchild, or grandchild or with a married (must be a dependent[5]) child, stepchild, or grandchild.

Such child, stepchild, or grandchild must reside with the taxpayer in the United States for more than six months of the tax year (the entire tax year in the case of a surviving spouse). Married individuals must file a joint return to receive the benefits of the credit.

The earned income credit is a form of negative income tax (a refundable credit to the extent it exceeds the tax liability). An eligible individual may elect to receive advance payments of the earned income credit from his or her employer (rather than to receive the credit from the IRS upon filing of the tax return). If this election is made, the taxpayer must file a certificate of eligibility (Form W–5) with his or her employer and *must* file a tax return for the year the income is earned.

Tax Credit for Elderly or Disabled Taxpayers

The credit for the elderly was originally enacted in 1954 as the retirement income credit to provide tax relief for those who were not receiving substantial benefits from tax-free Social Security payments.

EXAMPLE 18   X is a retired taxpayer who received $8,000 of Social Security benefits as his only income in 1990. X's Social Security benefits are excluded from gross income. Therefore, his income tax is $0. In 1990, Y, a single taxpayer 66 years of age, has $8,000 of income from a pension plan funded by his former employer. Assuming Y has no itemized deductions or deductions *for* adjusted gross income, his income tax for 1990 (before credits) is $285. The retirement income credit was enacted to mitigate this inequity.   □

The credit for the elderly rules apply to taxpayers age 65 or over and to individuals under age 65 who are retired with a permanent and total disability and who have disability income from a public or private employer on account of the disability.

---

5. § 32(c)(1). The credit can also be claimed by a custodial parent who is not entitled to a dependency exemption for a child. This situation de-velops when the exemption is released through a written agreement or in a pre-1985 divorce or separation.

The *maximum* allowable credit is $1,125 (15% × $7,500 of qualifying income), but this amount is reduced for taxpayers who receive Social Security benefits as well as for taxpayers whose adjusted gross income exceeds specified amounts. Many taxpayers receive Social Security benefits or adjusted gross income high enough to reduce the base for the credit to zero.

The eligibility requirements and the tax computation are somewhat complicated. Because of this complexity, an individual may elect to have the IRS compute his or her tax and the amount of the tax credit.

The credit is based on an initial amount (referred to as the *base amount*) and filing status in accordance with Figure 11–2. For taxpayers under age 65 who are retired on permanent and total disability, the base amounts could be less than those stated because such amounts are limited to taxable disability income.

This initial base amount is *reduced* by (1) Social Security, Railroad Retirement, and certain excluded pension benefits and (2) one-half of the taxpayer's adjusted gross income in excess of $7,500 for a single taxpayer, a head of household, or a surviving spouse. The adjusted gross income factor is $10,000 for married taxpayers filing jointly. It is generally $5,000 for married taxpayers filing separately. The credit is equal to 15 percent of the base amount after subtracting the adjustments just described.

EXAMPLE 19

H and his wife W are both over age 65 and received Social Security benefits of $2,400 in 1990. On a joint return, H and W reported adjusted gross income of $14,000.

Base amount		$ 7,500
Less: Social Security benefits	$2,400	
One-half of the excess of adjusted gross income of $14,000 over $10,000	2,000	(4,400)
Balance subject to credit		$ 3,100
Tax credit allowed ($3,100 × 15%)		$ 465

☐

The credit for the elderly may not offset any alternative minimum tax. Schedule R of Form 1040 is used to calculate and report the credit.

FIGURE 11—2 Base Amounts for Tax Credit for Elderly and Disabled

Status	Base Amount
Single, head of household, or surviving spouse	$ 5,000
Married, joint return, only one spouse qualifies	5,000
Married, joint return, both spouses qualify	7,500
Married, separate return, spouses live apart the entire year	3,750

Foreign Tax Credit

Both individual taxpayers and corporations may claim a tax credit for foreign income tax paid on income earned and subject to tax in another country or a U.S. possession.[6] As an alternative, a taxpayer may claim a deduction instead of a credit. In most instances the tax credit is advantageous since it is a direct offset against the tax liability.

The purpose of the foreign tax credit is to mitigate double taxation since income earned in a foreign country is subject to both U.S. and foreign taxes. However, the operation of the ceiling limitation formula may result in some form of double taxation or taxation at rates in excess of U.S. rates when the foreign tax rate is in excess of U.S. rates. This is a distinct possibility because U.S. tax rates have been lowered whereas many foreign countries have not reduced their rates.

Computation.   Taxpayers are required to compute the (FTC) foreign tax credit based upon an overall limitation. The foreign tax credit allowed is the *lesser* of the foreign taxes imposed or the overall limitation determined according to the following formula:

$$\frac{\text{Foreign-source taxable income}}{\text{Worldwide taxable income}} \times \frac{\text{U.S. tax}}{\text{before FTC}}$$

For individual taxpayers, worldwide taxable income in the overall limitation formula is determined before personal and dependency exemptions are deducted.

EXAMPLE 20   In 1990, T, a calendar year corporation, has $10,000 of income from Country Y, which imposes a 15% tax, and $20,000 from Country Z, which imposes a 50% tax. T has taxable income of $61,800 from within the United States, is married filing a joint return, and claims two dependency exemptions. Thus, although T's taxable income for purposes of determining U.S. tax is $91,800, taxable income amounts used in the limitation formula are not reduced by personal and dependency exemptions. Thus, for this purpose, taxable income is 100,000 [$91,800 + (4 × $2,050)]. Assume that T's U.S. tax before the credit is $22,156. The overall limitation is computed as follows:

$$\frac{\text{Foreign-source taxable income}}{\text{Worldwide taxable income}} = \frac{\$30,000}{\$100,000} \times \$22,156 = \$6,647$$

In this case, $6,647 is the amount allowed as the foreign tax credit because this amount is less than the $11,500 of foreign taxes imposed [$1,500 (Country Y) + $10,000 (Country Z)]. □

Thus, the overall limitation may result in some of the foreign income being subjected to double taxation. Unused foreign tax credits can be carried back two years and forward five years. Form 1116, Computation of Foreign Tax Credit, is used to compute the limitation on the amount of foreign tax credit for individuals and Form 1118 for corporations.

---

6. Section 27 provides for the credit, but the qualifications and calculation procedure for the credit are contained in §§ 901–908.

Only foreign income taxes, war profits taxes, and excess profits taxes (or taxes paid in lieu of such taxes) qualify for the credit. In determining whether or not the tax is an income tax, U.S. criteria are applied. Thus, value added taxes (VAT), severance taxes, property taxes, and sales taxes do not qualify because they are not regarded as taxes on income. Such taxes may be deductible, however.

The foreign earned income exclusion was discussed in chapter 4, and expenses of employees working outside the United States were discussed in chapter 9.

Credit for Child and Dependent Care Expenses

A credit is allowed to taxpayers who incur employment-related expenses for child or dependent care.[7] The credit is a specified percentage of expenses incurred to enable the taxpayer to work or to seek employment. Expenses on which the credit is based are subject to limitations.

Eligibility. An individual must maintain a household for either of the following:

- A dependent under age 13.

- A dependent or spouse who is physically or mentally incapacitated.

Generally, married taxpayers must file a joint return to obtain the credit. The credit may also be claimed by the custodial parent for a nondependent child under age 13 if the noncustodial parent is allowed to claim the child as a dependent under a pre-1985 divorce agreement or under a waiver in the case of a post-1984 agreement.

Eligible Employment-Related Expenses. Eligible expenses include amounts paid for household services and care of a qualifying individual that are incurred to enable the taxpayer to be employed. Child and dependent care expenses include expenses incurred in the home, such as payments for a housekeeper. Out-of-the-home expenses that qualify for the credit include those for the care of a dependent under the age of 13 and those incurred for an older dependent or spouse who is physically or mentally incapacitated as long as he or she regularly spends at least eight hours each day in the taxpayer's household. This makes the credit available to taxpayers who keep handicapped or older children and elderly relatives in the home instead of institutionalizing them. Out-of-the-home expenses incurred for services provided by a dependent care center will qualify only if the center complies with all applicable laws and regulations of a state or unit of local government.

Child care payments to a relative are eligible for the credit unless the relative is a dependent of the taxpayer or the taxpayer's spouse or is a child (under age 19) of the taxpayer.

EXAMPLE 21   M is an employed mother of an eight-year-old child. M pays her mother, G, $1,500 per year to care for the child after school. M does not claim G as a dependent. M also pays her daughter D, age 17, $900 for the child's care during the summer. Of these amounts, only the $1,500 paid to G qualifies as employment-related child care expenses. □

---

7. § 21.

The total for qualifying employment-related expenses is limited to an individual's earned income. For married taxpayers, this limitation applies to the spouse with the *lesser* amount of earned income. Special rules are provided for taxpayers with nonworking spouses who are disabled or are full-time students. If a nonworking spouse is physically or mentally disabled or is a full-time student, such spouse is *deemed* to have earned income. The deemed amount is $200 per month if there is one qualifying individual in the household or $400 per month if there are two or more qualifying individuals in the household.

Allowable Amounts.   In general, the credit is equal to a percentage of unreimbursed employment-related expenses up to $2,400 for one qualifying individual and $4,800 for two or more individuals. The maximum rate is 30 percent, reduced 1 percent for each $2,000 (or fraction thereof) of adjusted gross income in excess of $10,000 (but not below 20 percent). The following chart shows the applicable percentage for taxpayers with adjusted gross income greater than $10,000:

Adjusted Gross Income in Excess of	Applicable Rate of Credit
$10,000	29%
12,000	28%
14,000	27%
16,000	26%
18,000	25%
20,000	24%
22,000	23%
24,000	22%
26,000	21%
28,000	20%

EXAMPLE 22

W, who has two children under age 13, worked full-time while her spouse, H, was attending college for 10 months during the year. W earned $21,000 and incurred $5,000 of child care expenses. H is deemed to be fully employed and to have earned $400 for each of the 10 months (or a total of $4,000). Since H and W have adjusted gross income of $21,000, they are allowed a credit rate of 24%. H and W are limited to $4,000 in qualified child care expenses (the lesser of $4,800 or $4,000). They are entitled to a tax credit of $960 (24% × $4,000) for the year. □

Dependent Care Assistance Program.   Recall from chapter 4 that an exclusion from gross income is allowed for a limited amount reimbursed to the taxpayer for child or dependent care expenses. The taxpayer is not allowed both an exclusion from income and a child and dependent care credit on the same amount. The allowable child and dependent care expenses are reduced dollar for dollar by the amount of reimbursement.

EXAMPLE 23

Assume the same facts as in Example 22, except that of the $5,000 paid for child care, W was reimbursed $2,500 by her employer under a qualified

dependent care assistance program. The reimbursement reduces W's taxable wages. Thus, H and W have AGI of $18,500, so the credit rate is 25%. The maximum amount of child care expenses for two or more dependents of $4,800 is reduced by the $2,500 reimbursement, resulting in a tax credit of $575 [25% × ($4,800 − $2,500)]. □

In any case, the child and dependent care credit will not be allowed unless, at the time the credit is claimed, the taxpayer reports the correct name, address, and tax identification number (either Social Security number or Employer Identification number) of the care provider. If the care provider is a tax-exempt organization, the name and address but not the tax identification number are required.

The credit is claimed by completing and filing Form 2441, Credit for Child and Dependent Care Expenses. A copy of this form appears in Appendix B.

Credit for Mortgage Interest Paid

Qualified home buyers are allowed to claim a tax credit for a portion of mortgage interest paid.[8] Under this program, qualified first-time home buyers are issued *mortgage credit certificates*. Such certificates can be issued only by state or local political subdivisions with authority to issue qualified mortgage bonds to provide funds for home financing. The mortgage credit certificate specifies both the portion of the debt that qualifies for the credit and the percentage rate for the credit.

The taxpayer's credit is the product of the certificate credit rate and the mortgage interest paid during the year on the certified indebtedness amount. The certificate credit rate must be at least 10 percent but not more than 50 percent. However, if the credit rate exceeds 20 percent, the credit may not exceed $2,000 per year. The interest deduction on the qualifying mortgage is reduced by the amount of the credit claimed. The mortgage interest credit is nonrefundable, but excess credits may be carried over for three years.

EXAMPLE 24   W, who holds a mortgage credit certificate specifying a 50% credit rate, paid qualifying mortgage interest of $4,400 during the year. Because the credit rate exceeds 20%, W's credit is limited to $2,000, and his interest deduction is $2,400 ($4,400 interest paid − $2,000 mortgage interest credit). □

The authority of qualified governmental units to issue mortgage credit certificates expires after 1990. In any event, a mortgage credit certificate, once issued, remains in effect as long as the residence being financed continues to be the certificate recipient's principal residence.

Priority of Credits

Refundable versus Nonrefundable Credits

Certain credits are refundable; others are nonrefundable. Refundable credits include taxes withheld on wages (§ 31), the earned income credit (§ 32), tax withheld at the source on nonresident aliens and foreign corporations (§ 33), and the credit for certain uses of gasoline and special fuels (§ 34). *Refundable credits* are refunded to the taxpayer even if the amount of the credit (or credits) exceeds the taxpayer's tax liability.

8. § 25.

EXAMPLE 25   T, who is single, had taxable income of $27,000 in 1990. His income tax from the 1990 Tax Rate Schedule is $5,032. During 1990, T's employer withheld income tax of $5,349. T is entitled to a refund of $317 ($5,349 − $5,032) because the credit for tax withheld on wages is a refundable credit. □

Nonrefundable credits are not refunded if they exceed the taxpayer's tax liability.

EXAMPLE 26   T is single, age 67, and retired. T's taxable income for 1990 is $1,320, and the tax on this amount is $198. T's tax credit for the elderly is $225. This credit can be used to reduce T's net tax liability to zero, but it will not result in a refund, even though the credit ($225) exceeds the tax liability ($198). This result occurs because the tax credit for the elderly is a nonrefundable credit. □

Some nonrefundable credits, such as the foreign tax credit, are subject to carryover provisions if they exceed the amount allowable as a credit in a given year. Other nonrefundable credits, such as the tax credit for the elderly (refer to Example 26), are not subject to carryover provisions and are lost if they exceed the limitations. Because some credits are subject to carryover provisions while others are not, it is important to determine the order in which credits are offset against the tax liability. The Code provides that nonrefundable credits are to be offset against a taxpayer's income tax liability in the following order:

- Nonrefundable personal credits:
  - Child and dependent care credit.
  - Credit for the elderly and disabled.
  - Mortgage certificate credit.
- Foreign tax credit.
- Orphan drugs testing credit.
- Nonconventional source fuel credit.
- General business credit, which is the sum of the following:
  - Investment tax credit.
  - Jobs credit.
  - Alcohol fuels credit.
  - Research activities credit.
  - Low-income housing credit.

General Business Credit

Two special rules apply to the general business credit. First, any unused credit must first be carried back 3 years, then forward 15 years. Second, for any tax year, the general business credit is limited. The components of the ceiling amount are defined below:

Regular tax liability is the tax liability determined from the appropriate tax table or tax rate schedule, based on taxable income. The following are *not* included in regular tax liability:

- Alternative minimum tax (see chapter 14).

- Additional taxes imposed on excess benefits and premature distributions from retirement plans and from IRAs.

- Pass-through taxes of S corporations (see chapter 20).

Net regular tax liability is the regular tax liability reduced by the following nonrefundable tax credits:

- Child and dependent care expenses credit.

- Credit for the elderly and the permanently and totally disabled.

- Credit for mortgage interest paid.

- Foreign tax credit.

- Orphan drug testing credit.

- Credit for producing fuel from nonconventional sources.

Net income tax is the sum of the regular tax liability and the alternative minimum tax reduced by the nonrefundable tax credits that enter into the calculation of net regular tax liability.

Tentative minimum tax is reduced by the foreign tax credit allowed.

With the above definitions clearly in mind, the general business credit is limited to the taxpayer's *net income tax* reduced by the greater of

- The *tentative minimum tax.*

- 25 percent of *net regular tax liability* that exceeds $25,000.[9]

EXAMPLE 27

T's general business credit for 1990 is $70,000, consisting of $30,000 regular ITCs and $40,000 of other general business credits. His net income tax is $150,000, tentative minimum tax is $130,000, and net regular tax liability is $150,000. He has no other tax credits. The computation of T's general business credit allowed for the tax year is computed as follows:

Net income tax	$150,000
Less: The greater of	
• $130,000 (tentative minimum tax)	
• $31,250 [25% × ($150,000 − $25,000)]	130,000
Amount of general business credit allowed for tax year	$ 20,000

T then has $50,000 ($70,000 − $20,000) of unused general business credits. □

Treatment of Unused General Business Credits

Unused credits are initially carried back three years (to the earliest year in the sequence) and are applied to reduce tax during these years. Thus, the taxpayer may receive a

---

9. This amount is $12,500 for married taxpayers filing separately unless one of the spouses is not entitled to the general business credit.

refund of tax from the benefits of such carryback. Any remaining unused credits are then carried forward 15 years. A FIFO method is applied to the carryovers, carrybacks, and utilization of credits earned during a particular year. The oldest credits are used first in determining the amount of the general business credit.

The FIFO method minimizes the potential for loss of a general business credit benefit because of the expiration of credit carryovers, since the earliest years are used before the current credit for the taxable year.

EXAMPLE 28   This example illustrates the use of general business credit carryovers.

• General business credit carryovers		
1987	$ 4,000	
1988	6,000	
1989	2,000	
Total carryovers	$12,000	
• 1990 general business credit		$ 40,000
• Total credit allowed in 1990 (based on tax liability)	$50,000	
Less: Utilization of carryovers		
1987	(4,000)	
1988	(6,000)	
1989	(2,000)	
• Remaining credit allowed	$38,000	
Applied against		
1990 general business credit		(38,000)
1990 unused amount carried forward to 1991		$ 2,000

CONCEPT SUMMARY 11–1

Tax Credits

Credit	Computation	Comments
Tax withheld on wages (§ 31)	Amount is reported to employee on W–2 form.	Refundable credit.
Earned income (§ 32)	Amount is determined by reference to Earned Income Credit Table published by IRS. Computations underlying amounts in Earned Income Credit Table are illustrated in Example 17. $953.40 maximum credit in 1990.	Refundable credit. A form of negative income tax to assist low-income taxpayers. Earned income and AGI must be less than $20,264 in 1990. Child (must be dependent in most cases) must live with taxpayer.
Child and dependent care (§ 21)	Rate ranges from 20% to 30% depending on AGI. Maximum base for credit is $2,400 for one qualifying individual, $4,800 for two or more.	Nonrefundable personal credit. No carryback or carryforward. Benefits taxpayers who incur employment-related child or dependent care expenses in order to work or seek employment. Eligible dependents include children under age 13 or dependent (any age) or spouse who is physically or mentally incapacitated.

Credit	Computation	Comments
Elderly and disabled (§ 22)	15% of sum of base amount minus reductions for (a) Social Security and other nontaxable benefits and (b) excess AGI. Base amount is fixed by law (e.g., $5,000 for a single taxpayer).	Nonrefundable personal credit. No carryback or carryforward. Provides relief for taxpayers not receiving substantial tax-free retirement benefits.
Mortgage certificate (§ 25)	Specified certificate rate (from 10% to 50%) times qualified interest paid. Limited to $2,000 if credit rate exceeds 20%.	Nonrefundable personal credit. Unused credits may be carried forward three years. Provides tax break for qualified first-time home buyers.
Foreign tax (§ 27)	Foreign income/total worldwide taxable income × U.S. tax = overall limitation. Lesser of foreign taxes imposed or overall limitation.	Nonrefundable credit. Unused credits may be carried back two years and forward five years. Purpose is to prevent double taxation on foreign income.
General business (§ 38)	May not exceed net income tax minus the greater of tentative minimum tax or 25% of net regular tax liability that exceeds $25,000.	Nonrefundable credit. Components include investment tax credit, jobs credit, alcohol fuels credit, research activities credit, and low-income housing credit. Unused credit may be carried back 3 years and forward 15 years. FIFO method applies to carryovers, carrybacks, and credits earned during current year.
Investment (§ 46)	Qualifying investment times regular percentage, energy percentage, or rehabilitation percentage, depending on type of property. Part of general business credit and subject to limitations thereon.	Nonrefundable credit. Part of general business credit and therefore subject to same carryback, carryover, and FIFO rules. Regular percentage applies to transition property. Energy percentages range from 10% to 15%. Regular rehabilitation rate is 10%; rate for certified historic structures is 20%.
Jobs credit (§ 51)	Regular credit is 40% of first $6,000 of wages paid to each eligible employee. Qualified summer youth employee (QSYE) credit is 40% of first $3,000 of wages paid to QSYE. Eligible employees must begin work before October 1, 1990.	Nonrefundable credit. Part of general business credit and therefore subject to same carryback, carryover, and FIFO rules. Purpose is to encourage employment of specified groups. QSYE generally must be age 16 or 17 on hiring date.
Research activities (§ 41)	Incremental credit is 20% of excess of computation year expenditures minus the base amount. Basic research credit is allowed to certain corporations for 20% of cash payments to qualified organizations that exceed a specially calculated base amount.	Nonrefundable credit. Part of general business credit and therefore subject to same carryback, carryover, and FIFO rules. Purpose is to encourage high-tech research in the United States.
Low-income housing (§ 42)	Appropriate rate times eligible basis (portion of project attributable to low-income units).	Nonrefundable credit. Part of general business credit and therefore subject to same carryback, carryover, and FIFO rules. Credit is available each year for 10 years. Recapture may apply.

TAX PLANNING CONSIDERATIONS

Foreign Tax Credit

A U.S. citizen or resident working abroad (commonly referred to as an *expatriate*) may elect to claim either a foreign tax credit or the foreign earned income exclusion. In cases where the income tax of a foreign country is higher than the U.S. income tax, the credit choice usually is preferable. If, however, the reverse is true, election of the foreign earned income exclusion probably reduces the overall tax burden.

Unfortunately, the choice between the credit and the earned income exclusion is not without some limitations. The election of the foreign earned income exclusion, once made, can be revoked for a later year. However, once revoked, the earned income exclusion will not be available for a period of five years unless the IRS consents to an earlier date. This will create a dilemma for expatriates whose job assignments over several years shift between low and high bracket countries.

EXAMPLE 29   In 1989, T, a calendar year taxpayer, is sent by his employer to Saudi Arabia (a low-tax country). For 1989, therefore, T elects the foreign earned income exclusion. In 1990, T's employer transfers him to France (a high-tax country). Accordingly, T revokes the foreign earned income exclusion for 1990 and chooses instead to use the foreign income tax credit. If T is transferred back to Saudi Arabia (or any other low-tax country) within five years, he no longer has access to the foreign earned income exclusion.   □

Credit for Child and Dependent Care Expenses

A taxpayer might incur employment-related expenses that also qualify as medical expenses (e.g., a nurse is hired to provide in-the-home care for an ill and incapacitated dependent parent). Such expenses may be either deducted as medical expenses (subject to the 7.5 percent limitation) or utilized in determining the child and dependent care credit. If the choice is to take the dependent care credit and the employment-related expenses exceed the limitation ($2,400, $4,800, or earned income, as the case may be), the excess may be considered a medical expense. If, however, the choice is made to deduct such qualified employment-related expenses as medical expenses, any portion that is not deductible because of the 7.5 percent limitation may not be used in computing the child and dependent care credit.

EXAMPLE 30   T, a single individual, has the following tax position for tax year 1990:

Adjusted gross income		$30,000
Itemized deductions *from* adjusted gross income—		
Other than medical expenses	$2,500	
Medical expenses	6,000	$ 8,500

All of T's medical expenses were incurred to provide nursing care for her disabled father while she was working. The father lives with T and qualifies as T's dependent. □

What should T do in this situation? One approach would be to use $2,400 of the nursing care expenses to obtain the maximum dependent care credit allowed of $480 (20% × $2,400). The balance of these expenses should be claimed as medical expenses. After a reduction of 7.5 percent of adjusted gross income, this would produce a medical expense deduction of $1,350 [$3,600 (remaining medical expenses) − (7.5% × $30,000)].

Another approach would be to claim the full $6,000 as a medical expense and forgo the dependent care credit. After the 7.5 percent adjustment of $2,250 (7.5% × $30,000), a deduction of $3,750 remains.

The choice, then, is between a credit of $480 plus a deduction of $1,350 and a credit of $0 plus a deduction of $3,750. Which is better, of course, depends upon the relative tax savings involved.

PROBLEM MATERIALS

Discussion Questions

1. If investment tax credit property is prematurely disposed of or ceases to be qualified property, how is the tax liability affected in the year of the disposition?

2. The regular investment tax credit was repealed for property placed in service after December 31, 1985. Is there any way a taxpayer can benefit from unused ITC related to investment tax credit property placed in service on or before that date? Explain.

3. V is considering the purchase and renovation of an old building. He has heard about the tax credit for rehabilitation expenditures but does not know the specific rules applicable to the credit. He has asked you to explain the most important details to him. What will you tell V?

4. On August 1, 1990, Z hired C, who is certified as a member of a targeted group for purposes of the jobs credit. C was paid $900 per month. He worked for eight months. How much is Z's jobs credit for wages paid to C during 1990? For 1991?

5. The research activities credit has two components: the incremental research credit and the basic research credit. What types of expenditures are eligible for the incremental research credit? What types of expenditures are eligible for the basic research credit?

6. For purposes of determining the incremental research activities tax credit, the base period for determining the fixed-base percentage is not the same as the base period for determining average annual gross receipts. Explain.

7. Which of the following taxpayers are eligible for the earned income credit for the tax year 1990?
   a. H and W are married and have a dependent child. H earned $7,600 and W earned $7,000.
   b. A, who is divorced from B, maintains a household for her son J. Under a pre-1985 divorce agreement, J is claimed as a dependent by B, his father, who contributes $2,000 toward his support. A earns $14,000 and has no other income.

c. P, an unmarried taxpayer, earns $12,000 and has no other income. He claims a dependency exemption for his aunt under a multiple support agreement.

8. Individuals who receive substantial Social Security benefits are usually not eligible for the tax credit for the elderly because these benefits effectively eliminate the base upon which the credit is computed. Explain.

9. What purpose is served by the overall limitation to the foreign tax credit?

10. Do all foreign taxes qualify for the U.S. foreign tax credit? Explain.

11. T was divorced in 1987 and was awarded custody of her 6-year-old son. During 1990, T and her current husband file a joint return in which they waive the dependency exemption in favor of the natural father and ex-husband. Under these circumstances, can T claim the child care credit for the expenses she paid for her son's care while she works? Explain.

12. T is not concerned with the child and dependent care credit because his adjusted gross income is considerably in excess of $20,000. Is T under a misconception regarding the tax law? Explain.

13. Some employers sponsor a child care assistance program. If an unmarried taxpayer pays $6,000 for the care of one child under the age of 13 and receives $4,000 in reimbursement from a qualified program, how is the child care credit affected? What if the $6,000 covers the care of three children under age 13?

14. J and K are married and have a dependent child eight years of age. J earned $15,000 during 1990. K, a full-time student for the entire year, was not employed. J and K believe they are not entitled to the credit for child and dependent care because K was not employed. Is this correct? Explain your answer.

15. Discuss the underlying rationale for the enactment of the following tax credits:
   a. Low-income housing credit.
   b. Foreign tax credit.
   c. Tax credit for the elderly or disabled.
   d. Earned income credit.
   e. Credit for child and dependent care expenses.
   f. Jobs credit.

16. What is a refundable credit? Give examples. What is a nonrefundable credit? Give examples.

17. In determining the maximum amount of general business credit allowed an individual taxpayer for a tax year, net income tax, tentative minimum tax, and net regular tax liability are important concepts.
   a. Define each term.
   b. Using these terms, state the general business credit limitation for an individual taxpayer for 1990.

18. The FIFO method is applied to general business credit carryovers, carrybacks, and the utilization of credits generated during a particular year. What effect does the FIFO method have on the utilization of general business credit carryovers?

19. Discuss the order in which credits are offset against the tax liability. Why is the order in which credits are utilized important?

Problems

20. M, a calendar year taxpayer, entered into a written contract, binding on December 31, 1985, to purchase new industrial equipment. This property cost $150,000 and

had a class life of 22 years. Compute M's tentative regular investment tax credit and determine the basis of the equipment for purposes of cost recovery if the equipment is placed in service:

a. In 1986.

b. In 1987.

c. In 1989.

21. B claimed the investment tax credit on the following property acquired in December 1985:

Asset	Recovery Period	Cost
Truck	3 years	$20,000
Machinery	5 years	80,000

a. Compute B's maximum tentative investment tax credit for 1985.

b. Assume B sells both assets in 1990 after holding them for four full years. What is the amount of investment tax credit B must recapture in 1990?

22. T acquired an office building that had originally been placed in service in 1930. The building cost $50,000, and T spent $60,000 to rehabilitate it. The building was placed in service on July 1, 1990. Compute T's credit for rehabilitation expenditures, basis in the building, and cost recovery allowance for 1990.

23. Z Corporation acquired an office building for $100,000 in 1990. The building originally had been placed in service in 1930. Z spent $50,000 for qualified rehabilitation expenditures. Compute Z's rehabilitation credit for the year.

24. On August 1, 1984, R acquired and placed in service a pre-1936 office building. The cost was $250,000, of which $50,000 applied to the land. The building is 18-year real property. In order to keep tenants, R spent $140,000 renovating the building in 1990. The expenses were of the type that qualify for the rehabilitation credit. These improvements were placed in service on May 1.

a. Compute R's rehabilitation tax credit for 1990.

b. Determine cost recovery for the year.

c. What is R's basis in the property at the end of 1990?

25. X Company hired six handicapped individuals (qualifying X Company for the jobs credit) in March 1990. Each of these individuals received wages of $7,000 during 1990.

a. Calculate the amount of the jobs credit for 1990.

b. Assume X Company paid total wages of $120,000 to its employees during the year. How much of this amount is deductible in 1990 if the jobs credit is elected?

26. On May 15, 1990, Y Corporation hired four individuals (A, B, C, and D), all of whom qualified Y Corporation for the jobs credit. A and B also were certified as qualified summer youth employees. D moved out of state in September, quitting his job after earning $4,000 in wages. A, B, and C all continued as employees of Y Corporation. During 1990 C earned $6,500. A and B each earned $3,500 during their first 90 days of employment. Beginning on August 15, A and B were certified for participation in the company's cooperative education program. In this capacity, A earned $2,000 to December 31 and $2,500 to the end of school on May 15, 1991. B also earned an additional $2,000 to December 31, at which time he quit school and left the program. Compute Y Corporation's jobs credit, without regard to the tax liability ceiling limitation, for 1990. Also compute Y's deduction for wages paid to A, B, C, and D during 1990. Will Y receive any benefit in 1991?

27. In July 1990, X Corporation hired two handicapped workers who qualify as targeted employees for purposes of the jobs credit. Each employee was paid $10,000 in 1990. Compute X's allowable jobs credit for 1990 with respect to these two employees.

28. Which of the following individuals qualify for the earned income credit for 1990?
    a. T is single and has no dependents. His income consisted of $7,000 wages and taxable interest of $1,000.
    b. T maintains a household for a dependent unmarried child and is eligible for head-of-household tax rates. Her income consisted of $10,000 salary and $800 taxable interest.
    c. T is married and files a joint return with his wife. T and his wife have no dependents. Their combined income consisted of $8,000 salary and $600 taxable interest. Adjusted gross income is $8,600.

29. T, a widower, lives in an apartment with his three minor children whom he supports. T earned $17,100 during 1990. He contributed $1,000 to an IRA and uses the standard deduction. Calculate the amount, if any, of T's earned income credit.

30. H, age 67, and W, age 66, are married retirees who received the following income and retirement benefits during 1990:

Fully taxable pension from H's former employer	$ 8,000
Dividends and interest	2,500
Social Security benefits	4,000
	$14,500

    Assume H and W file a joint return and have no deductions *for* adjusted gross income and do not itemize. Are they eligible for the tax credit for the elderly? If so, calculate the amount of the credit, assuming the credit is not limited by their tax liability.

31. H, age 67, and W, age 66, are married retirees who received the following income and retirement benefits during 1990:

Fully taxable pension from H's former employer	$ 5,000
Dividends and interest	8,000
Social Security benefits	1,750
	$14,750

    Assume H and W file a joint return, have no deductions *for* adjusted gross income, and do not itemize. Are they eligible for the tax credit for the elderly? If so, calculate the amount of the credit assuming their actual tax liability (before credits) is $323.

32. T, a U.S. citizen and resident, owns and operates a novelty goods business. During 1990, T has taxable income of $200,000, made up as follows: $50,000 from foreign sources and $150,000 from U.S. sources. The income from foreign sources is subject to foreign income taxes of $26,000. For 1990, T files a joint return claiming his three children as dependents. Assuming, T chooses to claim the foreign taxes as an income tax credit, what is his income tax liability for 1990?

33. Q Corporation, a U.S. corporation, is a manufacturing concern that sells most of its products in the United States. It does, however, do some business in Europe through various branches. During 1990, Q Corporation has taxable income of $500,000, of which $400,000 is U.S.-sourced and $100,000 is foreign-sourced. Foreign income taxes paid are $20,000. Q Corporation's U.S. income tax liability before any foreign tax credit is $170,000. What is Q Corporation's U.S. income tax net of the allowable foreign tax credit?

34. H and W are husband and wife, and both are gainfully employed. They have three children under the age of 13. During 1990, H earned $25,000, while W earned $30,000. In order for them to work, they paid $5,800 to various unrelated parties to care for their children. Assuming H and W file a joint return, what, if any, is their child and dependent care credit for 1990?

35. R and T are husband and wife and have two dependent children under the age of 13. Both R and T are gainfully employed and during 1990 earned salaries as follows: $12,000 (R) and $10,000 (T). To care for their children while they work, R and T pay M (R's mother) $3,600. M does not qualify as the dependent of R and T. Assuming R and T file a joint return, what, if any, is their child and dependent care credit?

36. K and J are husband and wife and have one dependent child, age 9. K is a full-time student for all of 1990, while J earns $18,000 as a nurse's aid. In order to provide care for their child while K attends classes and J is working, they pay S (J's 17-year-old sister) $2,300. S is not the dependent of K and J. Assuming K and J file a joint return, what, if any, is their child and dependent care credit?

37. F spent $500,000 to build a qualified low-income housing project in January 1990 when the credit rate was 8.89%. He financed the project partly from savings and partly from funds borrowed from First National Bank. All units are rented to families that qualify on the basis of income. Compute F's low-income housing credit for all relevant years.

38. B has a tentative general business credit of $110,000 for 1990. B's net regular tax liability before the general business credit is $125,000; tentative minimum tax is $100,000. Compute B's allowable general business credit for 1990.

Cumulative Problems

39. H and W, ages 38 and 36, are married and file a joint return. Their household includes S, their 10-year-old son, and F, who is H's 76-year-old father. F is very ill and has been confined to bed for most of the year. He has no income of his own and is fully supported by H and W. H and W had the following income and expenses during 1990:

H's wages	$ 9,800
W's salary	17,200
Interest from First National Bank	250
Unemployment compensation received by H, who was laid off for five months during the year	4,000
Dividends received on January 3, 1991; the corporation mailed the check on December 31, 1990	250
Amounts paid to N, H's niece, for household help and caring for S and F while H and W were working	3,000
Unreimbursed travel expenses (including meals of $200) incurred by W in connection with her job	750
Total itemized deductions (not including any potential deductions mentioned elsewhere in the problem)	4,600
Federal income taxes withheld by their employers	2,300

Compute net tax payable or refund due for H and W for 1990. Suggested software (if available): *WEST–TAX Planner.*

40. Ray Jones (Social Security number 265–33–1982) lives at 960 Elm Street, Franklin, KY 40601. He is the sole proprietor of Ray's Plumbing Repair, located at 1420 Main Street. Since Ray's business is confined to plumbing repairs, he maintains only a nominal amount of plumbing supplies.

Ray generally works alone. On occasion, however, his brother handles some calls. For this help, the brother is paid an agreed-upon rate per hour, and Ray withholds and matches FICA taxes.

Ray's widowed mother is disabled and lives with him. Ray provides all of her support and maintains the household in which they live. The mother qualifies as Ray's dependent. Because of the mother's disability, Ray pays various housekeepers $2,800 during the year to care for her while he works.

Ray's business records for 1990 reflect the following information:

Gross income from business	$28,900
Plumbing supplies	2,100
Rent paid on shop	5,100
Utilities paid on shop	2,200
Advertising	870
Depreciation	1,100
Salaries	10,100
Employer's share of FICA	773

Other transactions occurring during 1990 are summarized below:

- Medical expenses of Ray ($200) and his mother ($400). All of these expenses were paid by Ray, and none were covered by insurance.
- Real estate taxes on personal residence of $2,100.
- Interest on home mortgage of $3,700.
- Charitable contributions of $500.
- Dividends received from a Canadian corporation of $2,000. The checks Ray received total $1,700 after $300 of Canadian income tax was withheld at the source.

Based on his tax liability (including self-employment tax) for 1989, Ray made estimated tax payments of $1,100 during 1990.

Determine the amount of tax due (or refund) for 1990. Suggested software (if available): *TurboTax*, if tax return solutions are desired, WEST-TAX Planner, if tax return solutions are not desired.

41. James R. Jordan lives at 2322 Branch Road, Mesa, AZ 85202. He is a tax accountant with Mesa Manufacturing Company. He also writes computer software programs for tax practitioners and has a part-time tax practice. James, age 35, is single and has no dependents. His Social Security number is 111–35–2222. He wants to contribute one dollar to the Presidential Election Campaign Fund.

During 1989, James earned a salary of $45,680 from his employer. He received interest of $890 from Home Federal Savings and Loan and $435 from Home State Bank. He received dividends of $620 from Acme Corporation, $470 from Jason Corporation, and $360 from General Corporation.

James received a $1,600 income tax refund from the state of Arizona on May 12, 1989. On his 1988 Federal income tax return, he reported total itemized deductions of $6,700, which included $2,000 of state income tax withheld by his employer.

Fees earned from his part-time tax practice in 1989 totaled $4,200. He paid $500 to have the tax returns processed by a computerized tax return service.

On February 1, 1989, James bought 500 shares of Acme Corporation common stock for $17.60 a share. On July 16, James sold the stock for $15 a share.

James bought a used pickup truck for $3,000 on June 5, 1989. He purchased the truck from his brother-in-law, who was unemployed and was in need of cash. On November 2, 1989, he sold the truck to a friend for $3,400.

On January 2, 1980, James acquired 100 shares of Jason Corporation common stock for $30 a share. He sold the stock on December 19, 1989, for $75 a share.

During 1989, James received royalties of $15,000 on a software program he had written. James incurred the following expenditures in connection with his software writing activities:

Cost of microcomputer (100% business use)	$8,000
Cost of printer (100% business use)	2,000
Supplies	650
Fee paid to computer consultant	3,500

James elected to expense the maximum portion of the cost of the microcomputer and printer allowed under the provisions of § 179.

Although his employer suggested that James attend a convention on current developments in corporate taxation, James was not reimbursed for the travel expenses of $1,360 he incurred in attending the convention. The $1,360 included $200 for the cost of meals.

During 1989, James paid $300 for prescription medicines and $2,875 in doctor bills, hospital bills, and medical insurance premiums. His employer withheld state income tax of $1,954. James paid real property taxes of $1,766 on his home. Interest on his home mortgage was $3,845, and interest to credit card companies was $320. James contributed $20 each week to his church and $10 each week to the United Way. Professional dues and subscriptions totaled $350.

James's employer withheld Federal income taxes of $9,500 during 1989. James paid estimated taxes of $1,600. What is the amount of James Jordan's net tax payable or refund due for 1989? If James has a tax refund due, he wants to have it credited toward his 1990 income tax. If you use tax forms for your solution, you will need Forms 1040, 2106, and 4562 and Schedules A, B, C, D, and SE. Suggested software (if available): *TurboTax* for tax return solutions, *WEST–TAX Planner* if tax return solutions are not desired.

12

PROPERTY TRANSACTIONS: DETERMINATION OF GAIN OR LOSS, BASIS CONSIDERATIONS, AND NONTAXABLE EXCHANGES

OBJECTIVES

Explain the computation of realized gain or loss on property dispositions.

Define the terms "amount realized" and "adjusted basis."

Distinguish between realized and recognized gain or loss.

Discuss the recovery of capital doctrine.

Explain how basis is determined for various methods of asset acquisition.

Present various loss disallowance provisions.

Describe provisions for postponement or exclusion of gain on the sale of a personal residence.

Discuss the rationale for nonrecognition (postponement) of gain in certain property transactions.

Identify the different types of nontaxable exchanges.

Examine the nonrecognition provisions available on the involuntary conversion of property and like-kind exchanges.

Identify tax planning opportunities related to selected property transactions and the nonrecognition provisions discussed in the chapter.

12–1

This chapter and the following chapter are concerned with the income tax consequences of property transactions (the sale or other disposition of property). The following questions are to be considered with respect to the sale or other disposition of property:

- Is there a realized gain or loss?
- If so, is the gain or loss recognized?
- If the gain or loss is recognized, is it ordinary or capital?
- What is the basis of replacement property, if any, that is acquired?

This chapter is concerned with the determination of realized and recognized gain or loss and the basis of property. Chapter 13 covers the classification of the recognized gain or loss as ordinary or capital.

DETERMINATION OF GAIN OR LOSS

Realized Gain or Loss

Realized gain or loss is measured by the difference between the amount realized from the sale or other disposition of property and the property's adjusted basis on the date of disposition. If the amount realized exceeds the property's adjusted basis, the result is a *realized gain*. Conversely, if the property's adjusted basis exceeds the amount realized, the result is a *realized loss*.

EXAMPLE 1   T sells X Corporation stock with an adjusted basis of $3,000 for $5,000. T's realized gain is $2,000. If T had sold the stock for $2,000, he would have had a $1,000 realized loss.   □

Sale or Other Disposition.   The term *sale or other disposition* is defined broadly in the tax law and includes virtually any disposition of property. Thus, transactions such as trade-ins, casualties, condemnations, thefts, and bond retirements are treated as dispositions of property. The most common disposition of property arises from a sale or exchange. The key factor in determining whether a disposition has taken place usually is whether an identifiable event has occurred[1] as opposed to a mere fluctuation in the value of the property.

EXAMPLE 2   T owns X Corporation stock that cost $3,000. The stock has appreciated in value by $2,000 since T purchased it. T has no realized gain, since mere fluctuation in value is not a disposition or identifiable event for tax purposes. Nor would T have a realized loss had the stock declined in value by $2,000.   □

Amount Realized.   The *amount realized* from a sale or other disposition of property is the sum of any money received plus the fair market value of other property received. The amount realized also includes amounts representing real property taxes treated as imposed on the seller if such amounts are to be paid by the buyer (refer to chapter 10). The reason for including these taxes in the amount

---

1.   Reg. § 1.1001–1(c)(1).

realized is that their payment by the purchaser is, in effect, an additional amount paid to the seller of the property.

The amount realized also includes any liability on the property disposed of, such as a mortgage debt, if the buyer assumes the mortgage or the property is sold subject to the mortgage.[2] The amount of such liability is included in the amount realized even if the debt is nonrecourse and the amount of the debt is greater than the fair market value of the mortgaged property.[3]

EXAMPLE 3   T sells property on which there is a mortgage of $20,000 to U for $50,000 cash. T's amount realized from the sale is $70,000 if the mortgage is assumed by U or if U takes the property subject to the mortgage. □

The *fair market value* of property received in a sale or other disposition has been defined by the courts as the price at which property will change hands between a willing seller and a willing buyer when neither is compelled to sell or buy.[4] Fair market value is determined by considering the relevant factors in each case. An expert appraiser is often required to evaluate these factors in arriving at fair market value. When the fair market value of the property received cannot be determined, the value of the property surrendered may be used.[5]

In calculating the amount realized, selling expenses such as advertising, commissions, and legal fees relating to the disposition are deducted. The amount realized is the net amount received directly or indirectly by the taxpayer from the disposition of property regardless of whether it is in the form of cash.

Adjusted Basis.   The *adjusted basis* of property disposed of is the property's original basis adjusted to the date of disposition. Original basis is the cost or other basis of the property on the date the property is acquired by the taxpayer. *Capital additions* increase and *recoveries of capital* decrease the original basis so that on the date of disposition the adjusted basis reflects the unrecovered cost or other basis of the property. Adjusted basis is determined as follows:

Cost (or other adjusted basis) on date of acquisition
+ Capital additions
− Capital recoveries
= Adjusted basis on date of disposition

Capital Additions.   Capital additions include the cost of capital improvements and betterments made to the property by the taxpayer. These expenditures are distinguishable from expenditures for the ordinary repair and maintenance of the property that are neither capitalized nor added to the original basis (refer to chapter 5). The latter expenditures are deductible in the current taxable year if they are related to business or income-producing property. Amounts representing real property taxes treated as imposed on the seller but paid or assumed by the buyer are part of the cost of the property. Any liability on property that is assumed by the

---

2. *Crane v. Comm.*, 47–1 USTC ¶9217, 35 AFTR 776, 67 S.Ct. 1047 (USSC, 1947). Although a legal distinction exists between the direct assumption of a mortgage and taking property subject to a mortgage, the tax consequences in calculating the amount realized are the same.

3. *Tufts v. Comm.*, 83–1 USTC ¶9328, 51 AFTR2d

83–1132, 103 S.Ct. 1826 (USSC, 1983).

4. *Comm. v. Marshman*, 60–2 USTC ¶9484, 5 AFTR2d 1528, 279 F.2d 27 (CA–6, 1960).

5. *U.S. v. Davis*, 62–2 USTC ¶9509, 9 AFTR2d 1625, 82 S.Ct. 1190 (USSC, 1962).

buyer is also included in the buyer's original basis of the property. The same rule applies if property is acquired subject to a liability. Amortization of the discount on bonds increases the adjusted basis of the bonds.

Capital Recoveries.   The following are examples of capital recoveries:

1. *Depreciation and Cost Recovery Allowances.* The original basis of depreciable property is reduced by the annual depreciation charges (or cost recovery allowances) while the property is held by the taxpayer. The amount of depreciation that is subtracted from the original basis is the greater of the *allowed* or *allowable* depreciation on an annual basis. In most circumstances, the allowed and allowable depreciation amounts are the same (refer to chapter 8).

2. *Investment Tax Credit.* For property placed in service after 1982 and before 1986, the taxpayer may be required to reduce the adjusted basis of the property by 50 percent of the available investment tax credit. Such reduction in the adjusted basis of the property is required unless the taxpayer has elected to take a reduced investment tax credit (refer to chapters 8 and 11).

3. *Casualties and Thefts.* A casualty or theft may result in the reduction of the adjusted basis of property. The adjusted basis is reduced by the amount of the deductible loss. In addition, the adjusted basis is reduced by the amount of insurance proceeds received. However, the receipt of insurance proceeds may result in a recognized gain rather than in a deductible loss. Such gain increases the adjusted basis of the property.

EXAMPLE 4

An insured truck used in a trade or business is destroyed in an accident. The adjusted basis is $8,000, and the fair market value is $6,500. Insurance proceeds of $6,500 are received. The amount of the casualty loss is $1,500 ($6,500 insurance proceeds − $8,000 adjusted basis). The adjusted basis is reduced by the $1,500 casualty loss and the $6,500 of insurance proceeds received.   □

EXAMPLE 5

An insured truck used in a trade or business is destroyed in an accident. The adjusted basis is $6,500, and the fair market value is $8,000. Insurance proceeds of $8,000 are received. The amount of the casualty gain is $1,500 ($8,000 insurance proceeds − $6,500 adjusted basis). The adjusted basis is increased by the $1,500 casualty gain and is reduced by the $8,000 of insurance proceeds received ($6,500 basis before casualty + $1,500 casualty gain − $8,000 insurance proceeds = $0 basis).   □

4. *Certain Corporate Distributions.* A corporate distribution to a shareholder that is not taxable is treated as a return of capital, and it reduces the basis of the shareholder's stock in the corporation.[6] For example, if a corporation makes a cash distribution to its shareholders and has no earnings and profits, such distributions are treated as a return of capital. If the corporation does have earnings and profits but makes a distribution in excess of such earnings and profits, the excess distribution is treated as a return of capital. Once the basis

---

6. § 1016(a)(4) and Reg. § 1.1016–5(a). See chapter 17 for further discussion of corporate distributions.

of the stock is reduced to zero, the amount of any subsequent distributions is a capital gain if the stock is a capital asset.

EXAMPLE 6

U Corporation has accumulated earnings and profits of $140,000 at the beginning of 1990. For 1990, U Corporation generates current earnings and profits of $30,000. During 1990, U Corporation makes cash distributions to its only shareholder, T, in the amount of $200,000. T's basis for his U Corporation stock is $20,000. Of the $200,000 cash distributed to T, $170,000 is classified as dividend income (to the extent of current earnings and profits of $30,000 and beginning accumulated earnings and profits of $140,000). The next $20,000 is treated as a return of capital and reduces T's basis for his U Corporation stock to zero. The remaining $10,000 is a capital gain. ☐

5. *Amortizable Bond Premium.* The basis in a bond purchased at a premium is reduced by the amortizable portion of the bond premium. Investors in taxable bonds may *elect* to amortize the bond premium, but the premium on tax-exempt bonds *must be* amortized. The amount of the amortized premium on taxable bonds is permitted as an interest deduction. Therefore, the election produces the opportunity for an annual interest deduction to offset ordinary income in exchange for a larger capital gain or smaller capital loss on the disposition of the bond. No such interest deduction is permitted for tax-exempt bonds.

The amortization deduction is allowed for taxable bonds because the premium is viewed as a cost of earning the taxable interest from the bonds. The reason the basis of taxable bonds is reduced is that the amortization deduction is a recovery of the cost or basis of the bonds. The basis of tax-exempt bonds is reduced even though the amortization is not allowed as a deduction. No amortization deduction is permitted on tax-exempt bonds, since the interest income is exempt from tax and the amortization of the bond premium merely represents an adjustment of the effective amount of such income.

EXAMPLE 7

T purchases S Corporation taxable bonds with a face value of $100,000 for $110,000, thus paying a premium of $10,000. The annual interest rate is 7%, and the bonds mature 10 years from the date of purchase. The annual interest income is $7,000 (7% × $100,000). If T elects to amortize the bond premium, the $10,000 premium is deducted over the 10-year period. T's basis for the bonds is reduced each year by the amount of the amortization deduction. Note that if the bonds were tax-exempt, amortization of the bond premium and the basis adjustment would be mandatory. However, no deduction would be allowed for the amortization. ☐

Recognized Gain or Loss

Recognized gain is the amount of the realized gain included in the taxpayer's gross income. A *recognized loss*, on the other hand, is the amount of a realized loss that is deductible for tax purposes. As a general rule, the entire amount of a realized gain or loss is recognized.

Concept Summary 12–1 summarizes the realized gain or loss and recognized gain or loss concepts.

CONCEPT SUMMARY 12–1

Recognized Gain or Loss

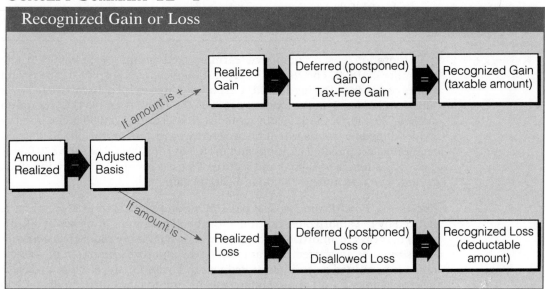

Nonrecognition of Gain or Loss

In certain cases, a realized gain or loss is not recognized upon the sale or other disposition of property. One of the exceptions to the recognition of gain or loss involves nontaxable exchanges, which are covered later in this chapter. Additional exceptions include losses realized upon the sale, exchange, or condemnation of personal use assets (as opposed to business or income-producing property) and gains realized upon the sale of a residence by taxpayers 55 years of age or older (discussed later in this chapter). In addition, realized losses from the sale or exchange of business or income-producing property between certain related parties are not recognized.

Sale, Exchange, or Condemnation of Personal Use Assets.   A realized loss from the sale, exchange, or condemnation of personal use assets (e.g., a personal residence or an automobile not used at all for business or income-producing purposes) is not recognized for tax purposes. An exception exists for casualty or theft losses from personal use assets (see chapter 7). In contrast, any gain realized from the sale or other disposition of personal use assets is, generally, fully taxable. The following examples illustrate the tax consequences of the sale of personal use assets.

EXAMPLE 8   T sells an automobile, which is held exclusively for personal use, for $6,000. The adjusted basis of the automobile is $5,000. T has a realized and recognized gain of $1,000. □

EXAMPLE 9   T sells the automobile in Example 8 for $4,000. T has a realized loss of $1,000, but the loss is not recognized. □

Recovery of Capital Doctrine

Doctrine Defined.   The *recovery of capital doctrine* pervades all the tax rules relating to property transactions and is very significant with respect to these

transactions. The doctrine derives its roots from the very essence of the income tax—a tax on income. Therefore, as a general rule, a taxpayer is entitled to recover the cost or other original basis of property acquired and is not taxed on that amount.

The cost or other original basis of depreciable property is recovered through annual depreciation deductions. The basis is reduced as the cost is recovered over the period the property is held. Therefore, when property is sold or otherwise disposed of, it is the adjusted basis (unrecovered cost or other basis) that is compared to the amount realized from the disposition to determine realized gain or loss.

Relationship of the Recovery of Capital Doctrine to the Concepts of Realization and Recognition. If a sale or other disposition results in a realized gain, the taxpayer has recovered more than the adjusted basis of the property. Conversely, if a sale or other disposition results in a realized loss, the taxpayer has recovered less than the adjusted basis.

The general rules for the relationship between the recovery of capital doctrine and the realized and recognized gain and loss concepts are summarized as follows:

Rule 1. A realized gain that is *never recognized* results in the *permanent recovery* of more than the taxpayer's cost or other basis for tax purposes. For example, all or a portion of the realized gain on the sale of a personal residence by taxpayers 55 years of age or older can be excluded from gross income under § 121.

Rule 2. A realized gain on which *recognition is postponed* results in the *temporary recovery* of more than the taxpayer's cost or other basis for tax purposes. For example, an exchange of like-kind property under § 1031, an involuntary conversion under § 1033, or a replacement of a personal residence under § 1034 are all eligible for postponement treatment.

Rule 3. A realized loss that is *never recognized* results in the *permanent recovery* of less than the taxpayer's cost or other basis for tax purposes. For example, a loss on the sale of an automobile held for personal use is not deductible.

Rule 4. A realized loss on which *recognition is postponed* results in the *temporary recovery* of less than the taxpayer's cost or other basis for tax purposes. For example, the realized loss on the exchange of like-kind property under § 1031 is postponed.

These rules are illustrated in discussions to follow in this chapter.

BASIS CONSIDERATIONS

Determination of Cost Basis

The basis of property is generally the property's cost. Cost is the amount paid for the property in cash or other property. This general rule follows logically from the recovery of capital doctrine; that is, the cost or other basis of property is to be recovered tax-free by the taxpayer.

A *bargain purchase* of property is an exception to the general rule for determining basis. A bargain purchase may result when an employer transfers property to an employee at less than the property's fair market value (as compensation for services) or when a corporation transfers property to a shareholder at less than the property's fair market value (a dividend). The basis of property acquired in a bargain purchase is the property's fair market value. If the basis of the property were not increased by the bargain amount, the taxpayer would be taxed on this amount again at disposition.

EXAMPLE 10   T buys a machine from her employer for $10,000 on December 30, 1990. The fair market value of the machine is $15,000. T must include the $5,000 difference between cost and the fair market value of the machine in gross income for the taxable year 1990. The bargain element represents additional compensation to T. T's basis for the machine is $15,000, the machine's fair market value. □

Identification Problems.   Cost identification problems are frequently encountered in securities transactions. For example, the Regulations require that the taxpayer adequately identify the particular stock that has been sold.[7] A problem arises when the taxpayer has purchased separate lots of stock on different dates or at different prices and cannot adequately identify the lot from which a particular sale takes place. In this case, the stock is presumed to come from the first lot or lots purchased (a FIFO presumption).[8] When securities are left in the custody of a broker, it may be necessary to provide specific instructions and receive written confirmation as to which securities are being sold.

EXAMPLE 11   T purchases 100 shares of Q Corporation stock on July 1, 1988, for $5,000 ($50 a share) and another 100 shares of the same stock on July 1, 1989, for $6,000 ($60 a share). She sells 50 shares of the stock on January 2, 1990. The cost of the stock sold, assuming T cannot adequately identify the shares, is $50 a share, or $2,500. This is the cost T will compare to the amount realized in determining the gain or loss from the sale. □

Allocation Problems.   When a taxpayer acquires multiple assets in a lump-sum purchase, it is necessary to allocate the total cost among the individual assets. Allocation is necessary because some of the assets acquired may be depreciable (e.g., buildings) and others not (e.g., land). In addition, only a portion of the assets acquired may be sold, or some of the assets may be capital or § 1231 assets that receive special tax treatment upon subsequent sale or other disposition. A lump-sum cost is allocated on the basis of the fair market values of the individual assets acquired.

EXAMPLE 12   T purchases a building and land for $800,000. Because of the depressed nature of the industry in which the seller was operating, T was able to negotiate a very favorable purchase price. Appraisals of the individual assets indicate that the fair market value of the building is $600,000 and that of the land is $400,000. T's basis for the building is $480,000 ($600,000/$1,000,000 × $800,000), and the basis for the land is $320,000 ($400,000/$1,000,000 × $800,000). □

If a business is purchased and *goodwill* is involved, a special allocation rule applies. Initially, the purchase price is assigned to the assets, excluding goodwill, to the extent of the total fair market value of the assets. This assigned amount is then allocated among these assets on the basis of the fair market value of the individual assets acquired. Goodwill is then assigned the residual amount of the purchase price. The resultant allocation is applicable to both the buyer and the seller.[9]

---

7. Reg. § 1.1012–1(c)(1).
8. *Kluger Associates, Inc.*, 69 T.C. 925 (1978).
9. § 1060.

EXAMPLE 13   T sells his business to P. T and P agree that the values of the individual assets are as follows:

Inventory	$ 50,000
Building	500,000
Land	200,000
Goodwill	150,000

Negotiations conducted by T and P result in a sales price of $1 million. The application of the residual method with respect to goodwill results in the following allocation of the $1 million purchase price:

Inventory	$ 50,000
Building	500,000
Land	200,000
Goodwill	250,000

The residual method requires that all of the excess of the purchase price over the fair market value of the assets ($1,000,000 − $900,000 = $100,000) be allocated to goodwill. Absent this requirement, the purchaser could allocate the excess pro rata to all of the assets, including goodwill, based on their respective fair market values. This would have resulted in only $166,667 [$150,000 + ($150,000 ÷ $900,000 × $100,000)] being assigned to goodwill. □

In the case of *nontaxable stock dividends*, the allocation depends upon whether the dividend is a common stock dividend on common stock or a preferred stock dividend on common stock. If the dividend is common on common, the cost of the original common shares is allocated to the total shares owned after the dividend. The holding period of the new shares includes the holding period of the old shares.

EXAMPLE 14   T owns 100 shares of R Corporation common stock for which he paid $1,100. He receives a 10% common stock dividend, giving him a new total of 110 shares. Before the stock dividend, T's basis was $11 per share ($1,100 divided by 100 shares). The basis of each share after the stock dividend is $10 ($1,100 divided by 110 shares). □

If the dividend is preferred stock on common, the cost of the original common shares is allocated between the common and preferred shares on the basis of their relative fair market values on the date of distribution.

EXAMPLE 15   S owns 100 shares of X Corporation common stock for which she paid $1,000. She receives a stock dividend of 50 shares of preferred stock on her common stock. The fair market values on the date of distribution of the preferred stock dividend are $30 a share for common stock and $40 a share for preferred stock.

Thus, the total fair market value is $3,000 ($30 × 100) for common stock and $2,000 ($40 × 50) for preferred stock. The basis of S's common stock after the dividend is $600, or $6 a share ($3,000/$5,000 × $1,000), and the basis of the preferred stock is $400, or $8 a share ($2,000/$5,000 × $1,000). □

Gift Basis

When a taxpayer receives property as a gift, there is no cost to the recipient. Thus, under the cost basis provision, the donee's basis would be zero. However, this would violate the statutory intent that gifts are not subject to the income tax. With a zero basis, a sale by the donee would result in all of the amount realized being treated as realized gain. Therefore, a basis is assigned to the property received depending on the following:

- The date of the gift.
- The basis of the property to the donor.
- The amount of the gift tax paid.
- The fair market value of the property.

Gifts Prior to 1921.   If property was acquired by gift before 1921, its basis for income tax purposes is its fair market value on the date of the gift.

Gift Basis Rules if No Gift Tax Is Paid.   Property received by gift can be referred to as *dual basis* property; that is, the basis for gain and the basis for loss might not be the same amount. The present basis rules for gifts of property can be described as follows:

- If the donee subsequently disposes of gift property in a transaction that results in a gain, the basis to the donee is the same as the donor's adjusted basis.[10] The donee's basis in this case is referred to as the *gain basis*. Therefore, a *realized gain* results if the amount realized from the disposition exceeds the donee's gain basis.

EXAMPLE 16   T purchased stock in 1989 for $10,000. He gave the stock to his son, S, in 1990, when the fair market value was $15,000. Assuming no gift tax was paid on the transfer and the property is subsequently sold by S for $15,000, S's basis would be $10,000, and S would have a realized gain of $5,000. □

- If the donee subsequently disposes of gift property in a transaction that results in a loss, the basis to the donee is the lower of the donor's adjusted basis or fair market value on the date of the gift. The donee's basis in this case is referred to as the *loss basis*. Therefore, a *realized loss results* if the amount realized from the disposition is less than the donee's loss basis.

EXAMPLE 17   T purchased stock in 1989 for $10,000. He gave the stock to his son, S, in 1990, when the fair market value was $7,000. S later sold the stock for $6,000. S's basis would be $7,000 (fair market value is less than donor's adjusted basis of $10,000), and the loss from the sale would be $1,000 ($6,000 amount realized − $7,000 basis). □

---

10. § 1015(a) and Reg. § 1.1015–1(a)(1). See Reg. § 1.1015–1(a)(3) for cases in which the facts necessary to determine the donor's adjusted ba- sis are unknown. Refer to Example 22 for the effect of depreciation deductions by the donee.

The amount of the loss basis will differ from the amount of the gain basis only if at the date of the gift the adjusted basis of the property exceeds the property's fair market value. Note that the loss basis rule prevents the donee from receiving a tax benefit from the decline in value while the donor held the property. Therefore, in Example 17, S had a loss of only $1,000 rather than a loss of $4,000. The $3,000 difference represents the decline in value while T held the property. It is perhaps ironic, however, that the gain basis rule may eventually result in the donee's being subject to income tax on the appreciation that occurs while the donor held the property, as illustrated in Example 16.

If the amount realized from sale or other disposition is between the basis for loss and the basis for gain, no gain or loss is realized.

EXAMPLE 18	Assume the same facts as in Example 17, except that S sold the stock for $8,000. The application of the gain basis rule produces a loss of $2,000 ($8,000 − $10,000). The application of the loss basis rule produces a gain of $1,000 ($8,000 − $7,000). Therefore, neither a gain nor a loss is recognized because the amount realized is between the gain basis and the loss basis. □

Adjustment for Gift Tax. If gift taxes are paid by the donor, the donee's gain basis may exceed the adjusted basis of the property to the donor. This will occur only if the fair market value of the property at the date of the gift is greater than the donor's adjusted basis (the property has appreciated in value). The portion of the gift tax paid that is related to the appreciation is added to the donor's basis in calculating the donee's gain basis for the property. In this circumstance, the formula for calculating the donee's gain basis is as follows:

$$\text{Donee's gain basis} = \text{Donor's adjusted basis} + \left(\frac{\text{Unrealized appreciation}}{\text{Fair market value at date of gift}} \times \text{Gift tax paid} \right)$$

EXAMPLE 19	F made a gift of stock to S in 1990, when the fair market value of the stock was $40,000. F had purchased the stock in 1978 for $10,000. Because the unrealized appreciation is $30,000 ($40,000 fair market value less $10,000 adjusted basis) and the fair market value is $40,000, three-fourths ($30,000/$40,000) of the gift tax paid is added to the basis of the property. If the gift tax is $4,000, S's basis in the property is $13,000 [$10,000 + $3,000 (¾ of the $4,000 gift tax)]. □

EXAMPLE 20	F made a gift of stock to S in 1990, when the fair market value of the stock was $40,000. Gift tax of $4,000 was paid by F, who had purchased the stock in 1978 for $45,000. Because there is no unrealized appreciation at the date of the gift, none of the gift tax paid is added to the donor's basis in calculating the donee's gain basis. Therefore, the donee's gain basis is $45,000. □

For *gifts made before 1977*, the full amount of the gift tax paid may be added to the donor's basis. However, the ceiling on this total is the fair market value of the property at the date of the gift. Thus, in Example 19, if the gift was made before 1977, the basis of the property would be $14,000 ($10,000 + $4,000). In Example 20, the basis would still be $45,000 ($45,000 + $0).

Holding Period.   The *holding period* for property acquired by gift begins on the date the property was acquired by the donor if the gain basis rule applies. The holding period starts on the date of the gift if the loss basis rule applies.[11] The significance of the holding period for capital assets is discussed in chapter 13.

The following example summarizes the basis and holding period rules for gift property:

EXAMPLE 21   T acquires 100 shares of X Corporation stock on December 30, 1978, for $40,000. On January 3, 1990, when the stock has a fair market value of $38,000, T gives it to S. Gift tax of $4,000 is paid by the donor. There is no increase in basis for a portion of the gift tax paid because the property had not appreciated in value at the time of the gift. Therefore, S's gain basis is $40,000. S's basis for determining loss is $38,000 (fair market value) because the fair market value on the date of the gift is less than the donor's adjusted basis.

- If S sells the stock for $45,000, he has a recognized gain of $5,000. The holding period for determining whether the capital gain is short term or long term begins on December 30, 1978, the date the property was acquired by the donor.

- If S sells the stock for $36,000, he has a recognized loss of $2,000. The holding period for determining whether the capital loss is short term or long term begins on January 3, 1990, the date of the gift.

- If S sells the property for $39,000, there is no gain or loss since the amount realized is less than the gain basis of $40,000 and more than the loss basis of $38,000. □

Basis for Depreciation.   The basis for depreciation on depreciable gift property is the donee's gain basis. This rule is applicable even if the donee later sells the property at a loss and uses the loss basis rule in calculating the amount of the realized loss.

EXAMPLE 22   F gave a machine to D in 1990, when the adjusted basis was $32,000 (cost of $40,000 − accumulated depreciation of $8,000) and the fair market value was $26,000. No gift tax was paid. D's gain basis at the date of the gift is $32,000, and D's loss basis is $26,000. During 1990, D deducts depreciation (cost recovery) of $10,240 ($32,000 × 32%). Therefore, at the end of 1990, D's gain basis is $21,760 ($32,000 − $10,240), and D's loss basis is $15,760 ($26,000 − $10,240). □

Property Acquired from a Decedent

General Rules.   The basis of property acquired from a decedent is generally the property's fair market value at the date of death (referred to as the *primary valuation amount*). The property's basis is the fair market value six months after the date of death if the executor or administrator of the estate *elects* the alternate valuation date for estate tax purposes. This amount is referred to as the *alternate valuation amount*. If an estate tax return does not have to be filed because the estate is below the threshold amount for taxability, the alternate valuation date and

---

11.   Rev.Rul. 59–86, 1959–1 C.B. 209.

amount are not available. Even if an estate tax return is filed and the executor elects the alternate valuation date, the six months after death date is available only for property that the executor has not distributed before this date. Any property distributed or otherwise disposed of during this six-month period will have an adjusted basis equal to the fair market value on the date of distribution or other disposition.

For inherited property, both unrealized appreciation and decline in value are taken into consideration in determining the basis of the property for income tax purposes. Contrast this with the carryover basis rules for property received by gift.

The alternate valuation date can be elected only if the election results in the reduction of both the value of the gross estate and the estate tax liability below the amounts they would have been if the primary valuation date had been used. Thus, the planning opportunity of increasing the basis of the property to the beneficiary for income tax purposes by electing the alternate valuation amount while not increasing the estate tax liability (because of estate tax deductions or credits) is negated.

EXAMPLE 23   D inherited property from her father, who died in 1989. Her father's adjusted basis for the property at date of death was $35,000. The property's fair market value at date of death was $50,000. The alternate valuation date was not elected. D's basis for income tax purposes is $50,000. This is commonly referred to as a *stepped-up basis*.   □

EXAMPLE 24   Assume the same facts as in Example 23, except the property's fair market value at date of death was $20,000. D's basis for income tax purposes is $20,000. This is commonly referred to as a *stepped-down basis*.   □

EXAMPLE 25   D inherited property from her father, who died in 1990. Her father's adjusted basis for the property at date of death was $35,000. The property's fair market value was $250,000 at date of death and was $260,000 six months after death. The alternate valuation date cannot be elected because the value of the gross estate has increased during the six-month period. D's basis for income tax purposes is $250,000.   □

EXAMPLE 26   Assume the same facts as in Example 25, except the property's fair market value six months after death was $245,000. If the executor elects the alternate valuation date, D's basis for income tax purposes is $245,000.   □

EXAMPLE 27   Assume the same facts as in the previous example, except the property is distributed four months after the date of the decedent's death. At the distribution date, the property's fair market value is $247,500. Since the executor elected the alternate valuation date, D's basis for income tax purposes is $247,500.   □

The Code contains a provision designed to eliminate a tax avoidance technique referred to as *deathbed gifts*. If the time period between the date of the gift of appreciated property and the date of the donee's death is not greater than one year, the usual basis rule (stepped-up basis) for inherited property may not apply. The adjusted basis of such property inherited by the donor or his or her spouse from

the donee shall be the same as the decedent's adjusted basis for the property rather than the fair market value at the date of death or the alternate valuation date.

EXAMPLE 28   N gives stock to his uncle, U, in 1990. N's basis for the stock is $1,000, and the fair market value is $9,000. No gift tax is paid. Eight months later, N inherits the stock from U. At the date of U's death, the fair market value of the stock is $12,000. N's adjusted basis for the stock is $1,000. □

Survivor's Share of Property.   Both the decedent's share and the survivor's share of *community property* have a basis equal to fair market value on the date of the decedent's death.[12] This result applies to the decedent's share of the community property because the property flows to the surviving spouse from the estate (fair market value basis for inherited property). Likewise, the surviving spouse's share of the community property is deemed to be acquired by bequest, devise, or inheritance from the decedent. Therefore, it will also have a basis equal to fair market value.

EXAMPLE 29   H and W reside in a community property state. H and W own community property (200 shares of XYZ stock) that was acquired in 1973 for $100,000. Assume that H dies in 1990, when the securities are valued at $300,000. One-half of the XYZ stock is included in H's estate. If W inherits H's share of the community property, the basis for determining gain or loss is $300,000 [$150,000 (W's share of one-half of the community property) plus $150,000 (½ × $300,000, the value of XYZ stock at the date of H's death)] for the 200 shares of XYZ stock. □

In a *common law* state, only one-half of jointly held property of spouses (tenants by the entirety or joint tenants with rights of survivorship) is includible in the estate.[13] In such a case, no adjustment of the basis is permitted for the excluded property interest.

EXAMPLE 30   Assume the same facts as in the previous example, except that the property is jointly held by H and W who reside in a common law state. Also assume that H purchased the property and made a gift of one-half of the property when the stock was acquired, with no gift tax being paid. Only one-half of the XYZ stock is included in H's estate, and W's basis for determining gain or loss in the excluded half is not adjusted upward for the increase in value to date of death. Therefore, W's basis would be $200,000 ($50,000 + $150,000). □

Holding Period of Property Acquired from a Decedent.   The holding period of property acquired from a decedent is *deemed to be long term* (held for the required long-term holding period). This provision is applicable regardless of whether the property is disposed of at a gain or a loss.

Disallowed Losses

Related Taxpayers.   Section 267 provides that realized losses from sales or exchanges of property, directly or indirectly, between certain related parties are not recognized. This loss disallowance provision applies to several types of related-

---

12. § 1014(b)(6).   13. § 2040(a).

party transactions. The most common involve (1) members of a family and (2) transactions between an individual and a corporation in which the individual owns, directly or indirectly, more than 50 percent in value of the corporation's outstanding stock. Refer to chapter 5 for a detailed discussion of the related-party provisions.

Wash Sales.   Section 1091 stipulates that in certain cases, a realized loss on the sale or exchange of stock or securities is not recognized. Specifically, if a taxpayer sells or exchanges stock or securities and within 30 days before *or* after the date of such sale or exchange acquires substantially identical stock or securities, any loss realized from the sale or exchange is not recognized. The term *acquire* means acquire by purchase or in a taxable exchange and includes an option to purchase substantially identical securities. *Substantially identical* means the same in all important particulars. Corporate bonds and preferred stock are normally not considered substantially identical to the corporation's common stock. However, if the bonds and preferred stock are convertible into common stock, they may be considered substantially identical under certain circumstances. Attempts to avoid the application of the wash sales rules by having a related taxpayer repurchase the securities have been unsuccessful. These wash sales provisions do *not* apply to gains.

Recognition of the loss is disallowed because the taxpayer is considered to be in substantially the same economic position after the sale and repurchase as before the sale and repurchase. However, this rule does not apply to taxpayers engaged in the business of buying and selling securities. Investors, however, are not allowed to create losses through wash sales to offset income for tax purposes.

Realized loss that is not recognized is added to the basis of the substantially identical stock or securities whose acquisition resulted in the nonrecognition of loss. In other words, the basis of the replacement stock or securities is increased by the amount of the unrecognized loss. If the loss were not added to the basis of the newly acquired stock or securities, the taxpayer would never recover the entire basis of the old stock or securities.

The basis of the new stock or securities includes the unrecovered portion of the basis of the formerly held stock or securities. Therefore, the holding period of the new stock or securities begins on the date of acquisition of the old stock or securities.

EXAMPLE 31   T owns 100 shares of A Corporation stock (adjusted basis of $20,000), 50 shares of which she sells for $8,000. Ten days later, T purchases 50 shares of the same stock for $7,000. T's realized loss of $2,000 ($8,000 amount realized less $10,000 adjusted basis of 50 shares) is not recognized because it resulted from a wash sale. T's basis in the newly acquired stock is $9,000 ($7,000 purchase price plus $2,000 unrecognized loss from the wash sale). □

The taxpayer may acquire less than the number of shares sold in a wash sale. In this case, the loss from the sale is prorated between recognized and unrecognized loss on the basis of the ratio of the number of shares acquired to the number of shares sold.

Conversion of Property from Personal Use to Business or Income-Producing Use

As discussed previously, losses from the sale of personal use assets are not recognized for tax purposes, but losses from the sale of business and income-producing assets are deductible. Can a taxpayer convert a personal use asset that has declined in value to business use and then sell the asset to recognize a business loss? The law prevents this by requiring that the *original basis for loss* on personal use assets

converted to business or income-producing use is the lower of the property's adjusted basis or fair market value on the date of conversion. The *gain basis* for converted property is the property's adjusted basis on the date of conversion. The law is not concerned with gains on converted property because gains are recognized regardless of whether property is business, income producing, or personal use.

EXAMPLE 32   T's personal residence has an adjusted basis of $75,000 and a fair market value of $60,000. T converts the personal residence to rental property. His basis for loss is $60,000 (lower of $75,000 adjusted basis and fair market value of $60,000). The $15,000 decline in value is a personal loss and can never be recognized for tax purposes. T's basis for gain is $75,000. □

The basis for loss is also the basis for depreciating the converted property.[14] This is an exception to the general rule that provides that the basis for depreciation is the gain basis (e.g., property received by gift). This exception prevents the taxpayer from recovering a personal loss indirectly through depreciation of the higher original basis. After the property is converted, both its basis for loss and its basis for gain are adjusted for depreciation deductions from the date of conversion to the date of disposition. These rules apply only if a conversion from personal to business or income-producing use has actually occurred.

EXAMPLE 33   At a time when her personal residence (adjusted basis of $40,000) is worth $50,000, T converts one-half of it to rental use. The property is not ACRS recovery property. At this point, the estimated useful life of the residence is 20 years and there is no estimated salvage value. After renting the converted portion for five years, T sells the property for $44,000. All amounts relate only to the building; the land has been accounted for separately. T has a $2,000 realized gain from the sale of the personal use portion of the residence and a $7,000 realized gain from the sale of the rental portion. These gains are computed as follows:

	Personal Use	Rental
Original basis for gain and loss—adjusted basis on date of conversion (fair market value is greater than the adjusted basis)	$20,000	$20,000
Depreciation—five years	None	5,000
Adjusted basis—date of sale	$20,000	$15,000
Amount realized	22,000	22,000
Realized gain	$ 2,000	$ 7,000

As discussed later in this chapter, T may be able to defer recognition of part or all of the $2,000 gain from the sale of the personal use portion of the residence under § 1034. The $7,000 gain from the rental portion is recognized. □

EXAMPLE 34   Assume the same facts as in the previous example, except that the fair market value on the date of conversion is $30,000 and the sales proceeds are $16,000. T has a $12,000 realized loss from the sale of the personal use portion of the

---

14. Reg. § 1.167(g)–1.

residence and a $3,250 realized loss from the sale of the rental portion. These losses are computed as follows:

	Personal Use	Rental
Original basis for loss—fair market value on date of conversion (fair market value is less than the adjusted basis)	*	$15,000
Depreciation—five years	None	3,750
Adjusted basis—date of sale	$20,000	$11,250
Amount realized	8,000	8,000
Realized loss	$12,000	$ 3,250

*Not applicable.

The $12,000 loss from the sale of the personal use portion of the residence is not recognized. The $3,250 loss from the rental portion is recognized. □

Summary of Basis Adjustments

Some of the more common items that either increase or decrease the basis of an asset appear in Concept Summary 12−2.

CONCEPT SUMMARY 12−2

Adjustments to Basis

Item	Effect	Refer to Chapter	Explanation
Amortization of bond discount.	Increase	13	Amortization is mandatory for certain taxable bonds and elective for tax-exempt bonds.
Amortization of bond premium.	Decrease	12	Amortization is mandatory for tax-exempt bonds and elective for taxable bonds.
Amortization of covenant not to compete.	Decrease	13	Covenant must be for a definite and limited time period.
Amortization of intangibles.	Decrease	8	Not all intangibles can be amortized (e.g., goodwill).
Assessment for local benefits.	Increase	10	To the extent not deductible as taxes (e.g., assessment for streets and sidewalks that increase the value of the property versus one for maintenance or repair or for meeting interest charges).
Bad debts.	Decrease	7	Only the specific charge-off method is permitted.
Capital additions.	Increase	12	Certain items, at the taxpayer's election, can be capitalized or deducted (e.g., selected indirect moving expenses and medical expenses).
Casualty.	Decrease	7	For a casualty loss, the amount of the adjustment is the summation of the deductible loss and the insurance proceeds received. For a casualty gain, the amount of the adjustment is the insurance proceeds received reduced by the recognized gain.
Cost recovery.	Decrease	8	§ 168 is applicable to tangible assets placed in service after 1980 whose useful life is expressed in terms of years. ·

Item	Effect	Refer to Chapter	Explanation
Condemnation.	Decrease	12	See casualty explanation.
Depletion.	Decrease	8	Use the greater of cost or percentage depletion. Percentage depletion can still be deducted when the basis is zero.
Depreciation.	Decrease	8	§ 167 is applicable to tangible assets placed in service before 1981 and to tangible assets not depreciated in terms of years.
Easement.	Decrease		If no use of the land is retained by the taxpayer, all of the basis is allocable to the easement transaction. However, if only part of the land is affected by the easement, only part of the basis is allocable to the easement transaction.
Improvements by lessee to lessor's property.	Increase	4	Adjustment occurs only if the lessor is required to include the fair market value of the improvements in gross income under § 109.
Imputed interest.	Decrease	15	Amount deducted is not part of the cost of the asset.
Investment tax credit.	Decrease	11	Amount is 50% (100% for transition property) of the investment tax credit. If the election to reduce the investment tax credit is made, no adjustment is required.
Investment tax credit recapture.	Increase	11	Amount is 50% (100% for transition property) of the investment tax credit recaptured. If the election to reduce the investment tax credit was made, no adjustment is required.
Limited expensing under § 179.	Decrease	8	Occurs only if the taxpayer elects § 179 treatment.
Medical capital expenditure permitted as a medical expense.	Decrease	10	Adjustment is the amount of the deduction (the effect on basis is to increase it by the amount of the capital expenditure net of the deduction).
Moving capital expenditure permitted as a moving expense.	Decrease	9	Adjustment is for the amount the taxpayer elects to deduct as an indirect moving expense (the effect on basis is to increase it by the amount of the capital expenditure net of the deduction).
Real estate taxes; apportionment between the buyer and seller.	Increase or Decrease	10	To the extent the buyer pays the seller's pro rata share, the buyer's basis is increased. To the extent the seller pays the buyer's pro rata share, the buyer's basis is decreased.
Rebate from manufacturer.	Decrease		Since the rebate is treated as an adjustment to the purchase price, it is not included in the buyer's gross income.
Stock dividend.	Decrease	4	Adjustment occurs only if the stock dividend is nontaxable.
Stock rights.	Decrease	12	Adjustment occurs only for nontaxable stock rights and only if the fair market value of the rights is at least 15% of the fair market value of the stock or, if less than 15%, the taxpayer elects to allocate the basis between the stock and the rights.
Theft.	Decrease	7	See casualty explanation.

In discussing the topic of basis, a number of specific techniques for determining basis have been presented. Although the various techniques are responsive to and mandated by transactions occurring in the marketplace, they do possess enough common characteristics to be categorized as follows:

- The basis of the asset may be determined by reference to the asset's cost.

- The basis of the asset may be determined by reference to the basis of another asset.

- The basis of the asset may be determined by reference to the asset's fair market value.

- The basis of the asset may be determined by reference to the basis of the asset to another taxpayer.

NONTAXABLE EXCHANGES

A taxpayer who is going to replace a productive asset (e.g., machinery) used in a trade or business might structure the transactions as a sale of the old asset and the purchase of a new asset. Under this circumstance, any realized gain on the asset sale is recognized. The basis of the new asset is its cost. Conversely, the taxpayer may be able to trade the old asset for the new asset. This exchange of assets may qualify for nontaxable exchange treatment.

The tax law recognizes that nontaxable exchanges result in a change in the *form* but not in the *substance* of the taxpayer's relative economic position. The replacement property received in the exchange is viewed as substantially a continuation of the old investment. Additional justification for nontaxable exchange treatment is that this type of transaction does not provide the taxpayer with the wherewithal to pay the tax on any realized gain. The nonrecognition provisions do not apply to realized losses from the sale or exchange of personal use assets. Such losses are not recognized because they are personal in nature and not because of any nonrecognition provision.

In a *nontaxable exchange*, realized gains or losses are not recognized. However, the nonrecognition is usually temporary. The recognition of gain or loss is merely *postponed* (deferred) until the property received in the nontaxable exchange is subsequently disposed of in a taxable transaction. This is accomplished by assigning a carryover basis to the replacement property.

EXAMPLE 35   T exchanges property with an adjusted basis of $10,000 and a fair market value of $12,000 for property with a fair market value of $12,000. The transaction qualifies for nontaxable exchange treatment. T has a realized gain of $2,000 ($12,000 amount realized − $10,000 adjusted basis). His recognized gain is $0. His basis in the replacement property is a carryover basis of $10,000. Assume the replacement property is nondepreciable. If T subsequently sells the replacement property for $12,000, his realized and recognized gain will be the $2,000 gain that was postponed (deferred) in the nontaxable transaction. If the replacement property is depreciable, the carryover basis of $10,000 is used in calculating depreciation.   □

In some nontaxable exchanges, only part of the property involved in the transaction will qualify for nonrecognition treatment. If the taxpayer receives cash or other nonqualifying property, part or all of the realized gain from the exchange is recognized. In these instances, gain is recognized because the taxpayer has

changed or improved his or her relative economic position and has the where-withal to pay income tax to the extent of cash or other property received.

It is important to distinguish between a nontaxable disposition, as the term is used in the statute, and a tax-free transaction. First, a direct exchange is not required in all circumstances (e.g., replacement of involuntarily converted prop-erty or sale and replacement of a personal residence). Second, as previously mentioned, the term *nontaxable* refers to postponement of recognition via a carryover basis. In a tax-free transaction, the nonrecognition is permanent (e.g., see the discussion later in the chapter of the § 121 election by a taxpayer age 55 or over to exclude gain on the sale of a residence). Therefore, the basis of any property acquired is not dependent on that of the property disposed of by the taxpayer.

LIKE-KIND EXCHANGES—§ 1031

Section 1031 provides for nontaxable exchange treatment if the following require-ments are satisfied:

- The form of the transaction is an exchange.

- Both the property transferred and the property received are held either for productive use in a trade or business or for investment.

- The property is like-kind property.

Like-kind exchanges include business for business, business for investment, investment for business, or investment for investment property. Property held for personal use, inventory, and partnership interests (both limited and general) do not qualify under the like-kind exchange provisions. Securities, even though held for investment, do not qualify for like-kind exchange treatment.

The nonrecognition provision for like-kind exchanges is *mandatory* rather than elective. That is, a taxpayer who wants to recognize a realized gain or loss will have to structure the transaction in a form that does not satisfy the statutory requirements for a like-kind exchange. This topic is discussed further under Tax Planning Considerations.

Like-Kind Property

"The words 'like-kind' refer to the nature or character of the property and not to its grade or quality. One kind or class of property may not . . . be exchanged for property of a different kind or class."[15]

Although the term *like-kind* is intended to be interpreted very broadly, three categories of exchanges are not included in this broad definition. First, livestock of different sexes do not qualify as like-kind property. Second, real estate can be exchanged only for other real estate, and personalty can be exchanged only for other personalty. For example, the exchange of a machine (personalty) for an office building (realty) is not a like-kind exchange. *Real estate* includes principally rental buildings, office and store buildings, manufacturing plants, warehouses, and land. It is immaterial whether real estate is improved or unimproved. Thus, unimproved land can be exchanged for an apartment house. *Personalty* includes principally machines, equipment, trucks, automobiles, furniture, and fixtures. Third, real property located in the United States exchanged for foreign real property (and vice versa) does not qualify as like-kind property.

---

15. Reg. § 1.1031(a)–1(b).

EXAMPLE 36   T made the following exchanges during the taxable year:

a.   Inventory for a machine used in business.

b.   Land held for investment for a building used in business.

c.   Stock held for investment for equipment used in business.

d.   A business truck for a business machine.

e.   An automobile used for personal transportation for a machine used in business.

f.   Livestock for livestock of a different sex.

g.   Land held for investment in New York for land held for investment in London.

Exchanges (b), investment real property for business real property, and (d), business personalty for business personalty, qualify as exchanges of like-kind property. Exchanges (a), inventory; (c), stock; (e), personal use automobile (not held for business or investment purposes); (f), livestock of different sexes; and (g), U.S. and foreign real estate, do not qualify. □

A special provision applies if the taxpayers involved in the exchange are related parties under § 267(b). To qualify for like-kind exchange treatment, the taxpayer and the related party must not dispose of the like-kind property received in the exchange within the two-year period following the date of the exchange. If such an early disposition does occur, the postponed gain will be recognized as of the date of the early disposition. Dispositions due to death, involuntary conversions, and certain non-tax avoidance transactions are not treated as early dispositions.

Exchange Requirement

The transaction must actually involve a direct exchange of property to qualify as a like-kind exchange. Thus, the sale of old property and the purchase of new property, even though like-kind, is generally not an exchange. However, if the two transactions are mutually dependent, the IRS may treat the two interdependent transactions as a like-kind exchange. For example, if the taxpayer sells an old business machine to a dealer and purchases a new one from the same dealer, like-kind exchange treatment could result.[16]

The taxpayer might want to avoid nontaxable exchange treatment. Recognition of gain gives the taxpayer a higher basis for depreciation (see Example 62). To the extent that such gains would, if recognized, be passive activity income that could offset passive activity losses, it may be preferable to avoid the nonrecognition provisions through an indirect exchange transaction. For example, a taxpayer may sell property to one individual and follow the sale with a purchase of similar property from another individual. The taxpayer may also want to avoid nontaxable exchange treatment so that a realized loss can be recognized.

Boot

If the taxpayer in a like-kind exchange gives or receives some property that is not like-kind property, recognition may occur. Property that is not like-kind property,

---

16.   Rev.Rul. 61–119, 1961–1 C.B. 395.

including cash, is referred to as *boot*. Although the term "boot" does not appear in the Code, tax practitioners commonly use it rather than using "property that is not like-kind property."

The *receipt* of boot will trigger recognition of gain if there is realized gain. The amount of the recognized gain is the *lesser* of the boot received or the realized gain (realized gain serves as the ceiling on recognition).

EXAMPLE 37

T and S exchange machinery, and the exchange qualifies as like-kind under § 1031. Since T's machinery (adjusted basis of $20,000) is worth $24,000 and S's machine has a fair market value of $19,000, S also gives T cash of $5,000. T's recognized gain is $4,000, the lesser of the realized gain ($24,000 amount realized – $20,000 adjusted basis = $4,000) or the fair market value of the boot received ($5,000). □

EXAMPLE 38

Assume the same facts as in the previous example, except that S's machine is worth $21,000 (not $19,000). Under these circumstances, S gives T cash of $3,000 to make up the difference. T's recognized gain is $3,000, the lesser of the realized gain ($24,000 amount realized – $20,000 adjusted basis = $4,000) or the fair market value of the boot received ($3,000). □

The receipt of boot does not result in recognition if there is realized loss.

EXAMPLE 39

Assume the same facts as in Example 37, except the adjusted basis of T's machine is $30,000. T's realized loss is $6,000 ($24,000 amount realized – $30,000 adjusted basis = $6,000 realized loss). The receipt of the boot of $5,000 does not trigger recognition. Therefore, the recognized loss is $0. □

The *giving* of boot usually does not trigger recognition. If the boot given is cash, any realized gain or loss will not be recognized.

EXAMPLE 40

T and S exchange equipment in a like-kind exchange. T receives equipment with a fair market value of $25,000. T transfers equipment worth $21,000 (adjusted basis of $15,000) and cash of $4,000. T's realized gain is $6,000 ($25,000 amount realized – $15,000 adjusted basis – $4,000 cash). However, none of the realized gain is recognized. □

If, however, the boot given is appreciated or depreciated property, gain or loss is recognized to the extent of the differential between the adjusted basis and the fair market value of the boot. For this purpose, *appreciated or depreciated property* is defined as property for which the adjusted basis is not equal to the fair market value.

EXAMPLE 41

Assume the same facts as in the previous example, except that T transfers equipment worth $10,000 (adjusted basis of $12,000) and boot worth $15,000 (adjusted basis of $9,000). T's realized gain appears to be $4,000 ($25,000 amount realized – $21,000 adjusted basis). Since realization previously has

served as a ceiling on recognition, it appears that the recognized gain is $4,000 (lower of realized gain of $4,000 or amount of appreciation on boot of $6,000). However, the recognized gain actually is $6,000 (full amount of the appreciation on the boot). In effect, T must calculate the like-kind and boot parts of the transaction separately. That is, the realized loss of $2,000 on the like-kind property is not recognized ($10,000 fair market value – $12,000 adjusted basis), and the $6,000 realized gain on the boot is recognized ($15,000 fair market value – $9,000 adjusted basis). □

One other similar circumstance exists in which realization does not serve as a ceiling on recognition.

EXAMPLE 42

T and S exchange equipment in a like-kind exchange. T receives from S like-kind equipment with a fair market value of $25,000 and boot with a fair market value of $6,000. T gives up like-kind equipment with an adjusted basis of $12,000 and boot with an adjusted basis of $8,000. Although T's realized gain appears to be $11,000 ($25,000 + $6,000 – $12,000 – $8,000), T must report the like-kind and boot elements separately. It is therefore necessary to know the fair market value of the like-kind property and the boot transferred by T. Assume the fair market value of the like-kind equipment given up by T is $9,000 and that of the boot is $22,000. The realized loss of $3,000 on the like-kind property is not recognized ($9,000 fair market value – $12,000 adjusted basis), and the $14,000 realized gain on the boot is recognized ($22,000 fair market value – $8,000 adjusted basis). □

Basis of Property Received

If an exchange does not qualify as nontaxable under § 1031, gain or loss is recognized, and the basis of property received in the exchange is the property's fair market value. If the exchange qualifies for nonrecognition, the basis of property received must be adjusted to reflect any postponed (deferred) gain or loss. The *basis* of *like-kind property* received in the exchange is the property's fair market value less postponed gain or plus postponed loss. If the exchange partially qualifies for nonrecognition (if there is recognition associated with boot), the basis of like-kind property received in the exchange is the property's fair market value less postponed gain or plus postponed loss. The *basis* of any *boot* received is the boot's fair market value.

If there is a postponed loss, nonrecognition creates a situation in which the taxpayer has recovered *less* than the cost or other basis of the property exchanged in an amount equal to the unrecognized loss. If there is a postponed gain, the taxpayer has recovered *more* than the cost or other basis of the property exchanged in an amount equal to the unrecognized gain.

EXAMPLE 43

T exchanges a building (used in his business) with an adjusted basis of $30,000 and fair market value of $38,000 for land with a fair market value of $38,000. The land is to be held as an investment. The exchange qualifies as like-kind (an exchange of business real property for investment real property). Thus, the basis of the land is $30,000 (the land's fair market value of $38,000 less the $8,000 postponed gain on the building). If the land is later sold for its fair market value of $38,000, the $8,000 postponed gain will be recognized. □

EXAMPLE 44   Assume the same facts as in the previous example, except that the building has an adjusted basis of $48,000 and fair market value of only $38,000. The basis in the newly acquired land is $48,000 (fair market value of $38,000 plus the $10,000 postponed loss on the building). If the land is later sold for its fair market value of $38,000, the $10,000 postponed loss will be recognized. □

The Code provides an alternative approach for determining the basis of like-kind property received:
Adjusted basis of like-kind property surrendered

+ Adjusted basis of boot given
+ Gain recognized
− Fair market value of boot received
− Loss recognized
= Basis of like-kind property received

This approach is logical in terms of the recovery of capital doctrine. That is, the unrecovered cost or other basis is increased by additional cost (boot given) or decreased by cost recovered (boot received). Any gain recognized is included in the basis of the new property. The taxpayer has been taxed on this amount and is now entitled to recover it tax-free. Any loss recognized is deducted from the basis of the new property. The taxpayer has received a tax benefit on that amount.

The *holding period* of the property surrendered in the exchange carries over and *tacks on* to the holding period of the like-kind property received. The logic of this rule is derived from the basic concept of the new property as a continuation of the old investment. For the boot received, there will be a new holding period (from the date of exchange) rather than a carryover holding period.

Depreciation recapture potential also carries over to the property received in a like-kind exchange. See chapter 13 for a discussion of this topic.

The following comprehensive example illustrates the like-kind exchange rules.

EXAMPLE 45   T exchanged the following old machines for new machines in five independent like-kind exchanges:

Exchange	Adjusted Basis of Old Machine	Fair Market Value of New Machine	Adjusted Basis of Boot Given	Fair Market Value of Boot Received
1	$4,000	$9,000	$ –0–	$ –0–
2	4,000	9,000	3,000	–0–
3	4,000	9,000	6,000	–0–
4	4,000	9,000	–0–	3,000
5	4,000	3,500	–0–	300

T's realized and recognized gains and losses and the basis of each of the like-kind properties received are as follows:

				New Basis Calculation				
Exchange	Realized Gain (Loss)	Recognized Gain (Loss)	Old Adj. Basis	+ Boot Given	+ Gain Recognized	– Boot Received	= New Basis
1	$ 5,000	$ –0–	$4,000	+ $ –0–	+ $ –0–	– $ –0–	= $ 4,000*
2	2,000	–0–	4,000	+ 3,000	+ –0–	– –0–	= 7,000*
3	(1,000)	–(0)–	4,000	+ 6,000	+ –0–	– –0–	= 10,000**
4	8,000	3,000	4,000	+ –0–	+ 3,000	– 3,000	= 4,000*
5	(200)	–(0)–	4,000	+ –0–	+ –0–	– 300	= 3,700**

*Basis may be determined in gain situations under the alternative method by subtracting the gain not recognized from the fair market value of the new property,

> $9,000 – $5,000 = $4,000 for exchange 1.
> $9,000 – $2,000 = $7,000 for exchange 2.
> $9,000 – $5,000 = $4,000 for exchange 4.

**In loss situations, basis may be determined by adding the loss not recognized to the fair market value of the new property,

> $9,000 + $1,000 = $10,000 for exchange 3.
> $3,500 + $200 = $3,700 for exchange 5.

The basis of the boot received is the boot's fair market value.

☐

If a buyer either assumes a liability or takes property subject to a liability, the amount of the liability is treated as boot received by the seller. Example 46 illustrates the effect of such a liability. In addition, the example illustrates the tax consequences for both parties involved in the like-kind exchange.

EXAMPLE 46   X and Y exchange real estate investments. X gives up property with an adjusted basis of $250,000 (fair market value $400,000) that is subject to a mortgage of $75,000 (assumed by Y). In return for this property, X receives property with a fair market value of $300,000 (adjusted basis $200,000) and cash of $25,000.

- X's realized gain is $150,000. X gave up property with an adjusted basis of $250,000. X received $400,000 from the exchange ($300,000 fair market value of like-kind property plus $100,000 boot received). The boot received consists of the cash of $25,000 received from Y and X's mortgage of $75,000 that is assumed by Y.

- X's recognized gain is $100,000. The realized gain of $150,000 is recognized to the extent of boot received.

- X's basis in the real estate received from Y is $250,000. This basis can be computed by subtracting the postponed gain ($50,000) from the fair market value of the real estate received ($300,000). It can also be computed by adding the recognized gain ($100,000) to the adjusted basis of the real estate given up ($250,000) and subtracting the boot received ($100,000).

- Y's realized gain is $100,000. Y gave up property with an adjusted basis of $200,000 plus boot of $100,000 ($75,000 mortgage assumed plus $25,000 cash) or a total of $300,000. Y received $400,000 from the exchange (fair market value of like-kind property received).

- Y has no recognized gain because he did not receive any boot. The entire gain of $100,000 is postponed.

- Y's basis in the real estate received from X is $300,000. This basis can be computed by subtracting the postponed gain ($100,000) from the fair market value of the real estate received ($400,000). It can also be computed by adding the boot given ($75,000 mortgage assumed by Y plus $25,000 cash) to the adjusted basis of the real estate given up ($200,000).[17] □

Involuntary Conversions—§ 1033

General Scheme

Section 1033 provides that a taxpayer who suffers an involuntary conversion of property may postpone recognition of *gain* realized from the conversion. The objective of this provision is to provide relief to the taxpayer who has suffered hardship and who does not have the wherewithal to pay the tax on any gain realized from the conversion. Postponement of realized gain is permitted to the extent that the taxpayer reinvests the amount realized from the conversion in replacement property. The rules for nonrecognition of gain are as follows:

- If the amount reinvested in replacement property *equals or exceeds* the amount realized, realized gain is *not recognized.*

- If the amount reinvested in replacement property is *less than* the amount realized, realized gain *is recognized* to the extent of the deficiency.

If a *loss* occurs on an involuntary conversion, § 1033 does not modify the normal rules for loss recognition. That is, if realized loss otherwise would be recognized, § 1033 does not change the result.

Involuntary Conversion Defined

An *involuntary conversion* results from the destruction (complete or partial), theft, seizure, requisition or condemnation, or the sale or exchange under threat or imminence of requisition or condemnation of the taxpayer's property. To prove the existence of a threat or imminence of condemnation, the taxpayer must obtain confirmation that there has been a decision to acquire the property for public use. In addition, the taxpayer must have reasonable grounds to believe the property will be taken.[18] The property does not have to be sold to the authority threatening to condemn it to qualify for § 1033 postponement. The taxpayer can sell the property to another party if he or she satisfies the previously mentioned confirmation and reasonable grounds requirements.[19] Likewise, the sale of property to a condemning authority by a taxpayer who acquired the property from its former owner with the knowledge that the property was under threat of condemnation also qualifies as an involuntary conversion under § 1033.[20] A voluntary act, such as an act of arson by a taxpayer involving his or her own property, is not an involuntary conversion.[21]

---

17. Example (2) of Reg. § 1.1031(d)–2 illustrates a special situation where both the buyer and the seller transfer liabilities that are assumed or property is acquired subject to a liability by the other party.

18. Rev.Rul. 63–221, 1963–2 C.B. 332, and *Joseph P.*

Balistrieri, 38 TCM 526, T.C.Memo. 1979–115.

19. Rev.Rul. 81–180, 1981–2 C.B. 161.

20. Rev.Rul. 81–181, 1981–2 C.B. 162.

21. Rev.Rul. 82–74, 1982–1 C.B. 110.

Although most involuntary conversions are casualties or condemnations, some special situations are included within the definition. Involuntary conversions, for example, include livestock destroyed by or on account of disease or exchanged or sold because of disease or solely on account of drought.

Computing the Amount Realized

The amount realized from the condemnation of property usually includes only the amount received as compensation for the property.[22] Any amount received that is designated as severance damages by both the government and the taxpayer is not included in the amount realized. Severance awards usually occur when only a portion of the entire property is condemned (e.g., a strip of land is taken to build a highway). Severance damages are awarded because the value of the taxpayer's remaining property has declined as a result of the condemnation. Such damages reduce the basis of the property. However, if either of the following requirements is satisfied, the nonrecognition provision of § 1033 applies to the severance damages.

- Severance damages are used to restore the usability of the remaining property.

- The usefulness of the remaining property is destroyed by the condemnation, and the property is sold and replaced at a cost equal to or exceeding the sum of the condemnation award, severance damages, and sales proceeds.

Replacement Property

The requirements for replacement property generally are more restrictive than those for like-kind property under § 1031. The basic requirement is that the replacement property be similar or related in service or use to the involuntarily converted property.

Different interpretations of the phrase *similar or related in service or use* apply if the involuntarily converted property is held by an *owner-user* rather than an *owner-investor* (e.g., lessor). The taxpayer who uses the property in his or her trade or business is subject to a more restrictive test in terms of acquiring replacement property. For the owner-user, the *functional use test* applies, and for the owner-investor, the *taxpayer use test* applies.

Taxpayer Use Test.   The taxpayer use test for owner-investors provides the taxpayer with more flexibility in terms of what qualifies as replacement property than does the functional use test for owner-users. Essentially, the properties must be used by the taxpayer (the owner-investor) in similar endeavors. For example, rental property held by an owner-investor will qualify if replaced by other rental property, regardless of the type of rental property involved. This test would be met if an investor replaced a manufacturing plant with a wholesale grocery warehouse if both properties were held for the production of rental income.[23] A rental residence replaced by a personal residence does not meet this test.[24]

Functional Use Test.   This test requires that the taxpayer's use of the replacement property and of the involuntarily converted property be the same. A rental residence replaced by a personal residence does not meet this test. A manufactur-

22. *Pioneer Real Estate Co.*, 47 B.T.A. 886 (1942), *acq.* 1943 C.B. 18.

23. *Loco Realty Co. v. Comm.*, 62–2 USTC ¶ 9657, 10

AFTR2d 5359, 306 F.2d 207 (CA–8, 1962).

24. Rev.Rul. 70–466, 1970–2 C.B. 165.

ing plant replaced by a wholesale grocery warehouse, whether rented or not, does not meet this test; but as indicated above, the IRS applies the taxpayer use test to owner-investors. However, the functional use test still applies to owner-users (e.g., a manufacturer whose manufacturing plant is destroyed by fire is required to replace the plant with another facility of similar functional use).

Special Rules.   Under one set of circumstances, the broader replacement rules for like-kind exchanges are substituted for the narrow replacement rules normally used for involuntary conversions. This beneficial provision applies if business real property or investment real property is condemned. Therefore, the taxpayer has substantially more flexibility in terms of his or her selection of replacement property. For example, improved real property can be replaced with unimproved real property. Another special rule provides that proceeds from the involuntary conversion of livestock due to soil or other environmental contamination need be expended only for any property to be used for farming, including real property. Finally, another special rule permits an indirect replacement approach. Under this rule, the taxpayer can acquire controlling interest (80 percent) in a corporation that owns property that qualifies as replacement property in lieu of purchasing the replacement property directly. However, the aforementioned special rule that substitutes the broader replacement rules for like-kind exchanges cannot be used in conjunction with this indirect replacement approach.

The rules concerning the nature of replacement property are illustrated in Concept Summary 12–3.

Time Limitation on Replacement

The taxpayer has a two-year period after the close of the taxable year in which any gain is realized from the involuntary conversion to replace the property.[25] This rule

CONCEPT SUMMARY 12–3

Replacement Property Tests

Type of Property and User	Like-Kind Test	Taxpayer Use Test	Functional Use Test
Land used by a manufacturing company is condemned by a local government authority.	X		
Apartment and land held by an investor are sold due to the threat or imminence of condemnation.	X		
An investor's rented wholesale grocery warehouse is destroyed by fire; the warehouse may be replaced by other rental properties (e.g., an apartment building).		X	
A manufacturing plant is destroyed by fire; replacement property must consist of another manufacturing plant that is functionally the same as the property converted.			X
Personal residence of taxpayer is condemned by a local government authority; replacement property must consist of another personal residence.			

---

25. §§ 1033(a)(2)(B) and (g)(4) and Reg. §§ 1.1033(a)–2(c)(3) and (f)–1(b).

affords as much as three years from the date of realization of gain to replace the property if the realization of gain took place on the first day of the taxable year.[26] If the form of the involuntary conversion is the condemnation of real property used in a trade or business or held for investment, a three-year period is substituted for the normal two-year period. Thus, the taxpayer could actually have as much as four years from the date of realization of gain to replace the property in this case.

EXAMPLE 47   T's warehouse is destroyed by fire on December 16, 1989. The adjusted basis is $325,000. Proceeds of $400,000 are received from the insurance company on January 10, 1990. T is a calendar year taxpayer. The latest date for replacement is December 31, 1992 (the end of the taxable year in which realized gain occurred plus two years). The critical date is not the date the involuntary conversion occurred, but rather the date of gain realization. □

EXAMPLE 48   Assume the same facts as in the previous example, except T's warehouse is condemned. The latest date for replacement is December 31, 1993 (the end of the taxable year in which realized gain occurred plus three years). □

The earliest date for replacement typically is the date the involuntary conversion occurs. However, if the property is condemned, it is possible to replace the condemned property before this date. In this case, the earliest date is the date of the threat or imminence of requisition or condemnation of the property. The purpose of this provision is to enable the taxpayer to make an orderly replacement of the condemned property.

Nonrecognition of Gain

Nonrecognition of gain can be either mandatory or elective, depending upon whether the conversion is direct (into replacement property) or into money.

Direct Conversion.   If the conversion is directly into replacement property rather than into money, nonrecognition of realized gain is *mandatory*. In this case, the basis of the replacement property is the same as the adjusted basis of the converted property. Direct conversion is rare in practice and usually involves condemnations. The following example illustrates the application of the rules for direct conversions.

EXAMPLE 49   T's property with an adjusted basis of $20,000 is condemned by the state. T receives property with a fair market value of $50,000 as compensation for the property taken. Since the nonrecognition of realized gain is mandatory for direct conversions, T's realized gain of $30,000 is not recognized, and the basis of the replacement property is $20,000 (adjusted basis of the condemned property). □

---

26. The taxpayer can apply for an extension of this time period anytime before its expiration [Reg. § 1.1033(a)–2(c)(3)]. Also, the period for filing the application for extension can be extended if the taxpayer shows reasonable cause.

Conversion into Money. If the conversion is into money, "at the election of the taxpayer the gain shall be recognized only to the extent that the amount realized upon such conversion . . . exceeds the cost of such other property or such stock."[27] This is the usual case, and nonrecognition (postponement) is *elective*.

The basis of the replacement property is the property's cost less postponed (deferred) gain. The holding period of the replacement property, if the election to postpone gain is made, includes the holding period of the converted property.

Section 1033 applies *only to gains* and *not to losses*. Losses from involuntary conversions are recognized if the property is held for business or income-producing purposes. Personal casualty losses are recognized, but condemnation losses related to personal use assets (e.g., a personal residence) are neither recognized nor postponed.

Examples 50 and 51 illustrate the application of the involuntary conversion rules.

EXAMPLE 50

T's building (used in his trade or business), with an adjusted basis of $50,000, is destroyed by fire in 1990. T is a calendar year taxpayer. In 1990, T receives an insurance reimbursement for the loss in the amount of $100,000. T invests $80,000 in a new building.

- T has until December 31, 1992, to make the new investment and qualify for the nonrecognition election.

- T's realized gain is $50,000 ($100,000 insurance proceeds less $50,000 adjusted basis of old building).

- Assuming the replacement property qualifies as similar or related in service or use, T's recognized gain is $20,000. T reinvested $20,000 less than the insurance proceeds ($100,000 proceeds minus $80,000 reinvested). Therefore, his realized gain is recognized to that extent.

- T's basis in the new building is $50,000. This is the building's cost of $80,000 less the postponed gain of $30,000 (realized gain of $50,000 less recognized gain of $20,000).

- The computation of realization, recognition, and basis would apply even if T were a real estate dealer and the building destroyed by fire were part of his inventory. Section 1033 does not generally exclude inventory, as does § 1031. □

EXAMPLE 51

Assume the same facts as in the previous example, except that T receives only $45,000 (instead of $100,000) of insurance proceeds. T would have a realized and recognized loss of $5,000. The basis of the new building would be the building's cost of $80,000. If the building destroyed were held for personal use, the recognized loss would be subject to other limitations. The loss of $5,000 would be limited to the decline in fair market value of the property, and the amount of the loss would be reduced first by $100 and then by 10% of adjusted gross income (refer to chapter 7). □

Although the previous discussion describes an indirect conversion as a conversion into money, § 1033 refers to indirect conversions as conversions "into

---

27. § 1033(a)(2)(A) and Reg. § 1.1033(a)–2(c)(1).

money or other property not similar or related in service or use to the converted property . . . ."[28] An indirect conversion into other than money would be rare, but it could occur and is treated the same as a conversion into money.

Involuntary Conversion of a Personal Residence

The tax consequences of the involuntary conversion of a personal residence depend upon whether the conversion is a casualty or condemnation and whether a realized loss or gain results.

Loss Situations.   If the conversion is a condemnation, the realized loss is not recognized. Loss from the condemnation of a personal use asset is never recognized. If the conversion is a casualty (a loss from fire, storm, etc.), the loss is recognized subject to the personal casualty loss limitations.

Gain Situations.   If the conversion is a condemnation, the gain may be postponed under either § 1033 or § 1034. That is, the taxpayer may elect to treat the condemnation as a sale under the deferral of gain rules relating to the sale of a personal residence under § 1034 (presented subsequently). If the conversion is a casualty, the gain can be postponed only under the involuntary conversion provisions.

Reporting Considerations

An election to postpone gain normally is made on the return for the taxable year in which gain is realized. The taxpayer should attach to the return a statement that includes supportive details. If the property has not been replaced before filing the tax return, the taxpayer should also attach a supporting statement to the return for the taxable year in which the property is replaced.

If the property either is not replaced within the prescribed period or is replaced at a cost less than anticipated, an amended return must be filed for the taxable year in which the election was made. A taxpayer who has elected § 1033 postponement and makes an appropriate replacement may not later revoke the election. In addition, once the taxpayer has designated qualifying property as replacement property, he or she cannot later change the designation.[29] If no election is made on the return for the taxable year in which gain is realized, an election may still be made within the prescribed time period by filing a claim for credit or refund.[30]

Involuntary conversions from casualty and theft are reported first on Form 4684, Casualties and Thefts. Casualty and theft losses on personal use property for the individual taxpayer are carried from Form 4684 to Schedule A of Form 1040. For other casualty and theft items, the Form 4684 amounts are generally reported on Form 4797, Sales of Business Property, unless Form 4797 is not required. In the latter case, the amounts are reported directly on the tax return involved.

Except for personal use property, recognized gains and losses from involuntary conversions other than by casualty and theft are reported on Form 4797. As stated previously, if the property involved in the involuntary conversion (other than by casualty and theft) is personal use property, any loss is not recognized. Any gain is treated as gain on a voluntary sale.

---

28. § 1033(a)(2).

29. Rev.Rul. 83–39, 1983–1 C.B. 190.

30. Reg. § 1.1033(a)–2(c)(2).

SALE OF A RESIDENCE—§ 1034

A realized loss from the sale of a personal residence is not recognized because the residence is personal use property. A realized gain is, however, subject to taxation. There are two provisions in the tax law whereby all or part of the realized gain is either postponed or excluded from taxation. The first of these, § 1034, is discussed below. The second, § 121, is discussed later in the chapter.

Section 1034 provides for the *mandatory* nonrecognition of gain from the sale or exchange of a personal residence if the sales proceeds are reinvested in a replacement residence within a prescribed time period. Both the old and new residences must qualify as the taxpayer's principal residence. A houseboat or house trailer qualifies if used by the taxpayer as his or her principal residence.[31]

The reason for not recognizing gain when a residence is replaced by a new residence within the prescribed time period (discussed below) is that the new residence is viewed as a continuation of the investment. Also, if the proceeds from the sale are reinvested, the taxpayer does not have the wherewithal to pay tax on the gain. Beyond these fundamental concepts, Congress, in enacting § 1034, was concerned with the hardship of involuntary moves and the socially desirable objective of encouraging the mobility of labor.

Replacement Period

For the nonrecognition treatment to apply, the old residence must be replaced by a new residence within a period *beginning two years before* the sale of the old residence and *ending two years after* such sale. This four-year period applies regardless of whether the new residence is purchased or constructed. In addition to acquiring the residence during this period, the taxpayer must *occupy* and use the new residence as the principal residence during this same time period. The occupancy requirement has been strictly construed by both the IRS and the courts, and even circumstances beyond a taxpayer's control do not excuse noncompliance.[32]

EXAMPLE 52   T sells her personal residence from which she realizes a gain of $50,000. The construction of a new residence begins immediately after the sale. However, unstable soil conditions and a trade union strike cause unforeseen delays in construction. The new residence ultimately is completed and occupied by T 25 months after the sale of the old residence. Since the occupancy requirement has not been satisfied, § 1034 is inapplicable, and T must recognize a gain of $50,000 on the sale of the old residence. □

Taxpayers might be inclined to make liberal use of § 1034 as a means of speculating when the price of residential housing is rising. Without any time restriction on its use, § 1034 would permit deferral of gain on multiple sales of principal residences, each one of which would result in an economic profit. The Code curbs this approach by precluding the application of § 1034 to any sales occurring within two years of its last use.

---

31. Reg. § 1.1034–1(c)(3)(i).
32. *James A. Henry*, 44 TCM 844, T.C.Memo. 1982–

469; and *William F. Peck*, 44 TCM 1030, T.C.Memo. 1982–506.

EXAMPLE 53

After T sells his principal residence (subsequently designated as the first residence) in March of 1989 for $150,000 (realized gain of $60,000), he buys and sells the following (all of which qualify as principal residences):

	Date of Purchase	Date of Sale	Amount Involved
Second residence	April 1989		$160,000
Second residence		May 1990	180,000
Third residence	June 1990		200,000

Because multiple sales have occurred within a period of two years, § 1034 does not apply to the sale of the second residence. Thus, the realized gain of $20,000 [$180,000 (selling price) – $160,000 (purchase price)] must be recognized. □

The two-year rule precluding multiple use of § 1034 could work a hardship where a taxpayer has been transferred by his or her employer and therefore has little choice in the matter. For this reason, § 1034 was amended to provide an exception to the two-year rule when the sale results from a change in the location of employment. To qualify for the exception, a taxpayer must meet the distance and length-of-employment requirements specified for the deduction of moving expenses under § 217.

EXAMPLE 54

Assume the same facts as in the previous example, except that in February of 1990, T's employer transfers T to a job in another state. Consequently, the sale of the second residence and the purchase of the third residence were due to the relocation of employment. If T satisfies the distance and length-of-employment requirements of § 217, no gain will be recognized on the sale of the first and second residences. □

Principal Residence

As indicated, both the old and new residences must qualify as the taxpayer's principal residence. Whether property is the taxpayer's principal residence is dependent ". . . upon all the facts and circumstances in each case."[33]

EXAMPLE 55

T sells his principal residence and moves to Norfolk, Virginia, where he is employed. He decides to rent an apartment in Norfolk because of its proximity to his place of employment. He purchases a beach house at Virginia Beach that he occupies most weekends. T does not intend to live in the beach house other than on weekends. The apartment in Norfolk is his principal place of residence. Therefore, the purchase of the beach house does not qualify as an appropriate replacement. □

If the old residence ceases to be the taxpayer's principal residence before its sale, the nonrecognition provision does not apply. For example, if the taxpayer

---

33. Reg. § 1.1034–1(c)(3).

abandons the old residence before its sale, the residence no longer qualifies as a principal residence.[34] If the old residence is converted to other than personal use (e.g., rental) before its sale, the nonrecognition provision does not apply. If only partially converted to business use, gain from the sale of the personal use portion still qualifies for nonrecognition. It is possible to convert part of a principal residence to business use and later to convert that part back to being part of the principal residence (e.g., a home office).[35]

Temporarily renting out the old residence before sale does not necessarily terminate its status as the taxpayer's principal residence,[36] nor does temporarily renting out the new residence before it is occupied by the taxpayer. An issue associated with temporarily renting out the old residence while attempting to sell it is whether a taxpayer is entitled to deduct expenses in excess of income relating to the rental of a residence before its sale. That is, is the old residence subject to the loss deduction rules for hobby loss activities? If it is, the deductions associated with the rental activity are limited to the rental income generated. The Tax Court concluded that since the property was considered to be the taxpayer's principal residence and as a result qualifies for § 1034 postponement of gain, the property was subject to the hobby loss limitations. The Court of Appeals reversed the Tax Court and held that the hobby loss provisions did not apply.[37]

Nonrecognition of Gain Requirements

Realized gain from the sale of the old residence is not recognized if the taxpayer reinvests an amount *at least equal* to the adjusted sales price of the old residence. Realized gain is recognized to the extent the taxpayer does not reinvest the adjusted sales price in a new residence. Therefore, the amount not reinvested is treated similarly to boot received in a like-kind exchange.

The *adjusted sales price* is the amount realized from the sale of the old residence less fixing-up expenses. The *amount realized* is calculated by reducing the selling price by the selling expenses. *Selling expenses* include items such as advertising the property for sale, real estate broker commissions, legal fees in connection with the sale, and loan placement fees paid by the taxpayer as a condition of the arrangement of financing for the buyer. To the extent that the selling expenses are deducted as moving expenses, they are not allowed as deductions in the computation of the amount realized (refer to chapter 9).

Fixing-up expenses are personal in nature and are incurred by the taxpayer to assist in the sale of the old residence. Fixing-up expenses include such items as ordinary repairs, painting, and wallpapering. To qualify as a fixing-up expense, the expense must (1) be incurred for work performed during the 90-day period ending on the date of the contract of sale, (2) be paid within 30 days after the date of the sale, and (3) not be a capital expenditure.

Although selling expenses are deductible in calculating the amount realized, fixing-up expenses are not. Therefore, fixing-up expenses do not have an impact on the calculation of realized gain or loss. However, since fixing-up expenses are deductible in calculating the adjusted sales price, they do have the potential for

---

34. *Richard T. Houlette*, 48 T.C. 350 (1967), and *Stolk v. Comm.*, 64-1 USTC ¶9228, 13 AFTR2d 535, 326 F.2d 760 (CA-2, 1964).
35. Rev.Rul. 82-26, 1982-1 C.B. 114.
36. *Robert W. Aagaard*, 56 T.C. 191 (1971), *acq.*

1971-2 C.B. 1; *Robert G. Clapham*, 63 T.C. 505 (1975); Rev.Rul. 59-72, 1959-1 C.B. 203; and Rev.Rul. 78-146, 1978-1 C.B. 260.
37. *Bolaris v. Comm.*, 85-2 USTC ¶9822, 56 AFTR2d 85-6472, 776 F.2d 1428 (CA-9, 1985).

producing tax benefit in that they reduce the amount of the reinvestment required to qualify for nonrecognition treatment. Conversely, if a replacement residence is not acquired, the fixing-up expenses produce no tax benefit.

Reducing the amount of the required reinvestment by the amount of fixing-up expenses is another application of the wherewithal to pay concept. To the extent that the taxpayer has expended part of the funds received on the sale in preparing the old residence for sale, he or she does not have the funds available to reinvest in the new residence.

As previously mentioned, fixing-up expenses are not considered in determining realized gain. They are considered only in determining how much realized gain is to be postponed. In addition, fixing-up expenses have no direct effect on the basis of the new residence. Indirectly, through their effect on postponed gain, they can bring about a lesser basis for the new residence. The effects of fixing-up expenses on the computation of gain realized and recognized and on the basis of the new residence are illustrated in Concept Summary 12–4 and in Example 56.

Capital Improvements

Capital improvements are added to the adjusted basis of a personal residence. The adjusted basis is used in computing gain or loss on a subsequent sale or other

CONCEPT SUMMARY 12–4

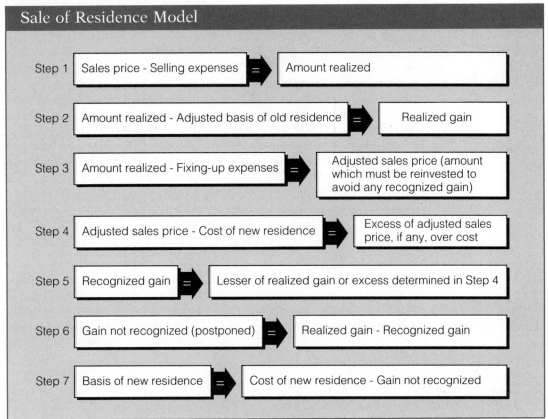

Sale of Residence Model

Step 1 | Sales price - Selling expenses = Amount realized

Step 2 | Amount realized - Adjusted basis of old residence = Realized gain

Step 3 | Amount realized - Fixing-up expenses = Adjusted sales price (amount which must be reinvested to avoid any recognized gain)

Step 4 | Adjusted sales price - Cost of new residence = Excess of adjusted sales price, if any, over cost

Step 5 | Recognized gain = Lesser of realized gain or excess determined in Step 4

Step 6 | Gain not recognized (postponed) = Realized gain - Recognized gain

Step 7 | Basis of new residence = Cost of new residence - Gain not recognized

disposition of the property. However, in calculating the cost of a replacement residence (for determining the nonrecognition of gain under § 1034), only capital improvements made during a certain time period are counted. The time period begins two years before the date of sale of the old residence and ends two years after such date (the time period during which the old residence can be replaced).[38]

If the taxpayer receives a residence by gift or inheritance, such residence will not qualify as a replacement residence. However, if the taxpayer makes substantial capital expenditures (e.g., reconstruction or additions) to such property within the replacement time period, these expenditures do qualify.

Basis of the New Residence

The *basis* of the new residence is the cost of the new residence less the realized gain not recognized (postponed gain). If there is any postponed gain, the *holding period* of the new residence includes the holding period of the old residence.

Concept Summary 12–4 summarizes the sale-of-residence concepts. Example 56 illustrates these concepts and the application of the nonrecognition provision.

EXAMPLE 56

T sells her personal residence (adjusted basis of $36,000) for $44,000. She receives only $41,400 after payment of a brokerage fee of $2,600. Ten days before the sale, T incurred and paid for qualified fixing-up expenses of $1,400. Two months later, T acquires a new residence. Determine the gain, if any, T must recognize and the basis of the new residence under each of the following circumstances:

- The new residence cost $60,000. The cost of the new residence has no effect on determining the realized gain from the sale of the old residence. The realized gain is $5,400 ($41,400 amount realized less $36,000 adjusted basis of old residence). None of the gain is recognized because T reinvested at least $40,000 ($41,400 amount realized − $1,400 fixing-up expenses = $40,000 adjusted sales price) in the new residence. The $5,400 realized gain is postponed, and the basis of the new residence is $54,600 ($60,000 cost less $5,400 postponed gain).

- The new residence cost $38,000. Of the realized gain of $5,400, $2,000 is recognized because T reinvested $2,000 less than the adjusted sales price of $40,000. The remaining gain of $3,400 is not recognized and is postponed. The basis of the new residence is $34,600 ($38,000 cost less $3,400 postponed gain).

- The new residence cost $32,000. All of the realized gain of $5,400 is recognized because T reinvested $8,000 less than the adjusted sales price of $40,000. Since the amount not reinvested exceeds the realized gain, the entire gain is recognized and § 1034 does not apply. The basis of the new residence is simply the residence's cost of $32,000 because there is no postponed gain. □

---

38. *Charles M. Shaw*, 69 T.C. 1034 (1978); Reg. § 1.1034–1(c)(4)(ii); and Rev.Rul. 78–147, 1978– 1 C.B. 261.

Reporting Procedures

The taxpayer is required to report the details of the sale of the residence on the tax return for the taxable year in which gain is realized, even if all of the gain is postponed. If a new residence is acquired and occupied before filing, a statement should be attached to the return showing the purchase date, the cost, and date of occupancy. Form 2119, Sale or Exchange of Principal Residence, is used to show the details of the sale and replacement, and a copy should be retained permanently by the taxpayer as support for the basis of the new residence. If a replacement residence has not been purchased when the return is filed, the taxpayer should submit the details of the purchase on the return of the taxable year during which it occurs. If the old residence is not replaced within the prescribed time period, or if some recognized gain results, the taxpayer must file an amended return for the year in which the sale took place.

SALE OF A RESIDENCE—§ 121

Taxpayers age 55 or older who sell or exchange their principal residence may *elect to exclude* up to $125,000 ($62,500 for married individuals filing separate returns) of realized gain from the sale or exchange. The election can be made *only once.* This provision is contrasted with § 1034 where nonrecognition is mandatory and may occur many times during a taxpayer's lifetime. Section 121 also differs from § 1034 in that it does not require the taxpayer to purchase a new residence. The excluded gain is never recognized, whereas the realized gain not recognized under § 1034 is postponed by subtracting it from the cost of the new residence in calculating the adjusted basis.

This provision is the only case in the tax law where a realized gain from the disposition of property that is not recognized is excluded rather than merely postponed. In other words, the provision allows the taxpayer a permanent recovery of more than the cost or other basis of the residence tax-free.

The reason for § 121 is simply the desire of Congress to relieve older citizens of the large tax they might incur from the sale of a personal residence. The dollar and age limitations restrict the benefit of § 121 to taxpayers who presumably have a greater need for increased tax-free dollars.

Requirements

The taxpayer must be at least age 55 before the date of the sale and have *owned* and *used* the residence as a principal residence for at least *three years* during the *five-year* period ending on the date of sale. The ownership and use periods do not have to be the same period of time. Short temporary absences (e.g., vacations) count as periods of use. If the residence is owned jointly by husband and wife, only one of the spouses is required to meet these requirements if a joint return is filed for the taxable year in which the sale took place.

In determining whether the ownership and use period requirements are satisfied, transactions affecting prior residences may be relevant. If a former residence is involuntarily converted and any gain is postponed under § 1033, the holding period of the former residence is added to the holding period of the replacement residence for § 121 purposes. However, if the realized gain is postponed under § 1034 (sale of residence provision), the holding period of the former residence is not added to the holding period of the replacement residence for § 121 purposes. In this instance, the holding period of the replacement residence begins with the acquisition date of the replacement residence.

EXAMPLE 57   T has lived in his residence since 1983. The residence is involuntarily converted in July 1990. T purchases a replacement residence in August 1990. In determining whether T can satisfy the ownership and use requirements at the time of the subsequent sale of the replacement residence purchased in 1990, he includes the holding period of the involuntarily converted residence.   □

EXAMPLE 58   Assume the same facts as in the previous example, except that T's residence was not involuntarily converted. Instead, T sold it so that he could move into a larger house. In determining whether T can satisfy the ownership and use requirements at the time of the subsequent sale of the replacement residence purchased in 1990, T is not permitted to include the holding period of the old residence.   □

Relationship to Other Provisions

The taxpayer can treat an involuntary conversion of a principal residence as a sale for purposes of § 121(a). Any gain not excluded under § 121 is then subject to postponement under § 1033 or § 1034 (condemnation only), assuming the requirements of those provisions are met.

Any gain not excluded under § 121 from the sale of a residence is subject to postponement under § 1034, assuming the requirements of that provision are met. This relationship is illustrated in Examples 59 and 60.

Making and Revoking the Election

The election not to recognize gain under § 121 may be made or revoked at any time before the statute of limitations expires. Therefore, the taxpayer generally has until the *later* of (1) three years from the due date of the return for the year the gain is realized or (2) two years from the date the tax is paid to make or revoke the election. Making the election is accomplished by attaching a signed statement (showing all the details of the sale) to the return for the taxable year in which the sale took place. Form 2119 is used for this purpose. Revocation is accomplished by filing a signed statement (showing the taxpayer's name, Social Security number, and taxable year for which the election was made) indicating such revocation.

Computation Procedure

The following examples illustrate the application of both the § 121 and § 1034 provisions.

EXAMPLE 59   T sells his personal residence (adjusted basis of $32,000) for $205,000, of which he receives only $195,400 after the payment of selling expenses. Ten days before the sale, T incurred and paid for qualified fixing-up expenses of $6,400. T is age 55 and elects the exclusion of gain under § 121. He does not acquire a replacement residence.   □

EXAMPLE 60   Assume the same facts as in the previous example, except that T acquires a new residence for $40,000 within the prescribed time period.

The solutions to Examples 59 and 60 are as follows:

	Example 59	Example 60
Amount realized ($205,000 − $9,600)	$195,400	$195,400
Adjusted basis	32,000	32,000
Realized gain	$163,400	$163,400
§ 121 exclusion	125,000	125,000
Realized gain after exclusion	$ 38,400	$ 38,400
Amount realized	$195,400	$195,400
Fixing-up expenses	6,400	6,400
Adjusted sales price	$189,000	$189,000
§ 121 exclusion	125,000	125,000
Adjusted sales price after exclusion	$ 64,000	$ 64,000
Cost of new residence	−0−	40,000
Excess of adjusted sales price after the exclusion over reinvestment	$ 64,000	$ 24,000
Recognized gain (lower of realized gain after exclusion or above excess)	$ 38,400	$ 24,000
Realized gain after exclusion	$ 38,400	$ 38,400
Recognized gain	38,400	24,000
Postponed gain	$ −0−	$ 14,400
Cost of new residence	$ −0−	$ 40,000
Postponed gain	−0−	14,400
Basis of new residence	$ −0−	$ 25,600

Comparing the results of Examples 59 and 60 provides insight into the relationship between § 1034 and § 121. If T had not made the election to postpone gain under § 121 in Example 59, his recognized gain would have been $163,400 (the realized gain). Thus, the election resulted in the permanent exclusion of the $125,000 of realized gain by reducing the recognized gain to $38,400. Further documentation of the permanent nature of the § 121 exclusion is provided in the calculation of the basis of the new residence in Example 60. The $40,000 cost of the residence is reduced only by the postponed gain of $14,400. That is, it is not reduced by the amount of the § 121 exclusion. To postpone all of the $38,400 realized gain after the exclusion, T would have needed to reinvest $64,000 (the adjusted sales price after the exclusion). Also, note that the Example 59 results demonstrate that the realized gain after the exclusion is the ceiling on recognition.

OTHER NONRECOGNITION PROVISIONS

In terms of impacting on the typical taxpayer, sales of residences and involuntary conversions occur more frequently than the other types of nontaxable exchanges. Several additional nonrecognition provisions that are not as common are treated briefly in the remainder of this chapter.

Exchange of Stock for Property—§ 1032

Under this Section, no gain or loss is recognized to a corporation on the receipt of money or other property in exchange for its stock (including treasury stock). In other words, no gain or loss is recognized by a corporation when it deals in its own stock. This provision is consistent with the accounting treatment of such transactions.

Certain Exchanges of Insurance Policies—§ 1035

Under this provision, no gain or loss is recognized from the exchange of certain insurance contracts or policies. The rules relating to exchanges not solely in kind and the basis of the property acquired are the same as under § 1031. Exchanges qualifying for nonrecognition include the following:

- The exchange of life insurance contracts.

- The exchange of a life insurance contract for an endowment or annuity contract.

- The exchange of an endowment contract for another endowment contract that provides for regular payments beginning at a date not later than the date payments would have begun under the contract exchanged.

- The exchange of an endowment contract for an annuity contract.

- The exchange of annuity contracts.

Exchange of Stock for Stock of the Same Corporation—§ 1036

No gain or loss is recognized by a shareholder on the exchange of common stock solely for common stock in the same corporation or from the exchange of preferred stock for preferred stock in the same corporation. Exchanges between individual shareholders as well as between a shareholder and the corporation are included. The rules relating to exchanges not solely in kind and the basis of the property acquired are the same as under § 1031. For example, a nonrecognition exchange occurs when common stock with different rights, such as voting for nonvoting, is exchanged. Gain or loss from the exchange of common for preferred or preferred for common usually is recognized even though the stock exchanged is in the same corporation.

Certain Reacquisitions of Real Property—§ 1038

Under this provision, no loss is recognized from the repossession of real property sold on an installment basis. Gain is recognized to a limited extent.

Transfers of Property between Spouses or Incident to Divorce—§ 1041

Section 1041 provides that transfers of property *between spouses or former spouses incident to divorce* are nontaxable transactions. Therefore, the basis to the recipient is a carryover basis. To be treated as incident to the divorce, the transfer must be related to the cessation of marriage or occur within one year after the date on which the marriage ceases.

Section 1041 also provides for nontaxable exchange treatment on property transfers *between spouses during marriage*. The basis to the recipient spouse is a carryover basis.

Sale of Stock to Stock Ownership Plans or Certain Cooperatives—§ 1042

Section 1042 provides that the realized gain will be postponed if the taxpayer (or his or her executor) sells qualified securities to a qualified entity and, within a

specified time period, such seller purchases qualified replacement property. Qualified entities include an employee stock ownership plan (ESOP) and an eligible worker-owned cooperative. To qualify for this treatment, several statutory requirements must be satisfied.

TAX PLANNING CONSIDERATIONS

Cost Identification and Documentation Considerations

The allocation of the contract price for multiple assets acquired in a single transaction is needed for several reasons. First, some of the assets may be depreciable although others are not. From the different viewpoints of the buyer and the seller, this may produce a tax conflict that will need to be resolved. That is, the seller will prefer a high allocation for nondepreciable assets, whereas the purchaser will prefer a high allocation for depreciable assets (see chapter 13). Second, the seller will need to know the amount realized on the sale of the capital assets and the ordinary income assets to classify the recognized gains and losses as capital or ordinary. For example, whether the allocation is to goodwill or a covenant not to compete (see chapter 13) will produce different tax consequences to the seller. Third, the buyer will need the adjusted basis of each asset to calculate the realized gain or loss on the sale or other disposition of each asset.

Selection of Property for Making Gifts

A donor can achieve several tax advantages by making gifts of appreciated property. Income tax on the unrealized gain that would have occurred had the donor sold the property is avoided by the donor. A portion of this amount can be permanently avoided as the result of the donee's adjusted basis being increased by a part of the gift tax paid by the donor. Even absent this increase in basis, the income tax liability on the sale of the property by the donee can be less than the income tax liability that would have resulted from the donor's sale of the property. Such reduced income tax liability will occur if the donee is in a lower tax bracket than the donor. In addition, any subsequent appreciation during the time the property is held by the lower tax bracket donee will result in a tax savings on the sale or other disposition of the property. Such gifts of appreciated property can be an effective tool in family tax planning.

Taxpayers should generally not make gifts of depreciated property (property that, if sold, would produce a realized loss) because the donor does not receive an income tax deduction for the unrealized loss element. In addition, the donee will receive no benefit from this unrealized loss upon the subsequent sale of the property because of the loss basis rule. The loss basis rule provides that the donee's basis is the lower of the donor's basis or fair market value at the date of the gift. If the donor anticipates that the donee will sell the property upon receiving it, the donor should sell the property and take the loss deduction, assuming the loss is deductible. The donor can then give the proceeds from the sale to the donee.

Selection of Property for Making Bequests

A decedent's will should generally make bequests of appreciated property. Doing so enables income tax to be avoided by the decedent and the inheritor of the property on the unrealized gain because the recipient takes the fair market value as his or her basis.

Taxpayers generally should not make bequests of depreciated property (property that, if sold, would produce a realized loss) because the decedent does not receive an income tax deduction for the unrealized loss element. In addition, the inheritor will receive no benefit from this unrealized loss upon the subsequent sale of the property.

EXAMPLE 61   On the date of her death, W owned land held for investment purposes. The land had an adjusted basis of $600,000 and a fair market value of $100,000. If W had sold the property before her death, the recognized loss would have been $500,000. If H inherits the property and sells it for $50,000, the recognized loss will be $50,000 (the decline in value since W's death). In addition, regardless of the period of time the property is held by H, the holding period is long term (see chapter 13). ☐

From an income tax perspective, it is preferable to transfer appreciated property as a bequest rather than as a gift.[39] This results from the step-up in basis for inherited property, whereas for property received by gift, the donee has a carryover basis. However, in making this decision, consideration must also be given to the estate tax consequences of the bequest versus the gift tax consequences of the gift.

Wash Sales.   The wash sales provisions can be avoided if the security is replaced within the statutory time period with a similar rather than a substantially identical security. For example, the sale of Bethlehem Steel common stock and a purchase of Inland Steel common stock would not be treated as a wash sale. Such a procedure can enable the taxpayer to use an unrealized capital loss to offset a recognized capital gain. The taxpayer can sell the security before the end of the taxable year, offset the recognized capital loss against the capital gain, and invest the sales proceeds in a similar security.

Because the wash sales provisions do not apply to gains, it may be desirable to engage in a wash sale before the end of the taxable year. This recognized capital gain may be used to offset capital losses or capital loss carryovers from prior years.

Like-Kind Exchanges

Since application of the like-kind provisions is mandatory rather than elective, in certain instances it may be preferable to avoid qualifying for § 1031 nonrecognition. If the like-kind provisions do not apply, the end result may be the recognition of capital gain in exchange for a higher basis in the newly acquired asset. Also, the immediate recognition of gain may be preferable in certain situations. Examples of immediate recognition being beneficial include the following:

- Taxpayer has unused net operating loss carryovers.
- Taxpayer has unused investment tax credit carryovers.
- Taxpayer has suspended or current passive activity losses.
- Taxpayer expects his or her effective tax rate to increase in the future.

---

39. Consideration must also be given to the estate tax consequences of the bequest versus the gift tax consequences of the gift.

EXAMPLE 62   T disposes of a machine (used in his business) with an adjusted basis of $3,000 for $4,000. T also acquires a new business machine for $9,000. If § 1031 applies, the $1,000 realized gain is not recognized, and the basis of the new machine is reduced by $1,000 (from $9,000 to $8,000). If § 1031 does not apply, a $1,000 gain is recognized and may receive capital gain treatment to the extent that the gain is not recognized as ordinary income due to the depreciation recapture provisions (see chapter 13). In addition, the basis for depreciation on the new machine is $9,000 rather than $8,000 since there is no unrecognized gain. □

Another time for avoiding the application of § 1031 nonrecognition treatment is when the adjusted basis of the property being disposed of exceeds the fair market value.

EXAMPLE 63   Assume the same facts as in the previous example, except the fair market value of the machine is $2,500. If § 1031 applies, the $500 realized loss is not recognized. Therefore, to recognize the loss, T should sell the old machine and purchase the new one. The purchase and sale transactions should be with different taxpayers. □

On the other hand, the like-kind exchange procedure can be utilized to control the amount of recognized gain.

EXAMPLE 64   S has property with an adjusted basis of $40,000 and a fair market value of $100,000. P wants to buy S's property, but S wants to limit the amount of recognized gain on the proposed transaction. P acquires other like-kind property (from an outside party) for $80,000. P then exchanges this property and $20,000 cash for S's property. S has a realized gain of $60,000 ($100,000 amount realized − $40,000 adjusted basis). S's recognized gain is only $20,000, the lower of the boot received of $20,000 or the realized gain of $60,000. S's basis for the like-kind property is $40,000 ($40,000 adjusted basis + $20,000 gain recognized − $20,000 boot received). If S had sold the property to P for its fair market value of $100,000, the result would have been a $60,000 recognized gain ($100,000 amount realized − $40,000 adjusted basis) to S. It is permissible for S to identify the like-kind property that he wants P to purchase.[40] □

Involuntary Conversions

In certain cases, a taxpayer may prefer to recognize gain from an involuntary conversion. Keep in mind that § 1033, unlike § 1031 (dealing with like-kind exchanges), generally is an elective provision.

EXAMPLE 65   T has a $40,000 realized gain from the involuntary conversion of an office building. The entire proceeds of $450,000 are reinvested in a new office

---

40. *Franklin B. Biggs*, 69 T.C. 905 (1978); Rev.Rul. 57–244, 1957–1 C.B. 247; Rev.Rul. 73–476, 1973–2 C.B. 300; *Starker vs. U.S.*, 79–2 USTC ¶9541, 44 AFTR2d 79–5525, 602 F.2d 1341 (CA–9, 1979); and *Baird Publishing Co.*, 39 T.C. 608 (1962).

building. T, however, does not elect to postpone gain under § 1033 because of an expiring net operating loss carryover that is offset against the gain. Therefore, none of the realized gain of $40,000 is postponed. By not electing § 1033 postponement, T's basis in the replacement property will be the property's cost of $450,000 rather than $410,000 ($450,000 reduced by the $40,000 realized gain). □

Sale of a Personal Residence

Replacement Period Requirements.   Several problems arise in avoiding the recognition of gain on the sale of a principal residence. Most of these problems can be resolved favorably through appropriate planning procedures. However, a few represent situations where the taxpayer has to accept the adverse tax consequences and possesses little, if any, planning flexibility. One pitfall concerns the failure to reinvest *all* of the proceeds from the sale of the residence into a new principal residence.

EXAMPLE 66

R sells her principal residence in January 1988 for $150,000 (adjusted basis of $40,000). Shortly thereafter, R purchases for $100,000 a 50-year-old house in a historical part of the community that she uses as her principal residence. It was R's intention to significantly renovate the property over a period of time and thereby make it more suitable to her living needs. In December 1990, R enters into a contract with a home improvement company to carry out the renovation at a cost of $60,000. It is clear that only $100,000 of the proceeds from the sale of the old residence has been reinvested in a new principal residence on a *timely* basis. Of the realized gain of $110,000, therefore, $50,000 ($150,000 adjusted sales price − $100,000 reinvested) must be recognized.[41] □

Principal Residence Requirement.   Section 1034 will not apply unless the property involved is the taxpayer's principal residence. In this connection, one potential hurdle can arise in cases where the residence has been rented and therefore has not been occupied by the taxpayer for an extended period of time. Depending on the circumstances, the IRS might contend that the taxpayer has abandoned the property as his or her principal residence. The *key* to the abandonment issue is whether or not the taxpayer intended to reoccupy the property and use it as a principal residence upon his or her return to the locale. If the residence is, in fact, not reoccupied, the taxpayer should have a good reason to explain why it is not.

EXAMPLE 67

T is transferred by her employer to another office out of the state on a three-year assignment. It is the understanding of the parties that the assignment is temporary, and upon its completion, T will return to the original job site. During her absence, T rents her principal residence and lives in an apartment at the new location. T has every intention of reoccupying her residence. However, when she returns from the temporary assignment, she finds that the residence no longer suits her needs. Specifically, the public school located nearby where she had planned to send her children has been

---

41. It has been assumed that § 121 did not apply.

closed. As a consequence, T sells the residence and replaces it with one more conveniently located to a public school. Under these circumstances, it would appear that T is in an excellent position to show that she has not abandoned the property as her principal residence. She can satisfactorily explain why she did not reoccupy the residence before its sale.[42] □

The principal residence requirement could cause difficulty where a taxpayer works in two places and maintains more than one household. In such cases, the principal residence will be the location where the taxpayer lives most of the time.[43]

EXAMPLE 68

E is a vice president of Z Corporation and in this capacity spends about an equal amount of time in the company's New York City and Miami offices. E owns a house in each location and expects to retire in about five years. At that time, he plans to sell his New York home and use some of the proceeds to make improvements on the Miami property. Both homes have appreciated in value since their acquisition, and such appreciation can be expected to continue. From a tax planning standpoint, E should be looking toward the use of §§ 121 and 1034 to shelter some or all of the gain he will realize on the future sale of the New York City home.[44] To do this, he should arrange his affairs so as to spend more than six months each year at that location. Upon its sale, therefore, the New York home will be his principal residence. □

Section 121 Considerations.   Older individuals who may be contemplating a move from their home to an apartment should consider the following possibilities for minimizing or deferring taxes:

- Wait until age 55 to sell the residence and elect under § 121 to exclude up to $125,000 of the realized gain.

- Sell the personal residence under an installment contract to spread the gain over several years.[45]

- Sell the personal residence and purchase a condominium instead of renting an apartment, thereby permitting further deferral of the unrecognized gain.

The use of § 121 should be carefully considered. Although such use avoids the immediate recognition of gain, the election expends the full $125,000 allowed.

EXAMPLE 69

In 1990 T, age 55, sells his personal residence for an amount that yields a realized gain of $5,000. Presuming T does not plan to reinvest the sales proceeds in a new principal residence (take advantage of the deferral possibility of § 1034), should he avoid the recognition of this gain by utilizing § 121? Electing § 121 would mean that T would waste $120,000 of his lifetime exclusion. □

---

42. Rev.Rul. 78–146, 1978–1 C.B. 260. Compare *Rudolph M. Stucchi*, 35 TCM 1052, T.C.Memo. 1976–242.

43. Rev.Rul. 77–298, 1977–2 C.B. 308.

44. If E qualifies, § 121′ would allow the first $125,000 of gain to be nontaxable. Further gain recognition might be avoided under § 1034 to the extent the sales proceeds are applied toward improvements on the Miami home.

45. § 453(a). See the discussion of the installment method in chapter 15.

In this connection, the use of § 121 by one spouse precludes the other spouse from later taking advantage of the exclusion.

EXAMPLE 70   Assume the same facts as in the previous example, except that T was married to W at the time of the sale. Later, T and W are divorced and W marries R. If T has used the § 121 exclusion, it is unavailable to W and R even though either one of them may otherwise qualify. This result occurs because for T to make the election for the 1990 sale, it was necessary for W to join with him in making the election even if the residence was owned separately by T. For W and R to be able to make the § 121 election, it would be necessary for W and T to revoke their prior election. Another planning approach would be for R to sell his residence before the marriage to W and to elect the exclusion on that sale. ☐

A taxpayer who is eligible to elect § 121 exclusion treatment may choose not to do so in order to remain eligible to elect it in the future. In arriving at this decision, consideration must be given to the probability that the taxpayer will satisfy the three-out-of-five year ownership and use period requirements associated with a residence sale in the future. As previously mentioned, the holding period for the occupancy and use requirements does carry over for a § 1033 involuntary conversion but does not carry over for a § 1034 sale.

Taxpayers should maintain records of both the purchase and sale of personal residences since the sale of one residence results in an adjustment of the basis of the new residence if the deferral provisions of § 1034 apply. Form 2119 should be filed with the tax return and a copy retained as support for the basis of the new residence. Detailed cost records should be retained for an indefinite period.

PROBLEM MATERIALS

Discussion Questions

1. If a taxpayer sells property for cash, the amount realized consists of the net proceeds from the sale. For each of the following, indicate the effect on the amount realized:
    a. The property is sold on credit.
    b. A mortgage on the property is assumed by the buyer.
    c. The purchaser pays property taxes that are treated as imposed on the seller.

2. T is negotiating to buy some land. Under the first option, T will give S $70,000 and assume S's mortgage on the land for $30,000. Under the second option, T will give S $100,000, and S will immediately pay off the mortgage. T would like for his basis for the land to be as high as possible. Given this objective, which option should T select?

3. If the buyer of property assumes the seller's mortgage, why is the amount of the mortgage included in the amount realized by the seller? What effect does the mortgage assumption have on the seller's (a) adjusted basis for the mortgaged property and (b) realized gain or loss?

4. C and D each own an automobile that each uses exclusively in his respective trade or business. The adjusted basis of each automobile is $17,000, and the fair market value is $11,000. Both automobiles are destroyed in accidents. C's automobile is

insured, and C receives insurance proceeds of $11,000. D's automobile is uninsured. Explain how the adjusted basis for each automobile is reduced to zero, even though one is insured and the other is uninsured.

5. T owns stock in X Corporation and Y Corporation. He receives a $1,000 distribution from both corporations. The instructions from X Corporation state that the $1,000 is a dividend. The instructions from Y Corporation state that the $1,000 is not a dividend. What could cause the instructions to differ as to the tax consequences?

6. A taxpayer who acquires a taxable bond at a premium may elect to amortize the premium, whereas a taxpayer who acquires a tax-exempt bond at a premium must amortize the premium. Why would a taxpayer make the amortization election for taxable bonds? What effect does the mandatory amortization of tax-exempt bonds have on taxable income?

7. T's building is condemned and his realized loss is $5,000. U's building is condemned and her realized loss is $6,000. U deducts her realized loss of $6,000 on her tax return whereas T is unable to deduct his realized loss of $5,000 on his tax return. Explain why only U is permitted to deduct her realized loss.

8. T owns 300 shares of Z Corporation stock. He acquired the shares as follows:
   - On February 16, he purchased 100 shares.
   - On June 3, he inherited 100 shares.
   - On October 12, he received 100 shares as a gift.

   T decides to sell 200 shares prior to the end of the year. How will he determine the adjusted basis for the 200 shares sold?

9. R makes a gift of an appreciated building to E. E dies three months later, and R inherits the building from E. During the period that E held the building, he deducted depreciation and made a capital expenditure. What effect might these items have on R's basis for the inherited building?

10. Immediately before his death in 1990, H sells securities (adjusted basis of $100,000) for their fair market value of $20,000. The sale was not to a related party. The securities were community property, and H is survived by his wife, W.
    a. Did H act wisely? Why or why not?
    b. Suppose the figures are reversed (sale for $100,000 of property with an adjusted basis of $20,000). Would the sale be wise? Why or why not?

11. For the executor to elect the alternate valuation date, what requirements must be satisfied? What is the Congressional justification for this limitation on the election?

12. R owns 100 shares of stock in Z Corporation. His adjusted basis for the stock is $5,000. On December 21, R sells the stock in the marketplace for $12,000. R purchases 100 shares of stock in Z Corporation in the marketplace on January 5 of the following year for $12,200.
    a. What is R trying to achieve from a tax perspective?
    b. Will he succeed?
    c. Using the same data, except that R's adjusted basis for the stock is $15,000, respond to (a) and (b).

13. What is the basis for property converted from personal use to business or income-producing use when there is a loss? When there is a gain? Why is there a difference? How does conversion affect depreciation and why?

14. Which of the following qualify as like-kind exchanges under § 1031?
    a. Improved for unimproved real estate.
    b. Crane (used in business) for inventory.

    c. Rental house for truck (used in business).

    d. Business equipment for securities.

    e. Delicatessen for bakery (both used for business).

    f. Personal residence for apartment building (held for investment).

    g. Rental house for land (both held for investment).

    h. Ten shares of stock in X Corporation for 10 shares of stock in Y Corporation.

15. If a taxpayer exchanges his or her personal use car for another car to be held for personal use, any realized loss is not recognized. However, if realized gain occurs, the realized gain is recognized. Why?

16. T is planning on selling a machine used in his business so that he can recognize the realized loss. He will use the sales proceeds to purchase a replacement machine. Are there any circumstances under which T will not be able to recognize the realized loss?

17. A taxpayer's property is involved in an involuntary conversion. Are there any circumstances under which neither the functional use test nor the taxpayer use test is the appropriate test with respect to qualifying replacement property?

18. Taxpayer's warehouse is destroyed by fire. What are the different tax options available to the taxpayer (a) if he has a realized gain and (b) if he has a realized loss?

19. Discuss the tax options available to the taxpayer when the form of the transaction is (a) a direct involuntary conversion and (b) an indirect involuntary conversion.

20. Z is notified by the city public housing àuthority on April 5, 1990, that his apartment building is going to be condemned as part of an urban renewal project. On April 12, 1990, S offers to buy the building from Z. Z sells the building to S on April 30, 1990. Condemnation occurs on June 1, 1990, and S receives the condemnation proceeds from the city. Assume both Z and S are calendar year taxpayers.

    a. What is the earliest date that Z can dispose of the building and qualify for § 1033 postponement treatment?

    b. Does the sale to S qualify as a § 1033 involuntary conversion?

    c. What is the latest date that S can acquire qualifying replacement property and qualify for postponement of the realized gain?

    d. What type of property will be qualifying replacement property?

21. Discuss the justification for nonrecognition of gain on the sale or exchange of a principal residence. Discuss the justification for disallowance of loss.

22. What effect does the renting of a house that has been the taxpayer's principal residence have on the qualification of the house as a principal residence?

23. The personal residence of C is destroyed by fire. C receives insurance proceeds. His realized gain exceeds the amount of the § 121 exclusion of $125,000. C satisfies the age, ownership, and occupancy requirements associated with the § 121 exclusion.

    a. Can an involuntary conversion qualify for the § 121 exclusion?

    b. If C is not going to acquire a replacement residence, should he elect the § 121 exclusion? What factors should he consider in making this decision?

    c. If C is going to acquire a replacement residence, should he elect the § 121 exclusion? What factors should he consider in making this decision?

    d. Assume all the facts are the same, except that C sells his personal residence. Respond to (b) and (c).

24. A and B, both age 60, are sisters who live in the house they inherited from their parents 20 years ago. H and W, age 60, are married. They purchased their

principal residence 7 years ago. Comment on any differences in the application of the § 121 exclusion to the sisters and the married couple.

25. Distinguish between the effect of the § 121 exclusion and the § 1034 postponement on the basis of a replacement residence.

Problems

26. R bought a rental house at the beginning of 1985 for $80,000, of which $10,000 is allocated to the land and $70,000 to the building. Early in 1987, he had a tennis court built in the backyard at a cost of $5,000. R has deducted $32,200 for depreciation on the house and $1,300 for depreciation on the court. At the beginning of 1990, R sells the house and tennis court for $125,000 cash.

    a. What is R's realized gain or loss?

    b. If an original mortgage of $20,000 is still outstanding and the buyer assumes the mortgage in addition to the cash payment, what is R's realized gain or loss?

    c. If the buyer takes the property subject to the mortgage, what is R's realized gain or loss?

27. D's residence, with a basis of $80,000 and a fair market value of $100,000, is damaged by fire. After the fire, the fair market value is $45,000. D receives insurance proceeds of $55,000. His adjusted gross income is $40,000.

    a. What effect does the casualty have on the adjusted basis?

    b. What effect does the casualty have on the adjusted basis if the residence is uninsured?

28. T's warehouse, which has an adjusted basis of $250,000, is destroyed by a hurricane. T receives insurance proceeds of $400,000. Because T has excess warehouse space in his business, he invests the $400,000 in X Corporation stock.

    a. Calculate T's realized gain or loss.

    b. Calculate T's recognized gain or loss.

    c. Calculate T's basis for the X Corporation stock.

29. C owns all of the stock of a corporation. The earnings and profits of the corporation are $25,000. C's adjusted basis for his stock is $40,000. He receives a cash distribution of $70,000 from the corporation.

    a. What effect does the distribution have on the adjusted basis of C's stock?

    b. What effect would the distribution have on the adjusted basis of C's stock if the earnings and profits of the corporation were $80,000?

30. B paid $270,000 for bonds with a face value of $250,000 at the beginning of 1986. The bonds mature in 10 years and pay 9% interest per year.

    a. If B sells the bonds for $255,000 at the beginning of 1990, does she have a realized gain or loss? If so, how much?

    b. If B trades the bonds at the beginning of 1991 for stock worth $262,500, does she have a realized gain or loss? If so, how much?

31. Which of the following would definitely result in a recognized gain or loss?

    a. K sells his lakeside cabin, which has an adjusted basis of $10,000, for $15,000.

    b. A sells his personal residence, which has an adjusted basis of $15,000, for $10,000.

    c. C's personal residence is on the site of a proposed airport and is condemned by the city. C receives $55,000 for the house, which has an adjusted basis of $65,000.

   d. B sells his personal residence, which has an adjusted basis of $80,000, for $90,000.

   e. J gives stock to his niece. J's adjusted basis is $8,000, and the fair market value is $5,000.

32. L owns 30% of the stock of LJ Corporation. He purchases undeveloped land from the corporation for $45,000. The fair market value of the land is $60,000.

   a. Calculate the amount of income, if any, that L must recognize.

   b. Calculate L's basis for the land.

33. P purchases the assets of a sole proprietorship from S. The adjusted basis of each of the assets on S's books and the fair market value of each asset as agreed to by P and S are as follows:

Asset	S's Adjusted Basis	FMV
Accounts receivable	$ –0–	$ 10,000
Notes receivable	15,000	20,000
Machinery and equipment	85,000	100,000
Building	100,000	300,000
Land	200,000	350,000

The purchase price is $900,000. Determine P's basis for each of the assets of the sole proprietorship.

34. During the year, F received the following dividends on her stock portfolio:

   a. Five shares of common stock in U Company on 10 shares of common stock she already owns. F paid $30 a share for the original 10 shares.

   b. Twenty shares of preferred stock in X Company on 200 shares of common stock for which F paid $10,000. The fair market value of the preferred stock on the date of distribution was $40, and the fair market value of the common stock was $60.

What is the basis per share for each of the common shares and the preferred shares?

35. T received various gifts over the years. He has decided to dispose of the following assets that he received as gifts:

   a. In 1920, he received a Rolls Royce worth $22,000. The donor's adjusted basis for the auto was $16,000. T sells the auto for $35,000 in 1990.

   b. In 1928, he received land worth $20,000. The donor's adjusted basis was $24,000. T sells the land for $150,000 in 1990.

   c. In 1935, he received stock in G Company. The donor's adjusted basis was $1,000. The fair market value on the date of the gift was $2,000. T sells the stock for $2,500 in 1990.

   d. In 1951, he received land worth $12,000. The donor's adjusted basis was $15,000. T sells the land for $4,000 in 1990.

   e. In 1987, he received stock worth $30,000. The donor's adjusted basis was $40,000. T sells the stock in 1990 for $33,000.

What is the realized gain or loss from each of the preceding transactions? Assume in each of the gift transactions that no gift tax was paid.

36. R receives a gift of property (after 1976) that has a fair market value of $100,000 on the date of gift. The donor's adjusted basis for the property was $60,000. Assume the donor paid gift tax of $16,000 on the gift.

   a. What is R's basis for gain and loss and for depreciation?

   b. If R had received the gift of property before 1977, what would his basis be for gain and loss and for depreciation?

37. T is planning to make a charitable contribution of stock worth $20,000 to the Boy Scouts. The stock T is considering contributing has an adjusted basis of $15,000. A friend has suggested that T sell the stock and contribute the $20,000 in proceeds rather than contribute the stock.

　　a. Should T follow the friend's advice? Why?

　　b. Assume the fair market value is only $13,000. In this case, should T follow the friend's advice? Why?

　　c. Rather than make a charitable contribution to the Boy Scouts, T is going to make a gift to N, his niece. Advise T regarding (a) and (b).

38. D inherits property from M, her mother. M's adjusted basis for the property is $100,000, and the fair market value is $125,000. Six months after M's death the fair market value is $140,000. D is the sole beneficiary of M's estate.

　　a. Can the executor of M's estate elect the alternate valuation date?

　　b. What is D's basis for the property?

39. Q's estate includes the following assets available for distribution to R, one of Q's beneficiaries:

	Decedent's Adjusted Basis	FMV at Date of Death	FMV at Alternate Valuation Date
Cash	$ 10,000	$ 10,000	$ 10,000
Stock	40,000	125,000	60,000
Apartment building	60,000	300,000	325,000
Land	75,000	100,000	110,000

The fair market value of the stock six months after Q's death was $60,000. However, believing that the stock would continue to decline in value, the executor of the estate distributed the stock to R one month after Q's death. R immediately sold the stock for $85,000.

　　a. Determine R's basis for the assets if the primary valuation date and amount apply.

　　b. Determine R's basis for the assets if the executor elects the alternate valuation date and amount.

40. C inherited land from her grandfather, whose basis in the land was $150,000. At the date of the grandfather's death, the fair market value of the land was $200,000. Six months thereafter the land had appreciated to $220,000. According to the executor, $4,000 of the estate tax payable is allocable to the land. In filing the estate tax return, the executor is willing to make any elections that will produce beneficial income tax consequences to the taxpayer.

　　a. What is C's basis in the inherited property?

　　b. What is C's basis in the inherited property if the grandfather's basis was $300,000?

　　c. What is C's basis in the inherited property if the fair market value of the land on the date of the grandfather's death was $220,000 and the fair market value six months thereafter was $200,000?

41. W purchased 50 shares of A Corporation common stock for $2,500 on May 12, 1990. On August 12, 1990, W purchased 25 additional shares for $1,375; on August 27, 1990, W purchased 10 additional shares for $500. On September 3, 1990, he sold the 50 shares purchased on May 12, 1990, for $2,000.

　　a. What is W's realized gain or loss on September 3, 1990?

　　b. What is W's recognized gain or loss?

　　c. What is the basis of W's remaining shares after the sale on September 3?

42. T owns land and building with an adjusted basis of $125,000 and a fair market value of $250,000. T exchanges the land and building for land with a fair market value of $160,000 that T will use as a parking lot. In addition, T receives stock worth $90,000.

    a. What is T's realized gain or loss?

    b. His recognized gain or loss?

    c. The basis of the land and the stock received?

43. T owns investment land with an adjusted basis of $35,000. P has offered to purchase the land from T for $175,000 for use in a real estate development. The amount offered by P is $10,000 in excess of what T perceives as the fair market value of the land. T would like to dispose of the land to P but does not want to incur the tax liability that would result. T identifies an office building with a fair market value of $175,000 that he would like to acquire. P purchases the office building and then exchanges the office building for T's land.

    a. Calculate T's realized and recognized gain on the exchange and T's basis for the office building.

    b. Calculate P's realized and recognized gain on the exchange and P's basis in the land.

44. What is the basis of the new property in each of the following exchanges?

    a. Apartment building held for investment (adjusted basis $160,000) for lake-front property held for investment (fair market value $180,000).

    b. Barber shop (adjusted basis $30,000) for grocery store (fair market value $27,000), both held for business use.

    c. Drug store (adjusted basis $30,000) for bulldozer (fair market value $35,000), both held for business use.

    d. IBM common stock (adjusted basis $4,000) for shoe shine stand used in business (fair market value $5,000).

    e. Rental house (adjusted basis $20,000) for land held for investment (fair market value $32,000).

45. G exchanges real estate held for investment plus stock for real estate to be held for investment. The stock transferred has an adjusted basis of $5,000 and a fair market value of $2,500. The real estate transferred has an adjusted basis of $12,500 and a fair market value of $13,750. The real estate acquired has a fair market value of $16,250.

    a. What is G's realized gain or loss?

    b. His recognized gain or loss?

    c. The basis of the newly acquired real estate?

46. H exchanges a machine (adjusted basis of $25,000 and fair market value of $45,000) and undeveloped land held for investment (adjusted basis of $50,000 and fair market value of $300,000) for land worth $290,000 to be used in her business. The undeveloped land has a mortgage of $55,000 that the other party to the exchange assumes.

    a. What is H's realized gain or loss?

    b. Her recognized gain or loss?

    c. The basis of the newly acquired real estate?

47. E converted her personal residence to rental property on January 1, 1989. At that time, the adjusted basis was $80,000 and the fair market value was $100,000. During the interim rental period, E deducted depreciation of $5,576. The rental property is condemned on December 31, 1990, in connection with an urban renewal project, and E receives condemnation proceeds of $60,000.

    a. What is the adjusted basis at the condemnation date?

    b. What is the recognized gain or loss on the condemnation?

48. Do the following qualify for involuntary conversion treatment?

    a. Purchase of a sporting goods store as a replacement for a bookstore (used in a business) that was destroyed by fire.

    b. Sale of a home because a neighbor converted his residence into a nightclub.

    c. Purchase of an airplane to replace a shrimp boat (used in a business) that was wrecked by a hurricane.

    d. Taxpayer's residence destroyed by a tornado and replaced with another residence.

    e. Purchase of an apartment building to replace a rental house by an investor. The rental house was destroyed by a flood.

49. R's office building, which is used in his business, is destroyed by a hurricane in September 1990. The adjusted basis is $225,000. R receives insurance proceeds of $350,000 in October 1990.

    a. Calculate R's realized gain or loss, recognized gain or loss, and basis for the replacement property if R acquires an office building for $390,000 in October 1990.

    b. Calculate R's realized gain or loss, recognized gain or loss, and basis for the replacement property if R acquires a warehouse for $330,000 in October 1990.

    c. Calculate R's realized gain or loss and recognized gain or loss if R does not acquire replacement property.

50. T, age 42, has lived in her residence for three years. Her adjusted basis is $130,000. Knowing that she is going to move to another city, she lists her residence for sale in February 1988. When she moves in May 1988, she purchases another residence for $190,000. Due to market conditions, she does not sell her original residence until July 1990. The selling price is $225,000, selling expenses are $13,000, and fixing-up expenses are $4,000.

    a. What is T's realized gain or loss?

    b. The recognized gain or loss?

    c. The basis of the new residence?

51. What are the realized, recognized, and postponed gain or loss, the new basis, and the adjusted sales price for each of the following? Assume that none of the taxpayers is 55 years of age or older.

    a. R sells her residence for $90,000. The adjusted basis was $55,000. The selling expenses were $5,000. The fixing-up expenses were $3,000. She did not reinvest in a new residence.

    b. D sells his residence for $170,000. The adjusted basis was $120,000. The selling expenses were $4,000. The fixing-up expenses were $6,000. D reinvested $160,000 in a new residence.

    c. M sells her residence for $65,000. The adjusted basis was $35,000. The selling expenses were $1,000. The fixing-up expenses were $2,000. She reinvested $40,000.

    d. B sells his residence for $70,000. The adjusted basis was $65,000. The selling expenses were $6,000. He reinvested $80,000.

    e. C sells his residence for $100,000, and his mortgage is assumed by the buyer. The adjusted basis was $80,000; the mortgage, $50,000. The selling expenses were $4,000. The fixing-up expenses were $2,000. He reinvested $120,000.

52. H, age 60, and W, age 45, have been married for two years. H sells the personal residence in which H and W reside for $180,000. W has no ownership interest in the house. Legal fees and realtor's commissions are $15,000. Fixing-up expenses are $4,000. H's adjusted basis is $55,000. H has owned and occupied the house for the past 7 years and plans to elect the § 121 exclusion. H purchases a replacement residence 22 months after the sale for $135,000. Before her marriage to H, W was married to P. While married to W, P had sold his personal residence and elected § 121 treatment to exclude the realized gain. W joined P in making the election, even though she had no ownership interest in the house. P and W were divorced five years ago.

    a. Calculate H's realized gain, recognized gain, and basis for the replacement residence if H and W file a joint return.

    b. Calculate H's realized gain, recognized gain, and basis for the replacement residence if H and W file separate returns.

    c. Calculate H's realized gain, recognized gain, and basis for the replacement residence in (a) and (b) if P and W had filed separate returns during the taxable year that P elected § 121 treatment.

    d. Advise H on what action is necessary to maximize the § 121 exclusion.

Cumulative Problems

53. Ada Johnson, age 28, is single and has no dependents. Her Social Security number is 444–11–3333, and she resides at 210 Avenue G, Kentwood, LA 70444. Her salary in 1990 was $25,000. She incurred unreimbursed expenses of $800 for travel and $500 for entertainment in connection with her job as an assistant personnel director. In addition, she had the following items of possible tax consequence in 1990:

    a. Itemized deductions (not including any potential deductions mentioned previously), $5,800.

    b. Proceeds from the October 8, 1990, sale of land inherited from her father on June 15, 1990 (fair market value on June 15 was $35,000; her father's adjusted basis was $15,000), $38,000.

    c. Proceeds from the November 1, 1990, sale of 50 shares of X Corporation stock received as a gift from her father on October 5, 1976, when the fair market value of the stock was $6,000 (her father's adjusted basis in the stock was $5,500, and he paid gift tax of $800 on the transfer), $7,500.

    d. Proceeds from the November 5, 1990, sale of her personal automobile, for which she had paid $4,500 in 1982, $3,100.

    e. Proceeds from the December 3, 1990, sale of 10 shares of Y Corporation stock to her brother (she had paid $85 per share for the stock on February 7, 1990), $600.

    f. Dividends received from a domestic corporation, $120.

Part 1—Tax Computation

Ada's employer withheld Federal income tax of $3,880. Compute Ada's net tax payable or refund due for 1990. Suggested software (if available): *WEST–TAX Planner* or *BNA Individual Income Tax Spreadsheet.*

Part 2—Tax Planning

As of the beginning of 1991, Ada is promoted to the position of personnel director. The promotion will result in a salary increase. Her new position will result in an

estimated increase in her expenses for travel from $800 to $3,000 and in her expenses for entertainment from $500 to $4,000. Her employer has offered her the following options.

a. Salary increase of $20,000.

b. Salary increase of $12,000 and reimbursement for all travel and entertainment expenses not in excess of $7,000.

Ada estimates that her itemized deductions (excluding any potential deductions for travel and entertainment) will remain at $5,800. She anticipates that no dividends will be received and no proceeds from asset sales will be received.

Calculate Ada's tax liability for 1991 under both option (a) and option (b) so she can decide which option to select. Suggested software (if available): *WEST–TAX Planner* or *BNA Individual Income Tax Spreadsheet*.

 54. Tammy Walker, age 37, is a self-employed accountant. Tammy's Social Security number is 333–40–1111. Her address is 101 Glass Road, Richmond, VA 23236. Her income and expenses associated with her accounting practice for 1990 are as follows:

Revenues (cash receipts during 1990)	$95,000
Expenses	
Salaries	$23,000
Office supplies	1,100
Postage	500
Depreciation of equipment	12,000
Telephone	650
	$37,250

Since Tammy is a cash method taxpayer, she does not record her receivables as revenue until she receives cash payment. At the beginning of 1990, her accounts receivable were $12,000, and the balance had increased to $16,000 by the end of the year. The balance at December 31, 1990, would have been $18,500, except that an account for $2,500 had become uncollectible in November.

Tammy used one room in her eight-room house as an office (400 square feet out of a total square footage of 4,000). She paid the following expenses related to the house during 1990:

Utilities	$ 3,000
Insurance	400
Property taxes	3,000
Repairs	1,400

Tammy had purchased the house on September 1, 1989, for $200,000. She sold her previous house on November 15, 1989, for $105,000. Her selling expenses had been $9,000, and qualified fixing-up expenses were $1,100. Tammy and her former husband, Lou, had purchased the house in 1988 for $80,000. Tammy had received Lou's 50% ownership interest as part of their divorce settlement in August 1988. Tammy had not used any part of the former residence as a home office.

Tammy has one child, Thomas, age 17. Thomas lives with his father during the summer and with Tammy for the rest of the year. Tammy can document that she spent $6,000 during 1990 for the child's support. The father normally provides about $1,000 per year, but this year he gave the child a new car for Christmas. The cost of the car was $15,000. The divorce decree is silent regarding the dependency exemption for the child.

Under the terms of the divorce decree, Tammy is to receive alimony of $800 per month. The payments will terminate at Tammy's death or if Tammy should remarry.

Tammy provides part of the support of her mother, age 67. The total support for 1990 for her mother was as follows:

Social Security benefits	$ 4,800
From Tammy	1,900
From Bob, Tammy's brother	1,300
From Susan, Tammy's sister	2,000

Bob and Susan have both indicated their willingness to sign a multiple support waiver form if it will benefit Tammy.

Tammy's deductible itemized deductions during 1990, excluding any itemized deductions related to the house, were $6,000. She made estimated tax payments of $18,500.

Part 1—Tax Computation

Compute Tammy's lowest net tax payable or refund due for 1990. Suggested software (if available): *WEST–TAX Planner* or *BNA Individual Income Tax Spreadsheet.*

Part 2—Tax Planning

Tammy and her former husband have had discussions regarding the $800 alimony he pays her each month. Due to a health problem of his new wife, he does not feel that he can afford to continue to pay the $800 each month. He is in the 15% tax bracket. If Tammy will agree to decrease the amount by 25%, he will agree that the amount paid is not alimony for tax purposes. Assume that the other data used in calculating Tammy's taxable income for 1990 will apply for her 1991 tax return. Advise Tammy as to whether she should agree to her former husband's proposal. Suggested software (if available): *WEST–TAX Planner* or *BNA Individual Income Tax Spreadsheet.*

13

PROPERTY TRANSACTIONS: CAPITAL GAINS AND LOSSES, SECTION 1231, AND RECAPTURE PROVISIONS

OBJECTIVES

Define a capital asset, apply the definition, and examine its statutory expansions.

Discuss the rules relating to capital gain treatment and retirement of corporate obligations.

Discuss and apply the holding period rules for determining whether capital gain or loss is long term or short term.

Explain the differences in the tax treatment of capital gains and losses of corporate versus noncorporate taxpayers.

Define § 1231 assets and compute § 1231 gains and losses.

Discuss §§ 1245 and 1250 recapture and certain recapture provisions.

Explain the treatment of gains and losses from dispositions of passive activity property.

Develop tax planning ideas related to §§ 1231, 1245, and 1250.

GENERAL CONSIDERATIONS

Rationale for Separate Reporting of Capital Gains and Losses

Currently, capital gains are not taxed at a lower rate than ordinary gains. Therefore, the tax on a net capital gain and the tax on the same amount of net ordinary income are identical. Despite this result, however, the tax law requires that capital gains and losses be very carefully separated from other types of gains and losses.

Why does the Code still require separate reporting of gains and losses and a determination of their tax character although this appears to have no effect on the tax liability? The reason is that significant differences in taxable income may occur when ordinary gains and losses are present versus when capital gains and losses are present. Capital losses must initially be offset against capital gains. After this offset, any remaining capital loss is deductible only to the extent of $3,000 per tax year. Net capital loss exceeding this limit is carried over and may be deductible in future tax years. Since capital losses are offset against capital gains to determine whether a net capital loss exists, a separate netting of capital gains and losses is required. The netting procedure is discussed in the Tax Treatment of Capital Gains and Losses of Noncorporate Taxpayers portion of this chapter.

Historically, capital gains were taxed at a significantly lower rate than ordinary gains. This preferential treatment of capital gains is likely to return if Congress raises ordinary income tax rates.[1] If the capital gain and loss provisions of the current tax law did not require separate reporting, it would probably be very difficult for Congress to reenact preferential treatment for capital gains. Thus, Congress deliberately retained the separate reporting of capital gains and losses even though it felt current tax rates do not justify preferential treatment of net capital gains.

As a result of the factors discussed above, the individual income tax forms include very extensive reporting requirements for capital gains and losses. The material in this chapter will help you understand the tax principles underlying those forms.

In addition to the capital gains provisions, this chapter is concerned with § 1231 provisions, which apply to the sale or exchange of business properties and to certain involuntary conversions. The chapter also covers the recapture provisions that treat as ordinary income certain gains that otherwise would be treated as long-term capital gain. The impact of the passive loss provisions (refer to chapter 6) on the taxation of property gains and losses is discussed briefly in the chapter.

General Scheme of Taxation

Recognized gains and losses must be properly classified. Proper classification depends upon three characteristics:

* The tax status of the property.
* The manner of the property's disposition.
* The holding period of the property.

---

1. The national budget deficit, low tax rates for wealthy taxpayers, and Congressional support for preferential capital gain rates will probably combine to raise tax rates on ordinary income. Since the current law contains an alternative tax on long-term capital gains (although it currently does not yield a lower tax), raising ordinary tax rates will probably make a lower tax on long-term capital gains a reality.

The three possible tax statuses are capital asset, § 1231 asset, or ordinary asset. Property disposition may be by sale, exchange, casualty, theft, or condemnation. The two holding periods are one year or less (short term) and more than one year (long term).[2]

The major focus of this chapter is capital gains and losses. Capital gains and losses usually result from the disposition of a capital asset. The most common disposition is a sale of the asset. Capital gains and losses can also result from the disposition of § 1231 assets. Except in very limited circumstances, capital gains and losses cannot result from the disposition of ordinary assets.

CAPITAL ASSETS

Definition of a Capital Asset

Personal use assets and investment assets are the most common capital assets owned by individual taxpayers. Personal use assets usually include items such as clothing, recreation equipment, a residence, and automobiles. Investment assets usually include corporate stocks and bonds, government bonds, and vacant land. Remember, however, that losses from the sale or exchange of personal use assets are not recognized. Therefore, the classification of such losses as capital losses can be ignored.

Due to the historical preferential treatment of capital gains, taxpayers have preferred that gains be capital gains rather than ordinary gains. As a result, a great many statutes, cases, and rulings have accumulated in the attempt to define what is and what is not a capital asset. Unfortunately, capital assets are not directly defined in the Code. Instead, § 1221 defines what is *not* a capital asset. A capital asset is property held by the taxpayer (whether or not it is connected with the taxpayer's business) that is *not* any of the following:

- Inventory or property held primarily for sale to customers in the ordinary course of a business. The Supreme Court, in *Malat v. Riddell*, defined *primarily* as meaning *of first importance* or *principally*.[3]

- Accounts and notes receivable acquired from the sale of inventory or acquired for services rendered in the ordinary course of business.

- Depreciable property or real estate used in a business.

- Certain copyrights; literary, musical, or artistic compositions; or letters, memoranda, or similar property held by (1) a taxpayer whose efforts created the property; (2) in the case of a letter, memorandum, or similar property, a taxpayer for whom it was produced; or (3) a taxpayer in whose hands the basis of such property is determined, for purposes of determining gain from a sale or exchange, in whole or part by reference to the basis of such property in the hands of a taxpayer described in (1) or (2).

- U.S. government publications that are (1) received by a taxpayer from the U.S. government other than by purchase at the price at which they are offered for sale to the public or (2) held by a taxpayer whose basis, for purposes of determining gain from a sale or exchange, is determined by reference to a taxpayer described in (1).

---

2. For assets acquired prior to January 1, 1988, the short-term holding period was six months or less, and the long-term holding period was more than six months. See the discussion under Hold-ing Period later in this chapter.

3. 66–1 USTC ¶9317, 17 AFTR2d 604, 86 S.Ct. 1030 (USSC, 1966).

The Code defines what is *not* a capital asset. From the preceding list, it is apparent that inventory, accounts and notes receivable, and most fixed assets of a business are not capital assets. The following discussion provides further detail on each part of the capital asset definition.

Inventory.   What constitutes inventory is determined by the taxpayer's business.

EXAMPLE 1   T Company buys and sells used cars. Its cars would be inventory. Its gains from sale of the cars would be ordinary income. □

Accounts and Notes Receivable.   Usually no gain or loss results from the collection of a business receivable of an accrual basis taxpayer because the basis of the receivable is equal to the amount collected. However, if such a taxpayer sells his or her receivables, an ordinary gain or loss may result. A cash basis taxpayer usually does not have a basis for his or her receivables. Thus, a gain will result from the sale of the receivables.

EXAMPLE 2   T Company has accounts receivable of $100,000. Because it needs working capital, it sells the receivables for $83,000 to a financial institution. T Company would have a $17,000 ordinary loss if it were an accrual basis taxpayer (it would have earlier recorded $100,000 of revenue when the receivable was established). T Company would have $83,000 of ordinary income if it were a cash basis taxpayer because it would not have recorded any revenue earlier and because the receivable has no tax basis. □

Business Fixed Assets.   Depreciable property and real estate (both depreciable and nondepreciable) used by a business are not capital assets. The Code has a very complex set of rules pertaining to such property. One of these rules is discussed under the Real Property Subdivided for Sale heading. This chapter also discusses the potential capital gain treatment under § 1231 for business fixed assets.

Copyrights and Creative Works.   Generally, the person whose efforts led to the copyright or creative work has an ordinary asset, not a capital asset. *Creative works* include the works of authors, composers, and artists. Also, the person for whom a letter, memorandum, or other similar property was created has an ordinary asset. Finally, a person receiving a copyright or a creative work by gift from the creator or the person for whom the work was created has an ordinary asset.

EXAMPLE 3   T is a part-time music composer. One of her songs was purchased by a music publisher for $5,000. T would have a $5,000 ordinary gain from the sale of an ordinary asset. □

EXAMPLE 4   T received a letter from the President of the United States in 1944. In the current year, T sells the letter to a collector for $300. T has a $300 ordinary gain from the sale of an ordinary asset (because the letter was created for T). □

EXAMPLE 5   T gives a song she composed to her son. The son sells the song to a music publisher for $5,000. The son has a $5,000 ordinary gain from the sale of an ordinary asset. ☐

(Patents are subject to special statutory rules discussed later in the chapter.)

U.S. Government Publications.   U.S. government publications received from the U.S. government (or its agencies) for a reduced price are not capital assets. This prevents a taxpayer from later donating the publications to charity and claiming a charitable contribution equal to the fair market value of the publications. A charitable contribution of a capital asset generally yields a deduction equal to the fair market value. A charitable contribution of an ordinary asset generally yields a deduction equal to less than the fair market value. If such property is received by gift from the original purchaser, the property is not a capital asset to the donee. (For a more comprehensive explanation of charitable contributions of property, refer to chapter 10.)

Effect of Judicial Action

Court decisions play an important role in the definition of capital assets. Because the Code only lists categories of what are *not* capital assets, judicial interpretation is sometimes required to determine whether a specific item fits into one of those categories. The Supreme Court follows a literal interpretation of the categories.[4] For instance, corporate stock is not mentioned in § 1221. Thus, corporate stock is usually a capital asset. However, what if corporate stock is purchased for resale to customers? Then it is *inventory* and is not a capital asset because inventory is one of the categories in § 1221. (See the discussion of Dealers in Securities below.) A Supreme Court decision was required to make the distinction between capital asset and noncapital asset status when a taxpayer who did not normally acquire stock for resale to customers acquired stock with the intention of resale. The Court decided that since the stock was not acquired primarily for sale to customers (the taxpayer did not sell the stock to its regular customers), the stock was a capital asset.

Often the outcome of the capital asset determination hinges on whether the asset is held for investment purposes (capital asset) or business purposes (ordinary asset). The taxpayer's *use* of the property often provides objective evidence.

EXAMPLE 6   T buys an expensive painting for his business. If T depreciates the painting, the painting is depreciable property and, therefore, not a capital asset. If T is in the business of buying and selling paintings, the painting is inventory and, therefore, an ordinary asset. If T simply uses the painting to decorate his business and does not depreciate it, it is a capital asset. ☐

Statutory Expansions

Because of the uncertainty associated with the capital asset definition, Congress has enacted several Code Sections to clarify the definition. These statutory expansions of the capital asset definition are discussed in the following sections.

---

4. *Arkansas Best v. Comm.*, 88−1 USTC ¶9210, 61 AFTR2d 88−655, 108 S.Ct. 971 (USSC, 1988).

Dealers in Securities.   As a general rule, securities (stocks, bonds, and other financial instruments) held by a dealer are considered to be inventory and are not, therefore, subject to capital gain or loss treatment. A *dealer in securities* is a merchant (e.g., a brokerage firm) that regularly engages in the purchase and resale of securities to customers. The dealer must identify any securities being held for investment. Generally, if a dealer clearly identifies certain securities as held for investment purposes by the close of business on the date of acquisition, gain from the sale of such securities will be capital gain. However, the gain will not be capital gain if the dealer ceases to hold the securities for investment prior to the sale. Losses are capital losses if at any time the securities have been clearly identified by the dealer as held for investment.

Real Property Subdivided for Sale.   Substantial development activities relative to real property may result in the owner being considered a dealer for tax purposes. Income from the sale of real estate property lots is treated as the sale of inventory (ordinary income) if the owner is considered to be a dealer. However, § 1237 allows real estate investors capital gain treatment if they engage in limited development activities. To be eligible for § 1237 treatment, the following requirements must be met:

- The taxpayer may not be a corporation.
- The taxpayer may not be a real estate dealer.
- No substantial improvements may be made to the lots sold. *Substantial* generally means more than a 10 percent increase in the value of a lot. Shopping centers and other commercial or residential buildings are considered substantial, while filling, draining, leveling, and clearing operations are not.
- The taxpayer must hold the lots sold for at least five years, except for inherited property. The substantial improvements test is less stringent if the property is held at least 10 years.

If the preceding requirements are met, all gain is capital gain until the tax year in which the sixth lot is sold. Sales of contiguous lots to a single buyer in the same transaction count as the sale of one lot. In the tax year the sixth lot is sold, some of the gain may be ordinary income. Five percent of the revenue from lot sales is potential ordinary income. That potential ordinary income is offset by any selling expenses from the lot sales. Practically, sales commissions often are at least 5 percent of the sales price, so none of the gain is treated as ordinary income.

If the requirements for § 1237 treatment are not met (e.g., the seller is a corporation), the gain still may not necessarily be ordinary income. The gain may be capital gain under § 1221 or § 1231 if the requirements of either of these sections are met.

Section 1237 does not apply to losses. A loss from the sale of subdivided real property is an ordinary loss unless the property qualifies as a capital asset under § 1221.

Sale or Exchange

Recognition of capital gain or loss requires a sale or exchange of a capital asset. The Code uses the term *sale or exchange*, but does not define it. Generally, a sale involves the receipt of money and/or the assumption by the purchaser of liabilities for property. An exchange involves the transfer of property for other property.

Thus, an involuntary conversion (casualty, theft, or condemnation) is not a sale or exchange. In several situations, the determination of whether a sale or exchange has taken place has been clarified by the enactment of Code Sections that specifically provide for sale or exchange treatment.

Recognized gains or losses from the cancellation, lapse, expiration, or any other termination of a right or obligation with respect to personal property (other than stock) that is or would be a capital asset in the hands of the taxpayer are capital gains or losses.[5] See the discussion under Options later in the chapter for more details.

Worthless Securities

Occasionally, securities such as stock and, especially, bonds may become worthless due to the insolvency of their issuer. If such a security is a capital asset, the loss is deemed to have occurred as the result of a sale or exchange on the *last day* of the tax year.[6] This last-day rule may have the effect of converting what otherwise would have been a short-term capital loss into a long-term capital loss. See Treatment of Capital Losses later in this chapter.

Section 1244 allows an ordinary deduction on disposition of stock at a loss. The stock must be that of a small business company, and the ordinary deduction is limited to $50,000 ($100,000 for married individuals filing jointly) per year. For a more detailed discussion, refer to chapter 7.

Special Rule—Retirement of Corporate Obligations

A debt obligation (e.g., a bond or note payable) may have a tax basis in excess of or less than its redemption value because it may have been acquired at a premium or discount. Consequently, the collection of the redemption value may result in a loss or gain. Generally, the collection of a debt obligation is *not* a sale or exchange. Therefore, any loss or gain cannot be a capital loss or gain because no sale or exchange has taken place. However, if the debt obligation was issued by a corporation or certain government agencies, the collection of the redemption value is treated as a sale or exchange.[7]

EXAMPLE 7	T acquires $1,000 of XYZ Corporation bonds for $980 in the open market. If the bonds are held to maturity, the $20 difference between T's collection of the $1,000 maturity value and T's cost of $980 is treated as capital gain. If the obligation were issued to T by an individual instead of by a corporation, T's $20 gain would be ordinary since there is no sale or exchange of the debt by T. □

Options

Generally, the sale or exchange of an option to buy or sell property results in capital gain or loss if the subject property is (or would be) a capital asset to the option holder.[8]

---

5. § 1234A.
6. § 165(g)(1).
7. § 1271.

8. § 1234(a) and Reg. § 1.1234–1(a)(1). See the Glossary of Tax Terms in Appendix C for a definition of stock options.

EXAMPLE 8   T wants to buy some vacant land for investment purposes. She cannot afford the full purchase price. Instead, she convinces the landowner to sell her the right to purchase the land for $100,000 anytime in the next two years. T pays $3,000 to obtain this option to buy the land. The option is a capital asset for T because if she actually purchased the land, the land would be a capital asset. Three months after purchasing the option, T sells it for $7,000. T would have a $4,000 short-term capital gain on this sale since she held the option for one year or less.   □

Failure to Exercise Options.   If an option holder (grantee) fails to exercise the option, the lapse of the option is considered a sale or exchange on the option expiration date. Thus, the loss is a capital loss if the property subject to the option is (or would be) a capital asset in the hands of the grantee.

The grantor of an option on stocks, securities, commodities, or commodity futures receives short-term capital gain treatment upon the expiration of the option. Options on property other than stocks, securities, commodities, or commodity futures result in ordinary income to the grantor when the option expires. For example, an individual investor who owns certain stock (a capital asset) may sell a call option, entitling the buyer of the option to acquire the stock at a specified price higher than the value at the date the option is granted. The writer of the call receives a premium (e.g., 10 percent) for writing the option. If the price of the stock does not increase during the option period, the option will expire unexercised. Upon the expiration of the option, the grantor must recognize short-term capital gain. These provisions do not apply to options held for sale to customers (the inventory of a securities dealer).

Exercise of Options by Grantee.   If the option is exercised, the amount paid for the option is added to the selling price of the property subject to the option. This increases the gain to the grantor upon the sale of the property. The gain is capital or ordinary depending on the nature of the property sold. The grantee, of course, adds the cost of the option to the basis of the property acquired.

EXAMPLE 9   On September 1, 1978, X purchases 100 shares of Y Company stock for $5,000. On April 1, 1990, he writes a call option on the stock, giving the option holder the right to buy the stock for $6,000 during the following six-month period. X receives a call premium of $500 for writing the call.

- If the call is exercised by the option holder on August 1, 1990, X has $1,500 ($6,000 + $500 − $5,000) of long-term capital gain from the sale of the stock.

- Assume that X decides to sell his stock prior to exercise for $6,000 and enters into a closing transaction by purchasing a call on 100 shares of Y Company stock for $5,000. Since the Y stock is selling for $6,000, X must pay a call premium of $1,000. He recognizes a $500 short-term capital loss [$1,000 (call premium paid) – $500 (call premium received)] on the closing transaction. On the actual sale of the Y Company stock, X has a long-term capital gain of $1,000 [$6,000 (selling price) – $5,000 (cost)].

- Assume that the original option expired unexercised. X has a $500 short-term capital gain equal to the call premium received for writing the option. This gain is not recognized until the option expires.   □

CONCEPT SUMMARY 13–1

Options

	Effect on	
Event	Grantor	Grantee
Option is granted.	Receives value and has a contract obligation (a liability).	Pays value and has a contract right (an asset).
Option expires.	Has a short-term capital gain if the option property is stocks, securities, commodities, or commodity futures. Otherwise, gain is ordinary income.	Has a loss (capital loss if option property would have been a capital asset for the grantee).
Option is exercised.	Amount received for option increases proceeds from sale of the option property.	Amount paid for option becomes part of basis of the option property purchased.
Option is sold or exchanged.	Result depends upon whether option later expires or is exercised (see above).	Could have gain or loss (capital gain or loss if option property would have been a capital asset for the grantee).

Patents

Rationale for Capital Gain Treatment.   The sale of a patent may result in long-term capital gain treatment whether or not the patent is a capital asset.[9] The encouragement of technological progress is the primary reason for this provision. Ironically, authors, composers, and artists are not eligible for capital gain treatment on their creations because such works are not capital assets. The Code allows special treatment for patents, but not for copyrights or trademarks. Presumably, Congress chose not to use the tax law to encourage cultural endeavors. The following example illustrates the special treatment for patents.

EXAMPLE 10   T, a druggist, invents a pill-counting machine, which she patents. In consideration of a lump-sum payment of $200,000 plus $10 per machine sold, T assigns the patent to Drug Products, Inc. Assuming T has transferred all substantial rights, the question of whether the transfer is a sale or exchange of a capital asset is not relevant. T automatically has a long-term capital gain from both the lump-sum payment and the $10 per machine royalty to the extent these proceeds exceed her basis for the patent.   □

Statutory Requirements.   The following are key issues for the transfer of patent rights:

* Whether the patent is a capital asset.

* Whether the transfer is a sale or exchange.

* Whether all substantial rights to the patent (or an undivided interest in it) are transferred.

---

9.   § 1235.

Section 1235 resolves whether the transfer is a sale or exchange of a capital asset. The statute provides that

> a transfer . . . of property consisting of all substantial rights to a patent, or an undivided interest therein which includes a part of all such rights, by any holder shall be considered the sale or exchange of a capital asset held for [the long-term holding period], regardless of whether or not payments in consideration of such transfer are (1) payable periodically over a period generally coterminous with the transferee's use of the patent, or (2) contingent on the productivity, use, or disposition of the property transferred.[10]

If the transfer meets the requirements, any gain or loss is *automatically* a long-term capital gain or loss regardless of whether the patent is a capital asset, whether the transfer is a sale or exchange, and how long the patent was held by the transferor.

Substantial Rights.   To receive favorable capital gain treatment, all *substantial rights* to the patent must be transferred. All substantial rights have not been transferred when the transfer is limited geographically within the issuing country or the transfer is for a period that is less than the remaining life of the patent. [11]

EXAMPLE 11   Assume T, the druggist in Example 10, only licensed Drug Products, Inc. to manufacture and sell the invention in Michigan. She retained the right to license the machine elsewhere in the United States. T has retained a substantial right and is not eligible for automatic long-term capital gain treatment.

□

Holder Defined.   The *holder* of a patent is usually the creator of the invention. A holder may also be a person who purchases the patent rights from the creator before the patented invention is reduced to practice. However, the creator's employer and certain parties related to the creator do not qualify as holders. Thus, in the common situation where an employer has all rights to an employee's inventions, the employer would not be eligible for long-term capital gain treatment. More than likely, the employer would have an ordinary asset because the patent was developed as part of its business.

Franchises

A mode of operation, a widely recognized brand name, and a widely known business symbol are all valuable assets. These assets may be licensed (commonly known as franchising) by their owner for use by other businesses. Many fast-food restaurants are franchises. The franchisee usually pays the owner (franchisor) an initial fee plus a contingent fee. The contingent fee is often based upon the franchisee's sales volume.

For Federal income tax purposes, a *franchise* is an agreement that gives the franchisee the right to distribute, sell, or provide goods, services, or facilities within a specified area.[12] A franchise transfer includes granting a franchise, transfers by one franchisee to another person, or renewal of a franchise.

---

10. § 1235(a) and Reg. § 1.1235–1(a).
11. Reg. § 1.1235–2(b)(1).
12. § 1253(b)(1). See the Glossary of Tax Terms in

Appendix C for a definition of the term "franchise."

A franchise transfer is generally not a sale or exchange of a capital asset. Section 1253 provides that

> a transfer of a franchise, trademark, or trade name shall not be treated as a sale or exchange of a capital asset if the transferor retains any significant power, right, or continuing interest with respect to the subject matter of the [transfer].

Significant Power, Right, or Continuing Interest. *Significant powers, rights, or continuing interests* include control over assignment, quality of products and services, sale or advertising of other products or services, and the right to require that substantially all supplies and equipment be purchased from the transferor. Also included are the right to terminate the franchise at will and the right to substantial contingent payments. Most modern franchising operations involve some or all of these powers, rights, or continuing interests.

Transferee Deduction. Contingent franchise payments are ordinary income for the franchisor and an ordinary deduction for the franchisee. A noncontingent lump-sum payment must be deducted by the franchisee over the shorter of the franchise period or 10 years. Noncontingent equal periodic payments required by the franchise agreement may be deducted when paid if the payment period equals the franchise period or the payment period exceeds 10 years. For each type of noncontingent payment discussed above, the transferor's income is ordinary and is generally recognized when received.

EXAMPLE 12	T grants a franchise to U to sell fast foods. Payments to T are contingent on the sales of the franchise outlet. The payments are ordinary income to T and deductible as a business expense by U. □

EXAMPLE 13	T, a franchisee, sells the franchise to a third party. Payments to T are not contingent, and all significant powers, rights, and continuing interests are transferred. The payments are capital gain to T. □

Sports Franchises. Section 1253 does not apply to professional sports franchises.[13] However, § 1056 imposes certain restrictions upon the allocation of the costs of acquiring a sports franchise to the cost basis of player contracts. In addition, if a sports franchise is sold, gain from the sale of the player contracts is subject to depreciation recapture as ordinary income under § 1245.[14]

Lease Cancellation Payments

The tax treatment of payments received for cancelling a lease depends on whether the recipient is the lessor or the lessee and whether the lease is a capital asset or not.[15]

Lessee Treatment. Payments received by a lessee for a lease cancellation are capital gains if the lease is a capital asset or § 1231 asset.[16] Generally, a lessee's lease would be a capital asset if the property (either personalty or realty) is used for

---

13. § 1253(e).
14. See the discussion of recapture provisions later in the chapter.

15. See the Glossary of Tax Terms in Appendix C for definitions of the terms "lessor" and "lessee."
16. § 1241 and Reg. § 1.1241–1(a).

the lessee's personal use (e.g., his or her residence). A lessee's lease would be an ordinary asset if the property is used in the lessee's trade or business.[17]

Lessor Treatment.   Payments received by a lessor for a lease cancellation are always ordinary income because they are considered to be in lieu of rental payments.[18]

EXAMPLE 14   T owns an apartment building that he is going to convert into an office building. S is one of the apartment tenants and receives $1,000 from T to cancel the lease. S would have a capital gain of $1,000 (which would be long term or short term depending upon how long S had held the lease). T would have an ordinary deduction of $1,000.   □

EXAMPLE 15   M owns an apartment building near a university campus. P is one of the tenants. P is graduating early and offers M $800 to cancel P's lease. M accepts the offer. M has ordinary income of $800. P has a nondeductible payment since the apartment was personal use property.   □

HOLDING PERIOD

Property must be held more than one year to qualify for long-term capital gain or loss treatment.[19] Property not held for the required long-term period will result in short-term capital gain or loss. To compute the holding period, start counting on the day after the property was acquired. In subsequent months, this same day is the start of a new month.[20] The following examples illustrate the computation of the holding period.

EXAMPLE 16   T purchases a capital asset on January 15, 1989, and sells it on January 16, 1990. T's holding period is more than one year. If T had sold the asset on January 15, 1990, the holding period would have been exactly one year, and the gain or loss would have been short term.   □

A capital asset acquired on the last day of any month must not be disposed of until on or after the first day of the thirteenth succeeding month to be held for more than one year.[21]

EXAMPLE 17   T purchases a capital asset on February 28, 1989. If T sells the asset on February 28, 1990, the holding period is one year, and T will have a short-term capital gain or loss. If T sells the asset on March 1, 1990, the holding period is more than one year, and T will have a long-term capital gain or loss.   □

---

17. Reg. § 1.1221–1(a).
18. *Hort v. Comm.*, 41–1 USTC ¶9354, 25 AFTR 1207, 61 S.Ct. 757 (USSC, 1941).
19. § 1222.

20. *Caspe v. U.S.*, 82–2 USTC ¶9714, 51 AFTR2d 83–353, 694 F.2d 1116 (CA–8, 1982).
21. Rev.Rul. 66–7, 1966–1 C.B. 188.

Review of Special Holding Period Rules

There are several special holding period rules.[22] The application of these rules depends on the type of asset and how it was acquired.

Tax-Free Exchanges.   The holding period of property received in a nontaxable exchange includes the holding period of the former asset if the property that has been exchanged is a capital asset or a § 1231 asset. In certain nontaxable transactions involving a substituted basis, the holding period of the former property is *tacked on* to the holding period of the newly acquired property.

EXAMPLE 18   X exchanges a business truck for another truck in a like-kind exchange. The holding period of the truck exchanged tacks on to the holding period of the new truck. □

EXAMPLE 19   T sells her former personal residence and acquires a new residence. If the transaction qualifies for nonrecognition of gain on the sale of a residence, the holding period of the new residence includes the holding period of the former residence. □

Certain Nontaxable Transactions Involving a Carryover of Another Taxpayer's Basis.   The holding period of a former owner of property is tacked on to the present owner's holding period if the transaction is nontaxable and the basis of the property to the former owner carries over to the new owner.

EXAMPLE 20   T acquires 100 shares of A Corporation stock for $1,000 on December 31, 1983. The shares are transferred by gift to S on December 31, 1989, when the stock is worth $2,000. S's holding period begins with the date the stock was acquired by T since the donor's basis of $1,000 becomes the basis for determining gain or loss on a subsequent sale by S. □

EXAMPLE 21   Assume the same facts as in Example 20, except that the fair market value of the shares is only $800 on the date of the gift. The holding period begins on the date of the gift if S sells the stock for a loss since the value of the shares at the date of the gift is used in the determination of basis. If the shares are sold for $500 on April 1, 1990, S has a $300 recognized capital loss and the holding period is from December 31, 1989, to April 1, 1990 (thus, the loss is short term). □

Certain Disallowed Loss Transactions.   Under several Code provisions, realized losses are disallowed. When a loss is disallowed, there is no carryover of holding period. Losses can be disallowed under § 267 (sale or exchange between related taxpayers), § 707(b)(1) (sale or exchange involving controlled partnerships), and § 262 (sale or exchange of personal use assets) as well as other Code sections. Taxpayers who acquire property in a disallowed loss transaction will have a new holding period begin and will have a basis equal to the purchase price.

---

22. § 1223.

EXAMPLE 22 J sold her principal residence at a loss. J may not deduct the loss because it arises from the sale of personal use property. J purchases a replacement residence for more than the selling price of her former residence. J will have a basis equal to the cost of the replacement residence, and her holding period will begin when she acquires the replacement residence. ☐

Inherited Property. The holding period for inherited property is treated as long term no matter how long the property is actually held by the heir.

EXAMPLE 23 S inherits XYZ stock from her father. She receives the stock on April 1, 1990, and sells it on November 1, 1990. Even though the stock was not held more than one year, S receives long-term capital gain or loss treatment on the sale. ☐

Special Rules for Short Sales

The holding period of property sold short is determined under special rules provided in § 1233. A *short sale* occurs when a taxpayer sells borrowed property and repays the lender with substantially identical property either held on the date of the sale or purchased after the sale. Short sales usually involve corporate stock. The seller's objective is to make a profit in anticipation of a decline in the price of the stock. If the price declines, the seller in a short sale recognizes a profit equal to the difference between the sales price of the borrowed stock and the price paid for the replacement stock.

EXAMPLE 24 C does not own any shares of Z Corporation. However, C sells 30 shares of Z. The shares are borrowed from C's broker, and the borrowed shares must be replaced within 45 days. C has a short sale because he was short the shares he sold. C will *close* the short sale by purchasing Z shares and delivering them to his broker. If the original 30 shares were sold for $10,000 and C later purchases 30 shares for $8,000, C would have a gain of $2,000. C's hunch that the price of Z stock would decline was correct. C was able to profit from selling high and buying low. If C had to purchase Z shares for $13,000 to close the short sale, he would have a loss of $3,000. In this case, C has sold low and bought high—not the result he wanted! C also would be making a short sale (a *short sale against the box*) if he borrowed shares from his broker to sell and then closed the short sale by delivering other Z shares he owned at the time of making the short sale. ☐

A short sale gain or loss is a capital gain or loss to the extent that the short sale property constitutes a capital asset of the taxpayer. The gain or loss is not recognized until the short sale is closed. Generally, the holding period of the short sale property is determined by how long the property used to close the short sale was held. However, if *substantially identical property* (e.g., other shares of the same stock) is held by the taxpayer, the short-term or long-term character of the short sale gain or loss may be affected:

- If substantially identical property has *not* been held for the long-term holding period on the short sale date, the short sale *gain or loss* is short term.

- If substantially identical property has *been* held for the long-term holding period on the short sale date, the short sale *gain* is long term if the substantially identical property is used to close the short sale and short term if it is not used to close the short sale.

- If substantially identical property has *been* held for the long-term holding period on the short sale date, the short sale *loss* is long term whether or not the substantially identical property is used to close the short sale.

- If substantially identical property is acquired *after* the short sale date and on or before the closing date, the short sale *gain or loss* is short term.

Concept Summary 13–2 summarizes the short sale rules.

The short sale rules are intended to prevent the conversion of short-term capital gains into long-term capital gains and long-term capital losses into short-term capital losses. The following examples illustrate the application of the short sale rules.

CONCEPT SUMMARY 13–2

Short Sales of Securities

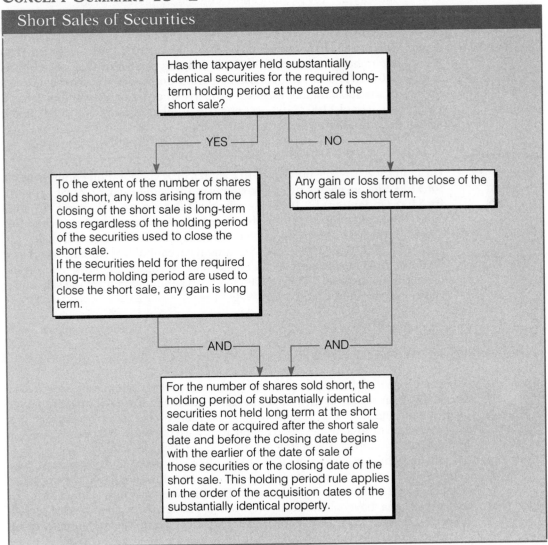

Has the taxpayer held substantially identical securities for the required long-term holding period at the date of the short sale?

— YES —   — NO —

To the extent of the number of shares sold short, any loss arising from the closing of the short sale is long-term loss regardless of the holding period of the securities used to close the short sale.
If the securities held for the required long-term holding period are used to close the short sale, any gain is long term.

Any gain or loss from the close of the short sale is short term.

— AND —   — AND —

For the number of shares sold short, the holding period of substantially identical securities not held long term at the short sale date or acquired after the short sale date and before the closing date begins with the earlier of the date of sale of those securities or the closing date of the short sale. This holding period rule applies in the order of the acquisition dates of the substantially identical property.

EXAMPLE 25   On January 2, 1990, T purchases five shares of Y Corporation common stock for $100. On April 14, 1990, she engages in a short sale of five shares of the same stock for $150. On August 15, T closes the short sale by repaying the borrowed stock with the five shares purchased on January 2. T has a $50 short-term capital gain from the short sale because she had not held substantially identical shares for the long-term holding period on the short sale date.   □

EXAMPLE 26   Assume the same facts as in the previous example, except that T closes the short sale on January 30, 1991, by repaying the borrowed stock with five shares purchased on January 29, 1991, for $200. The stock used to close the short sale was not the property purchased on January 2, 1990, but since T held short-term property at the April 14, 1990, short sale date, the gain or loss from closing the short sale is short term. T has a $50 short-term loss ($200 cost of stock purchased January 29, 1991, and a short sale selling price of $150).   □

EXAMPLE 27   Assume the same facts as in Example 26. On January 31, 1991, T sells for $200 the stock purchased January 2, 1990. T's holding period for that stock begins January 30, 1991, because the holding-period portion of the short sale rules applies to the substantially identical property in order of acquisition. T has a short-term gain of $100 ($100 cost of stock purchased January 2, 1990, and a selling price of $200).   □

EXAMPLE 28   On January 2, 1990, T purchases five shares of X Corporation common stock for $100. She purchases five more shares of the same stock on April 14, 1990, for $200. On January 17, 1991, she sells short five shares of the same stock for $150. On September 30, 1991, she repays the borrowed stock with the five shares purchased on April 14, 1990, and sells the five shares purchased on January 2, 1990, for $200. T has a $50 long-term capital loss from the short sale because she held substantially identical shares for more than one year on the date of the short sale. T has a $100 long-term capital gain from the sale of the shares purchased on January 2, 1990.   □

TAX TREATMENT OF CAPITAL GAINS
AND LOSSES OF NONCORPORATE TAXPAYERS

All taxpayers net their capital gains and losses. Short-term gains and losses (if any) are netted against one another, and long-term gains and losses (if any) are netted against one another. The results will be net short-term gain or loss and net long-term gain or loss. If these two net positions are of opposite sign (one is a gain and one is a loss), they are netted against one another.

Six possibilities exist for the result after all possible netting has been completed. Three of these final results are gains, and three are losses. One possible result is a net long-term capital gain (NLTCG). Net long-term capital gains of noncorporate taxpayers historically were subject to beneficial treatment. A second possibility is a net short-term capital gain (NSTCG). Third, the netting may result

in both NLTCG and NSTCG. For each of these possibilities, the gain is treated the same as ordinary income and is taxable in full.

The last three results of the capital gain and loss netting process are losses. Thus, a fourth possibility is a net long-term capital loss (NLTCL). A fifth result is a net short-term capital loss (NSTCL). Finally, a sixth possibility includes both an NLTCL and an NSTCL. Neither NLTCLs nor NSTCLs are treated as ordinary losses. Treatment as an ordinary loss generally is preferable to capital loss treatment since ordinary losses are deductible in full while the deductibility of capital losses is subject to certain limitations. An individual taxpayer may deduct a maximum of $3,000 of net capital losses for a taxable year.[23]

Treatment of Capital Gains

Computation of Net Capital Gain. As just discussed, the first step in the computation is to net all long-term capital gains and losses and all short-term capital gains and losses. The result is the taxpayer's net long-term capital gain (NLTCG) or loss (NLTCL) and net short-term capital gain (NSTCG) or loss (NSTCL).

EXAMPLE 29

Some possible results of the *first step* in netting capital gains and losses are shown below. Assume that each case is independent (assume the taxpayer's only capital gains and losses are those shown in the given case).

Case	STCG	STCL	LTCG	LTCL	Result of Netting	Description of Result
A	$8,000	($5,000)			$3,000	NSTCG
B	2,000	(7,000)			(5,000)	NSTCL
C			$9,000	($1,000)	8,000	NLTCG
D			8,800	(9,800)	(1,000)	NLTCL

☐

The *second step* in netting capital gains and losses requires offsetting any positive and negative amounts that remain after the first netting step. This procedure is illustrated in the following examples.

EXAMPLE 30

Assume that T had all the capital gains and losses specified in Cases B and C in Example 29:

Case C ($9,000 LTCG − $1,000 LTCL)	$ 8,000	NLTCG
Case B ($2,000 STCG − $7,000 STCL)	(5,000)	NSTCL
Excess of NLTCG over NSTCL	$ 3,000	

☐

---

23. § 1211(b).

The excess of NLTCG over NSTCL is defined as *net capital gain (NCG)*. There is a $3,000 NCG in Example 30. The maximum tax rate on NCG is 28 percent, but since the maximum regular tax rate is also 28 percent, the tax on NCG does not differ from the tax on ordinary income. The current law does contain a special NCG alternative tax. The NCG alternative tax was last beneficial to taxpayers in 1987.[24] If Congress reduces the maximum tax on NCG or increases the ordinary income tax rate, this alternative tax computation will probably be beneficial again. In the meantime, the alternative tax can be ignored, and all capital gains are taxed the same as ordinary income.

There is no special name for the excess of NSTCG over NLTCL, nor is there any special tax treatment. The nature of the gain is short term, and the gain is treated the same as ordinary gain and is included in U's gross income.

Treatment of Capital Losses

Computation of Net Capital Loss.   A *net capital loss* results if capital losses exceed capital gains for the year. A net capital loss may be all long term, all short term, or part long and part short term.[25] The characterization of a net capital loss as long or short term is important in determining the capital loss deduction (discussed later in this chapter).

CONCEPT SUMMARY 13–3

Noncorporate Taxpayer's Treatment of Net Capital Gain or Loss

Net Capital Gain Treatment Summarized

1. All long-term capital gain	Taxable in full as ordinary income. 28% alternative tax is available, but is not beneficial.
2. All short-term capital gain	Taxable in full as ordinary income.
3. Part long-term and part short-term capital gain	Taxable in full as ordinary income. 28% alternative tax is available for long-term capital gain portion, but is not beneficial.

Net Capital Loss Treatment Summarized

4. All long-term capital loss	$1 of loss used to make $1 of deduction. Deduction is *for* AGI and limited to $3,000 per year. Portion of loss not used to make deduction carries forward indefinitely.
5. All short-term capital loss	$1 of loss used to make $1 of deduction. Deduction is *for* AGI and limited to $3,000 per year. Portion of loss not used to make deduction carries forward indefinitely.
6. Part long-term and part short-term capital loss	Short-term losses used first to make $3,000 deduction.

---

24. § 1(j). In 1987, the maximum regular rate was 38.5%, whereas the NCG alternative rate was 28%.

25. § 1222(10) defines a net capital loss as the net loss after the capital loss deduction. However, that definition confuses the discussion of net capital loss. Therefore, net capital loss is used here to mean the result after netting capital gains and losses and before considering the capital loss deduction. The capital loss deduction is discussed under Treatment of Net Capital Loss in this chapter.

EXAMPLE 31

Three different individual taxpayers have the following capital gains and losses during the year:

Taxpayer	LTCG	LTCL	STCG	STCL	Result of Netting	Description of Result
R	$1,000	($2,800)	$1,000	($500)	($1,300)	NLTCL
S	1,000	(500)	1,000	(2,800)	(1,300)	NSTCL
T	400	(1,200)	500	(1,200)	(1,500)	NLTCL ($800)
						NSTCL ($700)

R's net capital loss of $1,300 is all long term. S's net capital loss of $1,300 is all short term. T's net capital loss is $1,500, $800 of which is long term and $700 of which is short term. ☐

Treatment of Net Capital Loss. A net capital loss (NCL) is deductible from gross income to the extent of $3,000 per tax year.[26] Capital losses exceeding the loss deduction limits carry forward indefinitely.[27] Notice that net capital gain is taxed the same as ordinary income, but net capital loss is deductible only to the extent of $3,000. Thus, although there is no beneficial treatment for capital gains, there is *unfavorable* treatment for capital losses in terms of the $3,000 annual limitation on deducting NCL against ordinary income. If the net capital loss includes both long-term and short-term capital loss, the short-term capital loss is counted first toward the $3,000 annual limitation.

EXAMPLE 32

T has an NCL of $5,000, of which $2,000 is STCL and $3,000 is LTCL. T has a capital loss deduction of $3,000 ($2,000 of STCL and $1,000 of LTCL) with an LTCL carryforward of $2,000. ☐

Carryovers. Taxpayers are allowed to carry over unused capital losses indefinitely. The STCL and LTCL carried over retain their character as STCL or LTCL.

EXAMPLE 33

In 1989, T incurred $1,000 of STCL and $11,000 of LTCL. In 1990, T has a $400 LTCG.

- T's net capital loss for 1989 is $12,000. T deducts $3,000 ($1,000 STCL and $2,000 LTCL). T has $9,000 of LTCL carried forward to 1990.

- T combines the $9,000 LTCL carryforward with the $400 LTCG for 1990. T has an $8,600 NLTCL for 1990. T deducts $3,000 of LTCL in 1990 and carries forward $5,600 of LTCL to 1991. ☐

---

26. § 1211(b)(1). Married persons filing separate returns are limited to a $1,500 deduction per taxable year.

27. § 1212(b).

When a taxpayer has both a capital loss deduction and negative taxable income, a special computation of the capital loss carryover is required. Specifically, the capital loss carryover is the net capital loss minus the lesser of the following:

- The capital loss deduction claimed on the return.

- The negative taxable income increased by the capital loss deduction claimed on the return and the personal and dependency exemption deduction.

Without this provision, some of the tax benefit of the capital loss deduction would be wasted when the deduction drives taxable income below zero.

EXAMPLE 34

In 1990, J has a $13,000 net capital loss (all long term), a $2,050 personal exemption deduction, and a $4,000 negative taxable income. The negative taxable income includes a $3,000 capital loss deduction. The capital loss carryover to 1991 is $11,950 computed as follows:

- The $4,000 negative taxable income is treated as a negative number, but the capital loss deduction and personal exemption deduction are treated as positive numbers.

- $13,000 − the lesser of $3,000 (capital loss deduction) or $1,050 [− $4,000 (negative taxable income) + $3,000 (capital loss deduction) + $2,050 (personal exemption deduction)] = $13,000 − $1,050 = $11,950 carryover. □

Tax Treatment of Capital Gains and Losses of Corporate Taxpayers

The treatment of a corporation's net capital gain or loss differs from the rules for individuals. Briefly, the differences are as follows:

- There is a NCG alternative tax rate of 34 percent. However, since the maximum corporate tax rate is 34 percent, the alternative tax is not beneficial unless Congress raises regular tax rates or enacts favorable capital gain treatment.

- Capital losses offset only capital gains. No deduction is permitted against ordinary taxable income (whereas a $3,000 deduction is allowed to individuals).[28]

- There is a three-year carryback and a five-year carryover period for net capital losses.[29] Corporate carryovers and carrybacks are always treated as short term, regardless of their original nature.

EXAMPLE 35

X Corporation has a $15,000 NLTCL for the current year and $57,000 of ordinary taxable income. X Corporation may not offset the $15,000 NLTCL against its ordinary income by taking a capital loss deduction. The $15,000 NLTCL becomes a $15,000 STCL for carryback and carryover purposes. This amount may be offset by capital gains in the three-year carryback period or, if not absorbed there, offset by capital gains in the five-year carryforward period. □

The rules applicable to corporations are discussed in greater detail in chapter 16.

---

28. § 1211(a).   29. § 1212(a)(1).

SECTION 1231 ASSETS

Relationship to Capital Assets

Depreciable property and real property used in business are not capital assets. Thus, the recognized gains from the disposition of such property (principally machinery, equipment, buildings, and land) would appear to be ordinary income rather than capital gain. Due to § 1231, however, *net gain* from the disposition of such property is sometimes *treated* as *long-term capital gain*. A long-term holding period requirement must be met; the disposition must generally be from a sale, exchange, or involuntary conversion; and certain recapture provisions must be satisfied for this result to occur. Section 1231 may also apply to involuntary conversions of capital assets. Since an involuntary conversion is not a sale or exchange, such a disposition would not normally result in a capital gain.

If the disposition of depreciable property and real property used in business results in a *net loss*, § 1231 *treats* the *loss* as an *ordinary loss* rather than as a capital loss. Ordinary losses are fully deductible *for* adjusted gross income. Capital losses are offset by capital gains, and, if any loss remains, the loss is deductible to the extent of $3,000 per year for individuals and is not deductible currently at all by regular corporations. It seems, therefore, that § 1231 provides the *best* of both potential results: net gain is treated as long-term capital gain and net loss is treated as ordinary loss.

EXAMPLE 36

R sells business land and building at a $5,000 gain and business equipment at a $3,000 loss. Both properties were held for the long-term holding period. R's net gain is $2,000, and that net gain may (depending on various recapture rules discussed later in this chapter) be treated as a long-term capital gain under § 1231. □

EXAMPLE 37

S sells business equipment at a $10,000 loss and business land at a $2,000 gain. Both properties were held for the long-term holding period. S's net loss is $8,000, and that net loss is an ordinary loss. □

Justification for Favorable Tax Treatment

The favorable capital gain/ordinary loss treatment sanctioned by § 1231 can be explained by examining several historical developments. Before 1938, business property had been included in the definition of capital assets. Thus, if such property was sold for a loss (not an unlikely possibility during the depression years), a capital loss resulted. If, however, such property was depreciable and could be retained for its estimated useful life, much (if not all) of its costs could be recovered in the form of depreciation. Because the allowance for depreciation was fully deductible whereas capital losses were not, the tax law favored those who did not dispose of an asset. Congress recognized this inequity when it removed business property from the capital asset classification. During the period 1938–1942, therefore, all such gains and losses were ordinary gains and losses.

With the advent of World War II, two principal conditions forced Congress to reexamine the situation regarding business assets. First, the sale of business assets at a gain was discouraged because the gain would be ordinary income. Gains were

common because the war effort had inflated prices. Second, taxpayers who did not want to sell their assets often were required to because of government acquisitions through condemnation. Often the condemnation awards resulted in large gains to those taxpayers who were forced to part with their property and deprived them of the benefits of future depreciation deductions. Of course, the condemnations constituted involuntary conversions, the gain from which could be deferred through timely reinvestment in property that was "similar or related in service or use." But where was such property to be found in view of wartime restrictions and other governmental condemnations? The end product did not seem equitable: a large ordinary gain due to government action and no deferral possibility due to government restrictions.

In recognition of these two conditions, in 1942 Congress eased the tax bite on the disposition of some business property by allowing preferential capital gain treatment. Thus, the present scheme of § 1231 and the dichotomy of capital gain/ordinary loss treatment evolved from a combination of economic considerations existing in 1938 and in 1942.

The rules regarding § 1231 treatment do not apply to *all* business property. Important in this regard are the holding period requirements and the fact that the property must be either depreciable property or real estate used in business. Nor is § 1231 necessarily limited to business property. Transactions involving certain capital assets may fall into the § 1231 category. Thus, § 1231 singles out only some types of business property.

As discussed previously, for 1988 and later years, there is no beneficial tax rate for long-term capital gains. Why, then, is § 1231 still beneficial? As we will see, § 1231 requires netting of § 1231 gains and losses. If the result is a gain, the gain is treated as a long-term capital gain. The gain will therefore be available to absorb capital losses and help prevent the unfavorable net capital loss result. Also, if a special tax rate for long-term capital gains is reenacted, the § 1231 procedure would still be available and would allow net § 1231 gains to be taxed at the favorable long-term capital gain rate. Finally, § 1231 assets can create an ordinary loss and yet be treated the same as capital assets for purposes of the appreciated property charitable contribution provisions (refer to chapter 10).

Property Included

Section 1231 property includes the following:

- Depreciable or real property used in business (principally machinery and equipment, buildings, and land).
- Timber, coal, or domestic iron ore to which § 631 applies.
- Livestock held for draft, breeding, dairy, or sporting purposes.
- Unharvested crops on land used in business.
- Certain nonpersonal use capital assets.

Property Excluded

Section 1231 property does *not* include the following:

- Property not held for the long-term holding period. Since the benefit of § 1231 is long-term capital gain treatment, the holding period must correspond to the more-than-one-year holding period that applies to capital assets. Livestock must be held at least 12 months (24 months in some cases). Unharvested crops

do not have to be held for the required long-term holding period, but the land must be held for the long-term holding period.

- Property where casualty losses exceed casualty gains for the taxable year. If a taxpayer has a net casualty loss, the individual casualty gains and losses are treated as ordinary gains and losses.

- Inventory and property held primarily for sale to customers.

- Copyrights; literary, musical, or artistic compositions, etc.; and certain U.S. government publications.

Notice that the last two items (inventory and copyrights, etc.) are also not capital assets.

Special Rules for Nonpersonal Use Capital Assets

Nonpersonal use property disposed of by casualty or theft may receive § 1231 treatment. Nonpersonal use property includes capital assets held for the production of income, such as an investment painting or investment land. Nonpersonal use property also includes business property. The casualty or theft *long-term* gains and losses from nonpersonal use property are combined (see Concept Summary 13–4). If the result is a gain, the gains and losses are treated as § 1231 transactions. If the result is a loss, § 1231 does not apply. Instead, the gains are treated as ordinary (even though some of them may initially be capital gains), the business losses are deductible *for* AGI, and the other losses (even though some of them may initially be capital losses) are deductible *from* AGI as miscellaneous losses subject to the 2 percent of AGI limitation. Thus, a nonpersonal use capital asset that is disposed of by casualty or theft may or may not be a § 1231 asset, depending on the result of the netting process. For simplicity, the rest of this chapter will use the term *casualty* to mean casualty *or* theft.

Personal use property casualty gains and losses are not subject to the § 1231 rules. If the result of netting these gains and losses is a gain, the net gain is a capital gain. If the netting results in a loss, the net loss is a deduction *from* adjusted gross income to the extent it exceeds 10 percent of AGI.

Casualties, thefts, and condemnations are *involuntary conversions*. Notice that condemnation gains and losses are not included in the netting processes discussed above. Long-term *recognized* condemnation gains and losses from the disposition of property held for business use and for the production of income are treated as § 1231 gains and losses. Involuntary conversion gains may be deferred if conversion proceeds are reinvested, but involuntary conversion losses are recognized (refer to chapter 12) regardless of whether the conversion proceeds are reinvested.

This variation in treatment between casualty and condemnation gains and losses sheds considerable light on what § 1231 is all about. Section 1231 has no effect on whether realized gain or loss is recognized. Instead, it merely dictates how such gain or loss might be *classified* (ordinary or capital) under certain conditions.

Gains and losses from *condemnations* of personal use property are not subject to the § 1231 rules. The gains are capital gains and the losses are nondeductible because they arise from the disposition of personal use property.

General Procedure for § 1231 Computation

The tax treatment of § 1231 gains and losses depends on the results of a rather complex *netting* procedure. The steps in this netting procedure are as follows.

CONCEPT SUMMARY 13–4

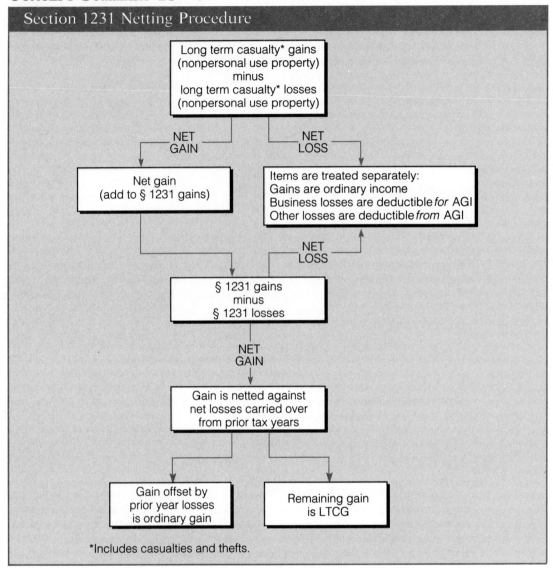

Section 1231 Netting Procedure

*Includes casualties and thefts.

Step 1: Casualty Netting.   Net all long-term gains and losses from casualties of nonpersonal use property. Casualty gains result when insurance proceeds exceed the adjusted basis of the property.

    a.   If the casualty gains exceed the casualty losses, add the excess to the other § 1231 gains for the taxable year.

    b.   If the casualty losses exceed the casualty gains, exclude all losses and gains from further § 1231 computation. If this is the case, all casualty gains are ordinary income. Business casualty losses are deductible *for* adjusted gross income. Other casualty losses are deductible *from* adjusted gross income.

Step 2: § 1231 Netting.   After adding any net casualty gain from Step 1a to the other § 1231 gains and losses (including recognized condemnation gains and losses), net all § 1231 gains and losses.

a. If the gains exceed the losses, the net gain is offset by the nonrecaptured § 1231 losses (see § 1231 Lookback below) from prior tax years. To the extent of this offset, the net § 1231 gain is classified as ordinary gain. Any remaining gain is long-term capital gain.

b. If the losses exceed the gains, all gains are ordinary income. Business losses are deductible *for* adjusted gross income. Other casualty losses are deductible *from* adjusted gross income.

Step 3: § 1231 Lookback.   The net § 1231 gain from Step 2a is offset by the nonrecaptured net § 1231 losses for the five preceding taxable years. For 1990, the lookback years are 1985, 1986, 1987, 1988, and 1989. To the extent of the nonrecaptured net § 1231 loss, the current year net § 1231 gain is ordinary income. The *nonrecaptured* net § 1231 losses are those that have not already been used to offset net § 1231 gains. Only the net § 1231 gain exceeding this net § 1231 loss carryforward is given long-term capital gain treatment. Concept Summary 13−4 summarizes the § 1231 computational procedure. Examples 40 and 41 illustrate the lookback procedure.

Examples 38 through 41 illustrate the application of the § 1231 computation procedure.

EXAMPLE 38   During 1990, T had $125,000 of AGI before considering the following recognized gains and losses:

Capital Gains and Losses	
Long-term capital gain	$3,000
Long-term capital loss	(400)
Short-term capital gain	1,000
Short-term capital loss	(200)

Casualties	
Theft of diamond ring (owned four months)	$ (800)*
Fire damage to personal residence (owned 10 years)	(400)*
Gain from insurance recovery on accidental destruction of business truck (owned two years)	200

§ 1231 Gains and Losses from Depreciable Business Assets Held Long Term	
Asset A	$ 300
Asset B	1,100
Asset C	(500)

Gains and Losses from Sale of Depreciable Business Assets Held Short Term	
Asset D	$ 200
Asset E	(300)

* As adjusted for the $100 floor on personal casualty losses.

T had no net § 1231 losses in tax years before 1990.

Disregarding the recapture of depreciation and passive loss offset possibilities (discussed later in the chapter), the tax treatment of the above gains and losses is as follows:

- The diamond ring and the residence are personal use assets. Therefore, these casualties are not § 1231 transactions. The $800 (ring) plus $400 (residence) losses are potentially deductible *from* adjusted gross income. However, the total loss of $1,200 does not exceed 10 percent of AGI. Thus, only the business casualty remains. The $200 gain is added to the § 1231 gains.

- The gains from § 1231 transactions (Assets A, B, and C and the business casualty gain) exceed the losses by $1,100 ($1,600 less $500). This excess is a long-term capital gain and is added to T's other long-term capital gains.

- T's net long-term capital gain is $3,700 ($3,000 plus $1,100 from § 1231 transactions less the long-term capital loss of $400). T's net short-term capital gain is $800 ($1,000 less $200). The result is capital gain net income of $4,500 that is subject to tax as ordinary income.[30]

- The gain and loss from Assets D and E (depreciable business assets held for less than the long-term holding period) are treated as ordinary gain and loss by T.

Results of the Gains and Losses on T's Tax Computation	
NLTCG	$ 3,700
STCG	800
Ordinary gain from sale of Asset D	200
Ordinary loss from sale of Asset E	(300)
AGI from other sources	125,000
AGI	$129,400

- T would have personal casualty losses of $800 (diamond ring) + $400 (personal residence). A personal casualty loss is deductible only to the extent it exceeds 10% of AGI. Thus, none of the $1,200 is deductible ($129,400 × 10% = $12,940). □

EXAMPLE 39

Assume the same facts as in Example 38, except the loss from Asset C was $1,700 instead of $500.

- The treatment of the casualty losses is the same as in Example 38.

- The losses from § 1231 transactions now exceed the gains by $100 ($1,700 less $1,600). The result is that the gains from Assets A and B and the business casualty gain are ordinary income and the loss from Asset C is a

---

30. The $3,700 qualifies for the *alternative tax* on long-term capital gains. However, for 1990 this alternative tax rate is the same as the maximum ordinary tax rate, so no benefit results. The long-term capital gain in Examples 39, 40, and 41 also qualifies for the alternative tax, but there would be no benefit from using this tax.

deduction *for* adjusted gross income (a business loss). The same result can be achieved by simply treating the $100 net loss as a deduction *for* AGI.

- Capital gain net income is $3,400 ($2,600 long-term plus $800 short-term) and is subject to tax as ordinary income.

Results of the Gains and Losses on T's Tax Computation	
NLTCG	$ 2,600
STCG	800
Net ordinary loss on Assets A, B, and C and business casualty gain	(100)
Ordinary gain from sale of Asset D	200
Ordinary loss from sale of Asset E	(300)
AGI from other sources	125,000
AGI	$128,200

- None of the personal casualty losses would be deductible since $1,200 does not exceed 10% of $128,200. □

EXAMPLE 40   Assume the same facts as in Example 38, except that T has a $700 nonrecaptured net § 1231 loss from 1989.

- The treatment of the casualty losses is the same as in Example 38.

- The 1990 net § 1231 gain of $1,100 is treated as ordinary income to the extent of the 1989 nonrecaptured § 1231 loss of $700. The remaining $400 net § 1231 gain is a long-term capital gain and is added to T's other long-term capital gains.

- T's net long-term capital gain is $3,000 ($3,000 plus $400 from § 1231 transactions less the long-term capital loss of $400). T's short-term capital gain is still $800 ($1,000 less $200). The result is capital gain net income of $3,800 and is subject to tax as ordinary income.

Results of the Gains and Losses on T's Tax Computation	
NLTCG	$ 3,000
STCG	800
Ordinary gain from recapture of § 1231 losses	700
Ordinary gain from sale of Asset D	200
Ordinary loss from sale of Asset E	(300)
AGI from other sources	125,000
AGI	$129,400

- None of the personal casualty losses would be deductible since $1,200 does not exceed 10% of $129,400. □

EXAMPLE 41

Assume the same facts as in Example 38, except that in 1988 T had a net § 1231 loss of $2,700 and in 1989 a net § 1231 gain of $300.

- The treatment of the casualty losses is the same as in Example 38.

- The 1988 net § 1231 loss of $2,700 would have been carried over to 1989 and offset against the 1989 net § 1231 gain of $300. Thus, the $300 gain would have been ordinary income, and $2,400 of nonrecaptured 1988 net § 1231 loss would carry over to 1990. The 1990 net § 1231 gain of $1,100 would be offset against this loss, resulting in $1,100 of ordinary income. The nonrecaptured net § 1231 loss of $1,300 ($2,400 − $1,100) would carry over to 1991.

- Capital gain net income is $3,400 ($2,600 net long-term capital gain plus $800 net short-term capital gain) and is subject to tax as ordinary income.

**Results of the Gains and Losses
on T's Tax Computation**

NLTCG	$ 2,600
STCG	800
Ordinary gain from recapture of § 1231 losses	1,100
Ordinary gain from sale of Asset D	200
Ordinary loss from sale of Asset E	(300)
AGI from other sources	125,000
AGI	$129,400

- None of the personal casualty losses would be deductible since $1,200 does not exceed 10% of $129,400. □

SECTION 1245 RECAPTURE

Section 1245 prevents taxpayers from receiving the dual benefits of depreciation deductions that offset ordinary income plus § 1231 long-term capital gain treatment on the disposition of the depreciated property. Section 1245 applies primarily to non-real estate property and requires that gain recognized be treated as ordinary income to the extent of depreciation taken on the property disposed of. Section 1245 does not apply if property is disposed of at a loss. Generally, the loss will be a § 1231 loss unless the form of the disposition is a casualty.

EXAMPLE 42

T purchased a $100,000 business machine and deducted $70,000 depreciation before selling it for $80,000. If it were not for § 1245, the $50,000 § 1231 gain ($80,000 less $30,000 adjusted basis) would be treated as a long-term capital gain. Section 1245 prevents this potentially favorable result by recapturing as ordinary income (not as § 1231 gain) any gain to the extent of depreciation taken. In this example, the entire $50,000 gain would be ordinary income. □

Section 1245 provides, in general, that the portion of recognized gain from the sale or other disposition of § 1245 property that represents depreciation (including § 167 depreciation, § 168 cost recovery, § 179 immediate expensing, and the

investment tax credit 50 percent basis reduction) is recaptured as ordinary income. The method of depreciation (e.g., accelerated or straight-line) does not matter. All depreciation taken is potentially subject to recapture. Thus, § 1245 recapture is often referred to as *full recapture*. Any remaining gain after subtracting the amount recaptured as ordinary income will usually be § 1231 gain. The remaining gain would be casualty gain if it were disposed of in a casualty event.

Although § 1245 applies primarily to non-real estate property, it does apply to certain real estate. Nonresidential real estate acquired after 1980 and before 1987 and for which accelerated depreciation (the statutory percentage method of the accelerated cost recovery system) is used is subject to the § 1245 recapture rules. Such property includes 15-year, 18-year, and 19-year nonresidential real estate.

The following examples illustrate the general application of § 1245.

EXAMPLE 43 On January 1, 1990, T sold for $13,000 a machine acquired several years ago for $12,000. She had taken $10,000 of depreciation on the machine.

- The recognized gain from the sale is $11,000. This is the amount realized of $13,000 less the adjusted basis of $2,000 ($12,000 cost less $10,000 depreciation taken).

- Depreciation taken is $10,000. Therefore, $10,000 of the $11,000 recognized gain is ordinary income, and the remaining $1,000 gain is § 1231 gain.

- The § 1231 gain is also equal to the excess of the sales price over the original cost of the property ($13,000 − $12,000 = $1,000 § 1231 gain). □

EXAMPLE 44 Assume the same facts as in the previous example, except the asset is sold for $9,000 instead of $13,000.

- The recognized gain from the sale is $7,000. This is the amount realized of $9,000 less the adjusted basis of $2,000.

- Depreciation taken is $10,000. Therefore, since the $10,000 depreciation taken exceeds the recognized gain of $7,000, the entire $7,000 recognized gain is ordinary income. □

EXAMPLE 45 Assume the same facts as in Example 43, except the asset is sold for $1,500 instead of $13,000.

- The recognized loss from the sale is $500. This is the amount realized of $1,500 less the adjusted basis of $2,000.

- Since there is a loss, there is no depreciation recapture. All of the loss is § 1231 loss. □

The application of § 1245 recapture rules does not mean the depreciation deductions are lost. It means only that to the extent of depreciation taken, the gain does not qualify for potential long-term capital gain treatment under § 1231.

If § 1245 property is disposed of in a transaction other than a sale, exchange, or involuntary conversion, the maximum amount recaptured is the excess of the property's fair market value over its adjusted basis. See the discussion under Considerations Common to §§ 1245 and 1250 later in the chapter.

Section 1245 Property

Generally, § 1245 property includes all depreciable personal property (e.g., machinery and equipment), including livestock. Buildings and their structural components generally are not § 1245 property. The following property is *also* subject to § 1245 treatment:

* Amortizable personal property such as patents, copyrights, and leaseholds of § 1245 property. Professional baseball and football player contracts are § 1245 property.

* Amortization of reforestation expenditures and expensing of costs to remove architectural and transportation barriers to the handicapped and elderly.

* Immediate expensing of costs of depreciable tangible personal property under § 179.

* Elevators and escalators acquired before January 1, 1987.

* Certain depreciable tangible real property (other than buildings and their structural components) employed as an integral part of certain activities such as manufacturing and production. For example, a natural gas storage tank where the gas is used in the manufacturing process is § 1245 property.

* Pollution control facilities, railroad grading and tunnel bores, on-the-job training, and child care facilities on which amortization is taken.

* Single-purpose agricultural and horticultural structures and petroleum storage facilities (e.g., a greenhouse or silo).

* As noted above, 15-year, 18-year, and 19-year nonresidential real estate for which accelerated cost recovery is used is subject to the § 1245 recapture rules, although it is technically not § 1245 property. Such property would have been placed in service after 1980 and before 1987.

EXAMPLE 46

T acquired nonresidential real property on January 1, 1986, for $100,000. She used the statutory percentage method to compute the ACRS depreciation. She sells the asset on January 15, 1990, for $120,000. The amount and nature of T's gain are determined as follows:

Amount realized		$120,000
Adjusted basis		
Cost	$100,000	
Less cost recovery: 1986	(8,800)	
1987	(8,400)	
1988	(7,600)	
1989	(6,900)	
1990	(263)	
January 15, 1990, adjusted basis		(68,037)
Gain realized and recognized		$ 51,963

The gain of $51,963 is treated as ordinary income to the extent of *all* depreciation taken because the property is 19-year nonresidential real estate

for which accelerated depreciation was used. Thus, T reports ordinary income of $31,963 ($8,800 + $8,400 + $7,600 + $6,900 + $263) and § 1231 gain of $20,000 ($51,963 − $31,963).   □

Observations on § 1245

* In most instances, the total depreciation taken will exceed the recognized gain. Therefore, the disposition of § 1245 property usually results in ordinary income rather than § 1231 gain. Thus, generally, no § 1231 gain will occur unless the § 1245 property is disposed of for more than its original cost. Refer to Example 43.

* Recapture applies to the total amount of depreciation allowed or allowable regardless of the depreciation method used.

* Recapture applies regardless of the holding period of the property. Of course, the entire recognized gain would be ordinary income if the property were held for less than the long-term holding period, because § 1231 would not apply.

* Section 1245 does not apply to losses, which receive § 1231 treatment.

* As discussed later in the chapter, gains from the disposition of § 1245 assets may also be treated as passive gains.

SECTION 1250 RECAPTURE

Section 1250 was enacted in 1964 for depreciable real property and has been revised many times. The provision prevents taxpayers from receiving the benefits of both *accelerated* depreciation (or cost recovery) deductions and subsequent long-term capital gain treatment upon the sale of real property. If straight-line depreciation is taken on the property, § 1250 does not apply. Nor does § 1250 apply if the real property is sold at a loss. The loss would generally be a § 1231 loss unless the property was disposed of by casualty.

Section 1250 as originally enacted required recapture of a percentage of the additional depreciation deducted by the taxpayer. *Additional depreciation* is the excess of accelerated depreciation actually deducted over depreciation that would have been deductible if the straight-line method had been used. Since only the additional depreciation is subject to recapture, § 1250 recapture is often referred to as *partial recapture*.

Post-1969 additional depreciation on nonresidential real property is subject to 100 percent recapture (see Example 47). Post-1969 additional depreciation on residential property may be subject to less than 100 percent recapture (see Example 48).

The following discussion describes the computational steps prescribed in § 1250 and reflected on Form 4797 (Gains and Losses from Sales or Exchanges of Assets Used in a Trade or Business and Involuntary Conversions).

If § 1250 property is disposed of in a transaction other than a sale, exchange, or involuntary conversion, the maximum amount recaptured is the excess of the property's fair market value over the adjusted basis. For example, if a corporation distributed property to its shareholders as a dividend, the property would be disposed of by the corporation at a gain if the fair market value is greater than the adjusted basis. The maximum amount of § 1250 recapture would be the amount of the gain.

Generally, *§ 1250 property* is depreciable real property (principally buildings and their structural components) that is not subject to § 1245.[31] Intangible real property, such as leaseholds of § 1250 property, is also included.

The recapture rules under § 1250 are substantially less punitive than the § 1245 recapture rules since only the amount of additional depreciation is subject to recapture. Straight-line depreciation (except for property held one year or less) is not recaptured.

Computing Recapture on Nonresidential Real Property

For § 1250 property other than residential rental property, the potential recapture is equal to the amount of additional depreciation taken since December 31, 1969. This nonresidential real property includes buildings such as offices, warehouses, factories, and stores. (The definition of and rules for residential rental housing are discussed later in the chapter.) The lower of the potential § 1250 recapture amount or the gain is ordinary income. The following general rules apply:

- Post-1969 additional depreciation is depreciation taken in excess of straight-line after December 31, 1969.

- If the property is held for one year or less (usually not the case), all depreciation taken, even under the straight-line method, is additional depreciation.

- Special rules apply to dispositions of substantially improved § 1250 property. These rules are rather technical, and the reader should consult the examples in the Regulations for illustrations of their application.[32]

The following procedure is used to compute recapture on nonresidential real property under § 1250:

- Determine the gain from the sale or other disposition of the property.

- Determine post-1969 additional depreciation.

- The lower of the gain or the post-1969 additional depreciation is ordinary income.

- If any gain remains (total gain less recapture), it is § 1231 gain. However, it would be casualty gain if the disposition was by casualty.

The following example shows the application of the § 1250 computational procedure.

EXAMPLE 47   On January 3, 1980, T, an individual, acquired a new building at a cost of $200,000 for use in his business. The building had an estimated useful life of 50 years and no estimated salvage value. Depreciation has been taken under the double-declining balance method through December 31, 1989. Pertinent information with respect to depreciation taken follows:

---

31. As previously discussed, in one limited circumstance, § 1245 does apply to depreciable realty. If nonresidential realty is placed in service after 1980 and before 1987 and the statutory percentage method of cost recovery is used, § 1245 recapture rules apply rather than § 1250 recapture rules.

32. § 1250(f) and Reg. § 1.1250–5.

Year	Undepreciated Balance (Beginning of the Year)	Current Depreciation Provision	Straight-line Depreciation	Additional Depreciation
1980	$200,000	$ 8,000	$ 4,000	$ 4,000
1981	192,000	7,680	4,000	3,680
1982	184,320	7,373	4,000	3,373
1983	176,947	7,079	4,000	3,079
1984	169,868	6,795	4,000	2,795
1985	163,073	6,523	4,000	2,523
1986	156,550	6,262	4,000	2,262
1987	150,288	6,012	4,000	2,012
1988	144,276	5,771	4,000	1,771
1989	138,505	5,540	4,000	1,540
Total 1980–1989		$67,035	$40,000	$27,035

On January 2, 1990, the building was sold for $180,000. Compute the amount of § 1250 ordinary income and § 1231 gain.

- The recognized gain from the sale is $47,035. This is the difference between the $180,000 amount realized and the $132,965 adjusted basis ($200,000 cost less $67,035 depreciation taken).
- Post-1969 additional depreciation is $27,035.
- The amount of post-1969 ordinary income is $27,035. Since the post-1969 additional depreciation of $27,035 is less than the recognized gain of $47,035, the entire gain is not recaptured.
- The remaining $20,000 ($47,035 – $27,035) gain is § 1231 gain. □

Computing Recapture on Residential Rental Housing

Section 1250 recapture applies to the sale or other disposition of residential rental housing. Property qualifies as *residential rental housing* only if at least 80 percent of gross rental income is rental income from dwelling units.[33] The rules are the same as for other § 1250 property, except that only the post-1975 additional depreciation is recaptured in full. The post-1969 through 1975 recapture percentage is 100 percent less one percentage point for each full month the property is held over 100 months.[34] Therefore, the additional depreciation for periods after 1975 is initially applied against the recognized gain, and such amounts are recaptured in full as ordinary income. Any remaining recognized gain is then tested under the percentage rules applicable to the post-1969 through 1975 period. If any of the recognized gain is not absorbed by the recapture rules pertaining to the post-1969 period, the remaining gain is § 1231 gain.

---

33. § 167(j)(2)(B) and Reg. § 1.167(j)–3(b)(1)(i).
34. §§ 1250(a)(1) and (2) and Reg. § 1.1250–1(d)(1)(i)(c).

EXAMPLE 48	Assume the same facts as in the previous example, except the building is residential rental housing.

- Post-1975 ordinary income is $27,035 (post-1975 additional depreciation of $27,035).

- Since the building was acquired in 1980, the post-1969 through 1975 recapture rules do not apply.[35]

- The remaining $20,000 ($47,035 − $27,035) gain is § 1231 gain. ☐

Under § 1250, when straight-line depreciation is used, there is no § 1250 recapture potential unless the property is disposed of in the first year of use. Before 1987, accelerated depreciation on real estate generally was available. For real property placed in service after 1986, however, only straight-line depreciation is allowed. Therefore, the § 1250 recapture rules will have no application to such property unless the property is disposed of in the first year of use.

EXAMPLE 49	T acquires a residential rental building on January 1, 1989, for $300,000. He receives an offer of $450,000 for the building in 1990 and sells it on December 23, 1990.

- T would take $20,909 [($300,000 × .03485) + ($300,000 × .03636 × 11.5/12) = $20,909] of total depreciation for 1989 and 1990, and the adjusted basis of the property would be $279,091 ($300,000 − $20,909).

- T's gain would be $170,909 ($450,000 − $279,091).

- All of the gain would be § 1231 gain. ☐

The § 1250 recapture rules apply to the following property for which accelerated depreciation was used:

- Residential real estate acquired before 1987.

- Nonresidential real estate acquired before 1981.

- Real property used predominantly outside the United States.

- Certain government-financed or low-income housing described in § 1250(a)(1)(B).

CONSIDERATIONS COMMON TO §§ 1245 AND 1250

Exceptions

Recapture under §§ 1245 and 1250 does not apply to the following transactions.

Gifts.   The recapture potential does carry over to the donee.[36]

EXAMPLE 50	T gives his daughter, D, § 1245 property with an adjusted basis of $1,000. The amount of recapture potential is $700. D uses the property in her business and

---

35. If the building had been acquired on January 3, 1975, and sold on January 2, 1990, it would have been held 180 months. The recapture percentage for the 1975 additional depreciation would be

20% [100% less (180% less 100%)].

36. §§ 1245(b)(1) and 1250(d)(1) and Reg. §§ 1.1245–4(a)(1) and 1.1250–3(a)(1).

claims further depreciation of $100 before selling it for $1,900. D's recognized gain is $1,000 (amount realized of $1,900 less $900 adjusted basis), of which $800 is recaptured as ordinary income ($100 depreciation taken by D plus $700 recapture potential carried over from T). The remaining gain of $200 is § 1231 gain. Even if D used the property for personal purposes, the $700 recapture potential would still be carried over. □

Death.   Although not a very attractive tax planning approach, death eliminates all recapture potential. In other words, any recapture potential does not carry over from a decedent to an estate or heir.

EXAMPLE 51   Assume the same facts as in the previous example, except T's daughter receives the property as a result of T's death. The $700 recapture potential from T is extinguished. D would have a basis for the property equal to the property's fair market value (assume $1,800) at T's death. D would have a $200 gain when the property is sold because the selling price ($1,900) exceeds the property's adjusted basis ($1,800 original basis to D less $100 depreciation) by $200. Because of § 1245, $100 would be ordinary income. The remaining gain of $100 would be § 1231 gain. □

Charitable Transfers.   The recapture potential reduces the amount of the charitable contribution deduction under § 170.[37]

EXAMPLE 52   T donates to his church § 1245 property with a fair market value of $10,000 and an adjusted basis of $7,000. Assume that the amount of recapture potential is $2,000 (the amount of recapture that would occur if the property were sold). T's charitable contribution deduction (subject to the limitations discussed in chapter 10) is $8,000 ($10,000 fair market value less $2,000 recapture potential). □

Certain Tax-Free Transactions.   These are transactions in which the transferor's adjusted basis of property carries over to the transferee.[38] The recapture potential also carries over to the transferee.[39] Included in this category are transfers of property pursuant to

- Tax-free incorporations under § 351.

- Certain liquidations of subsidiary companies under § 332.

- Tax-free contributions to a partnership under § 721.

- Tax-free reorganizations.

Gain may be recognized in these transactions if boot is received. If gain is recognized, it is treated as ordinary income to the extent of the recapture potential or recognized gain, whichever is lower.[40]

---

37. § 170(e)(1)(A) and Reg. § 1.170A–4(b)(1). In certain circumstances, § 1231 gain also reduces the amount of the charitable contribution. See § 170(e)(1)(B).

38. §§ 1245(b)(3) and 1250(d)(3) and Reg. §§ 1.1245–4(c) and 1.1250–3(c).

39. Reg. §§ 1.1245–2(a)(4) and –2(c)(2) and 1.1250–2(d)(1) and (3) and –3(c)(3).

40. §§ 1245(b)(3) and 1250(d)(3) and Reg. §§ 1.1245–4(c) and 1.1250–3(c). Some of these special corporate problems are discussed in chapter 16. Partnership contributions are discussed in chapter 21.

Like-kind Exchanges (§ 1031) and Involuntary Conversions (§ 1033).   Gain may be recognized to the extent of boot received under § 1031. Gain also may be recognized to the extent the proceeds from an involuntary conversion are not reinvested in similar property under § 1033. Such recognized gain is subject to recapture as ordinary income under §§ 1245 and 1250. The remaining recapture potential, if any, carries over to the property received in the exchange.

EXAMPLE 53

T exchanges § 1245 property with an adjusted basis of $300 for § 1245 property with a fair market value of $6,000. The exchange qualifies as a like-kind exchange under § 1031. T also receives $1,000 cash (boot). T's realized gain is $6,700 [amount realized of $7,000 less $300 (adjusted basis of property)]. Assuming the recapture potential is $7,500, gain of $1,000 is recognized because boot of $1,000 is received. The remaining recapture potential of $6,500 carries over to the like-kind property received. □

SPECIAL RECAPTURE PROVISIONS

Special Recapture for Corporations

Corporations (other than S corporations) selling depreciable real estate may have ordinary income in addition to that required by § 1250. The *ordinary gain adjustment* is 20 percent of the excess of the § 1245 potential recapture over the § 1250 recapture.[41] The result is that the § 1231 gain is correspondingly decreased by this increase in ordinary income.

EXAMPLE 54

A corporation purchased a residential building on January 1, 1986, for $100,000. Accelerated depreciation of $31,963 was taken before the building was disposed of on January 15, 1990. The straight-line depreciation for the same period would have been $21,121. The selling price was $120,000. Section 1250 would recapture $10,842 ($31,963 − $21,121). Section 1245 would have recaptured the entire $31,963. The ordinary gain adjustment is computed as follows:

Section 1245 recapture (lower of depreciation taken or total gain)	$ 31,963
Less: Gain recaptured by § 1250	(10,842)
Excess of § 1245 gain over § 1250 gain	$ 21,121
Percentage that is ordinary gain	20%
Ordinary gain adjustment	$ 4,224
Section 1231 gain [$120,000 selling price − ($100,000 cost − $31,963 depreciation taken) = $51,963 gain; $51,963 gain − $10,842 § 1250 gain − $4,224 ordinary gain adjustment]	$ 36,897

□

---

41. § 291(a)(1).

CONCEPT SUMMARY 13–5

Depreciation Recapture and § 1231 Netting Procedure Flowchart

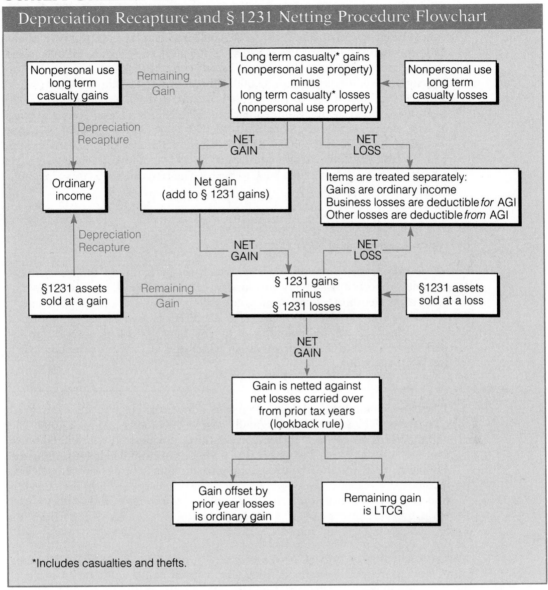

*Includes casualties and thefts.

Recapture of Investment Credit Basis Reduction

The investment tax credit has been repealed for property placed in service after December 31, 1985. However, on property eligible for investment tax credit under the prior law, a basis reduction was sometimes required (refer to the discussion in chapter 11). This basis reduction amount is subject to § 1245 recapture. However, if an investment credit recapture takes place upon disposition of the property, one-half of the investment credit recapture is added back to the property's basis before computing gain or loss.

EXAMPLE 55

B purchased business machinery in December 1985 for $100,000. B took $10,000 of investment tax credit ($100,000 × 10%) and $95,000 of depreciation [$100,000 − ($10,000 × .5) = $95,000; $95,000 × 1.00 (the sum of the 1985 through 1989 depreciation rates) = $95,000]. In February 1990, B found that the machine was ineffective and sold it for $105,000. B would have an investment credit recapture of $2,000. B's recomputed credit is $8,000 (8% × $100,000). The balance of the credit is recaptured. One-half of the $2,000 recaptured credit would be added back to the machine's basis. Thus, the basis at sale would be $1,000 ($100,000 − $5,000 − $95,000 + $1,000). B's gain would be $104,000 ($105,000 − $1,000). Gain recaptured by § 1245 would be $99,000 (the $95,000 of depreciation plus the $4,000 of investment credit basis reduction that was not added back to basis). The remaining $5,000 gain would be § 1231 gain. □

Gain from Sale of Depreciable Property between Certain Related Parties

When the sale or exchange of property, which in the hands of the *transferee* is depreciable property (principally machinery, equipment, and buildings, but not land), is between certain related parties, any gain recognized is ordinary income.[42] This provision is applicable to both direct and indirect sales or exchanges. A *related party* is defined as an individual and his or her controlled corporation or partnership or a taxpayer and any trust in which the taxpayer (or the taxpayer's spouse) is a beneficiary.

EXAMPLE 56

T sells a personal automobile (therefore nondepreciable) to her controlled corporation. The automobile originally cost $5,000 and is sold for $7,000. The automobile is to be used in the corporation's business. If the related-party provision did not exist, T would realize a long-term capital gain (assuming the asset was held for the required long-term holding period) of $2,000. The income tax consequences would be favorable because T's controlled corporation is entitled to depreciate the automobile (assuming business use) based upon the purchase price of $7,000. Under the related-party provision, T's $2,000 gain is ordinary income. □

The related-party provision was enacted to prevent certain related parties from enjoying the dual benefits of long-term capital gain treatment (transferor) and a step-up in basis for depreciation (transferee). Recapture under §§ 1245 and 1250 applies first before recapture under the related-party provision.

Control means ownership of more than 50 percent in value of the corporation's outstanding stock or more than 50 percent of the capital interest or profits interest of a partnership. In determining the percentage of stock owned or partnership interest owned, the taxpayer must include that stock or partnership interest owned by related taxpayers as determined under the constructive ownership rules of § 267(c).

Section 267(a)(1) disallows a loss on the sale of property between certain related taxpayers. Therefore, a sale of property between certain related parties may

---

42. § 1239.

result in ordinary income (if the property is depreciable in the hands of the transferee) or a nondeductible loss.

The related-party provision applies regardless of whether the transfer is from a shareholder or partner to the entity or from the entity to a shareholder or partner. Ordinary income treatment also applies to transfers between two corporations controlled by the same shareholder.

EXAMPLE 57

T, the sole shareholder of X Corporation, sells a building (adjusted basis of $40,000) for $100,000 to the corporation for use in its business. Since the building was depreciated by T using the straight-line method, none of the depreciation will be recaptured under § 1250. Nevertheless, the related-party provision applies to convert T's § 1231 gain of $60,000 to ordinary income. The basis of the building to X Corporation is $100,000 (the building's cost).   □

Intangible Drilling Costs and Depletion

Taxpayers may elect to either *expense or capitalize* intangible drilling and development costs for oil, gas, or geothermal properties.[43] *Intangible drilling and development costs* (IDC) include operator (one who holds a working or operating interest in any tract or parcel of land) expenditures for wages, fuel, repairs, hauling, and supplies. These expenditures must be incident to and necessary for the drilling of wells and preparation of wells for production. In most instances, taxpayers elect to expense IDC to maximize tax deductions during drilling.

Intangible drilling costs are subject to § 1254 recapture when the property is disposed of. The gain on the disposition of the property is subject to recapture as ordinary income as follows:

- For properties acquired before 1987, the IDC expensed after 1975 in excess of what cost depletion would have been had the IDC been capitalized.

- For properties acquired after 1986, the IDC expensed.

For properties acquired after 1986, depletion on oil, gas, geothermal, and other mineral properties is subject to recapture to the extent the depletion reduced the basis of the property. The combined IDC and depletion recapture may not exceed the recognized gain from disposition of the property. If the property is disposed of at a loss, no recapture occurs.

EXAMPLE 58

X acquired a working interest in certain oil and gas properties for $50,000 during 1989. He incurred $10,000 of intangible development and drilling costs. X elected to expense these costs in 1989. In January 1990, the properties were sold for $60,000. Disregard any depreciation on tangible depreciable properties and assume that cost depletion would have amounted to $2,000 had the IDC been capitalized. The gain realized and recognized is $10,000 ($60,000 − $50,000). The gain is recaptured as ordinary income to the extent of the expensed IDC ($10,000), which is equal to the recognized gain ($10,000). Therefore, $10,000 is recaptured.   □

---

43. § 263(c).

Special rules are provided for determining recapture upon the sale or other disposition of a portion or an undivided interest in oil, gas, geothermal, and other mineral properties.

Passive Activity Losses

Passive activity losses may result in current losses that are not deductible against nonpassive activity income.[44] If there is insufficient current passive income to absorb the passive losses, the losses are *suspended* until such time as sufficient passive income is available to absorb them. (Passive activity losses are discussed in chapter 6.) When a passive activity is disposed of, the suspended and current year losses of that activity are fully deductible. However, they also reduce the recognized gain, if any, from disposition of the activity. Any remaining gain is then available to allow other passive activity current and suspended losses to be currently deductible. The recognized gain still receives treatment under the normal property disposition rules discussed earlier in this chapter. If a passive activity is disposed of at a recognized loss, the loss is treated under the normal property disposition provisions. Thus, recognized *gains* from passive activity dispositions have a dual purpose: to allow deductibility of passive losses to the extent of the gain and to be treated under the normal property disposition rules. Recognized *losses* from passive activity dispositions do not have a dual purpose.

Example 59   S disposes of a passive activity during 1990 at a $36,000 gain. The passive activity asset was a § 1231 asset, and the gain is a § 1231 gain. However, S has a current passive loss of $6,000 from this activity, no suspended losses from the activity, and $21,000 of current losses from another passive activity. The $36,000 gain allows the $6,000 and $21,000 passive losses to be fully deductible in 1990 as *for* AGI deductions. For purposes of computing S's net § 1231 gain, the full $36,000 of § 1231 gain is used. □

Example 60   Assume the same facts as in the previous example, except that S has a $36,000 § 1231 loss rather than a gain. The § 1231 loss would be included in S's net § 1231 computation. The $6,000 current loss from the passive activity disposed of would be deductible in full as a deduction *for* AGI. The $21,000 loss from the other passive activity would not be deductible unless the phase-in of nondeductibility rules apply to it. □

Reporting Procedures

Noncapital gains and losses are reported on Form 4797, Sales of Business Property. Before filling out Form 4797, however, Form 4684, Casualties and Thefts, must be completed to determine whether or not such transactions will enter into the § 1231 computation procedure. Recall that this will occur only if a net gain results from casualties and thefts of nonpersonal use property held for the long-term holding period.

---

44.   § 469.

Importance of Capital Asset Status

Why is capital asset status still important if long-term capital gains are no longer eligible for special tax treatment? Nearly all tax experts agree that the current taxation of long-term capital gains at ordinary tax rates is a temporary situation. Regular tax rates are probably going to rise, and the historical lower taxation of long-term capital gains will again be in place.

In the meantime, capital asset status is still important because capital gains must be offset by capital losses. If a net capital loss results, the maximum deduction is $3,000 per year. Also, because the capital asset structure remains in the Code, capital gains and losses must still be reported separately on Schedule D of Form 1040. Consequently, capital gains and losses must be segregated from other types of gains and losses.

Planning for Capital Asset Status

It is important to keep in mind that capital asset status often is a question of objective evidence. Thus, property that is not a capital asset to one party may qualify as a capital asset to another party.

EXAMPLE 61

T, a real estate dealer, transfers by gift a tract of land to S, her son. The land was recorded as part of T's inventory (it was held for resale) and was therefore not a capital asset to T. S, however, treats the land as an investment. The land is a capital asset in S's hands, and any later taxable disposition of the property by S will yield a capital gain or loss. □

If proper planning is carried out, even a dealer may obtain long-term capital gain treatment on the sale of the type of property normally held for resale.

EXAMPLE 62

T, a real estate dealer, segregates tract A from the real estate he regularly holds for resale and designates such property as being held for investment purposes. The property is not advertised for sale and is disposed of several years later. The negotiations for the sale were initiated by the purchaser and not by T. Under these circumstances, it would appear that any gain or loss from the sale of tract A should be a capital gain or loss.[45] □

When a business is being sold, one of the major decisions usually concerns whether a portion of the sales price is goodwill. For the seller, goodwill generally represents the disposition of a capital asset. Goodwill has no basis and represents a residual portion of the selling price that cannot be allocated reasonably to the known assets. The amount of goodwill thus represents capital gain. The buyer purchasing goodwill has a capitalizable, nonamortizable asset—a very disadvantageous situation.

---

45. *Toledo, Peoria & Western Railroad Co.*, 35 TCM 1663, T.C.Memo. 1976–366.

The buyer would prefer that the residual portion of the purchase price be allocated to a covenant not to compete (a promise that the seller will not compete against the buyer by conducting a business similar to the one that the buyer has purchased). Payments for a covenant not to compete are ordinary income to the seller, but are ordinary deductions for the buyer over the life of the covenant.

The case law requires a covenant not to compete to be clearly specified in the sales contract.[46] Otherwise, unallocated payments will be regarded as payments for goodwill.[47] The parties should therefore bargain for the nature of this portion of the sales price and clearly specify its nature in the sales contract.

EXAMPLE 63

M is buying J's dry cleaning proprietorship. An appraisal of the assets indicates that a reasonable purchase price would exceed the value of the known assets by $30,000. If the purchase contract does not specify the nature of the $30,000, the amount will be goodwill, and J will have a long-term capital gain of $30,000. M will have a nonamortizable $30,000 asset. If M is paying the extra $30,000 to prevent J from conducting another dry cleaning business in the area, J will have $30,000 of ordinary income. M will have a $30,000 deduction over the life of the covenant if the contract specifies the purpose for the payment. □

Effect of Capital Asset Status in Other Than Sale Transactions

The nature of an asset (capital or ordinary) is important in determining the tax consequences that result when a sale or exchange occurs. It may, however, be just as significant absent a taxable sale or exchange. When a capital asset is disposed of, the result is not always a capital gain or loss. Rather, in general, the disposition must be a sale or exchange. Collection of a debt instrument having a basis less than the face value would result in an ordinary gain rather than a capital gain even though the debt instrument is a capital asset. The collection is not a sale or exchange. Sale of the debt shortly before the due date for collection will not produce a capital gain.[48] If selling the debt in such circumstances could produce a capital gain but collecting could not, the narrow interpretation of what constitutes a capital gain or loss would be frustrated. Another illustration of the sale or exchange principle could involve a donation of certain appreciated property to a qualified charity. Recall that in certain circumstances, the measure of the charitable contribution is fair market value when the property, if sold, would have yielded a long-term capital gain [refer to chapter 10 and the discussion of § 170(e)].

EXAMPLE 64

T wants to donate a tract of unimproved land (basis of $40,000 and fair market value of $200,000) held for the required long-term holding period to State University (a qualified charitable organization). However, T currently is under audit by the IRS for capital gains she reported on certain real estate transactions during an earlier tax year. Although T is not a licensed real estate broker, the IRS agent conducting the audit is contending that she has achieved dealer status by virtue of the number and frequency of the real estate

---

46. See, for example, *James A. Patterson*, 49 TCM 670, T.C.Memo. 1985–53.

47. § 1060(a)(2).

48. *Comm. v. Percy W. Phillips*, 60–1 USTC ¶ 9294, 5 AFTR2d 855, 275 F.2d 33 (CA–4, 1960).

transactions she has conducted. Under these circumstances, T would be well-advised to postpone the donation to State University until such time as her status is clarified. If she has achieved dealer status, the unimproved land may be inventory (refer to Example 62 for another possible result), and T's charitable contribution deduction would be limited to $40,000. If not, and if the land is held as an investment, T's deduction becomes $200,000 (the fair market value of the property). □

Stock Sales

The following rules apply in determining the date of a stock sale:

- The date the sale is executed is the date of the sale. The execution date is the date the broker completes the transaction on the stock exchange.

- The settlement date is the date the cash or other property is paid to the seller of the stock. This date is *not* relevant in determining the date of sale.

EXAMPLE 65

T, a cash basis taxpayer, sells stock that results in a gain. The sale was executed on December 29, 1989. The settlement date is January 5, 1990. The date of sale is December 29, 1989 (the execution date). The holding period for the stock sold ends with the execution date. □

Maximizing Benefits

Ordinary losses generally are preferable to capital losses because of the limitations imposed on the deductibility of net capital losses and the requirement that capital losses be used to offset capital gains. The taxpayer may be able to convert what would otherwise have been capital loss to ordinary loss. For example, business (but not nonbusiness) bad debts, losses from the sale or exchange of small business investment company stock, and losses from the sale or exchange of small business company stock all result in ordinary losses.[49]

Although capital losses can be carried over indefinitely, *indefinite* becomes definite when a taxpayer dies. Any loss carryovers not used by such taxpayer are permanently lost. That is, no tax benefit can be derived from the carryovers subsequent to death.[50] Therefore, the potential benefit of carrying over capital losses diminishes when dealing with older taxpayers.

It is usually beneficial to spread gains over more than one taxable year. In some cases, this can be accomplished through the installment sales method of accounting.

Year-End Planning

The following general rules can be applied for timing the recognition of capital gains and losses near the end of a taxable year:

- If the taxpayer already has recognized over $3,000 of capital loss, sell assets to generate capital gain equal to the excess of the capital loss over $3,000.

---

49. §§ 166(d), 1242, and 1244. Refer to the discussion in chapter 7.

50. Rev.Rul. 74−175, 1974−1 C.B. 52.

EXAMPLE 66   T has already incurred a $6,000 LTCL. T should generate $3,000 of capital gain. The gain will offset $3,000 of the loss. Thus, the remaining loss of $3,000 can be deducted against ordinary income.   □

- If the taxpayer already has recognized capital gain, sell assets to generate capital loss equal to the capital gain. The gain will not be taxed, and the loss will be fully *deductible* against the gain.

Timing of § 1231 Gain

Although §§ 1245 and 1250 recapture much of the gain from the disposition of business property, sometimes § 1231 gain is still substantial. For instance, land held as a business asset will generate either § 1231 gain or § 1231 loss. If the taxpayer already has a capital loss for the year, the sale of land at a gain should be postponed so that the net § 1231 gain is not netted against the capital loss. The capital loss deduction will therefore be maximized for the current tax year, and the capital loss carryforward (if any) may be offset against the gain when the land is sold. If the taxpayer already has a § 1231 loss, § 1231 gains might be postponed to maximize the ordinary loss deduction this year. However, the carryforward of nonrecaptured § 1231 losses will make the § 1231 gain next year an ordinary gain.

EXAMPLE 67   T has a $2,000 net STCL for 1990. He could sell business land for a $3,000 § 1231 gain. He will have no other capital gains and losses or § 1231 gains and losses in 1990 or 1991. He has no nonrecaptured § 1231 losses from prior years. T is in the 28% tax bracket in 1990 and 1991. If he sells the land in 1990, he will have a $1,000 net LTCG ($3,000 § 1231 gain − $2,000 STCL) and will pay a tax of $280 ($1,000 × 28%). If T sells the land in 1991, he will have a 1990 tax savings of $560 ($2,000 capital loss deduction × 28% tax rate on ordinary income). In 1991, he will pay tax of $840 ($3,000 gain × 28%). By postponing the sale for a year, T will have the use of $840 ($560 + $280).   □

EXAMPLE 68   S has a $15,000 § 1231 loss in 1990. He could sell business equipment for a $20,000 § 1231 gain and a $12,000 § 1245 gain. S is in the 28% tax bracket in 1990 and 1991. He has no nonrecaptured § 1231 losses from prior years. If he sells the equipment in 1990, he will have a $5,000 net § 1231 gain and $12,000 of ordinary gain. His tax would be $4,760 [($5,000 § 1231 gain × 28%) + ($12,000 ordinary gain × 28%)].

If S postpones the equipment sale until 1991, he would have a 1990 ordinary loss of $15,000 and tax savings of $4,200 ($15,000 × 28%). In 1991, he would have $5,000 of § 1231 gain (the 1990 § 1231 loss carries over and recaptures $15,000 of the 1991 § 1231 gain as ordinary income) and $27,000 of ordinary gain. His tax would be $8,960 [($5,000 § 1231 gain × 28%) + ($27,000 ordinary gain × 28%)]. By postponing the equipment sale, S has the use of $8,960 ($4,200 + $4,760).   □

Timing of Recapture

Since recapture is usually not triggered until the property is sold or disposed of, it may be possible to plan for recapture in low bracket or in loss years. If a taxpayer

has net operating loss carryovers that are about to expire, the recognition of ordinary income from recapture may be advisable to absorb the loss carryovers.

EXAMPLE 69

T has a $15,000 net operating loss carryover that will expire this year. He owns a machine that he plans to sell in the early part of next year. The expected gain of $17,000 from the sale of the machine will be recaptured as ordinary income under § 1245. T sells the machine before the end of this year and offsets $15,000 of the ordinary income against the net operating loss carryover.   □

Postponing and Shifting Recapture

It is also possible to postpone recapture or to shift the burden of recapture to others. For example, recapture is avoided upon the disposition of a § 1231 asset if the taxpayer replaces the property by entering into a like-kind exchange. In this instance, recapture potential is merely carried over to the newly acquired property (refer to Example 53).

Recapture can be shifted to others through the gratuitous transfer of § 1245 or § 1250 property to family members. A subsequent sale of such property by the donee will trigger recapture to the donee rather than the donor (refer to Example 50). Such procedure would be advisable only if the donee is in a lower income tax bracket than the donor.

Avoiding Recapture

The immediate expensing election (§ 179) is subject to § 1245 recapture. If the election is not made, the § 1245 recapture potential will accumulate more slowly (refer to chapter 8). Since using the immediate expense deduction complicates depreciation and book accounting for the affected asset, not taking the deduction may make sense even though the time value of money might indicate it should be taken.

Disposing of Passive Activities

Taxpayers with suspended or current passive losses may wish to dispose of passive activities. The current and suspended losses of the activity disposed of will be fully deductible. If there is a recognized loss on the disposition, the loss will not be subject to the passive activity loss limitations. Rather, it will be classified and treated as a normal property disposition loss (refer to Example 60). If there is a recognized gain on the disposition, the gain will first absorb the current and suspended losses of the activity disposed of and any remaining gain will absorb losses from other passive activities. The gain will also be treated under the normal property disposition rules (refer to Example 59).

PROBLEM MATERIALS

Discussion Questions

1. Why did Congress leave the structure of the capital asset Code sections in place even though there is no beneficial tax rate for long-term capital gains?

2. T owns the following assets. Which of them are capital assets?
   a. Ten shares of Standard Motors common stock.
   b. A copyright on a song T wrote.
   c. A U.S. government savings bond.
   d. A note T received when he loaned $100 to a friend.
   e. A very rare copy of "Your Federal Income Tax" (a U.S. government publication that T purchased many years ago from the U.S. Government Printing Office).
   f. T's personal use automobile.
   g. A letter T received from a former U.S. President. T received the letter because he had complained to the President about the President's foreign policy.

3. Under what circumstances are copyrights capital assets?

4. Can a dealer in securities have investments (as opposed to inventory) in securities? Explain.

5. In what circumstances may real estate held for resale receive capital gain treatment?

6. What are the two general requirements for the recognition of a capital gain or loss?

7. A corporate bond is worthless due to a bankruptcy on May 10. At what date does the tax loss occur? (Assume the bond was held by an individual for investment purposes.)

8. R, a single individual, has a $25,000 loss from the sale of § 1244 small business company stock. How may R treat this loss?

9. M, a real estate dealer, purchased for $25,000 a one-year option on 40 acres of farm land. If M is able to get the property rezoned for single-family residential development, she will exercise the option and purchase the land for $800,000. The rezoning effort is unsuccessful, and the option expires. How should the $25,000 be treated?

10. An individual pays a $100 premium to acquire an option to buy stock. The individual does not exercise the option, and it lapses. What may the individual do with the $100 loss?

11. If a grantee of an option exercises the option, do the grantor's proceeds from the sale of the option property increase? Why?

12. When does the transfer of a patent result in long-term capital gain? Short-term capital gain? Ordinary income?

13. What is a franchise? In practice, does the transfer of a franchise usually result in capital gain or loss treatment? Why or why not?

14. When are lease cancellation payments received by a lessee capital in nature? When are lease cancellation payments received by a lessor capital in nature?

15. W owns A Corporation stock purchased on April 15, 1989, for $8,000 and B Corporation stock purchased on August 3, 1990, for $20,000. Both stocks are sold on December 5, 1990, for $30,000 each. What are the amount and character of the income recognized from these transactions?

16. X owns A Corporation stock purchased on June 10, 1989, for $8,000 and B Corporation stock purchased on October 23, 1989, for $20,000. Both stocks are sold on April 23, 1990, for $30,000 each. What is X's adjusted gross income for 1990 if she also had wages of $80,000?

17. H exchanges a computer used in her business for another computer that she will use in her business. The transaction qualifies as a like-kind exchange. H had held the computer given up in the exchange for four years. The computers are § 1231

assets. What is the holding period of the computer received in the exchange on the day of its acquisition?

18. What is the general rule used to determine the holding period of property sold short? What is an exception to this rule, and why was the exception enacted?

19. Is there any reason a taxpayer would prefer to recognize a loss as a capital loss rather than as an ordinary loss?

20. Differentiate between the capital loss carryover rules for unused capital losses of individuals and corporations.

21. What type of transactions involving capital assets are included under § 1231? Why wouldn't they qualify for long-term capital gain treatment without § 1231?

22. Do casualty gains from disposition of personal use assets receive § 1231 treatment?

23. Under what circumstances is a nonpersonal use casualty gain treated as ordinary income? Why?

24. Describe the treatment that results if a taxpayer has net § 1231 losses.

25. Fully depreciated business equipment purchased for $75,000 was stolen from V. It was not recovered, and the insurance reimbursement was $10,000. Is this $10,000 gain subject to depreciation recapture? Why?

26. What is recapture potential under § 1245? What factors limit it?

27. Differentiate between the types of property covered by §§ 1245 and 1250.

28. If depreciable real property is sold at a loss after being held long term, does § 1250 apply?

29. How does depreciation recapture under § 1245 differ from depreciation recapture under § 1250?

30. S bought a building in 1985 for $100,000 and insisted on using accelerated depreciation because she did not intend to sell it for 30 years. In 1990, she sold the building for $200,000 and moved to a different state. Assume the depreciation taken was $37,000 and straight-line depreciation for the same time period would have been $26,000. What would be the amount of depreciation recapture if the building were a retail store? An apartment building?

31. What happens to recapture potential when a like-kind exchange is made?

32. If a taxpayer has a § 1231 gain from disposition of a passive loss activity, what may happen to the gain before it is treated under the normal § 1231 gain and loss netting process?

Problems

33. N had three property transactions during the year. She sold a vacation home used for personal purposes at a $35,000 gain. The home had been held for five years and had never been rented. N also sold an antique clock for $3,500 that she had inherited from her grandmother. The clock was valued in N's grandmother's estate at $2,000. N owned the clock for only four months. N sold these assets to finance her full-time occupation as a songwriter. Near the end of the year, N sold one of the songs she had written two years earlier. She received cash of $15,000 and a royalty interest in revenues derived from the merchandising of the song. N had no tax basis for the song. N had no other income and $18,000 in deductible songwriting expenses. Assume the maximum tax rate applies to N.
    a. Assuming the year is 1990, what is N's adjusted gross income?
    b. What is N's tax on capital gains in 1990?

34. F, a college art student, made a humorous drawing of his school's mascot. He silk-screened the drawing on 1,000 T-shirts he purchased for $3 each. The silk screening cost $1 per T-shirt. F sold the T-shirts for $8 each at a booth on his lawn near the college football stadium. All the T-shirts were sold during the fall. F incurs $150 of marketing costs. What is F's adjusted gross income? What is the character of his gain from selling the T-shirts?

35. L, an accrual basis taxpayer, is a component parts manufacturer. L's major customer is very slow to pay L's invoices. To generate cash, L sells $250,000 of accounts receivable to O, an unrelated individual, for $210,000. O then collects the full amount of the receivables from the customer. What are the tax consequences of these events for L and O?

36. T is looking for vacant land to buy. She would hold the land as an investment. For $1,000, she is granted an 11-month option on January 1, 1990, to buy 10 acres of vacant land for $25,000. The owner (who is holding the land for investment) paid $10,000 for the land several years ago.

   a. Does the land owner have gross income when $1,000 is received for granting the option?

   b. Does T have an asset when the option is granted?

   c. If the option lapses, does the land owner have a recognized gain? If so, what type of gain? Does T have a recognized loss? If so, what type of loss?

   d. If the option is exercised and an additional $25,000 is paid for the land, how much recognized gain does the seller have? What type of gain? What is T's tax basis for the property?

37. In 1990, A sells to Z a three-month option to buy 1,000 shares of X Corporation stock for $10,000. The option premium is $1,000. A originally purchased the stock in 1980 for $8,000.

   a. What are the tax consequences to A if Z exercises the option?

   b. If Z allows the option to lapse?

38. In each of the following independent situations, determine whether the sale at a gain of all substantial rights in a patent qualifies for capital gain treatment:

   a. The creator sells the patent to a manufacturing company. The creator is not an employee of the manufacturing company.

   b. A manufacturing company owns a patent developed by one of its employees. It has been using the patent in its manufacturing process. The company sells the patent along with the assets of the manufacturing process.

   c. An investor buys a patent that has not been reduced to practice from the creator. After holding it for three months, she sells it to a retail company.

39. F, Inc., sells a franchise to R. The franchise contains many restrictions on how R may operate his store. For instance, R cannot use less than Grade 10 Idaho potatoes, must fry the potatoes at a constant 410 degrees, dress store personnel in F-approved uniforms, and have an F sign that meets detailed specifications on size, color, and construction. F receives a $40,000 franchise fee from R during the current year. What is the nature of this payment?

40. D is a student at State University. He is graduating in June but has an apartment lease that expires at the end of August. He cannot find someone to lease the apartment for the summer. D's landlord offers to cancel D's lease for $900 (one-half of the July and August rent). D accepts the offer. What are the tax consequences for D and his landlord?

41. E acquires 200 Z Corporation common shares at $10 per share on October 13, 1987. On August 10, 1989, E gives the shares to her son, B. At the time of the gift,

the shares are worth $40 each. On May 11, 1990, B sells the shares for $45 each. What is B's gain? Is it short or long term?

42. T sells short 100 shares of A stock at $20 per share on January 15, 1990. He buys 200 shares of A stock on April 1, 1990, at $25 per share. On May 2, 1990, he closes the short sale by delivering 100 of the shares purchased April 1.

   a. What are the amount and nature of T's loss upon closing the short sale?

   b. When does the holding period for the remaining 100 shares begin?

   c. If T sells (at $27 per share) the remaining 100 shares on January 20, 1991, what will be the nature of his gain or loss?

43. U (single with no dependents) has the following transactions in 1990:

Adjusted gross income (exclusive of capital gains and losses)	$200,000
Long-term capital gain	900
Long-term capital loss	(5,000)
Short-term capital gain	1,000
Short-term capital loss	(1,900)

What is U's net capital gain or loss?

44. In 1990, B (single with no dependents) had a recognized $18,000 LTCG from an installment sale of a personal residence that was sold in 1986. She also purchased from an inventor for $8,000 (and resold in two months for $7,000) a patent on a rubber bonding process. The patent was purchased as an investment. Additionally, she had the following capital gains and losses from stock transactions:

Long-term capital loss	($3,000)
Long-term capital loss carryover from 1989	(12,000)
Short-term capital gain	11,000
Short-term capital loss	(6,000)

What is B's net capital gain or loss?

45. In 1990, W (single with no dependents) engaged in various stock transactions. W purchased R, Inc., common stock on January 10, for $8,000. The price began to plummet almost immediately. W sold the stock short on March 31, 1990, for $3,000. On June 11, 1990, W closed the short sale by delivering identical stock that she had purchased on June 10, 1990, for $10,000. On June 11, 1990, the price of the R stock was $12,000. A very favorable first-quarter earnings report (contrary to rumored large losses) accounted for the swings in the stock price. W also had the following stock transaction results: $500 STCG, $6,300 STCL, $700 LTCL, $43,500 LTCG. W has $210,000 of taxable income from sources other than those previously mentioned. What is W's net capital gain or loss? What is W's total tax liability?

46. For several years, K had rented a $3,000 per month apartment. In 1990, a fire destroyed the apartment building. Under local law, the landlord was required to find comparable housing for K within five days. The landlord offered K $10,000 in lieu of suitable housing and in cancellation of the remaining two years of K's lease. K accepted. K's belongings were destroyed in the fire. All the belongings had been owned more than one year. K's insurance covered everything for replacement value. K received a check for $76,000. She prepared the following schedule to aid in your analysis:

Item	Adjusted Basis	FMV	Insurance Award	Action Taken	Amount Spent
Clothing	$25,000	$ 3,000	$25,000	Replaced	$40,000
Piano	8,000	12,000	10,000	Not replaced	—
Furniture	45,000	33,000	41,000	Replaced	38,000

K wishes to defer gains if possible. K's salary is $120,000. What is K's net capital gain or loss? K's adjusted gross income? K's basis for the replacement assets?

47. Q has a 1990 net long-term capital gain of $35,000 and a short-term capital loss carryover from 1989 of $47,300. Q has other taxable income of $134,000. What should Q do with these items?

48. R Corporation has $16,800 of long-term capital loss for 1990 and $5,000 of other taxable income. What is its 1990 taxable income and the amount (if any) of its capital loss carryover?

49. T owns an airplane that she uses only for pleasure. T's insurance company did not cover $6,000 of damage to T's plane resulting from a tornado. T had paid $35,000 for the plane. T also had a $3,800 casualty gain on a personal use piano as a result of the same tornado. T has $22,500 of wages, is single, and has no dependents. She has $4,000 of real estate taxes, $3,000 of qualified residence interest, and $2,000 of other personal interest for the year. Compute T's taxable income for 1990.

50. V has the following net § 1231 results for each of the years shown. What would be the nature of the net gains in 1989 and 1990?

Tax Year	Net § 1231 Loss	Net § 1231 Gain
1985	$ –0–	
1986	15,000	
1987	35,000	
1988		$10,000
1989		30,000
1990		15,000

51. T had the following transactions during 1990:

- Damage from wreck of a sailboat held more than one year due to hurricane ($15,000 loss).
- Sale of mechanical rake bought on April 1 and sold on September 1 ($600 gain). (Disregard recapture.)
- Sale of farm land with unharvested crops, held four years ($12,000 gain).
- Recovery on theft of family brooch owned for 10 years ($10,000 gain).
- Fire in silo on December 6, purchased May 8 ($1,000 loss).
- Sale of grist mill owned 11 years ($30 loss).
- Sale of 15 shares of Q Corporation stock held three years ($1,800 gain).

a. How is each transaction treated?

b. What is T's 1990 AGI?

52. R owned a number of parking lots throughout the city. In 1990, R sold two parcels of unimproved real estate that he had used since 1978 in his parking lot business. The sale of parcel A resulted in a $6,000 recognized loss, and the sale of parcel B generated a $10,000 recognized gain. R also had a long-term capital gain of $7,000 from a sale of stock he had held for investment. R's adjusted gross income was $50,000 before taking the previous transactions into consideration. Compute R's 1990 adjusted gross income after including the described transactions.

53. S Corporation sold machines A and B during the current year. The machines had been purchased for $180,000 and $240,000, respectively. The machines were purchased eight years ago and were depreciated to zero. Machine A was sold for $40,000 and machine B for $260,000. What amount of gain is recognized by S, and what is the nature of the gain?

54. On June 1, 1987, T acquired a retail store for $400,000. The store was 31.5-year real property, and the statutory percentage cost recovery method was used. The store was sold on June 21, 1990, for $130,000. Depreciation taken totaled $38,000. What are the amount and nature of T's gain or loss from disposition of the store?

55. D is the sole proprietor of a trampoline shop. During 1990, the following transactions occurred:

- Unimproved land adjacent to the store was condemned by the city on February 1. The condemnation proceeds were $25,000. The land, acquired in 1982, had an allocable basis of $15,000. D has additional parking across the street and plans to use the condemnation proceeds to build his inventory.

- A truck used to deliver trampolines was sold on January 2 for $3,500. The truck was purchased on January 2, 1986, for $6,000. On the date of sale, the adjusted basis was $2,667.

- D sold an antique rowing machine at an auction. Net proceeds were $3,900. The rowing machine was purchased as used equipment 17 years ago for $5,200 and is fully depreciated.

- D sold an apartment building for $200,000 on September 1. The rental property was purchased on September 1, three years ago, for $150,000 and was being depreciated over a 35-year life using the straight-line method. At the date of sale, the adjusted basis was $135,000. This is D's only passive activity loss, and D has no current or suspended losses from this activity.

- D's personal yacht was stolen September 5. The yacht had been purchased in August at a cost of $25,000. The fair market value immediately preceding the theft was $20,000. D's yacht was insured for 50% of the original cost, and D received $12,500 on December 1.

- D sold a Buick on May 1 for $9,600. The vehicle had been used exclusively for personal purposes. It was purchased on September 1, 1985, for $10,800.

- An adding machine used by D's bookkeeper was sold on June 1. Net proceeds of the sale were $135. The machine was purchased on June 2, four years ago, for $350. It was being depreciated over a five-year life employing the straight-line method. The adjusted basis on the date of sale was $70.

- D's trampoline stretching machine (owned two years) was stolen on May 5, but the business's insurance company will not pay any of the machine's value because D failed to pay the insurance premium. The machine had a fair market value of $8,000 and an adjusted basis of $6,000 at the time of theft.

- D had AGI of $4,000 from sources other than those described above.

    For each transaction, what is the amount and nature of recognized gain or loss?

b. What is D's 1990 adjusted gross income?

56. R purchased a building in April 1989 for $200,000. He sold the building on December 23, 1990, for $235,000. What would be the nature and amount of R's gain assuming the following:

a. The building is residential rental real estate, and total cost recovery of $12,121 was taken?

b. The building is a retail store, and total cost recovery of $10,583 was taken?

57. P owned a § 1245 asset with an adjusted basis of $5,000. The amount of depreciation deducted by P was $6,000 ($5,000 adjusted basis + $6,000 depreciation = $11,000 original cost). On May 1, 1988, P made a gift of the asset to his child, C, when the fair market value was $22,500. C used the asset for two years (deducting an additional $2,000 of depreciation) in her business. On November 7, 1990, C sold the asset for $36,000.

    a. What is C's basis for the asset on November 7, 1990?

    b. What are the amount and character of C's recognized gain?

    c. How would your answers in (a) and (b) differ if C had received the asset as a result of P's death?

58. E organizes a corporation of which she is the sole shareholder. She transfers to the corporation a business machine that cost $18,000 and has an adjusted basis of $5,000 and a fair market value of $15,500. Several years later, the corporation sells the machine for $12,000 after taking cost recovery deductions of $3,000 on it. What are the tax ramifications of this transfer?

59. J sold an apartment building she had owned for three years for $35,000 in 1990. The building had an adjusted basis of $40,000 and was sold to J's brother at its FMV. The furniture in the building was sold to an unrelated party, and a $28,000 § 1245 gain resulted. J sold the land to her brother for a gain of $20,000. J had other income of $78,000 and $75,000 of expenses deductible for AGI. What is J's 1990 AGI? Assume the real estate was not a passive activity and J had no nonrecaptured § 1231 losses.

60. In 1990, M disposes of passive activity A for a $15,000 § 1245 gain and a $30,000 § 1231 gain. M has no suspended losses from this activity but has a current operating loss of $3,000. M also has a current operating loss of $8,700 from passive activity B, but has no suspended losses from that activity. M has no other property transactions during 1990 and has no nonrecaptured § 1231 losses. What is the treatment of the gains from the disposition of activity A?

61. Refer to the facts of Problem 60. Assume that M has a $45,000 § 1231 loss rather than a gain from the disposition of the passive activity. What is the treatment of the loss from the disposition of activity A?

Cumulative Problems

62. Tom Tenor, age 28, is an automobile mechanic. Tom lives at 518 Marigold Lane, Okemos, MI 48864. His Social Security number is 393–86–4502. He is single and has no dependents. In April 1990, while tinkering with his automobile, Tom devised a carburetor modification kit that increases gas mileage by 20%. He patented the invention and in June 1990 sold it to X Corporation for a lump-sum payment of $250,000 plus $5 per kit sold. Other information of potential tax consequence is as follows:

    a. Cash received from X Corporation, which sold 20,000 kits in 1990, $100,000.

    b. Wages earned as a mechanic from January 1 through June 17, $4,300.

    c. Points paid on a $200,000 mortgage Tom incurred to buy a luxurious new home (he had previously lived in an apartment), $6,000.

    d. State sales taxes paid on four new automobiles Tom acquired in 1990, $2,200.

    e. Costs Tom incurred (including rent paid for a garage, materials, supplies, etc.) during the time he has continued his experimental activities and has worked on several potentially patentable automotive devices, $14,000.

    f. Interest on home mortgage, $7,500.

g. Various miscellaneous itemized deductions (not including any potential deductions above), $9,400.

h. Interest income on savings account, $6,200.

Compute Tom's lowest legal tax liability, before prepayments or credits, for 1990. Suggested software (if available): *WEST–TAX Planner* or *BNA Individual Income Tax Spreadsheet*.

63. Margaret Gill, age 33, is single with no dependents. Margaret is an insurance adjuster. She resides at 2510 Grace Avenue, Richmond, VA 23100. Her Social Security number is 666–88–1000. The following information is for Margaret's 1989 tax year. She earned a $40,000 salary. On March 1, 1982, she purchased 500 shares of People's Power Company for $10,000. She sold those shares on October 14, 1989, for $8,500 after receiving nontaxable dividends totaling $2,600 (including $700 in 1989). She also received $300 in taxable dividends in 1989 from People's Power Company. On November 7, 1983, Margaret purchased 1,000 shares of XYZ Corporation for $22,000. On February 12, 1989, she received an additional 100 shares in a nontaxable 10% stock dividend. On February 13, 1989, she sold those 100 shares for $2,500. During 1989, she paid $6,000 in deductible home mortgage interest, $1,200 in property taxes, $2,000 in state income taxes, $600 in sales tax, and $1,500 in professional dues and subscriptions. Her employer withheld Federal income tax of $6,200. Compute Margaret's net tax payable or refund due for 1989. If you use tax forms for your computations, you will need Form 1040 and Schedules A, B, and D. Suggested software (if available): *TurboTax* for tax return solutions, *WEST–TAX Planner* or *BNA Individual Income Tax Spreadsheet* if tax return solutions are not desired.

64. Glen and Diane Okumura are married, file a joint return, and live at 39 Kaloa Street, Honolulu, Hawaii 56790. Glen's Social Security number is 777–88–2000 and Diane's is 888–77–1000. The Okumuras have two dependent children, Amy (age 15) and John (age 9). Glen works for the Hawaii Public Works Department, and Diane owns a retail dress shop. The Okumuras had the following transactions during 1990:

a. Glen earned $57,000 in wages and had Federal income tax withholding of $14,000.

b. Diane had net income of $98,000 from the dress shop and made Federal income tax estimated payments of $24,000.

c. The Okumuras sold a small apartment building for $165,000. The building was acquired in 1986 for $300,000, accelerated cost recovery of $74,400 was taken, and $46,800 of straight-line cost recovery would have been taken for the same time period. The apartment building was a passive activity, with a $2,000 1990 operating loss, and $4,500 of prior-year suspended passive losses.

d. Diane sold a delivery truck used in her business. The truck cost $35,000, $21,700 of cost recovery had been taken, and it was sold for $18,000.

e. The Okumuras received $13,000 in dividends on various domestic corporation stock that they own.

f. The Okumuras sold stock for a $15,000 long-term capital gain and other stock at a $6,000 short-term capital loss.

g. The Okumuras had the following itemized deductions: $1,000 unreimbursed medical expenses; $10,500 personal use property taxes; $7,000 qualified residence interest; $3,000 personal interest; $1,500 of Glen's unreimbursed employee business expenses; $535 of investment-related expenses; and $6,300 of state income taxes paid.

Compute the Okumuras' 1990 net tax payable or refund due. (Ignore self-employment tax.) Suggested software (if available): *WEST–TAX Planner.*

14

ALTERNATIVE MINIMUM TAX

Once gross income has been determined (refer to chapters 3 and 4) and various deductions accounted for (refer to chapters 5–10), the income tax liability can be computed. Generally the computation procedure requires only familiarity with use of the Tax Table or Tax Rate Schedules. Some taxpayers, however, may be subject to taxes in addition to the regular income tax. One such additional tax is the alternative minimum tax. Any taxpayer who is subject to the regular income tax may be subject to the alternative minimum tax. This chapter explains the provisions of the alternative minimum tax and the determination of tax liability under its terms.

INDIVIDUAL ALTERNATIVE MINIMUM TAX

The tax law contains many incentives that are intended to influence the economic and social behavior of taxpayers (refer to chapter 1). Some of the more prominent incentives to influence *economic* behavior permit rapid write-offs of certain costs, including the following:

- Accelerated depreciation write-offs for realty (buildings) and personalty (e.g., machinery and equipment).

- Immediate expensing of intangible drilling costs, circulation expenditures, mining exploration and development costs, and research and development expenditures.

Tax incentives designed to provide relief for taxpayers also include provisions that allow for deferral of income. For example, in limited circumstances taxpayers may use the completed contract method for income tax purposes.

Other tax incentives that are intended to influence social or economic behavior include the following:

- Charitable contribution deductions based on the fair market value of appreciated long-term capital gain property.

- Deduction of certain personal expenditures, including personal interest and state and local taxes.

- Exclusion of interest on debt obligations of state and local governmental units.

Statistical data compiled by the Department of the Treasury revealed that some taxpayers with large economic incomes were able to minimize or even avoid the payment of income tax by taking advantage of the incentive provisions that Congress had enacted.

Although taxpayers were reducing taxes legally through various investments that resulted in preferential treatment for income tax purposes, Congress was distressed by the resulting inequity. This point is made clear in the following extract from the Report by the Ways and Means Committee of the House of Representatives on the Tax Reform Act of 1969:

> This is obviously an unfair situation. In view of the tax burden on our citizens, at this time, it is particularly essential that our taxes be distributed in a fair manner. Your committee believes that no one should be permitted to avoid his fair share of the tax burden—to shift his tax load to the backs of other taxpayers.[1]

---

1. 1969–3 C.B. 249.

To ensure that taxpayers who benefit from such special provisions pay at least a minimum amount of tax, Congress enacted a special tax, called the *alternative minimum tax* (*AMT*), that applies to corporations, individuals, trusts, and estates. Because it is referred to as a *minimum* tax, it is easy to misinterpret the nature of the tax. The AMT is *not* beneficial to taxpayers. Instead of saving (or minimizing) tax dollars through special computation procedures, it could result in additional tax liability.

Originally, the minimum tax was a special tax of 10 percent levied against specified items of tax preference in excess of $30,000 and was added on to the regular income tax; thus, it was commonly referred to as the add-on minimum tax. The present AMT, however, applies only if it exceeds the regular income tax.

In expanding the scope of the AMT in TRA of 1986, Congress reaffirmed the position taken in enacting the original minimum tax in 1969.

> [T]he minimum tax should serve one overriding objective: to ensure that no taxpayer with substantial economic income can avoid significant tax liability by using exclusions, deductions, and credits. Although these provisions may provide incentives for worthy goals, they become counterproductive when taxpayers are allowed to use them to avoid virtually all tax liability. The ability of high-income taxpayers to pay little or no tax undermines respect for the entire tax system and, thus, for the incentive provisions themselves. In addition, even aside from public perceptions . . . it is inherently unfair for high-income taxpayers to pay little or no tax due to their ability to utilize tax preferences.[2]

Overview of the Alternative Minimum Taxable Income (AMTI) Computation

The original minimum tax and previous versions of the AMT were based on tax preferences. For example, if a taxpayer deducted percentage depletion in excess of the basis of a mineral property, the excess depletion was treated as a tax preference and became a part of the minimum tax base. The *current* AMT is based on preferences *and* adjustments to regular taxable income.

The concept of *AMT adjustments* to taxable income was introduced in TRA of 1986. Adjustments arise because Congress has prescribed AMT treatment for certain income and deduction items that differs from the regular income tax treatment of these items. The alternative minimum taxable income (AMTI) computation starts with taxable income and makes adjustments to reflect these differences between income tax and AMT treatment of the specified items. Tax preferences are then added and the total is labeled AMTI. The first step in the calculation of the AMT is the determination of AMTI:

> Taxable income
> **Plus:** Positive AMT adjustments
> **Minus:** Negative AMT adjustments
> **Plus:** Tax preferences
> **Equals:** Alternative minimum taxable income

In order to comprehend the structure of the AMT, it is important to understand the nature of adjustments and preferences.

---

2. *General Explanation of the Tax Reform Act of 1986 ("Blue Book"),* prepared by The Staff of the Joint Committee on Taxation, May 4, 1987, H.R. 3838, 99th Cong., pp. 432–433.

Adjustments.   As shown in the AMTI formula above, taxable income is increased by *positive adjustments* and decreased by *negative adjustments*. Many of the positive adjustments arise as a result of timing differences related to deferral of income or acceleration of deductions. When these timing differences reverse, *negative adjustments* are made.

Adjustments to taxable income that arise as a result of timing differences related to the acceleration of deductions for regular tax purposes include the following:

- Difference between modified ACRS depreciation deducted for income tax purposes and ADS (alternative depreciation system) depreciation deductible for AMT purposes.

- Difference between the amount allowed under *immediate expensing* provisions applicable for income tax purposes and the amount that would be allowed if the expenditures were *amortized* as prescribed for AMT purposes.

In addition, there are timing differences that relate to deferrals allowed for regular tax purposes but not for AMT purposes. Included in this category of adjustments is the difference between income reported under the completed contract method for income tax purposes and income that would be reported under the percentage of completion method prescribed for AMT purposes.

There are several other adjustments that do not relate to timing differences. The "adjustments" in question are more like preferences than adjustments in that they are always positive, never negative (they always increase and never decrease AMTI). Included in this category of adjustments are the following:

- Itemized deductions allowed for regular tax purposes but not for AMT purposes (e.g., consumer interest and state and local taxes).

- The standard deduction if the taxpayer does not itemize.

- The deduction for personal and dependency exemptions.

These adjustments, and their effect on AMTI, are discussed in detail under AMT Adjustments.

Preferences.   Some deductions allowed to taxpayers for regular income tax purposes provide extraordinary tax savings. Congress has chosen to single out these items, which are referred to as tax preferences. The AMT is designed to take back the tax benefits derived through the use of preferences in the computation of taxable income for regular income tax purposes. This is why taxable income, which is the starting point in computing AMTI, is increased by tax preference items. The effect of adding these preference items is to disallow for alternative minimum tax purposes those preferences that were allowed in the regular income tax computation. Tax preferences include the following items:

- Percentage depletion in excess of the property's adjusted basis.

- Intangible drilling costs in excess of 65 percent of the net income from oil, gas, and geothermal properties.

- Net appreciation on contributed long-term capital gain property.

- Interest on certain private activity bonds.

- Excess of accelerated over straight-line depreciation on real property placed in service before 1987.

- Excess of accelerated over straight-line depreciation on *leased* personal property placed in service before 1987.

- Excess of amortization allowance over depreciation on pre-1987 certified pollution control facilities.

These preferences are discussed in detail under AMT Preferences.

AMT Adjustments

Circulation Expenditures.   For income tax purposes, circulation expenditures, other than those the taxpayer elects to charge to a capital account, may be expensed in the year incurred.[3] Such expenditures include those made to establish, maintain, or increase the circulation of a newspaper, magazine, or other periodical.

Circulation expenditures are not deductible in the year incurred for AMT purposes. In computing AMTI, these expenditures must be capitalized and amortized ratably over the three-year period beginning with the year in which the expenditures were made.[4]

The AMT adjustment for circulation expenditures is the amount expensed for income tax purposes minus the amount that can be amortized for AMT purposes. The adjustment can be either positive or negative, as shown in Example 1 below. The *nature* of AMT adjustments can be understood by examining the adjustments required for circulation expenditures.

EXAMPLE 1 | In 1990, T incurs $24,000 of deductible circulation expenditures. This amount is deducted for income tax purposes. For AMT purposes, the circulation expenditures must be deducted over a three-year period. This results in a deduction for AMT purposes of $8,000 ($24,000 ÷ 3). T's schedule of positive and negative adjustments is shown as follows:

Year	Income Tax Deduction	AMT Deduction	AMT Adjustment
1990	$24,000	$ 8,000	+$16,000
1991	–0–	8,000	–8,000
1992	–0–	8,000	–8,000
Total	$24,000	$24,000	$ –0–

□

The AMT adjustments can be avoided if the taxpayer elects to write off the circulation expenditures over a 3-year period for regular income tax purposes.[5]

Depreciation of Post-1986 Real Property.   For real property placed in service after 1986, AMT depreciation is computed under the alternative depreciation system, which uses the straight-line method over a 40-year life. The depreciation lives for regular tax purposes are 27.5 years for residential rental property and 31.5 years for all other real property. The difference between AMT depreciation and

---

3. § 173(a).
4. § 56(b)(2)(A)(i).

5. § 59(e)(2)(A).

regular tax depreciation is treated as an adjustment in computing the AMT. The differences will be positive during the regular tax life of the asset because the asset is written off over a shorter period for regular tax purposes. For example, during the income tax life of real property, the regular tax depreciation will exceed the AMT depreciation, because AMT depreciation is computed over a 40-year period.

Table 8–7 is used to compute regular income tax depreciation on real property placed in service after 1986. For alternative minimum tax purposes, depreciation on real property placed in service after 1986 is computed under the alternative depreciation system (refer to Table 8–12).

EXAMPLE 2   In January 1990, V placed in service a nonresidential building that cost $100,000. Depreciation for 1990 for income tax purposes is $3,042 ($100,000 cost × 3.042% from Table 8–7). For AMT purposes, depreciation is $2,396 ($100,000 cost × 2.396% from Table 8–12). In computing AMTI for 1990, V has a positive adjustment of $646 ($3,042 income tax depreciation − $2,396 AMT depreciation). ☐

After real property has been held for the entire depreciation period for income tax purposes, income tax depreciation will be zero. However, the depreciation period under ADS is 40 years, so depreciation will continue for AMT purposes. This will cause negative adjustments after the property has been fully depreciated for income tax purposes.

EXAMPLE 3   Assume the same facts as in the previous example, and compute the AMT adjustment for 2022 (the thirty-third year of the asset's life). Income tax depreciation will be zero (refer to Table 8–7). AMT depreciation will be $2,500 ($100,000 cost × 2.500% from Table 8–12). Therefore, V will have a negative AMT adjustment of $2,500 ($0 income tax depreciation − $2,500 AMT depreciation). ☐

After real property has been fully depreciated for income tax and AMT purposes, the positive and negative adjustments that have been made for AMT purposes will net to zero.

For real property and leased personal property placed in service before 1987, the difference between accelerated depreciation for regular income tax and straight-line depreciation for the AMT results in a tax preference rather than an AMT adjustment. These situations are explained later in the chapter under AMT Preferences.

Depreciation of Post-1986 Personal Property.   For most personal property placed in service after 1986, the modified ACRS (MACRS) deduction for regular income tax purposes is based on the 200 percent declining-balance method with a switch to straight-line when that method produces a larger depreciation deduction for the asset. Refer to Table 8–2 for computing income tax depreciation.

For AMT purposes, the taxpayer must use the alternative depreciation system (ADS). This method is based on the 150 percent declining-balance method with a similar switch to straight-line for all personal property. Refer to Table 8–10 for percentages to be used in computing AMT depreciation.

All personal property placed in service after 1986 may be taken into consideration in computing one net adjustment. Using this netting process, the AMT

adjustment for a tax year is the difference between the total MACRS depreciation for all personal property computed for regular tax purposes and the total ADS depreciation computed for AMT purposes. When the total of MACRS deductions exceeds the total of ADS deductions, the amount of the adjustment is positive. When the total of ADS deductions exceeds the total of MACRS deductions, the adjustment for AMTI is negative.

The MACRS deduction for personal property will be larger than the ADS deduction in the early years of an asset's life, but the ADS deduction will be larger in the later years. This is so because ADS lives (based on class life) are longer than MACRS lives (based on recovery period).[6] Over the ADS life of the asset, the same amount of depreciation will be deducted for both regular tax and AMT purposes. In the same manner as other timing adjustments, the AMT adjustments over the ADS life of the asset will net to zero.

The taxpayer may elect to use ADS for regular income tax purposes.[7] If this election is made, no AMT adjustment is required because the depreciation deduction will be the same for regular tax and for the AMT.

Pollution Control Facilities.   For regular tax purposes, the cost of certified pollution control facilities may be amortized over a period of 60 months. For AMT purposes, the cost of these facilities placed in service after 1986 must be depreciated under the ADS over the appropriate class life, determined as explained above for depreciation of post-1986 property. The required adjustment (either positive or negative) for AMTI is equal to the difference between the amortization deduction allowed for regular tax and the depreciation deduction computed under ADS.

In the case of pre-1987 facilities, a similar calculation results in an AMT preference, as discussed later in the chapter.

Mining Exploration and Development Costs.   In computing taxable income, taxpayers are allowed to deduct certain mining exploration and development expenditures. The deduction is allowed for expenditures paid or incurred during the taxable year for exploration[8] (ascertaining the existence, location, extent, or quality of a deposit or mineral) and for development of a mine or other natural deposit, other than an oil or gas well. Mining development expenditures are those paid or incurred after the existence of ores and minerals in commercially marketable quantities has been disclosed.[9]

For AMT purposes, however, mining exploration and development costs must be capitalized and amortized ratably over a 10-year period.[10] The AMT adjustment for mining exploration and development costs that are expensed is equal to the amount expensed minus the allowable expense if the costs had been capitalized and amortized ratably over a 10-year period. This provision does not apply to costs relating to an oil or gas well.

EXAMPLE 4   In 1990, M incurs $150,000 of mining exploration expenditures. This amount is deducted for income tax purposes. For AMT purposes, these mining exploration expenditures must be amortized over a 10-year period. M must make a positive adjustment for AMTI of $135,000 [$150,000 (allowed for

---

6. Class lives and recovery periods are established for all assets in Rev.Proc. 87–56, 1987–2 C.B. 674.

7. § 168(g)(7).

8. § 617(a).

9. § 616(a).

10. § 56(a)(2).

income tax) − $15,000 (for AMT)] for 1990, the first year. In each of the next nine years for AMT purposes, M is required to make a negative adjustment of $15,000 [$0 (allowed for regular tax) − $15,000 (for AMT)]. □

To avoid the AMT adjustments for mining exploration and development costs, a taxpayer may elect to write off the expenditures over a 10-year period for regular income tax purposes.[11]

Research and Experimentation Expenditures.   For income tax purposes, research and experimentation expenditures (see chapter 7) may be deducted by the taxpayer in the year paid or incurred.[12] However, for AMT purposes, such expenditures must be capitalized and amortized ratably over a 10-year period.[13] For research and experimentation expenditures that are expensed, the AMT adjustment is equal to the amount expensed minus the amount that would have been allowed if the expenditures had been capitalized and amortized ratably over a 10-year period. The AMT adjustment for research and experimentation expenditures can be avoided if the taxpayer elects to write the expenditures off over a 10-year period.

EXAMPLE 5   T incurred research and experimentation expenditures of $100,000 in 1990 and elected to expense that amount for regular tax purposes. Since research and experimentation expenditures must be amortized over a 10-year period for AMT purposes, T's AMT deduction is $10,000 each year ($100,000 ÷ 10 years) for 1990 and the succeeding nine years. T has a positive adjustment for 1990 of $90,000 ($100,000 allowed for regular tax − $10,000 allowed for AMT purposes). The adjustment reverses in each of the following nine years ($0 deduction for regular tax − $10,000 for AMT purposes = $10,000 negative adjustment). □

Assume that T in Example 5 elects to claim a tax credit amounting to $10,000 in regard to the research and experimentation expenditures (see chapter 11 for choices), the amount expensed currently must be reduced by 100 percent of the credit.[14] Thus, in this situation, T would be allowed a current deduction of $90,000 [$100,000 (amount of expenditures) − $10,000 (100 percent of the $10,000 credit taken)] for regular tax purposes. For AMTI, T has a positive adjustment for 1990 of $81,000 [$90,000 allowed for regular tax − $9,000 ($90,000 ÷ 10 years) for AMT purposes]. In each of the next nine years, the AMT adjustment is a negative $9,000 [$0 (deduction for regular tax) − $9,000 (for AMT)].

Although the research and experimentation expenditures tax credit cannot be used in the year of election if a taxpayer is liable for the AMT, the credit is subject to the general carryover rules applicable to unused business tax credits. Thus, the benefit of the credit will be realized in a year when the taxpayer is liable for the regular tax instead of the AMT.

Passive Activity Losses.   Losses on passive activities acquired *after* October 22, 1986, are not deductible in computing either the income tax or the AMT.[15]

---

11. §§ 59(e)(2)(D) and (E).

12. § 174(a).

13. § 56(b)(2)(A)(ii). For tax years beginning after 1990, a special rule applies to individuals who materially participate in an activity. Such indi-viduals are not required to capitalize and amor-tize research and experimentation expenditures generated by such activity.

14. § 280C(c).

15. §§ 469(a) and 58(b)(3).

However, for income tax purposes, losses incurred on passive activities acquired *before* October 23, 1986, are deductible as follows: 65 percent in 1987, 40 percent in 1988, 20 percent in 1989, 10 percent in 1990, and 0 percent thereafter. These percentages are referred to as transition percentages. Rules for the deductibility of passive losses are summarized below.

Date Activity Acquired	AMT Deduction	Income Tax Deduction
After 10/22/86	Zero	Zero
Before 10/23/86	Zero	Amount allowed under transition percentages

Passive activity losses on pre–October 23, 1986, passive activities that are deducted for income tax purposes are not deductible in arriving at alternative minimum taxable income (AMTI).[16] Consequently, an AMT adjustment is required.

EXAMPLE 6 In 1990, W has a $100,000 loss on a passive activity that she acquired in 1985. Assume that none of the loss is attributable to adjustments or preferences. Under the transition rules, 10% of the passive activity loss is allowed, so W may deduct $10,000 for income tax purposes. For AMT purposes, the entire passive activity loss is disallowed in 1990. As a result, W has a positive adjustment to AMTI of $10,000. □

The passive loss that can be used to offset passive income for income tax purposes may be different from the passive loss used to offset passive income for AMT purposes, as it is in Example 6. Consequently, the suspended passive loss for income tax purposes may be different from the suspended passive loss for AMT purposes. In Example 6, the suspended passive loss for regular income tax is $90,000 ($100,000 − $10,000 used). For AMT purposes, the suspended passive loss is $100,000 ($100,000 − $0 used).

The passive loss limitations of § 469 apply in computing AMTI,[17] except that in applying these limitations:

1. The AMT adjustments to taxable income apply.

2. Any deduction, to the extent such deduction is an item of tax preference for AMT purposes, is not taken into account.

Due to the lack of Regulations or other IRS pronouncements, there is considerable uncertainty as to how the AMT passive loss provisions are to be interpreted. The only guidance at this point appears in the material prepared by the Staff of the Joint Committee on Taxation, as reflected in Example 7.[18]

---

16. § 58(b)(3).

17. §§ 58(b)(1) and (2).

18. *General Explanation of the Tax Reform Act of 1986 ("Blue Book"),* prepared by The Staff of the Joint Committee on Taxation, May 4, 1987, H.R. 3838, 99th Cong., p. 448. The example is quoted verbatim, except for the material enclosed within brackets [ ].

EXAMPLE 7

A taxpayer has $200,000 of salary income and $50,000 of gross income from passive activities. The taxpayer's deductions with respect to the passive activities equal $120,000 for regular [income] tax purposes and $80,000 for minimum tax purposes. [Assume all passive activities were acquired after October 22, 1986.] For regular tax purposes, the taxpayer has income of $200,000 [salary] and a suspended passive loss in the amount of $70,000 [$50,000 gross income from passive activities − $120,000 deductions from passive activities]. For minimum tax purposes, the taxpayer has income of $200,000 [salary] and a suspended passive loss of $30,000 [$50,000 income from passive activities − $80,000 deductions from passive activities]. □

The Staff of the Joint Committee on Taxation provides another clue as to the interpretation of the provisions related to AMT passive losses:

... where a Code provision refers to a 'loss' of the taxpayer from an activity, for purposes of the alternative minimum tax the existence of a loss is determined with regard to the items that are includable and deductible for minimum tax, not regular tax, purposes. ... With respect to the passive loss provision, for example, section 58 provides expressly that, in applying the limitation for minimum tax purposes, all minimum tax adjustments to income and expense *are made* and regular tax deductions that are items of tax preference *are disregarded*.

Until regulations are issued, Example 7, along with the language of § 58(b) and the above explanation by the Staff of the Joint Committee, leads to the interpretations in Examples 8 and 9.

EXAMPLE 8

T acquired two passive activities in 1990. Activity A had net passive income of $10,000, and there were no AMT adjustments or preferences in connection with the activity. Activity B had gross income of $28,000 and operating expenses (not affected by AMT adjustments or preferences) of $20,000. T claimed MACRS depreciation of $20,000 for Activity B; depreciation under the alternative depreciation system (ADS) would have been $15,000. In addition, T deducted $10,000 of percentage depletion in excess of basis. The following comparison illustrates the differences in the computation of the passive loss for income tax and AMT purposes.

	Income Tax	AMT
Gross income	$28,000	$28,000
Deductions:		
Operating expenses	$20,000	$20,000
Depreciation	20,000	15,000
Depletion	10,000	–0–
Total deductions	$50,000	$35,000
Passive loss	$22,000	$ 7,000

Because the adjustment for depreciation ($5,000) applies and the preference for depletion ($10,000) is not taken into account in computing AMTI, the regular tax passive activity loss of $22,000 for Activity B must be reduced by these amounts, resulting in a passive activity loss for AMT purposes of $7,000, as shown. □

For income tax purposes, T would offset the $10,000 of net passive income from Activity A with $10,000 of the passive loss from Activity B. For AMT purposes, T would offset the $10,000 of net passive income from Activity A with the $7,000 passive activity loss allowed from Activity B, resulting in passive activity income of $3,000. Thus, in computing AMTI, T must make a positive passive loss adjustment of $3,000 [$10,000 (passive activity loss allowed for regular tax) − $7,000 (passive activity loss allowed for the AMT)]. To avoid duplication, the AMT adjustment for depreciation and the preference for depletion are *not* separately reported. They are accounted for in determining the AMT passive loss adjustment.

EXAMPLE 9   Assume the same facts as in the previous example. For regular tax purposes, T has a suspended passive loss of $12,000 [$22,000 (amount of loss) − $10,000 (used in 1990)]. This suspended passive loss can offset passive income in the future or can offset active or portfolio income when T disposes of the loss activity (see chapter 7). For AMT purposes, T's suspended passive loss is $0 [$7,000 (amount of loss) − $7,000 (amount used in 1990)]. □

Passive Farm Losses.   A passive farm loss is defined as any loss from a tax shelter farming activity (a farming syndicate or any other activity consisting of farming unless the taxpayer materially participates in the activity). For regular tax purposes, losses from passive farm activities are subject to the phase-in rules for passive losses (refer to chapter 6).

The limitations for passive farm losses are more severe than the limitations for passive losses in general. Each farming activity is treated separately for purposes of applying the limitation, and there is no netting of passive losses from one farming activity against passive income from a different farming activity. For AMT purposes, the passive farm loss limitations are applied before application of the general passive loss limitations. Thus, even though passive income from a farming activity cannot be offset by passive losses from other farming activities, such income can be offset by passive loss from nonfarm activities.[19]

If a nonfarm passive activity results in a suspended loss, the suspended loss can offset passive income from other nonfarm activities. However, if a farm passive activity results in a suspended loss, the suspended loss can offset income only from the *same* activity in a subsequent year for AMTI. This rule does not apply, however, in the year of termination of the taxpayer's entire interest in the farm shelter activity. In this case, the amount of loss is allowed in determining AMTI and is not treated as a loss from a farm tax shelter activity.[20]

If a taxpayer is insolvent at the end of the taxable year, the amount of recomputed passive activity loss (both farm and nonfarm) for AMTI is reduced by the amount of insolvency. For this purpose, the taxpayer is insolvent to the extent that liabilities exceed the fair market value of assets.

Use of Completed Contract Method of Accounting.   For any long-term contract entered into after March 1, 1986, taxpayers are required to use the percentage of completion method for AMT purposes. However, in limited circumstances, taxpayers can use the completed contract method for income tax

---

19. *General Explanation of the Tax Reform Act of 1986 ("Blue Book"),* prepared by The Staff of the Joint Committee on Taxation, May 4, 1987, H.R.

3838, 99th Cong., pp. 446–447.
20. § 58(c)(2).

purposes.[21] Thus, a different amount of income will be recognized for income tax purposes than is recognized for AMT purposes. The resulting AMT adjustment is equal to the difference between income reported under the percentage of completion method and the amount reported using the completed contract method. The adjustment can be either positive or negative, depending on the amount of income recognized under the different methods.

An AMT adjustment on long-term contracts can be avoided by using the percentage of completion method for regular income tax purposes rather than the completed contract method.

Incentive Stock Options. The exercise of an incentive stock option does not increase regular taxable income.[22] However, for AMT purposes, the excess of the fair market value of stock over the exercise price is treated as an adjustment in the first taxable year in which the rights in the stock are freely transferable or are not subject to a substantial risk of forfeiture.

EXAMPLE 10 | In 1990, M exercised an incentive stock option that had been granted by his employer, X Corporation. M acquired 1,000 shares of X Corporation stock for the option price of $20 per share. The stock is freely transferable. The fair market value of the stock at the date of exercise was $50 per share. For AMT purposes, M has a positive gain or loss adjustment (see below) for 1990 of $30,000 ($50,000 fair market value − $20,000 option price). The transaction does not affect regular taxable income. □

The income tax basis of stock acquired through the exercise of incentive stock options is different from the AMT basis. The income tax basis of such stock is equal to its cost, while the AMT basis is equal to the fair market value on the date the options were exercised. Consequently, the gain or loss upon disposition of the stock will be different for income tax purposes and AMT purposes.

EXAMPLE 11 | Assume the same facts as in the previous example and that M sells the stock for $60,000 in 1992. M's gain for income tax purposes will be $40,000 ($60,000 amount realized − $20,000 income tax basis). For AMT purposes, the gain will be $10,000 ($60,000 amount realized − $50,000 AMT basis). Therefore, M will have a $30,000 negative adjustment in computing AMT in 1992 ($40,000 income tax gain − $10,000 AMT gain). Note that the $30,000 negative adjustment upon disposition in 1992 offsets the $30,000 positive adjustment upon exercise of the incentive stock option in 1990. □

Adjusted Gain or Loss. When property is sold during the year or a casualty occurs to business or income-producing property, gain or loss reported for regular income tax may be different than gain or loss determined for the AMT. This is so because the adjusted basis of the property for AMT purposes must reflect any current and prior AMT adjustments for the following:

• Depreciation

• Circulation expenditures

---

21. See chapter 15, Accounting Periods and Methods, for a detailed discussion of the completed contract and percentage of completion methods of accounting.

22. § 421(a).

- Research and experimentation expenditures
- Mining exploration and development costs
- Amortization of certified pollution control facilities.

If the gain computed for AMT purposes is less than the gain computed for regular income tax *or* if the loss for AMT purposes is more than the loss for income tax purposes *or* if a loss is computed for AMT purposes and a gain for income tax, the difference is a negative gain or loss adjustment in determining AMTI. Otherwise, the AMT gain or loss adjustment is positive.

EXAMPLE 12   In January 1990, K paid $100,000 for a duplex acquired for rental purposes. Income tax depreciation in 1990 was $3,485 ($100,000 cost × 3.485% from Table 8–7). AMT depreciation was $2,396 ($100,000 cost × 2.396% from Table 8–12). For AMT purposes, K made a positive adjustment of $1,089 ($3,485 income tax depreciation − $2,396 AMT depreciation). ☐

EXAMPLE 13   K sold the duplex on December 20, 1991, for $105,000. Income tax depreciation for 1991 is $3,485 [($100,000 cost × 3.636% from Table 8–7) × (11.5/12)]. AMT depreciation for 1991 is $2,396 [($100,000 cost × 2.500% from Table 8–12) × (11.5/12)]. K's AMT adjustment for 1991 was $1,089 ($3,485 income tax depreciation − $2,396 AMT depreciation). ☐

Because depreciation on the duplex differs for income tax and AMT purposes, the adjusted bases also will differ. Consequently, the gain or loss on disposition of the duplex will be different for income tax and AMT purposes.

EXAMPLE 14   The adjusted basis of K's duplex for income tax purposes is $93,030 ($100,000 cost − $3,485 depreciation for 1990 − $3,485 depreciation for 1991). For AMT purposes, the adjusted basis is $95,208 ($100,000 cost − $2,396 depreciation for 1990 − $2,396 depreciation for 1991). The income tax gain is $11,970 ($105,000 amount realized − $93,030 income tax basis). The AMT gain is $9,792 ($105,000 amount realized − $95,208 AMT basis). Because the income tax and AMT gain on the sale of the duplex differ, K must make a negative AMT adjustment of $2,178 ($11,970 income tax gain − $9,792 AMT gain). Note that this negative adjustment offsets the $2,178 total of the two positive adjustments for depreciation ($1,089 in 1990 + $1,089 in 1991). ☐

Alternative Tax Net Operating Loss Deduction.   In computing taxable income, taxpayers are allowed to deduct net operating loss (NOL) carryovers and carrybacks (refer to chapter 7). The income tax NOL must be modified, however, in computing AMTI. The starting point in computing the alternative tax NOL is the regular NOL computed for income tax purposes. The AMT NOL, however, is determined by applying AMT adjustments and ignoring tax preferences. Thus, preferences that have been deducted in computing the income tax NOL will be added back, thereby reducing or eliminating the AMT NOL.

EXAMPLE 15   In 1990, T incurred a net operating loss of $100,000. T had no AMT adjustments, but his deductions included tax preferences of $18,000. His AMT

NOL carryover to 1991 will be $82,000 ($100,000 regular tax NOL − $18,000 tax preferences deducted in computing the NOL).   □

In Example 15, if the adjustment was not made to the income tax NOL, the $18,000 in tax preference items deducted in 1990 would have the effect of reducing AMTI in the year the 1990 NOL is utilized. This would weaken the entire concept of the AMT.

If a taxpayer has an alternative tax NOL that is carried back or over to another year, such alternative tax NOL must be used against AMTI in the carryback or carryover year even if the regular tax, rather than the alternative minimum tax, applies.

EXAMPLE 16   K's alternative tax NOL for 1991 (carried over from 1990) is $10,000. AMTI before considering the alternative tax NOL is $25,000. If K's regular income tax exceeds the AMT, the AMT does not apply. Nevertheless, K's alternative tax NOL of $10,000 is "used up" in 1991 and is not available for carryover to a later year.   □

Itemized Deductions.   Taxes (state, local, foreign income, and property taxes) and miscellaneous itemized deductions that are subject to the 2 percent of AGI floor are not allowed in computing AMT. A positive AMT adjustment in the total amount for each is required. Moreover, if the taxpayer's gross income includes the recovery of any tax deducted as an itemized deduction, a negative AMT adjustment in the amount of the recovery is allowed for AMTI. This is so even though the deduction occurred in a prior tax year.

Itemized deductions that are allowed for AMT purposes include the following:

- Casualty losses.
- Gambling losses.
- Charitable contributions.
- Medical expenses in excess of 10 percent of AGI.
- Estate tax on income in respect of a decedent.
- Qualified interest.

Medical Expenses.   The rules for determining the AMT deductions for medical expenses are sufficiently complex to require further explanation. For income tax purposes, medical expenses are deductible to the extent they exceed 7.5 percent of AGI. However, for AMT purposes, medical expenses are deductible only to the extent they exceed 10 percent of AGI.

EXAMPLE 17   K, who had AGI of $100,000 in 1990, incurred medical expenses of $12,000 during the year. For income tax purposes, K can deduct $4,500 [$12,000 medical expenses − .075($100,000 AGI)]. In computing the AMT, K can deduct only $2,000 [$12,000 medical expenses − .10($100,000 AGI)]. Because taxable income is the starting point in computing AMTI, K must make a positive adjustment of $2,500 ($4,500 income tax deduction − $2,000 AMT deduction).   □

Interest in General.   The AMT itemized deduction allowed for interest expense includes only qualified housing interest and investment interest to the extent of net investment income that is included in the determination of AMTI.

In computing regular taxable income, taxpayers who itemize can deduct the following types of interest (refer to chapter 10):

- Personal (consumer) interest, subject to the transition rules.

- Qualified residence interest.

- Investment interest, subject to the investment interest limitations.

Personal Interest.   For AMT purposes, personal (consumer) interest is not deductible. Therefore, taxpayers who deduct the limited amount of personal interest allowed under transition rules for regular income tax purposes are required to make a positive AMT adjustment in that amount in computing AMTI.

EXAMPLE 18   In 1990, B paid interest of $500 on credit cards and $1,200 on an automobile loan. For income tax purposes, B can deduct $170 ($1,700 total interest × .10) under the transition rules. However, personal interest is not deductible for AMT purposes. Therefore, B must make a positive adjustment of $170 in computing AMT for 1990. □

Housing Interest.   Under current income tax rules, taxpayers who itemize can deduct qualified residence interest on up to two residences. However, the deduction is limited to interest on acquisition indebtedness up to $1,000,000 and home equity indebtedness up to $100,000. Acquisition indebtedness is debt that is incurred in acquiring, constructing, or substantially improving a qualified residence of the taxpayer and secured by the residence of the taxpayer. Home equity indebtedness is indebtedness secured by a qualified residence of the taxpayer, but does not include acquisition indebtedness.

EXAMPLE 19   G, who used the proceeds of a mortgage to acquire a personal residence, paid mortgage interest of $112,000 in 1990. Of this amount, $14,000 was attributable to acquisition indebtedness in excess of $1,000,000. G may deduct mortgage interest of $98,000 ($112,000 total − $14,000 disallowed). □

The mortgage interest deduction for AMT purposes is limited to *qualified housing interest,* rather than *qualified residence interest.* Qualified housing interest includes only interest incurred to acquire, construct, or substantially improve the taxpayer's principal residence. It also includes such interest on one other dwelling used for personal purposes. Upon refinancing a loan, interest paid will be deductible as qualified housing interest for AMT purposes only if:

- The proceeds are used to acquire or substantially improve a qualified residence.
- Interest on the prior loan was qualified housing interest.
- The amount of the loan was not increased.

Further, a special rule applies to indebtedness incurred before July 1, 1982, and secured at that time by a qualified residence. Qualified housing interest

includes interest on all such debt even if it does not fall under the definition of acquisition indebtedness.

A positive AMT adjustment is required in the amount of the difference between qualified *residence* interest allowed as an itemized deduction for regular tax purposes and qualified *housing* interest allowed in the determination of AMTI.

Investment Interest. Investment interest is deductible for income tax purposes to the extent of net investment income plus the lesser of excess investment interest or $10,000 multiplied by the applicable transition percentage. Excess investment interest is the excess of investment interest incurred over net investment income before deducting investment interest.

EXAMPLE 20   In 1990, J had net investment income of $15,000 before deducting investment interest. She incurred investment interest expense of $30,000 during the year. Her investment interest deduction is $16,000 [$15,000 net investment income + .10($10,000)]. ☐

The investment interest deduction for AMT purposes does not include interest deductible under the transition rules ($1,000 in Example 20). Therefore, J in Example 20 would make a positive adjustment of $1,000 in computing AMTI.

If a taxpayer pays or incurs interest expense on an investment in specified private activity bonds,[23] such interest expense is not deductible for regular tax purposes because the income from these bonds is not included in taxable income. For AMT purposes, though, the interest income is a preference item (explained later in the chapter); thus it is included in net investment income for AMT purposes, as are other related AMT adjustments and preferences. This results in an allowable itemized deduction in determining AMTI for the interest expense related to this investment.

The AMT deduction for investment interest may be larger than for regular income tax purposes because of the inclusion in AMTI of preferences, such as the interest income from specified private activity bonds.

EXAMPLE 21   Assume the same facts as in Example 20, except that J also has $10,000 of interest income from specified private activity bonds. She has no interest expense or other deductions related to the bonds. J's itemized deduction for investment interest expense for regular tax purposes remains the same ($16,000) as in Example 20. For AMT purposes, the itemized deduction allowed for investment interest expense now becomes $25,000, the amount of net investment income ($15,000 + $10,000). In determining AMTI, J would make a negative adjustment of $9,000 [$16,000 (amount allowed for regular tax) − $25,000 (amount allowed for the AMT)]. ☐

Qualified net investment income is the excess of qualified investment income over qualified investment expenses. Qualified investment income includes the following to the extent that such amounts are not derived from the conduct of a trade or business:

• Gross income from interest, dividends, rents, and royalties.

• Any net gain attributable to the disposition of property held for investment.

---

23. § 57(a)(5).

Qualified investment expenses include deductions directly connected with the production of qualified net investment income to the extent that such deductions are allowable in computing adjusted gross income and are not items of tax preference.

Other Adjustments.   The standard deduction is not allowed as a deduction in computing AMTI. Although it would be rare for a person who does not itemize to be subject to the AMT, it is possible. In such a case, the taxpayer would be required to enter a positive adjustment for the standard deduction in computing the AMT.

The exemption amount deducted for income tax purposes is not allowed in computing AMTI.[24] Therefore, taxpayers must enter a positive AMT adjustment for the exemption amount claimed in computing the income tax. A separate exemption (discussed below) is allowed for AMT purposes. To allow both the income tax exemption amount and the AMT exemption amount would result in extra benefits for taxpayers.

EXAMPLE 22   T, who is single, has no dependents and does not itemize deductions. He earned a salary of $105,300 in 1990. Based on this information, T's taxable income for 1990 is $100,000 ($105,300 − $3,250 standard deduction − $2,050 exemption). □

EXAMPLE 23   Assume the same facts as in Example 22. In addition, assume T's tax preferences for the year totaled $150,000. T's AMTI is $255,300 ($100,000 taxable income + $3,250 adjustment for standard deduction + $2,050 adjustment for exemption + $150,000 tax preferences). □

AMT Preferences

Percentage Depletion.   Congress originally enacted the percentage depletion rules to provide taxpayers with incentives to invest in the development of specified natural resources. Percentage depletion is computed by multiplying a rate specified in the Code times the gross income from the property (refer to chapter 8). The percentage rate is based on the type of mineral involved. The basis of the property is reduced by the amount of percentage depletion taken until the basis reaches zero. However, once the basis of the property reaches zero, it is possible to continue taking percentage depletion deductions. Thus, over the life of the property, depletion deductions may greatly exceed the cost of the property.

The percentage depletion preference is equal to the excess of the regular tax deduction for percentage depletion over the adjusted basis of the property at the end of the taxable year. Basis is determined without regard to the depletion deduction for the taxable year.

EXAMPLE 24   T owns a mineral property that qualifies for a 22% depletion rate. The basis of the property at the beginning of 1990 was $10,000. Gross income from the property in 1990 was $100,000. For regular tax purposes, T's percentage depletion deduction (assume it is not limited by taxable income from the property) is $22,000. For AMT purposes, T has a tax preference of $12,000 ($22,000 − $10,000). □

---

24.   § 56(b)(1)(E).

Intangible Drilling Costs.   In computing the income tax, taxpayers are allowed to deduct certain intangible drilling and development costs in the year incurred, although such costs are normally capital in nature.[25] The deduction is allowed for costs incurred in connection with oil and gas wells and geothermal wells. A geothermal deposit is defined as a geothermal reservoir consisting of natural heat that is stored in rock or in an aqueous liquid or vapor.[26]

For AMT purposes, excess intangible drilling costs (IDC) for the year are treated as a preference. The preference for excess IDC is computed as follows:

> Intangible drilling costs expensed in the year incurred
> **Minus:** Deduction if IDC were capitalized and amortized over 10 years
> **Equals:** Excess of IDC expense over amortization
> **Minus:** 65% of net oil and gas income
> **Equals:** Tax preference item

EXAMPLE 25   J, who incurred IDC of $50,000 in 1990, elected to expense that amount. J's net oil and gas income for the year was $60,000. J's tax preference for IDC for 1990 is $6,000 [($50,000 IDC − $5,000 amortization) − (.65 × $60,000 income)].   □

Charitable Contributions of Appreciated Property.   For income tax purposes, taxpayers who contribute appreciated long-term capital gain property to a qualified charity are allowed to compute their itemized deduction based on the fair market value of the property (refer to chapter 10). This can result in a generous tax benefit if the property is greatly appreciated because the unrealized appreciation is not taxable.

EXAMPLE 26   T contributed X Corporation stock to the United Fund, a qualified charitable organization. T's basis in the stock was $5,000, and its fair market value at the date of contribution was $100,000. T's charitable contribution deduction is based on the $100,000 fair market value, even though the $95,000 of appreciation has never been included in income.   □

For AMT purposes the contribution of appreciated long-term capital gain property to charity results in a tax preference item. Unrealized gain on such property is offset by unrealized loss on other long-term capital gain property contributed to charity. Thus, only the net amount of appreciation on all long-term capital gain properties contributed to charity becomes a preference.

EXAMPLE 27   H made two property contributions of long-term assets to charity during 1990. Asset A had a fair market value of $60,000 and an adjusted basis of $25,000. Asset B had a fair market value of $40,000 and an adjusted basis of $56,000. H's tax preference on the contributions is $19,000 ($35,000 appreciation on Asset A − $16,000 decline in value on Asset B).   □

It is interesting to note that Congress first considered including unrealized appreciation on contributed property (as well as tax-exempt interest discussed

---

25.   § 263(c).   26.   § 613(e).

below) as tax preference items in 1969.[27] However, it was not until TRA of 1986 that these items were treated as preferences. Thus, a proposal is not necessarily dead if it is not enacted when originally considered by Congress. The Code contains numerous examples of proposals that were enacted many years after they no longer appeared to be a threat.

Interest on Private Activity Bonds. An important theme underlying TRA of 1986 was a broadening of the base for the AMT. Congress concluded that certain items not treated as tax preferences under pre-1986 law should be added to the AMT base. Such action was necessary so that the AMT could serve its intended purpose of requiring taxpayers with substantial incomes to pay some tax.

One of the items added to the AMT base is tax-exempt interest on newly issued private activity bonds. For income tax purposes, the interest on these specified private activity bonds is exempt under § 103. For AMT purposes, interest on these bonds is treated as a tax preference if the bonds were issued on or after August 7, 1986. The relevant date for bonds that would not have been industrial development bonds under prior law is September 1, 1986. Section 141 of the Code contains a lengthy, complex definition of private activity bonds.[28] In general, private activity bonds are bonds where more than 10 percent of the proceeds are used for private business use and certain other tests under §§ 141(b)(2) and (c) are met.

Although the interest on private activity bonds is treated as an AMT preference, it continues to be tax-exempt for income tax purposes. In addition, expenses related to purchasing or carrying tax-exempt private activity bonds are treated differently for AMT purposes and income tax purposes. Such expenses continue to be disallowed for income tax purposes, but they are allowed in computing AMT. Therefore, the required adjustment is equal to the interest on private activity bonds minus any deduction that would have been allowed for income tax purposes if the interest had been included in gross income.

Depreciation. For real property and leased personal property placed in service before 1987, there is an AMT preference for the excess of accelerated depreciation over straight-line depreciation. The following discussion will focus on leased personal property, rather than real property, to illustrate the nature of this depreciation preference.

Accelerated depreciation on pre-1987 leased personal property was computed using specified ACRS percentages. Percentages for five-year cost recovery property (refer to Table 8-1, chapter 8) were as follows: 15 percent, 22 percent, 21 percent, 21 percent, and 21 percent. For AMT purposes, depreciation on pre-1987 leased personal property that was five-year property under ACRS was computed over an AMT life of eight years using the straight-line method. As a result, in the early years of the life of the asset, the cost recovery allowance used in computing income tax was greater than the straight-line depreciation deduction allowed in computing AMT. The excess depreciation was treated as a tax preference item.

EXAMPLE 28   P acquired personal property on January 1, 1986, at a cost of $10,000. The property, which was placed in service as leased personal property on January 1, was five-year ACRS property. P's 1986 depreciation deduction for regular tax purposes was $1,500 ($10,000 cost × 15% rate). For AMT purposes, the asset

---

27. Treasury Tax Reform Studies and Proposals (Part 2), pp. 132 and 142 (1969).

28. Before TRA of 1986, private activity bonds were known as industrial development bonds.

was depreciated over the AMT life of eight years using the straight-line method. Thus, AMT depreciation for 1986 was $625 [($10,000 ÷ 8) × ½ year convention]. P's tax preference for 1986 was $875 ($1,500 − $625). ACRS depreciation for 1990 is $2,100 ($10,000 × .21 ACRS rate), and straight-line depreciation is $1,250 ($10,000 ÷ 8). Therefore, the tax preference for 1990 is $850 ($2,100 − $1,250). P's tax preferences for excess depreciation are summarized below:

Year	ACRS Allowance	AMT Deduction	Preference
1986	$1,500	$ 625	$875
1987	2,200	1,250	950
1988	2,100	1,250	850
1989	2,100	1,250	850
1990	2,100	1,250	850

□

Amortization of Certified Pollution Control Facilities.   For income tax purposes, § 169 of the Code provides an election that allows taxpayers to amortize the cost of certified pollution control facilities over a period of 60 months. For pre-1987 facilities, excess amortization is a tax preference item. Excess amortization equals the amortization deducted by the taxpayer minus the amount that would have been deducted if the asset were depreciated over its longer useful life or cost recovery period. A similar calculation for certified pollution control facilities placed in service *after* 1986, is treated as an *adjustment*, discussed in a prior section of the chapter.

Other Components of the AMT Formula

Alternative minimum taxable income is a somewhat confusing term. For income tax purposes, once *taxable income* has been computed, it is possible to compute the income tax. However, after *AMTI* has been computed, it is not possible to compute the AMT until the *AMT base* has been determined. An additional step is necessary to arrive at the AMT base. This procedure is shown in the AMT formula in Figure 14–1.

Exemption Amount.   The exemption amount is $40,000 for married taxpayers filing joint returns, $30,000 for single taxpayers, and $20,000 for married taxpayers filing separate returns. The exemption is phased out at a rate of 25 cents on the dollar when AMTI exceeds the levels listed below:

- $112,500 for single taxpayers.
- $150,000 for married taxpayers filing jointly.
- $75,000 for married taxpayers filing separately.

The following example explains the calculation of the phase-out of the AMT exemption.

EXAMPLE 29   G, who is single, has AMTI of $192,500 in 1990. Her $30,000 exemption is reduced by $20,000 [($192,500 − $112,500) × .25 phase-out rate]. G's AMT exemption for 1990 is $10,000 ($30,000 exemption − $20,000 reduction). □

FIGURE 14−1 Alternative Minimum Tax Formula

Regular taxable income

Plus or minus: Adjustments

Plus: Tax preferences

Equals: Alternative minimum taxable income

Minus: Exemption

Equals: Alternative minimum tax base

Times: 21% rate

Equals: Tentative minimum tax before foreign tax credit

Minus: Alternative minimum tax foreign tax credit

Equals: Tentative minimum tax

Minus: Regular tax liability*

Equals: Alternative minimum tax (if amount is positive)

* This is the regular tax liability for the year reduced by any allowable foreign tax credit. It does not
include any tax on lump-sum distributions from pension plans, any investment tax credit recapture,
or any low-income credit recapture. See § 55(c).

The following table shows the beginning and end of the AMT exemption
phase-out range for each filing status.

Status	Exemption	Phase-Out	
		Begins at	Ends at
Married, joint	$40,000	$150,000	$310,000
Single or head of household	30,000	112,500	232,500
Married, separate	20,000	75,000	155,000

To preclude the tax saving that might result when married taxpayers file separate
returns, a special rule applies to these taxpayers. The AMTI of a married person
filing a separate return is increased by the lesser of

• 25 percent of the AMTI that exceeds $155,000 (the amount at which the
exemption phases out on a separate return), or

• $20,000 (the maximum exemption amount of the taxpayer's spouse).

AMT Rate.   The rate for the AMT is a flat 21 percent.

Illustration of the AMT Computation

The provisions for computation of the AMT are illustrated in the following
example.

EXAMPLE 30   T, who is single, had taxable income for 1990 as follows:

Salary		$192,000
Interest		8,000
Adjusted gross income .		$200,000
Less itemized deductions:		
Medical expenses ($35,000 − 7.5% of $200,000 AGI)†	$20,000*	
State income taxes	12,000	
Interest††		
Home mortgage (for qualified housing)	30,000*	
Investment interest	5,300*	
Contributions	7,000*	
Casualty losses	4,000*	(78,300)
		$121,700
Less exemption		(2,050)
Taxable income		$119,650

† Total medical expenses were $35,000, reduced by 7.5% of AGI, resulting in an itemized deduction of $20,000. However, for AMT purposes, the reduction is 10%, which leaves an AMT itemized deduction of $15,000 ($35,000 − 10% of $200,000 AGI). Therefore, an adjustment of $5,000 is required for medical expenses disallowed for AMT purposes.

†† In this illustration, all interest is deductible in computing alternative minimum taxable income. Qualified housing interest is deductible. Investment interest ($5,300) is deductible to the extent of net investment income included in the minimum tax base. For this purpose, the $8,000 of interest income is treated as net investment income.

Deductions marked by an asterisk are allowed as *alternative tax itemized deductions*. Alternative minimum taxable income is computed as follows (assume T had exclusion preferences of $150,000):

Taxable income	$119,650
Plus: Adjustments	
State income taxes	12,000
Medical expenses	5,000
Personal exemption	2,050
Plus: Tax preferences	150,000
Equals: Alternative minimum taxable income	$288,700
Minus: AMT exemption (phased down to zero)	−0−
Equals: Minimum tax base	$288,700
Times: AMT rate	.21
	$ 60,627
Minus: Regular tax on taxable income	(34,076)
Equals: Alternative minimum tax	$ 26,551

□

AMT Credit

As discussed previously, timing differences will give rise to adjustments to the minimum tax base. In later years, the timing differences will reverse, as was illustrated in several of the preceding examples. To provide equity for the taxpayer when timing differences reverse, the regular tax liability may be reduced by a tax credit for prior years' minimum tax liability attributable to timing differences. The minimum tax credit may be carried over indefinitely. Therefore, there is no need to keep track of when the minimum tax credit arose.

EXAMPLE 31 Assume the same facts as in Example 1. Also assume that in 1990, T paid AMT as a result of the $16,000 adjustment arising from the circulation expenditures. In 1991, $8,000 of the timing difference reverses, resulting in regular taxable income that is $8,000 greater than AMTI. Because T has already paid AMT as a result of the write-off of circulation expenditures, he is allowed an AMT credit in 1991. □

The AMT credit is applicable only for the AMT that results from timing differences. It is not available in connection with the adjustment for itemized deductions or with exclusion preferences. Exclusion preferences include excess percentage depletion, the charitable contribution preference, and the specified private activity bond interest preference.

EXAMPLE 32 D, who is single, has zero taxable income in 1990. He also has positive timing adjustments of $300,000 and exclusion preferences of $100,000. His AMTI is $400,000 because his AMT exemption is phased out completely due to the level of AMTI. D's AMT is $84,000 ($400,000 × 21% AMT rate). □

To determine the amount of AMT credit to carry over, the AMT must be recomputed reflecting only the exclusion preferences and the AMT exemption amount.

EXAMPLE 33 Assume the same facts as in the previous example. If there had been no positive timing adjustments in 1990, D's AMT liability would have been $14,700 [($100,000 exclusion preferences − $30,000 exemption) × 21% AMT rate]. D may carry over an AMT credit of $69,300 ($84,000 AMT − $14,700 related to exclusion preferences). □

Concept Summary 14-1 presents an expanded version of the AMT formula, with brief descriptions of the components of the formula. Form 8801 should be used to calculate the credit for prior year minimum tax.

CONCEPT SUMMARY 14–1

Expanded Alternative Minimum Tax Formula

Taxable income

Plus: Income tax net operating loss deduction

Plus or minus: Adjustments to taxable income that are required to compute AMTI, including the following:

Standard deduction (if taxpayer did not itemize).

Personal and dependency exemption amounts.

Itemized deductions allowed for income tax purposes but not for AMT:

Medical expenses deducted for income tax purposes minus amount deductible for AMT.

Miscellaneous itemized deductions in excess of 2% of AGI.

Taxes (includes state and local income taxes, real estate taxes, and personal property taxes).

Refund of taxes deducted in previous year if such taxes were not allowed for AMT (enter as negative amount).

Personal interest (to the extent that it was deductible under the transition rules).

Mortgage interest that is not qualified housing interest.

Difference between investment interest expense allowed for income tax purposes and deduction allowed for AMT.

Excess of ACRS over ADS depreciation on real property placed in service after 1986 (AMT alternative period is 40 years vs. regular tax periods of 27.5 years for residential rental property and 31.5 years for all other rental property).

Excess of ACRS depreciation over alternative depreciation on all personal property placed in service after 1986 (AMT requires 150% declining-balance method, switching to straight-line, over the asset's ADR midpoint or class life).

Circulation expenditures (AMT requires amortization over three years vs. immediate expensing allowed for income tax).

Research and experimentation expenditures (AMT requires amortization over 10 years vs. immediate expensing allowed for income tax).

Mining and exploration expenditures (AMT requires amortization over 10 years vs. immediate expensing allowed for income tax).

Income on long-term contracts (AMT requires percentage of completion method; completed contract method is allowed in limited circumstances for income tax purposes).

Pollution control facilities placed in service after 1986 (AMT requires ADS depreciation using the ADR class life; the straight-line method, 60-month amortization is allowed for income tax purposes).

Adjusted gain or loss:

Incentive stock options (excess of fair market value over option price is a positive adjustment in the year the options are freely transferable).

Dispositions of assets (if gain or loss for AMT purposes differs from gain or loss for income tax purposes—refer to Examples 12 through 14).

Tax shelter farm loss if the farm activity is not a passive activity (difference between the amount reported for AMT purposes and income tax purposes).

Passive activity loss (recompute gains and losses for AMT by taking into account all AMT adjustments, preferences, and AMT prior year unallowed losses that apply to the activity; enter difference between AMT amounts and income tax amounts; also, passive activity loss allowed for income tax purposes under transition rules is not allowed for AMT purposes).

Beneficiary's share of AMTI from an estate or trust.

Plus: Preferences that must be added to compute alternative minimum taxable income (AMTI), including the following:

Net appreciation on contribution of long-term capital gain property (considering all contributions, whether the property has appreciated or declined in value).

Tax-exempt interest on private activity bonds issued after August 7, 1986.

Percentage depletion in excess of the property's adjusted basis.

Excess of accelerated over straight-line depreciation on real property placed in service before 1987.

Excess of accelerated over straight-line depreciation on leased personal property placed in service before 1987.

Excess intangible drilling costs (IDC) minus 65% of the net income from oil, gas, and geothermal properties (AMT requires amortization over 120 months vs. immediate expensing of IDC allowed for income tax purposes).

Equals: Alternative minimum taxable income (AMTI) before deduction of AMT net operating loss (AMT NOL).

Minus: The allowable AMT net operating loss (which cannot exceed more than 90% of AMTI before deduction of AMT NOL).

Equals: Alternative minimum taxable income.

Minus: Exemption ($40,000 for married joint, $30,000 for single, $20,000 for married separate; exemption is subject to phase-out rules).

Equals: Alternative minimum tax base.

Times: 21% rate.

Equals: Tentative minimum tax before allowable AMT foreign tax credit.

Minus: Allowable AMT foreign tax credit (may not reduce tentative minimum tax before allowable AMT foreign tax credit by more than 90%).

Equals: Tentative minimum tax.

Minus: Regular income tax liability before credits (other than foreign tax credit allowed for income tax purposes).

Equals: Alternative minimum tax (if positive).

TAX PLANNING CONSIDERATIONS

Avoiding Preferences and Adjustments

Several strategies and elections are available that enable taxpayers to avoid having preferences and adjustments.

- A taxpayer who is in danger of incurring AMT liability should not invest in tax-exempt private activity bonds unless such strategy makes good investment sense. Any AMT triggered by interest on private activity bonds will reduce the yield on an investment in these bonds. Other tax-exempt bonds or taxable corporate bonds might yield a better after-tax return.

- A taxpayer may elect to expense certain costs in the year incurred or to capitalize and amortize the costs over some specified period. The decision should be based on the present discounted value of after-tax cash flows under the available alternatives. Costs subject to elective treatment include circulation expenditures, mining exploration and development costs, and research and experimentation expenditures.

Controlling the Timing of Preferences and Adjustments

The AMT exemption often will keep items of tax preference from being subject to the AMT. To use the AMT exemption effectively, taxpayers should avoid bunching

preferences and positive adjustments in any one year. To avoid bunching of preferences and adjustments, taxpayers should attempt to control the timing of such items when possible. For example, the contribution of appreciated long-term capital gain property will result in a tax preference item. The timing of such a contribution is usually subject to the control of the taxpayer. Before making a substantial contribution of such property, the taxpayer should assess his or her position relative to the AMT.

Taking Advantage of the AMT/Regular Tax Rate Differential

A taxpayer who cannot avoid triggering the AMT in a given year can usually save taxes by taking advantage of the rate differential between the AMT and the regular tax.

EXAMPLE 34   T, who expects to be in the 28% tax bracket in 1991, is subject to the AMT in 1990. He is considering the sale of a parcel of land at a gain of $100,000. If he sells the land in 1991, he will have to pay tax of $28,000 ($100,000 gain × .28 regular tax rate). However, if he sells the land in 1990, he will pay tax of $21,000 ($100,000 gain × .21 AMT rate). Thus, accelerating the sale into 1990 will save T $7,000 in tax.   □

EXAMPLE 35   B, who expects to be in the 28% tax bracket in 1991, is subject to the AMT in 1990. He is going to contribute $10,000 in cash to his alma mater, State University. If he makes the contribution in 1991, he will save tax of $2,800 ($10,000 contribution × .28 regular tax rate). However, if he makes the contribution in 1990, he will save tax of $2,100 ($10,000 contribution × .21 AMT rate). Thus, deferring the contribution until 1991 will save B $700 in tax.   □

This deferral/acceleration strategy should be considered with regard to any income or expenses for which the taxpayer can control the timing.

PROBLEM MATERIALS

Discussion Questions

1. Why did Congress enact the alternative minimum tax?

2. T incurred $30,000 of circulation expenditures in 1990 and expensed that amount. Compute T's AMT adjustments for 1990, 1991, and 1992 and indicate whether the adjustments are positive or negative.

3. A wealthy acquaintance of yours is concerned about the alternative minimum tax and is thinking about selling all of his municipal bonds to prevent the interest from being subject to the AMT. What information should you give him?

4. M, a corporate executive, plans to exercise an incentive stock option granted by his employer to purchase 1,000 shares of the corporation's stock for an option price of $50 per share. The stock is currently selling for $125 per share. Explain the possible consequences of this action on M's regular tax and alternative minimum tax.

5. Two elements in the alternative minimum tax formula are tax preferences and alternative minimum tax adjustments. Explain how these elements differ.

6. Adjustments that are considered in computing the alternative minimum tax can be either positive or negative. Give an example of such an adjustment, including amounts. Explain the rationale behind the concept of positive and negative adjustments.

7. How can an individual taxpayer avoid having an alternative minimum tax adjustment for research and experimentation expenditures?

8. What is a passive loss? How is it treated for regular tax purposes? How is it treated for alternative minimum tax purposes?

9. T, an equipment dealer who will be subject to the alternative minimum tax in 1990, has an opportunity to make a large sale of equipment in December 1990 or January 1991. Discuss tax planning strategies T should consider in connection with the sale.

10. Certain taxpayers have the option of using either the percentage of completion method or the completed contract method for reporting profit on long-term contracts. What impact could the alternative minimum tax have on this decision?

11. Does computation of the alternative minimum tax ever require an adjustment for the standard deduction?

12. H, who had adjusted gross income of $100,000 in 1990, incurred medical expenses of $14,000 during the year. Compute H's medical expense deductions for income tax and AMT purposes. How much is H's AMT adjustment, and is it positive or negative?

13. Are all itemized deductions that are allowed in computing taxable income also allowed in computing alternative minimum taxable income? Explain any differences.

14. In computing the alternative tax itemized deduction for interest, it is possible that some interest allowed as an itemized deduction for income tax purposes will not be allowed. Explain.

15. The net operating loss for computing taxable income differs from the alternative tax net operating loss. Explain.

16. What is the purpose of the AMT credit? Briefly describe how the credit is computed.

17. Discuss tax planning strategies for minimizing the alternative minimum tax.

Problems

18. D placed an apartment building in service in January 1990. The apartment building cost $1,000,000, and she computed depreciation using the appropriate modified (post-1986) ACRS table (refer to chapter 8). Compute D's AMT adjustments for 1990 and 2020, and indicate whether the adjustments are positive or negative.

19. Assume the same facts as in Problem 18 *and* that D sells the building on December 20, 1992, for $1,100,000. How will this transaction affect D's income tax and alternative minimum tax computations in 1992?

20. In 1990, M incurred $200,000 of mining and exploration expenditures. He elects to deduct the expenditures as quickly as the tax law allows for income tax purposes.

    a. How will M's treatment of mining and exploration expenditures affect his income tax and AMT computations for 1990?

    b. How can M avoid having AMT adjustments related to the mining and exploration expenditures?

21. In 1990, C has a $50,000 loss on a passive activity she acquired in 1984. None of the loss is attributable to AMT adjustments or preferences. How will the loss be treated for income tax purposes? For AMT purposes?

22. F acquired a passive activity in 1990. Gross income from operations of the activity was $100,000. Operating expenses, not including depreciation, were $90,000. Income tax depreciation of $25,000 was computed under the modified accelerated cost recovery system (post-1986 ACRS). AMT depreciation, computed under the alternative depreciation system (ADS), was $16,000. Compute F's passive loss for income tax purposes and for AMT purposes.

23. In March 1990, M exercised incentive stock options granted by his employer. He paid $20 per share for 1,000 shares of stock with a fair market value of $50 per share. The stock was not subject to restrictions and was freely transferable. M sold the stock for $60 per share in December 1991. What are the income tax and alternative minimum tax consequences of these transactions for 1990 and 1991?

24. In 1990, J incurred circulation expenditures of $60,000. The entire amount was deducted in 1990 for income tax purposes. On March 1, J placed in service a warehouse that cost $100,000. He computed depreciation on the warehouse using the appropriate modified (post 1986) ACRS table (refer to chapter 8). Compute J's net adjustments for alternative minimum tax purposes in 1990, 1991, and 1992.

25. In 1990, J made two charitable contributions of property that he had acquired in 1985. He contributed common stock that had a basis of $50,000 and a fair market value of $76,000. In addition, he contributed land to be used as a park by the city. The basis of the land was $30,000, and its fair market value was $21,000. What effect will these contributions have on J's alternative minimum taxable income in 1990?

26. P, who is single and has no dependents, had taxable income of $150,000 and tax preferences of $50,000 in 1990. P did not itemize deductions for income tax purposes. Compute P's alternative minimum tax exemption for 1990.

27. S, who is single and has no dependents, had taxable income of $250,000 and tax preferences of $50,000 in 1990. S did not itemize deductions for income tax purposes. What is the largest amount that S can deduct for the alternative minimum tax exemption?

28. T, who is single, has no dependents and does not itemize. She has the following items relative to her tax return for 1990:

Bargain element from the exercise of an incentive stock option (no restrictions apply to the stock)	$ 50,000
Accelerated depreciation on equipment acquired before 1987 (straight-line depreciation would have yielded $60,000)	80,000
Percentage depletion in excess of property's adjusted basis	90,000
Taxable income for regular tax purposes	150,000

    a. Determine T's AMT adjustments and preferences for 1990.

    b. Calculate the alternative minimum tax (if any) for 1990.

29. B, who is single, has the following items for 1990:

Income:

Salary	$150,000
Interest from bank	5,000
Interest on corporate bonds	10,000
Dividends	4,000
Short-term capital gain	12,000
Long-term capital gain	20,000

Expenses:

Unreimbursed employee business expenses (no meals or entertainment)	3,000
Total medical expenses	40,000
State income taxes	8,000
Real property taxes	7,000
Home mortgage (qualified housing) interest	5,000

Casualty loss on vacation home:

Decline in value	20,000
Adjusted basis	70,000
Insurance proceeds	12,000
Tax preferences	100,000

Compute B's tax liability for 1990 before credits or prepayments.

30. In 1990, T incurred a net operating loss of $40,000. He deducted total tax preference items of $16,000 in arriving at the NOL and elected to carry the NOL forward. Compute T's alternative minimum tax net operating loss carryover.

31. During the course of your interview with Jim, who is one of your tax clients, you obtain the following information:

a. Jim, age 52, is single and has no dependents. He is independently wealthy and lives in Aspen, Colorado. In 1990, he earned $18,000 as a ski instructor.

b. Jim's savings account at First National Bank was credited with $45,000 of interest during the year. In addition, he received $126,000 of dividends from General Motors.

c. On March 15, 1990, Jim sold 10,000 shares of Widgets, Inc., stock for $45 per share. He had acquired 15,000 shares of Widgets stock on April 1, 1982, at a cost of $35 per share.

d. An examination of Jim's personal financial documents yields the following information:

   • IRA contribution, $2,000 (Jim is not covered by his employer's pension plan).
   • State income taxes withheld and estimated payments, $2,500.
   • Real estate taxes on his residence, $8,800.
   • Home mortgage interest, $45,500.
   • Credit card interest, $900.
   • Cash contributions to qualified (50% limit) charities, $10,000.
   • Professional dues and subscriptions, $500.
   • Tax return preparation fee, $2,500.

e. Jim owns several condominiums at Snowmass Ski Resort. Throughout the year, the condominiums are rented to vacationers for short periods on a weekly or monthly basis. Jim acquired the condos in 1983. There was a net

loss on the condos of $180,000 in 1990. Jim is not involved in the management of the condos. He pays Snowmass Property Management, Inc., to handle all management aspects of the properties.

f. In 1985, Jim invested in an equipment leasing deal. Income from this investment was $140,000 in 1990. The following expenses were incurred: interest, $50,000; management fees, $21,000; equipment expenses, $33,000; and depreciation, $225,000.

g. In 1985, Jim acquired an Aspen apartment complex, which he manages. Rental income in 1990 was $240,000. Expenses were $275,000.

h. In 1990, Jim invested in MNO Realty, a limited partnership. His share of the partnership's loss in 1990 was $300,000.

i. Jim's employer withheld $3,500 of Federal income tax in 1990. In addition, Jim made estimated payments of $45,000.

Analyze Jim's tax information and compute his tax liability for 1990. Suggested software (if available): *WEST–TAX Planner* or *BNA Individual Income Tax Spreadsheet.*

Cumulative Problems

32. X, who is single and age 46, has no dependents. In 1990, he earned a salary of $150,000 as vice president of ABC Manufacturing Corporation. Over the years, he has invested wisely and owns several thousand shares of stock and an apartment complex.

In January 1990, X sold 500 shares of stock for a gain of $50,000. He had owned the stock for 12 years. X received dividends of $15,000 on the stock he retained.

On May 20, 1990, X exercised his rights under ABC's incentive stock option plan. For an option price of $26,000, he acquired stock worth $53,000. The stock is freely transferable.

On September 15, X contributed 100 shares of JKL stock to the American Red Cross. The basis of the stock was $50 per share, and its fair market value was $70 per share.

Gross rental income from the apartment complex, which was acquired in 1982, was $140,000. Deductible expenses for the complex were $240,000. X does not participate in the management of the complex.

X received $10,000 interest on corporate bonds in 1990. His itemized deductions were as follows: state and local income taxes, $3,300; property taxes on residence, $3,200; mortgage interest on home (qualified housing), $18,000.

Compute X's lowest legal tax liability, before prepayments or credits, for 1990.

 33. R, age 38, is single and has no dependents. He is independently wealthy as a result of having inherited sizable holdings in real estate and corporate stocks and bonds. R is a minister at First Methodist Church, but he accepts no salary from the church. However, he does reside in the church's parsonage free of charge. The rental value of the parsonage is $400 a month. The church also provides R a cash grocery allowance of $50 a week. Examination of R's financial records provides the following information for 1990:

a. On January 16, 1990, R sold 2,000 shares of stock for a gain of $100,000. The stock was acquired four years ago.

b. R received $120,000 of interest on private activity bonds in 1990.

c. R received gross rental income of $160,000 from an apartment complex he owns and manages.

d. Expenses related to the apartment complex, which he acquired in 1983, were $280,000.

e. R's dividend and interest income was $40,000.

f. R had the following itemized deductions *from* adjusted gross income:

  - $80,000 fair market value of stock contributed to Methodist church (basis of stock was $20,000).
  - $2,000 interest on consumer purchases.
  - $8,500 state and local income taxes.
  - $9,000 medical expenses.
  - $1,000 casualty loss (in excess of the $100 floor and the 10% limitation).

Compute R's tax, including alternative minimum tax if applicable, before prepayments or credits, for 1990. Suggested software (if available): *BNA Individual Income Tax Spreadsheet.*

34. Michael Young, a 36-year-old architect, is single and has no dependents. He lives at 8685 Midway Road, Kent, OH 44240. His Social Security number is 857–97–2873.

Michael reported adjusted gross income of $100,000 and taxable income of $84,500 on Form 1040 for 1989. His itemized deductions reported on Schedule A included the following:

  - Total medical expenses, $12,000.
  - State and local income taxes, $3,400.
  - Real property taxes on personal residence, $2,500.
  - Interest on charge accounts ($1,000 total × .20 allowed), $200.
  - Miscellaneous itemized deductions in excess of 2% floor, $800.

In February 1989, Michael exercised an incentive stock option and acquired 1,000 shares of his employer's stock for the option price of $20 per share. The fair market value of the stock at the date of exercise was $85 per share. The stock is freely transferable.

Michael acquired private activity bonds on January 2, 1989. He earned interest of $4,000 on the bonds during 1989.

Determine whether Michael is subject to the alternative minimum tax. Use Form 6251, Alternative Minimum Tax—Individuals, for your computations.

15

ACCOUNTING PERIODS AND METHODS

OBJECTIVES   Review the requirements for adoption and change of the tax year.

Describe the rules of income and expense recognition for the cash and accrual methods of tax accounting.

Analyze the procedures for changing accounting methods.

Explain and illustrate the installment method of accounting.

Explain the alternative methods of accounting for long-term contracts.

Analyze the imputed interest rules applicable to installment sales.

OUTLINE

Earlier chapters discussed the types of income subject to tax (gross income and exclusions) and allowable deductions. This chapter focuses on the related issue of determining the periods in which income and deductions are reported. Generally, a taxpayer's income and deductions must be assigned to particular 12-month periods—calendar years or fiscal years.

Income and deductions are placed within particular years through the use of tax accounting methods. The basic accounting methods are the cash method, accrual method, and the hybrid method. Other special purpose methods are available for specific circumstances or types of transactions such as the installment method and the methods used for long-term construction contracts.

An entire subchapter of the Code, Subchapter E, is devoted to accounting periods and accounting methods. Over the long run, the accounting period used by a taxpayer will not affect the aggregate amount of reported taxable income. However, taxable income for any particular year may vary significantly due to the use of a particular reporting period. Also, through the choice of accounting methods or periods, it is possible to postpone the recognition of taxable income and to enjoy the benefits from such deferral of the related tax. This chapter discusses the taxpayer's alternatives for accounting periods and accounting methods.

ACCOUNTING PERIODS

In General

A taxpayer who keeps adequate books and records may be permitted to elect to use a *fiscal year*, a 12-month period ending on the last day of a month other than December. Otherwise, a *calendar year* must be used. Frequently, corporations can satisfy the recordkeeping requirements and elect to use a fiscal year. Often the fiscal year conforms to a natural business year (e.g., a summer resort's fiscal year may end on September 30, after the close of the season). Individuals seldom use a fiscal year because they do not maintain the necessary books.

Generally, a taxable year may not exceed 12 calendar months. However, if certain requirements are met, a taxpayer may elect to use an annual period that varies from 52 to 53 weeks. In such case, the year-end must be on the same day of the week (e.g., the Tuesday falling closest to October 31 or the last Tuesday in October). The day of the week selected for ending the year would depend upon business considerations. For example, a retail business that is not open on Sundays may end its tax year on a Sunday so that an inventory can be taken without interrupting business operations.

EXAMPLE 1   T is in the business of selling farm supplies. His natural business year terminates at the end of October with the completion of harvesting. At the end of the fiscal year it is necessary to take an inventory, and it is most easily accomplished on a Tuesday. Therefore, T could adopt a 52–53 week tax year ending on the Tuesday closest to October 31. If this method is selected, the year-end date may fall in the following month if that Tuesday is closer to October 31. The tax year ending in 1990 will contain 52 weeks beginning on Wednesday, November 1, 1989, and ending on Tuesday, October 30, 1990. The tax year ending in 1991 will have 52 weeks beginning on Wednesday, October 31, 1990, and ending on Tuesday, October 29, 1991. □

Partnerships and S Corporations. Partnerships are subject to additional restrictions to prevent partners from deferring partnership income by selecting a different year-end for the partnership. For example, if the tax year for the partnership ended on January 31 and the partners used a calendar year, partnership profits for the first 11 months would not be reported by the partners until the following year. In general, the partnership tax year must be the same as the tax year of the majority interest partners. The *majority interest partners* are the partners who own a greater than 50 percent interest in the partnership capital and profits. If the majority owners do not have the same tax year, the partnership must adopt the same tax year as its principal partners. A *principal partner* is a partner with a 5 percent or more interest in the partnership capital or profits. If the principal partners do not have the same tax year and no majority of partners have the same tax year, the partnership must use a calendar year for tax reporting.

EXAMPLE 2

The XYZ Partnership is owned equally by X Corporation, Y Corporation, and individual Z. The partners have the following tax years.

	Partner's Tax Year Ending
X	June 30
Y	June 30
Z	December 31

The partnership's tax year must end on June 30. If Y as well as Z's year ended on December 31, the partnership would be required to adopt a calendar year. □

Similarly, S corporations must adopt a calendar year. However, partnerships and S corporations may *elect* an otherwise *impermissible year* under any of the following conditions:

- A business purpose for the year can be demonstrated.

- The partnership's or S corporation's year results in a deferral of not more than three months' income, and the entity agrees to make required tax payments.

- The entity retains the same year as was used for the fiscal year ending in 1987, provided the entity agrees to make required tax payments.

Business Purpose. The only business purpose for a fiscal year that the IRS has acknowledged is the need to conform the tax year to the natural business year of a business.[1] Generally, only seasonal businesses have a natural business year. For example, the natural business year for a department store may end on January 31, after Christmas returns have been processed and clearance sales have been completed.

Required Tax Payments. Under this system, the partnership or S corporation has required tax payments due by April 15 of each tax year. The amount due is

---

1. Rev.Rul. 87–57, 1987–2 C.B. 117.

computed by applying the highest individual tax rate plus 1 percent to an estimate of the deferral period income. The deferral period runs from the close of the fiscal year to the end of the calendar year. Estimated income for this period is based on the average monthly earnings for the previous fiscal year. The amount due is reduced by the amount of required tax payments for the previous year.

EXAMPLE 3

S, Inc., an S corporation, elected a fiscal year ending September 30. R is the only shareholder. For the fiscal year ending September 30, 1991, S, Inc., earned $100,000. The required tax payment for the previous year was $5,000. The corporation must pay $2,250 by April 15, 1992, calculated as follows:

$$(\$100,000 \times {}^{3}\!/_{12} \times 29\%*) - \$5,000 = \$2,250$$

* Maximum § 1 rate of 28% + 1%.   □

Personal Service Corporations (PSCs).   A PSC is a corporation whose shareholder-employees provide personal services (e.g., medical, dental, legal, accounting, actuarial, consulting, or performing arts). Generally, a PSC must use a calendar year. However, a fiscal year can be *elected* by a PSC under any of the following conditions:

- A business purpose for the year can be demonstrated.

- The PSC year results in a deferral of not more than three months' income, the corporation pays the shareholder-employee's salary during the portion of the calendar year after the close of the fiscal year, and the salary for that period is at least proportionate to the shareholder-employee's salary received for such fiscal year.

- The PSC retains the same year as was used for the fiscal year ending in 1987, provided the latter two requirements contained in the preceding option are satisfied.

EXAMPLE 4

Y's corporation paid Y $120,000 of salary during its fiscal year ending September 30, 1990. The corporation cannot satisfy the business purpose test for a fiscal year. The corporation can continue to use its fiscal year without any negative tax effects, provided Y receives as salary during the period October 1 through December 31, 1990, at least $30,000 (3 months/12 months × $120,000).   □

If the salary test is not satisfied, the PSC can retain the fiscal year, but the corporation's deduction for salary for the fiscal year is limited to the following:

A + A(F/N)

Where A = Amount paid after the close of the fiscal year

F = Number of months in fiscal year minus number of months from the end of the fiscal year to the end of the ongoing calendar year

N = Number of months from the end of the fiscal year to the end of the ongoing calendar year.

EXAMPLE 5 | Assume the corporation in the previous example paid Y $10,000 of salary during the period October 1 through December 31, 1990. The deduction for Y's salary for the corporation's fiscal year ending September 30, 1991, is thus limited to $40,000 calculated as follows:

$$\$10,000 + \left[\$10,000 \left(\frac{12 - 3}{3} \right) \right] =$$
$$\$10,000 + \$30,000 = \$40,000$$

□

Making the Election

A taxpayer elects to use a calendar or fiscal year by the timely filing of his or her initial tax return. For all subsequent years, this same period must be used unless approval for change is obtained from the IRS.

Changes in the Accounting Period

A taxpayer must obtain consent from the IRS before changing the tax year. This power to approve or not to approve a change is significant in that it permits the IRS to issue authoritative administrative guidelines that must be met by taxpayers who wish to change their accounting period. An application for permission to change tax years must be made on Form 1128, Application for Change in Accounting Period, and must be filed on or before the fifteenth day of the second calendar month following the close of the short period that results from the change in accounting period.

EXAMPLE 6 | Beginning in 1990, T Corporation, a calendar year taxpayer, would like to switch to a fiscal year ending March 31. The corporation must file Form 1128 by May 15, 1990. □

IRS Requirements.   The IRS will not grant permission for the change unless the taxpayer can establish a substantial business purpose for the change. One substantial business purpose is a request to change to a tax year that coincides with the *natural business year* (the completion of an annual business cycle). The IRS applies an objective gross receipts test to determine if the entity has a natural business year. Twenty-five percent of the entity's gross receipts for the 12-month period must be realized in the final 2 months of the 12-month period for three consecutive years.

EXAMPLE 7 | A Virginia Beach motel had gross receipts as follows:

	1988	1989	1990
July–August receipts	$300,000	$250,000	$325,000
September 1–August 31 receipts	1,000,000	900,000	1,250,000
Receipts for 2 months divided by receipts for 12 months	30.0%	27.8%	26.0%

Since the natural business year test is satisfied, the entity will be allowed to use a fiscal year ending August 31. □

The IRS usually will establish certain conditions that the taxpayer must accept if the approval for change is to be granted. In particular, if the taxpayer has a net operating loss for the short period, the IRS may require that the loss be carried forward and allocated equally over the 6 following years. As you may recall (refer to chapter 7), net operating losses are ordinarily carried back for 3 years and forward for 15 years.

EXAMPLE 8   X Corporation changed from a calendar year to a fiscal year ending September 30. The short period return for the nine months ending September 30, 1990, reflected a $60,000 net operating loss. The corporation had taxable income for 1987, 1988, and 1989. As a condition for granting approval, the IRS will require X Corporation to allocate the $60,000 loss over the next six years. Thus, X Corporation will reduce its taxable income by $10,000 each year ending September 30, 1991, through September 30, 1996.   □

Taxable Periods of Less Than One Year

A *short year* (or short period) is a period of less than 12 calendar months. A taxpayer may have a short year for (1) the first tax reporting period, (2) the final income tax return, or (3) a change in the tax year. If the short period results from a change in the taxpayer's annual accounting period, the taxable income for such period must be annualized. Due to the progressive tax rate structure, taxpayers could reap benefits from a short-period return if some adjustments were not required. Thus, the taxpayer is required to do the following:

Annualize the short-period income.

$$\text{Annualized income} = \text{Short-period income} \times \frac{12}{\substack{\text{Number of months} \\ \text{in the short period}}}$$

Compute the tax on the annualized income.

Convert the tax on the annualized income to a short-period tax.

$$\text{Short-period tax} = \text{Tax on annualized income} \times \frac{\substack{\text{Number of months} \\ \text{in the short period}}}{12}$$

EXAMPLE 9   B Corporation obtained permission to change from a calendar year to a fiscal year ending September 30, beginning in 1990. For the short period January 1 through September 30, 1990, the corporation's taxable income was $48,000. The relevant tax rates and the resultant short-period tax are as follows:

Amount of Taxable Income	Tax Calculation
$1–$50,000	15% of taxable income
$50,001–$75,000	$7,500 plus 25% of taxable income in excess of $50,000
Annualized income ($48,000 × 12/9) = $64,000	

Tax on annualized income

$$\$7,500 + .25 \,(\$64,000 - \$50,000) =$$
$$\$7,500 + \$3,500 = \$11,000$$

Short-period tax = ($\$11,000 \times 9/12$) = $8,250

Annualizing the income increased the tax by $1,050:

Tax with annualizing	$8,250
Tax without annualizing (.15 × $48,000)	7,200
	$1,050

☐

Rather than annualize the short-period income, the taxpayer can elect to (1) calculate the tax for a 12-month period beginning on the first day of the short period and (2) convert the tax in (1) to a short-period tax as follows:

$$\frac{\text{Taxable income for short period}}{\text{Taxable income for the 12-month period}} \times \text{Tax on the 12 months of income}$$

EXAMPLE 10   Assume B Corporation's taxable income for the calendar year 1990 was $60,000. The tax on the full 12 months of income would have been $10,000 [$7,500 + .25 ($60,000 − $50,000)]. The short-period tax would be $8,000 ($48,000/$60,000 × $10,000). Thus, if the corporation utilized this option, the tax for the short period would be $8,000 (rather than $8,250, as calculated in Example 9).   ☐

For individuals, annualizing requires some special adjustments:

• Deductions must be itemized for the short period (the standard deduction is not allowed).

• Personal and dependency exemptions must be prorated.

Fortunately, individuals rarely change tax years.

Mitigation of the Annual Accounting Period Concept

Several provisions in the Code are designed to give the taxpayer relief from the seemingly harsh results that may be produced by the combined effects of an arbitrary accounting period and a progressive rate structure. For example, under the net operating loss carryback and carryover rules, a loss in one year can be carried back and offset against taxable income for the preceding 3 years. Unused net operating losses are then carried over for 15 years. In addition, the Code provides special relief provisions for casualty losses pursuant to a disaster and for the reporting of insurance proceeds from destruction of crops.[2]

Restoration of Amounts Received under a Claim of Right.   The court-made *claim of right doctrine* applies when the taxpayer has received as income property that he or she treats as his or her own but the taxpayer's rights to the income are

---

2. §§ 165(i) and 451(d). Refer to chapter 7.

disputed.[3] According to the doctrine, the taxpayer must include the amount as income in the year of receipt. The rationale for the doctrine is that the Federal government cannot await the resolution of all disputes before exacting a tax. As a corollary to the doctrine, if the taxpayer is later required to repay the funds, generally a deduction is allowed in the year of repayment.[4]

EXAMPLE 11   In 1990, T received a $5,000 bonus computed as a percentage of profits. In 1991, it was determined that the 1990 profits had been incorrectly computed, and T had to refund the $5,000 to his employer in 1991. T was required to include the $5,000 in his 1990 income, but he can claim a $5,000 deduction in 1991. ☐

In Example 11 the transactions were a wash; that is, the income and deduction were the same ($5,000). Suppose, however, T was in the 28 percent tax bracket in 1990 but in the 15 percent bracket in 1991. Without some relief provision, the mistake would be costly to T. T paid $1,400 tax in 1990 (.28 × $5,000), but the deduction reduced his tax liability in 1991 by only $750 (.15 × $5,000). The Code does provide the needed relief in such cases. Under § 1341, when income has been taxed under the claim of right doctrine but must later be repaid, in effect, the taxpayer gets the deduction in the year he or she can receive the greater tax benefit. Thus, in Example 11, the repayment in 1991 would reduce T's 1991 tax liability by the greater 1990 rate (.28) applied to the $5,000. However, relief is provided only for cases in which there is a significant difference in the tax, that is, when the deduction for the amount previously included in income exceeds $3,000.

ACCOUNTING METHODS

Permissible Methods

Section 446 requires that taxable income be computed under the method of accounting regularly employed by the taxpayer in keeping his or her books, provided the method clearly reflects income. The Code recognizes the following as generally permissible methods:

- The cash receipts and disbursements method.
- The accrual method.
- A hybrid method (a combination of cash and accrual).

The Regulations refer to these alternatives as *overall methods* and add that the term *method of accounting* includes not only the overall method of accounting of the taxpayer but also the accounting treatment of any item.[5]

Generally, any of the three methods of accounting may be used if the method is consistently employed and clearly reflects income. However, the taxpayer is required to use the accrual method for sales and cost of goods sold if inventories are an income-producing factor to the business. Other situations in which the

---

3. *North American Consolidated Oil Co. v. Burnet,* 49 USTC ¶943, 11 AFTR 16, 52 S.Ct. 613 (USSC, 1932). See the Glossary of Tax Terms in Appendix C for a discussion of the term "claim of right doctrine."

4. *U.S. v. Lewis,* 51–1 USTC ¶9211, 40 AFTR 258, 71 S.Ct. 522 (USSC, 1951).

5. Reg. § 1.446–1(a)(1).

accrual method is required are discussed later. Special methods are also permitted for installment sales, for long-term construction contracts, and for farmers.

A taxpayer who has more than one trade or business may use a different method of accounting for each trade or business activity. Furthermore, a different method of accounting may be used to determine income from a trade or business than is used to compute nonbusiness items of income and deductions.

EXAMPLE 12   T operates a grocery store and owns stock and bonds. The income from the grocery store must be computed by the accrual basis because inventories are material. However, T can report his dividends and interest under the cash method.   ☐

The Code grants the IRS broad powers to determine whether the taxpayer's accounting method *clearly reflects income*. Thus, if the method employed does not clearly reflect income, the IRS has the power to prescribe the method to be used by the taxpayer.

Cash Receipts and Disbursements Method—Cash Basis

Most individuals and many businesses use the cash basis to report income and deductions. The popularity of this method can largely be attributed to its simplicity and flexibility.

Under the cash method, income is not recognized until the taxpayer actually receives, or constructively receives, cash or its equivalent. Cash is constructively received if it is available to the taxpayer. Deductions are generally permitted in the year of payment. Thus, year-end accounts receivable, accounts payable, and accrued income and deductions are not included in the determination of taxable income.

The cash method permits a taxpayer in many cases to choose the year in which he or she claims the deduction by simply postponing or accelerating the payment of expenses. However, for fixed assets, the cash basis taxpayer claims deductions through depreciation or amortization, the same as an accrual basis taxpayer does. In addition, prepaid expenses must be capitalized and amortized if the life of the asset extends substantially beyond the end of the tax year. Most courts have applied the one-year rule to determine whether capitalization and amortization are required. According to this rule, capitalization is required only if the asset has a life that extends beyond the tax year following the year of payment.

Restrictions on Use of the Cash Method.   The use of the cash method to measure income from a merchandising or manufacturing operation would often yield a distorted picture of the results of operations. Income for the period would largely be a function of when payments were made for goods or materials. Thus, the Regulations prohibit the use of the cash method (and require the accrual method) to measure sales and cost of goods sold if inventories are material to the business.[6]

The prohibition on the use of the cash method if inventories are material and the rules regarding prepaid expenses (discussed above) are intended to assure that annual income is clearly reflected. However, certain taxpayers may not use the

---

6. Reg. § 1.446–1(a)(4)(i).

cash method of accounting for Federal income tax purposes regardless of whether inventories are material. The accrual basis must be used to report the income earned by (1) a corporation (other than an S corporation), (2) a partnership with a corporate partner, and (3) a tax shelter. This accrual basis requirement has three exceptions:

- A farming business.

- A qualified personal service corporation (e.g., a corporation performing services in health, law, engineering, architecture, accounting, actuarial science, performing arts, or consulting).

- An entity that is not a tax shelter whose average annual gross receipts for the most recent three-year period are $5,000,000 or less.

Farming.   Although inventories are material to farming operations, the IRS long ago created an exception to the general rule and has allowed farmers to use the cash method of accounting. The purpose of the exception is to relieve the small farmer from the bookkeeping burden of accrual accounting. However, tax shelter promoters recognized, for example, that by deducting the costs of a crop in one tax year and harvesting the crop in a later year, income could be deferred from tax. Thus, §§ 447 and 464 were enacted to prevent the use of the cash method by certain farming corporations and limited partnerships (farming syndicates).

Farmers who are allowed to use the cash method of accounting must nevertheless capitalize their costs of raising trees when the preproduction period is greater than two years. Thus, a cash basis apple farmer must capitalize the cost of raising trees until the trees produce in merchantable quantities. Cash basis farmers can elect not to capitalize these costs, but if the election is made, the alternative depreciation system (refer to chapter 8) must be used for all farming property.

Generally, the cost of purchasing an animal must be capitalized. However, the cash basis farmer's cost of raising the animal can be expensed.

Accrual Method

All Events Test for Income.   Under the accrual method, an item is generally included in gross income for the year in which it is earned, regardless of when the income is collected. An item of income is earned when (1) all the events have occurred to fix the taxpayer's right to receive the income and (2) the amount of income (the amount the taxpayer has a right to receive) can be determined with reasonable accuracy. [7]

Example 13   A, a calendar year taxpayer who uses the accrual basis of accounting, was to receive a bonus equal to 6% of B Corporation's net income for its fiscal year ending each June 30. For the fiscal year ending June 30, 1990, B Corporation had net income of $240,000, and for the six months ending December 31, 1990, the corporation's net income was $150,000. A will report $14,400 (.06 × $240,000) for 1990 because her rights to the amount became fixed when B Corporation's year closed. However, A would not accrue income based on the corporation's profits for the last six months of 1990 since her right to the income does not accrue until the close of the corporation's tax year.   □

---

7. Reg. § 1.451–1(a). Refer to chapter 3 for further discussion of the accrual basis.

In a situation where the accrual basis taxpayer's right to income is being contested and the income has not yet been collected, generally no income is recognized until the dispute has been settled.[8] Before the settlement, "all of the events have not occurred that fix the right to receive the income."

All Events and Economic Performance Tests for Deductions.   An all events test applies to accrual basis deductions. A deduction cannot be claimed until (1) all the events have occurred to create the taxpayer's liability and (2) the amount of the liability can be determined with reasonable accuracy. Once these requirements are satisfied, the deduction will be permitted only if economic performance has occurred.

The economic performance test addresses situations in which the taxpayer's obligation is either of the following:

To pay for services or property to be provided in the future.

To provide services or property (other than money) in the future.

Regarding services or property to be provided to the taxpayer in the future (situation 1), economic performance occurs when the property or services are actually provided by the other party.

EXAMPLE 14   An accrual basis calendar year taxpayer, PS, Inc., promoted a boxing match held in the company's arena on December 31, 1990. AM, Inc., had contracted to clean the arena for $5,000, but the work was not actually performed until January 1, 1991. PS, Inc., did not pay the $5,000 until 1992. Although financial accounting would require PS, Inc., to accrue the $5,000 cleaning expense to match the revenues from the fight in 1990, the economic performance test has not been satisfied until 1991, when AM, Inc., performed the service. Thus, the expense must be deducted by PS, Inc., in 1991.   □

If the taxpayer is obligated to provide property or services (situation 2), economic performance occurs (and thus the deduction is allowed) in the year the taxpayer provides the property or services.

EXAMPLE 15   T Corporation, an accrual basis taxpayer, is in the strip mining business. According to the contract with the landowner, the company must reclaim the land. The estimated cost of reclaiming land mined in 1990 was $500,000, but the land was not actually reclaimed until 1992. The all events test was satisfied in 1990. The obligation existed, and the amount of the liability could be determined with reasonable accuracy. However, the economic performance test was not satisfied until 1992. Therefore, the deduction is not allowed until 1992.   □

The economic performance test is waived, and thus year-end accruals can be deducted, if all the following conditions are met:

• The obligation exists and the amount of the liability can be reasonably estimated.

• Economic performance occurs within a reasonable period (but not later than 8½ months after the close of the taxable year).

---

8. *Burnet v. Sanford & Brooks Co.*, 2 USTC ¶636, 9 AFTR 603, 51 S.Ct. 150 (USSC, 1931).

- The item is recurring in nature.

- Either the accrued item is not material, or accruing it results in a better matching of revenues and expenses.

EXAMPLE 16   M Corporation often sells goods that are on hand but cannot be shipped for another week. Thus, the sales account usually includes revenues for some items that have not been shipped at year-end. M Corporation is obligated to pay shipping costs. Although the company's obligation for shipping costs can be determined with reasonable accuracy, economic performance will not be satisfied until M Corporation (or its agent) actually delivers the goods. However, accruing shipping costs on sold items will better match expenses with revenues for the period. Therefore, the company should be allowed to accrue the shipping costs on items sold but not shipped at year-end.   □

It should be noted that the economic performance test does not address all possible accrued expenses. For example, an accrual for state income taxes or payroll taxes is not a liability for property or services received. In such cases, the taxpayer applies the all events test without considering economic performance.

Reserves.   Generally, the all events and economic performance tests will prevent the use of reserves (e.g., for product warranty expense) frequently used in financial accounting to match expenses with revenues. However, small banks are allowed to use a bad debt reserve. Furthermore, an accrual basis taxpayer in a service business is permitted to not accrue revenue that appears uncollectible based on experience. In effect, this is an indirect approach to allowing a reserve.

Hybrid Method

A *hybrid method* of accounting involves the use of more than one method. For example, a taxpayer who uses the accrual basis to report sales and cost of goods sold but uses the cash basis to report other items of income and expense is employing a hybrid method. The Code permits the use of a hybrid method provided the taxpayer's income is clearly reflected.[9] A taxpayer who uses the accrual method for business expenses must also use the accrual method for business income (a cash method for income items may not be used if the taxpayer's expenses are accounted for under the accrual basis.)

It may be preferable for a business that is required to report sales and cost of sales on the accrual method to report other items of income and expense under the cash method. The cash method permits greater flexibility in the timing of income and expense recognition.

Change of Method

The taxpayer, in effect, makes an election to use a particular accounting method when an initial tax return is filed using a particular method. If a subsequent change in method is desired, the taxpayer must obtain the permission of the IRS. The request for change is made on Form 3115, Application for Change in

---

9. § 446(c).

Accounting Method. Generally, the form must be filed within the first 180 days of the taxable year of the desired change.

As previously mentioned, the term *accounting method* encompasses not only the overall accounting method used by the taxpayer (the cash or accrual method) but also the treatment of any material item of income or deduction. Thus, a change in the method of deducting property taxes from a cash basis to an accrual basis that results in a deduction for taxes in a different year would constitute a change in an accounting method. Another example of accounting method change is a change involving the method or basis used in the valuation of inventories. However, a change in treatment resulting from a change in underlying facts does not constitute a change in the taxpayer's method of accounting. For example, a change in employment contracts so that an employee accrues one day of vacation pay for each month of service rather than 12 days of vacation pay for a full year of service is a change in the underlying facts and is not, therefore, an accounting method change.

Correction of an Error.   A change in accounting method should be distinguished from the *correction of an error*. An error can be corrected (by filing amended returns) by the taxpayer without special permission, and the IRS can simply adjust the taxpayer's liability if an error is discovered on audit of the return. Some examples of errors are incorrect postings, errors in the calculation of tax liability or tax credits, deductions of business expense items that are actually personal, and omissions of income and deductions. Unless the taxpayer or the IRS corrects the error within the statute of limitations, the taxpayer's total lifetime taxable income will be overstated or understated by the amount of the error.

Change from an Incorrect Method.   An *incorrect accounting method* is the consistent (year-after-year) use of an incorrect rule to report an item of income or expense. The incorrect accounting method generally will not affect the taxpayer's total lifetime income (unlike the error). That is, an incorrect method has a self-balancing mechanism. For example, deducting freight on inventory in the year the goods are purchased, rather than when the inventory is sold, is an incorrect accounting method. The total cost of goods sold over the life of the business is not affected, but the year-to-year income is incorrect.

If a taxpayer is employing an erroneous method of accounting, permission must be obtained from the IRS to change to a correct method. An erroneous method is not treated as a mechanical error that can be corrected by merely filing an amended tax return.

It should be noted that the tax return preparer as well as the taxpayer will be subject to penalties if the tax return is prepared using an incorrect method of accounting and permission for a change to a correct method has not been requested.

Net Adjustments Due to Change in Accounting Method.   In the year of change in accounting method, certain adjustments may be required to items of income and expense to prevent a distortion of taxable income resulting from the change.

EXAMPLE 17	In 1990, Z Corporation, with consent from the IRS, switched from the cash to the accrual basis for reporting sales and cost of goods sold. The corporation's accrual basis gross profit for the year was computed as follows:

Sales		$100,000
Beginning inventory	$ 15,000	
Purchases	60,000	
Less: Ending inventory	(10,000)	
Cost of goods sold		(65,000)
Gross profit		$ 35,000

At the end of the previous year, Z Corporation had accounts receivable of $25,000 and accounts payable for merchandise of $34,000. The accounts receivable from the previous year in the amount of $25,000 were never included in gross income since the taxpayer was on the cash basis and did not recognize the uncollected receivables. In the current year, the $25,000 was not included in the accrual basis sales since the sales were made in a prior year. Therefore, a $25,000 adjustment to income would be required to prevent the omission of the receivables from income.

The corollary of failure to recognize a prior year's receivables is the failure to recognize a prior year's accounts payable. The beginning of the year's accounts payable were not included in the current or prior year's purchases. Thus, a deduction for the $34,000 was not taken in either year and is therefore included as an adjustment to income for the period of change.

An adjustment is also required to reflect the $15,000 beginning inventory that was deducted (due to the use of a cash method of accounting) by the taxpayer in the previous year. In this instance, the cost of goods sold during the year of change was increased by the beginning inventory and resulted in a double deduction.

The net adjustment due to the change in accounting method would be computed as follows:

Beginning inventory (deducted in prior and current year)	$ 15,000
Beginning accounts receivable (omitted from income)	25,000
Beginning accounts payable (omitted from deductions)	(34,000)
Net increase in taxable income	$ 6,000

☐

Disposition of the Net Adjustment.   Generally, if the IRS *requires* the taxpayer to change an accounting method, the net adjustment is added to or subtracted from the income for the year of the change. In cases of positive (an increase in income) adjustments in excess of $3,000, the taxpayer is allowed to calculate the tax by spreading the adjustment over one or more previous years.

To encourage taxpayers to *voluntarily* change from incorrect methods and to facilitate changes from one correct method to another, the IRS generally allows the taxpayer to spread the adjustment into future years. Assuming the taxpayer files a timely request for change (Form 3115), the allocation periods that appear in Concept Summary 15–1 generally apply.

CONCEPT SUMMARY 15–1

Adjustment Periods

Change	Type of Adjustment	Allocation Period
Incorrect to correct method	Positive	Three years—year of change and the two succeeding years
Incorrect to correct method	Negative	Year of change
Correct to correct	Positive	Six years—year of change and the five succeeding years
Correct to correct	Negative	Six years—year of change and the five succeeding years

SPECIAL ACCOUNTING METHODS

Generally, accrual basis taxpayers recognize income when goods are sold and shipped to the customer. Cash basis taxpayers generally recognize income from a sale on the collection of cash from the customer. The tax law provides special accounting methods for certain installment sales and long-term contracts. These special methods were enacted, in part, to assure that the tax will be due when the taxpayer is best able to pay the tax.

Installment Method

Under the general rule for computing the gain or loss from the sale of property, the entire amount of gain or loss is recognized upon the sale or other disposition of the property.

EXAMPLE 18

A sold property to B for $10,000 cash plus B's note (fair market value and face amount of $90,000). A's basis in the property was $40,000. Gain or loss computed under the cash or accrual basis would be as follows:

Amount realized		
	Cash down payment	$ 10,000
	Note receivable	90,000
		$100,000
Basis in the property		(40,000)
Realized gain		$ 60,000

□

In Example 18, the general rule for recognizing gain or loss requires A to pay a substantial amount of tax on the gain in the year of sale even though only $10,000 cash was received. Congress enacted the installment sales provisions to prevent

this sort of hardship by allowing the taxpayer to spread the gain from installment sales over the collection period. The installment method is a very important planning tool because of the tax deferral possibilities.

Overview of the Installment Sales Provisions.   The relevant Code provisions are summarized as follows:

Section	Subject
453	General rules governing the installment method (e.g., when applicable), related-party transfers, and special situations (e.g., certain corporate liquidations).
453A	Special rules for nondealers of real property.
453B	Gain or loss recognition upon the disposition of installment obligations.
1038	Rules governing the repossession of real estate sold under the installment method.
483 1272 1274	Calculation and amortization of imputed interest.

Eligibility and Calculations.   The installment method applies to *gains* (but not losses) from the sale of property where the seller will receive at least one payment after the year of sale. For many years, practically all gains from the sale of property were eligible for the installment method. However, in recent years, the Code has been amended to deny the use of the installment method for the following:[10]

- Gains on property held for sale in the ordinary course of business.
- Depreciation recapture under § 1245 or § 1250.
- Gains on stocks or securities traded on an established market.

As an exception to the first item, the installment method may be used to report gains from sales of the following:

- Timeshare units (e.g., the right to use real property for two weeks each year).
- Residential lots (if the seller is not to make any improvements).
- Any property used or produced in the trade or business of farming.

The Nonelective Aspect.   Regardless of the taxpayer's method of accounting, as a general rule, eligible sales *must* be reported by the installment method. A special election is required to report the gain by any other method of accounting (see further discussion in a subsequent section of this chapter).

Computing the Gain for the Period.   The gain reported on each sale is computed by the following formula:

$$\frac{\text{Total gain}}{\text{Contract price}} \times \text{Payments received} = \text{Recognized gain}$$

The taxpayer must compute each variable as follows:

---

10. §§ 453(b), (i), and (l).

1. *Total gain* is the selling price reduced by selling expenses and the adjusted basis of the property. The selling price is the total consideration received by the seller, including notes receivable from the buyer and the seller's liabilities assumed by the buyer.

2. *Contract price* is the selling price less the seller's liabilities that are assumed by the buyer. Generally, the contract price is the amount, other than interest, the seller will receive from the purchaser.

3. *Payments received* are the collections on the contract price received in the tax year. This generally is equal to the cash received less the interest income collected for the period. If the buyer pays any of the seller's expenses, the amount paid is considered as received by the seller.

EXAMPLE 19   The seller is not a dealer, and the facts are as follows:

Sales price		
Cash down payment	$ 1,000	
Seller's mortgage assumed	3,000	
Notes payable to the seller	13,000	$ 17,000
Selling expenses		(500)
Seller's basis		(10,000)
Total gain		$ 6,500

The contract price is $14,000 ($17,000 − $3,000). Assuming the $1,000 is the only payment in the year of sale, the gain in that year is computed as follows:

$$\frac{\$6,500 \text{ (total gain)}}{\$14,000 \text{ (contract price)}} \times \$1,000 = \$464 \text{ (gain recognized in year of sale)}$$

☐

If the sum of the seller's basis and selling expenses is less than the liabilities assumed by the buyer, the difference must be added to the contract price and to the payments (treated as *deemed payments*) received in the year of sale. This adjustment to the contract price is required so that the ratio of total gain divided by contract price will not be greater than one.

EXAMPLE 20   Assume the same facts as in Example 19, except that the seller's basis in the property is only $2,000. The total gain, therefore, is $14,500 [$17,000 − ($2,000 + $500)]. Payments in the year of sale are $1,500 and are calculated as follows:

Down payment	$1,000
Excess of mortgage assumed over seller's basis and expenses ($3,000 − $2,000 − $500)	500
	$1,500

The contract price is $14,500 [$17,000 (selling price) − $3,000 (seller's mortgage assumed) + $500 (excess of mortgage assumed over seller's basis and seller's expenses)]. The gain in the year of sale is computed as follows:

$$\frac{\$14,500 \text{ (total gain)}}{\$14,500 \text{ (contract price)}} \times \$1,500 = \$1,500$$

In subsequent years, all amounts the seller collects on note principal ($13,000) will be recognized gain. □

As previously discussed, gain attributable to ordinary income recapture under §§ 1245 and 1250 is *ineligible* for installment reporting. Therefore, the § 1245 or § 1250 gain realized must be recognized in the year of sale, and the installment sale gain is the remaining gain.

EXAMPLE 21

T sold an apartment building for $50,000 cash and a $75,000 note due in two years. T's basis in the property was $25,000, and there was $40,000 ordinary income recapture under § 1250.

The realized gain is $100,000 ($125,000 − $25,000), and the $40,000 recapture must be recognized in the year of sale. Of the $60,000 remaining § 1231 gain, $24,000 must be recognized in the year of sale:

$$\frac{\S\,1231 \text{ gain}}{\text{Contract price}} \times \text{Payments received}$$

$$= \frac{\$125,000 - \$25,000 - \$40,000}{\$125,000} \times \$50,000$$

$$= \frac{\$60,000}{\$125,000} \times \$50,000 = \$24,000$$

The remaining realized gain of $36,000 ($60,000 − $24,000) will be recognized as the $75,000 note is collected. □

Other Amounts Considered Payments Received.   Congress and the IRS have added the following items to be considered as payments received in the year of sale:[11]

- Purchaser's evidence of indebtedness payable on demand and certain other readily tradable obligations (e.g., bonds traded on a stock exchange).

- Purchaser's evidence of indebtedness secured by cash or its equivalent.

In the absence of the first adjustment, the seller would have control over the year the gain is reported—whenever he or she demands payment or sells the tradable obligations. The seller receiving the obligations secured by cash can often post them as collateral for a loan and have the cash from the sale. Thus, there would be no justification for deferring the tax.

Imputed Interest.   Sections 483 and 1274 provide that if a deferred payment contract for the sale of property with a selling price greater than $3,000 does not contain a reasonable interest rate, a reasonable rate is imputed. The imputing of interest effectively restates the selling price of the property to equal the sum of the

---

11. § 453(f)(4) and Temp.Reg. § 15a.453–1(e).

payments at the date of the sale and the discounted present value of the future payments. The difference between the present value of a future payment and the payment's face amount is taxed as interest income, as discussed in the following paragraphs. Thus, the imputed interest rules prevent sellers of capital assets from increasing the selling price to reflect the equivalent of unstated interest on deferred payments and thereby converting ordinary (interest) income into long-term capital gains. Although the capital gain versus ordinary income distinction has lost much of its significance as a result of changes in the Code made by TRA of 1986, the imputed interest rules are important because of their effect on the timing of income recognition.

Generally, if the contract does not charge at least the Federal rate, interest will be imputed at the Federal rate. The Federal rate is the interest rate the Federal government pays on new borrowing and is published monthly by the IRS.[12]

As a general rule, the buyer and seller must account for interest on the accrual basis with semiannual compounding. The purpose of the accrual basis requirement is to assure that the seller's interest income and the buyer's interest expense are reported in the same tax year. Under pre-1984 law, the cash basis seller would not report interest income until it was actually collected, but an accrual basis buyer could deduct the interest as it accrued. The calculation and amortization of imputed interest are illustrated as follows:

EXAMPLE 22

T, a cash basis taxpayer, sold land on January 1, 1990, for $100,000 cash and $3,000,000 due on December 31, 1991, with 5% interest payable December 31, 1990, and December 31, 1991. At the time of the sale, the Federal rate was 12% (compounded semiannually). Because T did not charge at least the Federal rate, interest will be imputed at 12% (compounded semiannually).

Date	Payment	Present Value (at 12%) on 1/1/1990	Imputed Interest
12/31/1990	$ 150,000	$ 133,500	$ 16,500
12/31/1991	3,150,000	2,495,095	654,905
	$3,300,000	$2,628,595	$671,405

Thus, the selling price will be restated to $2,728,595 ($100,000 + $2,628,595) rather than $3,100,000 ($100,000 + $3,000,000), and T will recognize interest income in accordance with the following amortization schedule:

	Beginning Balance	Interest Income (at 12%)*	Received	Ending Balance
1990	$2,628,595	$324,895	$ 150,000	$2,803,490
1991	2,803,490	346,510	3,150,000	–0–

* Compounded semiannually.

---

12. § 1274(d)(1). There are three Federal rates: short-term (not over three years), mid-term (over three years but not over nine years), and long-term (over nine years).

CONCEPT SUMMARY 15–2

Interest on Installment Sales

	Imputed Interest Rate
General rule	Federal rate
Exceptions	
● Principal amount not over $2.8 million.[a]	Lesser of Federal rate or 9%
● Sale of land (with a calendar year ceiling of $500,000) between family members (the seller's spouse, brothers, sisters, ancestors, or lineal descendants).[b]	Lesser of Federal rate or 6%

	Method of Accounting for Interest	
	Seller's Interest Income	**Buyer's Interest Expense**
General rule[c]	Accrual	Accrual
Exceptions		
● Total payments under the contract are $250,000 or less.[d]	Taxpayer's overall method	Taxpayer's overall method
● Sale of a farm (sales price of $1 million or less).[e]	Taxpayer's overall method	Taxpayer's overall method
● Sale of a principal residence.[f]	Taxpayer's overall method	Taxpayer's overall method
● Sale for a note with a principal amount of not over $2 million, the seller is on the cash basis, the property sold is not inventory, and the buyer agrees to report expense by the cash method.[g]	Cash	Cash

a § 1274A.
b §§ 1274(c)(3)(F) and 483(e).
c §§ 1274(a) and 1272(a)(3).
d §§ 1274(c)(3)(C) and 483.
e §§ 1274(c)(3)(A) and 483.
f §§ 1274(c)(3)(B) and 483.
g § 1274A(c).

Congress has created several exceptions regarding the rate at which interest is imputed and the method of accounting for the interest income and expense. The general rules and exceptions are summarized in Concept Summary 15–2.

Related-Party Sales of Nondepreciable Property.   Because of favorable judicial authority, it was possible (with proper planning) to use the installment sales approach in sales between related parties.

EXAMPLE 23   F and D (father and daughter) each own substantial investment properties. F would like to sell a capital asset that has a basis of $20,000 and a value of $100,000. He could easily sell the property for cash, but that would result in a

taxable gain for the year. To defer the tax while enjoying the proceeds of the sale, F and D could structure transactions as follows:

First Disposition. F sells the asset to D for $100,000 and receives $10,000 cash and a $90,000 interest-bearing long-term note. In the year of the sale, he reports a gain of $8,000, computed as follows:

$$\frac{\$100{,}000 - \$20{,}000}{\$100{,}000} \times \$10{,}000 = \$8{,}000$$

F has a $72,000 deferred gain.

Second Disposition. D has a basis in the asset of $100,000 (cost). Soon after purchasing the asset from F, D sells it on the open market for $100,000. The net result of the two transactions is that the family unit (F and D) has $100,000 cash and a deferred tax liability that will not come due until the future, when D pays F the principal on the note. The interest payments will be a wash within the family, that is, F's income will be offset by D's deduction. □

Although transactions as depicted in Example 23 had to be carefully planned, before 1980 they could succeed. Obviously, this scheme was too good to be true. Thus, Congress added a provision to the Code to close this loophole. The basic approach of the related-party installment sales rules is to assume that the proceeds of the second sale are used to pay the note owed to the first seller. Thus, the deferred gain from the first disposition is accelerated to the date of the second disposition.

EXAMPLE 24   Assume the same facts as in Example 23, except D sold the asset for $110,000. D realized and must recognize a $10,000 gain, and F must recognize his previously deferred $72,000 gain, even though D did not retire the note payable to F. □

A realized loss from the second sale complicates the analysis. The first seller is deemed to have received in the year of the second sale the *lesser* of the following:

- The total amount realized from the second disposition.
- The total contract price reduced by the total amount already received.

However, even with this modification of the rules, Congress did not eliminate the benefits of all related-party installment sales:

- Related parties include the first seller's brothers, sisters, ancestors, lineal descendants, controlled corporations, and partnerships, trusts, and estates in which the seller has an interest.
- There is no acceleration if the second disposition occurs more than two years after the first sale.

Thus, if the taxpayer can sell the property to an unrelated party (not a related party) or patient family member, the intrafamily installment sale is still a powerful tax planning tool. There are other exceptions that can be applied in some circumstances.

Related-Party Sales of Depreciable Property.   The installment method cannot be used to report a gain on the sale of depreciable property to a controlled entity. The purpose of this rule is to prevent the seller from deferring gain (until collections are received) while the related purchaser is enjoying a stepped-up basis for depreciation purposes.

The prohibition on the use of the installment method applies to sales between the taxpayer and a partnership or corporation in which the taxpayer holds a more-than-50 percent interest. Constructive ownership rules must be considered in applying the ownership test (e.g., the taxpayer is considered to own stock owned by a spouse and certain other family members). However, if the taxpayer can establish that tax avoidance was not a principal purpose of the transaction, the installment method can be used to report the gain.

EXAMPLE 25   P purchased an apartment building from his controlled corporation, S Corporation. P was short of cash at the time of the purchase (December 1990), but was to collect a large cash payment in January 1991. The agreement required P to pay the entire arm's length price in January 1991. There were good business reasons for P's acquiring the building. S Corporation should be able to convince the IRS that tax avoidance was not a principal purpose for the installment sale because the tax benefits are not overwhelming. The corporation will report all of the gain in the year following the year of sale, and the building must be expensed over 27.5 years (the cost recovery period). □

Disposition of Installment Obligations

The law prevents taxpayers from avoiding the recognition of deferred gross profit on installment obligations through various means (e.g., the sale of installment notes or the distribution of such notes to shareholders). The taxpayer must pay the tax on the portion of gross profits that was previously deferred as follows:

If an installment obligation is satisfied at other than its face value or distributed, transmitted, sold, or otherwise disposed of, gain or loss shall result to the extent of the difference between the basis of the obligation and either of the following:

• The amount realized, in the case of satisfaction at other than face value or in a sale or exchange.

• The fair market value of the obligation at the time of distribution, transmission, or disposition, in the case of the distribution, transmission, or disposition other than by sale or exchange.

The gift of an installment note will be treated as a taxable disposition by the donor. The amount realized from the cancellation is the face amount of the note if the parties (obligor and obligee) are related to each other.

EXAMPLE 26   F cancels a note issued by D (F's daughter) that arose in connection with the sale of property. At the time of the cancellation, the note had a basis to F of $10,000, a face amount of $25,000, and a fair market value of $20,000. Presuming the initial sale by F qualified as an installment sale, the cancellation would result in gain of $15,000 ($25,000 − $10,000) to F. □

Certain exceptions to the recognition of gain provisions are provided for transfers of installment obligations pursuant to tax-free incorporations under § 351, contributions of capital to a partnership, certain corporate liquidations, transfers due to the taxpayer's death, and transfers between spouses or incident to divorce. In such instances, the deferred profit is merely shifted to the transferee, who is responsible for the payment of tax on the subsequent collections of the installment obligations.

Pledging Installment Obligations

Borrowing and using installment obligations as security for the loan may be a means of receiving the cash from installment obligations without recognizing income. However, the Code specifically requires that a seller of property (other than farming property) must treat amounts borrowed as collections on the contract, where the installment obligations serve as security for the debt.[13] This acceleration of gain applies to an amount borrowed when the indebtedness is secured by an installment obligation arising from the sale of property (realty and personalty) for more than $150,000 and the property was either used in the taxpayer's trade or business or held for the production of rental income.

EXAMPLE 27	In 1990, T sold land used in his business for $500,000 (basis of $150,000). T received $200,000 cash and an interest-bearing note for $300,000 due in 1993. In 1991, T borrowed $250,000 using the note as security. The receipt of the loan proceeds will cause T to recognize gain of $175,000 [($500,000 − $150,000)/$500,000 × $250,000]. When T collects the note in 1993, he must recognize the balance of the realized gain of $35,000 (.70 × $50,000). ☐

Interest on Deferred Taxes

With the installment method, the seller earns interest on the receivable. The receivable includes the deferred gain. Thus, one could reason that the seller is earning interest on the deferred taxes. Some commentators reason that the government is, in effect, making interest-free loans to taxpayers who report gains by the installment method. Following the line of reasoning that the amount of the deferred taxes is a loan, in some situations, the taxpayer is required to pay interest on the deferred taxes.[14]

Electing Out of the Installment Method

A taxpayer can *elect not to use* the installment method. The election is made by reporting on a timely filed return the gain computed by the taxpayer's usual method of accounting (cash or accrual). However, the Regulations provide that the amount realized by a cash basis taxpayer cannot be less than the value of the property sold. This rule differs from the usual cash basis accounting rules (discussed earlier),[15] which measure the amount realized in terms of the fair market value of the property received. The net effect of the Regulations is to allow the cash basis taxpayer to report his or her gain as an accrual basis taxpayer. The election has frequent application to year-end sales by taxpayers who expect to be in a higher tax bracket in the following year.

---

13. §§ 453A(b) and (d).
14. See § 453A for details.

15. Refer to chapter 3, Example 9.

EXAMPLE 28
On December 31, 1990, T sold land to B for $20,000 (fair market value). The cash was to be paid on January 4, 1991. T is a cash basis taxpayer, and his basis in the land is $8,000. He expects to have substantially greater taxable income in 1991 than he did in 1990.

The transaction constitutes an installment sale because a payment will be received in a tax year after the tax year of disposition. B's promise to pay T is an installment obligation, and under the Regulations, the value of the installment obligation is equal to the value of the property sold ($20,000). If T were to elect out of the installment method, he would report a $12,000 gain ($20,000 − $8,000) in 1990 rather than in 1991. □

Permission of the IRS is required to revoke an election not to use the installment method.

Long-Term Contracts

A *long-term contract* is a building, installation, construction, or manufacturing contract that is entered into but not completed within the same tax year. Furthermore, a manufacturing contract is long term only if the contract is to manufacture (1) a unique item not normally carried in finished goods inventory or (2) items that normally require more than 12 calendar months to complete.

EXAMPLE 29
T, a calendar year taxpayer, entered into two contracts during the year. One contract was to construct a building foundation. Work was to begin in October 1989 and was to be completed by June 1990. The contract is long term because it will not be entered into and completed in the same tax year. The fact that the contract requires less than 12 calendar months to complete is not relevant because the contract is not for manufacturing. The second contract was for architectural services to be performed over two years. These services will not qualify for long-term contract treatment because the taxpayer will not build, install, construct, or manufacture a product. □

Generally, the taxpayer must accumulate all of the direct and indirect costs incurred under a contract. This will require the accumulation of production costs and the allocation of these costs to individual contracts. Furthermore, mixed services costs, costs that benefit contracts as well as the general administrative operations of the business, must be allocated to production. Concept Summary 15–3 (see page 15–26) contains a list of the types of costs that must be accumulated and allocated to contracts. Reasonable bases for cost allocations must be developed by the taxpayer.

EXAMPLE 30
C, Inc., uses detailed cost accumulation records to assign labor and materials to its contracts in progress. The total cost of fringe benefits is allocated to a contract on the following basis:

$$\frac{\text{Labor on the contract}}{\text{Total salaries and labor}} \times \text{Total cost of fringe benefits}$$

CONCEPT SUMMARY 15–3

Contract Costs, Mixed Services Costs, and Current Expense Items for Contracts

	Contracts Eligible for the Completed Contract Method	Other Contracts
Contract costs		
Direct materials (a part of the finished product).	Capital	Capital
Indirect materials (consumed in production but not in the finished product, e.g., grease and oil for equipment).	Capital	Capital
Storage, handling, and insurance on materials.	Expense	Capital
Direct labor (worked on the product).	Capital	Capital
Indirect labor (worked in the production process but not directly on the product, e.g., a construction supervisor).	Capital	Capital
Fringe benefits for direct and indirect labor (e.g., vacation, sick pay, unemployment, and other insurance).	Capital	Capital
Pension costs for direct and indirect labor:		
• Current cost.	Expense	Capital
• Past service costs.	Expense	Capital
Depreciation on production facilities:		
• For financial statements.	Capital	Capital
• Tax depreciation in excess of financial statements.	Expense	Capital
Depreciation on idle facilities.	Expense	Expense
Property taxes, insurance, rent, and maintenance on production facilities.	Capital	Capital
Bidding expenses—successful.	Expense	Capital
Bidding expenses—unsuccessful.	Expense	Expense
Interest to finance real estate construction.	Capital	Capital
Interest to finance personal property:		
• Construction period of one year or less.	Expense	Expense
• Construction period exceeds one year and costs exceed $1,000,000.	Capital	Capital
• Construction period exceeds two years.	Capital	Capital
Mixed services costs		
Personnel operations.	Expense	Allocate
Data processing.	Expense	Allocate
Purchasing.	Expense	Allocate
Selling, general, and administrative expenses (including an allocated share of mixed services)	Expense	Expense
Losses	Expense	Expense

Similarly, storage and handling costs for materials are allocated to contracts on the following basis:

$$\frac{\text{Contract materials}}{\text{Materials purchases}} \times \text{Storage and handling cost}$$

The cost of the personnel operations, a mixed services cost, is allocated between production and general administration based on the number of employees in each function. The personnel cost allocated to production is allocated to individual contracts on the basis of the formula used to allocate fringe benefits. □

The accumulated costs are deducted when the revenue from the contract is recognized. Generally, two methods of accounting are used in varying circumstances to determine when the revenue from a contract is recognized. These are as follows:

1. The completed contract method.

2. The percentage of completion method.

The completed contract method may be used for (1) home construction contracts (contracts in which at least 80 percent of the estimated costs are for dwelling units in buildings with four or fewer units) and (2) certain other real estate construction contracts. Other real estate contracts can qualify for the completed contract method if the following requirements are satisfied:

• The contract is expected to be completed within the two-year period beginning on the commencement date of the contract.

• The contract is performed by a taxpayer whose average annual gross receipts for the three taxable years preceding the taxable year in which the contract is entered into do not exceed $10 million.

All other contractors must use the percentage of completion method.

Completed Contract Method.   Under the *completed contract method*, no revenue from the contract is recognized until the contract is completed and accepted. However, a taxpayer may not delay completion of a contract for the principal purpose of deferring tax.

In some instances, the original contract price may be disputed or the buyer may want additional work to be done on a long-term contract. If the disputed amount is substantial (it is not possible to determine whether a profit or loss will ultimately be realized on the contract), the Regulations provide that no amount of income or loss is recognized until the dispute is resolved. In all other cases, the profit or loss (reduced by the amount in dispute) is recognized in the current period on completion of the contract. However, additional work may need to be performed with respect to the disputed contract. In this case, the difference between the amount in dispute and the actual cost of the additional work will be recognized in the year such work is completed rather than in the year in which the dispute is resolved.[16]

EXAMPLE 31   B, a calendar year taxpayer utilizing the completed contract method of accounting, constructed a building for C pursuant to a long-term contract. The

---

16.   Reg. § 1.451–3(d)(2)(ii)–(vii), Example (2).

gross contract price was $500,000. B finished construction in 1990 at a cost of $475,000. When C examined the building, he insisted that the building be repainted or the contract price be reduced. The estimated cost of repainting is $10,000. Since under the terms of the contract, B would be assured of a profit of at least $15,000 ($500,000 − $475,000 − $10,000) even if the dispute was ultimately resolved in favor of C, B must include $490,000 ($500,000 − $10,000) in gross income and is allowed deductions of $475,000 for 1990.

In 1991, B and C resolved the dispute, and B repainted certain portions of the building at a cost of $6,000. B must include $10,000 in 1991 gross income and may deduct the $6,000 expense in that year. □

EXAMPLE 32   Assume the same facts as in the previous example, except the estimated cost of repainting the building is $50,000. Since the resolution of the dispute completely in C's favor would mean that there would be a net loss on the contract ($500,000 − $475,000 − $50,000 = $25,000 loss), no income or loss would be recognized until the year in which the dispute is resolved. □

Frequently the contractor will receive payment at various stages of completion. For example, when the contract is 50 percent complete, the contractor may receive 50 percent of the contract price less a retainage. The taxation of these payments is generally governed by Regulation § 1.451–5 "advance payments for goods and long-term contracts" (discussed in chapter 3). Generally, contractors are permitted to defer the advance payments until such payments are recognized as income under the taxpayer's method of accounting.

Percentage of Completion Method.   In 1986, Congress began limiting the circumstances under which the completed contract method could be used. However, rather than totally disallowing the use of the completed contract method, Congress created the *percentage of completion-capitalized cost method.* Under this method, 40 percent of the items produced under a contract were accounted for by the percentage of completion method, and the remaining 60 percent could be accounted for under the completed contract method. Subsequent legislation increased the 40 percent initially to 70 percent and finally to 90 percent. The Revenue Reconciliation Act of 1989 effectively repealed the percentage of completion-capitalized cost method. Therefore, only the percentage of completion method can be used to account for long-term contracts unless the taxpayer qualifies for one of the two exceptions which permit the completed contract method to be used (home construction contracts and certain other real estate construction contracts).

Under the *percentage of completion method,* a portion of the gross contract price is included in income during each period. The revenue accrued each period is computed as follows:

$$\frac{C}{T} \times P$$

Where C = Contract costs incurred during the period
T = Estimated total cost of the contract
P = Contract price

All of the costs allocated to the contract during the period are deductible from the accrued revenue. Because T in the above formula is an estimate that frequently differs from total actual costs, which are not known until the contract has been completed, the profit on a contract for a particular period may be overstated or understated.

EXAMPLE 33   B, Inc., entered into a contract that was to take two years to complete, with estimated total costs of $225,000. The contract price was $300,000. Costs of the contract for 1990, the first year, totaled $135,000. The gross profit reported by the percentage of completion method for 1990 was $45,000 [($135,000/$225,000 × $300,000) − $135,000]. The contract was completed at the end of 1991 at a total cost of $270,000. In retrospect, 1990 profit should have been $15,000 [($135,000/$270,000 × $300,000) − $135,000]. Thus, taxes were overpaid in 1990. □

A *de minimis* rule enables the contractor to delay the recognition of income for a particular contract under the percentage of completion method. If less than 10 percent of the estimated contract costs have been incurred by the end of the taxable year, the taxpayer can elect to defer the recognition of income and the related costs until the taxable year in which cumulative contract costs are at least 10 percent of the estimated contract costs.

Lookback Provisions.   In the year a contract is completed, a *lookback* provision requires the recalculation of annual profits reported on the contract accounted for by the percentage of completion method. Interest is paid to the taxpayer if there was an overpayment of taxes, and interest is payable by the taxpayer if there was an underpayment.

EXAMPLE 34   Assume B, Inc., in Example 33, was in the 34% tax bracket in both years and the relevant interest rate was 10%. For 1990, the company paid excess taxes of $10,200 [($45,000 − $15,000) × .34]. When the contract is completed at the end of 1991, B, Inc., should receive interest of $1,020 for one year on the tax overpayment ($10,200 × .10). □

TAX PLANNING CONSIDERATIONS

Taxable Year

Under the general rules for tax years, partnerships and S corporations frequently will be required to use a calendar year. However, if the partnership or S corporation can demonstrate a business purpose for a fiscal year, the IRS will allow the entity to use the requested year. The advantage to the fiscal year is that the calendar year partners and S corporation shareholders may be able to defer from tax the income earned from the close of the fiscal year until the end of the calendar year. Tax advisers for these entities should apply the IRS's gross receipts test described in Rev.Proc. 87–32 to determine if permission for the fiscal year will be granted.

Cash Method of Accounting

The cash method of accounting gives the taxpayer considerable control over the recognition of expenses and some control over the recognition of income. This method can be used by proprietorships, partnerships, and small corporations (gross receipts of $5 million or less) that provide services (inventories are not material to the service business). Farmers (except certain farming corporations) can also use the cash method.

Installment Method

Unlike the accrual and cash methods, the installment method results in an interest-free loan (of deferred taxes) from the government. Thus, the installment method is a powerful tax planning tool and should be considered when a sale of eligible property is being planned. Note, however, that the provision that requires interest to be paid on the deferred taxes on certain installment obligations reduces this benefit.

Related Parties. Intrafamily installment sales can still be a useful family tax planning tool. If the related party holds the property more than two years, a subsequent sale will not accelerate the gain from the first disposition. Patience and forethought are rewarded.

The 6 percent limitation on imputed interest on sales of land between family members enables the seller to convert ordinary income into capital gain, or make what is, in effect, a nontaxable gift. If the selling price is raised to adjust for the low interest rate charges on an installment sale, the seller has more capital gain but less ordinary income than would be realized from a sale to an unrelated party. If the selling price is not raised and the specified interest of 6 percent is charged, the seller enables the relative to have the use of the property without having to pay for its full market value. Moreover, this bargain sale is not a taxable gift.

Disposition of Installment Obligations. A disposition of an installment obligation is also a serious matter. Gifts of the obligations will accelerate income to the seller. The list of taxable and nontaxable dispositions of installment obligations should not be trusted to memory. In each instance where transfers of installment obligations are contemplated, the practitioner should conduct research to be sure he or she knows the consequences.

PROBLEM MATERIALS

Discussion Questions

1. X recently began conducting an office supply business as a corporation. Z began conducting his law practice through a corporation. Neither corporation has made an S election. What tax year alternatives are available to the X business that are not available to the Z business?

2. Z Company's tax return indicated that it was for the period beginning June 28, 1990, and ending July 3, 1991. How could a tax return include a period of more than 12 months?

3. What do you think of a proposed change in the tax law to allow S corporations and partnerships to select a tax year independent of the tax years of the shareholders

and partners? The change is supposedly justified on the basis that tax accountants should be allowed to spread their work more evenly throughout the year.

4. D is an orthopedic surgeon who practices in a ski area. He recently incorporated his practice and elected S corporation treatment. D's brother has recommended that the corporation elect a year ending April 30th, right after the close of the ski season. What is your advice to D?

5. T Corporation began business on October 29, 1989. The end of July would be a convenient time for the company to close its tax year. In July 1990, the president of the company informs you of his desired tax year. Can T adopt a July 31 year-end and, if so, is annualization required?

6. In 1990, T, a cash basis taxpayer, erroneously reported as dividend income an amount received from a corporation. The payment was actually a recovery of capital. In 1991, T discovered the error and amended her 1990 Federal and state income tax returns. As a result, T received a refund of state taxes that she had deducted as an itemized deduction on her Federal income tax return in 1990. T was in the 33% marginal bracket in 1990 when the state taxes were deducted, but she is only in the 15% bracket in 1991 when the state tax refund is received. Will T be allowed to claim the erroneous deduction in the high-bracket year (1990) and treat the refund as income for the lower-bracket year (1991)?

7. X Corporation is a retailer, and its annual gross receipts have never exceeded $5,000,000. Y Corporation is a retailer whose gross receipts have never been less than $5,000,000 for a tax year. X and Y are C corporations and have been in existence for more than four years. What accounting method options are available to each corporation for the following types of income and deductions?
    a. Inventories.
    b. Accrued payroll taxes.
    c. Sales of merchandise.
    d. Income from repair services.

8. X owns bonds and stocks that pay interest and dividends. He is also a partner in a partnership in the rental business and is the sole shareholder of a grocery store that is operated as an S corporation. If the S corporation uses the accrual method, does this mean that X's interest, dividends, and partnership income must be determined by the accrual method?

9. B, a certified public accountant, recently obtained a new client. The client is a retail grocery store that has used the cash method to report its income since it began doing business. Will B incur any liability if he prepares the tax return in accordance with the cash method and does not advise the client of the necessity of seeking the IRS's permission to change to the accrual method?

10. In December 1990, a cash basis taxpayer paid January through June 1991 management fees in connection with his rental properties. The fees were $4,000 per month. Compute the 1990 expense under the following assumptions:
    a. The fees were paid by an individual who derived substantially all of his income from the properties.
    b. The fees were paid by a tax-shelter partnership.

11. Why is the accrual method required for sales and cost of goods sold when inventories are material to the business?

12. Compare the cash basis and accrual basis of accounting as applied to the following:
    a. Fixed assets.
    b. Prepaid rental income.
    c. Prepaid interest expense.

d. A note received for services performed if the market value and face amount of the note differ.

13. When are reserves for estimated expenses allowed for tax purposes? What is the role of the matching concept in tax accounting?

14. What difference does it make whether the taxpayer or the IRS initiates the change in accounting method?

15. X has made Y an offer on the purchase of a capital asset. X will pay (1) $200,000 cash or (2) $50,000 cash and a 12% installment note for $150,000 guaranteed by City Bank of New York. If Y sells for $200,000 cash, she will invest the after-tax proceeds in certificates of deposit yielding 12% interest. Y's cost of the asset is $25,000. Why would Y prefer the installment sale?

16. Which of the following are eligible for installment reporting? Assume some payments are received after the year of sale and the sales are for gains.
    a. Fully depreciated equipment sold for $50,000. The original cost of the equipment was $75,000.
    b. Sale of a tractor by a farm equipment dealer.
    c. Sale of stock in a family controlled corporation.
    d. Sale of residential lots.

17. In 1990, the taxpayer sold some real estate and received an installment note. The sale met all of the requirements for using the installment method, but the taxpayer did not know that the installment method could be used. Thus, the entire gain was reported in the year of sale. In 1991, the taxpayer learns that he could have used the installment method. Is there anything he can do? Explain.

18. T, a cash basis taxpayer, sold land in December 1990. At the time of the sale, T received $10,000 cash and a note for $90,000 due in 90 days. T expects to be in a much higher tax bracket in 1991. Can T report the entire gain in 1990?

19. In 1990, S, a cash basis taxpayer, sold land to P, an accrual basis taxpayer. The principal and interest were due in two years, and the interest was equal to the Federal rate. Neither the buyer nor the seller is a dealer in real estate. Indicate when the buyer and seller will report their interest expense and income in each of the following cases:
    a. The selling price is $2.5 million.
    b. The selling price is $200,000.
    c. The selling price is $600,000.

20. On June 1, 1988, Father sold land to Son for $100,000. Father reported the gain by the installment method, with the gain to be spread over five years. In May 1990, Son received an offer of $150,000 for the land, to be paid over three years. What would be the tax consequences of Son's sale?

21. In 1989, T sold a building to his 100% controlled corporation. The entire purchase price is to be paid in 1990. When should T report the gain on the sale of the building?

22. T is considering selling his stock in a family-owned corporation for $6 million. The buyer would prefer to pay the price in installments. What is the minimum amount T should receive in the year of sale?

23. The taxpayer began work on a contract in June 1990 and completed the contract in April 1991.
    a. Can the percentage of completion method be used to report the income from the contract?
    b. If the taxpayer in (a) uses the accrual basis to report income, assuming no advance payments are received, when will the income be recognized?

Problems

24. L, M, and N are unrelated corporations engaged in real estate development. The three corporations formed a joint venture (treated as a partnership) to develop a tract of land. Assuming the venture does not have a natural business year, what tax year must the joint venture adopt under the following circumstances?

		Tax Year Ending	Interest in Joint Venture
a.	L	Sept. 30	33%
	M	June 30	33%
	N	March 31	34%
b.	L	Sept. 30	20%
	M	June 30	60%
	N	March 31	20%
c.	L	Jan. 31	30%
	M	Jan. 31	25%
	N	Dec. 31	45%

25. Z conducted his professional practice through Z, Inc. The corporation uses a fiscal year ending September 30 even though the business purpose test for a fiscal year cannot be satisfied. For the year ending September 30, 1990, the corporation paid Z a salary of $150,000, and during the period January through September 1990, the corporation paid Z a salary of $120,000.

    a. How much salary should Z receive during the period October 1 through December 31, 1990?

    b. Assume Z received only $30,000 salary during the period October 1 through December 31, 1990. What would be the consequences to Z, Inc.?

26. P Corporation is in the business of sales and home deliveries of fuel oil and currently uses a calendar year for reporting its taxable income. However, P's natural business year ends April 30. For the short period, January 1, 1990, through April 30, 1990, the corporation earned $30,000. Assume the corporate tax rates are as follows: 15% on taxable income of $50,000 or less, 25% on taxable income over $50,000 but not over $75,000, and 34% on taxable income over $75,000.

    a. What must P Corporation do to change its taxable year?

    b. Compute P Corporation's tax for the short period.

27. L, a cash basis taxpayer, owned a building that he leased to T. In 1990, T prepaid the 1991 rent. During 1990, the building was destroyed by fire. Under the lease agreement, L was required to refund $6,000 to T. Also, in June 1990, L paid the insurance premium on the property for the next 12 months. After the building was destroyed, in 1991 L got a $600 refund on the insurance premium. L was in the 33% marginal tax bracket in 1990 and in the 15% marginal bracket in 1991. What are the effects of the refunds on L's 1991 tax liability?

28. Compute the taxpayer's income or deductions for 1990 using (1) the cash basis and (2) the accrual basis for each of the following:

    a. In 1990, the taxpayer purchased new equipment for $100,000. The taxpayer paid $25,000 in cash and gave a $75,000 interest-bearing note for the balance. The equipment has an ACRS life of five years, the mid-year convention applies, and the § 179 election was not made.

    b. In December 1990, the taxpayer collected $10,000 for January rents. In January 1991, the taxpayer collected $2,000 for December 1990 rents.

c. In December 1990, the taxpayer paid office equipment insurance premiums for January–June 1991 of $30,000.

29. Which of the following businesses must use the accrual method of accounting?

   a. A corporation with annual gross receipts of $12 million from equipment rentals.

   b. A partnership (not a tax shelter) engaged in farming and with annual gross receipts of $8 million.

   c. A corporation that acts as an insurance agent, with annual gross receipts of $1 million.

   d. A manufacturer with annual gross receipts of $600,000.

   e. A retailer with annual gross receipts of $250,000.

30. When is the economic performance test satisfied in the following cases?

   a. R Corporation sponsored a contest to promote the company's products. In 1990, the winner was announced. The winner is to receive $10,000 each year for 10 years.

   b. S Corporation is a strip miner and is liable for reclaiming the land. The estimated reclamation cost for land mined in 1990 was $200,000. The company hired Z Corporation to perform the work. Z reclaimed the land in 1991, and S Corporation paid Z in 1992.

   c. T Corporation guarantees its products against all defects for 12 months. At the end of 1990, several customers had returned products for corrections of defects. The estimated cost of servicing the goods was $150,000. All claims were valid, and the claims were satisfied in 1991.

   d. P Corporation had state taxable income of $100,000 for 1990. However, the taxes on the income were not actually paid until the company filed its tax return in March 1991.

31. In 1990, the taxpayer was required to switch from the cash to the accrual basis of accounting for sales and cost of goods sold. Taxable income for 1990 computed under the cash basis was $40,000. Relevant account balances were as follows:

	Beginning of the Year	End of the Year
Accounts receivable	$27,000	$30,000
Accounts payable	12,000	9,000
Inventory	6,000	4,000

Compute the following:

   a. The adjustment due to the change in accounting method.

   b. The accrual basis taxable income for 1990.

32. In 1990, the taxpayer changed from the cash to the accrual basis of accounting for sales, cost of goods sold, and accrued expenses. Taxable income for 1990 computed under the cash method was $45,000. Relevant account balances are as follows:

	Beginning of the Year	End of the Year
Accounts receivable	$ 3,000	$12,000
Accounts payable	–0–	–0–
Accrued expenses	2,000	1,000
Inventory	10,000	16,000

   a. Compute the accrual basis taxable income for 1990 and the adjustment due to the change in accounting method.

   b. Assuming the changes were voluntary, how will the adjustment due to the change be treated?

33. T, a cash basis taxpayer, has agreed to sell land to Z, Inc., a well-established and highly profitable company. Z is willing to (1) pay $100,000 cash or (2) pay $25,000 cash and the balance ($75,000) plus interest at 10% (the Federal rate) in two years. T is in the 35% marginal tax bracket (combined Federal and state) for all years, and he believes he can reinvest the sales proceeds and earn a 14% before-tax rate of return.

    a. Should T accept the deferred payments option if his basis in the land is $10,000?

    b. Do you think your results would change if T's basis in the land is $90,000?

34. S, who is not a dealer, sold an apartment house to P during 1991. The closing statement for the sale is as follows:

Total selling price		$100,000
Add: P's share of property taxes (6 months) paid by S		2,500
Less: S's 11% mortgage assumed by P	$55,000	
P's refundable binder ("earnest money") paid in 1990	1,000	
P's 11% installment note given to S	30,000	
S's real estate commissions and attorney's fees	7,500	(93,500)
Cash paid to S at closing		$ 9,000
Cash due from P = $9,000 + $7,500 expenses		$ 16,500

During 1991, S collected $4,000 in principal on the installment note and $2,000 interest. S's basis in the property was $70,000 [$85,000 − $15,000 (depreciation)], and there was $9,000 in potential depreciation recapture under § 1250. The Federal rate is 9%.

    a. Compute the following:

       1. Total gain.
       2. Contract price.
       3. Payments received in the year of sale.
       4. Recognized gain in the year of sale and the character of such gain.

    (*Hint:* Think carefully about the manner in which the property taxes are handled before you begin your computations.)

    b. Same as (a)(2) and (3), except S's basis in the property was $45,000.

    c. Assume that S was considering selling the apartment house but there was no mortgage on the property. Would there be any tax benefits if S borrowed on the property before the sale?

35. On June 30, 1990, T sold property for $250,000 cash on the date of sale and a $750,000 note due on September 30, 1991. No interest was stated in the contract. The present value of the note (using 13.2%, which was the Federal rate) was $640,000. T's basis in the property was $400,000, and $40,000 of the gain was depreciation recapture under § 1245. Expenses of the sale totaled $10,000, and T was not a dealer in the property sold.

    a. Compute T's gain to be reported in 1990.

    b. Compute T's interest income for 1991.

36. On July 1, 1989, a cash basis taxpayer sold land for $400,000 due on the date of the sale and $3,000,000 principal and $763,200 interest (12%) due on June 30, 1991. The seller's basis in the land was $500,000. The Federal short-term rate was 13%, compounded semiannually.

    a. Compute the seller's interest income and gain in 1989, 1990, and 1991.

    b. Same as (a), except that the amount due in two years was $1,000,000 principal and $254,400 interest and the purchaser will use the cash method to account for interest.

37. On December 30, 1990, Father sold land to Son for $10,000 cash and a 7% installment note with a face amount of $190,000. In 1991, after paying $30,000 on the principal of the note, Son sold the land. In 1992, Son paid Father $25,000 on the note principal. Father's basis in the land was $50,000. Assuming Son sold the land for $250,000, compute Father's taxable gain in 1991.

38. X sold land to an unrelated party in 1989. X's basis in the land was $40,000, and the selling price was $100,000: $25,000 payable at closing and $25,000 (plus 10% interest) due January 1, 1990, 1991, and 1992. What would be the tax consequences of the following? [Treat each part independently and assume (1) X did not elect out of the installment method and (2) the installment obligations have values equal to their face amounts.]

    a. In 1990, X gave to his daughter the right to collect all future payments on the installment obligations.

    b. In 1990, after collecting the payment due on January 1, X transferred the installment obligation to his 100% controlled corporation in exchange for additional shares of stock.

    c. X received on December 31, 1990, the payment due on January 1, 1991. On December 15, 1991, X died, and the remaining installment obligation was transferred to X's estate. The estate collected the amount due on January 1, 1992.

39. The R Construction Company reports its income by the completed contract method. At the end of 1990, the company completed a contract to construct a building at a total cost of $980,000. The contract price was $1,200,000. However, the customer refused to accept the work and would not pay anything on the contract because he claimed the roof did not meet specifications. R's engineers estimated it would cost $140,000 to bring the roof up to the customer's standards. In 1991, the dispute was settled in the customer's favor; the roof was improved at a cost of $170,000, and the customer accepted the building and paid the $1,200,000.

    a. What would be the effects of the above on R's taxable income for 1990 and 1991?

    b. Same as (a), except R had $1,100,000 accumulated cost under the contract at the end of 1990.

40. X Company is a real estate construction company with average annual gross receipts of $3 million. X uses the completed contract method, and the contracts require 18 months to complete. Which of the following costs would be allocated to construction in progress by X?

    a. The payroll taxes on direct labor.

    b. The current services pension costs for employees whose wages are included in direct labor.

    c. Accelerated depreciation on equipment used on contracts.

    d. Sales tax on materials assigned to contracts.

    e. The past service costs for employees whose wages are included in direct labor.

    f. Bidding expenses for contracts awarded.

41. Indicate the accounting method that should be used to compute the income from the following contracts:

    a. A contract to build six jet aircraft.

    b. A contract to build a new home. The contractor's average annual gross receipts are $15 million.

    c. A contract to manufacture 3,000 pairs of boots for a large retail chain. The manufacturer has several contracts to produce the same boot for other retailers.

    d. A contract to pave a parking lot. The contractor's average annual gross receipts are $2 million.

42. The A Construction Company reports its income by the percentage of completion method. In 1990, the company entered into a contract to build a warehouse for $1,500,000. A estimated that the total cost of the contract would be $900,000. At the end of 1990, the total accumulated cost on the contract was $750,000. An architect estimated that the contract was 80% complete at the end of 1990. In 1991, the contract was completed at a total cost of $1,050,000.

    a. Determine A's profit on the contract that should be reported for 1990.

    b. Determine A's profit on the contract that should be reported for 1991.

    c. Under the lookback provisions, what are the consequences to A of having incorrectly estimated the costs of the contract?

16

CORPORATIONS: OPERATING RULES, ORGANIZATION, AND CAPITAL STRUCTURE

OBJECTIVES Summarize the income tax treatment of various forms of conducting a business.
Review the general income tax provisions applicable to individuals.
Establish the tax rules peculiar to corporations.
Describe the tax consequences of incorporating a new or existing business.
Describe the capital structure of a corporation and explain what it means for tax purposes.
Evaluate the corporate form as a means of conducting a trade or business.

Tax Treatment of Various Business Forms

Business operations can be conducted in a number of different forms. Among the various possibilities are the following:

- Sole proprietorships.
- Partnerships.
- Trusts and estates.
- Subchapter S corporations (also known as S corporations).
- Regular corporations (also called Subchapter C or C corporations).

For Federal income tax purposes, the distinction between these forms of business organizations becomes very important. A summary of the tax treatment of each form will highlight these distinctions:

1. Sole proprietorships are not separate taxable entities from the individual who owns the proprietorship. The owner of the business will therefore report all business transactions on his or her individual income tax return.

2. Partnerships are not subject to the income tax. Under the conduit concept, the various tax attributes of the partnership's operations flow through to the individual partners to be reported on their personal income tax returns (see Example 1). Although a partnership is not a tax-paying entity, it is a reporting entity. Form 1065 is used to aggregate partnership transactions for the tax year and to allocate their pass-through to the individual partners. The tax consequences of the partnership form of business organization are outlined in Subchapter K of the Internal Revenue Code and are the subject of chapter 21.

3. The income tax treatment of trusts and estates is in some respects similar and in others dissimilar to the partnership approach. In terms of similarity, income is taxed only once. However, tax may be imposed on the entity. Unlike a partnership, therefore, a trust or an estate may be subject to the Federal income tax. Whether the income will be taxed to a trust or an estate or to its beneficiaries generally depends on whether the income is retained by the entity or distributed to the beneficiaries. In the event of distribution, a modified form of the conduit principle is followed to preserve for the beneficiary the character of certain income (e.g., nontaxable interest on municipal bonds). The income taxation of trusts and estates is treated in chapter 26.

4. Subchapter S of the Code permits certain corporations to elect special tax treatment. Such special treatment generally means avoidance of any income tax at the corporate level. Subchapter S corporations, called S corporations, are treated like partnerships in that the owners of the entity report most of the corporate tax attributes (e.g., income, losses, capital gains and losses, § 1231 gains and losses, charitable contributions, tax-exempt interest) on their individual returns. S corporations and their shareholders are the subject of chapter 20.

5. The regular corporate form of doing business carries with it the imposition of the corporate income tax. For Federal income tax purposes, therefore, the corporation is recognized as a separate tax-paying entity. This produces what is known as a double tax effect. Income is taxed to the corporation as earned and taxed again to the shareholders as dividends when distributed. Also, the tax attributes of various types of income lose their identity as they pass

through the corporate entity. In other words, the corporation does not act as a conduit when making distributions to its shareholders.

EXAMPLE 1

During the current year, X Company receives tax-exempt interest, which is distributed to its owners. If X Company is a regular corporation, the distribution to the shareholders constitutes a dividend. The fact that it originated from tax-exempt interest is of no consequence. On the other hand, if X Company is a partnership or an S corporation, the tax-exempt interest retains its identity and passes through to the individual partners or owners. □

The tax consequences of operating a business in the regular corporate form fall within Subchapter C of the Code and are the subject of this chapter and chapters 17 and 18. Corporations that either accumulate earnings unreasonably or meet the definition of a personal holding company may be subject to further taxation. These so-called penalty taxes are imposed in addition to the corporate income tax and are discussed in chapter 19.

Clearly, then, the form of organization chosen to carry on a trade or business has a significant effect on Federal income tax consequences. Though tax considerations may not control the choice, it could be unfortunate if they are not taken into account.

WHAT IS A CORPORATION?

The first step in any discussion of the Federal income tax treatment of corporations must be definitional. More specifically, what is a corporation? At first glance, the answer to this question would appear to be quite simple. Merely look to the appropriate state law to determine whether the entity has satisfied the specified requirements for corporate status. Have articles of incorporation been drawn up and filed with the state regulatory agency? Has a charter been granted? Has stock been issued to shareholders? These are all points to consider.

Compliance with state law, although important, may not tell the full story as to whether or not an entity is to be recognized as a corporation for tax purposes. On the one hand, a corporation qualifying under state law may be disregarded as a taxable entity if it is a mere "sham." On the other hand, an organization not qualifying as a regular corporation under state law may be taxed as a corporation under the association approach. These two possibilities are discussed in the following sections.

Disregard of Corporate Entity

In most cases, the IRS and the courts will recognize a corporation legally constituted under state law. In exceptional situations, however, the corporate entity may be disregarded because it lacks substance.[1] The key to such treatment rests with the degree of business activity conducted at the corporate level. Thus,

---

1. The reader should bear in mind that the textual discussion relates to the classification of an entity for *Federal* income tax purposes. State corporate income taxes or other corporate taxes (e.g., franchise taxes) may still be imposed. An entity may quite possibly be treated as a corporation for state tax purposes and not for Federal, and vice versa. This will become even more apparent when dealing with S corporations (chapter 20) because such status is not recognized by some states.

the more the corporation does in connection with its trade or business, the less likely it will be treated as a sham and disregarded as a separate entity.[2]

Whether the IRS or the taxpayers will attempt to disregard the corporate entity must depend on the circumstances of each particular situation. More often than not, the IRS may be trying to disregard (or "collapse") a corporation to make the corporation's income taxable directly to the shareholders. In other situations, a corporation might be trying to avoid the corporate income tax or to permit its shareholders to take advantage of excess corporate deductions and losses.[3]

Theoretically, the disregard-of-corporate-entity approach should be equally available to both the IRS and the taxpayers. From a practical standpoint, however, taxpayers have enjoyed considerably less success than has the IRS. Courts generally conclude that since the taxpayers created the corporation in the first place, they should not be permitted to later disregard it in order to avoid taxes.

Associations Taxed as Corporations

Section 7701(a)(3) defines a corporation as including "associations, joint stock companies, and insurance companies." What Congress intended by the inclusion of associations in the definition has never been entirely clear. Judicial decisions have clarified the status of associations and the relationship between associations and corporations.

The designation given to the entity under state law is not controlling. In one case, what was a business trust under state law was deemed to be an association (and therefore taxable as a corporation) for Federal income tax purposes.[4] In another case, a partnership of physicians was held to be an association even though state law in the tax year in question prohibited the practice of medicine in the corporate form.[5] Therefore, the partnership was subject to the Federal income tax rules applicable to corporations.

Whether or not an entity will be considered an association for Federal income tax purposes depends upon the number of corporate characteristics it possesses. According to court decisions and Reg. § 301.7701–2(a), corporate characteristics include the following:

1. Associates.

2. An objective to carry on a business and divide the gains therefrom.

3. Continuity of life.

4. Centralized management.

5. Limited liability.

6. Free transferability of interests.

The Regulations state that an unincorporated organization shall not be classified as an association unless it possesses more corporate than noncorporate characteristics. In making the determination, the characteristics common to both corporate and noncorporate business organizations shall be disregarded.

---

2. A classic case in this area is *Paymer v. Comm.*, 45–2 USTC ¶9353, 33 AFTR 1536, 150 F.2d 334 (CA–2, 1945). Here, two corporations were involved. The Court chose to disregard one corporate entity but to recognize the other.

3. An election under Subchapter S would accom-

plish this if it were timely and the parties qualified. See chapter 20.

4. *Morrissey v. Comm.*, 36–1 USTC ¶9020, 16 AFTR 1274, 56 S.Ct. 289 (USSC, 1936).

5. *U.S. v. Kintner*, 54–2 USTC ¶9626, 47 AFTR 995, 216 F.2d 418 (CA–9, 1954).

Both corporations and partnerships generally have associates (shareholders and partners) and an objective to carry on a business and divide the gains. In testing whether a particular partnership is an association, these criteria would be disregarded. It then becomes a matter of determining whether the partnership possesses a majority of the remaining corporate characteristics (items 3 through 6). Does the partnership terminate upon the withdrawal or death of a partner (no continuity of life)? Is the management of the partnership centralized, or do all partners participate therein? Are all partners individually liable for the debts of the partnership, or is the liability of some limited to their actual investment in the partnership (a limited partnership)? May a partner freely transfer his or her interest without the consent of the other partners? Courts have ruled that any partnership lacking two or more of these characteristics will not be classified as an association. Conversely, any partnership having three or more of these characteristics will be classified as an association.

For trusts, the first two characteristics would have to be considered in testing for association status. The conventional type of trust often does not have associates and usually restricts its activities to handling investments rather than carrying on a trade or business. These characteristics, however, are common to corporations. Consequently, whether a trust qualifies as an association depends upon the satisfaction of the first two corporate characteristics.

From a taxpayer's standpoint, the desirability of association status turns on the tax implications involved. In some cases, the parties may find it advantageous to have the entity taxed as a corporation, while in others they may not. These possibilities are explored at length under Tax Planning Considerations in this chapter.

An Introduction to the Income Taxation of Corporations

An Overview of Corporate versus Individual Income Tax Treatment

In any discussion of how corporations are treated under the Federal income tax, the best approach is to compare such treatment with that applicable to individual taxpayers.

Similarities. Gross income of a corporation is determined in much the same manner as it is for individuals. Thus, gross income includes compensation for services rendered, income derived from a business, gains from dealings in property, interest, rents, royalties, and dividends—to name only a few such items [§ 61(a)]. Both individuals and corporations are entitled to exclusions from gross income, although fewer exclusions are allowed for corporate taxpayers. Interest on municipal bonds is excluded from gross income whether the bondholder is an individual or a corporate taxpayer.

Gains and losses from property transactions are handled similarly. For example, whether a gain or loss is capital or ordinary depends upon the nature of the asset in the hands of the taxpayer making the taxable disposition. In defining what is not a capital asset, Code § 1221 makes no distinction between corporate and noncorporate taxpayers. In the area of nontaxable exchanges, corporations are like individuals in that they do not recognize gain or loss on a like-kind exchange (§ 1031) and they may defer recognized gain on an involuntary conversion of property (§ 1033). The nonrecognition of gain provisions dealing with the sale of a personal residence (§§ 121 and 1034) do not apply to corporations. Both corporations and individuals are vulnerable, however, to the disallowance of losses on

sales of property to related parties [§ 267(a)(1)] or on the wash sales of securities (§ 1091). The wash sales rules do not apply to individuals who are traders or dealers in securities or to corporations that are dealers if the sales of the securities are in the ordinary course of the corporation's business.

Upon the sale or other taxable disposition of depreciable property, the recapture rules (e.g., §§ 1245 and 1250) generally make no distinction between corporate and noncorporate taxpayers. [However, § 291(a) does cause a corporation to have more recapture on § 1250 property. This difference is discussed later in the chapter.]

The business deductions of corporations also parallel those available to individuals. Therefore, deductions will be allowed for all ordinary and necessary expenses paid or incurred in carrying on a trade or business under the general rule of § 162(a). Specific provision is made for the deductibility of interest, certain taxes, losses, bad debts, accelerated cost recovery, charitable contributions, net operating losses, research and experimental expenditures, and other less common deductions. No deduction will be permitted for interest paid or incurred on amounts borrowed to purchase or carry tax-exempt securities. The same holds true for expenses contrary to public policy and certain unpaid expenses and interest between related parties.

Many of the tax credits available to individuals can also be claimed by corporations. This is the case with the foreign tax credit. Not available to corporations are certain credits that are personal in nature, such as the child care credit, the credit for the elderly, and the earned income credit.

Dissimilarities.   Significant variations also exist in the income taxation of corporations and individuals. A major variation is that different tax rates apply to corporations (§ 11) and to individuals (§ 1). Corporate tax rates are discussed later in the chapter.

All allowable corporate deductions are treated as business deductions. Thus, the determination of adjusted gross income (AGI), so essential for individual taxpayers, has no relevance to corporations. Taxable income is simply computed by subtracting from gross income all allowable deductions and losses. Corporations thus need not be concerned with itemized deductions or the standard deduction. Likewise, the deduction for personal and dependency exemptions is not available to corporations.

Because corporations can have only business deductions and losses, they are not subject to the $100 floor on the deductible portion of casualty and theft losses and the limitation that nonbusiness casualty losses will be deductible only to the extent such losses exceed 10 percent of AGI.

EXAMPLE 2   During the current year, X, a calendar year taxpayer with AGI of $10,000, suffers a casualty loss of $4,000. If X is an individual, only $2,900 ($4,000 − $100 − $1,000) of the casualty loss can be deducted (assuming the loss is personal and there has been no actual insurance recovery and none is reasonably anticipated). Chances are the casualty loss can only be claimed as an itemized deduction and would not be available if X chose not to itemize. On the other hand, if X is a corporation, the item would be deductible in full as a business expense under § 162. □

Specific Provisions Compared

In comparing the tax treatment of individuals and corporations, the following areas warrant special discussion:

- Accounting periods and methods.
- Capital gains and losses.
- Recapture of depreciation.
- Passive losses.
- Charitable contributions.
- Net operating losses.
- Special deductions available only to corporations.

Accounting Periods and Methods

Accounting Periods. Corporations generally have the same choices of accounting periods as do individual taxpayers. Like an individual, a corporation may choose a calendar year or a fiscal year for reporting purposes. Corporations, however, enjoy greater flexibility in the selection of a tax year. For example, corporations usually can have different tax years from those of their shareholders. Also, newly formed corporations (as new taxpayers) usually have a choice of any approved accounting period without having to obtain the consent of the IRS.

Personal service corporations (PSCs) and S corporations are subject to severe restrictions in the use of fiscal years. The rules applicable to S corporations are discussed in chapter 20.

A PSC, often an association treated as a corporation (refer to the earlier discussion in this chapter), has as its principal activity the performance of personal services. Such services must be substantially performed by owner-employees and must be in the fields of health, law, engineering, architecture, accounting, actuarial science, performing arts, or consulting.[6]

Barring certain exceptions, PSCs must adopt a calendar year for tax purposes. The exceptions that permit the use of a fiscal year are discussed in chapter 15.[7]

Accounting Methods. As a general rule, the cash method of accounting is unavailable to regular corporations.[8] Exceptions apply in the following situations:

- S corporations.
- Corporations engaged in the trade or business of farming and timber.
- Qualified personal service corporations.
- Corporations with average annual gross receipts of $5 million or less. (In determining the $5 million or less test, the corporation would use the average of the three prior taxable years.)

Both individuals and corporations that maintain inventory for sale to customers are required to use the accrual method of accounting for determining sales and cost of goods sold.

Capital Gains and Losses

Capital gains and losses result from the taxable sales or exchanges of capital assets. Whether such gains and losses would be long term or short term depends upon the holding period of the assets sold or exchanged. Each year a taxpayer's long-term capital gains and losses are combined, and the result is either a *net* long-term

---

6. § 448(d).

7. §§ 444 and 280H.

8. § 448.

capital gain or a *net* long-term capital loss. A similar aggregation is made with short-term capital gains and losses, the result being a *net* short-term capital gain or a *net* short-term capital loss. The following combinations and results are possible:

1. A net long-term capital gain and a net short-term capital loss. These are combined, and the result is either a net capital gain or a net capital loss.

2. A net long-term capital gain and a net short-term capital gain. No further combination is made.

3. A net long-term capital loss and a net short-term capital gain. These are combined, and the result is either capital gain net income or a net capital loss.

4. A net long-term capital loss and a net short-term capital loss. No further combination is made.

Capital Gains.   Before the TRA of 1986, long-term capital gains (combination 2 and, possibly, combination 1) enjoyed favorable tax treatment. Individuals were allowed a 60 percent deduction, which meant that only 40 percent of net capital gains were subject to the income tax. For corporations, the gains were subject to either the applicable corporate rate or an alternative rate of 28 percent.

While retaining the capital gain and loss classification, the TRA of 1986 eliminated the preferential treatment previously allowed for net capital gains. Such gains are taxed at ordinary income tax rates. However, in the fall of 1989, the Bush administration attempted to reinstate favorable capital gains provisions. Although these provisions were not passed by Congress, it appears that the administration will continue to push for the changes.

Capital Losses.   Differences exist between corporate and noncorporate taxpayers in the income tax treatment of net capital losses (refer to combinations 3 and 4 and, possibly, to combination 1). Generally, *noncorporate* taxpayers (e.g., individuals) can deduct up to $3,000 of such net losses against other income.[9] Any remaining capital losses can be carried forward to future years until absorbed by capital gains or by the $3,000 deduction.[10] Carryovers do not lose their identity but remain either long term or short term.

EXAMPLE 3   T, an individual, incurs a net long-term capital loss of $7,500 for calendar year 1990. Assuming adequate taxable income, T may deduct $3,000 of this loss on his 1990 return. The remaining $4,500 ($7,500 − $3,000) of the loss is carried to 1991 and years thereafter until completely deducted. The $4,500 will be carried forward as a long-term capital loss. □

Unlike individuals, corporate taxpayers are not permitted to claim any net capital losses as a deduction against ordinary income. Capital losses, therefore, can be used only as an offset against capital gains. Corporations may, however, carry back net capital losses to three preceding years, applying them first to the earliest year in point of time. Carryforwards are allowed for a period of five years from the year of the loss. When carried back or forward, a long-term capital loss becomes a short-term capital loss.

---

9. The limitations on capital losses for both corporate and noncorporate taxpayers are contained in § 1211.

10. Carryback and carryover rules for both corporate and noncorporate taxpayers can be found in § 1212.

EXAMPLE 4   Assume the same facts as in Example 3, except that T is a corporation. None of the $7,500 long-term capital loss incurred in 1990 can be deducted in that year. T Corporation may, however, carry back the loss to years 1987, 1988, and 1989 (in this order) and apply it to any capital gains recognized in these years. If the carryback does not exhaust the loss, the loss may be carried forward to calendar years 1991, 1992, 1993, 1994, and 1995 (in this order). Either a carryback or a carryforward of the long-term capital loss converts it to a short-term capital loss. □

Recapture of Depreciation

Corporations have more recapture of depreciation under § 1250 than do individuals. Depreciation recapture for § 1245 property is computed in the same manner for individuals and for corporations. However, § 291(a)(1) provides for additional recapture on sales of depreciable real estate that is § 1250 property. The additional amount recaptured is equal to 20 percent of the excess of any amount that would be treated as ordinary income under § 1245 over the amount treated as ordinary income under § 1250.

EXAMPLE 5   A corporation purchased an office building on January 3, 1984, for $300,000. Accelerated depreciation was taken in the amount of $156,000 before the building was sold on January 5, 1990, for $250,000. Straight-line depreciation would have been $120,000 (using a 15-year recovery period under ACRS). Because the building is 15-year real estate, it is treated as § 1245 recovery property. The gain of $106,000 [$250,000 − ($300,000 − $156,000)] is recaptured to the extent of all depreciation taken. Thus, all gain is ordinary income under § 1245. □

EXAMPLE 6   Assume the building in Example 5 is residential rental property, making it § 1250 property. Gain recaptured under § 1250 is $36,000 ($156,000 depreciation taken − $120,000 straight-line depreciation). For an individual taxpayer, the remaining gain of $70,000 would be § 1231 gain. However, for a corporate taxpayer, § 291(a)(1) causes additional § 1250 ordinary income of $14,000, computed as follows:

Section 1245 recapture	$106,000
Less: Gain recaptured under § 1250	(36,000)
Excess § 1245 gain	$ 70,000
Percentage that is ordinary gain	20%
Additional § 1250 gain	$ 14,000
Ordinary income ($36,000 + $14,000)	$ 50,000
Section 1231 gain ($106,000 − $36,000 − $14,000)	56,000
Total gain	$106,000

□

EXAMPLE 7   Assume the building in Example 5 is commercial property and straight-line depreciation was used. An individual would report all gain of $70,000 [$250,000 sales price − ($300,000 cost of building − $120,000 straight-line depreciation)] as § 1231 gain. However, a corporate taxpayer would recapture as ordinary income (under § 291) 20% of the depreciation recapture under § 1245 (20% of $70,000). Thus, $14,000 would be ordinary income, and $56,000 would be § 1231 gain.   □

Passive Losses

The passive loss rules apply to noncorporate taxpayers and to closely held C corporations and personal service corporations. For S corporations and partnerships, passive income or loss flows through to the owners, and the passive loss rules are applied at the owner level. The passive loss rules are applied to closely held corporations and to personal service corporations to prevent taxpayers from incorporating to aviod the passive loss limitations.

A corporation is closely held if, at any time during the taxable year, more than 50 percent of the value of the corporation's outstanding stock is owned, directly or indirectly, by or for not more than five individuals. A personal service corporation is classified as such for purposes of the passive loss provisions if the following requirements are met:

- The principal activity of the corporation is the performance of personal services.

- Such services are substantially performed by owner-employees.

- More than 10 percent of the stock (in value) is held by owner-employees. *Any* stock held by an employee on *any* one day causes the employee to be an owner-employee.

For the personal service corporation, the general passive activity loss rules apply. Passive activity losses cannot be offset against either active income or portfolio income. For the closely held corporation, the application of the passive activity rules is less harsh. Closely held corporations may offset passive losses against active income, but not against portfolio income.

EXAMPLE 8   T Corporation, a closely held corporation, has $300,000 of passive losses from a rental activity, $200,000 of active business income, and $100,000 of portfolio income. The corporation may offset $200,000 of the $300,000 passive loss against the $200,000 active business income, but may not offset the remainder against the $100,000 of portfolio income.   □

Individual taxpayers are not allowed to offset passive losses against *either* active or portfolio income.

Charitable Contributions

No deduction will be allowed to either corporate or noncorporate taxpayers for a charitable contribution unless the recipient is a qualified charitable organization. Generally, a deduction will be allowed only for the year in which the payment is

made. However, an important exception is made for accrual basis corporations. Here the deduction may be claimed in the year *preceding* payment if the contribution has been authorized by the board of directors by the end of that year and is, in fact, paid on or before the fifteenth day of the third month of the next year.[11]

EXAMPLE 9

On December 28, 1990, XYZ Company, a calendar year accrual basis partnership, authorizes a $5,000 donation to the Atlanta Symphony Association (a qualified charitable organization). The donation is made on March 14, 1991. Because XYZ Company is a partnership, the contribution can be deducted only in 1991.[12] □

EXAMPLE 10

Assume the same facts as in Example 9, except that XYZ Company is a corporation. Presuming the December 28, 1990, authorization was made by its board of directors, XYZ Company may claim the $5,000 donation as a deduction for calendar year 1990. If it was not, the deduction may still be claimed for calendar year 1991. □

Property Contributions.   For both corporate and noncorporate taxpayers, the amount that can be claimed as a charitable deduction for a noncash contribution generally is measured by the fair market value of the property contributed. If the property has appreciated in value, however, the tax law makes a distinction between ordinary income property and capital gain property. If the property had been sold and would have yielded ordinary income, the deduction is limited to the adjusted basis of the property contributed. Only when the property would have yielded a long-term capital gain is a deduction allowed for any appreciation thereon. Section 1231 property (depreciable property and real estate used in a trade or business and held for the long-term holding period) would not be ordinary income property except to the extent of its recapture potential under §§ 1245 and 1250.

All capital gain property is not treated alike for purposes of the charitable contribution deduction. The appreciation is not deductible in the following two situations:

1. Tangible personal property is involved, and the use of the property by the charitable organization is unrelated to the purpose or function constituting the basis for exemption under § 501.

2. The donation is to a private foundation [as defined in § 509(a)].

In situation 1, tangible personalty does not include real estate and intangible property (e.g., stocks and bonds).

EXAMPLE 11

In the current year, X (a retail grocer) contributes the following items to qualified charitable organizations:

---

11. § 170(a)(2).
12. Each partner will pick up his or her allocable portion of the charitable contribution deduction as of December 31, 1991 (the end of the partnership's tax year). See chapter 21.

	Adjusted Basis	Fair Market Value
Canned food products given to the local Salvation Army soup kitchen	$ 4,000	$ 4,400
Rare gem collection given to the Civic Symphony Association	50,000	120,000
Texaco stock held for two years as an investment and given to the Methodist Church building fund	20,000	25,000

Since the canned food products were inventory to X (ordinary income property), the deduction is limited to $4,000. Because of situation 1, none of the appreciation on the rare gem collection can be claimed. Thus, the deduction is limited to $50,000. As to the Texaco stock, it is a capital asset and if sold would have yielded a long-term capital gain of $5,000. Consequently, the $5,000 appreciation is allowable, resulting in a deduction of $25,000. Situation 1 does not apply since stock is an intangible. □

Corporations enjoy two special exceptions where 50 percent of the appreciation (but not to exceed twice the basis) on property will be allowed on certain contributions. The first exception concerns inventory if the property is used in a manner related to the exempt purpose of the donee and the donee uses the property solely for the care of the ill, the needy, or infants.

EXAMPLE 12   Assume the same facts as in Example 11, except that X is a regular corporation. Under the exception, the donation to the Salvation Army would increase by $200 [50% × ($4,400 − $4,000)] for a total of $4,200. All other allowable contribution amounts would remain the same. □

The second exception involves gifts of scientific property to colleges and certain scientific research organizations for use in research, provided certain conditions are met.[13] As was true of the inventory exception, 50 percent of the appreciation on such property will be allowed as an additional deduction.

Limitations Imposed on Charitable Contribution Deductions.   Like individuals, corporations are not permitted an unlimited charitable contribution deduction. For any one year, a corporate taxpayer is limited to 10 percent of taxable income, computed without regard to the charitable contribution deduction, any net operating loss carryback or capital loss carryback, and the dividends received deduction. Any contributions in excess of the 10 percent limitation may be carried forward to the five succeeding tax years. Any carryforward must be added to subsequent contributions and will be subject to the 10 percent limitation. In applying this limitation, the current year's contributions must be deducted first, with excess deductions from previous years deducted in order of time.[14]

---

13. These conditions are set forth in § 170(e)(4). For the inventory exception, see § 170(e)(3).

14. The carryover rules relating to all taxpayers are in § 170(d).

EXAMPLE 13   During 1990, T Corporation (a calendar year taxpayer) had the following income and expenses:

Income from operations	$140,000
Expenses from operations	110,000
Dividends received	10,000
Charitable contributions made in May 1990	5,000

For purposes of the 10% limitation *only*, T Corporation's taxable income is $40,000 [$140,000 − $110,000 + $10,000]. The dividends received deduction (see page 16–14) is not considered in computing income for this purpose. Consequently, the allowable charitable deduction for 1990 is $4,000 (10% × $40,000). The $1,000 unused portion of the contribution can be carried forward to 1991, 1992, 1993, 1994, and 1995 (in that order) until exhausted. □

EXAMPLE 14   Assume the same facts as in Example 13. In 1991, T Corporation has taxable income (for purposes of the 10% limitation) of $50,000 and makes a charitable contribution of $4,500. The maximum deduction allowed for 1991 would be $5,000 (10% × $50,000). The first $4,500 of the allowed deduction must be allocated to the contribution made in 1991, and $500 of the $1,000 unused contribution is carried over from 1990. The remaining $500 of the 1990 contribution may be carried over to 1992, etc. □

Net Operating Losses

The net operating loss of a corporation may be carried back 3 years and forward 15 to offset taxable income for those years and is not subject to the adjustments required for individual taxpayers. A corporation does not adjust its tax loss for the year for capital losses as do individual taxpayers. This is true because a corporation is not permitted a deduction for net capital losses. A corporation does not make adjustments for nonbusiness deductions as do individual taxpayers. Further, a corporation is allowed to include the dividends received deduction (see page 16–14) in computing its net operating loss.[15]

EXAMPLE 15   In 1990, X Corporation has gross income (including dividends) of $200,000 and deductions of $300,000 excluding the dividends received deduction. X Corporation had received taxable dividends of $100,000 from Exxon stock. X Corporation has a net operating loss computed as follows:

---

15. The modifications required to arrive at the amount of net operating loss that can be carried back or forward are in § 172(d).

Gross income (including dividends)		$ 200,000
Less: Business deductions	$300,000	
Dividends received deduction		
(70% of $100,000)*	70,000	(370,000)
Taxable income (or loss)		($ 170,000)

*See the discussion of the dividends received deduction in the next section of this chapter.

The net operating loss is carried back three years to 1987. (X Corporation may *elect* to forgo the carryback option and instead carry forward the loss.) Assume X Corporation had taxable income of $40,000 in 1987. The carryover to 1988 is computed as follows:

Taxable income for 1987	$ 40,000
Less: Net operating loss carryback	(170,000)
Taxable income for 1987 after net operating loss carryback (carryover to 1988)	($ 130,000)

Deductions Available Only to Corporations

Dividends Received Deduction.   The purpose of the dividends received deduction is to prevent triple taxation. Absent the deduction, income paid to a corporation in the form of a dividend would be subject to taxation for a second time (once to the distributing corporation) with no corresponding deduction to the distributing corporation. Later, when the recipient corporation paid the income to its individual shareholders, such income would again be subject to taxation with no corresponding deduction to the corporation. The dividends received deduction alleviates this inequity by causing only some or none of the dividend income to be subject to taxation at the corporate level.

The amount of the dividends received deduction depends upon the percentage of ownership the recipient corporate shareholder holds in a domestic corporation making the dividend distribution.[16] For dividends received (or accrued) after 1987, the deduction percentages are as follows:

Percentage of Ownership by Corporate Shareholder	Deduction Percentage
Less than 20%	70%
20% or more (but less than 80%)	80%
80% or more*	100%

*The payor corporation must be a member of an affiliated group with the recipient corporation.

---

16. § 243(a).

The dividends received deduction is limited to a percentage of the taxable income of a corporation computed without regard to the net operating loss, the dividends received deduction, and any capital loss carryback to the current tax year. The percentage of taxable income limitation corresponds to the deduction percentage. Thus, if a corporate shareholder owns less than 20 percent of the stock in the distributing corporation, the dividends received deduction is limited to 70 percent of taxable income. However, the taxable income limitation does not apply if the corporation has a net operating loss for the current taxable year.[17]

In working with these myriad rules, the following steps need to be taken:

1. Multiply the dividends received by the deduction percentage.

2. Multiply the taxable income by the deduction percentage.

3. Limit the deduction to the lesser of Step 1 or Step 2, unless subtracting the amount derived in Step 1 from 100 percent of taxable income generates a loss. If so, use the amount derived in Step 1.

EXAMPLE 16   P, R, and T Corporations are three unrelated calendar year corporations. For 1990 they have the following transactions:

	P Corporation	R Corporation	T Corporation
Gross income from operations	$ 400,000	$ 320,000	$ 260,000
Expenses from operations	(340,000)	(340,000)	(340,000)
Dividends received from domestic corporations (less than 20% ownership)	200,000	200,000	200,000
Taxable income before the dividends received deduction	$ 260,000	$ 180,000	$ 120,000

In determining the dividends received deduction, use the step procedure just described:

	P Corporation	R Corporation	T Corporation
Step 1 (70% × $200,000)	$140,000	$140,000	$140,000
Step 2			
70% × $260,000 (taxable income)	$182,000		
70% × $180,000 (taxable income)		$126,000	
70% × $120,000 (taxable income)			$ 84,000
Step 3			
Lesser of Step 1 or Step 2	$140,000	$126,000	
Generates a net operating loss			$140,000

R Corporation is subject to the 70 percent of taxable income limitation. It does not qualify for loss rule treatment since subtracting $140,000 (Step 1)

---

17. §§ 246(b)(1) and (2).

from $180,000 (100 percent of taxable income) does not yield a negative figure. T Corporation does qualify for loss rule treatment because subtracting $140,000 (Step 1) from $120,000 (100 percent of taxable income) does yield a negative figure. In summary, each corporation is allowed the following dividends received deduction for 1990: $140,000 for P Corporation, $126,000 for R Corporation, and $140,000 for T Corporation. □

If a corporation already has a net operating loss before any dividends received deduction is claimed, the taxable income limitation would not apply. Consequently, the full dividends received deduction is allowed.

Deduction of Organizational Expenditures.   Expenses incurred in connection with the organization of a corporation normally are chargeable to a capital account. That they benefit the corporation during its existence seems clear. But how can they be amortized when most corporations possess unlimited life? The lack of a determinable and limited estimated useful life would therefore preclude any tax write-off. Code § 248 was enacted to solve this problem.

Under § 248, a corporation may elect to amortize organizational expenditures over a period of 60 months or more. The period begins with the month in which the corporation begins business.[18] Organizational expenditures subject to the election include legal services incident to organization (e.g., drafting the corporate charter, bylaws, minutes of organizational meetings, terms of original stock certificates), necessary accounting services, expenses of temporary directors and of organizational meetings of directors or shareholders, and fees paid to the state of incorporation.

Expenditures that do not qualify include those connected with issuing or selling shares of stock or other securities (e.g., commissions, professional fees, and printing costs) or with the transfer of assets to a corporation. Such expenditures reduce the amount of capital raised and are not deductible at all.

To qualify for the election, the expenditures must be *incurred* before the end of the taxable year in which the corporation begins business. In this regard, the corporation's method of accounting is of no consequence. Thus, an expense incurred by a cash basis corporation in its first tax year but not paid until a subsequent year would qualify.

The election is made in a statement attached to the corporation's return for its first taxable year. The return and statement must be filed no later than the due date of the return (including any extensions). The statement must set forth the description and amount of the expenditures involved, the date such expenditures were incurred, the month in which the corporation began business, and the number of months (not less than 60) over which such expenditures are to be deducted ratably.

If the election is not made on a timely basis, organizational expenditures cannot be deducted until the corporation ceases to do business and liquidates. These expenditures will be deductible if the corporate charter limits the life of the corporation.

EXAMPLE 17   T Corporation, an accrual basis taxpayer, was formed and began operations on May 1, 1990. The following expenses were incurred during its first year of operations (May 1 through December 31, 1990):

---

18. The month in which a corporation begins business may not be immediately apparent. See Reg. § 1.248–1(a)(3). For a similar problem in the Subchapter S area, see chapter 20.

Expenses of temporary directors and of organizational meetings	$500
Fee paid to the state of incorporation	100
Accounting services incident to organization	200
Legal services for drafting the corporate charter and bylaws	400
Expenses incident to the printing and sale of stock certificates	300

Assume T Corporation makes a timely election under § 248 to amortize qualifying organizational expenses over a period of 60 months. The monthly amortization would be $20 [($500 + $100 + $200 + $400) ÷ 60 months], and $160 ($20 × 8 months) would be deductible for tax year 1990. Note that the $300 of expenses incident to the printing and sale of stock certificates does not qualify for the election. These expenses cannot be deducted at all but reduce the amount of the capital realized from the sale of stock. □

DETERMINING THE CORPORATE INCOME TAX LIABILITY

Corporate Income Tax Rates

Although corporate income tax rates have fluctuated widely over past years, the general trend of the changes has been downward. Current corporate income tax rates are as follows:

Taxable Income	Tax Rate
$50,000 or less	15%
Over $50,000 but not over $75,000	25%
Over $75,000	34%

For a corporation that has taxable income in excess of $100,000 for any taxable year, the amount of the tax shall be increased by the lesser of (1) 5 percent of such excess or (2) $11,750. In effect, the additional tax means a 39 percent rate for every dollar of taxable income from $100,000 to $335,000.[19]

EXAMPLE 18	X Corporation, a calendar year taxpayer, has taxable income of $90,000 for 1990. Its income tax liability will be $18,850, determined as follows: $7,500 (15% × $50,000) + $6,250 (25% × $25,000) + $5,100 (34% × $15,000). □

EXAMPLE 19	Y Corporation, a calendar year taxpayer, has taxable income of $335,000 for 1990. Its income tax liability will be $113,900, determined as follows: $7,500 (15% × $50,000) + $6,250 (25% × $25,000) + $88,400 (34% × $260,000) + $11,750 (5% × $235,000). Note that the tax liability of $113,900 is 34% of $335,000. Thus, the benefits of the lower rates on the first $75,000 of taxable income completely phase out at $335,000. □

19. § 11(b).

Qualified personal service corporations are taxed at a flat 34 percent rate on all taxable income. Thus, they do not enjoy the tax savings of the 15 percent (on the first $50,000) and 25 percent (on the next $25,000) lower brackets. For this purpose, a qualified personal service corporation is one that is substantially employee owned and engages in one of the following activities: health, law, engineering, architecture, accounting, actuarial science, performing arts, or consulting.

Alternative Minimum Tax

Corporations are subject to an alternative minimum tax (AMT) that is structured in the same manner as that applicable to individuals. The AMT for corporations, as for individuals, involves a more expansive tax base than does the regular tax. Like individuals, the corporation is required to apply a minimum tax rate to the expanded base and to pay the difference between the AMT tax liability and the regular tax. Many of the adjustments and tax preference items necessary to arrive at alternative minimum taxable income (AMTI) are the same for the individual and the corporation. Although the objective of the AMT is the same for the individual and for the corporation, the rate and exemptions are different. Computation of the AMT for corporations is discussed in chapter 19.

PROCEDURAL MATTERS

Filing Requirements for Corporations

A corporation must file a return whether it has taxable income or not.[20] A corporation that was not in existence throughout an entire annual accounting period is required to file a return for that fraction of the year during which it was in existence. In addition, the corporation must file a return even though it has ceased to do business if it has valuable claims for which it will bring suit. It is relieved of filing returns once it ceases business and dissolves, retaining no assets, whether or not it is treated as a corporation under state law for certain limited purposes connected with the winding up of its affairs, such as for suing and being sued.

The corporate return is filed on Form 1120 unless the corporation is a small corporation entitled to file the shorter Form 1120–A. Corporations may file Form 1120–A if all the following requirements are met:

- Gross receipts or sales do not exceed $250,000.

- Total income (gross profit plus other income including gains on sales of property) does not exceed $250,000.

- Total assets do not exceed $250,000.

- The corporation is not involved in a dissolution or liquidation.

- The corporation is not a member of a controlled group under §§ 1561 and 1563.

- The corporation does not file a consolidated return.

- The corporation does not have ownership in a foreign corporation.

---

20. § 6012(a)(2).

- The corporation does not have foreign shareholders who directly or indirectly own 50 percent or more of its stock.

Corporations electing under Subchapter S (see chapter 20) file on Form 1120S. Forms 1120, 1120–A, and 1120S are reproduced in Appendix B.

The return must be filed on or before the fifteenth day of the third month following the close of a corporation's tax year. Corporations can receive an automatic extension of six months for filing the corporate return by filing Form 7004 by the due date for the return.[21] However, the IRS may terminate the extension by mailing a 10-day notice to the taxpayer corporation.

A corporation must make payments of estimated tax unless its tax liability can reasonably be expected to be less than $500. The payments must be at least 90 percent of the corporation's final tax. These payments can be made in four installments due on or before the fifteenth day of the fourth month, the sixth month, the ninth month, and the twelfth month of the corporate taxable year. The full amount of the unpaid tax is due on the due date of the return.

Failure to make the required estimated tax prepayments will result in a nondeductible penalty being imposed on the corporation. The penalty can be avoided, however, if any of various exceptions apply.[22]

Reconciliation of Taxable Income and Financial Net Income

Taxable income and financial net income for a corporation are seldom the same amount. For example, a difference may arise if the corporation uses the accelerated cost recovery system (ACRS) for tax purposes and straight-line depreciation for financial purposes. Consequently, cost recovery allowable for tax purposes may differ from book depreciation.

Many items of income for accounting purposes, such as proceeds from a life insurance policy on the death of a corporate officer and interest on municipal bonds, may not be taxable income. Some expense items for financial purposes, such as expenses to produce tax-exempt income, estimated warranty reserves, a net capital loss, and Federal income taxes, may not be deductible for tax purposes.

Schedule M–1 on the last page of Form 1120 is used to reconcile financial net income (net income after Federal income taxes) with taxable income (as computed on the corporate tax return before the deduction for a net operating loss and for the dividends received deduction). In the left-hand column of Schedule M–1, net income per books is added to the Federal income tax liability for the year, the excess of capital losses over capital gains (which cannot be deducted in the current year), taxable income that is not income in the current year for financial purposes, and expenses recorded on the books that are not deductible on the tax return. In the right-hand column, income recorded on the books that is not currently taxable or is tax-exempt and deductions for tax purposes that are not expenses for financial purposes are deducted from the left-hand column total to arrive at taxable income (before the net operating loss deduction and the dividends received deduction).

---

21. § 6081.
22. See § 6655 for the penalty involved and the various exceptions thereto.

EXAMPLE 20   During 1990, T Corporation had the following transactions:

Net income per books (after tax)	$92,400
Taxable income	50,000
Federal income tax liability (15% × $50,000)	7,500
Interest income from tax-exempt bonds	5,000
Interest paid on loan, the proceeds of which were used to purchase the tax-exempt bonds	500
Life insurance proceeds received as a result of the death of a key employee	50,000
Premiums paid on keyman life insurance policy	2,600
Excess of capital losses over capital gains	2,000

For book and tax purposes, T Corporation determines depreciation under the straight-line method. T Corporation's Schedule M–1 for the current year is as follows:

Schedule M-1	**Reconciliation of Income per Books With Income per Return** (You are not required to complete this schedule if the total assets on line 15, column (d), of Schedule L are less than $25,000.)		
1 Net income per books	92,400	7 Income recorded on books this year not included on this return (itemize):	
2 Federal income tax	7,500		
3 Excess of capital losses over capital gains . .	2,000	**a** Tax-exempt interest $ 5,000	
4 Income subject to tax not recorded on books this year (itemize): _____		Life insurance proceeds on keyman $50,000	55,000
		8 Deductions on this return not charged against book income this year (itemize):	
5 Expenses recorded on books this year not deducted on this return (itemize):		**a** Depreciation . . . $_____	
a Depreciation . . . $_____		**b** Contributions carryover $_____	
b Contributions carryover $_____			
c Travel and entertainment . $_____			
Int. on tax exempt bonds $500			
Prem. on keyman ins. $2,600	3,100	9 Total of lines 7 and 8	55,000
6 Total of lines 1 through 5	105,000	10 Income (line 28, page 1)—line 6 less line 9 .	50,000

Schedule M–2 reconciles unappropriated retained earnings at the beginning of the year with unappropriated retained earnings at year-end. Beginning balance plus net income per books, as entered on line 1 of Schedule M–1, less dividend distributions during the year equals ending retained earnings. Other sources of increases or decreases in retained earnings are also listed on Schedule M–2.

EXAMPLE 21   Assume the same facts as in Example 20. T Corporation's beginning balance in unappropriated retained earnings is $125,000. During the year, T Corporation distributed a cash dividend of $30,000 to its shareholders. Based on these further assumptions, T Corporation's Schedule M–2 for the current year is as follows:

Schedule M-2	**Analysis of Unappropriated Retained Earnings per Books (line 25, Schedule L)** (You are not required to complete this schedule if the total assets on line 15, column (d), of Schedule L are less than $25,000.)		
1 Balance at beginning of year	125,000	5 Distributions: **a** Cash	30,000
2 Net income per books	92,400	**b** Stock	
3 Other increases (itemize): _____		**c** Property	
_____		6 Other decreases (itemize): _____	
_____		_____	
		7 Total of lines 5 and 6	30,000
4 Total of lines 1, 2, and 3	217,400	8 Balance at end of year (line 4 less line 7)	187,400

CONCEPT SUMMARY 16—1

Income Taxes of Individuals and Corporations Compared

	Individuals	Corporations
Computation of gross income	§ 61.	§ 61.
Computation of taxable income	§ 62 and §§ 63(b) through (h).	§ 63(a). Concept of AGI has no relevance.
Deductions	Trade or business (§ 162); nonbusiness (§ 212); some personal and employee expenses (generally deductible as itemized deductions).	Trade or business (§ 162).
Charitable contributions	Limited in any tax year to 50 percent of AGI; 30 percent for long-term capital gain property unless election is made to reduce fair market value of gift.	Limited in any tax year to 10 percent of taxable income computed without regard to the charitable contribution deduction, net operating loss, and dividends received deduction.
	Excess charitable contributions carried over for five years.	Same as for individuals.
	Amount of contribution is the fair market value of the property; if lower, ordinary income property will be limited to adjusted basis; capital gain property will be treated as ordinary income property if certain tangible personalty is donated to a nonuse charity or a private foundation is the donee.	Same as individuals, but exceptions allowed for certain inventory and for scientific property where one-half of the appreciation will be allowed as a deduction.
	Time of deduction is the year in which payment is made.	Time of deduction is the year in which payment is made unless accrual basis taxpayer. Accrual basis corporation can take deduction in year preceding payment if contribution was authorized by board of directors by end of year and contribution is paid by fifteenth day of third month of following year.
Casualty losses	$100 floor on personal casualty and theft losses; personal casualty losses deductible only to extent losses exceed 10 percent of AGI.	Deductible in full.
Depreciation recapture under § 1250	Recaptured to extent accelerated depreciation exceeds straight-line.	20 percent of excess of amount that would be recaptured under § 1245 over amount recaptured under § 1250 is additional ordinary income.
Net operating loss	Adjusted for nonbusiness deductions over nonbusiness income and personal exemptions.	Generally no adjustments.
	Carryback period is three years and carryforward period is 15 years.	Same as for individuals.
Dividend exclusion and deduction	None.	Generally 70 percent of dividends received.
Net capital gains	Taxed in full.	Taxed in full.

	Individuals	**Corporations**
Capital losses	Only $3,000 of capital loss per year can offset ordinary income; loss is carried forward indefinitely to offset capital gains or ordinary income up to $3,000; carryovers remain long term or short term (as the case may be).	Can offset only capital gains; carried back three years and forward five; carryovers and carrybacks are short-term losses.
Passive losses	Passive activity losses cannot be offset against either active income or portfolio income.	Passive loss rules apply to closely held C corporations and personal service corporations. For personal service corporations, the rule is the same as for individuals. For closely held corporations, passive losses may offset active income but not portfolio income.
Tax rates	Mildly progressive with two rates for 1989 (15 percent and 28 percent); phase-out of 15 percent bracket begins as taxpayers (depending on filing status) reach a certain level of taxable income.	Mildly progressive with three rates (15 percent, 25 percent, and 34 percent); lower brackets phased out between $100,000 and $335,000 of taxable income.
Alternative minimum tax	Applied at a 21 percent rate to AMTI; exemption allowed depending on filing status (e.g., $40,000 for married filing jointly); exemption phases out when AMTI reaches a certain amount (e.g., $150,000 for married filing jointly).	Applied at a 20 percent rate on AMTI (taxable income as modified by certain adjustments plus preference items); $40,000 exemption allowed but phases out once AMTI reaches $150,000; adjustments and tax preference items similar to those applicable to individuals but also include 75% of adjusted current earnings over AMTI.

ORGANIZATION OF AND TRANSFERS TO CONTROLLED CORPORATIONS

In General

Absent special provisions in the Code, a transfer of property to a corporation in exchange for stock would be a sale or exchange of property and would constitute a taxable transaction. Gain or loss would be measured by the difference between the tax basis of the property transferred and the value of the stock received. Section 351 provides for the nonrecognition of gain or loss upon the transfer of property to a corporation solely in exchange for stock if the persons transferring such property are in control of the corporation immediately after the transfer.

The nonrecognition of gain or loss reflects the principle of continuity of the taxpayer's investment. There is no real change in the taxpayer's economic status. The investment in certain properties carries over to the investment in corporate stock. The same principle governs the nonrecognition of gain or loss on like-kind exchanges under § 1031. Gain is postponed until a substantive change in the taxpayer's investment occurs (i.e., a sale to or a taxable exchange with outsiders). This approach can be justified under the wherewithal to pay concept.

EXAMPLE 22   R is considering incorporating his donut shop. If R incorporates, he would transfer the following assets to the corporation:

	Tax Basis	Fair Market Value
Cash	$10,000	$ 10,000
Furniture and fixtures	20,000	60,000
Building	40,000	100,000
	$70,000	$170,000

R will receive stock in the newly formed corporation worth $170,000 in exchange for the assets. Absent the nonrecognition provisions of § 351, R would recognize a taxable gain of $100,000 on the transfer. This would deter R from incorporating his business. But under § 351, there is no recognition of gain because there is no real change in R's economic status. R's investment in the assets of his unincorporated donut shop carries over to his investment in the incorporated donut shop. □

Section 351(a) provides that gain or loss is not recognized upon the transfer by one or more persons of property to a corporation solely in exchange for stock in that corporation if, immediately after the exchange, such person or persons are in control of the corporation to which the property was transferred.

EXAMPLE 23

Individuals A and B form X Corporation. A transfers property with an adjusted basis of $30,000, fair market value of $60,000, for 50% of the stock. B transfers property with an adjusted basis of $40,000, fair market value of $60,000, for the remaining 50% of the stock. Gain is not recognized on the transfer because it qualifies under § 351. The basis of the stock to A is $30,000, and the basis of the stock to B is $40,000. X Corporation has a basis of $30,000 in the property transferred by A and a basis of $40,000 in the property transferred by B. □

Section 351(b) provides that if property or money, other than stock or securities, is received by the transferors, gain will be recognized to the extent of the lesser of the gain realized or boot received (the amount of money and the fair market value of other property received). Loss is never recognized. The nonrecognition of gain or loss is accompanied by a carryover of basis.

EXAMPLE 24

A and B, individuals, form X Corporation. A transfers property with an adjusted basis of $30,000, fair market value of $60,000, for 50% of the stock. B transfers property with an adjusted basis of $40,000, fair market value of $70,000, for the remaining 50% of the stock, plus $10,000 cash. The transfer qualifies under § 351. Thus, A recognizes no gain on the transfer. However, because B received boot of $10,000, B will recognize gain of $10,000, which is the lesser of the gain realized of $30,000 [$60,000 (fair market value of the stock) + $10,000 (boot) − $40,000 (adjusted basis of the property transferred)] or the boot received of $10,000. The basis of the stock to A is $30,000 while the basis of the stock to B is $40,000 [$40,000 (basis of the property transferred) + $10,000 (gain recognized) − $10,000 (boot received)]. □

There are three requirements for nonrecognition of gain or loss: (1) a transfer of property for (2) stock in the transferee corporation if (3) the transferors are in control of the transferee corporation.

Transfer of Property

Questions concerning exactly what constitutes property for purposes of § 351 have arisen. Services rendered are specifically excluded by the Code from the definition of property. With this exception, the definition of property is comprehensive. Unrealized receivables for a cash basis taxpayer are considered property, for example. Secret processes and formulas, as well as secret information in the general nature of a patentable inventory, also qualify as property under § 351.

Stock

If property is transferred to a corporation in exchange for any property other than stock, the property constitutes boot. Such property is taxable to the transferor shareholder to the extent of any realized gain. The Regulations state that stock rights and stock warrants are not included in the term "stock."[23] Generally, however, the term "stock" needs no clarification. Currently securities constitute boot under § 351. Thus, the receipt of securities in exchange for the transfer of appreciated property to a controlled corporation will cause recognition of gain. Prior to the amendments to § 351 occasioned by the Revenue Reconciliation Act of 1989, transfers were subject to nonrecognition of gain or loss under § 351 when there was a transfer of property for stock *or securities* if the transferors were in control of the transferee corporation.[24] Thus, for transfers occurring on or before October 2, 1989, securities do not constitute boot.

Control of the Transferee Corporation

To qualify as a nontaxable transaction under § 351, the transferor must be in control of the transferee corporation immediately after the exchange. *Control* for these purposes requires the person or persons transferring the property to own, immediately after the transfer, stock possessing at least 80 percent of the total combined voting power of all classes of stock entitled to vote and at least 80 percent of the total *number* of shares of all other classes of stock of the corporation [§ 368(c)]. Control can apply to a single person or to several individuals if they are all parties to an integrated transaction. If more than one person is involved, the Regulations affirm that the exchange does not necessarily require simultaneous exchanges by two or more persons. They do, however, comprehend situations in which the rights of the parties have been previously defined and the execution of the agreement proceeds ". . . with an expedition consistent with orderly procedure."[25]

EXAMPLE 25

A exchanges property, which cost him $60,000 but which has a fair market value of $100,000, for 70% of the stock of X Corporation. The other 30% is owned by B, who acquired it several years ago. The fair market value of the stock is $100,000. A realizes a taxable gain of $40,000 on the transfer. If A and B had transferred property to X Corporation in a simultaneous transaction or in separate transactions, both of which related to the execution of a previous

---

23. Reg. § 1.351–1(a)(1)(ii).
24. The Revenue Reconciliation Act of 1989 amended § 351 by deleting "or securities". The

result is that securities are treated as boot for transfers after October 2, 1989.

25. Reg. § 1.351–1(a)(1).

agreement, with A receiving 70% of the stock and B receiving 30%, gain would not have been recognized by either party. □

Section 351 treatment will be lost if stock is transferred to persons who did not contribute property, causing those who did to lack control immediately after the exchange. However, a person who performs services for the corporation in exchange for stock and also transfers some property is treated as a member of the transferring group, although he or she is taxed on the value of the stock issued for services.

Control is not lost if stock received by shareholders in a § 351 exchange is sold to persons who are not parties to the exchange shortly after the transaction, unless the plan for ultimate sale of the stock existed before the exchange.

Section 351 is mandatory and not elective. If a transaction falls within the provisions of § 351, neither gain nor loss is recognized on the transfer (except that realized gain is recognized to the extent of boot received), and there is a carryover of basis.

Assumption of Liabilities—§ 357

Absent § 357 of the Code, the transfer of mortgaged property to a controlled corporation could trigger gain to the extent of the mortgage whether the controlled corporation assumed the mortgage or took property subject to it. This is the case in nontaxable like-kind exchanges under § 1031. Liabilities assumed by the other party are considered the equivalent of cash and treated as boot. Section 357(a) provides, however, that the assumption of a liability by the acquiring corporation or the corporation taking property subject to a liability will not produce boot to the transferor shareholder in a § 351 transaction. Nevertheless, liabilities assumed by the transferee corporation are treated as "other property or money" as far as the basis of stock received in the transfer is concerned. The basis of the stock received must be reduced by the amount of the liabilities assumed by the corporation.

EXAMPLE 26

C transfers property with an adjusted basis of $60,000, fair market value of $100,000, to X Corporation for 100% of the stock in X. The property is subject to a liability of $25,000 that X Corporation assumes. The exchange is tax-free under §§ 351 and 357. However, under § 358(d), the basis to C of the stock in X Corporation is only $35,000 ($60,000 basis of property transferred − $25,000 mortgage assumed). The basis of the property to X Corporation is $60,000. □

The rule of § 357(a) has two exceptions. Section 357(b) provides that if the principal purpose of the assumption of the liabilities is to avoid tax *or* if there is no bona fide business purpose behind the exchange, the liabilities, in total, will be treated as money received and taxed as boot. Further, § 357(c) provides that if the sum of the liabilities exceeds the adjusted basis of the properties transferred, the excess is taxable gain.

Tax Avoidance or No Bona Fide Business Purpose Exception.   Section 357(b)(1)(A) generally poses few problems. A tax avoidance purpose for transferring liabilities to a controlled corporation would seem unlikely in view of the basis adjustment necessitated by § 358(d). Since the liabilities transferred reduce the

basis of the stock received for the property, any realized gain is merely deferred and not avoided. Such gain would materialize when and if the stock is disposed of in a taxable sale or exchange.

Satisfying the bona fide business purpose will not be difficult if the liabilities were incurred in connection with the transferor's normal course of conducting his or her trade or business. But the bona fide business purpose requirement will cause difficulty if the liability is taken out shortly before the property is transferred and the proceeds therefrom are utilized for personal purposes. This type of situation seems akin to a distribution of cash by the corporation that would be taxed as boot.

EXAMPLE 27

D transfers real estate (basis of $40,000 and fair market value of $90,000) to a controlled corporation in return for stock in such corporation. Shortly before the transfer, D mortgages the real estate and uses the $20,000 proceeds to meet personal obligations. Along with the real estate, the mortgage is transferred to the corporation. In this case, it would appear that the assumption of the mortgage lacks a bona fide business purpose within the meaning of § 357(b)(1)(B). Because the amount of the liability is considered boot, D has a taxable gain on the transfer of $20,000.[26] □

Liabilities in Excess of Basis Exception.   Unlike § 357(b), § 357(c) has posed numerous problems in § 351 transfers. Much litigation has centered around this provision of the Code in recent years, particularly with respect to cash basis taxpayers who incorporate their businesses. Section 357(c) states that if the sum of liabilities assumed and the liabilities to which transferred property is subject exceeds the total of the adjusted bases of the properties transferred, the excess is taxable gain. Absent this provision, if liabilities exceed basis in property exchanged, a taxpayer would have a negative basis in the stock received in the controlled corporation. Section 357(c) alleviates the negative basis problem; the excess over basis is gain to the transferor.

EXAMPLE 28

A, an individual, transfers assets with an adjusted tax basis of $40,000 to a newly formed corporation in exchange for 100% of the stock. The corporation assumes liabilities on the transferred properties in the amount of $50,000. Absent § 357(c), A's basis in the stock of the new corporation would be a negative $10,000 ($40,000 basis of property transferred + $0 gain recognized − $0 boot received − $50,000 liabilities assumed). Section 357(c) causes A to recognize a gain of $10,000. The stock will have a zero basis in A's hands, and the negative basis problem is eliminated ($40,000 basis of property transferred + $10,000 gain recognized − $0 boot received − $50,000 liabilities assumed.) □

If §§ 357(b) and (c) both apply to the same transfer (i.e., the liability is not supported by a bona fide business purpose and also exceeds the basis of the properties transferred), § 357(b) predominates. This could be significant because § 357(b) does not create gain on the transfer, as does § 357(c), but merely converts

---

26. § 351(b). The effect of the application of § 357(b) is to taint *all* liabilities transferred even though some may be supported by a bona fide business purpose.

the liability to boot. Thus, the realized gain limitation continues to apply to § 357(b) transactions.

Basis Determination

Recall that § 351(a) postpones gain until the taxpayer's investment changes substantially. Postponement of the realized gain is accomplished through a carryover of basis pursuant to §§ 358(a) and 362(a).

Section 358(a).   For a taxpayer transferring property to a corporation in a § 351 transaction, basis of stock received in the transfer is the same as the basis the taxpayer had in the property transferred, increased by any gain recognized on the exchange and decreased by boot received. For this purpose, liabilities transferred usually constitute boot.

Section 362(a).   The basis of properties received by the corporation is determined under § 362(a), which provides that basis to the corporation is the basis in the hands of the transferor, increased by the amount of any gain recognized to the transferor shareholder.

EXAMPLE 29	C and D form Y Corporation with the following investment: C transfers property (basis of $30,000 and fair market value of $70,000), and D transfers cash of $60,000. Each receives 50 shares of Y Corporation stock, but C also receives $10,000 in cash. Assume each share of the Y Corporation stock is worth $1,200. Although C's realized gain is $40,000 ($60,000 value of 50 shares of Y Corporation stock + $10,000 cash received − $30,000 basis of the property transferred), only $10,000 (the amount of the boot) is recognized. C's basis in the Y Corporation stock becomes $30,000 ($30,000 basis of the property transferred + $10,000 gain recognized by C − $10,000 cash received). Y Corporation's basis in the property transferred by C is $40,000 ($30,000 basis of the property to C + $10,000 gain recognized to C). D neither realizes nor recognizes gain or loss and will have a basis in the Y Corporation stock of $60,000. ☐

EXAMPLE 30	Assume the same facts as in Example 29, except that C's basis in the property transferred is $68,000 (instead of $30,000). Because recognized gain cannot exceed realized gain, the transfer generates only $2,000 of gain to C. The basis of the Y Corporation stock to C becomes $60,000 ($68,000 basis of property

FIGURE 16–1 Shareholder's Basis in Stock Received

Adjusted basis of property transferred	$xx,xxx
Plus: Gain recognized	x,xxx
Minus: Boot received (including any liabilities transferred)	(x,xxx)
Equals: Basis of stock received	$xx,xxx

FIGURE 16–2 Corporation's Basis in Properties Received

Adjusted basis of property transferred	$xx,xxx
Plus: Gain recognized by transferor shareholder	xxx
Equals: Basis of property to corporation	$xx,xxx

transferred + $2,000 gain recognized − $10,000 cash received). Y Corporation's basis in the property received from C is $70,000 ($68,000 basis of the property to C + $2,000 gain recognized by C). ☐

Recapture Considerations

Recapture of Accelerated Cost Recovery (Depreciation).   In a pure § 351(a) nontaxable transfer (no boot involved) to a controlled corporation, the recapture of accelerated cost recovery rules do not apply.[27] Moreover, any recapture potential of the property carries over to the corporation as it steps into the shoes of the transferor-shareholder for purposes of basis determination.

EXAMPLE 31   T transfers to a controlled corporation equipment (basis of $30,000 and a fair market value of $100,000) in return for additional stock. If sold by T, the property would have yielded a gain of $70,000, all of which would be recaptured as ordinary income under § 1245. If the transfer comes within § 351(a) because of the absence of boot, T has no recognized gain and no accelerated cost recovery to recapture. Should the corporation later dispose of the equipment in a taxable transaction, it will have to take into account the § 1245 recapture potential originating with T. ☐

Tax Benefit Rule.   A taxpayer may have to take into income the recovery of an item previously expensed. Such income, however, will be limited to the amount of the deduction that actually produced a tax savings. The relevance of the tax benefit rule to transfers to controlled corporations under § 351 was first apparent in connection with accounts receivable and the reserve for bad debts.

EXAMPLE 32   T, an accrual basis individual, incorporates her sole proprietorship. In return for all of the stock of the corporation, T transfers, among other assets, accounts receivable with a face amount of $100,000 and a reserve for bad debts of $10,000 (book value of $90,000). T had previously deducted the addition to the reserve. The $10,000 deduction resulted in a tax benefit to T. ☐

The IRS took the position that § 351 did not insulate the transfer from the tax benefit rule. Since T had previously deducted the reserve for bad debts and such reserve was no longer necessary to her, the full $10,000 should be taken into

---

27. §§ 1245(b)(3) and 1250(d)(3).

income. In *Nash v. U.S.*,[28] the Supreme Court disagreed. Operating on the assumption that the stock T received must be worth only $90,000 (the book value of the receivables), the situation was compared to a sale. Because no gain would have resulted had the receivables been sold for $90,000, why should it matter that they were transferred to a controlled corporation under § 351?

The Supreme Court decision in *Nash*, however, does not imply that the tax benefit rule is inapplicable to transfers to controlled corporations when no gain is otherwise recognized under § 351(a). Returning to the facts in Example 32, suppose T was one of several transferors and the value of the stock she received exceeded the book value of the receivables ($90,000). Could the excess be subject to income recognition by virtue of the application of the tax benefit rule? The answer to this question has not been specifically passed upon by the courts.

CAPITAL STRUCTURE OF A CORPORATION

Capital Contributions

The receipt of money or property in exchange for capital stock (including treasury stock) produces neither gain nor loss to the recipient corporation (§ 1032). Gross income of a corporation also does not include shareholders' contributions of money or property to the capital of the corporation (§ 118). Additional funds received from shareholders through voluntary pro rata payments are not income to the corporation even though there is no increase in the outstanding shares of stock of the corporation. Such payments represent an additional price paid for the shares held by the shareholders and are treated as additions to the operating capital of the corporation.

Contributions by nonshareholders, such as land contributed to a corporation by a civic group or a governmental group to induce the corporation to locate in a particular community, are also excluded from the gross income of a corporation. Property that is transferred to a corporation by a nonshareholder for services rendered or for merchandise *does* constitute taxable income to the corporation.

The basis of property received by a corporation from a shareholder as a contribution to capital is the basis of the property in the hands of the shareholder increased by any gain recognized to the shareholder. For property transferred to a corporation by a nonshareholder as a contribution to capital, the basis of the property is zero. If money is received by a corporation as a contribution to capital from a nonshareholder, the basis of any property acquired with the money during a 12-month period beginning on the day the contribution was received is reduced by the amount of the contribution. The excess of money received over the cost of new property is used to reduce the basis of other property held by the corporation. The excess is applied in reduction of basis in the following order:

- Depreciable property.
- Property subject to amortization.
- Property subject to depletion.
- All other remaining properties.

The reduction of the basis of property within each category is made in proportion to the relative bases of the properties.

---

28. 70-1 USTC ¶9405, 25 AFTR2d 1177, 90 S.Ct. 1550 (USSC, 1970).

EXAMPLE 33   A city donates land to X Corporation as an inducement for X to locate in the city. The receipt of the land does not represent taxable income. However, the land's basis to the corporation is zero. Assume the city also pays the corporation $10,000 in cash. The money is not taxable income to the corporation. However, when the corporation purchases property with the $10,000 (within the next 12 months), the basis of such property is reduced by $10,000. ☐

Debt in the Capital Structure

Advantages of Debt.   Shareholders should consider the relationship between debt and equity in the capital structure. The advantages of receiving long-term debt are numerous. Interest on debt is deductible by the corporation, whereas dividend payments are not. Further, the shareholders are not taxed on loan repayments made to them unless the repayments exceed basis. As long as a corporation has earnings and profits (see chapter 17), an investment in stock cannot be withdrawn tax-free. Any withdrawals will be deemed to be taxable dividends to the extent of earnings and profits of the distributing corporation.

EXAMPLE 34   A, an individual, transfers $100,000 to a newly formed corporation for 100% of the stock. In the first year of operations, the corporation has net income of $40,000. Such earnings are credited to the earnings and profits account of the corporation. If the corporation distributes $10,500 to A, the distribution will be a taxable dividend with no corresponding deduction to the corporation. Assume A transferred cash of $50,000 for stock. In addition, A loans the corporation $50,000, transferring cash of $50,000 to the corporation for a note in the amount of $50,000, payable in equal annual installments of $5,000 and bearing interest at the rate of 11%. At the end of the year, the corporation would pay A $5,500 interest, which would be tax deductible. The $5,000 principal repayment on the loan would not be taxed to A. ☐

Reclassification of Debt as Equity.   In certain instances, the IRS will contend that debt is really an equity interest and will deny the shareholders the tax advantages of debt financing. If the debt instrument has too many features of stock, it may be treated as a form of stock, and principal and interest payments will be considered dividends. Pursuant to § 385, the IRS has the authority to characterize corporate debt wholly as equity or as part debt and part equity.

Though the form of the instrument will not ensure debt treatment, the failure to observe certain formalities in the creation of the debt may lead to an assumption that the purported debt is, in fact, a form of stock. The debt should be in proper legal form, should bear a legitimate rate of interest, should have a definite maturity date, and should be repaid on a timely basis. Payments should not be contingent upon earnings. Further, the debt should not be subordinated to other liabilities, and proportionate holdings of stock and debt should be avoided.

Section 385 lists several factors that *may* be used to determine whether a debtor-creditor relationship or a shareholder-corporation relationship exists. The main thrust of § 385, however, is to turn the matter over to the U.S. Treasury Department to prescribe Regulations that would provide more definite guidelines as to when a corporation is or is not thinly capitalized.

Regulations that were proposed and scheduled to be finalized in 1980 were repeatedly modified and finally withdrawn. The Treasury concluded that neither

the final regulations, as published in December 1980, nor the proposed revisions, as published in January 1982, fully reflected the position of either the IRS or the Treasury on debt/equity matters. Consequently, the final regulations and the proposed revisions were withdrawn. It is uncertain when the Treasury will adopt a new set of regulations.

TAX PLANNING CONSIDERATIONS

Corporate versus Noncorporate Forms of Business Organization

The decision to use the corporate form in conducting a trade or business must be weighed carefully. Besides the nontax considerations attendant to the corporate form (limited liability, continuity of life, free transferability of interest, centralized management), tax ramifications will play an important role in any such decision. Close attention should be paid to the following:

1. The regular corporate form means the imposition of the corporate income tax. Corporate-source income will be taxed twice—once as earned by the corporation and again when distributed to the shareholders. Since dividends are not deductible, a strong incentive exists in a closely held corporation to structure corporate distributions in a deductible form. Thus, profits may be bailed out by the shareholders in the form of salaries, interest, or rents. Such procedures lead to a multitude of problems, one of which, the reclassification of debt as equity, is discussed in this chapter. The problems of unreasonable salaries and rents are covered in chapter 17 in the discussion of constructive dividends.

2. Assuming the current tax rates remain in effect, the top rates definitely favor the noncorporate taxpayer over the corporate taxpayer. For example, the top rate for individuals is 28 percent for 1989. For corporations, the top rate is 34 percent. The differential is not so pronounced, however, if one presumes a shareholder with a top rate of 28 percent and a corporation that limits its taxable income to $100,000 to avoid the phase-out of the 15 percent and 28 percent lower brackets. Here, the time value of the taxes saved (by not distributing dividends and postponing the effect of the double tax that otherwise results) could make operating a business in the corporate form advantageous.

3. Corporate source income loses its identity as it passes through the corporation to the shareholders. Thus, items possessing preferential tax treatment (e.g., interest on municipal bonds) are not taxed as such to the shareholders.

4. As noted in chapter 17, it may be difficult for shareholders to recover some or all of their investment in the corporation without an ordinary income result since most corporate distributions are treated as dividends to the extent of the corporation's earnings and profits.

5. Corporate losses cannot be passed through to the shareholders.[29]

6. The liquidation of a corporation will normally generate tax consequences to both the corporation and its shareholders (see chapter 18).

---

29. Points 1, 2, and 5 could be resolved through a Subchapter S election (see chapter 20), assuming the corporation qualifies for such an election. In part, the same can be said for point 3.

7. The corporate form provides the shareholders with the opportunity to be treated as employees for tax purposes if the shareholders, in fact, render services to the corporation. Such status makes a number of attractive tax-sheltered fringe benefits available. They include, but are not limited to, group term life insurance (§ 79), the $5,000 death gratuity [§ 101(b)(1)], and meals and lodging (§ 119). These benefits are not available to partners and sole proprietors.

The Association Route

Consideration 7 in the preceding section led to the popularity of the professional association. The major tax incentive involved was to cover the shareholder-employees under a qualified pension plan. Professionals, particularly physicians, who were not permitted to form regular corporations because of state law prohibitions or ethical restrictions, created organizations with sufficient corporate attributes to be classified as associations. The position of the IRS on the status of these professional associations (whether or not they should be treated as corporations for tax purposes) vacillated over a period of years. After a series of judicial losses, however, the IRS has accepted their association status, assuming certain conditions are satisfied.

Over recent years, the popularity of the association approach has diminished significantly. Changes in the tax law have curtailed the deferral opportunities of qualified pension and profit sharing plans available to employees. At the same time, improvements were made to H.R. 10 (Keogh) plans available to self-employed taxpayers. By placing the two types of plans on a parity with each other, one of the major incentives to achieve employee status through association status no longer exists.

Operating the Corporation

Tax planning to reduce corporate income taxes should occur before the end of the tax year. Effective planning can cause income to be shifted to the next tax year and can produce large deductions by incurring expenses before year-end. Attention should especially be focused on the following.

Charitable Contributions.   Recall that accrual basis corporations may claim a deduction for charitable contributions in the year preceding payment if the contribution has been authorized by the board of directors by the end of the tax year and is paid on or before the fifteenth day of the third month of the following year. Even though the contribution may not ultimately be made, it might well be authorized. A deduction cannot be thrown back to the previous year (even if paid within the two and a half months) if it has not been authorized.

Timing of Capital Gains and Losses.   The corporation should consider offsetting profits on the sale of capital assets by selling some of the depreciated securities in the corporate portfolio. In addition, any already realized capital losses should be carefully monitored. Recall that corporate taxpayers are not permitted to claim any net capital losses as deductions against ordinary income. Capital losses can be used only as an offset against capital gains. Further, net capital losses can only be carried back three years and forward five. Gains from the sales of capital assets should be timed to offset any capital losses. The expiration of the carryover period for any net capital losses should be watched carefully so that sales of appreciated securities occur before that date.

Net Operating Losses. In some situations, the election to forgo a net operating loss carryback and utilize the carryforward option might generate greater tax savings. In this regard, one must take into account three considerations. First, the time value of the tax refund that is lost by not using the carryback procedure must be considered. Second, the election to forgo a net operating loss carryback is irrevocable. Thus, one cannot later choose to change if the future predicted high profits do not materialize. Third, one must consider the future increases (or decreases) in corporate income tax rates that can reasonably be anticipated. This last consideration undoubtedly will be the most difficult to work with. Although corporate tax rates have remained relatively stable in past years, the changes made by TRA of 1986 and projected budget deficits do little to assure taxpayers that future rates will remain constant.

Dividends Received Deduction. Although the dividends received deduction is normally limited to the lesser of 70 percent of the qualifying dividends or 70 percent of taxable income, an exception is made when the full deduction yields a net operating loss. In close situations, therefore, the proper timing of income or deductions may yield a larger dividends received deduction.

Organizational Expenditures. To qualify for the 60-month amortization procedure of § 248, only organizational expenditures incurred in the first taxable year of the corporation can be considered. This rule could prove to be an unfortunate trap for corporations formed late in the year.

EXAMPLE 35 T Corporation is formed in December 1990. Qualified organizational expenditures are incurred as follows: $2,000 in December 1990 and $3,000 in January 1991. If T Corporation uses the calendar year for tax purposes, only $2,000 of the organizational expenditures can be written off over a period of 60 months. □

The solution to the problem posed by Example 35 is for T Corporation to adopt a fiscal year that ends beyond January 31. All organizational expenditures will then have been incurred before the close of the first taxable year.

Shareholder-Employee Payment of Corporate Expenses. In a closely held corporate setting, shareholder-employees often pay corporate expenses (e.g., travel and entertainment) for which they are not reimbursed by the corporation. The IRS often disallows the deduction of these expenses by the shareholder-employee since the payments are voluntary on the part of such shareholder-employee. If the deduction is more beneficial at the shareholder-employee level, a corporate policy against reimbursement of such expenses should be established. Proper planning in this regard would be to decide before the beginning of each tax year where the deduction would do the most good. Any corporate policy regarding reimbursement of such expenses could be modified on a year-to-year basis depending upon the varying circumstances.

In deciding whether corporate expenses should be kept at the corporate level or shifted to the shareholder-employee, the impact of TRA of 1986 will have to be considered. One important point is the treatment of unreimbursed employee expenses after 1986. First, since employee expenses are now itemized deductions, they will be of no benefit to the taxpayer who chooses the standard deduction option. Second, these expenses will be subject to the 2 percent of AGI limitation. No such limitation will be imposed if the expenses are claimed by the corporation.

Working with § 351

In using § 351(a), one should ensure that all parties transferring property (which includes cash) receive control of the corporation. Although simultaneous transfers are not necessary, a long period of time between transfers could be vulnerable if the transfers are not properly documented as part of a single plan.

EXAMPLE 36   C, D, and E form X Corporation with the following investment: cash of $100,000 from C, real estate worth $100,000 (basis of $20,000) from D, and a patent worth $100,000 (basis of zero) from E. In return for this investment, each party is to receive one-third of the corporation's authorized stock of 300 shares. On June 1, 1990, after the corporate charter is granted, C transfers cash of $100,000 in return for 100 shares. Two months later, D transfers the real estate for another 100 shares. On December 3, 1990, E transfers the patent for the remaining 100 shares. ☐

Taken in isolation, the transfers by D and E would result in recognized gain to each. Section 351 would not be applicable because neither D nor E achieves the required 80 percent control. If, however, the parties are in a position to prove that all transfers were part of the same plan, C's transfer can be counted, and the 80 percent requirement is satisfied. To do this, the parties should document and preserve evidence of their intentions. Also, it would be helpful to have some reasonable explanation for the delay in D's and E's transfers.

To meet the requirements of § 351, mere momentary control on the part of the transferor may not suffice if loss of control is compelled by a prearranged agreement.

EXAMPLE 37   For many years, T operated a business as a sole proprietor, employing R as manager. To dissuade R from quitting and going out on her own, T promised her a 30% interest in the business. To fulfill this promise, T transfers the business to newly formed X Corporation in return for all its stock. Immediately thereafter, T transfers 30% of the stock to R. Section 351 probably would not apply to the transfer by T to X Corporation. It appears that T was under an obligation to relinquish control. If this is not the case and such loss of control was by voluntary act on the part of T, momentary control would suffice.[30]

☐

Later transfers of property to an existing corporation must satisfy the control requirement if recognition of gain is to be avoided. In this connection, a transferor's interest cannot be counted if the value of stock received is relatively small compared with the value of stock already owned and the primary purpose of the transfer is to qualify other transferors for § 351 treatment. For purposes of issuing advance rulings, the IRS policy is to treat the amount transferred as *not* being relatively small in value if such amount is equal to, or in excess of, 10 percent of the fair market value of the stock already owned by such person.[31]

---

30. Compare *Fahs v. Florida Machine and Foundry Co.*, 48–2 USTC ¶9329, 36 AFTR 1151, 168 F.2d 957 (CA–5, 1948), with *John C. O'Connor*, 16 TCM 213, T.C.Memo. 1957–50, *aff'd.* in 58–2 USTC ¶9913, 2 AFTR2d 6011, 260 F.2d 358 (CA–6, 1958).

31. Rev.Proc. 77–37, 1977–2 C.B. 568.

EXAMPLE 38   At a point when R Corporation has 800 shares outstanding (owned equally by T and her son) and worth $1,000 each, it issues an additional 200 shares to T in exchange for land (basis of $20,000 and fair market value of $200,000). Presuming the son makes no contribution, T's transfer does not meet the requirements of § 351. Since the son's ownership interest cannot be counted (he was not a transferor), T must satisfy the control requirement on her own. In this regard, she falls short since she ended up with 600 shares (400 shares originally owned + 200 shares newly received) out of 1,000 shares now outstanding for only a 60% interest.[32] Thus, T must recognize a gain of $180,000 on the transfer. □

To make the transfer in Example 38 fall under § 351, what needs to be done? One possibility would be to include the son as a transferor so that his ownership interest can be counted in meeting the control requirement. In using the IRS guidelines to avoid the "relatively small in value" hurdle, this would entail an investment on the part of the son (for additional stock) of at least $40,000 in cash or property (10% × $400,000 fair market value of the shares already owned). If this approach is taken, § 351 will apply to T, and none of her realized gain of $180,000 will be recognized.

To keep the matter in perspective, one should be in a position to recognize when § 351 is not relevant.

EXAMPLE 39   Assume the same facts as in Example 38, except that T receives no additional shares in R Corporation in exchange for the transfer of the land. Because T has made a contribution to capital, compliance with § 351 is of no consequence. No gain will be recognized by T owing to such contribution, although a basis adjustment is in order as to her original 400 shares. Other tax consequences may materialize however.[33] □

Avoiding § 351.   Because § 351(a) provides for the nonrecognition of gain on transfers to controlled corporations, it is often regarded as a relief provision favoring taxpayers. There could be situations, however, where the avoidance of § 351(a) produces a more advantageous tax result. The transferors might prefer to recognize gain on the transfer of property if they cannot be particularly harmed by the gain because they are in low tax brackets. Further, the gain might be capital gain from which the transferors may be able to offset substantial capital losses.

Another reason that a particular transferor might wish to avoid § 351 concerns possible loss recognition. Recall that § 351(a) refers to the nonrecognition of both gains and losses. In a boot situation, § 351(b)(2) specifically states: "No loss to such recipient shall be recognized." The course of action for a transferor who wishes to recognize loss on the transfer of property with a basis in excess of fair market value could be any of several alternatives:

---

32. The stock attribution rules of § 318 (see chapter 17) do not apply to § 351 transfers. Consequently, the shares held by the son are not treated as being constructively owned by the mother.

33. Because the son has benefited from T's capital

contribution (his shares are worth more as a result), a gift has taken place. Therefore, T's capital contribution could lead to the imposition of a gift tax liability. In this connection, see chapter 25.

- Sell the property to the corporation for its stock. However, the IRS could attempt to collapse the "sale" by taking the approach that the transfer really falls under § 351(a). If the sale is disregarded, the transferor ends up with a realized, but unrecognized, loss.

- Sell the property to the corporation for other property or boot. Because the transferor receives no stock, § 351 is inapplicable.

- Transfer the property to the corporation in return for securities. Recall that § 351 does not apply to a transferor who receives only securities. In both this and the previous alternatives, one would have to watch for the possible disallowance of the loss under § 267.

Suppose, however, the loss property is to be transferred to the corporation and no loss is recognized by the transferor due to § 351(a). This could present an interesting problem in terms of assessing the economic realities involved.

EXAMPLE 40

E and F form X Corporation with the following investment: property by E (basis of $40,000 and fair market value of $50,000) and property by F (basis of $60,000 and fair market value of $50,000). Each receives 50% of the X Corporation stock. Has F acted wisely in settling for only 50% of the stock? At first blush, it would appear so, since E and F each invested property of the same value ($50,000). But what about the tax considerations? Due to the basis carryover of § 362(b), the corporation now has a basis of $40,000 in E's property and $60,000 in F's property. In essence, then, E has shifted a possible $10,000 gain to the corporation while F has transferred a $10,000 potential loss. (The higher basis in F's property has value to the corporation either in the form of higher depreciation deductions or less gain on a later sale.) With this in mind, an equitable allocation of the X Corporation stock would call for F to receive a greater percentage interest than E. □

PROBLEM MATERIALS

Discussion Questions

1. Briefly discuss the income tax consequences of the various forms of business organization in relation to the following:
   a. The tax treatment of sole proprietorships.
   b. Partnerships and the conduit concept.
   c. Partnerships as reporting entities.
   d. The similarities and dissimilarities between the tax treatment of partnerships, trusts, and estates.
   e. The similarities between S corporations and partnerships.
   f. The dissimilarities between S corporations and regular corporations.
   g. The similarities and dissimilarities between the tax treatment of individuals and regular corporations.

2. What effect does state law have in determining whether an entity is to be treated as a corporation for Federal income tax purposes?

3. Under what circumstances may a corporation legally constituted under state law be disregarded for Federal income tax purposes?

4. A building and lot situated in a favorable location in a large city is owned by individuals X and Y. X and Y want to sell the property but do not want the potential purchaser to know their identities. Thus, X and Y transfer the building and lot to a newly organized corporation, T Corporation, in exchange for all the stock of T Corporation. T Corporation sells the building and lot, collects the proceeds from the sale, distributes the proceeds to X and Y, and liquidates. T Corporation conducts no other activities. In all respects T Corporation meets the requirements of a corporation under applicable state law. Would T Corporation be recognized as a separate entity for tax purposes? Why or why not?

5. Why might the IRS attempt to disregard a legally constituted corporate entity? Why might the shareholders attempt such?

6. Evaluate the disadvantages of using the corporate form in carrying on a trade or business in light of the following:
   a. No deduction is permitted for dividend distributions.
   b. The conduit concept does not apply.

7. Under what circumstances might the owners of a business wish to have the business classified as an association? To have it not be so classified?

8. In testing for association status, what criteria are considered in the case of partnerships? In the case of trusts?

9. Compare the income tax treatment of corporations and individuals in the following respects:
   a. Applicable tax rates.
   b. Adjusted gross income determination.
   c. Deduction for casualty losses.
   d. Allowable tax credits.
   e. Recapture of depreciation.
   f. Dividends received from domestic corporations.
   g. Net operating losses.

10. Compare the tax treatment of corporate and noncorporate taxpayers' capital gains and losses with respect to the following:
    a. Net capital gains.
    b. A net long-term capital loss.
    c. A net short-term capital loss.
    d. Capital loss carrybacks.
    e. Capital loss carryovers.

11. What is the justification for the dividends received deduction?

12. Compare the tax treatment of corporate and noncorporate taxpayers' charitable contributions with respect to the following:
    a. The year of the deduction for an accrual basis taxpayer.
    b. The percentage limitations on the maximum deduction allowed for any one year.
    c. The amount of the deduction allowed for the donations of certain inventory.

13. In connection with organizational expenditures, comment on the following:
    a. Those that qualify for amortization.
    b. Those that do not qualify for amortization.
    c. The period over which amortization can take place.
    d. Expenses incurred but not paid by a cash basis corporation.
    e. Expenses incurred by a corporation in its second year of operation.

    f. The alternative if no election to amortize is made.

    g. The timing of the election to amortize.

14. The corporate income tax can be expressed by use of the following formula: $13,750 + 34% of taxable income in excess of $75,000.

    a. Do you agree? Explain.

    b. When would the formula work?

15. Qualified personal service corporations need not be concerned about keeping taxable income at $100,000 or less. Please comment.

16. What are the conditions for filing a Form 1120–A?

17. What purpose is served by Schedule M–1 of Form 1120? By Schedule M–2?

18. In terms of justification and effect, § 351 (transfer to corporation controlled by transferor) and § 1031 (like-kind exchanges) are much alike. Explain.

19. What does the term "property" include for purposes of § 351?

20. In arriving at the basis of stock received by a shareholder in a § 351 transfer, describe the effect of the following:

    a. The receipt of other property (boot) in addition to stock by the shareholder.

    b. Transfer of a liability to the corporation, along with the property, by the shareholder.

    c. The shareholder's basis in the property transferred to the corporation.

21. How does a corporation determine its basis in property received pursuant to a § 351 transfer?

22. What is the control requirement of § 351? Describe the effect of each of the following in satisfying this requirement:

    a. A shareholder renders services to the corporation for stock.

    b. A shareholder both renders services and transfers property to the corporation for stock.

    c. A shareholder has only momentary control after the transfer.

    d. A long period of time elapses between the transfers of property by different shareholders.

23. Assuming a § 351(a) nontaxable transfer, explain the tax effect, if any, of each of the following transactions:

    a. The transfer of depreciable property with recapture potential under § 1245 or § 1250.

    b. The later sale of such property by the corporation.

24. At a point when X Corporation has been in existence for six years, shareholder T transfers real estate (adjusted basis of $20,000 and fair market value of $100,000) to the corporation for additional stock. At the same time, P, the only other shareholder, purchases one share of stock for cash. After the two transfers, the percentages of stock ownership are as follows: 79% by T and 21% by P.

    a. What were the parties trying to accomplish?

    b. Will it work? Explain.

    c. Would the result change if T and P are father and son?

25. Assume the same facts as in Question 24, except that T receives nothing from X Corporation for the transfer of the real estate to the corporation. Does this change the tax result as to T?

26. Before incorporating her apartment rental business, B takes out second mortgages on several of the units. B uses the mortgage funds to make capital improvements to her personal residence. Along with all of the rental units, B

transfers the mortgages to the newly formed corporation in return for all of its stock. Discuss the tax consequences to B of the procedures followed.

27. In structuring the capitalization of a corporation, what are the advantages of utilizing debt rather than equity?

Problems

28. XYZ Corporation incurred net short-term capital gains of $30,000 and net long-term capital losses of $80,000 during 1990. Taxable income from other sources was $400,000. Prior years' transactions included the following:

1986	Net long-term capital gains	$80,000
1987	Net short-term capital gains	20,000
1988	Net long-term capital gains	10,000
1989	Net long-term capital gains	10,000

    a. How are the capital gains and losses treated on the 1990 tax return?
    b. Compute the capital loss carryback to the carryback years.
    c. Compute the amount of capital loss carryover, if any, and designate the years to which the loss may be carried.

29. X Corporation acquired residential rental property on January 3, 1984, for $100,000. The property was depreciated using the accelerated method and a 15-year recovery period under ACRS. Depreciation in the amount of $52,000 was claimed. X Corporation sold the property on January 1, 1990, for $110,000. What is the gain on the sale, and how is it taxed?

30. Assume the property in Problem 29 was a commercial building and X Corporation used the straight-line method of depreciation with a 15-year recovery period under ACRS. What would be the gain on the sale, and how would it be taxed?

31. During 1990, T Corporation, a calendar year taxpayer, had the following income and expenses:

Income from operations	$225,000
Expenses from operations	165,000
Qualifying dividends from domestic corporations	15,000
Net operating loss carryover from 1989	4,500

    On June 3, 1990, T Corporation made a contribution to a qualified charitable organization of $10,500 in cash (not included in any of the above items).
    a. Determine T Corporation's charitable contribution deduction for 1990.
    b. What happens to any excess charitable contribution deduction not allowable for 1990?

32. Pursuant to a resolution adopted by its board of directors, X Corporation, a calendar year accrual basis taxpayer, authorizes a $50,000 donation to City University (a qualified charitable organization) on December 20, 1989. The donation is made on March 10, 1990. Is the corporation correct in claiming a deduction (subject to statutory limitations) in 1989? What if the donation were made on April 10, 1990?

33. During 1990, a corporation has $100,000 of gross income and $125,000 in allowable business deductions. Included in gross income is $30,000 in qualifying dividends from domestic corporations (less than 20% owned).
    a. Determine the corporation's net operating loss for 1990.
    b. What happens to the loss if the corporation was newly created in 1990? In 1987?

34. In each of the following independent situations, determine the dividends received deduction. Assume that none of the corporate shareholders owns 20% or more of the stock in the corporations paying the dividends.

	E Corporation	F Corporation	G Corporation
Income from operations	$ 700,000	$ 800,000	$ 700,000
Expenses from operations	(600,000)	(900,000)	(740,000)
Qualifying dividends	100,000	200,000	200,000

35. T Corporation was formed on December 1, 1990. Qualifying organizational expenses were incurred and paid as follows:

Incurred and paid in December 1990	$10,000
Incurred in December 1990 but paid in January 1991	5,000
Incurred and paid in February 1991	3,000

Assume T Corporation makes a timely election under § 248 to amortize organizational expenditures over a period of 60 months. What amount may be amortized in the corporation's first tax year under each of the following assumptions?

a. T Corporation adopts a calendar year and the cash basis of accounting for tax purposes.

b. Same as (a), except that T Corporation chooses a fiscal year of December 1 through November 30.

c. T Corporation adopts a calendar year and the accrual basis of accounting for tax purposes.

d. Same as (c), except that T Corporation chooses a fiscal year of December 1 through November 30.

36. T Corporation, an accrual basis taxpayer, was formed and began operations on July 1, 1990. The following expenses were incurred during the first tax year of operations (July 1 through December 31, 1990):

Expenses of temporary directors and of organizational meetings	$2,500
Fee paid to the state of incorporation	300
Accounting services incident to organization	600
Legal services for drafting the corporate charter and bylaws	1,400
Expenses incident to the printing and sale of stock certificates	500
	$5,300

Assume T Corporation makes an appropriate and timely election under § 248(c) and the Regulations thereunder.

a. What is the maximum organizational expense T may write off for tax year 1990?

b. What would have been the result if a proper election had not been made?

37. In each of the following independent situations, determine the corporation's income tax liability. Assume that all corporations use a calendar year for tax purposes and that the tax year involved is 1990.

	Taxable Income
J Corporation	$ 40,000
K Corporation	120,000
L Corporation	380,000
M Corporation	70,000

38. A regular corporation did not distribute any dividends in tax year 1990. It had no capital gains or losses. What is its 1990 income tax liability under the following independent situations?

    a. Its taxable income was $30,000.

    b. Its taxable income was $70,000.

    c. Its taxable income was $130,000.

    d. Its taxable income was $2,000,000.

    e. Same as (a) except that the corporation distributed $20,000 in dividends to its sole shareholder.

    f. Same as (a) except that the corporation had a $20,000 capital loss.

39. For 1990, T Corporation, an accrual basis calendar year taxpayer, had net income per books of $172,750 and the following special transactions:

Life insurance proceeds received through the death of the corporation president	$100,000
Premiums paid on the life insurance policy on the president	10,000
Prepaid rent received and properly taxed in 1989 but credited as rent income in 1990	15,000
Rent income received in 1990 ($10,000 is prepaid and relates to 1991)	25,000
Interest income on tax-exempt bonds	5,000
Interest on loan to carry tax-exempt bonds	3,000
ACRS depreciation in excess of straight-line (straight-line was used for book purposes)	4,000
Capital loss in excess of capital gains	6,000
Federal income tax liability for 1990	22,250

    Using Schedule M–1 of Form 1120 (the most recent version available), compute T Corporation's taxable income for 1990.

40. Using the legend provided, classify each of the following statements:

    Legend

    I = Applies only to individual taxpayers
    C = Applies only to corporate taxpayers
    B = Applies to both individual and corporate taxpayers
    N = Applies to neither individual nor corporate taxpayers

    a. A net capital loss can be carried back.

    b. Net long-term capital losses are carried forward as short-term capital losses.

    c. A $4,000 net short-term capital loss in the current year can be deducted against ordinary income only to the extent of $3,000.

    d. The carryforward period for net capital losses is five years.

    e. The alternative minimum tax does not apply.

    f. Net operating losses are not allowed to be carried back.

    g. The credit for the elderly applies.

    h. The carryback period for excess charitable contributions is three years.

    i. Excess charitable contributions can be carried forward indefinitely.

    j. On the disposition of certain depreciable real estate, more ordinary income may result.

    k. Percentage limitations may restrict the amount of charitable deductions that can be claimed in any one tax year.

l. Casualty losses are deductible in full.

m. More adjustments are necessary to arrive at a net operating loss deduction.

41. G and H form Z Corporation with the following investment:

	Property Transferred		Number of Shares Issued
	Basis to Transferor	Fair Market Value	
From G—			
Cash	$60,000	$ 60,000	
Unrealized receivables	–0–	140,000	50
From H—			
Cash	25,000	25,000	
Machinery	50,000	75,000	50
Equipment	80,000	100,000	

a. How much gain, if any, must G recognize?

b. What will be G's basis in the Z Corporation stock?

c. What will be Z Corporation's basis in the unrealized receivables?

d. How much gain, if any, must H recognize?

e. What will be H's basis in the Z Corporation stock?

f. What will be Z Corporation's basis in the machinery and equipment?

42. A, B, C, and D (all individuals) form W Corporation with the following investment:

	Property Transferred		Number of Shares Issued
	Basis to Transferor	Fair Market Value	
From A—			
Personal services rendered to W Corporation	$ –0–	$ 10,000	10
From B—			
Equipment	115,000	100,000	90*
From C—			
Cash	20,000	20,000	
Unrealized accounts receivable	–0–	30,000	50
From D—			
Land and building	70,000	150,000	
Mortgage on land and building	100,000	100,000	50

*B receives $10,000 in cash in addition to the 90 shares.

The mortgage transferred by D is assumed by W Corporation. The value of each share of W Corporation stock is $1,000.

a. What, if any, is A's recognized gain or loss?

b. What basis will A have in the W Corporation stock?

c. How much gain or loss must B recognize?

d. What basis will B have in the W Corporation stock?

e. What basis will W Corporation have in the equipment?

f. What, if any, is C's recognized gain or loss?

g. What basis will C have in the W Corporation stock?

h. What basis will W Corporation have in the unrealized accounts receivable?

i. How much gain or loss must D recognize?

j. What basis will D have in the W Corporation stock?

k. What basis will W Corporation have in the land and building?

43. A and B organize X Corporation by transferring the following property:

| | Property Transferred | | Number of |
	Basis to Transferor	Fair Market Value	Shares Issued
From A—			
Unimproved land	$10,000	$100,000	
Mortgage on land	50,000	50,000	50
From B—			
Receivables	60,000	50,000	50

Assume the value of each share of X Corporation stock is $1,000.

a. What, if any, is A's recognized gain or loss?

b. What basis will A have in the X Corporation stock?

c. What basis will X Corporation have in the land?

d. What, if any, is B's recognized gain or loss?

e. What basis will B have in the X Corporation stock?

f. What basis will X Corporation have in the receivables?

44. A organized Y Corporation 10 years ago by contributing property worth $500,000, basis of $100,000, for 2,000 shares of stock in Y, representing 100% of the stock in Y Corporation. A later gave each of his children, B and C, 500 shares of stock in Y Corporation. In the current year, A transfers property worth $160,000, basis of $50,000, to Y Corporation for 500 shares in Y Corporation. What gain, if any, will A recognize on this transfer?

45. A forms T Corporation transferring land with a basis of $50,000, fair market value of $300,000. The land is subject to a mortgage of $150,000. Two weeks prior to incorporating T, A borrowed $50,000 for personal purposes and gave the lender a second mortgage on the land. T Corporation issues stock worth $100,000 to A and assumes the mortgages on the land.

a. What are the tax consequences to A and to T Corporation?

b. Assume that A does not borrow the $50,000 prior to incorporating T. A transfers the land to T Corporation for all the stock in T. T Corporation then borrows $50,000 and gives the lender a mortgage on the land. T Corporation distributes the $50,000 to A. What are the tax consequences to A and to T Corporation?

46. A city donates land to X Corporation as an inducement for X to locate there. The land is worth $100,000. The city also donates $50,000 in cash to X.

a. What income, if any, must X recognize as a result of the transfer of land and cash to it by the city?

b. What basis will X have in the land?

c. If X purchases property six months later with the $50,000 cash, what basis will X have in the property?

17

CORPORATIONS: DISTRIBUTIONS NOT IN COMPLETE LIQUIDATION

OBJECTIVES

Distinguish between corporate distributions not in complete liquidation and those in complete liquidation of the corporation.

Explain the concept of earnings and profits and its importance in measuring dividend income.

Discuss the tax consequences of a property dividend to the recipient shareholder and to the corporation making the distribution.

Illustrate the types of constructive dividend situations that could materialize in a closely held corporate setting.

Differentiate between taxable and nontaxable stock dividends.

Describe the various stock redemptions that qualify for sale or exchange treatment and thereby avoid dividend treatment.

OUTLINE

A working knowledge of the rules pertaining to corporate distributions is essential for anyone dealing with the tax problems of corporations and their shareholders. The form of such distributions is important because it can produce varying tax results to shareholders. Dividends are taxed as ordinary income to the recipient shareholder (however, stock dividends may not be taxed at all), while stock redemptions generally receive capital gain or loss treatment after allowing the shareholder to recover basis in the redeemed stock.

DIVIDEND DISTRIBUTIONS

Taxable Dividends—In General

Distributions by a corporation to its shareholders are presumed to be dividends unless the parties can prove otherwise. Section 316 treats such distributions, whether in the form of cash or other property, as ordinary dividend income to a shareholder to the extent of the distribution's pro rata share of earnings and profits (E & P) of the distributing corporation accumulated since February 28, 1913, or to the extent of corporate E & P for the current year.

Under § 301(c), the portion of a corporate distribution that is not taxed as a dividend (because of insufficient E & P) will be nontaxable to the extent of the shareholder's basis in the stock and will reduce that basis accordingly. The excess of the distribution over the shareholder's basis is treated as a capital gain if the stock is a capital asset.

EXAMPLE 1

At the end of the year, Y Corporation (a calendar year taxpayer) has E & P of $30,000. On this date, the corporation distributes cash of $40,000 to its two equal shareholders, C and D. The adjusted basis of the shareholders' stock investment is $8,000 for C and $4,000 for D. The $40,000 distribution should be accounted for as follows:

	C	D
Amount distributed	$ 20,000	$ 20,000
Portion from E & P (taxed as a dividend)	− 15,000	− 15,000
	$ 5,000	$ 5,000
Return of capital (reduction of basis)	− 5,000	− 4,000
	$ −0−	$ 1,000
Capital gain	− −0−	− 1,000
	$ −0−	$ −0−

Thus, of the $20,000 C receives, $15,000 is dividend income and $5,000 is a nontaxable return of capital. After the distribution, C will have a basis in the Y Corporation stock of $3,000 ($8,000 original adjusted basis − $5,000 return of capital). As to D, the result is $15,000 of dividend income, $4,000 of nontaxable return of capital, and $1,000 of capital gain. After the distribution, D will have a basis in the Y Corporation stock of $0 ($4,000 original adjusted basis − $4,000 return of capital). □

Since E & P is the key to dividend treatment of corporate distributions, its importance cannot be emphasized enough. Beginning in 1990, E & P will assume added importance since a concept based on adjusted E & P will replace pretax book income in the determination of business untaxed reported profits for purposes of the alternative minimum tax (refer to the discussion in chapter 12).

Earnings and Profits—§ 312

The term "earnings and profits" is not defined by the Code. Although § 312 lists certain transactions that affect E & P, it stops short of a complete definition. E & P does possess similarities to the accounting concept of retained earnings (earnings retained in the business), but E & P and retained earnings are often not the same. For example, although a stock dividend is treated as a capitalization of retained earnings for financial accounting purposes (i.e., it is debited to the retained earnings account and credited to a capital stock account), it does not decrease E & P. Similarly, the elimination of a deficit in a "quasi-reorganization" increases retained earnings but does not increase E & P.

To fully understand the concept of E & P, it is helpful to keep several observations in mind. First, E & P might well be described as the factor that fixes the upper limit on the amount of dividend income shareholders would have to recognize as a result of a distribution by the corporation. In this sense, E & P represents the corporation's economic ability to pay a dividend without impairing its capital. Therefore, the effect of a specific transaction on the E & P account may be determined simply by considering whether or not the transaction increases or decreases the corporation's capacity to pay a dividend.

Computation of E & P.   Barring certain important exceptions, E & P is increased by earnings for the taxable year computed in the same manner as taxable income is determined. If the corporation uses the cash method of accounting in computing taxable income, it must also use the cash method to determine the changes in E & P.[1]

E & P is increased for all items of income. Interest on municipal bonds, for example, though not taxed to the corporation, would increase the corporation's E & P. Gains and losses from property transactions generally affect the determination of E & P only to the extent they are recognized for tax purposes. Thus, a gain on an involuntary conversion not recognized by the corporation because the insurance proceeds are reinvested in property that is similar or related in service or use to the property converted (§ 1033) would not affect E & P. However, the E & P account can be affected by both deductible and nondeductible items. Consequently, excess capital losses, expenses incurred to produce tax-exempt income, and Federal income taxes all reduce E & P, although such items do not enter into the calculation of taxable income.

The E & P account can be reduced only by cost depletion, even though the corporation may be using percentage (statutory) depletion for income tax purposes. E & P cannot be reduced by accelerated depreciation.[2] However, if a depreciation method such as units-of-production or machine hours is used, the adjustment to E & P can be determined on this basis.

The alternative ACRS system must be used for purposes of computing E & P. Thus, if cost recovery is figured under ACRS, E & P must be computed using the

---

1. Regulations relating to E & P begin at Reg. § 1.312–6.

2. § 312(k).

straight-line recovery method over a recovery period equal to the asset's Asset Depreciation Range (ADR) midpoint life. Later, when the asset is sold, the increase or decrease in E & P is determined by using the adjusted basis of the asset for E & P purposes.

A corporation's E & P for the year in which it sells property on the installment basis will be increased by the amount of any deferred gain. This is accomplished by treating all principal payments as having been received in the year of sale.[3]

A corporation that accounts for income and expenses attributable to a long-term contract on the completed contract method of accounting must use the percentage of completion basis in arriving at E & P.[4]

Intangible drilling costs [allowable as a deduction under § 263(c)] and mineral exploration and development costs [allowable under § 616(a) or § 617] are required to be capitalized for purposes of computing E & P. Once capitalized, these expenditures can be charged to E & P over a specified period: 60 months for intangible drilling costs and 120 months for mine exploration and development costs.[5]

EXAMPLE 2   A corporation sells property (basis of $10,000) to its sole shareholder for $8,000. Because of § 267 (disallowance of losses on sales between related parties), the $2,000 loss cannot be deducted in arriving at the corporation's taxable income for the year. But since the overall economic effect of the transaction is a decrease in the corporation's assets by $2,000, the loss will reduce the current E & P for the year of sale. □

EXAMPLE 3   A corporation pays a $10,000 premium on a keyman life insurance policy (the corporation is the owner and beneficiary of the policy) covering the life of its president. As a result of the payment, the cash surrender value of the policy is increased by $7,000. Although none of the $10,000 premium would be deductible for tax purposes, current E & P would be reduced by $3,000. □

EXAMPLE 4   A corporation collects $100,000 on a keyman life insurance policy. At the time the policy matured on the death of the insured employee, it possessed a cash surrender value of $30,000. None of the $100,000 will be included in the corporation's taxable income [see § 101(a)], but $70,000 would be added to the current E & P account. □

EXAMPLE 5   During 1990, a corporation makes charitable contributions, $12,000 of which cannot be deducted in arriving at the taxable income for the year because of the 10% limitation. However, pursuant to § 170(d)(2), the $12,000 is carried

---

3. Under prior law, gains from installment sales were not included in E & P until recognized for purposes of computing taxable income for the year. Thus, gain deferred for purposes of computing taxable income was also deferred for purposes of computing E & P.

4. Under prior law, income from long-term contracts accounted for under the completed con-

tract method of accounting was included in E & P when such income was recognized for tax purposes, generally in the year in which the contract was completed.

5. Under prior law, these costs were charged against E & P in the same manner as they were treated for purposes of computing taxable income.

over to 1991 and fully deducted in that year. The excess charitable contribution would reduce the corporation's current E & P for 1990 by $12,000 and increase its current E & P for 1991, when the deduction is allowed, by a like amount. The increase in E & P in 1991 is necessitated by the fact that the charitable contribution carryover reduces the taxable income for that year (the starting point for computing E & P) and already has been taken into account in determining the E & P for 1990. □

EXAMPLE 6

On January 2, 1988, X Corporation purchased for $30,000 equipment with an ADR midpoint life of 10 years that was then depreciated under MACRS. The asset was sold on January 2, 1990, for $27,000. For purposes of determining taxable income and E & P, cost recovery claimed on the machine and the machine's adjusted basis are summarized as follows:

	Cost Recovery	Adjusted Basis
Taxable Income		
1988: $30,000 × 14.29%	$4,287	$25,713
1989: $30,000 × 24.49%	7,347	18,366
E & P		
1988: $30,000 ÷ 10-year recovery period × ½ (half year for first year of service)	$1,500	$28,500
1989: $30,000 ÷ 10-year recovery period	3,000	25,500

Gain on the sale for purposes of determining taxable income and increase (decrease) in E & P is computed as follows:

	Taxable Income	E & P
$27,000 − $18,366 adjusted basis	$8,634	
$27,000 − $25,500 adjusted basis		$1,500

EXAMPLE 7

In 1990, X Corporation, a calendar year taxpayer, sells unimproved real estate (basis of $20,000) for $100,000. Under the terms of the sale, X Corporation will receive two annual payments, beginning in 1991, of $50,000 each with interest of 12%. X Corporation does not elect out of the installment method. Although X Corporation's taxable income for 1990 will not reflect any of the gain from the sale, the corporation must increase E & P for 1990 by $80,000 (the deferred profit component). □

Summary of E & P Adjustments. Recall that E & P serves as a measure of the earnings of the corporation that are treated as available for distribution as taxable dividends to the shareholders. Although E & P is initially increased by the

corporation's taxable income, certain adjustments must be made to taxable income with respect to various transactions in determining the corporation's current E & P. Those adjustments are reviewed in Concept Summary 17–1. Other items that affect E & P, such as property dividends and stock redemptions, are covered later in the chapter and are not incorporated in Concept Summary 17–1.

The Source of the Distribution.   In determining the source of a dividend distribution, a dividend is deemed to have been made first from current E & P and then from E & P accumulated since February 28, 1913.

EXAMPLE 8   At the beginning of the current year, Y Corporation has a deficit in accumulated E & P of $30,000. For the year, it has current E & P of $10,000 and distributes $5,000 to its shareholders. The $5,000 distribution will be treated as a taxable dividend since it is deemed to have been made from current E & P. This will be the case even though Y Corporation will still have a deficit in its accumulated E & P at the end of the current year.   □

CONCEPT SUMMARY 17–1

E & P Adjustments

Nature of the Transaction	Effect on Taxable Income in Arriving at Current E & P
Tax-exempt income.	Add
Federal income taxes.	Subtract
Disallowed loss on sale between related parties.	Subtract
Payment of premiums on insurance policy on life of corporate officer.	Subtract
Collection of proceeds of insurance policy on life of corporate officer.	Add
Excess charitable contribution (over 10% limitation).	Subtract
Deduction of excess charitable contribution in succeeding taxable year (increase E & P because deduction reduces taxable income while E & P was reduced in a prior year).	Add
Realized gain (not recognized) on an involuntary conversion.	No effect
Percentage depletion (only cost depletion can reduce E & P).	Add
Accelerated depreciation (E & P is reduced only by straight-line, units-of-production, or machine hours depreciation).	Add
Deferred gain on installment sale (all gain is added to E & P in year of sale).	Add
Long-term contract reported on completed contract method (use percentage of completion method).	Add
Intangible drilling costs deducted currently (reduce E & P in future years by amortizing costs over 60 months).	Add
Mining exploration and development costs (reduce E & P in future years by amortizing costs over 120 months).	Add

If distributions made during the year exceed the current year's E & P, the portion of each distribution deemed to have been made from current E & P is the percentage that the total E & P for the year bears to the total distributions for that year. This can make a difference if any of the shareholders sell their stock during the year and total current distributions exceed current E & P.

Distinguishing between Current and Accumulated E & P.   Accumulated E & P can be defined as the total of all previous years' current E & P as computed on the first day of each taxable year in accordance with the tax law in effect during that year. The factors that affect the computation of the current E & P for any one year have been discussed previously. Why must the distinction be drawn between current and accumulated E & P when it is clear that distributions are taxable if and to the extent that current *and* accumulated E & P exist?

1. When there is a deficit in accumulated E & P and a positive amount in current E & P, distributions will be regarded as dividends to the extent of the current E & P. Refer to Example 8.

2. Current E & P is allocated on a pro rata basis to the distributions made during the year; accumulated E & P is applied (to the extent necessary) in chronological order beginning with the earliest distributions.

3. Unless and until the parties can show otherwise, it is presumed that any distribution is covered by current E & P.

4. When a deficit in current E & P (a current loss) and a positive balance in accumulated E & P exist, the accounts are netted at the date of distribution. If the resulting balance is zero or a deficit, the distribution is a return of capital. If a positive balance results, the distribution will represent a dividend to such extent. Any loss is allocated ratably during the year unless the parties can show otherwise.

Distinctions 3 and 4 are illustrated as follows:

EXAMPLE 9   Q Corporation uses a fiscal year of July 1 through June 30 for tax purposes. T, Q Corporation's only shareholder, uses a calendar year. As of July 1, 1990, Q Corporation had a zero balance in its accumulated E & P account. For fiscal year 1990–91, the corporation has suffered a $5,000 operating loss. On August 1, 1990, Q Corporation distributed $10,000 to T. The distribution represents dividend income to T and must be reported as such when T files her income tax return for calendar year 1990 on or before April 15, 1991. Because T cannot prove until June 30, 1991, that the corporation had a deficit for fiscal year 1990–91, she must assume the $10,000 distribution was fully covered by current E & P. When T learns of the deficit, she can file an amended return for 1990 showing the $10,000 as a return of capital. □

EXAMPLE 10   At the beginning of the current year, R Corporation (a calendar year taxpayer) had accumulated E & P of $10,000. During the year, the corporation incurred a $15,000 net loss from operations that accrued ratably. On July 1, R Corporation distributed $6,000 in cash to H, its sole shareholder. The balance of both accumulated and current E & P as of July 1 must be determined and netted because of the deficit in current E & P. The balance at this date would

be $2,500 [$10,000 (accumulated E & P) − $7,500 (one-half of the current deficit of $15,000)]. Of the $6,000 distribution, $2,500 would be taxed as a dividend and $3,500 would represent a return of capital. □

Property Dividends—Effect on the Shareholder

When a corporation distributes property rather than cash to a shareholder, the amount distributed is measured by the fair market value of the property on the date of distribution. Section 301(c) is applicable to such distributions. Thus, the portion of the distribution covered by existing E & P is a dividend, and any excess is treated as a return of capital.

If the fair market value of the property distributed exceeds the corporation's E & P and the shareholder's basis in the stock investment, a capital gain would result. The amount distributed is reduced by any liabilities to which the distributed property is subject immediately before and immediately after the distribution and by any liabilities of the corporation assumed by the shareholder in connection with the distribution.[6] The basis in the distributed property is the fair market value of the property on the date of the distribution.

EXAMPLE 11

P Corporation has E & P of $60,000. It distributes land with a fair market value of $50,000 (adjusted basis of $30,000) to its sole shareholder, T. The land is subject to a liability of $10,000, which T assumes. T would have a taxable dividend of $40,000 ($50,000 fair market value − $10,000 liability). The basis of the land to T is $50,000. □

EXAMPLE 12

Ten percent of X Corporation is owned by Y Corporation. X Corporation has ample E & P to cover any distributions made during the year. One such distribution made to Y Corporation consists of a vacant lot with an adjusted basis of $5,000 and a fair market value of $3,000. Y Corporation has a taxable dividend of $3,000, and its basis in the lot becomes $3,000. □

Property that has depreciated in value is usually not a suitable subject for distribution as a property dividend. Note what has happened in Example 12. The loss of $2,000 (adjusted basis $5,000, fair market value $3,000), in effect, disappears. If, instead, the lot had first been sold and the $3,000 proceeds distributed, the loss would have been preserved for X Corporation.

Property Dividends—Effect on the Corporation

A property distribution by a corporation to its shareholders poses two questions. Does the distribution result in recognized gain or loss to the corporation making the distribution? What effect will the distribution have on the corporation's E & P? These questions are answered in the following discussion.

Recognition of Gain or Loss.   All distributions of appreciated property cause gain to the distributing corporation.[7] In effect, the corporation that makes a property

---

6. § 301(b)(2).

7. Section 311 covers taxability of a corporation on distributions.

dividend will be treated as if it had sold the property to the shareholder for its fair market value. However, no loss is recognized to the distributing corporation on distributions of property with a tax basis in excess of fair market value.

EXAMPLE 13   X Corporation distributes land (basis of $10,000 and fair market value of $30,000) to T, an individual shareholder. X Corporation must recognize a gain of $20,000. □

EXAMPLE 14   Assume the property in Example 13 has a fair market value of $10,000 and a basis of $30,000. X Corporation would not recognize a loss on the distribution. □

If the distributed property is subject to a liability in excess of basis or the shareholder assumes such a liability, the fair market value of the property for purposes of determining gain on the distribution is treated as not being less than the amount of the liability.

EXAMPLE 15   Assume the land in Example 13 is subject to a liability of $35,000. X Corporation must recognize a gain of $25,000 on the distribution. □

Effect of Corporate Distributions on E & P.   In the event of a corporate distribution, the E & P account is reduced by the amount of money distributed or by the greater of the fair market value or the adjusted basis of property distributed, less the amount of any liability on the property.[8] E & P is increased by gain recognized on appreciated property distributed as a property dividend.

EXAMPLE 16   M Corporation distributes property (basis of $10,000 and fair market value of $20,000) to T, its shareholder. M Corporation recognizes a gain of $10,000, which would be added to its E & P, which would be reduced by $20,000, the fair market value of the property. T would have dividend income of $20,000. □

EXAMPLE 17   Assume the same facts as in Example 16, except that the fair market value of the property is $15,000 and the adjusted basis in the hands of M Corporation is $20,000. Because the loss is not recognized and the adjusted basis is greater than fair market value, E & P is reduced by $20,000. T must report dividend income of $15,000. □

EXAMPLE 18   Assume the same facts as in Example 17, except that the property is subject to a liability of $6,000. E & P would now be reduced by $14,000 ($20,000 adjusted basis − $6,000 liability). T would have a dividend of $9,000 ($15,000 amount of the distribution − $6,000 liability), and T's basis in the property is $15,000. □

---

8.   §§ 312(a), (b), and (c).

Under no circumstances can a distribution, whether cash or property, either generate a deficit in E & P or add to a deficit in E & P. Deficits can arise only through corporate losses.

Constructive Dividends

A distribution by a corporation to its shareholders can be treated as a dividend for Federal income tax purposes even though it is not formally declared or designated as a dividend or issued pro rata to all shareholders. Nor must the distribution satisfy the legal requirements of a dividend as set forth by applicable state law. The key factor determining dividend status is a measurable economic benefit conveyed to the shareholder. This benefit, often described as a constructive dividend, is distinguishable from actual corporate distributions of cash and property in form only.

Constructive dividend situations usually arise in the context of the closely held corporation. Here, the dealings between the parties are less structured, and, frequently, formalities are not preserved. The constructive dividend serves as a substitute for actual distributions and is intended to accomplish some tax objective not available through the use of direct dividends. The shareholders may attempt to bail out corporate profits in a form deductible to the corporation. Recall that dividend distributions do not provide the distributing corporation with an income tax deduction, although they do reduce E & P. Alternatively, the shareholders may be seeking benefits for themselves while avoiding the recognition of income. Constructive dividends are, in reality, disguised dividends.

Do not conclude, however, that all constructive dividends are deliberate attempts to avoid actual and formal dividends. Often, constructive dividends are inadvertent, and, consequently, a dividend result may come as a surprise to the parties. For this reason, if for none other, an awareness of the various constructive dividend situations is essential to protect the parties from unanticipated tax consequences. The types of constructive dividends most frequently encountered are summarized below.

Shareholder Use of Corporate-Owned Property.   A constructive dividend can occur when a shareholder uses corporation property for personal purposes at no cost. Personal use of corporate-owned automobiles, airplanes, yachts, fishing camps, hunting lodges, and other entertainment facilities is commonplace in some closely held corporations. Such use will cause the shareholder to have dividend income to the extent of the fair rental value of the property for the period of its personal use.[9]

Bargain Sale of Corporate Property to a Shareholder.   Shareholders often purchase property from a corporation at a cost that is less than the fair market value of the property. These bargain sales produce dividend income to the extent of the difference between the property's fair market value on the date of sale and the amount paid for the property by the shareholder. Such questionable situations might be avoided by appraising the property on or about the date of the sale. The appraised value becomes the price to be paid by the shareholder.

---

9. This result presumes the ownership of the property to be in the corporation. If not, and if the ownership can be attributed to the shareholder, the measure of the constructive dividend would be the cost of the property. In this regard, bare legal title at the corporate level may not suffice. See, for example, *Raymond F. Daly*, 37 TCM 15, T.C.Memo. 1978–5.

Bargain Rental of Corporate Property. A bargain rental of corporate property by a shareholder also produces dividend income. Here the measure of the constructive dividend is the excess of the property's fair rental value over the rent actually paid. Again, the importance of appraisal data in avoiding any questionable situations should be readily apparent.

Payments for the Benefit of a Shareholder. If a corporation pays an obligation of a shareholder, the payment is treated as a constructive dividend. The obligation involved need not be legally binding on the shareholder; it may, in fact, be a moral obligation. Forgiveness of shareholder indebtedness by the corporation can create an identical problem. Excessive rentals paid by a corporation for the use of shareholder property are treated as constructive dividends.

Excessive Compensation. A salary payment of a shareholder-employee that is deemed to be unreasonable is frequently treated as a constructive dividend and therefore is not deductible by the corporation. In determining the reasonableness of salary payments, the following factors are to be considered:

- The employee's qualifications.

- A comparison of salaries with dividend distributions.

- The prevailing rates of compensation for comparable positions in comparable business concerns.

- The nature and scope of the employee's work.

- The size and complexity of the business.

- A comparison of salaries paid with both gross and net income.

- The salary policy of the taxpayer with respect to all employees.

- For small corporations with a limited number of officers, the amount of compensation paid the particular employee in previous years.

Loans to Shareholders. Advances to shareholders that are not bona fide loans are also deemed to be constructive dividends. Whether an advance qualifies as a bona fide loan is a question of fact to be determined in light of the particular circumstances. Factors considered in determining whether the advance is a bona fide loan include the following:

- Whether the advance is on open account or is evidenced by a written instrument.

- Whether the shareholder furnished collateral or other security for the advance.

- How long the advance has been outstanding.

- Whether any payments have been made, excluding dividend sources.

- The shareholder's financial capability to repay the advance.

- The shareholder's use of the funds (e.g., payment of routine bills versus nonrecurring, extraordinary expenses).

- The regularity of such advances.

- The dividend-paying history of the corporation.

If a corporation succeeds in getting past the hurdle of proving that an advance to a shareholder is a bona fide loan so that the advance is not deemed to be a

constructive dividend, the shareholder will still have a constructive dividend in the amount of any forgone interest. Interest-free or below-market loans by a corporation to a shareholder cause the shareholder to have a constructive dividend to the extent of "imputed interest," which is the difference between the rate the Federal government pays on new borrowings, compounded semiannually, and the interest charged on the loan. The corporation is deemed to have made a dividend distribution to the shareholder to the extent of the forgone interest. The shareholder is then deemed to have made an interest payment to the corporation for the same amount. Although the shareholder may be permitted to deduct the deemed interest payment, the corporation has interest income with no corresponding deduction since the imputed interest element is a constructive dividend.

EXAMPLE 19   T Corporation loans its principal shareholder, S, $100,000 on January 2, 1990. The loan is interest-free. On December 31, 1990, T Corporation is deemed to have made a dividend distribution to S in the amount of the imputed interest on the loan, determined by using the Federal rate and compounded semiannually. Assume the Federal rate is 12%. T Corporation is deemed to have paid a dividend to S in the amount of $12,360.

Although S has dividend income of $12,360, he may be permitted to offset the income with a $12,360 deemed interest payment to T Corporation. T Corporation has deemed interest income of $12,360, but has no corresponding deduction because the deemed payment from T Corporation to S is a nondeductible dividend. □

Loans to a Corporation by Shareholders.   When shareholder loans to a corporation are reclassified as equity because the debt has too many features of stock, any interest and principal payments made by the corporation to the shareholder are treated as constructive dividends.

Tax Treatment of Constructive Dividends.   Constructive distributions possess the same tax attributes as actual distributions. Thus, a corporate shareholder would be entitled to the dividends received deduction of § 243. The constructive distribution would be a taxable dividend only to the extent of the corporation's current and accumulated E & P. As usual, the task of proving that the distribution constitutes a return of capital because of inadequate E & P rests with the taxpayer.

Stock Dividends and Stock Rights

Stock Dividends—§ 305.   Because no change occurs in a shareholder's proportionate interest in a corporation upon receipt of a stock dividend, such distributions were initially accorded tax-free treatment. The current provisions of § 305 are based on the proportionate interest concept.

Stock dividends are not taxable if they are pro rata distributions of stock, or stock rights, on common stock. Section 305(b) contains five exceptions to the general rule that stock dividends are nontaxable. These exceptions deal with various disproportionate distribution situations. If stock dividends are not taxable, there is no reduction in the corporation's E & P.[10] If the stock dividends are taxable, the distribution is treated by the distributing corporation in the same manner as any other taxable property dividend.

---

10.   § 312(d)(1).

If a stock dividend is taxable, basis to the shareholder-distributee is fair market value, and the holding period starts on the date of receipt. If a stock dividend is not taxable, § 307 requires that the basis of the stock on which the dividend is distributed be reallocated. If the dividend shares are identical to these formerly held shares, basis in the old stock is reallocated by dividing the taxpayer's cost in the old stock by the total number of shares. If the dividend stock is not identical to the underlying shares (a stock dividend of preferred on common, for example), basis is determined by allocating cost of the formerly held shares between the old and new stock according to the fair market value of each. Holding period will include the holding period of the formerly held stock.[11]

skip

EXAMPLE 20   A, an individual, bought 1,000 shares of stock two years ago for $10,000. In the current tax year, A received 10 shares of common stock as a nontaxable stock dividend. A's basis of $10,000 would be divided by 1,010. Consequently, each share of stock would have a basis of $9.90 instead of the pre-dividend $10 basis. ☐

EXAMPLE 21   Assume A received, instead, a nontaxable preferred stock dividend of 100 shares. The preferred stock has a fair market value of $1,000, and the common stock, on which the preferred is distributed, has a fair market value of $19,000. After the receipt of the stock dividend, the basis of the common stock is $9,500, and the basis of the preferred is $500, computed as follows:

Fair market value of common	$19,000
Fair market value of preferred	1,000
	$20,000
Basis of common: 19/20 × $10,000	$ 9,500
Basis of preferred: 1/20 × $10,000	$ 500

☐

Stock Rights.   The rules for determining taxability of stock rights are identical to those for determining taxability of stock dividends. If the rights are taxable, the recipient has income to the extent of the fair market value of the rights. The fair market value then becomes the shareholder-distributee's basis in the rights. If the rights are exercised, the holding period for the new stock is the date the rights (whether taxable or nontaxable) are exercised. The basis of the new stock is the basis of the rights plus the amount of any other consideration given.

If stock rights are not taxable and the value of the rights is less than 15 percent of the value of the old stock, the basis of the rights is zero unless the shareholder elects to have some of the basis in the formerly held stock allocated to the rights.[12] If the fair market value of the rights is 15 percent or more of the value of the old stock and the rights are exercised or sold, the shareholder must allocate some of the basis in the formerly held stock to the rights. Assume the value of the stock rights is less than 15 percent of the value of the stock and the shareholder makes an election to allocate basis to the rights. The election is made in the form of a statement attached to the shareholder's return for the year in which the rights are received.

---

11. § 1223(5).   12. § 307(b)(1).

EXAMPLE 22   A corporation with common stock outstanding declares a nontaxable dividend payable in rights to subscribe to common stock. Each right entitles the holder to purchase one share of stock for $90. One right is issued for every two shares of stock owned. T owns 400 shares of stock purchased two years ago for $15,000. At the time of the distribution of the rights, the market value of the common stock is $100 per share, and the market value of the rights is $8 per right. T receives 200 rights. He exercises 100 rights and sells the remaining 100 rights three months later for $9 per right. T need not allocate the cost of the original stock to the rights because the value of the rights is less than 15% of the value of the stock ($1,600 ÷ $40,000 = 4%).

If T does not allocate his original stock basis to the rights, his basis in the new stock will be $9,000 ($90 × 100). Sale of the rights would produce long-term capital gain of $900 ($9 × 100). The holding period of the rights starts with the date the original 400 shares of stock were acquired. The holding period of the new stock begins on the date the stock was purchased.

If T elects to allocate basis to the rights, his basis in the rights would be $577, computed as follows: $1,600 value of rights ÷ $41,600 value of rights and stock × $15,000 = $577. His basis in the stock would be $14,423 [($40,000 ÷ $41,600) × $15,000 = $14,423]. When he exercises the rights, his basis in the new stock would be $9,288.50 ($9,000 cost + $288.50 basis in 100 rights). Sale of the rights would produce a long-term capital gain of $611.50 ($900 selling price − $288.50 basis in the remaining 100 rights). □

STOCK REDEMPTIONS

Overview

In a stock redemption a corporation purchases some of its stock from a shareholder. The reacquired stock can be cancelled, held as treasury stock, or otherwise disposed of. Redemptions take place for various reasons. Some of the more common reasons are summarized below.

1. A shareholder may wish to withdraw some or all of his or her investment in the corporation. Perhaps the shareholder wants to take advantage of other investment opportunities or retire or disagrees with current management policies.

2. The corporation may want to reacquire some of its stock to pass on to key nonshareholder employees or to fund employee stock ownership plans.

3. The corporation may feel that its own stock is an attractive investment. Thus, it chooses to "invest in itself."

Reason 1 above arises most often in the context of a closely held corporation. Because no market probably exists for the stock, the withdrawing shareholder's choices are limited to selling the stock to the other shareholders or to the corporation. If the other shareholders lack the funds to purchase the stock, the withdrawing shareholder must resort to the corporation.

Presuming a shareholder sells all or part of his or her stock investment to the issuing corporation, what tax consequences result? Two possibilities exist. First, the transaction will be classified as a dividend if it does not qualify for *exchange* treatment under the tax law. In this regard, the *Internal Revenue Code* controls, and the classification of the transaction under state law is immaterial. Second, if exchange treatment requirements are satisfied, the shareholder will recognize *gain*

or loss measured by the difference between the consideration received and the basis of the stock redeemed. Such gain or loss will usually be capital because stock held as an investment is a capital asset.

EXAMPLE 23   T redeems stock (basis of $40,000) in X Corporation for its fair market value of $100,000. The stock was acquired by T five years ago as an investment. If the redemption *does not* qualify as an exchange and assuming X Corporation has adequate E & P, the $100,000 T receives is dividend income. If the redemption *does* qualify as an exchange, the result is as follows:

Redemption proceeds	$100,000
Less basis in the stock redeemed	40,000
Long-term capital gain	$ 60,000

□

In Example 23 note the advantage of having the redemption qualify for exchange treatment. By allowing the shareholder to recover the basis in the stock, $40,000 of income is avoided. Thus, stock redemptions should be structured so as to satisfy the exchange requirements of the tax law.

Under the present Code, the following major types of stock redemptions qualify for exchange treatment and will, as a result, avoid dividend income consequences:

- Distributions not essentially equivalent to a dividend [§ 302(b)(1)].

- Distributions substantially disproportionate in terms of shareholder effect [§ 302(b)(2)].

- Distributions in complete termination of a shareholder's interest [§ 302(b)(3)].

- Distributions to pay a shareholder's death taxes (§ 303).

Stock Attribution Rules

In order to obtain exchange treatment, most redemptions require a reduction in the redeeming shareholder's relative ownership in the corporation. To deter the use of certain qualifying stock redemptions in related-party situations, § 318 imposes constructive ownership of stock (stock attribution) rules. In testing for exchange treatment, therefore, a shareholder may be required to take into account the stock owned by others who fall within the definition of related parties. Related parties include immediate family, specifically spouses, children, grandchildren, and parents. Attribution also takes place *from* and *to* partnerships, estates, trusts, and corporations (50 percent or more ownership required in the case of corporations).

EXAMPLE 24   T, an individual, owns 30% of the stock in X Corporation, the other 70% being held by her children. For purposes of § 318, T is treated as owning 100% of the stock in X Corporation. She owns 30% directly and, because of the family attribution rules, 70% indirectly. □

EXAMPLE 25   C, an individual, owns 50% of the stock in Y Corporation. The other 50% is owned by a partnership in which C has a 20% interest. C is deemed to own 60% of Y Corporation: 50% directly and, because of the partnership interest, 10% indirectly.   □

The stock attribution rules of § 318 do not apply to stock redemptions to pay death taxes. Under certain conditions, the *family* attribution rules (refer to Example 24) do not apply to stock redemptions in complete termination of a shareholder's interest.

Not Essentially Equivalent to a Dividend Stock Redemption— § 302(b)(1)

Section 302(b)(1) provides that a redemption will be treated as a distribution in part or full payment in exchange for the stock if it is "not essentially equivalent to a dividend." A distribution is not essentially equivalent to a dividend when there has been a meaningful reduction of the shareholder's proportionate interest in the redeeming corporation. The facts and circumstances of each case will determine whether a distribution in redemption of stock is essentially equivalent to a dividend within the meaning of § 302(b)(1). Courts have considered a decrease in the redeeming shareholder's voting control to be the most significant indicator of a meaningful reduction. Other factors considered are reductions in the rights of redeeming shareholders to share in corporate earnings or to receive corporate assets upon liquidation.

EXAMPLE 26   A, an individual, owns 58% of the common stock of Y Corporation. After a redemption of part of A's stock, A owns 51% of the stock of Y Corporation. A would continue to have dominant voting rights in Y; thus, the redemption would be treated as "essentially equivalent to a dividend," and A would have ordinary income on the entire amount of the distribution.   □

EXAMPLE 27   X Corporation redeems 2% of the stock of B, a minority shareholder. Before the redemption, B owned 10% of X Corporation. In this case, the redemption may qualify as "not essentially equivalent to a dividend." B experiences a reduction in her voting rights, her right to participate in current earnings and accumulated surplus, and her right to share in net assets upon liquidation.   □

There are few objective tests to determine when a redemption is or is not essentially equivalent to a dividend. Section 302(b)(1) was specifically added to provide for redemptions of preferred stock. Often, such stock is called in by the corporation without the shareholder's exercising any control over the redemption. Some courts interpreted § 302(b)(1) to mean that a redemption would be granted exchange treatment if there was a business purpose for the redemption and there was no tax avoidance scheme to bail out dividends at favorable tax rates. The real question was whether the stock attribution rules of § 318(a) applied to this provision. However, some courts appeared to be less concerned with the application of § 318(a) and more concerned with the presence of a business purpose for the redemption.

These issues were resolved by the U.S. Supreme Court in *U.S. v. Davis*.[13] First, the Court found that the presence or absence of a business purpose was not determinative in the application of § 302(b)(1). For a redemption to be not essentially equivalent to a dividend, there must be "a meaningful reduction of the shareholder's proportionate interest in the corporation." Second, the attribution rules of § 318(a) must be considered in resolving the meaningful reduction test.

What the Supreme Court had in mind when it promulgated the meaningful reduction test has been the subject of much controversy. It should be clear, however, that a meaningful reduction will require a smaller change in ownership than is needed for a § 302(b)(2) redemption (see the discussion below of substantially disproportionate redemptions). Likewise, a shareholder that maintains voting control of the corporation after the redemption is not apt to qualify under § 302(b)(1).

EXAMPLE 28

W Corporation has 100 shares of stock outstanding. Of these shares, 58 are owned by S and 42 by other *unrelated* individuals. If W Corporation redeems 7 of S's shares, the redemption will not qualify under § 302(b)(1) because S continues to have voting control after the redemption. □

If a redemption is treated as an ordinary dividend, the shareholder's basis in the stock redeemed attaches to the remaining stock. According to the Regulations, this basis would attach to other stock held by the taxpayer (or to stock he or she owns constructively).[14]

EXAMPLE 29

A husband and wife each own 50 shares in X Corporation, representing 100% of the stock of X. All the stock was purchased for $50,000. The corporation redeems the husband's 50 shares. Assuming the rules governing the complete termination of a shareholder's interest under § 302(b)(3) do not apply, such a redemption would be treated as a taxable dividend. The husband's basis in the stock, $25,000, would attach to his wife's stock so that she would have a basis of $50,000 in the 50 shares she currently owns in X Corporation. □

Substantially Disproportionate Redemptions—§ 302(b)(2)

A redemption of stock qualifies for capital gain treatment under § 302(b)(2) if two conditions are met:

The distribution must be substantially disproportionate. To be substantially disproportionate, the shareholder must own, after the distribution, less than 80 percent of his or her total interest in the corporation before the redemption. For example, if a shareholder has a 60 percent ownership in a corporation that redeems part of the stock, the redemption is substantially disproportionate only if the percentage of ownership after the redemption is less than 48 percent (80 percent of 60 percent).

The shareholder must own, after the distribution, less than 50 percent of the total combined voting power of all classes of stock entitled to vote.

---

13.   70−1 USTC ¶9289, 25 AFTR2d 70−827, 90 S.Ct. 1041 (USSC, 1970).   14.   Reg. § 1.302−2(c).

In determining the percentage of ownership of the shareholder, it must be remembered that the constructive ownership rules of § 318(a) apply.

EXAMPLE 30

A, B, and C, unrelated individuals, own 30 shares, 30 shares, and 40 shares, respectively, in X Corporation. X Corporation has E & P of $200,000. The corporation redeems 20 shares of C's stock for $30,000. C paid $200 a share for the stock two years ago. After the redemption, C has a 25% interest in the corporation [20 shares of a total of 80 shares (100 − 20)]. This represents less than 80% of his original ownership (40% × 80% = 32%) and less than 50% of the total voting power. Consequently, the distribution qualifies as a stock redemption. C has a long-term capital gain of $26,000 [$30,000 − $4,000 (20 shares × $200)]. □

EXAMPLE 31

Given the situation in Example 30, assume instead that B and C are father and son. The redemption described previously would not qualify for exchange treatment. C is deemed to own the stock of B, so that after the redemption, he would have 50 shares of a total of 80 shares, more than 50% ownership. He would also fail the 80% test. Before the redemption, C is deemed a 70% owner (40 shares owned by him and 30 shares owned by B, his son). After the redemption, he is deemed a 62.5% owner (20 shares owned directly by him and 30 shares owned by B from a total of 80 shares). C has a taxable dividend of $30,000. □

Complete Termination of a Shareholder's Interest Redemptions—§ 302(b)(3)

If a shareholder terminates his or her entire stock ownership in a corporation through a stock redemption, the redemption will qualify for exchange treatment. Such a complete termination may not meet the substantially disproportionate rules of § 302(b)(2) if the constructive ownership rules are applied. The difference in the two provisions is that the constructive ownership rules of § 318(a)(1) do not apply to § 302(b)(3) if (1) the former shareholder has no interest, other than that of a creditor, in the corporation after the redemption (including an interest as an officer, director, or employee) for at least 10 years, and (2) the former shareholder files an agreement to notify the IRS of any acquisition within the 10-year period and to retain all necessary records pertaining to the redemption during this time period. A shareholder can reacquire an interest in the corporation by bequest or inheritance, but in no other manner.

The required agreement should be in the form of a separate statement signed by the shareholder and attached to the return for the year in which the redemption occurred. The agreement should recite that the shareholder agrees to notify the appropriate District Director within 30 days of a reacquisition of an interest in the corporation occurring within 10 years from the redemption.

EXAMPLE 32

The stock of X Corporation is held as follows: 40 shares by D (basis of $30,000), 30 shares by S (D's son), and 30 shares by H (D's husband). At a time when each share is worth $2,000, X Corporation redeems D's 40 shares for $80,000. Although D filed the necessary agreement with the IRS, she remains

an employee of X Corporation at a salary of $12,000. Section 302(b)(3) does not apply to this redemption because of D's continued employment status. Consequently, and to the extent of X Corporation's E & P, the distribution proceeds are a dividend to D. □

Redemptions to Pay Death Taxes—§ 303

Section 303 provides an executor the opportunity to redeem stock in a closely held corporation when the stock represents a substantial amount of the gross estate of the shareholder-decedent. The redemption is effected to provide the estate with liquidity. Stock in a closely held corporation is generally not readily marketable. However, it could be redeemed if § 302 would not cause ordinary dividend treatment. Section 303, to an extent, alleviates this problem.

Section 303 is, in effect, an exception to § 302(b). If a stock redemption qualifies under § 303, the rules of § 302(b) do not apply. The distribution will qualify as a stock redemption regardless of whether it is substantially disproportionate or not essentially equivalent to a dividend.

In a § 303 redemption, the redemption price generally equals the basis of the stock that qualifies. This is so because under § 1014, the income tax basis of property owned by a decedent becomes the property's fair market value on the date of death (or alternate valuation date if available and if elected). If, as is usually the case, this so-called step-up or step-down in basis that occurs at death (refer to chapter 12) equals the redemption price, the exchange is free of any income tax consequences to the shareholder's estate.

Section 303 applies when a distribution is made with respect to stock of a corporation, the value of which stock, in the gross estate of a decedent, is in excess of 35 percent of the value of the adjusted gross estate of the decedent. (For a definition of "gross estate" and "adjusted gross estate," see the Glossary of Tax Terms in Appendix C.) In determining the 35 percent requirement, stock of two or more corporations is treated as the stock of a single corporation if 20 percent or more in value of the outstanding stock of each corporation is included in the decedent's gross estate.[15]

EXAMPLE 33

The adjusted gross estate of a decedent is $300,000. The gross estate includes stock in X and Y Corporations valued at $100,000 and $80,000, respectively. Unless the two corporations can be treated as a single corporation, § 303 will not apply to a redemption of the stock. Assume the decedent owned all the stock of X Corporation and 80% of the stock of Y. Section 303 would then apply because 20% or more of the value of the outstanding stock of both corporations would be included in the decedent's estate. The 35% test would be met when the stock is treated as that of a single corporation. □

EXAMPLE 34

The adjusted gross estate of D, decedent, was $900,000. The death taxes and funeral and administration expenses of the estate totaled $200,000. Included in the estate was stock in X Corporation, a closely held corporation, valued at $340,000. D had acquired the stock years ago at a cost of $60,000. X Corporation redeems $200,000 of the stock from D's estate. The redemption

---

15. § 303(b)(2)(B).

would qualify under § 303 and thus would not represent a dividend to D's estate. In addition, § 1014 would apply to give the stock a step-up in basis. Consequently, there would be no tax on the redemption. □

The use of § 303 is subject to time limitations. Section 303 applies only to redemptions made within 90 days after the expiration of the period of limitations for the assessment of the Federal estate tax. If a timely petition for a redetermination of an estate tax deficiency is filed with the U.S. Tax Court, the applicable period for a § 303 redemption is extended to 60 days after the decision of the Court becomes final.[16]

Section 303 applies only to the extent of the sum of the estate, inheritance, legacy, and succession taxes imposed by reason of the decedent's death and to the extent of the amount of funeral and administration expenses allowable as deductions to the estate.[17]

Effect on the Corporation Redeeming Its Stock

Having considered the different types of stock redemptions that will receive exchange treatment, what is the tax effect to the corporation redeeming its stock? If the corporation uses property to carry out the redemption, is gain or loss recognized on the distribution? Furthermore, one needs to determine what effect, if any, the redemption will have on the corporation's E & P. These matters are discussed in the following paragraphs.

Recognition of Loss by the Corporation.   The purchase of stock, including the repurchase by an issuing corporation of its own stock, is generally treated as a capital transaction that does not give rise to a loss. In addition, all expenses a corporation incurs in redeeming its stock are nonamortizable capital expenditures. Payments that are not deductible include stock purchase premiums; amounts paid to a shareholder for the shareholder's agreement not to reacquire stock in the corporation for a specified time; and legal, accounting, transfer agent, brokerage, and appraisal fees.

Recognition of Gain by the Corporation.   Section 311 provides that corporations will be taxed on all distributions of appreciated property whether in the form of a property dividend or a stock redemption.

EXAMPLE 35   To carry out a § 303 redemption, Y Corporation transfers land (basis of $80,000, fair market value of $300,000) to a shareholder's estate. Y Corporation has a recognized gain of $220,000 ($300,000 − $80,000). □

Effect on Earnings and Profits.   A stock redemption reduces the E & P account of a corporation in an amount not in excess of the ratable share of the distributing corporation's E & P that is attributable to the stock redeemed.[18]

---

16. § 303(b)(1).

17. § 303(a).

18. § 312(n)(7).

EXAMPLE 36   X Corporation has 100 shares of stock outstanding. It redeems 30 shares for $100,000 at a time when it has paid-in capital of $120,000 and E & P of $150,000. The charge to E & P would be 30% of the amount in the E & P account ($45,000), and the remainder of the redemption price ($55,000) would be a reduction of the capital account. ☐

OTHER CORPORATE DISTRIBUTIONS

Partial liquidations of a corporation, if in compliance with the statutory requirements of § 302(e), will result in exchange treatment to the shareholders. Distributions of stock and securities of a controlled corporation to the shareholders of the parent corporation will be free of any tax consequences if they fall under § 355. Both of these types of corporate distributions possess similarities to stock redemptions and dividend distributions but are not discussed here because of their limited applicability.

CONCEPT SUMMARY 17–2

Corporate Distributions

1. Without a special provision, corporate distributions are taxed as dividend income to the recipient shareholders to the extent of the distributing corporation's E & P accumulated since February 28, 1913, or to the extent of current E & P. Any excess is treated as a return of capital to the extent of the shareholder's basis in the stock and, thereafter, as capital gain. See §§ 301 and 316.

2. Property distributions are considered dividends (taxed as noted in item 1) in the amount of their fair market value. The amount deemed distributed is reduced by any liabilities on the property distributed. The shareholder's basis in such property is the fair market value.

3. Earnings and profits of a corporation are increased by corporate earnings for the taxable year computed in the same manner as the corporation computes its taxable income. As a general rule, the account is increased for all items of income, whether taxed or not, and reduced by all items of expense, whether deductible or not. See § 312. Refer to Concept Summary 17–1 for a summary of the effect of certain transactions on taxable income and current E & P.

4. A corporation recognizes gain, but not loss, on distributions of property to its shareholders. E & P of the distributing corporation is reduced by the amount of money distributed or by the greater of the fair market value or the adjusted basis of property distributed less the amount of any liability applicable to the distributed property.

5. As a general rule, stock dividends or stock rights (representing stock in the distributing corporation) are not taxed, with certain exceptions.

6. Stock redemptions that qualify under § 302(b) are given exchange treatment. Section 302(b) requires that such distributions either be substantially disproportionate or be not essentially equivalent to a dividend. In making a determination of substantially disproportionate or not essentially equivalent to a dividend under §§ 302(b)(1), (2), and (3), the rules of § 318(a) determining the constructive ownership of stock apply, unless the shareholder redeems all of his or her interest in the corporation and does not reacquire (other than by bequest or inheritance) any interest (except as a creditor) for 10 years after the redemption.

7. If stock included in a decedent's estate represents more than 35 percent of the adjusted taxable estate, it may upon redemption qualify for exchange treatment separate and apart from § 302(b). Section 303 provides automatic exchange treatment on the redemption of such stock.

8. A corporation is taxed on the appreciation of property distributed in redemption of its stock.

9. The E & P account of the distributing corporation is reduced in a stock redemption in proportion to the amount of the corporation's outstanding stock that is redeemed.

TAX PLANNING CONSIDERATIONS

Corporate Distributions

In connection with the preceding discussion of corporate distributions, the following points might well need reinforcement:

- Because E & P is the measure of dividend income, its periodic determination is essential to corporate planning. Thus, an E & P account should be established and maintained, particularly if the possibility exists that a corporate distribution might represent a return of capital.

- Accumulated E & P is the sum of all past years' current E & P. No statute of limitations exists on the computation of E & P. The IRS could, for example, redetermine a corporation's current E & P for a tax year long since passed. Such a change would affect accumulated E & P and would have a direct impact on the taxability of current distributions to shareholders.

- Taxpayers should be aware that manipulating distributions to avoid or minimize dividend exposure is possible.

EXAMPLE 37

After several unprofitable years, Y Corporation has a deficit in accumulated E & P of $100,000 as of January 1, 1990. Starting in 1990, Y Corporation expects to generate annual E & P of $50,000 for the next four years and would like to distribute this amount to its shareholders. The corporation's cash position (for dividend purposes) will correspond to the current E & P generated. Compare the following possibilities:

1. On December 31 of 1990, 1991, 1992, and 1993, Y Corporation distributes a cash dividend of $50,000.

2. On December 31 of 1991 and 1993, Y Corporation distributes a cash dividend of $100,000.

The two alternatives are illustrated as follows:

Year	Accumulated E & P (First of Year)	Current E & P	Distribution	Amount of Dividend
		Alternative 1		
1990	($100,000)	$50,000	$50,000	$50,000
1991	(100,000)	50,000	50,000	50,000
1992	(100,000)	50,000	50,000	50,000
1993	(100,000)	50,000	50,000	50,000
		Alternative 2		
1990	($100,000)	$50,000	$ –0–	$ –0–
1991	(50,000)	50,000	100,000	50,000
1992	(50,000)	50,000	–0–	–0–
1993	–0–	50,000	100,000	50,000

Alternative 1 leads to an overall result of $200,000 in dividend income since each $50,000 distribution is fully covered by current E & P. Alternative 2, however, results in only $100,000 of dividend income to the shareholders. The remaining $100,000 is a return of capital. Why? At the time Y Corporation made its first distribution of $100,000 on December 31, 1991, it had a deficit of $50,000 in accumulated E & P (the original deficit of $100,000 is reduced by the $50,000 of current E & P from 1990). Consequently, the $100,000 distribution yields a $50,000 dividend (the current E & P for 1991) and $50,000 as a return of capital. As of January 1, 1992, Y Corporation's accumulated E & P now has a deficit balance of $50,000 (a distribution cannot increase a deficit in E & P). Add in $50,000 of current E & P from 1992, and the balance as of January 1, 1993, is zero. Thus, the second distribution of $100,000 made on December 31, 1993, also yields $50,000 of dividends (the current E & P for 1993) and $50,000 as a return of capital. □

Constructive Dividends

Tax planning can be particularly effective in avoiding constructive dividend situations.

● Shareholders should try to structure their dealings with the corporation on an arm's length basis. For example, reasonable rent should be paid for the use of corporate property, or a fair price should be paid for its purchase. Needless to say, the parties should make every effort to support the amount involved with appraisal data or market information obtained from reliable sources at or close to the time of the transaction.

● Dealings between shareholders and a closely held corporation should be formalized as much as possible. In the case of loans to shareholders, for example, the parties should provide for an adequate rate of interest, written evidence of the debt, and a realistic repayment schedule that is not only arranged but also followed.

● If corporate profits are to be bailed out by the shareholders in a form deductible to the corporation, a balanced mix of the different alternatives could lessen the risk of disallowance by the IRS. Rent for the use of shareholder property, interest on amounts borrowed from shareholders, or salaries for services rendered by shareholders are all feasible substitutes for dividend distributions. But overdoing any one approach may well attract the attention of the IRS. Too much interest, for example, might mean the corporation is thinly capitalized and some of the debt therefore really represents equity investment.

● Much can be done to protect against the disallowance of corporate deductions for compensation that is determined to be unreasonable in amount. Example 38 is an illustration, all too common in a family corporation, of what *not* to do.

EXAMPLE 38   Z Corporation is wholly owned by T. Corporate employees and annual salaries include Mrs. T ($15,000), T, Jr. ($10,000), T ($80,000), and E ($40,000). The operation of Z Corporation is shared about equally between T and E (an unrelated party). Mrs. T (T's wife) performed significant services for the corporation during the corporation's formative years but now merely attends the annual meeting of the board of directors. T, Jr. (T's son), is a full-time student and occasionally signs papers for the corporation in his capacity as

treasurer. Z Corporation has not distributed a dividend for 10 years, although it has accumulated substantial E & P. What is wrong with this situation?

- Mrs. T's salary seems vulnerable unless one can prove that some or all of the $15,000 annual salary is payment for services rendered to the corporation in prior years (i.e., she was underpaid for those years).[19]

- T, Jr.'s, salary is also vulnerable; he does not appear to earn the $10,000 paid to him by the corporation. True, neither T, Jr., nor Mrs. T is a shareholder, but each one's relationship to T is enough of a tie-in to raise the unreasonable compensation issue.

- T's salary appears susceptible to challenge. Why, for instance, is he receiving $40,000 more than E when it appears each shares equally in the operation of the corporation?

- No dividends have been distributed by Z Corporation for 10 years, although the corporation is capable of distributing dividends.   □

Stock Redemptions

Several observations come to mind in connection with tax planning for stock redemptions:

- The § 302(b)(1) variety (not essentially equivalent to a dividend) provides minimal utility and should be relied upon only as a last resort. Instead, the redemption should be structured to fit one of the safe harbors of either § 302(b)(2) (substantially disproportionate), § 302(b)(3) (complete termination), or § 303 (to pay death taxes).

- For a family corporation in which all of the shareholders are related to each other, the only hope of a successful redemption might lie in the use of § 302(b)(3) or § 303. But in using § 302(b)(3), be careful that the family stock attribution rules are avoided. Here, strict compliance with § 302(c)(2) (i.e., the withdrawing shareholder does not continue as an employee of the corporation, etc., and does not reacquire an interest in the corporation within 10 years) is crucial.

- The alternative to a successful stock redemption is dividend treatment of the distribution under § 301. But do not conclude that a dividend is always undesirable from a tax standpoint. Suppose the distributing corporation has little, if any, E & P. Or the distributee-shareholder is another corporation. In this latter regard, dividend treatment might well be preferred because of the availability of the dividends received deduction.

- When using the § 303 redemption, the amount to be sheltered from dividend treatment is the sum of death taxes and certain estate administration expenses. Nevertheless, a redemption in excess of the limitation will not destroy the applicability of § 303.

- The timing and sequence of a redemption should be carefully handled.

EXAMPLE 39   P Corporation's stock is held as follows: R (60 shares), S (20 shares), and T (20 shares). R, S, and T are all individuals and are not related to each other. The

---

19. See, for example. *R. J. Nicoll Co.*, 59 T.C. 37 (1972).

corporation redeems 24 of R's shares. Shortly thereafter, it redeems 5 of S's shares. Does R's redemption qualify as substantially disproportionate? Taken in isolation, it would appear to meet the requirements of § 302(b)(2)—the 80% and 50% tests have been satisfied. Yet, if the IRS takes into account the later redemption of S's shares, R has not satisfied the 50% test; he still owns $^{36}/_{71}$ of the corporation after both redemptions.[20] A greater time lag between the two redemptions would therefore have placed R in a better position to argue against collapsing the series of redemptions into one. □

PROBLEM MATERIALS

Discussion Questions

1. What is meant by the term "earnings and profits"?

2. Why is it important to distinguish between "current" and "accumulated" E & P?

3. Describe the effect of a distribution in a year when the distributing corporation has any of the following:
   a. A deficit in accumulated E & P and a positive amount in current E & P.
   b. A positive amount in accumulated E & P and a deficit in current E & P.
   c. A deficit in both current and accumulated E & P.
   d. A positive amount in both current and accumulated E & P.

4. Five years ago, a corporation determined its current E & P to be $100,000. In the current year, it makes a distribution to its shareholders of $200,000. The IRS contends that the current E & P of the corporation five years ago was really $150,000.
   a. Can the IRS successfully make this contention?
   b. What difference would the additional $50,000 in E & P make?

5. If a corporation is chartered in a state that prohibits the payment of dividends that impair paid-in capital, is it possible for the corporation to pay a dividend that is a return of capital for tax purposes and yet comply with state law? Discuss.

6. The suggestion is made that any distributions to shareholders by a calendar year corporation should take place on January 1 before the corporation has developed any current E & P. Assess the validity of this suggestion.

7. T, an individual shareholder, receives a distribution from X Corporation and treats it as a return of capital. Upon audit by the IRS, he tells the agent: "Show me that X Corporation had adequate E & P to cover the distribution, and I will report the distribution as dividend income." Please comment.

8. A corporation with no E & P distributes a property dividend. Can it be said that the shareholders need not recognize any dividend income? Explain.

9. A corporation distributed property (adjusted basis of $100,000 and fair market value of $80,000) to its shareholders. Has the corporation acted wisely? Why or why not?

10. Does the distributing corporation recognize gain or loss when it distributes property as a dividend to its shareholders? Explain.

11. When are stock dividends taxable?

12. How are nontaxable stock rights handled for tax purposes? Taxable stock rights?

---

20. § 302(b)(2)(D).

13. X Corporation sells its plant and equipment to its shareholders. Shortly thereafter, X Corporation enters into a long-term lease for the use of these assets. In connection with the possible tax ramifications of these transactions, consider the following:

    a. The sale of the assets for less than their adjusted basis to X Corporation.

    b. The amount of rent X Corporation has agreed to pay.

14. Why is it important that an advance from a corporation to a shareholder be categorized as a bona fide loan? With regard to the resolution of this issue, comment on the relevance of the following factors:

    a. The corporation has never paid a dividend.

    b. The advance is on open account.

    c. The advance provides for 2% interest.

    d. No date is specified for the repayment of the advance.

    e. The advance was used by the shareholder to pay personal bills.

    f. The advance is repaid by the shareholder immediately after the transaction was questioned by the IRS on audit of the corporate income tax return.

15. How can shareholders bail out corporate profits in such a manner as to provide the corporation with a deduction? What are the risks involved?

16. Whether compensation paid to a corporate employee is reasonable is a question of fact to be determined from the surrounding circumstances. How would the resolution of this problem be affected by each of the following factors?

    a. The employee is not a shareholder but is related to the sole owner of the corporate employer.

    b. The employee-shareholder never completed high school.

    c. The employee-shareholder is a full-time college student.

    d. The employee-shareholder was underpaid for her services during the formative period of the corporate employer.

    e. The corporate employer pays a nominal dividend each year.

    f. Year-end bonuses are paid to all shareholder-employees.

17. Under what circumstances does § 303 apply to a stock redemption? What is the tax effect of the application of § 303?

18. "A § 303 stock redemption usually results in no gain or loss being recognized by the estate." Evaluate this statement.

19. A corporation distributes $100,000 to a shareholder in complete redemption of the shareholder's stock. Can the corporation reduce its E & P by this amount? Explain.

Problems

20. Complete the following schedule for each case.

	Accumulated E & P Beginning of Year	Current E & P	Cash Distributions (All on Last Day of Year)	Amount Taxable	Return of Capital
a.	$40,000	($10,000)	$50,000	$30000	$—
b.	(50,000)	30,000	40,000	—30000	10000
c.	30,000	50,000	70,000	70000	—
d.	60,000	(20,000)	45,000	40000	5000
e.	Same as (d), except the distribution of $45,000 is made on June 30 and the corporation uses the calendar year for tax purposes.			—	—

21. Complete the following schedule for each case.

	Accumulated E & P Beginning of Year	Current E & P	Cash Distributions (All on Last Day of Year)	Amount Taxable	Return of Capital
a.	$75,000	$20,000	$60,000	$—	$—
b.	(20,000)	40,000	45,000	—	—
c.	(90,000)	50,000	30,000	—	—
d.	60,000	(55,000)	40,000	—	—
e.	Same as (d), except the distribution of $40,000 is made on June 30 and the corporation uses the calendar year for tax purposes.			—	—

22. Indicate in each of the following independent situations the effect on taxable income and E & P, stating the amount of any increase (or decrease) as a result of the transaction. (In determining the effect on E & P, assume E & P has already been increased by current taxable income.)

Transaction	Taxable Income Increase (Decrease)	E & P Increase (Decrease)
a. Receipt of $15,000 tax-exempt income	0	↑
b. Payment of $15,150 Federal income taxes	0	↓
c. Collection of $100,000 on life insurance policy on corporate president	0	↑
d. Charitable contribution, $30,000, with $20,000 allowable as a deduction in the current tax year	↓20K	↓10K
e. Deduction of remaining $10,000 charitable contribution in succeeding year	↓	↑
f. Realized gain on involuntary conversion of $200,000 ($30,000 of gain is recognized)	↑30	0

23. Indicate in each of the following independent situations the effect on taxable income and E & P, stating the amount of any increase (or decrease) as a result of the transaction. (In determining the effect on E & P, assume E & P has already been increased by current taxable income.)

Transaction	Taxable Income Increase (Decrease)	E & P Increase (Decrease)
a. Intangible drilling costs deductible from current taxable income in the amount of $50,000	—	—
b. Sale of unimproved real estate, basis of $200,000, fair market value of $800,000 (no election out of installment basis; payments in year of sale total $40,000)	—	—

Transaction	Taxable Income Increase (Decrease)	E & P Increase (Decrease)
c. Accelerated depreciation of $70,000 (straight-line would have been $40,000)	_____	_____
d. Long-term contract begun in current year (income to be reported on completed contract method; estimated profit on total contract is $350,000; percentage completed in current tax year is 30%)	_____	_____
e. Sale of equipment to 100% owned corporation (adjusted basis was $120,000 and selling price was $50,000)	_____	_____

24. Equipment with a useful life of 7 years under MACRS and an ADR midpoint life of 10 years was purchased on January 3, 1988, at a cost of $100,000. The § 179 deduction to expense part of the cost was not elected. The equipment had an adjusted basis of $61,220 on January 3, 1990, when it was sold for $70,000. What are the tax consequences on the sale, and what adjustment is made to E & P?

25. X Corporation sells property, adjusted basis of $200,000, fair market value of $180,000, to its sole shareholder for $160,000. How much loss can the corporation deduct as a result of this transaction? What is the effect on the corporation's E & P for the year of sale?

26. X Corporation, with E & P of $300,000, distributes property worth $70,000, adjusted tax basis of $100,000, to Y, a corporate shareholder. The property is subject to a liability of $15,000, which Y assumes.

   a. What is the amount of dividend income to Y.

   b. What is Y's basis in the property received?

   c. How does the distribution affect X Corporation's E & P account?

27. R & D Corporation had E & P of $45,000 when it made a current distribution of inventories with a cost of $60,000 and a fair market value of $105,000. Determine a sole shareholder's taxable income from the distribution.

28. AB Corporation distributes to its shareholders real property with an adjusted basis of $5,000 and fair market value of $10,000. The realty is subject to a liability of $17,500. What is the effect of this distribution on the taxable income of the corporation?

29. At the beginning of its taxable year 1990, T Corporation had E & P of $50,000. T Corporation sold an asset at a loss of $50,000 on June 30, 1990. T Corporation incurred a total deficit for the calendar year 1990 of $55,000. Assume T Corporation made a distribution of $15,000 to its sole shareholder, A, an individual, on July 1, 1990. How will A be taxed on the $15,000?

30. At the beginning of its taxable year 1990, X Corporation had a deficit in E & P of $60,000. Its net profits for the period January 1, 1990, through June 30, 1990, were $75,000, but its E & P for the entire taxable year 1990 was only $5,000. If X Corporation made a distribution of $15,000 to its sole shareholder A, an individual, how would A be taxed on the distribution?

31. The stock in XY Corporation is owned equally by X, an individual, and Y Corporation. On January 1, 1990, XY had a deficit of $50,000. Its current E & P (for taxable year 1990) was $35,000. In 1990, XY distributed cash of $15,000 to

both X and Y Corporation. How will X and Y Corporation be taxed on the distribution? What will be the accumulated E & P of XY Corporation at the end of 1990?

32. A paid $30,000 for 15 shares of stock in XY Corporation five years ago. In November 1989, she received a nontaxable stock dividend of five additional shares in XY Corporation. She sells the five shares in March 1990 for $10,000. What is her gain, and how is it taxed?

33. AB Corporation declares a nontaxable dividend payable in rights to subscribe to common stock. One right and $60 entitle the holder to subscribe to one share of stock. One right is issued for each share of stock owned. T, a shareholder, owns 100 shares of stock that she purchased two years ago for $3,000. At the date of distribution of the rights, the market value of the stock was $80 per share, and the market value of the rights was $20 per right. T received 100 rights. She exercises 60 rights and purchases 60 additional shares of stock. She sells the remaining 40 rights for $750. What are the tax consequences of these transactions to T?

34. X Corporation has 200 shares of common stock outstanding. A owns 100 of the shares, A's father owns 30 shares, A's brother owns 20 shares, and A's daughter owns 30 shares. Y Corporation owns the remaining 20 shares. A owns 60% of the stock in Y Corporation.

   a. In applying the stock attribution rules of § 318, how many shares does A own in X Corporation?

   b. Assume A owns only 40% of Y Corporation. How many shares does A own, directly or indirectly, in X Corporation?

35. V Corporation has 1,000 shares of common stock outstanding. The shares are owned by unrelated shareholders as follows: H, 400 shares; J, 400 shares; and K, 200 shares. The corporation redeems 100 shares of the stock owned by K for $45,000. K paid $100 per share for her stock two years ago. The E & P of V Corporation was $400,000 on the date of redemption. What is the tax effect to K of the redemption?

36. In Problem 35, assume H is the father of K. How would this affect the tax status of the redemption? What if H were K's brother instead of her father?

37. The gross estate of D, decedent, is $900,000. The gross estate includes stock in A and B Corporations valued at $150,000 and $250,000, respectively. D owned 30% of A stock and 60% of B stock. Death taxes and funeral and administration expenses for D's estate were $100,000. D had a basis of $60,000 in the A stock and $90,000 in the B stock. What are the tax consequences to D's estate if A Corporation redeems one-third of D's stock for $50,000 and B Corporation redeems one-fifth of D's stock for $50,000?

38. X Corporation has 500 shares of stock outstanding. It redeems 50 shares for $90,000 when it has paid-in capital of $300,000 and E & P of $400,000. What is the reduction in the E & P of X Corporation as a result of the redemption?

18

CORPORATIONS: DISTRIBUTIONS IN COMPLETE LIQUIDATION AND AN OVERVIEW OF REORGANIZATIONS

OBJECTIVES

Contrast property dividends and stock redemptions with distributions in complete liquidation of a corporation.

Review the tax effect on the shareholders of a corporation being liquidated.

Review the tax effect of a complete liquidation on the corporation being liquidated.

Recognize the tax planning opportunities available to minimize the income tax result in the complete liquidation of a corporation.

Present an overview of corporate reorganizations.

LIQUIDATIONS—IN GENERAL

When a stock redemption occurs or a dividend is distributed, the assumption usually is that the corporation will continue as a separate entity. With complete liquidation, however, corporate existence terminates. A complete liquidation, like a qualified stock redemption, is afforded exchange treatment. However, the tax effects of a liquidation vary somewhat from those of a stock redemption.

The Liquidation Process

A complete liquidation exists for tax purposes when a corporation ceases to be a going concern and exists solely to wind up its affairs, pay its debts, and distribute any remaining assets to its shareholders.[1] Legal dissolution under state law is not required for the liquidation to be complete for tax purposes, however. A transaction will be treated as a liquidation even though the corporation retains a nominal amount of assets to pay any remaining debts and to preserve its legal status.[2]

A liquidation may occur for several different reasons. The corporate business may have been unsuccessful. In some instances, even when a corporation has been profitable, the shareholders may nonetheless decide to terminate the corporate existence and acquire the assets of the corporation.

A liquidation frequently occurs when another person or corporation wants to purchase the assets of the corporation. The purchaser may buy the stock of the shareholders and then liquidate the corporation to acquire the assets. On the other hand, the purchaser may buy the assets directly from the corporation. After the sale of its assets, the corporation will distribute the sales proceeds to its shareholders and be liquidated. The different means used to liquidate a corporation will produce varying tax results.

Liquidations and Other Distributions Compared

Recall that a property distribution, whether in the form of a dividend or a stock redemption, produces gain (but not loss) to the distributing corporation. For the shareholder, the fair market value of a property dividend produces ordinary income to the extent of the corporation's E & P. On the other hand, a stock redemption qualifying under § 302 or § 303 is afforded exchange treatment.

The tax effects to the corporation in a complete liquidation are somewhat like those in a stock redemption in that a liquidation is also afforded exchange treatment. Still the tax consequences of a complete liquidation differ in several respects from the consequences of a stock redemption. Except for certain distributions of so-called disqualified property and some distributions to related parties (in which case loss recognition is limited) and the liquidation of an 80 percent or more controlled subsidiary, a liquidating corporation recognizes gain *and* loss upon distribution of its assets. The shareholders receive exchange treatment on receipt of the property from the liquidating corporation. The distribution of assets is treated as payment for the shareholder's stock, resulting in either a gain or a loss.

Liquidations and stock redemptions parallel each other as to the effect of E & P on such distributions. For the corporation undergoing liquidation, E & P has no tax impact on the gain or loss to be recognized by the shareholders. This is so

---

1.   Reg. § 1.332–2(c).   2.   Rev.Rul. 54–518, 1954–2 C.B. 142.

because § 301 (governing dividend distributions) is specifically made inapplicable to complete liquidations.[3]

EXAMPLE 1

Z Corporation, with E & P of $40,000, makes a cash distribution of $50,000 to its sole shareholder. Assume the shareholder's basis in the Z Corporation stock is $20,000 and the stock is held as an investment. If the distribution is not in complete liquidation or if it does not qualify as a stock redemption, the shareholder must recognize dividend income of $40,000 (the amount of Z Corporation's E & P) and must treat the remaining $10,000 of the distribution as a return of capital. On the other hand, if the distribution is pursuant to a complete liquidation or qualifies for exchange treatment as a stock redemption, the shareholder will have a recognized capital gain of $30,000 [$50,000 (the amount of the distribution) – $20,000 (the basis in the stock)]. In the latter case, note that Z Corporation's E & P is of no consequence to the tax result. □

In the event the distribution results in a *loss* to the shareholder, an important distinction could exist between stock redemptions and liquidations. The distinction could arise because § 267 (disallowance of losses between related parties) is applicable to stock redemptions but generally not to liquidations.

With reference to the basis of noncash property received from the corporation, the rules governing liquidations and stock redemptions are identical. Section 334(a) specifies that the basis of such property distributed pursuant to a complete liquidation under § 331 shall be the fair market value on the date of distribution.

The tax consequences of a complete liquidation of a corporation are examined in this chapter from the standpoint of the effect on the distributing corporation and on the shareholder. Tax rules differ when a controlled subsidiary is liquidated. Thus, the rules relating to the liquidation of a controlled subsidiary receive separate treatment.

LIQUIDATIONS—EFFECT ON THE DISTRIBUTING CORPORATION

For the corporation in the process of complete liquidation, §§ 336 and 337 govern the tax results. The general rules relating to complete liquidations are covered in § 336, wherein gain or loss is recognized to the distributing corporation. However, for certain distributions of disqualified property and some distributions to related shareholders, loss is not recognized. Under § 337, no gain or loss is recognized by a subsidiary corporation for distributions to a parent corporation that owns 80 percent or more of the stock of the subsidiary.

Background

Originally, a corporate distribution of property, whether a liquidating or a nonliquidating distribution, produced neither gain nor loss to the distributing corporation. This nonrecognition concept was sometimes referred to as the *General Utilities* rule.[4] However, over the years, statutory and judicial modifications and interpretations significantly increased the number of recognition situa-

---

3. § 331(b).

4. The doctrine was attributed to the 1935 Supreme Court decision in *General Utilities & Oper-* *ating Co. v. Helvering*, 36–1 USTC ¶9012, 16 AFTR 1126, 56 S.Ct. 185 (USSC, 1935).

tions. For example, depreciation and the investment tax credit were recaptured on distributed assets. Further, under the tax benefit rule, a corporation had to take into income any assets distributed to the shareholders for which it had previously claimed a deduction. In addition, the assignment of income doctrine was applied to distributions in liquidation and to sales by the liquidating corporation. Gain resulted from the distribution or sale of LIFO inventory and installment notes receivable. The sale of inventory produced income to the corporation unless the inventory was sold in bulk to one person in one transaction. Because of the many modifications, a liquidating corporation was not shielded from recognition of all income.

With the many statutory and judicial inroads, not much was actually left of the *General Utilities* doctrine when it was repealed in 1986. Foremost among the remaining transfers in which the doctrine insulated the liquidating corporation from a recognition result were the following: distributions in kind and sale of investment assets (e.g., marketable securities and land), distributions in kind and bulk sales of non-LIFO inventory, and the § 1231 element as to assets used in a trade or business. The repeal of the *General Utilities* rule now causes a liquidating corporation to recognize, as a general rule, all gains and most losses on distributions of property.

EXAMPLE 2   Pursuant to a complete liquidation, R Corporation (not a closely held corporation) distributes the following assets to its shareholders: land held as an investment (basis of $150,000, fair market value of $300,000), non-LIFO inventory (basis of $50,000, fair market value of $40,000), and marketable securities (basis of $100,000, fair market value of $120,000). If the liquidation were completed in 1985, R Corporation would recognize no gain or loss as a result of the distribution. However, if the liquidation were completed in 1987 or thereafter, R Corporation would have a gain of $170,000 ($150,000 + $20,000) and a loss of $10,000. □

General Rule

Section 336 provides that with the exception of property distributed to a parent in complete liquidation of a subsidiary (covered by § 337 discussed later in the chapter), gain or loss is recognized by a liquidating corporation on the distribution of property in complete liquidation as if such property were sold to the distributee at the fair market value. Section 336, which has repealed the *General Utilities* doctrine, strengthens the notion of double taxation that is inherent in operating a business in the corporate form. As a result, liquidating distributions are subject to tax both at the corporate level and at the shareholder level.

When property distributed in a complete liquidation is subject to a liability of the liquidating corporation, the deemed fair market value of that property cannot be less than the amount of the liability.

EXAMPLE 3   Pursuant to a complete liquidation, T Corporation distributes to its shareholders land held as an investment (basis of $200,000, fair market value of $300,000). The land is subject to a liability in the amount of $350,000. T Corporation has a gain of $150,000 on the distribution. □

Limitation on Losses.   As a general rule, losses on the distribution of property in a complete liquidation are recognized. There are two exceptions, however. The

first exception applies to certain distributions to related parties as defined under § 267. The second exception prevents a loss deduction on certain distributions of property with a built-in loss that was contributed to the corporation shortly before the adoption of a plan of liquidation. In this instance, the built-in loss may be disallowed as a deduction upon liquidation even if the distribution is to an unrelated party.

Because the abolition of the *General Utilities* rule opens the door for recognition of losses in a liquidation, Congress was concerned that taxpayers might attempt to avoid the repeal of the rule by creating artificial losses at the corporate level. Taxpayers could accomplish this by contributing property with built-in losses to the corporation before a liquidation. Recall from chapter 16 that in § 351 transfers (nontaxable transfers to a corporation in exchange for stock when the transferor is in control of the corporation) and contributions to capital, the transferor's income tax basis carries over to the transferee corporation. Thus, high basis, low fair market value property could be transferred to a corporation contemplating liquidation with the expectation that such built-in losses might neutralize expected gains from appreciated property distributed or sold in the liquidation process.

Section 336(d) closes the possibility of utilizing built-in losses to neutralize the gain upon liquidation by imposing restrictions on the deductibility of losses in related-party situations (those covered by § 267) and in certain sales and distributions to unrelated parties of built-in loss property. A corporation and a shareholder are related parties if the shareholder owns (directly or indirectly) more than 50 percent in value of the corporation's outstanding stock.

Once the related-party situation is present, losses will be disallowed on distributions to the related parties in either of the following cases: (1) the distribution is not pro rata or (2) the property distributed is disqualified property (property acquired by the liquidating corporation in a § 351 transaction or as a contribution to capital during a five-year period ending on the date of the distribution).

EXAMPLE 4

Z Corporation's stock is held equally by three brothers. One year before Z's liquidation, the shareholders transfer property (basis of $150,000, fair market value of $100,000) to Z Corporation in return for stock (a § 351 transaction). In liquidation, Z Corporation transfers the property (still worth $100,000) to the brothers. Because § 267 applies (each brother owns directly and indirectly 100% of the stock) and disqualified property is involved, none of the $50,000 realized loss may be recognized by Z Corporation. □

EXAMPLE 5

Assume that Z Corporation stock is owned by A and B, who are unrelated. A owns 80% and B owns 20% of the stock in Z Corporation. Z Corporation had the following assets that were distributed in complete liquidation of Z Corporation:

	Adjusted Basis	Fair Market Value
Cash	$600,000	$600,000
Equipment	150,000	200,000
Building	400,000	200,000

Assume Z Corporation distributes the equipment to B and the cash and the building to A. Z Corporation will recognize a gain of $50,000 on the distribution of the equipment; however, the loss of $200,000 on the building will be disallowed. This is because the distribution was not pro rata, and the loss property was distributed to a related party. ☐

EXAMPLE 6   Assume that Z Corporation in Example 5 distributed the cash and equipment to A and the building to B. Again, Z Corporation would recognize the $50,000 gain on the equipment; however, it could now also recognize the $200,000 loss on the building. The distribution of the loss property was not to a related party because B did not own more than 50% of the stock in Z Corporation. ☐

The loss limitation provisions are extended to distributions to unrelated parties when loss property is transferred to a corporation shortly before the corporation is liquidated. This second exception to the general rule that a corporation can recognize losses on a complete liquidation was imposed to prevent the doubling of losses, or the so-called "stuffing" of a corporation.

EXAMPLE 7   Assume A, a shareholder in T Corporation, transfers property with a basis of $10,000, fair market value of $3,000, to T Corporation in a transaction that qualifies under § 351. A's basis in the additional stock acquired in T Corporation, in exchange for the property, is $10,000. T Corporation's basis in the property will also be $10,000. A few months after the transfer, T Corporation adopts a plan of complete liquidation. Upon liquidation, T Corporation distributes the property to A. If T Corporation were permitted a loss deduction of $7,000, there would be a double loss because A would also recognize a loss of $7,000 upon receipt of the property [$10,000 (basis in A's stock) − $3,000 (fair market value of the property)]. To prevent the doubling of losses, § 336(d) prohibits T Corporation from taking a loss on the distribution even if A is an unrelated party. ☐

Losses are disallowed on a distribution to shareholders who are not related parties when the property distributed was acquired in a § 351 transaction or as a contribution to capital and was contributed as part of a plan, the principal purpose of which was to recognize loss by the corporation in connection with the liquidation. Such a purpose will be presumed if the transfer occurs within two years of the adoption of the plan of liquidation.

The prohibition against a loss deduction on distributions to unrelated parties is broader than the first exception, which disallows losses on certain distributions to related parties, in that it applies regardless of whether the shareholder is a related party under § 267. However, the prohibition is narrower than the first exception in that it applies only to property that had a built-in loss upon acquisition by the corporation and only as to the amount of the built-in loss.

EXAMPLE 8   On January 2, 1990, in a transaction that qualifies under § 351 T Corporation acquires property with a basis of $10,000, fair market value of $3,000. T Corporation adopts a plan of liquidation on July 1, 1990, and distributes the property to A, an unrelated party, on November 10, 1990, when the property is

worth $1,000. T Corporation can recognize a loss of $2,000, the difference between the value of the property on the date of acquisition and the fair market value of the property on the date of distribution. Only the built-in loss of $7,000 [$10,000 (basis) − $3,000 (fair market value on date of acquisition)] is disallowed. ☐

EXAMPLE 9

Assume the property in Example 8 was worth $12,000 on the date T Corporation acquired the property. However, the property is worth only $2,000 when T Corporation distributes the property upon the complete liquidation of the corporation. If the distribution is to an unrelated shareholder, T Corporation will recognize the entire $8,000 loss [$10,000 (basis) − $2,000 (fair market value on date of distribution)]. However, if the distribution is to a related party, T Corporation cannot recognize any of the loss because the property is disqualified property (e.g., property acquired in a § 351 transaction within five years of the distribution). (Note: The loss limitation applies even though the property was worth more than its basis when it was transferred to the corporation. When the distribution is to a related party, the loss is disallowed even though the decline in value occurred entirely during the period the corporation held the property. However, if the property is distributed to an unrelated party, only the built-in loss [e.g., the loss that occurred prior to the transfer to the corporation] is disallowed.) ☐

For liquidation loss purposes, the basis of disqualified property that is later sold or distributed to an unrelated party is reduced by the excess of the property's basis on the contribution date over the property's fair market value on such date.[5] Thus, any subsequent decline in value to the point of the liquidating distribution results in a deductible loss as long as the property is not distributed to a related party.

The loss limitation can apply regardless of how long the corporation has held the property prior to liquidation; however, if the period is two years or less, a tax avoidance purpose is presumed. Still, if there is a clear and substantial relationship between the contributed property and the business of the corporation, a loss will be permitted on the distribution of such property if the distribution is to an unrelated party. Under this circumstance (i.e., there was a business reason for transferring the loss property to the liquidating corporation), a loss will also be permitted on the sale of the property.

EXAMPLE 10

Z Corporation's stock is held 60% by A and 40% by B. One year before Z's liquidation, property (basis of $150,000, fair market value of $100,000) is transferred to Z Corporation as a contribution to capital. There is no business reason for the transfer. In liquidation, Z Corporation transfers the property (now worth $90,000) to B. Because the distribution was to an unrelated party, the basis is reduced to $100,000 for liquidation purposes [$150,000 (carryover basis under § 362) − $50,000 (difference between carryover basis of $150,000 and fair market value of $100,000)]. A loss of $10,000 ($100,000 − $90,000) can be recognized. (If the property had been distributed to A, a related party, even the $10,000 loss would be disallowed.) ☐

---

5. § 336(d)(2).

EXAMPLE 11   Assume in Example 10, that the property was transferred to Z Corporation because a bank required the additional capital investment as a condition to making a loan to Z Corporation. Because there was a business purpose for the transfer, presumably the loss of $50,000 will be recognized if the property is distributed to B in liquidation. However, if the property is distributed to A, a related party, the loss would still be disallowed. □

Distributions of loss property by a liquidating corporation are summarized in Figure 18–1.

Expenses of Liquidation.   The general expenses involved in liquidating a corporation are deductible by the corporation as business expenses under § 162.

FIGURE 18–1 Distributions of Loss Property by a Liquidating Corporation

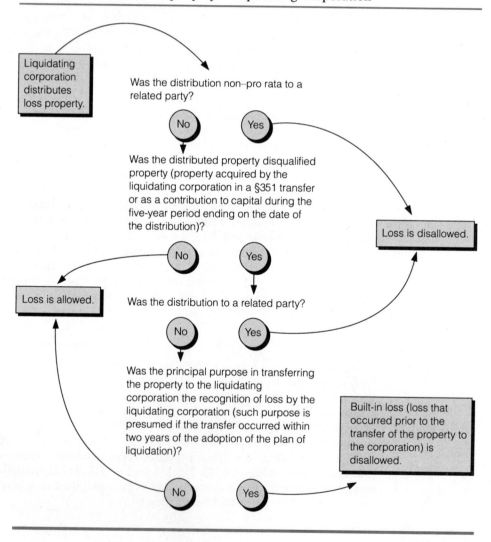

Examples include the legal and accounting cost of drafting a plan of liquidation and the cost of revocation of the corporate charter. Liquidation expenses relating to the disposition of corporate assets are also deductible. Expenses relating to the sale of corporate assets, including a brokerage commission for the sale of real estate and a legal fee to clear title, are offset against the selling price of the assets.

EXAMPLE 12

During its liquidation, R Corporation incurs the following expenses:

General liquidation expenses	$12,000
Legal expenses to effect a distribution of property	200
Sales commissions to sell inventory	3,000
Brokerage fee on sale of real estate	8,000

R Corporation can deduct $12,200 ($12,000 + $200). The $3,000 commission and the $8,000 brokerage fee are applied against the selling price of the inventory and the real estate. □

LIQUIDATIONS—EFFECT ON THE SHAREHOLDER

The tax consequences to the shareholders of a corporation in the process of liquidation are governed by the general rule under § 331 and two exceptions under §§ 332 and 338 (both exceptions relate to the liquidation of a subsidiary).

The General Rule under § 331

In the case of a complete liquidation, the general rule under § 331(a)(1) provides for exchange treatment. Since § 1001(c) requires the recognition of gain or loss on the sale or exchange of property, the end result is to treat the shareholder as having sold his or her stock to the corporation being liquidated. Thus, the difference between the fair market value of the assets received from the corporation and the adjusted basis of the stock surrendered (realized gain or loss) becomes the amount that is recognized. If the stock is a capital asset in the hands of the shareholder, capital gain or loss results. As is usually true, the burden of proof is on the taxpayer to furnish evidence on the adjusted basis of the stock. In the absence of such evidence, the stock will be deemed to have a zero basis, and the full amount of the liquidation proceeds represents the amount of the gain to be recognized.[6]

Section 334(a) provides that under the general rule of § 331, the income tax basis to the shareholder of property received in a liquidation will be the property's fair market value on the date of distribution. The general rule follows the same approach taken with stock redemptions that qualify for exchange treatment.

Special Rule for Certain Installment Obligations

Section 453(h) provides some relief from the bunching of gain problem encountered when a liquidating corporation sells its assets. Although the liquidating corporation must recognize all gain on such sales, the shareholders' gain on the

---

6. *John Calderazzo*, 34 TCM 1, T.C. Memo. 1975–1.

receipt of notes obtained by the corporation on the sale of its assets may be deferred to the point of collection.[7] Such treatment will require the shareholders to allocate their bases in the stock among the various assets received from the corporation.

EXAMPLE 13

In 1990, after a plan of complete liquidation has been adopted, X Corporation sells its only asset—unimproved land held as an investment that has appreciated in value—to P (an unrelated party) for $100,000. Under the terms of the sale, X Corporation receives cash of $25,000 and P's notes for the balance of $75,000. The notes are payable over 10 years ($7,500 per year) and carry an 11% rate of interest. Immediately after the sale, X Corporation distributes the cash and notes to S, an individual and sole shareholder. Assume that S has an adjusted basis in the X Corporation stock of $20,000 and that the installment notes possess a value equal to the face amount ($75,000). The tax result of these transactions is summarized as follows:

- X Corporation will recognize gain on the sale of the land, measured by the difference between the $100,000 selling price and the basis X Corporation had in the land.

- S may defer the gain on the receipt of the notes for $75,000 to the point of collection.

- S must allocate the adjusted basis in the stock ($20,000) between the cash and the installment notes. Using the relative fair market value approach, 25% [$25,000 (amount of cash)/$100,000 (total distribution)] of $20,000 (adjusted basis in the stock), or $5,000, is allocated to the cash, and 75% [$75,000 (FMV of notes)/$100,000 (total distribution)] of $20,000 (adjusted basis in the stock), or $15,000, is allocated to the notes.

- S must recognize $20,000 [$25,000 (cash received) − $5,000 (allocated basis of the cash)] in the year of the liquidation.

- Since S's gross profit on the notes is $60,000 [$75,000 (contract price) − $15,000 (allocated basis of the notes)], the gross profit percentage is 80% [$60,000 (gross profit)/$75,000 (contract price)]. Thus, S must report a gain of $6,000 [$7,500 (amount of note) × 80% (gross profit percentage)] on the collection of each note over the next 10 years. The interest element would be accounted for separately. □

If distributions are received by the shareholder in more than one taxable year, basis reallocations may necessitate the filing of amended returns.[8]

Special rules apply if the installment obligations arise from sales between certain related parties.[9]

---

7. Section 453(h) does not apply to the sale of inventory property and property held by the corporation primarily for sale to customers in the ordinary course of its trade or business unless such property is sold in bulk to one person.

8. § 453(h)(2). For an example of such a possibility,

see the Finance Committee Report on H.R. 6883 (reported with amendments on September 26, 1980), the Installment Sales Revision Act of 1980.

9. §§ 453(h)(1)(C) and (D). For this purpose, related parties are defined in § 1239(b).

LIQUIDATIONS—PARENT–SUBSIDIARY SITUATIONS

Section 332 is an exception to the general rule that the shareholder recognizes gain or loss on a corporate liquidation. If a parent corporation liquidates a subsidiary corporation in which it owns at least 80 percent of the voting stock, no gain or loss is recognized for distributions to the parent.[10]

The requirements for application of § 332 are as follows:

- The parent must own at least 80 percent of the voting stock of the subsidiary and at least 80 percent of the total value of the subsidiary's stock.

- The subsidiary must distribute all its property in complete redemption of all its stock within the taxable year or within three years from the close of the tax year in which a plan was adopted and the first distribution occurred.

- The subsidiary must be solvent.[11]

If these requirements are met, § 332 becomes mandatory.

When a series of distributions occurs in the liquidation of a subsidiary corporation, the parent corporation must own the required amount of stock (80 percent) on the date of adoption of a plan of liquidation and at all times until all property has been distributed.[12] If the parent fails to qualify at any time, the provisions for nonrecognition of gain or loss do not apply to any distribution.

Tax Treatment When a Minority Interest Exists

A distribution to a minority shareholder in a § 332 liquidation is treated in the same manner as one made pursuant to a nonliquidating redemption. Accordingly, gain (but not loss) is recognized by the distributing corporation on the property distributed to the minority shareholder.

EXAMPLE 14

The stock of S Corporation is held as follows: 80% by P Corporation and 20% by T, an individual. S Corporation is liquidated on December 10, 1990, pursuant to a plan adopted on January 10, 1990. At the time of its liquidation, S Corporation had assets with a basis of $100,000 and fair market value of $500,000. S Corporation will have to recognize gain of $80,000 [($500,000 fair market value − $100,000 basis) × 20% minority interest]. The remaining gain of $320,000 will be sheltered by § 337(a). □

The minority shareholder is subject to the general rule of § 331. Accordingly, the difference between the fair market value of the assets distributed and the basis of the minority shareholder's stock is the amount of gain or loss recognized by the minority shareholder. The tax basis of property received by the minority shareholder will be the property's fair market value as of the date of distribution.[13]

---

10. § 337(a).
11. Reg. §§ 1.332–2(a) and (b).
12. The date of the adoption of a plan of complete liquidation could be crucial in determining whether § 332 applies. See, for example, *George L. Riggs, Inc.*, 64 T.C. 474 (1975).

13. § 334(a).

Indebtedness of Subsidiary to Parent

If a subsidiary satisfies a debt owed to the parent with appreciated property, it must recognize gain on the transaction unless § 332 applies. When § 332 is applicable, gain or loss is not recognized by the subsidiary upon the transfer of properties to the parent even though some properties are transferred to satisfy the subsidiary's indebtedness to the parent.[14]

EXAMPLE 15   S Corporation owes its parent, P Corporation, $20,000. It satisfies the obligation by transferring land (worth $20,000 with a tax basis of $8,000). Normally, S Corporation would recognize a gain of $12,000 on the transaction. However, if the transfer is made pursuant to a liquidation under § 332, S Corporation would not recognize a gain. □

Realized gain or loss is recognized by the parent corporation on the satisfaction of indebtedness, even though property is received during liquidation of the subsidiary. The special provision noted above does not apply to the parent corporation.

EXAMPLE 16   P Corporation purchased bonds of its subsidiary S at a discount. Upon liquidation of the subsidiary pursuant to § 332, P received payment in the face amount of the bonds. The transaction has no tax effect on S Corporation. However, P Corporation must recognize gain in the amount of the difference between its basis in the bonds and the amount received in payment. □

If a parent corporation does not receive at least partial payment for its stock in a subsidiary corporation upon liquidation of the subsidiary, § 332 will not apply.[15] The parent corporation would then have a bad debt deduction for the difference between the value of any properties received from the subsidiary and its basis in the subsidiary debt.

Section 332 does not apply to the liquidation of an insolvent subsidiary corporation. If the subsidiary is insolvent, the parent corporation would have a loss deduction for its worthless stock in the subsidiary. The loss would be ordinary if more than 90 percent of the gross receipts for all tax years of the subsidiary were from sources other than passive sources.[16] Otherwise, the loss would be a capital loss.

EXAMPLE 17   P Corporation paid $100,000 for all the stock of S Corporation 15 years ago. At present, S has a deficit of $600,000 in E & P. If P liquidates S, § 332 would not apply because S is insolvent. P Corporation would have a loss deduction for its worthless stock in S Corporation. If more than 90% of the gross receipts of S Corporation for all tax years were from sources other than passive sources, the loss would be ordinary. Otherwise, it would be a capital loss. Assume P also loaned S Corporation $50,000. Since the assets are not sufficient to pay the

---

14. § 337(b).

15. Reg. § 1.332–2(b).

16. See § 165(g) and Reg. § 1.165–5.

liabilities, P would also have a loss on the note. Upon liquidation, the basis of the assets of S to P would be the fair market value. P's loss would be measured by the fair market value of S's assets less the liabilities payable to third parties less P's basis in the S stock and note.   □

Basis of Property Received by the Parent Corporation—The General Rule of § 334(b)(1)

Unless a parent corporation elects under § 338, property received by the parent corporation in a complete liquidation of its subsidiary under § 332 has the same basis it had in the hands of the subsidiary.[17] The parent's basis in stock of the liquidated subsidiary disappears. This is true even though some of the property was transferred to the parent in satisfaction of debt owed the parent by the subsidiary.

EXAMPLE 18   P, the parent corporation, has a basis of $20,000 in stock in S Corporation, a subsidiary in which it owns 85% of all classes of stock. P Corporation purchased the stock of S Corporation 10 years ago. In the current year, P Corporation liquidates S Corporation and acquires assets worth $50,000 with a tax basis to S Corporation of $40,000. P Corporation would have a basis of $40,000 in the assets, with a potential gain upon sale of $10,000. P Corporation's original $20,000 basis in S Corporation's stock disappears.   □

EXAMPLE 19   P Corporation has a basis of $60,000 in stock in S Corporation, a subsidiary acquired 10 years ago. It liquidates S Corporation and receives assets worth $50,000 with a tax basis to S Corporation of $40,000. P Corporation again has a basis of $40,000 in the assets it acquired from S Corporation. If it sells the assets for $50,000, it will have a gain of $10,000 in spite of the fact that its basis in S Corporation stock was $60,000. P Corporation's loss will never be recognized.   □

Because the parent corporation takes the subsidiary's basis in its assets, the carryover rules of § 381 apply. The parent would acquire a net operating loss of the subsidiary, any investment credit carryover, capital loss carryover, and a carryover of E & P of the subsidiary. (Section 381 applies to most tax-free reorganizations and to a tax-free liquidation under § 332 if the subsidiary's bases in its assets carry over to the parent.)

Basis of Property Received by the Parent Corporation—The Exception of § 338

Background.   Under the general rule of § 332(b)(1), problems developed when a subsidiary was liquidated shortly after acquisition by a parent corporation.

1. When the basis of the subsidiary's assets was in excess of the purchase price of the stock, the parent received a step-up in basis in such assets at no tax cost.

---

17. § 334(b)(1) and Reg. § 1.334–1(b).

If, for example, the parent paid $100,000 for the subsidiary's stock and the basis of the assets transferred to the parent was $150,000, the parent enjoyed a $50,000 benefit without any gain recognition. The $50,000 increase in basis of the subsidiary's assets could have led to additional depreciation deductions and either more loss or less gain upon the later disposition of the assets by the parent.

2. If the basis of the subsidiary's assets was below the purchase price of the stock, the parent suffered a step-down in basis in such assets with no attendant tax benefit. Return to Example 19. If the situation is changed slightly—the subsidiary's stock is not held for 10 years, but the subsidiary is liquidated shortly after acquisition—the basic inequity of the "no loss" situation is apparent. (Any number of reasons that one corporation would pay more for the stock in another corporation than the latter's basis in the assets could exist. For one, the basis of the assets has no necessary correlation to the fair market value. For another, the acquiring corporation might have no choice in the matter if it really wants the assets. The shareholders in the acquired corporation might prefer to sell their stock rather than the assets of the corporation. Tax consequences would undoubtedly have some bearing on such a decision.)

In the landmark decision of *Kimbell-Diamond Milling Co. v. Comm.*,[18] the courts finally resolved these problems. When a parent corporation liquidates a subsidiary shortly after the acquisition of its stock, the parent is really purchasing the assets of the subsidiary. Consequently, the basis of such assets should be the cost of the stock. Known as the "single transaction" approach, the basis determination is not made under the general rule of § 334(b)(1). The *Kimbell-Diamond* problem ultimately led to the enactment of § 338.

Requirements for Application.   Section 338 provides that for a qualified stock purchase as defined below, an acquiring corporation may, by the fifteenth day of the ninth month beginning after the month in which the qualified stock purchase occurs, make an irrevocable election to treat the acquisition as a purchase of the assets of the acquired corporation.

A purchasing corporation makes a qualified stock purchase if it acquires at least 80 percent of the voting power and at least 80 percent of the value of the acquired corporation within a 12-month period beginning with the first purchase of stock. The stock must be acquired in a taxable transaction (e.g., § 351 and other nonrecognition provisions do not apply). An acquisition of stock by any member of an affiliated group, including the purchasing corporation, is considered to be an acquisition by the purchasing corporation.

Tax Consequences.   If the parent makes a qualified election under § 338, the purchasing corporation will have a basis in the subsidiary's assets equal to its basis in the subsidiary's stock. The subsidiary need not be liquidated.

Under § 338, the acquired corporation is deemed to have sold its assets for an amount equal to the purchasing corporation's grossed-up basis in the subsidiary's stock adjusted for liabilities of the subsidiary corporation. The grossed-up basis is the basis in the subsidiary stock multiplied by a fraction having 100 percent as its numerator and the percentage of value of the subsidiary's stock held by the

---

18. 14 T.C. 74 (1950), *aff'd.* in 51–1 USTC ¶ 9201, 40 AFTR 328, 187 F.2d 718 (CA–5, 1951), *cert. den.* 72 S.Ct. 50 (USSC, 1951).

purchasing corporation on the acquisition date as its denominator.[19] This amount is allocated among the subsidiary's assets using the residual method described below.

The election of § 338 produces gain or loss to the subsidiary being purchased. The subsidiary is treated as having sold all of its assets at the close of the acquisition date in a single transaction at the fair market value.[20] The subsidiary is then treated as a new corporation that purchased all of the assets as of the beginning of the day after the acquisition date.

EXAMPLE 20

S Corporation has an $800,000 basis in its assets and liabilities totaling $500,000. It has E & P of $200,000 and assets worth $2,000,000. P Corporation purchases 80% of the stock of S on March 10, 1990, for $1,200,000 [($2,000,000 less liabilities of $500,000) × 80%]. Because the purchase price of the S stock exceeds S's basis in its assets, and to eliminate S's E & P, P may choose to elect by December 15, 1990, to treat the acquisition as a purchase of the assets of S under § 338. S need not be liquidated for § 338 to apply. If P elects § 338, the tax consequences are as follows:

- S will be deemed to have sold its assets for an amount equal to the grossed-up basis in the S stock.

- The grossed-up basis in the S stock would be computed as follows: the basis of the S stock would be multiplied by a fraction, with 100% the numerator and 80% the denominator. Thus, the basis of the S stock, $1,200,000, is multiplied by 100/80. The result is $1,500,000, which is adjusted for liabilities of S Corporation of $500,000 for a deemed selling price of $2,000,000.

- The selling price of $2,000,000 less the basis of S's assets of $800,000 produces a recognized gain to S Corporation of $1,200,000. □

Because P did not purchase 100 percent of the stock of S, different results occur depending on whether or not S is liquidated. If S is not liquidated, it is treated as a new corporation as of March 11, 1990. The basis of S's assets would be $2,000,000, and the E & P would be eliminated. If S Corporation is liquidated, P Corporation would have a basis of $1,600,000 in S's assets, representing 80 percent of S's assets. S's E & P would not carry over to P.

Note the results of the § 338 election. The assets of S Corporation receive a stepped-up basis but at a substantial tax cost. S Corporation must recognize all of its realized gain. Because of the tax liability to S Corporation on its recognized gain, P Corporation should reduce the amount paid for the assets of S Corporation.

Allocation of Purchase Price.   The new stepped-up basis of the assets of a subsidiary when a § 338 election is in effect is allocated among the assets by use of the residual method.[21] This requires that the amount of the purchase price of the assets that exceeds the aggregate fair market values of the tangible and identifiable intangible assets (other than goodwill and going concern value) must be allocated to goodwill or going concern value. Neither goodwill nor going concern value can be amortized for tax purposes.

---

19. § 338(b)(4).

20. § 338(a).

21. § 1060

EXAMPLE 21   For $4,000,000, P Corporation acquires all of the stock of S Corporation and elects to liquidate under § 338. If the fair market value of S Corporation's physical assets is $3,500,000, P must allocate $500,000 of the purchase price either to goodwill or to going concern value.   □

In Example 21, none of the purchase price would have to be allocated to goodwill or going concern value if the physical assets were worth $4,000,000. However, the burden of proof of showing no residual amount will be on the taxpayer and not on the IRS.

Consistency Requirement.   A consistency requirement under § 338 ensures that the acquiring corporation does not pick and choose which of the acquired subsidiary corporations are to be covered by the § 338 election. For a one-year period before and after the acquisition of the subsidiary (the consistency period), the parent is deemed to have made an election under § 338 if it makes a direct purchase of assets from the subsidiary or from an affiliate of the subsidiary during that period.[22] (Exceptions exist, such as for asset purchases in the ordinary course of a business.)

EXAMPLE 22   On June 15, 1990, P Corporation purchases all of the stock of T Corporation. Shortly thereafter, P Corporation purchases all of the assets of S Corporation, a subsidiary of T Corporation. P Corporation will be deemed to have made the election as to T Corporation.   □

In addition, during the consistency period, tax treatment of acquisitions of stock of two or more other companies that are members of an affiliated group must be consistent.[23]

EXAMPLE 23   On June 1, 1990, P Corporation purchases all of the stock in T Corporation and makes a timely election under § 338. If T Corporation owns all the stock in S Corporation, the § 338 election also applies to S Corporation. This is so even though P Corporation never made an election as to S Corporation. On the other hand, if P Corporation does not make an election as to T Corporation, it cannot make the election as to S Corporation.   □

A Comparison of §§ 334(b)(1) and 338.   Under the general rule of § 334(b)(1), a subsidiary's basis in its assets carries over to the parent corporation upon liquidation. The recapture rules of §§ 1245, 1250, and 1252 do not apply to liquidations of subsidiary corporations when basis is determined under § 334(b)(1). These Sections except such liquidations from their provisions.[24] Consequently, a subsidiary liquidation pursuant to §§ 332 and 334(b)(1) is completely tax-free (except for any minority interest). On the other hand, a liquidation pursuant to § 338, while tax-free to the parent, is taxable to the subsidiary.

If a liquidation under § 332 qualifies under § 338 and a timely election is made, the holding period of the property received by the parent corporation begins

22. § 338(e).
23. § 338(f).

24. See, for example, §§ 1245(b)(3), 1250(d)(3), and 47(b)(2).

CONCEPT SUMMARY 18-1

Summary of Liquidation Rules

Effect on the Shareholder	Basis of Property Received	Effect on the Corporation
§ 331—The general rule provides for capital gain treatment on the difference between the FMV of property received and the basis of the stock in the corporation. (Gain on installment obligations resulting from sales of noninventory property or inventory property sold in bulk to one person by the corporation may, however, be deferred to the point of collection.)	§ 334(a)—Basis of assets received by the shareholder will be the FMV on the date of distribution (except for installment obligations in which gain is deferred to the point of collection).	§ 336—Gain or loss is recognized for distributions in kind and for sales by the liquidating corporation. Losses are not recognized for distributions to related parties (shareholders who own, directly or indirectly, more than 50% of the corporation's stock) if the distribution is not pro rata or if disqualified property is distributed. Losses may be disallowed on distributions of disqualified property even if made to unrelated parties.
§ 332—Liquidation of a subsidiary in which the parent owns 80% of the voting stock and 80% of the value of the subsidiary stock. No gain or loss is recognized to the parent corporation. Subsidiary must distribute all of its property within the taxable year or within three years from the close of the taxable year in which the plan is adopted.	§ 334(b)(1)—Property has the same basis as it had in the hands of the subsidiary. Parent's basis in the stock disappears. Carryover rules of § 381 apply.	§ 337—No gain or loss is recognized by the subsidiary on distributions to an 80% or more parent. Gain (but not loss) is recognized on distributions to minority shareholders.
	§ 338—Basis of assets takes the basis that the parent held in the stock in the subsidiary. Basis is allocated to assets using the residual method. Carryover rules of § 381 do not apply. (Subsidiary need not be liquidated.)	§ 338—Gain or loss is recognized by the subsidiary corporation.

on the date the parent acquired the subsidiary's stock. If the corporation is not liquidated, the holding period of the assets to the subsidiary would start anew on the acquisition date because the subsidiary is treated as having sold the assets as of that date.[25] In a liquidation under § 334(b)(1), the holding period of the subsidiary carries over to the parent.

CORPORATE REORGANIZATIONS

A corporate combination, usually referred to as a reorganization, can be either a taxable or a nontaxable transaction. Assuming a business combination is taxable, § 1001 of the Code provides that the seller's gain or loss is measured by the difference between the amount realized and the basis of property surrendered. The purchaser's basis for the property received is the amount paid for such property, and the holding period begins on the date of purchase.

---

25. § 338(a).

Certain exchanges are specifically excepted from tax recognition by the Code. For example, § 1031 provides that no gain or loss shall be recognized if property held for productive use or for investment is exchanged solely for ". . . . property of a like kind . . . ." Section 1033, if elected by the taxpayer, provides for partial or complete nonrecognition of gain if property destroyed, seized, or stolen is compulsorily or involuntarily converted into similar property. Further, § 351 provides for nonrecognition of gain upon the transfer of property to a controlled corporation. Finally, §§ 361 and 368 provide for nonrecognition of gain in certain corporate reorganizations. The Regulations state the underlying assumption behind such nonrecognition of gain or loss as follows:

> . . . the new property is substantially a continuation of the old investment still unliquidated; and, in the case of reorganizations, . . . the new enterprise, the new corporate structure, and the new property are substantially continuations of the old still unliquidated.[26]

Summary of the Different Types of Reorganizations

Section 368(a) of the Code specifies seven corporate restructures or reorganizations that will qualify as nontaxable exchanges. It is important that the planner of a nontaxable business combination determine well in advance that the proposed transaction falls specifically within one of these seven described types. If the transaction fails to qualify, it will not be granted special tax treatment.

Section 368(a)(1) states that the term "reorganization" means the following:

(A)   A statutory merger or consolidation.

(B)   The acquisition by one corporation, in exchange solely for all or a part of its voting stock (or in exchange solely for all or a part of the voting stock of a corporation that is in control of the acquiring corporation), of stock of another corporation if, immediately after the acquisition, the acquiring corporation has control of such other corporation (whether or not such acquiring corporation had control immediately before the acquisition).

(C)   The acquisition by one corporation, in exchange solely for all or a part of its voting stock (or in exchange solely for all or a part of the voting stock of a corporation that is in control of the acquiring corporation), of substantially all of the properties of another corporation, but in determining whether the exchange is solely for stock, the assumption by the acquiring corporation of a liability of the other, or the fact that property acquired is subject to a liability, shall be disregarded.

(D)   A transfer by a corporation of all or a part of its assets to another corporation if immediately after the transfer the transferor, or one or more of its shareholders (including persons who were shareholders immediately before the transfer), or any combination thereof, is in control of the corporation to which the assets are transferred, but only if, in pursuance of the plan, stock and securities of the corporation to which the assets are transferred are distributed in a transaction that qualifies under § 354, § 355, or § 356.

(E)   A recapitalization.

---

26.   Reg. § 1.1011–2(c).

(F)   A mere change in identity, form, or place of organization, however effected.

(G)   A transfer by a corporation of all or a part of its assets to another corporation in a bankruptcy or receivership proceeding, but only if, in pursuance of the plan, stock and securities of the transferee corporation are distributed in a transaction that qualifies under § 354, § 355, or § 356.

These seven different types of tax-free reorganizations are designated by the letters identifying each: "Type A," "Type B," "Type C," "Type D," "Type E," "Type F," and "Type G" reorganizations. Basically, excepting the recapitalization (E), the change in form (F), and the insolvent corporation (G) provisions, a tax-free reorganization is (1) a statutory merger or consolidation, (2) an exchange of stock for voting stock, (3) an exchange of assets for voting stock, or (4) a divisive reorganization (the so-called spin-off, split-off, or split-up).

General Consequences of Tax-Free Reorganizations

Generally, no gain or loss is recognized to the security holders of the various corporations involved in tax-free reorganizations in the exchange of their stock and securities[27] except when they receive cash or other consideration in addition to stock and securities.[28] As far as securities (long-term debt) are concerned, however, gain is not recognized if securities are surrendered in the same principal amount (or a greater principal amount) as the principal amount of the securities received.

If additional consideration is received, gain is recognized but not in excess of the sum of money and the fair market value of other property received. If the distribution has the effect of the distribution of a dividend, any recognized gain is a taxable dividend to the extent of the shareholder's share of the corporation's E & P. The remainder is treated as an exchange of property.[29] Loss is never recognized. The tax basis of stock and securities received by a shareholder pursuant to a tax-free reorganization will be the same as the basis of those surrendered, decreased by the amount of boot received and increased by the amount of gain and dividend income, if any, recognized on the transaction.

EXAMPLE 24

T, an individual, exchanges stock she owns in Target Corporation for stock in Acquiring Corporation plus $2,000 cash. The exchange is pursuant to a tax-free reorganization of both corporations. T paid $10,000 for the stock in Target two years ago. The stock in Acquiring possesses a fair market value of $12,000. T has a realized gain of $4,000 ($12,000 + $2,000 − $10,000), which is recognized to the extent of the boot received, $2,000. Assume the distribution has the effect of a dividend. If T's share of E & P in Target is $1,000, that amount would be a taxable dividend. The remaining $1,000 would be treated as a gain from the exchange of property. T's basis in the Aquiring stock would be $10,000 ($10,000 basis in stock surrendered − $2,000 boot received + $2,000 gain and dividend income recognized).   □

---

27.   The term "securities" includes bonds and long-term notes. Short-term notes are not considered to be securities. The problem of drawing a line between short-term and long-term notes is, to say the least, troublesome. Some courts include

notes with a 5-year maturity date as long term; others, 10 years.

28.   § 358(a).

29.   § 356(a).

EXAMPLE 25   Assume T's basis in the Target stock was $15,000. T would have a realized loss of $1,000 on the exchange, none of which would be recognized. Her basis in the Acquiring stock would be $13,000 ($15,000 basis in stock surrendered – $2,000 boot received). □

Because there is a substituted basis in tax-free reorganizations, the unrecognized gain or loss will be recognized when the new stock or securities are disposed of in a taxable transaction.

No gain or loss is recognized by the acquired corporation on the exchange of property pursuant to a tax-free reorganization.[30] If the acquired corporation receives cash or other property in the exchange, as well as stock or securities in the acquiring corporation, gain is recognized by the corporation on such other property only if the corporation fails to distribute the other property to its shareholders. If the acquired corporation distributes boot received in a tax-free reorganization, the shareholders, and not the corporation, are taxed on any recognized gain occasioned by the receipt of boot.[31]

Gain or loss also is not recognized by the acquiring corporation. Property received from the acquired corporation retains the basis it had in the hands of the acquired corporation, increased by the amount of gain recognized by the acquired corporation on the transfer.[32]

If a corporate exchange qualifies as a tax-free reorganization under one of the seven types mentioned, the tax consequences described are automatic regardless of the intent of the parties involved.

TAX PLANNING CONSIDERATIONS

Effect of a Liquidating Distribution on the Corporation

Assets that have depreciated in value should not be distributed in the form of a property dividend before liquidation. Although losses on disqualified property and non-pro rata distributions to related shareholders are not recognized, losses are otherwise recognized in *complete liquidations*. Thus, potential loss from such assets can be used to offset gains recognized upon a complete liquidation. On the other hand, if assets that have depreciated in value are distributed as *property dividends*, the corporation will receive no tax benefit from the potential loss. Recall that losses on nonliquidating distributions are not recognized.

Effect of a Liquidating Distribution on the Shareholder

Under the general rule of § 331, shareholders will have recognized gain or loss measured by the difference between the liquidation proceeds and the basis of the stock given up. In cases of a large gain, a shareholder may wish to consider shifting the gain to others. One approach is to give the stock to family members or donate it to charity. Whether this procedure will be successful depends on the timing of

---

30. § 361(a).

31. § 361(b). If the acquired corporation has sufficient E & P and the shareholders receive pro rata distributions as boot, the boot is treated as a dividend and taxed as ordinary income and

not as capital gain. See *Shimberg v. U.S.*, 78–2 USTC ¶9607, 42 AFTR2d 78–5575, 577 F.2d 283 (CA–5, 1978).

32. § 362(b).

the transfer. If the donee of the stock is not in a position to prevent the liquidation of the corporation, the donor will be deemed to have made an anticipatory assignment of income. As a result, the gain will still be taxed to the donor. Hence, advance planning becomes crucial in arriving at the desired tax result.

Recall that § 453(h) provides some relief from the general rule of § 331 that all gain is to be recognized by the shareholder upon the shareholder's receipt of the liquidation proceeds. If the payment for the sale of § 337 corporate assets after a plan of liquidation has been adopted is by installment notes, the shareholders receiving such notes as liquidation distributions may be able to report the gain on the installment method. Hence, some gain can be deferred to the point of collection of such notes.

The use of § 332 for the liquidation of a subsidiary is not elective. Nevertheless, some flexibility may be available.

- Whether § 332 applies depends on the 80 percent stock ownership test. Given some substance to the transaction, § 332 may well be avoided if a parent corporation reduces its stock ownership in the subsidiary below this percentage. On the other hand, the opposite approach may be desirable. A parent could make § 332 applicable by acquiring enough additional stock in the subsidiary to meet the 80 percent test.

- Once § 332 becomes operative, less latitude is present in determining the parent's basis in the subsidiary's assets. If § 334(b)(1) applies, the subsidiary's basis carries over to the parent. If § 338 applies and a timely election is made, the parent's basis becomes the cost of the stock. (If the subsidiary is not liquidated, the basis of the assets to the subsidiary is the parent's cost of the stock.) Presumably, § 338 can be avoided by failing to make a timely election.

- If a timely election is made under § 338, the parent corporation's basis in the stock of the subsidiary is allocated among the assets of the subsidiary.

PROBLEM MATERIALS

Discussion Questions

1. Compare stock redemptions and liquidations with other corporate distributions in terms of the following:
   a. Recognition of gain to the shareholder.
   b. Recognition of gain or loss by the distributing corporation.
   c. Effect on the distributing corporation's E & P.
2. Compare stock redemptions with liquidations in terms of the following:
   a. Possible disallowance of a loss (§ 267) to a shareholder.
   b. Basis of noncash property received from the corporation.
3. What losses are not recognized by the liquidating corporation in a complete liquidation?
4. What are related-party situations?
5. What is disqualified property in a liquidating distribution?
6. Can losses ever be recognized in a complete liquidation if disqualified property is involved? Explain.

7. Discuss the tax treatment of liquidation expenses in connection with the following:

    a. General liquidation expenses.

    b. Expenses relating to a distribution of assets in kind.

    c. Expenses relating to a sale of assets.

8. Explain the tax consequences to a shareholder of a corporation in the process of liquidation under the general rule of § 331.

9. In terms of the applicability of § 332, describe the effect of each of the following:

    a. The adoption of a plan of complete liquidation.

    b. The period of time in which the corporation must liquidate.

    c. The amount of stock held by the parent corporation.

    d. The solvency of the subsidiary being liquidated.

10. What are the tax consequences of a § 332 liquidation when a minority interest is involved?

11. Under § 332, how is the satisfaction by a subsidiary of a debt owed to its parent treated for tax purposes?

12. Could a liquidation of one corporation involve §§ 331 and 332?

13. Describe the problem that led to the enactment of § 338.

14. What are the requirements for the application of § 338?

15. Under what circumstances could the application of § 338 be beneficial to the parent corporation? Detrimental?

16. Compare §§ 334(b)(1) and 338 with respect to the following:

    a. Carryover to the parent of the subsidiary's corporate attributes.

    b. Recognition by the subsidiary of gain or loss on distributions to its parent.

17. Will the application of § 331 to a liquidation always result in capital gain or loss being recognized by a shareholder? Why or why not?

18. "The E & P of the corporation being liquidated will disappear."

    a. Do you agree with this statement?

    b. Why or why not?

19. Is it possible to have a complete liquidation where the existence of the corporation being liquidated is not terminated? Elaborate.

Problems

20. S Corporation distributes to its shareholders land held as an investment (basis of $100,000, fair market value of $600,000) pursuant to a complete liquidation. The land is subject to a liability of $700,000. How much gain does S Corporation have on a distribution of the land in 1990?   600,000

21. On July 1, 1990, T Corporation's stock is held equally by F and D, father and daughter. One year before liquidation, F transfers property (basis of $200,000, fair market value of $60,000) to T Corporation in return for stock. In liquidation, T Corporation transfers the property to D. At the time of the liquidation, the property is worth $50,000. How much loss would T Corporation recognize on the distribution?   0

22. T Corporation has the following assets on January 10, 1990:

	Basis to T Corporation	Fair Market Value
Cash	$ 300,000	$300,000
Inventory	100,000	300,000
Equipment	1,060,000	600,000
Building	400,000	760,000
Land	40,000	40,000

The inventory had been purchased by T Corporation; the remaining assets were acquired seven years ago. T Corporation adopted a plan of liquidation in January 1990 and distributed its assets that same year to its shareholders, A (70%) and B (30%). A and B are unrelated. What are the tax consequences to T Corporation under the following independent circumstances:

a. The assets are distributed to A and B in proportion to their stock interests (70% interest in each asset to A and 30% interest in each asset to B).

b. The equipment, building, and land are distributed to A, and the cash and inventory are distributed to B.

c. The equipment is distributed to B, and the remaining assets are distributed to A.

d. What is the result in (a) if the equipment had been transferred to T Corporation in a § 351 transaction 10 months before the liquidation when the equipment had a basis of $1,060,000 and a fair market value of $660,000?

23. On January 10, 1990, in a transaction that qualifies under § 351, X Corporation acquired land with a basis to the contributing shareholder of $400,000. The land had a value on that date of $250,000. X Corporation adopts a plan of liquidation on July 1, 1990. On December 10, 1990, when the value of the land has declined to $200,000, X Corporation distributes the land to A, a shareholder who owns 30% of the stock in X Corporation. X Corporation never used the land for any business purpose during the time it owned the land. How much loss can X Corporation recognize on the distribution of the land?

24. Assume in Problem 23 that X Corporation distributed the land to B, a shareholder who owns 60% of its stock. How much loss can X Corporation recognize on the distribution of the land?

25. In 1989, after a plan of complete liquidation has been adopted, W Corporation sells its only asset, unimproved land, to T (an unrelated party) for $200,000. Under the terms of the sale, W Corporation receives cash of $40,000 and T's note in the amount of $160,000. The note is payable in five years ($32,000 per year) and carries an interest rate of 12%. In 1989, immediately after the sale, W Corporation distributes the cash and notes to S, an individual and sole shareholder. Assume that S has an adjusted basis in the W Corporation stock of $40,000 and that the installment notes possess a value equal to the face amount. What are the tax results to S if the choice is to defer as much gain as possible on the transaction?

26. T Corporation acquired land in a § 351 exchange in 1988. The land had a basis of $600,000 and a fair market value of $650,000 on the date of the transfer. T Corporation has two shareholders, A and B, unrelated individuals. A owns 80% of the stock in T Corporation, and B owns 20%. T Corporation adopts a plan of liquidation in 1990. On this date the value of the land has decreased to $200,000. In distributing the land either to A or to B, or to both, as part of the liquidating distributions from T Corporation, should T Corporation

    a. distribute all the land to A?
    b. distribute all the land to B?
    c. distribute 80% of the land to A and 20% to B?
    d. distribute 50% of the land to A and 50% to B?
    e. sell the land and distribute the proceeds of $200,000 proportionately to A and to B?

27. Assume in Problem 26 that the plan of liquidation is not adopted until 1991. In addition, assume the land had a fair market value of $500,000 on the date of the transfer of the land to the corporation. Its fair market value on the date of the liquidation has decreased to $200,000. How would your answers to Problem 25 change?

28. The stock of S Corporation is held as follows: 85% by P Corporation and 15% by T, an individual. S Corporation is liquidated on October 1, 1990, pursuant to a plan of liquidation adopted on January 15, 1990. At the time of its liquidation, S Corporation's assets had a basis of $2,000,000 and fair market value of $18,000,000. P Corporation has a basis of $800,000 in its S Corporation stock. The basis of the stock in S Corporation to T is $80,000.
    a. How much gain, if any, must S Corporation recognize on the liquidation?
    b. How much gain, if any, is recognized by the receipt of property from S Corporation to P Corporation? To T?

29. At the time of its liquidation under § 332, S Corporation had the following assets and liabilities:

	Basis to S Corporation	Fair Market Value
Cash	$480,000	$ 480,000
Marketable securities	360,000	960,000
Unimproved land	600,000	1,200,000
Unsecured bank loan	(120,000)	(120,000)
Mortgage on land	(360,000)	(360,000)

P Corporation, the sole shareholder of S Corporation, has a basis in its stock investment of $1,440,000. At the time of its liquidation, S Corporation's E & P was $1,920,000.
    a. How much gain (or loss) will S Corporation recognize if it distributes all of its assets and liabilities to P Corporation?
    b. How much gain (or loss) will P Corporation recognize?
    c. If § 334(b)(1) applies, what will be P Corporation's basis in the marketable securities it receives from S Corporation?
    d. What will be P's basis in the unimproved land?

30. S Corporation, owned by two individual shareholders, has a basis of $450,000 (fair market value of $1,000,000) in its assets and has E & P of $80,000. Its liabilities total $100,000. If the assets were sold, all gain would be long-term capital gain or § 1231 gain. P Corporation purchases 20% of all the stock of S Corporation for $180,000 on March 1, 1990; 15% for $135,000 on September 20, 1990; and 60% for $540,000 on December 1, 1990, or a total consideration of $855,000.
    a. Is P Corporation entitled to make an election under § 338?
    b. Assume P Corporation may make an election under § 338. Should P do so? When must P make such an election?

c. What are the tax consequences to S Corporation and to P Corporation if P Corporation makes a valid election under § 338 but does not liquidate S Corporation?

d. What is the tax result if S Corporation is liquidated four months after a valid § 338 election? A, an individual who holds the 5% minority interest in S Corporation, has a $10,000 basis in his stock in S. What is the tax result to A upon the liquidation?

31. P Corporation paid $900,000 for all the stock of S Corporation 10 years ago. S Corporation's balance sheet is as follows:

Assets

Cash	$	22,500
Inventory		67,500
Accounts receivable		45,000
Equipment		180,000
Land		225,000
	$	540,000

Liabilities and Shareholders' Equity

Accounts payable	$	360,000
Payable to P Corporation		540,000
Common stock		900,000
Deficit		(1,260,000)
	$	540,000

What are the tax consequences to P Corporation if it liquidates S Corporation?

19

CORPORATE ACCUMULATIONS

Chapter 20 discusses one major technique for minimization of the tax liability of closely held corporations: the S corporation election. However, some of the corporations that fall into the closely held category either may not qualify for the election or may find it unattractive. For these other taxpayers, how can corporate earnings be transmitted to the shareholders while ensuring a deduction for the corporation? One method is to reduce the amount of equity capital invested in a controlled corporation by increasing the debt obligations. In other words, convert dividends into interest payments deductible by the corporation. This method has limits. The Internal Revenue Service may contend that the capital structure is unrealistic and the debt is not bona fide. For these reasons, the IRS may disallow the corporate deduction for interest expense (refer to chapter 16).

An alternative possibility is to convert the earnings of the closely held corporation into compensation to the officers, generally the major shareholders. The compensation is a deductible expense. If it were not for the reasonableness requirement, officer-shareholders could withdraw all corporate profits as salaries and thereby eliminate the corporate tax (refer to chapter 17). However, the reasonableness requirement prevents a corporation from deducting as salaries what are, in fact, nondeductible dividends.

Another approach entails the lease of shareholder-owned property to the corporation. The corporation (the lessee) deducts the lease payment from gross income and saves taxes at the corporate level. Although the shareholders must recognize the rental payments as ordinary income, there is an overall tax savings, because the corporation obtains deductions for what are essentially dividend payments. However, the IRS may classify such payments as disguised dividends and disallow the rental deductions (refer to chapter 17).

A fourth method is simply to accumulate the earnings at the corporate level. A temporary or permanent accumulation of earnings in a corporation results in a deferral of the second tax at the shareholder level. Further, the corporation can invest in funds that are tax-free (e.g., state and local bonds) or buy stock in other domestic corporations to take advantage of the dividends received deduction. Congress took steps to stem such accumulations as early as the first income tax law enacted under the Sixteenth Amendment. Today, in addition to the usual corporate income tax, an extra tax is imposed on earnings accumulated beyond the reasonable needs of the business. Also, a penalty tax may be imposed on undistributed personal holding company income.

This chapter demonstrates how the accumulation of earnings can be employed without leading to adverse tax consequences—the imposition of additional taxes.

Penalty Tax on Unreasonable Accumulations

One method of optimizing the distribution of earnings in a corporation is to accumulate the earnings until the most advantageous time to distribute them to shareholders is reached. If the board of directors is aware of the tax problems of the shareholders, it can channel earnings into the shareholders' pockets with a minimum of tax cost by using any of several mechanisms. The corporation can distribute dividends only in years when the major shareholders are in lower tax brackets. Alternatively, dividend distributions might be curtailed, causing the value of the stock to increase, in a manner similar to that of a savings account, as the retained earnings (and the earnings and profits account) increase. Later, the shareholders can sell their stock in the year of their choice at an amount that reflects the increased retained earnings. In this manner, the capital gain could be

postponed to years when less tax ensues (e.g., the shareholders have capital losses to offset the gains). Or, the shareholders can choose to retain their shares. Upon death, the estate or heirs would receive a step-up in basis equal to the fair market value of the stock on the date of death or, if elected, on the alternate valuation date. As a result, the increment in value represented by the step-up in basis would be largely attributable to the earnings retained by the corporation and would not be subject to income taxation.

However, there are problems involved in any situation in which corporate earnings are accumulated. As previously mentioned, a penalty tax may be imposed on accumulated taxable earnings, or a personal holding company tax may be levied on certain accumulated passive income. Consider first the accumulated earnings tax. Accumulation can be accomplished. However, the tax law is framed to discourage the retention of earnings that are unrelated to the business needs of the company. Earnings retained in the business to avoid the imposition of the tax that would have been imposed on distributions to the shareholder are subject to a penalty tax.

EXAMPLE 1	T operated a consulting business as a sole proprietor in 1989. Assume she is in the 28% tax bracket in 1990, and she incorporates her business at the beginning of the year. Her business earns $120,000 in 1990, before her salary of $60,000. Since $60,000 of the income is accumulated, $6,800 of taxes are "saved" ($16,800 individual tax versus $10,000 corporate tax on the $60,000 accumulated). This accumulated savings could occur each year with the corporation reinvesting the saved taxes. Thus, without an accumulated earnings tax or personal holding company tax, T could use her corporation like a savings account. For example, the corporation could take advantage of the 70% dividends received deduction for dividend–paying stocks. With the top individual tax rate (28% for 1990) below the top corporate tax rate (34% for 1990), it is less attractive to hold investment property in a C corporation than in a flow-through entity (partnership, S corporation, or sole proprietor). Further, the earnings are still at the corporate level, and T might be in a higher individual rate when the accumulated earnings are distributed. □

The Element of Intent

Although the penalty tax is normally applied against closely held corporations, a corporation is not exempt from the tax merely because its stock is widely held.[1] For example, in a Second Court of Appeals decision,[2] the tax was imposed upon a widely held corporation with over 1,500 shareholders. However, a much smaller group of shareholders actually controlled the corporation. As a practical matter, the presence of the required tax avoidance purpose may not exist in the case of a widely held corporation in which no small group has legal or effective control of the corporation.

The key to imposition of the tax is not the number of the shareholders in the corporation but whether a shareholder group controls corporate policy. If such a group does exist and withholds dividends to protect its own tax position, an accumulated earnings tax (§ 531) problem might materialize.

---

1. § 532(c).
2. *Trico Products v. Comm.*, 43–2 USTC ¶9540, 31

AFTR 394, 137 F.2d 424 (CA–2, 1943).

When a corporation is formed or availed of to shield its shareholders from individual taxes by accumulating rather than distributing earnings and profits, the "bad" purpose for accumulating earnings is considered to exist under § 532(a). This subjective test, in effect, asks, Did the corporation and/or shareholder(s) *intend* to retain the earnings in order to avoid the tax on dividends? According to the Supreme Court, this tax avoidance motive need *not* be the dominant or controlling purpose for accumulating the earnings to trigger application of the penalty tax; it need only be a contributing factor to the retention of earnings.[3] If a corporation accumulates funds beyond its reasonable needs, such action is determinative of the existence of a "bad" purpose, unless the contrary can be proven by the preponderance of the evidence. The fact that the business is a mere holding or investment company is *prima facie* evidence of this tax avoidance purpose.[4]

Imposition of the Tax and the Accumulated Earnings Credit

The tax is imposed in addition to the regular corporate tax and the 20 percent alternative minimum tax. For taxable years beginning after December 31, 1987, the rate is 28 percent. Previously, the rates were 27½ percent on the first $100,000 of accumulated taxable income and 38½ percent on all accumulated taxable income in excess of $100,000.

Most corporations are allowed a minimum $250,000 credit against accumulated taxable income, even though they might be accumulating earnings beyond their reasonable business needs. However, certain personal service corporations in health, law, engineering, architecture, accounting, actuarial science, performing arts, and consulting are limited to a $150,000 accumulated earnings credit. Moreover, a nonservice corporation (other than a holding or investment company) may retain more than $250,000 (and a service organization may retain more than $150,000) of accumulated earnings if the company can justify that the accumulation is necessary to meet the reasonable needs of the business.[5]

The accumulated earnings credit is the greater of the following:

1. The current earnings and profits for the tax year that are needed to meet the reasonable needs of the business (see the subsequent discussion) *less* the net long-term capital gain for the year (net of any tax thereon). In determining the reasonable needs for any one year, the accumulated earnings and profits of past years must be taken into account.

2. The amount by which $250,000 exceeds the accumulated earnings and profits of the corporation at the close of the preceding tax year (designated the "minimum credit").

EXAMPLE 2   T Corporation, a calendar year manufacturing concern, has accumulated E & P of $120,000 as of December 31, 1989. For 1990, it has no capital gains and has current E & P of $140,000. A realistic estimate places T Corporation's reasonable needs of the business for 1990 at $200,000. Under item 1, T Corporation's accumulated earnings credit based on the reasonable needs of

---

3. *U.S. v. The Donruss Co.,* 69–1 USTC ¶9167, 23 AFTR2d 69–418, 89 S.Ct. 501 (USSC, 1969).

4. § 533. See, for example, *H. C. Cockrell Warehouse Corp.,* 71 T.C. 1036 (1979).

5. §§ 535(c) and 537 and Reg. § 1.537–1.

the business would be $80,000 ($200,000 reasonable needs of the business – $120,000 accumulated E & P). Pursuant to item 2, the minimum accumulated earnings credit would be $130,000 ($250,000 minimum credit allowed for nonservice corporations – $120,000 accumulated E & P as of the close of the preceding tax year). Thus, the credit becomes $130,000 (the greater of $80,000 or $130,000). □

Several observations should be made about the accumulated earnings credit. First, the minimum credit of $250,000 is of no consequence as long as the prior year's ending balance in accumulated E & P is $250,000 or more. Second, when the credit is based on reasonable needs, the credit is the amount that exceeds accumulated E & P. Third, a taxpayer must choose between the reasonable needs credit (item 1) or the minimum credit (item 2). Combining the two in the same year is not permissible. Fourth, although the § 531 tax is not imposed on accumulated E & P, the amount of the credit depends upon the balance of this account as of the end of the preceding year.

Reasonable Needs of the Business

It has been firmly established that if a corporation's funds are invested in assets essential to the needs of the business, the IRS will have a difficult time imposing the accumulated earnings tax. "Thus, the size of the accumulated earnings and profits or surplus is not the crucial factor; rather it is the reasonableness and nature of the surplus."[6] What are the reasonable business needs of a corporation? This is precisely the point upon which difficulty arises and which creates controversy with the IRS.

Justifiable Needs—In General. The reasonable needs of a business include the business's reasonably anticipated needs.[7] These anticipated needs must be specific, definite, and feasible. A number of court decisions illustrate that indefinite plans referred to only briefly in corporate minutes merely provide a false feeling of security for the taxpayer.[8]

The Regulations list some legitimate reasons that could indicate that the earnings of a corporation are being accumulated to meet the reasonable needs of the business. Earnings may be allowed to accumulate to provide for bona fide expansion of the business enterprise or replacement of plant and facilities as well as to acquire a business enterprise through the purchase of stock or assets. Provision for the retirement of bona fide indebtedness created in connection with the trade or business (e.g., the establishment of a sinking fund for the retirement of bonds issued by the corporation) is a legitimate reason for accumulating earnings under ordinary circumstances. Providing necessary working capital for the business (e.g., to acquire inventories) and providing for investment or loans to suppliers or customers (if necessary to maintain the business of the corporation) are valid grounds for accumulating earnings.[9] Funds may be retained for self-insurance[10] and realistic business contingencies (e.g., lawsuits, patent infringement).[11] Accumulations to

6. *Smoot Sand & Gravel Corp. v. Comm.*, 60–1 USTC ¶9241, 5 AFTR2d 626, 274 F.2d 495 (CA–4, 1960).

7. § 537(a)(1).

8. See, for example, *Fine Realty, Inc. v. U.S.*, 62–2 USTC ¶9758, 10 AFTR2d 5751, 209 F.Supp. 286 (D.Ct. Minn., 1962).

9. Reg. § 1.537–2(b).

10. *Halby Chemical Co., Inc. v. U.S.*, 67–2 USTC ¶9500, 19 AFTR2d 1589 (Ct.Cls., 1967).

11. *Dielectric Materials Co.*, 57 T.C. 587 (1972).

avoid an unfavorable competitive position[12] and to carry keyman life insurance policies[13] are justifiable.

The reasonable business needs of a company also include the post-death § 303 redemption requirements of a corporation.[14] Accumulations for such purposes are limited to the amount needed (or reasonably anticipated to be needed) to effect a redemption of stock included in the gross estate of the decedent-shareholder.[15] This amount may not exceed the sum of the death taxes and funeral and administration expenses allowable under §§ 2053 and 2106.[16]

Section 537(b) provides that reasonable accumulations to pay future product liability losses shall represent a reasonable anticipated need of the business. Guidelines for the application of this change are prescribed in Proposed Regulations.

Justifiable Needs—Working Capital Requirements for Inventory Situations.
For many years, the penalty tax on accumulated earnings was based upon the concept of retained earnings. The courts generally looked at retained earnings alone to determine whether there was an unreasonable accumulation. However, a corporation may have a large retained earnings balance and yet possess no liquid assets with which to pay dividends. Therefore, the emphasis should more appropriately be placed upon the liquidity of a corporation. Does the business have liquid assets *not* needed that could be used to pay dividends? It was not, however, until 1960 that the courts began to use this liquidity approach.[17]

Over the years, greater recognition has been placed on the liquidity needs of the corporation. The reasonable needs of the business can be divided into two categories:

1. Working capital needed for day-to-day operations.

2. Expenditures of a noncurrent nature (extraordinary expenses).

The operating cycle of a business is the average time interval between the acquisition of materials (or services) entering the business and the final realization of cash. The courts seized upon the operating cycle because it had the advantage of objectivity for purposes of determining working capital. A normal business has two distinct cycles:

1. Purchase of inventory → the production process → finished goods inventory

2. Sale of merchandise → accounts receivable → cash collection

A systematic operating cycle formula was developed in *Bardahl Manufacturing Co.* and *Bardahl International Corp.*[18] The technique became known as the *Bardahl* formula.

---

12. *North Valley Metabolic Laboratories*, 34 TCM 400, T.C.Memo, 1975–79.

13. *Emeloid Co. v. Comm.*, 51–1 USTC ¶66,013, 40 AFTR 674, 189 F.2d 230 (CA–3, 1951). Keyman life insurance is a policy on the life of a key employee that is owned by and made payable to the employer. Such insurance would enable the employer to recoup some of the economic loss that could materialize upon the untimely death of the key employee.

14. The § 303 redemption to pay death taxes and administration expenses of a deceased share-holder is discussed in chapter 17.

15. §§ 537(a)(2) and (b)(1).

16. § 303(a).

17. See *Smoot Sand & Gravel Corp. v. Comm.*, cited in Footnote 6.

18. *Bardahl Manufacturing Co.*, 24 TCM 1030, T.C.Memo. 1965–200; *Bardahl International Corp.*, 25 TCM 935, T.C.Memo. 1966–182. See also *Apollo Industries, Inc. v. Comm.*, 66–1 USTC ¶9294, 17 AFTR2d 518, 358 F.2d 867 (CA–1, 1966).

The standard method now used to determine the reasonable working capital needs for a corporation can be outlined as follows:

$$\text{Inventory cycle} = \frac{\text{Average inventory}}{\text{Cost of goods sold}}$$

Plus

$$\text{Accounts receivable cycle} = \frac{\text{Average accounts receivable}}{\text{Net sales}}$$

Minus

$$\text{Accounts payable cycle} = \frac{\text{Average accounts payable}[19]}{\text{Purchases}}$$

Equals

A decimal percentage

These formulas assume that working capital needs are computed on a yearly basis. However, this may not provide the most favorable result. A business that experiences seasonally based high and low cycles illustrates this point. For example, a construction company can justify a greater working capital need if computations are based on a cycle that includes the winter months only and not on an annual average.[20] In the same vein, an incorporated CPA firm would choose a cycle during the slow season.

Both of the original *Bardahl* decisions used the so-called peak cycle approach, whereby the inventory and accounts receivable figures are the amounts for the month-end during which the total amounts in inventory and accounts receivable were the greatest. In fact, the *Bardahl International* decision specifically rejected the average cycle approach. However, some courts have rejected the peak cycle approach,[21] which probably should be used where the business of the corporation is seasonal.[22]

The decimal percentage derived above, when multiplied by the cost of goods sold plus general, administrative, and selling expenses (not including Federal income taxes and depreciation),[23] equals the working capital needs of the business.

If the statistically computed working capital needs plus any extraordinary expenses are more than the current year's net working capital, no penalty tax is imposed. Working capital is the excess of current assets over current liabilities. This amount is the relatively liquid portion of the total business capital that is a buffer for meeting obligations within the normal operating cycle of the business.

However, if working capital needs plus any extraordinary expenses are less than the current year's net working capital, the possibility of the imposition of a penalty tax does exist.[24]

In *Bardahl Manufacturing Corp.*, the costs and expenses used in the formula were those of the following year, whereas in *Bardahl International Corp.*, costs and expenses of the current year were used. Use of the subsequent year's expected costs seems to be the more equitable position.

The IRS normally takes the position that the operating cycle should be reduced by the accounts payable cycle since the payment of such expenses may be

---

19. The accounts payable cycle was developed in *Kingsbury Investments, Inc.*, 28 TCM 1082, T.C.Memo. 1969–205.

20. See *Audits of Construction Contracts*, AICPA, 1965, p. 25.

21. See, for example, *W. L. Mead, Inc.*, 34 TCM 924, T.C.Memo. 1975–215.

22. *Magic Mart, Inc.*, 51 T.C. 775 (1969).

23. In *W. L. Mead, Inc.*, cited in Footnote 21, the Tax Court allowed depreciation to be included in the

expenses of a service firm with no inventory. Likewise, in *Doug-Long, Inc.*, 72 T.C. 158 (1979), the Tax Court allowed a truck stop to include quarterly estimated tax payments in operating expenses.

24. *Electric Regulator Corp. v. Comm.*, 64–2 USTC ¶9705, 14 AFTR2d 5447, 336 F.2d 339 (CA–2, 1964) used "quick assets" (current assets less inventory).

postponed by various credit arrangements that will reduce the operating capital requirements. However, a number of court decisions have omitted such a reduction. In any case, a corporate tax planner should not have to rely on creditors to avoid the accumulated earnings penalty tax. The corporation with the most acute working capital problem will probably have a large accounts payable balance. If the previously outlined formula for determining reasonable working capital needs is used, a large accounts payable balance will result in a sizable reduction in the maximum working capital allowable before the tax is imposed. For tax planning purposes, a corporation should hold accounts payable at a reduced level.

EXAMPLE 3

Q, an accountant for a local appliance store, is asked by his president to determine if the corporation is susceptible to the accumulated earnings tax. Q calculates, as a fraction of the year, the inventory cycle (.08), the receivables cycle (.12), and the payables cycle (.13). The three ratios are combined to determine the operating cycle ratio of .07 (.08 + .12 − .13). Since the operating expenses are $525,000, Q calculates the working capital needs to be $36,750 (.07 times $525,000).

Next Q calculates the actual working capital, using current assets at fair market value less current liabilities. Thus, $285,000 less $200,000 results in $85,000 of actual working capital. Comparing actual working capital ($85,000) with the working capital needs of $36,750, Q determines that the corporation has excess working capital of $48,250. If this appliance store has no other reasonable business needs, the corporation may be subject to the accumulated earnings tax. ☐

No Justifiable Needs.   Certain situations do *not* call for the accumulation of earnings. For example, accumulating earnings to make loans to shareholders[25] or brother-sister corporations is not considered within the reasonable needs of the business.[26] Accumulations to retire stock without curtailment of the business and for unrealistic business hazards (e.g., depression of the U.S. economy) are invalid reasons for accumulating funds,[27] as are accumulations made to carry out investments in properties or securities unrelated to the corporation's activity.[28]

Concept Summary 19–1 reviews the previous discussion regarding what does and does not constitute a reasonable need of the business.

Measuring the Accumulation.   Should the cost or fair market value of assets be used to determine whether a corporation has accumulated earnings and profits beyond its reasonable needs? This issue remains unclear. The Supreme Court has indicated that fair market value is to be used when dealing with marketable securities.[29] Although the Court admitted that the concept of earnings and profits does not include unrealized appreciation, it asserted that to determine if accumulated earnings are reasonable, the current asset ratio must be considered. Thus, the Court looked to the economic realities of the situation and held that fair market value is to be used with respect to readily marketable securities. The Court's opinion did not address the proper basis for valuation of assets other than marketable securities. However, the IRS may assert that this rule should be extended to include other assets. Therefore, tax advisers and corporate personnel

---

25. Reg. §§ 1.537–2(c)(1), (2), and (3).
26. See *Young's Rubber Corp.*, 21 TCM 1593, T.C. Memo. 1962–300.
27. *Turnbull, Inc. v. Comm.*, 67–1 USTC ¶9221, 19 AFTR2d 609, 373 F.2d 91 (CA–5, 1967), and Reg.

§ 1.537–2(c)(5).
28. Reg. § 1.537–2(c)(4).
29. *Ivan Allen Co. v. U.S.*, 75–2 USTC ¶9557, 36 AFTR2d 75–5200, 95 S.Ct. 2501 (USSC, 1975).

✓ CONCEPT SUMMARY 19—1

Reasonable Business Needs

Legitimate Reasons	Invalid Reasons
Expansion of a business.	Loans to shareholders.
Replacement of capital assets.	Loans to brother-sister corporations.
Replacement of plant.	Future depression.
Acquisition of a business.	Unrealistic contingencies.
Working capital needs.	Investment in assets unrelated to the business.
Product liability loss.	Retirement of stock without a curtailment of the business.
Loans to suppliers or customers.	
Redemption under § 303 to pay death taxes and administration expenses of a shareholder.	
Realistic business hazards.	
Loss of a major customer or client.	
Reserve for actual lawsuit.	
Protection of a family business from takeover by outsiders.	
Debt retirement.	
Self-insurance.	

should regularly check all security holdings to guard against accumulations caused by the appreciation of investments.

EXAMPLE 4   C Company had accumulated earnings and profits of approximately $2,000,000. Five years ago, the company invested $150,000 in various stocks and bonds. At the end of the current tax year, the fair market value of these securities approximated $2,500,000. Two of C Company's shareholders, father and son, owned 75% of the stock. If these securities are valued at cost, current assets minus current liabilities are deemed to be equal to the reasonable needs of the business. However, if the marketable securities are valued at their $2,500,000 fair market value, the value of the liquid assets would greatly exceed the corporation's reasonable needs. Under the Supreme Court's economic reality test, the fair market value must be used. Consequently, the corporation would be subject to the § 531 penalty tax.   □

Mechanics of the Penalty Tax

The taxable base for the accumulated earnings tax is a company's accumulated taxable income (ATI). Taxable income of the corporation is modified as follows:[30]

ATI ➡ Taxable income ± Certain adjustments – Dividends

paid deduction – Accumulated earnings credit

---

30.   § 535(a).

For a corporation that is not a mere holding or investment company, the "certain adjustments" include the following items as deductions:

1. Corporate income tax accrued.
2. Charitable contributions in excess of 10 percent of adjusted taxable income.
3. Capital loss adjustment.[31]
4. Excess of net long-term capital gain over net short-term capital loss, diminished by the capital gain tax and reduced by net capital losses from earlier years.

and the following items as additions:

5. Capital loss carryovers and carrybacks.
6. Net operating loss deduction.
7. Dividends received deduction.

The purpose of each of these adjustments is to produce an amount that more closely represents the dividend-paying capacity of the corporation. For example, the corporate income tax is deducted from taxable income since the corporation does not have this money to pay dividends. Conversely, the dividends received deduction is added to taxable income because the deduction has no impact upon the ability to pay a dividend. Note that item 4, in effect, allows a corporation to accumulate any capital gains without a penalty tax.

Payment of dividends reduces the amount of accumulated taxable income subject to the penalty tax. The dividends paid deduction includes any dividends paid during the tax year that the shareholders must report as ordinary income *and* any dividends paid within two and one-half months after the close of the tax year.[32] A nontaxable stock dividend under § 305(a) does not affect the dividends paid deduction. Further, a shareholder may file a consent statement to treat as a dividend the amount specified in such consent. A consent dividend is taxed to the shareholder even though it is not actually distributed. However, the consent dividend is treated as a contribution to the capital of the corporation (paid-in capital) by the shareholder.[33]

EXAMPLE 5   A nonservice closely held corporation that had no capital gains or losses in prior years has the following financial transactions for calendar year 1990:

Taxable income	$300,000
Tax liability	100,250
Excess charitable contributions	22,000
Short-term capital loss	(40,000)
Dividends received (less than 20% owned)	100,000
Research and development expenses	46,000
Dividends paid in 1990	40,000
Accumulated earnings (1/1/90)	220,000

---

31. This deduction (item 3) and item 4 are either/or deductions since a corporation would not have both in the same year. For the capital loss adjustment, see § 535(b)(5).
32. §§ 535(a), 561(a), and 563(a).
33. §§ 565(a) and (c)(2). The consent dividend procedure would be appropriate if the corporation is not in a position to make a cash or property distribution to its shareholders. The dividends paid deduction is discussed more fully later in the chapter.

Presuming the corporation is subject to the § 531 tax and has *no* reasonable business needs that would justify its accumulations, the accumulated taxable income is calculated as follows:

Taxable income		$ 300,000
Plus: 70% dividends received deduction		70,000
		$ 370,000
Less: Tax liability	$100,250	
Excess charitable contributions	22,000	
Net short-term capital loss adjustment	40,000	
Dividends paid	40,000	
Accumulated earnings minimum credit ($250,000 − $220,000)	30,000	(232,250)
Accumulated taxable income		$ 137,750

Thus, the accumulated earnings penalty tax for 1990 would be $38,570 ($137,750 × 28%). ☐

EXAMPLE 6
In Example 5, assume that the reasonable needs of the business of § 535(c) amount to $270,000 in 1990. The current year's accumulated earnings would be reduced by $50,000, rather than the $30,000, of accumulated earnings minimum credit. Thus, accumulated taxable income would be $117,750, and the penalty tax would be $32,970. Note that the first $220,000 of accumulated earnings *cannot* be omitted in determining whether taxable income for the current year is reasonably needed by the enterprise. ☐

PERSONAL HOLDING COMPANY PENALTY TAX

The personal holding company (PHC) tax was enacted to discourage the sheltering of certain types of passive income in corporations owned by high tax bracket individuals. These "incorporated pocketbooks" were frequently found in the entertainment and construction industries. For example, a taxpayer could shelter the income from securities in a corporation, which would pay no dividends, and allow the corporation's stock to increase in value. Thus, as with the accumulated earnings tax, the purpose of the PHC tax is to force the distribution of corporate earnings to the shareholders. However, in any one year, the IRS cannot impose both the PHC tax and the accumulated earnings tax.[34]

EXAMPLE 7
If the personal holding company tax did not exist, a significant tax savings could be achieved by "incorporating a pocketbook." Assume that a taxpayer in the 28% bracket owns investments that yield $50,000 a year. Tax on the investment income will be $14,000 ($50,000 × 28%). If the taxpayer transfers these investments to a corporation, the corporate tax will be only $7,500 ($50,000 × .15). Transferring the investments to an incorporated pocketbook would save $6,500 in taxes ($14,000 individual tax − $7,500 corporate tax). ☐

---

34. § 532(b)(1) and Reg. § 1.541−1(a).

Whether a corporation will be included within the statutory definition of a personal holding company for any particular year depends upon the facts and circumstances in evidence during that year.[35] Therefore, PHC status may be conferred even in the absence of any such active intent on the part of the corporation. In one situation,[36] a manufacturing operation adopted a plan of complete liquidation, sold its business, and invested the proceeds of the sale in U.S. Treasury bills and certificates of deposit. During the liquidating corporation's last tax year, 100 percent of the corporation's adjusted ordinary gross income was interest income. Since the corporation was owned by one shareholder, the corporation was a PHC, even though in the process of liquidation.

Certain types of corporations are expressly excluded from PHC status in § 542(c):

- Tax-exempt organizations under § 501(a).
- Banks and domestic building and loan associations.
- Life insurance companies.
- Surety companies.
- Foreign personal holding companies.
- Lending or finance companies.
- Foreign corporations.
- Small business investment companies.

Absent these exceptions, the business world could not perform necessary activities without a high rate of taxation. For example, a legitimate finance company should not be burdened by the personal holding company tax because it is performing a valuable business function of loaning money, whereas an incorporated pocketbook's major purpose is to shelter the investment income from possible higher individual tax rates.

Definition of a Personal Holding Company

Two tests are incorporated within the PHC provisions:

1. Was more than 50 percent of the *value* of the outstanding stock owned by five or fewer individuals at any time during the *last half* of the taxable year?

2. Is a substantial portion (60 percent or more) of the corporate income (adjusted ordinary gross income) composed of passive types of income such as dividends, interest, rents, royalties, or certain personal service income?

If the answer to both of these questions is affirmative, the corporation is classified as a PHC. Once classified as a PHC, the corporation is required to pay a penalty tax in addition to the regular corporate income tax. This penalty tax is 50 percent before 1987, 38.5 percent for taxable years beginning in 1987, and 28 percent for taxable years beginning after 1987.

Stock Ownership Test. To meet the stock ownership test, more than 50 percent *in value* of the outstanding stock must be owned, directly or indirectly, by

---

35. *Affiliated Enterprises, Inc. v. Comm.*, 44–1 USTC ¶9178, 32 AFTR 153, 140 F.2d 647 (CA–10, 1944).

36. *Weiss v. U.S.*, 75–2 USTC ¶9538, 36 AFTR2d 75–

5186 (D.Ct. Ohio, 1975). See also *O'Sullivan Rubber Co. v. Comm.*, 41–2 USTC ¶9521, 27 AFTR 529, 120 F.2d 845 (CA–2, 1941).

or for not more than five individuals sometime during the last half of the tax year. Thus, if the corporation has 9 or fewer shareholders, it automatically meets this test. If 10 unrelated individuals own *equal* portions of the value of the outstanding stock, the stock ownership requirement would not be met. However, if these 10 individuals do not hold equal value, the test would be met.

Note that this ownership test is based on fair market value and not on the number of shares outstanding. Fair market value is determined in light of all the circumstances and is based on the company's net worth, earning and dividend-paying capacity, appreciation of assets, and other relevant factors. If there are two or more classes of stock outstanding, the total value of all the stock should be allocated among the various classes according to the relative value of each class.

In determining the stock ownership of an individual, very broad constructive ownership rules are applicable. Under § 544, the following attribution rules determine indirect ownership:

1. Any stock owned by a corporation, partnership, trust, or estate is considered to be owned proportionately by the shareholders, partners, or beneficiaries.

2. The stock owned by the members of an individual's family (brothers, sisters, spouse, ancestors, and lineal descendants) or by the individual's partner is considered to be owned by such individual.

3. If an individual has an option to purchase stock, such stock is regarded as owned by that person.

4. Convertible securities are treated as outstanding stock.

Attribution rules 2, 3, and 4 are applicable only for the purpose of classifying a corporation as a PHC and cannot be used to avoid the application of the PHC provisions. Basically, these broad constructive ownership rules make it difficult for a closely held corporation to avoid application of the stock ownership test.

Gross Income Test.   The gross income test is met if 60 percent or more of the corporation's adjusted ordinary gross income (AOGI) is composed of certain passive income items (PHC income). AOGI is calculated by subtracting certain items from gross income (as defined by § 61).[37] The adjustments required to arrive at AOGI appear in Concept Summary 19–2.

In Concept Summary 19–2 the deduction of (a) and (b) from gross income results in the intermediate concept, ordinary gross income (OGI), the use of which is noted subsequently. The starting point, gross income, is not necessarily synonymous with gross receipts. In fact, for transactions in stocks, securities, and commodities, the term "gross income" includes only the excess of gains over any losses.[38]

PHC income includes income from dividends; interest; royalties; annuities;[39] rents; mineral, oil, and gas royalties; copyright royalties; produced film rents; and amounts from certain personal service contracts.

EXAMPLE 8	M Corporation has four shareholders, and its AOGI is $95,000, composed of gross income from a merchandising operation of $40,000, interest income of $15,000, dividend income of $25,000, and adjusted income from rents of

---

37. §§ 543(b)(1) and (2).

38. Reg. § 1.542–2. See also Reg. § 1.543–2(b) wherein net gain on transactions in stocks and securities is not reduced by a net loss on commodities futures transactions.

39. § 543(a)(1).

CONCEPT SUMMARY 19–2

Adjusted Ordinary Gross Income Determination

Gross income

Less:	a.	Capital gains.
	b.	Section 1231 gains.
Equals:		Ordinary gross income (OGI)
Less:	c.	Depreciation, property taxes, interest expense, and rental expenses directly related to gross income from rents (not to exceed such income from rents).
	d.	Depreciation, property and severance taxes, interest expense, and rental expenses directly related to gross income from mineral, oil, and gas royalties (not to exceed gross income from such royalties).
	e.	Interest on a condemnation award, a judgment, a tax refund, and an obligation of the United States held by a dealer.
Equals:		Adjusted ordinary gross income (AOGI)

$15,000. Total passive income is $55,000 ($15,000 + $25,000 + $15,000). Since 60% of AOGI ($57,000) is greater than the passive income ($55,000), this corporation is not a personal holding company. □

EXAMPLE 9   Assume in Example 8 that the corporation received $21,000 in interest income rather than $15,000. Total passive income is now $61,000 ($21,000 + $25,000 + $15,000). Since 60% of AOGI ($60,600) is less than the passive income of $61,000, this corporation is a personal holding company. □

Most passive types of income such as dividends, interest, royalties, and annuities cause few classification problems. Certain income items, however, may or may not be classified as PHC income. Special rules apply to rental income, mineral, oil, and gas royalties, and personal service contracts.

Rental Income.   Although rental income is normally classified as PHC income, it can be excluded from that category if two tests are met. The first test is met if a corporation's adjusted income from rents is 50 percent or more of the corporation's AOGI. The second test is satisfied if the total dividends paid for the tax year, dividends considered as paid on the last day of the tax year, and consent dividends are equal to or greater than the amount by which the nonrent PHC income exceeds 10 percent of OGI.[40] The taxpayer wishes to meet both tests so that the rent income can be excluded from PHC income for purposes of the gross income test referred to above. (See Figure 19–2 on page 19–22.)

With respect to this 50 percent test, "adjusted income from rents" is defined as gross income from rents reduced by the deductions allowable under § 543(b)(3). These deductions are depreciation, property taxes, interest, and rent. Generally, compensation is not included in the term "rents" and is not an allowable deduction. The final amount included in AOGI as adjusted income from rents cannot be less than zero.

---

40. § 543(a)(2).

EXAMPLE 10

Assume that Z Corporation has rental income of $10,000 and the following business deductions:

Depreciation on rental property	$1,044
Interest on mortgage	2,504
Real property taxes	1,504
Salaries and other business expenses (§ 162)	3,015

The adjusted income from rents included in AOGI is $5,000 ($10,000 − $1,000 − $2,500 − $1,500). Salaries and other § 162 expenses do not affect the calculation of AOGI. ☐

A company deriving its income primarily from rental activities can avoid PHC status by merely distributing as dividends the amount of nonrental PHC income that exceeds 10 percent of its OGI.

EXAMPLE 11

During the tax year, N Corporation receives $15,000 in rental income, $4,000 in dividends, and a $1,000 long-term capital gain. Corporate deductions for depreciation, interest, and real estate taxes allocable to the rental income amount to $10,000. The company paid a total of $2,500 in dividends to its eight shareholders. To determine whether or not rental income is PHC income, OGI, AOGI, and adjusted income from rents must be calculated.

Rental income	$ 15,000
Dividends	4,000
Long-term capital gain	1,000
Gross income	$ 20,000
Deduct: Gains from sale or disposition of capital assets	(1,000)
OGI	$ 19,000
Deduct: Depreciation, interest, and real estate taxes	(10,000)
AOGI	$ 9,000

First, adjusted income from rents must be 50% or more of AOGI.

Rental income	$ 15,000
Deduct: Depreciation, interest, and real estate taxes	(10,000)
Adjusted income from rents	$ 5,000
50% of AOGI	$ 4,500

N Corporation has satisfied the first test.

Second, total dividends paid for the year amount to $2,500. This figure must be equal to or greater than the amount by which nonrent PHC income exceeds 10% of OGI.

Nonrent PHC income	$ 4,000
Less: 10% of OGI	(1,900)
Excess	$ 2,100

N Corporation meets both tests; the adjusted income from rents is not classified as PHC income. □

Mineral, Oil, and Gas Royalties.   Similar to rental income, adjusted income from mineral, oil, and gas royalties can be excluded from PHC income classification if three tests are met.[41] First, adjusted income from such royalties must constitute 50 percent or more of AOGI. Second, nonroyalty PHC income may not exceed 10 percent of OGI. Note that this 10 percent test is not accompanied by the dividend escape clause previously described in relation to rental income. Therefore, corporations receiving income from mineral, oil, or gas royalties must be careful to minimize nonroyalty PHC income. Furthermore, adjusted income from rents and copyright royalties is considered to be nonroyalty PHC income whether or not treated as such by §§ 543(a)(2) and (4). Third, the company's business expenses under § 162 (other than compensation paid to shareholders) must be at least 15 percent of AOGI.

EXAMPLE 12   P Corporation has gross income of $4,000, which consists of gross income from oil royalties in the amount of $2,500, $400 of dividends, and $1,100 from the sale of merchandise. The total amount of the deductions for depletion, interest, and property and severance taxes allocable to the gross income from oil royalties equals $1,000. Deductions allowable under § 162 amount to $450. P Corporation's adjusted income from oil royalties will not be PHC income if the three tests are met. Therefore, OGI, AOGI, and adjusted income from oil royalties must be determined:

Oil royalties income	$ 2,500
Dividends	400
Sale of merchandise	1,100
Gross income (*and* OGI)	$ 4,000
Deduct: Depletion, interest, and property and severance taxes	(1,000)
AOGI	$ 3,000

Adjusted income from oil royalties must be 50% or more of AOGI.

Oil royalties income	$ 2,500
Deduct: Depletion, interest, and property and severance taxes	(1,000)
Adjusted income from oil royalties	$ 1,500
50% of AOGI	$ 1,500

---

41. § 543(a)(3).

Test one is met. Since nonroyalty PHC income is $400 (composed solely of the $400 of dividends) and this amount is not more than 10% of OGI, the second test is also satisfied. The third requirement is satisfied if deductible expenses under § 162 amount to at least 15% of AOGI.

§ 162 expenses	$450
15% of $3,000 (AOGI)	$450

P Corporation's adjusted income from oil royalties is not PHC income. □

As in the case of income from mineral, oil, and gas royalties and rents, copyright royalties and produced film rents are not categorized as PHC income if certain tests are met.[42]

Royalties received from licensing computer software are excluded from the definition of PHC income if the following conditions are satisfied:[43]

- The corporation must be actively engaged in the business of developing computer software.
- The royalties must constitute at least 50 percent of OGI.
- Business-related deductions must equal or exceed 25 percent of OGI.
- Passive income (other than computer software royalties) in excess of 10 percent of OGI must be distributed as a dividend.

Personal Service Contracts.   Any amount from personal service contracts is classified as PHC income only if (1) some person other than the corporation has the right to designate, by name or by description, the individual who is to perform the services and (2) the person so designated owns, directly or indirectly, 25 percent or more in value of the outstanding stock of the corporation at some time during the taxable year.[44]

EXAMPLE 13   B, C, and D (all attorneys) are equal shareholders in X Company, a professional association engaged in the practice of law. E, a new client, retains X Company to pursue a legal claim. Under the terms of the retainer agreement, E designates B as the attorney who will perform the legal services. The suit is successful, and 30% of the judgment E recovers is paid to X Company as a fee. Since the parties have met all of the requirements of § 543(a)(7), the fee received by X Company is PHC income.[45] □

The result reached in Example 13 could have been avoided if the retainer agreement had not specifically designated B as the party to perform the services.

Calculation of the PHC Tax

To this point, the discussion has focused on the determination of personal holding company status. If an entity is classified as a PHC, a new set of computations is

---

42. §§ 543(a)(4) and (5).
43. Section 543(d).
44. § 543(a)(7). For an application of the "right to designate," see *Thomas P. Byrnes, Inc.,* 73 T.C. 416 (1979).

45. The example presumes X Company will be treated as a corporation for Federal tax purposes. As noted in chapter 16, this is the usual result of professional association status.

relevant in determining the amount upon which the penalty tax is imposed. This tax base is called undistributed PHC income (UPHC income). Basically, this amount is taxable income, subject to certain adjustments, minus the dividends paid deduction.

The starting point is corporate taxable income, but the adjustments arrive at UPHC income, which more clearly represents the corporation's dividend-paying capacity. Concept Summary 19–3 shows how this amount is determined.

Dividends Paid Deduction.   Since the purpose of the PHC penalty tax is to force a corporation to pay dividends, five types of dividends paid deductions reduce the amount subject to the penalty tax. First, dividends actually paid during the tax year ordinarily reduce UPHC income.[46] However, such distributions must be pro rata. They must exhibit no preference to any shares of stock over shares of the same class or to any class of stock over other classes outstanding. This prohibition is especially harsh when portions of an employee-shareholder's salary are declared unreasonable and classified as a disguised or constructive dividend. In the case of a dividend of appreciated property, the dividends paid deduction should be the fair market value of the property (not the adjusted basis to the distributing corporation). The Regulations, however, hold to the contrary.[47]

EXAMPLE 14   Three individuals are equal shareholders in a personal holding company. A property dividend with an adjusted basis of $20,000 (FMV of $30,000) is paid to the three shareholders in the following proportion: 25%, 35%, and 40%. This is not a pro rata distribution, and the dividends are not deductible from UPHC income. □

CONCEPT SUMMARY 19–3

Undistributed PHC Income Determination

Taxable income

Plus: a. Dividends received deduction.
          b. Net operating loss (NOL), other than the NOL from the preceding year (computed without the dividends received deduction).
          c. Certain business expenses and depreciation attributable to nonbusiness property owned by the corporation that exceed the income derived from such property (unless the taxpayer proves that the rent was the highest obtainable and the rental business was a bona fide business activity).*

Less: d. Federal income tax accrual (other than the PHC tax and the accumulated earnings tax).
          e. Excess charitable contributions beyond the 10 percent corporate limitation (with a maximum of the 20 percent, 30 percent, or 50 percent limitation imposed on individuals). **
          f. Excess of long-term capital gain over short-term capital loss (net of tax).

Equals: Adjusted taxable income

Less: Dividends paid deduction

Equals: Undistributed PHC income

*§ 545(b).

**Reg. § 1.545–2.

---

46. §§ 561(a)(1) and 562.
47. Reg. § 1.562–1(a). This Regulation was promul-

gated when most property dividends were non-taxable to the distributing corporation.

A two and one-half month grace period exists following the close of the tax year. Dividends paid during this period may be treated as paid during the tax year just closed. However, the amount allowed as a deduction from UPHC income cannot exceed either (1) the UPHC income for the tax year or (2) 20 percent of the total dividends distributed during the tax year.[48]

The consent dividend procedure involves a hypothetical distribution of the corporate income taxed to the shareholders. Since the consent dividend is taxable, a dividends paid deduction is allowed. The shareholder's basis in his or her stock is increased by the consent dividend (a contribution to capital), and a subsequent actual distribution of the consent dividend might be taxed. The consent election is filed by the shareholders at any time not later than the due date of the corporate tax return. The consent dividend is considered distributed by the corporation on the last day of the tax year and is included in the gross income of the shareholder in the tax year in which or with which the tax year of the corporation ends. The disadvantage of this special election is that the shareholders must pay taxes on dividends they do not actually receive. However, if cash is not available for dividend distributions, the consent dividend route is a logical alternative.

EXAMPLE 15

Q Corporation, a calendar year taxpayer solely owned by T, is a PHC. Dividends of $30,000 must be paid to avoid the PHC tax, but the company has a poor cash position. T elects the consent dividend treatment under § 565 and is taxed on $30,000 of dividends. The shareholder's basis in Q Corporation stock is increased by $30,000 as a result of this special election. Thus, the corporation does not incur the PHC tax, but T is taxed even though he receives no cash from the corporation with which to pay such tax. □

Even after a corporation has been classified as a PHC, a belated dividend distribution made in a subsequent tax year can avoid the PHC penalty tax. This deficiency dividend provision allows the payment of a dividend within 90 days after the determination of the PHC tax deficiency for a prior tax year.[49] A determination occurs when a decision of a court is final, a closing agreement under § 7121 is signed, or a written agreement is signed between the taxpayer and a District Director. Note that the dividend distribution cannot be made before the determination or after the running of the 90-day time period. Furthermore, the deficiency dividend procedure does not relieve the taxpayer of interest, additional amounts, or assessable penalties computed with respect to the PHC tax.

A dividend carryover from two prior years may be available to reduce the UPHC income. When the dividends paid by a company in its prior years exceed the company's UPHC income for such years, the excess amount may be deducted in the current year. See § 564(b) for the manner of computing this dividend carryover.

Personal Holding Company Planning Model. Some of the complex PHC provisions may be developed into a flow chart format. Figure 19—1 and Figure 19—2 provide a PHC planning model and the rules for the rent exclusion test, respectively.

Computations Illustrated. After the appropriate adjustments have been made to corporate taxable income and the sum of the dividends paid has been subtracted, the resulting figure is UPHC income, which is multiplied by the appropriate penalty tax rate to obtain the PHC tax. Although the tax revenue from

---

48. §§ 563(b) and 543(a)(2)(B)(ii).   49. § 547.

FIGURE 19–1   Personal Holding Company Planning Model

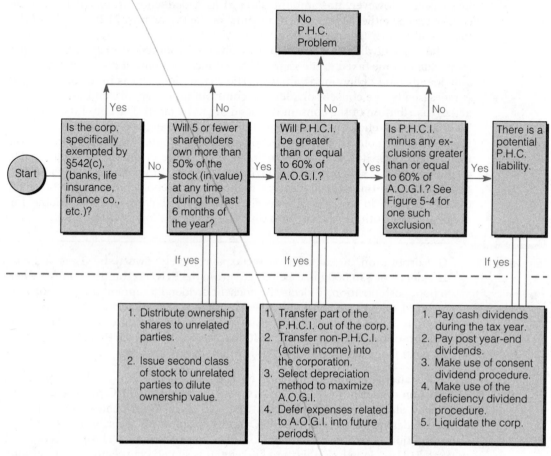

From "Understanding and Avoiding the Personal Holding Company Tax: A Tax Planning Model," by Pratt and Whittenburg, which appeared in the June 1975 issue of *Taxes — the Tax Magazine* published and copyrighted 1975 by Commerce Clearing House, Inc., and appears here with their permission.

the PHC tax may be small, the mere threat of this confiscatory tax prompts owners to monitor their corporations and take the necessary steps to avoid the tax.

EXAMPLE 16   X Corporation had the following items of income and expense in 1990:

Dividend income (from **IBM** stock investment)	$ 40,000
Rent income	150,000
Depreciation expense	40,000
Mortgage interest	30,000
Real estate taxes	30,000
Salaries	20,000
Dividends paid (three shareholders)	20,000
Corporate income tax liability (§ 11)	6,300

FIGURE 19–2   Rent Exclusion Test

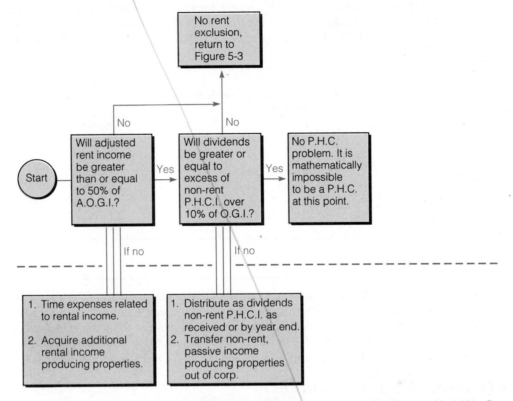

From "Understanding and Avoiding the Personal Holding Company Tax: A Tax Planning Model," by Pratt and Whittenburg, which appeared in the June 1975 issue of *Taxes — the Tax Magazine* published and copyrighted 1975 by Commerce Clearing House, Inc., and appears here with their permission.

OGI would be $190,000 ($40,000 + $150,000), and AOGI would be $90,000 ($190,000 − $40,000 − $30,000 − $30,000). Taxable income is $42,000, computed as follows:

Rent income		$ 150,000
Dividend income		40,000
		$ 190,000
Less: Depreciation expense	$40,000	
Mortgage interest	30,000	
Real estate taxes	30,000	
Salaries	20,000	(120,000)
		$ 70,000
Less: Dividends received deduction		
($40,000 × 70%)		(28,000)
Taxable income		$ 42,000

The adjusted income from rents is $50,000 ($150,000 − $100,000). The corporation does meet the 50% rental income test since $50,000 is greater than

50% of AOGI ($90,000 × 50% = $45,000). But the corporation did not pay at least $21,000 of dividends ($40,000 nonrental PHC income − $19,000 = $21,000). Therefore, the 10% rental income test is not met, and the rental income is classified as PHC income. Since all income is passive, this corporation is a PHC. The PHC tax of $12,236 would be calculated as follows:

Taxable income	$ 42,000
Plus: Dividends received deduction ($40,000 × 70%)	28,000
	$ 70,000
Less: § 11 tax	(6,300)
	$ 63,700
Less: Dividends paid	(20,000)
UPHC income	$ 43,700
	× .28
PHC tax liability	$ 12,236

□

EXAMPLE 17   Assume that in Example 16, $22,000 of dividends are paid to the shareholders (instead of $20,000). In this case, the rental income is not PHC income because the 10% test is met ($22,000 is equal to or greater than the nonrental PHC income in excess of 10% of OGI). Thus, an increase of at least $2,000 in the dividends paid in Example 16 avoids the $12,236 PHC tax liability.   □

COMPARISON OF §§ 531 AND 541

A review of several important distinctions between the penalty tax on the unreasonable accumulation of earnings (§ 531) and the tax on personal holding companies (§ 541) will set the stage for the presentation of tax planning considerations applicable to both taxes.

- Unlike § 531, there is no element of intent necessary for the imposition of the § 541 (PHC) tax. This makes § 541 a real trap for the unwary.

- The imposition of the § 541 tax is not affected by the past history of the corporation. Thus, it could be just as applicable to a newly formed corporation as to one that has been in existence for many years. This is not the case with the § 531 tax. Past accumulations have a direct bearing on the determination of the accumulated earnings credit. In this sense, younger corporations are less vulnerable to the § 531 tax since complete insulation generally is guaranteed until accumulations exceed $250,000.

- Although one could conclude that both taxes pose threats for closely held corporations, the stock ownership test of § 542(a)(2) makes this threat very explicit with regard to the § 541 tax. However, publicly held corporations can be subject to the § 531 tax if corporate policy is dominated by certain shareholders who are using the corporate form to avoid income taxes on dividends through the accumulation of corporate profits.[50]

---

50. § 532(c).

- Sufficient dividend distributions can negate both taxes. In the case of § 531, however, such dividends must be distributed on a timely basis. Both taxes allow a two and one-half month grace period and provide for the consent dividend procedure.[51] Only the § 541 tax allows the deficiency dividend procedure.

- Differences in reporting procedures arise because the § 541 tax is a self-assessed tax and the § 531 tax is not. For example, if a corporation is a personal holding company, it must file a Schedule PH along with its Form 1120 (the corporate income tax return) for the year involved. Failure to file the Schedule PH can result in the imposition of interest and penalties and also brings into play a special six-year statute of limitations for the assessment of the § 541 tax.[52] On the other hand, the § 531 tax is assessed by the IRS and consequently requires no reporting procedures on the part of the corporate taxpayer.

TAX PLANNING CONSIDERATIONS

The elimination of favorable capital gain rates has made most corporate distributions less attractive, and many companies will prefer permanent deferral of accumulated earnings rather than temporary deferral. Even with higher corporate rates than individual rates, a corporation can invest accumulated funds in tax-free vehicles or purchase high-yield corporate stocks to take advantage of the dividends received deduction. Thus, the threat of the accumulated earnings tax and the personal holding company tax continues to be a prime concern of many corporations.

The § 531 Tax

Justifying the Accumulations. The key defense against imposition of the § 531 tax is a successful assertion that the accumulations are necessary to meet the reasonable needs of the business. Several points should be kept in mind:

- To the extent possible, the justification for the accumulation should be documented. If, for example, the corporation plans to acquire additional physical facilities for use in its trade or business, the minutes of the board of directors' meetings should reflect the decision. Furthermore, such documentation should take place during the period of accumulation. This planning may require some foresight on the part of the taxpayer, but meaningful planning to avoid a tax problem should not be based on what happens after the issue has been raised by an agent as the result of an audit. In the case of a profitable closely held corporation that accumulates some or all of its profits, the parties might well operate under the assumption that § 531 is always a potential issue. Recognition of a tax problem at an early stage is the first step in a satisfactory resolution.

  - Keep in mind that multiple reasons for making an accumulation are not only permissible but invariably advisable. Suppose, for example, a manufacturing

---

51. Under the § 531 tax, dividends paid within the first two and one-half months of the succeeding year *must* be carried back to the preceding year. In the case of the § 541 tax, the carryback is optional—some or all of the dividends can be

deducted in the year paid. The 20% limit on carrybacks applicable to § 541 [see § 563(a)] does not cover § 531 situations.

52. § 6501(f). See also chapter 24.

corporation plans to expand its plant. It would not be wise to stop with the cost of such expansion as the only justification for all accumulations. What about further justification based on the corporation's working capital requirements as determined under the *Bardahl* formula or some variation thereof? Other reasons for making the accumulation may well be present and should be recognized.

- The reasons for the accumulation should be sincere and, once established, pursued to the extent feasible.

EXAMPLE 18   In 1985, the board of directors of W Corporation decide to accumulate $1,000,000 to fund the replacement of W's plant. Five years pass, and no steps are taken to initiate construction. ☐

EXAMPLE 19   In 1985, the board of directors of Y Corporation decide to accumulate $1,000,000 to fund the replacement of Y's plant. In the ensuing five-year period, the following steps are taken: a site selection committee is appointed (1985); a site is chosen (1986); the site (land) is purchased (1987); an architect is retained, and plans are drawn up for the new plant (1988); bids are requested and submitted for the construction of the new plant (1990). ☐

Compare Examples 18 and 19. Y Corporation is in a much better position to justify the accumulation. Even though the plant has not yet been replaced some five years after the accumulations began, the progress toward its ultimate construction speaks for itself. On the other hand, W Corporation may be hard pressed to prove the sincerity of its objective for the accumulations in light of its failure to follow through on the projected replacement.

- The amount of the accumulation should be realistic under the circumstances.

EXAMPLE 20   W Corporation plans to replace certain machinery at an estimated cost of $500,000. The original machinery was purchased for $300,000 and, because of $250,000 in depreciation deducted for tax purposes, possesses a present book value of $50,000. How much of an accumulation can be justified for the replacement to avoid the § 531 tax? At first blush, one might consider $500,000 as the appropriate amount since this represents the estimated replacement cost of the machinery. But what about the $250,000 in depreciation that W Corporation has already deducted? If it is counted again as part of a reasonable accumulation, a double tax benefit results. Only $250,000 ($50,000 unrecovered cost of the old machinery + $200,000 additional outlay necessary) can be justified as the appropriate amount for an accumulation.[53] ☐

EXAMPLE 21   During the current year, a competitor files a $2,000,000 patent infringement suit against Z Corporation. Competent legal counsel advises Z Corporation

---

53. *Battelstein Investment Co. v. U.S.*, 71–1 USTC ¶9227, 27 AFTR2d 71–713, 442 F.2d 87 (CA–5, 1971).

that the suit is groundless. Under such conditions, the corporation can hardly justify accumulating $2,000,000 because of the pending lawsuit. □

- Since the § 531 tax is imposed on an annual basis, justification for accumulations may vary from year to year.[54]

EXAMPLE 22

For calendar years 1988 and 1989, R Corporation was able to justify large accumulations owing to a pending additional income tax assessment. In early 1990, the assessment is settled and paid. After the settlement, R Corporation can no longer consider the assessment as a reasonable anticipated need of the business. □

Danger of Loans to Shareholders. The presence of loans made by a corporation to its shareholders often raises the § 531 issue. If this same corporation has a poor dividend-paying record, it becomes particularly vulnerable. When one recalls that the avowed goal of the § 531 tax is to force certain corporations to distribute dividends, the focus becomes clear. If a corporation can spare funds for loans to shareholders, it certainly has the capacity to pay dividends. Unfortunately, the presence of such loans can cause other tax problems for the parties.

EXAMPLE 23

During the year in question, Q Corporation made advances of $120,000 to its sole shareholder, T. Although prosperous and maintaining substantial accumulations, Q Corporation has never paid a dividend. Under these circumstances, the IRS could move in either of two directions. It could assess the § 531 tax against Q Corporation for its unreasonable accumulation of earnings. Alternatively, the IRS could argue that the advances were not bona fide loans but, instead, taxable dividends. Such a dual approach places the taxpayers in a somewhat difficult position. If, for example, they contend that the advance was a bona fide loan, T avoids dividend income but Q Corporation becomes vulnerable to the imposition of the § 531 tax.[55] On the other hand, a concession that the advance was not a loan hurts T but helps Q Corporation avoid the penalty tax. □

Role of Dividends. The relationship between dividend distribution and the § 531 tax needs further clarification. It would be helpful to pose and answer several questions. First, can the payment of enough dividends completely avoid the § 531 tax? The answer must be affirmative because of the operation of § 535. Recall that this provision defines accumulated taxable income as *taxable income* (adjusted by certain items) *minus the sum of the dividends paid deduction and the accumulated earnings credit*. Since the § 531 tax is imposed on accumulated taxable income, no tax would be due if the dividends paid and the accumulated earnings credit are large enough to offset taxable income. Sufficient *taxable* dividends, therefore, will avoid the tax.[56] Second, can the payment of *some* dividends completely avoid the

---

54. Compare *Hardin's Bakeries, Inc. v. Martin, Jr.*, 67–1 USTC ¶9253, 19 AFTR2d 647, 293 F.Supp. 1129 (D.Ct.Miss., 1967), with *Hardin v. U.S.*, 70–2 USTC ¶9676, 26 AFTR2d 70–5852 (D.Ct.Miss., 1970), *aff'd., rev'd., rem'd.* by 72–1 USTC ¶9464, 29 AFTR2d 72–1446, 461 F.2d 865 (CA–5, 1972).

55. *Ray v. U.S.*, 69–1 USTC ¶9334, 23 AFTR2d 69–1141, 409 F.2d 1322 (CA–6, 1969).

56. As noted earlier, nontaxable stock dividends issued under § 305(a) do not affect the dividends paid deduction.

§ 531 tax? As the question is worded, the answer must be *no*. Theoretically, even significant dividend distributions will not insulate a corporation from the tax. From a practical standpoint, however, the payment of dividends indicates that the corporation is not being used exclusively to shield its shareholders from tax consequences. To the extent that this reflects the good faith of the parties and the lack of tax avoidance motivation, it is a factor the IRS will consider with regard to the § 531 issue.

Avoiding the § 541 Tax

The classification of a corporation as a personal holding company requires the satisfaction of *both* the stock ownership and the gross income tests. Failure to meet either of these two tests will avoid PHC status and the § 541 tax.

- The stock ownership test can be handled through a dispersion of stock ownership. Success might not be achieved, however, unless the tax planner watches the application of the stock attribution rules.

- Remember the following relationship when working with the gross income test:

$$\frac{\text{PHC income}}{\text{AOGI}} = 60\% \text{ or more}$$

  Decreasing the numerator (PHC income) or increasing the denominator (AOGI) of the fraction will reduce the resulting percentage. Keeping the resulting percentage below 60 percent precludes classification as a personal holding company. To control PHC income, investments in low-yield growth securities are preferable to those that generate heavy interest or dividend income. Capital gains from the sale of such securities will not affect PHC status since they are not included in either the numerator or the denominator of the fraction. Investments in tax-exempt securities are also attractive because the interest income therefrom, like capital gains, carries no effect in applying the gross income test.

- Income from personal service contracts may, under certain conditions, constitute PHC income. Where a 25 percent or more owner of a PHC is specifically designated in a retainer agreement as the party to perform the services, the personal service contract income will be PHC income. See Example 13 earlier in the chapter.

- Rent income may or may not be PHC income. The relative amount of rent income is the key consideration. If

$$\frac{\text{Adjusted income from rents}}{\text{AOGI}} = 50\% \text{ or more}$$

  and nonrent PHC income less 10 percent of OGI is distributed as a dividend, rent income will not be PHC income. Maximizing adjusted income from rents clearly will improve the situation for taxpayers. Since adjusted income from rents represents gross rents less expenses attributable thereto, a conservative approach in determining such expenses would be helpful. The taxpayer should be encouraged to minimize depreciation (e.g., choose straight-line over accelerated cost recovery method). This approach to the handling of expenses attributable to rental property has to be confusing to many taxpayers because it contradicts what is normally done to reduce income tax consequences.

PHC status need not carry tragic tax consequences if the parties are aware of the issue and take appropriate steps. Since the tax is imposed on UPHC income, properly timed dividend distributions will neutralize the tax and avoid interest and penalties. Also, as long as a corporation holds PHC status, the § 531 tax cannot be imposed.

EXAMPLE 24

X Corporation is owned entirely by two sisters, R and S (ages 86 and 88, respectively). X Corporation's major assets comprise investments in low-yield and high-growth securities, unimproved real estate, and tax-exempt bonds, all of which have a realizable value of $500,000. The basis of the stock in X Corporation to each sister is $50,000. □

The liquidation of X Corporation (a frequent solution to undesired PHC status) would be disastrous to the two sisters. As noted in the discussion of § 331 in chapter 18, such liquidation would result in the recognition of a capital gain of $400,000. In this case, therefore, it would be preferable to live with PHC status. Considering the nature of the assets held by X Corporation, this may not be difficult to do. Keep in mind that the interest from the tax-exempt bonds is not PHC income. Should X Corporation wish to sell any of its investments, the long-term capital gain that would result is not PHC income. The PHC tax on any other income (the dividends from the securities) can be controlled through enough dividend distributions to reduce UPHC income to zero. Furthermore, as long as X Corporation remains a PHC, it is insulated from the § 531 tax (the imposition of which would be highly probable in this case).

The liquidation of X Corporation should await the deaths of R and S and consequently should be carried out by their estates or heirs. By virtue of the application of § 1014 (refer to chapter 12), the income tax basis in the stock would be stepped up to the fair market value of the stock on the date of death. Much, if not all, of the capital gain potential currently existing at the shareholder level would thus be eliminated.

PROBLEM MATERIALS

Discussion Questions

1. List some valid business reasons for accumulating funds in a closely held corporation.

2. Explain the purpose(s) underlying the creation of the accumulated earnings penalty tax and the personal holding company tax.

3. A merger of two corporations could result in the imposition of the accumulated earnings tax on the surviving corporation. Is this possible? Explain.

4. Explain the *Bardahl* formula. How could it be improved?

5. Can the IRS impose both the PHC tax and the accumulated earnings tax upon a construction company?

6. ATI = Taxable income ± Certain adjustments + The dividends paid deduction − The accumulated earnings credit. Please comment.

7. In making the "certain adjustments" (refer to Question 6) necessary in arriving at ATI, which of the following items should be added (+), should be subtracted (−), or will have no effect (NE) on taxable income?

    a. A nontaxable stock dividend distributed by the corporation to its shareholders.

    b. Corporate income tax incurred and paid.

    c. Charitable contributions paid in the amount of 10% of taxable income.

    d. Deduction of a net operating loss carried over from a prior year.

    e. The dividends received deduction.

8. Ms. J (a widow) and Mr. K (a bachelor) are both shareholders in H Corporation (closely held). If they elope during the year, what possible effect, if any, could it have on H Corporation's vulnerability to the PHC tax?

9. M Corporation is a consulting firm. Its entire outstanding stock is owned by three individuals. M Corporation entered into a contract with T Corporation to perform certain consulting services in consideration of which T was to pay M $65,000. The individual who was to perform the services was not designated by name or description in the contract, and no one but M had the right to designate such person. Does the $65,000 constitute PHC income?

10. Which of the following income items could be PHC income?

    a. Dividends.

    b. Interest.

    c. Rental income.

    d. Sales of merchandise.

    e. Annuities.

    f. Mineral royalties.

    g. Copyright royalties.

    h. Produced film rents.

    i. Gain from sale of securities.

11. D, a shareholder in H Corporation, dies, and under his will, the stock passes to his children. If H Corporation is a personal holding company, what effect, if any, will D's death have on the continuation of this status?

12. How is AOGI calculated?

13. The election to capitalize (rather than to depreciate) certain expenses to rental property could make a difference in determining whether or not the corporate lessor is a personal holding company. How could this be so?

14. If the 50% test as to rents is satisfied, the PHC tax cannot be imposed upon the corporation. Do you agree? Why or why not?

15. General Motors Corporation has no difficulty avoiding either the accumulated earnings tax or the PHC tax. Explain.

16. The payment of enough dividends can avoid either the accumulated earnings tax or the PHC tax. Explain.

17. Explain the deficiency dividend procedure.

18. Relate the following points to the avoidance of the accumulated earnings tax:

    a. Documentation of justification for the accumulation.

    b. Multiple justifications for the accumulation.

    c. Follow-up on the established justification for the accumulation.

    d. Loans by the corporation to its shareholders.

    e. The corporation's record of substantial dividend payments.

19. Relate the following points to the avoidance of the PHC tax:

    a. Sale of stock to outsiders.

    b. An increase in AOGI.

    c. A decrease in PHC income.

    d. Long-term capital gains recognized by the corporation.

    e. Corporate investment in tax-exempt bonds.

    f. Income from personal service contracts.

g. The choice of straight-line depreciation for rental property owned by the corporation.

20. Compare the accumulated earnings tax to the PHC tax on the basis of the following items:

   a. The element of intent.

   b. Applicability of the tax to a newly created corporation.

   c. Applicability of the tax to a publicly held corporation.

   d. The two and one-half month rule with respect to the dividends paid deduction.

   e. The availability of the deficiency dividend procedure.

   f. Procedures for reporting and paying the tax.

Problems

21. A calendar year consulting corporation has accumulated earnings and profits of $80,000 on January 1, 1990. For the calendar year 1990, the corporation has taxable income of $100,000. This corporation has no reasonable needs that justify an accumulation of its earnings and profits. Calculate the amount vulnerable to the accumulated earnings penalty tax. ꓔꓵ50

22. In 1990, P Corporation, a manufacturing company, retained $60,000 for its reasonable business needs. The company had a long-term capital gain of $20,000 and a net short-term capital loss of $15,000, with a resulting capital gain tax of $1,250. The accumulated earnings and profits amount at the end of 1989 was $260,000. On January 25, 1990, a taxable dividend of $90,000 was paid. Calculate the accumulated earnings credit for 1990.

23. A retail corporation had accumulated earnings and profits on January 1, 1990, of $250,000. Its taxable income for the year 1990 was $75,000. The corporation paid no dividends during the year. There were no other adjustments to determine accumulated taxable income. Assume a court determined that the corporation is subject to the accumulated earnings tax and that the reasonable needs of the business required earnings and profits in the total amount of $266,500. Determine the accumulated earnings tax and explain your calculations.

24. A construction corporation is accumulating a significant amount of earnings and profits. Although the corporation is closely held, it is not a personal holding company. The following facts relate to the tax year 1990:

Taxable income	$450,000
Federal income tax	153,000
Dividend income from a qualified domestic corporation (less than 20% owned)	30,000
Dividends paid in 1990	70,000
Consent dividends	35,000
Dividends paid on 2/1/91	5,000
Accumulated earnings credit	10,000
Excess charitable contributions (the portion in excess of the amount allowed as a deduction in computing the corporate income tax)	9,000
Net capital loss adjustment	3,000

Compute the accumulated earnings tax, if any.

25. The following facts relate to a closely held legal services corporation's 1990 tax year:

Net taxable income	$400,000
Federal income taxes	136,000
Excess charitable contributions	20,000
Capital loss adjustment	20,000
Dividends received (less than 20% owned)	140,000
Dividends paid	60,000
Accumulated earnings, 1/1/90	130,000

Assume that this is not a personal holding company. Calculate any accumulated earnings tax.

26. Which of the following purposes can be used by a corporation to justify accumulations to meet the reasonable needs of the business?

a. X Corporation creates a reserve for a depression that might occur in 1992.

b. P Corporation has an extraordinarily high working capital need.

c. Q Corporation, a manufacturing company, invests in several oil and gas drilling funds.

d. N, a hotel, is being sued because of a structural accident that injured 32 people.

e. M Corporation is considering establishing a sinking fund to retire some bonds.

f. Z Corporation carries six keyman life insurance policies.

g. T Corporation makes loans to R Corporation, an unrelated party who is having financial problems and who is a key customer.

h. B Corporation agrees to retire 20% of its outstanding stock without curtailment of its business.

27. A wholly owned motor freight corporation has permitted its earnings to accumulate. The company has no inventory but wishes to use the *Bardahl* formula to determine the amount of operating capital required for a business cycle. The following facts are relevant:

Yearly revenues	$3,300,000
Average accounts receivable	300,000
Yearly expenses	3,500,000
Average accounts payable	213,000

a. Determine the turnover rate of average accounts receivable.

b. Determine the number of days in the accounts receivable cycle.

c. Determine the expenses for one accounts receivable cycle.

d. Determine the number of days in the accounts payable cycle.

e. Determine the operating capital needed for one business cycle.

f. Explain why the time allowed a taxpayer for the payment of accounts payable should be taken into consideration in applying the *Bardahl* formula.

28. N Corporation is having accumulated earnings problems but has no accounts receivable. C, the corporate controller, provides you with the following information:

Year-end balances:	
Current assets	
Cash	$25,000
Inventory (average)	72,000
	$97,000
Current liabilities	17,000
Working capital available	$80,000

Income statement:

Gross sales		$330,000
Less: Sales returns and allowances		30,000
		$300,000
Less: Cost of goods sold	$170,000	
Sales and administrative expenses	45,000	
Depreciation	20,000	
Income taxes	9,000	244,000
Net income		$ 56,000

Calculate the working capital *required* for the corporation if purchases total $120,000.

29. Determine whether the following factors or events will increase (+), decrease (–), or have no effect (NE) on the working capital needs of a corporation when calculating the *Bardahl* formula:

a. Decrease in depreciation deduction.

b. Use of peak inventory figure rather than average inventory.

c. Increase in the annual cost of goods sold.

d. Purchase of a tract of land for a future parking lot.

e. Use of average receivables rather than peak receivables.

f. Increase in annual net sales.

g. Increase in accounts payable.

h. Increase in the annual expenses.

i. Gain on the sale of treasury stock.

30. A corporation has gross income of $20,000, which consists of $11,000 of rental income and $9,000 of dividend income. The corporation has $3,000 of rental income adjustments and pays $8,000 of dividends to its nine shareholders.

a. Calculate adjusted income from rents.

b. Calculate AOGI.

c. Is the so-called 50% test met? Show calculations.

d. Is the 10% rental income test met? Show calculations.

e. Is the corporation a personal holding company?

31. Assume one change in the situation in Problem 30. Rental income adjustments are decreased from $3,000 to $2,000. Answer the same questions as in Problem 30.

32. X Corporation has $10,000 of dividend income, $40,000 of gross income from rents, and $30,000 of personal service income (not PHC income). Expenses in the amount of $30,000 relate directly to the rental income. Assume there are eight shareholders and the 10% test is met. Is this corporation a PHC? Explain.

33. C Corporation has gross income of $200,000, which consists of gross income from rent of $150,000, dividends of $15,000, a capital gain from the sale of securities of $10,000, and $25,000 from the sale of merchandise. Deductions directly related to the rent income total $100,000.

a. Calculate OGI.

b. Calculate AOGI.

c. Calculate adjusted income from rents.

d. Does the rental income constitute PHC income? Explain.

e. Is this corporation a PHC (assuming there are five shareholders)?

34. Assume the same facts as in Problem 33, except that dividend income is $25,000 (rather than $15,000) and the corporation pays $5,000 of dividends to its shareholders. Answer the same questions as in Problem 33.

35. X Corporation has the following financial data for the tax year 1990:

Rental income	$430,000
Dividend income	2,900
Interest income	50,000
Operating income	9,000
Depreciation (rental warehouses)	100,000
Mortgage interest	125,000
Real estate taxes	35,000
Officers' salaries	85,000
Dividends paid	2,000

   a. Calculate OGI.

   b. Calculate AOGI.

   c. Does X Corporation's adjusted income from rents meet the 50% or more of AOGI test?

   d. Does X Corporation meet the 10% dividend test?

   e. How much in dividends could X Corporation pay within the two and one-half month grace period during 1991?

   f. If the 1990 corporate income tax return has not been filed, what would you suggest for X Corporation?

36. Using the legend provided, classify each of the following statements accordingly:

Legend

A = Relates only to the tax on unreasonable accumulation of earnings (the § 531 tax)

P = Relates only to the personal holding company tax (the § 541 tax)

B = Relates to both the § 531 tax and the § 541 tax

N = Relates to neither the § 531 tax nor the § 541 tax

   a. The tax is applied to taxable income of the corporation after adjustments are made.

   b. The tax is a self-assessed tax.

   c. An accumulation of funds for reasonable business purposes will help avoid the tax.

   d. A consent dividend mechanism can be used to avoid the tax.

   e. If the stock of the corporation is equally held by 10 unrelated individuals, the tax cannot be imposed.

   f. Any charitable deduction in excess of the 10% limitation is allowed as a deduction before the tax is imposed.

   g. Gains from the sale or disposition of capital assets are not subject to the tax.

   h. A sufficient amount of rental income will cause the tax not to be imposed.

   i. A life insurance company would not be subject to the tax.

   j. A corporation with only dividend income would avoid the tax.

37. Indicate in each of the following independent situations whether the corporation involved is a PHC (assume the stock ownership test is met):

	A Corporation	B Corporation	C Corporation	D Corporation
Sales of merchandise	$ 8,000	$ –0–	$ –0–	$ 2,500
Capital gains	–0–	–0–	–0–	1,000
Dividend income	15,000	5,000	1,000	2,500
Gross rental income	10,000	5,000	9,000	15,000
Expenses related to rents	8,000	2,500	8,000	10,000
Dividends paid	–0–	–0–	–0–	500
Personal holding company? (Circle Y for yes or N for no.)	Y N	Y N	Y N	Y N

38. Indicate in each of the following independent situations whether the corporation involved is a PHC (assume the stock ownership test is met):

	E Corporation	F Corporation	G Corporation	H Corporation
Sales of merchandise	$ –0–	$3,000	$ –0–	$ –0–
Capital gains	–0–	–0–	1,000	–0–
Interest income	20,000	4,800	2,000	60,000
Gross rental income	80,000	1,200	20,000	50,000
Expenses related to rents	60,000	1,000	10,000	–0–
Dividends paid	12,000	–0–	–0–	20,000
Personal holding company? (Circle Y for yes or N for no.)	Y N	Y N	Y N	Y N

39. Calculate in each of the following independent situations the PHC tax liability in 1990:

	M Corporation	N Corporation
Taxable income	$140,000	$580,000
Dividends received deduction	37,000	70,000
Contributions in excess of 10%	4,000	10,000
Federal income taxes	37,850	197,200
Net capital gain	70,000	40,000
Capital gain tax	25,350	13,600
NOL under § 172		12,000
Current year dividends	12,000	120,000
Consent dividends		25,000
Two and one-half month dividends	4,000	

20

S CORPORATIONS

GENERAL CONSIDERATIONS

Subchapter S of the Internal Revenue Code of 1986 allows for the unique treatment of certain corporations for Federal income tax purposes.[1] This election essentially results in a tax treatment of the S corporation that resembles that of a partnership, but the entity is still a corporation under state law and for many other tax purposes. Special provisions pertain to the entity, however, under the operational provisions of §§ 1361 through 1379. Since individual tax rates are now generally lower than corporate rates, both Subchapter S and Subchapter K (partnerships) of the Code have taken on an added importance. Most businesses should reevaluate the desirability of using a C corporation as the means of conducting a trade or business.

An S corporation is largely a tax-reporting, rather than a tax-paying, entity. In this respect, the entity is treated much like a partnership. Similar to the partnership conduit concept, the taxable income of an S corporation flows through to the shareholders, regardless of whether such income is distributed in the form of actual dividends. There is, in general, no S corporation corporate-level tax, and the income is taxed to the shareholders immediately. As Example 1 demonstrates, with an entity earning $300,000 in 1989, an S corporation would generate more than $73,000 of additional after-tax earnings compared to a C corporation.

EXAMPLE 1	Assume that a flow-through business entity earns $300,000, the applicable marginal individual tax rate is 28%, the applicable marginal corporate tax rate is 34%, and all after-tax income is distributed currently. Its available after-tax earnings compared with those of a similar C corporation are as follows:	

	C Corporation	S Corporation or Partnership
Earnings	$ 300,000	$300,000
Less: Corporate tax	(102,000)	–0–
Available for distribution	$ 198,000	$300,000
Less: Tax at shareholder level	(55,440)	(84,000)
Available after-tax earnings	$ 142,560	$216,000

The flow-through business entity generates an extra $73,440 of after-tax earnings ($216,000 − $142,560) compared with a similar C corporation. Moreover, the flow-through business entity avoids the corporate alternative minimum tax and the business untaxed reported profits AMTI adjustment. The C corporation might be able to reduce this disadvantage by paying out its earnings as compensation, rents, or interest expense. Tax at the owner level also can be avoided by not distributing after-tax earnings. □

Losses of C corporations do not flow through to the shareholders. However, losses of an S corporation *are* allocated to the shareholders, who deduct them on

---

1. The Subchapter S Revision Act of 1982 labels a Subchapter S corporation as an "S corporation." It also designates regular corporations (those that have not elected S status) as "C corporations." C corporations are those governed by Subchapter C of the Code (§§ 301–386).

their individual tax returns. Other corporate transactions that flow through separately under the conduit concept include net long-term capital gains and losses, charitable contributions, tax-exempt interest, foreign tax credits, and business credits. Each shareholder of an S corporation separately takes into account his or her pro rata share of certain items of income, deductions, and credits. The character of any item of income, expense, gain, loss, or credit is determined at the corporate level. These tax items pass through as such to each shareholder, based on the prorated number of days during the relevant S year that each shareholder held stock in the corporation.

Subchapter S in Perspective

Subchapter S permits certain corporations to avoid the corporate income tax and enables them to pass through operating losses to their shareholders. It represents an attempt to achieve a measure of tax neutrality in resolving the difficult problem of whether a business should be conducted as a sole proprietorship, partnership, or corporation.

In dealing with the provisions of Subchapter S, certain observations should be kept in mind:

1. S corporation status is an elective provision. Failure to make the election will mean that the rules applicable to the taxation of C corporations and shareholders will apply (refer to chapter 16).

2. S corporations are regular corporations in the legal sense. The S election affects only the Federal income tax consequences of electing corporations. A few states, including Louisiana and New Jersey, do not recognize the S election, and in such cases, such corporations are subject to the state corporate income tax and whatever other state corporate taxes are imposed.

3. Federal income tax law treats S corporations neither as partnerships nor as regular corporations. The tax treatment is almost like partnership taxation, but it involves a unique set of tax rules. However, Subchapter C controls unless Subchapter S otherwise provides an applicable tax effect.

4. Because Subchapter S is an elective provision, strict compliance with the applicable Code requirements generally has been demanded by both the IRS and the courts. An unanticipated deviation from the various governing requirements may therefore lead to an undesirable and often unexpected tax result (e.g., the loss of the S election).

Although not generally regarded as a taxable entity, an S corporation may be subject to the following taxes:

- Preelection built-in gains tax.

- Tax on certain long-term capital gains.

- Passive investment income penalty tax.

An S corporation is *not* subject to the following taxes:

- Corporate income tax under § 11.

- Accumulated earnings tax.

- Personal holding company tax.

- Alternative minimum tax.

- Environmental excise tax on alternative minimum taxable income.

QUALIFICATION FOR S CORPORATION STATUS

Definition of a Small Business Corporation

A small business corporation must possess the following characteristics:[2]

- Is a domestic corporation (is incorporated or organized in the United States).
- Is not otherwise ineligible for the election.
- Has no more than 35 shareholders.
- Has as its shareholders only individuals, estates, and certain trusts.
- Issues only one class of stock.
- Does not have a nonresident alien shareholder.

Ineligible Corporation.   Banks, insurance companies, Puerto Rico or possession corporations, and members of an affiliated group (as defined in § 1504) are not eligible to make an S election. Thus, an S corporation cannot own 80 percent or more of the stock of another corporation. Under certain conditions, however, a corporation can establish one or more inactive affiliates, looking to the possibility that such companies may be needed in the future. The *affiliated group* prohibition does not apply, though, as long as none of the affiliated corporations engages in business or produces gross income.

Number of Shareholders Limitation.   An electing corporation is limited to 35 shareholders. This number corresponds to the private placement exemption under Federal securities law. In testing for the 35-shareholder limitation, a husband and wife are treated as one shareholder as long as they remain married. Furthermore, the estate of a husband or wife and the surviving spouse are treated as one shareholder.

EXAMPLE 2   H and W (husband and wife) jointly own 10 shares in S Corporation, with the remaining 90 shares outstanding owned by 34 other unmarried persons. H and W are divorced, and pursuant to the property settlement approved by the court, the 10 shares held by H and W are divided between them (5 to each). Before the divorce settlement, S Corporation had only 35 shareholders. After the settlement, it has 36 shareholders and no longer can qualify as a small business corporation.   □

Type of Shareholder Limitation.   All of an S corporation's shareholders must be either individuals, estates, or certain trusts. Stated differently, none of the shareholders may be partnerships, corporations, or nonqualifying trusts. The justification for this limitation is related to the 35-shareholder restriction. If, for example, a partnership with 40 partners were qualified to be a shareholder, could it not be said that there would be at least 40 owners of the corporation? If this interpretation were permitted, the 35-shareholder restriction could easily be circumvented by indirect ownership. Keep in mind, though, that an S corporation can be a partner in a partnership and can own stock of another corporation or all the stock of an inactive subsidiary corporation.

---

2. § 1361(b)(1). Note that the definition of "small" for purposes of Subchapter S relates chiefly to the number of shareholders and not to the size of the corporation.

One Class of Stock Limitation.   An S corporation can have only one class of stock issued and outstanding.[3] Congress apparently felt that the capital structure of a small business corporation should be kept relatively simple. Allowing more than one class of stock (e.g., common and preferred) would complicate the pass-through to the shareholders of various corporate tax attributes. Authorized and unissued stock or treasury stock of another class does not disqualify the corporation. Likewise, unexercised stock options, warrants, and convertible debentures do not constitute a second class of stock.

Nonresident Alien Prohibition.   An S corporation cannot have a nonresident alien as a shareholder. In a community property jurisdiction where one of the spouses is married to a nonresident alien, this rule could be a trap for the unwary. A resident alien or a nonresident U.S. citizen is, however, a permissible S corporation shareholder.

Making the Election

If the corporation satisfies the definition of a small business corporation, the next step to achieving S status is a valid election. In this regard, key factors include who must make the election and when the election must be made.

Who Must Elect.   The election is made by filing Form 2553, and all shareholders must consent thereto.[4] For this purpose, both husband and wife must file consents even if their stock is held as joint tenants, tenants in common, tenants by the entirety, or community property. Since the husband and wife are generally considered as one shareholder for purposes of the 35-shareholder limitation, this inconsistency in treatment has led to considerable taxpayer grief—particularly in community property states where the spouses may not realize that their stock is jointly owned as a community asset.

   The consent of a minor shareholder can be made by the minor or the legal or natural guardian (e.g., parent). If the stock is held under a state Uniform Gifts to Minors Act, the custodian of the stock may consent for the minor but only if the custodian is also the minor's legal or natural guardian. The minor would not be required to issue a new consent when he or she comes of age and the custodianship terminates.[5]

When the Election Must Be Made.   To be effective for the following year, the election can be made at any time during the current year. To be effective for the current year, however, the election must be made on or before the fifteenth day of the third month of such current year. An election can be effective for a short tax year of less than two months and fifteen days, even if it is not made until the following tax year.[6]

EXAMPLE 3	In 1989, X Corporation, a calendar year C corporation, decides to become an S corporation beginning January 1, 1990. An election made at any time during 1989 will accomplish this objective. If, however, the election is made in 1990, it must be made on or before March 15, 1990. An election after March 15, 1990, will not make X Corporation an S corporation until 1991. □

---

3. § 1361(b)(1)(D).
4. § 1362(a)(2).

5. Rev.Rul. 71–287, 1971–2 C.B. 317.
6. § 1362(b).

Although no statutory authority exists for obtaining an extension of time for filing an election or consent, permission may be obtained for an extension of time to file a consent if a timely election is filed, reasonable cause is given, and the interests of the government are not jeopardized.

An election cannot be made for an entity that does not yet exist.[7] In the case of a newly created corporation, the question may arise as to when the 2½-month election period begins to run. Regulation § 1.1372–2(b)(1) specifies that the first month begins at the earliest occurrence of any of the following events: (1) when the corporation has shareholders, (2) when it acquires assets, or (3) when it begins doing business.

EXAMPLE 4   Several individuals acquire assets on behalf of T Corporation on June 29, 1990, and begin doing business on July 3, 1990. They subscribe to shares of stock, file articles of incorporation for T Corporation, and become shareholders on July 7, 1990. The S election must be filed no later than 2½ months from June 29, 1990 (on or before September 12) to be effective for 1990. □

Even if the 2½-month rule is met, a current election will not be valid until the following year under either of the following conditions:

- The eligibility requirements were not met during any part of the taxable year before the date of election.

- Persons who were shareholders during any part of the taxable year before the election date, but were not shareholders when the election was made, did not consent.

These rules prevent the allocation of income or losses to preelection shareholders who either were ineligible to hold S corporation stock or did not consent to the election.

EXAMPLE 5   As of January 15, 1989, the stock of X Corporation (a calendar year C corporation) was held equally by three individual shareholders: U, V, and Z. On that date, Z sold its interest to U and V. On March 14, 1989, U and V make the S election by filing Form 2553. X Corporation cannot become an S corporation until 1990. Although the election filing was timely, Z did not consent thereto. Had all individuals who were shareholders during the year (U, V, and Z) signed Form 2553, S status would have taken effect as of January 1, 1989. □

Once an election is made, it does not have to be renewed; it remains in effect unless otherwise lost.

Loss of the Election

An S election can be lost in any of the following ways:

- A new shareholder owning more than one-half of the stock affirmatively refuses to consent to the election.

---

7. See, for example, *T.H. Campbell & Bros., Inc.,* 34 TCM 695, T.C.Memo. 1975–149.

- Shareholders owning a majority of shares (voting and nonvoting) voluntarily revoke the election.

- The number of shareholders exceeds the maximum allowable limitation.

- A class of stock other than voting or nonvoting common stock is created.

- A subsidiary (other than a nonoperating entity) is acquired.

- The corporation fails the passive investment income limitation.

- A nonresident alien becomes a shareholder.

Voluntary Revocation. Section 1362(d)(1) permits a voluntary revocation of the election if shareholders owning a majority of shares consent. A revocation filed up to and including the fifteenth day of the third month of the tax year is effective for the entire tax year unless a prospective effective date is specified. A revocation made after the fifteenth day of the third month of the tax year is effective on the first day of the following tax year. However, if a prospective date is specified, the termination is effective as of the specified date.

EXAMPLE 6 The shareholders of T Corporation, a calendar year S corporation, elect to revoke the election on January 5, 1990. Assuming the election is duly executed and its filing is timely, T Corporation will become a regular corporation for calendar year 1990. If, on the other hand, the election is not made until June 1990, T Corporation will not become a regular corporation until calendar year 1991. □

A revocation that designates a prospective effective date results in the splitting of the year into a short S corporation taxable year and a short C corporation taxable year. The day *before* the day on which the revocation occurs is treated as the last day of a short S corporation taxable year, and the day on which the revocation occurs is treated as the first day of the short regular corporate taxable year. The corporation allocates the income or loss for the entire year on a pro rata basis.

EXAMPLE 7 Assume the same facts as in Example 6, except that the corporation designates July 1, 1990, as the revocation date. Accordingly, June 30, 1990, is the last day of the S corporation taxable year. The regular corporate taxable year runs from July 1, 1990, to December 31, 1990. Any income or loss for the entire year is allocated between the short years on a prorated basis. □

Rather than elect a pro rata allocation, the corporation can elect (with the consent of *all* who were shareholders at any time during the S short year) to report the income or loss on each return on the basis of income or loss as shown on the corporate permanent records. Under this method, items are attributed to the short S corporation and C corporation years according to the time they were incurred (as reflected in the records).[8]

Cessation of Small Business Corporation Status. A corporation not only must be a small business corporation to make the S election but also must continue to qualify as such to keep the election. In other words, meeting the

---

8. §§ 1362(e)(1), (2), and (3).

definition of a small business corporation is a continuing requirement for maintaining the S status. In the case of an involuntary termination, the loss of the election applies as of the date on which the disqualifying event occurs.

Passive Investment Income Limitation.   The Code provides a passive investment income limitation for S corporations that possess accumulated earnings and profits from years in which the entity was a C corporation. If such a corporation has passive income in excess of 25 percent of its gross receipts for three consecutive taxable years, the S election is terminated as of the beginning of the following taxable year.[9]

EXAMPLE 8

For 1987, 1988, and 1989, B Corporation, a calendar year S corporation, derived passive income in excess of 25% of its gross receipts. If B holds accumulated earnings and profits from years in which it was a C corporation, its S election is terminated as of January 1, 1990. □

Such damaging C corporation earnings and profits could be acquired by an S corporation from a regular corporation where earnings and profits carry over, in a reorganization (e.g., due to a merger), or they could be earned in years before the S election. S corporations themselves, however, never generate earnings and profits.

Although passive investment income appears to parallel that of personal holding company income (refer to chapter 19), the two types of income are not identical. For example, long-term capital gain from the sale of securities would be passive investment income but would not be personal holding company income. Moreover, there are no relief provisions for rent income similar to the personal holding company rules. The inclusion of gains from the sale of securities within the definition of passive investment income generally has made it difficult, if not impossible, for corporations that deal chiefly in security transactions to achieve S status if the harmful C corporation earnings and profits exist.

Rents present a unique problem. Although rents are classified by the Code as passive investment income, Regulation § 1.1372−4(b)(5)(vi) states that rents will not fall into this category if the corporation (landlord) renders significant services to the occupant (tenant).

EXAMPLE 9

T Corporation owns and operates an apartment building. Although the corporation provides utilities for the building, maintains the lobby in the building, and furnishes trash collection for the tenants, this does not constitute the rendering of significant services for the occupants.[10] Thus, the rents paid by the tenants of the building constitute passive investment income to T Corporation. □

EXAMPLE 10

Assume the same facts as in Example 9, with one addition—T Corporation also furnishes maid services to its tenants. Now the services rendered are significant, in that they go beyond what one might normally expect the landlord of an apartment building to provide. Under these circumstances, the rental income no longer constitutes passive investment income. □

---

9. § 1362(d)(3)(A)(ii).

10. *Bramlette Building Corp., Inc.*, 52 T.C. 200

(1969), *aff'd.* in 70−1 USTC ¶9361, 25 AFTR2d 70−1061, 424 F.2d 751 (CA−5, 1970).

Reelection after Termination. After the election has been terminated, § 1362(g) enforces a five-year waiting period before a new election can be made. The Code does, however, allow for the IRS to make exceptions to this rule (to permit an earlier reelection by the corporation).

OPERATIONAL RULES

An S corporation is largely a tax-reporting, rather than a tax-paying, entity. In this respect, the entity is treated much like a partnership. Similar to the partnership conduit concept, the taxable income of an S corporation flows through to the shareholders, whether or not such income is distributed in the form of actual dividends. Likewise, losses of the entity are allocated to the shareholders, who deduct them on their individual tax returns. Other corporate transactions that flow through separately under the conduit concept include net long-term capital gains and losses, charitable contributions, tax-exempt interest, foreign tax credits, and business credits. Similar to the partnership rules, each shareholder of an S corporation takes into account separately his or her pro rata share of certain items of income, deductions, and credits. Under § 1366(b), the character of any item of income, expense, gain, loss, or credit is determined at the corporate level. These tax items pass through as such to each shareholder based on the prorated number of days during the relevant S year that each held stock in the corporation.

Choice of Tax Year

Since S corporation shareholders report their share of S items as of the entity's year-end, the selection of a corporate tax year is an important tax decision. An S corporation might use a calendar year or a fiscal year, but for tax deferral purposes, a corporate fiscal year ending January 31 and a calendar year shareholder would be ideal.

After 1986, however, S corporations must conform to the taxable years of their shareholders (this is the calendar year in most instances). There are two exceptions to this general rule. First, an S corporation may use a taxable year for which it can establish a business purpose.[11] Second, an S corporation may make a one-time election under § 444 to establish a fiscal year, provided that a corporate-level payment is made on any income deferred by the shareholders.

An S corporation can establish an acceptable business purpose for a fiscal year in three ways:

- The fiscal year is a natural business year.

- The fiscal year serves an acceptable business purpose.

- An existing S corporation meets certain grandfathering requirements.[12]

Meeting the natural business year exception involves a simple quantitative test. If 25 percent or more of a corporation's gross receipts for the 12-month period is recognized in the last two months of such period, and such requirement has been met for three consecutive 12-month periods, the S corporation may adopt, retain, or change to a noncalendar year. If the entity is to establish a natural business year, it must have at least a 47-month gross receipt history.

Other business purposes may be used to establish that a fiscal year is acceptable to the IRS. However, the fiscal year must be close to its natural business

---

11. § 1378(a).

12. Rev.Proc. 87–32, 1987–2 C.B. 396.

year (the entity barely fails the 25 percent test). The IRS lists the following factors that do *not* constitute such a valid business purpose:[13]

- The use of a particular fiscal year for regulatory or financial accounting purposes.

- The hiring practices of a particular corporation.

- Tax deferral for the shareholders.

- Use of a fiscal year for administrative purposes (e.g., awarding bonuses or promotions).

- Use of model years, price lists, or other items that change on a noncalendar annual basis.

In general, a taxable year under the § 444 election may not result in a deferral period of more than three months. However, an S corporation in existence before 1987 may elect to retain its previous taxable year for years after 1986, even though such a year results in a deferral period exceeding three months.

The penalty for a fiscal year under § 444 is that the S corporation must make a required payment on April 15 for any tax year for which the election is in effect. This required payment is equal to the highest rate of tax under § 1 plus one percentage point. Thus, for election years beginning in 1988 the required payment rate is 29 percent (28% + 1%). Such payments are not deductible by the S corporation (or by any person) for Federal income tax purposes. They are refundable deposits that do not earn interest and do not pass through to the S shareholders.[14]

EXAMPLE 11   An S corporation is organized on October 5, 1990. Its Subchapter S ordinary income for the next 15 months is as follows:

October 5–December 31, 1990	$ 30,000
January 1991	20,000
February–September 30, 1991	180,000
October–December 31, 1991	60,000

If the S corporation elects a calendar year, the shareholders recognize $30,000 of income in 1990. But if a January 31 fiscal year were available, the calendar year shareholders recognize no income for 1990. Furthermore, only $50,000 would be taxable to the shareholders in 1991. This deferral of income caused Congress to legislate calendar year treatment for most S corporations. If this S corporation could select a September 30 fiscal year, no income is taxable to the shareholders in 1990, and only $230,000 is taxable in 1991. □

EXAMPLE 12   X was a C corporation in 1986 with a September 30 fiscal year. During 1987, X elects S status and is unable to meet the business purpose exception for maintaining a fiscal year. For X Corporation to maintain a fiscal year, it must

---

13. Rev.Rul. 87–57, 1987–2 C.B. 117.   14. § 7519.

elect under § 444 and make a required payment under § 7519 by April 15. A failure to make this payment would result in the termination of the § 444 election, effective for the year in which the failure occurred. An electing corporation need not make a required payment until the amount for the current and all preceding election years exceeds $500. If X Corporation had made an S election in 1986, § 444 would not be available. However, the entity would be allowed to change to a taxable year under § 444 by treating the deferral period of the tax year being changed as the same as the deferral period of the last tax year of the C corporation. ☐

The required payment to be made by an S corporation under a § 444 election should approximate the tax that would be payable if a calendar year were used. Although the § 444 election is complex, there still may be valid business reasons to select a fiscal year. A company may have difficulty closing the books, preparing statements, and issuing its Schedules K–1 on a timely basis under a calendar year.

Computation of Taxable Income

Subchapter S taxable income or loss is generally determined in a manner similar to the tax rules that apply to partnerships, except that the amortization of organization expenditures under § 248 is an allowable deduction. Also, S corporations must recognize any gains (but not losses) on distributions of appreciated property to the shareholders.

Certain deductions not allowable for a partnership are not allowable for an S corporation, including the standard deduction, personal exemptions, alimony deductions, personal moving expenses, and expenses for the care of certain dependents. Furthermore, provisions of the Code governing the computation of taxable income applicable only to corporations, such as the dividends received deduction, do not apply.[15]

In general, S corporation items are divided into (1) nonseparately computed income or losses and (2) separately stated income, losses, deductions, and credits that uniquely could affect the tax liability of any shareholders. In essence, nonseparate items are lumped together into an undifferentiated amount that constitutes Subchapter S taxable income or loss. For example, any net gains from the recapture provisions of § 1245 and §§ 1250 through 1255 constitute nonseparately computed income.

Each shareholder receives a pro rata portion of this nonseparately computed amount. For a shareholder who dies during the year, the share of the pro rata items up to the date of death must be reported on the shareholder's final individual income tax return. Tax accounting and other elections are generally made at the corporate level, except for elections that partners may make separately (e.g., foreign tax credit election).

The following items, among others, are separately stated on Schedule K of Form 1120S, and each shareholder takes into account his or her pro rata share (the share is passed through on a Schedule K–1):[16]

- Tax-exempt income.[17]

- Long-term and short-term capital gains and losses.

---

15. § 703(a)(2).
16. §§ 1366(a) and (b).
17. Tax-exempt income passes through to the share-

holders and increases their tax basis in the stock. A subsequent distribution does not result in taxation of the tax-exempt income.

- Section 1231 gains and losses.
- Charitable contributions.
- Passive gains, losses, and credits under § 469.
- Certain portfolio income.
- Section 179 expense deduction.
- Tax preferences.
- Depletion.
- Foreign income or losses.
- Wagering gains or losses.
- Nonbusiness income or loss (§ 212).
- Recoveries of tax benefit items.
- Intangible drilling costs.
- Investment interest, income, and expenses.
- Total property distributions.
- Total dividend distributions from accumulated earnings and profits.

This pro rata method assigns an equal amount of each of the S items to each day of the year. If a shareholder's interest changes during the year, this per-day method assigns the shareholder a pro rata share of each item for *each* day the stock is owned:

S Corporation item		Percentage of shares owned		Percentage of year owned		Amount of item to be reported

This per-day method must be used unless the shareholder disposes of his or her entire interest in the entity.[18]

If there is a complete termination of a shareholder's interest during the tax year, all shareholders may elect to treat the S taxable year as two taxable years, with the first year ending on the date of the termination. Under this election, an interim closing of the books is undertaken, and the owners report their shares of the S corporation items as they occurred during the year.

A comparison of Schedule K for Form 1120S and Schedule K for Form 1065 (see chapter 21) indicates several major differences. The S corporation's Schedule K contains a section for reporting distributions from both S and C corporation earnings. In addition, the S corporation form includes no listing of guaranteed salaries or self-employment income.

EXAMPLE 13   The following is the income statement for B Company, an S corporation:

---

18. §§ 1366(a)(1) and 1377(a)(1).

Sales		$ 40,000
Less: Cost of sales		(23,000)
Gross profit on sales		$ 17,000
Less: Interest expense	$1,200	
Charitable contributions	400	
Advertising expenses	1,500	
Other operating expenses	2,000	(5,100)
		$ 11,900
Plus: Tax-exempt income	$ 300	
Dividend income	200	
Long-term capital gain	500	
	$1,000	
Less: Short-term capital loss	(150)	850
Net income per books		$ 12,750

Subchapter S taxable income for B Company is calculated as follows, using net income for book purposes as a point of departure:

Net income per books			$12,750
Separately computed items:			
Deduct: Tax-exempt interest	$ 300		
Dividend income	200		
Long-term capital gain	500		
	($1,000)		
Add: Charitable contributions	$400		
Short-term capital loss	150	550	
Net effect of separately computed items			(450)
Subchapter S taxable income			$12,300

The $12,300 of Subchapter S taxable income, as well as the separately computed items, are divided among the shareholders, based upon their stock ownership. ☐

EXAMPLE 14

Assume in Example 13 that shareholder P owned 10% of the stock for 100 days and 12% for the remaining 265 days. Using the required per-day allocation method, P's share of the S corporation items is as follows:

	Schedule K Totals	P's Share		P's Schedule K–1 Totals
		10%	12%	
Subchapter S taxable income	$12,300	$337	$1,072	$1,409
Tax-exempt interest	300	8	26	34
Dividend income	200	5	17	22
LTCG	500	14	44	58
Charitable contributions	400	11	35	46
STCL	150	4	13	17

P's share of the Subchapter S taxable income is the total of $12,300 × .10 × 100/365 plus $12,300 × .12 × 265/365, or $1,409. P's Schedule K–1 totals would flow through to his Form 1040. ☐

EXAMPLE 15   If, in Example 14, P dies after owning the stock 100 days, his share of the S corporation items would be reported on the final Form 1040. Thus, the items in the column labeled 10% in Example 14 would be reported on P's final tax return. S corporation items that occur after the shareholder's death would appear on the Form 1041 (the estate's income tax return). ☐

Tax Treatment of Distributions to Shareholders

The amount of any distribution to an S corporation shareholder is equal to the cash plus the fair market value of any other property distributed. Either of two sets of distribution rules applies, depending upon whether the electing corporation has accumulated earnings and profits (e.g., from Subchapter C years).

A distribution by an S corporation having no accumulated earnings and profits is not includible in gross income to the extent that it does not exceed the shareholder's adjusted basis in stock. When the amount of the distribution exceeds the adjusted basis of the stock, such excess is treated as a gain from the sale or exchange of property (capital gain in most cases).

EXAMPLE 16   P, a calendar year S corporation, has no accumulated earnings and profits. During the year, J, an individual shareholder, receives a cash dividend of $12,200 from P Corporation. J's basis in his stock is $9,700. From the cash distribution J recognizes a capital gain of $2,500, the excess of the distribution over the stock basis ($12,200 − $9,700). The remaining $9,700 is tax-free, but it reduces J's basis in the stock to zero. ☐

An S corporation should maintain an accumulated adjustments account (AAA). Essentially, the AAA is a cumulative total of undistributed net income items for S corporation taxable years beginning after 1982. The AAA is adjusted in a similar fashion to the shareholder's stock basis, except there is no adjustment for tax-exempt income and related expenses or for Federal taxes attributable to a C corporation tax year. Further, any decreases in stock basis have no impact on the AAA when the AAA balance is negative.

The AAA is a corporate account, whereas the shareholder's basis in his or her stock investment is calculated at the shareholder level. Therefore, the AAA (unlike the stock basis) can have a negative balance. The AAA is determined at the end of the year of a distribution rather than at the time such distribution is made. A pro rata portion of each distribution is treated as made out of the AAA when more than one distribution occurs in the same year. The AAA is important in maintaining the treatment of a property distribution as tax-free. This AAA procedure provides the mechanism for taxing the income of an S corporation only once.

A shareholder has a proportionate interest in the AAA, regardless of the size of his or her stock basis. However, since the AAA is a corporate account, there is no connection between the prior accumulated S corporation income and any particular shareholder. The AAA is not a personal right. Thus, the benefits of the AAA can be shifted from one shareholder to another shareholder. For example, when one S

shareholder transfers stock to another shareholder, any AAA on the purchase date is fully available to the purchaser. Similarly, the issuance of additional stock to a new shareholder in an S corporation having an AAA would cause a dilution of the AAA in relationship to the existing shareholders.

The treatment of a distribution from an S corporation with accumulated earnings and profits is summarized as follows:

1. Distributions are tax-free up to the amount in the AAA (limited to stock basis).

2. Any previously taxed income (PTI)[19] in the corporation under prior-law rules can be distributed on a tax-free basis. However, PTI probably cannot be distributed in property other than in cash [according to Reg. § 1.1375–4(b), effective under prior law].

3. The remaining distribution constitutes a dividend to the extent of accumulated earnings and profits. With the consent of all of its shareholders, an S corporation can elect to have a distribution treated as made from accumulated earnings and profits rather than from the AAA. This is known as an AAA bypass election. Otherwise, no adjustments are made to accumulated earnings and profits during S years except for distributions taxed as dividends; investment tax credit recapture applicable to the corporation; and adjustments from redemptions, liquidations, reorganizations, and divisions. For example, accumulated earnings and profits can be acquired in a reorganization.

4. Any residual amount is applied against the shareholder's remaining basis in his or her stock. Such amount is considered to be a return of capital, which is not taxable. In this context, basis is reduced by the fair market value of the distributed asset.

5. Distributions that exceed the shareholder's tax basis for the stock are taxable as capital gains.

These rules apply regardless of the manner in which the shareholder acquired the stock.

EXAMPLE 17

T, a calendar year S corporation, distributes a $1,200 cash dividend to its only shareholder, X, on December 31, 1990. The shareholder's basis in her stock is $100 on December 31, 1989, and the corporation has no accumulated earnings and profits. For 1990, T Corporation had $1,000 of nonseparately computed income from operations, $500 capital loss, and $400 of tax-exempt income.

X must report $1,000 of income and $500 of capital loss. The tax-exempt income retains its character and is not taxed to the shareholder. X's stock basis is increased by the $400 tax-exempt income and the $1,000 taxable income, and it is decreased by the $500 capital loss. The results of current operations affect the shareholder's basis before the application of the distribution rule.

Immediately before the cash dividend, X's stock basis is $1,000. Thus, $1,000 of the dividend is tax-free (a tax-free recovery of basis), but X has a $200 gain from the sale or exchange of stock. X's basis in the AAA and stock is zero as of December 31, 1990, determined as follow:

---

19. §§ 1368(c)(1) and (e)(1). Before 1983, an account similar to an AAA was called previously taxed income (PTI). Any S corporations in existence before 1983 may have PTI, which, at this point, can be distributed tax-free.

	Corporate AAA	X's Stock Basis
Balance 1/1/90	–0–	$ 100
Income	$1,000	1,000
Capital loss	(500)	(500)
Tax-exempt income	—	400
Subtotal	$ 500	$ 1,000
Distribution	(500)	(1,000)
Balance 12/31/90	$ –0–	$ –0–

□

EXAMPLE 18   Assume the same facts as in Example 17, except that T Corporation had Subchapter C earnings and profits of $750. T has an AAA of $500 ($1,000 − $500), which does not include the tax-exempt income. X's basis in the stock immediately before the distribution is $1,000 since X's basis is increased by the tax-exempt income. Therefore, X is not taxed on the first $500, which is a recovery of the AAA. The next $700 is a taxable dividend from the accumulated earnings and profits account. (Refer to the first column of Concept Summary 20–1.) X's basis in the stock is $500 ($1,000 − $500). Although the taxable portion of the distribution does not reduce X's basis in the stock, the nontaxable AAA distribution does. □

Schedule M.   Schedule M on page 4 of Form 1120S (see below) contains a column labeled "Other adjustments account." Essentially, this account includes items not used in the calculation of the AAA, such as tax-exempt income and any related nondeductible expenses. However, distributions from this account are not taxable. Once the earnings and profits account reaches zero, distributions fall under the two-tier system: (1) nontaxable to the extent of basis, then (2) capital gain. Moreover, there is no need for an "other adjustments account" when there are no accumulated earnings and profits.

EXAMPLE 19   During 1990, S Corporation incurred the following items:

Accumulated adjustments account, beginning of year	$ 8,500
Prior-taxed income, beginning of year	6,250
Ordinary income	25,000
Tax-exempt interest	4,000
Key-employee life insurance proceeds received	5,000
Payroll penalty expense	2,000
Charitable contributions	3,000
Unreasonable compensation	5,000
Premiums on key-employee life insurance	2,000
Distributions to shareholders	16,000

S Corporation's Schedule M for the current year appears as follows:

| Schedule M | Analysis of Accumulated Adjustments Account, Other Adjustments Account, and Shareholders' Undistributed Taxable Income Previously Taxed (If Schedule L, column (c), amounts for lines 24, 25, or 26 are not the same as corresponding amounts on line 9 of Schedule M, attach a schedule explaining any differences. See instructions.) |

	Accumulated adjustments account	Other adjustments account	Shareholders' undistributed taxable income previously taxed
1 Balance at beginning of year	8,500		6,250
2 Ordinary income from page 1, line 21 . . .	25,000		
3 Other additions		9,000**	
4 Total of lines 1, 2, and 3	33,500	9,000	
5 Distributions other than dividend distributions	16,000		
6 Loss from page 1, line 21			
7 Other reductions	10,000*	2,000	
8 Add lines 5, 6, and 7	26,000	2,000	
9 Balance at end of tax year—subtract line 8 from line 4	7,500	7,000	6,250

* $2,000 payroll penalty + $3,000 charitable contributions + $5,000 unreasonable compensation
** $4,000 tax-exempt interest + $5,000 life insurance proceeds

Any distribution of cash by the corporation with respect to the stock during a post-termination transition period of approximately one year is applied against and reduces the adjusted basis of the stock to the extent that the amount of the distribution does not exceed the AAA.[20] Thus, a terminated S corporation should make a cash distribution during the one-year period following termination to the extent of all previously undistributed net income items for all S tax years.

EXAMPLE 20 The sole shareholder of P, a calendar year S corporation during 1989, elects to terminate the S election, effective January 1, 1990. As of the end of 1989, P has

CONCEPT SUMMARY 20-1

Classification Procedures for Distributions from an S Corporation*

Where Earnings and Profits Exist	Where No Earnings and Profits Exist
1. Distributions are tax-free to the extent of the accumulated adjustments account.**	1. Distributions are nontaxable to the extent of adjusted basis in stock.
2. Any PTI from pre-1983 tax years can be distributed tax-free.	2. Excess distributions are treated as gain from the sale or exchange of property (capital gain in most cases).
3. The remaining distribution constitutes ordinary dividend from accumulated earnings and profits.***	
4. Any residual amount is applied as a tax-free reduction in basis of stock.	
5. Any excess distributions are treated as gain from the sale or exchange of stock (capital gain in most cases).	

* A distribution of appreciated property by an electing corporation results in a gain that first is allocated to and reported by the shareholders.

** Once stock basis reaches zero, any distribution from the AAA is treated as a gain from the sale or exchange of stock. Thus, basis is an upper limit on what a shareholder may receive tax-free.

*** An AAA bypass election is available to pay out accumulated E & P before reducing the AAA [§ 1368(e)(3)].

20. §§ 1371(e) and 1377(b).

an AAA of $1,300. P's sole shareholder, Q, can receive a nontaxable distribution of cash during a post-termination transition period of approximately one year to the extent of P's AAA. Although a cash dividend of $1,300 during 1990 would be nontaxable to Q, it would reduce the adjusted basis of Q's stock.   □

Alternative Minimum Tax.   An S corporation is not directly subject to the alternative minimum tax (AMT). Under the conduit approach, all tax preference items flow through the S corporation to be included in the shareholders' AMT calculations. The allocation of the tax preference items is based upon the pro rata daily allocation method, unless the corporation has elected the interim closing-of-the-books method. Each shareholder includes the proper portion of each tax preference item in his or her AMT calculations. For a list of tax preference items, see chapter 14.

An S corporation has the advantage of calculating tax preference items using individual, rather than corporate, rules. Thus, the S corporation has no business untaxed reported profits (BURP) or accumulated current earnings (ACE) adjustment. For corporations with large BURP or ACE adjustments, an S election can be quite attractive. Recall, though, that the individual AMT rate is 1 percent higher than the corporate rate.

EXAMPLE 21   During 1990, an S corporation has an excess mining exploration costs preference item of $45,000, an excess depletion tax preference of $70,000, and untaxed appreciation on a charitable contribution of $10,000. The ACE adjustment is $80,000. If T is a 10% shareholder, T would be assigned 10% of $45,000, $70,000, and $10,000 as tax preference items ($4,500 + $7,000 + $1,000), but T is assigned no ACE adjustment.   □

Corporate Treatment of Certain Property Distributions

An S corporation recognizes a gain on any distribution of appreciated property (other than in a reorganization) in the same manner as if the asset had been sold to the shareholder at its fair market value.[21] The corporate gain is passed through to the shareholders. There is an important reason for this rule. Otherwise, property might be distributed tax-free (other than for certain recapture items) and later sold without income recognition to the shareholder because of the stepped-up basis equal to the asset's fair market value.

The S corporation will not recognize a loss relative to assets that are worth less than their basis. Furthermore, when such depreciated property is distributed, the shareholder receives a basis in the asset equal to the asset's fair market value. Thus, the potential loss is postponed until the shareholder sells the stock of the S corporation. Since loss property receives a step-down in basis without any loss recognition, such dividend distributions should be avoided. The character of the gain—capital gain or ordinary income—will depend upon the type of asset being distributed.

EXAMPLE 22   Q, an S corporation for 10 years, distributes a tract of land held as an investment to its majority shareholder. The land was purchased for $22,000

---

21. § 1363(d).

many years ago and is currently worth $82,000. Q Corporation recognizes a capital gain of $60,000, which increases the AAA by $60,000. Then the property dividend reduces AAA by $82,000 (the fair market value). The tax consequences are the same for appreciated property, whether it is distributed to the shareholders and they dispose of it, or the property is sold by the corporation and the proceeds are distributed to the shareholders.

If the land were purchased for $80,000 many years ago and is currently worth $30,000, the $50,000 realized loss would not be recognized at the corporate level, and the shareholder receives a $30,000 basis in the land. The $50,000 realized loss disappears from the corporate level. Since loss is not recognized on the distribution of depreciated property, the AAA is not reduced. To recognize the loss on depreciated property, the property must be sold by the S corporation. □

EXAMPLE 23

Assume the same facts as in Example 22, except that Q is a regular corporation or a partnership. Assume the partner's basis in the partnership is $25,000. The tax consequences may be summarized as follows.

| | Appreciated Property | | |
	C Corporation	S Corporation	Partnership
Entity gain/loss	$60,000	$60,000	$ –0–
Owner's gain/loss	60,000	60,000	–0–
Owner's basis	82,000	82,000	25,000
	Depreciated Property		
	C Corporation	S Corporation	Partnership
Entity gain/loss	$ –0–	$ –0–	$ –0–
Owner's gain/loss	–0–	–0–	–0–
Owner's basis	30,000	30,000	25,000

□

Shareholder's Tax Basis

The initial tax basis of stock in an S corporation is calculated similarly to the basis of stock in a regular corporation, dependent upon the manner in which shares are acquired (e.g., gift, inheritance, purchase). Once the initial tax basis is determined, various transactions during the life of the corporation affect the shareholder's basis in the stock.

A shareholder's basis is increased by further stock purchases and capital contributions. Operations during the year also cause the following upward adjustments to basis:[22]

• Nonseparately computed income.

• Separately stated income items (nontaxable income).

• Depletion in excess of basis in the property.

---

22. § 1367(a).

The following items cause a downward adjustment to basis (but not below zero):

- Nonseparately computed loss.
- Separately stated loss and deduction items.
- Distributions not reported as income by the shareholder (AAA distributions).
- Nondeductible expenses of the corporation.

A shareholder's basis in the stock can never be reduced below zero, and any further downward adjustment (losses or deductions) is applied to reduce (but not below zero) the shareholder's basis in any indebtedness from the electing corporation. Once the basis of any debt is reduced, it is later increased (only up to the original amount) by subsequent net income items. The adjustment is made *before* any increase to the basis in the stock.[23]

EXAMPLE 24   T, a sole shareholder, has a $7,000 stock basis and a $2,000 basis in a loan that he made to a calendar year S corporation at the beginning of 1990. Subchapter S net income during 1990 is $8,200. The corporation incurred a short-term capital loss of $2,300 and received $2,000 of tax-exempt interest income. Cash of $15,000 is distributed to T on November 15, 1990. As a result, T's basis in his stock is zero, and his loan basis is $1,900 ($2,000 − $100) at the end of 1990:

Beginning basis in the stock	$ 7,000
Separately computed income	8,200
Short-term capital loss	(2,300)
Tax-exempt interest income	2,000
	$ 14,900
Distribution received (to extent of basis)	(14,900)
Final basis in the stock	$ –0–

Because stock basis cannot be reduced below zero, the $100 excess distribution reduces T's loan basis.   □

Treatment of Losses

Net Operating Loss.   One major advantage of an S election is the ability to pass through any net operating loss (NOL) of the corporation directly to the shareholders. A shareholder can deduct such a loss for the year in which the corporation's tax year ends. The corporation is not entitled to any deduction for the NOL. The loss is deducted in arriving at adjusted gross income (it is a deduction *for* AGI). A shareholder's basis in the stock is reduced to the extent of any pass-through of the net operating loss, and the shareholder's AAA is reduced by the same deductible amount.[24]

Net operating losses are allocated among shareholders in the same manner as income is. NOLs are allocated on a daily basis to all shareholders.[25] Presumably,

---

23. § 1367(b)(2).   25. § 1377(a)(1).
24. § 1368(e)(1)(A).

transferred shares are considered to be held by the transferee (not the transferor) on the date of the transfer.

EXAMPLE 25

An S corporation incurs a $20,000 NOL for the current year. At all times during the tax year, the stock was owned equally by the same 10 shareholders. Each shareholder is entitled to deduct $2,000 *for* adjusted gross income for the tax year in which the corporate tax year ends. □

Deductions for an S corporation's NOL pass-through cannot exceed a shareholder's adjusted basis in the stock plus the basis of any loans made by the shareholder to the corporation. If a taxpayer is unable to prove the tax basis, the NOL pass-through can be denied. In essence, a shareholder's stock or loan basis cannot go below zero. As noted previously, once a shareholder's adjusted stock basis has been eliminated by an NOL, any excess net operating loss is used to reduce the shareholder's basis for any loans made to the corporation (but never below zero). The basis for loans is established by the actual advances made to the corporation, and not by indirect loans.[26]

Except in the Eleventh Circuit, the fact that a shareholder has guaranteed a loan made to the corporation by a third party has no effect upon the shareholder's loan basis unless payments actually have been made as a result of that guarantee. If the corporation defaults on an indebtedness and the shareholder makes good on the guarantee, the shareholder's indebtedness basis is increased to that extent. Such a subsequent increase in basis has no influence on the results of a prior year in which an NOL exceeded a shareholder's adjusted basis. The Eleventh Circuit has held that a shareholder's guarantee of a loan to an S corporation may be treated as equity where the lender looks to the shareholder as the primary debtor.[27] The Tax Court has rejected this increase in debt basis in a reviewed decision.[28]

A shareholder's share of an NOL may be greater than both the basis in the stock and the basis of the indebtedness. A shareholder is entitled to carry forward a loss to the extent that the loss for the year exceeds both the stock basis and the loan basis. Any loss carried forward may be deducted *only* by the same shareholder if and when the basis in the stock of or loans to the corporation is restored.[29]

Any loss carryover remaining at the end of a one-year post-termination transition period is lost forever.[30] The post-termination transition period ends on the later of (1) one year after the effective date of the termination of the S election or the due date for the last S return (whichever is later) or (2) 120 days after the determination that the corporation's S election had terminated for a previous year. Thus, a shareholder who has a loss carryover should increase the stock or loan basis and flow through the loss before disposing of the stock.

EXAMPLE 26

T, an individual, has a stock basis of $4,000 in an S corporation. He has loaned $2,000 to the corporation and has guaranteed another $4,000 loan made to the corporation by a local bank. Although his share of the S corporation's NOL for

---

26. *Ruth M Prashker,* 59 T.C. 172 (1972); *Frederick G. Brown v. U. S.,* 83–1 USTC ¶9364, 52 AFTR2d 82–5081, 706 F.2d 756 (CA–6, 1983).

27. *Selfe v. U.S.,* 86–1 USTC ¶9115, 57 AFTR2d 86–464, 778 F.2d 769 (CA–ll, 1985).

28. *Estate of Leavitt,* 90 T.C. 206 (1988), *aff'd —*

F.2d— (CA–4, 1989). See also *James K. Calcutt,* 91 T.C. — , No. 2 (1988).

29. § 1366(d).

30. § 1377(b).

the current year is $9,500, T may deduct only $6,000 of the NOL on his individual tax return. T may carry forward $3,500 of the NOL, to be deducted when the basis in his stock or loan to the corporation is restored. T has a zero basis in both the stock and loan after the flow-through of the $6,000 NOL. □

Net operating losses from regular-corporation years cannot be utilized at the corporate level (except with respect to built-in gains), nor can they be passed through to the shareholders. Further, the running of the carryforward period continues during S status.[31] Consequently, it may not be appropriate for a corporation that has unused net operating losses to make this election. When a corporation is expecting losses in the future, an election should be made before the loss year.

If a loan's basis has been reduced and is not restored, income will result when the loan is repaid. If the corporation issued a note as evidence of the debt, repayment constitutes an amount received in exchange for a capital asset, and the amount that exceeds the shareholder's basis is entitled to capital gain treatment.[32] However, if the loan is made on open account, the repayment constitutes ordinary income to the extent that it exceeds the shareholder's basis for the loan. Each repayment must be prorated between the gain portion and the repayment of the debt. Thus, a note should be given to ensure capital gain treatment for the income that results from a loan's repayment.

Passive Losses and Credits.   There are three major classes of income and losses: active, portfolio, and passive. Section 469 provides that net passive losses and credits are not deductible and must be carried over to a year when there is passive income. S corporations are not directly subject to these limits, but shareholders who do not materially participate in operating the business will be able to apply the corporate losses and credits only against income from other

CONCEPT SUMMARY 20–2

Treatment of Losses

Step 1.   Allocate total loss to the shareholder on a daily basis, based upon stock ownership.

Step 2.   If the shareholder's loss exceeds his or her stock basis, apply any excess to any adjusted basis of any indebtedness owned directly by the shareholder. Losses from distributions do not reduce debt basis.

Step 3.   Where loss exceeds the debt basis, any excess is suspended and carried over to succeeding tax years.

Step 4.   In succeeding tax years, any net increase (resulting from *all* positive and negative basis adjustments) restores the debt basis first, up to its original amount.

Step 5.   Once debt basis is restored, any net increase remaining is used to increase any stock basis.

Step 6.   Any suspended loss from a previous year now reduces stock basis first and debt basis second.

Step 7.   If the S election terminates, any suspended loss carryover may be deducted during the post-termination transition period to the extent of the *stock* basis at the end of such period. Any loss remaining at the end of this period is lost forever.

---

31. § 1371(b).

32. *Joe M. Smith*, 48 T.C. 872 (1967), *aff'd.* and *rev'd.* in 70–1 USTC ¶9327, 25 AFTR2d 70–936, 424

F.2d 219 (CA–9, 1970), and Rev.Rul. 64–162, 1964–1 C.B. 304.

passive activities. In other words, flow-through income and deductions from an S corporation are considered as arising from a passive activity, unless the shareholder materially participates in the corporate business. For example, a passive loss at the S corporation level could not be offset against the earned income of a nonparticipating shareholder. Regular, continuous, and substantial involvement in the S corporation is necessary to meet the material participation requirement.

EXAMPLE 27   N is a 50% owner of an S corporation engaged in a passive activity under § 469. N, a nonparticipating shareholder, receives a salary of $6,000 for services as a result of the passive activity. This deduction creates a $6,000 passive loss at the corporate level. N will have $6,000 earned income as a result of the salary. The $6,000 salary creates a $6,000 deduction/passive loss, which flows through to the shareholders. N's $3,000 share of the loss may not be deducted against the $6,000 earned income; § 469(e)(3) indicates that earned income shall not be taken into account in computing the income or loss from a passive activity. □

At-Risk Provisions.   The at-risk rules generally apply to S corporation shareholders. Essentially, the amount at risk is determined separately for each shareholder, and the amount of the losses of the corporation that are passed through and deductible by the shareholders are not affected by the amount the S corporation has at risk. A shareholder usually is considered at risk with respect to an activity to the extent of cash and the adjusted basis of other property contributed to the electing corporation, any amount borrowed for use in the activity with respect to which the taxpayer has personal liability for payment from personal assets, and the net fair market value of personal assets that secure nonrecourse borrowing.

Hobby Loss Rules.   The hobby loss provisions of § 183 preclude the pass-through of losses to the shareholders when an S corporation is not deemed to be engaged in a trade or business. Thus, if the corporation would have difficulty in establishing that its activities do constitute an active trade or business, its shareholders may be precluded from deducting the full amount of the flow-through loss.

Tax on Preelection Built-in Gains

Because Congress was concerned that certain C corporations would elect S status to avoid the corporate income tax on the sale or exchange of appreciated property (avoiding a tax on such built-in gains), it completely revamped § 1374. A regular corporation converting to S corporation status after 1986 generally incurs a corporate level tax on any built-in gains when an asset is disposed of at a gain by the S corporation in a taxable disposition within 10 years after the date on which the S election took effect.

General Rules.   The tax is applied to any unrealized gain attributable to appreciation in the value of an asset (e.g., real estate, cash basis receivables, goodwill) or other income items while held by the C corporation. The highest corporate tax rate (applicable to that type of income) is applied to the lesser of (1) the recognized built-in gains of the S corporation for the tax year or (2) the amount that would be the taxable income of the corporation for such tax year if it were a

C corporation. Any built-in gain that escapes taxation due to the taxable income limitation is carried forward to future tax years, when it is treated as recognized built-in gain. Thus, given a low or negative taxable income in any year when built-in gain assets are sold, the taxpayer defers the payment of the built-in gains penalty tax liability. The total amount of gain that must be recognized is limited to the aggregate net built-in gains of the corporation at the time of conversion to S status. Thus, it may be advisable to obtain an independent appraisal when converting a C corporation to an S corporation.

EXAMPLE 28   M is a former C corporation whose first S corporation year began on January 1, 1990. At such time, it had two assets: X, with a value of $1,000 and a basis of $400, and Y, with a value of $400 and a basis of $600. Thus, net unrealized built-in gains as of January 1, 1990, are $400. If asset X is sold for $1,000 during 1990, while asset Y is retained, the recognized built-in gain is limited to $400.   □

EXAMPLE 29   Assume the same facts as in Example 28, except that taxable income in 1990 is $300. The new § 1374 tax is assessed only on $300. However, the $100 recognized built-in gain that circumvents the tax in 1990 is carried forward and treated as recognized built-in gain in 1991. There is no statutory limit on the carryforward period, but the gain would effectively expire at the end of the 10-year recognition period applicable to all built-in gains.   □

Gains on sales or distributions of all assets by an S corporation are presumed to be built-in gains unless the taxpayer can establish that the appreciation accrued after the conversion. This § 1374 tax is generally avoided if the S election was made before 1987.[33] The old § 1374 tax may still apply to many grandfathered S corporations in each of the first three S years after the conversion.

To the extent that a tax is imposed on any built-in gain, under § 1366(f)(2), such tax reduces proportionately the amount of any built-in gain to pass through to the shareholder. Post-conversion appreciation is subject to the regular S corporation pass-through rules.

EXAMPLE 30   M Corporation elects S status, effective for calendar year 1989. As of January 1, 1989, one of M Corporation's assets has a basis of $50,000 and a fair market value of $110,000. Early in 1990, the asset is sold for $135,000. M Corporation incurs a realized gain of $85,000, of which $60,000 is subject to the § 1374 penalty tax of 34%. The entire $85,000 gain is subject to the corporate pass-through rules (reduced by the § 1374 tax itself), but only $25,000 of the gain fully bypasses the corporate income tax.   □

Normally, tax attributes of a C corporation do not carry over to a converted S corporation. For purposes of the tax on built-in gains, however, certain carryovers are allowed. An S corporation can offset any gain by related attributes from prior C corporation years, such as unexpired net operating losses or business credit carryforwards.

---

33. § 1362.

EXAMPLE 31   Assume the same facts as in Example 30, except that M also had a $10,000 net operating loss carryover when it elected S status. The NOL reduces M Corporation's built-in gain from $60,000 to $50,000. Thus, only $50,000 is subject to the § 1374 penalty tax. ☐

LIFO Recapture Tax.   When a corporation uses the FIFO method for its last year before making the S election, any built-in gain is recognized and taxed as the inventory is sold. This is not true for a LIFO-basis corporation, unless it invades the LIFO layer during the 10-year period. To preclude deferral of gain recognition under LIFO, the law requires a LIFO recapture amount for an S election made after December 17, 1987.

A C corporation using LIFO for its last year before making an S election must include in income the excess of the inventory's value under FIFO over the LIFO value. The increase in tax liability resulting from LIFO recapture is payable in four equal installments, with the first payment due on or before the due date for the corporate return for the last C corporation year (without regard to any extensions). The remaining three installments must be paid on or before the due dates of the succeeding corporate returns. No interest is due if payments are made by the due dates. The basis of the LIFO inventory is adjusted to take into account this LIFO recapture amount.

EXAMPLE 32   Q Corporation converts from a C corporation to an S corporation for the beginning of 1990. Q used the LIFO inventory method in 1989, with its ending LIFO inventory at $110,000 (with a FIFO value of $190,000). Q must add $80,000 of LIFO recapture amount to its 1989 taxable income, resulting in an increased tax liability of $27,200. Thus, Q must pay one-fourth or $6,800 with its 1989 corporate tax return. The three succeeding installments of $6,800 each must be paid with Q's three succeeding tax returns. ☐

Tax Treatment of Long-Term Capital Gains

An old § 1374 tax may be incurred if a C corporation made a valid S election before 1987. Under old § 1374(a), an S corporation is taxed on capital gains if it meets all of the following requirements: First, the taxable income of the corporation must exceed $25,000. Second, the excess of the net long-term capital gain over the net short-term capital loss must exceed $25,000. Third, this amount must exceed 50 percent of the corporation's taxable income for the year. This penalty tax is the smaller of (1) the alternative capital gain tax rate (34 percent in 1989 and 1990) times the amount of the net capital gain in excess of $25,000 or (2) the regular corporate tax if the corporation were a C corporation. Any tax applied at the corporate level reduces the amount of the long-term capital gain to be passed through to the shareholders.

EXAMPLE 33   An S corporation has four equal shareholders. It is not subject to the new § 1374 penalty tax, and it fails to meet any of the exemptions from old § 1374. For the current year, it has taxable income of $90,000. The corporation also has a $100,000 net long-term capital gain taxable under old § 1374. The capital gains tax at the corporate level is $25,500, and each shareholder would include $18,625 in long-term capital gain, as calculated below:

Corporate level	
Capital gain	$100,000
Exempt amount	−25,000
Tax base	$ 75,000
Capital gain rate	× .34
Old § 1374 tax	$ 25,500
Shareholder level	
Capital gain flow-through	$100,000
Old § 1374 tax	−25,500
Total Schedule K item	$ 74,500
	÷ 4
Each Schedule K–1 amount	$ 18,625

☐

Fringe Benefit Rules

An S corporation cannot deduct its expenditures in providing certain fringe benefits to an employee-shareholder owning more than 2 percent of the stock of the S corporation. The constructive ownership rules of § 318 (refer to chapter 17) are applicable in applying the 2 percent ownership test.[34] Such a shareholder-employee is restricted from receiving the following benefits, among others:

- Excludible group term life insurance.

- The $5,000 death benefit exclusion.

- The exclusion from income of amounts paid for an accident and health plan.

- The exclusion from income of amounts paid by an employer to an accident and health plan.

- The exclusion from income of meals and lodging furnished for the convenience of the employer.

- Workers' compensation payments on behalf of the shareholder-employee.

EXAMPLE 34   P Corporation, an S corporation, pays for the medical care of two shareholder-employees during the current year. T, an individual owning 2% of the stock, receives $1,700 for this purpose. S, an individual owning 20% of the stock, receives $3,100. The $1,700 is deducted as a business expense by P Corporation. The $3,100 paid on behalf of S is not deductible by the corporation because S owns more than 2% of the stock. S can deduct the $3,100 herself, but only to the extent that personal medical expenses are allowable as an itemized deduction under § 213. ☐

Other Operational Rules

Investment Tax Credit.   Although the investment tax credit (ITC) was eliminated as of 1986, S corporations may still have ITC recapture potential. An S election is treated as a mere change in the form of conducting a trade or business

---

34. §§ 1372(a) and (b).

for purposes of ITC recapture. However, an S corporation still continues to be liable for any ITC recapture for Subchapter C taxable years upon early disposition of property.[35] Any premature disposition of the property results in ITC recapture at the shareholder level.

Since the investment in qualified property passes through to the shareholders, recapture falls upon the shareholders when the corporation prematurely disposes of the property (or ceases to use it as ITC property). Recapture may also be required of any shareholder who prematurely disposes (by sale or otherwise) of too much of the stock. Any change in the shareholder's proportionate ownership below 66⅔ percent and 33⅓ percent of original investment triggers proportionate recapture at the shareholder level. The purchaser of the stock is *not* allowed to claim the ITC on the amount of the purchase price of the stock allocated to the ITC property. Since the S corporation is still the user of the ITC property, this may be inequitable, but no ITC is available to the purchaser of the stock.

Oil and Gas Producers.   Oil and gas producers seldom choose S status. The election by a C corporation of Subchapter S is treated as a transfer of oil and gas properties under § 613A(c)(13)(C). Therefore, as of the date of the election, neither the shareholders nor the electing corporation will be allowed to claim percentage depletion on production from proven oil or gas wells.

Miscellaneous Rules.   Other possible effects of various Code provisions on S corporations include the following:

- An S corporation may own stock in another corporation, but an S corporation may not have a corporate shareholder. An S corporation is not eligible for a dividends received deduction.

- An S corporation is not subject to the 10 percent of taxable income limitation applicable to charitable contributions made by a C corporation.

- Foreign taxes paid by an electing corporation will pass through to the shareholders and should be claimed as either a deduction or a credit (subject to the applicable limitations).[36]

- Any family member who renders services or furnishes capital to an electing corporation must be paid reasonable compensation, or the IRS can make adjustments to reflect the value of such services or capital.[37] This rule may make it more difficult for related parties to shift Subchapter S taxable income to children or other family members.

EXAMPLE 35

F and M each own one-third of a fast-food restaurant, and their 14-year-old son owns the other shares. Both parents work full-time in the restaurant operations, but the son works infrequently. Neither parent receives a salary during 1990, when the taxable income of the S corporation is $160,000. The IRS can require that reasonable compensation be paid to the parents to prevent the full one-third of the $160,000 from being taxed to the son. Otherwise, this would be an effective technique to shift earned income to a family member to reduce total family tax burden. With the new procedure for taxing the unearned income of children, this shifting technique becomes much more valuable. □

---

35. § 1371(d).

36. § 1373(a).

37. § 1366(e). In addition, beware of an IRS search

for the "real owner" of the stock, under Reg. § 1.1373–1(a)(2).

- The depletion allowance is computed separately by each shareholder. Each shareholder is treated as having produced his or her pro rata share of the production of the electing corporation, and each is allocated a respective share of the adjusted basis of the electing corporation as to oil or gas property held by the corporation.[38]

- An S corporation is placed on the cash method of accounting for purposes of deducting business expenses and interest owed to a cash basis related party (including a shareholder who owns at least 2 percent of the stock in the corporation).[39] Thus, the timing of the shareholder's income and the corporate deduction must match.

- Although § 1366(a)(1) provides for a flow-through of S items to a shareholder, it does not apply to self-employment income. Thus, a shareholder's portion of S income is not self-employment income and is not subject to the self-employment tax. Compensation for services rendered to an S corporation is, however, subject to FICA taxes.

TAX PLANNING CONSIDERATIONS

Determining When the Election Is Advisable

Effective tax planning with S corporations begins with determining whether the election is appropriate. In light of changes made by the TRA of 1986, a reevaluation of the desirability of using a C corporation as a means of conducting a trade or business should be considered. In this context, one should consider the following factors:

- Are losses from the business anticipated? If so, the S election may be highly attractive because these losses pass through to the shareholders.

- What are the tax brackets of the shareholders? If the shareholders are in high individual income tax brackets, it may be desirable to avoid S corporation status and have profits taxed to the corporation at lower rates (e.g., 15 percent or 25 percent).

- When the immediate pass-through of Subchapter S taxable income is avoided, profits of the corporation may later be taken out by the shareholders as capital gain income through stock redemptions, some liquidating distributions, or sales of stock to others; received as dividend distributions in low-tax-bracket years; or negated by a partial or complete step-up in basis upon the death of the shareholder. On the other hand, if the shareholders are in low individual income tax brackets, the pass-through of corporate profits does not affect the decision so forcefully, and the avoidance of the corporate income tax becomes the paramount consideration. Under these circumstances, the S election could be highly attractive. Although an S corporation usually escapes Federal taxes, it may not be immune from state and local taxes imposed on corporations or from several Federal penalty taxes.

- Does a C corporation have a net operating loss carryover from a prior year? Such a loss cannot be used in an S year (except for purposes of the § 1374 tax).

---

38. § 613A(c)(13).   39. § 267(b).

Even worse, S years count in the 15-year carryover limitation. Thus, even if the S election is made, one might consider terminating the election before the carryover limitation expires. This would permit utilization of the loss by (what is again) a C corporation.

- Both individuals and C corporations are subject to the alternative minimum tax. Many of the tax preference items are the same, but some apply only to corporate taxpayers, while others are limited to individuals. The minimum tax adjustment relating to business untaxed reported profits or accumulated current earnings could create havoc with some C corporations (refer to chapter 14). S corporations themselves are not subject to this tax.

- Some C corporations must convert from the cash method to the accrual method of accounting (refer to chapter 15).

- S corporations and partnerships have lost most of the flexibility in the choice of their accounting period (see also chapter 21).

- By taxing C corporations on nonliquidating and liquidating distributions of appreciated property (refer to chapters 17 and 18), the effect of double taxation is reinforced.

The choice of the form of doing business often is dictated by other factors. For example, many businesses cannot qualify for the S election or would find the partnership form impractical. Therefore, freedom of action based on tax considerations may not be an attainable goal.

Making a Proper Election

Once the parties have decided the election is appropriate, it becomes essential to ensure that the election is made properly.

- Make sure all shareholders consent thereto. If any doubt exists concerning the shareholder status of an individual, it would be wise to have such party issue a consent anyway. Not enough consents will be fatal to the election; the same cannot be said for too many consents.

- Be sure that the election filing is timely and proper. Along this line, either hand carry the election to an IRS office or send it by certified or registered mail. A copy of the election should become part of the corporation's permanent files.

- Regarding the above, be careful to ascertain when the timely election period begins to run for a newly formed corporation. Remember that an election made too soon (before the corporation is in existence) is worse than one made too late. If serious doubts exist concerning when this period begins, more than one election might be considered a practical means of guaranteeing the desired result.

- Because of the § 1374 built-in gains provision, proper tax planning dictates that all corporate properties be appraised on or about the effective date of the S election. With such appraisals in hand, an S corporation can provide evidence as to the appreciation of any assets after the effective date of the election. Especially for inventory items or goods in process on the conversion date, the S corporation has an incentive to maximize the portion of overall gain attributable to the post-conversion period. The corporation must keep records to show the assets that were purchased in a taxable acquisition after the election.

EXAMPLE 36   X Corporation elects S status effective for calendar year 1989. As of January 1, 1990, X Corporation's only asset has a basis of $40,000 and a fair market value of $100,000. If, in 1990, this asset is sold for $120,000, X Corporation recognizes an $80,000 gain, of which $60,000 is subject to the corporate income tax. The other $20,000 of gain is subject to the S corporation pass-through rules and bypasses the corporate income tax. Unless the taxpayer can show otherwise, any appreciation existing at the sale or exchange will be presumed to be preconversion built-in gain. Therefore, X Corporation incurs a taxable gain of $80,000 unless it can prove that the $20,000 gain developed after the effective date of the election. □

Preserving the Election

Recall how an election can be lost and that a five-year waiting period generally is imposed before another S election is available. To preserve an election, the following points should be kept in mind:

- As a starting point, make sure all parties concerned are aware of the various transactions that lead to the loss of an election.

- Watch for possible disqualification as a small business corporation. For example, the divorce of a shareholder, accompanied by a property settlement, could violate the 35-shareholder limitation. The death of a shareholder could result in a nonqualifying trust becoming a shareholder. The latter circumstance might be avoided by utilizing a buy/sell agreement, binding the deceased shareholder's estate to turn in the stock to the corporation for redemption or, as an alternative, to sell it to the surviving shareholders.

- Make sure a new majority shareholder (including the estate of a deceased shareholder) does not file a refusal to continue the election.

- Watch for the passive investment income limitation. Avoid a consecutive third year with excess passive income if a corporation has accumulated Subchapter C earnings and profits. In this connection, assets that produce passive investment income (e.g., stocks and bonds, certain rental assets) might be retained by the shareholders in their individual capacities and thereby kept out of the corporation.

- Do not transfer stock to a nonresident alien.

Planning for the Operation of the Corporation

Operating an S corporation to achieve optimum tax savings for all parties involved requires a great deal of care and, most important, an understanding of the applicable tax rules.

AAA Considerations.   Although the corporate-level accumulated adjustments account (AAA) is used primarily by an S corporation with accumulated earnings and profits from a Subchapter C year, all S corporations should maintain an accurate record of the AAA. Because there is a grace period for distributing the AAA after termination of the S election, the parties must be in a position to determine the balance of the account.

EXAMPLE 37   Y is an S corporation during 1989, with no accumulated earnings and profits from a Subchapter C year. Over the years, no attempt was made to maintain an

accurate accounting for the AAA. In 1990, the S election is terminated, and the entity has a grace period for distributing the AAA tax-free to its shareholders. A great deal of time and expense may be necessary to reconstruct the AAA balance in 1990. ☐

The AAA bypass election may be used to avoid the accumulated earnings tax or personal holding company tax in the year preceding the first tax year under Subchapter S. This bypass election allows the accumulated earnings and profits to be distributed instead.

EXAMPLE 38

Z is an S corporation during 1989, with a significant amount in its accumulated earnings and profits account. The shareholders are subject to low income tax rates for 1990 and expect to terminate the election in that year. Since the new C corporation may be subject to the accumulated earnings penalty tax in 1990, the shareholders may wish to use the AAA bypass election to distribute some or all of the accumulated earnings and profits. Of course, any distributions of the accumulated earnings and profits account in 1989 would be taxable to the shareholders. ☐

A net loss allocated to a shareholder reduces the AAA. This required adjustment should encourage an electing corporation to make annual distributions of net income to avoid the reduction of an AAA by a future net loss.

Salary Structure. The amount of salary that a shareholder-employee of an S corporation is paid can have varying tax consequences and should be considered carefully. Larger amounts might be advantageous if the maximum contribution allowed under the retirement plan has not been reached. Smaller amounts may be beneficial if the parties are trying to shift taxable income to lower-bracket shareholders, lessen payroll taxes, curtail a reduction of Social Security benefits, or reduce losses that do not pass through because of the basis limitation. Many of the problems that do arise in this area can be solved with proper planning. Most often, such planning involves making before-the-fact projections of the tax positions of the parties involved.

The IRS can require that reasonable compensation be paid to family members who render services or provide capital to the S corporation. Section 1366(e) allows the IRS to make adjustments in the items taken into account by family-member shareholders to reflect the value of services or capital provided by such parties.

Loss Considerations. A net loss in excess of tax basis may be carried forward and deducted only by the same shareholder in succeeding years. Thus, before disposing of the stock, one should increase the basis of such stock/loan to flow through the loss. The next shareholder does not obtain the carryover loss.

Any unused carryover loss in existence upon the termination of the S election may be deducted only in the next tax year and is limited to the individual's *stock* basis (not loan basis) in the post-termination year.[40] The shareholder may wish to purchase more stock to increase the tax basis in order to absorb the loss.

The NOL provisions create a need for sound tax planning during the last election year and the post-termination transition period. If it appears that the S corporation is going to sustain a net operating loss or use up any loss carryover,

---

40. § 1366(d)(3).

each shareholder's basis should be analyzed to determine if it can absorb the share of the loss. If basis is insufficient to absorb the loss, further investments should be considered before the end of the post-termination transition year. Such investments can be accomplished through additional stock purchases from the corporation or from other shareholders to increase basis. This action will ensure the full benefit from the net operating loss or loss carryover.

EXAMPLE 39   A calendar year C corporation has a net operating loss in 1989 of $20,000. A valid S election is made in 1990, and there is another $20,000 NOL in that year. At all times during 1990, the stock of the corporation was owned by the same 10 shareholders, each of whom owned 10% of the stock. T, one of the 10 shareholders, has an adjusted basis of $1,800 at the beginning of 1990. None of the 1989 NOL may be carried forward into the S year. Although T's share of the 1990 NOL is $2,000, the deduction for the loss is limited to $1,800 in 1990 with a $200 carryover. ☐

Controlling Adjustments and Preference Items.   The individual alternative minimum tax (AMT) affects more taxpayers because of tax base expansion, the personal exemption phase-out, and a narrowing of the difference between regular tax rates and the individual AMT rate. In an S corporation setting, tax preferences flow through proportionately to the shareholders. In computing the individual AMT, a shareholder treats these preferences as if they were directly realized.

A flow-through of tax preferences can be a tax disaster for a shareholder who is an "almost-AMT" taxpayer. Certain steps can be taken to protect such a shareholder from being pushed into the AMT. For example, a large donation of appreciated property by an S corporation could adversely affect an "almost-AMT" taxpayer. Certain adjustment and preference items are subject to elections that can remove them from the shareholder's AMT computation. Preferences can be removed from a shareholder's AMTI base by the S corporation's electing to capitalize and amortize certain expenditures over a prescribed period of time. These include excess intangible drilling and development expenditures, research and experimental costs, mining exploration and development expenditures, and circulation expenses.

Other corporation choices can protect an "almost-AMT" shareholder. Using the percentage of completion method of accounting (rather than the completed contract method) or the accrual method of tax accounting (rather than the installment method) can be beneficial to certain shareholders. However, many of these decisions and elections may generate conflicts of interest when some shareholders are not so precariously situated and would not suffer from the flow-through of adjustments and tax preference items.

Termination Aspects.   If the shareholders of an S corporation decide to terminate the election through voluntary means, they should make sure that the disqualifying act possesses substance. When the intent of the parties is obvious and the act represents a technical noncompliance rather than a real change, the IRS may be able to disregard it and keep the parties in S status.[41]

Liquidation of an S Corporation.   S corporations are subject to the same liquidation rules applicable to C corporations (refer to chapter 18). The distribu-

---

41. See *Clarence L. Hook,* 58 T.C. 267 (1972).

tion of appreciated property to S shareholders in complete liquidation is treated as if the property were sold to the shareholders in a taxable transaction. Unlike a C corporation, however, the S corporation incurs no tax on the liquidation gains because the gains flow through to the shareholders, subject only to the built-in gains tax of § 1374. Any corporate gain increases the shareholder's stock basis by a like amount, and it reduces any gain realized by the shareholder when he or she receives the liquidation proceeds. Thus, an S corporation usually avoids the double tax that is imposed on C corporations.

PROBLEM MATERIALS

Discussion Questions

1. What are the major advantages and disadvantages of an S election?
2. Which of the following items could be considered to be disadvantageous (or potential hazards) for S elections?
    a. The dividends received deduction is lost.
    b. Foreign tax credit is not available.
    c. Net operating loss at the corporate level cannot be utilized.
    d. Constructive dividends are not actually distributed.
    e. A locked-in AAA occurs after termination.
    f. An AAA is a personal right that cannot be transferred.
    g. Basis in stock is increased by constructive dividends.
    h. A trust is treated as a shareholder.
    i. Salaries of certain shareholders are not high enough.
3. On February 23, 1990, the two 50% shareholders of a calendar year corporation decide to elect to be an S corporation. One of the shareholders had purchased her stock from a previous shareholder on January 18, 1990. Discuss any potential problems.
4. Q is the sole owner of a calendar year S corporation that manufactures water heaters. On March 9, Q realizes that the corporation is going to make a very large profit. Discuss how Q can terminate his corporation's S election.
5. In which of the following situations is a termination of a calendar year S corporation's election effective as of the first day of the following tax year?
    a. A partnership becomes a shareholder on April 2.
    b. There is a failure of the passive investment income limitation.
    c. A new 45% shareholder affirmatively refuses to consent to the S election.
    d. Shareholders owning 57% of the outstanding stock file a formal revocation on February 23.
    e. A fatal second class of stock is issued on March 3.
    f. The electing corporation becomes a member of an affiliated group on March 10.
6. An S corporation recently had its S election involuntarily terminated. Must the corporation wait five years before making a new election?
7. K is considering creating an S corporation for her interior decorating business. She has a friend who has an S corporation with a January 31 fiscal year. She wishes to set up a similar fiscal year. Advise K.
8. In the current year, an S corporation distributes land worth $88,000 to a shareholder. The land cost $22,000 three years ago. Discuss any tax impact on the

corporation or the shareholder from this distribution. The corporation has no accumulated earnings and profits, and the stock basis is $102,000.

9. Y's basis in his S corporation is $5,500, and he anticipates that his share of the net operating loss for this year will be $7,400. The tax year is not closed. Advise Y.

10. How do the new passive loss limitations in § 469 affect an S corporation?

11. One of your clients is considering electing S corporation status. T, Inc., is a six-year-old company with two equal shareholders who paid $30,000 each for their stock. In 1989, T, Inc., has a $90,000 NOL carryforward. Estimated income is $40,000 for 1989 and approximately $25,000 for each of the next three years. Should T, Inc., make an S election for 1989?

Problems

12. An S corporation's profit and loss statement for 1990 shows net profits (book income) of $90,000. The corporation has three equal shareholders. From supplemental data, you obtain the following information about the corporation for 1990:

Selling expense	$11,500
Tax-exempt interest	2,000
Dividends received	9,000
Section 1231 gain	6,000
Section 1245 gain	10,000
Recovery of bad debts	3,400
Capital losses	6,000
Salary to owners (each)	9,000
Cost of goods sold	95,000

   a. Compute Subchapter S taxable income or (loss) for 1990.

   b. What would be one of the shareholders' portion of taxable income (or loss)?

13. P owned 10% of the outstanding stock of a calendar year S corporation. P sold all of his stock to Q on July 1, 1990. At the end of 1990, the total AAA was $800,000 before considering any distributions, and the amount in the accumulated earnings and profits account was $800,000. The S corporation made a distribution of $600,000 to the shareholders on April 1, 1990, which included a distribution of $60,000 to P. On October 1, 1990, another distribution of $600,000 was made to the shareholders, including $60,000 to Q. Determine the amounts taxable to P and Q.

14. A calendar year S corporation has no accumulated earnings and profits in the current year. The corporation makes a cash dividend of $90,000 to Q, an individual shareholder. Q's AAA is $40,000, and the adjusted basis in his stock is $70,000. Determine how this distribution should be taxed.

15. Assume the same facts as in Problem 14, except that Q's share of accumulated earnings and profits is $10,000. Would your answer change?

16. Using the following legend, classify the transaction as a plus (+) or minus (−) on Schedule M on page 4 of Form 1120S:

Legend

PTI	=	Shareholders' undistributed taxable income previously taxed
AAA	=	Accumulated adjustments account
OAA	=	Other adjustments account
NA	=	No direct impact on Schedule M

a. Receipt of tax-exempt interest income.

b. Unreasonable compensation determined.

c. Ordinary income.

d. Distribution of nontaxable income (PTI) from 1981.

e. Nontaxable life insurance proceeds.

f. Expenses related to tax-exempt securities.

g. Charitable contributions.

h. Gifts in excess of $25.

i. Nondeductible fines.

j. Organizational expenses.

17. X, an individual, owns 50% of an S corporation's stock with a basis of $40,000. X receives a corporate distribution of appreciated property with a fair market value of $18,000 (adjusted basis of $4,000). Calculate X's stock basis *after* the property distribution.

18. A calendar year S corporation has AAA of $30,000 and accumulated earnings and profits of $25,000. The corporation distributes land worth $8,000 (adjusted basis of $20,000) to its sole shareholder whose stock basis is $32,000.

a. Discuss all tax aspects, assuming the shareholder holds the land for five months and sells it for $7,500.

b. Assume the land is sold for $8,000 by the S corporation and the cash is distributed to the shareholder. Discuss all tax aspects.

c. Suppose in (a) that the AAA is $5,000.

d. Suppose in (a) that an AAA bypass election is in effect.

19. Form 1120S of an S corporation shows a net loss of $8,200 for 1990. G, an individual, owns 30% of the stock during the year. While auditing the corporate books, you obtain the following information for 1990:

Salaries paid to the three owners	$46,000
Charitable contributions	7,000
Tax-exempt interest	2,000
Dividends received ($6,000 was from a foreign company)	9,000
Section 1231 losses	3,000
Section 1250 gain	20,000
Recoveries of prior property taxes	3,000
Cost of goods sold	66,000
Capital losses	5,000
Advertising expenses	4,200
Long-term capital gains	16,000

a. Compute book income (or loss).

b. If G's tax basis in his stock is $2,100 at year-end, what amount may he deduct in 1990 on his individual tax return?

20. Form 1120S of an S corporation shows taxable income of $80,000 for 1990. P, an individual, owns all of the stock during the year. The corporate books show the following information for 1990:

P's beginning stock basis	$ 3,000
Cash dividends to P	20,000
Tax-exempt interest	3,000
Net sales	191,000
Section 1250 gain	10,000

Section 1231 loss	6,000
Charitable contributions	7,000
Cost of goods sold	72,000
Capital loss	8,000
Overhead expenses	12,000
Long-term capital gain	7,000
Political contributions	2,000
P's loan to S corporation	16,000
P's additional stock purchases	6,000
P's beginning AAA	15,000

    a. Compute P's stock basis at the end of 1990.

    b. Compute P's ending AAA.

21. In the following independent statements, indicate whether the transaction will increase (+), decrease (−), or have no effect (NE) on the adjusted basis of a shareholder's stock in an S corporation:

    a. Tax-exempt income.

    b. Long-term capital gain.

    c. Net operating loss.

    d. Section 1231 gain.

    e. Excess of percentage depletion over the basis of the property.

    f. Separately computed income.

    g. Nontaxable return-of-capital distribution by the corporation.

    h. Charitable contributions.

    i. Business gift in excess of $25.

    j. Section 1245 gain.

    k. Dividends received by the S corporation.

    l. Short-term capital loss.

    m. Recovery of a bad debt.

    n. Long-term capital loss.

22. T owns stock in an S corporation that sustains a net operating loss during 1990. T's share of the loss is $45,000, and her adjusted basis in the stock is $24,000. T also has a $5,000 loan outstanding to the corporation. What amount, if any, is T entitled to deduct with respect to the NOL?

23. A calendar year corporation has a net operating loss in 1989 of $20,000. A valid S election is made in 1990, and again there is a $20,000 NOL. At all times during 1990, the stock of the corporation was owned by the same 10 shareholders, each of whom owned 10% of the stock. If W, one of the 10 shareholders, has an adjusted basis of $1,500 at the beginning of 1990, what amount, if any, may she deduct for 1990?

24. M owns 50% of the stock in an S corporation. The corporation sustains a $12,000 net operating loss and a $4,000 capital loss during 1990. M's adjusted basis in the stock is $4,000, and she has a loan outstanding to the corporation for $3,000. What amount, if any, is M entitled to deduct with respect to these losses for 1990?

25. An S corporation had a net operating loss of $36,600 in 1990. E and B were the equal and only shareholders of the corporation from January 1 to January 21, 1990. On January 21, 1990, E sold his stock to B for $41,000. At the beginning of 1990, both E and B had a basis of $40,000 in the stock of the corporation. (Note: On the date of the sale, stock is regarded as being held by the transferee.)

    a. What amount, if any, of the NOL will pass through to E?

    b. What amount of the NOL will pass through to B?

    c. What gain, if any, will be taxable to E on the sale of his stock?

26. During February 1988, W, Inc., a C corporation, elects to become an S corporation at a time when its building and land are worth $2.2 million. The adjusted basis of the land is $200,000, and the tax book value of the building is $400,000. The company has some securities valued as of February at $260,000 (with an $80,000 cost basis). You are the accountant for a 40% shareholder. What happens at both the corporate and shareholder level in the following events (show calculations)?

    a. In November 1990, W, Inc., moves into a new building and sells the land and old building for $2.3 million (total tax basis of $500,000).

    b. In February 1991, the company sells one-half of the securities for $145,000.

 27. N Corporation elects S corporation status, effective for tax year 1989. As of January 1, 1989, N's assets were appraised as follows:

	Adjusted Basis	Fair Market Value
Cash	$ 16,010	$ 16,010
Accounts receivable	–0–	55,400
Inventory (FIFO)	70,000	90,000
Investment in land	110,000	195,000
Building	220,000	275,000
Goodwill	–0–	93,000

In the following situations, calculate any § 1374 tax, assuming that the highest corporate rate is 34%.

    a. During 1989, N Corporation collects $45,000 of the accounts receivable and sells 80% of the inventory for $96,000.

    b. In 1990, N Corporation sells the land held for investment for $197,000.

    c. In 1996, the building is sold for $310,000.

28. A cash basis S corporation has the following assets and liabilities on January 1, 1990, the date its S election is made.

	Adjusted Basis	Fair Market Value
Cash	$ 200,000	$ 200,000
Accounts receivable	–0–	100,000
Equipment	110,000	100,000
Land	1,800,000	2,500,000
Accounts payable	–0–	110,000

During 1990, the S corporation collects the accounts receivable and pays the accounts payable. The land is sold for $3 million, and the taxable income for the year is $600,000. Calculate any § 1374 penalty tax.

21

PARTNERSHIPS

Overview of Partnership Taxation

Partnerships and S corporations are flow-through operating tax entities in which business income is taxed at the owner level. They are commonly used in activities such as real estate development, property rentals, ship building, movie making, stage play production, computer software development, construction, farming, natural resource mining, and the rendering of services in accounting, dentistry, engineering, medicine, and law.

One reason partnerships and S corporations are used is to avoid the double tax on C corporation income. An S corporation rather than a partnership may be used to limit the owner's ultimate legal liability. When this limitation is needed and the partnership form is desired, a limited partnership may be used.

The recent surge in popularity of partnerships and S corporations can be traced to two major factors. Foremost among these is the owners' opportunity to obtain a lower tax rate. Since the maximum rate for individuals is 28 percent, versus 34 percent for C corporations, the use of a flow-through entity can reduce the applicable tax liability. Moreover, the owners may find that a flow-through entity will facilitate a desire to own passive activity income generators. Taxpayers who invested in tax shelter loss generators were caught short when the passive activity limitation (PAL) rules were enacted. Under the PAL rules, the use of tax shelter losses to offset other income was either curtailed or substantially restricted. To counteract these rules, activities were sought whose positive passive income could offset shelter losses. For new investors, publicly traded limited partnerships that place passive activity income and loss generators under one roof were formed.

Since partnership and S corporation usage is so widespread, a study of related tax problems will prove useful to students, business persons, and consultants. This chapter addresses partnership formations, operations, and nonliquidating distributions. Dispositions of partnership interests, liquidating and disproportionate distributions, optional basis adjustments, and special problems associated with family and limited partnerships are beyond the coverage of this text. Chapter 20 is concerned with S Corporations.

Tax Consequences of Partnership Activities

A partnership is not a taxable entity. Rather, the taxable income or loss of the entity, and any other receipts or expenditures that receive special tax treatment under the Code when they relate to an individual taxpayer, flow through to the partners at the end of the entity's tax year. Each partner receives his or her allocable share of the partnership's ordinary income for the year, and of any other such specially treated items. As a result, the partnership itself pays no Federal income tax on its income, but the partners' own individual tax liabilities are affected by the activities of the entity. For instance, if the partnership enjoys a profitable year and generates ordinary taxable income of $100,000, 25 percent partners must increase their adjusted gross income for the year by $25,000, regardless of the extent of property distributions that they received from the partnership during the year.

EXAMPLE 1   A is a 40% partner in the ABC Partnership. Both A's and the partnership's tax years end on December 31. In 1990, the partnership generates $200,000 of ordinary taxable income. However, because the partnership needs capital for expansion and debt reduction, A makes no cash withdrawals during 1990. He

meets his living expenses by reducing his investment portfolio. A is taxed on his $80,000 allocable share of the partnership's 1990 income, even though he received no property distributions from the entity during 1990. In exchange for the partners' avoidance of double taxation, the Code violates the wherewithal to pay principle with respect to partnerships. ☐

EXAMPLE 2

Assume the same facts as in Example 1, except that the partnership recognizes a 1990 taxable loss of $100,000. A's 1990 adjusted gross income is reduced by $40,000, and his proportionate share of the loss flows through to him from the partnership. He claims a $40,000 partnership loss for the year and reduces his basis in his partnership interest by the same amount. ☐

In allocating the ordinary taxable income of a partnership to the partners, the profit- and loss-sharing ratios that are included in the partnership agreement typically are used. When income flows through to a partner from the entity, his or her basis in the partnership increases accordingly, and when a partner receives the flow-through of a loss, basis is reduced.

Many items of income and expense retain their tax character as they flow through to the partners. Generally, if an item of income or expense could affect a partner's taxable income in a special manner if it retained its character, then such character applies to the partner. The item is withheld from the computation of the entity's ordinary taxable income and is reported separately by the partnership to the partners and to the IRS. All other items are netted at the partnership level before they flow through to the partners.

EXAMPLE 3

B is a 25% partner in the SS Partnership. The cash basis entity collected sales income of $60,000 during 1990, and it spent $15,000 on business expenses in generating such income. In addition, it sold a corporate bond for a $9,000 long-term capital gain. The bond had been contributed by a partner to provide collateral for a loan that the partnership had incurred. When the loan was paid off, the partnership no longer needed the bond. Finally, the partnership made a $1,000 contribution to the local Performing Arts Fund drive. The fund is a qualifying charity. SS and all of its partners use a calendar tax year.

B receives ordinary taxable income from the partnership for 1990 of $11,250 [($60,000 − $15,000) × 25%]. She also receives a flow-through of a $2,250 long-term capital gain and a $250 charitable contribution deduction. The ordinary income increases B's gross income outright, and the capital gain and charitable contribution are combined with her other similar activities for the year as though she had incurred them herself. These items could be treated differently on the individual tax returns of the various partners (e.g., because one of the partners may be subject to a percentage limitation on his or her charitable contribution deduction in 1990), so they are withheld from the computation of ordinary partnership income and flow through to the partners separately. ☐

Other items that are allocated separately to the partners include recognized gains and losses from property transactions; dividend income; tax preferences and adjustments for the alternative minimum tax; expenditures that qualify for the jobs credit and the foreign tax credit; expenses that would be itemized by the partners or other nonbusiness deductions; and other items that are allocated to certain partners by the partnership agreement. If such special allocations are to be

recognized for tax purposes, however, they must have a substantial economic effect aside from the corresponding tax consequences.[1] Finally, partnerships are allowed neither the special corporate dividends received deduction nor the deduction for net operating losses.

EXAMPLE 4   When the GH Partnership was formed, G contributed cash and H contributed some City of Helena bonds that she had held for investment purposes. The partnership agreement allocates all of the tax-exempt interest income from the bonds to H as an inducement for her to remain a partner. This is a special allocation of an item to a partner that is acceptable for income tax purposes because it reflects the differing economic circumstances that underlie the partners' contributions to the capital of the entity. Since H would have received the exempt income if she had not joined the partnership, she can retain such tax-favored treatment via the special allocation.   □

EXAMPLE 5   Assume the same facts as in Example 4. Three years after it was formed, GH purchased some City of Butte bonds. The municipal bond interest income flows through to the partners as a separately stated item, so that it retains its tax-exempt status. However, the partnership agreement allocates all of this income to G because he is subject to a higher marginal income tax bracket than is H. This allocation is not effective for income tax purposes, as it has no substantial economic effect other than the reduction of the partners' income tax liability.   □

Conceptual Basis for Partnership Taxation

The unique tax treatment of partners and partnerships can be traced to two legal concepts that evolved long ago: the *entity concept* and the *aggregate* or *conduit concept*. Both concepts have been used in civil and common law, and their influence can be seen in practically every related tax rule.

Entity Concept.   The entity concept treats partners and partnerships as separate units and gives the partnership its own tax "personality" by (1) requiring a partnership to file an information tax return and (2) treating partners as separate and distinct parties from the partnership in certain transactions between them.

Aggregate or Conduit Concept.   The aggregate or conduit concept treats the partnership as a channel through which income, credits, deductions, etc., flow to the partners for their own tax consideration. Under this concept, the partnership is considered as a collection of taxpayers joined in an agency relationship with one another. Imposition of the income tax on individual partners and the disallowance of certain deductions and tax credits reflect the influence of this doctrine. This same concept has influenced the tax treatment of other pass-through units, such as S corporations (chapter 20) and certain trusts (chapter 26).

Combined Concepts.   Rules that contain a blend of both the entity and aggregate concepts include provisions concerning the formation, operation, and liquidation of a partnership.

---

1.   § 704(b).

What Is a Partnership?

A partnership is an association of two or more persons to carry on a trade or business, with each contributing money, property, labor, or skill, and with all expecting to share in profits and losses. For Federal income tax purposes, a partnership includes a syndicate, group, pool, joint venture, or other unincorporated organization, through which any business, financial operation, or venture is carried on, and which is not otherwise classified as a corporation, trust, or estate. If an association is used for the following purposes, however, it may by election be excluded wholly or partially from the partnership rules:

- Investment motivations, rather than the active conduct of a trade or business.
- Joint production, extraction, or use of property.
- Underwriting, selling, or distributing a specific security issue.

Special Definitions

When a partnership is used to conduct a service business, such as public accounting, law, medicine, etc., very likely it will be a *general partnership*, so that creditors are protected by partnership and partner assets. On the other hand, the *limited partnership* form will likely be used for real estate development activities, so that investors are protected against losses in excess of their investment. Unless special rules apply, only the general partners are liable to creditors. When a limited partnership uses nonrecourse debt to finance the purchase of property and pledges the property as collateral, usually no partner is liable on the debt. *Nonrecourse debt* is debt for which no party is personally liable. Lenders on nonrecourse debt generally require that collateral be pledged against the loan. Upon default, the lender merely recalls the collateral or the secured property, rather than the partners' personal assets.

Throughout this chapter, reference is made to a partner's inside interest basis and outside interest basis. *Inside basis* refers to the partner's share of the adjusted basis of the aggregate partnership assets, as determined from the partnership's tax accounts. *Outside basis* accounts for the actual investment of after-tax dollars that he or she has made in the partnership. Differences between inside and outside basis arise when a partner's interest is sold to another person for more or less than the selling partner's inside basis. The buying partner's outside basis equals the price paid for the interest, but his or her share of the entity's inside basis is derived from historical cost considerations.

EXAMPLE 6

Q purchases a one-fourth interest in the AB Partnership. AB owns one asset, a paid-up office building that it actively manages. AB bought the building for $200,000, and it properly has claimed $120,000 in cost recovery deductions. Q bought into the partnership by paying X, the selling partner, $60,000 in cash.

Because of its attractive location near the interstate highway, the fair market value of the building is now $240,000. Q's *outside basis* in the partnership—the tax basis in the partnership interest that she owns—is $60,000 (her purchase price). Her share of the partnership's *inside basis* in the building is $20,000 (1/4 partnership interest × $80,000 entity's adjusted basis in the building). □

OPERATIONS OF THE PARTNERSHIP

An individual, corporation, trust, estate, or partnership can hold an ownership interest and become a partner. Thus, the income, deductions, credits, and preferences of a partnership can be reported and taxed on any of a number of tax liability returns (e.g., Forms 1040 [individuals], 1041 [fiduciaries], 1120 [C corporations], and 1120S [S corporations]).

A partnership is subject to all other taxes, in the same manner as any other business. Thus, the partnership files returns and pays the outstanding amount of pertinent sales and property taxes, wealth taxes, and unemployment, Social Security, and other payroll taxes. A partnership generally is a tax-reporting, rather than a taxpaying, entity for purposes of its Federal (and state) income tax computations only.

Measuring and Reporting Income

The partnership's Form 1065 organizes and reports the transactions of the entity for the tax year, and each of the partnership's tax items is reported on Schedule K of that return. Each partner, and the IRS, receives a Schedule K-1, on which is reported the partner's allocable share of partnership income, credits, and preferences for the year. The Form 1065 is due on the fifteenth day of the fourth month following the close of the partnership's tax year; for a calendar year partnership, this is April 15.

Income Measurement.   The measurement and reporting of partnership income requires a two-step approach. Certain items must be segregated and reported separately on the partnership return and each partner's Schedule K-1.

Items that are not separately reported are netted at the partnership level. Items passed through separately include the following:

- Partner's share of ordinary income items.
- Short- and long-term capital gains and losses.
- Charitable contributions.
- Portfolio income items (dividends, interest, and royalties).
- Fully and partially tax-exempt interest.
- Immediately expensed tangible personal property.
- Items allocated differently from the general profit and loss ratio.
- Recovery of items previously deducted (tax benefit items).
- AMT preference items.
- Passive activity items (rental real estate income or loss).
- Intangible drilling and development costs.
- Credit items for taxes to foreign countries and U.S. possessions.
- Nonbusiness and personal items (e.g., alimony, medical, and dental).

The reason for separately reporting the preceding items is rooted in the aggregate or conduit concept. Here, items that affect various exclusions, deductions, and credits at the partner level must pass through without loss of identity so that the proper tax for each partner may be determined.

A partnership is not allowed the following deductions:

- Personal exemptions.
- Taxes paid to foreign countries or U.S. possessions.
- Net operating losses.
- Alimony, medical expense, moving expense, and individual retirement savings.
- Depletion of oil and gas interests.

EXAMPLE 7

Z is a one-third partner in the XYZ Partnership. This year, the entity entered into the following transactions:

Fees received	$ 100,000
Salaries paid	30,000
Cost recovery deductions	11,000
Supplies, repairs	3,000
Payroll taxes paid	9,000
Contribution to art museum	5,000
Short-term capital gain recognized	12,000
Net income from passive rental operations	7,000
Dividends received	1,500
City of Albuquerque bond interest received	2,300
AMT adjustment—installment sale	(44,000)
Payment of Y's alimony obligations	4,000

The entity experienced a $20,000 net loss from operations last year, its first year of operations.

The two-step computational process that is used to determine partnership income is applied in the following manner:

Nonseparately Stated Items (Ordinary Income)	
Fee income	$ 100,000
Salary deduction	− 30,000
Cost recovery deductions	− 11,000
Supplies, repairs	− 3,000
Taxes paid	− 9,000
Ordinary income	$ 47,000

Separately Stated Items	
Charitable contributions	$ 5,000
Short-term capital gain	12,000
Passive income	7,000
Portfolio income	1,500
Exempt income	2,300
AMT adjustment—installment sale	(44,000)

Each of the separately stated items passes through proportionately to each partner and is included on the appropriate schedule or netted with similar items that the partner generated for the year. Thus, Z's Form 1040 includes an additional $1,667 charitable contribution, a $4,000 short-term capital gain, a $14,667 adjustment in computing alternative minimum taxable income, and so on, as though Z had generated these items himself. In addition, Z reports $15,667 as his share of the partnership's ordinary income, the combination of the nonseparately stated items.

The partnership is not allowed a deduction for last year's $20,000 net operating loss—this item was passed through to the partners' own income tax returns for the previous year. Moreover, no deduction is allowed for personal expenditures (payment of Y's alimony), and no personal exemption is allowed on the Form 1065. □

Withdrawals.   Capital withdrawals by partners during the year do not affect the partnership's income measuring and reporting process. Such items are treated as distributions made on the last day of the partnership's tax year. Furthermore, when withdrawals exceed the partners' shares of partnership income, the excess may generate additional gross income, unless repayment is required.

Tax Accounting Elections.   The entity concept governs elections by the partnership and its partners. Such elections affect the measurement and reporting of partnership income and loss, the basis of property items, and the avoidance of the partnership rules. Elections related to the following items are made:

By the partnership

- Inventory method.
- Cost or percentage depletion method, excluding oil and gas wells.
- Accounting method (cash, accrual, or hybrid method).
- Capitalizing or expensing of fixed assets.
- Cost recovery methods and assumptions.
- Tax year (when a required year is not followed).
- Amortization of organizational cost and period.
- Amortization of start-up expenditures and period.
- Optional basis adjustments for property.
- Immediate expensing of certain tangible personal property.
- Nonrecognition treatment for involuntary conversion gains.
- Avoidance of partnership rules.

By the partners

- Income from discharge of indebtedness.
- Cost or depletion percentage method for oil and gas wells.
- Deductions and credits for foreign countries and U.S. possessions.

Penalties.   Each partner's share of partnership items should be reported on the partner's individual tax return in the same manner as presented on Schedule K–1, Form 1065. If such reporting is not followed, the IRS must be notified of any

inconsistent treatment. A partnership with 10 or fewer partners, where each partner's share of partnership items is the same for all items, is automatically excluded from this rule. If a partner fails to comply with this requirement because of negligence or intentional disregard of rules or regulations, a negligence penalty may be added to the tax due.

To encourage the filing of a partnership return, a penalty is imposed on the partnership of $50 per month (or fraction thereof), but not to exceed five months, for failure to file a complete and timely information return without reasonable cause. Every general partner is personally liable for the penalty.

Loss Limitations

Partnership losses flow through to the partners for use on their tax returns. However, the amount and nature of the losses that may be used by a partner for tax computational purposes may be limited. When limitations apply, all or a portion of the losses are held in suspension until a triggering condition occurs. At that time, the losses can be used to determine the partner's tax liability.

Overall Limitation.   A partner's deduction of flow-through partnership losses is limited to the adjusted basis of the partner's ownership interest at the end of the partnership year, before considering any losses for that year. Distributions during the year are taken into account before losses are applied against basis.

Losses that cannot be deducted because of this rule are suspended and carried forward for use against future increases in the partner's interest basis. Such increases might result from additional capital contributions, additional debts, or future income.

EXAMPLE 8   C and D do business as the CD Partnership, sharing profits and losses equally. All parties use the calendar year. At the start of the current year, the basis of C's partnership interest is $25,000. The partnership sustained an operating loss of $80,000 in the current year and earned a profit of $70,000 in the next year. For the current year, only $25,000 of C's $40,000 allocable share of the partnership loss (one-half of $80,000 loss) can be deducted. As a result, the basis of C's partnership interest is zero as of January 1 of the following year, and C must carry forward the remaining $15,000 of partnership losses.   □

EXAMPLE 9   Assume the same facts as in Example 8. Since the partnership earned a profit of $70,000 for the next calendar year, C reports net partnership income of $20,000 ($35,000 distributive share of income less the $15,000 carryover loss). The basis of C's partnership interest becomes $20,000.   □

In Example 8, C's entire $40,000 share of the current year partnership loss could have been deducted in the current year if C had contributed an additional $15,000 or more in capital by December 31. If the partnership had incurred additional debt of $30,000 or more by the end of the current year, C's basis would have been increased to permit the loss to be deducted in that year. Thus, if partnership losses are projected for a given year, careful tax planning can ensure their deductibility.

Effects of Loss Limitations.   Several points should be noted about losses and carryover limitations. The first guidepost is the partner's interest basis at year-end

CONCEPT SUMMARY 21–1

Tax Reporting of Partnership Activities

Event	Partnership Level	Partner Level
1. Compute partnership ordinary income.	Form 1065, Line 21, Page 1.	Schedule K–1, (Form 1065), Line 1, Page 1.
	Schedule K, Form 1065, Line 1, Page 3.	Each partner's share is passed through for separate reporting.
		Each partner's basis is increased.
2. Compute partnership ordinary loss.	Form 1065, Line 21, Page 1.	Schedule K–1 (Form 1065), Line 1, Page 1.
	Schedule K, Form 1065, Line 1, Page 3.	Each partner's share is passed through for separate reporting.
		Each partner's basis is decreased.
		The amount of a partner's loss deduction may be limited.
		Losses that may not be deducted are carried forward for use in future years.
3. Separately reported items like portfolio income, capital gain and loss, and immediately expensed amounts for personal property.	Schedule K, Form 1065, Various Lines, Page 3.	Schedule K–1 (Form 1065), Various Lines, Pages 2–3. Each partner's share is passed through for separate reporting.
4. Net earnings from self-employment.	Schedule K, Form 1065, Line 14, Page 3.	Schedule K–1 (Form 1065), Line 14, Page 2.

before considering any losses. Losses that exceed this basis are carried forward indefinitely, awaiting the time when the partner has a positive year-end basis.

Second, the partner's separate limitation rules come into play. These rules may relate to limits on the use of capital, casualty, passive, or portfolio losses to reduce taxable income.

Finally, special at-risk and passive activity limitations may apply. Generally, a partner is at risk to the extent of his or her economic investment in a partnership (adjusted basis of contributed property, cash contributions, debt for which the partner is personally liable or has pledged other property as security, and the earnings share that has not been withdrawn or used to absorb losses). The at-risk and passive activity rules are discussed in chapter 6.

Review Form 1065, reproduced in Appendix B to this text, in light of Concept Summary 21–1.

FORMATION OF A PARTNERSHIP: TAX EFFECTS

Several times in this chapter reference has been made to the partner's basis in his or her partnership interest. A determination of the basis of this asset is critical to an understanding of the tax treatment of partners and partnerships that is included in Subchapter K of the Code. As is the case in several other contexts, including a transfer of assets to a controlled corporation and the treatment of so-called like-kind exchanges, the Code allows a deferral of the recognition of a

gain or loss when the wherewithal to pay principle is violated (if the party receives no cash with which to pay the tax that is generated by the gain). This deferral is implemented, however, by manipulating the basis of the property that the transferor receives in the exchange. If a realized gain is deferred, the basis of the asset that is received by the taxpayer is reduced, and if a realized loss is deferred, the basis of that asset is increased.

Partner's Gain or Loss on Contributions to Entity

When a partner transfers an asset to a partnership, an exchange occurs between two parties. An exchange of this nature is sufficient to trigger the recognition of any increase or decrease in the fair market value of the assets that are transferred to the new entity. Thus, a recognized gain or loss should be produced for the partner.

Generally, however, no such gain or loss is recognized by the partner, relative to a contribution to the capital of the partnership, either when the partnership is formed or subsequent to the creation thereof.[2] Although Congress has related its grounds for this deferral to a belief that the partner's economic status remains unchanged after the assets are placed into the partnership, the rationale for such a deferral is attributable to the wherewithal to pay principle. The partner typically receives no liquid asset when he or she contributes property to a partnership, and payment of a resulting tax could present cash-flow difficulties.

EXAMPLE 10

A transfers two assets to the LM Partnership, on the day that the entity is created, in exchange for a 60% profit and loss interest therein. This 60% partnership interest is worth $60,000. She contributes cash of $40,000 and retail display equipment (basis to her as a sole proprietor, $8,000; fair market value, $20,000). Since an exchange has occurred between two entities, A should recognize a $12,000 gain on this transaction. The gain realized is the fair market value of the partnership interest of $60,000 less the basis of the assets that A surrendered to the partnership [$40,000 (cash) + $8,000 (equipment)].

A's $12,000 realized gain is not recognized by her in the year of contribution, however. Under § 721, such a transfer is exempt from tax. A might have been pressed for cash if she had been required to recognize the $12,000 gain. All that she received from the partnership was an illiquid interest therein; she received no cash with which to pay any resulting tax liability. □

EXAMPLE 11

Assume the same facts as in Example 10, except that the equipment that A contributed to the partnership had an adjusted basis of $25,000. She has a $5,000 realized loss [$60,000 − ($40,000 + $25,000)], but she cannot deduct any portion of this loss. Realized losses, as well as realized gains, are deferred by § 721.

If it were not critical that the partnership receive A's display equipment in lieu of other such property that could be purchased from an outside supplier, A should have sold the equipment to such a supplier, which would have allowed her to deduct a $5,000 loss in the year of the sale. On the day of the sale, then, A could have contributed $60,000 cash (including the proceeds from the sale) for her interest in the partnership. □

---

2. § 721.

EXAMPLE 12   Assume the same facts as in Example 10. Five years after the partnership was created, A contributes another piece of equipment to the entity from her sole proprietorship. This property has a basis of $35,000 and a fair market value of $50,000. A can defer the recognition of this $15,000 realized gain. Section 721 is effective *whenever* a partner makes a contribution to the capital of the partnership.   □

The nonrecognition provisions of § 721 have two exceptions, however. First, if the partner receives the partnership interest without contributing any property to the entity, the fair market value of the related interest is taxable to the partner. In effect, the partner purchases the interest with the (pre-tax) proceeds of the services that he or she rendered in exchange for the ownership rights in the entity.

EXAMPLE 13   When they formed the BCD Partnership, B, C, and D each received a 33⅓% interest in the entity. D became a one-third partner to compensate him for the accounting and tax planning services that he rendered relative to the forma-tion of the partnership. The value of a one-third interest in the partnership (for each of the parties) is $20,000. D must recognize a $20,000 gain with respect to his share of the partnership, probably in the form of consulting fees received. This treatment resembles the results that would occur if the partner-ship had paid D $20,000 for his services and D had immediately contributed that amount to the entity for a one-third ownership interest.   □

Second, when the partner contributes property to the entity, and the other partners assume a liability that is associated with the property, the partner recognizes a gain to the extent of the excess of the partners' new liability over his or her basis in the asset.

EXAMPLE 14   B, C, and D formed the BCD Partnership as equal partners. D contributed a building to the partnership (basis to him, $50,000; fair market value, $200,000). The building is subject to a $180,000 mortgage, which the partner-ship assumed. Since D's partners have, through the partnership arrangement, accepted responsibility for $120,000 of the mortgage (⅔ × $180,000), D must recognize a gain of $70,000 upon the creation of the partnership [$120,000 (liabilities assumed by the entity) − $50,000 (D's basis in the building)].   □

Collapsible Transactions.   The nonrecognition provisions will not apply if the partnership is used to effect a tax-free exchange of assets. For example, two partners in the same partnership have appreciated assets they wish to exchange free of tax. Assume that the assets cannot qualify under any other nonrecognition rules for tax-free treatment (e.g., a like-kind exchange). Each partner contributes his or her appreciated property to the partnership. Then, each receives what is hoped to be a nontaxable distribution of the property contributed by the other. Unless five years pass between the contribution and distribution dates, the IRS will collapse the transactions and require each partner to recognize any realized gain (but not loss) on the assets that he or she contributed. This gain is recognized on the date of the asset distribution.

Investment Companies.   There is another exception to the nonrecognition of gain rule on the contribution of property to a partnership. The contributing

partner must recognize gain realized on the transfer of property to a partnership that would be treated as an investment company if the partnership were incorporated. A partnership will be considered an investment company if, after the transfer, more than 80 percent of the value of its assets (excluding cash and nonconvertible debt obligations) is held for investment and consists of readily marketable stocks or securities. The purpose of this provision is to prevent investors from using the partnership form to diversify their investment portfolios or exchange stocks or securities on a tax-free basis.

Contributed ITC Property.   An early disposal of contributed investment tax credit (ITC) property will trigger the related credit recapture provisions, which are still in effect. However, the ITC is not recaptured by reason of a mere change in the form of conducting the trade or business, as long as the property is retained in such trade or business as ITC property and the taxpayer retains a substantial interest in such trade or business.

Basis of Partnership Interest

The original tax basis of a partnership interest acquired in a § 721 contribution of property to a partnership generally equals the sum of money contributed plus the partner's adjusted basis of any other transferred property. However, if gain is recognized under the investment company rule discussed above, the partner's original interest basis is increased accordingly.

After the partnership begins its trade or business operations, the partner's basis is adjusted almost daily. The most important of these adjustments are (1) an increase in the basis of the interest, to the extent of the net income items that flow through to the partner at the end of the entity's tax year, or a decrease in the interest (but not below zero), to the extent of the net deductible losses that flow through to the partner; and (2) an adjustment to reflect changes in the liabilities of the partnership (basis is increased when partnership liabilities increase, and basis decreases to the extent of any reduction in such partnership debts).

The former adjustment is in accord with the taxability or deductibility of partnership income or losses. Since the partner's share of the entity's income already has been taxed to him or her, basis is increased so that a subsequent distribution from the partnership will not produce another tax. The latter adjustment to the partner's basis is made with respect to *any* form of debt that the partnership accepts during its operation, be it a long-term mortgage or bond or simple trade accounts payable.

Several other adjustments are made to the partners' bases in their ownership interests. (3) Additional capital contributions increase the basis in one's partnership interest, to the extent of the cash and adjusted basis (to the partner) of the noncash assets that are contributed, and withdrawals of capital from the entity reduce basis, but never below zero. (4) Basis is increased by the amount of the partner's share of tax-exempt income that the entity receives, and it is decreased to the extent of the nondeductible expenditures that the partnership makes. Thus, when the exempt income is withdrawn by the partner from the entity, its nontaxable status is retained, via a return of the partner's capital.

EXAMPLE 15	E is a one-third partner in the FM Partnership. On January 1, 1990, E's basis in his partnership interest was $50,000. During 1990, the calendar year, cash basis partnership generated ordinary taxable income of $200,000. It also received $60,000 of interest income from City of Buffalo bonds, and it paid

$2,000 in nondeductible bribes to local law enforcement officials, so that the police would not notify the IRS about the products that the entity had imported without paying the proper $15,000 in tariffs. On July 1, 1990, E contributed $20,000 cash and a computer (zero basis to him) to the partnership. E's monthly draw from the partnership is $3,000; this is not a guaranteed payment. The only liabilities that the partnership has incurred are trade accounts payable. On January 1, 1990, there were $45,000 of such liabilities; this account included $21,000 on January 1, 1991.

E's basis in the partnership on December 31, 1990, is $112,000 [$50,000 (beginning balance) + $66,667 (share of ordinary partnership income) + $20,000 (share of exempt income) − $667 (share of nondeductible expenditures) + $0 (basis to E of additional noncash capital contribution) + $20,000 (additional cash contributions to partnership capital) − $36,000 (capital withdrawal) − $8,000 (share of net decrease in partnership liabilities)]. □

EXAMPLE 16   Assume the same facts as in Example 15. If E withdraws cash of $112,000 from the partnership on January 1, 1991, the withdrawal reduces his basis to zero. He has recognized his share of the partnership's corresponding income throughout his association with the entity, via the annual flow-through of his share of the partnership's income and expense items. In addition, the $20,000 municipal bond interest retains its nontaxable character in this distribution. E receives such assets as a part of his capital withdrawal because his basis was increased in 1990 when the partnership received the interest income.

Review the pertinent corresponding sections of chapter 17. When a corporation receives tax-exempt income, the receipts are excluded from its gross income, but the earnings and profits account is increased by the amount of such income. Accordingly, when the interest is distributed to the shareholders, a taxable dividend results. □

The flow-through of partnership losses reduces the partner's basis to, but not below, zero. To the extent that such losses cannot be deducted by the partner, they can be carried forward to a subsequent year and deducted when the partner has generated some basis to be reduced by the deductible loss. There is no time limit on this carryforward of the partner's excess losses, but from a present-value standpoint, unnecessary delays in the use of these deductions should be avoided.

Figure 21–1 summarizes the application of these rules in computing a partner's interest basis.

Partnership Basis in Contributed Assets

When a partner contributes an asset to the capital of a partnership, the entity assigns a carryover basis to the property. The entity's basis in the asset is equal to that which the partner held in the property prior to its transfer to the partnership. This basis is increased by the amount of any gain that the partner recognized as a result of the formation of the partnership. Thus, two assets are created out of one when a partnership is formed, namely, the property in the hands of the new entity and the new asset (the partnership interest) in the hands of the partner. Both assets are assigned a basis that is derived from the partner's existing basis in the contributed property.

No step-up in the basis of the asset, perhaps to fair market value, is allowed relative to the partnership's cost recovery deductions or its subsequent computa-

FIGURE 21–1   Partner's Basis in Partnership Interest

Inside Basis	**Outside Basis**
Original contribution that created the partnership interest (including share of partnership debt)	Price paid for interest as an original contribution to the partnership or to a partner or former partner (including share of partnership debt) or gift or inherited basis
+ Since interest acquired, partner's share of partnership's	+ Since interest acquired, partner's share of partnership's
• Debt increase	• Debt increase
• Income items	• Income items
• Exempt income items	• Exempt income items
• Excess of depletion deductions over adjusted basis of property subject to depletion	• Excess of depletion deductions over adjusted basis of property subject to depletion
+ Partner's contributions	+ Partner's contributions
± Optional basis adjustments*	
− Since interest acquired, partner's share of partnership's	− Since interest acquired, partner's share of partnership's
• Debt decrease	• Debt decrease
• Loss items	• Loss items
• Nondeductible items not chargeable to a capital account	• Nondeductible items not chargeable to a capital account
• Special depletion deduction for oil and gas wells	• Special depletion deduction for oil and gas wells
− Partner's distributions and withdrawals	− Partner's distributions and withdrawals

The basis of a partner's interest can never be negative.

*Optional basis adjustments are not covered in this text. See chapter 8 of *West's Federal Taxation: Corporations, Partnerships, Estates, and Trusts* (1991 edition).

tion of gain or loss realized upon the disposition of the asset. Typically, the partnership merely continues with the same cost recovery method that the partner had been using.

The holding period for the contributed asset also carries over to the partnership. Thus, the partnership's holding period for the asset includes the period during which the partner owned the asset individually.

EXAMPLE 17   G contributed some machinery to the WM Partnership in exchange for a one-third partnership interest. The machinery had a basis to her of $20,000. Its fair market value, and that of the partnership interest, was $35,000. G's basis in the partnership interest is $20,000, and the entity's basis in the machinery is also $20,000. □

EXAMPLE 18   Assume the same facts as in Example 17, except that the asset that G contributed to the partnership was a painting. The painting is a capital asset to both G and the partnership. G had purchased the painting six years ago

from the artist. Since G's holding period relative to the asset carries over to the partnership, the painting is a long-term capital asset to the entity from the first day of its operations. □

Depreciation Method and Period.   Although the contributing partner's property basis and holding period carry over to the partnership, the transfer of certain depreciable property could result in unfavorable tax consequences to the partnership. For instance, a partnership is not allowed to expense immediately any part of the cost of § 179 property that it receives from the transferor partner. In addition, a partnership is prohibited from using an accelerated cost recovery method or holding period that differs from that of the transferor partner.

Receivables, Inventory, and Losses.   To prevent the conversion of ordinary income into capital gain, gain or loss is treated as ordinary if it occurs on the disposal of either of the following:

• Contributed receivables that were unrealized in the (cash basis) contributing partner's hands at the contribution date. Such receivables include the right to receive payment for goods or services delivered (or to be delivered) at the contribution date. The cash basis contributing partner would not have reported income arising from the receivables.

• Contributed property that was inventory in the contributor's hands on the contribution date, *when the disposal occurs within five years of this date.* Inventory includes all property except capital and § 1231 assets.

To prevent the conversion of a capital loss into an ordinary loss, capital treatment is assigned to a loss on the disposal of the following:

• Contributed property that was capital loss property in the contributor's hands on the contribution date, *when the disposal occurs within five years of this date.*

EXAMPLE 19   T operates a cash basis retail electronics and television store as a sole proprietor. R is an enterprising individual who likes to invest in small businesses. On January 2 of the current year, T and R form the TR Partnership. Their partnership contributions are as follows:

	Adjusted Basis	Fair Market Value
From T:		
Receivables	$ –0–	$ 2,000
Land used as parking lot*	1,200	3,000
Inventory	2,500	5,000
From R:		
Cash	10,000	10,000

*Parking lot had been held for five months at contribution date.

Within 30 days of forming the partnership, TR collects the receivables and sells the inventory for cash. It uses the land for the next 10 months as a parking lot, then sells it for $3,500 cash. TR realized the following income in the current year from these transactions:

- Ordinary income of $2,000 from collecting receivables.

- Ordinary income of $5,000 from sale of inventory.

- § 1231 gain of $2,300 from sale of land.

The land takes a carryover holding period. Thus, it is classified as long term at the sale date. □

EXAMPLE 20   Assume the same facts as Example 19, except for the following:

- The land contributed by T was held for investment and had a fair market value of $800 at the contribution date.

- TR used the land as a parking lot for 11 months and sold it for $650.

TR realizes the following income and loss from these transactions:

- Ordinary income of $2,000 from collecting receivables.

- Ordinary income of $5,000 from sale of inventory.

- Capital loss of $400 from sale of land.

- § 1231 loss of $150 from sale of land.

Since the land was sold within five years of the contribution date, $400 of the realized loss is a capital loss. The remaining loss of $150 is a § 1231 loss since TR used the property in its business. □

Concept Summary 21–2 summarizes the operation of the rules that apply to partnership asset contributions and basis adjustments.

CONCEPT SUMMARY 21–2

Partnership Formation and Basis Computation

1. The *entity concept* treats partners and partnerships as separate units. The nature of gains and losses is determined at the partnership level.

2. The *aggregate concept* is used to connect partners and partnerships. It allows income, gains, losses, credits, deductions, etc. to flow through to the partners for separate tax reporting.

3. Sometimes both the *aggregate* and *entity* concepts apply, but one usually dominates. When land used as a parking lot is sold for a gain within five years of its contribution date, and the land was held by the contributing partner as inventory, the resulting gain is ordinary.

4. Generally, gain or loss is not recognized by partners or partnerships when property is contributed for capital interests. Gain could be recognized when excessive debt is contributed with the property.

5. Partners contributing property for partnership interests generally take the contributed property's adjusted basis for their *inside basis* and *outside basis*.

6. The holding period of a partner's interest includes that of contributed property when the property was a § 1231 asset or capital asset in the partner's hands. If not, the holding period starts on the day the interest is acquired. The holding period of an interest acquired by a cash contribution starts at acquisition.

7. Contributed property generally takes a carryover adjusted basis.

8. The partnership's holding period for contributed property includes the contributing partner's holding period.

DISTRIBUTIONS FROM THE PARTNERSHIP

The previous sections of this chapter introduced the tax treatment of distributions from a partnership to its partners. This section will expand that discussion by addressing the allocation of such distributions that are incurred in the course of the normal operations of the partnership. Distributions to partners that are in complete liquidation of their ownership interests are not discussed in this text. See chapter 8 of *West's Federal Taxation: Corporations, Partnerships, Estates, and Trusts* (1991 edition).

A partner annually recognizes all of his or her share of the taxable income or loss of the partnership via the flow-through of such items in proportion to the partner's ownership interest. As a result, distributions of assets from the entity generally are not taxable to the recipients. Rather, just as the flow-through of a pro rata share of partnership income increased the partner's basis in the entity, subsequent nonliquidating distributions of partnership assets to the partner are nontaxable and reduce his or her basis in the interest.

EXAMPLE 21   J is a one-fourth partner in the SP Partnership. His basis in the ownership interest is $40,000 on January 1, 1990. The partnership distributes $25,000 cash to him on January 2, 1990. This distribution is not taxable to J. It reduces his basis in the partnership to $15,000. □

When noncash property is distributed to a partner, the entity generally does not recognize any of its realized gain or loss on the asset at the date of the distribution. However, just as the partnership is assigned a carryover basis when a partner contributes property to it, the partner assumes the entity's basis in an asset that he or she receives in a distribution from the partnership. Thus, following the wherewithal to pay principle, any realized gain or loss is deferred until the asset is sold or exchanged in a manner that generates cash with which to pay the applicable tax liability.

EXAMPLE 22   Assume the same facts as in Example 21, except that the partnership distributes to J some land with a $25,000 fair market value. The entity has a $13,000 basis in the land at the date of the distribution. J receives the land tax-free, and the partnership does not recognize its $12,000 realized gain thereon. However, J reduces his partnership basis by $13,000 (the entity's basis in the asset) and assigns a $13,000 basis to the land when he receives it. If J sells the land on January 13, 1990, for its $25,000 fair market value, he then recognizes the $12,000 realized gain that accrued while the land was held by the partnership. □

A problem arises when the partner's basis in his or her ownership interest is insufficient to allow a full allocation of the partnership's carryover basis to the distributed property. Since a distribution cannot reduce the partner's basis in the interest below zero, the basis of the property that is received is limited to the existing basis in the interest. When nonliquidating distributions to a partner exceed his or her basis in the partnership interest, such basis is allocated among the distributed assets according to the relative adjusted bases of the assets in the hands of the partnership.

In this procedure basis first is assigned to any cash that is received by the partner. The partner recognizes gross income from a nonliquidating distribution only to the extent that the cash that he or she has received exceeds the basis of his or her partnership interest. Following the wherewithal to pay principle, however, the partner recognizes no gain from such a distribution in the absence of this excess of cash received over the basis in the entity. By adopting a carryover basis approach to this procedure, any deferred gain that was realized by the partnership will be recognized by the partner upon the sale or taxable exchange of the distributed asset.

EXAMPLE 23   K is a one-third partner in the SF Partnership. Her basis in this ownership interest is $50,000 on December 31, 1990, after accounting for the calendar year entity's 1990 operations and for K's 1990 capital contributions and withdrawals. On December 31, 1990, the partnership distributes $60,000 cash to K. K must recognize a $10,000 gain from this distribution by the partnership ($60,000 cash received − $50,000 basis in her partnership interest). Most likely, this distribution from the entity will be recognized by K as a capital gain.[3] □

EXAMPLE 24   Assume the same facts as in Example 23, except that the partnership distributes cash of $12,000 and land (basis to the entity $20,000; fair market value $45,000) to K. Although she realizes a $7,000 gain as a result of this distribution [$57,000 amount realized ($12,000 cash + $45,000 fair market value of the land) − $50,000 adjusted basis of the partnership interest], K recognizes no gross income therefrom.

The $12,000 cash is employed first, to reduce K's basis in the partnership. Second, the partnership's $20,000 adjusted basis in the land is allocated to K, and her basis in the partnership is reduced accordingly. Thus, her basis in the ownership interest is $18,000 on January 1, 1991 ($50,000 beginning balance − $12,000 basis assigned to the cash distribution − $20,000 basis assigned to the noncash asset). If K sells the land to a third party early in 1991 for its $45,000 fair market value, she will recognize the gain that had accrued during the period the partnership owned the asset ($45,000 sales proceeds − $20,000 substituted basis in the land). □

EXAMPLE 25   Assume the same facts as in Example 24, except that the partnership also distributes to K two parcels of land. One of these parcels had a basis to the partnership of $15,000, and the entity's basis in the other was $45,000. The fair market value of each parcel was $50,000. Since the $12,000 cash that K received in the distribution does not exceed her basis in the partnership interest, she need recognize none of the $62,000 gain that she realized on the transfer ($112,000 amount realized − $50,000 basis in the partnership interest).

K first assigns a $12,000 basis to the cash that she received from the partnership. Her remaining $38,000 basis in the entity is allocated, in full, to

---

3. § 731(a). Depending upon the composition of the partnership's assets, however, the $10,000 gain could be recognized as ordinary income. See §§ 741 and 751.

CONCEPT SUMMARY 21-3

Nonliquidating Distributions

1. Generally, no gain or loss is recognized on a nonliquidating (current) distribution that is proportional as to assets of the partnership. However, if the distributed cash exceeds the partner's outside basis, gain is recognized.

2. Distributed property usually takes the same basis that it had to the partnership. With respect to a current distribution where the adjusted basis of distributed property exceeds the partner's outside basis (and ordinary income assets are not present), the basis is allocated among the assets.

the two parcels of land, so that K's basis in the partnership on January 1, 1991, is zero. She assigns bases to the land parcels pro rata to their adjusted bases in the hands of the partnership (and *not* according to their relative market values). Thus, the former parcel of land receives a $9,500 basis in K's hands [$38,000 basis to be allocated to the parcels × ($15,000 basis to the partnership of the first parcel ÷ $60,000 basis to the partnership of both parcels)]. K assigns a $28,500 basis to the latter parcel [$38,000 × ($45,000 ÷ $60,000)].

If K were to sell both of the parcels early in 1991 at their fair market values, she would receive sales proceeds of $100,000. Thus, she would recognize all of the $62,000 gain that she deferred upon receiving the property from the partnership [$100,000 amount realized − $38,000 adjusted basis in the two parcels ($9,500 + $28,500)]. □

EXAMPLE 26

Review the tax results of Examples 24 and 25. Although K need recognize none of the gain that she realizes from the distributions, she has been assigned a low or zero basis in the partnership interest. This basis adjustment is not attractive to K if she anticipates that the partnership will be generating net losses in the near future. Since her tax basis in the entity is zero, she will be unable to deduct her share of such losses when they flow through to her on the last day of the partnership's tax year.

The low basis that K has assigned to the parcels of land are of no tax detriment to her if she does not intend to sell the land in the near future. Since land does not generate cost recovery deductions, the substituted basis will be used only to determine K's gain or loss upon her disposition of the asset in a taxable sale or exchange. □

Concept Summary 21-3 summarizes the rules that apply to nonliquidating partnership distributions.

OTHER MATTERS

Transactions between Partner and Partnership

Guaranteed Payments.   When a partner makes a voluntary withdrawal from the partnership, no taxable income results to the partner. Such a distribution is treated as a recovery of the capital that the partner previously had contributed, after paying taxes thereon, to the entity. Thus, the partner's basis is decreased by the amount of cash (or by the partnership's basis in the distributed asset) that was

withdrawn. The partner must pay tax on the income of the partnership when it is earned, even if it is not distributed to him or her. Thus, if a tax were levied on asset withdrawals of this sort, a true form of double taxation on the income of the partnership would result.

Some distributions to a partner resemble a salary, however. Guaranteed payments are those distributions to partners that are computed without regard to the income or other activities of the entity. For instance, if the amount of a distribution is a fixed dollar amount, or if it is expressed as a percentage of the capital that the partner has invested in the partnership, it is a guaranteed payment.

EXAMPLE 27

P, R, and S formed the PRS Partnership in 1984. According to the partnership agreement, P is to receive a $21,000 distribution from the entity every year, payable in 12 monthly installments. R is to receive an amount that is equal to 18% of his capital account, as it is computed by the firm's accountant at the beginning of the year, payable in 12 monthly installments. S is the partnership's advertising specialist. He withdraws 3% of the partnership's gross sales every month for his personal use. P and R have received guaranteed payments from the partnership, but S has not. ☐

Guaranteed payments resemble the salary, interest, or rental expense payments of other businesses and receive similar treatment under partnership tax law.[4] Thus, in contrast to the provision that usually applies to withdrawals of assets by partners from their partnerships, guaranteed payments are deductible by the entity, and, on the last day of the partnership's tax year, the recipients must report such income separately from their usual partnership distributions.

EXAMPLE 28

Continue with the situation that was introduced in Example 27. For calendar year 1990, P received the $21,000 that was provided by the partnership agreement, R's guaranteed payment for 1990 was $18,000, and S withdrew $20,000 under his personal expenditures clause. Before considering these amounts, the partnership's ordinary income for 1990 was $650,000.

The partnership can deduct its payments to P and R, so the final amount of its 1990 ordinary income is $611,000 ($650,000 − $21,000 − $18,000). Thus, each of the equal partners is allocated $203,667 of ordinary partnership income for their 1990 individual income tax returns ($611,000 ÷ 3). In addition, P must report $21,000 of salary income, and R must include the $18,000 interest in his 1990 gross income. S's partnership draw is deemed to have come from his allocated $203,667 (or from the accumulated partnership income that was taxed to him in prior years) and is not taxed separately to him. ☐

EXAMPLE 29

Assume the same facts as in Example 28, except that S's withdrawals total $1,000, and ordinary partnership income (before considering the partners' distributions) was $30,000. The deductions for the guaranteed payments reduce the final ordinary income of the partnership to a $9,000 loss ($30,000 − $21,000 − $18,000). Thus, P's 1990 individual income tax return includes her $21,000 salary and the $3,000 partnership loss. R's gross income includes the $18,000 interest and his

---

4. § 707(c).

allocable $3,000 partnership loss. S's return merely includes his $3,000 share of the partnership loss. Guaranteed payments, like any other deductible expenses of a partnership, can create an ordinary loss for the entity. In this manner, the partners can allocate a higher or lower proportion of the tax benefits among them. □

EXAMPLE 30

Assume the same facts as in Example 27, except that the partnership's tax year ends on March 31, 1991. The total amount of the guaranteed payments is taxable to the partners on that date. Thus, even though 9 of P's 12 payments for fiscal 1990 were received in calendar 1990, all of her salary is recognized in 1991. Similarly, all of R's interest income is taxable to him in 1991 and not when it is received. The deduction for, and the gross income from, guaranteed payments are allowed on the same date that all of the other income and expense items relative to the partnership are allocated to the partners (on the last day of the entity's tax year). □

Gain or Loss between Partner and Entity.   Some types of transactions between partners and their partnership are scrutinized closely by the IRS because of the possibility that the transactions are not conducted at arm's length. Thus, whenever possible, the partner who conducts business with the partnership should document the transaction completely, providing for adequate consideration and valid debt or sale agreements, so that the IRS's suspicions can be quelled, if necessary. The disallowance of realized losses between related parties applies to such transactions, however, when the partner controls a greater than 50 percent capital or profits interest in the partnership. In accordance with the § 267 provisions, though, the purchaser may use the disallowed loss to offset the subsequent gain that is recognized when the asset is sold to an unrelated party.

EXAMPLE 31

W sells land (adjusted basis to him, $30,000; fair market value, $45,000) to a partnership in which he controls a 60% capital interest. The partnership pays him $20,000 for the land. W's $10,000 realized loss is not deductible by him. The sale apparently was not at arm's length, but the taxpayer's intentions are irrelevant. W and the partnership are related parties, and the loss is disallowed.

When the partnership sells the land to an outsider at a later date, it receives a sales price of $44,000. The partnership can offset the recognition of its realized gain on the subsequent sale ($44,000 sales proceeds − $20,000 adjusted basis = $24,000) by the amount of the prior disallowed loss ($30,000 − $20,000 = $10,000). Thus, it recognizes a $14,000 gain on its sale of the land. □

Using a similar rationale, any gain that is realized on a sale or exchange between a partner and a partnership in which the partner controls a capital or profit interest of 50 percent or more must be recognized as ordinary income, unless the asset is a capital asset in the hands of the purchaser.

EXAMPLE 32

Z purchases some land (adjusted basis, $30,000; fair market value, $45,000) from a partnership in which he controls a 90% profit interest, for $45,000. The land was a capital asset to the partnership. If the land is held for investment purposes by Z, the partnership recognizes a $15,000 capital gain. However, if Z is a land developer and the property is not a capital asset to him, the

partnership must recognize $15,000 ordinary income from the same sale, even though the property was a capital asset to the entity. □

Partners as Employees.   A partner generally does not qualify as an employee for tax purposes. Thus, a partner receiving guaranteed payments will not be regarded as an employee for purposes of withholding taxes or for qualified pension and profit sharing plans.

Close of Final Tax Year

When does a partnership's final tax year end? Technically, it ends when the partnership terminates, which is either of the following events:

* No part of the business continues to be carried on by any of the partners in a partnership.

* Within a 12-month period, there is a sale or exchange of 50 percent or more of the partnership's capital and profits.

A partnership's tax year generally does not close upon the death of a partner; the entry of a new partner; or the liquidation, sale, or exchange of an existing partnership interest. In the case of the sale or liquidation of an entire interest, the partnership's tax year closes only for the partner who disposed of the partnership interest. Additionally, the taxable year of the partnership closes for a deceased partner if there is a buy-sell agreement among the partners under which the partner's interest is immediately sold to the remaining partners for a formula or fixed price on the date of death.

Such an agreement is not without problems. If the deceased partner owned 50 percent or more of the total interest in capital and profits, the entire partnership would terminate when the interest is sold. Termination also occurs under the buy-sell agreement if the deceased partner's interest in capital and profits, when added to the other interests sold or exchanged within a 12-month period, equals or exceeds 50 percent of total capital and profits interests.

An unplanned close of the partnership's tax year should be avoided because of the bunching problem (partnership income from more than 12 months being included in one taxable year).

EXAMPLE 33   Partner R, who held a one-third interest in the RST Partnership, died on November 20 of the last calendar year. The partnership uses an approved fiscal year ending September 30. R used a calendar year. The partnership agreement does not contain a buy-sell provision that is triggered upon the death of a partner. Thus, the partnership's tax year does not close with R's death. Instead, income from the fiscal year ending September 30 of the current calendar year will be taxed to R's estate or other successor. Income from the fiscal year ending September 30 of the last year must be reported on R's final income tax return, which covers the period from January 1 to November 20.

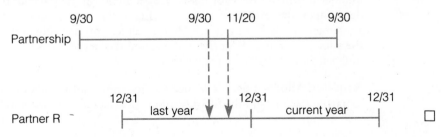

CONCEPT SUMMARY 21–4

Partner/Partnership Transactions and Close of Partnership Year

1. Partners can transact business with their partnerships in a nonpartner capacity. These transactions include such things as the sale and exchange of property, rentals, etc.

2. Losses are disallowed between a partner or related party and a partnership when the partner or related party owns more than a 50 percent interest in the partnership's capital or profits. When there is income from a related sale, it is ordinary if the property is a capital asset to the transferor, but not to the transferee.

3. Guaranteed payments to partners generally are deductible to the partnership in determining the partnership's taxable income (ordinary income) and includible in the receiving partner's gross income for the partnership year that ends with or within the partner's tax year under the partnership's method of accounting.

4. A partnership's final tax year closes when no part of the business continues to be carried on by any of the partners in a partnership or when, within a 12-month period, there is a sale or exchange of 50 percent or more of the total interests in capital and profits.

5. Generally, the partnership tax year of a deceased partner does not close with the partner's death. If the partners have a formula or fixed price buy-sell agreement to purchase the deceased partner's interest at death, the partnership's tax year could close.

EXAMPLE 34   Assume the same facts as in Example 33, except that the partnership agreement contained a buy-sell provision that triggered the sale of R's interest to the remaining partners for a fixed price at his or her death. Although R's death will not affect the surviving partners, it will close the partnership's tax year for R. Thus, R's final income tax return for the last calendar year must include R's share of partnership income both for the fiscal year ending September 30 of last year and for the period from October 1 to R's death. □

Special Allocations of Income

A partner's distributive share of partnership items is determined by the partnership agreement. This agreement may provide different ratios for sharing items. However, retroactive allocations to partners according to their interests at year-end are not permitted. When there is a change in any partner's ownership interest during the year, the partnership can use an allocation method that takes into account the varying interests of the partners. Partnerships that do not use an interim closing but prorate partnership items are required to use a daily convention.

Substantial Economic Effect.   If the partnership agreement does not provide for determining a partner's distributive share of income, gain, loss, deduction, or credit, or an allocation lacks substantial economic effect, a partner's share is determined in accordance with the partner's interest in the partnership. The manner in which profits or losses are recorded on the partnership books generally determines the profit and loss sharing ratios in the absence of a partnership agreement. In determining whether an allocation has substantial economic effect, the allocation must affect the dollar amount of a partner's share of income or loss, independent of the tax consequences.

Required Allocations.   A special allocation that results in shifting tax benefits to partners who can take full advantage of selected items would be subject to close

IRS scrutiny. However, allocations of income, gain, loss, and deductions with respect to contributed property are required to mitigate inequities that might arise because of the differing nature of the property.

EXAMPLE 35

M and X formed an equal profit and loss sharing partnership on January 1 of the current year. M contributed cash of $10,000, and X contributed land purchased two years ago and held for investment. The land had adjusted basis and fair market value at the contribution date of $6,000 and $10,000, respectively. For accounting purposes, the partnership recorded the land at its fair market value of $10,000. For tax purposes, the partnership took a carryover basis in the land of $6,000. After using the land as a parking lot for five months, MX sold it for $10,600. Assume no other transactions took place. The accounting and tax gain from the land sale are computed as follows:

	Accounting	Tax
Amount realized	$10,600	$10,600
Adjusted basis	10,000	6,000
Gain realized	$ 600	$ 4,600
Gain to X at contribution date	–0–	4,000
Remaining gain (split equally)	$ 600	$ 600

M recognizes $300 of the gain ($600/2), and X recognizes $4,300 [$4,000 + ($600/2)]. □

Organization and Syndication Costs

Amounts paid or incurred to organize a partnership or promote the sale of a partnership interest are not deductible. However, the Code permits a ratable amortization of some of these costs.[5]

Organization Costs.   By election, organization costs may be amortized ratably over a period of 60 months or more, starting with the month in which the partnership began business. The election must be made by the due date (including extensions) of the partnership return for the year it began business.

Organizational costs include expenditures that are (1) incident to the creation of the partnership; (2) chargeable to a capital account; and (3) of a character that, if incident to the creation of a partnership with an ascertainable life, would be amortized over such a life. These expenditures include accounting fees and legal fees incident to the partnership's organization. To be amortizable, such expenditures must be incurred within the period that starts a reasonable time before the partnership begins business. The period ends with the due date (without extensions) of the tax return for that beginning year.

Cash method partnerships are not allowed to deduct *in the year incurred* the portion of such expenditures that are paid after the beginning year's end. The portion of such expenditures that would have been deductible in a prior year, if paid before that year's end, is deductible in the year of payment.

---

5.   § 709.

Expenditures related to the following items are not organization costs:

- Acquiring assets for the partnership.
- Transferring assets to the partnership.
- Admitting partners, other than at formation.
- Removing partners, other than at formation.
- Negotiating operating contracts.
- Syndication costs.

EXAMPLE 36   The ABC Partnership was formed on May 15 of the current year and immediately started business. ABC uses a calendar tax year. ABC incurred $720 in legal fees for drafting the partnership agreement and $480 in accounting fees for tax advice of an organizational nature. The legal fees were paid in October of the current year. The accounting fees were paid in January of the following year. The partnership selected the cash method of accounting and elected to amortize its organization costs.

On its first tax return, ABC deducts $96 of organization costs [($720 legal fees/60 months) × 8 months]. No deduction was taken for the accounting fees since they were paid the following year. On its tax return for next year, ABC deducts organization costs of $304 {[($720 legal fees/60 months) × 12 months] + [($480 accounting fees/60 months) × 20 months]}. The $64 of accounting fees [($480/60) × 8] that could have been deducted on ABC's first tax return if paid by that year's end are deducted on the return for the second year.   □

Syndication Costs.   Unlike organization costs, syndication costs are capitalized without an amortization election. Such costs include the following expenditures incurred for promoting and marketing partnership interests:

- Brokerage fees.
- Registration fees.
- Legal fees related to the underwriter, placement agent, and issuer (general partner or the partnership) for security advice or advice on the adequacy of tax disclosures in the prospectus or placement memo for securities law purposes.
- Accounting fees related to offering materials.
- Printing costs of prospectus, placement memos, and other selling materials.

Fees for tax advice about partnership operations and forecasts used to plan operations and structure transactions are not syndication costs. These costs should be deductible either as organization costs or as general business start-up expenditures. In either case, they can be amortized over a period of 60 months or more.

Taxable Year of the Partnership

In computing a partner's taxable income for a specific year, the partner's distributive share of partnership income and guaranteed payments for the partnership year that ends with or within the partner's taxable year must be included.

When all partners use the calendar year, it would be beneficial in present value terms if the partnership would adopt a fiscal year ending with January 31. Why? As Figure 21–2 illustrates, when January 31 is the adopted year, the reporting of

FIGURE 21–2 Deferral Benefit When Fiscal Year Is Used and All Partners Are on the Calendar Year

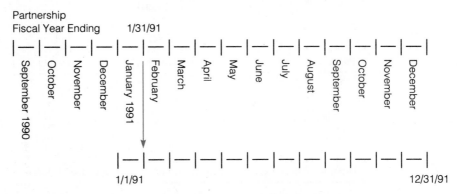

income from the partnership and payment of related taxes can be deferred an additional 11 months. For instance, income earned by the partnership in March 1991 is not taxed to the partners until January 31, 1992, and the related tax return is not due until April 15, 1993. Even though each partner may be required to file quarterly tax returns and make estimated tax payments, some deferral is still possible.

Under the general rules for determining a partnership's tax year, reference is made to the partners' tax years in the order presented in Figure 21–3.[6]

EXAMPLE 37 A and B will be equal partners in the AB Partnership. A uses the calendar year, and B uses the fiscal year ending August 31. Since neither A nor B will be a majority partner, and since as principal partners they will not have the same tax year, the general rules indicate that the partnership's required tax year must be determined by the "least aggregate deferral" method. The computa-

FIGURE 21–3 Required Tax Year of Partnership

In Order, Partnership Must Use	Requirements
Majority partners' tax year	• Own more than 50% of capital *and* profits.
	• Have a common tax year.
Principal partners' tax year	• All of those who own more than 5% of capital *or* profits.
	• Have a common tax year.
Year with smallest amount of income deferred	• "Least aggregate deferral" method.

6. § 706.

tions below support August 31 as AB's tax year since the 2.0 months of deferral using that year-end is less than the 4.0 months of deferral when December 31 is used.

Test for 12/31 Year-End

Partner	Year Ends	Profit Interest		Deferral		Product
A	12/31	50%	×	–0–	=	0.0
B	8/31	50%	×	8	=	4.0
Aggregate number of deferral months						4.0

Test for 8/31 Year-End

Partner	Year Ends	Profit Interest		Months of Deferral		Product
A	12/31	50%	×	4	=	2.0
B	8/31	50%	×	–0–	=	0.0
Aggregate number of deferral months						2.0

When a required year is unacceptable to the entity, three other alternative tax years are available.

- Elect a tax year so that taxes on partnership income are not deferred for more than *three months* from the required tax year. Then, have the partnership maintain with the IRS a prepaid, non-interest-bearing deposit of estimated taxes deferred.[7]

- Follow IRS procedures to obtain approval for using a *natural business tax year*, under which 25 percent or more of the partnership's gross receipts were recognized during the last two months of the same 12-month period for three consecutive years.[8]

- Establish to the IRS's satisfaction that a *business purpose* exists for a different tax year (a natural business year at the end of a peak season or shortly thereafter, such as a Maine or Minnesota fishing resort that closes every fall).

To use the three-month-or-less deferral rule, the partnership must file an election on Form 8716 by the *earlier of* the following:

- The fifteenth day of the fifth month following the month that includes the first day of the tax year for which the election is effective.

- The due date (without extensions) of the partnership return resulting from the election.

Required tax deferral deposits are computed at the highest individual tax rate plus one percentage point. The first payment is due on April 15 (plus extensions)

---

7. Partnerships that used a fiscal year immediately prior to 1987 could have elected to retain this year, even though the deferral was greater than three months.

8. Rev. Proc. 74–33, 1974–2 C.B. 489, Rev. Rul. 87–57, 1987–2 C.B. 117, and Rev. Proc. 87–32, 1987–1 C.B. 396.

of the calendar year following the calendar year in which the first tax year begins. Future payments are also due on April 15 (plus extensions). When the required tax deferral deposit increases, the partnership makes additional payments. When it decreases, the partnership can get a refund. In summary, the partnership maintains an annually adjusted prepaid tax deferral balance with the IRS.[9]

TAX PLANNING CONSIDERATIONS

Choosing Partnership Taxation

Concept Summary 21-5 enumerates various factors that the owners of a business should consider in making decisions as to the appropriate use of C corporations, S corporations, and partnerships as a means of doing business.

CONCEPT SUMMARY 21-5

Advantages and Disadvantages of the Partnership Form

The partnership form may be attractive when one or more of the following factors are present:

- The entity is generating net taxable losses and/or valuable tax credits, which will be of use directly to the owners.
- The entity does not generate material amounts of tax preference and adjustment items, which would increase the alternative minimum tax liabilities of its owners.
- The entity is generating net passive income, which its owners can use to claim immediate deductions for net passive losses that they have generated from other sources.
- Other means by which to reduce the effects of the double taxation of business income (e.g., compensation to owners, interest, and rental payments) have been exhausted.
- Given the asset holdings and distribution practices of the entity, the possibility of liability under the accumulated earnings and personal holding company taxes is significant.
- Restrictions relative to S corporation status (e.g., the 35-shareholder maximum or the restriction to one class of outstanding stock) are not attractive, perhaps because of elaborate executive compensation arrangements or an anticipated public offering of stock.
- The owners wish to make special allocations of certain income or deduction items—such allocations are not possible under the C or S corporation forms.
- The owners anticipate liquidation of the entity within a period of less than 10 years—such transactions would generate entity-level recognized gains relative to appreciated property sold or distributed because of the liquidation, and they could make the entity subject to S corporation penalty taxes.
- Adequate basis amounts in the partnership exist; these facilitate the deduction of flow-through losses and the assignment of an adequate basis to assets distributed in-kind to the partners.

The partnership form may be less attractive when one or more of the following factors are present:

- The entity is generating net taxable income, which will be taxed directly to the owners who do not necessarily receive any funds with which to pay the tax.
- The type of income that the entity is generating (e.g., business and portfolio income) is not as attractive to its owners as would be net passive income because such income could be used to offset the net passive losses that the owners have generated on their own.
- Congress enacts tax legislation raising the maximum marginal tax rate applicable to individuals above that applicable to C corporations.

---

9. Reg. § 1.1245-4(c)(4) (Ex. 3).

Formation and Operation of a Partnership

Potential partners should be cautious in contributing assets to a partnership, so that they are not required to recognize any gain upon the creation of the entity. The exceptions to the nonrecognition provisions of § 721 are relatively straightforward and resemble the corresponding portions of § 351. However, a partner whose capital or profits interest in the entity does not exceed 80 percent can contribute additional assets to the entity after the inception of the partnership. This possibility is not available to less-than-controlling shareholders in a corporation.

The partners should anticipate the tax benefits and pitfalls that are presented in Subchapter K and should take appropriate actions to resolve any resulting problems and arrange the flow-through procedure in a satisfactory manner. Typically, these adjustments simply require an appropriate provision in the partnership agreement (e.g., with respect to differing allocation percentages for gain and loss years). Recall, however, that special allocations of income, expense, or credit items must be accompanied by a substantial economic effect.

Notice the dangers that accompany an unplanned termination of the partnership's tax year (e.g., when 50 percent or more of the partnership's ownership interests change hands within a 12-month period). If the partnership employs a fiscal tax year, the partners may be forced to include more than one year's worth of partnership income in their individual income tax returns. Accordingly, the partnership agreement might include a provision that requires a committee of the partners (and its tax adviser) to approve all sales or exchanges of partnership interests in excess of, for example, a 5 percent capital or profit interest floor amount. In this manner, although the committee would not be empowered to exercise any veto power over such sales or exchanges, it could suggest that the transfers be delayed to an appropriate date, so as not to create an unnecessary bunching of income problem.

In a similar vein, the partners might consider the acquisition of several insurance policies on each others' lives via a buy-sell agreement. These policies would ensure that in the event of the unexpected death of one of the partners, the survivors would possess enough liquid assets to maintain the entity in its present condition. For instance, the partnership agreement could provide that such policy proceeds be used to redeem the partner's interest from his or her estate or beneficiaries. Alternatively, the partners could use the insurance proceeds to conduct a search-and-interview procedure and identify a likely successor to the partner's ownership interest. Buy-sell agreements also provide the partners with essential estate tax planning opportunities.

Distributions to Partners

The carryover basis approach to the nonliquidating distributions of a partnership places a premium on the knowledge that the partners should have concerning the basis of the partnership's assets to the entity and their own basis amounts in the partnership interest. For instance, the only situation in which a nonliquidating distribution triggers recognized gain to the partner is when the cash that the partner receives exceeds his or her basis in the partnership interest. Thus, a partner who is unaware of the present basis in his or her partnership interest may arrange a nonliquidating distribution that generates an unwanted increase in his or her individual gross income for the year. Such gain usually is capital in nature. The partner never can recognize a loss from a nonliquidating partnership distribution.

Similarly, a knowledge of the basis in one's partnership interest is critical because this amount may be substituted as the basis in the property that the

partner receives in the nonliquidating distribution. Thus, if the basis in the partnership interest is relatively low at the date of the distribution, the partner should consider a delay of any distribution of depreciable assets. The base for the partner's subsequent cost recovery purposes will not allow him or her to generate deductions that are commensurate with those that would have been allocated to the partner had the distribution not occurred.

EXAMPLE 38

B is a 50% partner in the TS Partnership. The entity purchased some depreciable property in 1990 for $60,000. B's basis in his partnership interest on December 31, 1990, is $4,000. If the partnership distributes the property to him on that date, he will assign a $4,000 basis to the asset, and his total cost recovery deductions relative to the property will be limited to that amount. However, if the distribution is postponed until some later date, B will receive an allocable portion of the cost recovery deductions that are generated by the partnership, computed with reference to its $60,000 depreciable base in the asset. Thus, his total deductions with respect to the asset may be greater if the distribution does not take place in 1990. □

For similar reasons, if the partner anticipates a sale or other taxable exchange of the property received in a nonliquidating distribution, it is critical that the basis that he or she assigns to the asset, as it is substituted from the partner's basis in his or her ownership interest, is as large as possible. This minimizes the partner's subsequent recognized gain, or maximizes such recognized loss, upon the transfer to the third party.

Preserving Cost Recovery Deductions on Contributed Property

The contribution of property to a partnership subject to debt in excess of its basis may result in gain to the contributing partner. If the contributed property were subject to depreciation recapture, ordinary income would result. Unless the partnership is considered the original user of depreciable property, it will not be allowed to deviate from the contributing partner's recovery period or method. Thus, consideration should be given to retaining ownership of the property and leasing it to the partnership.

Drafting the Partnership Agreement

Although a written partnership agreement is not required, many rules governing the tax consequences to partners and their partnerships refer to such an agreement. Remember that a partner's distributive share of income, gain, loss, deduction, or credit is determined in accordance with the partnership agreement. Consequently, if taxpayers operating a business in partnership form want a measure of certainty as to the tax consequences of their activities, a carefully drafted partnership agreement is crucial. If such an agreement contains the obligations, rights, and powers of the partners, it should prove invaluable in settling controversies among them and provide some degree of certainty as to the tax consequences of the partners' actions.

Overall Comparison: Forms of Doing Business

See Concept Summary 21–6 for a detailed comparison of the tax consequences of the following forms of doing business: sole proprietorship, partnership, S corporation, and corporation.

CONCEPT SUMMARY 21–6

Tax Attributes of Different Forms of Business (Assume Partners and Shareholders Are All Individuals)

	Sole Proprietorship	Partnership	S Corporation*	Regular Corporation**
Restrictions on type or number of owners	One owner. The owner must be an individual.	Must have at least 2 owners.	Only individuals, estates, and certain trusts can be owners. Maximum number of shareholders limited to 35.	None, except some states require a minimum of 2 shareholders.
Incidence of tax	Sole proprietorship's income and deductions are reported on Schedule C of the individual's Form 1040. A separate Schedule C is prepared for each business.	Entity not subject to tax. Partners in their separate capacity subject to tax on their distributive share of income. Partnership files Form 1065.	Except for certain capital gains, built-in gains, and violations of passive investment income tests when accumulated earnings and profits are present from Subchapter C tax years, entity not subject to Federal income tax. S corporation files Form 1120S. Shareholders are subject to tax on income attributable to their stock ownership. C corporations that claimed an investment tax credit and elect S status remain liable for any ITC recapture potential.	Income subject to double taxation. Entity subject to tax, and shareholder subject to tax on any corporate dividends received. Corporation files Form 1120.
Maximum tax rate	33 percent at individual level.	33 percent at partner level.	33 percent at shareholder level.	39 percent at corporate level plus 33 percent on any corporate dividends at shareholder level.
Choice of tax year	Same tax year as owner.	Selection generally restricted to coincide with tax year of majority partners or principal partners, or to calendar year.	Restricted to a calendar year unless IRS approves a different year for business purposes or other exceptions apply.	Unrestricted selection allowed at time of filing first tax return.

	Sole Proprietorship	Partnership	S Corporation[*]	Regular Corporation[**]
Timing of taxation	Based on owner's tax year.	Partners report their share of income in their tax year with or within which the partnership's tax year ends. Partners in their separate capacity are subject to payment of estimated taxes.	Shareholders report their share of income in their tax year with or within which the corporation's tax year ends. Generally, the corporation uses a calendar year; but see "Choice of tax year" above. Shareholders may be subject to payment of estimated taxes.	Corporation subject to tax at close of its tax year. May be subject to payment of estimated taxes. Dividends will be subject to tax at the shareholder level in the tax year received.
Basis for allocating income to owners	Not applicable (only one owner).	Profit and loss sharing agreement. Cash basis items of cash basis partnerships are allocated on a daily basis. Other partnership items are allocated after considering varying interests of partners.	Pro rata share based on stock ownership. Shareholder's pro rata share is determined on a daily basis according to the number of shares of stock held on each day of the corporation's tax year.	Not applicable.
Contribution of property to the entity	Not a taxable transaction.	Generally, not a taxable transaction.	Is a taxable transaction unless the § 351 requirements are satisfied.	Is a taxable transaction unless the § 351 requirements are satisfied.
Character of income taxed to owners	Retains source characteristics.	Conduit—retains source characteristics.	Conduit—retains source characteristics.	All source characteristics are lost when income is distributed to owners.
Basis for allocating a net operating loss to owners	Not applicable (only one owner).	Profit and loss sharing agreement. Cash basis items of cash basis partnerships are allocated on a daily basis. Other partnership items are allocated after considering varying interests of partners.	Prorated among shareholders on a daily basis.	Not applicable.
Limitation on losses deductible by owners	Investment plus liabilities.	Partner's investment plus share of liabilities.	Shareholder's investment plus loans made by shareholder to corporation.	Not applicable.

	Sole Proprietorship	Partnership	S Corporation*	Regular Corporation**
Subject to at-risk rules	Yes, at the owner level. Indefinite carryover of excess loss.	Yes, at the partner level. Indefinite carryover of excess loss.	Yes, at the shareholder level. Indefinite carryover of excess loss.	Yes, for closely held corporations. Indefinite carryover of excess loss.
Subject to passive activity loss rules	Yes, at the owner level. Indefinite carryover of excess loss.	Yes, at the partner level. Indefinite carryover of excess loss.	Yes, at the shareholder level. Indefinite carry over of excess loss.	Yes, for closely held corporations and personal service corporations. Indefinite carryover of excess loss.
Tax consequences of earnings retained by entity	Taxed to owner when earned and increases his or her investment in the sole proprietorship.	Taxed to partners when earned and increases their respective interests in the partnership.	Taxed to shareholders when earned and increases their respective basis in stock.	Taxed to corporation as earned and may be subject to penalty tax if accumulated unreasonably.
Nonliquidating distributions to owners	Not taxable.	Not taxable unless money received exceeds recipient partner's basis in partnership interest. Existence of § 751 assets may cause tax problems.	Generally not taxable unless the distribution exceeds the shareholder's AAA or stock basis. Existence of accumulated earnings and profits could cause some distributions to be dividends.	Taxable in year of receipt to extent of earnings and profits or if exceeds basis in stock.
Distribution of appreciated property	Not taxable.	No recognition at the partnership level.	Recognition at the corporate level to the extent of the appreciation. Conduit—amount of recognized gain is passed through to shareholders.	Taxable at the corporate level to the extent of the appreciation.
Splitting of income among family members	Not applicable (only one owner).	Difficult—IRS will not recognize a family member as a partner unless certain requirements are met.	Rather easy—gift of stock will transfer tax on a pro rata share of income to the donee. However, IRS can make adjustments to reflect adequate compensation for services.	Same as an S corporation, except that donees will be subject to tax only on earnings actually or constructively distributed to them. Other than unreasonable compensation, IRS generally cannot make adjustments to reflect adequate compensation for services and capital.

	Sole Proprietorship	**Partnership**	**S Corporation**[*]	**Regular Corporation**[**]
Organizational costs	Amortizable over 60 months.	Same as sole proprietorship.	Same as sole proprietorship.	Same as sole proprietorship.
Charitable contributions	Limitations apply at owner level.	Conduit—partners are subject to deduction limitations in their own capacity.	Conduit—shareholders are subject to deduction limitations in their own capacity.	Limited to 10 percent of taxable income before certain deductions.
Tax preference items	Apply at owner level in determining alternative minimum tax.	Conduit—passed through to partners who must account for such items in their separate capacity.	Conduit—passed through to shareholders who must account for such items in their separate capacity.	Subject to alternative minimum tax at corporate level.
Capital gains	Taxed at owner level using ordinary income rates. Alternative tax rates do not produce beneficial results.	Conduit—partners must account for their respective shares.	Conduit, with certain exceptions (a possible penalty tax)—shareholders must account for their respective shares.	Taxed at corporate level using ordinary income rates. Alternative rates do not produce beneficial results.
Capital losses	Only $3,000 of capital losses can be offset each tax year against ordinary income. Indefinite carryover.	Conduit—partners must account for their respective shares.	Conduit—shareholders must account for their respective shares.	Carried back three years and carried forward five years, deductible only to the extent of capital gains.
§ 1231 gains and losses	Taxable or deductible at owner level. Five-year lookback rule for § 1231 losses.	Conduit—partners must account for their respective shares.	Conduit—shareholders must account for their respective shares.	Taxable or deductible at corporate level only. Five-year lookback rule for § 1231 losses.
Foreign tax credits	Available at owner level.	Conduit—passed through to partners.	Generally conduit—passed through to shareholders.	Available at corporate level only.
§ 1244 treatment of loss on sale of interest	Not applicable.	Not applicable.	Available.	Available.
Basis treatment of entity liabilities	Includible in interest basis.	Includible in interest basis.	Not includible in stock basis.	Not includible in stock basis.
Built-in gains	Not applicable.	Not applicable.	Possible corporate tax.	Not applicable.
Special allocations to owners	Not applicable (only one owner).	Available if supported by substantial economic effect.	Not available.	Not applicable.
Availability of fringe benefits to owners	None.	None.	None unless a 2 percent or less shareholder.	Available within antidiscrimination rules.

	Sole Proprietorship	Partnership	S Corporation[*]	Regular Corporation[**]
Effect of liquidation/redemption/reorganization on basis of entity assets	Not applicable.	Usually carried over from entity to partner unless a § 754 election is made, excessive cash is distributed, or more than 50 percent of the capital interests are transferred within 12 months.	Taxable step-up to fair market value.	Taxable step-up to fair market value.
Sale of ownership interest	Treated as the sale of individual assets. Classification of recognized gain or loss is dependent on the nature of the individual assets.	Treated as the sale of a partnership interest. Recognized gain or loss is classified as capital under § 741 subject to ordinary income treatment under § 751.	Treated as the sale of corporate stock. Recognized gain is classified as capital gain. Recognized loss is classified as capital loss subject to ordinary loss treatment under § 1244.	Treated as the sale of corporate stock. Recognized gain is classified as capital gain. Recognized loss is classified as capital loss subject to ordinary loss treatment under § 1244.
Investment tax credit recapture	Occurs at owner level.	Conduit—passed through to partners.	Conduit—passed through to shareholders.	Occurs at corporate level.

[*]Refer to chapter 20 for additional details on S corporations.
[**]Refer to chapters 16 through 19 for additional details on regular corporations.

PROBLEM MATERIALS

Discussion Questions

1. Distinguish between the entity concept and the aggregate or conduit concept of a partnership.

2. What is a partnership for Federal income tax purposes?

3. Under what circumstances can organizations elect to be excluded from the partnership tax provisions? Why would an organization wish to be excluded?

4. Compare the nonrecognition of gain or loss provision on contributions to a partnership with the similar provision found in corporate formation. What are the major differences and similarities?

5. When a partner transfers property with a fair market value of $1,000 to a partnership and receives a cash distribution of $1,000, will the transfer be treated as a contribution to capital?

6. How is the basis of a contributing partner's interest determined?

7. If appreciated property is contributed to a partnership in exchange for a partnership interest, what basis does the partnership take in such property?

8. How is the holding period of a partnership interest determined? The partnership's holding period in contributed property?

9. What effect does the contribution of property subject to a liability have on the basis of the contributing partner's interest? What is the effect on the basis of the other partners' interests?

10. Why is a partnership required to file any tax return?

11. What are guaranteed payments?

12. To what extent can partners deduct their distributive share of partnership losses? What happens to any unused losses?

13. Under what circumstances will a partnership's tax year close?

Problems

14. L and K form an equal partnership with a cash contribution of $60,000 from L and a property contribution (adjusted basis of $30,000 and a fair market value of $60,000) from K.

   a. How much gain, if any, must L recognize on the transfer? Must K recognize any gain?

   b. What is L's interest basis in the partnership?

   c. What is K's interest basis in the partnership?

   d. What basis will the partnership have in the property transferred by K?

15. L, B, and R form the LBR Partnership on January 1 of the current year. In return for a 30% capital interest, L transfers property (basis of $24,000, fair market value of $37,500) subject to a liability of $15,000. The liability is assumed by the partnership. B transfers property (basis of $37,500, fair market value of $22,500) for a 30% capital interest, and R transfers cash of $30,000 for the remaining 40% interest.

   a. How much gain must L recognize on the transfer?

   b. What is L's interest basis in the partnership?

   c. How much loss may B recognize on the transfer?

   d. What is B's interest basis in the partnership?

   e. What is R's interest basis in the partnership?

   f. What basis will the LBR Partnership have in the property transferred by L?

   g. What is the partnership's basis in the property transferred by B?

16. Assume the same facts as in Problem 15, except that the property contributed by L has a fair market value of $67,500 and is subject to a mortgage of $45,000.

   a. How much gain must L recognize on the transfer?

   b. What is L's interest basis in the partnership?

   c. What is B's interest basis in the partnership?

   d. What is R's interest basis in the partnership?

   e. What basis will the LBR Partnership have in the property transferred by L?

   f. If the partnership borrows $200,000 to purchase an office building, what effect, if any, will the loan have on each partner's interest in the partnership? What effect will the loan *repayment* have on each partner's interest?

17. X and Y are equal members of the XY Partnership. They are real estate investors who formed the partnership two years ago with equal cash contributions. The XY Partnership purchased a piece of land. On January 1 of the current year, Z contributed to the partnership some land he held for investment with a fair market value of $20,000 for a one-third interest. Z purchased the land three years ago for $25,000. No special allocation agreements were in effect before or after Z

was admitted to the partnership. The XYZ Partnership holds all land for investment. Immediately before Z's property contribution, the balance sheet of the XY Partnership was as follows:

	Basis	FMV		Basis	FMV
Land	$5,000	$40,000	X, Capital	$2,500	$20,000
			Y, Capital	2,500	20,000
	$5,000	$40,000		$5,000	$40,000

a. At the contribution date, what is Z's date basis and interest basis in the XYZ Partnership?

b. On June 30 of the current year, the partnership sold the land contributed by Z for $20,000. How much is the loss, and how is it allocated among the partners?

c. Prepare a balance sheet for the XYZ Partnership immediately after the land sale.

18. Assume the same facts as in Problem 17, with the following exceptions:

- The fair market value of the land contributed by Z declined after Z joined the partnership.
- XYZ sold the land contributed by Z for $17,000.

a. How much is the loss, and how is it allocated among the partners?

b. Prepare a balance sheet for the XYZ Partnership immediately after the land sale, along with schedules that support the amount in each partner's account.

19. Assume the same facts as in Problem 17, with the following exceptions:

- The fair market value of the land not contributed by Z declined after Z joined the partnership.
- XYZ sold the land for $17,000.

a. How much is the gain, and how is it allocated among the partners?

b. Prepare a balance sheet for the XYZ Partnership immediately after the land sale, along with schedules that support the amount in each partner's account.

20. Q is a cash basis sole proprietor whose business is the buying, holding, and selling of real estate. S is a small cash basis manufacturer of specialty candies. Last year, S served as a consultant to a small candy manufacturer in another state and billed the manufacturer $10,000 for her services. B is employed by a local manufacturer and is a casual investor in real estate. Q, S, and B form the QSB Partnership, which will buy, hold, and sell real estate parcels. On January 2 of the current year, the three individuals contributed the following items to the newly formed partnership, each for a one-third interest in capital and profits:

	Adjusted Basis	Fair Market Value
Q contributes land held as inventory	$ 5,000	$10,000
S contributes the receivable for her consulting activities	–0–	10,000
B contributes land held as a long-term capital asset	15,000	10,000

Since the partnership needs cash for working capital, shortly after formation it sells both land parcels for their contribution date fair market values and collects the receivable contributed by S.

a. What is the nature of the gain on the sale of the land contributed by Q, and how is the gain allocated among the partners?

b. What is the nature of the income from the collection of the receivable contributed by S, and how is the income allocated among the partners?

c. What is the nature of the loss on the sale of the land contributed by B, and how is the loss allocated among the partners?

21. As of January 1 of last year, the basis of D's 25% capital interest in the DEF Partnership was $24,000. D and the partnership use the calendar year for tax purposes. The partnership incurred an operating loss of $100,000 for last year and a profit of $8,000 for the current year.

a. How much loss, if any, may D recognize for last year?

b. How much net reportable income must D recognize for the current year?

c. What is D's interest in the partnership as of January 1 of the current year?

d. What is D's interest in the partnership as of January 1 of the next year?

e. What year-end tax planning would you suggest to ensure that the partners can deduct their share of partnership losses?

22. LM and KM are equal partners in the calendar year M & M Partnership. For the current year, the partnership had an operating loss of $60,000, a long-term capital loss of $4,000, and a short-term capital gain of $9,000. The partnership had no other transactions for the current year. At the start of the current year, LM's interest basis in the M & M Partnership was $28,000 and KM's was $19,500.

a. How much short-term capital gain must LM report on her tax return for the current year?

b. How much short-term capital gain must KM report on her tax return for the current year?

c. How much of the operating loss and the long-term capital loss must LM report on her tax return for the current year?

d. How much of the operating loss and the long-term capital loss must KM report on her tax return for the current year?

e. What is LM's partnership interest at the start of the next calendar year? KM's partnership interest at the start of the next calendar year?

23. R, P, and M form an equal partnership on January 1 of the current year. Each partner and RPM use the cash method of accounting. For reporting purposes, R uses a calendar year, P uses an August 31 fiscal year, and M uses a June 30 fiscal year.

a. What is RPM's required tax year under the least aggregate deferral method?

b. Assuming that RPM cannot establish a natural business year that differs from your answer in (a), what tax year can RPM elect that provides the partners with the greatest aggregate additional deferral?

24. Four Lakes Partnership is owned by four sisters (25% interest each). One sister sells investment property to the partnership for its fair market value of $54,000 (basis of $72,000).

a. How much loss, if any, may this sister recognize?

b. If the partnership later sells the property for $81,000, how much gain must it recognize?

c. If the sister's basis in the investment property were $20,000 instead of $72,000, how much, if any, capital gain would she recognize on the sale?

25. E and Z are equal partners in the accrual basis EZ Partnership. At the beginning of the current year, E's capital account has a balance of $10,000, and the partnership has debts of $30,000 payable to unrelated parties. The following

information about EZ's operations for the current year is obtained from the partnership's records:

Taxable income	$48,000
Tax-exempt interest income	5,000
§ 1245 gain	4,000
§ 1231 gain	6,200
Long-term capital gain	500
Long-term capital loss	100
Short-term capital loss	250
Charitable contribution to Girl Scouts	800
Cash distribution to E	10,000

Assume none of the property was contributed by the partners and year-end partnership debt payable to unrelated parties is $24,000.

a. What is E's basis in the partnership interest at the beginning of the year?

b. What is E's basis in the partnership interest at the end of the current year?

26. N, an equal partner in the MN Partnership, is to receive a payment of $20,000 for services plus 50% of the partnership's profits or losses. After deducting the $20,000 payment to N, the partnership has a loss of $12,000.

a. How much, if any, of the $12,000 partnership loss will be allocated to N?

b. What is the net income from the partnership that N must report on his personal income tax return?

27. D is a 50% owner of Philadelphia Cheese Treets, Inc., a C corporation. She receives a $5,000 monthly salary from the corporation, and Cheese Treets generates $200,000 taxable income for its tax year ending January 31, 1991.

a. How do these activities affect D's 1990 adjusted gross income?

b. Same as (a), except that Cheese Treets is an S corporation.

c. Same as (a), except that Cheese Treets is a partnership. Treat D's salary as a guaranteed payment.

28. G holds a 75% interest in the FG Partnership. Both of the partners, and the partnership, use the calendar year for tax purposes. On January 1, 1990, G's basis in the partnership was $30,000. The entity's 1990 activities are summarized as follows:

Partnership's ordinary income	$20,000
Municipal bond interest income	4,000
G's 1990 draws	30,000
FG's accounts payable, 1–1–90	27,000
FG's accounts payable, 12–31–90	20,000
Cash distribution to the partners, 12–31–90	15,000
Distribution of land to G, 12–31–90:	
Fair market value	6,000
Basis to FG	5,000

a. The partnership's distributions were not in liquidation of the entity. What is G's basis in his ownership interest just *prior* to the distributions on December 31, 1990?

b. What is his basis in the partnership interest *after* accounting for the distributions?

c. What is G's basis in the land that he received?

d. How do your answers to (a) and (b) change if the cash distribution to the partners is $35,000?

e. How do your answers to (a) and (b) change if the cash distribution to the partners is $3,500?

29. FM and FT are equal partners in the calendar year F & F Partnership. FM uses a fiscal year ending June 30, and FT uses a calendar year. FM is paid an annual calendar year salary of $50,000. For the last calendar year, F & F Partnership's taxable income was $40,000. For the current calendar year, the partnership's taxable income is $50,000.

   a. What is the aggregate amount of income from the partnership that must be reported by FM for his tax year that ends within the current calendar year?

   b. What is the aggregate amount of income from the partnership that must be reported by FT for the current calendar year?

   c. If FM's annual salary is increased to $60,000 starting on January 1 of the current calendar year and the taxable income of the partnership for the last year and the current year are the same (i.e., $40,000 and $50,000), what is the aggregate amount of income from the partnership that must be reported by FM for his tax year that ends within the current calendar year?

30. On October 1 of the last calendar year, T is invited to join the partnership of PFK & Associates, a local certified public accounting firm. In exchange for a cash contribution of $10,000 to the partnership, T receives a 5% partnership interest. Before admission, T was employed as one of the partnership's salaried managers and received $2,500 monthly as compensation. As a new partner, T is entitled to monthly cash drawings of $4,000. The partnership has an October 1 to September 30 fiscal year, which the IRS has approved as appropriate for business purposes. It reports profits of $800,000 and $1,000,000, respectively, for its fiscal years ending September 30 of the current and next calendar years.

   a. Assuming partner T is a cash basis calendar year taxpayer who withdraws $4,000 per month, how much income from the partnership must he report for the last calendar year?

   b. For the current calendar year?

31. Assume that the PFK & Associates partnership described in Problem 30 purchased $100,000 of new equipment on December 1 of the last calendar year and the property was to be assigned a five-year cost recovery life. No other § 179 assets were acquired.

   a. If the partnership properly elects to treat $10,000 of the investment in the new equipment as a § 179 deduction, what will be T's share of the qualifying investment in § 179 property?

   b. On which personal income tax returns of T must the above item be reported?

32. Indicate whether the following statements are true or false:

   a. Since a partnership is not a taxable entity, it is not required to file any type of tax return.

   b. Each partner can choose a different method of accounting and depreciation computation in determining his or her gross income from the entity.

   c. A partnership may not choose a tax year that is different from that of all of its principal partners.

   d. Generally, a transfer of appreciated property to a partnership results in recognized gain to the contributing partner.

   e. The period of time that a partner held the asset prior to its transfer to the partnership is included in the holding period of the asset for the partnership.

   f. A partner can carry forward, for an unlimited period of time, any operating losses that exceed his or her basis in the entity.

   g. Cash distributions in excess of the partner's basis generate income to the partner.

h. Property that the partner receives in a nonliquidating distribution always is assigned a carryover basis.

i. When a partner renders services to the entity in exchange for an interest therein, he or she does not recognize any gross income.

j. Losses on sales between a partner and the partnership always are disallowed.

33. For each of the following independent statements, indicate whether the tax attribute is applicable to regular corporations (C), partnerships (P), both business forms (B), or neither business form (N):

a. Restrictions are placed on the type and number of owners.

b. Business income will be taxable to the owners rather than to the entity.

c. Distributions of earnings to the owners will result in a tax deduction to the entity.

d. The source characteristics of an entity's income flow through to the owners.

e. Capital gains are subject to tax at the entity level.

f. Organization costs can be amortized over a period of 60 months or more.

34. S and F are CPAs. Each operates a practice within a sole proprietorship. S enjoys working with small businesses, rendering financial and tax planning advice, and she has developed an extensive consulting practice. F enjoys completing tax returns and assisting clients in IRS audits. His practice is oriented toward tax-compliance activities. S and F believe that they will be able to serve all of their clients in a more effective manner if they join in a new partnership.

S has accumulated the following assets in her proprietorship. These assets have a current market value of $100,000.

Automobile, used predominantly for the business—cost	$20,000
Accumulated depreciation	8,000
Computer system—cost	7,000
Accumulated depreciation	3,000
Computer software, newly purchased—cost	12,000
Tax library materials, newly purchased—cost	30,000
Office furniture—cost	50,000
Accumulated depreciation	24,000
Supplies, fully expensed	2,000

In addition, S holds a $45,000 bank note, which is secured by the computer system and office furniture. F has operated his business out of his home. Thus, he has few business assets. He intends to contribute cash to the partnership in an amount that is sufficient to give him a 50% capital interest.

a. How much cash should F invest in the partnership?

b. Discuss the tax and nontax factors that S and F should consider with respect to the use of a partnership for their new business.

c. Should S contribute all of her business assets to the partnership?

d. Discuss the immediate tax consequences of the contributions to the partnership.

Comprehensive Tax Return Problem

35. James R. Wesley (297–19–9261), Rita B. Healthy (284–74–7832), Susan C. Yourez (257–62–3544), and Frank T. Bizzano (219–75–3822) are equal partners in WHYB, a small business management advisory partnership. The partnership

uses the cash basis and calendar year and began operations on January 1 two years before the start of the current year. Since that time, it has experienced a 30% growth rate each year. Its current address is 2937 Skyline Speedway, Bloomington, IN 47401. During the current year, each partner withdrew $40,000. The following information was taken from the partnership's income statement for the current year.

Receipts	
Fees collected	$75,000
Tax-exempt interest	1,600
Payments	
Advertising	5,000
Contribution to Boy Scouts	800
Employee salaries	42,000
Equipment rental	6,000
Office rent	24,000
Salary, James R. Wesley	12,000
Taxes	4,600
Utilities	3,700
Insurance premiums	2,200

a. Prepare Form 1065 and Schedule K for WHYB Partnership, leaving blank any items where insufficient information has been provided.

b. Prepare Schedule K–1 for James R. Wesley.

22

TAX-EXEMPT ENTITIES

OBJECTIVES

Identify the different types of exempt organizations.

Differentiate between the tax consequences of public charities and private foundations.

Discuss the taxes imposed on the prohibited transactions of private foundations.

Explain the tax on unrelated business income and debt-financed income.

GENERAL CONSIDERATIONS

Ideally, any entity that generates profit would prefer not to be subject to the Federal income tax. All of the types of entities discussed thus far are subject to the Federal income tax at one (e.g., sole proprietorship, partnership, and S corporation forms generally are only subject to single taxation) or more (e.g., corporate form is subject to double taxation) levels. However, organizations classified as exempt organizations may be able to escape Federal income taxation.

As discussed in chapter 1, the major objective of the Federal tax law is to raise revenue. If revenue raising were the only objective, the Code would not contain provisions that permit certain organizations to be either partially or completely exempt from Federal income taxation. However, among the other objectives discussed in chapter 1 are social considerations. This objective bears directly on the decision by Congress to provide for exempt organization tax status. The House Report on the Revenue Act of 1938 provides as follows:[1]

> The exemption from taxation of money or property devoted to charitable and other purposes is based upon the theory that the Government is compensated for the loss of revenue by its relief from the financial burden which would otherwise have to be met by appropriations from public funds, and by the benefits resulting from the promotion of the general welfare.

In recognition of this social consideration objective, Subchapter F (Exempt Organizations) of the Code (§§ 501–528) provides the statutory authority for certain organizations to be exempt from Federal income taxation. Such exempt status is not open-ended in that two general limitations exist. First, the nature or scope of the organization may result in it being only partially exempt from tax (the organization generates unrelated business income).[2] Second, the organization may engage in activities (or fail to act in certain circumstances) that are subject to special taxation (prohibited transactions).[3]

Types of Exempt Organizations

An organization qualifies for exempt status *only* if it fits into one of the categories provided for in the Code (for Section numbers, see Concept Summary 22–1).[4] Included are the following:

1. Corporation that is organized under an act of Congress and is an instrumentality of the United States exempt from Federal income tax.

2. Corporation organized to hold title to property for an exempt organization and to pay the net income to the exempt organization.

3. Entity organized and operated exclusively for the following purposes: religious, charitable, scientific, literary, educational, testing for public safety, fostering national or international amateur sports, or prevention of cruelty to children or animals.

---

1. See 1939–1 (Part 2) C.B. 742 for a reprint of H.R. No. 1860, 75th Congress, 3rd Session.
2. See the subsequent discussion of Unrelated Business Taxable Income.
3. See the subsequent discussion of Taxes Imposed on Private Foundations.
4. Section 501(a) provides for exempt status for organizations described in §§ 401 and 501. The orientation of this chapter is toward organizations that conduct business activities. Therefore, the exempt organizations described in § 401 (qualified pension, profit sharing, and stock bonus trusts) are outside the scope of the chapter and are not discussed. Likewise, organizations described in § 501 that are not involved in the conduct of business activities are excluded.

4. Civic leagues operated exclusively for the promotion of social welfare and local associations of employees whose association net earnings are used exclusively for charitable, educational, or recreational purposes.

5. Labor, agricultural, and horticultural organizations.

6. Business leagues, chambers of commerce, real estate boards, boards of trade, and professional football leagues.

7. Social clubs organized and operated exclusively for pleasure, recreation, and other nonprofitable purposes.

8. Fraternal beneficiary societies operating under the lodge system and having a system for the payment of insurance benefits to members and their dependents.

9. Voluntary employees' beneficiary associations having a system for the payment of insurance benefits to members, their dependents, or their designated beneficiaries.

10. Domestic fraternal societies not providing for the payment of insurance benefits, but whose net earnings are devoted exclusively to the following purposes: religious, charitable, scientific, literary, educational, or fraternal.

11. Local teachers' retirement fund associations.

12. Local benevolent life insurance associations, mutual ditch or irrigation companies, mutual or cooperative telephone companies, or like organizations.

13. Cemetery companies owned and operated exclusively for the benefit of their members.

14. Credit unions without capital stock organized for mutual purposes.

15. Insurance companies or associations, other than life, whose net written premiums (or direct written premiums, if greater) do not exceed $350,000.

16. Corporation organized by a farmers' cooperative for the purpose of financing crop operations.

17. Armed forces members' posts or organizations.

18. Group legal service plans' organizations or trusts.

19. Religious and apostolic organizations.

20. Cooperative hospital service organizations.

21. Cooperative service organizations of operating educational organizations.

Requirements for Exempt Status

Exempt status frequently requires more than mere classification in one of the categories of exempt organizations. Several items tend to permeate the definitional requirements of many of the organizations that qualify for exempt status. These are as follows:

1. The organization serves some type of *common good.*[5]

2. The organization is *not* a *for profit* entity.[6]

---

5. See, for example, §§ 501(c)(3) and (4).
6. See, for example, §§ 501(c)(3), (4), (6), (13), and (14).

CONCEPT SUMMARY 22-1

Types of Exempt Organizations

Statutory Authority	Brief Description	Examples or Comments
§ 501(c)(1)	Corporations that are instrumentalites of the United States.	Commodity Credit Corporation, Federal Deposit Insurance Corporation, Federal Land Bank.
§ 501(c)(2)	Corporations holding title to property for and paying income to exempt organizations.	Corporation holding title to college fraternity house.
§ 501(c)(3)	Religious, charitable, educational, etc., organizations.	Boy Scouts of America, Red Cross, Salvation Army, Episcopal Church, United Fund, University of Richmond.
§ 501(c)(4)	Civic leagues.	Garden club, tenants' association promoting tenants' legal rights in entire community, anti-abortion organization, League of Women Voters.
§ 501(c)(5)	Labor, agricultural, and horticultural organizations.	Teachers' association, organization formed to promote effective agricultural pest control, organization formed to test soil and to educate community members in soil treatment, garden club.
§ 501(c)(6)	Business leagues, chambers of commerce, real estate boards, etc.	Chambers of commerce, American Plywood Association, medical association peer review board, organization promoting acceptance of women in business and professions.
§ 501(c)(7)	Social clubs.	Country club, rodeo and riding club, press club, bowling club, college fraternities.
§ 501(c)(8)	Fraternal beneficiary societies.	Must operate under the lodge system *and* must provide for the payment of life, sickness, accident, or other benefits to members or their dependents.
§ 501(c)(9)	Voluntary employees' beneficiary associations	Purpose is to provide for the payment of life, sickness, accident, or other benefits to members, their dependents, or their designated beneficiaries.
§ 501(c)(10)	Domestic fraternal societies.	Must operate under the lodge system; must not provide for the payment of life, sickness, accident, or other benefits; and must devote the net earnings exclusively to religious, charitable, scientific, literary, educational, and fraternal purposes.
§ 501(c)(11)	Local teachers' retirement fund associations.	Only permitted sources of income are amounts received from (1) public taxation, (2) assessments on teaching salaries of members, and (3) income from investments.
§ 501(c)(12)	Local benevolent life insurance associations, etc.	Local cooperative telephone company, local mutual water company, local mutual electric company.
§ 501(c)(13)	Cemetery companies.	Must be operated exclusively for the benefit of lot owners who hold the lots for burial purposes.
§ 501(c)(14)	Credit unions.	Excludes Federal credit unions that are exempt under § 501(c)(1).

Statutory Authority	Brief Description	Examples or Comments
§ 501(c)(15)	Mutual insurance companies.	Mutual fire insurance company, mutual automobile insurance company.
§ 501(c)(16)	Corporations organized by farmers' cooperatives for financing crop operations.	Related farmers' cooperative must be exempt from tax under § 521.
§ 501(c)(19)	Armed forces members' posts or organizations.	Veterans of Foreign Wars (VFW), Reserve Officers Association.
§ 501(c)(20)	Group legal service plans' organizations.	Group legal service plan provided by a corporation for its employees.
§ 501(d)	Religious and apostolic organizations.	Communal organization. Members must include pro rata share of the net income of the organization in their gross income as dividends.
§ 501(e)	Cooperative hospital service organizations.	Centralized purchasing organization for 5 exempt hospitals.
§ 501(f)	Cooperative service organization of educational institutions.	Organization formed to manage 10 universities' endowment funds.

3. *Net earnings* do not benefit the members of the organization.[7]

4. The organization does not exert *political influence.*[8]

Serving the Common Good.   The underlying rationale for all exempt organizations is that they serve some type of *common good.* However, depending on the type of the exempt organization, the term *common good* may be interpreted broadly or narrowly. If interpreted broadly, the group being served is the general public or some large subset thereof. Conversely, if interpreted narrowly, the group is the specific group referred to in the statutory language. This breadth of common good is a factor in classifying the exempt organization as a private foundation (see the subsequent discussion).

Not for Profit Entity.   The organization is not organized or operated for the purpose of making a profit. For some types of exempt organizations, the *for profit prohibition* appears in the statutory language. For other types, the prohibition is implied.

Net Earnings and Members of the Organization.   The underlying issue is what uses are appropriate for the net earnings of the organization. The logical answer would seem to be that the earnings should be used for the exempt purpose of the organization. However, where the organization exists for the good of a specific group of members, such an open-ended interpretation could permit net earnings to benefit specific group members. In addition, even where the organization exists for the common good, unreasonable payments could be made to insiders and others for goods and services. Therefore, the Code contains statutory language prohibiting such use for certain types of exempt organizations. For these types of exempt organizations, the statutory language is, or is similar to, the following:

---

7. See, for example, §§ 501(c)(3), (6), (7), (9), (10), (11), and (19).

8. See, for example, § 501(c)(3).

> . . . no part of the net earnings . . . inures to the benefit of any private shareholder or individual . . . [9]

In some cases, the statutory prohibition does not appear in the Code, but appears in the Regulations instead. Certain types of exempt organizations do not need to have such a prohibition included in the statutory language because the statutory language defining the exempt organization effectively prevents such use. For example, the statutory language for domestic fraternal societies is as follows:

> . . . the net earnings of which are devoted exclusively to religious, charitable, scientific, literary, educational, and fraternal purposes . . . [10]

Political Influence.   Religious, charitable, educational, etc., organizations are generally prohibited from attempting to influence legislation or participate in political campaigns. Participation in political campaigns includes both participation *on behalf of* a candidate and participation *in opposition to* a candidate.

In a limited circumstance, such exempt organizations are permitted to attempt to influence legislation. See the subsequent discussion under Prohibited Transactions.

Tax Consequences of Exempt Status

An organization that is appropriately classified as one of the types of exempt organizations is generally exempt from Federal income tax. However, if the exempt organization engages in a prohibited transaction, it will be subject to tax. Second, if the organization is a so-called feeder organization (see definition in subsequent discussion entitled Feeder Organizations), it is subject to tax. Third, if the organization is classified as a private foundation, it may be partially subject to tax. Finally, an exempt organization is subject to tax on its unrelated business taxable income (which includes unrelated debt-financed income).

Prohibited Transactions.   The Code contains a separate section on prohibited transactions (§ 503). However, this Code section should not be viewed as all-inclusive. If the organization fails to continue to qualify as one of the types of exempt organizations, it will have effectively engaged in a prohibited transaction.

Engaging in a prohibited transaction can produce two potential results. First, it can result in the organization being subject to Federal income taxation on part or all of its income. Even worse, the exempt organization may forfeit its exempt status. It is imperative that a distinction be made between the two different tax consequences. Prohibited transactions will be discussed in the following sequence:

1. Failure to continue to qualify as one of the types of exempt organizations.

2. Election not to forfeit exempt status associated with lobbying activities.

3. Violation under § 503.

Exempt organizations initially qualify for such tax status only if they qualify as a type of exempt organization under § 501. The initial qualification requirements then effectively become maintenance requirements. Failure to satisfy these maintenance requirements results in the loss of exempt status.

Organizations exempt under § 501(c)(3) (religious, charitable, educational, etc., organizations) generally are prohibited from attempting to influence legisla-

---

9. § 501(c)(6).   10. § 501(c)(10).

tion (lobbying activities) or from participating in political campaigns.[11] Since this is both a qualification and a maintenance requirement, its violation can result in the forfeiture of exempt status.

Certain § 501(c)(3) exempt organizations are permitted to engage in lobbying activities on a limited basis.[12] Eligible for such treatment are most § 501(c)(3) exempt organizations (educational institutions, hospitals, and medical research organizations; organizations supporting government schools; organizations publicly supported by charitable contributions; certain organizations that are publicly supported by various sources including admissions, sales, gifts, grants, contributions, or membership fees; and certain organizations that support certain types of public charities). Specifically excluded from eligibility are churches or an integrated auxiliary of a church. Also excluded are private foundations. Organizations not permitted to engage in lobbying activities are referred to as *disqualified* organizations.

For qualifying § 501(c)(3) organizations, an *affirmative election* is required in order to be eligible to participate in lobbying activities on a limited basis. If the election is made, a ceiling is placed on such expenditures. Exceeding the ceiling amount will result in the violation of a maintenance requirement and thus can lead to the forfeiture of exempt status. Even though the ceiling is not exceeded, as discussed subsequently, a tax may be imposed on some of the lobbying expenditures.

Two terms are key to the calculation of the ceiling amount: *lobbying expenditures* and *grass roots expenditures*. Lobbying expenditures are those made for the purpose of influencing legislation through either of the following:

- Attempting to affect the opinions of the general public or any segment thereof.

- Communicating with any legislator or staff member or with any government official or staff member who may participate in the formulation of legislation.

Grass roots expenditures are those made for the purpose of influencing legislation through attempting to affect the opinions of the general public or any segment thereof.

The statutory ceiling is imposed on both lobbying expenditures and grass roots expenditures. The ceiling on lobbying expenditures is computed as follows:

$$150\% \times \text{Lobbying nontaxable amount} = \text{Lobbying expenditures ceiling}$$

The ceiling on grass roots expenditures is computed as follows:

$$150\% \times \text{Grass roots nontaxable amount} = \text{Grass roots expenditures ceiling}$$

The lobbying nontaxable amount and the grass roots nontaxable amount are defined subsequently.

The election by a § 501(c)(3) organization to be eligible to make lobbying expenditures on a limited basis is not without adverse tax consequences. The election also subjects the exempt organization to tax on the *excess lobbying expenditures* as follows:[13]

$$25\% \times \text{Excess lobbying expenditures} = \text{Tax liability}$$

---

11. § 501(c)(3).

12. § 501(h).

13. § 4911(a)(1).

The excess lobbying expenditures are the greater of the following:[14]

- Excess of the lobbying expenditures for the taxable year over the lobbying nontaxable amount.

- Excess of the grass roots expenditures for the taxable year over the grass roots nontaxable amount.

The *lobbying nontaxable amount* is the lesser of (1) $1,000,000 or (2) the amount determined in Figure 22–1.[15] The *grass roots nontaxable amount* is 25 percent of the lobbying nontaxable amount.[16]

| EXAMPLE 1 | F, a qualifying § 501(c)(3) organization, incurs lobbying expenditures for the taxable year of $500,000 and grass roots expenditures of $0. Exempt purpose expenditures for the taxable year are $5,000,000. F makes the election to be eligible to make lobbying expenditures on a limited basis. |

Applying the data in Figure 22–1, the lobbying nontaxable amount is $400,000 [$225,000 + 5% ($5,000,000 − $1,500,000)]. The ceiling on lobbying expenditures is $600,000 (150% × $400,000). Therefore, the $500,000 of lobbying expenditures are within the permitted ceiling of $600,000. However, the election results in the imposition of tax on the excess lobbying expenditures of $100,000 ($500,000 lobbying expenditures − $400,000 lobbying nontaxable amount). The resultant tax liability is $25,000 ($100,000 × 25%). □

A § 501(c)(3) organization that makes disqualifying lobbying expenditures is subject to a tax on the lobbying expenditures for the taxable year. A tax may also be levied on the organization management. The rate of the tax on the organization is 5 percent, and the rate on management is also 5 percent. The tax is imposed on management only if management knew that making the expenditures was likely to result in the organization no longer being described in § 501(c)(3) and if management's actions were willful and not due to reasonable cause. Such tax does not apply to private foundations (see the subsequent discussion of private foundations).[17]

FIGURE 22–1   Calculation of Lobbying Nontaxable Amount

Exempt Purpose Expenditures	Lobbying Nontaxable Amount Is
Not over $500,000	20% of exempt purpose expenditures*
Over $500,000 but not over $1,000,000	$100,000 + 15% of the excess of exempt purpose expenditures over $500,000
Over $1,000,000 but not over $1,500,000	$175,000 + 10% of the excess of exempt purpose expenditures over $1,000,000
Over $1,500,000	$225,000 + 5% of the excess of exempt purpose expenditures over $1,500,000

* Exempt purpose expenditures generally are the amounts paid or incurred for the taxable year to accomplish the following purposes: religious, charitable, scientific, literary, educational, fostering national or international amateur sports competition, or the prevention of cruelty to children or animals.

14. § 4911(b).
15. § 4911(c)(2).
16. § 4911(c)(4).
17. § 4912.

CONCEPT SUMMARY 22-2

Exempt Organizations and Influencing Legislation

Factor	Tax Result
Type to which applicable	§ 501(c)(3) organization.
Effect of influencing legislation	Subject to tax on lobbying expenditures under § 4912.
	Forfeit exempt status under § 501(c)(3).
	Not eligible for exempt status under § 501(c)(4).
Effect of electing § 501(h) treatment	Limited ability to make lobbying expenditures.
	Subject to tax under § 4911.

The tax result of exempt organizations influencing legislation is reviewed in Concept Summary 22-2.

Section 503 results in the exempt organization losing its exempt status, at least temporarily, if it engages in a prohibited transaction. Since none of the exempt organizations subject to § 503 treatment are among the types of exempt organizations being examined in this chapter, § 503 is not discussed further.[18]

Feeder Organizations. A *feeder organization* carries on a trade or business for the benefit of an exempt organization (remits its profits to the exempt organization). Such organizations are not exempt from Federal income taxation. This provision is intended to prevent an entity whose primary purpose is to conduct a trade or business for profit from escaping taxation merely because all of its profits are payable to one or more exempt organizations.[19]

For purposes of the feeder organization rules, three types of activities are defined as not comprising the activities of a trade or business. Therefore, such types of activities are *not* subject to the feeder organization rules. These excluded activities are as follows:[20]

- An activity that generates rental income that would be excluded from the definition of the term *rent* for purposes of the unrelated business income tax (discussed subsequently).

- Activities that normally would constitute a trade or business, but for which substantially all the work is performed by volunteers.

- Activities that normally would constitute the trade or business of selling merchandise, but for which substantially all the merchandise has been received as contributions or gifts.

PRIVATE FOUNDATIONS

Tax Consequences of Private Foundation Status

Certain exempt organizations are classified as private foundations. This classification produces two negative consequences. First, this may have an adverse impact on the contributions received by the donee exempt organization because the tax consequences to the donor may not be as favorable as they would be if the exempt

---

18. §§ 503(a) and (c).

19. § 502(a).

20. § 502(b).

organization were not a private foundation.[21] Second, the classification may result in taxation at the exempt organization level. The reason for this less beneficial tax treatment is that this type of exempt organization envisions a more narrow definition of the common good and therefore less broad donor support. In other words, § 501(c)(3) organizations that are not classified as private foundations—the so-called *public charities*—generally do have broad public support (or actively function in a supporting relationship to such organizations).

Definition of a Private Foundation.   The Code defines a private foundation by enumerating the § 501(c)(3) exempt organizations that are not private foundations. Thus, only § 501(c)(3) exempt organizations so enumerated are not private foundations. Included as being *outside* the definition of a private foundation are the following § 501(c)(3) organizations:[22]

1. Churches; educational institutions; hospitals and medical research organizations; charitable organizations receiving a major portion of their support from the general public or the United States, a state, or a political subdivision thereof; and governmental units.

2. Organizations that are broadly supported by the general public (excluding disqualified persons), by governmental units, or by organizations described in (1) above.

3. Organizations organized and operated exclusively for the benefit of organizations described in (1) or (2) [a supporting organization].

4. Organizations organized and operated exclusively for testing for public safety.

To satisfy the broadly supported provision in (2) above, both the following tests must be satisfied:

• One-third support test.

• Not more than one-third support test.

Under the *one-third support test*, the organization *normally* must receive more than one-third of its support each taxable year from the three aforementioned groups in the form of the following:

• Gifts, grants, contributions, and membership fees.

• Gross receipts from admissions, sales of merchandise, performance of services, or the furnishing of facilities in an activity that is not an unrelated trade or business for purposes of the unrelated business income tax (discussed subsequently). However, such gross receipts from any person or governmental agency in excess of the greater of $5,000 or 1 percent of the organization's support for the taxable year are not counted.

The *not more than one-third support test* limits the amount of support *normally* received from the following sources to one-third of the organization's support for the taxable year:

• Gross investment income (gross income from interest, dividends, rents, and royalties).

• Unrelated business taxable income (discussed subsequently) minus the related tax.

---

21. § 170(e)(1)(B)(ii).   22. § 509(a).

For this purpose, the term *normally* refers to the tests being satisfied for the four taxable years preceding the current taxable year. Satisfying the test for the current taxable year will result in the subsequent taxable year being treated as satisfying the test.[23]

EXAMPLE 2

P, a § 501(c)(3) organization, received the following support during the taxable year:

Governmental unit A for services rendered	$30,000
Governmental unit B for services rendered	20,000
General public for services rendered	20,000
Gross investment income	15,000
Contributions from individual substantial contributors (disqualified persons)	15,000

For purposes of the *one-third support test*, the support from governmental unit A is counted only to the extent of $5,000 (greater of $5,000 or 1% of $100,000 support). Likewise, for governmental unit B, only $5,000 is counted as support. Thus, the total countable support is only $30,000 ($20,000 from the general public + $5,000 + $5,000), and the related percentage is only 30% ($30,000/$100,000). The $15,000 received from disqualified persons is excluded from the numerator but is included in the denominator. Thus, the test for the taxable year is failed.

In calculating the *not more than one-third support test*, only the gross investment income of $15,000 is included in the numerator. Thus, the test is satisfied ($15,000/$100,000 = 15%) for the taxable year.

Since both tests were not satisfied, P does not qualify as an organization that is broadly supported. □

The intent of the two tests is to exclude from private foundation status those § 501(c)(3) organizations that are responsive to the general public rather than to the private interests of a limited number of donors or other persons.

Examples of § 501(c)(3) organizations that are properly classified as private foundations receiving broad public support include the United Fund, the Boy Scouts, university alumni associations, symphony orchestras, and the PTA.

Taxes Imposed on Private Foundations

In general, a private foundation is exempt from Federal income taxation. However, because it is a private foundation, as contrasted with a more broadly, publicly supported organization, it may be subject to the following taxes, which are levied only on private foundations:

- Tax based on investment income.
- Tax on self-dealing.
- Tax on failure to distribute income.
- Tax on excess business holdings.

---

23. Reg. § 1.509(a)–3(c).

- Tax on investments that jeopardize charitable purposes.
- Tax on taxable expenditures.

These taxes serve to restrict the permitted activities of private foundations. The taxes may be imposed on the private foundation and the foundation manager and may be imposed in the form of both an initial tax and an additional tax. The initial taxes (first-level), with the exception of the tax based on investment income, are imposed because the private foundation engages in so-called *prohibited* transactions. Such acts include both certain actions and certain failures to act. The additional taxes (second-level) are imposed only if the prohibited transactions are not corrected within a statutory time period. The additional taxes are effectively waived (not assessed, abated, or refunded) if the prohibited transactions are corrected during a statutory correction period.[24] See Concept Summary 22–3 for additional details.

The tax on failure to distribute income will be used to illustrate how expensive these taxes can be and the related importance of avoiding the imposition of such taxes.

CONCEPT SUMMARY 22–3

Taxes Imposed on Private Foundations

Type of Tax	Code Section	Purpose	Private Foundation		Foundation Manager	
			Initial Tax	Additional Tax	Initial Tax	Additional Tax
On investment income	§ 4940	Audit fee to defray IRS expenses.	2%*			
On self-dealing	§ 4941	Engaging in transactions with disqualified persons.	5%**	200%	2.5%†	50%†
On failure to distribute income	§ 4942	Failing to distribute adequate amount of income for exempt purposes.	15%	100%		
On excess business holdings	§ 4943	Investments that enable the private foundation to control unrelated businesses.	5%	200%		
On jeopardizing investments	§ 4944	Speculative investments that put the private foundation's assets at risk.	5%	25%	5%††	5%†
On taxable expenditures	§ 4945	Expenditures that should not be made by private foundations.	10%	100%	2.5%††	50%†

  *   May be possible to reduce the tax rate to 1%. In addition, an exempt operating foundation [see §§ 4940(d)(2) and 4942(j)(3)] is not subject to the tax.

 **   Imposed on the disqualified person rather than the foundation.

  †   Subject to a statutory ceiling of $10,000.

 ††   Subject to a statutory ceiling of $5,000.

---

24. § 4961.

For failure to distribute all of its income, a tax may be imposed on a nonoperating private foundation in the form of an initial tax (first-level) and an additional tax (second-level). The initial tax is imposed at a rate of 15 percent on the income for the taxable year that is not distributed during the current or the following taxable year. The initial tax will continue to be imposed on such undistributed income for each year until the IRS assesses the tax.

The additional tax is imposed at a rate of 100 percent on the amount of the inadequate distribution that is not distributed by the assessment date. The additional tax is effectively waived if the undistributed income is distributed within 90 days after the mailing of the deficiency notice for the additional tax. Extensions of this period may be obtained.

Undistributed income is the excess of the distributable amount (in effect, the amount that should have been distributed) over qualifying distributions made by the entity. The distributable amount is the excess of the minimum investment return over the sum of the (1) unrelated business income tax and (2) the excise tax based on net investment income under § 4940. The minimum investment return is 5 percent of the excess of the fair market value of the foundation's assets over the unpaid debt associated with acquiring or improving these assets. Assets of the foundation that are employed directly in carrying on the foundation's exempt purpose are not used in making this calculation.

EXAMPLE 3

P, a private foundation, has undistributed income of $80,000 for its taxable year 1987. Fifteen thousand dollars of this amount is distributed during 1988, and an additional $45,000 is distributed during 1989. The IRS deficiency notice is mailed to P on August 5, 1990. The initial tax is $12,750 [($65,000 × 15%) + ($20,000 × 15%)].

At the date of the deficiency notice, no additional distributions have been made with respect to the 1987 undistributed income. Therefore, since the remaining undistributed income of $20,000 has not been distributed by August 5, 1990, an additional tax of $20,000 ($20,000 × 100%) is imposed.

If the $20,000 of undistributed income for 1987 were distributed within 90 days of the IRS deficiency notice for the additional tax, the additional tax would be waived. Lacking this distribution, however, $32,750 ($12,750 + $20,000) in taxes are payable by the foundation. □

UNRELATED BUSINESS INCOME PROBLEMS

As discussed in the previous section, private foundations are subject to excise taxes for certain actions or failures to act. One of these excise taxes penalizes the private foundation for using the foundation to gain control of unrelated businesses (tax on excess business holdings). However, the term *unrelated business* for purposes of that excise tax is different from the term *unrelated business* as used in the discussion of the unrelated business income tax that follows.

The general objective of the tax on unrelated business income is to tax such income as if the entity were subject to the corporate income tax. Thus, the tax rates that are used are those applicable to a corporate taxpayer.[25] The alternative minimum tax also applies with respect to the tax preferences that enter into the computation of unrelated business taxable income.[26] In general, *unrelated business*

---

25. § 511(a)(1).   26. § 511(d)(1).

income is income from activities not related to the exempt purpose of the exempt organization, and the tax is levied because the organization is engaging in substantial commercial activities.[27] Absent such a tax, the nonexempt organization (a regular taxable business entity) would be placed at a substantial disadvantage when trying to compete with the exempt organization. Thus, the unrelated business income tax is intended to neutralize the tax differences.[28]

EXAMPLE 4   C is an exempt private foundation. The exempt activity of C is to maintain a restoration of eighteenth-century colonial life (houses, public buildings, taverns, businesses, and craft demonstrations) that is visited by over 1 million people per year. A fee is charged for admission to the "restored area." In addition to this "museum" activity, C operates two hotels and three restaurants that are available to the general public. The earnings from the hotel and restaurant business are used to defray the costs of operating the "museum" activity.

   The "museum" activity is not subject to the Federal income tax, except to the extent of any tax liability for any of the aforementioned excise taxes that are levied on private foundations. However, even though the income from the hotel and restaurant business is used for exempt purposes, such income is unrelated business income and is subject to the tax on unrelated business income. □

The tax on unrelated business income applies to all organizations that are exempt from Federal income taxation under § 501(c), except those exempt under § 501(c)(1). In addition, the tax applies to state colleges and universities (educational institutions above the secondary level operated by any governmental agency or political subdivision thereof).[29]

A materiality exception generally exempts an entity from being subject to the unrelated business income tax if such income is insignificant. See the later discussion of the $1,000 statutory deduction generally available to all exempt organizations.

Unrelated Trade or Business

For an exempt organization to be subject to the tax on unrelated business income, the following factors must be present:[30]

- The organization conducts a trade or business.

- The trade or business is not substantially related to the exempt purpose of the organization.

- The trade or business is regularly carried on by the organization.

The first two factors are discussed below, and the third factor is included in the discussion entitled Unrelated Business Income.

   The Code does contain the following statutory exceptions to classification as an unrelated trade or business; that is, even if all of the above factors are present, the activity will not be classified as an unrelated trade or business.[31]

---

27. § 512(a)(1).
28. Reg. § 1.513–1(b).
29. § 511(a)(2) and Reg. § 1.511–2(a)(2).

30. § 513(a) and Reg. § 1.513–2(a).
31. § 513(a).

- The individuals performing substantially all the work of the trade or business do so without compensation (e.g., an orphanage operates a retail store for sales to the general public, and all the work is done by volunteers).

- The trade or business consists of merchandise sales, and substantially all of the merchandise has been received as gifts or contributions (e.g., thrift shops).

- For § 501(c)(3) organizations and for state colleges or universities, the trade or business is conducted primarily for the convenience of the organization's members, students, patients, officers, or employees (e.g., a laundry operated by the college for laundering dormitory linens and students' clothing).

- For local associations of employees under § 501(c)(4), the trade or business consists of selling to association members, at their usual place of employment, work-related clothing and equipment and items normally sold through vending machines, snack bars, or food dispensing facilities. However, such association must have been organized before May 27, 1969.

Definition of Trade or Business.   Trade or business, for this purpose, is broadly defined. It includes any activity conducted for the production of income through the sale of merchandise or the performance of services. To be treated as a trade or business, it is not necessary that the activity generate a profit. The activity may be part of a larger set of activities conducted by the organization, some of which may be related to the exempt purpose. Such inclusion in a larger set does not result in the activity losing its identity as an unrelated trade or business.[32]

EXAMPLE 5   H is an exempt hospital that operates a pharmacy. The pharmacy provides medicines and supplies to the patients in the hospital (contributes to the conduct of the hospital's exempt purpose). In addition, the pharmacy sells medicines and supplies to the general public. The activity of selling to the general public constitutes a trade or business for purposes of the unrelated business income tax. □

Not Substantially Related to the Exempt Purpose.   Exempt organizations frequently conduct unrelated trades or business in order to provide income to help defray the costs of conducting the exempt purpose (see the hotel and restaurant business in Example 4). Providing such financial support for the exempt purpose has no effect in preventing such business from being classified as an unrelated trade or business and thereby being subject to the tax on unrelated business income.

Determining whether a trade or business is substantially related to the accomplishment of an organization's exempt purpose requires an examination of the relationship, if any, between the trade or business and the accomplishment of the exempt purpose. Not only must the trade or business contribute to the accomplishment of the exempt purpose, but it must also contribute *importantly* to such accomplishment. To be related to the accomplishment of the exempt purpose, the conduct of the business activities must have a causal relationship to such accomplishment. The determination of the causal relationship and the related importance are to be based on an examination of the facts and circumstances. In evaluating the importance of the contribution, the size and extent of the activities in relation to the nature and extent of the exempt function that such activities serve must be considered.[33]

---

32. Reg. § 1.513–1(b).   33. Reg. § 1.513–1(d).

EXAMPLE 6   D, an exempt organization, operates a school for training children in the performing arts. As an essential part of that training, the children participate in performances for the general public. The children are paid at the minimum wage for the actual performances, and D derives gross income by charging for admission to the performances.

The income derived from admissions is not income from an unrelated trade or business because the performances by the children contribute importantly to the accomplishment of the exempt purpose of providing training in the performing arts. □

EXAMPLE 7   Assume the facts are the same as in Example 6, except that four performances are conducted each weekend of the year. Assume that this number of performances far exceeds that required for the training of the children. Thus, the part of the income derived from admissions for these excess performances is income from an unrelated trade or business. □

The trade or business may sell merchandise that has been produced as part of the accomplishment of the exempt purpose. The sale of such merchandise is normally treated as substantially related. However, if the merchandise is not sold in substantially the same state it was in at the completion of the exempt purpose, then the gross income subsequently derived from the sale of the merchandise is income from an unrelated trade or business.[34]

EXAMPLE 8   H, an exempt organization, conducts programs for the rehabilitation of the handicapped. One of the programs includes training in the repair of radios and televisions. H derives gross income by selling the repaired items. The income so derived is substantially related to the accomplishment of the exempt purpose. □

An asset or facility used in the exempt purpose may also be used in a nonexempt purpose. Income derived from the use in the nonexempt purpose is income from an unrelated trade or business. Related expense allocations for assets and employees used in both an exempt and a nonexempt purpose are to be made on a reasonable basis.[35]

EXAMPLE 9   M, an exempt organization, operates a museum. As part of the exempt purpose of the museum, educational lectures are given in the museum's theater during the operating hours of the museum. In the evening, when the museum is closed, the theater is leased to an individual who operates a movie theater. The lease income received from the individual who operates the movie theater is income from an unrelated trade or business. □

Special Rule for Bingo Games.   A special provision applies in determining whether income from bingo games is from an unrelated trade or business. Under

---

34. Reg. § 1.513−1(d)(4)(ii).   35. Reg. § 1.513−1(d)(4)(iii).

this provision, a *qualified bingo game* is not an unrelated trade or business. However, in order to be a qualified bingo game, both of the following requirements must be satisfied:[36]

- The bingo game is legal under both state and local law.

- Commercial bingo games (conducted for a profit motive) ordinarily are not permitted in the jurisdiction.

EXAMPLE 10   B, an exempt organization, conducts weekly bingo games. The laws of the state and municipality in which B conducts the bingo games expressly provide that bingo games may be conducted by exempt organizations. Such laws do not permit bingo games to be conducted by profit-oriented entities. Since both of the requirements for bingo games are satisfied, the bingo games conducted by B are not an unrelated trade or business. □

EXAMPLE 11   B, an exempt organization, conducts weekly bingo games in City X and City Y. State law expressly permits exempt organizations to conduct bingo games. State law also provides that profit-oriented entities may conduct bingo games in City X, which is a resort community. Several businesses regularly conduct bingo games there.

The bingo games conducted by B in City Y are not an unrelated trade or business. However, the bingo games that B conducts in City X are an unrelated trade or business because commercial bingo games are regularly permitted to be conducted there. □

Special Rule for Distribution of Low-Cost Articles.   If an exempt organization distributes low-cost items and such distributions are incidental to the organization's solicitation for charitable contributions, such distributions may not be considered an unrelated trade or business. A low-cost article is one that costs $5 (to be indexed) or less. Examples of such items are pens, stamps, stickers, stationery, and address labels. If more than one item is distributed to a person during the calendar year, the costs of the items are combined. The following requirements must be satisfied for the distributions to be *incidental*:[37]

- The person receiving the low-cost article did not request it.

- The person receiving the low-cost article receives it without having given express consent.

- The distribution of the article is accompanied by a request for a charitable contribution.

- The person receiving the low-cost article is notified at the time of receipt that the article may be retained even if a charitable contribution is not made.

Special Rule for Rental or Exchange of Membership Lists.   If an exempt organization conducts a trade or business that consists of either exchanging with or renting to other exempt organizations the organization's donor or membership list (mailing lists), such trade or business is not an unrelated trade or business.[38]

---

36. § 513(f).
37. § 513(h)(1)(A).

38. § 513(h)(1)(B).

Other Special Rules.   Other special rules are used in determining whether each of the following activities is an unrelated trade or business:[39]

- Qualified public entertainment activities (e.g., a state fair).
- Qualified convention and trade show activities.
- Certain services provided at cost or less by a hospital to other small hospitals.
- Certain pole rentals by telephone companies.

Discussion of these special rules is beyond the scope of this text.

Unrelated Business Income

If an exempt organization conducts an unrelated trade or business, taxation will result only if the exempt organization regularly conducts such business and such business produces unrelated business income.

Regularly Carried on by the Organization.   An activity will not be classified as unrelated business income unless it is regularly carried on by the exempt organization. The purpose of this provision is to assure that only those activities that are actually competing with taxable organizations are subject to the unrelated business income tax. With this objective in mind, factors to be considered in assessing *regularly carried on* include the frequency of the activity, the continuity of the activity, and the manner in which the activity is pursued. In other words, is the activity generally being conducted similarly to the conduct of the activity by a taxable organization?[40]

EXAMPLE 12

E, an exempt organization, owns land that is located next to the state fairgrounds. During the 10 days of the state fair, E uses the land as a parking lot and charges individuals attending the state fair for parking there. Under these circumstances, the activity is not regularly carried on. □

EXAMPLE 13

F, an exempt organization, has its offices in the downtown area. It owns a parking lot adjacent to its offices on which its employees park during the week. On Saturdays, it rents the spaces in the parking lot to individuals shopping or working in the downtown area. In this case, F is conducting a business activity on a year-round basis, even though it is only for one day per week. Thus, an activity is regularly being carried on. □

Unrelated Business Income Defined.   Unrelated business income is generally the income derived from the unrelated trade or business. To convert it from a gross income measure to a net income measure, it must be reduced by the deductions directly connected with the conduct of the unrelated trade or business.[41]

Unrelated Business Taxable Income

General Tax Model.   The model for unrelated business taxable income appears in Figure 22–2.

---

39. §§ 513(d), (e), and (g).
40. § 512(a)(1) and Reg. § 1.513–1(c).

41. § 512(a)(1).

FIGURE 22–2 Tax Formula for Unrelated Business Taxable Income

> Gross unrelated business income
> − Deductions
> = Net unrelated business income
> ± Modifications
> = Unrelated business taxable income

The modifications that must be made to convert net unrelated business income to unrelated business taxable income are grouped for presentation purposes into a positive adjustment category and a negative adjustment category. The positive adjustments require that certain items that either were not included in the gross unrelated business income category or were included in the deductions category be added in calculating unrelated business taxable income. The negative adjustments require that certain items that either were included in the gross unrelated business income category or were not included in the deductions category be deducted in calculating unrelated business taxable income. This pedagogical approach provides an effective technique for dealing with income and deduction items that receive special treatment.

Positive adjustments:[42]

1. The charitable contribution deduction is permitted without regard to whether the charitable contributions are associated with the unrelated trade or business. However, to the extent the charitable contributions deducted in calculating net unrelated business income (see Figure 22–2) exceed 10 percent of unrelated business taxable income (without regard to the charitable contribution deduction), such excess is treated as a positive adjustment.

EXAMPLE 14 E, an exempt organization, has unrelated business taxable income of $100,000 (excluding the charitable contribution deduction). Total charitable contributions (all associated with the unrelated trade or business) are $13,000. Assuming that the $13,000 is deducted in calculating net unrelated business income, the excess of $3,000 [$13,000 − 10% ($100,000)] is a positive adjustment in calculating unrelated business taxable income. □

2. Unrelated debt-financed income [including debt-financed income associated with items (1) through (4) in the subsequent discussion of negative adjustments] net of the unrelated debt-financed deductions (see the subsequent discussion on Unrelated Debt–Financed Income).

3. Certain interest, annuity, royalty, and rental income received by the exempt organization from an organization it controls (80 percent test) are included in unrelated business taxable income. Such amounts are included regardless of whether such activity on the part of the controlling organization is a trade or business or is regularly conducted. Therefore, to the extent such amounts are not included in net unrelated business income (see Figure 22–2), a positive adjustment is required in calculating unrelated business taxable income. Note

---

42. §§ 512(a)(1) and (b) and Reg. § 1.512(b)–1.

that this provision overrides the modifications for these types of income (discussed subsequently under negative adjustments).

Negative adjustments:

1. Income from dividends, interest, and annuities net of all deductions directly related to producing such income.

2. Royalty income, regardless of whether it is measured by production, gross income, or taxable income from the property, net of all deductions directly related to producing such income. However, if the income is from a working interest and the exempt organization is responsible for its share of the development costs, the resultant income is not considered to be royalty income.

3. Rental income from real property and from certain personal property net of all deductions directly related to producing such income. Personal property rents are included in the negative adjustment only if the personal property is leased with the real property and the amount of the personal property rental income is incidental (determined at the time the personal property is placed in service by the lessee) when compared with the total rental income under the lease. Under the Regulations, personal property rental income is not incidental if it exceeds 10 percent of total rental income under the lease. However, none of the rental income (from real property and personal property) will be treated as a negative adjustment if either of the following conditions is present:

   a. More than 50 percent of the rental income under the lease is from personal property.

   b. Rental income is calculated completely, or in part, based on the profits of the lessee (unless such calculation is based on a fixed percentage of sales or receipts).

EXAMPLE 15   E, an exempt organization, leases land and a building (realty) and computers (personalty) housed in the building. Forty-six thousand dollars of the lease is identified as being for the land and building and $4,000 for the computers. Expenses that are properly allocable to the land and building are $10,000. The net rental income from the land and building of $36,000 ($46,000 − $10,000) and that from the computers of $4,000 are treated as negative adjustments. □

EXAMPLE 16   Assume the facts are the same as in Example 15, except the rental income from the land and building is $35,000 and that from the computers is $15,000. Since the rental income from the computers is not incidental, such rental income is not treated as a negative adjustment. □

EXAMPLE 17   Assume the facts are the same as in Example 15, except the rental income from the land and building is $20,000 and that from the computers is $30,000. Since over 50% of the rental income under the lease is from the computers, neither the rental income from the land and building nor that from the computers is treated as a negative adjustment. □

Note that if the lessor of real property provides significant services to the lessee, such income, for this purpose, is not rental income.

4. Gains and losses from the sale, exchange, or other disposition of property *except for* inventory.

EXAMPLE 18   Assume E, the owner of the land, building, and computers in Example 15 sells these assets for $450,000. The adjusted basis for these assets is $300,000. The recognized gain of $150,000 is treated as a negative adjustment in calculating unrelated business taxable income (it is included in gross unrelated business income and then is deducted as a modification).   □

5. Certain research income net of all deductions directly related to producing such income.

6. The charitable contribution deduction is permitted without regard to whether the charitable contributions are associated with the unrelated trade or business. Therefore, to the extent that the charitable contributions exceed those deducted in calculating net unrelated business income (see Figure 22–2), such excess is treated as a negative adjustment in calculating unrelated business taxable income. Note, however, that the total deductions for charitable contributions may not exceed 10 percent of unrelated business taxable income (without regard to the charitable contribution deduction) [see positive adjustment (1)].

EXAMPLE 19   E, an exempt organization, has unrelated business taxable income of $100,000 (excluding the charitable contribution deduction). The total charitable contributions are $9,000, of which $7,000 (those associated with the unrelated trade or business) have been deducted in calculating net unrelated business income. Therefore, the other $2,000 of charitable contributions are deducted as a negative adjustment in calculating unrelated business taxable income.   □

7. A specific deduction of $1,000 is permitted.

Unrelated Debt-Financed Income

In the calculation model for the tax on unrelated business income (see Figure 22–2), unrelated debt-financed income is one of the modifications in the positive adjustment category. Because of the importance of this item, it is discussed separately here.

Definition of Debt-Financed Income.   *Debt-financed income* is the gross income generated from debt-financed property. *Debt-financed property* is all property of the exempt organization that is held to produce income and on which there is acquisition indebtedness *except* for the following:[43]

1. Property for which substantially all the use is for the achievement of the exempt purpose of the exempt organization.

2. Property whose gross income is otherwise treated as unrelated business income.

3. Property whose gross income is from the following sources and is not otherwise treated as unrelated business income:

---

43. § 514(b).

    a.   Income from research performed for the United States or an agency thereof or a state or a political subdivision thereof.

    b.   For a college, university, or hospital, income from research.

    c.   For an organization that performs fundamental (as distinguished from applied) research for the benefit of the general public, income from research.

4.   Property used in a trade or business that is treated as not being an unrelated trade or business under one of the statutory exceptions.

    For purposes of the first exception, the term *substantially all* requires that the use in the exempt purpose be at least 85 percent of the use of the property by the exempt organization. If the 85 percent test is not satisfied, but a portion of the use of the property is for the exempt purpose, then that portion of the property is not debt-financed property.[44]

EXAMPLE 20

F, an exempt organization, owns a five-story office building on which there is acquisition indebtedness. Three of the floors are used for F's exempt purpose. The two other floors are leased to X Corporation. In this case, the *substantially all* test is not satisfied. Therefore, 40% of the office building is debt-financed property, and 60% is not. □

    In addition to the four above exceptions, a special rule provides that certain land that is acquired for exempt use within 10 years (property acquired for prospective exempt use) may be excluded from being debt-financed property. To qualify for exclusion under this special rule, the following requirements must be satisfied:[45]

1.   The exempt organization acquires real property for the principal purpose of using the land (substantially all its use) for the achievement of the exempt purpose of the exempt organization.

2.   Such use is to commence within 10 years of the acquisition date.

3.   At the acquisition date, the acquired property is located in the *neighborhood* of other property of the exempt organization for which substantially all the use is for the achievement of the exempt purpose of the exempt organization.

    Even if the third requirement is not satisfied (the property is not located in the neighborhood), it may still be possible to have the land excluded from being debt-financed property. Such exclusion will result if the acquired land is actually converted to being used for the achievement of the exempt purpose of the exempt organization within the 10-year period. Qualification under this provision will result in a refund of taxes previously paid. If the exempt organization is a church, the 10-year period is replaced with a 15-year period, and the neighborhood requirement is waived.

    Examples of income from debt-financed property include the rental of real estate, rental of tangible personal property, and investments in corporate stock, including gains from the disposition of such property. Gains from property that is unrelated business income property are also included to the extent such gains are not otherwise treated as unrelated business income.

---

44. Reg. § 1.514(b)–1(b)(1)(ii).   45. § 514(b)(3).

In determining whether there is acquisition indebtedness on property, the relevant time period for the determination is any time during the taxable year. However, for property disposed of during the taxable year, the period is the 12-month period ending on the date of disposition.[46]

Definition of Acquisition Indebtedness.   In general terms, acquisition indebtedness is debt sustained by the exempt organization in association with the acquisition of property (but see the earlier discussion of exclusions from the definition of property for this purpose under Definition of Unrelated Debt-Financed Income). More precisely, *acquisition indebtedness* consists of the unpaid amounts of the following for debt-financed property:[47]

1. Debt incurred in acquiring or improving the property.

2. Debt incurred prior to the acquisition or improvement of the property, but which would not have been incurred absent such acquisition or improvement.

3. Debt incurred subsequent to the acquisition or improvement of the property, but which would not have been incurred absent such acquisition or improvement and whose incurrence was reasonably foreseeable at the time of acquisition or improvement.

EXAMPLE 21

F, an exempt organization, acquires land for $100,000. In order to finance the acquisition, F mortgages the land with a bank and receives loan proceeds of $80,000. F leases the land to X Corporation. The mortgage is acquisition indebtedness. □

EXAMPLE 22

G, an exempt organization, makes improvements to an office building that it rents to X Corporation. Excess working capital funds are used to finance the improvements. G is later required to mortgage its laboratory building, which it uses for its exempt purpose, to replenish the working capital. The mortgage is acquisition indebtedness. □

Portion of Debt-Financed Income and Deductions Treated as Unrelated Business Taxable Income.   Once the amount of the debt-financed income and deductions is determined, it is necessary to ascertain what portion of the debt-financed income and deductions is unrelated debt-financed income and deductions. Unrelated debt-financed income increases unrelated business taxable income, and unrelated debt-financed deductions decrease unrelated business taxable income (see the earlier discussion under Unrelated Business Taxable Income).

The calculation is made for each debt-financed property. The gross income from the property is multiplied by the following percentage:[48]

$$\frac{\text{Average acquisition indebtedness for the property}}{\text{Average adjusted basis of the property}} = \frac{\text{Debt/basis}}{\text{percentage}}$$

---

46. § 514(b)(1).
47. § 514(c)(1). Under a special rule, educational organizations in certain limited circumstances can exclude debt incurred for real property acquisi-

tions from classification as acquisition indebtedness.
48. § 514(a)(1).

This percentage has a statutory ceiling of 100 percent. If debt-financed property is disposed of during the taxable year at a gain, average acquisition indebtedness in the formula is replaced with highest acquisition indebtedness. *Highest acquisition indebtedness* is defined as the largest amount of acquisition indebtedness with respect to the property for the 12-month period preceding the date of disposition.[49]

The allowable deductions are those that are directly related to the debt-financed property and the income therefrom. However, depreciation deductions are limited to the amount that would have been calculated using the straight-line method. Once the amount of the allowable deductions is determined, this amount is multiplied by the debt/basis percentage.[50]

EXAMPLE 23

F, an exempt organization, owns an office building that it leases to X Corporation for $120,000 per year. The average acquisition indebtedness is $300,000, and the average adjusted basis is $500,000. Since the office building is debt-financed property, the unrelated debt-financed income is calculated as follows:

$$\frac{\$300,000}{\$500,000} \times \$120,000 = \$72,000 \qquad \square$$

Once a capital loss has been multiplied by the debt/basis percentage in the year of the loss, any amount carried back or forward is not adjusted by the debt/basis percentage of the taxable year to which it is carried. If the debt-financed property is disposed of during the taxable year at a loss, average acquisition indebtedness in the formula is replaced with highest acquisition indebtedness.

Average Acquisition Indebtedness.   The *average acquisition indebtedness* for a debt-financed property is the average amount of the outstanding debt for the taxable year (ignoring interest) during the portion of the year the property is held by the exempt organization. This amount is calculated by summing the outstanding debt on the first day of each calendar month the property is held by the exempt organization and dividing this summation by the number of months the property is held by the organization. Part of a month is treated as a full month.[51]

EXAMPLE 24

On August 12, F, an exempt organization, acquires an office building that is debt-financed property for $500,000. The initial mortgage on the property is $400,000. The principal amount of the debt on the first of each month is as follows:

Month	Principal Amount
August	$ 400,000
September	380,000
October	360,000
November	340,000
December	320,000
	$1,800,000

---

49. § 514(c)(7).
50. § 514(a)(3).

51. § 514(c)(7) and Reg. § 1.514(a)–1(a)(3).

The average acquisition indebtedness is $360,000 ($1,800,000 ÷ 5 months). Note that even though August is only a partial month, it is treated as a full month. □

Average Adjusted Basis. The *average adjusted basis* of debt-financed property is calculated by summing the adjusted basis of the property on the first day during the taxable year the property is held by the exempt organization and the adjusted basis on the last day during the taxable year the property is so held and dividing by two.[52]

EXAMPLE 25   Assume the facts are the same as in Example 24. In addition, during the taxable year, depreciation of $5,900 is deducted. The average adjusted basis is $497,050 [($500,000 + $494,100) ÷ 2]. □

TAX PLANNING CONSIDERATIONS

Exempt organizations can provide two potential tax benefits. First, the entity may be exempt from Federal income taxation. Second, contributions to the entity may be deductible by the donor.

An organization will be exempt from taxation only if it fits into one of the categories enumerated in the Code. Thus, particular attention must be given to the qualification requirements. Since these requirements, in effect, become maintenance requirements, these requirements must continue to be satisfied to avoid termination of exempt status.

Exempt organizations that can qualify as public charities receive more beneficial tax treatment than do those that qualify as private foundations. Thus, if possible, the organization should be structured to qualify as a public charity.

If the organization is a private foundation, care must be exercised to avoid the assessment of tax liability on prohibited transactions. If such assessment does occur in the form of an initial tax, corrective actions should be implemented to avoid the assessment of an additional tax.

If the exempt organization conducts an unrelated trade or business, it may be subject to taxation on the unrelated business income. Worse yet, the unrelated trade or business could result in the loss of exempt status if the magnitude of the trade or business activity is ascertained to be the primary purpose of the organization. Thus, caution and planning should be used to eliminate the latter possibility and to minimize the former.

PROBLEM MATERIALS

Discussion Questions

1. Why are certain organizations either partially or completely exempt from Federal income taxation?

2. Under what circumstances may an exempt organization be subject to Federal income tax?

---

52. § 514(a)(1) and Reg. § 1.514(a)–1(a)(2).

3. How can a § 501(c)(3) organization engage in lobbying without engaging in a prohibited transaction?

4. What is a feeder organization, and why is it not exempt from Federal income taxation?

5. What is a private foundation, and what are the disadvantages of an exempt organization being classified as a private foundation?

6. What types of taxes may be levied on a private foundation? Why are the taxes levied?

7. A private foundation has net investment income of $50,000, yet its tax liability on net investment income is zero. Explain.

8. What is the purpose of the tax on unrelated business income?

9. Under what circumstances can an exempt organization conduct bingo games and not have the income be treated as unrelated business income?

10. Passive income (e.g., interest, royalties, and annuities) generally is not unrelated business income. Under what circumstances do such items increase the amount of unrelated business taxable income?

11. What effect does unrelated debt-financed income have on unrelated business income?

12. Define each of the following with respect to unrelated debt-financed property:
   a. Debt-financed income.
   b. Debt-financed property.
   c. Acquisition indebtedness.
   d. Average acquisition indebtedness.
   e. Average adjusted basis.

Problems

13. E, a § 501(c)(3) educational institution, makes lobbying expenditures of $95,000. E incurs exempt purposes expenditures of $400,000 in carrying out its educational mission.
   a. Determine the tax consequences to E if it does not elect to be eligible to participate in lobbying activities on a limited basis.
   b. Determine the tax consequences to E if it does elect to be eligible to participate in lobbying activities on a limited basis.

14. P, a § 501(c)(3) organization, received support from the following sources:

Governmental unit A for services rendered	$ 4,000
General public for services rendered	60,000
Gross investment income	30,000
Contributions from disqualified persons	20,000
Contributions from other than disqualified persons	86,000

   a. Does P satisfy the test for receiving broad public support?
   b. Is P a private foundation?

15. P is a private foundation that has been in existence for 10 years. During this period, it has been unable to satisfy the requirements for classification as a private operating foundation. At the end of 1989, it had undistributed income of $100,000. Of this amount, $40,000 was distributed in 1990, and $60,000 was

distributed during the first quarter of 1991. The IRS deficiency notice was mailed on August 1, 1992.

    a. Calculate the initial tax for 1989, 1990, and 1991.

    b. Calculate the additional tax for 1992.

16. F, is the foundation manager of P, a private foundation. D, a substantial contributor to P, engages in an act of self-dealing with P. F is aware that the act is an act of self-dealing. The amount involved is $100,000.

    a. Calculate the amount of the initial tax.

    b. Calculate the amount of the additional tax if the act of self-dealing is not corrected within the correction period.

17. A museum that is an exempt organization operates a gift shop. The annual operations budget of the museum is $2.5 million. Gift shop sales generate a profit of $750,000. Another $500,000 of endowment income is generated. Both the income from the gift shop and the endowment income are used to support the exempt purpose of the museum. The balance of $1.25 million required for annual operations is provided through admission fees.

    a. Calculate the amount of unrelated business income.

    b. Assume that the endowment income is reinvested rather than being used to support annual operations. Calculate the amount of unrelated business income.

18. F, an exempt organization, has unrelated business taxable income of $400,000 (excluding the deduction for charitable contributions). During the year, it makes charitable contributions of $45,000, of which $38,000 are associated with the unrelated trade or business.

    a. Calculate unrelated business taxable income.

    b. Assume that the charitable contributions are $39,000, of which $38,000 are associated with the unrelated trade or business. Calculate unrelated business taxable income.

19. G, an exempt organization, leases a factory building, machinery, and equipment to Y Corporation. The annual lease rental amount for the building is $150,000, and the amount for the machinery and equipment is $200,000. Depreciation on the building is $5,500, and depreciation on the machinery and equipment is $40,000.

    a. Calculate the amount of unrelated business taxable income to G.

    b. Assume that the rental income from the machinery and equipment is only $20,000 and the related depreciation is $4,000. Calculate the amount of unrelated business taxable income to G.

20. T, an exempt organization, leases a building to Q Corporation. The annual rental income is $150,000, and the annual depreciation expense is $30,000. A mortgage was used to finance the initial acquisition of the building by T. Average acquisition indebtedness is $800,000. The adjusted basis of the building at the beginning of the taxable year is $900,000.

    a. Calculate the unrelated debt-financed income and deductions.

    b. Assume that rather than leasing the building, T uses it in the performance of its exempt purpose. Calculate the unrelated debt-financed income and deductions.

23

Taxation of International Transactions

OVERVIEW OF INTERNATIONAL TAXATION

Three major elements of international taxation that may be of concern to U.S. taxpayers are U.S. Federal taxation, U.S. state taxation, and foreign jurisdiction taxation. Each of these tax jurisdictions may levy taxes on two different categories of transactions: (1) transactions involving U.S. persons and foreign investment and (2) transactions involving foreign persons and U.S. investment. This chapter will cover U.S. Federal taxation as it applies to these two categories of transactions.

Problems Encountered

Taxation usually involves two parties, the taxpayer and the taxing authority. In the international arena, each of these parties faces problems. For example, the taxpayer may encounter double or even multiple taxation of the same income. Also, the taxpayer may have deductions disallowed because of the differences in tax law from country to country. Conversely, tax authorities may have to deal with the problem of tax jurisdiction. When taxes are due on income earned within a particular country, legal barriers make it difficult for the tax authorities of that country to access funds in foreign banks or property situated in foreign jurisdictions when taxes have not been paid. Furthermore, tax authorities have to contend with taxpayers shifting the source of income to other jurisdictions in order to avoid taxation.

Objectives of the Law

Congress has enacted legislation and entered into bilateral treaties to deal with these and other problems encountered in the taxation of international transactions. Some primary objectives of U.S. tax legislation and treaties have been to alleviate double taxation, limit the shifting of the income source, and prevent unwarranted deferral of the taxation of foreign-source income. Another reason for certain tax provisions in this area is to provide equal tax treatment for resident and nonresident taxpayers.

THE FOREIGN TAX CREDIT

The United States retains the right to tax its citizens and residents on their worldwide taxable income. This provision can result in what is referred to as double taxation.

EXAMPLE 1   R, a U.S. resident, has a business in Mexico. This business earns him taxable income of $75,000 in 1990. He pays income tax of $20,000 on these earnings to the Mexican tax authorities. He also must include the $75,000 in gross income for U.S. tax purposes. Absent any consideration of the foreign taxes paid, assume he would owe $21,000 in U.S. income taxes on this foreign-source income. This would result in total taxes on the $75,000 of $41,000, or 55%. ☐

To reduce the possibility of double taxation, the U.S. Congress enacted the foreign tax credit (FTC) provisions. Under these provisions, a qualified taxpayer is allowed a tax credit for foreign income taxes paid. This credit is a dollar for dollar reduction of U.S. income tax liability.

EXAMPLE 2   R, in Example 1 above, takes an FTC of $20,000, reducing his U.S. tax liability on the foreign-source income to $1,000. Therefore, R's total taxes on the $75,000 are $21,000, or 28%. □

The Credit Provisions

The Direct Credit.   The FTC is available to U.S. taxpayers who pay or incur a foreign income tax. This is referred to as a direct credit.[1] R, in Example 1 above, would be eligible for the direct credit.

For purposes of the direct credit, only the taxpayer who bears the legal incidence of the foreign tax is eligible for the credit. Generally, tax incidence has been an issue only with regard to taxes withheld on income either by the foreign tax authorities or by the payor of the income for remittance to the foreign tax authorities. In some cases, there has been disagreement regarding whether the legal obligation to pay the tax was that of the payor or the payee.[2]

The Indirect Credit.   Section 902 provides for an indirect credit for certain foreign income taxes paid by foreign corporations. The indirect credit is available to U.S. *corporate* taxpayers who receive actual or constructive dividends from foreign corporations that have borne the legal incidence of the foreign tax. These foreign taxes are deemed paid by the corporate shareholders in the same proportion as the dividends actually or constructively received bear to the foreign corporation's post-1986 undistributed earnings. A domestic corporation that chooses the FTC for deemed-paid foreign taxes must "gross up" dividend income by the amount of deemed-paid taxes.

EXAMPLE 3   D, a domestic corporation, owns 50 percent of F, a foreign corporation. D receives a dividend of $120,000 from F. F's foreign taxes paid on post-1986 earnings were $500,000. F's post-1986 earnings (after taxes) total $1,200,000. D's deemed-paid foreign taxes for FTC purposes are $50,000 [$500,000 × ($120,000/$1,200,000)]. D must include the $50,000 in gross income for the gross-up adjustment if the FTC is elected. □

Certain ownership requirements must be met before the indirect credit is available to a domestic corporation. The domestic corporation must own 10 percent or more of the voting stock of the foreign corporation. The credit is also available for deemed-paid foreign taxes of second- and third-tier foreign corporations if the 10 percent ownership requirement is met at the second- and third-tier level and a 5 percent indirect ownership requirement is met from tier to tier. The § 902 ownership requirements are summarized in Figure 23–1.

FTC Limitations.   In order to prevent foreign taxes from being credited against U.S. taxes levied on U.S.-source taxable income, the FTC is subject to a limitation. Section 904 provides that the FTC for any taxable year shall not exceed the lesser of the actual foreign taxes paid or accrued, or the U.S. taxes (before the FTC) on foreign-source taxable income (the general limitation). The general limitation formula is as follows:

---

1. § 901.
2. See *Biddle v. Comm.*, 38–1 USTC ¶9040, 19

AFTR 1253, 58 S.Ct. 379 (USSC, 1938).

FIGURE 23–1   Section 902 Ownership Requirements

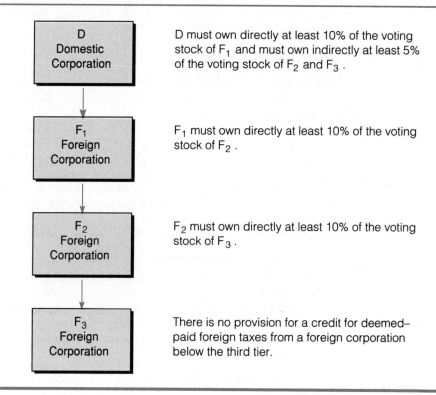

D must own directly at least 10% of the voting stock of F_1 and must own indirectly at least 5% of the voting stock of F_2 and F_3.

F_1 must own directly at least 10% of the voting stock of F_2.

F_2 must own directly at least 10% of the voting stock of F_3.

There is no provision for a credit for deemed-paid foreign taxes from a foreign corporation below the third tier.

$$\frac{\text{U.S. tax}}{\text{before FTC}} \times \frac{\text{Foreign-source taxable income}^3}{\text{Worldwide taxable income}}$$

EXAMPLE 4

S, a U.S. resident, owns a boutique in Paris, France, that earns her $50,000 foreign-source taxable income for 1990. This is her total worldwide taxable income for the tax year. She pays $20,000 in foreign taxes. Assume her U.S. tax before the FTC is $14,000. The FTC allowed for 1990 is $14,000 [$14,000 × ($50,000/$50,000)]. Thus, her net U.S. tax liability is zero. □

EXAMPLE 5

T, a U.S. resident, invests in foreign securities. His worldwide taxable income for 1990 is $120,000, consisting of $100,000 in salary from a U.S. employer and $20,000 of income from foreign sources. Foreign taxes of $6,000 were withheld by foreign tax authorities. Assume that T's U.S. tax before the FTC is $33,600. His FTC for 1990 is $5,600 [$33,600 × ($20,000/$120,000)]. Thus, his net U.S. tax liability is $28,000. □

---

3.   The taxable income of an individual, estate, or trust is computed without any deduction for per-sonal exemptions. § 904(b)(1).

As Example 5 illustrates, the limitation can prevent some portion of foreign taxes paid in high tax jurisdictions from being credited. Taxpayers could overcome this problem, however, by generating additional foreign-source income that is subject to no, or low, foreign taxation.

EXAMPLE 6   ABC, Inc., a domestic corporation, earns $500,000 of foreign-source taxable income from manufacturing operations. The foreign taxes on this income amount to $275,000. ABC's U.S.-source taxable income is $700,000. Its U.S. tax before the FTC is $408,000. Its FTC is limited to $170,000 [$408,000 × ($500,000/$1,200,000)]. □

EXAMPLE 7   If ABC invested enough funds to generate $100,000 of foreign-source interest income that was taxed at 5% by foreign tax jurisdictions, its U.S. tax before the FTC would be $442,000, and its FTC would be $204,000 [$442,000 × ($600,000/$1,300,000)]. ABC's foreign taxes would increase only $5,000, while its FTC would increase $34,000. □

In order to prevent this "cross-crediting" of foreign taxes illustrated in Example 7, Congress has enacted legislation providing for several separate limitation "baskets." These provisions require that a separate limitation be calculated for certain categories of foreign-source taxable income and the foreign taxes attributable to such income. Currently, § 904(d) provides separate limitation baskets for the following:

- Passive income.
- High withholding tax income.
- Financial services income.
- Shipping income.
- Dividends from each noncontrolled § 902 corporation.
- Dividends from a domestic international sales corporation (DISC) or former DISC to the extent they are treated as foreign-source income.
- Taxable income attributable to foreign trade income under § 923(b).
- Distributions from a foreign sales corporation (FSC) or former FSC out of E & P attributable to foreign trade income or qualified interest and carrying charges under § 263(c).

All other foreign-source income is included in a general (or overall) limitation basket.

A separate limitation under § 907 applies to foreign taxes paid on foreign oil and gas extraction income. This limitation is applied before consideration of the general limitation. Special provisions define the various categories of income, particularly with regard to the possibility that a certain item of income could fall in more than one basket, such as passive income and high withholding tax interest.

In addition, there are *look-through* rules in the case of controlled foreign corporations (CFCs) that require the U.S. shareholder receiving, for example, dividend income to "look through" to the source (classification) of the income at the CFC level.

EXAMPLE 8

D, a domestic corporation, receives foreign-source dividend income from three noncontrolled § 902 foreign corporations, X, Y, and Z. D's worldwide taxable income is $3,300,000, and its U.S. tax liability before the FTC is $1,122,000. The FTC would be determined as follows:

Payor	Dividend	Foreign Taxes Paid and Deemed Paid	FTC Limitation	FTC
X	$ 50,000	$ 4,000	$17,000*	$4,000**
Y	100,000	40,000	34,000	34,000
Z	150,000	7,500	51,000	7,500
	$300,000	$51,500		$45,500

*$1,122,000 × ($50,000/$3,300,000).
**Lesser of $4,000 or $17,000.

Without the separate basket limitation, D would have an FTC of $51,500 ($4,000 + $40,000 + $7,500). □

The limitations can result in unused (noncredited) foreign taxes for the tax year. Section 904 provides for a two-year carryback and five-year carryover of excess foreign taxes. The taxes can be credited in years when the formula limitation for that year exceeds the foreign taxes attributable to the same tax year. The carryback and carryover provision is available only within the separate baskets. In other words, excess foreign taxes in one basket cannot be carried over unless there is an excess limitation in the same basket for the carryover year.

The Alternative Minimum Tax FTC.   For purposes of the alternative minimum tax, the FTC is limited to the lesser of the credit for regular tax purposes or 90 percent of the tentative minimum tax before the credit.[4] The 10 percent cutback is calculated on the tentative minimum tax without regard to the alternative tax NOL deduction. Moreover, the general FTC limitation is calculated by using alternative minimum taxable income rather than taxable income in the denominator of the formula and the tentative minimum tax rather than the regular tax. The source of alternative minimum taxable income must be determined for the purpose of foreign-source taxable income.

Other Considerations.   In order for a foreign levy to qualify for the FTC, it must be a tax, and its predominant character must be that of an income tax in the U.S. sense.[5] A levy is a tax if it is a compulsory payment, as contrasted with a payment for a specific economic benefit such as the right to extract oil. A tax's predominant character is that of an income tax in the U.S. sense if it reaches realized net gain and is not dependent on its creditability against the income tax of another country (not a "soak-up" tax). A tax that is levied in lieu of an income tax is also creditable.[6]

4. § 59.
5. Reg. § 1.901–2.

6. § 903 and Reg. § 1.903–1.

EXAMPLE 9   D, a domestic corporation, receives oil extraction income from operations in a foreign country. The tax laws of the foreign country levy a 50% tax on extraction income and a 30% tax on all other taxable income derived within the country. If D pays $700,000 in taxes to the foreign country with regard to its extraction income, only $420,000 [$700,000 $\times$ (30% $\div$ 50%)] of that amount is creditable as an income tax. $\square$

EXAMPLE 10   X, a domestic corporation, generates $2 million of taxable income from operations in F, a foreign country. Under F's tax laws, a tax is levied on income generated in F by foreign residents only in those cases in which the country of residence (such as the United States) allows a tax credit for foreign taxes paid. X will not be allowed an FTC for taxes paid to F because the foreign tax is a soak-up tax. $\square$

Certain foreign taxes, even though meeting the definition of creditable, are not creditable because of a prohibition under § 901(j) on such credit for taxes paid to foreign governments that the United States does not recognize. Furthermore, the FTC is required to be reduced by multiplying the otherwise allowable FTC under § 901 by the International Boycott Factor.[7] This provision applies where a person, or a member of a controlled group that includes such person, participates in or cooperates with an international boycott during the taxable year.

For purposes of the FTC, foreign taxes are attributable to the year in which they are paid or accrued. For taxpayers using the cash method of accounting for tax purposes, an election to take the FTC in the year in which the foreign taxes accrue is available. Such an election is binding on the taxpayer for the year in which it is made and for all subsequent years. Taxes paid in a foreign currency are translated to U.S. dollars for FTC purposes at the exchange rate in effect when the taxes are actually paid.[8] Any adjustment of foreign taxes paid by a foreign corporation is translated at the rate in effect at the time of adjustment, except that any refund or credit is translated at the rate in effect at the time of original payment of the foreign taxes.

The FTC is elective for any particular tax year. If the taxpayer does not "choose" to take the FTC, a deduction may be allowed for foreign taxes paid or incurred. However, a taxpayer cannot take a credit and a deduction for the same foreign income taxes.[9] A taxpayer can take a deduction in the same year as an FTC for foreign taxes that are not creditable (e.g., for "soak-up" taxes).

Possessions Corporations

To encourage the economic development of U.S. possessions, a credit provision was enacted for income from operations in U.S. possessions. Since 1976, domestic corporations may elect to receive a § 936 credit against U.S. taxes equal to 34 percent of possession-source taxable income and qualified investment income whether any tax is paid or due to the possession. This is what is referred to as a "tax-sparing" credit. No additional credit or deduction is allowed for income taxes actually paid to the possession.

---

7. §§ 908 and 999.

8. §§ 986(b) and 987.

9. §§ 164 and 275.

The credit is allowed against the U.S. tax attributable to foreign-source taxable income from the active conduct of a trade or business in a U.S. possession, or the sale or exchange of substantially all the assets used by the domestic corporation in such active trade or business, and qualified possession-source investment income. The credit is not allowed against certain taxes such as the accumulated earnings tax under § 531 and the personal holding company tax under § 541.

In order to elect the credit, the domestic corporation must meet certain conditions. Eighty percent or more of its gross income for the three-year period immediately preceding the taxable year for which the credit is taken must be derived from sources within a U.S. possession, and 75 percent or more of its gross income for such period must have been derived from the active conduct of a trade or business within a U.S. possession. The credit is not available for income received in the United States unless it is possession-source income received from an unrelated person and is attributable to an active trade or business conducted in a possession.

Specific rules apply regarding intangible property income. The credit is not available for such income. Intangible property income is includible in taxable income by a domestic corporation as U.S.-source income unless all of its shareholders who are U.S. persons elect to include their pro rata share of such income in their gross income as U.S.-source income.

EXAMPLE 11   A qualified possessions corporation has the following foreign-source income on which it pays the following foreign taxes:

Taxable Income	Source	Foreign Taxes
$400,000 active trade or business income	Possession	$40,000
50,000 qualified investment income	Possession	–0–
10,000 passive nonqualified income	Possession	–0–
40,000 investment income	Nonpossession	16,000

Assume that the taxpayer's worldwide taxable income is $500,000 and its U.S. tax before the FTC is $170,000. The § 936 possessions corporation credit is $153,000 (34% × $450,000), and the § 901 FTC is $13,600 {lesser of $16,000 or [$170,000 × ($40,000/$500,000)]}. □

SOURCING OF INCOME AND ALLOCATION OF DEDUCTIONS

The sourcing of income within or without the United States has a direct bearing on a number of tax provisions. The numerator of the FTC limitation formula is foreign-source taxable income. Generally, nonresident aliens and foreign corporations are subject to Federal taxation only on U.S.-source income. The foreign earned income exclusion is available only for foreign-source income.

Income Sourced within the United States

The determination of source depends on the type of income realized. This makes the classification of income an important consideration (e.g., income from the sale of property versus income for the use of property). A detailed discussion of the

characterization of income, however, is beyond the scope of this chapter. Section 861 contains source rules for most types of income. Other rules pertaining to the source of income are found in §§ 862–865.

Interest.   Interest income received from the U.S. government, or the District of Columbia, and from noncorporate U.S. residents or domestic corporations is sourced within the United States. There are a few exceptions to this rule, most notably interest received from a resident alien individual or domestic corporation where an 80 percent foreign business requirement is met, and interest received on amounts deposited with a foreign branch of a U.S. corporation, if the branch is engaged in the commercial banking business.

EXAMPLE 12

J holds a bond issued by X, a domestic corporation. For the immediately preceding three tax years, 82% of X's gross income was active foreign business income. The interest income that J receives for the tax year from X Corporation will be foreign-source income.[10] □

Dividends.   Dividends received from domestic corporations (other than certain possessions corporations) are sourced within the United States. Generally, dividends paid by a foreign corporation will be foreign-source income. However, if 25 percent or more of a foreign corporation's gross income for the immediately preceding three tax years was effectively connected with the conduct of a U.S. trade or business, the dividends received in the taxable year will be U.S.-source income to the extent of the proportion of gross income that was effectively connected with the conduct of a U.S. trade or business for the immediately preceding three-year period. Dividends from foreign sales corporations (FSCs) and domestic international sales corporations (DISCs) can be treated as U.S.-source income.

EXAMPLE 13

T receives dividend income from the following corporations for the tax year:

Amount	Corporation	Effectively Connected Income for Past 3 Years	Active Foreign Business Income for Past 3 Years
$500	X, domestic	85%	15%
600	Y, domestic	13%	87%
300	Z, foreign	80%	20%

T has $1,340 of U.S.-source income, $500 from X, $600 from Y, and $240 from Z. The 80% active foreign business requirement would affect only interest income received from Y Corporation, not dividend income. Only 80% of the dividend from Z Corporation is U.S.-source income. □

Personal Services Income.   The source of income from personal services is determined by the location in which the services are performed (within or without

---

10. § 861(c). As will be subsequently discussed, certain interest income, even though U.S.-source income, is not taxable if earned by nonresident aliens or foreign corporations.

the United States). A limited "commercial traveler" exception is available to nonresident aliens who are in the United States for 90 days or less during the taxable year. The compensation cannot exceed $3,000 in total for the services performed in the United States. In addition, the services must be performed on behalf of a nonresident alien, foreign partnership, or foreign corporation that is not engaged in a U.S. trade or business, or on behalf of an office or place of business maintained in a foreign country or possession of the United States by an individual who is a citizen or resident of the United States, a domestic partnership, or a domestic corporation.

EXAMPLE 14   M, a nonresident alien, is an engineer employed by a foreign oil company. M spent four weeks in the United States arranging the purchase of field equipment for his company. His salary for the four weeks was $3,500. Even though the oil company is not engaged in a U.S. trade or business, and M was in the United States for less than 90 days during the taxable year, the income is U.S.-source income because it exceeds $3,000. □

The issue of whether income is derived from the performance of personal services is important in determining the income's source. It has been held that a corporation can perform personal services[11] and that, in the absence of capital as an income-producing factor, personal service income can arise even though there is no recipient of such services.[12]

Rents and Royalties.   The source of income received for the use of tangible property is the country in which the property producing the income is located. The source of income received for the use of intangible property (e.g., patents, copyrights, secret processes and formulas) is the country in which the property producing the income is used.

Sale or Exchange of Property.   Income from the disposition of U.S. real property interests is U.S.-source income. The definition of a U.S. real property interest is discussed subsequently in regard to the Foreign Investment in Real Property Tax Act (FIRPTA). Generally, the location of real property determines the source of any income derived from such property.

The source of income from the sale of personal property (property other than real property) will depend on several factors, including whether the property was produced by the seller, the type of property sold (e.g., inventory or a capital asset), and the residence of the seller. The general rule under § 865 provides that the income, gain, or profit from the sale of personal property is sourced according to the residence of the seller. Income from the sale of purchased inventory, however, is sourced in the country in which the sale takes place.[13]

When the seller has produced the property, the income must be apportioned between the country of production and the country of sale. The regulations provide

---

11. See *British Timken Limited*, 12 T.C. 880 (1949), and Rev.Rul. 60–55, 1960–1 C.B. 270.

12. See *Robida v. Comm.*, 72–1 USTC ¶9450, 29 AFTR2d 72–1223, 460 F.2d 1172 (CA–9, 1972). The taxpayer was employed in military PXs around the world. He had large slot machine winnings and claimed the foreign earned income exclusion. The IRS challenged the exclusion on the grounds that the winnings were not earned income because there was no recipient of Robi-

da's services. The Court, however, found, that in the absence of capital, the winnings were earned income.

13. § 861(a)(6).The sale is deemed to take place where title passes. See Reg. § 1.861–7(c) regarding title passage. This is an area of tax law in which there has been considerable conflict. See, for example, *Kates Holding Company, Inc.*, 79 T.C. 700 (1982) and *Miami Purchasing Service Corporation*, 76 T.C. 818 (1981).

guidelines for allocating such income between production and sales.[14] If the manufacturer or producer regularly sells to wholly independent distributors, this can establish an "independent" factory or production price that can be used to determine the split between production and sales income. However, if an independent price has not been established, one-half of the taxable income from production and sales must be apportioned between U.S. and foreign sources in proportion to the value of the taxpayer's property within and without the United States that was used to produce such income. The remaining one-half is apportioned between U.S. and foreign sources in proportion to the taxpayer's gross sales (within and without the United States) of such property produced and sold.

Losses from the sale of personal property are sourced according to the source of any income that may have been generated by the property prior to its disposition. This provision discourages the manipulation of the source of losses for tax purposes.

There are several exceptions to the general rule for the sourcing of income from the sale of personal property:

1. Gain on the sale of depreciable personal property is sourced according to prior depreciation deductions to the extent thereof.

2. Gain attributable to an office or fixed place of business maintained outside the United States by a U.S. resident is foreign-source income.

3. Gain attributable to an office or fixed place of business maintained in the United States by a nonresident alien is U.S.-source income. This exception does not apply to a sale of inventory where a foreign office materially participates in the sale.

4. Gain on the sale of intangibles is sourced according to prior amortization deductions to the extent thereof. Contingent payments, however, are sourced as royalty income.

5. Gain from the sale of goodwill is sourced where the goodwill was generated.

6. Gain from the sale of stock of an 80 percent–owned foreign affiliate is foreign-source income if the affiliate is engaged in an active trade or business and the stock is sold in the foreign country in which the affiliate derives more than 50 percent of its gross income for the immediately preceding three-year period.

Transportation and Communication Income.   Income from transportation beginning *and* ending in the United States is U.S.-source income. Fifty percent of the income from transportation beginning *or* ending in the United States is U.S.-source income, unless the U.S. point is only an intermediate stop. This rule does not apply to personal service income unless the transportation is between the United States and a possession.[15] Income from space and ocean activities conducted outside the jurisdiction of any country is sourced according to the residence of the person conducting the activity.

International communication income derived by a U.S. person is sourced 50 percent within the United States where transmission is between the United States and a foreign country. International communication income derived by foreign persons is foreign-source income unless it is attributable to an office or other fixed place of business within the United States, in which case it is U.S.-source income.

---

14. § 863(b)(2) and Reg. § 1.863–3.   15. §§ 863(c) and (d).

Income Sourced without the United States

The provisions for sourcing income without the United States are not as detailed and specific as are those for determining U.S.-source income. Basically, § 862 provides that if interest, dividends, compensation for personal services, income from the use or sale of property, and other income is not U.S.-source income, then it is sourced without the United States (foreign-source income).

Allocation and Apportionment of Deductions

Since the United States levies a tax on *taxable income*, deductions and losses must be allocated and apportioned between U.S.- and foreign-source gross income to determine U.S.- and foreign-source taxable income. A detailed discussion of Treasury Regulation § 1.861–8, which provides the basis for such allocation and apportionment, is beyond the scope of this chapter. Briefly, the regulation calls for allocation of deductions directly related to an activity or property to classes of income, followed by apportionment between the statutory and residual groupings on some reasonable basis. For FTC purposes, foreign-source income is the statutory grouping, and U.S.-source income is the residual grouping.

EXAMPLE 15   ABC, Inc., a domestic corporation, has $2,000,000 gross income, all generated by real estate activity. Of this amount, $1,500,000 is sales income and $500,000 is rental income. A $50,000 deductible item, directly related to real estate activity, is allocated $37,500 to sales income and $12,500 to rental income. These allocations would then be apportioned between U.S.- and foreign-source income (the statutory groupings) in each class. For example, if 80% of the rental income is from foreign sources, a reasonable apportionment of the $12,500 would be $10,000, or 80%, to foreign-source income. If, however, it could be shown that $45,000 of the deductible item was directly related to sales income, the $45,000 would be allocated to that class of gross income, with the remainder allocated ratably. ☐

Specific rules apply to interest expense. Allocation and apportionment of interest expense is based on the theory that money is fungible; thus, with limited exceptions, interest expense is attributable to all the activities and property of the taxpayer regardless of any specific purpose for incurring the debt on which interest is paid.[16] Generally, taxpayers must allocate and apportion interest expense on the basis of assets, using either the fair market value or the tax book value of assets.[17] Once the fair market value is used, the taxpayer must continue to use such method. Special rules apply in allocating and apportioning interest expense in the case of an affiliated group of corporations.

EXAMPLE 16   X, a domestic corporation, generates U.S.-source and foreign-source gross income for 1990. X's assets (tax book value) are as follows:

---

16. Prop.Reg. § 1.861–8(e)(2)(iv) describes circumstances in which interest expense can be directly allocated to specific debt. This exception to the fungibility concept is limited to those cases in which specific property is purchased or improved with nonrecourse debt.

17. Reg. §§ 1.861–9T and 1.861–10T.

Generating U.S.-source income	$18,000,000
Generating foreign-source income	5,000,000
	$23,000,000

X incurs interest expense of $800,000 for 1990. Using the asset method and the tax book value, interest expense is apportioned to foreign-source income as follows:

$$\frac{\$5,000,000 \text{ (foreign assets)}}{\$23,000,000 \text{ (total assets)}} \times \$800,000 = \underline{\$173,913} \qquad \square$$

Specific rules also apply to research and development expenditures, certain stewardship expenses, legal and accounting fees and expenses, income taxes, and losses.

A deduction not definitely related to any class of gross income is ratably allocated to all classes of gross income and apportioned between U.S.- and foreign-source income.

Section 482 Considerations

It is evident from the preceding discussions of the FTC and the relevance of income sourcing that taxpayers may be tempted to manipulate the source of income and the allocation of deductions arbitrarily to minimize taxation. This manipulation is more easily accomplished between or among related persons. The IRS uses § 482 to counter such actions. Under this provision, the IRS has the power to reallocate gross income, deductions, credits, or allowances between or among organizations, trades, or businesses owned or controlled directly or indirectly by the same interests whenever it determines that this is necessary to prevent the evasion of taxes or to reflect income more clearly. Section 482 is a "one-edged" sword available only to the IRS. The taxpayer cannot invoke it to reallocate income and expenses.[18]

The reach of § 482 is quite broad. It is the IRS's position that a corporation and its sole shareholder who works full-time for the corporation can be treated as two separate trades or businesses for purposes of § 482.[19] Two unrelated shareholders who each owned 50 percent of a corporation were held to be acting in concert for their common good and, thus, together controlled the corporation.[20]

Section 482 is supplemented by legislative regulations that provide rules for safe harbor charges in regard to loans, services, and the use of tangible property. The regulations provide little specific guidance in the area of intangibles. Several court decisions in recent years have addressed this issue.[21]

The regulations also provide three specific methods for determining an arm's-length price on the sale of tangible property: the comparable uncontrolled

---

18. Reg. § 1.482–1(b)(3).
19. Rev.Rul. 88–38, 88–1 C.B. 246. But see *Foglesong v. Comm.*, 82–2 USTC ¶9650, 50 AFTR2d 82–6016, 691 F.2d 848 (CA–7, 1982), *rev'g* 77 T.C. 1102 (1981).
20. See *Comm. v. B. Forman Company, Inc.*, 72–1 USTC ¶9182, 29 AFTR2d 72–405, 453 F.2d 1144 (CA–2, 1972).

21. See *Eli Lilly & Company and Subsidiaries v. Comm.*, 88–2 USTC ¶9502, 62 AFTR2d 88–5569, 856 F.2d 855 (CA–7, 1988), *aff'g.* in part, *rev'g.* in part, and *rem'g.* 84 T.C. 996 (1985); *Bausch & Lomb, Inc. & Consolidated Subsidiaries*, 92 T.C. _____, No. 33(1989); and *G.D. Searle*, 88 T.C. 252 (1987).

price method, the resale price method, and the cost plus method. These methods are to be relied on in the order given, with the regulations allowing for various undefined methods when none of the above methods is appropriate.

After 1986, payments made by related parties for the sale or use of intangible property must be commensurate with the income attributable to the intangibles. Furthermore, the basis or inventory cost of imported property purchased from a related party cannot exceed the value declared for customs duty purposes.[22]

On October 19, 1988, the Treasury released its *Study of Intercompany Pricing* (the "White Paper"). It concluded that the market-based approach to intercompany pricing reflected in the current § 482 regulations cannot be applied effectively due to the integration of the tangible property and the marketing and manufacturing intangibles in income generation. Thus, the Treasury concluded that the market-based approach should be supplemented by an alternative pricing approach that considers the return earned in the marketplace on a firm's factors of production. It is anticipated that regulations will be proposed in line with the findings of the White Paper.

U.S. Taxation of Nonresident Aliens and Foreign Corporations

Generally, only the U.S.-source income of nonresident aliens (NRAs) and foreign corporations is subject to U.S. taxation. This reflects the reach of U.S. tax jurisdiction. This constraint, however, does not prevent the United States from also taxing the foreign-source income of NRAs and foreign corporations, when that income is effectively connected with the conduct of a U.S. trade or business.[23] The income of NRAs and foreign corporations subject to U.S. taxation can therefore be divided into two classifications: effectively connected and noneffectively connected income. In some respects foreign corporations enjoy preferential income tax treatment compared with NRA individuals. In addition, NRA individuals can be subject to the Federal estate and gift tax.

Nonresident Alien Individuals

An NRA individual is an individual who is not a citizen or resident of the United States. Citizenship is determined under the immigration and naturalization laws of the United States. Basically, the citizenship statutes are broken down into two categories, nationality at birth and nationality through naturalization.

Residency.   For many years, the definition of residency for Federal income tax purposes was very subjective, requiring an evaluation of a person's intent and actions with regard to the length and nature of stay in the United States. In 1984, Congress enacted a more objective test of residency. A person is a resident of the United States for income tax purposes if such person meets either the "green card" test or the substantial presence test. If either of these tests is met for the calendar year, the individual is deemed a U.S. resident for the year.[24]

An alien issued a green card is considered a U.S. resident on the first day he or she is physically present in the United States after issuance. The green card is Immigration Form I–551, which, in reality, is now blue and white, but is still referred to as the "green card." Status as a U.S. resident remains in effect until the

---

22. § 1059A.
23. §§ 871, 881, and 882.

24. § 7701(b). See also Prop.Reg. § 301.7701(b).

green card has been revoked or the individual has abandoned lawful permanent resident status.

The substantial presence test will apply to an alien without a green card. It is a mathematical test involving physical presence in the United States. An individual who is physically present in the United States for at least 183 days during the calendar year is a U.S. resident for income tax purposes. This 183-day requirement can also be met over a three-year period that includes the two immediately preceding years and the current year. For this purpose, each day of the current calendar year is counted as a full day, each day of the first preceding year as one-third day, and each day of the second preceding year as one-sixth day.

EXAMPLE 17   N, an alien, was present in the United States for 90 days in 1988, 180 days in 1989, and 110 days in 1990. For Federal income tax purposes, N is a U.S. resident for 1990 since her physical presence for the three-year period consisted of 185 days [(90 days × 1/6) + (180 days × 1/3) + (110 days × 1)]. □

Several exceptions are provided under the substantial presence test. Commuters from Mexico and Canada who are employed in the United States, but return home each day, are excepted, as are those individuals who are prevented from leaving the United States due to a medical condition that arose while in the United States. Some individuals are exempt from the substantial presence test, including foreign government–related individuals (e.g., diplomats), qualified teachers, trainees and students, and certain professional athletes.

If an individual meets the substantial presence requirement under the three-year test period, but was not in the United States for at least 31 days in the current calendar year, the individual is not a resident under the substantial presence test. Also, if the requirement is met under the three-year test period, but the individual was not present in the United States for 183 days in the current year, classification as a U.S. resident for the year can be avoided by showing a closer connection (for example, home, family, social and professional ties) to another country. This exception will apply only if the individual's tax home[25] is in a foreign country and the person has taken no steps toward establishing permanent residence in the United States.

Residence, under the substantial presence test, begins the first day the individual is physically present in the United States and ends the last day of physical presence for the calendar year, assuming the substantial presence test is not satisfied for the next calendar year. Nominal presence of 10 days or less can be ignored in determining whether or not the substantial presence test is met.

The application of the income tax treaties that the United States has in force with other countries depends on the residence of the taxpayer. Most of the treaties have "tie breaker" provisions for those situations in which a person may qualify as a resident of both treaty countries under each country's laws. Certain treaties override § 7701(b) for the purpose of income tax status (as resident or nonresident), but may not override residence under § 7701(b) for purposes of other tax provisions, such as the sourcing of income.

Nonresident Aliens Not Engaged in a U.S. Trade or Business.   Section 871(a) subjects certain U.S. source income that is not effectively connected with

---

25. Tax home has the same meaning as under § 911(d)(3), but without regard to whether the individual's place of abode is in the United States.

the conduct of a U.S. trade or business to a 30 percent tax. This income includes dividends, interest, rents, royalties, certain compensation, premiums, annuities, and other fixed, determinable, annual or periodic (FDAP) income. The 30 percent tax rate is generally applied to gross income since deductions for expenses incurred in earning such income are not allowed.[26] NRAs are allowed a deduction for casualty and theft losses with regard to property located within the United States, a deduction for qualified charitable contributions, and one personal exemption. Residents of countries contiguous to the United States are allowed dependency exemptions as well. Generally the tax is collected through withholding by the U.S. payor.[27] Interest received from certain portfolio debt investments, even though U.S.-source income, is exempt from taxation as is interest earned on deposits with banking institutions as long as such interest is not effectively connected with the conduct of a U.S. trade or business.

Capital gains not effectively connected with the conduct of a U.S. trade or business are exempt from tax as long as the NRA individual was not present in the United States for 183 days or more during the taxable year. If an NRA has not established a taxable year, the calendar year will be treated as the taxable year. Capital loss carryforwards are not allowed to NRAs.[28]

Even though an NRA is not *actually* engaged in the conduct of a U.S. trade or business, any gains from the sale of U.S. real property interests are treated as effectively connected income. This is discussed in more detail subsequently. Furthermore, the taxpayer can elect to treat income from certain passive real estate activities (for example, a net lease arrangement) as effectively connected income. This will allow the taxpayer to deduct any expenses incurred in earning the income attributable to the real estate in determining taxable income. Once made, the election is irrevocable.

Nonresident Aliens Engaged in a U.S. Trade or Business.   As long as FDAP income and capital gains are not effectively connected income, the tax treatment of these income items is the same for NRAs engaged in a U.S. trade or business as for NRAs who are not so engaged. Effectively connected income, however, is taxed at the same rates that apply to U.S. citizens and residents, and deductions for expenses attributable to such income are allowed.

Two important definitions determine the U.S. tax consequences to NRAs with U.S.-source income: *the conduct of a U.S. trade or business* and *effectively connected income*. Section 864 and the accompanying regulations contain guidelines for making these determinations.

General criteria for determining if a U.S. trade or business exists include the location of production activities, management, distribution activities, and other business functions. Trading in commodities and securities ordinarily will not constitute a trade or business. Dealers, however, need to avoid maintaining a U.S. trading office and trading for their own account. Corporations (other than certain personal holding companies) that are not dealers can trade for their own account as long as their principal office is located outside the United States. There are no restrictions on individuals who are not dealers. An NRA individual who performs services in the United States for a foreign employer is not engaged in a U.S. trade or business.

A U.S. trade or business is a prerequisite to having effectively connected income. Section 864(c) provides a dual test for determining if income, such as

---

26. § 873.
27. § 1441.

28. § 871(a)(2).

FDAP income and capital gains, is effectively connected income. Income is effectively connected with a U.S. trade or business if it is derived from assets used in, or held for use in, the trade or business (asset-use test) or if the activities of the trade or business were a material factor in the production of the income (business-activities test).

EXAMPLE 18   N, an NRA, operates a U.S. business. During the year excess cash funds accumulate. N invests these funds on a short-term basis so that they remain available to meet business needs. Any income earned from such investment is effectively connected income under the asset-use test. □

Estate and Gift Taxes.   The value of property situated in the United States shall be included in a deceased NRA's gross estate for U.S. estate tax purposes.[29] Thus, the question of situs (location) of property owned by the decedent at the time of death is important.

Generally, the situs of real property is not subject to conflict. One probably would not question the conclusion that a piece of land in Kansas is situated in the United States. Also, the situs of tangible personal property is easily determined (e.g., jewelry in a safe deposit box located in a bank in New York City).

Specific rules are provided for certain intangible property. Stock owned and held by an NRA at the time of death is deemed situated in the United States only if issued by a domestic corporation.[30] Debt obligations of a U.S. person or the United States, a state or any political subdivision thereof, or the District of Columbia are deemed property situated within the United States. However, the proceeds of life insurance on the life of an NRA are not property situated within the United States. Furthermore, amounts on deposit in U.S. banks are not property situated within the United States if the interest income earned on such deposits would be foreign-source income. A similar rule applies to portfolio debt obligations where the interest income earned on such debt would be exempt from U.S. income taxation.

The tax rates applicable to the taxable estate of a deceased NRA differ from those applicable to the taxable estate of a U.S. citizen or resident. Furthermore, the Code allows a unified credit against the estate tax imposed on an NRA's taxable estate of only $3,600. In fact, the credit is not "unified" since, for gift tax purposes, taxable gifts made by NRAs are subject to the same rates imposed on U.S. citizens and residents[31] and a unified credit against the gift tax is not allowed to NRAs.[32] The gift tax is imposed only on an NRA's transfer of tangible property situated in the United States.[33]

For purposes of the estate and gift tax, an individual is a *nonresident* if such person's domicile is not within the United States at the time of death or on the date the gift is transferred.[34] A person acquires a domicile in a place by living there with no definite present intention to change domicile at a later date. In other words, *action* and *intent* are required to establish domicile. Intent is subject to question more often than action. It is easy to determine whether an individual has actually lived and acquired permanent physical ties, such as a personal residence, in the United States. Some factors that the courts have considered in determining intent

---

29. The estate tax provisions of the Code applicable to NRAs are contained in §§ 2101–2108.

30. § 2104(a).

31. § 2502.

32. § 2505.

33. § 2501(a)(2) and § 2511.

34. Reg. § 20.0–1.

are participation in local affairs, payment of taxes, voting status, location of personal property, and statements concerning residence.

Foreign Corporations

Definition.   The classification of an entity as a foreign corporation for U.S. tax purposes is an important consideration. Section 7701(a)(5) defines a foreign corporation as one that is not domestic. A domestic corporation is a corporation that is created or organized in the United States.

The IRS looks at the corporate characteristics outlined in the regulations under § 7701 to determine whether a foreign entity should be treated as an association taxable as a corporation. See the discussion of these characteristics in chapter 16. In determining the presence or absence of any of these characteristics, the IRS looks at the rights and duties of the foreign entity under the laws of the jurisdiction in which it resides. Classification of the foreign entity as a corporation, an association taxable as a corporation, a partnership, or some other form of entity can affect the U.S. tax consequences with regard to the entity and its owners. For example, stock in a foreign corporation is not included in the U.S. gross estate of an NRA individual even where all the assets of the corporation are located in the United States. Also, individuals expecting the pass-through of losses of a foreign partnership will be denied those losses if the foreign entity is deemed to be an association taxable as a corporation for U.S. tax purposes.

Income Not Effectively Connected with a U.S. Trade or Business.   Under § 881, U.S.-source FDAP income of foreign corporations is taxed by the United States in the same manner as that of NRA individuals—at a flat 30 percent rate. The exemptions from U.S. taxation for certain portfolio interest, interest on deposits (where such interest is not effectively connected with the conduct of a U.S. trade or business), and U.S.-source dividends from domestic corporations meeting the 80 percent foreign business requirement are available for foreign corporations. The U.S.-source capital gains of foreign corporations are exempt from the Federal income tax if they are not effectively connected with the conduct of a U.S. trade or business.

Effectively Connected Income.   Section 882 subjects foreign corporations conducting a trade or business within the United States to Federal income taxation on effectively connected income. Additionally, any U.S.-source income other than noneffectively connected FDAP and capital gains is deemed effectively connected (e.g., casual sales of items by the home office).

Branch Profits Tax.   In addition to the income tax imposed under § 882 on effectively connected income of a foreign corporation, a tax equal to 30 percent of the *dividend equivalent amount* for the taxable year is imposed on any foreign corporation.[35] The objective of the branch profits tax is to afford equal tax treatment to income generated by a domestic corporation controlled by a foreign corporation and to income generated by other U.S. operations controlled by foreign corporations. If the foreign corporation operates through a U.S. subsidiary (a domestic corporation), the income of the subsidiary is taxable by the United States when derived and also subject to a withholding tax when repatriated (returned as dividends to the foreign parent). Before enactment of the branch

---

35. § 884.

profits tax, the foreign corporation with a branch in the United States paid only the initial tax on its U.S. earnings; remittances were not taxed.

The dividend equivalent amount (DEA) is the foreign corporation's effectively connected earnings for the taxable year, adjusted for increases and decreases in the foreign corporation's U.S. net equity (investment in the U.S. operations) for the taxable year. The DEA is limited to current E & P and post-1986 accumulated E & P that is effectively connected, or treated as effectively connected, with the conduct of a U.S. trade or business and that has not been previously subject to the branch profits tax. E & P for this purpose does not include income otherwise exempt from U.S. taxation, certain FSC income, gain on sale of stock of a domestic corporation that is a U.S. real property holding corporation, and income that the taxpayer elects to treat as effectively connected under Subpart F. U.S. net equity is the sum of money and the aggregate adjusted basis of assets and liabilities directly connected to U.S. operations that generate effectively connected income. A decrease in net equity as the result of a deficit for the tax year is not subject to the branch profits tax.

EXAMPLE 19   F, a foreign corporation and calendar year taxpayer, had a deficit in effectively connected E & P of $200 for 1988 and 1989. F has $180 of effectively connected E & P for 1990. F had $2,000 U.S. net equity at the end of 1989 and has $2,000 U.S. net equity at the end of 1990. F has a DEA of $180 for 1990, its effectively connected E & P for the year, even though it has a net deficit of $220 in effectively connected E & P for the period 1988–1990. ☐

EXAMPLE 20   At the end of 1990, F, a foreign corporation and calendar year taxpayer, has $300 of accumulated effectively connected E & P that has not been previously taxed under § 884 and has a $180 deficit in effectively connected E & P for 1991. F has U.S. net equity of $450 at the end of 1990 and U.S. net equity of $250 at the end of 1991, a decrease of $200. F has a DEA of $20 for 1991, resulting from F's deficit of $180 in effectively connected E & P for 1991, increased by the $200 decrease in U.S. net equity during the year.[36] ☐

The 30 percent rate of the branch profits tax may be reduced or eliminated by a treaty provision. A lower rate specified in a treaty applies where the treaty provides for a branch profits tax or withholding on dividends paid by a corporation resident in the treaty country. The rate reduction will not apply if the foreign corporation is not a qualified resident of the treaty country (for example, a foreign corporation owned by persons nonresident in the treaty country). The branch profits tax does not apply where prohibited by treaty under a nondiscrimination clause. If a foreign corporation is subject to the branch profits tax, no other tax will be levied on the dividend actually paid by the corporation during the taxable year.

The Foreign Investment in Real Property Tax Act

Before the enactment of the Foreign Investment in Real Property Tax Act (FIRPTA) in 1980, NRAs and foreign corporations could avoid U.S. taxation on gains from the sale of U.S. real estate if such gains were treated as capital gains and were not

---

36. Reg. § 1.884–1T, Examples (5) and (6).

effectively connected with the conduct of a U.S. trade or business. Furthermore, persons who were residents of a country that had an income tax treaty with the United States that allowed for an annual election to treat real estate operations as a trade or business could take advantage of the election for tax years prior to the year of sale and then revoke the election for the year in which the sale took place.

Under FIRPTA, gains and losses realized by NRAs and foreign corporations from the sale or other disposition of U.S. real property interests are treated as effectively connected with the conduct of a U.S. trade or business even where such persons are not actually so engaged.[37] NRA individuals must pay a tax equal to at least 21 percent of the lesser of such individual's alternative minimum taxable income (AMTI) or net U.S. real property gain for the taxable year.

EXAMPLE 21

N, an NRA individual, has a NOL of $500,000 from the conduct of a U.S. trade or business, an $800,000 gain on the disposition of a U.S. real property interest that, absent § 897, is not effectively connected with the U.S. business, and AMTI of $450,000. N's U.S.-source taxable income is $300,000, and regular tax liability would be $84,000 ($300,000 × 28%). N is subject to the AMT and must pay a tax of $94,500 [the lesser of $168,000 (21% × $800,000) or $94,500 (21% × $450,000)]. This $94,500 consists of the regular tax liability of $84,000 plus an AMT of $10,500 ($94,500 − $84,000). □

For these purposes, losses of individual taxpayers are taken into account only to the extent they are deductible under § 165(c) (business losses, losses on transactions entered into for profit, and losses from casualties and thefts).

U.S. Real Property Interest.   Any direct interest in real property situated in the United States and any interest in a domestic corporation (other than solely as a creditor) are U.S. real property interests unless the taxpayer can establish that a domestic corporation was not a U.S. real property holding corporation during the shorter of the period after June 18, 1980, during which the taxpayer held an interest in such corporation, or the five-year period ending on the date of disposition of such interest (the base period). A domestic corporation is not a U.S. real property holding corporation if it holds no U.S. real property interests on the date of disposition of its stock and any U.S. real property interests held by the corporation during the base period were disposed of in a transaction in which gain, if any, was fully recognized. This exception also applies if the U.S. real property interest disposed of by the corporation was stock of a second U.S. real property holding corporation that ceased to be a real property holding corporation by way of a taxable disposition of its U.S. real property interests.

EXAMPLE 22

From January 1, 1985, through January 1, 1990, F (a foreign investor) holds shares in D, a U.S. corporation. During this period, D holds two parcels of U.S. real estate and stock of S, another U.S. corporation. S also owns U.S. real estate. The two parcels of real estate held directly by D were disposed of on December 15, 1986, in a like-kind exchange in which D acquired foreign realty. S disposed of its U.S. real estate in a taxable transaction on January 1, 1990. An interest in D will be treated as an interest in U.S. real property

---

37. § 897.

because D did not recognize gain on the December 15, 1986, exchange of the U.S. real property interests. Had D's ownership of U.S. real estate been limited to its indirect ownership through S, as of January 2, 1990, an interest in D would not constitute an interest in U.S. real property, since S disposed of its interests in U.S. real property in a taxable transaction in which gain was fully recognized. □

A real property holding corporation is any corporation (whether foreign or domestic) where the fair market value of the corporation's U.S. real property interests equals or exceeds 50 percent of the sum of fair market value of its U.S. real property interests, its interests in real property located outside the United States, plus any other of its assets that are used or held for use in a trade or business. Stock regularly traded on an established securities market is not treated as a U.S. real property interest where a person holds no more than 5 percent of such stock.

Withholding Provisions. Any purchaser or agent acquiring a U.S. real property interest from a foreign person must withhold 10 percent of the amount realized on the disposition.[38] The payment of such amount must be submitted along with Form 8288 within at least 20 days after the transfer. The amount withheld need not exceed the transferor's maximum tax liability with regard to the transfer. A domestic partnership, trust, or estate with a foreign partner, foreign grantor treated as owner, or foreign beneficiary must withhold 34 percent (or 28 percent where allowed by the IRS) of the gain allocable to such person on a disposition of a U.S. real property interest. Foreign corporations are also subject to withholding provisions on certain distributions.

Failure to withhold can subject the purchaser or the purchaser's agent to interest on any unpaid amount. A civil penalty of 100 percent of the amount required to be withheld and a criminal penalty of up to $10,000 or five years in prison can be imposed for willful failure to withhold.[39]

Certain exemptions from withholding are provided. An agent for the purchaser or seller is liable to withhold only to the extent of compensation received by such agent for handling the transaction.

Special Provisions

Taxpayers Married to Nonresident Aliens. A citizen or resident of the United States, who is married to an NRA at the close of the taxable year, may elect to file a joint return with the NRA spouse.[40] Both spouses must consent to the election, and, once made, the election applies for the current year and all subsequent years unless revoked. Such an election results in the treatment of the NRA as a U.S. resident for income tax purposes. Thus, the election subjects such NRA's worldwide taxable income to U.S. taxation.

Dual Resident Taxpayers. A taxpayer who is a dual resident (an NRA for a portion of the tax year and a U.S. resident for a portion of the tax year) can elect to file a joint return if such person is a U.S. resident at the close of the taxable year and is married to a U.S. citizen or resident.[41] Both spouses must consent to the election, which can be made only one time by a married couple. This election also

---

38. § 1445.
39. §§ 6672 and 7202.

40. § 6013(g).
41. § 6013(h).

subjects the dual resident's worldwide taxable income for the entire tax year to U.S. taxation.

Community Income.   Special rules prescribe the tax treatment of community income in the case of a married couple one or both of whom are NRAs.[42] Earned income, other than trade or business income and a partner's distributive share of partnership income, is treated as income of the spouse who rendered the personal services. Trade or business income and a partner's distributive share of partnership income are treated as income of the husband. However, if the wife exercises substantially all of the management and control of a trade or business, all the gross income and deductions attributable to such trade or business are treated as hers. A partner's distributive share of partnership income is treated as income of the partner. Other community income derived from separate property owned by one spouse will be treated as that spouse's income. All other community income is treated as the applicable community property law provides.

EXAMPLE 23   H, a U.S. citizen, is married to W, an NRA. H and W do not elect to file a joint return. Under the laws of F, their country of residence, dividends from stock owned jointly by married couples are considered the property of the husband. If H and W receive dividends on stock they own jointly, H must include the entire dividend in gross income for U.S. tax purposes even where it is foreign-source income. □

Expatriation to Avoid Tax.   An NRA individual who lost U.S. citizenship after March 8, 1965, and within 10 years immediately preceding the close of the current tax year, will be subject to U.S. taxation under § 877 unless such loss of citizenship did not have as one of its principal purposes the avoidance of the U.S. income, estate, or gift tax. Under § 877, only U.S.-source taxable income is subject to tax and only if the tax under § 877 is greater than the tax that the expatriate would otherwise owe with regard to U.S.-source taxable income. For this purpose, gain on the sale or exchange of property (other than stock or debt obligations) located in the United States is U.S.-source income, as is gain on the sale or exchange of stock issued by a domestic corporation and debt obligations of U.S. persons or of the United States, a state or political subdivision thereof, or the District of Columbia. This source rule also applies to the sale or exchange of property that takes its basis in whole or in part by reference to the property described above.

Tax Treaties

Income Tax.   Over 30 income tax treaties between the United States and other countries are in effect. These treaties generally provide *taxing rights* with regard to the taxable income of residents of one treaty country who have income sourced in the other treaty country. For the most part, neither country is prohibited from taxing the income of its residents. The treaties generally provide for primary taxing rights that require the other treaty partner to allow a credit for the taxes paid on income that is taxed under the primary taxing rights of one treaty partner and is also taxed by the other treaty partner.

---

42. § 879.

EXAMPLE 24   T, a resident of F, a country with which the United States has an income tax treaty, earns income attributable to a permanent establishment (e.g., place of business) in the United States. Under the treaty, the United States has primary taxing rights with regard to this income. F can also require that the income be included in gross income and subject to F's income tax, but must allow a credit for the taxes paid to the United States on such income. ☐

Primary taxing rights generally depend on the residence of the taxpayer or the presence of a permanent establishment in a treaty country, to which the income is attributable. Generally, a permanent establishment is a branch, office, factory, workshop, warehouse, or other fixed place of business.

The United States developed a Model Income Tax Treaty[43] as the starting point for negotiating income tax treaties with other countries. The most controversial of the articles in the model treaty is Article 16, Limitation On Benefits. This article is meant to prevent what is known as "treaty shopping." Treaty shopping occurs when an entity resident in a treaty country takes advantage of the provisions of the treaty even though the majority of the owners of the entity are not residents of the treaty country. Article 16 disallows treaty benefits to an entity unless more than 75 percent of the beneficial interest in the entity is owned, directly or indirectly, by one or more individual residents of the same treaty country in which the entity is resident. Furthermore, the entity cannot be a conduit for meeting liabilities, such as interest or royalty payments, to persons who are not residents in either treaty country and who are not U.S. citizens. The United States' negotiating position with regard to Article 16 of the Model Income Tax Treaty has led to the termination of some treaties.[44]

Several code provisions override the income tax treaties to some extent, for example § 884 (the branch profits tax) and § 897 (FIRPTA). The U.S. Treasury Department is currently considering the impact of the Tax Reform Act of 1986 on tax treaties that have been negotiated. In addition, several international trade organizations have expressed concern that treaty override provisions inhibit treaty negotiations and international trade.

Estate and Gift Tax.   The United States has estate tax treaties with fewer than 20 countries. Some of these treaties are combined estate and gift tax treaties. Like the income tax treaties, they provide primary taxing rights and a credit for taxes paid to the treaty country with the primary taxing rights. Primary taxing rights generally reside with the country of situs of the property (older treaties) or country of domicile of the donor or decedent (newer treaties). Primary taxing rights regarding immovable property and property of a permanent establishment for the most part reside with the country in which the property is situated.

U.S. TAXPAYERS ABROAD

Citizens and residents of the United States are subject to Federal taxation on their worldwide taxable income. U.S. taxpayers who operate in a foreign country as a sole proprietor, or through a foreign branch or foreign partnership, must include foreign-source income in gross income for U.S. tax purposes and are allowed a deduction for related expenses and losses.

---

43. Treasury Department Model Income Tax Treaty (June 16, 1981).

44. U.S.–Netherlands Antilles and U.S.-Aruba income tax treaties as of January 1, 1988.

Income tax treaties can reduce or eliminate the taxation of the income by the foreign country party to the treaty. Since, under the treaty, the United States reserves the right to tax its citizens and residents, relief from double taxation is achieved with the FTC. In addition to the FTC, there are other specific tax provisions regarding certain foreign-source income of U.S. citizens and residents.

The Foreign Earned Income Exclusion—§ 911

To allow U.S. multinational entities to be competitive in the world market, Congress enacted legislation granting an exclusion (from U.S. gross income) for a certain amount of qualified foreign earned income. This exclusion was meant to allow the multinational entities to employ U.S. citizens and residents for foreign operations without having to pay them a wage or salary far in excess of that paid to nationals of the particular foreign country or countries. Since the United States taxes worldwide taxable income of its citizens and residents, without the exclusion the tax burden on a U.S. taxpayer working abroad could be much greater than that on a native of the foreign country. Currently, § 911 allows a foreign earned income exclusion for (1) a qualified housing cost amount and (2) foreign earned income not in excess of $70,000.

The exclusion is elective and is made by filing Form 2555 with the income tax return, or with an amended return, for the first taxable year for which the election is to be effective. An election once made remains in effect for that year and for all subsequent years unless revoked. If the election is revoked for any taxable year, the taxpayer may not make the election again (without consent of the IRS) until the sixth taxable year following the taxable year for which revocation was first effective.

Qualified Individuals.   The exclusion is available to an individual whose tax home is in a foreign country and who is either (1) a U.S. citizen and bona fide resident of a foreign country or countries or (2) a citizen or resident of the United States who, during any 12 consecutive months, is physically present in a foreign country or countries for at least 330 full days. *Tax home* has the same meaning as under § 162(a)(2) relating to travel expenses while away from home. The issue of whether a stay abroad is temporary can be troublesome. If the stay abroad is deemed to be temporary, the taxpayer's tax home has not shifted to the foreign country. The IRS has held that an individual who worked in another city for 16 months was temporarily away from home.[45]

Only whole days count for the physical presence test. The taxpayer has some flexibility in choosing the 12-month period.

EXAMPLE 25   C, a U.S. citizen, arrived in Ireland from Boston at 3 P.M. on March 28, 1989. C remained in Ireland until 8 A.M. on March 1, 1990, at which time C departed for the United States. Among other possible 12-month periods, C is present in a foreign country an aggregate of 330 full days during each of the following 12-month periods: March 1, 1989, through February 28, 1990, and March 29, 1989, through March 28, 1990. □

Some factors considered in establishing a bona fide foreign residence are intention of the taxpayer, establishment of the taxpayer's home temporarily in a

45. Rev.Rul. 83–82, 1983–1 C.B. 45.

foreign country for an indefinite period, participation in community activities, and, in general, assimilation into the foreign environment.[46]

Section 911 is not available to a U.S. citizen or resident who resides and/or works in a foreign country in contravention of an executive order (countries with which the United States has broken diplomatic ties, such as Iran and Cuba). However, an exception is allowed for an individual who is required to leave a foreign country before meeting the bona fide residence or physical presence test because of war, civil unrest, or similar adverse conditions that preclude the normal conduct of business. Here, such individual may obtain a waiver on establishing to the satisfaction of the Secretary of the Treasury that the requirements would have been met under normal conditions.

If spouses both earn foreign earned income, each may be eligible for the foreign earned income exclusion. Each spouse would be subject to a separate limitation, even when the couple files a joint return. Community property laws are ignored, and the income is treated as that of the spouse who actually performed the services.

The General Exclusion.   The foreign earned income (general) exclusion is available for foreign earned income and is limited to the lesser of (1) $70,000 or (2) foreign earned income less the housing cost amount exclusion. The exclusion is available for the tax year in which income would be taken into account for tax purposes; the limitation, however, is determined for the tax year in which the services were performed. Income received after the close of the taxable year following the taxable year in which the services were performed does not qualify for the exclusion.

EXAMPLE 26

T, a U.S. resident, is present in a foreign country for all of 1989. T earns $100,000 from the performance of personal services. T returns to the United States on January 1, 1990, and remains there. Of the $100,000 foreign earned income, T receives $60,000 in 1989 and $40,000 in 1990. T can take a foreign earned income exclusion of $60,000 for 1989 and $10,000 for 1990 ($70,000 statutory limit minus the $60,000 excluded for 1989). If T did not receive the $40,000 until 1991, no exclusion would be allowed for 1991 because the $40,000 was received after the close of the taxable year following the taxable year in which the services were performed.   □

The statutory amount must be prorated on a daily basis where the taxpayer does not qualify for the exclusion for the full tax year. If T, in Example 26 qualified for only 11 months of the year, the statutory amount would be $64,055 [$70,000 × (334 days/365 days)].

Amounts paid by the United States, or any agency of the United States, to an employee do not qualify for the exclusion. This rule is attributable to the fact that such persons usually are not subject to the income tax of the country where they work. Thus, relief from double taxation is not necessary since it does not exist.

The Housing Cost Amount.   The housing cost amount is equal to the qualified housing expenses of an individual for the tax year less a base amount. The base amount is 16 percent of the salary of an employee of the United States for Step 1

---

46. *Sochurek v. Comm.*, 62–1 USTC ¶9293, 9
     AFTR2d 883, 300 F.2d 34 (CA–7, 1962).

Grade GS–14. The base amount is determined on a daily basis. For 1989, the base amount for a full year was $7,775. If a qualified individual was employed overseas for 250 days of the year, the applicable base amount would be $5,325 [$7,775 × (250 days/365 days)].

Qualified housing expenses include reasonable expenses paid or incurred during the taxable year for housing for the individual (and spouse and dependents where appropriate) in a foreign country. Qualified housing expenses are those provided by an employer and include utilities and insurance, but not interest and taxes deductible under §§ 163 or 164. Under certain conditions, housing expenses for a second household will be allowed for a spouse and dependents.

If the taxpayer is an employee, all housing expenses are treated as provided by the employer. However, only those housing expenses for which the employer actually incurs a cost are included in the taxpayer's gross income as foreign earned income. The housing cost amount exclusion is limited to foreign earned income.

EXAMPLE 27	C, a U.S. citizen, works as an engineer for a U.S. multinational company in Bahrain. C is a bona fide resident of Bahrain for the entire calendar and tax year and earns a salary of $80,000. In addition, C's employer provides housing costs in the amount of $16,000. If the base amount is $7,775 and C elects both exclusions, the housing cost amount exclusion is $8,225 ($16,000 − $7,775), and the foreign earned income exclusion is $70,000 (the lesser of foreign earned income of $96,000 minus the $8,225 housing cost amount exclusion, or the $70,000 statutory limit). C's taxable income will include $17,775 of foreign earned income ($80,000 + $16,000 − $8,225 − $70,000). □

A self-employed individual is not eligible to exclude housing expenses, but can elect to deduct them. It is possible that an individual could have housing expenses that must be allocated between employer-provided amounts and amounts incurred by the individual as a self-employed person. The § 911 regulations provide guidelines for such a situation. The deduction for housing expenses is limited to the lesser of the housing cost amount or foreign earned income less the foreign earned income exclusion.

EXAMPLE 28	T, a U.S. citizen, owns an architectural firm in Atlanta. T spends the year in Ireland overseeing a construction project. T's self-employment income from the project for the tax year that qualifies as earned income is $75,000. T's qualified housing expenses totaled $15,000. If T meets the physical presence test, or maintains a bona fide residence in Ireland for the entire tax year, T can exclude $70,000 of foreign earned income and deduct $5,000 of housing expenses (the lesser of $15,000 minus the base amount or $75,000 foreign earned income minus the foreign earned income exclusion of $70,000). □

Any housing cost expenses disallowed due to the limitation can be carried over to the subsequent tax year and deducted to the extent that the housing cost amount for the subsequent tax year does not exceed foreign earned income in excess of the foreign earned income exclusion for the tax year.

EXAMPLE 29	C, a U.S. citizen, qualifies as a bona fide resident of F, a foreign country, for the entire 1989 tax year. C is self-employed and earns $80,000 of foreign earned

income and incurs housing cost expenses of $12,000 in excess of the base amount. C is entitled to a foreign earned exclusion of $70,000 and may deduct housing cost expenses of $10,000 ($80,000 − $70,000). C can carry over $2,000 of the housing cost expenses to 1990. If C's foreign earned income for 1990 is $85,000 and housing cost expenses are $14,000 in excess of the base amount, C can take a foreign earned income exclusion of $70,000 and deduct housing cost expenses of $15,000 ($14,000 for 1990 and $1,000 carry over from 1989). The remaining $1,000 of housing cost expenses from 1989 expire. ☐

Effect on Foreign Taxes and Other Deductible Expenses.   The taxpayer who elects the § 911 exclusion must take this into consideration when calculating the FTC and certain deductions. The FTC is not allowed for foreign taxes attributable to excluded foreign earned income. A deduction is also disallowed for such foreign taxes.

EXAMPLE 30

R, a U.S. resident, who qualified for the foreign earned income exclusion for the tax year, excluded $70,000 of his $140,000 foreign earned income. Foreign taxes attributable to total foreign earned income are $60,000. After reduction for disallowed expenses attributable to excluded foreign earned income, the net excluded amount is $64,000. Foreign-source income less all expenses attributable to foreign-source income is $128,000. The foreign taxes that qualify for the FTC, or for a deduction against income for U.S. tax purposes, equal $30,000 [$60,000 − ($60,000 × $64,000/$128,000)]. ☐

Note that in determining the disallowed amount, net (or taxable) income amounts are used, rather than gross income amounts.

Certain deductible expenses of the taxpayer are attributable to foreign earned income. To the extent such income is excluded from gross income, these deductions must be reduced. For example, moving expenses to locate in a foreign country are attributable to foreign-source income.

EXAMPLE 31

S, a U.S. citizen, is a bona fide resident of Venezuela. For the tax year, S excludes $70,000 of his total foreign earned income of $100,000. S incurs moving expenses of $25,000, all of which are attributable to foreign-source income. The portion of the moving expenses attributable to the excluded income is $17,500 [$25,000 × ($70,000/$100,000)]. S may claim moving expenses of $7,500 on his tax return for the year. ☐

In the case where items other than income taxes are considered, gross income amounts are used in the ratio to determine disallowed deductions.

Other Considerations

Section 119 allows employees who are furnished lodgings in a "camp" in a foreign country to exclude the value of the lodgings and any meals provided to them by or on behalf of their employer. The lodgings must be furnished for the convenience of the employer because the services are rendered in a remote area where satisfactory housing is not otherwise available on the open market. The lodgings must be in a common area that normally accommodates 10 or more employees, is not available to the public, and is as near as practicable to the site where the individual performs services.

Taxpayers moving to a foreign country, who qualify for the moving expense deduction under § 217, are allowed up to $4,500 for temporary living expenses for any consecutive 90-day period after obtaining employment and an overall limitation on indirect moving expenses of $6,000. In addition, the cost of storing household goods and transporting goods to and from storage is deductible without limit. The increased amounts for moving abroad do not apply when the taxpayer moves back to the United States.

No Individual Retirement Account deduction is allowed if all the taxpayer's earned income is excluded under § 911. The replacement period is extended to four years under § 1034 for purposes of deferring gain on the sale of a personal residence. U.S. citizens and residents residing abroad when an income tax return is due are allowed an automatic two-month extension for filing their income tax return.

FOREIGN CORPORATIONS CONTROLLED BY U.S. PERSONS

In order to minimize current tax liability, taxpayers can attempt to defer the recognition of taxable income. One way by which taxpayers seek to defer income recognition is to shift the income-generating activity to a foreign entity that is not within the U.S. tax jurisdiction. A foreign corporation is the most suitable entity for such an endeavor since, unlike a partnership, it is not a conduit through which income is taxed directly to the owner.

Realizing that the above tax planning device would hinder the collection of Federal tax revenues, Congress enacted §§ 951–964 in the Revenue Act of 1962. This and subsequent legislation have led to the present provisions for corporations controlled by U.S. persons.

Controlled Foreign Corporations

Subpart F, §§ 951–964 of the Code, provides that certain types of income generated by controlled foreign corporations (CFCs) are currently included in gross income by its U.S. shareholders. For Subpart F to apply, the foreign corporation must have been a CFC for an uninterrupted period of 30 days or more during the taxable year. When this is the case, U.S. shareholders who own stock in the corporation on the last day of the tax year on which the corporation is a CFC must include their pro rata share of Subpart F income and increase in earnings invested in U.S. property for the tax year in gross income for their taxable year in which or with which the taxable year of the corporation ends.

EXAMPLE 32   F, a calendar year corporation, is a CFC for all of 1990. X, a U.S. resident, owns 60% of F's one class of stock for the entire year. Subpart F income is $100,000, there has been no increase in investment in U.S. property for the tax year, and no distributions have been made during the year. X, a calendar year taxpayer, must include $60,000 in gross income as a constructive dividend for 1990. □

EXAMPLE 33   F is a CFC until July 1, 1990. T, a U.S. citizen, owns 30% of its one class of stock for the entire year. Subpart F income is $100,000. T must include $14,877 [$100,000 × 30% × (181 days/365 days)] in gross income as a constructive dividend for 1990. □

A CFC is any foreign corporation in which more than 50 percent of the total combined voting power of all classes of stock entitled to vote or the total value of the stock of the corporation is owned by U.S. shareholders on any day during the taxable year of the foreign corporation. For purposes of determining if a foreign corporation is a CFC, a *U.S. shareholder* is defined as a U.S. person who owns, or is considered as owning, 10 percent or more of the total combined voting power of all classes of voting stock of the foreign corporation. Stock owned directly, indirectly, and constructively is counted.[47]

Indirect ownership involves stock held through a foreign entity, such as a foreign corporation, foreign partnership, or foreign trust. Such stock is considered as actually owned proportionately by the shareholders, partners, or beneficiaries. The constructive ownership rules under § 318(a), with certain modifications, apply in determining if a U.S. person is a U.S. shareholder, in determining whether a foreign corporation is a CFC, and for certain related party provisions of Subpart F. Some of the modifications are (1) stock owned by a nonresident alien individual is not considered constructively owned by a U.S. citizen or resident alien individual; (2) if a partnership, estate, trust, or corporation owns, directly or indirectly, more than 50 percent of the voting power of a corporation, it is deemed to own all of its stock; and (3) the threshold for corporate attribution is 10 percent rather than 50 percent.[48]

	Shareholders of Foreign Corporation	Voting Power	Classification
EXAMPLE 34	A	30%	U.S. person
	B	9%	U.S. person
	C	41%	Foreign person
	D	20%	U.S. person

B is A's son. A, B, and D are "U.S. shareholders." A owns 39%, 30% directly and 9% constructively through B. B also owns 39%, 9% directly and 30% constructively through A. Thus, B is a "U.S. shareholder." D owns 20% directly. F is a CFC because "U.S. shareholders" own 59% of the voting power. If B were not related to A or to any other U.S. persons who were shareholders, B would not be a "U.S. shareholder," and F would not be a CFC. ☐

U.S. shareholders must include their pro rata share of the applicable income in their gross income only to the extent of their actual ownership. Stock held indirectly is considered actually owned for this purpose.

EXAMPLE 35

B, in Example 34 above, would recognize only 9% of the Subpart F income as a constructive dividend. A would recognize 30% and D would recognize 20%. If B were a foreign corporation, wholly owned by A, A would recognize 39% as a constructive dividend. If C owned only 40% of the stock and E, a U.S. person, owned 1% and was not related to any of the other shareholders, E would not be a "U.S. shareholder" and would not have to include any of the Subpart F income in gross income. ☐

47. § 957.   48. § 958.

Subpart F Income.   Subpart F income consists of the following:

- Insurance income (§ 953).

- Foreign base company income (§ 954).

- International boycott factor income (§ 999).

- Illegal bribes.

- Income derived from a § 901(j) foreign country.

Insurance income is income attributable to any insurance or annuity contract in connection with property in, or liability arising out of activity in, or the lives or health of residents of a country other than the country under the laws of which the CFC is created or organized. Such income includes that from the reinsurance of such property, activity, or persons, and any arrangement with another corporation whereby such other corporation assumes such risks in exchange for the CFC's insurance of risks not described above.

EXAMPLE 36   X, a domestic corporation, owns 80% of F, a CFC organized in Country A. Y Corporation and Z Corporation are unrelated corporations, both of which were organized in Country B. F issues insurance on the property of Y and Z. The income derived from these insurance contracts is Subpart F income to F.   □

If the foreign corporation is a *captive insurance company,* the U.S. shareholders must include any related-person insurance income in gross income as a constructive dividend if the U.S. shareholders own 25 percent or more of the voting power of the foreign corporation. For this purpose, any U.S. person owning *any* stock of the foreign corporation is deemed a *U.S. shareholder.* Related-person insurance income is that attributable to insurance or reinsurance where the primary insured is a U.S. shareholder or a person related to a U.S. shareholder. Corporations in which such persons own less than 20 percent of the voting power and value are excluded, as are corporations for which the related-person insurance income for the taxable year is less than 20 percent of its total insurance income. Moreover, a foreign corporation can elect to treat its related-person insurance income as effectively connected with a U.S. trade or business and avoid Subpart F with regard to this income. By making such an election, the CFC waives the right to any income tax treaty benefits with regard to the related-person insurance income.

Foreign Base Company Income.   There are five categories of foreign base company income (FBCI):

- Foreign personal holding company income.

- Foreign base company sales income.

- Foreign base company services income.

- Foreign base company shipping income.

- Foreign base company oil-related income.

Each of these income categories is defined in § 954. A *de minimis* rule provides that, if the total amount of a foreign corporation's FBCI and gross insurance income for the taxable year is less than the lesser of 5 percent of gross income or $1 million, none of its gross income will be treated as FBCI for the tax year. The *de*

minimis rule does not apply to other types of income under Subpart F, such as increases in investment in U.S. property. However, if a foreign corporation's FBCI and gross insurance income exceed 70 percent of total gross income, all the corporation's gross income for the tax year is treated as FBCI or insurance income.

FBCI and insurance income subject to high foreign taxes are not included under Subpart F if the taxpayer establishes that such income was subject to an effective rate, imposed by a foreign country, of more than 90 percent of the maximum corporate rate under § 11. For 1989, this rate must be greater than 30.6 percent (90% × 34%).

Foreign personal holding company (FPHC) income is gross income that consists of the following:

- Dividends, interest, royalties, rents, and annuities;

- Excess gains over losses from the sale or exchange of property (including an interest in a trust, partnership, or REMIC) that gives rise to FPHC income as described above or that does not give rise to any income;

- Excess gains over losses from transactions in any commodities (other than bona fide hedging transactions as part of an active business as a producer, processor, merchant, or handler of commodities, or foreign currency gains or losses under § 988);

- Excess of foreign currency gains over foreign currency losses attributable to § 988 foreign currency transactions (other than any transaction directly related to the business needs of the CFC); and

- Any income equivalent to interest.

FPHC income does not include rents and royalties derived in the active conduct of a trade or business and received from an unrelated person or any export financing interest that is derived in the conduct of a banking business. FPHC income also does not include rent and royalty income received from a related person for the use of property within the foreign country in which the CFC is organized. Also excluded are dividends and interest income received from related persons created or organized in the same foreign country as the CFC and having a substantial part of their trade or business assets located in the foreign country. These exceptions will not apply where the interest, rent, or royalty reduces the payor's Subpart F income.

Foreign base company (FBC) sales income is income derived from the purchase of personal property from or on behalf of a related person, or from the sale of personal property to or on behalf of a related person.

EXAMPLE 37   F, a CFC owned 100% by X, a U.S. corporation, will generate FBC sales income in any one of the following situations:

- Purchase of widgets from anyone as commission agent for X Corporation.

- Purchase of widgets from X Corporation and sale to anyone.

- Purchase of widgets from anyone and sale to X Corporation.

- Sale of widgets to anyone as commission agent for X Corporation.   ☐

An exception applies to property that is manufactured, produced, grown, or extracted in the country in which the CFC was organized or created and also to property sold for use, consumption, or disposition within such country. Certain

income derived by a branch of the CFC in another country can be deemed FBC sales income if the effect of using the branch is the same as if the branch were a wholly owned subsidiary.

FBC services income is income derived from the performance of services for or on behalf of a related person and performed outside the country in which the CFC was created or organized. Income from services performed before and in connection with the sale of property by a CFC that has manufactured, produced, grown, or extracted such property is not FBC services income.

FBC shipping income includes several classifications of income, including dividends and interest received from a foreign corporation, to the extent such income is attributable to, or is derived from, or in connection with, the use of any aircraft or vessel in foreign commerce, the performance of services directly related to the use of such aircraft or vessel, or sale or exchange of any such aircraft or vessel.

FBC oil-related income is income, other than extraction income, derived in a foreign country and not sold by the CFC or a related person for use or consumption within the country in which the oil or gas was extracted. Only a corporation with production of at least 1,000 barrels per day will be treated as deriving FBC oil-related income.

Distributions of Previously Taxed Income.   Under § 959, distributions from a CFC are treated as first from E & P attributable to increases in investment in U.S. property previously taxed as a constructive dividend, second from E & P attributable to previously taxed Subpart F income other than that described above, and last from other E & P. Thus, distributions of previously taxed income will not be taxed as a dividend on distribution but will reduce E & P.

EXAMPLE 38   ABC, Inc., a U.S. shareholder that owns 100% of F, a CFC, receives a $100,000 distribution from F. F's E & P is composed of the following amounts:

- $50,000 attributable to previously taxed increases in investment in U.S. property,
- $30,000 attributable to previously taxed Subpart F income, and
- $40,000 attributable to other E & P.

ABC will have a taxable dividend of only $20,000, all attributable to other E & P. The remaining $80,000 is previously taxed income. F's E & P is reduced by $100,000. The remaining E & P of F is all attributable to other E & P.   □

A U.S. shareholder's basis in CFC stock is increased by constructive dividends included in income under Subpart F and decreased by subsequent distributions of previously taxed income. Under § 960, U.S. corporate shareholders who own at least 10 percent of the voting stock of a foreign corporation are allowed an indirect FTC for foreign taxes deemed paid on constructive dividends included in gross income under Subpart F. The indirect credit also is available for Subpart F income attributable to second- and third-tier foreign corporations as long as the 10 percent ownership requirement is met from tier to tier. Deemed-paid taxes for which an indirect FTC is allowed under § 960 are not creditable under § 902 when actual distributions of previously taxed income are made.

Foreign Sales Corporations

Prior to 1985, the Domestic International Sales Corporations (DISC) provisions (§§ 991–997) allowed for a deferral of the tax on a portion of the export income of a DISC until actual repatriation of the earnings. Over the years, Congress cut the amount of export income on which deferral was allowed. As the result of charges by the General Agreement on Trade and Tariffs (whose members include some of the United States' major trading partners) that the DISC provisions were a prohibited "export subsidy," the DISC provisions were curtailed, and the Foreign Sales Corporation (FSC) provisions (§§ 921–927) were enacted. The major short-term benefit of converting an export operation from a DISC to an FSC was that deferred DISC income that was forgiven would never be subject to U.S. taxation. The only remaining DISCs are interest charge ones—the price of deferral is an annual interest charge on the deferred taxes.[49] Only export sales up to $10 million qualify for deferral. Amounts in excess of $10 million are deemed distributed.

FSCs are not allowed a tax deferral on export income. Instead, a certain percentage (about 16 percent) of export income is exempt from U.S. taxation (exempt foreign trade income). Pricing methods are provided for determining exempt foreign trade income.

In order for a foreign corporation to elect FSC status, it must meet a foreign presence requirement. An exception to this requirement is provided if the foreign corporation's export receipts do not exceed $5 million (the small FSC exception). The foreign presence requirement includes maintaining a foreign office, operating under foreign management, keeping a permanent set of books at the foreign office, conducting foreign economic processes (e.g., selling activities), and being a foreign corporation (one organized or created under the laws of a foreign country or any U.S. possession). In addition, the corporation must have no more than 25 shareholders at any time during the taxable year and have no preferred stock outstanding at any time during the taxable year.

FOREIGN CURRENCY TRANSACTIONS

Changes in the relative value of a foreign currency and the U.S. dollar (the foreign exchange rate) affect the dollar value of foreign property held by the taxpayer, the dollar value of foreign debts, and the dollar amount of gain or loss on a transaction denominated in a foreign currency. The foreign currency exchange rates, however, have no effect on the transactions of a U.S. person who arranges all international transactions in U.S. dollars.

EXAMPLE 39   X, a domestic corporation, purchases goods from F, a foreign corporation, and pays for these goods in U.S. dollars. F then exchanges the U.S. dollars for the currency of the country in which it operates. X has no foreign exchange considerations with which to contend. If X purchased goods from F and was required to pay F in a foreign currency, X would have to exchange U.S. dollars for the foreign currency in order to make payment. If the exchange rate had changed from the date of purchase to the date of payment, X would have a foreign currency gain or loss on the currency exchange. □

---

49. § 995(f).

Taxpayers may find it necessary to translate amounts denominated in foreign currency into U.S. dollars for any of the following purposes:

- Purchase of goods, services, and property.
- Sale of goods, services, and property.
- Collection of foreign receivables.
- Payment of foreign payables.
- FTC calculations.
- Recognizing income or loss from foreign branch activities.

Tax Issues

The following concepts are important when dealing with the tax aspects of foreign exchange:

1. Foreign currency is treated as property other than money.
2. Gain or loss on the exchange of foreign currency is considered separately from the underlying transaction (e.g., the purchase or sale of goods).
3. No gain or loss is recognized until a transaction is closed.

EXAMPLE 40   D, a domestic corporation, purchases merchandise for resale from F, a foreign corporation, for 50,000K. On the date of purchase, 1K (a foreign currency) is equal to $1 U.S. (1K:$1). On the date of payment by D (the foreign exchange date), the exchange rate is 1.25K:$1. In other words, D paid to F 50,000K, which cost D $40,000. D must record the purchase of the merchandise at $50,000 and recognize a foreign currency gain of $10,000 ($50,000 − $40,000). □

EXAMPLE 41   If, in Example 40 above, the foreign exchange rate on the date of purchase was 1K:$1, 1.2K:$1 on a date between the purchase and payment dates, and 1K:$1 on the payment date, D realizes no foreign currency gain or loss. The transaction was not closed at the time of the foreign exchange rate fluctuation. □

The major tax issues that must be considered in the taxation of foreign currency exchange are the following:

1. The character of the gain or loss (ordinary or capital).
2. The date of recognition of any gain or loss.
3. The source (U.S. or foreign) of the foreign currency gain or loss.

Before 1987, there was little statutory authority dealing with the taxation of foreign currency transactions. The IRS rulings and the court decisions on the subject were not consistent. The Tax Reform Act of 1986 provided statutory rules for most business transactions involving foreign currency exchange. Many personal transactions involving foreign currency exchange are not covered by these provisions, however, and the law developed prior to the 1986 Act still applies. For individuals, the post-1986 statutory provisions apply only to the extent that

allocable expenses would qualify as trade or business expenses under § 162 or expenses of producing income under § 212.[50]

Functional Currency

Prior to 1987, the Code contained no provisions for determining tax results when foreign operations could be recorded in a foreign currency. However, in 1981, the Financial Accounting Standards Board adopted FAS 52 on foreign currency translation. FAS 52 introduced the *functional currency* approach (the currency of the economic environment in which the foreign entity operates generally is to be used as the monetary unit to measure gains and losses). The 1986 Act adopted this approach for the most part.

Under § 985, all income tax determinations are to be made in the taxpayer's functional currency. Generally, a taxpayer's functional currency will be the U.S. dollar. In certain circumstances, a qualified business unit (QBU) may be required to use a foreign currency as its functional currency. A QBU is a separate and clearly identified unit of a taxpayer's trade or business (e.g., a foreign branch). A corporation is a QBU. An individual is not a QBU; however, a trade or business conducted by an individual may be a QBU.

Section 988 Transactions

The disposition of a nonfunctional currency can result in a foreign currency gain or loss under § 988. Section 988 transactions include those in which gain or loss is determined with regard to the value of a nonfunctional currency, such as the following:

1. Acquisition of (or becoming obligor under) a debt instrument.

2. Accruing (or otherwise taking into account) any item of expense or gross income or receipts that is to be paid or received at a later date.

3. Entering into or acquiring any forward contract, futures contract, option or similar investment position unless such position is a regulated futures contract or nonequity option that would be marked-to-market under § 1256.[51]

4. Disposition of nonfunctional currency.

Section 988 generally treats exchange gain or loss falling within its provisions as ordinary income or loss. Certain exchange gain or loss will be apportioned in the same manner as interest income or expense. Capital gain or loss treatment may be elected with regard to forward contracts, futures contracts, and options that constitute capital assets in the hands of the taxpayer. These capital assets cannot be part of a straddle or marked-to-market under § 1256 and must meet certain identification requirements.

As under pre-1987 law, a closed or completed transaction is required. The residence of the taxpayer generally determines the source of a foreign exchange gain or loss. For this purpose, the residence of a QBU is the country in which its principal place of business is located.

---

50. § 988(e).
51. Section 988(c)(1)(D)(ii) provides for an election to bring positions in regulated futures contracts and nonequity options that would be marked-to-market under § 1256 within the provisions of § 988. The election, once made, is binding for all future years. Special provisions apply with regard to qualified funds as defined under § 988(c)(1)(E)(iii).

Branch Operations

Where a QBU (a foreign branch, in this case) uses a foreign currency as its functional currency, the profit or loss must be computed in the foreign currency each year and translated into U.S. dollars for tax purposes. Section 987 mandates use of the profit and loss method for this purpose. This method requires that the entire amount of profit or loss, without taking remittances into account, be translated using a weighted-average exchange rate for the taxable year. Exchange gain or loss is recognized on remittances from the QBU by comparing the U.S. dollar amount of the remittance at the exchange rate in effect on the date of remittance with the U.S. dollar value (at the appropriate weighted-average rate) of a pro rata portion of post-1986 accumulated earnings of the branch. Such gain or loss is ordinary and sourced according to the income to which the remittance is attributable.

EXAMPLE 42   D, a domestic corporation, began operation of a QBU (foreign branch) in 1988. The functional currency of the QBU is the K. The QBU's profits for 1988–1990 are as shown.

	Income (in Ks)	Exchange Rate	Income in U.S. Dollars
1988	200K	1K:$1	$200
1989	200K	1.25K:$1	160
1990	200K	1.6K:$1	125
	600K		$485

The income is taxed to D in the year earned regardless of whether any remittances take place. □

Distributions from Foreign Corporations

An actual distribution of E & P from a foreign corporation is included in income by the U.S. recipient at the exchange rate in effect on the date of distribution. Thus, no exchange gain or loss is recognized. Deemed dividend distributions under Subpart F must be translated at the weighted-average exchange rate for the CFC's tax year to which the deemed distribution is attributable. Exchange gain or loss can result when an actual distribution of this previously taxed income is made. The gain or loss is the difference in the exchange rates on the date the deemed distribution is included in income and the date of the actual distribution.

EXAMPLE 43   In 1990, the QBU (see Example 42) remits 300K to D when the exchange rate is 1.6K:$1. D has a foreign currency loss of $55, determined as follows:

		Difference
$62.50* from 1988 at 1K:$1 =	$100.00**	($37.50)
$62.50 from 1989 at 1.25K:$1 =	80.00	(17.50)
$62.50 from 1990 at 1.6K:$1 =	62.50	–0–
	$242.50	($55.00)

*[300K × (200K/600K)] at a rate of 1.6K:$1 = $62.50.
**[300K × (200K/600K)] at a rate of 1K:$1 = $100.

The loss is an ordinary loss for 1990. It is sourced by reference to the post-1986 accumulated earnings (1988–1990). The results would generally be the same if this was a distribution of previously taxed Subpart F income. □

For FTC purposes, foreign taxes are translated at the exchange rate in effect when the foreign taxes were paid. For purposes of the indirect FTC, any adjustment of foreign taxes paid by the foreign corporation is translated at the rate in effect at the time of adjustment. Any refund or credit is translated at the rate in effect at the time of original payment of the foreign taxes.

EXAMPLE 44

F, a foreign subsidiary of D, a U.S. corporation, has pre-tax income of 300K. F pays 100K in foreign taxes. The exchange rate was .5K:$1 when the income was earned and the foreign taxes paid. None of the income is Subpart F income. If the 200K net earnings are distributed when the exchange rate is .4K:$1, the deemed-paid taxes are $200 [($500/$500) × $200]. The effective tax rate is 40%. □

TAX PLANNING CONSIDERATIONS

Tax legislation tends progressively to reduce the ability to plan transactions and operations in a manner that minimizes tax liability. However, taxpayers who are not limited by the constraints of a particular transaction or operation can use the following suggestions to plan for the maximum tax benefits in any case.

The Foreign Tax Credit Limitation and Sourcing Provisions

Since the FTC limitation is driven by the amount of foreign-source taxable income in the numerator of the limitation ratio, the sourcing of income is extremely important in this regard. Income that is taxed by a foreign tax jurisdiction benefits from the FTC only to the extent that it is classified as foreign-source income under U.S. tax law. Thus, elements such as the place of title passage that affect the sourcing of income should be given careful consideration before a transaction is undertaken.

A taxpayer who can control the timing of income and loss recognition will want to avoid recognizing losses in years in which the loss will be apportioned among the FTC limitation baskets in such a way as to reduce the foreign taxes for which a credit is allowed for the tax year.

EXAMPLE 45

D, a U.S. person, has U.S.-source taxable income of $200,000, worldwide taxable income of $300,000, and a U.S. tax liability (before FTC) of $84,000. D receives foreign-source taxable income, pays foreign income taxes, and has an FTC as shown:

Basket	Amount	Foreign Taxes	FTC Limitation	FTC
Passive	$ 20,000	$ 800	$ 5,600	$ 800
General	50,000	20,500	14,000	14,000
Non-CFC § 902 corporation #1	15,000	3,000	4,200	3,000
Non-CFC § 902 corporation #2	15,000	4,500	4,200	4,200
	$100,000	$28,800		$22,000

If D had a foreign-source loss of $10,000 that would fall in the shipping limitation basket, this would reduce the FTC by $1,820. The U.S. tax liability before FTC would be $81,200; 50% of the loss would be apportioned to the general limitation basket reducing the FTC limitation for this basket to $12,600 [$81,200 × ($45,000/$290,000)]; and 15% would be apportioned to the non-CFC § 902 corporation #2 basket, reducing the FTC limitation for this basket to $3,780 [$81,200 × ($13,500/$290,000)]. D would avoid this result if he could defer recognition of the loss to a tax year in which it would not have a negative effect on the FTC. □

When negotiating the terms of the sale of an intangible, such as a patent, the taxpayer may be able to influence the source of the gain on the sale by controlling the amount of consideration that is contingent on the productivity or use of the intangible by the purchaser. Under § 865, contingent payments are sourced in the same manner as royalty income (where the intangible will be used). If the intangible will be used outside the United States, the greater the portion of the sales price that is contingent, the greater the foreign-source income. This will benefit the U.S. seller as long as any taxation of the contingent payments by the foreign tax authorities does not exceed the U.S. tax on such amounts.

The Foreign Corporation as a Tax Shelter

The NRA who is able to hold U.S. investments through a foreign corporation can accomplish much in the way of avoiding U.S. taxation. Any capital gains (other than dispositions of U.S. real property interests) are not subject to U.S. taxation as long as they are not effectively connected with a U.S. trade or business and are not gains from commodity transactions entered into by a foreign corporation with its principal place of business in the United States. The NRA can dispose of the stock of a foreign corporation that holds U.S. real property and not be subject to taxation under § 897 (FIRPTA). Furthermore, the stock of a foreign corporation is not included in the U.S. gross estate of a deceased NRA even if all the assets of the foreign corporation are located in the United States.

Caution is advised where the foreign corporation may generate income effectively connected with the conduct of a U.S. trade or business. This income may be taxed at a higher rate than if the NRA individually generated the income. The trade-off between a higher U.S. tax on this income and protection from the U.S. estate tax and § 897 must be weighed.

Planning under Subpart F

The *de minimis* rule will allow a CFC to avoid the classification of income as FBC income or insurance income and prevent the U.S. shareholder from having to include it in gross income as a constructive dividend. Thus, a CFC with total FBC income and insurance income in an amount close to the 5 percent or $1 million level should monitor income realization in order to assure that the *de minimis* rule applies for the tax year. At least as important is avoiding the classification of all the gross income of the CFC as FBC income or insurance income. This happens when the sum of the FBC income and gross insurance income for the taxable year exceeds 70 percent of total gross income.

Careful timing of increases in investment in U.S. property can reduce the potential for constructive dividend income to U.S. shareholders. The gross income of U.S. shareholders attributable to increases in investment in U.S. property is

limited to the E & P of the CFC.[52] E & P that is attributable to amounts that either in the current year or a prior tax year have been included in gross income as Subpart F income is not taxed again when invested in U.S. property.[53]

The Foreign Earned Income Exclusion

The tax benefit of the foreign earned income exclusion depends on the tax the income will incur in the country in which earned and the year in which received. If the foreign country levies little or no tax on the income, the U.S. taxpayer will be able to exclude the housing cost amount plus up to $70,000 of foreign earned income and pay little or no tax on the income to the foreign tax jurisdiction. Since foreign earned income qualifies for the exclusion only if received in the year in which earned or the immediately succeeding tax year, the timely payment of such income is necessary.

In high tax jurisdictions, the taxpayer may benefit more from taking the FTC than from excluding the earnings from gross income. The taxpayer earning income in a high tax jurisdiction should compare the tax result of taking the exclusion with the tax result of forgoing either or both exclusions for the FTC. If U.S. taxes on the income are eliminated under all options and the taxpayer has excess foreign taxes to carry back or carry forward, then the FTC generally is more beneficial than the exclusion.

Taxpayers must also carefully monitor their trips to the United States when attempting to qualify for the exclusion under the physical presence test. Taxpayers who are attempting to establish a bona fide foreign residence must make sure that their ties to the foreign country predominate over their ties to the United States for the period for which bona fide foreign residence is desired.

Tax Treaties

The value of treaty benefits should never be overlooked by a taxpayer planning to perform services in a foreign country, to enter into a transaction with a foreign person or in a foreign country, or to conduct operations in a foreign country. Such persons should review the appropriate tax treaties carefully to apprise themselves of any benefits that may be available. There are international treaties not expressly labeled tax treaties that also can contain provisions that are beneficial to U.S. or foreign persons entering into international transactions.[54]

Nonresident Aliens and U.S. Resident Status

An NRA who does not want worldwide income subject to U.S. taxation should not acquire a green card unless such NRA has decided that U.S. resident status is worth the price of U.S. income taxation on a worldwide basis. Furthermore, an NRA who does not intend to become a U.S. resident for the tax year should avoid being physically present in the United States under any of the conditions that would lead to U.S. resident status for income tax purposes. Even if a person becomes a U.S. resident for income tax purposes, this does not necessarily mean that domicile has been changed to the United States. A resident alien can avoid the U.S. estate and gift tax in part at least by avoiding U.S. domicile. The showing of an intention to retain domicile in a foreign country will suffice to retain foreign domicile for U.S. estate and gift tax purposes. Thus, to avoid U.S. domicile, the NRA or resident alien must maintain sufficient ties with a foreign country.

---

52. § 959(a)(1).
53. § 959(a)(2).

54. *Arthur A. Amaral*, 90 T.C. 802 (1988).

PROBLEM MATERIALS

Discussion Questions

1. What factors must a taxpayer consider in determining whether a foreign tax is creditable for foreign tax credit purposes?

2. What income tax consequences need to be considered by a corporate shareholder who takes the indirect credit?

3. What are some of the tax consequences affected by the sourcing of income as within or without the United States?

4. When will income from the performance of personal services within the United States be treated as foreign-source income?

5. In the apportionment of expenses and losses between U.S.-source and foreign-source income, what is the statutory grouping (U.S. or foreign) with regard to each of the following provisions?
   a. Foreign tax credit.
   b. Foreign earned income exclusion.
   c. Branch profits tax.

6. What requirements must be met and what tax consequences should be considered by a taxpayer and NRA spouse in making the election to file a joint return?

7. What is the difference in the definition of "residency" for U.S. income tax purposes and for U.S. estate tax purposes?

8. How can an NRA individual holding U.S. property (e.g., land and buildings) at the time of death avoid the U.S. estate tax?

9. Why can stock of a foreign corporation held by NRA individuals be considered a tax shelter for U.S. tax purposes?

10. How does the U.S. tax law attempt to assure that the tax will be paid when NRAs and foreign corporations dispose of U.S. real property interests at a gain?

11. Explain why the following statement is false: Income tax treaties between the United States and foreign countries allow only one of the treaty partners (either the United States or the foreign country) to tax income earned in one treaty country by residents of the other treaty country.

12. Why does the United States allow an exclusion for foreign earned income, but not for foreign unearned income such as dividends from foreign corporations?

13. Why is the § 936 possessions corporation credit referred to as a "tax-sparing" credit?

14. How does the tax law prevent Subpart F income from being taxed more than once to the U.S. shareholders?

15. When would a U.S. corporation conducting international transactions *not* have to consider foreign exchange consequences?

16. Why would the U.S. recipient of a dividend (actual or constructive) from a foreign corporation have no foreign exchange gain or loss?

17. When would the U.S. recipient of a constructive dividend (for example, under Subpart F) have a foreign exchange gain or loss?

Problems

18. For the tax year, J, a U.S. resident individual, has worldwide taxable income (without regard to personal exemptions) of $200,000, consisting of $160,000 U.S.-source income and $40,000 foreign-source dividend income. J's U.S. income tax liability before FTC is $56,000, and the foreign tax paid on the dividend income is $12,000. What is J's FTC for the tax year?

19. D, a domestic, calendar year corporation, has worldwide taxable income consisting of $400,000 U.S.-source income and a $100,000 foreign-source dividend received from F, a § 902 noncontrolled foreign corporation. F's post-1986 E & P after taxes is $2,000,000. F's foreign income taxes attributable to such E & P are $1,100,000.

    a. What is the amount of D's deemed-paid foreign taxes with regard to the dividend from F?

    b. What is D's FTC for the tax year?

20. How would the answers to Problem 19 change if the foreign tax authorities withheld $30,000 in taxes on the dividend from F and D received only $70,000 with regard to the dividend?

21. D, a domestic corporation, has the following FTC record for each tax year, without consideration of carrybacks and carryovers:

Year	1	2	3	4	5	6
Foreign taxes paid and deemed paid	$ 600	$ 500	$ 200	$ 150	$ 400	$ 300
FTC limitation	400	350	300	300	300	250
Excess foreign taxes (+)	+200	+150			+100	+50
Excess FTC limitation (−)			−100	−150		

    What is the amount of carryover remaining after Year 6, to which year(s) is it attributable, and when will it expire if unused? Assume that D takes advantage of the carryback and carryover provisions and elects the FTC for all tax years.

22. World, Inc., a U.S. multinational corporation, has the following taxable income and pays the following taxes for 1990:

Category	Amount	Source	Foreign Taxes
Manufacturing	$100,000	Foreign	$ 40,000
	500,000	U.S.	–0–
Interest	50,000	Foreign	2,000
	20,000	U.S.	–0–
Dividends	40,000	Foreign*	10,000
	30,000	U.S.	–0–
Shipping	260,000	Foreign	130,000

    *This is comprised of $20,000 from each of two § 902 noncontrolled foreign corporations. The foreign taxes attributable to the dividends were $8,000 and $2,000, respectively.

    U.S. taxes before FTC = $340,000.

    a. What is World's FTC allowed for the tax year?

    b. Are there any excess foreign taxes or excess limitations and, if so, how are they treated for FTC purposes?

23. T, a U.S. resident, received the following dividend and interest income for 1990. What is the source (U.S. or foreign) of each income item?

    a. $5,000 dividend income from C, a domestic corporation, that has gross income from the active conduct of a foreign trade or business for the immediately preceding three-year period of $1,700,000. C's total gross income for the same period was $2,000,000.

    b. $10,000 dividend from G, a foreign corporation, that has gross income effectively connected with the conduct of a U.S. trade or business for the immediately preceding three-year period of $500,000. G's total gross income for the same period was $1,500,000.

    c. $800 interest from N, an NRA individual, on a loan made by T to N.

    d. $15,000 interest on X Corporation bonds. X is a domestic corporation that derived $1,800,000 of its gross income for the immediately preceding three-year period from the active conduct of a foreign trade or business. X's total gross income for this same period was $2,100,000.

    e. $2,000 interest from a savings account in a Chicago bank.

24. T, a resident of France, is sent to the United States by F Corporation, a foreign employer, to arrange the purchase of some machine tools. T spends three weeks in the United States. This is T's only trip to the United States during the year. T's gross monthly salary is $3,500. T's pay check is deposited in his French bank account while he is in the United States. The salary is attributable to 15 U.S. and 6 French working days. T's foreign employer does not have a U.S. trade or business. What is the amount of T's U.S.-source income?

25. Determine the source of income from the following sales:

    a. Sale of widgets (inventory) purchased by a U.S. resident in Florida and sold to a Canadian company, title passing in Canada.

    b. Sale of widgets (inventory) manufactured in Texas by a U.S. resident and sold to a West German company, title passing in West Germany.

    c. Sale of machinery that had been used exclusively in a foreign trade or business by a domestic corporation to an unrelated foreign corporation, title passing in Japan.

    d. Sale of IBM stock by R, an NRA individual, sale taking place on the New York Stock Exchange.

26. F, a foreign corporation resident in country M, is owned 100% by X, a domestic corporation. F, therefore, is a CFC. Determine F's Subpart F income (before expenses and cost of goods sold) for the tax year, given the following items of income:

    a. $200,000 from the sale of merchandise (purchased from X) to customers in country N.

    b. $120,000 insurance income from the insurance of the risks of G, another foreign corporation owned by X and resident in country P.

    c. $75,000 commissions from the sale of merchandise on behalf of X to residents of country M for use within M.

    d. $80,000 from the sale of merchandise to X. The merchandise was purchased from an unrelated manufacturer resident in country P.

    e. $300,000 from performance on a construction contract entered into by X. The services were performed by F's personnel in country P.

27. T, a U.S. shareholder, owns 15% of the only class of stock of F, a CFC. F is a CFC until July 1 of the current tax year. T has held the stock since F was organized and continues to hold it for the entire year. T and F are both calendar year taxpayers.

If F's Subpart F income for the tax year is $200,000, E & P is $350,000, and no distributions have been made for the tax year, what is the amount, if any, that T must include in gross income under Subpart F for the tax year?

28. N, a citizen and resident of country A, comes to the United States for the first time on February 1, 1990, and remains until June 10 of the same year, at which time N returns to A. N comes back to the United States on September 11, 1990, and remains until November 30, 1990, when N again returns to country A. N does not possess a green card. Is N a U.S. resident for 1990 under the substantial presence test? If so, is there any way that N can overcome the presumption of residence?

29. A, an NRA, has the following U.S.-source income for 1990. Determine A's U.S. tax liability assuming that A is single, has no § 165 losses and makes no charitable contributions.

Dividend from D Corporation*	$10,000
Interest from U.S. bank account**	4,000
Net income from U.S. trade or business	50,000

*A owns 30% of the stock of D, a U.S. corporation.
**The interest is attributable to the deposit of idle funds of the U.S. trade or business.

30. W, a U.S. resident, is married to H, an NRA. W has taxable income of $70,000 for the tax year. H, who is retired, receives foreign-source investment income of $20,000 for the tax year. Can W and H file a joint return? If so, should they?

31. F, a foreign corporation, operates a trade or business in the United States. F's U.S.-source taxable income effectively connected with this trade or business is $300,000 for the current tax year. F's current E & P is $250,000. F's net U.S. equity at the beginning of the year was $1.5 million and at the end of the year was $1.4 million. F is resident in a country with which the United States does not have an income tax treaty. What is the effect of the branch profits tax on F for the current tax year?

32. Assume that T, a U.S. citizen, becomes a bona fide resident of F, a foreign country, on March 28, 1989, and remains a resident until January 1, 1991. T is on the calendar year and cash tax basis in the United States. T earns a salary of $73,000 in 1990, but receives $60,000 of this amount in 1990 and $13,000 in 1991. T has no other foreign-source income in either year. How much of her salary is excludible under § 911 for 1990? How much for 1991? What would be the result if T received the $13,000 in 1992?

33. Calculate net taxable foreign-source earned income using the housing cost amount exclusion and the general exclusion for foreign-source earned income, given the following facts:

Total foreign-source earned income	$98,000*
Housing expenses paid by employer	25,000
Tax year	1990

*Includes the $25,000.

For ease of calculation, use $7,500 as the base amount for purposes of the housing cost amount exclusion.

34. Assume, in Problem 33, that the foreign-source earned income is that of a self-employed individual and that the individual also incurs the same amount of housing expenses. What amount is excludible and what amount is deductible, if any? Is there any carryover to 1991?

35. R, a qualified individual, has $140,000 of foreign-source earned income for 1990, of which $90,500 is excludible ($70,000 general exclusion and $20,500 housing

cost amount exclusion). R incurs $26,000 of moving expenses (all attributable to foreign-source income) and pays $35,000 of foreign taxes attributable to the foreign-source earned income. R's moving expenses of $16,500 are disallowed as being allocable to excluded income. R has no other deductible expenses. How much would the creditable foreign taxes have to be reduced due to the exclusions?

36. Assume that D, a domestic corporation, organizes a foreign branch in 1988. The branch is a QBU and uses the K (a foreign currency) as its functional currency. The following income and taxes resulted in 1988–1990:

	Income	Foreign Taxes	Exchange Rate
1988	150K/$300	45K/$90	.5K:$1
1989	150K/$200	45K/$60	.75K:$1
1990	150K/$150	45K/$45	1K:$1

Assuming the maximum corporate rate of 34% applies for U.S. tax purposes, determine the net U.S. tax for each year, with respect to the branch income.

37. Referring to Problem 36, assume that in 1990, 300K is remitted to the home office of D in the United States. Does this remittance trigger a foreign currency gain or loss? If so, what is its character (ordinary or capital)?

38. D, a U.S. corporation, contracts to buy a supply of rubber from a Malaysian company. The rubber is purchased on 90-day credit terms. The contract was for 50,000 tons of rubber at 1,000,000M$. D paid for the rubber 90 days after purchase. At the date of purchase, the exchange rate was 5M$:$1. Ninety days later the exchange rate was 4M$:$1.

   a. At what cost should D record the rubber purchase?

   b. How much, in U.S. dollars, did D have to pay 90 days after purchase for the rubber?

   c. Was there any recognizable gain or loss on payment? If so, how much and what is its character?

24

TAX ADMINISTRATION AND PRACTICE

OBJECTIVES

Examine the various administrative pronouncements issued by the IRS and evaluate how they can be used in tax practice.

Summarize the administrative powers of the IRS including the examination of taxpayer records, the assessment and demand process, and collection procedures.

Review the audit process, including how returns are selected for audit and the various types of audits conducted by the IRS.

Explain and illustrate the taxpayer appeal process including various settlement options available.

Explain how interest on a deficiency or a refund is determined and when it is due.

Discuss the various penalties that can be imposed on acts of noncompliance by taxpayers.

Review the rules governing the statute of limitations on assessments and on refunds.

Summarize the statutory and nonstatutory prohibitions and guides for those engaged in tax practice.

OUTLINE

Tax Administration

To provide quality tax consulting services, it is necessary to understand how the IRS is organized and how its various administrative groups function. For example, the taxpayer may object to a proposed deficiency assessment resulting from an IRS audit. The tax specialist must be familiar with IRS administrative appeal procedures to make a fully informed decision concerning appeal of the deficiency.

The Federal tax structure is predicated on a system of self-assessment. Consequently, every taxpayer is expected to determine his or her tax liability periodically and to pay any amount due to the IRS on a timely basis. In order to ensure that the self-assessment features of the system function efficiently, Congress has made a vast array of penalties available to the IRS. These penalties, often described as additions to tax, cover various acts of taxpayer noncompliance. Understanding the operation of the major penalties is an integral part of effective tax administration and practice.

IRS Procedure—Letter Rulings

Rulings issued by the National Office represent a written statement of the position of the IRS concerning the tax consequences of a course of action contemplated by the taxpayer. Letter (individual) rulings do not have the force and effect of law, but they do provide guidance and support for taxpayers in similar transactions. The IRS will issue rulings only on uncompleted, actual (rather than hypothetical) transactions or on transactions completed before the filing of the tax return for the year in question.

The IRS will not issue a ruling in certain circumstances. It will not rule in cases that essentially involve a question of fact.[1] For example, no ruling will be issued to determine whether compensation paid to employees is reasonable in amount and therefore allowable as a deduction.[2]

A letter ruling simply represents the current opinion of the IRS on the tax consequences of a particular transaction with a given set of facts. IRS rulings are not immutable. They are frequently declared obsolete or are superseded by new rulings in response to tax law changes. However, revocation or modification of a ruling is usually not applied retroactively to the taxpayer who received the ruling if he or she acted in good faith in reliance upon the ruling and if the facts in the ruling request were in agreement with the completed transaction. The IRS may revoke any ruling if, upon subsequent audit, the agent finds a misstatement or omission of facts or substantial discrepancies between the facts in the ruling request and the actual situation. A ruling may be relied upon only by the taxpayer who requested and received it.

Issuance of letter rulings benefits both the IRS and the taxpayer. The IRS ruling policy is an attempt to promote a uniform application of the tax laws. In addition, other benefits may accrue to the government through the issuance of rulings. Rulings may reduce the volume of litigation or number of disputes with revenue agents that would otherwise result, and they give the IRS an awareness of the significant transactions being consummated by taxpayers. A nominal fee is charged for processing a ruling request.

From the taxpayer's point of view, an advance ruling reduces the uncertainty of potential tax consequences resulting from a proposed course of action. Taxpayers frequently request a ruling before the consummation of a tax-free corporate

---

1. Rev.Proc. 90–1, I.R.B. No. 1, 8.   2. Rev.Proc. 90–3, I.R.B. No. 1, 54.

reorganization because of the severe tax consequences that would result if the reorganization were subsequently deemed to be taxable. Liquidations, stock redemptions, and transfers to controlled corporations under § 351 are other sensitive areas in which taxpayers want confirmation.

Letter rulings that are of both sufficient importance and general interest may be published as Revenue Rulings (in anonymous form) and thus made available to all taxpayers.

In general, all unpublished letter rulings, determination letters, and technical advice memoranda are now open to public inspection once identifying details and certain confidential information have been deleted. Letter rulings and technical advice memoranda now are reprinted and published by Prentice-Hall and Commerce Clearing House and are available in computerized document retrieval services, including WESTLAW, LEXIS, and PHINet. The general availability of such materials assists in the conduct of tax research and planning.

IRS Procedure—Additional Issuances

In addition to issuing unpublished letter rulings and published rulings and procedures, the IRS issues determination letters and technical advices.

A determination letter is issued by the District Director for a completed transaction when the issue involved is covered by judicial or statutory authority, regulations, or rulings. A determination letter is issued for various death, gift, income, excise, and employment tax matters.

EXAMPLE 1 T Corporation recently opened a car clinic and has employed numerous mechanics. The corporation is not certain if the mechanics are to be treated as employees or as independent contractors for withholding and payroll tax purposes. T Corporation may request a determination letter from the appropriate District Director. □

EXAMPLE 2 Assume the same facts as in Example 1. T Corporation would like to establish a pension plan that qualifies for the tax advantages of §§ 401 through 404. To determine whether the plan qualifies, T Corporation can request and obtain a determination letter from the IRS. □

EXAMPLE 3 A group of physicians plans to form an association to construct and operate a hospital. The determination letter procedure is appropriate to ascertain the group's status—either subject to the Federal income tax or tax-exempt. □

Technical advice is rendered by the National Office to the District Director and/or Regional Commissioner in response to the specific request of an agent, Appellate Conferee, or District Director. The taxpayer may ask that a request for technical advice be made if an issue in dispute is not treated by the law or precedent and/or published rulings or regulations. Technical advice also is appropriate when there is reason to believe that the tax law is not being administered consistently by the IRS. For example, a taxpayer may inquire why an agent proposes to disallow a certain expenditure when agents in other districts permit the deduction.

Administrative Powers of the IRS

Examination of Records.   For the purpose of determining the correct amount of tax due, the Code authorizes the IRS to examine the taxpayer's books and records and to summon the persons responsible to appear before the IRS and, when they appear, to produce the necessary books and records.[3] Taxpayers are required to maintain certain recordkeeping procedures and retain the records that are necessary to facilitate the audit. Therefore, the taxpayer and not the IRS has the burden of proof to substantiate any item on the tax return that is under examination. It should be noted that the files, workpapers, and other memoranda of a tax practitioner may be subpoenaed, since the courts have not extended to CPAs the privileged communication doctors and lawyers sometimes possess with respect to their clients.

Assessment and Demand.   The Code permits the IRS to assess a deficiency and to demand payment for the tax.[4] However, no assessment or effort to collect the tax may be made until 90 days following the issuance of a statutory notice of a deficiency (the 90-day letter). The taxpayer is, therefore, given 90 days to file a petition to the U.S. Tax Court, which effectively prevents the deficiency from being assessed or collected pending the outcome of the case.[5]

Certain exceptions to this assessment procedure should be noted:

- The IRS may issue a deficiency assessment without waiting 90 days if mathematical errors on the return incorrectly state the tax at less than the true liability.

- If the IRS believes the assessment or collection of a deficiency is in jeopardy, it may assess the deficiency and demand immediate payment.[6] The taxpayer is able to stay the collection of the jeopardy assessment by filing a bond for the amount of the tax and interest. This action will prevent the sale of any property that has been seized by the IRS.

Following assessment of the tax, the IRS will issue a notice and demand for payment. The taxpayer is usually given 30 days following the notice and demand for payment to pay the tax.

Collection.   If the taxpayer neglects or refuses to pay the tax after the receipt of the 30-day notice and demand letter, a lien develops in favor of the IRS upon all property (whether it be realty or personalty, tangible or intangible) belonging to the taxpayer. This lien, commonly referred to as a statutory lien, is not valid until the IRS files Form 668 (Notice of Federal Tax Lien Under Internal Revenue Laws).

The levy power of the IRS is very broad. It allows the IRS to garnish (attach) wages and salary and to seize and sell all nonexempt property *by any means*. The IRS can also make successive seizures on any property owned by the taxpayer until the levy is satisfied.

For 1989 there was a $1,550 exemption from levy for fuel, provisions, furniture, and personal household effects. In addition, there was a $1,050 exemption from levy for books, tools, machinery, or equipment that is necessary for the trade, business, or profession of the taxpayer. These exemptions have increased to $1,650 and $1,100, respectively, for 1990 and subsequent years.

---

3. § 7602.   5. § 6213.
4. § 6212.   6. § 6861.

For levies issued on or after July 1, 1989, the amount of weekly wages that is exempt from a levy is an amount equal to the sum of the taxpayer's standard deduction and the aggregate amount of deductions for personal exemptions allowable for the tax year in which the levy occurs, divided by 52.[7]

In exceptional cases an extension in the payment of a deficiency will be granted to prevent "undue hardship."[8]

If property is transferred and the tax is not paid, the subsequent owners of the property may be liable for the tax. This pursuit of the tax liability against succeeding owners is referred to as transferee liability. For example, if an estate is insolvent and unable to pay the estate tax, the executor or the beneficiaries may be liable for its payment.[9]

The Audit Process

Selection of Returns for Audit.   The IRS uses the Discriminant Function System (DIF) as a starting point in the selection of tax returns for audit (examination). This selection procedure utilizes mathematical formulas to select tax returns that are most likely to contain errors and yield substantial amounts of additional tax revenues upon audit. Despite the use of computer selection processes, the ultimate selection of returns for audit is still conducted by the classification staff within the Audit Division of the IRS.

The IRS does not openly disclose all of its audit selection techniques. However, the following observations can be made regarding the probability of a return's selection for audit:

- Certain groups of taxpayers are subject to audit more frequently than others. These groups include individuals with gross income in excess of $50,000, self-employed individuals with substantial business income and deductions, and cash businesses where the potential for tax evasion is high.

EXAMPLE 4   T owns and operates a liquor store on a cash-and-carry basis. As all of T's sales are for cash, T might well be a prime candidate for an audit by the IRS. Cash transactions are easier to conceal than those made on credit.   □

- If a taxpayer has been audited in a past year and such audit led to the assessment of a substantial deficiency, a return visit by the IRS is to be expected.

- An audit might materialize if information returns (e.g., Form W-2, Form 1099) are not in substantial agreement with the income reported on a taxpayer's return. Over the years, the IRS has been able to correlate an increasing number of information returns with the returns filed by taxpayers. Obvious discrepancies do not necessitate formal audits (see below) but usually can be handled by correspondence with the taxpayer.

- If an individual's itemized deductions are in excess of norms established for various income levels, the probability of an audit is increased. Also, certain types of deductions (e.g., casualty and theft losses, office in the home, tax-sheltered investments) are sensitive areas since the IRS realizes that many

---

7. § 6334.   9. § 6901.
8. § 6161(b).

taxpayers will determine the amount of the deduction incorrectly or may not be entitled to the deduction at all.

- The filing of a refund claim by the taxpayer may prompt an audit of the return.

- Certain returns are selected on a random sample basis [known as the Taxpayer Compliance Measurement Program (TCMP)] to develop, update, and improve the DIF formulas (discussed earlier). TCMP is the long-range research effort of the IRS designed to measure and evaluate taxpayer compliance characteristics. TCMP audits are tedious and time-consuming because the taxpayer is generally asked to verify most or all items on the tax return.

- Information is often obtained from other sources (e.g., other government agencies, news items, informants). The IRS can pay rewards to persons who provide information that leads to the detection and punishment of those who violate the tax laws. Such rewards are discretionary by a District Director and will not exceed 10 percent of the taxes, fines, and penalties recovered as a result of such information.[10]

EXAMPLE 5   T reports to the police that while he was out of town his home was burglarized and one of the items taken was a shoe box containing cash of $25,000. A representative of the IRS reading the newspaper account of the burglary might well wonder why someone would keep such a large amount of cash in a shoe box at home. ☐

EXAMPLE 6   After 15 years, B is discharged by her employer, Dr. F. Shortly thereafter, the IRS receives a letter from B informing it that Dr. F keeps two sets of books, one of which substantially understates his cash receipts. ☐

Many individual taxpayers mistakenly assume that if they do not hear from the IRS within a few weeks following the filing of the return or if they have received a refund check, no audit will be forthcoming. As a practical matter, most individual returns are examined within two years from the date of filing. If not, they generally remain unaudited. All large corporations are subject to annual audits, and in many instances tax years will remain open for long periods since the taxpayer may agree to extend the statute of limitations pending settlement of unresolved issues.

Verification and Audit Procedures.   The tax return is initially checked for mathematical accuracy. A check is also made for deductions, exclusions, etc., that are clearly erroneous. An obvious error would be the failure to comply with the 7.5 percent limitation on the deduction for medical expenses. In such cases, the Service Center merely sends the taxpayer revised computations and a bill for the corrected amount of tax if the error results in additional tax liability. Taxpayers are usually able to settle such matters through direct correspondence with the IRS without the necessity of a formal audit.

Office audits are conducted by representatives of the District Director's Office (designated tax technicians) either in the office of the IRS or through correspondence. Individual returns with few or no items of business income are usually handled through an office audit. In most instances, the taxpayer will be required merely to substantiate a deduction, credit, or item of income that appears on the

---

10.   § 7623 and Reg. § 301.7623–1.

return. An individual may have claimed medical expenses that are in excess of a normal amount for taxpayers on a comparable income level. The taxpayer will be asked to present documentation in the form of cancelled checks, invoices, etc., for the items in question. Note the substantiation procedure here that is absent from the mathematical check and simple error discovery process mentioned above.

The field audit is commonly used for corporate returns and for returns of individuals engaged in business or professional activities. This type of audit generally entails a more complete examination of a taxpayer's transactions. By way of contrast, an office audit is usually directed toward fewer items and is therefore narrower in scope.

A field audit is conducted by IRS agents at the office or home of the taxpayer or at the office of the taxpayer's representative. It is common practice for a tax firm to hold conferences with IRS agents in the firm's office during the field audit of a corporate client. The agent's work may be facilitated by a review of certain tax workpapers and discussions with the taxpayer's representative relative to items appearing on the tax return.

Upon a showing of good cause, a taxpayer may request and obtain a reassignment of his or her case from an office to a field audit. The inconvenience and expense involved in transporting records and other supporting data to the agent's office may constitute good cause for reassignment.

Starting in 1989 the IRS must, prior to or at the initial interview, provide the taxpayer with an explanation of the audit process that is the subject of the interview and describe the taxpayer's rights under that process. If the taxpayer clearly states at any time during the interview that he or she wishes to consult with an attorney, CPA, enrolled agent, or any other person permitted to represent the taxpayer before the IRS, then the IRS representative must suspend the interview.[11]

Also, any officer or employee of the IRS must, upon advance request, allow a taxpayer to make an audio recording of any in-person interview with the officer or employee concerning the determination and collection of any tax. The recording of IRS audit conferences may have significant legal implications. For example, if any IRS employee recklessly or intentionally disregards regulatory rules in the collection of Federal tax, the taxpayer can bring a civil action for damages in a U.S. District Court.[12] An audio recording made during collection actions may have a bearing on the outcome of such a suit.

Settlement with the Revenue Agent.   Following the audit, the IRS agent may either accept the return as filed or recommend certain adjustments. The Revenue Agent's Report (RAR) is reviewed by the agent's group supervisor and the Review Staff within the IRS. In most instances, the agent's proposed adjustments are approved. However, it is not uncommon for the Review Staff or group supervisor to request additional information or to raise new issues.

Agents must adhere strictly to IRS policy as reflected in published rulings, Regulations, and other releases. The agent cannot settle an unresolved issue based upon the probability of winning the case in court. Usually, issues involving factual questions can be settled at the agent level, and it may be advantageous for both the taxpayer and the IRS to reach agreement at the earliest point in the settlement process. For example, it may be to the taxpayer's advantage to reach agreement at the agent level and avoid any further opportunity for the IRS to raise new issues.

A deficiency (an amount in excess of tax shown on the return or tax previously assessed) may be proposed at the agent level. The taxpayer might wish to pursue

11. § 7520(1).   12. § 7433.

to a higher level the disputed issues upon which this deficiency is based. The taxpayer's progress through the appeal process is discussed in subsequent sections of this chapter.

If agreement is reached upon the proposed deficiency, Form 870 (Waiver of Restrictions on Assessment and Collection of Deficiency in Tax) is signed by the taxpayer. One advantage to the taxpayer of signing Form 870 at this point is that interest stops accumulating on the deficiency 30 days after the form is filed.[13] When this form is signed, the taxpayer effectively waives his or her right to the receipt of a statutory notice of deficiency (the 90-day letter) and to subsequent petition to the Tax Court. In addition, it is no longer possible for the taxpayer to go to the Appeals Division. The signing of Form 870 at the agent level generally closes the case. However, since Form 870 does not have the effect of a closing agreement, even after the taxpayer pays the deficiency, the taxpayer may subsequently sue for refund of the tax in a Federal District Court or in the Claims Court. Further, the IRS is not restricted by Form 870 and may assess additional deficiencies if deemed necessary.

The Taxpayer Appeal Process

If agreement cannot be reached at the agent level, the taxpayer receives a copy of the Revenue Agent's Report and a transmittal letter, which is commonly referred to as the 30-day letter. The taxpayer is granted 30 days to request an administrative appeal. If an appeal is not requested, a statutory notice of deficiency will be issued (the 90-day letter).

If an appeal is desired, an appropriate request must be made to the Appeals Division. Such request must be accompanied by a written protest except in the following cases:

- The proposed tax deficiency does not exceed $10,000 for any of the tax periods involved in the audit.

- The deficiency resulted from a correspondence or office audit (not as a result of a field audit).

The Appeals Division is authorized to settle all tax disputes based on the hazards of litigation. Since the Appeals Division has final settlement authority until a statutory notice of deficiency (the 90-day letter) has been issued, the taxpayer may be able to obtain a percentage settlement. In addition, an overall favorable settlement may be reached through a "trading" of disputed issues. The Appeals Division occasionally may raise new issues if the grounds are substantial and of significant tax impact.

Both the Appeals Division and the taxpayer have the right to request technical advice from the National Office of the IRS. When technical advice is favorable to the taxpayer, the Appeals Division is bound by such advice. If the technical advice is favorable to the IRS, however, the Appeals Division may nevertheless settle the case based on other considerations.

If agreement cannot be reached with the Appeals Division, the IRS issues a statutory notice of deficiency (90-day letter), which gives the taxpayer 90 days to file a petition with the Tax Court. (See Figure 24–1 for a review of the income tax appeal procedure, including the consideration of claims for refund.) After the case has been docketed in the Tax Court, the taxpayer has the opportunity to arrange for possible pretrial settlement with the Regional Counsel of the IRS. The Appeals

---

13. § 6601(c).

FIGURE 24-1 Income Tax Appeal Procedure

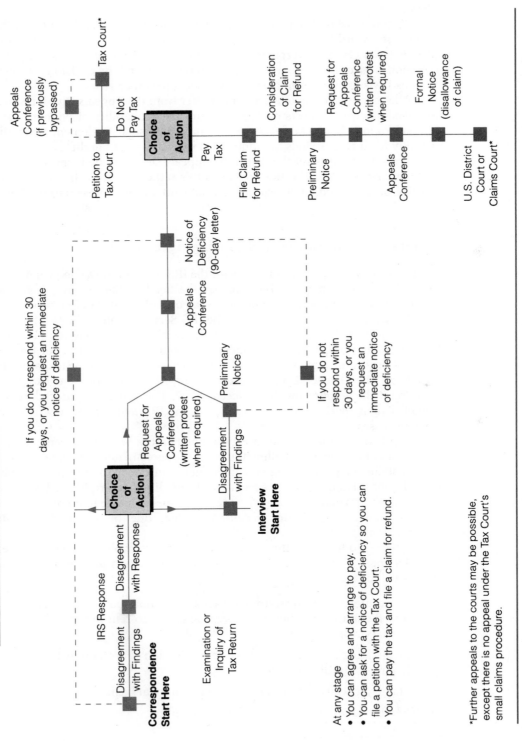

Division settlement power is transferred to the Regional Counsel when the case is docketed for a Tax Court trial after the issuance of the statutory notice of deficiency.

Taxpayers who file a petition with the U.S. Tax Court have the option of having their cases heard before the informal Small Claims Division if the amount of the deficiency or claimed overpayment does not exceed $10,000.[14] If the Small Claims Division is used, neither party may appeal the case, and the decisions of the Small Claims Division are not treated as precedents for other cases.

The economic costs of a settlement offer from the Appeals Division should be weighed against the costs of litigation and the probability of winning the case. Consideration should be given to the impact of such settlement upon the tax liability for future periods, in addition to the years under audit.

If a settlement is reached with the Appeals Division, the taxpayer is required to sign Form 870AD. The IRS considers this settlement to be binding upon both parties, absent fraud, malfeasance, concealment, or misrepresentation of material fact.

Offers in Compromise and Closing Agreements

The Code provides specific authority for the IRS to negotiate a compromise if there is doubt in the taxpayer's ability to pay the tax.[15] If the taxpayer is financially unable to pay the total amount of the tax, a Form 656 (Offer in Compromise) must be filed with the District Director or the IRS Service Center. The IRS investigates the claim by evaluating the taxpayer's financial ability to pay the tax. In some instances, the compromise settlement will include an agreement for final settlement of the tax through payments of a specified percentage of the taxpayer's future earnings. The District Director must obtain approval from the IRS Regional Counsel if the amount involved exceeds $500. This settlement procedure usually entails lengthy periods of negotiation with the IRS and is generally used only in extreme cases.

The IRS has statutory authority to enter into a written agreement allowing payment of taxes on an installment basis if the agreement will facilitate collection. The installment payment agreement remains in effect for the period that was initially agreed upon. The agreement may be modified or terminated because of (1) inadequate information or jeopardy; (2) subsequent change in financial condition; or (3) failure to pay any installment when due or to provide requested information.[16]

If there is doubt as to the amount of tax liability involved, a closing agreement may be appropriate. The IRS has enumerated situations in which closing agreements will be issued.[17]

1. An executor or administrator requires a determination of the tax liability either to facilitate the distribution of estate assets or to relieve himself or herself of fiduciary responsibility.

2. A liquidating corporation needs a determination of tax liability to proceed with the process of dissolution.

3. A taxpayer wishes to close returns on an annual basis.

4. Creditors demand evidence of the tax liability.

---

14. § 7463(a).
15. § 7122.

16. § 6159.
17. § 7121 and Rev.Proc. 68–16, 1968–1 C.B. 770.

A closing agreement is binding on both the taxpayer and the IRS, except upon a subsequent showing of fraud, malfeasance, or misrepresentation of a material fact.[18] The closing agreement may be added to Form 870 in reaching agreement upon the entire amount of tax due for a year under audit, used when disputed issues carry over to future years, and employed to dispose of a dispute involving a specific issue for a prior year or a proposed transaction involving future years. If, for example, the IRS is willing to make substantial concessions in the valuation of assets for death tax purposes, it may require a closing agreement from the recipient of the property to establish the tax basis of the assets for income tax purposes.

Interest

An important consideration for the taxpayer during negotiations with the IRS is the interest that accrues upon overpayments, deficiency assessments, and unpaid taxes. A taxpayer can effectively stop the accrual of interest upon a deficiency assessment by signing Form 870 and paying the tax. This action can then be followed by a suit in a Federal District Court or the Claims Court for recovery of the amount of the tax payment. If the Tax Court is selected as a forum, the tax usually is not paid and interest continues to accrue.

Determination of the Interest Rate.   Several years ago, Congress recognized that the interest rates applicable to Federal tax underpayments (deficiencies) and overpayments (refunds) should be more realistic in terms of what occurs in the business world. Currently, the Code provides for a quarterly determination of such rates.[19] For example, the rates that are determined during January are effective for the following April through June.

The interest rates are to be based on the Federal short-term rates as published periodically by the IRS in Revenue Rulings appearing in the Internal Revenue Bulletins. They are based on the average market yield on outstanding marketable obligations of the United States with remaining maturity of three years or less. This is the mechanism for arriving at short-term Federal rates, which are used to test the adequacy of interest in certain debt instruments issued for property and certain other obligations.

Underpayments are subject to the Federal short-term rates plus three percentage points, and overpayments carry the Federal short-term rates plus two percentage points. Consequently, the rate for tax deficiencies is one percentage point higher than the rate for tax refunds. For the first quarter of 1990, interest on tax deficiencies was set at 11 percent, and interest on refunds was 10 percent. Prior interest rates ranged from a low of 6 percent to a high of 20 percent.

In cases of deficiency assessments or claims for refund, interest is computed in accordance with the rates in effect during the periods involved. For assessments where the statute of limitations is not applicable (e.g., no return was filed or fraud was involved—see later section in the chapter), determining the interest element could prove to be a mathematical nightmare.

Computation of the Amount of Interest.   Prior law required that any interest on a deficiency or a refund be determined using the simple-interest method. For interest accruing after 1982, current law requires that the amount be compounded

---

18.   § 7121(b).   19.   § 6621.

daily.[20] Depending on the interest rate applicable, the daily compounding approach conceivably could double the principal amount over a period of five years or so. Consequently, this change in the method of computing interest should not be taken lightly.

The IRS has prepared and made available tables through which the daily compounded amount can be determined. Such tables will ease the burden of those who prepare late returns where additional taxes are due.[21]

The old rule (the simple-interest method) continues to apply in the calculation of the penalty on underpayments of estimated tax. However, the quarterly interest rate adjustments (discussed above) will have to be used in arriving at the amount of the penalty for underpayment of estimated tax.

IRS Deficiency Assessments.   Interest usually accrues from the unextended due date of the return until 30 days after the taxpayer agrees to the deficiency by signing Form 870. If the taxpayer does not pay the amount shown on the IRS's "notice and demand" (tax bill) within 30 days, interest again accrues on the deficiency. However, no interest is imposed upon the portion of the tax bill that represents interest on the previous deficiency.

Refund of Taxpayer's Overpayments.   If the overpayment is refunded to the taxpayer within 45 days after the date the return is filed or is due, no interest is allowed. Interest is authorized, however, when the taxpayer files an amended return or makes a claim for refund of a prior year's tax (e.g., when net operating loss or investment tax credit carrybacks result in refunds of a prior year's tax payments).

In the past and in light of high interest rates of up to 20 percent, it has proven advantageous for many taxpayers to delay filing various tax returns that lead to refunds. Thus, the IRS was placed in the unfortunate role of providing taxpayers with a high-yield savings account. Amendments to the tax law are intended to end this practice. The gist of the amendments is to preclude any interest accruing on a refund until such time as the IRS is properly notified of the refund.

Specifically the new law places taxpayers applying for refunds in the following described positions:

- When a return is filed after the due date, interest on any overpayment accrues from the date of filing. However, no interest will be due if the IRS makes the refund within 45 days of the date of filing.

EXAMPLE 7   T, a calendar year taxpayer, files her return for 1988 on December 1, 1989, such return reflecting an overwithholding of $2,500. On June 8, 1990, T receives a refund of her 1988 overpayment. Under these circumstances, the interest on T's refund began to accrue on December 1, 1989. □

EXAMPLE 8   Assume the same facts as in Example 7, except that the refund is paid to T on January 5, 1990 (rather than June 8, 1990). No interest would be due, since the refund was made within 45 days of the filing of the return. □

---

20. § 6622.
21. These tables can be found in Rev.Proc. 83–7, 1983–1 C.B. 583.

- In no event will interest accrue on an overpayment unless the return that is filed is in "processible form." Generally, this means that the return must contain enough information to enable the IRS to identify the taxpayer and to determine the tax (and overpayment) involved.

Penalties

A penalty may be defined as follows: "An adverse consequence imposed on a person for failure to comply with a Federal tax rule."

In the past few years, there has been a proliferation of tax penalties. In the interest of improving taxpayer compliance, Congress has modified existing penalties and imposed new penalties. Such legislation resulted in a maze of uncoordinated rules that confused both taxpayers and the IRS. For example, it was not uncommon for a single act of noncompliance to lead to the imposition of multiple penalties.

In the Revenue Reconciliation Act of 1989, Congress attempts to bring some order to the penalty area. Largely, the changes entail simplification, coordination, and combination of many existing penalties. This is particularly the case with the so-called "accuracy-related" penalties. These include the negligence, substantial understatement of income tax, substantial valuation overstatements, and substantial estate and gift tax valuation understatements penalties. Generally, the accuracy-related penalties are set at a common rate of 20 percent and the taxpayer defense to their imposition is now largely uniform.

In any tax text, it is confusing to the reader to add new rules without deleting the old rules. Wherever possible, therefore, the layering process should be avoided. Unfortunately, the complete omission of the old penalty rules is not possible for several reasons.

- The new rules are effective for returns due after December 31, 1989. Thus, the old rules continue to apply to pre-1990 situations.

- Many penalties result from IRS audits. Because there is often a considerable time lag between when the return was filed and when the audit takes place, most penalties imposed in the near future will be under the old rules.

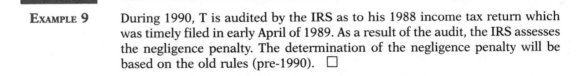

EXAMPLE 9   During 1990, T is audited by the IRS as to his 1988 income tax return which was timely filed in early April of 1989. As a result of the audit, the IRS assesses the negligence penalty. The determination of the negligence penalty will be based on the old rules (pre-1990). ☐

EXAMPLE 10   Assume the same facts as in Example 9 except that the time setting is advanced by one year. Thus, the audit occurs in 1991 of a 1989 return filed in 1990. The determination of the negligence penalty will be based on the new rules (post-1989). ☐

Failure to File and Failure to Pay.   For a failure to file a tax return by the due date (including extensions), a penalty of 5 percent per month (up to a maximum of 25 percent) is imposed on the amount of tax shown as due on the return.[22] If the failure to file is attributable to fraud, additional penalties can be imposed.

---

22. § 6651(a).

For a failure to pay the tax due as shown on the return, a penalty of one-half of 1 percent per month (up to a maximum of 25 percent) is imposed on the amount of the tax. A comparable penalty is assessed if the taxpayer fails to pay a deficiency assessment within 10 days.

In all of these cases, a fraction of a month counts as a full month. Also note that these penalties relate to the net amount of the tax due.

EXAMPLE 11 T, a calendar year self-employed taxpayer, prepays $18,000 for income taxes during 1989. Her total tax liability for 1989 proves to be $20,000. Without obtaining an extension from the IRS, she files her Form 1040 in early August of 1990 and encloses a check for the balance due of $2,000. The failure to file and the failure to pay penalties apply to the $2,000. □

During any month in which both the failure to file penalty and the failure to pay penalty apply, the failure to file penalty is reduced by the amount of the failure to pay penalty.

EXAMPLE 12 R files his tax return 10 days after the due date. Along with the return he remits a check for $3,000, which is the balance of the tax R owes. Disregarding the interest element, R's total penalties are as follows:

Failure to pay penalty (½ of 1% × $3,000)		$ 15
Plus:		
Failure to file penalty (5% × $3,000)	$150	
Less: Failure to pay penalty for the same period	(15)	
Failure to file penalty		135
Total penalties		$150

□

In Example 12, note that the penalties for one full month are imposed even though R was delinquent by only 10 days. Unlike the method used to compute interest, any part of a month is treated as a whole month.

An extension of time granted by the IRS will avoid the failure to file penalty. It will not, however, exonerate the taxpayer from the failure to pay penalty. But if a taxpayer, for whatever reason, is not in a position to complete the return, how is he or she able to determine the tax liability? The Regulations mercifully provide some latitude in resolving this quandary. If the extension is of the "automatic" four-month variety, the penalty for failure to pay will not be imposed if the additional tax liability due is no greater than 10 percent of the tax shown on the return.[23]

---

23. Reg. § 301.6651–1(c)(3)(i). The Regulation is premised on the assumption that satisfying the 10% rule constitutes reasonable cause.

EXAMPLE 13	S, a calendar year taxpayer, is self-employed and during 1989 makes quarterly payments of estimated taxes of $40,000. In early April of 1990, she applies for and obtains a four-month extension for filing her 1989 income tax return. In late May of 1990, S completes her 1989 return and delivers it to the IRS along with a check covering the additional tax that is due of $3,900. Under these circumstances, S has circumvented both the failure to file and the failure to pay penalties. She will, however, owe interest on the $3,900 that was paid late. □

When the 10 percent rule is not satisfied, the failure to pay penalty will be imposed on the *full* amount due.

EXAMPLE 14	Assume the same facts as in Example 13, except that S's additional tax liability proved to be $5,000 (rather than $3,900). In this event, a failure to pay penalty will be imposed on the full $5,000 that was paid late. □

Negligence Penalty.   The first of the accuracy-related penalties substantially changed by the Revenue Reconciliation Act of 1989 is the negligence penalty.[24] In brief, the changes are summarized below.

- The rate is raised from 5 percent to 20 percent.

- The penalty is imposed only on the portion of the tax underpayment attributable to negligence. Under pre-1990 rules, the penalty is imposed on the entire amount of the underpayment.

EXAMPLE 15	Upon audit by the IRS, it is determined that T underpaid her income tax by $10,000, of which $2,000 was attributable to negligence. Under pre-1990 rules, the negligence penalty is $500 (5% × $10,000). Under post-1989 rules, the penalty is $400 (20% × $2,000). As to which rules apply, see Examples 9 and 10 in this chapter. □

- The penalty no longer is automatic if a taxpayer fails to account for amounts reported on information returns (e.g., Form W–2, Form 1099).

As a practical matter, this last change is apt to have little effect since disregarding information returns in most situations would be indicative of negligence.

For purposes of the penalty, *negligence* includes any failure to make a reasonable attempt to comply with the provisions of the tax law. The penalty also applies to any disregard (whether careless, reckless, or intentional) of rules and regulations. The penalty can be avoided upon a showing of reasonable cause and that the taxpayer acted in good faith.

The negligence penalty is applicable to *all* taxes, but does not apply when fraud is involved.

---

24. All of the accuracy-related penalties have been consolidated in new § 6662. For the negligence penalty, see § 6662(b)(1). Pre-1990 law is contained in § 6653.

Fraud Penalty. A 75 percent penalty is imposed on any underpayment resulting from fraud on the part of the taxpayer.[25] Known as the civil fraud penalty, the burden of proof is upon the IRS to show by a preponderance of the evidence that the taxpayer had a specific intent to evade a tax.

Once the IRS has established that any portion of an underpayment is attributable to fraud, the entire underpayment is treated as so attributable except to the extent that the taxpayer establishes that any portion of the underpayment is not attributable to fraud. Thus, once the IRS has initially established that fraud has occurred, the taxpayer then bears the burden of proof to show by a preponderance of the evidence the portion of the underpayment that is not attributable to fraud.

Although the Code and the Regulations do not provide any assistance in ascertaining what constitutes civil fraud, it seems clear that mere negligence on the part of the taxpayer (however great) will not suffice. In this regard, consideration has to be given to the particular facts involved. Fraud has been found in cases where there have been manipulation of the books,[26] substantial omissions from income, and erroneous deductions.[27]

The penalty is imposed only on the portion of the underpayment attributable to fraud.

EXAMPLE 16   T underpaid his income tax for 1990 by $90,000. Assume that the IRS can prove that $60,000 of the underpayment was due to fraud. On the other hand, T can prove by a preponderance of the evidence that $30,000 of the underpayment was not due to fraud. The civil fraud penalty would be $45,000 (75% × $60,000). □

If the underpayment of tax is partly attributable to negligence and partly attributable to fraud, the negligence penalty (which may apply to the entire underpayment of tax) does not apply to any portion of the underpayment with respect to which a fraud penalty is imposed.

The Code contains, in addition to civil fraud penalties, numerous criminal sanctions that carry varying monetary fines and/or imprisonment. The difference between civil and criminal fraud is one of degree. A characteristic of criminal fraud is the presence of willfulness on the part of the taxpayer. Thus, § 7201 dealing with attempts to evade or defeat a tax contains the following language:

> Any person who *willfully* attempts in any manner to evade or defeat any tax imposed by this title or the payment thereof shall, in addition to other penalties provided by law, be guilty of a felony and, upon conviction thereof, shall be fined not more than $100,000 ($500,000 in the case of a corporation), or imprisoned not more than five years, or both, together with the costs of prosecution. [Emphasis added.]

As to the burden of proof, the IRS must show that the taxpayer was guilty of willful evasion "beyond the shadow of any reasonable doubt." Recall that in the civil fraud area, the standard applied to measure culpability is "by a preponderance of the evidence."

---

25. § 6653(b). Before TRA of 1986, the fraud penalty was 50%. Since the amendment to the fraud penalty applies only to returns due (determined without regard to extensions) after December 31, 1986, the 50% penalty amount will be used for some time. As noted later in the chapter, fraudu-

lent returns carry no statute of limitations.

26. *Dogget v. Comm.,* 60–1 USTC ¶9342, 5 AFTR2d 1034, 275 F.2d 823 (CA–4, 1960).

27. *Lash v. Comm.,* 57–2 USTC ¶9725, 51 AFTR 492, 245 F.2d 20 (CA–1, 1957).

Substantial Understatements of Tax Liability.   Another accuracy-related penalty deals with any substantial understatement of income tax. An understatement penalty is designed to strike at middle- and high-income taxpayers who play the so-called audit lottery. Some taxpayers take questionable and undisclosed positions on their tax returns in the hope that the return will not be selected for audit. A disclosure of such positions would have called attention to the return and increased the probability of audit.

A substantial understatement of a tax liability transpires when the understatement exceeds the larger of 10 percent of the tax due or $5,000. (Note: The monetary ceiling for corporations is $10,000.) The understatement to which the penalty applies is 10 percent of the difference between the amount of tax required to be shown on the return and the amount of tax actually shown on the return.

The Revenue Reconciliation Act of 1989 made several changes to this penalty.

- Consistent with the rates applicable to other accuracy-related penalties, the amount of the penalty is 20 percent of the amount of the underpayment attributable to the understatement. The pre-1990 rate is 25 percent.

- Congress directed that the list of what constitutes substantial authority (see the discussion below) be expanded by the IRS. Currently, the Regulations in point are not specific enough.[28]

- Somewhat related to the previous Congressional mandate, the IRS is directed to publish a list (at least annually) of positions *lacking* substantial authority.

The penalty can be avoided under any of the following circumstances:

- The taxpayer has *substantial authority* for such treatment.

- The relevant facts affecting the treatment are adequately disclosed in the return or in a statement attached thereto.

- The taxpayer has reasonable cause and acts in good faith.

Substantial authority is to be tested by looking to the taxpayer's position and not to the contrary authority. However, the existence of substantial authority does not necessarily mean that a taxpayer will prevail in a particular conflict with the IRS. It just means that the taxpayer has a defense to the imposition of the substantial understatement of tax liability penalty.

Penalty for Overvaluation.   An accuracy-related penalty significantly modified by the Revenue Reconciliation Act of 1989 relates to certain valuation (or basis) overstatements for income tax purposes. The objective of the penalty is to deter taxpayers from inflating values (or basis) usually charitable contributions of property, to reduce income taxes. The changes are summarized below.[29]

- All taxpayers are now subject to the penalty. Under pre-1990 rules, the penalty is limited to individuals, closely held corporations, or personal service corporations.

- The penalty is 20 percent of the tax that should have been paid had the correct valuation (or basis) been used. Under pre-1990 rules the penalty is as follows:

---

28.   Reg. § 1.6661-3(b).

29.   § 6662(b)(3), added by the Revenue Reconcilia-   tion Act of 1989. Pre-1990 law can be found in former § 6659.

If the valuation claimed is the following percentage of the correct valuation	Penalty rate
At least 150% but not more than 200%	10%
More than 200% but not more than 250%	20%
More than 250%	30%

- Regardless of the amount of overvaluation, charitable contributions automatically fall under the 30 percent penalty rate. Thus, post-1989 rules increase the *minimum* penalty from 10 percent to 20 percent but deletes the 30 percent *maximum* penalty.

- The penalty applies only when valuation (or basis) used is 200 percent or more of the correct valuation (or basis). Note that pre-1990 rules start with 150 percent.

- The penalty applies only to the extent that the resulting income tax underpayment exceeds $5,000 ($10,000 for most corporations). The pre-1990 threshold is $1,000.

EXAMPLE 17   In 1985, T (a calendar year taxpayer) purchased a painting for $10,000. In early 1989 when the painting is worth $18,000 (as later determined by the IRS), T donates the painting to an art museum. Based on the appraisal of a cousin who is an amateur artist, T deducts $40,000 for the donation on a timely filed return for 1989. Since T was in a 28% tax bracket, overstating the deduction by $22,000 results in a tax underpayment of $6,160 for 1989.

T's penalty for overvaluation is $1,232 [20% × $6,160 (the underpayment that resulted from using $40,000 instead of $18,000)]. Post-1989 rules govern the determination of the penalty because T's 1989 rules govern the determination of the penalty because T's 1989 income tax return is due after December 31, 1989. ☐

The substantial valuation overstatement penalty can be avoided if the taxpayer can show reasonable cause and good faith. However, when the overvaluation involves *charitable deduction property,* the taxpayer must show two *additional* facts.

- The claimed value of the property is based on a qualified appraisal made by a qualified appraiser.

- The taxpayer made a good faith investigation of the value of the contributed property.

Based on these criteria, T in Example 20 would be unlikely to avoid the penalty. A cousin who is an amateur artist does not meet the definition of a qualified appraiser. Likewise, T has not made a good faith investigation of the value of the contributed property.

Penalty for Undervaluation.   When attempting to minimize the income tax, it is to the benefit of taxpayers to *overvalue* deductions. When attempting to minimize transfer taxes (i.e., estate and gift taxes), however, executors and donors may be inclined to *undervalue* the assets transferred. By lessening the valuation chosen, estate and gift taxes are reduced. An accuracy-related penalty is imposed for substantial estate or gift tax valuation understatements.

The penalty is 20 percent of the transfer tax that would have been due had the correct valuation been used on Form 706 (estate tax return) or Form 709 (gift tax

return). The penalty only applies if the value of the property claimed on the return is 50 percent or less of the amount determined to be correct. The threshold amount for the application of the penalty is transfer tax liability in excess of $5,000. Thus, the penalty would not apply if the additional estate or gift tax due is $5,000 or less.

As is true with other accuracy-related penalties, reasonable cause and good faith on the part of the taxpayer is a defense.

Failure to Pay Estimated Taxes.   A penalty is imposed for a failure to pay estimated income taxes. The penalty applies to individuals and corporations and is based on the rate of interest in effect for deficiency assessments.[30] The penalty also applies to trusts and certain estates that are required to make estimated tax payments.

For individuals, the penalty is not imposed if the tax due for the year (less any amounts withheld) is less than $500. For corporations, the threshold amount is the same (refer to chapter 16).

The penalty generally can be avoided if the quarterly payments were based on one-fourth of the lesser of 90 percent of the current year's tax or 100 percent of the preceding year's tax (even if none was due). Quarterly payments are to be made on or before the fifteenth day of the fourth month (April 15 for a calendar year taxpayer), sixth month, and ninth month of the current year, and the first month of the following year. With corporations, the last quarterly payment is accelerated and must be made by the twelfth month of the same year.

The penalty is levied on the amount of the underpayment for the period of the underpayment. Payments of estimated tax are credited against unpaid installments in the order in which the installments are required to be paid.

EXAMPLE 18

T made the following payments of estimated tax during 1990 and had no income tax withheld:

April 16, 1990	$1,400
June 15, 1990	2,300
September 17, 1990	1,500
January 15, 1991	1,800

T's actual tax for 1990 is $8,000 and tax in 1989 was $10,000. Therefore, each installment should have been at least $1,800 [($8,000 × 90%) × 25%]. Of the payment on June 15, $400 will be credited to the unpaid balance of the first quarterly installment due on April 16, thereby effectively stopping the under-payment penalty for the first quarterly period. Of the remaining $1,900 payment on June 15, $100 is credited to the September 17 payment, resulting in this third quarterly payment being $200 short. Then $200 of the January 15 payment is credited to the September 17 shortfall, ending the period of underpayment for that portion due. The January 15, 1991, installment is now underpaid by $200, and a penalty will apply from January 15, 1991, to April 15, 1991 (unless paid sooner). T's underpayments for the periods of underpayment are as follows:

---

30. §§ 6654 and 6655.

1st installment due:	$400 from April 16–June 15
2nd installment due:	paid in full
3rd installment due:	$200 from September 17, 1990–January 15, 1991
4th installment due:	$200 from January 15–April 15, 1991

☐

As to employees, an equal part of withholding is deemed paid on each due date.

In computing the penalty, Form 2210 (Underpayment of Estimated Tax by Individuals) or Form 2220 (Underpayment of Estimated Tax by Corporations) is used.

Failure to Make Deposits of Taxes and Overstatements of Deposits.   When the business is not doing well or cash flow problems develop, there is a great temptation on the part of employers to "borrow" from Uncle Sam. One way this can be done is to fail to pay over to the IRS the amounts that have been withheld from the wages of employees for FICA and income tax purposes. The IRS does not appreciate being denied the use of such funds and has a number of weapons at its disposal to discourage the practice. Some of these penalties are summarized as follows:

• A penalty of up to 15 percent of any underdeposited amount not paid, unless it can be shown that the failure is due to reasonable cause and not to willful neglect.[31]

• A penalty of 25 percent of any overstated deposit claim unless such overstatement is due to reasonable cause and not to willful neglect.

• Various criminal penalties.[32]

• A 100 percent penalty if the employer's actions are willful.[33] The penalty is based on the amount of the tax evaded, not collected, or not accounted for or paid over. Since the penalty is assessable against the "responsible person" of the business, more than one party may be vulnerable (e.g., the president and treasurer of a corporation). Although the IRS might assess the penalty against more than one person, it cannot collect more than the 100 percent due.

In addition to these penalties the actual tax due must be remitted. An employer remains liable for the amount that should have been paid over even though the withholdings have not been taken out of the wages of its employees.[34]

The Statute of Limitations

A statute of limitations defines the period of time during which one party may pursue against another party a cause of action or other suit allowed under the governing law. Failure to satisfy any requirement provides the other party with an absolute defense should he or she see fit to invoke the statute. Inequity would result if there were no statute limiting action. Permitting the lapse of an extended period of time between the initiation of a claim and its pursuit could place the

---

31. § 6656.

32. See, for example, § 7202 (willful failure to collect or pay over a tax).

33. § 6672.

34. § 3403.

defense of such claim in jeopardy. Witnesses may have died or disappeared; records or other evidence may have been discarded or destroyed.

In terms of Federal tax consequences, it is important to distinguish between the statute of limitations on assessments by the IRS and the statute applicable to refund claims by a taxpayer.

Assessment and the Statute of Limitations.   In general, any tax that is imposed must be assessed within three years of the filing of the return (or, if later, the due date of the return).[35] Some exceptions to this three-year limitation follow:

- If no return is filed or a fraudulent return is filed, assessments can be made at any time. There is, in effect, no statute of limitations.

- If a taxpayer omits an amount of gross income in excess of 25 percent of the gross income stated on the return, the statute of limitations is increased to six years. The courts have interpreted this extended period of limitations rule to include only items affecting income and not the omission of items affecting cost of goods sold.[36] In addition, gross income includes capital gains in the *gross* income amount (not reduced by capital losses).

EXAMPLE 19

During 1985, T (an individual taxpayer) had the following income transactions (all of which were duly reported on his timely return):

Gross receipts		$ 480,000
Less: Cost of goods sold		(400,000)
Net business income		$ 80,000
Capital gains and losses—		
Capital gain	$ 36,000	
Capital loss	(12,000)	24,000
Total income		$ 104,000

T retains your services in 1990 as a tax consultant. It seems that he inadvertently omitted some income on his 1985 return and he wishes to know if he is "safe" under the statute of limitations. The six-year statute of limitations would apply, putting T in a vulnerable position only if he omitted more than $129,000 on his 1985 return [($480,000 + $36,000) × 25%]. □

- The statute of limitations may be extended by mutual consent of the District Director and the taxpayer.[37] This extension covers a definite period and is made by signing Form 872 (Consent to Extend the Time to Assess Tax). The extension is frequently requested by the IRS when the lapse of the statutory period is imminent and the audit has not been completed. In some situations, the extensions may apply only to unresolved issues. This practice often is applied to audits of corporate taxpayers and explains why many corporations have "open years."

---

35. §§ 6501(a) and (b)(1).

36. *The Colony, Inc. v. Comm.*, 58–2 USTC ¶9593, 1

AFTR2d 1894, 78 S.Ct. 1033 (USSC, 1958).

37. § 6501(c)(4).

Special rules relating to assessment are applicable in the following situations:

- Taxpayers (corporations, estates, etc.) may request a prompt assessment of the tax.

- The period for assessment of the personal holding company tax is extended to six years after the return is filed only if certain filing requirements are met.

- If a partnership or trust files a tax return (a partnership or trust return) in good faith and a later determination renders it taxable as a corporation, such return is deemed to be the corporate return for purposes of the statute of limitations.

- The assessment period for capital loss, net operating loss, and investment credit carrybacks is generally related to the determination of tax in the year of the loss or unused credit rather than in the carryback years.

If the tax is assessed within the period of limitations, the IRS has six years from the date of assessment to collect the tax.[38] However, if the IRS issues a statutory notice of deficiency to the taxpayer, who then files a Tax Court petition, the statute is suspended on both the deficiency assessment and the period of collection until 60 days after the decision of the Tax Court becomes final.[39]

Refund Claims and the Statute of Limitations.   To receive a tax refund, the taxpayer is required to file a valid refund claim. The official form for filing a claim is Form 1040X for individuals and Form 1120X for corporations. A refund claim must follow certain procedural requirements. If it does not, the claim may be rejected with no consideration of its merit. These procedural requirements include the following:

- A separate claim must be filed for each taxable period.

- The grounds for the claim must be stated in sufficient detail.

- The statement of facts must be sufficient to permit IRS appraisal of the merits of the claim.

The refund claim must be filed within three years of the filing of the tax return or within two years following the payment of the tax if this period expires on a later date.[40] In most instances, the three-year period is relevant for determining running of the statute of limitations. To be allowed, a claim must be filed during this period.

Certain exceptions are incorporated in the Code that can inadvertently reduce the benefits of the refund claim.[41]

EXAMPLE 20   On March 10, 1987, T filed his 1986 income tax return reflecting a tax of $10,500. On July 10, 1988, he filed an amended 1986 return showing an additional $3,000 of tax that was then paid. On May 18, 1990, he filed a claim for refund of $4,500. Assuming T is correct concerning the claim for refund, how much tax can he recover? The answer is only $3,000. Because the claim was not filed within the three-year period, T is limited to the amount he actually paid during the last two years. One might note that T would be entitled to interest on the $3,000 from July 10, 1988 (the date of the

---

38. § 6502(a).
39. § 6503(a)(1).
40. §§ 6511(a) and 6513(a).
41. § 6511(b).

overpayment), to a date not more than 30 days before the date of the refund check (subject to the 45-day rule discussed earlier in the chapter). ☐

EXAMPLE 21   D had $10,000 withheld in 1986. Because of heavy itemized deductions, D assumed she had no further tax to pay for the year. For this reason, and because of the exigencies of business, and without securing an extension, she did not file her 1986 return until June 9, 1987. Actually, the return showed a refund of $600, which D ultimately received. On May 3, 1990, D filed a $4,000 claim for refund of her 1986 taxes. How much, if any, of the $4,000 may D recover? None. Although the time limitation was met (the claim was filed within three years of the filing of the return), the amount limitation was not. A refund cannot exceed the amount paid within three years preceding the filing of the claim, and for this purpose, D's withholdings were deemed paid as of April 15, 1987. Had D requested and obtained an extension covering the filing of her 1986 return, the claim for refund would have been timely, and taxes paid would have exceeded the refund claimed. ☐

The tax law sets forth special rules for claims relating to bad debts and worthless securities. A seven-year period of limitations applies in lieu of the normal three-year rule.[42] The extended period is provided in recognition of the inherent difficulty associated with identification of the exact year a bad debt or security becomes worthless.

Refund claims relative to capital or net operating loss carrybacks may be filed within three years after the time for filing the tax return (including extensions) for the year of the loss. The IRS will accelerate the processing of a refund from a net operating loss carryback if Form 1045 (applicable to individuals) or Form 1139 (applicable to corporations) is utilized. But this special procedure is available only if the form is filed within the year following the year of the loss. In other cases, a Form 1040X or Form 1120X should be used.

If the taxpayer's refund claim is rejected by the IRS, a suit for refund generally may be filed six months after the filing of the claim.[43] This suit is filed in a Federal District Court or in the Claims Court.

TAX PRACTICE

The Tax Practitioner

Definition.   What is a tax practitioner? What service does the practitioner perform? To begin defining the term *tax practitioner*, one should consider whether the individual is qualified to practice before the IRS. Generally, practice before the IRS is limited to CPAs, attorneys, and persons who have been enrolled to practice before the IRS (termed "enrollees"). In most cases, enrollees are admitted to practice only if they take and successfully pass a special examination administered by the IRS. CPAs and attorneys are not required to take this examination and are automatically admitted to practice if they are in good standing with the appropriate licensing board regulating their profession.

Persons other than CPAs, attorneys, and enrollees may, however, be allowed to practice before the IRS in limited situations. Circular 230 (issued by the Treasury

---

42. § 6511(d)(1).   43. § 6532(a)(1).

Department and entitled "Rules Governing the Practice of Attorneys and Agents Before the Internal Revenue Service") permits the following notable exceptions:

- A taxpayer may always represent himself or herself. A person also may represent a member of his or her immediate family if no compensation is received for such services.

- Regular full-time employees may represent their employers.

- Corporations may be represented by any of their bona fide officers.

- Partnerships may be represented by any of the partners.

- Trusts, receiverships, guardianships, or estates may be represented by their trustees, receivers, guardians, or administrators or executors.

- A taxpayer may be represented by whoever prepared the return for the year in question. However, such representation cannot proceed beyond the agent level.

EXAMPLE 22   T, an individual, is currently undergoing audit by the IRS for tax years 1987 and 1988. She prepared the 1987 return herself but paid Z Company, a bookkeeping service, to prepare the 1988 return. Z Company may represent T in matters concerning only 1988. However, even with respect to 1988, Z Company would be unable to represent T at an Appeals Division proceeding. T could represent herself, or she could retain a CPA, attorney, or enrollee to represent her in matters concerning both years under examination. □

Rules Governing Tax Practice.   Circular 230 further prescribes the rules governing practice before the IRS. As applied to CPAs, attorneys, and enrollees, the following are imposed:

- A requirement to make known to a client any error or omission the client may have made on any return or other document submitted to the IRS.

- A duty to submit records or information lawfully requested by the IRS.

- An obligation to exercise due diligence as to accuracy in the preparation and filing of tax returns.

- A restriction against unreasonably delaying the prompt disposition of any matter before the IRS.

- A restriction against charging the client "an unconscionable fee" for representation before the IRS.

- A restriction against representing clients with conflicting interests.

Anyone can prepare a tax return or render tax advice, regardless of his or her educational background or level of competence. Likewise, there is nothing to preclude the "unlicensed" tax practitioner from advertising his or her specialty, from directly soliciting clients, or from otherwise violating any of the standards of conduct controlling CPAs, attorneys, or enrollees. Nevertheless, there do exist some restraints that govern all parties engaged in rendering tax advice or preparing tax returns for the general public.

- If the party holds himself or herself out to the general public as possessing tax expertise, he or she could be liable to the client if services are performed in a negligent manner. At a minimum, the measure of such damage would be any interest and penalties the client incurs because of the practitioner's failure to exercise due care.

- If someone agrees to perform a service (e.g., preparation of a tax return) and subsequently fails to do so, the aggrieved party may be in a position to obtain damages for breach of contract.

- The IRS requires all persons who prepare tax returns for a fee to sign as preparer of the return.[44] Failure to comply with this requirement could result in penalty assessment against the preparer.

- The Code prescribes various penalties for the deliberate filing of false or fraudulent returns. Such penalties are applicable to a tax practitioner who either was aware of the situation or actually perpetrated the false information or the fraud.[45]

- Penalties are prescribed for tax practitioners who disclose to third parties information they have received from clients in connection with the preparation of tax returns or the rendering of tax advice.

EXAMPLE 23

T operates a tax return preparation service. His brother-in-law, B, has just taken a job as a life insurance salesman. To help B find contacts, T furnishes B with a list of the names and addresses of all of his clients who report adjusted gross income of $10,000 or more. T is subject to penalties. □

- All nonattorney tax practitioners should avoid becoming engaged in activities that constitute the unauthorized practice of law. If they engage in this practice, action could be instituted against them in the appropriate state court by the local or state bar association. What actions constitute the unauthorized practice of law are undefined, and the issue remains an open question upon which reasonable minds can easily differ.

Legislative Penalties.   The following penalties also are provided under the Code:

1. A $250 penalty for understatements due to unrealistic positions.[46] Unless adequate disclosure is made, the penalty is imposed if two conditions are satisfied.

- Any part of any understatement of tax liability on any return or claim for refund is due to a position for which there was not a realistic possibility of being sustained on its merits.

- Any person who was an income tax return preparer to that return or claim knew (or should have known) of this position.

The penalty can be avoided by showing reasonable cause and by showing that the preparer acted in good faith.

2. A $1,000 penalty for willful and reckless conduct.[47] The penalty applies if any part of the understatement of a taxpayer's liability on a return or claim for refund is due to one of two causes.

- The preparer's willful attempt in any manner to understate the taxpayer's tax liability.

- Any reckless or intentional disregard of rules or regulations by the preparer.

---

44. Reg. § 1.6065–1(b)(1). Rev.Rul. 84–3, 1984–1 C.B. 264, contains a series of examples as to when a person will be deemed to be a preparer of the return.

45. § 7206.

46. § 6694(a) as amended by the Revenue Reconciliation Act of 1989.

47. § 6694(b) as amended by the Revenue Reconciliation Act of 1989.

Adequate disclosure can avoid the penalty. If both this penalty and the unrealistic position penalty (see item 1 above) apply to the same return, the total penalty cannot exceed $1,000.

3. A $1,000 ($10,000 for corporations) penalty per return or document is imposed against persons who aid in the preparation of returns or other documents that they know (or have reason to believe) would result in an understatement of the tax liability of another person. Aiding does not include clerical assistance in the preparation process.

   If this penalty applies, neither the unrealistic position penalty (item 1) nor the willful and reckless conduct penalty (item 2) applies.

4. A $50 penalty is assessed against the preparer for failure to sign a return or furnish the preparer's identifying number.[48]

5. A $50 penalty is assessed if the preparer fails to furnish a copy of the return or claim for refund to the taxpayer.

6. A $500 penalty may be assessed if a preparer endorses or otherwise negotiates a check for refund of tax issued to the taxpayer.

Ethical Considerations—Statements on Responsibilities in Tax Practice

Tax practitioners who are CPAs or attorneys must abide by the codes or canons of professional ethics applicable to their respective professions. The various codes and canons have much in common with and parallel the standards of conduct set forth in Circular 230. Tax practice is greatly affected by the prohibition against designation of a specialty. With some exceptions at the state bar association level, an attorney or a CPA cannot indicate on letterhead, business cards, or other approved listing that he or she specializes in tax matters or that his or her practice is limited to this field. From this standpoint, attorneys and CPAs are unlike physicians and dentists who have developed and effectively utilized an elaborate system of specialization.

In the belief that CPAs engaged in tax practice required further guidance in the resolution of ethical problems, the Tax Committee of the AICPA began issuing periodic statements on selected topics. The first of these Statements on Responsibilities in Tax Practice was released in 1964. All were revised in August of 1988. The statements that have been issued to date are discussed below.

Statement No. 1: Positions Contrary to the IRS Interpretations of the Code.   Under certain circumstances, a CPA may take a position that is contrary to that taken by the IRS. In order to do so, however, the CPA must have a good faith belief that the position, if challenged, has a realistic possibility of being sustained administratively or judicially on its merits.

The client should be fully advised of the risks involved and should know that certain penalties may result if the position taken by the CPA is not successful. The client should also be informed that disclosure on the return may avoid some or all of these penalties.

In no case should the CPA exploit the audit lottery approach; that is, to take a questionable position based on the probabilities that the client's return will not be chosen by the IRS for audit. Furthermore, the CPA should not "load" the return

---

48. § 6695.

with questionable items in the hope that they might aid the client in a later settlement negotiation with the IRS.

Statement No. 2: Answers to Questions on Returns.   A CPA should make a reasonable effort to obtain from the client, and provide, appropriate answers to all questions on a tax return before signing as preparer. Reasonable grounds may exist for omitting an answer. For example, reasonable grounds may include the following:

* The information is not readily available, and the answer is not significant taxwise.

* Genuine uncertainty exists regarding the meaning of the question as it applies to a particular situation.

* The answer to the question is voluminous.

The fact that an answer to a question could prove disadvantageous to the client does not justify omitting the answer.

Statement No. 3: Certain Procedural Aspects of Preparing Returns.   In preparing a return, a CPA may in good faith rely without verification on information furnished by the client or by third parties. However, the CPA should make reasonable inquiries if the information appears to be incorrect, incomplete, or inconsistent. In this regard, the CPA should refer to the client's prior returns whenever appropriate.

EXAMPLE 24   A CPA can normally take a client's word concerning the validity of dependency exemptions. But suppose a recently divorced client wants to claim his three children (of whom he does not have custody) as dependents. You must act in accordance with § 152(e)(2) in preparing the return, and this will require a waiver by the custodial parent. Without this waiver, you should not claim the dependency exemptions on your client's tax return. □

EXAMPLE 25   While preparing a client's income tax return for 1990, you review her income tax return for 1989. In comparing the dividend income reported on the 1989 Schedule B with that received in 1990, you note a significant decrease. Further investigation reveals the variation is due to a stock sale in 1990 that, until now, was unknown to you. Thus, the review of the 1989 return has unearthed a transaction that should be reported on the 1990 return. □

If the Code or the Regulations require certain types of verification (such as would be the case with travel and entertainment expenditures), the CPA must apprise the client of these rules. Further, inquiry must be made to ascertain whether the client has complied with the verification requirements.

Statement No. 4: Use of Estimates.   A CPA may prepare a tax return using estimates received from a taxpayer if it is impracticable to obtain exact data. The estimates must be reasonable under the facts and circumstances as known to the CPA. When estimates are used, they should be presented in such a manner as to avoid implying that greater accuracy exists.

Only in cases of unusual circumstances should the CPA disclose the use of estimates. Examples of unusual circumstances include the death or illness of the taxpayer, unavailability of an information return (e.g., a K–1 from a partnership), or destruction of taxpayer records.

Statement No. 5: Recognition of Administrative Proceeding of a Prior Year. Many positions that a CPA must take depend upon the facts and circumstances of a particular situation. Usually, in these cases the tax law sets forth a standard that is vague, and its satisfaction is a matter of individual judgment. As facts may vary from year-to-year, so may the position taken by a CPA. In these types of situations, the CPA is not bound by an administrative or judicial proceeding involving a prior year.

EXAMPLE 26

Upon audit of T Corporation's income tax return for 1989, the IRS disallowed $20,000 of the $100,000 salary paid to its president and sole shareholder on the grounds that it was unreasonable [§ 162(a)(1)]. You are the CPA who has been engaged to prepare T Corporation's income tax return for 1990. Again the corporation paid its president a salary of $100,000 and chose to deduct this amount. Because you are not bound in 1990 by what the IRS deemed reasonable for 1989, the full $100,000 can be claimed as a salary deduction. □

Besides the reasonable compensation issue, other problems that require a CPA's use of judgment include reclassification of corporate debt as equity (the thin capitalization possibility) and corporate accumulations beyond the reasonable needs of the business (the penalty tax under § 531).

Statement No. 6: Knowledge of Error—Return Preparation. A CPA should promptly advise a client upon learning of an error on a previously filed return or upon learning of a client's failure to file a required return. The advice can be oral or written and should include a recommendation of the corrective measures, if any, to be taken. The error or other omission should not be disclosed to the IRS without the client's consent.

If the past error is material and is not corrected by the client, the CPA may be unable to prepare the current year's tax return. Such might be true if the error has a carryover effect that precludes the correct determination of the tax liability for the current year.

EXAMPLE 27

In connection with the preparation of a client's 1990 income tax return, you discover the final inventory for 1989 was materially understated. First, you should advise the client to file an amended return for 1989 reflecting the correct amount in final inventory. Second, if the client refuses to make this adjustment, you should consider whether the error will preclude you from preparing a substantially correct return for 1990. Because this will probably be the case (the final inventory for 1989 becomes the beginning inventory for 1990), you should withdraw from the engagement. If the error is corrected by the client, you may proceed with the preparation of the tax return for 1990. You should, however, ensure that the error is not repeated. □

Statement No. 7: Knowledge of Error—Administrative Proceedings. When the CPA is representing a client in a return-related administrative proceeding in

which there is an error known to the CPA that has resulted or may result in a material understatement of tax liability, he or she should request the client's agreement to disclose the error to the IRS. Lacking such agreement, the CPA may be compelled to withdraw from the engagement.

Statement No. 8: Form and Content of Advice to Clients.   In providing tax advice to a client, the CPA must use judgment to ensure that the advice reflects professional competence and appropriately serves the client's needs. No standard format or guidelines can be established to cover all situations and circumstances involving written or oral advice by the CPA. The CPA may communicate with the client when subsequent developments affect advice previously provided with respect to significant matters. However, he or she cannot be expected to assume responsibility for initiating such communication, except while assisting a client in implementing procedures or plans associated with the advice provided. The CPA may undertake this obligation by specific agreement with his or her client.

The foregoing statements merely represent guides to action and are not part of the AICPA's Code of Professional Ethics. But because the statements are representative of standards followed by members of the profession, a violation thereof might indicate a deviation from the standard of due care exercised by most CPAs. The standard of due care is at the heart of any suit charging negligence that is brought against a CPA.

Tax Planning Considerations

Strategy in Seeking an Administrative Ruling

Determination Letters.   In many instances, the request for an advance ruling or a determination letter from the IRS is a necessary or desirable planning strategy. The receipt of a favorable ruling or determination reduces the risk associated with a transaction when the tax results are in doubt. For example, the initiation or amendment of a pension or profit sharing plan should be accompanied by a determination letter from the District Director. Otherwise, on subsequent IRS review, the plan may not qualify, and the tax deductibility of contributions to the plan will be disallowed. In some instances, the potential tax effects of a transaction are so numerous and of such consequence that to proceed without a ruling is unwise.

Letter Rulings.   It may not, in some cases, be necessary or desirable to request an advance ruling. For example, it is generally not desirable to request a ruling if the tax results are doubtful and the company is committed in any event to completion of the transaction. If a ruling is requested and negotiations with the IRS indicate that an adverse determination will be forthcoming, it is usually possible to have the ruling request withdrawn. However, the National Office of the IRS may forward its findings, along with a copy of the ruling request, to the District Director. In determining the advisability of a ruling request, consideration should be given to the potential exposure of other items in the tax returns of all "open years."

A ruling request may delay the consummation of a transaction if the issues are novel or complex. Frequently, a ruling can be processed within six months, although in some instances a delay of a year or more may be encountered.

Technical Advice.   In the process of contesting a proposed deficiency with the Appeals Division, consideration should be given to a request for technical advice from the National Office of the IRS. If such advice is favorable to the taxpayer, it is binding on the Appeals Division. The request may be particularly appropriate when the practitioner feels that the agent or Appeals Division has been too literal in the interpretation of an IRS ruling.

Considerations in Handling an IRS Audit

As a general rule, attempts should be made to settle disputes at the earliest possible stage of the administrative appeal process. New issues may be raised by IRS personnel if the case goes beyond the agent level. It is usually possible to limit the scope of the examination by furnishing pertinent information requested by the agent. Extraneous information or fortuitous comments may result in the opening of new issues and should therefore be avoided. Agents usually appreciate prompt and efficient response to inquiries, since their performance may in part be judged by their ability to close or settle assigned cases.

To the extent possible, it is advisable to conduct the investigation of field audits in the practitioner's office rather than in the client's office. This procedure permits greater control over the audit investigation and may facilitate the agent's review and prompt closure of the case.

Many practitioners feel that it is generally not advisable to have clients present at the scheduled conferences with the agent since the client may give emotional or gratuitous comments that impair prompt settlement. If the client is not present, however, he or she should be advised of the status of negotiations. It should be clear that the client is the final authority with regard to any proposed settlement.

The tax practitioner's workpapers should include all research memoranda, and a list of resolved and unresolved issues should be continually updated during the course of the IRS audit. Occasionally, agents will request access to excessive amounts of accounting data for the purpose of engaging in a so-called fishing expedition. Providing blanket access to workpapers should be avoided. Workpapers should be carefully reviewed to minimize opportunities for the agent to raise new issues not otherwise apparent. It is generally advisable to provide the agent with copies of specific workpapers upon request. An accountant's workpapers are not privileged and may therefore be subpoenaed by the IRS.

In unusual situations, a Special Agent may appear to gather evidence in the investigation of possible criminal fraud. When this occurs, the taxpayer should be advised to seek legal counsel to determine the extent of his or her cooperation in providing information to the agent. Also, it is frequently desirable for the tax adviser to consult personal legal counsel in such situations. If the taxpayer receives a Revenue Agent's Report (RAR), it generally indicates that the IRS has decided not to initiate criminal prosecution proceedings. The IRS usually does not take any action upon a tax deficiency until the criminal matter has been resolved.

Penalties

As previously discussed, penalties are imposed upon a taxpayer's failure to file a return or pay a tax when due. These penalties can be avoided if the failure is due to reasonable cause and not due to willful neglect. Reasonable cause, however, has not been liberally interpreted by the courts and should not be relied upon in the

routine type of situation.[49] A safer way to avoid the failure to file penalty would be to obtain from the IRS an extension of time for filing the return. Although an extension of time for filing does not normally excuse the failure to pay penalty, it will do so in the case of the automatic four-month variety if the 90 percent rule has been satisfied (refer to Example 13).

Since it is not deductible for income tax purposes, the penalty for failure to pay estimated taxes can become quite severe. Often trapped by this provision are employed taxpayers with outside income. Such persons may forget about such outside income and place undue reliance on the amount withheld from wages and salaries as being adequate to cover their liability. For such persons, not only does April 15 provide a real shock (in terms of the additional tax owed), but a penalty situation may have evolved. One possible way for an employee to mitigate this problem (presuming the employer is willing to cooperate) is described as follows:

EXAMPLE 28 — T, a calendar year taxpayer, is employed by X Corporation and earns (after withholding) a monthly salary of $4,000 payable at the end of each month. T also receives income from outside sources (interest, dividends, and consulting fees). After some quick calculations in early October of 1990, T determines that he has underestimated his tax liability for 1990 by $7,500 and will be subject to the penalty for the first two quarters of 1990 and part of the third quarter. T, therefore, completes a new Form W–4 in which he arbitrarily raises his income tax withholding by $2,500 a month. X Corporation accepts the Form W–4, and as a result, an extra $7,500 is paid to the IRS on T's account for the payroll period from October through December 1990. □

The reason T avoids any penalties for the underpayment in Example 28 for the first three quarters is that withholding of taxes is allocated over the year involved. Thus, a portion of the additional $7,500 withheld in October–December is assigned to the January 1–April 15 period, the April 16–June 15 period, etc. Had T merely paid the IRS an additional $7,500 in October, this would not have affected the penalty for the earlier quarters.

PROBLEM MATERIALS

Discussion Questions

1. Under what circumstances will a ruling be revoked by the IRS and applied retroactively to the detriment of the taxpayer?

2. During the course of your research of a tax problem, you find that another company received a favorable unpublished (letter) ruling approximately two years ago based on facts similar to your situation. What degree of reliance may be placed upon this ruling?

---

49. *Dustin v. Comm.*, 72–2 USTC ¶ 9610, 30
    AFTR2d 72–5313, 467 F.2d 47 (CA–9, 1972),
    aff'g. 53 T.C. 491 (1969).

3. Under what circumstances might the request for an advance ruling be considered a necessity? Are there situations in which a ruling should not be requested? If so, why?

4. In what situations might a taxpayer seek a determination letter?

5. What purpose does a request for technical advice serve?

6. What, if any, is the relationship between DIF and TCMP?

7. A taxpayer is fearful of filing a claim for refund for a prior year because he is convinced that the claim will cause an audit by the IRS of that year's return. Please comment.

8. In March of 1990, T receives a refund check from the IRS for the amount of overpayment she claimed when she filed her 1989 return in January. Does this mean that her 1989 return will not be audited? Explain.

9. Comment on the following:
   a. An RAR.
   b. Form 870.
   c. The 30-day letter.
   d. The 90-day letter.

10. If a taxpayer wishes to go to the Appeals Division of the IRS, when is a written protest required?

11. How may the running of interest on a deficiency assessment be stopped?

12. V, a calendar year taxpayer, files her 1989 income tax return on February 9, 1990, on which she claims a $1,200 refund. If V receives her refund check on May 2, 1990, will it include any interest? Explain.

13. Describe each of the following items:
    a. Closing agreement.
    b. Offer in compromise.

14. Frequently, tax litigation involves unresolved questions relating to several years before the current year. How is it possible for the IRS to assess a deficiency for these years, since the statute of limitations expires three years from the date of filing of the tax return?

15. T, a vice president of Z Corporation, prepared and filed the corporate Form 1120 for 1988. This return is being audited by the IRS in 1990.
    a. May T represent Z Corporation during the audit?
    b. Can such representation continue beyond the agent level (e.g., before the Appeals Division)?

16. On June 29, 1990, the IRS notifies T that his returns for 1983, 1984, and 1985 are under examination. The IRS issues a Form 870 for T to sign and agree to the proposed deficiencies for the years under examination. T signed the Form 870 on July 20, 1990. On December 1, 1990, the IRS notifies T that certain partnership losses that were reflected on T's 1983, 1984, and 1985 returns were disallowed, affecting the proposed deficiencies to T's returns as originally agreed to by T when he signed Form 870. Can the IRS reopen tax years that have been settled by a signed Form 870?

17. Z, a bookkeeper at H Corporation, embezzles $75,000 and spends it all in one memorable weekend at Lake Tahoe. Afterward, Z is arrested, sentenced, and jailed. Z has few prospects for future employment, and his property consists only of a $2,000 bank account and an automobile worth $1,200. The IRS assesses $30,000 in unpaid tax, penalties, and interest against Z. Is this an appropriate situation for an offer in compromise?

Problems

18. T, a calendar year taxpayer, does not file her 1989 return until June 4, 1990. At this point, she pays the $3,000 balance due on her 1989 tax liability of $30,000. T did not apply for and obtain any extension of time for filing the 1989 return. When questioned by the IRS on her delinquency, T asserts: "If I was too busy to file my regular tax return, I was too busy to request an extension."
    a. Is T liable for any penalties for failure to file and for failure to pay?
    b. If so, compute such penalties.

19. R, a calendar year taxpayer, was unable to file his 1989 income tax return on or before April 17, 1990. He did, however, apply for and obtain an automatic extension from the IRS. On May 12, 1990, R delivers his completed return to the IRS and remits the $5,000 balance due on his 1989 tax liability of $41,000.
    a. Determine R's penalty for failure to file.
    b. For failure to pay.
    c. Would your answers to (a) and (b) differ if R's tax liability for 1989 were $51,000 (instead of $41,000)? Explain.

20. R, a calendar year individual taxpayer, files her 1988 return on January 11, 1990. R did not obtain an extension for filing her return, and the return reflects additional income tax due of $3,800.
    a. What are R's penalties for failure to file and to pay?
    b. Would your answer change if R, before the due date of the return, had retained a CPA to prepare the return and it was the CPA's negligence that caused the delay?

21. Z underpaid her taxes by $15,000. Of this amount $7,500 was due to negligence on Z's part. Determine the amount of the negligence penalty that Z will have to pay based on the following assumptions:
    a. The tax year is 1988 and the return was timely filed in 1989.
    b. The tax year is 1989 and the reurn was timely filed in 1990.

22. V underpaid his taxes for 1987 in the amount of $100,000, of which $80,000 was attributable to civil fraud. What is V's civil fraud penalty?

23. A made a charitable contribution of property that he valued at $20,000. He deducted this amount as an itemized deduction on his tax return. The IRS can prove that the real value of the property is $8,000. A is in the 28% bracket. Determine A's overvaluation penalty based on the following assumptions:
    a. The tax year is 1988 and the return was timely filed in 1989.
    b. The tax year is 1989 and the return was timely filed in 1990.

24. R owns and operates an unincorporated business with three employees. On the due date, R takes the funds earmarked for his payroll tax deposit and uses them to satisfy personal expenses. Is R liable for penalties under § 6656 (under deposit of payroll tax)?

25. What is the applicable statute of limitations in each of the following independent situations?
    a. No return was filed by the taxpayer.
    b. A corporation is determined to have been a personal holding company for the year in question.
    c. For 1985, the XYZ Associates filed a Form 1065 (a partnership return). In 1990, the IRS determined that the organization was not a partnership in 1985 but was, in fact, a corporation.

    d. In 1985, T incurred a bad debt loss that she failed to claim.

    e. On his 1985 return, a taxpayer inadvertently omitted a large amount of gross income.

    f. Same as (e), except that the omission was deliberate.

    g. For 1985, a taxpayer innocently overstated her deductions by a large amount.

26. During 1985, T (an individual, calendar year taxpayer) had the following transactions, all of which were properly reported on a timely return:

Gross receipts		$ 960,000
Cost of goods sold		(800,000)
Gross profit		$ 160,000
Capital gains and losses—		
Capital gain	$ 72,000	
Capital loss	(24,000)	48,000
Total income		$ 208,000

    a. Presuming the absence of fraud on T's part, how much of an omission from gross income would be required to make the six-year statute of limitations apply?

    b. Would it matter in your answer to (a) if cost of goods sold had been inadvertently overstated by $100,000?

27. On April 2, 1987, X filed his 1986 income tax return, which showed a tax due of $40,000. X filed an amended return for 1986 that showed an additional tax of $12,000. X paid the additional amount. On May 18, 1990, X files a claim for a refund of $18,000.

    a. If X's claim for a refund is correct, how much tax will he recover?

    b. For what period will interest run in regard to X's claim for a refund?

28. Ms. T had $40,000 withheld in 1986. Because of heavy itemized deductions, she figured that she had no further tax to pay for the year. For this reason, and because of personal problems, and without securing an extension, she did not file her 1986 return until July 1, 1987. Actually, the return showed a refund of $2,400, which Ms. T ultimately received. On May 10, 1990, Ms. T filed a $16,000 claim for refund of her 1986 taxes.

    a. How much, if any, of the $16,000 may Ms. T recover?

    b. Would it have made any difference if Ms. T had requested and secured from the IRS an extension of time for filing her 1986 tax return?

29. R's Federal income tax returns (Form 1040) for the past three years (1987–89) were prepared by the following persons:

Preparer	1987	1988	1989
R	X		
S		X	
T			X

S is R's next-door neighbor and owns and operates a pharmacy. T is a licensed CPA and is engaged in private practice. In the event R is audited and all three returns are examined, comment on who may represent R before the IRS at the agent level. At the Appeals Division.

30. Indicate whether the following statements are true or false. (Note: SRTP= Statements on Responsibilities in Tax Practice.)

a. When a CPA has reasonable grounds for not answering an applicable question on a client's return, a brief explanation of the reason for the omission should not be provided because it would flag the return for audit by the IRS.

b. In preparing a taxpayer's return for 1989, a CPA finds out that the client had 50% of his medical expense deduction claimed for 1987 disallowed on audit by the IRS. The CPA should feel bound by the prior administrative proceeding in determining his client's medical expense deduction for 1989.

c. If the client tells you that she had contributions of $500 for unsubstantiated cash donations to her church, you should deduct an odd amount on her return (e.g., $499) because an even amount (i.e., $500) would indicate to the IRS that her deduction was based on an estimate.

d. Basing an expense deduction on the client's estimates is not acceptable under the SRTP.

e. If a CPA knows that his or her client has a material error on a prior year's return, he or she should not, without the client's consent, disclose the error to the IRS.

f. If a CPA's client will not correct a material error on a prior year's return, the CPA should not prepare the current year's return for the client.

g. If a CPA discovers during an IRS audit that his or her client has a material error on the return under examination, he or she should immediately withdraw from the engagement.

h. If a CPA renders tax advice to the client in early 1989, the client should be able to rely on such advice until April 16, 1990. (The client prepared her own tax return.)

i. The SRTP have the same force and effect as the AICPA's Code of Professional Ethics.

25

THE FEDERAL GIFT AND ESTATE TAXES

OBJECTIVES

Illustrate the mechanics of the unified transfer tax.

Establish which persons are subject to this tax.

Review the formulas for the Federal gift and estate taxes.

Set forth the transfers that are subject to the Federal gift or estate tax.

Describe the exclusions and the deductions available in arriving at a taxable gift or a taxable estate.

Illustrate the computation of the Federal gift or estate tax by making use of all available credits.

Explain the objective of a program of lifetime giving.

Show how the gift and estate taxes can be reduced.

TRANSFER TAXES—IN GENERAL

Until now, this text has dealt primarily with the various applications of the Federal income tax. Also important in the Federal tax structure are various excise taxes that cover transfers of property. Sometimes designated as transaction taxes, excise taxes are based on the value of the property transferred and not on the income derived therefrom. Two such taxes—the Federal estate tax and the Federal gift tax—are the central focus of this chapter.

Before the enactment of the Tax Reform Act of 1976, Federal law imposed a tax on the gratuitous transfer of property in one of two ways. If the transfer was during the owner's life, it was subject to the Federal gift tax. If, however, the property passed by virtue of the death of the owner, the Federal estate tax applied. Both taxes were governed by different rules including a separate set of tax rates. Because Congress felt that lifetime transfers of wealth should be encouraged, the gift tax rates were lower than the estate tax rates.

The Tax Reform Act of 1976 made significant changes to the approach taken by the Federal estate and gift taxes. Much of the distinction between life and death transfers was eliminated. Instead of subjecting these different types of transfers to two separate tax rate schedules, the Act substituted a unified transfer tax to cover all gratuitous transfers. Thus, gifts are subject to tax at the same rates as those applicable to transfers at death. In addition, current law eliminates the prior exemptions allowed under each tax and replaces them with a unified tax credit.

Nature of the Taxes

The Federal estate (or death) tax is designed to tax transfers at death. The tax differs, in several respects, from the typical inheritance tax imposed by many states and some local jurisdictions. First, the Federal death tax is imposed on the decedent's entire taxable estate. It is a tax on the right to pass property at death. Inheritance taxes are taxes on the right to receive property at death and are therefore levied on the heirs. Second, the relationship of the heirs to the decedent usually has a direct bearing on the inheritance tax determination. In general, the more closely related the parties, the larger the exemption and the lower the applicable rates.[1] Except for transfers to a surviving spouse that may result in a marital deduction, the Federal estate tax accords no difference in treatment based on the relationship of a decedent to his or her heirs.

The Federal gift tax, enacted several years after the enactment of the Federal estate tax, was designed to improve upon the effectiveness of the income and estate taxes. Apparently, Congress felt that one should not be able to give away property—thereby shifting the income tax consequences to others and further avoiding estate taxes on the death of the transferor—without incurring some tax liability. The answer, then, is the Federal gift tax, which covers inter vivos (lifetime) transfers.

The Federal gift tax is imposed on the right of one person (the donor) to transfer property to another (the donee) for less than full and adequate consideration. The tax is payable by the donor.[2] If, however, the donor fails to pay the tax

---

1. For example, one state's inheritance tax provides an exemption of $50,000 for surviving spouses, with rates ranging from 5% to 10% on the taxable portion. This is to be contrasted with an exemption of only $1,000 for strangers (persons unrelated to the deceased), with rates ranging

from 14% to 18% on the taxable portion. Other exemptions and rates fall between these extremes to cover beneficiaries variously related to the decedent.

2. § 2502(c).

when due, the donee may be held liable for the tax to the extent of the value of the property received.[3]

Persons Subject to the Taxes.   To determine whether a transfer is subject to the Federal gift tax, one must first ascertain if the donor is a citizen or resident of the United States. If the donor is not a citizen or a resident, it becomes important to determine whether the property involved in the gift was situated within the United States.

The Federal gift tax is applied to all transfers by gift of property wherever situated by individuals who, at the time of the gift, were citizens or residents of the United States. The term "United States" includes only the 50 states and the District of Columbia; it does not include U.S. possessions or territories.[4] For a U.S. citizen, the place of residence at the time of the gift is immaterial.

For individuals who are neither citizens nor residents of the United States, the Federal gift tax is applied only to gifts of property situated within the United States.[5] A gift of intangible personal property (e.g., stocks and bonds) usually is not subject to the Federal gift tax when made by nonresident aliens.[6]

A gift by a corporation is considered a gift by the individual shareholders. A gift to a corporation is generally considered a gift to the individual shareholders, except that in certain cases, a gift to a charitable, public, political, or similar organization may be regarded as a gift to the organization as a single entity.[7]

The Federal estate tax is applied to the entire taxable estate of a decedent who, at the time of his or her death, was a resident or citizen of the United States.[8] If the decedent was a U.S. citizen, the residence at death makes no difference for this purpose.

If the decedent was neither a resident nor a citizen of the United States at the time of death, the Federal estate tax will nevertheless be imposed on the value of any property situated within the United States. In such case, the tax determination is controlled by a separate subchapter of the Internal Revenue Code.[9] In certain instances, these tax consequences outlined in the Internal Revenue Code may have been modified by death tax conventions (treaties) between the United States and various foreign countries.[10] Further coverage of this area is beyond the scope of this text. The discussion to follow is limited to the tax treatment of decedents who were residents or citizens of the United States at the time of death.[11]

Formula for the Gift Tax.   Like the income tax, which uses taxable income (and not gross income) as a tax base, the gift tax rates do not usually apply to the full amount of the gift. Deductions and the annual exclusion may be allowed to

---

3. § 6324(b).
4. § 7701(a)(9).
5. § 2511(a).
6. §§ 2501(a)(2) and (3). But see § 2511(b) and Reg. §§ 25.2511–3(b)(2), (3), and (4) for exceptions.
7. Reg. §§ 25.0–1(b) and 25.2511–1(h)(1). But note the exemption from the Federal gift tax for certain transfers to political organizations discussed later.
8. § 2001(a).
9. Subchapter B (§§ 2101 through 2108) covers the estate tax treatment of decedents who are neither residents nor citizens. Subchapter A (§§ 2001 through 2057) covers the estate tax treatment of those who are either residents or citizens.

10. At present, the United States has death tax conventions with the following countries: Australia, Austria, Denmark, Federal Republic of Germany, Finland, France, Greece, Ireland, Italy, Japan, Netherlands, Norway, Republic of South Africa, Sweden, Switzerland, and the United Kingdom. The United States has gift tax conventions with Australia, France, Japan, the United Kingdom and West Germany.
11. Further information concerning Subchapter B (§§ 2101 through 2108) can be obtained by reading the Code Sections involved (and the Treasury Regulations thereunder). See also the Instructions to Form 706NA (U.S. Estate Tax Return of Nonresident Not a Citizen of the U.S.).

arrive at an amount called the *taxable gift*. However, unlike the income tax, which does not take into account taxable income from prior years, *prior taxable gifts* must be added to arrive at the tax base to which the unified transfer tax is applied. Otherwise, the donor could start over again each year with a new set of progressive rates.

EXAMPLE 1

D makes taxable gifts of $500,000 in 1985 and $500,000 in 1990. Presuming no other taxable gifts and disregarding the effect of the unified tax credit, D must pay a tax of $155,800 (see applicable tax rate schedule in Appendix A) on the 1985 transfer and a tax of $345,800 on the 1990 transfer (using a tax base of $1,000,000). If the 1985 taxable gift had not been included in the tax base for the 1990 gift, the tax would have been $155,800. One can easily see that the correct tax liability of $345,800 is more than twice $155,800. □

Because the gift tax is cumulative in effect, a credit is allowed for the gift taxes paid (or deemed paid) on prior taxable gifts included in the tax base. The deemed paid credit is explained later in the chapter.

EXAMPLE 2

Assume the same facts as in Example 1. D will be allowed a credit of $155,800 against the gift tax of $345,800. Thus, D's gift tax liability for 1990 becomes $190,000 ($345,800 − $155,800). □

The formula for the gift tax is summarized in Figure 25–1. [Note: Section (§) references are to the portion of the Internal Revenue Code involved.]

The annual exclusion before 1982 was $3,000. The change to $10,000 was made to allow larger gifts to be exempt from the Federal gift tax. The increase improves taxpayer compliance and thereby eases the audit function of the IRS. It also recognizes the inflationary trend in the economy.

FIGURE 25–1 Gift Tax Formula

Determine whether the transfers are or are not covered by referring to §§ 2511 through 2519; list the fair market value of only the covered transfers		$xxx,xxx
Determine the deductions allowed by § 2522 (charitable), § 2523 (marital)	$xx,xxx	
Claim the annual exclusion ($10,000 per donee) under § 2503(b), if available	xx,xxx	(xx,xxx)
Taxable gifts [as defined by § 2503(a)] for the current period		$ xx,xxx
Add: Taxable gifts from prior years		xx,xxx
Total of current and past taxable gifts		$ xx,xxx
Compute the gift tax on the total of current and past taxable gifts by using the rates in Appendix A		$ x,xxx
Subtract: Gift tax paid or deemed paid on past taxable gifts and the unified tax credit		(xxx)
Gift tax due on transfers during the current period		$ xxx

FIGURE 25-2   Estate Tax Formula

Gross estate (§§ 2031–2046)		$xxx,xxx
Subtract:		
Expenses, indebtedness, and taxes (§ 2053)	$xx	
Losses (§ 2054)	xx	
Charitable bequests (§ 2055)	xx	
Marital deduction (§ 2056)	xx	
ESOP deduction (§ 2057)	xx	(x,xxx)
Taxable estate (§ 2051)		$ xx,xxx
Add: Post-1976 taxable gifts		
[§ 2001(b)]		x,xxx
Tax base		$xxx,xxx
Tentative tax on total transfers		
[§ 2001(c)]		$ xx,xxx
Subtract:		
Unified transfer tax on post-1976 taxable gifts (gift taxes paid)	$xx	
Other tax credits (including the unified tax credit) [§§ 2010–2016]	xx	(x,xxx)
Estate tax due		$ xxx

Formula for the Federal Estate Tax.   The Federal unified transfer tax at death, commonly referred to as the Federal estate tax, is summarized in Figure 25–2. [Note: Section (§) references are to the portion of the Internal Revenue Code involved.]

The gross estate is determined by using the fair market value of the property on the date of the decedent's death (or on the alternate valuation date if applicable).

The reason for adding post-1976 taxable gifts to the taxable estate to arrive at the tax base goes back to the scheme of the unified transfer tax. Starting in 1977, all transfers, whether lifetime or by death, are to be treated the same. Consequently, taxable gifts made after 1976 must be accounted for upon the death of the donor. Note, however, that the double tax effect of including these gifts is eliminated by allowing a credit against the estate tax for the gift taxes previously paid.

Role of the Unified Tax Credit.   Before the unified transfer tax, the gift tax allowed a $30,000 specific exemption for the lifetime of the donor. A comparable $60,000 exemption was allowed for estate tax purposes. The justification for these exemptions was to allow donors and decedents to transfer modest amounts of wealth without being subject to the gift and estate taxes. Unfortunately, inflation took its toll, and more taxpayers were being subject to these transfer taxes than Congress felt was appropriate. The Congressional solution, therefore, was to rescind the exemptions and replace them with the unified tax credit.[12]

---

12.   §§ 2010 and 2505.

FIGURE 25-3   Unified Tax Credit Phase-In

Year of Death	Amount of Credit	Amount of Exemption Equivalent
1977	$ 30,000	$120,667
1978	34,000	134,000
1979	38,000	147,333
1980	42,500	161,563
1981	47,000	175,625
1982	62,800	225,000
1983	79,300	275,000
1984	96,300	325,000
1985	121,800	400,000
1986	155,800	500,000
1987 & thereafter	192,800	600,000

To curtail revenue loss, the credit was phased in as shown in Figure 25-3. The *exemption equivalent* is the amount of the transfer that will pass free of the gift or estate tax by virtue of the credit.

EXAMPLE 3   In 1990, D makes a taxable gift of $600,000. Presuming she has made no prior taxable gifts, D will not owe any gift tax. Under the applicable tax rate schedule (see Appendix A), the tax on $600,000 is $192,800, which is the exact amount of the credit allowed.[13]   □

The Tax Reform Act of 1976 allowed donors one last chance to use the $30,000 specific exemption on lifetime gifts. If, however, such use occurred on gifts made after September 8, 1976 (and before January 1, 1977), the unified tax credit must be reduced by 20 percent of the exemption so utilized.[14] The adjustment to the credit because of the use of the specific exemption applies whether the gift tax or the estate tax is involved. No adjustment is necessary for post-1976 gifts since the specific exemption was no longer available for such transfers.

EXAMPLE 4   Net of the annual exclusion, D, a widow, made gifts of $10,000 in June 1976 and $20,000 in December 1976. Assume D had never used any of her specific exemption and chose to use the full $30,000 to cover the 1976 gifts. Under these circumstances, the unified tax credit will be reduced by $4,000 (20% × $20,000). Note that the use of the specific exemption on transfers made before September 9, 1976, will have no effect on the credit.   □

Key Property Concepts

When property is transferred either by gift or by death, the form of ownership can have a direct bearing on any transfer tax consequences. Understanding the different forms of ownership is a necessary prerequisite to working with Federal gift and estate taxes.

---

13. The rate schedules are contained in § 2001(c).   14. §§ 2010(c) and 2505(c).

Undivided Ownership. Assume D and Y own an undivided but equal interest in a tract of land. Such ownership could fall into any of four categories: joint tenancy, tenancy by the entirety, tenancy in common, or community property.

If D and Y hold ownership as joint tenants or tenants by the entirety, the right of survivorship exists. This means that the last tenant to survive receives full ownership of the property. Thus, if D predeceases Y, the land belongs entirely to Y. None of the land, therefore, will pass to D's heirs or will be subject to administration by D's executor. A tenancy by the entirety is a joint tenancy between husband and wife.

If D and Y hold ownership as tenants in common or as community property, death does not defeat an owner's interest. Thus, if D predeceases Y, D's one-half interest in the land will pass to his or her estate or heirs.

Community property interests arise from the marital relationship. Normally, all property acquired after marriage, except by gift or inheritance, by husband and wife residing in a community property state will become part of the community. The following states have the community property system in effect: Louisiana, Texas, New Mexico, Arizona, California, Washington, Idaho, Nevada, and Wisconsin. All other states follow the common law system of ascertaining the rights of spouses to property acquired after marriage.

Partial Interests. Interests in assets can be divided in terms of rights to income and rights to principal. Particularly when property is placed in trust, it is not uncommon to carve out various income interests that have to be accounted for separately from the ultimate disposition of the property itself.

EXAMPLE 5   Under D's will, a ranch is to be placed in trust, life estate to S, D's son, with remainder to S's children (D's grandchildren). Under this arrangement, S is the life tenant and, as such, is entitled to the use of the ranch (including any income therefrom) during his life. Upon S's death, the trust will terminate, and its principal will pass to S's children. Thus, S's children will receive outright ownership of the ranch when S dies. □

THE FEDERAL GIFT TAX

General Considerations

Requirements for a Gift. For a gift to be complete under state law, the following elements must be present:

- A donor competent to make the gift.

- A donee capable of receiving and possessing the property.

- Donative intent on behalf of the donor.

- Actual or constructive delivery of the property to the donee or the donee's representative.

- Acceptance of the gift by the donee.

Whether transfers are or are not gifts under state law is important in applying the Federal gift tax. But state law does not always control in this matter. For example, the tax law makes it quite clear that the element of donative intent is not an essential factor in the application of the Federal gift tax to the transfer.

EXAMPLE 6   B (age 24) consents to marry D (age 62) if D transfers $200,000 of his property to her. The arrangement is set forth in a prenuptial agreement, D makes the transfer, and B and D are married. D lacked donative intent, and in most states no gift has been made from D to B. Nevertheless, the transfer would be subject to the Federal gift tax.   □

The key to the result reached in Example 6 and to the status of other types of transfers is whether full and adequate consideration in money or money's worth was given for the property transferred. Although such consideration is present in Example 6 (property for marriage) for purposes of state law, Reg. § 25.2512–8 reads: "A consideration not reducible to a value in money or money's worth, as love and affection, promise of marriage, etc., is to be wholly disregarded, and the entire value of the property transferred constitutes the amount of the gift."

Incomplete Transfers.   The Federal gift tax does not apply to transfers that are incomplete. Thus, if the transferor retains the right to reclaim the property or, for all intents and purposes, has not really parted with the possession of the property, a taxable event has not taken place.

EXAMPLE 7   D creates a trust with income payable to S for life, remainder to R. Under the terms of the trust instrument, D can revoke the trust at any time and repossess the trust principal and income therefrom. No gift takes place on the creation of the trust; D has not ceased to have dominion and control over the property.   □

EXAMPLE 8   Assume the same facts as in Example 7, except that one year after the transfer, D relinquishes his right to terminate the trust. At this point, the transfer becomes complete, and the Federal gift tax applies.   □

Business versus Personal Setting.   In a business setting, full and adequate consideration is apt to exist. Reg. § 25.2512–8 provides that "a sale, exchange, or other transfer of property made in the ordinary course of business (a transaction that is bona fide, at arm's length, and free of any donative intent) will be considered as made for an adequate and full consideration in money or money's worth." If the parties are acting in a personal setting, a gift is usually the result. Do not conclude, however, that the presence of *some* consideration may be enough to preclude Federal gift tax consequences. Again, the answer may rest on whether the transfer occurred in a business setting.

EXAMPLE 9   D sells S some real estate for $40,000. Unknown to D, the property contains valuable mineral deposits and is really worth $100,000. D may have made a bad business deal, but he has not made a gift to S of $60,000.   □

EXAMPLE 10   Assume the same facts as in Example 9, except that D and S are father and son. In addition, D is very much aware of the fact that the property is worth $100,000. D has made a gift of $60,000 to S.   □

Certain Excluded Transfers.   Transfers to political organizations are exempt from the application of the Federal gift tax.[15] This provision in the Code made unnecessary the previous practice whereby candidates for public office established multiple campaign committees to maximize the number of annual exclusions available to their contributors. As noted later, an annual exclusion of $10,000 (previously $3,000) for each donee passes free of the Federal gift tax.

The Federal gift tax does not apply to tuition payments made to an educational organization (e.g., a college) on another's behalf. Nor does it apply to amounts paid on another's behalf for medical care.[16] In this regard, perhaps, the law is realistic since most donors would not likely recognize these items as being transfers subject to the gift tax.

Lifetime versus Death Transfers.   Be careful to distinguish between lifetime (inter vivos) and death (testamentary) transfers.

EXAMPLE 11	D buys a U.S. savings bond, which he registers as follows: "D, payable to S upon D's death." No gift is made when D buys the bond; S has received only a mere expectancy (right to obtain ownership of the bond at D's death). Anytime before his death, D may redeem or otherwise dispose of the bond and thereby cut off S's interest. On D's death, no gift is made because the bond passes to S by testamentary disposition. As noted later, however, the bond will be included in D's gross estate as property in which the decedent had an interest (§ 2033). □

EXAMPLE 12	D purchases an insurance policy on his own life (face value of $100,000) and designates S as the beneficiary. Until his death, D remains the owner of the policy and pays all premiums thereon. In accordance with the reasoning set forth in Example 11, no gift to S is made either when the policy is purchased or when D pays any of the premiums thereon. On D's death, the $100,000 proceeds pass to S as a testamentary and not as an inter vivos transfer. As discussed later, the insurance proceeds will be included in D's gross estate under § 2042(2). □

Transfers Subject to the Gift Tax

Whether or not a transfer will be subject to the Federal gift tax will depend upon the application of §§ 2511 through 2519 and the Regulations thereunder.

Gift Loans.   To understand the tax ramifications of gift loans, an illustration is helpful.

EXAMPLE 13	Before his daughter (D) leaves for college, F lends her $300,000. D signs a note that provides for repayment in five years. The loan, however, contains no interest element, and neither F nor D expects any interest to be paid. Following F's advice, D invests the loan proceeds in income-producing securities. During her five years in college, D uses the income from the investments to pay for college costs and other living expenses. On the maturity date of the note, D repays the $300,000 she owes F. □

---

15. § 2501(a)(5).   16. § 2503(e).

In a gift loan arrangement, the following consequences ensue:

- F will have made a gift to D of the interest element. The amount of the gift will be determined by the difference between the amount of interest charged (in this case, none) and the market rate (as determined by the yield on certain U.S. government securities).

- The interest element must be included in F's gross income and will be subject to the Federal income tax.

- D may be allowed an income tax deduction as to the interest element. This result may benefit D only if she is in a position to itemize her deductions *from* adjusted gross income.

The Code defines a gift loan as "any below-market loan where the forgoing of interest is in the nature of a gift."[17] Unless tax avoidance was one of the principal purposes of the loan, special limitations apply if the gift loan does not exceed $100,000. In such a case, the interest element shall not exceed the borrower's net investment income.[18] Furthermore, if such net investment income does not exceed $1,000, it shall be treated as zero. Under the $1,000 *de minimis* rule, the interest element is to be disregarded.

Certain Property Settlements (§ 2516).   Normally, the settlement of certain marital rights is not regarded as being for consideration and is therefore subject to the Federal gift tax.[19] As a special exception to this general approach, Congress saw fit to enact § 2516. Under this provision, transfers of property interests made under the terms of a written agreement between spouses in settlement of their marital or property rights are deemed to be for adequate consideration. The transfers are thereby exempt from the Federal gift tax if a final decree of divorce is obtained within the three-year period beginning on the date one year before such agreement is entered into. Likewise excluded are transfers to provide a reasonable allowance for the support of minor children (including legally adopted children) of a marriage. The agreement need not be approved by the divorce decree.

Disclaimers (§ 2518).   A disclaimer is a refusal by a person to accept property that is designated to pass to him or her. The effect of the disclaimer is to pass the property to someone else.

EXAMPLE 14   D dies without a will and is survived by a son, S, and a grandson, GS. At the time of his death, D owned real estate that, under the applicable state law, passes to the closest lineal descendant, S in this case. If, however, S disclaims his interest in the real estate, state law provides that the property will pass to GS. At the time of D's death, S has considerable property of his own, and GS has none. □

Why might S want to consider issuing a disclaimer as to his inheritance and have the property pass directly from D to GS? By so doing, an extra transfer tax might be avoided. If the disclaimer does not take place (S accepts the inheritance),

---

17. § 7872(f)(3).
18. Net investment income has the same meaning given to the term by § 163(d). Generally, net investment income is investment income (e.g., interest, dividends) less related expenses.
19. See Reg. § 25.2512–8 and Example 6 in this chapter.

and the property eventually passes to GS (either by gift or by death), the later transfer will be subject to the application of either the gift tax or the estate tax.

For many years, whether or not a disclaimer was effective to avoid a Federal transfer tax depended on the application of state law. To illustrate by using the facts of Example 14, if state law determined that a disclaimer by S after D's death still meant that the real estate was deemed to have passed through S, the Federal gift tax would apply. In essence, S would be treated as if he had inherited the property from D and then given it to GS. As state law was not always consistent in this regard and sometimes was not even known, the application or nonapplication of Federal transfer taxes could depend on where the parties lived. To remedy this situation and provide some measure of uniformity to the area of disclaimers, §§ 2046 (relating to disclaimers for estate tax purposes) and 2518 were added to the Code.

In the case of the gift tax, meeting the requirements of § 2518 would treat a timely lifetime disclaimer by S (refer to Example 14) as if the property went directly from D to GS. Since it is not regarded as having passed through S (regardless of what state law holds), it will not be subject to the Federal gift tax.

The tax law also permits the avoidance of the Federal gift tax in cases of a partial disclaimer of an undivided interest.

EXAMPLE 15   Assume the same facts as in Example 14, except that S wishes to retain one-half of the real estate for himself. If S makes a timely disclaimer of an undivided one-half interest in the property, the Federal gift tax will not apply to the portion passing to GS. □

Other Transfers Subject to Gift Tax.   Other transfers that may carry gift tax consequences (e.g., the exercise of a power of appointment, the creation of joint ownership) are discussed and illustrated in connection with the Federal estate tax.

Annual Exclusion

The first $10,000 of gifts made to any one person during any calendar year (except gifts of future interests in property) is excluded in determining the total amount of gifts for the year.[20] The annual exclusion is applied to all gifts of a present interest made during the calendar year in the order in which they are made until the $10,000 exclusion per donee is exhausted. For a gift in trust, each beneficiary of the trust is treated as a separate person for purposes of the exclusion.

A future interest may be defined as one that will come into being (as to use, possession, or enjoyment) at some future date. Examples of future interests would include such possessory rights, whether vested or contingent, as remainder interests that are commonly encountered when property is transferred to a trust. On the other hand, a present interest is an unrestricted right to the immediate use, possession, or enjoyment of property or of the income therefrom.

EXAMPLE 16   During the current year, D makes the following cash gifts: $8,000 to R and $12,000 to S. D may claim an annual exclusion of $8,000 with respect to R and $10,000 with respect to S. □

---

20. § 2503(b).

EXAMPLE 17   By a lifetime gift, D transfers property to a trust with a life estate (with income payable annually) to R and remainder upon R's death to S. D has made two gifts: one to R of a life estate and one to S of a remainder interest. The life estate is a present interest and therefore qualifies for the annual exclusion. The remainder interest granted to S is a future interest and does not qualify for the exclusion. Note that S's interest does not come into being until some future date (on the death of R).   □

Although Example 17 indicates that the gift of an income interest is a present interest, this may not always prove to be the case. If a possibility exists that the income beneficiary may not receive the immediate enjoyment of the property, the transfer is one of a future interest.

EXAMPLE 18   Assume the same facts as in Example 17, except that the income from the trust need not be payable annually to R but may, at the trustee's discretion, be accumulated and added to corpus. Since R's right to receive the income from the trust is conditioned on the trustee's discretion, it is not a present interest and no annual exclusion will be allowed. The mere possibility of diversion is enough. It would not matter if the trustee never exercised his or her discretion to accumulate and did, in fact, distribute the trust income to R annually.   □

Trust for Minors.   Section 2503(c) offers an exception to the future interest rules just discussed. Under this provision, a transfer for the benefit of a person who has not attained the age of 21 years on the date of the gift may be considered a gift of a present interest even though the minor is not given the unrestricted right to the immediate use, possession, or enjoyment of the property. For the exception to apply, however, certain stringent conditions must be satisfied. One such condition is that all of the property and its income must be made available to the minor upon attaining age 21. Thus, the exception would allow a trustee to accumulate income on behalf of a minor beneficiary without converting the income interest to a future interest.

Deductions

In arriving at taxable gifts, a deduction is allowed for transfers to certain qualified charitable organizations. On transfers between spouses, a marital deduction may be available. Since both the charitable and marital deductions apply in determining the Federal estate tax, they are discussed later in the chapter.

Computing the Federal Gift Tax

 The Unified Transfer Tax Rate Schedule.   The top rates of the unified transfer tax rate schedule originally reached as high as 70 percent. To be consistent with the maximum income tax rate applicable to individuals which, until recently, was 50 percent, the top unified transfer tax rate was lowered to this amount. But the reduction was phased in, and the maximum of 50 percent will not be reached until 1993 (see applicable tax rate schedule in Appendix A). For transfers (by gift or death) made from 1984 through 1992, the top rate is 55 percent. As noted later in the chapter, the benefits of the graduated rates are to be phased out for larger gifts

beginning after 1987. Keep in mind that the unified transfer tax rate schedule applies to all transfers (by gift or death) after 1976. Different rate schedules applied for pre-1977 gifts and pre-1977 death transfers.

The Deemed-Paid Adjustment.   Reviewing the formula for the gift tax (refer to Figure 25–1), note that the tax base for a current gift includes *all* past taxable gifts. The effect of such inclusion is to force the current taxable gift into a higher bracket because of the progressive nature of the unified transfer tax rates (refer to Example 1). To mitigate such double taxation, the donor is allowed a credit for any gift tax previously paid (refer to Example 2).

To limit the donor to a credit for the gift tax *actually paid* on pre-1977 taxable gifts would be unfair. Pre-1977 taxable gifts were subject to a lower set of rates than those contained in the unified transfer tax rate schedule. As a consequence, the donor is allowed a "deemed-paid" credit on pre-1977 taxable gifts. This is the amount that would have been due under the unified transfer tax rate schedule had it been applicable. Post-1976 taxable gifts do not need the deemed-paid adjustment because the same rate schedule is involved in all gifts.

EXAMPLE 19   In early 1976, T made taxable gifts of $500,000, upon which a Federal gift tax of $109,275 was paid. Assume T makes further taxable gifts of $700,000 in 1990. The unified transfer tax on the 1990 gifts would be determined as follows:

Taxable gifts made in 1990		$ 700,000
Add: Taxable gifts made in 1976		500,000
Total of current and past taxable gifts		$1,200,000
Unified transfer tax on total taxable gifts per Appendix A [$345,800 + (41% × $200,000)]		$ 427,800
Subtract:		
Deemed paid tax on pre-1977 taxable gifts per Appendix A	$155,800	
Unified tax credit for 1990	192,800	(348,600)
Gift tax due on the 1990 taxable gift		$ 79,200

Note that the gift tax actually paid on the 1976 transfer was $109,275. Nevertheless, the deemed-paid credit allowed T on the gift was $155,800, considerably more than was paid.   □

The Election to Split Gifts by Married Persons.   To understand the reason for the gift-splitting election of § 2513, consider the following situations:

EXAMPLE 20   H and W are husband and wife and reside in Michigan, a common law state. H has been the only breadwinner in the family, and W has no significant amount of property of her own. Neither has made any prior taxable gifts or used the $30,000 specific exemption previously available for pre-1977 gifts. In 1990, H makes a gift to S of $1,220,000. Presuming the election to split gifts did not exist, H's gift tax would be as follows:

Amount of gift	$1,220,000
Subtract: Annual exclusion	(10,000)
Taxable gift	$1,210,000
Gift tax on $1,210,000 per Appendix A [$345,800 + (41% × $210,000)]	$ 431,900
Subtract: Unified tax credit for 1990	(192,800)
Gift tax due on the 1990 taxable gift	$ 239,100

□

EXAMPLE 21   Assume the same facts as in Example 20, except that H and W have always resided in California. Even though H is the sole breadwinner, since income from personal services generally is community property, the gift to S probably involves community property. If this is the case, the gift tax is worked out as follows:

	H	W
Amount of the gift (50% × $1,220,000)	$ 610,000	$ 610,000
Subtract: Annual exclusion	(10,000)	(10,000)
Taxable gifts	$ 600,000	$ 600,000
Gift tax on $600,000 per Appendix A	$ 192,800	$ 192,800
Subtract: Unified tax credit for 1990	(192,800)	(192,800)
Gift tax due on the 1990 taxable gifts	$ –0–	$ –0–

□

By comparing the results of Examples 20 and 21, one can see that married donors residing in community property jurisdictions possessed a significant gift tax advantage over those residing in common law states. To rectify this inequity, the Revenue Act of 1948 incorporated the predecessor to § 2513 into the Code. Under this Section, a gift made by a person to someone other than his or her spouse may be considered, for Federal gift tax purposes, as having been made one-half by each spouse. Returning to Example 20, this means H and W could treat the gift passing to S as being made one-half by each of them, even though the property may have belonged to H. Consequently, the parties would be able to achieve the same tax result as that outlined in Example 21.

To split gifts, the spouses must be legally married to each other at the time of the gift. If they are divorced later in the calendar year, they may still split the gift if neither marries anyone else during that year. They both must signify on their separate gift tax returns their consent to have all gifts made in that calendar year split between them. In addition, both must be citizens or residents of the United States on the date of the gift. A gift from one spouse to the other spouse cannot be split. Such a gift might, however, be eligible for the marital deduction.

The election to split gifts would not be necessary when husband and wife transfer community property to a third party. It would, however, be available if the subject of the gift consisted of the separate property of one of the spouses. Generally, separate property is property acquired before marriage and property acquired after marriage by gift or inheritance. The election, then, is not limited to residents of common law states.

CONCEPT SUMMARY 25–1

Federal Gift Tax

1. The Federal gift tax applies to all gratuitous transfers of property made by U.S. citizens or residents. In this regard, it does not matter where the property is located.

2. In the eyes of the IRS, a gratuitous transfer is one not supported by full and adequate consideration. If the parties are acting in a business setting, such consideration usually will exist. If purported sales are between family members, however, such transfers are suspect of a gift element.

3. If a lender loans money to another and intends some or all of the interest element to be a gift, the arrangement is categorized as a gift loan. To the extent that the interest provided for is less than the market rate, three tax consequences ensue. First, a gift has taken place between the lender and the borrower as to the interest element. Second, income may result to the lender. Third, an income tax deduction may be available to the borrower.

4. Property settlements can escape the gift tax if a divorce occurs within a prescribed period of time.

5. A disclaimer is a refusal by a person to accept property designated to pass to that person. The effect of a disclaimer is to pass the property to someone else. If certain conditions are satisfied, the issuance of a disclaimer will not be subject to the Federal gift tax.

6. Except for gifts of future interests, a donor will be allowed an annual exclusion of $10,000. The future interest limitation does not apply as to certain trusts created for minors.

7. By making the election to split a gift, a married couple will be treated as two donors. Such an election doubles the annual exclusion and makes available the unified tax credit to the nonowner spouse.

8. The election to split gifts will not be necessary if the property is jointly owned by the spouses. Such would be the case if the property is part of the couple's community.

9. In determining the tax base for computing the gift tax, all prior taxable gifts must be added to current taxable gifts. Thus, the gift tax is cumulative in nature.

10. Gifts are reported on Form 709 or Form 709–A. The return is due on April 15 following the year of the gift.

Procedural Matters

Having determined which transfers are subject to the Federal gift tax and the various deductions and exclusions available to the donor, consideration should be accorded to the procedural aspects of the tax. The sections to follow discuss the return itself, the due dates for filing and paying the tax, and other related matters.

The Federal Gift Tax Return.   For transfers by gift, a Form 709 (U.S. Gift Tax Return) must be filed whenever the gifts for any one calendar year exceed the annual exclusion or involve a gift of a future interest. Regardless of amount, however, transfers between spouses that are offset by the unlimited marital deduction do not require the filing of a Form 709.[21]

EXAMPLE 22   In 1990, D makes five gifts, each in the amount of $10,000, to his five children. If the gifts do not involve future interests, a Form 709 need not be filed to report the transfers. □

EXAMPLE 23   During 1990, M makes a gift of $20,000 cash of her separate property to her daughter. To double the amount of the annual exclusion allowed, F (M's

---

21. § 6019(a)(2).

husband) is willing to split the gift. Since the § 2513 election can be made only on a gift tax return, a form needs to be filed. This is so even though no gift tax will be due as a result of the transfer. Useful for this purpose is Form 709–A (U.S. Short Form Gift Tax Return), which is available to simplify the gift-splitting procedure. □

Presuming a gift tax return is due, it must be filed on or before the fifteenth day of April following the year of the gift.[22] As with other Federal taxes, when the due date falls on Saturday, Sunday, or a legal holiday, the date for filing the return is the next business day. Note that the filing requirements for Form 709 have no correlation to the accounting year used by a donor for Federal income tax purposes. Thus, a fiscal year taxpayer would have to follow the April 15 rule as to any reportable gifts.

Extensions of Time and Payment of Tax.   If sufficient reason is shown, the IRS is authorized to grant reasonable extensions of time for filing of the return.[23] Unless the donor is abroad, no extension in excess of six months may be granted. The application must be made before the due date of the return and must contain a full report of the causes for the delay. For a calendar year taxpayer, an extension of time for filing an income tax return also extends the time for filing the Form 709. An extension of time to file the return does not extend the time for payment of the tax.

THE FEDERAL ESTATE TAX

The discussion of the estate tax that follows is developed to coincide with the pattern of the formula appearing earlier in the chapter. In brief, the formula for the estate tax is summarized as follows (refer to page 25–5 for a more detailed presentation of the formula):

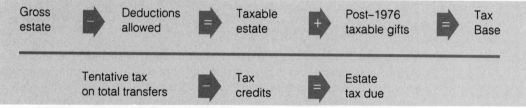

| Gross estate | − | Deductions allowed | = | Taxable estate | + | Post–1976 taxable gifts | = | Tax Base |

| Tentative tax on total transfers | − | Tax credits | = | Estate tax due |

The key components in the formula are the gross estate, the taxable estate, the tax base, and the credits allowed against the tentative tax.

Gross Estate

Simply stated, the gross estate comprises all property subject to the Federal estate tax. This in turn depends on the provisions of the Internal Revenue Code as supplemented by IRS pronouncements and the judicial interpretations of Federal courts.

Contrasted with the gross estate is the concept of the probate estate. Controlled by state (rather than Federal) law, the probate estate consists of all of a decedent's property subject to administration by the executor or administrator of the estate operating under the supervision of a local court of appropriate jurisdiction (usually designated as a probate court). An executor (or executrix) is

---

22. § 6075(b).   23. § 6081.

the decedent's personal representative as appointed under the decedent's will. An administrator (or administratrix) may be appointed by the local probate court of appropriate jurisdiction, usually because the decedent failed to appoint an executor in his or her will (or such designated person refused to serve) or the decedent died without a will.

The probate estate is frequently smaller than the gross estate because it contains only property owned by the decedent at the time of death and passing to heirs under a will or under the law of intestacy (the order of distribution for those dying without a will). As noted later, such items as the proceeds of many life insurance policies become part of the gross estate but are not included in the probate estate.

All states provide for an order of distribution in the event someone dies without a will. After the surviving spouse receives some or all of the estate, the preference is usually in the following order: down to lineal descendants (e.g., children, grandchildren), up to lineal ascendants (e.g., parents, grandparents), and out to collateral relations (e.g., brothers, sisters, aunts, and uncles).

Property Owned by the Decedent (§ 2033).   Property owned by the decedent at the time of death will be includible in the gross estate. The nature of the property or the use to which it was put during the decedent-owner's lifetime has no significance as far as the death tax is concerned. Thus, personal effects (such as clothing), stocks, bonds, furniture, jewelry, works of art, bank accounts, and interests in businesses conducted as sole proprietorships and partnerships are all included in the deceased's gross estate. In other words, no distinction is made between tangible or intangible, depreciable or nondepreciable, business or personal assets.

The application of § 2033 can be illustrated as follows:

EXAMPLE 24   D dies owning some City of Denver bonds. The fair market value of the bonds plus any interest accrued to the date of D's death is includible in D's gross estate. Although interest on municipal bonds is normally not taxable under the Federal income tax, it is, nevertheless, property owned by D at the time of D's death. However, any interest accrued after death is not part of D's gross estate. □

EXAMPLE 25   D dies on April 8, at a time when she owns stock in X Corporation and in Y Corporation. On March 1, both corporations had authorized a cash dividend payable on May 1. For X Corporation, the dividend was payable to shareholders of record as of April 1. Y Corporation's date of record is April 10. D's gross estate includes the following: the stock in X Corporation, the stock in Y Corporation, and the dividend on the X Corporation stock. It does not include the dividend on the Y Corporation stock. □

EXAMPLE 26   D dies holding some promissory notes issued to him by his son. In his will, D forgives these notes, relieving the son of any obligation to make payments thereon. The fair market value of these notes will be included in D's gross estate. □

Dower and Curtesy Interests (§ 2034).   In its common law (nonstatutory) form, dower generally gave a surviving widow a life estate in a portion of her husband's estate (usually the real estate he owned) with the remainder passing to their children. Most states have modified and codified these common law rules, and variations among jurisdictions are not unusual. In some states, for example, a widow's statutory share of her deceased husband's property may mean outright ownership in a percentage of both his real estate and personal property. Curtesy is a similar right held by the husband in his wife's property, taking effect in the event he survives her. Most states have abolished the common law curtesy concept and have, in some cases, substituted a modified statutory version.

Dower and curtesy rights are incomplete interests and may never materialize. Thus, if a wife predeceases her husband, her dower interest in her husband's property is lost.

EXAMPLE 27

D dies without a will, leaving an estate of $900,000. Under state law, W (D's widow) is entitled to one-third of D's property. The $300,000 W receives will be included in D's gross estate. Depending on the nature of the interest W receives in the $300,000, this amount could qualify D's estate for a marital deduction. (This possibility is discussed at greater length later in the chapter. For the time being, however, the focus is on what is or is not included as part of the decedent's gross estate.)   □

Adjustments for Gifts Made within Three Years of Death (§ 2035).   At one time, all taxable gifts made within three years of death were included in the donor's gross estate unless it could be shown that the gifts were not made in contemplation of death. The prior rule was designed to preclude tax avoidance since the gift tax and estate tax rates were separate and the former was lower than the latter. However, when the gift and estate tax rates were combined into the unified transfer tax, the reason for the rule for gifts in contemplation of death largely disappeared. The three-year rule has, however, been retained for the following items:

- Any gift tax paid on gifts made within three years of death. Called the gross-up procedure, this prevents the gift tax amount from escaping the estate tax.

- Any property interests transferred by gift within three years of death that would have been included in the gross estate by virtue of the application of § 2036 (transfers with a retained life estate), § 2037 (transfers taking effect at death), § 2038 (revocable transfers), and § 2042 (proceeds of life insurance). (All except § 2037 transfers are discussed later in the chapter.)

EXAMPLE 28

Before his death in 1990, D made the following taxable gifts:

| Year of Gift | Nature of the Asset | Fair Market Value | | Gift Tax Paid |
		Date of Gift	Date of Death	
1984	X Corporation stock	$100,000	$150,000	$ –0–
1988	Policy on D's life	40,000 (cash value)	200,000 (face value)	–0–
1989	Land	400,000	410,000	8,200

D's *gross estate* includes $208,200 ($200,000 life insurance proceeds + $8,200 gross-up for the gift tax on the 1989 taxable gift) as to these transfers. Referring to the formula for the estate tax (Figure 25–2), the other post-1976 taxable gifts are added to the *taxable estate* (at the fair market value on the date of the gift) in arriving at the tax base. D's estate will be allowed a credit for the $8,200 gift tax paid on the 1989 transfer. □

Transfers with a Retained Life Estate (§ 2036).   Code §§ 2036 through 2038 were enacted on the premise that the estate tax can be avoided on lifetime transfers only if the decedent does not retain control over the property. The logic of this approach is somewhat difficult to dispute—one should not be able to escape the tax consequences of property transfers at death while remaining in a position during life to enjoy some or all of the fruits of ownership.

Code § 2036 requires inclusion of the value of any property transferred by the deceased during lifetime for less than adequate consideration if either of the following was retained:

- The possession or enjoyment of, or the right to the income from, the property.

- The right, either alone or in conjunction with any person, to designate the persons who shall possess or enjoy the property or the income therefrom.

"The possession or enjoyment of, or the right to the income from, the property," as it appears in § 2036(a)(1), is considered to have been retained by or reserved to the decedent to the extent that such income, etc., is to be applied toward the discharge of a legal obligation of the decedent. The term "legal obligation" includes a legal obligation of the decedent to support a dependent during the decedent's lifetime.[24]

The practical application of § 2036 can best be explained by turning to two illustrations.

EXAMPLE 29   F's will passes all of F's property to a trust in which income goes to D for his life (D is given a life estate), and upon D's death, the principal goes to R (R is granted a remainder interest). On D's death, none of the trust property will be included in D's gross estate. Although D held a life estate, § 2036 is inapplicable because D was not the transferor (F was) of the property. Section 2033 (property owned by the decedent) would compel inclusion in D's gross estate of any income distributions D was entitled to receive at the time of his death. □

EXAMPLE 30   By deed, D transfers the remainder interest in her ranch to S, retaining for herself the right to continue occupying the property until death. Upon D's death, the fair market value of the ranch will be included in D's gross estate under § 2036(a)(1). Furthermore, D is subject to the gift tax. The amount of the gift would be the fair market value of the ranch on the date of the gift less the portion applicable to D's retained life estate. □

Revocable Transfers (§ 2038).   Another type of lifetime transfer that is drawn into a decedent's gross estate is covered by § 2038. Under this Section, the gross

---

24. Reg. § 20.2036–1(b)(2).

estate includes the value of property interests transferred by the decedent (except to the extent that the transfer was made for adequate and full consideration) if the enjoyment of the property transferred was subject, at the date of the decedent's death, to any power of the decedent to alter, amend, revoke, or terminate the transfer. This includes the power to change the beneficiaries or the power to accelerate or increase any beneficiary's enjoyment of the property.

The capacity in which the decedent could exercise the power is immaterial. If the decedent gave property in trust, making himself or herself the trustee with the power to revoke the trust, the property would be included in his or her gross estate. If the decedent named another person as trustee with the power to revoke but reserved the power to later appoint himself or herself trustee, the property would also be included in his or her gross estate. If, however, the power to alter, amend, revoke, or terminate was held at all times solely by a person other than the decedent and the decedent reserved no right to assume these powers, the property is not included in the decedent's gross estate under § 2038.

The Code and the Regulations make it quite clear that inclusion in the gross estate under § 2038 is not avoided by relinquishing a power within three years of death.[25] Recall from the previous discussion that § 2038 was one of several types of situations listed as exceptions to the usual rule excluding from the gross estate gifts made within three years of death.

In the event § 2038 applies, the amount includible in the gross estate is only the portion of the property transferred that is subject, at the decedent's death, to the decedent's power to alter, amend, revoke, or terminate.

The classic § 2038 type of situation results from the use of a revocable trust.

EXAMPLE 31   G creates a trust, life estate to her children, remainder to her grandchildren. Under the terms of the trust, G reserves the right to revoke the trust and revest the trust principal and income in herself. As noted earlier in Example 7, the creation of the trust will not result in a gift because the transfer is not complete. Furthermore, if G dies still retaining the power to revoke, the trust will be included in her gross estate under § 2038. □

More subtle applications of § 2038 result from the use of a state Uniform Gifts to Minors Act. The Uniform Gifts to Minors Act permits the ownership of securities to be transferred to a minor with someone designated as custodian. The custodian has the right to sell the securities, collect any income therefrom, and otherwise act on behalf of the minor without court supervision. The custodianship arrangement is convenient and inexpensive. Under state law the custodianship terminates automatically when the minor reaches a specified age (usually age 21). If the custodian also has the power to terminate the arrangement, § 2038 could create estate tax problems.

EXAMPLE 32   D transfers securities to S under the state's Uniform Gifts to Minors Act designating himself as the custodian. Under the Act, the custodian has the authority to terminate the custodianship at any time and distribute the proceeds to the minor. D dies four years later and before the custodianship is terminated. Although the transfer is effective for income tax purposes, it runs

---

25. § 2038(a)(1) and Reg. § 20.2038–1(e)(1).

afoul of § 2038.[26] Under this Section, the fair market value of the securities on the date of D's death will be included in D's gross estate for Federal estate tax purposes. ☐

EXAMPLE 33

Assume the same facts as in Example 32, except that D dissolves the custodianship (thereby turning the securities over to S) within three years of death. The fair market value of the securities on the date of D's death will be includible in D's gross estate.[27] ☐

EXAMPLE 34

Assume the same facts as in Example 32, except that S becomes of age and the custodianship terminates before D's death. Nothing will be included in D's gross estate upon D's death. ☐

EXAMPLE 35

G transfers securities to S under the state's Uniform Gifts to Minors Act designating D as the custodian. Nothing relating to these securities will be included in D's gross estate upon D's death during the term of the custodianship. Code § 2038 is not applicable because D was not the transferor. G's death during the custodianship should cause no estate tax consequences; G has retained no interest or control over the property transferred. ☐

In the area of incomplete transfers (§§ 2036 and 2038), there is much overlap in terms of application. It is not unusual, therefore, to find that either or both Sections apply to a particular transfer.

Annuities (§ 2039).   Annuities can be divided by their origin into commercial and noncommercial contracts. The noncommercial annuities are those issued by private parties and, in some cases, charitable organizations that do not regularly issue annuities. Although both varieties have much in common, noncommercial annuities present special income tax problems and are not treated further in this discussion.

Regulation § 20.2039–1(b)(1) defines an annuity as representing "one or more payments extending over any period of time." According to this Regulation, the payments may be equal or unequal, conditional or unconditional, periodic or sporadic. Most commercial contracts fall into one of four general patterns:

1. *Straight-life annuity.* The insurance company promises to make periodic payments to X (the annuitant) during his or her life. Upon X's death, the company has no further obligation under the contract.

2. *Joint and survivor annuity.* The insurance company promises to make periodic payments to X and Y during their lives with the payments to continue, usually in a diminished amount, for the life of the survivor.

3. *Self and survivor annuity.* The company agrees to make periodic payments to X during his or her life and, upon X's death, to continue these payments for the

---

26. If the minor is under the age of 14, net unearned income may be taxed at the parents' income tax rate. Net unearned income generally is passive income (e.g., dividends, interest) in excess of

$1,000. §§ 1(i) and (j).

27. § 2035(d)(2).

life of a designated beneficiary. This and the preceding type of annuity are most frequently used by married couples.

4. *Refund feature.* The company agrees to return to the annuitant's estate or other designated beneficiary a portion of the investment in the contract in the event of the annuitant's premature death.

In the case of a straight-life annuity, nothing will be included in the gross estate of the annuitant at death. Section 2033 (property in which the decedent had an interest) does not apply because the annuitant's interest in the contract is terminated by death. Section 2036 (transfers with a retained life estate) does not cover the situation; a transfer that is a "bona fide sale, for an adequate and full consideration in money or money's worth" is specifically excluded from § 2036 treatment. The purchase of a commercial annuity is presumed to entail adequate and full consideration unless some evidence exists to indicate that the parties were not acting at arm's length.

EXAMPLE 36   D purchases a straight-life annuity that will pay him $6,000 a month when he reaches age 65. D dies at age 70. Except for the payments he received before his death, nothing relating to this annuity will affect D's gross estate. ☐

In the case of a survivorship annuity (classifications 2 and 3), the estate tax consequences under § 2039(a) are usually triggered by the death of the first annuitant. The amount included in the gross estate is the cost from the same company of a comparable annuity covering the survivor at his or her attained age on the date of the deceased annuitant's death.

EXAMPLE 37   Assume the same facts as in Example 36, except that the annuity contract provides for W to be paid $3,000 a month for life as a survivorship feature. W is 62 years of age when D dies. Under these circumstances, D's gross estate will include the cost of a comparable contract that would provide an annuity of $3,000 per month for the life of a person (male or female, as the case may be) age 62. ☐

Full inclusion in the gross estate of the survivorship element is subject to the important exception of § 2039(b). Under this provision, the amount includible is to be based on the proportion of the deceased annuitant's contribution to the total cost of the contract. This can be expressed by the following formula:

$$\frac{\text{Decedent's contribution to purchase price}}{\text{Total purchase price of the annuity}}$$ $\times$ Value of the annuity (or refund) at decedent's death $=$ Amount includible in the deceased annuitant's gross estate

EXAMPLE 38   Assume ⌐ same facts as in Example 37, except that D and W are husband and wife and have always lived in a community property state. The premiums on the contract were paid with community funds. Because W contributed one-half of the cost of the contract, only one-half of the amount determined under Example 37 would be included in D's gross estate. ☐

The result reached in Example 38 is not unique to community property jurisdictions. For example, the outcome would have been the same in a noncommunity property state if W had furnished one-half of the consideration from her own funds.

Joint Interests (§§ 2040 and 2511).   Recall that joint tenancies and tenancies by the entirety are characterized by the right of survivorship. Thus, upon the death of a joint tenant, title to the property passes to the surviving tenant. Further, none of the property will be included in the *probate* estate of the deceased tenant. In the case of tenancies in common and community property, death does not defeat an ownership interest; rather, the deceased owner's interest will be part of the probate estate.

The *Federal estate tax treatment* of tenancies in common or of community property follows the logical approach of taxing only the portion of the property included in the deceased owner's probate estate. Thus, if D, X, and Z are tenants in common in a tract of land, each owning an equal interest, and D dies, only one-third of the value of the property is included in the gross estate. This one-third interest is also the same amount that will pass to D's heirs.

EXAMPLE 39   D, X, and Z acquire a tract of land with ownership listed as tenants in common, each party furnishing $20,000 of the $60,000 purchase price. At a point when the property is worth $90,000, D dies. If D's undivided interest in the property is 33⅓%, the gross estate *and* probate estate would each include $30,000. □

Unless the parties have provided otherwise, each tenant will be deemed to own an interest equal to the portion of the original consideration he or she furnished. On the other hand, the parties in Example 39 could have provided that D would receive an undivided half interest in the property although he contributed only one-third of the purchase price. In such case, X and Z have made a gift to D when the tenancy was created, and D's gross estate and probate estate would each include $45,000.

For certain joint tenancies, the tax consequences are different. All of the property is included in the deceased co-owner's gross estate unless it can be proven that the surviving co-owners contributed to the cost of the property.[28] If a contribution can be shown, the amount to be excluded is calculated by the following formula:

$$\frac{\text{Surviving co-owner's contribution}}{\text{Total cost of the property}} \times \text{Fair market value of the property}$$

In computing a survivor's contribution, any funds received as a gift *from the deceased co-owner* and applied to the cost of the property cannot be counted. However, income or gain from gift assets can be so counted.

If the co-owners receive the property as a gift *from another,* each co-owner will be deemed to have contributed to the cost of his or her own interest.

The preceding rules can be illustrated as follows:

EXAMPLE 40   D and Y (father and son) acquire a tract of land with ownership listed as joint tenancy with right of survivorship, D furnishing $40,000 and Y $20,000 of the

---

28. § 2040(a).

$60,000 purchase price. Of the $20,000 provided by Y, $10,000 had previously been received as a gift from D. At a point when the property is worth $90,000, D dies. Because only $10,000 of Y's contribution can be counted (the other $10,000 was received as a gift from D), Y has only furnished one-sixth ($10,000/$60,000) of the cost. Thus, D's gross estate must include five-sixths of $90,000, or $75,000. This presumes Y can prove that he did in fact make the $10,000 contribution. In the absence of such proof, the full value of the property will be included in D's gross estate. D's death makes Y the immediate owner of the property by virtue of the right of survivorship; therefore, none of the property will be part of D's probate estate.   □

EXAMPLE 41   F transfers property to D and Y as a gift listing ownership as joint tenancy with the right of survivorship. Upon D's death, one-half of the value of the property will be included in the gross estate. Since the property was received as a gift and the donees are equal owners, each will be considered as having furnished one-half of the consideration.   □

To simplify the joint ownership rules for *married persons*, § 2040(b) provides for an automatic inclusion rule upon the death of the first joint-owner spouse to die. Regardless of the amount contributed by each spouse, one-half of the value of the property will be included in the gross estate of the spouse that predeceases. This special rule eliminates the need to trace the source of contributions and recognizes that any inclusion in the gross estate will be neutralized by the marital deduction.

EXAMPLE 42   In 1986, H purchases real estate for $100,000 using his separate funds and listing title as "H and W, joint tenants with the right of survivorship." H predeceases W four years later when the property is worth $300,000. If H and W are husband and wife, H's gross estate must include $150,000 (½ of $300,000) as to the property.   □

EXAMPLE 43   Assume the same facts as in Example 42, except that it is W (instead of H) who dies first. Presuming the date of death value to be $300,000, W's gross estate must include $150,000 as to the property. In this regard, it is of no consequence that W did not contribute to the cost of the real estate.   □

In both Examples 42 and 43, inclusion in the gross estate of the first spouse to die will be neutralized by the unlimited marital deduction allowed for estate tax purposes (see the discussion of § 2056 later in the chapter). Recall that under the right of survivorship feature, the surviving joint tenant obtains full ownership of the property. The marital deduction generally is allowed for property passing from one spouse to another.

Whether or not a gift results when property is transferred into some form of joint ownership will depend on the consideration furnished by each of the contributing parties for the ownership interest thereby acquired.

EXAMPLE 44   D and S purchase real estate as tenants in common, each furnishing $20,000 of the $40,000 cost. If each is an equal owner in the property, no gift has occurred.   □

EXAMPLE 45

Assume the same facts as in Example 44, except that of the $40,000 purchase price, D furnishes $30,000 and S furnishes only $10,000. If each is an equal owner in the property, D has made a gift to S of $10,000. □

EXAMPLE 46

M purchases real estate for $240,000, the title to the property being listed as follows: "M, D, and S as joint tenants with the right of survivorship." If under state law the mother (M), the daughter (D), and the son (S) are deemed to be equal owners in the property, M will be treated as having made gifts of $80,000 to D and $80,000 to S. □

Several principal exceptions exist to the general rule that the creation of a joint ownership with disproportionate interests resulting from unequal consideration will trigger gift treatment. First, if the transfer involves a joint bank account, there is no gift at the time of the contribution.[29] If a gift occurs, it will be when the noncontributing party withdraws the funds provided by the other joint tenant. Second, the same rule applies to the purchase of U.S. savings bonds. Again, any gift tax consequences will be postponed until such time as the noncontributing party appropriates some or all of the proceeds for his or her individual use.

Life Insurance (§ 2042).   Under § 2042, the gross estate includes the proceeds of life insurance on the decedent's life if (1) they are receivable by the estate, (2) they are receivable by another for the benefit of the estate, or (3) the decedent possessed an incident of ownership in the policy.

Life insurance on the life of another owned by a decedent at the time of his or her death would be included in his or her gross estate under § 2033 (property in which the decedent had an interest) and not under § 2042. The amount includible is the replacement value of the policy.[30] Under these circumstances, inclusion of the face amount of the policy would be inappropriate; the policy has not yet matured.

EXAMPLE 47

At the time of his death, D owned a life insurance policy on the life of S, face amount of $100,000 and replacement value of $25,000, with W as the designated beneficiary. Since the policy had not matured at D's death, § 2042 would be inapplicable. However, § 2033 (property in which the decedent had an interest) would compel the inclusion of $25,000 (the replacement value) in D's gross estate. If the policy were owned by D and W as community property, only $12,500 would be included in D's gross estate. □

The term "life insurance" includes whole life policies, term insurance, group life insurance, travel and accident insurance, endowment contracts (before being paid up), and death benefits paid by fraternal societies operating under the lodge system.[31]

As just noted, proceeds of insurance on the life of the decedent receivable by the executor or administrator or payable to the decedent's estate are included in the gross estate. It is not necessary that the estate be specifically named as the

29. Reg. § 25.2511–1(h)(4).

30. Reg. § 20.2031–8(a)(1).

31. Reg. § 20.2042–1(a)(1). As to travel and accident insurance, see *Comm. v. Estate of Noel*, 65–1 USTC ¶12,311, 15 AFTR2d 1397, 85 S.Ct. 1238 (USSC, 1965).

beneficiary. For example, if the proceeds of the policy are receivable by an individual beneficiary and are subject to an obligation, legally binding upon the beneficiary, to pay taxes, debts, and other charges enforceable against the estate, the proceeds will be included in the decedent's gross estate to the extent of the beneficiary's obligation. If the proceeds of an insurance policy made payable to a decedent's estate are community assets and, under state law, one-half belongs to the surviving spouse, only one-half of the proceeds will be considered as receivable by or for the benefit of the decedent's estate.

Proceeds of insurance on the life of the decedent not receivable by or for the benefit of the estate are includible if the decedent possessed at his or her death any of the incidents of ownership in the policy, exercisable either alone or in conjunction with any other person, even if acting as trustee. In this connection, the term "incidents of ownership" means more than the ownership of the policy in a technical legal sense. Generally speaking, the term has reference to the right of the insured or his or her estate to the economic benefits of the policy. Thus, it also includes the power to change beneficiaries, to revoke an assignment, to pledge the policy for a loan, or to surrender or cancel the policy.[32]

EXAMPLE 48

At the time of death, D was the insured under a policy (face amount of $100,000) owned by S with W as the designated beneficiary. The policy was originally taken out by D five years ago and immediately transferred as a gift to S. Under the assignment, D transferred all rights in the policy except the right to change beneficiaries. D died without having exercised this right, and the policy proceeds are paid to W. Under § 2042(2), the retention of an incident of ownership in the policy (e.g., the right to change beneficiaries) by D forces $100,000 to be included in the gross estate.   □

Assuming that the deceased-insured holds the incidents of ownership in a policy, how much will be includible in the gross estate if the insurance policy is a community asset? Only one-half of the proceeds becomes part of the deceased spouse's gross estate.

In determining whether or not a policy is *community property* or what portion of it might be so classified, state law controls. In this regard, two general views appear to be followed. Under the inception of title approach, the key to classification depends on when the policy was originally purchased. If purchased before marriage, the policy will be separate property regardless of how many premiums were paid after marriage with community funds. However, in the event the noninsured spouse is not the beneficiary of the policy, he or she may be entitled to reimbursement from the deceased-insured spouse's estate for one-half of the premiums paid with community funds. The inception of title approach is followed in at least three states: Louisiana, Texas, and New Mexico.

In some community property jurisdictions, the classification of a policy follows the tracing approach: The nature of the funds used to pay the premiums controls. Thus, a policy paid for 20 percent with separate funds and 80 percent with community funds will be 20 percent separate property and 80 percent community property. At what point in time the policy was purchased should make no difference. Conceivably, a policy purchased after marriage with the premiums paid exclusively with separate funds would be classified entirely as separate property. The tracing approach appears to be the rule in California and Washington.

---

32. Reg. § 20.2042–1(c)(2).

The mere purchase of a life insurance contract with the designation of someone else as the beneficiary thereunder does not constitute a *gift*. As long as the purchaser still owns the policy, nothing has really passed to the beneficiary. Even on the death of the insured-owner, no gift takes place. The proceeds going to the beneficiary constitute a testamentary and not a lifetime transfer. But consider the following possibility:

EXAMPLE 49   D purchases an insurance policy on his own life and transfers the policy to S. D retains no interest in the policy (such as the power to change beneficiaries or to revest in himself or his estate the economic benefits of the policy). Under these circumstances, D has made a gift to S. Furthermore, if D continues to pay the premiums on the transferred policy, each payment will constitute a separate gift. □

Under certain conditions, the death of the insured might represent a gift to the beneficiary of part or all of the proceeds. This may prove true when the owner of the policy is not the insured.

EXAMPLE 50   D owns an insurance policy on the life of S, with T as the designated beneficiary. Up until the time of S's death, D retained the right to change the beneficiary of the policy. The proceeds paid to T by the insurance company by reason of S's death constitute a gift from D to T. □

Taxable Estate

After the gross estate has been determined, the next step is to arrive at the taxable estate. By virtue of § 2051, the taxable estate is the gross estate less the following: expenses, indebtedness, and taxes (§ 2053); losses (§ 2054); charitable transfers (§§ 2055 and 2522); the marital deduction (§§ 2056 and 2523); and the ESOP deduction (§ 2057). As previously noted, the charitable and marital deductions also carry gift tax ramifications.

Expenses, Indebtedness, and Taxes (§ 2053).   A deduction is allowed for funeral expenses; expenses incurred in administering property; claims against the estate; and unpaid mortgages and other charges against property, the value of which is included in the gross estate without reduction for the mortgage or other indebtedness.

Expenses incurred in administering community property are deductible only in proportion to the deceased spouse's interest in the community.[33]

Administration expenses include commissions of the executor or administrator, attorney's fees of the estate, accountant's fees, court costs, and certain selling expenses for disposition of estate property.

Claims against the estate include property taxes accrued before the decedent's death, unpaid income taxes on income received by the decedent in his or her lifetime, and unpaid gift taxes on gifts made by the decedent in his or her lifetime.

Amounts that may be deducted as claims against the estate are only for enforceable personal obligations of the decedent at the time of his or her death.

---

33. *U.S. v. Stapf,* 63–2 USTC ¶12,192, 12 AFTR2d
    6326, 84 S.Ct. 248 (USSC, 1963).

Deductions for claims founded on promises or agreements are limited to the extent that the liabilities were contracted in good faith and for adequate and full consideration. However, a pledge or subscription in favor of a public, charitable, religious, or educational organization is deductible to the extent that it would have constituted an allowable deduction had it been a bequest.[34]

Deductible funeral expenses include the cost of interment, the burial plot or vault, a gravestone, perpetual care of the grave site, and the transportation expense of the person bringing the body to the place of burial. If the decedent had, before death, acquired cemetery lots for himself or herself and his or her family, no deduction will be allowed, but such lots will not be included in the decedent's gross estate under § 2033 (property in which the decedent had an interest).

Losses (§ 2054).   Section 2054 permits an estate tax deduction for losses from casualty or theft incurred during the period of settlement of the estate. As is true with casualty or theft losses for income tax purposes, any anticipated insurance recovery must be taken into account in arriving at the amount of the deductible loss. Unlike the income tax, however, the deduction is not limited by a floor ($100) or a percentage amount (the excess of 10 percent of adjusted gross income). If the casualty occurs to property after it has been distributed to an heir, the loss belongs to the heir and not to the estate. If the casualty occurs before the decedent's death, it should be claimed on the appropriate Form 1040. The fair market value of the property (if any) on the date of death plus any insurance recovery would be included in the gross estate.

As is true of certain administration expenses, a casualty or theft loss of estate property can be claimed as an income tax deduction on the fiduciary return of the estate (Form 1041). But the double deduction prohibition of § 642(g) applies: claiming the income tax deduction requires a waiver of the estate tax deduction.

Transfers to Charity (§§ 2055 and 2522).   A deduction is allowed for the value of property in the decedent's gross estate that was transferred by the decedent through testamentary disposition to (or for the use of) any of the following:

1. The United States or any political subdivision therein.

2. Any corporation or association organized and operated exclusively for religious, charitable, scientific, literary, or educational purposes, as long as no benefit inures to any private individual and no substantial activity is undertaken to carry on propaganda or otherwise attempt to influence legislation or participate in any political campaign on behalf of any candidate for public office.

3. A trustee or trustees of a fraternal society, order, or association operating under the lodge system if the transferred property is to be used exclusively for religious, charitable, scientific, literary, or educational purposes, and no substantial activity is undertaken to carry on propaganda or otherwise attempt to influence legislation or participate in any political campaign on behalf of any candidate for public office.

4. Any veterans' organization incorporated by an Act of Congress (or any of its subdivisions) as long as no benefit inures to any private individual.

The organizations just described are identical to the ones that qualify for the Federal gift tax deduction under § 2522. With the following two exceptions, they

---

34.   § 2053(c)(1)(A) and Reg. § 20.2053-5.

are also the same organizations that will qualify a donee for an income tax deduction under § 170:

- Certain nonprofit cemetery associations qualify for income tax but not death and gift tax purposes.

- Foreign charities may qualify under the estate and gift tax but not under the income tax.

No deduction will be allowed unless the charitable bequest is specified by a provision in the decedent's will or the transfer was made before death and the property is subsequently included in the gross estate. Generally speaking, a deduction does not materialize when an individual dies intestate (without a will). The bequest to charity must be mandatory as to the amount involved and cannot be based on the discretion of another. It is, however, permissible to allow another, such as the executor of the estate, the choice of which charity will receive the specified donation. Likewise, a bequest may be expressed as an alternative and still be effective if the noncharitable beneficiary disclaims (refuses) the intervening interest before the due date for the filing of the estate tax return (nine months after the decedent's death plus any extensions of time granted for filing).

Marital Deduction (§§ 2056 and 2523).   The marital deduction originated with the Revenue Act of 1948 as part of the same legislation that permitted married persons to secure the income-splitting advantages of filing joint income tax returns. The purpose of these statutory changes was to eliminate the major tax variations that could develop between taxpayers residing in community property and common law states. The marital deduction was designed to provide equity in the estate and gift tax areas.

In a community property state, for example, no marital deduction generally was allowed since the surviving spouse already owned one-half of the community and such portion was not included in the deceased spouse's gross estate. In a common law state, however, most if not all of the assets often belonged to the breadwinner of the family. Upon such person predeceasing, all of these assets were included in his or her gross estate. (Recall that a dower or curtesy interest [regarding a surviving spouse's right to some of the deceased spouse's property] does not reduce the gross estate.) To equalize the situation, therefore, a marital deduction, usually equal to one-half of all separate assets, was allowed upon the death of the first spouse.

Ultimately, Congress decided to dispense with these historical justifications and recognize husband and wife as a single economic unit. Consistent with the approach taken under the income tax, spouses are to be considered as one for transfer tax purposes. By making the marital deduction unlimited in amount, neither the gift tax nor the estate tax will be imposed on outright interspousal transfers of property. Unlike prior law, the unlimited marital deduction even includes one spouse's share of the community property transferred to the other spouse.

Under § 2056, the marital deduction is allowed only for property that is included in the deceased spouse's gross estate and that passes or has passed to the surviving spouse. Property that passes from the decedent to the surviving spouse includes any interest received as (1) the decedent's legatee, devisee, heir, or donee; (2) the decedent's surviving tenant by the entirety or joint tenant; (3) the appointee under the decedent's exercise (or lapse or release) of a general power of appointment; or (4) the beneficiary of insurance on the life of the decedent.

EXAMPLE 51	At the time of his death in the current year, D owned an insurance policy on his own life (face amount of $100,000) with W (his wife) as the designated beneficiary. D and W also owned real estate (worth $250,000) as tenants by the entirety (D having furnished all of the purchase price). As to these transfers, $225,000 ($100,000 + $125,000) would be included in D's gross estate, and this amount represents the property that passes to W for purposes of the marital deduction.[35] □

Under certain conditions, disclaimers of property by the surviving spouse in favor of some other heir will affect the amount that passes and therefore qualifies for the marital deduction. Thus, if W is entitled to $400,000 of H's property but disclaims $100,000 in favor of S, the remainderperson under the will, the $100,000 will pass from H to S and not from H to W. Disclaimers by some other heir in favor of the surviving spouse may have a similar effect. Suppose W, as remainderperson, will receive $300,000 under H's will, but the will also provides that S is to receive a specific bequest of $100,000. If S issues a timely disclaimer in favor of W, the amount passing from H to W for purposes of the marital deduction will be increased from $300,000 to $400,000.

When a property interest passes to the surviving spouse, subject to a mortgage or other encumbrance, or when an obligation is imposed upon the surviving spouse in connection with the passing of a property interest, only the net value of the interest after reduction by the amount of the mortgage or other encumbrance qualifies for the marital deduction. To allow otherwise would result in a double deduction since liabilities of a decedent are separately deductible under § 2053.

EXAMPLE 52	In his will, H leaves real estate (fair market value of $200,000) to his wife. If the real estate is subject to a mortgage of $40,000 (upon which H was personally liable), the marital deduction is limited to $160,000 ($200,000 − $40,000). The $40,000 mortgage is deductible under § 2053 as an obligation of the decedent (H). □

However, if the executor is required under the terms of the decedent's will or under local law to discharge the mortgage or other encumbrance out of other assets of the estate or to reimburse the surviving spouse, the payment or reimbursement constitutes an additional interest passing to the surviving spouse.

EXAMPLE 53	Assume the same facts as in Example 52, except that H's will directs that the real estate is to pass to his wife free of any liabilities. Accordingly, H's executor pays off the mortgage by using other estate assets and distributes the real estate to the wife. The marital deduction now becomes $200,000. □

Federal estate taxes or other death taxes that are paid out of the surviving spouse's share of the gross estate are not included in the value of property passing to the surviving spouse. Therefore, it is usually preferable for the deceased spouse's

---

35. Inclusion in the gross estate would fall under § 2042 (proceeds of life insurance) and § 2040 (joint interests). Although D provided the full purchase price for the real estate, § 2040(b) re- quires inclusion of only one-half of the value of the property when one spouse predeceases the other.

will to provide that death taxes be paid out of the portion of the estate that does not qualify for the marital deduction.

Certain interests in property passing from the deceased spouse to the surviving spouse are referred to as *terminable interests*. Such an interest is one that will terminate or fail after the passage of time, upon the happening of some contingency, or upon the failure of some event to occur. Examples are life estates, annuities, estates for terms of years, and patents. A terminable interest will not qualify for the marital deduction if another interest in the same property passed from the deceased spouse to some other person for less than adequate and full consideration in money or money's worth and, by reason of its passing, such other person or his or her heirs may enjoy part of the property after the termination of the surviving spouse's interest.[36]

EXAMPLE 54

H's will places H's property in trust with a life estate to W, remainder to S or his heirs. The interest passing from H to W does not qualify for the marital deduction. It will terminate on W's death, and S or his heirs will thereafter possess or enjoy the property. □

EXAMPLE 55

Assume the same facts as in Example 54, except that the trust was created by H during his life. No marital deduction is available for gift tax purposes for the same reason given in Example 54.[37] □

EXAMPLE 56

During his life, H purchased a joint and survivor annuity providing for payments to himself for life and then to W for life should she survive him. All payments cease on the death of H or W, whoever dies last. If H dies first, the value of the survivorship annuity included in his gross estate under § 2039(a) and passing to W will qualify for the marital deduction. Although W's interest in the annuity will terminate on W's death, it is not a terminable interest. No other person may possess or enjoy the property after W's death. □

The justification for the terminable interest rule can be illustrated by examining the possible result of Examples 54 and 55 more closely. Without the rule, H could have passed property to W at no cost because of the marital deduction. Yet, on W's death, none of the property would have been included in W's gross estate. Section 2036 (transfers with a retained life estate) would not apply to W since she was not the original transferor of the property. Apparently, then, the marital deduction should not be available in situations where the surviving spouse can enjoy the property and still pass it to another without tax consequences. The marital deduction merely postpones the transfer tax on the death of the first spouse and operates to shift any such tax to the surviving spouse.

Consistent with the objective of the terminable interest rule, an alternative means for obtaining the marital deduction is available. Under this provision, the marital deduction will be allowed for transfers of *qualified terminable interest property* (commonly referred to as QTIP), defined as property that passes from one spouse to another by gift or at death and for which the transferee-spouse has a qualifying income interest for life.

---

36. §§ 2056(b)(1) and 2523(b)(1).
37. Both Examples 54 and 55 contain the potential for a qualified terminable interest property (QTIP) election discussed later in this section.

For a donee or a surviving spouse, a qualifying income interest for life exists under the following conditions:

- Such person is entitled for life to all of the income from the property (or a specific portion thereof), payable at annual or more frequent intervals.

- No person (including the spouse) has a power to appoint any part of the property to any person other than the surviving spouse during his or her life.[38]

If these conditions are met, an election can be made to claim a marital deduction as to the QTIP. For estate tax purposes, the election is made by the executor of the estate on Form 706 (estate tax return). For gift tax purposes, the election is made by the donor spouse on Form 709 (gift tax return). The election is irrevocable.

If the election is made, a transfer tax will be imposed upon the QTIP when the transferee-spouse disposes of it by gift or upon death. If the disposition occurs during life, the gift tax applies measured by the fair market value of the property as of that time.[39] If no lifetime disposition takes place, the fair market value of the property on the date of death (or alternate valuation date if applicable) will be included in the gross estate of the transferee-spouse.[40]

EXAMPLE 57   In 1990, H dies and provides in his will that certain assets (fair market value of $400,000) are to be transferred to a trust under which W (H's wife) is granted a life estate with the remainder passing to their children upon her death. Presuming all of the preceding requirements are satisfied and H's executor so elects, H's estate will receive a marital deduction of $400,000. □

EXAMPLE 58   Assume the same facts as in Example 57, with the further stipulation that W dies in 1995 when the trust assets are worth $900,000. This amount must be included in W's gross estate. □

Because the estate tax will be imposed on assets not physically included in the probate estate, the law provides for a shifting of the liability attributable thereto to the heirs. The amount that can be shifted is to be determined by comparing the estate tax liability both with and without the inclusion of the QTIP. This right of recovery can be negated by a provision in the deceased spouse's will.[41]

ESOP Deduction (§ 2057).   As amended by the Revenue Act of 1987, § 2057 allows an estate a deduction of 50 percent of the proceeds from the sale of employer securities to an employee stock ownership plan (ESOP) or an eligible worker-owned cooperative. The sale can be only of securities that are not publicly traded. The deduction is limited to 50 percent of the taxable estate (determined without regard to § 2057) and cannot reduce estate taxes by more than $750,000.

Holding period requirements are imposed to impede a planned sale in an imminent death situation. The deduction is not allowed unless the decedent has held the securities for at least the lesser of (1) five years before death or (2) the period from October 22, 1986, to the date of death.

38. §§ 2523(f) and 2056(b)(7).   40. § 2044.
39. § 2519.   41. § 2207A(a).

The purchaser of the employer securities (ESOP or qualified cooperative) must allocate them (or hold them for future allocation) to the plan participants. The purchaser may be subject to a special excise tax if the plan fails to make the allocation or disposes of the securities within a prescribed period of time.

Computing the Federal Estate Tax

Once the taxable estate has been determined, post-1976 taxable gifts are added to arrive at the tax base. Note that pre-1977 taxable gifts do not enter into the computation of the tax base.

EXAMPLE 59   D dies in 1990, leaving a taxable estate of $800,000. During her life, D made taxable gifts as follows: $50,000 in 1975 and $100,000 in 1982. For estate tax purposes, the Federal estate tax base becomes $900,000, determined as follows: $800,000 taxable estate + $100,000 taxable gift made in 1982. ☐

With the unified transfer tax rate schedule contained in § 2001(c), the tentative tax on the tax base is then computed. Using the facts in Example 59, the tax on $900,000 is $306,800 [$248,300 + (39% × $150,000)]—see Appendix A. (See the discussion below for the phase-out of the unified tax credit and the graduated tax rates for certain large estates.)

All available estate tax credits are subtracted from the tentative estate tax to arrive at the estate tax (if any) that is due.

Estate Tax Credits

Unified Tax Credit (§ 2010).   Recall, from previous discussion of this credit, that the amount of the credit allowed depends upon the year of the transfer. Returning to Example 59, the credit allowed on the gift in 1982 would be $62,800. Since the exemption equivalent of this amount is $225,000 (refer to Figure 25–3), no gift tax is due on the transfer. On D's death in 1990, however, the unified tax credit is $192,800, which is less than the tentative tax of $306,800 (refer to the discussion following Example 59). Disregarding the effect of any other estate tax credits, D's estate owes a tax of $114,000 ($306,800 tentative tax on a tax base of $900,000 − $192,800 unified tax credit for 1990).

Recall also that an adjustment to the unified tax credit will be necessary if any portion of the specific exemption was utilized on gifts made after September 8, 1976, and before January 1, 1977. In this regard, refer to Example 4.

Under the Revenue Act of 1987, the benefit of the unified tax credit and of the graduated unified tax rates is phased out for taxable transfers exceeding a certain amount. The gift and estate tax liability for taxable transfers in excess of $10 million is increased by 5 percent of such excess until the benefit of the credit and graduated brackets is recaptured.

Credit for State Death Taxes (§ 2011).   Section 2011 allows a limited credit for the amount of any death, inheritance, legacy, or succession tax actually paid to any state (or to the District of Columbia) attributable to any property included in the gross estate. Like the credit for foreign death taxes paid, this provision mitigates the harshness of subjecting the same property to multiple death taxes.

The credit allowed is limited to the lesser of the amount of tax actually paid or the amount provided for in a table contained in § 2011(b). (See Appendix A.) The

table amount is based on the adjusted taxable estate, which for this purpose is the taxable estate less $60,000. No credit is allowed if the adjusted taxable estate is $40,000 or less.

EXAMPLE 60   D's taxable estate is $98,000, and the state of appropriate jurisdiction imposes a death tax of $1,500 on this amount. Since the adjusted taxable estate is $38,000 ($98,000 − $60,000), none of the $1,500 paid qualifies for the death tax credit. □

EXAMPLE 61   D's taxable estate is $200,000, and the state of appropriate jurisdiction imposes a death tax of $3,000 on this amount. Because the adjusted gross estate is $140,000 ($200,000 − $60,000), the table amount limits the death tax credit to $1,200. □

As noted in Examples 60 and 61, the credit allowed by § 2011 may prove to be less than the amount of state death taxes paid. The reverse is, of course, possible but usually not the case. Most states ensure that the minimum tax payable to the jurisdiction is at least equal to the credit allowed by the table. Sometimes this result is accomplished by a sponge tax superimposed on the regular inheritance tax. Thus, if the regular inheritance tax yielded $2,500, but the maximum credit allowed by the table is $3,200, a sponge tax would impose an additional $700 in state death taxes. In other states, the whole state death tax liability depends entirely upon the amount allowed for Federal estate tax purposes as the credit under the table. Thus, in the previous illustration, the state death tax would be an automatic $3,200.

Credit for Gift Taxes (§ 2012).   A credit is allowed under § 2012 against the estate tax for any Federal gift tax paid on a gift of property subsequently included in the donor-decedent's gross estate.

EXAMPLE 62   In 1965, D transfers a remainder interest in a farm to her children, retaining for herself a life estate. As a result of the transfer, D incurred and paid a Federal gift tax of $45,000. D dies in 1990 when the property is worth $400,000. Since the application of § 2036 (retention of a life estate) forces the inclusion of the farm in D's gross estate, a double tax effect results. To mitigate this effect, § 2012 allows D's estate a credit for some or all of the $45,000 previously paid in gift taxes. □

The adjustments that might be necessary in working out the amount of the credit could become somewhat complicated and are not discussed further here.[42]

Only taxable gifts made after 1976 will be added to the donor's taxable estate in arriving at the base for the application of the unified transfer tax at death. To the extent these gifts have exceeded the unified tax credit and have generated a tax, such tax should be credited against the transfer tax due at death.

Credit for Tax on Prior Transfers (§ 2013).   Suppose D owns some property that he passes at death to S. Shortly thereafter, S dies and passes the property to R. Assuming both estates are subject to the Federal estate tax, one can easily

---

42. They are illustrated and explained in the instructions to Form 706 and in Reg. § 20.2012–1.

imagine the multiple effect involved in successive deaths. To mitigate the possible multiple taxation that might result, § 2013 provides relief in the form of a credit for a death tax on prior transfers. Thus, with regard to the preceding hypothetical case, S's estate may be able to claim as an estate tax credit some of the taxes paid by D's estate.

The credit is limited to the lesser of the following:

1. The amount of the Federal estate tax attributable to the transferred property in the transferor's estate.

2. The amount of the Federal estate tax attributable to the transferred property in the decedent's estate.

To apply the preceding limitations, certain adjustments must be made that are not covered in this text.[43] Note, however, that it is not necessary for the transferred property to be identified in the present decedent's estate or for it to be in existence at the time of the present decedent's death. It is sufficient that the transfer of property was subjected to the Federal estate tax in the estate of the transferor and that the transferor died within the prescribed period of time.

If the transferor died within two years before or after the present decedent's death, the credit is allowed in full (subject to the preceding limitations). If the transferor died more than two years before the decedent, the credit is a certain percentage: 80 percent if the transferor died within the third or fourth year preceding the decedent's death, 60 percent if within the fifth or sixth year, 40 percent if within the seventh or eighth year, and 20 percent if within the ninth or tenth year.

EXAMPLE 63   Pursuant to D's will, S inherits property. One year later S dies. Assume the estate tax attributable to the inclusion of the property in D's gross estate was $15,000 and that attributable to the inclusion of the property in S's gross estate is $12,000. Under these circumstances, S's estate may claim a credit against the estate tax of $12,000 (refer to limitation 2). □

EXAMPLE 64   Assume the same facts as in Example 63, except that S dies three years after D's death. The applicable credit is now 80% of $12,000, or $9,600. □

Credit for Foreign Death Taxes (§ 2014).   Under § 2014, a credit is allowed against the estate tax for any estate, inheritance, legacy, or succession tax actually paid to any foreign country. For purposes of this provision, the term "foreign country" not only means states in the international sense but also refers to possessions or political subdivisions of foreign states and to possessions of the United States.

Procedural Matters

A Federal estate tax return, if required, is due nine months after the date of the decedent's death.[44] This time limit applies to all estates regardless of the nationality or residence of the decedent. Frequently, however, an executor will request and obtain from the IRS an extension of time for filing Form 706 (estate tax return).

---

43. See the instructions to Form 706 and Reg. §§ 20.2013–2 and –3.

44. § 6075(a).

For the estate of a citizen or resident of the United States dying after 1976, Form 706 must be filed by the executor or administrator under the following conditions:[45]

Year of Death	Gross Estate in Excess of
1977	$120,000
1978	134,000
1979	147,000
1980	161,000
1981	175,000
1982	225,000
1983	275,000
1984	325,000
1985	400,000
1986	500,000
1987 & thereafter	600,000

Note that the filing requirements parallel the exemption equivalent amounts of the unified tax credit available for each year (refer to Figure 25–3). The filing requirements may be lower when the decedent has made taxable gifts after 1976 or has utilized any of the $30,000 specific gift tax exemption after September 8, 1976.

EXAMPLE 65   D dies in 1990, leaving a gross estate of $595,000. If D never made any post-1976 taxable gifts or used the specific gift tax exemption after September 8, 1976, Form 706 need not be filed by his estate.   □

EXAMPLE 66   Assume the same facts as in Example 65, except that D made a taxable gift of $20,000 in 1980. Since the filing requirement now becomes $580,000 ($600,000 regular filing requirement for 1990 − $20,000 post-1976 taxable gift), Form 706 must be filed by D's estate.   □

Form 706 must be filed with the IRS Service Center serving the district in which the decedent lived at the time of death. The return must be accompanied by various documents relevant to the determination of tax liability.

THE GENERATION-SKIPPING TRANSFER TAX

In order to preclude partial avoidance of Federal gift and estate taxes on large transfers, the tax law imposes an additional generation-skipping transfer tax.

45. § 6018(a).

The Problem

Previously, it was possible to bypass a generation of transfer taxes by structuring the transaction carefully.

EXAMPLE 67   Under his will, GF creates a trust, life estate to F (GF's son) and remainder to GD (GF's granddaughter) upon F's death. GF will be subject to the Federal estate tax, but no such tax comes about as a result of F's death. Although F held a life estate, § 2036 does not apply since F was not the grantor of the trust. Nor does § 2033 (property owned by the decedent) come into play because F's interest disappeared upon his death. The ultimate result, therefore, is that the property in trust skips a generation of transfer taxes. □

EXAMPLE 68   GM gives assets to GS (her grandson). Called a direct skip, the gift would circumvent any transfer taxes that would have resulted had the assets been channeled through GS's parents. □

The Solution

The generation-skipping transfer tax (GSTT) is imposed when a younger generation is bypassed in favor of a later generation.[46] The GSTT applies to lifetime transfers by gift made after September 25, 1985, and to transfers by death occurring after October 22, 1986. The tax rate imposed is the highest rate under the gift and estate tax schedule—55 percent through 1992 and 50 percent thereafter. Consequently, the GSTT does not permit the use of the graduated rate structure.

The application of the GSTT depends upon the type of arrangement involved. In Example 67 the GSTT would be imposed upon the death of F (the life tenant). The tax, however, would be levied against the trust. In effect, therefore, it reduces the amount that would be distributed to GD (the remainderperson).

In Example 68, the GSTT is imposed upon GM when the gift is made to GS. In this situation, not only will GM be subject to the GSTT, but the amount of such tax represents an additional gift to GS.[47] Thus, if a gift is a direct skip (such as Example 68), the total transfer tax (the GSTT plus the gift tax) might well exceed what the donee receives.

Though the GSTT may appear to yield a confiscatory result, every grantor is entitled to a $1 million exemption. The exemption can be applied to whichever transfers the grantor (or personal representative of the grantor) chooses. Any appreciation attributable to the exempted portion of the transfer will not be subject to the GSTT.

EXAMPLE 69   Assume the same facts as in Example 67 except that the trust created by GF contained assets valued at $1,000,000. Ten years later when F dies, the trust is now worth $3,000,000. If the exemption of $1,000,000 is used upon the creation of the trust, no GSTT results upon F's death. □

---

46. The generation-skipping transfer tax provisions are contained in §§ 2601-2663 of the Code.

47. § 2515.

CONCEPT SUMMARY 25-2

Federal Estate Tax

1. Both the Federal gift and estate taxes are excise taxes on the transfer of wealth.

2. The starting point for applying the Federal estate tax is to determine which assets are subject to tax. Such assets constitute a decedent's gross estate. The gross estate must be distinguished from the probate estate, since the latter classification includes assets subject to administration by the executor of the estate.

3. Although the gross estate generally will not include any gifts made by the decedent within three years of death, it will include any gift tax paid on such transfers.

4. Based on the premise that one should not continue to enjoy or control property and not have it subject to the estate tax, certain incomplete transfers are subject to inclusion in the gross estate.

5. Upon the death of a joint tenant, the full value of the property will be included in the gross estate unless the survivor(s) made a contribution toward the cost of the property. Spouses are subject to a special rule that calls for automatic inclusion of one-half of the value of the property in the gross estate of the first tenant to die. As to joint tenancies (or tenancies by the entirety) between husband and wife, it therefore makes no difference who furnished the original consideration. The creation of joint ownership will be subject to the gift tax when a tenant receives a lesser interest in the property than is warranted by the consideration furnished.

6. If the decedent is the insured, life insurance proceeds will be included in the gross estate if either of two conditions is satisfied. First, the proceeds are payable to the estate or for the benefit of the estate. Second, the decedent had possessed incidents of ownership (e.g., the right to change beneficiaries) over the policy. A transfer of an unmatured life insurance policy is subject to the gift tax. A gift also occurs when a policy matures and the owner of the policy is not the insured or the beneficiary.

7. In moving from the gross estate to the taxable estate, certain deductions are allowed. Under § 2053, deductions are permitted for various administration expenses (e.g., executor's commissions, funeral costs), debts of the decedent, and certain unpaid taxes. Casualty and theft losses incurred during the administration of an estate also can be deducted in arriving at the taxable estate.

8. Charitable transfers are deductible if the designated organization holds qualified status with the IRS at the time of the gift or upon death.

9. Transfers to a spouse qualify for the gift or estate tax marital deduction. Except as noted in (10), such transfers are subject to the terminable interest limitation.

10. The terminable interest limitation will not apply if the QTIP election is made. In the case of a lifetime transfer, the donor spouse makes the QTIP election. In the case of a testamentary transfer, however, the executor of the estate of the deceased spouse has the election responsibility.

11. Subject to limitations, a deduction of one-half of the selling price is allowed an estate for sale of employer stock to an ESOP.

12. The tax base for determining the estate tax is the taxable estate plus all post-1976 taxable gifts. From the tax so derived, all available credits are subtracted.

13. Of prime importance in the tax credit area is the unified tax credit. Except for large taxable transfers, the unified tax credit is $192,800 (exemption equivalent of $600,000).

14. Other Federal estate tax credits include credits for state death taxes, gift taxes, tax on prior transfers, and foreign death taxes.

15. If due, a Federal estate tax return (Form 706) must be filed within nine months of the date of the decedent's death. The IRS grants extensions for estates that encounter difficulty in complying with this deadline.

TAX PLANNING CONSIDERATIONS

The Federal Gift Tax

Before 1977, two sets of tax rates applicable to transfers for insufficient consideration existed. Since the gift tax rates were lower than the estate tax rates, this, by itself, placed a premium on lifetime giving as a means of reducing the overall tax burden. After 1976, however, the estate tax savings from a lifetime gift usually is limited to the appreciation on the property that develops after the transfer is made. This result materializes because transfers by gift and by death are now subject to the same set of rates [the uniform transfer tax of § 2001(c)]. Also, taxable gifts made after 1976 must be added to the taxable estate in arriving at the amount of the estate tax.

As to taxable gifts that generate a tax, consideration must be given to the time value to the donor of the gift taxes paid. Since the donor loses the use of these funds, the expected interval between a gift (the imposition of the gift tax) and death (the imposition of the death tax) might make the gift less attractive from an economic standpoint. On the plus side, however, are the estate tax savings that would result from any gift tax paid. Since these funds are no longer in the gross estate of the donor (except for gifts within three years of death), the estate tax thereon is avoided.

Gifts made after 1976 do, nevertheless, possess distinct advantages. First, and often most important, income from the property will generally be shifted to the donee. If the donee is in a lower bracket than the donor, the family unit will save on income taxes. Second, the proper spacing of gifts can further cut down the Federal gift tax by maximizing the number of annual exclusions available. Third, all states impose some type of death tax, but only a minority impose a gift tax. Thus, a gift might completely avoid a state transfer tax.

In minimizing gift tax liability in lifetime giving, the optimum use of the annual exclusion can have significant results. Important in this regard are the following observations:

1. Because the annual exclusion is available every year, space the gifts over as many years as possible. To carry out this objective, start the program of lifetime giving as soon as is feasible. As an illustration, a donor could give as much as $100,000 to a donee if equally spaced over a 10-year period without using any of the unified tax credit and incurring any gift tax.

2. To the extent consistent with the wishes of the donor, maximize the number of donees. For example, a donor could give $500,000 to five donees over a 10-year period ($100,000 apiece) without using any of the unified tax credit and incurring any gift tax.

3. For the married donor, make use of the election to split gifts. As an example, a married couple can give $1,000,000 to five donees over a 10-year period ($20,000 per donee each year) without using any of their unified tax credit and incurring any gift tax.

4. Watch out for gifts of future interests. As noted earlier in the chapter, the annual exclusion is available only for gifts of a present interest.

THE FEDERAL ESTATE TAX

Controlling the Amount of the Gross Estate.   Presuming an estate tax problem is anticipated, the starting point for planning purposes would be to

reduce the size of the potential gross estate. Aside from initiating a program of lifetime giving, several other possibilities exist.

Incomplete Transfers. If property is to be excluded from a donee's gross estate by means of a lifetime transfer, the consequences of transfers deemed incomplete for estate tax purposes must be recognized. In general, transfers are considered incomplete if the transferor continues to exercise control over the property or to enjoy its use.

EXAMPLE 70   Ten years ago, M transferred title to her personal residence to D, her daughter. Until the time of her death in the current year, M continued to live in the residence. □

In Example 70, the residence will be included in the gross estate of the donor (M) if an express or implied agreement exists between the donor and the donee for continued occupancy of the property.[48] This result is dictated by § 2036(a)(1): the transferor did not surrender the right to possession or enjoyment of the property.

If no express or implied agreement exists between the parties, may one be inferred by virtue of the fact that the transferor does not vacate the premises after the gift but continues to live there until his or her death? In this regard, the situation described in Example 70 could be precarious, to say the least.

An implied agreement will probably be found in Example 70 unless the parties can produce some strong proof to show otherwise. An affirmative answer to any of the following questions would be helpful, though not controlling, in excluding the residence from M's gross estate:

- Did M report the transfer on a gift tax return and, if appropriate, pay a Federal gift tax thereon?

- Did M pay a reasonable rental to D for her continued occupancy of the premises?

- Did D, as any owner might be expected to do, absorb the cost of maintaining the property?

- If the property was income producing (e.g., a farm or ranch), did D collect and report the income therefrom?[49]

Life Insurance. If the insured wants to keep the proceeds of a life insurance policy out of his or her gross estate, no incidents of ownership can be retained. All too often, a policy is transferred, but the transferor has unsuspectingly retained some incident of ownership that may cause inclusion in the gross estate. The only way to prevent this from happening is to carefully examine the policy itself and ensure that all incidents of ownership have been released.

Recall that a gift of a life insurance policy made within three years of the death of the owner-insured will be ineffective in terms of keeping the maturity value of the policy out of the gross estate. In this regard, refer to Example 28. To avoid this trap concerning gifts of life insurance policies, the sooner transferred the better since death usually is an unpredictable event.

---

48. See, for example, *Guynn v. U.S.,* 71–1 USTC ¶12,742, 27 AFTR2d 71–1653, 437 F.2d 1148 (CA–4, 1971).

49. Compare, for example, *Estate of Ethel R. Kerdolff,* 57 T.C. 643 (1972) with *Estate of Roy D. Barlow,* 55 T.C. 666 (1971).

Proper Handling of Estate Tax Deductions.   Estate taxes can be saved either by reducing the size of the gross estate or by increasing the total allowable deductions. Thus, the lower the taxable estate, the less the amount of estate tax generated. Planning in the deduction area generally involves the following considerations:

- Making proper use of the marital deduction.

- Working effectively with the charitable deduction.

- Properly handling other deductions and losses allowed under §§ 2053 and 2054.

The Marital Deduction in Perspective.   When planning for the estate tax marital deduction, both tax and nontax factors have to be taken into account. In the tax area, two major goals exist that guide planning. They are the equalization and the deferral approaches described as follows:

- Attempt to equalize the estates of both spouses. Clearly, for example, the estate tax on $2,000,000 is more than double the estate tax on $1,000,000 [compare $780,800 with $691,600 ($345,800 × 2)].

- Try to postpone estate taxation as long as possible. On a $1,000,000 amount, for example, what is the time value of $345,800 in estate taxes deferred for a period of, say, 10 years?

Barring certain circumstances, the deferral approach generally is preferable. By maximizing the marital deduction on the death of the first spouse to die, not only are taxes saved, but the surviving spouse is enabled to trim his or her future estate by entering into a program of lifetime giving. By making optimum use of the annual exclusion, considerable amounts can be gifted without incurring *any* transfer tax.

Tax planning must remain flexible and be tailored to the individual circumstances of the parties involved. Before the equalization approach is cast aside, therefore, consider the following variables:

- Both spouses are of advanced age and/or in poor health, and neither is expected to survive the other for a prolonged period of time.

- The spouse who is expected to survive has considerable assets of his or her own. To illustrate, a spouse that passes a $250,000 estate to a survivor who already has assets of $1,000,000 is trading a 32 percent bracket for a later 43 percent bracket.

- Because of appreciation, property worth $250,000 when it passes to the surviving spouse today may be worth $1,000,000 five years later when the survivor dies.

The Marital Deduction—Sophistication of the Deferral Approach.   When the saving of estate taxes for the family unit is the sole consideration, the equalization and deferral approaches can be combined with maximum effect.

EXAMPLE 71   At the time of his death in 1989, H had never made any post-1976 taxable gifts or used his specific exemption on any pre-1977 gifts. Under H's will, H's disposable estate of $1,100,000 passes to W, H's surviving spouse. For this purpose, the disposable estate means the gross estate less administration and other expenses and debts.   □

EXAMPLE 72   Assume the same facts as in Example 71, except that H's will provides as follows: $600,000 to the children and the remainder ($500,000) to W.   □

From a tax standpoint, which is the better plan? Although no estate tax results from either arrangement, Example 71 represents overkill in terms of the marital deduction. Why place an additional $600,000 in W's potential estate when it can pass free of tax to the children through the application of the $192,800 unified tax credit available for 1989? (Keep in mind that the exemption equivalent of $192,800 is $600,000.) Clearly, then, the arrangement in Example 72 is to be preferred, as it avoids unnecessary concentration of wealth in W's estate.

On occasion the disclaimer procedure can be used to maximize the deferral approach.

EXAMPLE 73   At the time of his death in 1989, H had never made any post-1976 gifts or used his specific exemption on pre-1977 gifts. Under H's will, H's disposable estate of $1,500,000 passes as follows: $700,000 to S (H's adult son) and the remainder ($800,000) to W (H's surviving spouse). Shortly after H's death, S issues a disclaimer as to $100,000 of his $700,000 bequest. Such amount, therefore, passes to W as the remainderperson under H's will.   □

Because the unified tax credit for 1989 is $192,800 (with an exemption equivalent of $600,000), S's disclaimer avoids an estate tax on $100,000. The end result is to increase the marital deduction by $100,000 and eliminate *any* estate tax upon H's death.

Effectively Working with the Charitable Deduction.   As a general guide to obtain overall tax savings, lifetime charitable transfers are to be preferred over testamentary dispositions. For example, an individual who gave $10,000 to a qualified charity during his or her life would secure an income tax deduction, avoid any gift tax, and reduce the gross estate by the amount of the gift. By way of contrast, if the $10,000 had been willed to charity, no income tax deduction would be available, and the amount of the gift would be includible in the decedent's gross estate (though later deducted for estate tax purposes). In short, the lifetime transfer provides a double tax benefit (income tax deduction plus reduced estate taxes) at no gift tax cost. The testamentary transfer merely neutralizes the effect of the inclusion of the property in the gross estate (inclusion under § 2033 and then deduction under § 2055).

On occasion, a charitable bequest may be dependent on the issuance of a disclaimer by a noncharitable heir. Such a situation frequently arises when special types of property or collections, which the decedent may feel a noncharitable heir should have a choice of receiving, are involved. If the charitable organization is the residuary legatee under a decedent's will, a disclaimer by a specific legatee passes the property by operation of the will to the holder of the residual interest and qualifies the estate for a charitable deduction under § 2055. Any exercise of such disclaimers in favor of charitable organizations should be carefully considered. Another course may be more advantageous from a tax standpoint.

EXAMPLE 74   D specified in his will that his valuable art collection is to pass to his son or, if the son refuses, to a designated and qualified art museum. At the time the will was drawn, D knew that his son was not interested in owning the art collection.

If, after D's death, the son issues a timely disclaimer, the art collection will pass to the designated museum, and D's estate will be allowed a charitable deduction for its death tax value. ☐

EXAMPLE 75

D's will specifies that one-half of his disposable estate is to pass to his wife and the remainder of his property to a designated and qualified charitable organization. If the wife issues a timely disclaimer after D's death, all of the property will pass to the charity and will qualify for the § 2055 charitable deduction. ☐

Did the son in Example 74 act wisely if he issued the disclaimer in favor of the museum? Although such a disclaimer would provide D's estate with a deduction for the value of the art collection, consider the income tax deduction alternative. If the son accepts the bequest, he can still dispose of the collection (and fulfill his father's philanthropic objectives) through lifetime donation to the museum and, at the same time, obtain for himself an income tax deduction under § 170. Whether this will save taxes for the family unit depends on a comparison of the father's estate tax bracket with the estimated income tax bracket of the son. If the value of the collection runs afoul of the percentage limitations of § 170(b)(1), the donations could be spread over more than one year. If this is done, and to protect against the contingency of the son's dying before donation of the entire collection, the son could neutralize any potential death tax consequences by providing in his will for the undonated balance to pass to the museum.

The use of a disclaimer in Example 75 would be sheer folly. It would not reduce D's estate tax; it would merely substitute a charitable deduction for the marital deduction. Whether the wife issues a disclaimer or not, no estate taxes will be due. The wife would be well-advised to accept her legacy and, if she is so inclined, to make lifetime gifts of it to a qualified charity. In so doing, she generates an income tax deduction for herself.

Proper Handling of Other Deductions and Losses under §§ 2053 and 2054. Many § 2053 and § 2054 deductions and losses may be claimed either as estate tax deductions or as income tax deductions of the estate on the fiduciary return (Form 1041), but a choice must be made.[50] In such a case, the deduction for income tax purposes will not be allowed unless the estate tax deduction is waived. It is possible for these deductions to be apportioned between the two returns. Certain expenses exist that do not follow this general rule. These variations are summarized as follows:

1. An expense deductible for estate tax purposes may not qualify as an income tax deduction. An example might be interest expense incurred to carry tax-exempt bonds that is disallowed for income tax purposes under § 265(a)(2). If this expense is not claimed under § 2053 for estate tax purposes, it will be completely lost.

2. Medical expenses incurred by the decedent but unpaid at the time of the decedent's death are covered by a special rule. If paid out of the estate during a one-year period beginning with the day after death, these expenses may be claimed as an income tax deduction in the year incurred or as an estate tax deduction, but not both.[51] Thus, the choice is between the decedent's appro-

---

50. § 642(g) and Reg. § 20.2053–1(d).   51. § 213(c).

priate Form 1040 and the estate's estate tax return. Such expenses may be split (divided in any way between Form 1040 and the estate tax return). Note that the estate's income tax return (Form 1041) is not involved.

3. Expenses in respect of a decedent fall into a special classification. Generally, they are expenses of a cash basis taxpayer, accrued at the time of the taxpayer's death but not deductible on the final Form 1040 by reason of the method of accounting.[52] Such deductions are allowed both for income tax and estate tax purposes. The deductions are available for income tax purposes to whoever is liable for and makes the payment. They include business and nonbusiness expenses (§§ 162 and 212), interest (§ 163), taxes (§ 164), and a possible credit for foreign taxes (§ 27). A deduction for depletion is allowed to the recipient of the income to which it relates.

4. Brokerage commissions and other expenses relating to the sale of estate property can be offset against the sale price of the property in computing taxable income of the estate or can be deducted on the estate tax return. A choice will have to be made whether these expenses will be claimed as income tax or estate tax deductions.

The preceding rules can be illustrated by the following examples:

EXAMPLE 76   The executor of D's estate is paid a proper commission (authorized under local law and approved by the probate court of appropriate jurisdiction) of $10,000 from estate assets. Such commission expense can be claimed on the estate tax return (Form 706) or on the income tax return of the estate (Form 1041), or split in any way between the two returns. However, no more than $10,000 can be claimed. □

EXAMPLE 77   The executor of D's estate pays $5,000 in burial expenses (authorized under local law and approved by the probate court of appropriate jurisdiction) from estate assets. The $5,000 expense should be claimed on the estate tax return; it is not an item properly deductible for income tax purposes. □

EXAMPLE 78   At the time of his death, D (a cash basis taxpayer) owed a local bank $10,000 on a loan due in several months. On the due date of the loan, the executor of D's estate pays the bank $10,800, which represents the principal amount of the loan ($10,000), interest accrued before D's death ($700), and interest accrued after D's death ($100). The amount deductible on the estate tax return (Form 706) is $10,700.[53] Because the interest accrued before D's death is an expense in respect of a decedent, it can also be claimed as an income tax deduction by whoever pays it. Since the interest was paid by the estate, it should be claimed on the estate's income tax return (Form 1041) along with the $100 of interest expense accrued after D's death. □

---

52. § 691(b).

53. The loan and interest accrued before death are deductible as a claim against the estate under § 2053(a)(3). This does not include any interest accrued after death. In this regard, it would not matter if the executor elected the alternate valuation date (see chapter 12) for the estate. See Reg. § 20.2053–4 and Rev.Rul. 77–461, 1977–2 C.B. 324. Compare *Estate of Jane deP. Webster*, 65 T.C. 968 (1976).

When a choice is available in the handling of §§ 2053 and 2054 expenses and losses, any decision must take into account different tax implications. A number of questions first have to be asked and satisfactorily resolved. Is the executor or executrix of the estate also the residuary legatee? If so, it would usually be rather pointless for him or her to claim any commissions due for serving in the capacity of executor or executrix. Although it would generate a § 2053 deduction (on Form 706) or an income tax deduction on the fiduciary return of the estate (on Form 1041), claiming the commission results in taxable income to the executor or executrix. If the commission is not claimed, the amount involved should pass through to the executor or executrix tax-free by virtue of his or her rights as residuary legatee.[54]

PROBLEM MATERIALS

Discussion Questions

1. The unified transfer tax adopts a different approach to the taxation of life and death transfers after 1976. Explain.

2. Why can the unified transfer tax be categorized as an excise tax? In this regard, how does it differ from an income tax?

3. Upon whom is the Federal gift tax imposed? Suppose such party is unable to pay the tax?

4. What are the major differences between the Federal estate tax and the typical inheritance tax levied by many states?

5. T, a resident and citizen of Canada, owns real estate located in Rochester, New York.
   a. Would T be subject to the U.S. gift tax if she transferred this property as a gift to her Canadian son?
   b. Would T be subject to the U.S. estate tax if she died and left the property to her Canadian son?

6. Explain what is meant by the statement that the Federal gift tax is cumulative in nature.

7. What effect, if any, do prior gifts made by a decedent have on the determination of the decedent's estate tax liability?

8. What effect, if any, does prior utilization of the $30,000 specific exemption have on the unified tax credit currently available?

9. What is meant by the exemption equivalent of the unified tax credit?

10. Reg. § 25.2512–8 states: "A consideration not reducible to a value in money or money's worth, as love and affection, promise of marriage, etc., is to be wholly disregarded, and the entire value of the property transferred constitutes the amount of the gift."
    a. What does this Regulation mean?
    b. When might it apply?

11. X sells property to Y for $50,000. If the property is really worth $100,000, has X made a gift to Y? What additional facts would you want to know before answering this question?

---

54. Section 102(a) specifies that a "bequest, devise, or inheritance" is excludible from gross income.

12. In connection with gift loans, comment on the following points:
    a. Since any interest element recognized by the lender as income can be deducted by the borrower, the income tax effect is neutralized for the family unit.
    b. The borrower's net investment income for the year is less than $1,000.
    c. The gift loan involved only $95,000.
    d. The lender charged the borrower interest of 2%.

13. In the absence of § 2516, why would certain property settlements incident to a divorce be subject to the Federal gift tax?

14. In connection with § 2518 dealing with disclaimers, comment on the following:
    a. The role of state law.
    b. The avoidance of a Federal gift tax or the Federal estate tax.
    c. The disclaimer of only a partial interest.

15. What is the justification for the annual exclusion? In what manner does it resemble the gift tax treatment of the following?
    a. Tuition payments to an educational organization on behalf of another.
    b. Medical care payments on behalf of another.

16. In connection with the gift-splitting provision of § 2513, comment on the following:
    a. What it was designed to accomplish.
    b. How the election is made.
    c. Its utility in a community property jurisdiction.

17. D makes the following taxable gifts: $200,000 in 1975 and $450,000 in 1990. On the 1975 gift, D incurred and paid a Federal gift tax of $40,000. How should the gift tax be determined on the 1990 gift?

18. In connection with the filing of a Federal gift tax return, comment on the following:
    a. No Federal gift tax is due.
    b. The § 2513 election to split gifts is to be used.
    c. A gift of a future interest is involved.
    d. The donor uses a fiscal year for Federal income tax purposes.
    e. The donor obtained from the IRS an extension of time for filing his or her Federal income tax return.

19. Distinguish between the following:
    a. The gross estate and the taxable estate.
    b. The gross estate and the probate estate.

20. No taxable gifts made within three years of death will be included in the gross estate of the donor. Evaluate the soundness of this statement.

21. D transfers a remainder interest in her residence to her adult son and continues to occupy the premises until her death five years later. Will the property be included in D's probate estate? Gross estate?

22. Using community property, H creates a trust with a life estate to W (H's wife), remainder to their children upon W's death.
    a. Is there any estate tax effect upon H's death four years later?
    b. Is there any estate tax effect upon W's death five years later?

23. It has been said that community property is much like a tenancy in common. Do you agree? Why or why not?

24. At the time of X's death, X was a joint tenant with Y in a parcel of real estate. With regard to the inclusion in X's gross estate under § 2040, comment on the following independent assumptions:
    a. The property was received by X and Y as a gift from D.
    b. Y provided all of the purchase price of the property.
    c. Y's contribution was received as a gift from X.
    d. X's contribution was derived from income generated by property received by X as a gift from Y.

25. T owns a policy on the life of S, with D as the designated beneficiary. Upon S's death, the insurance proceeds are paid to D.
    a. Are any of the proceeds included in S's gross estate?
    b. Does S's death generate any tax consequences to T?

26. For tax purposes, what difference does it make whether a casualty loss occurs before or after the death of the owner of the property?

27. In terms of the QTIP (qualified terminable interest property) election, comment on the following:
    a. Who makes the election.
    b. What the election accomplishes.
    c. The tax effect of the election upon the death of the surviving spouse.

Problems

28. In each of the following independent situations, indicate whether or not the transfer by D is, or could be, subject to the Federal gift tax:
    a. D makes a contribution to an influential political figure.
    b. D makes a contribution to B Corporation, of which he is not a shareholder.
    c. In consideration of his upcoming marriage to B, D establishes a savings account in B's name.
    d. Same as (c). After their marriage, D establishes a joint checking account in the names of "D and B."
    e. Same as (d). One year after the checking account is established, B withdraws all of the funds.
    f. D enters into an agreement with B whereby he will transfer property to her in full satisfaction of her marital rights. One month after the agreement, the transfer occurs. Later D and B are divorced.
    g. D purchases U.S. savings bonds, listing ownership as "D and B." Several years later, and after D's death, B redeems the bonds.

29. In each of the following independent situations, indicate whether or not the transfer by D is, or could be, subject to the Federal gift tax:
    a. D purchases real estate and lists title as "D and B as joint tenants." D and B are brothers.
    b. Same as (a), except that D and B are husband and wife.
    c. D creates a revocable trust with B as the designated beneficiary.
    d. Same as (c). One year after creating the trust, D releases all power to revoke the trust.
    e. D takes out an insurance policy on his life, designating B as the beneficiary.
    f. Same as (e). Two years later, D dies and the policy proceeds are paid to B.

g. D takes out an insurance policy on the life of W and designates B as the beneficiary. Shortly thereafter, W dies and the policy proceeds are paid to B.

h. D pays for B's college tuition.

30. In 1974, P purchased real estate for $400,000, listing ownership as follows: "P and U, equal tenants in common." P predeceases U in 1990, when the property is worth $600,000. Before 1974, P had not made any taxable gifts or utilized the $30,000 specific exemption. Assume P and U are brothers.

a. Determine P's gift tax consequences, if any, in 1974.

b. How much, if any, of the property should be included in P's gross estate?

31. In 1983, V purchased real estate for $400,000, listing title to the property as follows: "V and Z, joint tenants with the right of survivorship." Under applicable state law, both parties possess the right of severance. Z predeceases V in 1990, when the real estate is worth $600,000. Assume V and Z are brothers and that neither has made any other taxable gifts or utilized his $30,000 specific exemption.

a. Determine V's gift tax consequences, if any, in 1983.

b. How much, if any, of the property should be included in Z's gross estate?

32. Assume the same facts as in Problem 31, except that V and Z are husband and wife (rather than brothers).

a. Determine V's gift tax consequences, if any, in 1983.

b. How much, if any, of the property should be included in Z's gross estate? Will any such inclusion generate an estate tax liability? Explain.

33. In January 1990, H and W enter into a property settlement under which H agrees to pay $500,000 to W in return for the release of her marital rights. At the time the agreement is signed, H pays W $100,000 as a first installment. Although the parties intended to obtain a divorce, H dies in July 1990 before legal proceedings have been instituted. After H's death, the executor of H's estate pays to W the $400,000 remaining balance due under the property settlement.

a. What are the gift tax consequences of the $100,000 payment made upon the signing of the agreement? Why?

b. What are the estate tax consequences of the $400,000 paid to W from estate assets after H's death? Why?

34. In 1989, M makes a gift to her daughter of securities worth $700,000. M has never made any prior taxable gifts or utilized her $30,000 specific exemption. F (M's husband), however, made a taxable gift of $500,000 in early 1976 upon which he paid a gift tax of $109,275. At the time of F's gift, F was not married to M.

a. Determine M's gift tax liability on the 1989 transfer, assuming the parties chose not to make the election to split gifts under § 2513.

b. What would be the liability if the election to split the gift were made?

35. Before his death in 1990, E (a widower) made the following transfers:

- A gift of real estate (basis of $80,000 and fair market value of $300,000) to R (E's son). The gift was made in 1988 and resulted in a Federal gift tax of $10,000, which E paid. On the date of E's death, the property is worth $320,000.

- A gift of an insurance policy on E's life to S (the designated beneficiary). The policy was worth $10,000 but had a maturity value of $60,000. The gift was made in 1988 and resulted in no Federal gift tax liability.

- A gift of stock (basis of $20,000 and fair market value of $150,000) to T. The gift was made in 1980 and resulted in no Federal gift tax liability. On the date of E's death, the stock was worth $300,000.

Presuming the alternate valuation date is not elected, how much should be included in E's gross estate as to these transfers?

36. D dies on July 7, 1990, at a time when he owns stock in Z Corporation and W Corporation. On June 1 of the same year, both corporations authorized cash dividends payable on August 1. For Z Corporation, the dividend was payable to shareholders of record as of July 1, and W Corporation's date of record was July 10. After D's death, the executor of the estate received dividends in the following amounts: $6,000 from Z Corporation and $8,000 from W Corporation. D also owned some City of Minneapolis tax-exempt bonds. As of July 7, the accrued interest on the bonds was $7,500. On December 1, the executor of the estate received $10,000 in interest ($2,500 accrued since D's death) from the bonds. Concerning the dividends and interest, how much should be included in D's gross estate?

37. In each of the following independent situations, determine how much should be included in D's gross estate under § 2042 as to the various life insurance policies involved. Assume that none of the policies are community property.
    a. At the time of his death, D owned a paid-up policy on the life of B, with S as the designated beneficiary. The policy had a replacement cost of $80,000 and a maturity value of $300,000.
    b. W owns a policy on the life of D ($300,000 maturity value) with D's estate as the designated beneficiary. Upon D's death, the insurance company pays $300,000 to D's estate.
    c. Four years before his death, D transferred a policy on his life ($300,000 maturity value) to S as a gift. D retained the power to change beneficiaries. At the time of the transfer, the designated beneficiary was S. Because D had never exercised his right to change beneficiaries, the insurance company pays S $300,000 upon D's death.
    d. Same as (c), except that D releases the power to change beneficiaries one year before his death.

38. Comment on how each of the following independent situations should be handled for estate tax purposes:
    a. Before her death, D issued a note payable to her daughter in the amount of $100,000 for which no consideration was ever received by D. After D's death, the daughter files a claim against the estate and collects $100,000 on the note.
    b. At the time of her death, D (a widow) owned 10 cemetery lots (each worth $5,000), which she had purchased many years before for herself and her family.
    c. At the time of his death, D was delinquent in the payment of back Federal income taxes. Such taxes are paid by D's executor from assets of the estate.

39. Before his death in 1990, D donates stock held as an investment (basis of $8,000 and fair market value of $15,000) to his church. Under the same circumstances, E transfers an equal amount of property, except that such donation occurs pursuant to E's will. Assume that both taxpayers were in a 28% bracket for income tax purposes and that their estates will be subject to a death tax rate of 40%. Which taxpayer is in a better tax position? Why?

40. In 1990, H places in trust $500,000 worth of securities. Under the terms of the trust instrument, W (H's wife) is granted a life estate, and on W's death, the remainder interest passes to H and W's children. Upon W's death 18 years later, the trust assets are valued at $2,000,000.

a. How much, if any, marital deduction will be allowed on the gift made in 1990?

b. How much, if any, of the trust will be included in W's gross estate upon W's death?

41. In each of the following independent situations, determine the decedent's final estate tax liability (net of any unified tax credit):

	Decedent			
	A	**B**	**C**	**D**
Year of death	1984	1985	1986	1990
Taxable estate	$500,000	$700,000	$900,000	$800,000
Pre-1977 taxable gift*	–0–	250,000	100,000	–0–
Post-1976 taxable gift	200,000	–0–	–0–	250,000
Gift tax paid on pre-1977 taxable gift	–0–	49,725	15,525	–0–
Gift tax paid on post-1976 taxable gift	38,000	–0–	–0–	70,800

*The $30,000 specific exemption was used in full for each of these gifts; B's gift occurred on October 1, 1976, and C's took place in June 1976.

42. In each of the following independent situations, determine the decedent's final estate tax liability (net of any unified tax credit):

	Decedent			
	E	**F**	**G**	**H**
Year of death	1985	1986	1987	1990
Taxable estate	$900,000	$800,000	$1,000,000	$1,100,000
Pre-1977 taxable gift*	250,000	250,000	–0–	–0–
Post-1976 taxable gift	–0–	–0–	500,000	80,000
Gift tax paid on pre-1977 taxable gift	49,000	49,275	–0–	–0–
Gift tax paid on post-1976 taxable gift	–0–	–0–	155,800	18,200

*The $30,000 specific exemption was used in full for each of these gifts; E's gift occurred in December 1976, and F's took place in December 1975.

43. In each of the following independent situations, determine the decedent's final estate tax liability (net of any unified tax credit and credit for gift taxes paid) for 1990. (Note: In some cases, you will have to compute the gift tax that was paid.)

	Decedent			
	I	**J**	**K**	**L**
Taxable estate	$500,000	$300,000	$500,000	$600,000
Taxable gift made in:				
1979	–0–	200,000	–0–	–0–
1981	200,000	–0–	–0–	–0–
1982	–0–	–0–	300,000	–0–
1983	–0–	–0–	–0–	200,000

44. In each of the following independent situations, determine the decedent's final estate tax liability (net of any unified tax credit and credit for gift taxes paid) for 1990, the year of death. (Note: In some cases, you will have to compute the gift tax that was paid.)

	Decedent			
	M	**N**	**O**	**P**
Taxable estate	$800,000	$300,000	$700,000	$900,000
Taxable gift made in:				
1980	200,000	–0–	–0–	–0–
1981	–0–	300,000	–0–	–0–
1982	–0–	–0–	150,000	–0–
1983	–0–	–0–	–0–	300,000

45. Assume the filing requirement for 1990 is a gross estate in excess of $600,000. What effect would each of the following transactions before D's death in 1990 have on the filing requirement?

- Utilized $10,000 of the $30,000 specific gift tax exemption on a gift made in June 1976.
- Used the balance of the $30,000 specific gift tax exemption on a gift made in October 1976.
- Made a taxable gift of $100,000 in November 1976.
- Made a taxable gift of $100,000 in 1978.

26

INCOME TAXATION OF TRUSTS AND ESTATES

OBJECTIVES

Develop working definitions with respect to trusts, estates, beneficiaries, and other parties.

Identify steps by which to determine the accounting and taxable income of the trust or estate, and the related taxable income of the beneficiaries.

Illustrate the uses and implications of distributable net income.

Examine effects of statutory restrictions on accounting periods and methods available to trusts and estates, and on the taxation of distributions from accumulation trusts.

Review various tax planning procedures that can be used to minimize the tax consequences of trusts and estates and their beneficiaries.

AN OVERVIEW OF SUBCHAPTER J

Chapter 25 discussed the transfer tax provisions of the Internal Revenue Code. Several of the valuable income and estate tax planning techniques considered therein involved the use of the trust entity. Moreover, the very nature of estate taxation necessarily entails the estate of the decedent. It is now appropriate to cover the income tax treatment of trusts and estates.

The income taxation of trusts and estates is governed by Subchapter J of the Internal Revenue Code, §§ 641 through 692. Similarities will be apparent between Subchapter J and the income taxation of individuals (e.g., the definitions of gross income and deductible expenditures), partnerships (e.g., the conduit principle), and S corporations (e.g., the conduit principle and the trust as a separate taxable entity). Several important new concepts will be introduced, however, including the determination of distributable net income and the tier system of distributions to beneficiaries.

The primary concern of this chapter is the income taxation of estates and ordinary trusts. Grantor trusts and special trusts, such as alimony trusts, trusts to administer the requirements of a court in the context of a bankruptcy proceeding, and qualified retirement trusts, are beyond the scope of this text.

What Is a Trust?

The Code does not contain a definition of a trust. However, the Regulations explain that the term "trust," as used in the Code, refers to an arrangement created by a will or by an *inter vivos* (lifetime) declaration, through which trustees take title to property for the purpose of protecting or conserving it for the beneficiaries.[1]

Typically, then, the creation of a trust involves at least three parties: the *grantor* (sometimes referred to as the settlor or donor), whose selected assets are transferred to the trust entity; the *trustee*, who may be either an individual or a corporation and who is charged with the fiduciary duties associated with the trust agreement; and the *beneficiary*, whose rights to receive property from the trust are defined by applicable state law and by the trust document.

In some situations, however, fewer than three persons may be involved, as specified by the trust agreement. For instance, an elderly individual who can no longer manage his or her own property (e.g., because of ill health) could create a trust under which he or she was both the grantor and the beneficiary so that a corporate trustee could be charged with management of the grantor's assets.

In another situation, the grantor might designate himself or herself as the trustee of the trust assets. For example, a parent who wants to transfer selected assets to a minor child might use a trust entity to ensure that the minor does not waste the property. By identifying himself or herself as the trustee, the parent would retain virtual control over the property that is transferred.

Under the general rules of Subchapter J, however, the trusts just described are not recognized for income tax purposes. When only one party is involved (when the same individual is grantor, trustee, and sole beneficiary of the trust), Subchapter J rules do not apply, and the entity is ignored for income tax purposes.

Other Definitions

When the grantor transfers title of selected assets to a trust, those assets become the *corpus* (body), or principal, of the trust. Trust corpus, in most situations, earns

---

1. Reg. § 301.7701–4(a).

income, which may be distributed to the beneficiaries, or accumulated for the future by the trustee, as the trust instrument directs.

In the typical trust, the grantor creates two types of beneficiaries: one entitled to receive the accounting income of the trust and one who will receive trust corpus that remains at the termination of the trust entity. Beneficiaries in the first category hold an *income interest* in the trust, and those in the second category hold a *remainder interest* in the trust's assets. If the grantor retains the remainder interest, such interest is known as a *reversionary interest* (corpus reverts to the grantor when the trust entity terminates).

As identified by the trust document, the term of the trust may be for a specific number of years (for a *term certain*), or it may be until the occurrence of a specified event. For instance, a trust could be created that would exist (1) for the life of the income beneficiary—in this case, the income beneficiary is known as a *life tenant* in trust corpus; (2) for the life of some other individual; (3) until the income or remainder beneficiary reaches the age of majority; or (4) until the beneficiary, or another individual, marries, receives a promotion, or reaches some specified age.

The trustee may be required to distribute the accounting income of the entity according to a distribution schedule specified in the agreement. However, the trustee can be given a greater degree of discretion with respect to the timing and nature of such distributions. If the trustee can determine, within guidelines that may be included in the trust document, either the timing of the income or corpus distributions or the specific beneficiaries who will receive them (from among those identified in the agreement), the trust is referred to as a *sprinkling trust* (the trustee can "sprinkle" the distributions among the various beneficiaries). Family-wide income taxes can be reduced when such income is received by those who are subject to lower income tax rates. Thus, if the trustee is given a sprinkling power, the income tax liability of the family unit can be manipulated through the trust agreement.

For purposes of certain provisions of Subchapter J, a trust must be classified as either a *simple trust* or a *complex trust*. A simple trust is one that (1) is required to distribute its entire trust accounting income to designated beneficiaries every year, (2) has no beneficiaries that are qualifying charitable organizations, and (3) makes no distributions of trust corpus during the year. A complex trust is any trust that is not a simple trust.[2] These criteria are applied to the trust every year. Thus, every trust will be classified as a complex trust in the year in which it terminates (because it will be distributing all of its corpus during that year).

What Is an Estate?

An estate is created upon the death of every individual. This entity is charged to collect and conserve all of the individual's assets, satisfy all of his or her liabilities, and distribute the remaining assets to the heirs identified by state law or the will.

In the typical case, the creation of an estate involves at least three parties: the *decedent*, all of whose probate assets are transferred to the estate for disposition; the *executor* or *executrix*, who is appointed under the decedent's valid will (or the *administrator* or *administratrix*, if no valid will exists); and the *beneficiaries* of the estate, who are to receive assets or income from the entity, as the decedent indicated in the will. The executor or administrator holds the fiduciary responsibility to operate the estate as directed by the will, applicable state law, and the probate court.

---

2. Reg. § 1.651(a)–1.

It is important to recognize that the assets that constitute the probate estate are not identical to those that constitute the gross estate for transfer tax purposes (refer to chapter 25). Indeed, many of the gross estate assets do not enter the domain of the *probate estate* and thus are not subject to disposition by the executor or administrator. For instance, property held by the decedent as a joint tenant passes to the survivor(s) by operation of the applicable state's property law rather than through the probate estate. Proceeds of insurance policies on the life of the decedent, over which the decedent held the incidents of ownership, are not under the control of the executor or administrator. Rather, the designated beneficiaries of the policy receive the proceeds outright under the insurance contract.

An estate is a separate taxable entity. Thus, taxpayers may find it profitable, under certain circumstances, to prolong the estate's existence. This situation is likely to arise when the heirs are already in a high income tax bracket. Therefore, the heirs would prefer to have the income generated by the estate assets taxed at the estate's lower income tax rates. However, the tax authorities have recognized this possibility of shifting income to lower-bracket taxpayers. The Regulations caution that if the administration of an estate is unduly prolonged, the estate will be considered terminated for Federal income tax purposes after the expiration of a reasonable period for the performance of all duties of administration by the executor.[3]

NATURE OF TRUST AND ESTATE TAXATION

Estates and trusts are separate taxable entities, and their income taxation is governed by Subchapter J of the Internal Revenue Code. In general, the taxable income of a trust or an estate is taxed to the entity or to its beneficiaries to the extent that each has received the accounting income of the entity. Thus, Subchapter J creates a modified conduit principle relative to the income taxation of trusts, estates, and their beneficiaries: Whoever receives the accounting income of the entity, or some portion of it, is liable for the income tax thereon.

EXAMPLE 1   Beneficiary A receives 80% of the accounting income of Trust Z. The trustee accumulated the other 20% of the income at her discretion under the trust agreement and added it to trust corpus. A is liable for income tax only on the amount of the distribution, and Trust Z is liable for the income tax on the accumulated portion of the income.   □

The modified conduit principle of Subchapter J is subject to several exceptions. For instance, some trusts may be treated as associations and therefore will be subject to the corporate income tax.[4] In addition, part or all of the income of certain trusts must be taxed to the grantor if he or she retains too much control over the trust property or income.[5]

Filing Requirements

The fiduciary is required to file a Form 1041 (U.S. Fiduciary Income Tax Return) in the following situations:[6]

---

3. Reg. § 1.641(b)–3(a).

4. Refer to chapter 16 for a discussion of associations taxed as corporations; see also *Morrissey v. Comm.*, 36–1 USTC ¶9020, 16 AFTR 1274, 56 S.Ct. 289 (USSC, 1936).

5. §§ 671–679.

6. § 6012(a).

- In the case of an estate, if its gross income for the year is $600 or more.

- In the case of a trust, if there is any taxable income or, when there is no taxable income, if there is gross income of $600 or more.

Although the fiduciary is responsible for filing Form 1041 and paying any income tax due, he or she has no personal liability for the tax. In general, the IRS must look to the assets of the estate or the trust for the tax due. The fiduciary may become personally liable for such tax if excessive distributions of assets have been made (e.g., payment of debts, satisfaction of bequests) and have therefore rendered the entity unable to pay the tax due. An executor or administrator may obtain a discharge from such personal liability from the IRS. Taking advantage of this procedure would be highly advisable before making any substantial distributions of estate assets.

The fiduciary return (and any related tax liability) is due no later than the fifteenth day of the fourth month following the close of the entity's taxable year. The return should be filed with the Internal Revenue Service Center for the region in which the fiduciary resides or has his or her principal place of business.

Tax Accounting Periods, Methods, and Payments

An estate or trust may use many of the tax accounting methods available to individuals. The method of accounting used by the grantor of a trust or the decedent of an estate does not carry over to the entity.

An estate has the same election available to any new taxpayer regarding the choice of a tax year. Thus, the estate of a calendar year decedent dying on March 3 could select any fiscal year or report on a calendar year basis.[7] If the calendar year basis is selected, the estate's first taxable year would include the period from March 3 to December 31. If the first or last tax year of an estate is a short year (less than one calendar year), income for that year need not be annualized.

To eliminate the possibility of deferring the taxation of fiduciary-source income simply by the use of a fiscal tax year, the Code requires that all trusts (other than charitable and tax-exempt trusts) adopt a calendar tax year for taxable years that begin after 1986.[8]

Trusts and certain estates are required to make estimated Federal income tax payments, using the same quarterly schedule that applies to individual taxpayers.[9] This requirement applies to estates only with respect to tax years that end two or more years after the date of the decedent's death.

In addition, if the trustee so designates on the fiduciary income tax return that is filed on or before the sixty-fifth day following the close of the applicable trust tax year, an estimated income tax payment made by a trust can be assigned to a specified beneficiary of the entity. Under this rule, such a payment will be treated under § 643(g) as though it were a timely fourth-quarter estimated tax payment of the beneficiary. No such election is available with respect to an estate.

The two-year estimated tax exception for estates undoubtedly recognizes the liquidity problems that an executor often faces during the early months of the administration of the estate. Note, however, that the language of the Code does not ensure that an estate whose existence measures less than 24 months will never be required to make an estimated tax payment.

---

7. § 441.

8. See § 645.

9. § 6654(l).

EXAMPLE 2	X died on March 15, 1990. Her executor elected a fiscal year ending on July 31 for the estate. Estimated tax payments will be required from the estate commencing with the tax year that begins on August 1, 1991. □

Tax Rates and Personal Exemption

A compressed tax rate schedule applies to estates and trusts.[10] In addition to the regular income tax, an estate or trust may be subject to the alternative minimum tax imposed on tax preference items.[11] Trusts also may be subject to a special tax imposed by § 644 on gains from the sale or exchange of certain appreciated property. The rules with respect to this special tax are not discussed in the chapter.

Both trusts and estates are allowed a personal exemption in computing the fiduciary tax liability. All estates are allowed a personal exemption of $600. The exemption available to a trust depends upon the type of trust involved. A trust that is required to distribute all of its income currently is allowed an exemption of $300. All other trusts are allowed an exemption of only $100 per year.[12]

The classification of trusts as to the appropriate personal exemption is similar, but not identical, to the distinction between simple and complex trusts. The classification as a simple trust is more stringent.

EXAMPLE 3	Trust X is required to distribute all of its current accounting income to Ms. A. Trust Y is required to distribute all of its current accounting income, one-half to Mr. B and one-half to State University, a qualifying charitable organization. The trustee of Trust Z can, at her discretion, distribute the current accounting income or corpus of the trust to Dr. C. None of the trusts makes any corpus distributions during the year. All of the accounting income of Trust Z is distributed to Dr. C.
	Trust X is a simple trust; it will receive a $300 personal exemption. Trust Y is a complex trust; it will receive a $300 personal exemption. Trust Z is a complex trust; it will receive a $100 personal exemption. □

TAXABLE INCOME OF TRUSTS AND ESTATES

Generally, the taxable income of an estate or trust is computed in a manner similar to that used for an individual. Subchapter J does, however, present several important exceptions and special provisions that distinguish the computation of taxable income for such entities. Thus, a systematic approach to this taxable income calculation is necessary. Figure 26–1 illustrates the computation method followed in this chapter.

Entity Accounting Income

The first step in determining the taxable income of a trust or estate is to compute the entity's accounting income for the period. Although this prerequisite is not apparent from a cursory reading of Subchapter J, a closer look at the Code reveals a number of references to the income of the entity. Wherever the term "income" is used in Subchapter J without some modifier (e.g., *gross* income or *taxable* income),

---

10. § 1(e) (reproduced in Appendix A).

11. § 55.

12. § 642(b).

FIGURE 26–1 Accounting Income, Distributable Net Income, and the Taxable Income of the Entity and Its Beneficiaries (Five Steps)

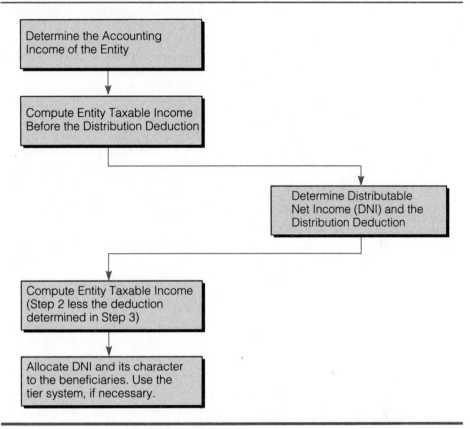

the statute is referring to the accounting income of the trust or estate for the appropriate tax year.

Thus, a definition of entity accounting income is critical to an understanding of the Subchapter J computation of fiduciary taxable income. Under state law, entity accounting income is the amount that the income beneficiary of the simple trust or estate is eligible to receive from the entity. Most importantly, the calculation of such accounting income is virtually under the control of the grantor or decedent (through a properly drafted trust agreement or will). If the document has been drafted at arm's length, a court will enforce a fiduciary's good faith efforts to carry out the specified computation of accounting income.

By allocating specific items of income and expenditure either to the income beneficiaries or to corpus, the desires of the grantor or decedent are put into effect. For instance, the typical document allocates to income any receipts of interest, dividends, rents, and royalties; the net profits from a business owned by the trust or estate; and most stock dividends, especially those less than or equal to 6 percent of the underlying stock. Moreover, the document usually allocates to income a portion of the fiduciary's fees and investment commissions and the operating expenses of the entity's business interests.

Conversely, the agreement or will typically allocates to corpus a portion of the fiduciary's fees and investment commissions, depreciation allowances relative to

the business assets of the entity, casualty losses associated with the entity property, and the capital gains and losses relative to the trust's investment assets. The treatment of such items of income and expenditure for taxable income purposes does not determine the treatment of such items in computing entity accounting income.

Where the controlling document is silent as to the proper allocation to income or corpus of one or more of the entity's items of income or expenditure, state law prevails. Thus, such allocations are an important determinant of the benefits received from the entity by its beneficiaries and the timing of such benefits.

EXAMPLE 4   The A Trust is a simple trust. Mrs. B is its sole beneficiary. In the current year the trust earns $20,000 in taxable interest and $15,000 in tax-exempt interest. In addition, the trust recognizes an $8,000 long-term capital gain. The trustee assesses a fee of $11,000 for the year. If the trust agreement allocates fees and capital gains to corpus, trust accounting income is $35,000, and Mrs. B receives that amount. Thus, the income beneficiary receives no immediate benefit from the trust's capital gain, and she bears none of the financial burden of the fiduciary's fees.

Interest income	$35,000
Long-term capital gain—allocable to corpus	± –0–
Fiduciary's fees—allocable to corpus	± –0–
Trust accounting income	$35,000

□

EXAMPLE 5   Assume the same facts as in Example 4, except that the trust agreement allocates the fiduciary's fees to income. The trust accounting income is $24,000, and Mrs. B receives that amount.

Interest income	$35,000
Long-term capital gain—allocable to corpus	± –0–
Fiduciary's fees	– 11,000
Trust accounting income	$24,000

□

EXAMPLE 6   Assume the same facts as in Example 4, except that the trust agreement allocates to income all capital gains and losses and one-half of the trustee's commissions. The trust accounting income is $37,500, and Mrs. B receives that amount.

Interest income	$35,000
Long-term capital gain	+8,000
Fiduciary's fees—one-half allocable to corpus	–5,500
Trust accounting income	$37,500

□

Gross Income

The gross income of an estate or trust is similar to that of an individual. In determining the gain or loss to be recognized by an estate or trust upon the sale or other taxable disposition of assets, the rules for basis determination are similar to those that apply to other taxpayers. Thus, the basis of property to an estate received from a decedent is determined under § 1014 (refer to chapter 12 for a more detailed discussion). Property received as a gift (the usual case in most trust arrangements) is controlled by § 1015. Property purchased by the trust from the grantor receives the grantor's basis, increased by any gain recognized by the grantor on the transfer.

Property Distributions. In general, no gain or loss is recognized by the entity upon its distribution of property to a beneficiary, pursuant to the provisions of the will or trust document. In this regard, the beneficiary of the distribution assigns to the distributed property a basis equal to that of the estate or trust. Moreover, the distribution absorbs distributable net income (DNI) and qualifies for a distribution deduction (both of which are explained in subsequent sections of this chapter) to the extent of the lesser of the distributed asset's basis to the beneficiary or the asset's fair market value as of the distribution date.

EXAMPLE 7	The H Trust distributes a painting, basis of $40,000 and fair market value of $90,000, to beneficiary K. K's basis in the painting is $40,000. The distribution absorbs $40,000 of H's DNI, and H may claim a $40,000 distribution deduction relative to the transaction. ☐
EXAMPLE 8	Assume the same facts as in Example 7, except that H's basis in the painting is $100,000. K's basis in the painting is also $100,000. The distribution absorbs $90,000 of H's DNI, and H may claim a $90,000 distribution deduction. ☐

A trustee or executor can elect to recognize gain or loss with respect to all of its in-kind property distributions for the year.[13] If such an election is made, the beneficiary's basis in the asset is equal to the asset's fair market value as of the distribution date. In addition, the distribution absorbs DNI and qualifies for a distribution deduction to the extent of the asset's fair market value. Note, however, that § 267 can restrict a trust's deduction for such losses.

EXAMPLE 9	The G Estate distributes an antique piano, basis to G of $10,000 and fair market value of $15,000, to beneficiary K. The executor elects that G recognize the related $5,000 gain on the distribution. Accordingly, K's basis in the piano is $15,000 ($10,000 basis to G + $5,000 gain recognized). Absent such an election, G would recognize no gain, and K's basis in the piano would be $10,000. ☐
EXAMPLE 10	Assume the same facts as in Example 9, except that G's basis in the piano is $18,000. The executor elects that G recognize the related $3,000 loss on the

---

13. § 643(e). The election applies to all distributions for the entity's tax year.

distribution. Accordingly, K's basis in the piano is $15,000 ($18,000 − $3,000). Absent such an election, G would recognize no loss, and K's basis in the piano would be $18,000. □

Income in Respect of a Decedent.   The gross income of a trust or estate includes income in respect of a decedent (IRD). For a cash basis decedent, IRD includes accrued salary, interest, rent, and other income items that were not constructively received before death. For both cash and accrual basis decedents, IRD includes, for instance, death benefits from qualified retirement plans and deferred pay contracts, income from a partnership whose tax year does not end with the death of the deceased partner, and collections of installment notes receivable.

The tax consequences of income in respect of a decedent can be summarized as follows:

- The fair market value of the right to IRD on the appropriate valuation date is included in the decedent's gross estate.[14] Thus, it is subject to the Federal estate tax.[15]

- The decedent's basis in the property carries over to the recipient (the estate or heirs). There is no step-up or step-down in the basis of IRD items.

- Gain or loss is recognized to the recipient of the income, measured by the difference between the amount realized and the adjusted basis of the IRD in the hands of the decedent. The character of such gain or loss depends upon the treatment that it would have received had it been realized by the decedent before death. Thus, if the decedent would have realized capital gain, the recipient must do likewise.[16]

- Expenses related to the IRD (such as interest, taxes, and depletion) that properly were not reported on the final income tax return of the decedent may be claimed by the recipient if the obligation is associated with the IRD. These items are known as *expenses in respect of a decedent*. They are deductible for both Federal estate and income tax purposes.

- If the IRD item would have created an alternative minimum tax (AMT) preference or adjustment for the decedent (e.g., with respect to the collection of certain tax-exempt interest by the entity), an identical AMT item is created for the recipient.

EXAMPLE 11   K died on July 13 of the current year. On August 2, K's estate received a check (before deductions) for $1,200 from K's former employer; this was K's compensation for the last pay period of his life. On November 23, K's estate received a $45,000 distribution from the qualified profit sharing plan of K's employer, the full amount to which K was entitled under the plan. Both K and the estate are calendar year cash basis taxpayers.

The last salary payment and the profit sharing plan distribution constitute IRD to K's estate; K had earned such items during his lifetime, and the estate had an enforceable right to receive each of them after K's death. Consequently,

---

14. § 2033. Refer to chapter 25.
15. To mitigate the effect of double taxation (imposition of both the death tax and income tax), § 691(c) allows the recipient an income tax de-

duction for the estate tax attributable to the income.

16. § 691(a)(3) and Reg. § 1.691(a)–3.

K's gross estate includes $46,200 with respect to these two items. However, the income tax basis to the estate for these items is not stepped up (from zero to $1,200 and $45,000, respectively) upon distribution to the estate.

The estate must report gross income of $46,200 with respect to the IRD items. Technically, the gain that is recognized upon the receipt of the IRD is $46,200 [($1,200 + $45,000) amounts realized − $0 adjusted basis].   □

Although this result (that the IRD is included both in K's gross estate and in the gross income of the estate) may appear to be harsh, recall that it is similar to that which applies to all of a taxpayer's earned income: The amount is subject to income tax upon its receipt, and to the extent that it is not consumed by the taxpayer before death, it constitutes an element of the gross estate.

EXAMPLE 12   Assume the same facts as in Example 11, except that K was an accrual basis taxpayer. IRD now includes only the $45,000 distribution from the qualified retirement plan. K's last paycheck was included in the gross income of his own last return (January 1 through date of death). Since the $1,200 salary already was recognized properly under K's usual method of tax accounting, it does not constitute IRD, and it is not gross income when it is received by the executor.   □

EXAMPLE 13   Assume the same facts as in Example 11. K's last paycheck was reduced by $165 for state income taxes that were withheld by the employer. The $165 tax payment is an expense in respect of a decedent, and it is allowed as a deduction *both* on K's estate tax return and on the estate's income tax return.   □

Ordinary Deductions

As a general rule, the taxable income of an estate or trust is similar to that of an individual. Thus, deductions are allowed for ordinary and necessary expenses paid or incurred in carrying on a trade or business; for the production or collection of income; for the management, conservation, or maintenance of property; and in connection with the determination, collection, or refund of any tax. Reasonable administration expenses, including fiduciary fees and litigation costs in connection with the duties of administration, also are deductible.

The trust or estate must apply the 2 percent of AGI floor to any § 212 expenses that it incurs. For this purpose, AGI appears to be the greater of (1) the pertinent-year AGI of the grantor of the trust or (2) the AGI of the trust or estate, computed as though the entity were an individual.

Expenses attributable to the production or collection of tax-exempt income are not deductible.[17] The amount of the disallowed deduction is found by using an apportionment formula, based upon the composition of the income elements of entity accounting income for the year of the deduction. This apportionment of the § 212 deduction is made without regard to the accounting income allocation of such expenses to income or to corpus. The deductibility of the fees is determined strictly by the Code (under §§ 212 and 265), and the allocation of expenditures to income and to corpus is controlled by the trust agreement or will or by state law.

---

17.   § 265.

Under § 642(g), amounts deductible as administration expenses or losses for death tax purposes (under §§ 2053 and 2054) cannot be claimed by the estate for income tax purposes unless the estate files a waiver of the death tax deduction. Although these expenses cannot be deducted twice, they may be allocated as the fiduciary sees fit between Forms 706 and 1041; they need not be claimed in their entirety on either return. The prohibition against double deductions does not extend to expenses in respect of a decedent, which are deductible both for estate tax purposes and on the income tax return of the recipient of the IRD.

Trusts and estates are allowed cost recovery deductions. However, such deductions are required to be apportioned among all of the parties involved. An estate is allowed a deduction for depreciation, depletion, and amortization, to be apportioned among the estate and the heirs on the basis of the estate's accounting income allocable to each.[18]

EXAMPLE 14   L and M are the equal income beneficiaries of the N Trust. Under the terms of the trust agreement, the trustee has complete discretion as to the timing of the distributions from N's current accounting income. The trust agreement allocates all depreciation expense to income. In the current year, the trustee distributes 40% of the current trust accounting income to L, and she distributes 40% of the income to M; thus, 20% of the income is accumulated. The depreciation deduction allowable to N is $100,000. This deduction is allocated among the trust and its beneficiaries on the basis of the distribution of current accounting income: L and M can each claim a $40,000 deduction, and the trust can deduct $20,000.   □

EXAMPLE 15   Assume the same facts as in Example 14, except that the trust agreement allocates all depreciation expense to corpus. L and M can each still claim a $40,000 depreciation deduction, and N retains its $20,000 deduction. The Code assigns the depreciation deduction proportionately to the recipients of current entity accounting income. Allocation of depreciation to income or to corpus is irrelevant in determining which party can properly claim the deduction.   □

On a sale by a trust of property received by transfer from the grantor, the amount of depreciation subject to recapture includes the depreciation claimed by the grantor before the transfer of the property to the trust. However, depreciation recapture potential disappears at death. Thus, when an entity receives depreciable property from a decedent, the recapture potential is reduced to zero.

EXAMPLE 16   J transferred an asset to the S Trust via a lifetime gift. The asset's total depreciation recapture potential was $40,000. If S sells the asset at a gain, ordinary income not to exceed $40,000 will be recognized by the trust. Had J transferred the asset after his death to his estate through a bequest, the $40,000 recapture potential would have disappeared.   □

---

18.   § 167(h) and §§ 611(b)(3) and (4).

Deductions for Losses

An estate or trust is allowed a deduction for casualty or theft losses not covered by insurance or other arrangement. Such losses may also be deductible by an estate for Federal death tax purposes under § 2054. As a result, an income tax deduction will not be allowed to an estate unless the death tax deduction is waived.

The net operating loss deduction is available for estates and trusts. The carryback of a net operating loss may reduce the distributable net income of the trust or estate for the carryback year and therefore affect the amount taxed to the beneficiaries for that year. In computing a net operating loss, the estate or trust cannot take into account deductions for charitable contributions or for distributions to beneficiaries.

Certain losses realized by an estate or trust may also be disallowed, as they are for all taxpayers. Thus, the wash sales provisions of § 1091 disallow losses on the sale or other disposition of stock or securities when substantially identical stock or securities are acquired by the estate or trust within the prescribed 30-day period. Likewise, § 267 disallows certain losses, expenses, and interest with respect to transactions between related taxpayers. Under § 267(b), the term "related taxpayers" includes, in addition to other relationships, the following:

- A grantor and a fiduciary of any trust.

- A fiduciary of a trust and a fiduciary of another trust, if the same person is a grantor of both trusts.

- A fiduciary of a trust and a beneficiary of such trust.

- A fiduciary of a trust and a beneficiary of another trust, if the same person is a grantor of both trusts.

- A fiduciary of a trust and a corporation, if more than 50 percent in value of the corporation's outstanding stock is owned, directly or indirectly, by or for the trust or by or for a person who is-a grantor of the trust.

Except for the possibility of unused losses in the year of termination, the net capital losses of an estate or trust cannot be deducted by a beneficiary.[19] They are to be used only on the fiduciary income tax return. The tax treatment of these losses is the same as that for individual taxpayers.

Charitable Contributions

An estate or complex trust is allowed a deduction for contributions to charitable organizations under the following conditions:

1. The contribution must be made pursuant to the will or trust instrument.

2. The recipient must be a qualified organization. For this purpose, qualified organizations include the same charities that qualify individual and corporate donors for the deduction, except that estates and trusts are permitted a deduction for contributions to certain foreign charitable organizations.

3. Generally, the contribution must be paid in the tax year claimed, but a fiduciary can treat amounts paid in the year immediately following as a

---

19. § 642(h).

deduction for the preceding year.[20] This rule treats estates and complex trusts more liberally than it does either individuals or corporations. For individuals, the year of payment always controls. Accrual basis corporations may, under certain conditions, claim a deduction for a pledge to a qualifying organization if the contribution is paid within two and one-half months of the end of the tax year.

4. In addition, estates are allowed a deduction for amounts permanently set aside for charitable purposes, regardless of when the charity actually receives the contribution.

Estates and complex trusts are not subject to a limitation on the extent of their deductible charitable contributions for the year (e.g., to a percentage of taxable or adjusted gross income), as are individuals and corporations. Nonetheless, a contribution may not fully qualify for a deduction by the entity. Specifically, the deduction is limited to amounts included in the gross income of the entity in the year of the contribution.

A contribution is deemed to have been made proportionately from each of the income elements of entity accounting income. Thus, in the event that the entity has tax-exempt income, the contribution is deductible only to the extent that the income elements of entity accounting income for the year of the deduction are included in the entity's gross income.

This rule is similar to that used to limit the § 212 deduction for fiduciary fees and other expenses incurred to generate tax-exempt income. However, if the will or trust agreement requires that the contribution be made from a specific type of income or from the current income from a specified asset, the document will control (the allocation of the contribution to taxable and tax-exempt income will not be required).

EXAMPLE 17   The K Trust has gross rental income of $80,000, expenses attributable to the rents of $60,000, and tax-exempt interest from state bonds of $20,000. Under the trust agreement, the trustee is directed to pay 30% of the annual trust accounting income to the United Way, a qualifying organization. Accordingly, the trustee pays $12,000 (30% × $40,000) to the charity in 1992. The charitable contribution deduction allowed for 1991 is $9,600 [($80,000/$100,000) × $12,000]. □

EXAMPLE 18   Assume the same facts as Example 17, except that the trust instrument also requires that the contribution be paid from the net rental income. The agreement controls, and the allocation formula need not be applied. Thus, the entire $12,000 is allowed as a charitable deduction. □

Deduction for Distributions to Beneficiaries

The modified conduit approach of Subchapter J is embodied in the deduction allowed to trusts and estates for the distributions made to beneficiaries during the year. When the beneficiary receives a distribution from the trust, some portion of that distribution may be subject to income tax on his or her own return. At the

---

20.   § 642(c)(1) and Reg. § 1.642(c)–1(b).

same time, the distributing entity is allowed a deduction for some or all of the distribution. Thus, the modified conduit principle of Subchapter J is implemented. A good analogy to this operation can be found in the taxability of corporate profits distributed to employees as taxable wages: The corporation is allowed a deduction for the payment, but the employee has received gross income in the form of compensation.

A critical value that is used in computing the amount of the entity's distribution deduction is *distributable net income* (DNI). DNI serves several functions as it is defined in Subchapter J:

- DNI is the maximum amount of the distribution on which the beneficiaries could be taxed.[21]

- DNI is the maximum amount that can be used by the entity as a distribution deduction for the year.[22]

- The makeup of DNI carries over to the beneficiaries (the items of income and expenses will retain their DNI character in the hands of the distributees).

Subchapter J presents a circular definition, however, with respect to DNI. The DNI value is necessary to determine the entity's distribution deduction and therefore its taxable income for the year. Nonetheless, the Code defines DNI as a modification of the entity's taxable income itself. Thus, using the systematic approach to determine the taxable income of the entity and of its beneficiaries, as enumerated in Figure 26–1 (earlier in the chapter), one first must compute *taxable income before the distribution deduction*, modify that amount to determine DNI and the distribution deduction, return to the calculation of *taxable income*, and apply the deduction that has been found.

Taxable income before the distribution deduction includes all of the entity's items of gross income, deductions, gains, losses, and exemptions for the year. Therefore, in computing this amount, one must (1) determine the appropriate personal exemption for the year and (2) account for all of the other gross income and deductions of the entity.

The next step in Figure 26–1 is the determination of *distributable net income*, computed by making the following adjustments specified to the entity's *taxable income before the distribution deduction:*

- Add back the personal exemption.

- Add back *net* tax-exempt interest. To arrive at this amount, reduce the total tax-exempt interest by any portion paid to or set aside for charitable purposes and by related expenses not deductible under § 265.

- Add back the entity's *net* capital losses.

- Subtract any net capital gains taxable to the entity (those allocable to corpus). In other words, the only net capital gains included in DNI are those attributable to income beneficiaries or to charitable contributions.

Since taxable income before the distribution deduction is computed by deducting all of the expenses of the entity (whether they were allocated to income or to corpus), DNI is reduced by expenses that are allocated to corpus. The effect of this procedure is to reduce the taxable income of the income beneficiaries, even though the actual distributions to them exceed DNI, because the distributions are not

---

21. §§ 652(a) and 662(a).   22. §§ 651(b) and 661(c).

reduced by expenses allocated to corpus. Aside from this shortcoming of Subchapter J, DNI offers a good approximation of the current-year economic income available for distribution to the entity's income beneficiaries.

Because DNI includes the net tax-exempt interest income of the entity, that amount must be removed from DNI in computing the distribution deduction. Moreover, with respect to estates and complex trusts, the amount actually distributed during the year may include discretionary distributions of income and distributions of corpus permissible under the will or trust instrument. Thus, the distribution deduction for estates and complex trusts is computed as the lesser of (1) the deductible portion of DNI or (2) the amount actually distributed to the beneficiaries during the year. In this regard, however, full distribution is always assumed by a simple trust, relative to both the entity and its beneficiaries, in a manner similar to the partnership and S corporation conduit entities.

EXAMPLE 19   The Z Trust is a simple trust. Because of severe liquidity problems, its 1990 accounting income was not distributed to its sole beneficiary, M, until early in 1991. Z is still allowed a full distribution deduction for, and M is still taxed upon, the entity's 1990 income in 1990. □

EXAMPLE 20   The P Trust is required to distribute its current accounting income annually to its sole income beneficiary, Mr. B. Capital gains and losses and all other expenses are allocable to corpus. In 1990, P incurs the following items:

Dividend income	$25,000
Taxable interest income	15,000
Tax-exempt interest income	20,000
Net long-term capital gains	10,000
Fiduciary's fees	6,000

1. Trust accounting income is $60,000; this includes the tax-exempt interest income, but not the fees or the capital gains, pursuant to the trust document. B receives $60,000 from the trust for 1990.

2. Taxable income before the distribution deduction is computed as follows:

Dividend income	$25,000
Interest income	15,000
Net long-term capital gains	10,000
Fiduciary's fees (40/60)	(4,000)
Personal exemption	(300)
Total	$45,700

The tax-exempt interest is excluded under § 103. Only a portion of the fees is deductible because some of the fees are traceable to the tax-exempt income. The trust receives a $300 personal exemption because it is required to distribute its annual trust accounting income.

3. DNI and the distribution deduction are computed in the following manner:

Taxable income before the distribution deduction (from above)		$45,700
Add back: Personal exemption		300
Subtract: Net long-term capital gains of the trust		(10,000)
Add back: Net tax-exempt income—		
Tax-exempt interest	$20,000	
Less: Disallowed fees	(2,000)	18,000
Distributable net income		$54,000
Distribution deduction		
($54,000 DNI – $18,000 net tax-exempt income)		$36,000

4. Finally, return to the computation of the taxable income of the P Trust. Simply, it is as follows:

Taxable income before the distribution deduction	$45,700
Less: Distribution deduction	(36,000)
Taxable income, P Trust	$9,700

A simple test should be applied at this point to ensure that the proper figure for the trust's taxable income has been determined. On what precisely is P to be taxed? P has distributed to Mr. B all of the trust's gross income except the $10,000 net long-term capital gains. The $300 personal exemption reduces taxable income to $9,700. □

EXAMPLE 21   The Q Trust is required to distribute all of its current accounting income equally to its two beneficiaries, Ms. F and the First Methodist Church, a qualifying charitable organization. Capital gains and losses and depreciation expenses are allocable to the income beneficiaries. Fiduciary fees are allocable to corpus. In the current year, Q incurs fiduciary fees of $18,000 and the following:

1. Rental income	$100,000
Depreciation expense (rental income property)	(15,000)
Other expenses related to rental income	(30,000)
Net long-term capital gains	20,000
Accounting income, Q Trust	$75,000
2. Taxable rental income	$100,000
Depreciation deduction	–0–
Rental expense deductions	(30,000)
Net long-term capital gains	20,000
Fiduciary's fees	(18,000)
Personal exemption	(300)
Charitable contribution deduction	(37,500)
Taxable income before the distribution deduction	$34,200

Since Q received no tax-exempt income, a deduction is allowed for the full amount of the fiduciary's fees. Q is a complex trust, but since it is required to distribute its full accounting income annually, a $300 exemption is allowed. The trust properly does not deduct any depreciation for the rental property. The depreciation deduction is available only to the recipients of the entity's accounting income for the period. Thus, the deduction will be split equally between Ms. F and the church. Such a deduction probably is of no direct value to the church, since the church is not subject to the income tax. The trust's charitable contribution deduction is based upon the $37,500 that the charity actually received (one-half of trust accounting income).

3.	Taxable income before the distribution deduction	$34,200
	Add back: Personal exemption	300
	Distributable net income	$34,500
	Distribution deduction	$34,500

The only adjustment necessary to compute DNI is the adding back of the trust's personal exemption, as there is no tax-exempt income. Furthermore, Subchapter J requires no adjustment relative to the charitable contribution. Thus, DNI is computed only from the perspective of Ms. F, who also received $37,500 from the trust.

4.	Taxable income before the distribution deduction	$34,200
	Less: Distribution deduction	(34,500)
	Taxable income, Q Trust	$ (300)

Perform the simple test (referred to above) to ensure that the proper taxable income for the Q Trust has been computed. All of the trust's gross income has been distributed to Ms. F and the charity. As is the case with most trusts that distribute all of their annual income, the personal exemption is "wasted" by the Q Trust. ☐

Tax Credits

An estate or trust may claim the foreign tax credit allowed under § 901 to the extent that it is not allocable to the beneficiaries. Similarly, other credits must be apportioned between the estate or trust and the beneficiaries on the basis of the entity accounting income allocable to each.

TAXATION OF BENEFICIARIES

The beneficiaries of an estate or trust receive taxable income from the entity under the modified conduit principle of Subchapter J. As just discussed, DNI determines the maximum amount that could be taxed to the beneficiaries for any tax year. In addition, the constitution of the elements of DNI carries over to the beneficiaries (e.g., net long-term capital gains retain their character when they are distributed from the entity to the beneficiary).

The timing of any tax consequences to the beneficiary of a trust or estate presents little problem, except when the parties involved use different tax years. A beneficiary must include in gross income an amount that is based upon the DNI of the trust for any taxable year or years of the trust or estate ending with or within his or her taxable year.[23]

EXAMPLE 22

An estate uses a fiscal year ending on March 31 for tax purposes. Its sole income beneficiary is a calendar year taxpayer. For the calendar year 1991, the beneficiary reports whatever income was assignable to her for the entity's fiscal year April 1, 1990, to March 31, 1991. If the estate is terminated by December 31, 1991, the beneficiary must also include any trust income assignable to her for the short year. This could result in a bunching of income in 1991. □

Distributions by Simple Trusts

The amount taxable to the beneficiaries of a simple trust is limited by the trust's DNI. However, since DNI includes net tax-exempt income, the amount included in the gross income of the beneficiaries could be less than DNI. Moreover, when there is more than one income beneficiary, the elements of DNI must be apportioned ratably according to the amount required to be distributed currently to each.

EXAMPLE 23

For the current calendar year, a simple trust has ordinary income of $40,000, a long-term capital gain of $15,000 (allocable to corpus), and a trustee commission expense of $4,000 (payable from corpus). Its two income beneficiaries, A and B, are entitled to the trust's annual accounting income, based on shares of 75% and 25%, respectively. Although A receives $30,000 as his share (75% × $40,000 trust accounting income), he will be allocated DNI of only $27,000 (75% × $36,000). Likewise, B is entitled to receive $10,000 (25% × $40,000), but she will be allocated DNI of only $9,000 (25% × $36,000). The $15,000 capital gain is taxed to the trust. □

Distributions by Estates and Complex Trusts

A problem arises with respect to distributions from estates and complex trusts when there is more than one beneficiary who receives a distribution from the entity during the year and the controlling document does not require a distribution of the entire accounting income of the entity.

EXAMPLE 24

The trustee of the W Trust may distribute the income or corpus of the trust at his discretion in any proportion between the two beneficiaries of the trust, Ms. K and Dr. L. Under the trust instrument, Ms. K must receive $15,000 from the trust every year. In the current year, the trust's accounting income is $50,000 and its distributable net income is $40,000. The trustee pays $35,000 to Ms. K and $25,000 to Dr. L for the current year. □

---

23. §§ 652(c) and 662(c).

How is W's DNI to be divided between Ms. K and Dr. L? Several arbitrary methods of allocating the DNI between the beneficiaries can be devised, but Subchapter J resolves the problem by creating a two-tier system to govern the taxation of beneficiaries in such situations.[24] The tier system determines precisely which distributions will be included in the gross income of the beneficiaries in full, which will be included in part, and which will not be included at all.

Income that is required to be distributed currently, whether or not it is distributed, is categorized as a *first-tier distribution*. All other amounts properly paid, credited, or required to be distributed are considered to be *second-tier distributions*. First-tier distributions are taxed in full to the beneficiaries to the extent that DNI is sufficient to cover these distributions. If the first-tier distributions exceed DNI, however, each beneficiary is taxed only on a proportionate part of the DNI. Second-tier distributions are not taxed if the first-tier distributions exceed DNI. However, if both first-tier and second-tier distributions are made and the first-tier distributions do not exceed DNI, the second-tier distributions are taxed to the beneficiaries proportionately to the extent of the "remaining" DNI.

The following formula is used to allocate DNI among the appropriate beneficiaries when only first-tier distributions are made and those amounts exceed DNI:

First–tier distributions to the beneficiary		
First–tier distributions to all noncharitable beneficiaries	X	Distributable net income (without deductions for charitable contributions) = Beneficiary's share of distributable net income

In working with this formula, amounts that pass to charitable organizations are not considered.

When both first-tier and second-tier distributions are made and the first-tier distributions exceed DNI, the above formula is applied to the first-tier distributions. In this case, none of the second-tier distributions are taxed because all of the DNI has been allocated to the first-tier beneficiaries.

If both first-tier and second-tier distributions are made and the first-tier distributions do not exceed the DNI, but the total of both first-tier and second-tier distributions does exceed DNI, the second-tier beneficiaries must recognize income as follows:

Second–tier distributions to the beneficiary		
Second–tier distributions to all beneficiaries	X	Remaining distributable net income (after first–tier distributions and charitable contributions) = Beneficiary's share of distributable net income

Charitable contributions are taken into account at this point.

EXAMPLE 25   The trustee of the G Trust is required to distribute $10,000 per year to both Mrs. H and Mr. U, the two beneficiaries of the entity. In addition, she is empowered to distribute other amounts of trust income or corpus at her sole discretion. In the current year, the trust has accounting income of $60,000 and DNI of $50,000. However, the trustee distributes only the required $10,000 each to H and to U. The balance of the income is accumulated, to be added to trust corpus.

---

24. §§ 662(a)(1) and (2).

In this case, only first-tier distributions have been made, but the total amount of such distributions does not exceed DNI for the year. Although DNI is the maximum amount that must be included by the beneficiaries for the year, no more can be included in gross income by the beneficiaries than is distributed by the entity. Thus, H and U each may be subject to tax on $10,000 as their proportionate shares of G's DNI. □

EXAMPLE 26   Assume the same facts in Example 25, except that DNI is $12,000. H and U each receive $10,000, but they cannot be taxed in total on more than DNI. Thus, each is taxed on $6,000 [$12,000 DNI × ($10,000/$20,000 of the first-tier distributions)]. □

EXAMPLE 27   Return to the facts described in Example 24. Ms. K receives a first-tier distribution of $15,000. Second-tier distributions include $20,000 to Ms. K and $25,000 to Dr. L. W's DNI is $40,000. The DNI is allocated between Ms. K and Dr. L as follows:

1. First-tier distributions	
To Ms. K	$15,000 DNI
To Dr. L	–0–
Remaining DNI = $25,000	
2. Second-tier distributions	
To Ms. K (20/45 × $25,000)	$11,111 DNI
To Dr. L (25/45 × $25,000)	$13,889 DNI

□

Separate Share Rule.   For the sole purpose of determining the amount of DNI for a complex trust with more than one beneficiary, the substantially separate and independent shares of different beneficiaries in the trust are treated as *separate trusts*. The reason for this special rule can be illustrated as follows:

EXAMPLE 28   Under the terms of the trust instrument, the trustee has the discretion to distribute or accumulate income on behalf of G and H (in equal shares). The trustee also has the power to invade corpus for the benefit of either beneficiary to the extent of that beneficiary's one-half interest in the trust. For the current year, the DNI of the trust is $10,000. Of this amount, $5,000 is distributed to G and $5,000 is accumulated on behalf of H. In addition, the trustee pays $20,000 from corpus to G. Without the separate share rule, G would be taxed on $10,000 (the full amount of the DNI). With the separate share rule, G is taxed on only $5,000 (his share of the DNI) and receives the $20,000 corpus distribution tax-free. The trust will be taxed on H's $5,000 share of the DNI that is accumulated. □

The separate share rule is designed to prevent the inequity that otherwise would result if the corpus payment were treated under the regular rules applicable to second-tier beneficiaries. Referring to Example 28, the effect of the separate share rule is to produce a two-trust result: one trust for G and one for H, each with DNI of $5,000.

Character of Income

Consistent with the modified conduit principle of Subchapter J, various classes of income (e.g., dividends, long-term capital gains, tax-exempt interest) retain the same character for the beneficiaries that they had when they were received by the entity. However, if there are multiple beneficiaries *and* if all of the DNI is distributed, a problem arises with respect to the allocation of the various classes of income among the beneficiaries.

Distributions are treated as consisting of the same proportion of each class of the items that enter into the computation of DNI as the total of each class bears to the total DNI of the entity. This allocation does not apply, however, if the terms of the governing instrument specifically allocate different classes of income to different beneficiaries or if local law requires such an allocation. Expressed as a formula, this generally means the following:

$$\frac{\text{Beneficiary's total share of DNI distributed}}{\text{Total DNI distributed}} \times \text{Total of DNI element deemed distributed (e.g., tax-exempt interest)} = \text{Beneficiary's share of the DNI element}$$

If the entity distributes only a part of its DNI, the amount of a particular class of DNI that is deemed distributed must first be determined. This is done as follows:

$$\frac{\text{Total distribution}}{\text{Total distributable net income}} \times \text{Total of a particular class of distributable net income} = \text{Total of the DNI element deemed distributed (e.g., tax-exempt interest)}$$

EXAMPLE 29   During the current year, a trust has DNI of $40,000, including the following: $10,000 of taxable interest, $10,000 of tax-exempt interest, and $20,000 of dividends. The trustee distributes, at her discretion, $8,000 to M and $12,000 to N, both noncharitable beneficiaries. The amount of each element of DNI that is deemed distributed will be $5,000 of taxable interest [($20,000 total distributed/$40,000 DNI) × $10,000 taxable interest in DNI], $5,000 of tax-exempt interest [($20,000/$40,000) × $10,000], and $10,000 of dividends [($20,000/$40,000) × $20,000]. M's share of this income is $8,000, made up of $2,000 of taxable interest [($8,000 DNI received by M/$20,000 total DNI distributed) × $5,000 taxable interest distributed], $2,000 of tax-exempt interest [($8,000/$20,000) × $5,000], and $4,000 of dividends [($8,000/$20,000) × $10,000]. The remaining amount of each income item deemed distributed is N's share: $3,000 of taxable interest, $3,000 of tax-exempt interest, and $6,000 of dividends. □

Special Allocations.   Under certain circumstances, the parties may modify the character-of-income allocation method set forth above. Such a modification is permitted only to the extent that the allocation is required in the trust instrument and only to the extent that it has an economic effect independent of the income tax consequences of the allocation.

EXAMPLE 30   Return to the facts described in Example 29. Assume that the beneficiaries are elderly individuals who have pooled their investment portfolios and avail

themselves of the trustee's professional asset management skills. Suppose that the trustee has the discretion to allocate different classes of income to different beneficiaries and that she designates all of N's $12,000 distribution as being from the tax-exempt income. Such a designation *would not be recognized* for tax purposes; the allocation method of Example 29 must be used.

Suppose, however, that the trust instrument stipulated that N was to receive all of the income from tax-exempt securities, because only N contributed the exempt securities to trust corpus. Pursuant to this provision, the $10,000 of the nontaxable interest is paid to N. This allocation is recognized, and $10,000 of N's distribution is tax-exempt. □

Losses in the Termination Year

The ordinary net operating and capital losses of a trust or estate do not flow through to the entity's beneficiaries, as would such losses from a partnership or an S corporation. However, in the year in which an entity terminates its existence, the beneficiaries do receive a direct benefit from the loss carryovers of the trust or estate.

Net operating losses and net capital losses are subject to the same carryover rules that otherwise apply to an individual (net operating losses can be carried back 3 years and then carried forward 15 years; net capital losses can be carried forward only, and for an indefinite period by the entity). However, if the entity incurs a net operating loss in the last year of its existence, the excess of deductions over the entity's gross income is allowed to the beneficiaries (it will flow through to them directly). This net loss will be available as a deduction *from* adjusted gross income in the beneficiary's tax year with or within which the entity's tax year ends in proportion to the relative amount of corpus assets that each beneficiary receives upon the termination of the entity but subject to the 2 percent of AGI floor.

Moreover, any carryovers of the entity's other net operating and net capital losses flow through to the beneficiaries in the year of termination in proportion to the relative amount of corpus assets that each beneficiary receives. The character of the loss carryforward is retained by the beneficiary, except that a carryover of a net capital loss to a corporate beneficiary is always deemed to be short term. Beneficiaries who are individuals can use these carryforwards as deductions *for* adjusted gross income.

EXAMPLE 31	The E Estate terminates on December 31, 1990. It had used a fiscal year ending July 31. For the termination year, the estate incurred a $15,000 net operating loss. In addition, the estate had an unused net operating loss carryforward of $23,000 from the year ending July 31, 1987, and an unused net long-term capital loss carryforward of $10,000 from the year ending July 31, 1989. Upon termination, D receives $60,000 of corpus, and Z Corporation receives the remaining $40,000. D and Z are calendar year taxpayers.

D can claim an itemized deduction of $9,000 [($60,000/$100,000) × $15,000] for the entity's net operating loss in the year of termination. This deduction is subject to the 2% of AGI floor on miscellaneous itemized deductions. In addition, she can claim a $13,800 deduction *for* adjusted gross income in 1990 (60% × $23,000) for the other net operating loss carryforward of E, and she can use $6,000 of E's net long-term capital loss carryforward with her other 1990 capital transactions.

Z Corporation receives ordinary business deductions in 1990 for E's net operating losses: $6,000 for the loss in the year of termination and $9,200 for the carryforward from fiscal year 1987. Moreover, Z can use the $4,000 carryforward of E's net capital losses to offset against its other 1990 capital transactions, although the loss must be treated as short term.

With respect to both D and Z, the losses flow through in addition to the other tax consequences of E that they received on July 31, 1990 (at the close of the usual tax year of the entity), under Subchapter J. Moreover, if the loss carryovers are not used by the beneficiaries in calendar year 1990, the short year of termination will exhaust one of the years of the usual carryforward period (e.g., D can use E's net operating loss carryforward through 15 years). □

The Throwback Rule

To understand the purpose and rationale of the throwback provision, one must review the general nature of taxation of trusts and their beneficiaries. The usual rule is that the income from trust assets will be taxed to the trust itself or to the beneficiary, but not to both. Generally, then, a beneficiary is not taxed on any distributions in excess of the trust's DNI. Thus, trustees of complex trusts might be tempted to arrange distributions in such a manner that would result in minimal income tax consequences to all of the parties involved. For instance, if the trust is subject to a lower income tax rate than are its beneficiaries, income could be accumulated at the trust level for several years before it is distributed to the beneficiaries. In this manner, the income that would be taxed to the beneficiaries in the year of distribution would be limited by the trust's DNI for that year. Further tax savings could be achieved by the use of multiple trusts because the income during the accumulation period would be spread over more than one taxpaying entity, thereby avoiding the graduated tax rates.

To discourage the use of these tax minimization schemes, the Code has, since 1954, contained some type of *throwback rule*. Because of this rule, a beneficiary's tax on a distribution of income accumulated by a trust in a prior year will approximate the increase in the beneficiary's tax for such a prior year that would have resulted had the income been distributed in the year that it was earned by the trust. The tax as so computed, however, is levied for the actual year of the distribution. In essence, the purpose of the throwback rule is to place the beneficiaries of complex trusts in the same nominal tax position as would have existed had they received the distributions during the years in which the trust was accumulating the income.

A detailed description of the application of the throwback rule is beyond the scope of this text.

Tax Planning Considerations

Many of the tax planning possibilities for estates and trusts have been discussed in chapter 25. However, there are several specific tax planning possibilities that should help to minimize the income tax effects on estates and trusts and their beneficiaries.

Income Tax Planning for Estates

As a separate taxable entity, an estate can select its own tax year and accounting methods. The executor of an estate should consider selecting a fiscal year because

CONCEPT SUMMARY 26—1

Taxation of Trusts and Estates

1. Estates and trusts are temporary entities, created to locate, maintain, and distribute assets and to satisfy liabilities according to the wishes of the decedent or grantor as expressed in the will or trust document.

2. Generally, the estate or trust acts as a conduit of the taxable income that it receives. Thus, to the extent that such income is distributed by the entity, it is taxable to the beneficiary. Taxable income retained by the entity is taxable to the entity itself.

3. The entity's accounting income must be determined first. Accounting conventions that are stated in the controlling document or, lacking such provisions, in state law allocate specific items of receipt and expenditure either to income or to corpus. Income beneficiaries typically receive payments from the entity that are equal to this accounting income amount.

4. The taxable income of the entity is computed using the computational scheme in Figure 26—1. The entity usually recognizes income in respect of a decedent. Deductions for fiduciary's fees and for charitable contributions may be reduced if the entity received any tax-exempt income during the year. Cost recovery deductions are assigned proportionately to the recipients of accounting income. Upon election, realized gain or loss on assets that properly are distributed in kind can be recognized by the entity.

5. A distribution deduction, computationally derived from distributable net income (DNI), is allowed to the entity. DNI is the maximum amount on which entity beneficiaries can be taxed. Moreover, the constitution of DNI is assigned to the recipients of the distributions.

this will determine when beneficiaries must include income distributions from the estate in their own tax returns. Beneficiaries must include the income for their tax year with or within which the estate's tax year ends. Proper selection of the estate's tax year thus could result in a smoothing out of income and a reduction of the income taxes for all parties involved.

Caution should be taken in determining when the estate is to be terminated. If a fiscal year had been selected for the estate, a bunching of income to the beneficiaries could occur in the year in which the estate is closed. Although prolonging the termination of an estate can be effective for income tax planning, keep in mind that the IRS carefully examines the purpose of keeping the estate open. Since the unused losses of an estate will pass through to the beneficiaries, the estate should be closed when the beneficiaries can enjoy the maximum tax benefit of such losses.

The timing and amounts of income distributions to the beneficiaries also present important tax planning opportunities. If the executor can make discretionary income distributions, he or she should evaluate the relative marginal income tax rates of the estate and its beneficiaries. By timing such distributions properly, the overall income tax liability can be minimized. Care should be taken, however, to time such distributions in light of the estate's DNI.

EXAMPLE 32   For several years before his death on March 7, D had entered into annual deferred compensation agreements with his employer. These agreements collectively called for the payment of $200,000 six months after D's retirement or death. To provide a maximum 12-month period within which to generate deductions to offset this large item of IRD, the executor or administrator of the estate should elect a fiscal year ending August 31. The election is made simply by filing the estate's first tax return for the short period of March 7 to August 31. □

EXAMPLE 33   B, the sole beneficiary of an estate, is a calendar year cash basis taxpayer. If the estate elects a fiscal year ending January 31, all distributions during the period of February 1 to December 31, 1989, will be reported on B's tax return for calendar year 1990 (due April 15, 1991). Thus, any income taxes that result from a $50,000 distribution made by the estate on February 20, 1989, will be deferred until April 15, 1991. □

EXAMPLE 34   Assume the same facts as in Example 33. If the estate is closed on December 15, 1990, the DNI for both the fiscal year ending January 31, 1990, and the final tax year ending December 15, 1990, will be included in B's tax return for the calendar year 1990. To avoid the effect of this bunching of income, the estate should not be closed until calendar year 1991. □

EXAMPLE 35   Assume the same facts as in Example 34, except that the estate has a substantial net operating loss for the period February 1 to December 15, 1990. If B is subject to a high income tax rate for calendar year 1990, the estate should be closed in that year so that the excess deductions will be passed through to its beneficiary. However, if B anticipates being in a higher tax bracket in 1991, the termination of the estate should be postponed. □

In general, beneficiaries who are subject to high tax rates should be made beneficiaries of second-tier (but not IRD) distributions of the estate. Most likely, these individuals will have less need for an additional steady stream of (taxable) income, and the income tax savings with respect to these parties can be relatively large. Moreover, a special allocation of tax-favored types of income and expenses should be considered so that, for example, tax-exempt income can be directed more easily to beneficiaries in higher income tax brackets.

Income Tax Planning with Trusts

The great variety of trusts provides the grantor, trustee, and beneficiaries with excellent opportunities for tax planning. Many of the same tax planning opportunities that are available to the executor of an estate are available to the trustee. For instance, the distributions from a trust are taxable to the trust's beneficiaries to the extent of the trust's DNI. Thus, if income distributions are discretionary, the trustee can time such distributions to minimize the income tax consequences to all parties. Remember, however, that the throwback rule applies to complex trusts. Consequently, the timing of distributions may prove to be of a more limited benefit than is available with respect to an estate, and it could result in a greater nominal tax than if the distributions had been made annually.

Tax Year and Payment Planning.   The TRA of 1986 reduced the benefits that arise from the traditional, tax-motivated use of trusts and estates through its revisions of the rate schedules that apply to such entities. Specifically, the familiar technique that encourages the accumulation within the entity of the otherwise taxable income of the trust or estate may no longer produce the same magnitude of tax benefits that were available under a more progressive tax rate schedule. Because the lower tax rates of the trust are exhausted more quickly and are very

similar to those that apply to the potential beneficiaries (indeed, they may be higher for the trust), the absolute and relative values of such an income shift are reduced.

Two other observations are pertinent with respect to the compressed tax rate schedule that applies to fiduciaries after 1986.

1. The effective value of the entity's 15 percent bracket is only $709 for 1990. Thus, the costs alone of planning to utilize this rate may exceed the eventual tax savings derived from such use. For example, there may no longer be a significant benefit to establishing a number of different trusts to take advantage of the graduated rates, since the costs associated with establishing and administering the trusts may exceed the per trust tax savings.

2. The timing of trust distributions themselves will continue to be important to the planner, however, since the rate differences between the entity and its beneficiaries might be as much as 18 percentage points at any one time (33% for the beneficiary – 15% for the entity). Consequently, it still may be a good idea to provide for a sprinkling power in the trust instrument.

Distributions of In-Kind Property

The ability of the trustee or executor to elect to recognize the realized gain or loss relative to a distributed noncash asset allows the gain or loss to be allocated to the optimal taxpayer.

EXAMPLE 36

The Y Estate distributed some stock, basis of $40,000 and fair market value of $50,000, to beneficiary L. Y is subject to a 15% income tax rate, and L is subject to a 28% tax rate. The executor of Y should elect that the entity recognize the related $10,000 realized gain, thereby subjecting the gain to Y's lower tax rate and reducing L's future capital gains income. □

EXAMPLE 37

Assume the same facts as in Example 36, except that Y's basis in the stock is $56,000. The executor of Y should *not* elect that the entity recognize the related $6,000 loss, thereby shifting the $56,000 basis and the potential loss to L's higher tax rates. □

PROBLEM MATERIALS

Discussion Questions

1. What is the importance of the accounting income of a trust or estate in determining its taxable income?

2. When must an income tax return be filed for an estate? A trust? When could the fiduciary be held liable for the income tax due from an estate or trust?

3. What is the general scheme of the income taxation of trusts and estates? How does the modified conduit principle relate to this general approach?

4. Under what circumstances could an estate or trust be taxed on a distribution of property to a beneficiary?

5. What is income in respect of a decedent? What are the tax consequences to a recipient of income in respect of a decedent?

6. How must an estate or trust treat its deductions for cost recovery? How does this treatment differ from the deductibility of administrative expenses or losses for estate tax purposes?

7. What happens to the net operating loss carryovers of an estate or trust if the entity is terminated before the deductions can be taken? How can this provision be used as a tax planning opportunity?

8. Discuss the income tax treatment of charitable contributions made by an estate or trust. How does this treatment differ from the requirements for charitable contribution deductions of individual taxpayers?

9. What is distributable net income? Why is this amount significant in the income taxation of estates and trusts and their beneficiaries?

10. Distinguish between first-tier and second-tier distributions from estates and complex trusts. Discuss the tax consequences to the beneficiaries receiving such distributions.

11. How must the various classes of income be allocated among multiple beneficiaries of an estate or trust?

12. What is the throwback rule? When is it applicable? Why was such a rule adopted?

13. Discuss the tax planning opportunities presented by the ability of an estate to select a noncalendar tax year.

Problems

14. The P Trust operates a welding business. Its current-year ACRS (accelerated cost recovery system) deductions properly amounted to $35,000. P's accounting income was $150,000, of which $80,000 was distributed to first-tier beneficiary Q, $60,000 was distributed to second-tier beneficiary R, and $10,000 was accumulated by the trustee. R also received a $15,000 corpus distribution. P's distributable net income was $52,000. Identify the treatment of P's cost recovery deductions.

15. The J Trust incurred the following items in 1990 using the cash basis of tax accounting:

Taxable interest income	$40,000
Tax-exempt interest income	35,000
Long-term capital gains	25,000
Fiduciary's fees	10,000

The trustee distributed $12,000 to a qualified charitable organization in 1991, designating such payment as from 1990 accounting income. The trust instrument allocates capital gains and fiduciary fees to income. Compute J's 1990 charitable contribution deduction.

16. The W Estate collected a $10,000 bonus from W's employer after W's death under a qualified deferred compensation plan. State income taxes due on the payment were $1,000, and the executor paid this amount during the first tax year of the estate. During this year, she also paid $1,200 for investment management fees relative to W's portfolio, which represented the bulk of the estate's assets. How is the estate's taxable income for the year affected by these transactions?

17. The M Estate, a calendar year taxpayer, earned $10,000 in portfolio income during 1990, and it paid $13,000 to the attorney who handled the probate and related matters for the estate. In addition, the estate deducted $3,000 of a $20,000 net captial loss that it had realized in 1988.

W, the sole beneficiary of the estate, generated $40,000 in adjusted gross income for 1990.
    a. How are the 1990 taxable incomes of M and W affected by these transactions?
    b. Same as (a), except that the estate is terminated as of the end of 1990.

18. The W Trust distributes $40,000 cash and a plot of land, basis of $15,000 and fair market value of $22,000, to its sole beneficiary, X. W's current-year distributable net income is $95,000. For each of the following independent cases, indicate (1) the amount of W's DNI deemed to be distributed to X, (2) W's distribution deduction for the land, and (3) X's basis in the land.
    a. No § 643(e) election is made.
    b. The trustee makes a § 643(e) election.
    c. Same as (a), except that W's basis in the land is $26,000.
    d. Same as (b), except that W's basis in the land is $26,000.

19. Assume the same facts as in Problem 18, except that W is an estate.

20. The Q Estate uses a fiscal year ending August 31 for Federal income tax purposes. For the year ending August 31, 1990, the estate had accounting income of $80,000 and distributable net income of $76,000. The estate has an unused net operating loss carryforward of $40,000 from 1984. Its sole beneficiary, Mrs. Q, recognized an unusually low amount of taxable income from her other 1990 activities. The IRS is applying pressure to terminate the estate on December 31, 1990. What would be the tax consequences of such a termination to the estate and to Mrs. Q? Should the executor attempt to keep the estate open into 1991?

21. The LMN Trust is a simple trust that correctly uses the calendar year for tax purposes. Its three income beneficiaries (L, M, and N) are entitled to the trust's annual accounting income in shares of one-third each. For the current calendar year, the trust has ordinary income of $60,000, a long-term capital gain of $18,000 (allocable to corpus), and a trustee commission expense of $6,000 (allocable to corpus).
    a. How much income is each beneficiary entitled to receive?
    b. What is the trust's distributable net income?
    c. What is the trust's taxable income?
    d. How much will be taxed to each of the beneficiaries?

22. Assume the same facts as in Problem 21, except that the trust instrument allocates the capital gain to income.
    a. How much income is each beneficiary entitled to receive?
    b. What is the trust's distributable net income?
    c. What is the trust's taxable income?
    d. How much will be taxed to each of the beneficiaries?

23. A trust is required to distribute $20,000 annually to its two income beneficiaries, A and B, in shares of 75% and 25%, respectively. If trust income is not sufficient to pay these amounts, the trustee is empowered to invade corpus to the extent necessary. During the current year, the trust has distributable net income of $12,000, and the trustee distributes $15,000 to A and $5,000 to B.
    a. How much of the $15,000 distributed to A must be included in A's gross income?

b. How much of the $5,000 distributed to B must be included in B's gross income?

c. Are these distributions considered to be first-tier or second-tier distributions?

24. Under the terms of the trust instrument, the trustee has discretion to distribute or accumulate income on behalf of W, S, and D in equal shares. The trustee is also empowered to invade corpus for the benefit of any of the beneficiaries to the extent of their respective one-third interest in the trust. In the current year, the trust has distributable net income of $48,000. Of this amount, $16,000 is distributed to W and $10,000 is distributed to S. The remaining $6,000 of S's share of DNI and D's entire $16,000 share are accumulated by the trust. Additionally, the trustee distributes $20,000 from corpus to W. How much income is taxed to W? To S? To D? To the trust?

25. The trustee of the M Trust is empowered to distribute accounting income and corpus to the trust's equal beneficiaries, Mr. P and Dr. G. In the current year, the trust incurs the following:

Taxable interest income	$40,000
Tax-exempt interest income	60,000
Long-term capital gains—allocable to corpus	35,000
Fiduciary's fees—allocable to corpus	12,000

The trustee distributed $25,000 to P and $28,000 to G.

a. What is M's trust accounting income?

b. What is M's distributable net income?

c. What is the amount of taxable income recognized by P from these activities? By G? By M?

26. For which tax year must each of the following entities first make estimated Federal income tax payments?

Entity	Date Created	Date of Tax Year-End
a. Trust	1/1/90	12/31
b. Trust	6/1/90	12/31
c. Estate	1/1/90	12/31
d. Estate	6/1/90	12/31
e. Estate	6/1/90	7/31

27

Working with the Tax Law

TAX SOURCES

Learning to work with the tax law involves acquiring skills in the following three basic areas:

- Familiarity with the sources of the law.
- Application of research techniques.
- Effective use of planning procedures.

Statutory, administrative, and judicial sources of the tax law are considered first in this chapter.

Statutory Sources of the Tax Law

Origin of the Internal Revenue Code.   Before 1939, the statutory provisions relating to Federal taxation were contained in the individual revenue acts enacted by Congress. Because of the inconvenience and confusion that resulted from dealing with many separate acts, in 1939 Congress codified all of the Federal tax laws. Known as the Internal Revenue Code of 1939, the codification arranged all Federal tax provisions in a logical sequence and placed them in a separate part of the Federal statutes. A further rearrangement took place in 1954 and resulted in the Internal Revenue Code of 1954.

Perhaps to emphasize the magnitude of the changes made by the Tax Reform Act (TRA) of 1986, Congress has redesignated the Internal Revenue Code of 1954 as the Internal Revenue Code of 1986. This is somewhat deceiving since a recodification of the tax law, as occurred in 1954, did not take place in 1986. The TRA of 1986 merely amends, deletes, or adds provisions to what was the Internal Revenue Code of 1954.

The following observations may help clarify the significance of the three codes:

- Neither the 1939, the 1954, nor the 1986 Code changed all of the tax law existing on the date of enactment. Much of the 1939 Code, for example, was incorporated into the 1954 Code. The same can be said for the transition from the 1954 to the 1986 Code. This point is important in assessing judicial and administrative decisions interpreting provisions under prior codes. For example, a decision interpreting § 121 of the Internal Revenue Code of 1954 will have continuing validity since § 121 is carried over unchanged to the Internal Revenue Code of 1986.

- Statutory amendments to the tax law are integrated into the existing code. Thus, future tax legislation will become part of the Internal Revenue Code of 1986.

The Legislative Process.   Federal tax legislation generally originates in the House of Representatives, where it is first considered by the House Ways and Means Committee. Tax bills originate in the Senate when they are attached as riders to other legislative proposals.[1] If acceptable to the Committee, the proposed bill is referred to the entire House of Representatives for approval or disapproval.

---

1. The Tax Equity and Fiscal Responsibility Act of 1982 originated in the Senate, and its constitutionality was unsuccessfully challenged in the courts. The Senate version of the Deficit Reduction Act of 1984 was attached as an amendment to the Federal Boat Safety Act.

Approved bills are sent to the Senate, where they are referred to the Senate Finance Committee for further consideration.

The next step involves referral from the Senate Finance Committee to the entire Senate. Assuming no disagreement between the House and Senate, passage by the Senate means referral to the President for approval or veto. If the bill is approved or if the President's veto is overridden, the bill becomes law and part of the Internal Revenue Code of 1986.

When the Senate version of the bill differs from that passed by the House, the Joint Conference Committee, including members of both the House Ways and Means Committee and the Senate Finance Committee, is called upon to resolve those differences. The result of the Joint Conference Committee, usually a compromise of the two versions, is then voted on by both the House and the Senate. If both bodies accept the bill, it is referred to the President for approval or veto.

The typical legislative process dealing with tax bills is summarized in Figure 27–1.

Referrals from the House Ways and Means Committee, the Senate Finance Committee, and the Joint Conference Committee are usually accompanied by Committee Reports. Because these Committee Reports often explain the provisions of the proposed legislation, they are a valuable source for ascertaining the intent of Congress. What Congress has in mind when it considers and enacts tax legislation is the key to interpreting such legislation. Since Regulations normally are not issued immediately after a statute is enacted, taxpayers and the courts look to legislative history materials to ascertain Congressional intent.

The role of the Joint Conference Committee indicates the importance of compromise to the legislative process. The practical effect of the compromise process is illustrated by reviewing what happened in the TRA of 1986 (H.R. 3838) with respect to the maximum income tax rates applicable to corporations beginning in 1988. See Figure 27–2.

Arrangement of the Code.   In working with the Code, it helps to understand the format followed. Note, for example, the following partial table of contents:

Subtitle A. Income Taxes

Chapter 1. Normal Taxes and Surtaxes

Subchapter A. Determination of Tax Liability

Part I. Tax on Individuals

Sections 1–5

Part II. Tax on Corporations

Sections 11–12

* * *

In referring to a provision of the Code, the key is usually the Section number involved. In designating Section 2(a) (dealing with the status of a surviving spouse), for example, it would be unnecessary to include Subtitle A, Chapter 1, Subchapter A, Part I. Merely mentioning Section 2(a) will suffice, since the Section numbers run consecutively and do not begin again with each new Subtitle, Chapter, Subchapter, or Part. However, not all Code Section numbers are used. Note that Part I ends with Section 5 and Part II starts with Section 11 (at present

FIGURE 27–1   Legislative Process for Tax Bills

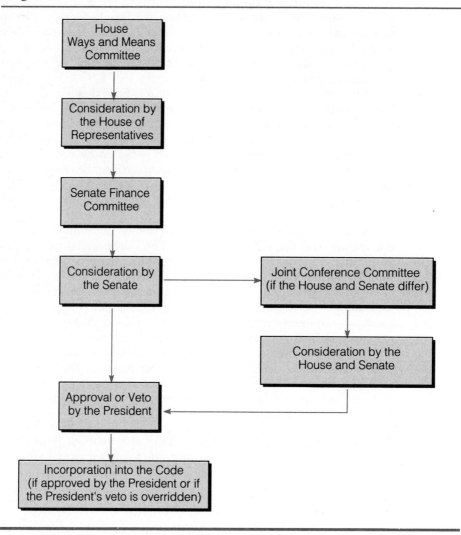

there are no Sections 6, 7, 8, 9, and 10). When the Code was drafted, the omission of Section numbers was intentional. This provides flexibility to incorporate later changes into the Code without disrupting the Code's organization. When Congress does not leave enough space, subsequent Code Sections are given A, B, C, etc., designations. A good example is the treatment of §§ 280A through 280H.

Tax practitioners commonly refer to some specific area of income taxation by Subchapter designation. More common Subchapter designations include Subchapter C ("Corporate Distributions and Adjustments"), Subchapter K ("Partners and Partnerships"), and Subchapter S ("Tax Treatment of S Corporations and Their Shareholders"). Particularly in the last situation, it is much more convenient to describe the effect of the applicable Code provisions involved (Sections 1361–1379) as "S corporation status" than as the "Tax Treatment of S Corporations and Their Shareholders."

FIGURE 27–2 Role of Joint Conference Committee

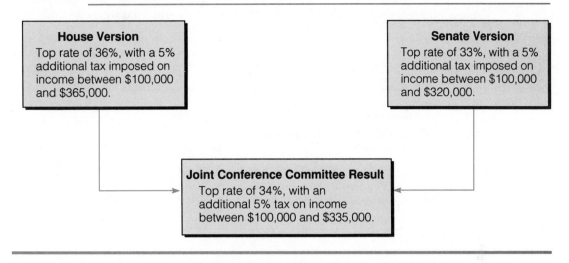

Citing the Code.   Code Sections are often broken down into subparts.[2] Section 2(a)(1)(A) serves as an example.

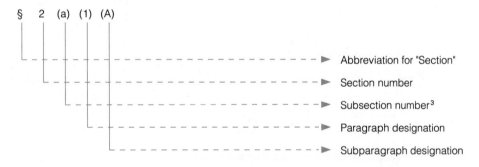

Broken down as to content, Section 2(a)(1)(A) appears as shown below.

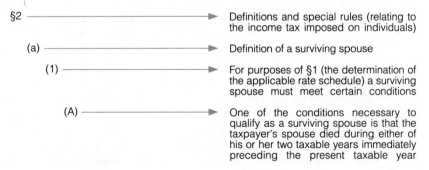

---

2. Some Code Sections do not necessitate subparts. See, for example, §§ 211 and 241.

3. Some Code Sections omit the subsection desig-nation and use, instead, the paragraph designa-tion as the first subpart. See, for example, §§ 212(1) and 1221(1).

Throughout the text, references to the Code Sections are in the form given above. The symbols "§" and "§§" are used in place of "Section" and "Sections." Unless otherwise stated, all Code references are to the Internal Revenue Code of 1986. The format followed in the text is summarized as follows:

Complete Reference	Text Reference
Section 2(a)(1)(A) of the Internal Revenue Code of 1986	§ 2(a)(1)(A)
Sections 1 and 2 of the Internal Revenue Code of 1986	§§ 1 and 2
Section 2 of the Internal Revenue Code of 1954	§ 2 of the Internal Revenue Code of 1954
Section 12(d) of the Internal Revenue Code of 1939[4]	§ 12(d) of the Internal Revenue Code of 1939

Effect of Treaties.   The United States signs certain tax treaties with foreign countries to render mutual assistance in tax enforcement and to avoid double taxation. Neither a tax law nor a tax treaty automatically takes precedence. Thus, when there is a direct conflict, the most recent item will take precedence. A taxpayer must disclose on the tax return any position where a treaty overrides a tax law. There is a $1,000 per failure to disclose penalty for individuals and a $10,000 per failure to disclose penalty for corporations.

Administrative Sources of the Tax Law

The administrative sources of the Federal tax law can be grouped as follows: Treasury Department Regulations, and Revenue Rulings and Revenue Procedures. All are issued either by the U.S. Treasury Department or by one of its instrumentalities (e.g., the Internal Revenue Service [IRS] or a District Director).

Treasury Department Regulations.   Regulations are issued by the U.S. Treasury Department under authority granted by Congress. Interpretative by nature, they provide taxpayers with considerable guidance on the meaning and application of the Code. Although not issued by Congress, Regulations carry considerable weight and are an important factor to consider in complying with the tax law.

Since Regulations interpret the Code, they are arranged in the same sequence. Regulations are, however, prefixed by a number that designates the type of tax or administrative, procedural, or definitional matter to which they relate. For example, the prefix 1 designates the Regulations under the income tax law. Thus, the Regulations under Code § 2 would be cited as Reg. § 1.2, with subparts added for further identification. The numbering pattern of these subparts often has no correlation with the Code subsections. The prefix 20 designates estate tax Regulations, 25 covers gift tax Regulations, 31 relates to employment taxes, and 301 refers to procedure and administration. This listing is not all-inclusive.

---

4. § 12(d) of the Internal Revenue code of 1939 is the predecessor to § 2 of the Internal Revenue Code of 1954 and the Internal Revenue Code of 1986.

New Regulations and changes to existing Regulations are usually issued in proposed form before they are finalized. The time interval between the proposal of a Regulation and its finalization permits taxpayers and other interested parties to comment on the propriety of the proposal. Proposed Regulations under Code § 2, for example, would be cited as Prop.Reg. § 1.2. The Tax Court indicates that proposed Regulations carry no more weight than a position advanced in a written brief prepared by a litigating party before the Tax Court. *Finalized* Regulations have the force and effect of law.

Sometimes temporary Regulations relating to elections and other matters where speed is important are issued by the Treasury. Such Regulations are issued without the comment period required for proposed Regulations. Temporary Regulations have the same authoritative value as final Regulations and may be cited as precedents. Temporary Regulations now must also be issued as proposed Regulations and automatically expire within three years after the date of issuance.

Proposed, temporary and final Regulations are published in the *Federal Register* and are reproduced in major tax services. Final Regulations are issued as Treasury Decisions (TD).

Regulations may also be classified as legislative, interpretative, or procedural. Refer to the subsequent discussion of this classification scheme under Assessing the Validity of a Treasury Regulation.

Revenue Rulings and Revenue Procedures. *Revenue Rulings* are official pronouncements of the National Office of the IRS as provided by § 7805(a). Like Regulations, they are designed to provide interpretation of the tax law. However, they do not carry the same legal force and effect of Regulations and usually deal with more restricted problems. In addition, Regulations are approved by the Secretary of the Treasury, whereas Revenue Rulings are not. Both Revenue Rulings and Revenue Procedures serve an important function in that they afford guidance to IRS personnel and taxpayers in handling routine tax matters.

A letter ruling is another type of ruling. Although letter rulings are not the same as Revenue Rulings, a Revenue Ruling often results from a specific taxpayer's request for a letter ruling. If the IRS believes that a taxpayer's request for a letter ruling deserves official publication because of its widespread impact, the holding will also be converted into a Revenue Ruling. Names, identifying descriptions, and money amounts are changed to conceal the identity of the requesting taxpayer.

In addition to arising from taxpayer requests, Revenue Rulings may arise from Technical Advice to District Offices of the IRS, court decisions, suggestions from tax practitioner groups, and various tax publications.

Revenue Procedures are issued in the same manner as Revenue Rulings, but they deal with the internal management practices and procedures of the IRS. Familiarity with these procedures can increase taxpayer compliance and assist the efficient administration of the tax laws by the IRS. The failure of a taxpayer to follow a Revenue Procedure can result in unnecessary delay or, in a discretionary situation, can cause the IRS to decline to act on behalf of a taxpayer.

Revenue Rulings and Revenue Procedures are published weekly by the U.S. Government in the *Internal Revenue Bulletin* (I.R.B.). Semiannually, the Bulletins for a six-month period are gathered together, reorganized by Code Section classification, and published in a bound volume called the *Cumulative Bulletin*

(C.B.).[5] The proper form for citing Rulings and Procedures depends on whether the item has been published in the *Cumulative Bulletin* or is available in I.R.B. form. Consider, for example, the following transition:

Temporary Citation $\left\{ \begin{array}{l} \text{Rev.Rul. 88–105, I.R.B. No. 51, 4.} \\ \textit{Explanation:}\ \text{Revenue Ruling Number 105, appearing on page 4 of the} \\ \text{51st weekly issue of the \textit{Internal Revenue Bulletin} for 1988.} \end{array} \right.$

Permanent Citation $\left\{ \begin{array}{l} \text{Rev.Rul. 88–105, 1988–2 C.B. 359.} \\ \textit{Explanation:}\ \text{Revenue Ruling Number 105, appearing on page 359 of} \\ \text{Volume 2 of the \textit{Cumulative Bulletin} for 1988.} \end{array} \right.$

Since the second volume of the 1988 *Cumulative Bulletin* was not published until August of 1989, the I.R.B. citation must be used until that time. After the publication of the *Cumulative Bulletin*, the C.B. citation is proper. The basic portion of both citations (Rev.Rul. 88–105) indicates that this was the 105th Revenue Ruling issued by the IRS during 1988.

Revenue Procedures are cited in the same manner, except that "Rev.Proc." is substituted for "Rev.Rul." Procedures, like Rulings, are published in the *Internal Revenue Bulletin* (the temporary source) and later transferred to the *Cumulative Bulletin* (the permanent source).

Letter Rulings.   Individual (letter) rulings are issued upon a taxpayer's request and describe how the IRS will treat a proposed transaction for tax purposes. They apply only to the taxpayer who asks for and obtains the ruling. Though this procedure may seem like the only real way to carry out effective tax planning, the IRS limits the issuance of individual rulings to restricted, preannounced areas of taxation. The main reason that the IRS will not rule in certain areas is that such areas involve fact-oriented situations. Thus, it is not possible to obtain a ruling on many of the problems that are particularly troublesome to taxpayers.

Although letter rulings once were private (not available to the public), the law now requires the IRS to make such rulings available for public inspection after identifying details are deleted. Published digests of private letter rulings can be found in *Private Letter Rulings* (published by Prentice-Hall), BNA *Daily Tax Reports*, and Tax Analysts and Advocates *Tax Notes*. IRS *Letter Rulings Reports* (published by Commerce Clearing House) contain both digests and full texts of all letter rulings. *Letter Ruling Review* (published by Tax Analysts and Advocates) is a monthly publication that selects and discusses the more important of the over 300 letter rulings issued each month.

Other Administrative Pronouncements.   Treasury Decisions (TDs) are issued by the Treasury Department to promulgate new Regulations, amend or otherwise change existing Regulations, or announce the position of the Government on selected court decisions.

---

5. Usually, only two volumes of the *Cumulative Bulletin* are published each year. However, when major tax legislation has been enacted by Congress, other volumes might be published containing the Congressional Committee Reports supporting the Revenue Act. See, for example, the two extra volumes for 1984 dealing with the Deficit Reduction Act of 1984. The 1984–3 *Cumulative Bulletin*, Volume 1, contains the text of the law itself; 1984–3, Volume 2, contains the Committee Reports. This makes a total of four volumes of the *Cumulative Bulletin* for 1984: 1984–1; 1984–2; 1984–3, Volume 1; and 1984–3, Volume 2.

CONCEPT SUMMARY 27–1

Administrative Sources

Source	Location	Authority
Regulations	Federal Register*	Force and effect of law.
Proposed Regulations	Federal Register* Internal Revenue Bulletin Cumulative Bulletin	Preview of final Regulations.
Temporary Regulations	Federal Register* Internal Revenue Bulletin Cumulative Bulletin	May be cited as a precedent.
Revenue Rulings Revenue Procedures	Internal Revenue Bulletin Cumulative Bulletin	Do not have the force and effect of law.
General Counsel's Memoranda Technical Memoranda Actions on Decisions	Tax Analysts' Tax Notes; P-H's Internal Memoranda of the IRS; CCH's IRS Position Reporter	May not be cited as a precedent.
Letter Ruling	Prentice-Hall and Commerce Clearing House loose-leaf services	Applicable only to taxpayer addressed. No precedential force.

*Finalized, proposed, and temporary Regulations are published in soft-cover form by several publishers.

The IRS publishes other administrative communications in the *Internal Revenue Bulletin,* such as Announcements, Notices, LRs (proposed Regulations), and Prohibited Transaction Exemptions.

The National Office of the IRS releases *Technical Advice Memoranda* (TAMs) weekly. Whereas letter rulings are responses to requests by taxpayers, TAMs are initiated by IRS personnel during IRS audits. A TAM is somewhat like a letter ruling in that it gives the IRS's determination of an issue. TAMs deal with completed rather than proposed transactions.

Like letter rulings, *determination letters* are issued at the request of taxpayers and provide guidance concerning the application of the tax law. They differ from letter rulings in that the issuing source is the District Director rather than the National Office of the IRS. Also, determination letters usually involve completed (as opposed to proposed) transactions. Determination letters are not published and are made known only to the party making the request.

The law now requires that several internal memoranda that constitute the working law of the IRS be released. These General Counsel's Memoranda (GCMs), Technical Memoranda (TMs), and Actions on Decisions (AODs) are not officially published, and the IRS indicates that they may not be cited as precedents by taxpayers. However, these working documents do explain the IRS's position on various issues.

Judicial Sources of the Tax Law

The Judicial Process in General. After a taxpayer has exhausted some or all of the remedies available within the IRS (no satisfactory settlement has been reached at the agent level or at the Appeals Division level), the dispute can be taken

to the Federal courts. The dispute is first considered by a court of original jurisdiction (known as a trial court), with any appeal (either by the taxpayer or the IRS) taken to the appropriate appellate court. In most situations the taxpayer has a choice of any of four trial courts: a Federal District Court, the U.S. Claims Court, the U.S. Tax Court, or the Small Claims Division of the U.S. Tax Court. The trial and appellate court scheme for Federal tax litigation is illustrated in Figure 27–3.

The broken line between the U.S. Tax Court and the Small Claims Division indicates that there is no appeal from the Small Claims Division. The jurisdiction of the Small Claims Division is limited to cases involving amounts of $10,000 or less.

American law, following English law, is frequently "made" by judicial decisions. Under the doctrine of *stare decisis*, each case (except in the Small Claims Division) has precedential value for future cases with the same controlling set of facts. Most Federal and state appellate court decisions and some decisions of trial courts are published. More than 3,000,000 judicial opinions have been published in the United States, and over 30,000 cases are published each year. Published court reports are organized by jurisdiction (Federal or state) and level of court (trial or appellate).

Trial Courts.   Differences between the various trial courts (courts of original jurisdiction) are summarized as follows:

• There is only one U.S. Claims Court and only one Tax Court, but there are many Federal District Courts. The taxpayer does not select the District Court that will hear the dispute but must sue in the one that has jurisdiction.

• Each District Court has only 1 judge, the Claims Court has 16 judges, and the Tax Court has 19 judges. In the case of the Tax Court, however, the entire court

FIGURE 27–3   Federal Judicial Tax Process

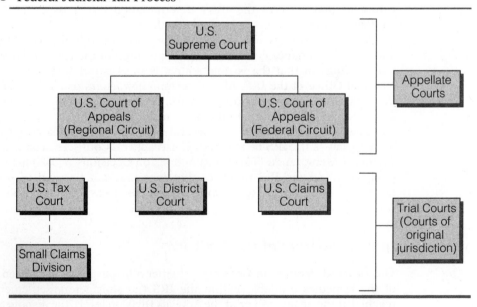

will decide a case (the court sits *en banc*) only when important or novel tax issues are involved. Most cases will be heard and decided by 1 of the 19 judges.

- The Claims Court meets most often in Washington, D.C., while a District Court meets at a prescribed seat for the particular district. Each state has at least one District Court, and many of the more populous states have more than one. Choosing the District Court usually minimizes the problem of travel inconvenience and expense for the taxpayer and his or her counsel.

- The Tax Court is officially based in Washington, D.C., but the various judges travel to different parts of the country and hear cases at predetermined locations and dates. Although this procedure eases the distance problem for the taxpayer, it could mean a delay before the case comes to trial and is decided.

- The Claims Court has jurisdiction in judgment upon any claim against the United States that is based upon the Constitution, any Act of Congress, or any regulation of an executive department. This forum appears to be more favorable for issues having an equitable or pro-business orientation (as opposed to purely technical issues) and those requiring extensive discovery.

- The Tax Court hears only tax cases and is the most popular forum. The Claims Court and District Courts hear nontax litigation as well as tax cases. Many Tax Court justices have been appointed from IRS or Treasury Department positions. Thus, some people suggest that the Tax Court has more expertise in tax matters.

    Some people believe that the Tax Court is more interested in protecting the revenues than are the other trial courts. For example, IRS statistics show that for the years 1987 and 1988, taxpayers won in the Tax Court in only 5.2 percent and 4.7 percent of the cases, respectively. During the same two years, taxpayers were successful 16.8 percent and 15.1 percent of the time in the District Courts and 11.1 and 2.4 percent of the time in the Claims Court.

- The only court in which a taxpayer can obtain a jury trial is a District Court. However, since juries can decide only questions of fact and not questions of law, even taxpayers who choose the District Court route often do not request a jury trial. If a jury trial is not elected, the judge will decide all issues. Note that a District Court decision is controlling only in the district in which the court has jurisdiction.

- For the Claims Court or a District Court to have jurisdiction, the taxpayer must pay the tax deficiency assessed by the IRS and sue for a refund. If the taxpayer wins (assuming no successful appeal by the Government), the tax paid plus appropriate interest thereon will be recovered. In the case of the Tax Court, however, jurisdiction is usually obtained without first paying the assessed tax deficiency. In the event the taxpayer loses in the Tax Court (and no appeal is taken or any such appeal is unsuccessful), the deficiency must be paid with appropriate interest. With the gradual elimination of the deduction for personal (consumer) interest, the Tax Court route of delaying payment of the deficiency can become expensive. For example, to earn 11 percent after tax, a taxpayer with a 33 percent marginal tax rate will have to earn 16.4 percent. By paying the tax, a taxpayer limits underpayment interest and penalties on underpayment interest.

Appellate Courts.   The following listing indicates the Court of Appeals of appropriate jurisdiction for appeals from a trial court.

CONCEPT SUMMARY 27–2

Federal Judicial System: Trial Courts

Issue	U.S. Tax Court	U.S. District Court	U.S. Claims Court
Number of judges per court	19	1	16
Payment of deficiency before trial	No	Yes	Yes
Jury trial available	No	Yes	No
Types of disputes	Tax cases only	Most criminal and civil issues	Claims against the United States
Jurisdiction	Nationwide	Location of taxpayer	Nationwide
IRS acquiescence policy	Yes	No	No
Appeal route	U.S. Court of Appeals	U.S. Court of Appeals	U.S. Court of Appeals for the Federal Circuit

COURT OF APPEALS JURISDICTIONS

First

Maine
Massachusetts
New Hampshire
Rhode Island
Puerto Rico

Second

Connecticut
New York
Vermont

Third

Delaware
New Jersey
Pennsylvania
Virgin Islands

District of Columbia

Washington, D.C.

Fourth

Maryland
North Carolina
South Carolina
Virginia
West Virginia

Fifth

Canal Zone
Louisiana
Mississippi
Texas

Sixth

Kentucky
Michigan
Ohio
Tennessee

Seventh

Illinois
Indiana
Wisconsin

Eighth

Arkansas
Iowa
Minnesota
Missouri
Nebraska
North Dakota
South Dakota

Ninth

Alaska
Arizona

California
Hawaii
Idaho
Montana
Nevada
Oregon
Washington
Guam

Tenth

Colorado
Kansas
New Mexico
Oklahoma
Utah
Wyoming

Eleventh

Alabama
Florida
Georgia

Federal Circuit

All of the jurisdictions
(where the case
originates in the Claims
Court)

If the Government loses at the trial court level (District Court, Tax Court, or Claims Court), it need not (and frequently does not) appeal. The fact that an appeal is not made, however, does not indicate that the IRS agrees with the result and will not litigate similar issues in the future. There could be a number of reasons for the Service's failure to appeal. First, the current litigation load may be heavy, and as a consequence, the IRS may decide that available personnel should be assigned to

other, more important, cases. Second, the IRS may determine that this is not a good case to appeal. Such might be true if the taxpayer is in a sympathetic position or the facts are particularly strong in his or her favor. In such event, the IRS may wait to test the legal issues involved with a taxpayer who has a much weaker case. Third, if the appeal is from a District Court or the Tax Court, the Court of Appeals of jurisdiction could have some bearing on whether or not the decision is made to go forward with an appeal. Based on past experience and precedent, the IRS may conclude that the chance for success on a particular issue might be more promising in another Court of Appeals. The IRS will wait for a similar case to arise in a different appellate court.

With the establishment of the Federal Circuit at the appellate level, a taxpayer has an alternative forum to the Court of Appeals of his or her home circuit for the appeal. Appeals from both the Tax Court and the District Court go to a taxpayer's home circuit. Now, where a particular circuit has issued an adverse decision, the taxpayer may wish to select the Claims Court route since any appeal will be to the Federal Circuit.

District Courts, the Tax Court, and the Claims Court must abide by the precedents set by the Court of Appeals of jurisdiction. A particular Court of Appeals need not follow the decisions of another Court of Appeals. All courts, however, must follow the decisions of the U.S. Supreme Court.

Because the Tax Court is a national court (it hears and decides cases from all parts of the country), the observation noted in the previous paragraph has caused problems. For many years the Tax Court followed a policy of deciding cases based on what it thought the result should be, even though the appeal of its decision might have been to a Court of Appeals that had previously decided a similar case differently. A number of years ago this policy was changed in the *Golsen*[6] decision. Now the Tax Court will still decide a case as it feels the law should be applied *only* if the Court of Appeals of appropriate jurisdiction has not yet passed on the issue or has previously decided a similar case in accord with the Tax Court's decision. If the Court of Appeals of appropriate jurisdiction has previously held otherwise, the Tax Court will conform under the *Golsen* rule even though it disagrees with the holding.

EXAMPLE 1

Taxpayer T lives in Texas and sues in the Tax Court on Issue A. The Fifth Court of Appeals is the appellate court of appropriate jurisdiction. The Fifth Court of Appeals has already decided, in a case based on similar facts and involving a different taxpayer, that Issue A should be resolved against the Government. Although the Tax Court feels that the Fifth Court of Appeals is wrong, under its *Golsen* policy it will render judgment for T. Shortly thereafter, Taxpayer U, a resident of New York, in a comparable case, sues in the Tax Court on Issue A. Assume that the Second Court of Appeals, the appellate court of appropriate jurisdiction, has never expressed itself on Issue A. Presuming the Tax Court has not reconsidered its position on Issue A, it will decide against Taxpayer U. Thus, it is entirely possible for two taxpayers suing in the same court to end up with opposite results merely because they live in different parts of the country. □

Appeal to the U.S. Supreme Court is by Writ of Certiorari. If the Court accepts jurisdiction, it will grant the Writ (*Cert. Granted*). Most often, it will deny

---

6. *Jack E. Golsen,* 54 T.C. 742 (1970).

jurisdiction (*Cert. Denied*). For whatever reason or reasons, the Supreme Court rarely hears tax cases. The Court usually grants certiorari to resolve a conflict among the Courts of Appeals (e.g., two or more appellate courts have assumed opposing positions on a particular issue). The granting of a Writ of Certiorari indicates that at least four members of the Supreme Court believe that the issue is of sufficient importance to be heard by the full court.

The role of appellate courts is limited to a review of the record of trial compiled by the trial courts. Thus, the appellate process usually involves a determination of whether or not the trial court applied the proper law in arriving at its decision. Rarely will an appellate court disturb a lower court's fact-finding determination.

The result of an appeal could be any of a number of possibilities. The appellate court could approve (affirm) or disapprove (reverse) the lower court's finding, and it could also send the case back for further consideration (remand). When many issues are involved, it is not unusual to encounter a mixed result. Thus, the lower court could be affirmed (*aff'd.*) on Issue A and reversed (*rev'd.*) on Issue B, and Issue C could be remanded (*rem'd.*) for additional fact finding.

When more than one judge is involved in the decision-making process, disagreement is not uncommon. In addition to the majority view, there could be one or more judges who concur (agree with the result reached but not with some or all of the reasoning) or dissent (disagree with the result). In any one case, it is the majority view that controls. But concurring and dissenting views can have influence on other courts or, at some subsequent date when the composition of the court has changed, even on the same court.

Having concluded a brief description of the judicial process, it is appropriate to consider the more practical problem of the relationship of case law to tax research. As previously noted, court decisions are an important source of tax law. The ability to cite a case and to locate it is therefore a must in working with the tax law. The usual pattern for a judicial citation is as follows: case name, volume number, reporter series, page or paragraph number, and court (where necessary).

Judicial Citations—The U.S. Tax Court.   A good starting point is with the U.S. Tax Court (formerly the Board of Tax Appeals). The Court issues two types of decisions: Regular and Memorandum. The distinction between the two involves both substance and form. In terms of substance, Memorandum decisions deal with situations necessitating only the application of already established principles of law. Regular decisions involve novel issues not previously resolved by the Court. In actual practice, however, this distinction is not always preserved. Not infrequently, Memorandum decisions will be encountered that appear to warrant Regular status, and vice versa. At any rate, do not conclude that Memorandum decisions possess no value as precedents. Both represent the position of the Tax Court and, as such, can be relied upon.

Another important distinction between the Regular and Memorandum decisions issued by the Tax Court arises in connection with form. Memorandum decisions are officially published in mimeograph form only. Regular decisions are published by the U.S. Government in a series called *Tax Court of the United States Reports*. Each volume of these *Reports* covers a six-month period (January 1 through June 30 and July 1 through December 31) and is given a succeeding volume number. But, as was true of the *Cumulative Bulletins*, there is usually a time lag between the date a decision is rendered and the date it appears in bound form. A temporary citation might be necessary to aid the researcher in locating a recent Regular decision. Consider, for example, the temporary and permanent citations for *Peter Pietanza*, a decision filed on March 30, 1989:

Temporary { *Peter Pietanza*, 92 T.C. ____, No. 41 (1989).
Citation   { *Explanation:* Page number left blank because not yet known.

Permanent { *Peter Pietanza*, 92 T.C. 729 (1989).
Citation   { *Explanation:* Page number now available.

Both citations tell us that the case will ultimately appear in Volume 92 of the *Tax Court of the United States Reports*. Until this volume is bound and made available to the general public, however, the page number must be left blank. Instead, the temporary citation identifies the case as being the 41st Regular decision issued by the Tax Court since Volume 91 ended. With this information, the decision can easily be located in either of the special Tax Court services published by Commerce Clearing House or Prentice-Hall. Once Volume 92 is released, the permanent citation can be substituted and the number of the case dropped.

Before 1943, the Tax Court was called the Board of Tax Appeals, and its decisions were published as the *United States Board of Tax Appeals Reports* (B.T.A.). These 47 volumes cover the period from 1924 to 1942. For example, the citation *Karl Pauli*, 11 B.T.A. 784 (1928) refers to the eleventh volume of the *Board of Tax Appeals Reports*, page 784, issued in 1928.

One further distinction between Regular and Memorandum decisions of the Tax Court involves the IRS procedure of acquiescence (A or Acq.) or nonacquiescence (NA or Nonacq.). If the IRS loses in a Regular decision, it will usually indicate whether it agrees or disagrees with the result reached by the Court. The acquiescence or nonacquiescence will be published in the *Internal Revenue Bulletin* and the *Cumulative Bulletin*. This procedure is not followed for Memorandum decisions or for the decisions of other courts. The IRS can retroactively revoke an acquiescence. In addition, the IRS sometimes issues an announcement that it will or will not follow a decision of another Federal court on similar facts. Such an announcement is not considered to be an acquiescence or nonacquiescence.

Although Memorandum decisions are not published by the U.S. Government, they are published by Commerce Clearing House (CCH) and Prentice-Hall (P-H). Consider, for example, the three different ways that *Jack D. Carr* can be cited:

Jack D. Carr, T.C. Memo. 1985–19
   The 19th Memorandum decision issued by the Tax Court in 1985.

Jack D. Carr, 49 TCM 507
   Page 507 of Vol. 49 of the *CCH Tax Court Memorandum Decisions*.

Jack D. Carr, P-H T.C.Mem.Dec. ¶85,019
   Paragraph 85,019 of the *P-H T.C. Memorandum Decisions*.

Note that the third citation contains the same information as the first. Thus, ¶ 85,019 indicates the following information about the case: year 1985, 19th T.C.Memo. Decision.[7] Although the Prentice-Hall citation does not include a specific volume number, the paragraph citation (85,019) indicates that the decision can be found in the 1985 volume of the P-H Memorandum Decision service. Note that the first two digits in the paragraph citation correspond to the year.

---

7. In this text, the Prentice-Hall citation for Memorandum decisions of the U.S. Tax Court is omit- ted. Thus, *Jack D. Carr* would be cited as 49 TCM 507, T.C.Memo. 1985–19.

Judicial Citations—The U.S. District Court, Claims Court, and Court of Appeals. District Court, Claims Court, Court of Appeals, and Supreme Court decisions dealing with Federal tax matters are reported in both the CCH *U.S. Tax Cases* (USTC), and the P-H *American Federal Tax Reports* (AFTR) series.

Federal District Court decisions, dealing with *both* tax and nontax issues, are also published by West Publishing Company in its *Federal Supplement Series*. Examples of how a District Court case can be cited in three different forms appear as follows:

> *Simons-Eastern Co. v. U.S.*, 73–1 USTC ¶9279 (D.Ct.Ga., 1972).
>
> *Explanation:* Reported in the first volume of the *U.S. Tax Cases* (USTC) published by Commerce Clearing House for calendar year 1973 (73–1) and located at paragraph 9279 (¶9279).
>
> *Simons-Eastern Co. v. U.S.*, 31 AFTR2d 73–640 (D.Ct.Ga., 1972).
>
> *Explanation:* Reported in the 31st volume of the second series of the *American Federal Tax Reports* (AFTR2d) published by Prentice-Hall and beginning on page 640. The "73" preceding the page number indicates the year the case was published but is a designation used only in recent decisions.
>
> *Simons-Eastern Co. v. U.S.*, 354 F.Supp. 1003 (D.Ct.Ga., 1972).
>
> *Explanation:* Reported in the 354th volume of the *Federal Supplement Series* (F.Supp.) published by West Publishing Company and beginning on page 1003.

In all of the above citations, note that the name of the case is the same (Simons-Eastern Co. being the taxpayer), as are the reference to the Federal District Court of Georgia (D.Ct.Ga.) and the year the decision was rendered (1972).[8]

Beginning in October 1982, decisions of the Claims Court (formerly the Court of Claims) are reported by West Publishing Company in a series designated *Claims Court Reporter*. Thus, the Claims Court decision in *Recchie v. U.S.* appears as follows:

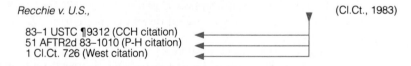

Decisions of the Court of Claims and the Courts of Appeals are published in the USTCs, AFTRs, and a West Publishing Company reporter designated as the *Federal Second Series* (F.2d). Illustrations of the different forms follow:

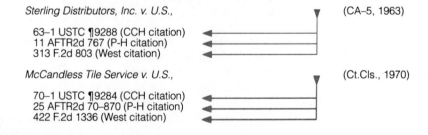

---

8. In this text, the case would be cited in the following form: *Simons-Eastern Co. v. U.S.*, 73–1 USTC ¶9279, 31 AFTR2d 73–640, 354 F.Supp. 1003 (D.Ct.Ga., 1972).

CONCEPT SUMMARY 27-3

Judicial Sources

Court	Location	Authority
U.S. Supreme Court`	S.Ct. Series (West) U.S. Series (U.S. Gov't.) L.Ed. (Lawyer's Co-Op.) AFTR (P-H) USTC (CCH)	Highest authority
U.S. Courts of Appeal	Federal 2nd (West) AFTR(P-H) USTC (CCH)	Next highest appellate court
Tax Court (Regular decisions)	U.S. Govt. Printing Office PH/CCH separate services	Highest trial court*
Tax Court (Memorandum decisions)	P-H Memo TC (P-H) TCM (CCH)	Less authority than regular T.C. decision
U.S. Claims Court	Claims Court Reporter (West) AFTR (P-H) USTC (CCH)	Similar authority as Tax Court
U.S. District Courts	F.Supp. Series (West) AFTR (P-H) USTC (CCH)	Lowest trial court
Small Claims Division of Tax Court	Not published	No precedent value

*Theoretically, the Tax Court, Claims Court, and District Courts are on the same level of authority. But some people believe that since the Tax Court hears and decides tax cases from all parts of the country (it is a national court),its decisions may be more authoritative than a Claims Court or District Court decision.

Note that *Sterling Distributors, Inc.*, is a decision rendered by the Fifth Court of Appeals in 1963 (CA–5, 1963), and *McCandless Tile Service* is one rendered by the Court of Claims in 1970 (Ct.Cls., 1970).

Judicial Citations—The U.S. Supreme Court.   Like all other Federal tax cases (except those rendered by the U.S. Tax Court), Supreme Court decisions are published by Commerce Clearing House in the USTCs and by Prentice-Hall in the AFTRs. The U.S. Government Printing Office also publishes these decisions in the *United States Supreme Court Reports* (U.S.), as do West Publishing Company in its *Supreme Court Reporter* (S.Ct.) and the Lawyer's Co-Operative Publishing Company in its *United States Reports, Lawyer's Edition* (L.Ed.). The following is an illustration of the different ways the same decision can be cited:

U.S. v. The Donruss Co.,   (USSC, 1969)

> 69–1 USTC ¶9167 (CCH citation)
> 23 AFTR2d 69–418 (P-H citation)
> 89 S.Ct. 501 (West citation)
> 393 U.S. 297 (U.S. Government Printing Office citation)
> 21 L.Ed.2d 495 (Lawyer's Co-Operative Publishing Co. citation)

The parenthetical reference (USSC, 1969) identifies the decision as having been rendered by the U.S. Supreme Court in 1969. The citations given in this text for Supreme Court decisions are limited to the CCH (USTC), P-H (AFTR), and West (S.Ct.) versions.

WORKING WITH THE TAX LAW—TAX RESEARCH

Tax research is the method whereby one determines the best available solution to a situation that possesses tax consequences. In other words, it is the process of finding a competent and professional conclusion to a tax problem. The problem might originate from either completed or proposed transactions. In the case of a completed transaction, the objective of the research is to determine the tax result of what has already taken place. For example, was the expenditure incurred by the taxpayer deductible or not deductible for tax purposes? When dealing with proposed transactions, however, the tax research process is directed toward the determination of possible tax consequences. To the extent that tax research leads to a choice of alternatives or otherwise influences the future actions of the taxpayer, it becomes the key to effective tax planning.

Tax research involves the following procedures:

- Identifying and refining the problem.
- Locating the appropriate tax law sources.
- Assessing the validity of the tax law sources.
- Arriving at the solution or at alternative solutions with due consideration given to nontax factors.
- Effectively communicating the solution to the taxpayer or the taxpayer's representative.
- Following up on the solution (where appropriate) in light of new developments.

These procedures are diagrammed in Figure 27–4. The broken lines reflect steps of particular interest when tax research is directed toward proposed, rather than completed, transactions.

Identifying the Problem

Problem identification must start with a compilation of the relevant facts involved. In this regard, *all* of the facts that might have a bearing on the problem must be gathered because any omission could modify the solution to be reached. To illustrate, consider what appears to be a very simple problem.

EXAMPLE 2

A widowed mother advances $52,000 to her son in 1983 to enable him to attend a private college. Seven years later, the mother claims a bad debt deduction for $42,000 that the son has not repaid. The problem: Is the mother entitled to a bad debt deduction? □

Refining the Problem.   Before a bad debt deduction can arise, it must be established that a debt really existed. In a related-party setting (e.g., mother and son), the IRS may contend that the original advance was not a loan but, in reality, a gift. Of key significance in this regard would be whether or not the lender (the mother) had an honest and real expectation of payment by the borrower (the son).[9]

---

9. *William F. Mercil,* 24 T.C. 1150 (1955), and *Evans Clark,* 18 T.C. 780 (1952), *aff'd.* 53–2 USTC ¶ 9452, 44 AFTR 70, 205 F.2d 353 (CA–2, 1953).

FIGURE 27–4   Tax Research Process

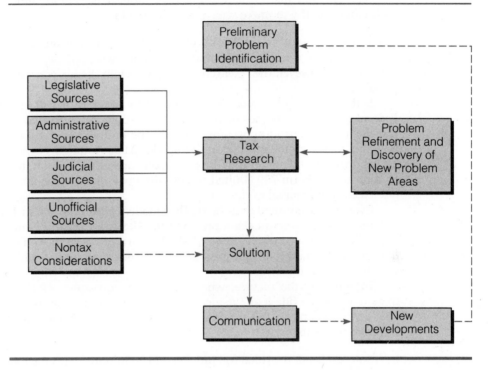

Indicative of this repayment expectation is whether or not the parties preserved the formalities of a loan, including the following:

- The borrower issued a written instrument evidencing the obligation.

- Interest was provided for as part of the loan arrangement.

- The note specified a set due date.

- Collateral was available to the lender in the event of default by the borrower.[10]

The very presence of some or all of the above formalities does not, however, guarantee that a bona fide loan will be found. By the same token, the absence of some or all of such formalities does not condemn the advance to a gift classification. Applying the formalities criteria to Example 2 is not possible since key facts (e.g., the presence or absence of a written note) are not given. Nevertheless, several inferences might be made that lead to a loan interpretation:

- It appears that the son has repaid at least $10,000 of the $52,000 that he borrowed. If the parties intended a gift of the full amount of the loan, why was partial repayment made?

- Although one would not expect a son on his way to college to have assets to serve as collateral for a loan, the obtaining of additional education could reinforce any expectation of repayment the mother might have. In most

---

10. *Arthur T. Davidson*, 37 TCM 725, T.C.Memo. 1978–167.

situations, the person with a college education would possess a higher earning potential than one without such education. This would improve the son's financial ability to make repayments on the loan.

Further Refinement of the Problem.   Whether the advance constitutes a loan or a gift may be a result that cannot be reached with any degree of certainty. In either event, however, the researcher must ascertain the tax consequences of each possibility.

If the advance ultimately is determined to be a gift, it will be subject to the Federal gift tax.[11] Whether or not a gift tax would be generated because of the transfer would depend upon how much of the unified tax credit the mother has available to absorb the gift tax on $42,000 [$52,000 (total gift) − $10,000 (annual exclusion)].[12] But whether the transfer results in a gift tax or not, it would have to be reported on Form 709 (United States Gift Tax Return) since the amount of the gift exceeds the annual exclusion.

Even if it is assumed that the mother made a gift to the son in 1983, does not the intervention of seven years preclude the IRS from assessing any gift tax that might be due as a result of such transfer?[13] Further research would indicate that the statute of limitations on assessments does not begin to run when a tax return was due but not filed.[14]

To complete the picture, what are the tax consequences if the advance is treated as a bona fide loan? Aside from the bad debt deduction aspects (covered later in the chapter), the tax law provides more immediate tax ramifications, summarized as follows:[15]

- If interest is not provided for, interest will be imputed with the following effect:
  a. The lender (the mother) must recognize interest income as to the imputed value.
  b. Since the lender has not received the interest, a gift of such interest is deemed to have taken place from the lender to the borrower.
  c. The borrower (son) is entitled to deduct (as an itemized expense) a portion of the amount of interest deemed paid to the lender (mother).

- If interest is provided for but the rate is lower than market (as determined by the yield on certain U.S. government securities), the differential will be treated as noted above.

- For gift loans of $100,000 or less, the imputed element cannot exceed the net investment income of the borrower.

Locating the Appropriate Tax Law Sources

Once the problem is clearly defined, what is the next step? This is a matter of individual judgment, but most involved tax research begins with the index volume

---

11. The transfer does not fall within the unlimited gift tax exclusion of § 2503(e)(2)(A) since the mother did not pay the amount directly to an educational institution. Besides, the exclusion covers only tuition payments and not other costs attendant on going to college (e.g., room and board).

12. This, in turn, depends upon the amount of taxable gifts the mother has made in the past. For a discussion of the mechanics of the Federal gift tax, see chapter 25.

13. Throughout the discussion of Example 2, the assumption has been made that if a gift occurred, it took place in 1983. Such need not be the case. Depending upon the mother's intent, she could have decided to make a gift of the unpaid balance anytime after the loan was made (e.g., 1984, 1985, etc.).

14. See § 6501(c)(3) and the discussion of the statute of limitations in chapter 24.

15. § 7872.

of the tax service. If the problem is not that complex, the researcher may bypass the tax service and turn directly to the Internal Revenue Code and the Treasury Regulations. For the beginner, this latter procedure saves time and will solve many of the more basic problems. If the researcher does not have a personal copy of the Code or Regulations, resorting to the appropriate volume(s) of a tax service will be necessary.

The major tax services available are as follows:

Standard Federal Tax Reporter, Commerce Clearing House.

Federal Taxes, Prentice-Hall.

Mertens, *Law of Federal Income Taxation*, Callaghan and Co.

Tax Coordinator, Research Institute of America.

Tax Management Portfolios, Bureau of National Affairs.

Rabkin and Johnson, *Federal Income, Gift and Estate Taxation*, Matthew Bender, Inc.

Bender's Federal Tax Service, Matthew Bender, Inc.

Working with Tax Services.   In this text, it is not feasible to explain the use of any particular tax service—this can be learned only by practice. However, several important observations can be made about the use of tax services that cannot be overemphasized. First, never forget to check for current developments. The main text of any service is not revised frequently enough to permit reliance on that portion as the *latest* word on any subject. Where such current developments can be found depends on which service is being used. Both the Commerce Clearing House and Prentice-Hall services contain a special volume devoted to current matters. Second, when dealing with a tax service synopsis of a Treasury Department pronouncement or a judicial decision, remember there is no substitute for the original source.

To illustrate, do not base a conclusion solely on a tax service's commentary on *Simons-Eastern Co. v. U.S.* If the case is vital to the research, look it up! It is possible that the facts of the case are distinguishable from those involved in the problem being researched. This is not to say that the case synopsis contained in the tax service is wrong—it might be just misleading or incomplete.

Tax Periodicals.   Additional sources of tax information are the various tax periodicals. The best means of locating a journal article pertinent to a tax problem is through Commerce Clearing House's *Federal Tax Articles*. This three-volume service includes a subject index, a Code Section number index, and an author's index. Also, the P-H tax service has a topical "Index to Tax Articles" section that is organized using the P-H paragraph index system.

The following are some of the more useful tax periodicals:

The Journal of Taxation
Warren, Gorham and Lamont
210 South Street
Boston, MA 02111

Trusts and Estates
Communication Channels, Inc.
6255 Barfield Road
Atlanta, GA 30328

Tax Law Review
Warren, Gorham and Lamont
210 South Street
Boston, MA 02111

Estate Planning
Warren, Gorham and Lamont
210 South Street
Boston, MA 02111

Taxation for Accountants Warren, Gorham and Lamont 210 South Street Boston, MA 02111	*The Practical Accountant* 1 Penn Plaza New York, NY 10119
The Tax Executive 1300 North 17th Street Arlington, VA 22209	*Journal of Corporate Taxation* Warren, Gorham and Lamont 210 South Street Boston, MA 02111
Oil and Gas Tax Quarterly Matthew Bender & Co. 235 East 45th Street New York, NY 10017	*Journal of Taxation for Individuals* Warren, Gorham and Lamont 210 South Street Boston, MA 02111
The International Tax Journal Panel Publishers 14 Plaza Road Greenvale, NY 11548	*The Tax Lawyer* American Bar Association 1800 M Street, N.W. Washington, DC 20036
TAXES—The Tax Magazine Commerce Clearing House, Inc. 4025 West Peterson Avenue Chicago, IL 60646	*Journal of the American Taxation Association* American Accounting Association 5717 Bessie Drive Sarasota, FL 33583
National Tax Journal 21 East State Street Columbus, OH 43215	*Tax Notes* 6830 Fairfax Drive Arlington, VA 22213
The Tax Adviser 1211 Avenue of the Americas New York, NY 10036	

Assessing the Validity of the Tax Law Sources

Once a source has been located, the next procedure is to assess such source in light of the problem at hand. Proper assessment involves careful interpretation of the tax law with consideration as to its relevance and validity. In connection with validity, an important step is to check for recent changes in the tax law.

Interpreting the Internal Revenue Code.   The language of the Code can be extremely difficult to comprehend fully. For example, one subsection [§ 341(e)] relating to collapsible corporations contains *one* sentence of more than 450 words (twice as many as in the Gettysburg Address). Within this same subsection are two other sentences of 270 and 300 words.

One author has noted 10 common pitfalls in interpreting the Code:[16]

1. Determine the limitations and exceptions to a provision. Do not permit the language of the Code Section to carry greater or lesser weight than was intended.

2. Just because a Section fails to mention an item does not necessarily mean that the item is excluded.

3. Read definitional clauses carefully.

---

16. H. G. Wong, "Ten Common Pitfalls in Reading the Internal Revenue Code," *The Practical Accountant* (July–August 1972), pp. 30–33.

Do not overlook small words such as "and" and "or." There is a world of difference between these two words.

Read the Code Section completely; do not jump to conclusions.

Watch out for cross-referenced and related provisions since many Sections of the Code are interrelated.

Congress is at times not careful when reconciling new Code provisions with existing Sections. Conflicts among Sections, therefore, do arise.

Be alert for hidden definitions; terms in a particular Code Section may be defined in the same Section *or in a separate Section*.

Some answers may not be found in the Code; therefore, a researcher may have to consult the Regulations and/or judicial decisions.

Take careful note of measuring words such as "less than 50%," "more than 50%," and "at least 80%."

Assessing the Validity of a Treasury Regulation.   It is often stated that Treasury Regulations have the force and effect of law. This is certainly true for most Regulations, but some judicial decisions that have held a Regulation or a portion thereof invalid, usually on the grounds that the Regulation is contrary to the intent of Congress upon the enactment of a particular Code Section. Most often the courts do not question the validity of Regulations because of the belief that "the first administrative interpretation of a provision as it appears in a new act often expresses the general understanding of the times or the actual understanding of those who played an important part when the statute was drafted."[17]

Keep in mind the following observations when assessing the validity of a Regulation:

- IRS agents must give the Code and the Regulations issued thereunder equal weight when dealing with taxpayers and their representatives.

- Proposed Regulations provide a preview of future final Regulations, but they are not binding on the IRS or taxpayers.

- In a challenge, the burden of proof is on the taxpayer to show that the Regulation is wrong. However, a court may invalidate a Regulation that varies from the language of the statute and has no support in the Committee Reports.

- If the taxpayer loses the challenge, the imposition of the negligence penalty can result. This provision deals with the "disregard of rules or regulations" on the part of the taxpayer.

- Final Regulations tend to be legislative, interpretative, or procedural. Procedural Regulations neither establish tax laws nor attempt to explain tax laws.

- Some interpretative Regulations merely reprint or rephrase what Congress has stated in its Committee Reports issued in connection with the enactment of tax legislation. Such Regulations are "hard and solid" and almost impossible to overturn because they clearly reflect the intent of Congress.

- In some Code Sections, Congress has given to the "Secretary or his delegate" the authority to prescribe Regulations to carry out the details of administration or

---

17. *Augustus v. Comm.*, 41–1 USTC ¶9255, 26 AFTR
    612, 118 F.2d 38 (CA–6, 1941).

to otherwise complete the operating rules. Under such circumstances, it could almost be said that Congress is delegating its legislative powers to the Treasury Department. Regulations issued pursuant to this type of authority truly possess the force and effect of law and are often called "legislative Regulations" (e.g., consolidated return Regulations).

Assessing the Validity of Other Administrative Sources of the Tax Law.   Revenue Rulings issued by the IRS carry less weight than Treasury Department Regulations. Rulings are important, however, in that they reflect the position of the IRS on tax matters. In any dispute with the IRS on the interpretation of tax law, therefore, taxpayers should expect agents to follow the results reached in any applicable Rulings.

Revenue Rulings further tell the taxpayer the IRS's reaction to certain court decisions. Recall that the IRS follows a practice of either acquiescing (agreeing) or nonacquiescing (not agreeing) with the *Regular* decisions of the U.S. Tax Court. This does not mean that a particular decision of the Tax Court is of no value if, for example, the IRS has nonacquiesced in the result. It does, however, indicate that the IRS will continue to litigate the issue involved.

Assessing the Validity of Judicial Sources of the Tax Law.   The judicial process as it relates to the formulation of tax law has already been described. How much reliance can be placed on a particular decision depends upon the following variables.

- The level of the court. A decision rendered by a trial court (e.g., a Federal District Court) carries less weight than one issued by an appellate court (e.g., the Fifth Court of Appeals). Unless Congress changes the Code, decisions by the U.S. Supreme Court represent the last word on any tax issue.

- The legal residence of the taxpayer. If, for example, a taxpayer lives in Texas, a decision of the Fifth Court of Appeals means more than one rendered by the Second Court of Appeals. This is the case because any appeal from a District Court or the Tax Court would be to the Fifth Court of Appeals and not to the Second Court of Appeals.[18]

- A Tax Court Regular decision carries more weight than a Memorandum decision because the Tax Court does not consider Memorandum decisions to be binding precedents. Furthermore, a Tax Court *reviewed* decision carries even more weight. All of the Tax Court judges participate in a reviewed decision.

- A Circuit Court decision where certiorari has been requested and denied by the Supreme Court carries more weight than a Circuit Court decision that was not appealed. A Circuit Court decision heard *en banc* (all the judges participate) carries more weight than a normal Circuit Court case.

- Whether the decision represents the weight of authority on the issue. In other words, is it supported by the results reached by other courts?

- The outcome or status of the decision on appeal. For example, was the decision appealed and, if so, with what result?

---

18. Before October 1, 1982, an appeal from the then-named U.S. Court of Claims (the other trial court) was directly to the U.S. Supreme Court.

In connection with the last two variables, the use of a citator is helpful to tax research.[19] The use of a citator is not illustrated in this text.

Assessing the Validity of Other Sources.   *Primary sources* of tax law include the Constitution, legislative history materials, statutes, treaties, Treasury Regulations, IRS pronouncements, and judicial decisions. The IRS considers only primary sources to constitute substantial authority. However, a researcher might wish to refer to *secondary materials* such as legal periodicals, treatises, legal opinions, general counsel memoranda, technical memoranda, and written determinations. In general, secondary sources are not authority. Reg. § 1.6661–3(b)(2) summarizes the opinion of the IRS as follows:

> In determining whether there is substantial authority . . . the following will be considered authority: Applicable provisions of the Internal Revenue Code and other statutory provisions; . . . regulations construing such statutes; court cases; administrative pronouncements (including revenue rulings and revenue procedures); tax treaties and regulations thereunder, and Treasury Department and other official explanations of such treaties; and Congressional intent as reflected in committee reports, . . . statements of managers . . . . Conclusions reached in treatises, legal periodicals, legal opinions or opinions rendered by other tax professionals, . . .general counsel memoranda. . ., technical memoranda, written determinations (except as provided in paragraph (b)(4)(i)). . . are not authority. The authorities underlying such expressions of opinions where applicable to the facts of a particular case, however, may give rise to substantial authority for the tax treatment of an item.

A letter ruling or determination letter is substantial authority only to the taxpayer to whom it is issued.

Upon the completion of major tax legislation, the staff of the Joint Committee on Taxation (in consultation with the staffs of the House Ways and Means and Senate Finance Committees) often will prepare a General Explanation of the Act, commonly known as the Bluebook because of the color of its cover. The IRS will not accept this detailed explanation as having legal effect. The Bluebook does, however, provide valuable guidance to tax advisers and taxpayers until Regulations are issued, and some letter rulings and General Counsel's Memoranda of the IRS cite such explanations.

Arriving at the Solution or at Alternative Solutions

Returning to Example 2, assume the researcher decides that the loan approach can be justified from the factual situation involved. Does this lead to a bad debt deduction for the mother? Before this question can be resolved, the loan needs to be classified as either a business or a nonbusiness debt. One of the reasons this classification is important is that a nonbusiness bad debt cannot be deducted until it becomes entirely worthless. Unlike a business debt, no deduction for partial worthlessness is allowed.[20]

It is very likely that the loan the mother made in 1983 falls into the nonbusiness category. Unless exceptional circumstances exist (e.g., the lender was in the trade or business of lending money), loans in a related-party setting invariably are treated as nonbusiness. The probability is therefore high that the mother would be relegated to nonbusiness bad debt status.

---

19. The major citators are published by Commerce Clearing House, Prentice-Hall, and Shepard's Citations, Inc.

20. § 166(d)(1)(A).

The mother has the burden of proving that the remaining unpaid balance of $42,000 is *entirely* worthless.[21] In this connection, what collection effort, if any, has the mother made? But would any such collection effort be fruitless? Perhaps the son is insolvent, ill, unemployed, or has disappeared for parts unknown.

Even if the debt is entirely worthless, one further issue remains to be resolved. In what year did the worthlessness occur? It could be, for example, that worthlessness took place in a year before it was claimed.[22]

A clear-cut answer may not be possible as to a bad debt deduction for the mother as to year 1990 (seven years after the advance was made). This does not, however, detract from the value of the research. Often a guarded judgment is the best possible solution to a tax problem.

Working with the Tax Law—Tax Planning

Tax research and tax planning are inseparable. The primary purpose of effective tax planning is to maximize the taxpayer's after-tax wealth. This does not mean that the course of action selected must produce the lowest possible tax under the circumstances. The minimization of tax liability must be considered in context with the legitimate business goals of the taxpayer.

A secondary objective of effective tax planning works toward a reduction or deferral of the tax in the current tax year. Specifically, this objective aims to accomplish any one or more of the following procedures: eradicating the tax entirely; eliminating the tax in the current year; deferring the receipt of income; proliferating taxpayers (i.e., forming partnerships and corporations or making lifetime gifts to family members); eluding double taxation; avoiding ordinary income; or creating, increasing, or accelerating deductions. However, this second objective should be accepted with considerable reservation. Although the maxim "A bird in the hand is worth two in the bush" has general validity, there are frequent cases in which the rule breaks down. For example, a tax election in one year, although it accomplishes a current reduction in taxes, could saddle future years with a disadvantageous tax position.

Nontax Considerations

An honest danger exists that tax motivations may take on a significance that does not conform with the true values involved. In other words, tax considerations can operate to impair the exercise of sound business judgment by the taxpayer. Thus, the tax planning process can become a medium through which to accomplish ends that are socially and economically objectionable. Ostensibly, a pronounced tendency exists for planning to go toward the opposing extremes of either not enough or too much emphasis on tax considerations. The happy medium—a balance that recognizes the significance of taxes, but not beyond the point at which planning serves to detract from the exercise of good business judgment—turns out to be the promised land that is seldom reached.

The remark is often made that a good rule to follow is to refrain from pursuing any course of action that would not be followed were it not for certain tax considerations. This statement is not entirely correct, but it does illustrate the desirability of preventing business logic from being "sacrificed at the altar of tax planning."

---

21. Compare *John K. Sexton*, 48 TCM 512, T.C.Memo. 1984–360, with *Stewart T. Oatman*, 45 TCM 214, T.C.Memo. 1982–684.

22. *Ruth Wertheim Smith*, 34 TCM 1474, T.C.Memo. 1975–339.

Tax Evasion and Tax Avoidance

A fine line exists between legal tax planning and illegal tax planning—tax avoidance versus tax evasion. Tax avoidance is merely tax minimization through legal techniques. In this sense, tax avoidance becomes the proper objective of all tax planning. Tax evasion, although also aimed at the elimination or reduction of taxes, connotes the use of subterfuge and fraud as a means to an end. Popular usage—probably because of the common goals involved—has linked these two concepts to the extent that any true distinctions have been obliterated in the minds of many. Consequently, the taint created by the association of tax avoidance and tax evasion has deterred some taxpayers from properly taking advantage of the planning possibilities. The now classic words of Judge Learned Hand in *Commissioner v. Newman* reflects the true values the individual should have:

> Over and over again courts have said that there is nothing sinister in so arranging one's affairs as to keep taxes as low as possible. Everybody does so, rich or poor; and all do right, for nobody owes any public duty to pay more than the law demands: taxes are enforced extractions, not voluntary contributions. To demand more in the name of morals is mere cant.[23]

Follow-up Procedures

Because tax planning usually involves a proposed (as opposed to a completed) transaction, it is predicated upon the continuing validity of the advice based upon the tax research. A change in the tax law (either legislative, administrative, or judicial) could alter the original conclusion. Additional research may be necessary to test the solution in light of current developments (refer to one set of broken lines depicted in Figure 27-4 on page 27-19).

Tax Planning—A Practical Application

Returning to the facts in Example 2, what should be done to help protect the mother's bad debt deduction?

- All formalities should be present as to the loan (e.g., written instrument, definite and realistic due date).

- Upon default, the lender (mother) should make a reasonable effort to collect from the borrower (son). If not, the mother should be in a position to explain why any such effort would be to no avail.

- If interest is provided for, it should be paid.

- Any interest paid (or imputed under § 7872) should be recognized as income by the mother.

- Because of the annual exclusion of $10,000, it appears doubtful that actual (or imputed) interest would necessitate the filing by the mother of a Federal gift tax return. But should one be due, it should be filed.

- If § 7872 applies (not enough or no interest is provided for), the son should keep track of his net investment income. This is advisable since the income the mother must recognize might be limited by such amount.

---

23. *Comm. v. Newman*, 47-1 USTC ¶ 9175, 35 AFTR 857, 159 F.2d 848 (CA-2, 1947).

Computer-Assisted Tax Research

The computer is being used more and more frequently in the day-to-day practice of tax professionals, students, and educators. Many software vendors offer tax return software programs for individual, corporate, partnership, and fiduciary returns. The use of computers, however, is not limited to the role of batch-processed tax returns and computer timesharing for quantitative tax and problem-solving planning and calculations.

Predictions are that the microcomputer will become the revolutionary tool of the future—much as the electronic calculator did in the 1970s. Electronic spreadsheets are being used to replace the 14-column worksheet. The electronic spreadsheet approach can be used for retirement planning, 1040 projections, real estate projections, partnership allocations, consolidated tax return problems, compensation planning—anything for which projections and calculations are needed. Internally prepared tax-related programs are used by many public accounting firms. Software is available for the microcomputer for estate planning calculations.

LEXIS, a computerized legal data bank, has been available since 1973 as a complement to the conventional research approach (available in at least one-half of the more than 70 graduate tax programs). WESTLAW, a competitive system from West Publishing Company, has been operational since 1975. Prentice-Hall has a national computer network, called PHINet, which makes its looseleaf service accessible by computer. WESTLAW, LEXIS, and PHINet are document retrieval systems only; they cannot interpret the law.

Users have access to these computerized data banks through special terminals and long-distance telephone lines. A user selects key words, phrases, or numbers and types the search request on the keyboard on the terminal. A display screen then shows the full text or portions of the various documents containing the words, phrases, or numbers in the search request. A printer can be used to obtain hard copy of any documents or portions of a document. For example, a researcher can obtain the decisions of a particular judge or court over a specified time period. It is also possible to access judicial opinions containing specific words or phrases of statutory language. These computer-assisted tax systems can be used as a citator by collecting all judicial decisions that have cited a particular decision or statute as well as all decisions that have a specific combination of two or more earlier decisions or statutes.

Computer-assisted tax research is useful in searching for facts because human indexing evolves around legal theories rather than fact patterns. Computer searching is also useful in finding new court decisions not yet in the printed indexes. Because computer searching probably does not find as many relevant cases as does manual searching, a combination of manual and computer searching can be quite effective.

PROBLEM MATERIALS

Discussion Questions

1. Where do the primary sources of tax information originate?
2. The Technical and Miscellaneous Revenue Act of 1988 became part of the Internal Revenue Code of 1986. Explain this statement.
3. In which legislative committee does a tax provision normally begin?

4. Why are Committee Reports of Congress important as a source of tax law?

5. Where may Proposed Regulations first be found? How would a Proposed Regulation under § 115 be cited?

6. How much reliance may be placed upon a Temporary Regulation?

7. Distinguish between the following:
    a. Treasury Regulations and Revenue Rulings.
    b. Revenue Rulings and Revenue Procedures.
    c. Revenue Rulings and letter rulings.
    d. Letter rulings and determination letters.

8. Rank the following items from the highest authority to the lowest in the Federal tax law system:
    a. Interpretative Regulation.
    b. Legislative Regulation.
    c. Letter ruling.
    d. Revenue Procedure.
    e. Internal Revenue Code.
    f. Proposed Regulation.

9. Interpret each of the following citations:
    a. Rev.Rul. 81–167, 1981–1 C.B. 45.
    b. Rev.Proc. 85–41, 1985–2 C.B. 482.
    c. Ltt.Rul. 8803020.

10. Which of the following statements would be considered advantages of the Small Claims Division of the Tax Court?
    a. Appeal to the Court of Appeals for the Federal Circuit is possible.
    b. A hearing of a deficiency of $11,200 is considered on a timely basis.
    c. Taxpayer can handle the litigation without using a lawyer or certified public accountant.
    d. Taxpayer can use other Small Claims decisions for precedent value.
    e. The actual hearing is held on an informal basis.
    f. Travel time will probably be reduced.

11. List an advantage and a disadvantage of using the U.S. Tax Court as the trial court for Federal tax litigation.

12. List an advantage and a disadvantage of using a U.S. District Court as the trial court for Federal tax litigation.

13. List an advantage and a disadvantage of using the U.S. Claims Court as the trial court for Federal tax litigation.

14. K lives in Michigan. In a controversy with the IRS, K loses at the trial court level. Describe the appeal procedure for each of the following trial courts:
    a. Small Claims Division of the U.S. Tax Court.
    b. U.S. Tax Court.
    c. U.S. District Court.
    d. U.S. Claims Court.

15. Suppose the U.S. Government loses a tax case in the U.S. District Court of Idaho and does not appeal the result. What does the failure to appeal signify?

16. To what court are decisions of each of the following courts first appealed?
    a. Small Claims Court.
    b. Federal District Court.

    c. U.S. Claims Court.

    d. U.S. Tax Court.

    e. Federal Court of Appeals.

17. A taxpayer from a U.S. District Court in which of the following states could appeal a decision to the Eighth Court of Appeals?

    a. Alaska.

    b. Arkansas.

    c. Arizona.

    d. Alabama.

    e. Maine.

    f. None of the above.

18. In assessing the validity of a prior court decision, discuss the significance of the following on the taxpayer's issue:

    a. The decision was rendered by the U.S. District Court of Wyoming. Taxpayer lives in Wyoming.

    b. The decision was rendered by the U.S. Claims Court. Taxpayer lives in Wyoming.

    c. The decision was rendered by the Second Court of Appeals. Taxpayer lives in California.

    d. The decision was rendered by the U.S. Supreme Court.

    e. The decision was rendered by the U.S. Tax Court. The IRS has acquiesced in the result.

    f. Same as (e), except that the IRS has nonacquiesced in the result.

19. What is the difference between a Regular and a Memorandum decision of the U.S. Tax Court?

20. Interpret each of the following citations:

    a. 54 T.C. 1514 (1970).

    b. 408 F.2d 117 (CA–2, 1969).

    c. 69–1 USTC ¶9319 (CA–2, 1969).

    d. 23 AFTR2d 69–1090 (CA–2, 1969).

    e. 293 F.Supp. 1129 (D.Ct., Miss., 1967).

    f. 67–1 USTC ¶9253 (D.Ct., Miss., 1967).

    g. 19 AFTR2d 647 (D.Ct., Miss., 1967).

    h. 56 S.Ct. 289 (USSC, 1935).

    i. 36–1 USTC ¶9020 (USSC, 1935).

    j. 16 AFTR 1274 (USSC, 1935).

    k. 422 F.2d 1336 (Ct.Cls., 1970).

21. Explain the following abbreviations:

a.	CA–2	i.	USTC
b.	Cls.Ct.	j.	AFTR
c.	*aff'd.*	k.	F.2d
d.	*rev'd.*	l.	F.Supp.
e.	*rem'd.*	m.	USSC
f.	*Cert. denied*	n.	S.Ct.
g.	*acq.*	o.	D.Ct.
h.	B.T.A.		

22. Give Prentice-Hall's citation for each of the following courts:
    a. Small Claims Division of the Tax Court.
    b. Federal District Court.
    c. Supreme Court.
    d. Tax Court Memorandum decision.

23. Where can you locate a published decision of the U.S. Claims Court?

24. A student friend majoring in sociology insists that tax advisers are immoral because they merely help people cheat the government. Defend tax planning by tax advisers.

Problems

25. T, an individual taxpayer, has just been audited by the IRS and, as a result, has been assessed a substantial deficiency (which he has not yet paid) in additional income taxes. In preparing his defense, T advances the following possibilities:
    a. Although a resident of Kentucky, T plans to sue in a U.S. District Court in Oregon that appears to be more favorably inclined toward taxpayers.
    b. If (a) is not possible, T plans to take his case to a Kentucky state court where an uncle is the presiding judge.
    c. Since T has found a B.T.A. decision that seems to help his case, he plans to rely on it under alternative (a) or (b).
    d. If he loses at the trial court level, T plans to appeal to either the U.S. Claims Court or the U.S. Second Court of Appeals. The reason for this choice is that he has relatives in both Washington, D.C., and New York. Staying with these relatives could save T lodging expense while his appeal is being heard by the court selected.
    e. Whether or not he wins at the trial court or appeals court level, T feels certain of success on an appeal to the U.S. Supreme Court.

    Evaluate T's notions concerning the judicial process as it applies to Federal income tax controversies.

26. Using the legend provided, classify each of the following statements (more than one answer per statement may be appropriate):

    Legend

D	=	Applies to the U.S. District Court
T	=	Applies to the U.S. Tax Court
C	=	Applies to the U.S. Claims Court
A	=	Applies to the U.S. Court of Appeals
U	=	Applies to the U.S. Supreme Court
N	=	Applies to none of the above

    a. Decides only Federal tax matters.
    b. Decisions are reported in the F.2d Series.
    c. Decisions are reported in the USTCs.
    d. Decisions are reported in the AFTRs.
    e. Appeal is by Writ of Certiorari.
    f. Court meets most often in Washington, D.C.
    g. Offers the choice of a jury trial.

h.   Is a trial court.

i.   Is an appellate court.

j.   Allows appeal to the Court of Appeals for the Federal Circuit and bypasses the taxpayer's particular Court of Appeals.

k.   Has a Small Claims Division.

l.   Is the only trial court where the taxpayer does not have to first pay the tax assessed by the IRS.

Research Problems

Chapter 2

Research Problem 1   Jerry, who is 13 years old, earned $1,200 from a paper route during 1990. In addition, he had two savings accounts. He earned interest of $1,200 on an account set up for him, in his name, by his grandparents. Jerry also earned $450 on a savings account he set up with earnings from his paper route over the last three years. How much of Jerry's interest income is treated as unearned income taxable at his parents' rate?

Research Problem 2   Emily's daughter, Sarah, graduated from high school on May 15, 1989. Emily and Sarah's father were divorced in 1987, and Emily was awarded custody of Sarah. Under the custody agreement, Sarah spent the last half of May and the entire months of June, July, and August with her father. Sarah returned to Emily's home on September 1, stayed there the first week of September, and then went away to college and lived on campus for the rest of the year. Can Emily file as a head of household for 1989?

Chapter 3

Research Problem 3   T is the vice president of a large publicly held corporation. As an officer, T has participated in the company's bonus plan for several years. In a previous year, the bonuses given were in the form of annuity contracts purchased from an insurance company. The contracts were nontransferable, and payments did not begin until the employee reached age 65. T's return was examined, and the revenue agent contended that T should include the purchase price of the annuity in income in the year the contract was received. Since the annuity is nontransferable and T does not have the option to receive cash, T does not think income should be recognized until collection on the annuity contract begins. The taxpayer asks your opinion on the matter.

Research Problem 4   Mr. A is a commissioned agent for a large insurance company. During the year he purchased a policy on his life and the lives of his children and received a commission. Mr. A treated the commission on these policies as a reduction in cost rather than as income. However, during an audit the revenue agent indicates that Mr. A must include the commission in his gross income. The taxpayer seeks your assistance in resolving the matter with the agent.

Partial list of research aids:

Ostheimer v. U.S., 59–1 USTC ¶ 9300, 3 AFTR2d 886, 264 F.2d 789 (CA–3, 1959).
Rev.Rul. 55–273, 1955–1 C.B. 221.

Chapter 4

Research Problem 5   S was asked by the M County School Board to resign her position as superintendent of public schools. She refused and submitted to the board

a list of grievances. She also alleged that the board had damaged her professional reputation. S was later fired, but after threatening suit she was paid $20,000 by the board. S has supplied a doctor's testimony clearly showing that the dispute with the board caused her to become physically and mentally ill. Is the $20,000 taxable?

Research Problem 6   E was recently hired as manager of Fertile Farm, Inc. E is required to live in the employer's house on the farm. E and the employer are trying to decide how to arrange terms with the electric company. The employer would like E to have the account with the utility in E's name, but the employer would reimburse E $200 each month. The $200 should be adequate to cover all charges. The employer requests this arrangement because the previous manager established the account in the company's name and left town without paying the bill. E has asked your tax advice on the matter.

Chapter 5

Research Problem 7   Taxpayer, a certified public accountant, gave the wrong advice to a client. As a result, the client incurred an additional $75,000 of costs. The CPA reimbursed the client and, although he had malpractice insurance, failed to file a claim for fear of either having his insurance cancelled or having the premiums drastically increased. Can the taxpayer deduct the $75,000 as a loss incurred in a trade or business under § 165(c) or as an ordinary and necessary business expense under § 162 of the Code?

Research Problem 8   S is a self-employed lawyer. One of his hobbies is songwriting. He had one song published in 1986. Over the next three years, S spent a considerable amount of time writing songs and meeting with producers. He has not shown a profit. He maintains a separate room in his house for the sole purpose of writing music, and he deducted a pro rata share of the utility bills and other home expenses. He incurred other expenses amounting to $4,000. Will his expenses for this endeavor be disallowed as a hobby loss?

Research aid:

§ 183

Chapter 6

Research Problem 9   H is a married individual who files a separate return for the taxable year. He is employed full-time as an attorney. H, who also owns an interest in a minor league baseball team, does no work in connection with the activity during the year. He anticipates that the activity will result in a loss for the taxable year. H pays his wife to work as an office receptionist in connection with the activity for an average of 20 hours a week during the year. Will H be allowed to deduct his share of the loss from the activity?

Research Problem 10   J owns interests in three business activities, X, Y, and Z. J does not materially participate in any of the activities considered separately, but he does participate for 110 hours in Activity X, 160 hours in Activity Y, and 125 hours in Activity Z. J does not own interests in any other businesses. J's net passive income (loss) for the taxable year from Activities X, Y, and Z is as follows:

	X	Y	Z
Gross income	$ 600	$ 700	$ 900
Deductions	(200)	($1,000)	(300)
Net income (loss)	$ 400	($ 300)	$ 600

How much of the gross income from the three activities is treated as income that is not from a passive activity?

Chapter 7

Research Problem 11   Joe Smith, the treasurer of X Corporation, has been embezzling company funds for the past three years. Joe has now been caught, and these embezzled amounts, which constitute taxable income, have created a very large tax deficiency for the prior three years. During the current year, Joe repaid a portion of the embezzled funds. This amount has been taken as a deduction on Joe's current year tax return. Discuss with Joe the possibility of the repayment of the embezzled funds creating a net operating loss that can be carried back and reduce some of the tax deficiency for the prior three years.

Research Problem 12   A and B have a winter home in Park City, Utah, where they take frequent skiing vacations. In the spring of the current year, after an unusually wet winter and a record-setting thaw, a mudslide came through the subdivision. The slide damaged the garage of the home. If adequate support had been given to the hill, the slide likely would have been avoided. The mudslide also caused damage to neighboring homes, resulting in a drop in value of all the homes in the area. The damage to the garage was $10,000, and the home decreased in value by $20,000. How much, if any, of the damage and/or the loss in value can be deducted as a § 165 casualty loss?

Chapter 8

Research Problem 13   H, one of your clients, is considering building a golf course in the resort area of Sun River, Oregon. Because the land is unimproved, all of the sand traps, greens, fairways, and tees will need to be constructed. Advise H as to whether any deductions can be taken on these landscaping improvements.

Research Problem 14   DJ operated several garbage dumps throughout the Chicago area. In 1990, DJ purchased a tract of land for $150,000. This land contained a pit that could accommodate 2,500,000 cubic yards of garbage. In 1990, the value of the land was reasonably estimated to be worth $55,000 without the pit. The sellers indicated that they had charged a premium for the land because they knew that DJ needed land with a pit for dumping garbage in that area. At the end of 1990 and several years thereafter, DJ had the property surveyed to determine the amount of space filled and the amount remaining. In 1990, 2,300,000 cubic yards remained to be filled. Discuss whether DJ would be able to depreciate the value of the air space that is now being reduced by the dumping of the garbage.

Chapter 9

Research Problem 15   T, an employee of X Corporation, is transferred overseas for a three-year duty assignment in Japan. In connection with the transfer, T incurs significant moving expenses, all of which were reimbursed by X Corporation. Since T did not want to take his household goods with him, he placed them in storage in the United States. X Corporation also reimbursed T for the storage charges he paid. After the three-year assignment, T returns to the United States. All moving expenses are again reimbursed by X Corporation. Because T is now 65 years of age, he retires upon reaching the United States.

a.   What are the special rules governing the moving expenses of expatriates (U.S. persons employed abroad)?

b.   Do the storage charges qualify for the deduction?

c.   Will T's moving expenses from the United States to Japan be treated the same as those for the return from Japan to the United States? Explain.

Research Problem 16   T, a heart specialist, left his job in Texas to accept a position in a California medical center. In addition to seeing patients, he was required to work on the hospital's heart transplant project under the supervision of Dr. H. Dr. H was an

impossible boss, who had already had two other doctors removed from the team. After 35 weeks of employment, Dr. H had T terminated from the project. Will T be able to deduct his moving expenses?

Research aid:

§ 217(c)(2)

Chapter 10

Research Problem 17   The taxpayer suffered from hypoglycemia, a condition caused by abnormally low blood sugar in the body. The taxpayer's doctor prescribed frequent feedings of a high protein diet as the major treatment for the condition. Taxpayer compared her food bills with those of her friends and estimated that the cost of her food with high protein supplements was much greater than that of ordinary food bought at the grocery store. In the current year, taxpayer paid $3,483 for food and estimated that 30% of this sum was attributable to extra protein required to treat her condition. Is this extra sum deductible as a medical expense?

Research Problem 18   Several years ago, R, a cash basis taxpayer, obtained a mortgage from State Bank to purchase a personal residence. In December 1990, $9,500 of interest was due on the mortgage, but R had only $75 in his checking account. On December 31, 1990, R borrowed $9,500 from State Bank, evidenced by a note, and the proceeds were deposited in R's checking account. On the same day, R issued a check in the identical amount of $9,500 to State Bank for the interest expense due. Is this interest expense deductible for the tax year 1990?

Partial list of research aids:

§ 163(h)(3).

William M. Roberts, 53 TCM 787, T.C.Memo. 1987–235.

Chapter 11

Research Problem 19   T is a CPA employed by an international accounting firm. In 1984, the accounting firm asked T to transfer to its Paris office. As part of the inducement to get T to accept the transfer, the accounting firm agreed to reimburse him for all expenses incurred in the move. The firm also agreed to pay all of T's moving expenses on his eventual return to the United States. Reimbursement of moving expenses for the return move was not contingent on T's continued employment by the firm. In 1990, T returned to the United States and was assigned to the firm's New York office. T properly included the reimbursement in gross income in 1990. In computing his foreign tax credit, T treated the reimbursement as income earned from personal services performed outside the United States. The IRS treated the income as earned from services performed within the United States and reduced T's foreign tax credit. Should T contest the IRS treatment of the moving expense reimbursement?

Chapter 12

Research Problem 20   S owned 3,000 acres of timberland in Oregon. CZ Corporation offered to purchase the property for $4.5 million. Since the adjusted basis for the land was only $400,000, S did not want to have the large recognized gain that would result. CZ Corporation offered to purchase the land on the installment method and thereby spread the recognized gain over the period of the installment payments. S rejected the proposal and countered with the following proposal.

- The land (fair market value of $4.5 million) would be transferred from S to CZ Corporation in exchange for a five-year contract under which S would have the right to identify real property that CZ Corporation would purchase and transfer to S.

- At the end of the five-year period, the remainder of the $4.5 million that had not been so expended would be transferred to S in cash.

- During the five-year period, the amount of the $4.5 million not expended by the end of each year was to be increased by a growth factor of 12% per year.

    a. Does the exchange qualify as a like-kind exchange under § 1031(a)?
    b. What is the appropriate treatment of the growth factor?
        Partial list of research aids:
        Starker v. U.S., 75–1 USTC ¶ 9443, 35 AFTR2d 75–1550 (D.Ct.Ore., 1975).

Research Problem 21   On January 1, 1990, X, a major shareholder in H Corporation, purchases land from the company for $300,000. The fair market value of the land is $1,200,000, and the adjusted basis in the hands of the corporation is $400,000.

    a. What are the possible tax consequences to X?
    b. What is the basis of the land to X?
    c. What is the tax consequence to H Corporation?

Research Problem 22   T owns real estate with an adjusted basis of $600,000 and a fair market value of $1,100,000. The amount of the nonrecourse mortgage on the property is $2,500,000. Because of substantial past and projected future losses associated with the real estate development (occupancy rate of only 37% after three years), T deeds the property to the creditor.

    a. What are the tax consequences to T?
    b. Assume the data are the same, except the fair market value of the property is $2,525,000. Therefore, T also receives $25,000 from the creditor when he deeds the property to the creditor. What are the tax consequences to T?

Partial list of research aids:

Rev.Rul. 76–111, 1976–1 C.B. 214.

Crane v. Comm., 47 USTC ¶9217, 35 AFTR 776, 67 S.Ct. 1047 (USSC, 1947).

Chapter 13

Research Problem 23   X Corporation has plants in a number of U.S. cities. It frequently transfers executives between those cities. If the executive cannot sell his or her home, the realty division of X Corporation will buy the home at its appraised value after 90 days. The realty division will then immediately attempt to resell the home. What is the nature of the gains and losses the realty division realizes when it sells the homes?

Research Problem 24   S owns a professional football franchise. He has received an offer of $80 million for the franchise, all the football equipment, the right to concession receipts, the rights to a stadium lease, and the rights to all the player contracts owned by S. Most of the players have been with the team for quite a long time and have contracts that were signed several years ago. The contracts have been substantially depreciated. S is concerned about potential § 1245 recapture when the contracts are sold. He has heard about "previously unrecaptured depreciation with respect to initial contracts" and would like to know more about it. Find a definition for that phrase and write an explanation of it.

    Partial list of research aids:
    § 1245(a)(4).

Research Problem 25   On May 10, 1984, D purchased a $160,000 building (but not the land) that was 60 feet wide, 80 feet deep, and two stories high. The front 60 feet of the 80-foot first-floor depth was rented as a retail store. The remaining 20 feet of the

first floor and all of the second floor were rented for residential use. D used the ACRS statutory percentages and sold the building for $140,000 in 1990. D is unsure whether all the depreciation is subject to recapture by § 1245, some of it is subject to recapture by § 1250, or none of it is subject to recapture.

Does § 1245 or § 1250 recapture apply in this situation?

Chapter 14

Research Problem 26   T is a full-time gambler whose only source of income is money that he wins from his gambling activities. IRS contends that T's gambling losses should be treated as itemized deductions for purposes of computing the alternative minimum tax. T argues that the gambling losses should be treated as trade or business expenses. Who is correct, T or the IRS?

Research Problem 27   B owns two warehouses that were placed in service before 1987. Accelerated depreciation for 1989 on Warehouse A was $12,000, and straight-line depreciation would have been $8,000. On Warehouse B, accelerated depreciation was $6,000, and straight-line depreciation would have been $7,500. What is the amount of B's tax preference for excess depreciation in 1989?

Chapter 15

Research Problem 28   In November 1990, A agreed to purchase stock from B for $1,000,000. The transaction was to be closed on December 28, 1990. In early December 1990, B became concerned about the taxes due on the sale in 1990. B suggested that the transaction be deferred until January 1991, but A insisted that the stock be transferred on December 28, 1990. A and B agreed that the cash paid by A on December 28, 1990, would be held by the First Bank as A's escrow agent, and the funds would be dispersed to B on January 4, 1991. The IRS agent insists that the escrow amount was constructively received by B in 1990 and that B therefore cannot defer his gain until 1991 under the installment sales rules. Is the agent correct?

Partial list of research aids:

Reed v. Comm., 83–2 USTC ¶ 9728, 53 AFTR2d 84–335, 723 F.2d 138 (CA–1, 1983).

Research Problem 29   In November 1990, M Corporation's accountant discovered that one of the company's warehouses was empty. The perpetual inventory records indicated that $200,000 of merchandise should have been in the warehouse. For 1990, the missing inventory was not included in the company's ending inventory. The stolen merchandise thus became a part of cost of goods sold for the year. The IRS claims the missing merchandise should have been deducted as a theft loss and under Reg. §§ 1.165–1(d)(2)(i) and 1.165–8(a)(2) is not deductible if there is a reasonable prospect for recovery. Moreover, the company had good prospects of recovery of the loss from the employees, insurance company, or auditors. Assuming the IRS is correct—that there is a reasonable prospect for recovery as of the end of the year—is the taxpayer foreclosed from deducting the $200,000 in 1990?

Partial list of research aids:

National Home Products, Inc., 71 T.C. 501 (1979).

Chapter 16

Research Problem 30   In 1980, several unrelated individuals created Joya Trust with a transfer of undeveloped real estate located near a large metropolitan area. In return for the transfer, the grantors received beneficial interests in Joya that were of a stated value and freely transferable. Under the trust instrument, the trust was to last 25 years or until dissolution by the trustees, whichever occurred sooner. The trust was not to terminate upon the death of a trustee, and the trustees were empowered to appoint

their own successors. The trustees were authorized to call annual meetings of the beneficiaries, but the votes of such beneficiaries were advisory only. Under applicable state law, the liability of the beneficiaries was limited to their investment in the trust.

Pursuant to authority granted by the trust instrument, Joya Trust arranged for the development of the real estate into recreational facilities (e.g., golf courses, tennis courts) and luxury housing units. When developed, the real estate was either sold or leased to the general public. Joya continued to manage the unsold and leased units as well as the recreational facilities until it was dissolved by action of its trustees in 1989. During its existence, how should Joya Trust be treated for Federal income tax purposes? Why?

Research Problem 31   A, a wealthy individual, had substantial income in 1989. A owned 80% of the common (voting) stock in AB Corporation and 100% of the preferred stock. The preferred stock, 65,000 shares, had a call value of $50,000. AB Corporation was required to pay a dividend of $2 per share on the preferred stock before any dividends could be paid on the common stock. On March 10, 1989, AB Corporation declared a dividend of $2 per share on the preferred stock and $1 per share on the common stock. The dividend was payable on April 10, 1989, to those shareholders on record as of April 1, 1989. On March 20, 1989, A gave all his preferred shares to his favorite charity, Y-Tech University. On April 10, 1989, AB Corporation paid Y-Tech a dividend of $130,000. On June 15, 1989, A offered to purchase the preferred shares from Y-Tech for the then value of the shares, $50,000. As Y-Tech had no desire to remain a shareholder in AB Corporation, it sold the stock to A for $50,000. On his 1989 tax return, A claimed a charitable contribution deduction of $180,000, the value of the preferred stock on the date of the gift. (The $180,000 value was reflected in the $50,000 call value of the stock plus the $130,000 dividend that had been declared on the stock.) A reported no income in connection with the transfer of the stock. Upon an audit of A's return in 1990, the IRS asserted a tax deficiency against A, contending that A had ordinary income of $130,000 as a result of the dividend payment to the charity. The IRS contended that the assignment of income doctrine caused the dividend income to be attributed to A. A contends that he should not be taxed on the dividend as Y-Tech University was "entitled" to the dividend payment. Should A be taxed on the dividend payment to the charity?

Chapter 17

Research Problem 32   J, the principal shareholder of X Corporation, diverted sums totaling $60,000 from the corporation during tax year 1987. Upon audit of J's return, the IRS contended these sums were taxable income to J under § 61 of the Code. J disagrees, stating that such sums represent constructive dividends and are taxable only to the extent of X Corporation's E & P, which J argues had a deficit in 1986. The IRS contends that should § 61 not apply, the $60,000 would still be taxable income because X Corporation had income in 1987. X Corporation is on the cash basis. It had a deficit in its E & P account as of January 1, 1987. However, it had E & P in 1987 of $65,000. Its income tax liability for 1987 was $31,500. The IRS argues that $31,500 cannot be a charge against current E & P because the tax was not paid until 1988 and the corporation was on the cash basis. Consequently, the $60,000 would be taxable income to J in 1987, regardless of whether it is income under § 61 or under § 301. J comes to you for advice. What advice would you give him?

Research Problem 33   A owns 40% of X Corporation; his father owns the remaining 60%. A also owns 70% of Y Corporation, with the remaining 30% being owned by his wife. A terminates his entire interest in X Corporation through a stock redemption that he reports as a long-term capital gain pursuant to § 302(b)(3). Three years later, Y Corporation enters into a contract with X Corporation whereby Y Corporation is given exclusive management authority over X Corporation's operations.

Upon audit, the IRS disallowed long-term capital gain treatment on the stock redemption in X Corporation contending that A acquired an interest in X within 10 years from the date of the redemption because of Y's management contract with X. What is the result?

Chapter 18

Research Problem 34   YZ Corporation was liquidated in 1987. In the year of liquidation, YZ Corporation reported taxable gain of $8,000,000, based upon a value in its assets of $10,000,000 and a basis of $2,000,000. After paying its tax liability of $2,720,000, YZ Corporation distributed its remaining assets, valued at $7,280,000 ($10,000,000 less the tax paid of $2,720,000), to its 10 shareholders. Shareholder A received $728,000 and reported a long-term capital gain in 1987 of $628,000 ($728,000 distribution – $100,000 stock basis). In 1989, the IRS audited YZ Corporation and determined that the corporation had an additional gain of $1,000,000 in the year of liquidation. The IRS assessed additional tax of $340,000 plus penalties and interest against YZ Corporation and then against A, based on transferee liability. A comes to you for advice. He is not certain where the other shareholders are located.

a. If A is required to pay all of the tax liability, will A be entitled to deduct the amount paid as a loss?

b. What is the nature of the loss—capital or ordinary?

c. Would § 1341 apply?

d. How can a shareholder be protected from the problem facing A?

Research Problem 35   A state-chartered savings and loan association merges with a Federal savings and loan association. The shareholders of the state-chartered savings and loan exchange their guaranty stock in the savings and loan for passbook savings accounts and certificates of deposit in the Federal savings and loan association. The savings accounts and certificates of deposit were the only form of equity in the Federal savings and loan association. Does the merger qualify as an "A" reorganization? Why or why not?

Chapter 19

Research Problem 36   Dr. B owns 90% of the stock of Dental Services, Inc. Dr. B performs medical services under an employment contract with the corporation. He is the only dentist employed and is the only officer of the corporation actively engaged in the production of income. Dental Services, Inc., furnishes office space and equipment and employs a dental hygienist and a receptionist to assist Dr. B.

a. Various patients receive dental care from Dr. B. Does Dental Services have PHC income under § 543(a)(7)?

b. Suppose Patient J secures an absolute binding promise from Dr. B that the dentist will personally perform a root canal operation and that the dentist has no right to substitute another dentist. Would your answer change?

Research Problem 37   In 1990, X Corporation lost a Tax Court decision upholding the following deficiencies in income tax and accumulated earnings tax:

Year	Deficiency in Income Tax	Accumulated Earnings Tax
1979	$360,000	–0–
1980	200,000	450,000
1981	201,000	600,000

May X Corporation deduct the deficiency in income taxes for 1980 and 1981 from accumulated taxable income in order to determine the accumulated earnings tax in 1980 and 1981?

Chapter 20

Research Problem 38   For several years, a father and son held some oil and gas working interests in a general partnership. These working interests incur some losses before they are transferred to a newly created S corporation in early 1989. The corporation acquires some other oil and gas working interests that incur losses, and the original oil and gas interests have both income and losses in 1989. Although the father does not materially participate in the corporation, he draws a salary of $7,000 during 1989. The son materially participates and receives a salary of $26,000 from the corporation. The corporation receives a small amount of interest and dividend income. Discuss the tax ramifications of these transactions under § 469.

Research Problem 39   On February 10, 1989, a calendar year S corporation mistakenly issues a second class of stock, thereby terminating the S election. During 1989, the corporation had nonseparately computed income of $200,000, nonseparately computed deductions of $60,000, tax-exempt income of $20,000, and tax credits of $30,000. The corporate records indicate that through February 9, 1989, the S corporation earned $20,000 of nonseparately computed income, incurred $5,000 of nonseparately computed deductions, and had no tax-exempt income or tax credits. Discuss the annualization procedure for this corporation, including the special election provided for in § 1362(e)(3).

Chapter 21

Research Problem 40   R contributed $50,000 for an interest in the RM Partnership. In its first year of operations, RM incurred legal fees of $2,000 for services incident to the organization of the partnership. R's share of these legal fees was $1,000. On its tax return for the first year of operations, RM did not elect to amortize the legal fees as an organization expense under § 709. Toward the end of the third year of operations, RM decided to wind up operations and liquidate. Based on R's capital account at the end of the third operating year, RM made a final liquidating distribution to R of $90,000. In determining RM's taxable income for its final tax year (the third year), its accountant deducted the $2,000 of organization legal fees on Form 1065 as a § 165 loss. R has asked you, her tax adviser, to determine how she should handle her $1,000 share of the write-off of these legal fees on her Form 1040.

Partial list of research aids:
§§ 165 and 709.
Reg. §§ 1.709–1(b)(2) and 1.709–1(c).

Research Problem 41   X is a partner in the two-person general partnership of XY, which started business five years ago. The partners have agreed to share all profits and losses equally. The partnership and the partners use the cash basis and calendar year. The accounting books and records of the partnership are maintained by an employee. All sales of the partnership are for cash. X and Y participate in the management and operations of the business, and each sells goods to customers and makes cash collections.

Two years ago, Y sold goods to customers and collected related cash that was not reported to the partnership's bookkeeper. These sales and collections amounted to $100,000. Y used some of the embezzled funds to cover his living expenses on a winter vacation to Mexico and Las Vegas. Y lost the remainder of the funds while gambling in Las Vegas. For the year of the embezzlement, the partnership's bookkeeper prepared the tax returns of the partnership and the two partners, and reviewed the returns with them before they were signed, dated, and filed. These returns did not include the embezzled funds.

In the current year, the IRS was auditing the records of the XY Partnership and its partners and discovered the unreported sales. The IRS claims that X must include $50,000 (50% of $100,000) in his income for the year the embezzlement took place. X does not feel that he is receiving fair treatment from the IRS and contacts you for tax

advice as to whether he must report $50,000 of additional partnership income from the embezzlement year.

Partial list of research aids:

U.S. v. Basye, 73-1 USTC ¶9250, 31 AFTR2d 73-802, 93 S.Ct. 1080 (USSC, 1973).

Chapter 23

Research Problem 42   J, a U.S. citizen, lives in Switzerland. He is an artist who sells his paintings throughout the world. As a U.S. citizen, he is subject to taxation on his worldwide income. J seeks to take a foreign earned income exclusion with regard to the income he receives from the sales of the paintings. An IRS agent questions the claim that the income from sale of the paintings is "earned" income for purposes of the exclusion. How would you advise J?

Partial list of research aids:

Mark Tobey, 60 T.C. 227 (1973), *acq.* 1979-1 C.B. 1.

Research Problem 43   George and Fred are both U.S. citizens who work on offshore oil rigs in territorial waters of country F. George works a shift of 28 days followed by 28 days off. On his off-duty days, he flies to his home in Florida where his wife and children live. George's employment prohibits him from living onshore in country F during his rest period. Fred works two out of every three weeks during the same period. He spends his free time in Z, the capital of country F, where he leases an apartment. He has a checking account and a savings account in Z. He also has an automobile, a boat, and other durable goods that he purchased in Z. He does not have a family in the United States, but has a girlfriend in Z. The issue is whether or not George and/or Fred have established a bona fide residence in a foreign country for purposes of the § 911 foreign earned income exclusion.

Partial list of research aids:

Robert C. Bujol, 53 TCM 762, T.C.Memo. 1987-230.

Kurt Van Yost, 44 TCM 1071, T.C.Memo. 1982-516.

Chesley O. James, 55 TCM 1112, T.C.Memo. 1988-266.

Chapter 24

Research Problem 44   Dr. and Mrs. L file a timely 1986 tax return on April 7, 1987. Just before the 3-year statute of limitations runs out, the IRS mails a notice of deficiency to the L's by certified mail, obtaining U.S. Postal Service Form 3877 as proof. Late in 1990 the IRS starts collection proceedings. The L's claim they never received the notice required under § 6212. The IRS is unable to locate the file containing its copy of the notice and Form 3877, but offers employees' testimony regarding regular IRS procedures in such cases as proof that the notice was sent. Would the employees' testimony be sufficient to satisfy the requirements of § 6212? What if the IRS was unable to locate its copy of the deficiency notice, but did have Form 3877?

Research Problem 45   The heirs of an estate engaged an attorney to handle its probate and relied upon him to perform all necessary acts. In turn, the attorney arranged to have his assistant named administrator and depended upon him to timely file the death tax return. Such return was not timely filed, and no explanation was presented for the failure to do so. Is the estate liable for the addition to tax under § 6651(a)?

Chapter 25

Research Problem 46   On October 1, 1976, H makes a gift of $66,000 to his son. In reporting the gift, W (H's wife) made the election under § 2513. As a result, no gift tax

was due. W dies in 1989, and in completing Form 706, her executor claims a unified tax credit of $192,800.

a.   Why was no gift tax due on the 1976 gift?

b.   Did the executor of W's estate act correctly in claiming a unified tax credit of $192,800 on Form 706? Why or why not?

Research Problem 47   H dies on April 24, 1988, and under his will a major portion of the estate passes to a trust. The provisions of the trust grant a life estate to W (H's surviving spouse), remainder to their adult children. The income is payable to W quarter-annually or at more frequent intervals. Income accrued or held undistributed by the trust at the time of W's death shall pass to the remainder interest.

On January 24, 1989, H's estate filed a Federal estate tax return and made the QTIP election thereon. On July 3, 1989, H's estate filed an amended return based on the premise that the QTIP election was improper. As a result of the loss of the marital deduction, the amended return was accompanied by a payment of additional estate taxes.

On February 11, 1989, W dies. All of her assets, including those in H's trust, pass to the childen.

a.   Why did H's estate file an amended return revoking the QTIP election?

b.   Is the revocation of the election proper procedure?

c.   Did H's estate ever qualify for the election?

Partial list of research aids:

Code §§ 2056 (b)(7) and 2013.

Estate of Rose D. Howard, 91 T.C. 329 (1988).

Chapter 26

Research Problem 48   At a recent seminar entitled "Estate and Income Tax Planning after Tax Reform," you heard a speaker assert, "The Clifford Trust is dead as of March 1, 1986." Because you had become quite familiar with the Clifford Trust and used it in conjunction with several of your clients, you wonder whether the speaker overstepped her bounds. Evaluate the propriety of the speaker's comment. Restrict your research to trusts created or assets transferred to such trusts after March 1, 1986.

Research Problem 49   Your client has come to you for some advice regarding gifts of property. She has just learned that she must undergo major surgery, and she would like to make certain gifts before entering the hospital. On your earlier advice, she had established a plan of lifetime giving for four prior years. Examine each of the following assets that she is considering using as gifts to family and friends. In doing so, evaluate the income tax consequences of having such property pass through her estate to the designated legatee.

a.   She plans to give a cottage to her son to fulfill a promise made many years ago. The cottage has been owned by your client for the past 15 years. It has a basis to her of $30,000 and a fair market value of $20,000.

b.   Since she has $100,000 of long-term capital losses that she has been carrying forward for the past few years, she is considering making a gift of $200,000 in installment notes to her daughter. Her basis in the notes is $100,000, and the notes' current fair market value is $190,000.

c.   She has promised to make a special cash bequest in her will of $25,000 to her grandson. However, she does not anticipate having that much cash immediately available after her death. She requests your advice concerning the income tax consequences to the estate if the cash bequest is settled with some other property.

APPENDIX A

Tax Rate Schedules and Tables

1989 Tax Rate Schedules

Caution: *Do not use these Tax Rate Schedules to figure your 1988 taxes. Use only to figure your 1989 estimated taxes.*

Schedule X—Single

If line 5 is: Over—	But not over—	The tax is:	of the amount over—
$0	$18,550	........15%	$0
18,550	44,900	**$2,782.50 + 28%**	**18,550**
44,900	93,130	**10,160.50 + 33%**	**44,900**
93,130	....	Use **Worksheet** below to figure your tax.	

Schedule Z— Head of household

If line 5 is: Over—	But not over—	The tax is:	of the amount over—
$0	$24,850	........15%	$0
24,850	64,200	**$3,727.50+ 28%**	**24,850**
64,200	128,810	**14,745.50 + 33%**	**64,200**
128,810	....	Use **Worksheet** below to figure your tax.	

Schedule Y-1—Married filing jointly or Qualifying widow(er)

If line 5 is: Over—	But not over—	The tax is:	of the amount over—
$0	$30,950	........15%	$0
30,950	74,850	**$4,642.50 + 28%**	**30,950**
74,850	155,320	**16,934.50 + 33%**	**74,850**
155,320	....	Use **Worksheet** below to figure your tax.	

Schedule Y-2— Married filing separately

If line 5 is: Over—	But not over—	The tax is:	of the amount over—
$0	$15,475	........15%	$0
15,475	37,425	**$2,321.25 + 28%**	**15,475**
37,425	117,895	**8,467.25 + 33%**	**37,425**
117,895	....	Use **Worksheet** below to figure your tax.	

Worksheet (Keep for your records)

1. If your filing status is: { Single, enter $26,076.40 / Head of household, enter $36,066.80 / Married filing jointly or Qualifying widow(er), enter $43,489.60 / Married filing separately, enter $35,022.35 } . . . . **1.** _____

2. Enter your taxable income from line 5 of the Form 1040-ES worksheet . . . . **2.** _____

3. If your filing status is: { Single, enter $93,130 / Head of household, enter $128,810 / Married filing jointly or Qualifying widow(er), enter $155,320 / Married filing separately, enter $117,895 } . . . . . **3.** _____

4. Subtract line 3 from line 2. Enter the result. (If the result is zero or less, use the schedule above for your filing status to figure your tax. DON'T use this worksheet.) . . . . **4.** _____

5. Multiply the amount on line 4 by 28% (.28). Enter the result . . . . **5.** _____

6. Multiply the amount on line 4 by 5% (.05). Enter the result . . . . **6.** _____

7. Multiply $560 by the number of exemptions claimed. (If married filing separately, see Note below.) Enter the result . . . . **7.** _____

8. Compare the amounts on lines 6 and 7. Enter the **smaller** of the two amounts . . . . **8.** _____

9. **Tax.** Add lines 1, 5, and 8. Enter the total here and on line 6 of the Form 1040-ES worksheet . . . . . . **9.** _____

Note: *If married filing separately and you did **not** claim an exemption for your spouse, multiply $560 by the number of exemptions claimed. Add $560 to the result and enter the total on line 7 above.*

1989 Tax Table

Use if your taxable income is less than $50,000. If $50,000 or more, use the Tax Rate Schedules.

Example: Mr. and Mrs. Brown are filing a joint return. Their taxable income on line 37 of Form 1040 is $25,300. First, they find the $25,300–25,350 income line. Next, they find the column for married filing jointly and read down the column. The amount shown where the income line and filing status column meet is $3,799. This is the tax amount they must write on line 38 of their return.

At least	But less than	Single	Married filing jointly *	Married filing separately	Head of a household
			Your tax is—		
25,200	25,250	4,652	3,784	5,051	3,833
25,250	25,300	4,666	3,791	5,065	3,847
25,300	25,350	4,680	(3,799)	5,079	3,861
25,350	25,400	4,694	3,806	5,093	3,875

If line 37 (taxable income) is— At least	But less than	And you are— Single	Married filing jointly *	Married filing separately	Head of a household
			Your tax is—		
$0	$5	$0	$0	$0	$0
5	15	2	2	2	2
15	25	3	3	3	3
25	50	6	6	6	6
50	75	9	9	9	9
75	100	13	13	13	13
100	125	17	17	17	17
125	150	21	21	21	21
150	175	24	24	24	24
175	200	28	28	28	28
200	225	32	32	32	32
225	250	36	36	36	36
250	275	39	39	39	39
275	300	43	43	43	43
300	325	47	47	47	47
325	350	51	51	51	51
350	375	54	54	54	54
375	400	58	58	58	58
400	425	62	62	62	62
425	450	66	66	66	66
450	475	69	69	69	69
475	500	73	73	73	73
500	525	77	77	77	77
525	550	81	81	81	81
550	575	84	84	84	84
575	600	88	88	88	88
600	625	92	92	92	92
625	650	96	96	96	96
650	675	99	99	99	99
675	700	103	103	103	103
700	725	107	107	107	107
725	750	111	111	111	111
750	775	114	114	114	114
775	800	118	118	118	118
800	825	122	122	122	122
825	850	126	126	126	126
850	875	129	129	129	129
875	900	133	133	133	133
900	925	137	137	137	137
925	950	141	141	141	141
950	975	144	144	144	144
975	1,000	148	148	148	148

1,000

At least	But less than	Single	Married filing jointly	Married filing separately	Head of a household
1,000	1,025	152	152	152	152
1,025	1,050	156	156	156	156
1,050	1,075	159	159	159	159
1,075	1,100	163	163	163	163
1,100	1,125	167	167	167	167
1,125	1,150	171	171	171	171
1,150	1,175	174	174	174	174
1,175	1,200	178	178	178	178
1,200	1,225	182	182	182	182
1,225	1,250	186	186	186	186
1,250	1,275	189	189	189	189
1,275	1,300	193	193	193	193
1,300	1,325	197	197	197	197
1,325	1,350	201	201	201	201
1,350	1,375	204	204	204	204
1,375	1,400	208	208	208	208

If line 37 (taxable income) is— At least	But less than	And you are— Single	Married filing jointly *	Married filing separately	Head of a household
			Your tax is—		
1,400	1,425	212	212	212	212
1,425	1,450	216	216	216	216
1,450	1,475	219	219	219	219
1,475	1,500	223	223	223	223
1,500	1,525	227	227	227	227
1,525	1,550	231	231	231	231
1,550	1,575	234	234	234	234
1,575	1,600	238	238	238	238
1,600	1,625	242	242	242	242
1,625	1,650	246	246	246	246
1,650	1,675	249	249	249	249
1,675	1,700	253	253	253	253
1,700	1,725	257	257	257	257
1,725	1,750	261	261	261	261
1,750	1,775	264	264	264	264
1,775	1,800	268	268	268	268
1,800	1,825	272	272	272	272
1,825	1,850	276	276	276	276
1,850	1,875	279	279	279	279
1,875	1,900	283	283	283	283
1,900	1,925	287	287	287	287
1,925	1,950	291	291	291	291
1,950	1,975	294	294	294	294
1,975	2,000	298	298	298	298

2,000

At least	But less than	Single	Married filing jointly	Married filing separately	Head of a household
2,000	2,025	302	302	302	302
2,025	2,050	306	306	306	306
2,050	2,075	309	309	309	309
2,075	2,100	313	313	313	313
2,100	2,125	317	317	317	317
2,125	2,150	321	321	321	321
2,150	2,175	324	324	324	324
2,175	2,200	328	328	328	328
2,200	2,225	332	332	332	332
2,225	2,250	336	336	336	336
2,250	2,275	339	339	339	339
2,275	2,300	343	343	343	343
2,300	2,325	347	347	347	347
2,325	2,350	351	351	351	351
2,350	2,375	354	354	354	354
2,375	2,400	358	358	358	358
2,400	2,425	362	362	362	362
2,425	2,450	366	366	366	366
2,450	2,475	369	369	369	369
2,475	2,500	373	373	373	373
2,500	2,525	377	377	377	377
2,525	2,550	381	381	381	381
2,550	2,575	384	384	384	384
2,575	2,600	388	388	388	388
2,600	2,625	392	392	392	392
2,625	2,650	396	396	396	396
2,650	2,675	399	399	399	399
2,675	2,700	403	403	403	403

If line 37 (taxable income) is— At least	But less than	And you are— Single	Married filing jointly *	Married filing separately	Head of a household
			Your tax is—		
2,700	2,725	407	407	407	407
2,725	2,750	411	411	411	411
2,750	2,775	414	414	414	414
2,775	2,800	418	418	418	418
2,800	2,825	422	422	422	422
2,825	2,850	426	426	426	426
2,850	2,875	429	429	429	429
2,875	2,900	433	433	433	433
2,900	2,925	437	437	437	437
2,925	2,950	441	441	441	441
2,950	2,975	444	444	444	444
2,975	3,000	448	448	448	448

3,000

At least	But less than	Single	Married filing jointly	Married filing separately	Head of a household
3,000	3,050	454	454	454	454
3,050	3,100	461	461	461	461
3,100	3,150	469	469	469	469
3,150	3,200	476	476	476	476
3,200	3,250	484	484	484	484
3,250	3,300	491	491	491	491
3,300	3,350	499	499	499	499
3,350	3,400	506	506	506	506
3,400	3,450	514	514	514	514
3,450	3,500	521	521	521	521
3,500	3,550	529	529	529	529
3,550	3,600	536	536	536	536
3,600	3,650	544	544	544	544
3,650	3,700	551	551	551	551
3,700	3,750	559	559	559	559
3,750	3,800	566	566	566	566
3,800	3,850	574	574	574	574
3,850	3,900	581	581	581	581
3,900	3,950	589	589	589	589
3,950	4,000	596	596	596	596

4,000

At least	But less than	Single	Married filing jointly	Married filing separately	Head of a household
4,000	4,050	604	604	604	604
4,050	4,100	611	611	611	611
4,100	4,150	619	619	619	619
4,150	4,200	626	626	626	626
4,200	4,250	634	634	634	634
4,250	4,300	641	641	641	641
4,300	4,350	649	649	649	649
4,350	4,400	656	656	656	656
4,400	4,450	664	664	664	664
4,450	4,500	671	671	671	671
4,500	4,550	679	679	679	679
4,550	4,600	686	686	686	686
4,600	4,650	694	694	694	694
4,650	4,700	701	701	701	701
4,700	4,750	709	709	709	709
4,750	4,800	716	716	716	716
4,800	4,850	724	724	724	724
4,850	4,900	731	731	731	731
4,900	4,950	739	739	739	739
4,950	5,000	746	746	746	746

* This column must also be used by a qualifying widow(er).

Continued on next page

1989 Tax Table—Continued

If line 37 (taxable income) is—		Single	Married filing jointly *	Married filing separately	Head of a household	If line 37 (taxable income) is—		Single	Married filing jointly *	Married filing separately	Head of a household	If line 37 (taxable income) is—		Single	Married filing jointly *	Married filing separately	Head of a household
At least	But less than					At least	But less than					At least	But less than				
		Your tax is—						Your tax is—						Your tax is—			

5,000 / **8,000** / **11,000**

5,000	5,050	754	754	754	754	8,000	8,050	1,204	1,204	1,204	1,204	11,000	11,050	1,654	1,654	1,654	1,654
5,050	5,100	761	761	761	761	8,050	8,100	1,211	1,211	1,211	1,211	11,050	11,100	1,661	1,661	1,661	1,661
5,100	5,150	769	769	769	769	8,100	8,150	1,219	1,219	1,219	1,219	11,100	11,150	1,669	1,669	1,669	1,669
5,150	5,200	776	776	776	776	8,150	8,200	1,226	1,226	1,226	1,226	11,150	11,200	1,676	1,676	1,676	1,676
5,200	5,250	784	784	784	784	8,200	8,250	1,234	1,234	1,234	1,234	11,200	11,250	1,684	1,684	1,684	1,684
5,250	5,300	791	791	791	791	8,250	8,300	1,241	1,241	1,241	1,241	11,250	11,300	1,691	1,691	1,691	1,691
5,300	5,350	799	799	799	799	8,300	8,350	1,249	1,249	1,249	1,249	11,300	11,350	1,699	1,699	1,699	1,699
5,350	5,400	806	806	806	806	8,350	8,400	1,256	1,256	1,256	1,256	11,350	11,400	1,706	1,706	1,706	1,706
5,400	5,450	814	814	814	814	8,400	8,450	1,264	1,264	1,264	1,264	11,400	11,450	1,714	1,714	1,714	1,714
5,450	5,500	821	821	821	821	8,450	8,500	1,271	1,271	1,271	1,271	11,450	11,500	1,721	1,721	1,721	1,721
5,500	5,550	829	829	829	829	8,500	8,550	1,279	1,279	1,279	1,279	11,500	11,550	1,729	1,729	1,729	1,729
5,550	5,600	836	836	836	836	8,550	8,600	1,286	1,286	1,286	1,286	11,550	11,600	1,736	1,736	1,736	1,736
5,600	5,650	844	844	844	844	8,600	8,650	1,294	1,294	1,294	1,294	11,600	11,650	1,744	1,744	1,744	1,744
5,650	5,700	851	851	851	851	8,650	8,700	1,301	1,301	1,301	1,301	11,650	11,700	1,751	1,751	1,751	1,751
5,700	5,750	859	859	859	859	8,700	8,750	1,309	1,309	1,309	1,309	11,700	11,750	1,759	1,759	1,759	1,759
5,750	5,800	866	866	866	866	8,750	8,800	1,316	1,316	1,316	1,316	11,750	11,800	1,766	1,766	1,766	1,766
5,800	5,850	874	874	874	874	8,800	8,850	1,324	1,324	1,324	1,324	11,800	11,850	1,774	1,774	1,774	1,774
5,850	5,900	881	881	881	881	8,850	8,900	1,331	1,331	1,331	1,331	11,850	11,900	1,781	1,781	1,781	1,781
5,900	5,950	889	889	889	889	8,900	8,950	1,339	1,339	1,339	1,339	11,900	11,950	1,789	1,789	1,789	1,789
5,950	6,000	896	896	896	896	8,950	9,000	1,346	1,346	1,346	1,346	11,950	12,000	1,796	1,796	1,796	1,796

6,000 / **9,000** / **12,000**

6,000	6,050	904	904	904	904	9,000	9,050	1,354	1,354	1,354	1,354	12,000	12,050	1,804	1,804	1,804	1,804
6,050	6,100	911	911	911	911	9,050	9,100	1,361	1,361	1,361	1,361	12,050	12,100	1,811	1,811	1,811	1,811
6,100	6,150	919	919	919	919	9,100	9,150	1,369	1,369	1,369	1,369	12,100	12,150	1,819	1,819	1,819	1,819
6,150	6,200	926	926	926	926	9,150	9,200	1,376	1,376	1,376	1,376	12,150	12,200	1,826	1,826	1,826	1,826
6,200	6,250	934	934	934	934	9,200	9,250	1,384	1,384	1,384	1,384	12,200	12,250	1,834	1,834	1,834	1,834
6,250	6,300	941	941	941	941	9,250	9,300	1,391	1,391	1,391	1,391	12,250	12,300	1,841	1,841	1,841	1,841
6,300	6,350	949	949	949	949	9,300	9,350	1,399	1,399	1,399	1,399	12,300	12,350	1,849	1,849	1,849	1,849
6,350	6,400	956	956	956	956	9,350	9,400	1,406	1,406	1,406	1,406	12,350	12,400	1,856	1,856	1,856	1,856
6,400	6,450	964	964	964	964	9,400	9,450	1,414	1,414	1,414	1,414	12,400	12,450	1,864	1,864	1,864	1,864
6,450	6,500	971	971	971	971	9,450	9,500	1,421	1,421	1,421	1,421	12,450	12,500	1,871	1,871	1,871	1,871
6,500	6,550	979	979	979	979	9,500	9,550	1,429	1,429	1,429	1,429	12,500	12,550	1,879	1,879	1,879	1,879
6,550	6,600	986	986	986	986	9,550	9,600	1,436	1,436	1,436	1,436	12,550	12,600	1,886	1,886	1,886	1,886
6,600	6,650	994	994	994	994	9,600	9,650	1,444	1,444	1,444	1,444	12,600	12,650	1,894	1,894	1,894	1,894
6,650	6,700	1,001	1,001	1,001	1,001	9,650	9,700	1,451	1,451	1,451	1,451	12,650	12,700	1,901	1,901	1,901	1,901
6,700	6,750	1,009	1,009	1,009	1,009	9,700	9,750	1,459	1,459	1,459	1,459	12,700	12,750	1,909	1,909	1,909	1,909
6,750	6,800	1,016	1,016	1,016	1,016	9,750	9,800	1,466	1,466	1,466	1,466	12,750	12,800	1,916	1,916	1,916	1,916
6,800	6,850	1,024	1,024	1,024	1,024	9,800	9,850	1,474	1,474	1,474	1,474	12,800	12,850	1,924	1,924	1,924	1,924
6,850	6,900	1,031	1,031	1,031	1,031	9,850	9,900	1,481	1,481	1,481	1,481	12,850	12,900	1,931	1,931	1,931	1,931
6,900	6,950	1,039	1,039	1,039	1,039	9,900	9,950	1,489	1,489	1,489	1,489	12,900	12,950	1,939	1,939	1,939	1,939
6,950	7,000	1,046	1,046	1,046	1,046	9,950	10,000	1,496	1,496	1,496	1,496	12,950	13,000	1,946	1,946	1,946	1,946

7,000 / **10,000** / **13,000**

7,000	7,050	1,054	1,054	1,054	1,054	10,000	10,050	1,504	1,504	1,504	1,504	13,000	13,050	1,954	1,954	1,954	1,954
7,050	7,100	1,061	1,061	1,061	1,061	10,050	10,100	1,511	1,511	1,511	1,511	13,050	13,100	1,961	1,961	1,961	1,961
7,100	7,150	1,069	1,069	1,069	1,069	10,100	10,150	1,519	1,519	1,519	1,519	13,100	13,150	1,969	1,969	1,969	1,969
7,150	7,200	1,076	1,076	1,076	1,076	10,150	10,200	1,526	1,526	1,526	1,526	13,150	13,200	1,976	1,976	1,976	1,976
7,200	7,250	1,084	1,084	1,084	1,084	10,200	10,250	1,534	1,534	1,534	1,534	13,200	13,250	1,984	1,984	1,984	1,984
7,250	7,300	1,091	1,091	1,091	1,091	10,250	10,300	1,541	1,541	1,541	1,541	13,250	13,300	1,991	1,991	1,991	1,991
7,300	7,350	1,099	1,099	1,099	1,099	10,300	10,350	1,549	1,549	1,549	1,549	13,300	13,350	1,999	1,999	1,999	1,999
7,350	7,400	1,106	1,106	1,106	1,106	10,350	10,400	1,556	1,556	1,556	1,556	13,350	13,400	2,006	2,006	2,006	2,006
7,400	7,450	1,114	1,114	1,114	1,114	10,400	10,450	1,564	1,564	1,564	1,564	13,400	13,450	2,014	2,014	2,014	2,014
7,450	7,500	1,121	1,121	1,121	1,121	10,450	10,500	1,571	1,571	1,571	1,571	13,450	13,500	2,021	2,021	2,021	2,021
7,500	7,550	1,129	1,129	1,129	1,129	10,500	10,550	1,579	1,579	1,579	1,579	13,500	13,550	2,029	2,029	2,029	2,029
7,550	7,600	1,136	1,136	1,136	1,136	10,550	10,600	1,586	1,586	1,586	1,586	13,550	13,600	2,036	2,036	2,036	2,036
7,600	7,650	1,144	1,144	1,144	1,144	10,600	10,650	1,594	1,594	1,594	1,594	13,600	13,650	2,044	2,044	2,044	2,044
7,650	7,700	1,151	1,151	1,151	1,151	10,650	10,700	1,601	1,601	1,601	1,601	13,650	13,700	2,051	2,051	2,051	2,051
7,700	7,750	1,159	1,159	1,159	1,159	10,700	10,750	1,609	1,609	1,609	1,609	13,700	13,750	2,059	2,059	2,059	2,059
7,750	7,800	1,166	1,166	1,166	1,166	10,750	10,800	1,616	1,616	1,616	1,616	13,750	13,800	2,066	2,066	2,066	2,066
7,800	7,850	1,174	1,174	1,174	1,174	10,800	10,850	1,624	1,624	1,624	1,624	13,800	13,850	2,074	2,074	2,074	2,074
7,850	7,900	1,181	1,181	1,181	1,181	10,850	10,900	1,631	1,631	1,631	1,631	13,850	13,900	2,081	2,081	2,081	2,081
7,900	7,950	1,189	1,189	1,189	1,189	10,900	10,950	1,639	1,639	1,639	1,639	13,900	13,950	2,089	2,089	2,089	2,089
7,950	8,000	1,196	1,196	1,196	1,196	10,950	11,000	1,646	1,646	1,646	1,646	13,950	14,000	2,096	2,096	2,096	2,096

* This column must also be used by a qualifying widow(er).

Continued on next page

1989 Tax Table—*Continued*

If line 37 (taxable income) is— At least	But less than	Single	Married filing jointly *	Married filing separately	Head of a house-hold
14,000					
14,000	14,050	2,104	2,104	2,104	2,104
14,050	14,100	2,111	2,111	2,111	2,111
14,100	14,150	2,119	2,119	2,119	2,119
14,150	14,200	2,126	2,126	2,126	2,126
14,200	14,250	2,134	2,134	2,134	2,134
14,250	14,300	2,141	2,141	2,141	2,141
14,300	14,350	2,149	2,149	2,149	2,149
14,350	14,400	2,156	2,156	2,156	2,156
14,400	14,450	2,164	2,164	2,164	2,164
14,450	14,500	2,171	2,171	2,171	2,171
14,500	14,550	2,179	2,179	2,179	2,179
14,550	14,600	2,186	2,186	2,186	2,186
14,600	14,650	2,194	2,194	2,194	2,194
14,650	14,700	2,201	2,201	2,201	2,201
14,700	14,750	2,209	2,209	2,209	2,209
14,750	14,800	2,216	2,216	2,216	2,216
14,800	14,850	2,224	2,224	2,224	2,224
14,850	14,900	2,231	2,231	2,231	2,231
14,900	14,950	2,239	2,239	2,239	2,239
14,950	15,000	2,246	2,246	2,246	2,246
15,000					
15,000	15,050	2,254	2,254	2,254	2,254
15,050	15,100	2,261	2,261	2,261	2,261
15,100	15,150	2,269	2,269	2,269	2,269
15,150	15,200	2,276	2,276	2,276	2,276
15,200	15,250	2,284	2,284	2,284	2,284
15,250	15,300	2,291	2,291	2,291	2,291
15,300	15,350	2,299	2,299	2,299	2,299
15,350	15,400	2,306	2,306	2,306	2,306
15,400	15,450	2,314	2,314	2,314	2,314
15,450	15,500	2,321	2,321	2,321	2,321
15,500	15,550	2,329	2,329	2,335	2,329
15,550	15,600	2,336	2,336	2,349	2,336
15,600	15,650	2,344	2,344	2,363	2,344
15,650	15,700	2,351	2,351	2,377	2,351
15,700	15,750	2,359	2,359	2,391	2,359
15,750	15,800	2,366	2,366	2,405	2,366
15,800	15,850	2,374	2,374	2,419	2,374
15,850	15,900	2,381	2,381	2,433	2,381
15,900	15,950	2,389	2,389	2,447	2,389
15,950	16,000	2,396	2,396	2,461	2,396
16,000					
16,000	16,050	2,404	2,404	2,475	2,404
16,050	16,100	2,411	2,411	2,489	2,411
16,100	16,150	2,419	2,419	2,503	2,419
16,150	16,200	2,426	2,426	2,517	2,426
16,200	16,250	2,434	2,434	2,531	2,434
16,250	16,300	2,441	2,441	2,545	2,441
16,300	16,350	2,449	2,449	2,559	2,449
16,350	16,400	2,456	2,456	2,573	2,456
16,400	16,450	2,464	2,464	2,587	2,464
16,450	16,500	2,471	2,471	2,601	2,471
16,500	16,550	2,479	2,479	2,615	2,479
16,550	16,600	2,486	2,486	2,629	2,486
16,600	16,650	2,494	2,494	2,643	2,494
16,650	16,700	2,501	2,501	2,657	2,501
16,700	16,750	2,509	2,509	2,671	2,509
16,750	16,800	2,516	2,516	2,685	2,516
16,800	16,850	2,524	2,524	2,699	2,524
16,850	16,900	2,531	2,531	2,713	2,531
16,900	16,950	2,539	2,539	2,727	2,539
16,950	17,000	2,546	2,546	2,741	2,546

If line 37 (taxable income) is— At least	But less than	Single	Married filing jointly *	Married filing separately	Head of a house-hold
17,000					
17,000	17,050	2,554	2,554	2,755	2,554
17,050	17,100	2,561	2,561	2,769	2,561
17,100	17,150	2,569	2,569	2,783	2,569
17,150	17,200	2,576	2,576	2,797	2,576
17,200	17,250	2,584	2,584	2,811	2,584
17,250	17,300	2,591	2,591	2,825	2,591
17,300	17,350	2,599	2,599	2,839	2,599
17,350	17,400	2,606	2,606	2,853	2,606
17,400	17,450	2,614	2,614	2,867	2,614
17,450	17,500	2,621	2,621	2,881	2,621
17,500	17,550	2,629	2,629	2,895	2,629
17,550	17,600	2,636	2,636	2,909	2,636
17,600	17,650	2,644	2,644	2,923	2,644
17,650	17,700	2,651	2,651	2,937	2,651
17,700	17,750	2,659	2,659	2,951	2,659
17,750	17,800	2,666	2,666	2,965	2,666
17,800	17,850	2,674	2,674	2,979	2,674
17,850	17,900	2,681	2,681	2,993	2,681
17,900	17,950	2,689	2,689	3,007	2,689
17,950	18,000	2,696	2,696	3,021	2,696
18,000					
18,000	18,050	2,704	2,704	3,035	2,704
18,050	18,100	2,711	2,711	3,049	2,711
18,100	18,150	2,719	2,719	3,063	2,719
18,150	18,200	2,726	2,726	3,077	2,726
18,200	18,250	2,734	2,734	3,091	2,734
18,250	18,300	2,741	2,741	3,105	2,741
18,300	18,350	2,749	2,749	3,119	2,749
18,350	18,400	2,756	2,756	3,133	2,756
18,400	18,450	2,764	2,764	3,147	2,764
18,450	18,500	2,771	2,771	3,161	2,771
18,500	18,550	2,779	2,779	3,175	2,779
18,550	18,600	2,790	2,786	3,189	2,786
18,600	18,650	2,804	2,794	3,203	2,794
18,650	18,700	2,818	2,801	3,217	2,801
18,700	18,750	2,832	2,809	3,231	2,809
18,750	18,800	2,846	2,816	3,245	2,816
18,800	18,850	2,860	2,824	3,259	2,824
18,850	18,900	2,874	2,831	3,273	2,831
18,900	18,950	2,888	2,839	3,287	2,839
18,950	19,000	2,902	2,846	3,301	2,846
19,000					
19,000	19,050	2,916	2,854	3,315	2,854
19,050	19,100	2,930	2,861	3,329	2,861
19,100	19,150	2,944	2,869	3,343	2,869
19,150	19,200	2,958	2,876	3,357	2,876
19,200	19,250	2,972	2,884	3,371	2,884
19,250	19,300	2,986	2,891	3,385	2,891
19,300	19,350	3,000	2,899	3,399	2,899
19,350	19,400	3,014	2,906	3,413	2,906
19,400	19,450	3,028	2,914	3,427	2,914
19,450	19,500	3,042	2,921	3,441	2,921
19,500	19,550	3,056	2,929	3,455	2,929
19,550	19,600	3,070	2,936	3,469	2,936
19,600	19,650	3,084	2,944	3,483	2,944
19,650	19,700	3,098	2,951	3,497	2,951
19,700	19,750	3,112	2,959	3,511	2,959
19,750	19,800	3,126	2,966	3,525	2,966
19,800	19,850	3,140	2,974	3,539	2,974
19,850	19,900	3,154	2,981	3,553	2,981
19,900	19,950	3,168	2,989	3,567	2,989
19,950	20,000	3,182	2,996	3,581	2,996

If line 37 (taxable income) is— At least	But less than	Single	Married filing jointly *	Married filing separately	Head of a house-hold
20,000					
20,000	20,050	3,196	3,004	3,595	3,004
20,050	20,100	3,210	3,011	3,609	3,011
20,100	20,150	3,224	3,019	3,623	3,019
20,150	20,200	3,238	3,026	3,637	3,026
20,200	20,250	3,252	3,034	3,651	3,034
20,250	20,300	3,266	3,041	3,665	3,041
20,300	20,350	3,280	3,049	3,679	3,049
20,350	20,400	3,294	3,056	3,693	3,056
20,400	20,450	3,308	3,064	3,707	3,064
20,450	20,500	3,322	3,071	3,721	3,071
20,500	20,550	3,336	3,079	3,735	3,079
20,550	20,600	3,350	3,086	3,749	3,086
20,600	20,650	3,364	3,094	3,763	3,094
20,650	20,700	3,378	3,101	3,777	3,101
20,700	20,750	3,392	3,109	3,791	3,109
20,750	20,800	3,406	3,116	3,805	3,116
20,800	20,850	3,420	3,124	3,819	3,124
20,850	20,900	3,434	3,131	3,833	3,131
20,900	20,950	3,448	3,139	3,847	3,139
20,950	21,000	3,462	3,146	3,861	3,146
21,000					
21,000	21,050	3,476	3,154	3,875	3,154
21,050	21,100	3,490	3,161	3,889	3,161
21,100	21,150	3,504	3,169	3,903	3,169
21,150	21,200	3,518	3,176	3,917	3,176
21,200	21,250	3,532	3,184	3,931	3,184
21,250	21,300	3,546	3,191	3,945	3,191
21,300	21,350	3,560	3,199	3,959	3,199
21,350	21,400	3,574	3,206	3,973	3,206
21,400	21,450	3,588	3,214	3,987	3,214
21,450	21,500	3,602	3,221	4,001	3,221
21,500	21,550	3,616	3,229	4,015	3,229
21,550	21,600	3,630	3,236	4,029	3,236
21,600	21,650	3,644	3,244	4,043	3,244
21,650	21,700	3,658	3,251	4,057	3,251
21,700	21,750	3,672	3,259	4,071	3,259
21,750	21,800	3,686	3,266	4,085	3,266
21,800	21,850	3,700	3,274	4,099	3,274
21,850	21,900	3,714	3,281	4,113	3,281
21,900	21,950	3,728	3,289	4,127	3,289
21,950	22,000	3,742	3,296	4,141	3,296
22,000					
22,000	22,050	3,756	3,304	4,155	3,304
22,050	22,100	3,770	3,311	4,169	3,311
22,100	22,150	3,784	3,319	4,183	3,319
22,150	22,200	3,798	3,326	4,197	3,326
22,200	22,250	3,812	3,334	4,211	3,334
22,250	22,300	3,826	3,341	4,225	3,341
22,300	22,350	3,840	3,349	4,239	3,349
22,350	22,400	3,854	3,356	4,253	3,356
22,400	22,450	3,868	3,364	4,267	3,364
22,450	22,500	3,882	3,371	4,281	3,371
22,500	22,550	3,896	3,379	4,295	3,379
22,550	22,600	3,910	3,386	4,309	3,386
22,600	22,650	3,924	3,394	4,323	3,394
22,650	22,700	3,938	3,401	4,337	3,401
22,700	22,750	3,952	3,409	4,351	3,409
22,750	22,800	3,966	3,416	4,365	3,416
22,800	22,850	3,980	3,424	4,379	3,424
22,850	22,900	3,994	3,431	4,393	3,431
22,900	22,950	4,008	3,439	4,407	3,439
22,950	23,000	4,022	3,446	4,421	3,446

* This column must also be used by a qualifying widow(er).

Continued on next page

1989 Tax Table—*Continued*

If line 37 (taxable income) is—		And you are—			
At least	But less than	Single	Married filing jointly *	Married filing sepa-rately	Head of a house-hold
		Your tax is—			
23,000					
23,000	**23,050**	4,036	3,454	4,435	3,454
23,050	**23,100**	4,050	3,461	4,449	3,461
23,100	**23,150**	4,064	3,469	4,463	3,469
23,150	**23,200**	4,078	3,476	4,477	3,476
23,200	**23,250**	4,092	3,484	4,491	3,484
23,250	**23,300**	4,106	3,491	4,505	3,491
23,300	**23,350**	4,120	3,499	4,519	3,499
23,350	**23,400**	4,134	3,506	4,533	3,506
23,400	**23,450**	4,148	3,514	4,547	3,514
23,450	**23,500**	4,162	3,521	4,561	3,521
23,500	**23,550**	4,176	3,529	4,575	3,529
23,550	**23,600**	4,190	3,536	4,589	3,536
23,600	**23,650**	4,204	3,544	4,603	3,544
23,650	**23,700**	4,218	3,551	4,617	3,551
23,700	**23,750**	4,232	3,559	4,631	3,559
23,750	**23,800**	4,246	3,566	4,645	3,566
23,800	**23,850**	4,260	3,574	4,659	3,574
23,850	**23,900**	4,274	3,581	4,673	3,581
23,900	**23,950**	4,288	3,589	4,687	3,589
23,950	**24,000**	4,302	3,596	4,701	3,596
24,000					
24,000	**24,050**	4,316	3,604	4,715	3,604
24,050	**24,100**	4,330	3,611	4,729	3,611
24,100	**24,150**	4,344	3,619	4,743	3,619
24,150	**24,200**	4,358	3,626	4,757	3,626
24,200	**24,250**	4,372	3,634	4,771	3,634
24,250	**24,300**	4,386	3,641	4,785	3,641
24,300	**24,350**	4,400	3,649	4,799	3,649
24,350	**24,400**	4,414	3,656	4,813	3,656
24,400	**24,450**	4,428	3,664	4,827	3,664
24,450	**24,500**	4,442	3,671	4,841	3,671
24,500	**24,550**	4,456	3,679	4,855	3,679
24,550	**24,600**	4,470	3,686	4,869	3,686
24,600	**24,650**	4,484	3,694	4,883	3,694
24,650	**24,700**	4,498	3,701	4,897	3,701
24,700	**24,750**	4,512	3,709	4,911	3,709
24,750	**24,800**	4,526	3,716	4,925	3,716
24,800	**24,850**	4,540	3,724	4,939	3,724
24,850	**24,900**	4,554	3,731	4,953	3,735
24,900	**24,950**	4,568	3,739	4,967	3,749
24,950	**25,000**	4,582	3,746	4,981	3,763
25,000					
25,000	**25,050**	4,596	3,754	4,995	3,777
25,050	**25,100**	4,610	3,761	5,009	3,791
25,100	**25,150**	4,624	3,769	5,023	3,805
25,150	**25,200**	4,638	3,776	5,037	3,819
25,200	**25,250**	4,652	3,784	5,051	3,833
25,250	**25,300**	4,666	3,791	5,065	3,847
25,300	**25,350**	4,680	3,799	5,079	3,861
25,350	**25,400**	4,694	3,806	5,093	3,875
25,400	**25,450**	4,708	3,814	5,107	3,889
25,450	**25,500**	4,722	3,821	5,121	3,903
25,500	**25,550**	4,736	3,829	5,135	3,917
25,550	**25,600**	4,750	3,836	5,149	3,931
25,600	**25,650**	4,764	3,844	5,163	3,945
25,650	**25,700**	4,778	3,851	5,177	3,959
25,700	**25,750**	4,792	3,859	5,191	3,973
25,750	**25,800**	4,806	3,866	5,205	3,987
25,800	**25,850**	4,820	3,874	5,219	4,001
25,850	**25,900**	4,834	3,881	5,233	4,015
25,900	**25,950**	4,848	3,889	5,247	4,029
25,950	**26,000**	4,862	3,896	5,261	4,043

If line 37 (taxable income) is—		And you are—			
At least	But less than	Single	Married filing jointly *	Married filing sepa-rately	Head of a house-hold
		Your tax is—			
26,000					
26,000	**26,050**	4,876	3,904	5,275	4,057
26,050	**26,100**	4,890	3,911	5,289	4,071
26,100	**26,150**	4,904	3,919	5,303	4,085
26,150	**26,200**	4,918	3,926	5,317	4,099
26,200	**26,250**	4,932	3,934	5,331	4,113
26,250	**26,300**	4,946	3,941	5,345	4,127
26,300	**26,350**	4,960	3,949	5,359	4,141
26,350	**26,400**	4,974	3,956	5,373	4,155
26,400	**26,450**	4,988	3,964	5,387	4,169
26,450	**26,500**	5,002	3,971	5,401	4,183
26,500	**26,550**	5,016	3,979	5,415	4,197
26,550	**26,600**	5,030	3,986	5,429	4,211
26,600	**26,650**	5,044	3,994	5,443	4,225
26,650	**26,700**	5,058	4,001	5,457	4,239
26,700	**26,750**	5,072	4,009	5,471	4,253
26,750	**26,800**	5,086	4,016	5,485	4,267
26,800	**26,850**	5,100	4,024	5,499	4,281
26,850	**26,900**	5,114	4,031	5,513	4,295
26,900	**26,950**	5,128	4,039	5,527	4,309
26,950	**27,000**	5,142	4,046	5,541	4,323
27,000					
27,000	**27,050**	5,156	4,054	5,555	4,337
27,050	**27,100**	5,170	4,061	5,569	4,351
27,100	**27,150**	5,184	4,069	5,583	4,365
27,150	**27,200**	5,198	4,076	5,597	4,379
27,200	**27,250**	5,212	4,084	5,611	4,393
27,250	**27,300**	5,226	4,091	5,625	4,407
27,300	**27,350**	5,240	4,099	5,639	4,421
27,350	**27,400**	5,254	4,106	5,653	4,435
27,400	**27,450**	5,268	4,114	5,667	4,449
27,450	**27,500**	5,282	4,121	5,681	4,463
27,500	**27,550**	5,296	4,129	5,695	4,477
27,550	**27,600**	5,310	4,136	5,709	4,491
27,600	**27,650**	5,324	4,144	5,723	4,505
27,650	**27,700**	5,338	4,151	5,737	4,519
27,700	**27,750**	5,352	4,159	5,751	4,533
27,750	**27,800**	5,366	4,166	5,765	4,547
27,800	**27,850**	5,380	4,174	5,779	4,561
27,850	**27,900**	5,394	4,181	5,793	4,575
27,900	**27,950**	5,408	4,189	5,807	4,589
27,950	**28,000**	5,422	4,196	5,821	4,603
28,000					
28,000	**28,050**	5,436	4,204	5,835	4,617
28,050	**28,100**	5,450	4,211	5,849	4,631
28,100	**28,150**	5,464	4,219	5,863	4,645
28,150	**28,200**	5,478	4,226	5,877	4,659
28,200	**28,250**	5,492	4,234	5,891	4,673
28,250	**28,300**	5,506	4,241	5,905	4,687
28,300	**28,350**	5,520	4,249	5,919	4,701
28,350	**28,400**	5,534	4,256	5,933	4,715
28,400	**28,450**	5,548	4,264	5,947	4,729
28,450	**28,500**	5,562	4,271	5,961	4,743
28,500	**28,550**	5,576	4,279	5,975	4,757
28,550	**28,600**	5,590	4,286	5,989	4,771
28,600	**28,650**	5,604	4,294	6,003	4,785
28,650	**28,700**	5,618	4,301	6,017	4,799
28,700	**28,750**	5,632	4,309	6,031	4,813
28,750	**28,800**	5,646	4,316	6,045	4,827
28,800	**28,850**	5,660	4,324	6,059	4,841
28,850	**28,900**	5,674	4,331	6,073	4,855
28,900	**28,950**	5,688	4,339	6,087	4,869
28,950	**29,000**	5,702	4,346	6,101	4,883

If line 37 (taxable income) is—		And you are—			
At least	But less than	Single	Married filing jointly *	Married filing sepa-rately	Head of a house-hold
		Your tax is—			
29,000					
29,000	**29,050**	5,716	4,354	6,115	4,897
29,050	**29,100**	5,730	4,361	6,129	4,911
29,100	**29,150**	5,744	4,369	6,143	4,925
29,150	**29,200**	5,758	4,376	6,157	4,939
29,200	**29,250**	5,772	4,384	6,171	4,953
29,250	**29,300**	5,786	4,391	6,185	4,967
29,300	**29,350**	5,800	4,399	6,199	4,981
29,350	**29,400**	5,814	4,406	6,213	4,995
29,400	**29,450**	5,828	4,414	6,227	5,009
29,450	**29,500**	5,842	4,421	6,241	5,023
29,500	**29,550**	5,856	4,429	6,255	5,037
29,550	**29,600**	5,870	4,436	6,269	5,051
29,600	**29,650**	5,884	4,444	6,283	5,065
29,650	**29,700**	5,898	4,451	6,297	5,079
29,700	**29,750**	5,912	4,459	6,311	5,093
29,750	**29,800**	5,926	4,466	6,325	5,107
29,800	**29,850**	5,940	4,474	6,339	5,121
29,850	**29,900**	5,954	4,481	6,353	5,135
29,900	**29,950**	5,968	4,489	6,367	5,149
29,950	**30,000**	5,982	4,496	6,381	5,163
30,000					
30,000	**30,050**	5,996	4,504	6,395	5,177
30,050	**30,100**	6,010	4,511	6,409	5,191
30,100	**30,150**	6,024	4,519	6,423	5,205
30,150	**30,200**	6,038	4,526	6,437	5,219
30,200	**30,250**	6,052	4,534	6,451	5,233
30,250	**30,300**	6,066	4,541	6,465	5,247
30,300	**30,350**	6,080	4,549	6,479	5,261
30,350	**30,400**	6,094	4,556	6,493	5,275
30,400	**30,450**	6,108	4,564	6,507	5,289
30,450	**30,500**	6,122	4,571	6,521	5,303
30,500	**30,550**	6,136	4,579	6,535	5,317
30,550	**30,600**	6,150	4,586	6,549	5,331
30,600	**30,650**	6,164	4,594	6,563	5,345
30,650	**30,700**	6,178	4,601	6,577	5,359
30,700	**30,750**	6,192	4,609	6,591	5,373
30,750	**30,800**	6,206	4,616	6,605	5,387
30,800	**30,850**	6,220	4,624	6,619	5,401
30,850	**30,900**	6,234	4,631	6,633	5,415
30,900	**30,950**	6,248	4,639	6,647	5,429
30,950	**31,000**	6,262	4,650	6,661	5,443
31,000					
31,000	**31,050**	6,276	4,664	6,675	5,457
31,050	**31,100**	6,290	4,678	6,689	5,471
31,100	**31,150**	6,304	4,692	6,703	5,485
31,150	**31,200**	6,318	4,706	6,717	5,499
31,200	**31,250**	6,332	4,720	6,731	5,513
31,250	**31,300**	6,346	4,734	6,745	5,527
31,300	**31,350**	6,360	4,748	6,759	5,541
31,350	**31,400**	6,374	4,762	6,773	5,555
31,400	**31,450**	6,388	4,776	6,787	5,569
31,450	**31,500**	6,402	4,790	6,801	5,583
31,500	**31,550**	6,416	4,804	6,815	5,597
31,550	**31,600**	6,430	4,818	6,829	5,611
31,600	**31,650**	6,444	4,832	6,843	5,625
31,650	**31,700**	6,458	4,846	6,857	5,639
31,700	**31,750**	6,472	4,860	6,871	5,653
31,750	**31,800**	6,486	4,874	6,885	5,667
31,800	**31,850**	6,500	4,888	6,899	5,681
31,850	**31,900**	6,514	4,902	6,913	5,695
31,900	**31,950**	6,528	4,916	6,927	5,709
31,950	**32,000**	6,542	4,930	6,941	5,723

* This column must also be used by a qualifying widow(er).

Continued on next page

1989 Tax Table—Continued

If line 37 (taxable income) is— At least	But less than	Single	Married filing jointly *	Married filing separately	Head of a household
32,000					
32,000	32,050	6,556	4,944	6,955	5,737
32,050	32,100	6,570	4,958	6,969	5,751
32,100	32,150	6,584	4,972	6,983	5,765
32,150	32,200	6,598	4,986	6,997	5,779
32,200	32,250	6,612	5,000	7,011	5,793
32,250	32,300	6,626	5,014	7,025	5,807
32,300	32,350	6,640	5,028	7,039	5,821
32,350	32,400	6,654	5,042	7,053	5,835
32,400	32,450	6,668	5,056	7,067	5,849
32,450	32,500	6,682	5,070	7,081	5,863
32,500	32,550	6,696	5,084	7,095	5,877
32,550	32,600	6,710	5,098	7,109	5,891
32,600	32,650	6,724	5,112	7,123	5,905
32,650	32,700	6,738	5,126	7,137	5,919
32,700	32,750	6,752	5,140	7,151	5,933
32,750	32,800	6,766	5,154	7,165	5,947
32,800	32,850	6,780	5,168	7,179	5,961
32,850	32,900	6,794	5,182	7,193	5,975
32,900	32,950	6,808	5,196	7,207	5,989
32,950	33,000	6,822	5,210	7,221	6,003
33,000					
33,000	33,050	6,836	5,224	7,235	6,017
33,050	33,100	6,850	5,238	7,249	6,031
33,100	33,150	6,864	5,252	7,263	6,045
33,150	33,200	6,878	5,266	7,277	6,059
33,200	33,250	6,892	5,280	7,291	6,073
33,250	33,300	6,906	5,294	7,305	6,087
33,300	33,350	6,920	5,308	7,319	6,101
33,350	33,400	6,934	5,322	7,333	6,115
33,400	33,450	6,948	5,336	7,347	6,129
33,450	33,500	6,962	5,350	7,361	6,143
33,500	33,550	6,976	5,364	7,375	6,157
33,550	33,600	6,990	5,378	7,389	6,171
33,600	33,650	7,004	5,392	7,403	6,185
33,650	33,700	7,018	5,406	7,417	6,199
33,700	33,750	7,032	5,420	7,431	6,213
33,750	33,800	7,046	5,434	7,445	6,227
33,800	33,850	7,060	5,448	7,459	6,241
33,850	33,900	7,074	5,462	7,473	6,255
33,900	33,950	7,088	5,476	7,487	6,269
33,950	34,000	7,102	5,490	7,501	6,283
34,000					
34,000	34,050	7,116	5,504	7,515	6,297
34,050	34,100	7,130	5,518	7,529	6,311
34,100	34,150	7,144	5,532	7,543	6,325
34,150	34,200	7,158	5,546	7,557	6,339
34,200	34,250	7,172	5,560	7,571	6,353
34,250	34,300	7,186	5,574	7,585	6,367
34,300	34,350	7,200	5,588	7,599	6,381
34,350	34,400	7,214	5,602	7,613	6,395
34,400	34,450	7,228	5,616	7,627	6,409
34,450	34,500	7,242	5,630	7,641	6,423
34,500	34,550	7,256	5,644	7,655	6,437
34,550	34,600	7,270	5,658	7,669	6,451
34,600	34,650	7,284	5,672	7,683	6,465
34,650	34,700	7,298	5,686	7,697	6,479
34,700	34,750	7,312	5,700	7,711	6,493
34,750	34,800	7,326	5,714	7,725	6,507
34,800	34,850	7,340	5,728	7,739	6,521
34,850	34,900	7,354	5,742	7,753	6,535
34,900	34,950	7,368	5,756	7,767	6,549
34,950	35,000	7,382	5,770	7,781	6,563

If line 37 (taxable income) is— At least	But less than	Single	Married filing jointly *	Married filing separately	Head of a household
35,000					
35,000	35,050	7,396	5,784	7,795	6,577
35,050	35,100	7,410	5,798	7,809	6,591
35,100	35,150	7,424	5,812	7,823	6,605
35,150	35,200	7,438	5,826	7,837	6,619
35,200	35,250	7,452	5,840	7,851	6,633
35,250	35,300	7,466	5,854	7,865	6,647
35,300	35,350	7,480	5,868	7,879	6,661
35,350	35,400	7,494	5,882	7,893	6,675
35,400	35,450	7,508	5,896	7,907	6,689
35,450	35,500	7,522	5,910	7,921	6,703
35,500	35,550	7,536	5,924	7,935	6,717
35,550	35,600	7,550	5,938	7,949	6,731
35,600	35,650	7,564	5,952	7,963	6,745
35,650	35,700	7,578	5,966	7,977	6,759
35,700	35,750	7,592	5,980	7,991	6,773
35,750	35,800	7,606	5,994	8,005	6,787
35,800	35,850	7,620	6,008	8,019	6,801
35,850	35,900	7,634	6,022	8,033	6,815
35,900	35,950	7,648	6,036	8,047	6,829
35,950	36,000	7,662	6,050	8,061	6,843
36,000					
36,000	36,050	7,676	6,064	8,075	6,857
36,050	36,100	7,690	6,078	8,089	6,871
36,100	36,150	7,704	6,092	8,103	6,885
36,150	36,200	7,718	6,106	8,117	6,899
36,200	36,250	7,732	6,120	8,131	6,913
36,250	36,300	7,746	6,134	8,145	6,927
36,300	36,350	7,760	6,148	8,159	6,941
36,350	36,400	7,774	6,162	8,173	6,955
36,400	36,450	7,788	6,176	8,187	6,969
36,450	36,500	7,802	6,190	8,201	6,983
36,500	36,550	7,816	6,204	8,215	6,997
36,550	36,600	7,830	6,218	8,229	7,011
36,600	36,650	7,844	6,232	8,243	7,025
36,650	36,700	7,858	6,246	8,257	7,039
36,700	36,750	7,872	6,260	8,271	7,053
36,750	36,800	7,886	6,274	8,285	7,067
36,800	36,850	7,900	6,288	8,299	7,081
36,850	36,900	7,914	6,302	8,313	7,095
36,900	36,950	7,928	6,316	8,327	7,109
36,950	37,000	7,942	6,330	8,341	7,123
37,000					
37,000	37,050	7,956	6,344	8,355	7,137
37,050	37,100	7,970	6,358	8,369	7,151
37,100	37,150	7,984	6,372	8,383	7,165
37,150	37,200	7,998	6,386	8,397	7,179
37,200	37,250	8,012	6,400	8,411	7,193
37,250	37,300	8,026	6,414	8,425	7,207
37,300	37,350	8,040	6,428	8,439	7,221
37,350	37,400	8,054	6,442	8,453	7,235
37,400	37,450	8,068	6,456	8,467	7,249
37,450	37,500	8,082	6,470	8,484	7,263
37,500	37,550	8,096	6,484	8,500	7,277
37,550	37,600	8,110	6,498	8,517	7,291
37,600	37,650	8,124	6,512	8,533	7,305
37,650	37,700	8,138	6,526	8,550	7,319
37,700	37,750	8,152	6,540	8,566	7,333
37,750	37,800	8,166	6,554	8,583	7,347
37,800	37,850	8,180	6,568	8,599	7,361
37,850	37,900	8,194	6,582	8,616	7,375
37,900	37,950	8,208	6,596	8,632	7,389
37,950	38,000	8,222	6,610	8,649	7,403

If line 37 (taxable income) is— At least	But less than	Single	Married filing jointly *	Married filing separately	Head of a household
38,000					
38,000	38,050	8,236	6,624	8,665	7,417
38,050	38,100	8,250	6,638	8,682	7,431
38,100	38,150	8,264	6,652	8,698	7,445
38,150	38,200	8,278	6,666	8,715	7,459
38,200	38,250	8,292	6,680	8,731	7,473
38,250	38,300	8,306	6,694	8,748	7,487
38,300	38,350	8,320	6,708	8,764	7,501
38,350	38,400	8,334	6,722	8,781	7,515
38,400	38,450	8,348	6,736	8,797	7,529
38,450	38,500	8,362	6,750	8,814	7,543
38,500	38,550	8,376	6,764	8,830	7,557
38,550	38,600	8,390	6,778	8,847	7,571
38,600	38,650	8,404	6,792	8,863	7,585
38,650	38,700	8,418	6,806	8,880	7,599
38,700	38,750	8,432	6,820	8,896	7,613
38,750	38,800	8,446	6,834	8,913	7,627
38,800	38,850	8,460	6,848	8,929	7,641
38,850	38,900	8,474	6,862	8,946	7,655
38,900	38,950	8,488	6,876	8,962	7,669
38,950	39,000	8,502	6,890	8,979	7,683
39,000					
39,000	39,050	8,516	6,904	8,995	7,697
39,050	39,100	8,530	6,918	9,012	7,711
39,100	39,150	8,544	6,932	9,028	7,725
39,150	39,200	8,558	6,946	9,045	7,739
39,200	39,250	8,572	6,960	9,061	7,753
39,250	39,300	8,586	6,974	9,078	7,767
39,300	39,350	8,600	6,988	9,094	7,781
39,350	39,400	8,614	7,002	9,111	7,795
39,400	39,450	8,628	7,016	9,127	7,809
39,450	39,500	8,642	7,030	9,144	7,823
39,500	39,550	8,656	7,044	9,160	7,837
39,550	39,600	8,670	7,058	9,177	7,851
39,600	39,650	8,684	7,072	9,193	7,865
39,650	39,700	8,698	7,086	9,210	7,879
39,700	39,750	8,712	7,100	9,226	7,893
39,750	39,800	8,726	7,114	9,243	7,907
39,800	39,850	8,740	7,128	9,259	7,921
39,850	39,900	8,754	7,142	9,276	7,935
39,900	39,950	8,768	7,156	9,292	7,949
39,950	40,000	8,782	7,170	9,309	7,963
40,000					
40,000	40,050	8,796	7,184	9,325	7,977
40,050	40,100	8,810	7,198	9,342	7,991
40,100	40,150	8,824	7,212	9,358	8,005
40,150	40,200	8,838	7,226	9,375	8,019
40,200	40,250	8,852	7,240	9,391	8,033
40,250	40,300	8,866	7,254	9,408	8,047
40,300	40,350	8,880	7,268	9,424	8,061
40,350	40,400	8,894	7,282	9,441	8,075
40,400	40,450	8,908	7,296	9,457	8,089
40,450	40,500	8,922	7,310	9,474	8,103
40,500	40,550	8,936	7,324	9,490	8,117
40,550	40,600	8,950	7,338	9,507	8,131
40,600	40,650	8,964	7,352	9,523	8,145
40,650	40,700	8,978	7,366	9,540	8,159
40,700	40,750	8,992	7,380	9,556	8,173
40,750	40,800	9,006	7,394	9,573	8,187
40,800	40,850	9,020	7,408	9,589	8,201
40,850	40,900	9,034	7,422	9,606	8,215
40,900	40,950	9,048	7,436	9,622	8,229
40,950	41,000	9,062	7,450	9,639	8,243

* This column must also be used by a qualifying widow(er).

Continued on next page

1989 Tax Table—*Continued*

If line 37 (taxable income) is— At least	But less than	Single	Married filing jointly *	Married filing separately	Head of a household
41,000					
41,000	41,050	9,076	7,464	9,655	8,257
41,050	41,100	9,090	7,478	9,672	8,271
41,100	41,150	9,104	7,492	9,688	8,285
41,150	41,200	9,118	7,506	9,705	8,299
41,200	41,250	9,132	7,520	9,721	8,313
41,250	41,300	9,146	7,534	9,738	8,327
41,300	41,350	9,160	7,548	9,754	8,341
41,350	41,400	9,174	7,562	9,771	8,355
41,400	41,450	9,188	7,576	9,787	8,369
41,450	41,500	9,202	7,590	9,804	8,383
41,500	41,550	9,216	7,604	9,820	8,397
41,550	41,600	9,230	7,618	9,837	8,411
41,600	41,650	9,244	7,632	9,853	8,425
41,650	41,700	9,258	7,646	9,870	8,439
41,700	41,750	9,272	7,660	9,886	8,453
41,750	41,800	9,286	7,674	9,903	8,467
41,800	41,850	9,300	7,688	9,919	8,481
41,850	41,900	9,314	7,702	9,936	8,495
41,900	41,950	9,328	7,716	9,952	8,509
41,950	42,000	9,342	7,730	9,969	8,523
42,000					
42,000	42,050	9,356	7,744	9,985	8,537
42,050	42,100	9,370	7,758	10,002	8,551
42,100	42,150	9,384	7,772	10,018	8,565
42,150	42,200	9,398	7,786	10,035	8,579
42,200	42,250	9,412	7,800	10,051	8,593
42,250	42,300	9,426	7,814	10,068	8,607
42,300	42,350	9,440	7,828	10,084	8,621
42,350	42,400	9,454	7,842	10,101	8,635
42,400	42,450	9,468	7,856	10,117	8,649
42,450	42,500	9,482	7,870	10,134	8,663
42,500	42,550	9,496	7,884	10,150	8,677
42,550	42,600	9,510	7,898	10,167	8,691
42,600	42,650	9,524	7,912	10,183	8,705
42,650	42,700	9,538	7,926	10,200	8,719
42,700	42,750	9,552	7,940	10,216	8,733
42,750	42,800	9,566	7,954	10,233	8,747
42,800	42,850	9,580	7,968	10,249	8,761
42,850	42,900	9,594	7,982	10,266	8,775
42,900	42,950	9,608	7,996	10,282	8,789
42,950	43,000	9,622	8,010	10,299	8,803
43,000					
43,000	43,050	9,636	8,024	10,315	8,817
43,050	43,100	9,650	8,038	10,332	8,831
43,100	43,150	9,664	8,052	10,348	8,845
43,150	43,200	9,678	8,066	10,365	8,859
43,200	43,250	9,692	8,080	10,381	8,873
43,250	43,300	9,706	8,094	10,398	8,887
43,300	43,350	9,720	8,108	10,414	8,901
43,350	43,400	9,734	8,122	10,431	8,915
43,400	43,450	9,748	8,136	10,447	8,929
43,450	43,500	9,762	8,150	10,464	8,943
43,500	43,550	9,776	8,164	10,480	8,957
43,550	43,600	9,790	8,178	10,497	8,971
43,600	43,650	9,804	8,192	10,513	8,985
43,650	43,700	9,818	8,206	10,530	8,999
43,700	43,750	9,832	8,220	10,546	9,013
43,750	43,800	9,846	8,234	10,563	9,027
43,800	43,850	9,860	8,248	10,579	9,041
43,850	43,900	9,874	8,262	10,596	9,055
43,900	43,950	9,888	8,276	10,612	9,069
43,950	44,000	9,902	8,290	10,629	9,083

If line 37 (taxable income) is— At least	But less than	Single	Married filing jointly *	Married filing separately	Head of a household
44,000					
44,000	44,050	9,916	8,304	10,645	9,097
44,050	44,100	9,930	8,318	10,662	9,111
44,100	44,150	9,944	8,332	10,678	9,125
44,150	44,200	9,958	8,346	10,695	9,139
44,200	44,250	9,972	8,360	10,711	9,153
44,250	44,300	9,986	8,374	10,728	9,167
44,300	44,350	10,000	8,388	10,744	9,181
44,350	44,400	10,014	8,402	10,761	9,195
44,400	44,450	10,028	8,416	10,777	9,209
44,450	44,500	10,042	8,430	10,794	9,223
44,500	44,550	10,056	8,444	10,810	9,237
44,550	44,600	10,070	8,458	10,827	9,251
44,600	44,650	10,084	8,472	10,843	9,265
44,650	44,700	10,098	8,486	10,860	9,279
44,700	44,750	10,112	8,500	10,876	9,293
44,750	44,800	10,126	8,514	10,893	9,307
44,800	44,850	10,140	8,528	10,909	9,321
44,850	44,900	10,154	8,542	10,926	9,335
44,900	44,950	10,169	8,556	10,942	9,349
44,950	45,000	10,185	8,570	10,959	9,363
45,000					
45,000	45,050	10,202	8,584	10,975	9,377
45,050	45,100	10,218	8,598	10,992	9,391
45,100	45,150	10,235	8,612	11,008	9,405
45,150	45,200	10,251	8,626	11,025	9,419
45,200	45,250	10,268	8,640	11,041	9,433
45,250	45,300	10,284	8,654	11,058	9,447
45,300	45,350	10,301	8,668	11,074	9,461
45,350	45,400	10,317	8,682	11,091	9,475
45,400	45,450	10,334	8,696	11,107	9,489
45,450	45,500	10,350	8,710	11,124	9,503
45,500	45,550	10,367	8,724	11,140	9,517
45,550	45,600	10,383	8,738	11,157	9,531
45,600	45,650	10,400	8,752	11,173	9,545
45,650	45,700	10,416	8,766	11,190	9,559
45,700	45,750	10,433	8,780	11,206	9,573
45,750	45,800	10,449	8,794	11,223	9,587
45,800	45,850	10,466	8,808	11,239	9,601
45,850	45,900	10,482	8,822	11,256	9,615
45,900	45,950	10,499	8,836	11,272	9,629
45,950	46,000	10,515	8,850	11,289	9,643
46,000					
46,000	46,050	10,532	8,864	11,305	9,657
46,050	46,100	10,548	8,878	11,322	9,671
46,100	46,150	10,565	8,892	11,338	9,685
46,150	46,200	10,581	8,906	11,355	9,699
46,200	46,250	10,598	8,920	11,371	9,713
46,250	46,300	10,614	8,934	11,388	9,727
46,300	46,350	10,631	8,948	11,404	9,741
46,350	46,400	10,647	8,962	11,421	9,755
46,400	46,450	10,664	8,976	11,437	9,769
46,450	46,500	10,680	8,990	11,454	9,783
46,500	46,550	10,697	9,004	11,470	9,797
46,550	46,600	10,713	9,018	11,487	9,811
46,600	46,650	10,730	9,032	11,503	9,825
46,650	46,700	10,746	9,046	11,520	9,839
46,700	46,750	10,763	9,060	11,536	9,853
46,750	46,800	10,779	9,074	11,553	9,867
46,800	46,850	10,796	9,088	11,569	9,881
46,850	46,900	10,812	9,102	11,586	9,895
46,900	46,950	10,829	9,116	11,602	9,909
46,950	47,000	10,845	9,130	11,619	9,923

If line 37 (taxable income) is— At least	But less than	Single	Married filing jointly *	Married filing separately	Head of a household
47,000					
47,000	47,050	10,862	9,144	11,635	9,937
47,050	47,100	10,878	9,158	11,652	9,951
47,100	47,150	10,895	9,172	11,668	9,965
47,150	47,200	10,911	9,186	11,685	9,979
47,200	47,250	10,928	9,200	11,701	9,993
47,250	47,300	10,944	9,214	11,718	10,007
47,300	47,350	10,961	9,228	11,734	10,021
47,350	47,400	10,977	9,242	11,751	10,035
47,400	47,450	10,994	9,256	11,767	10,049
47,450	47,500	11,010	9,270	11,784	10,063
47,500	47,550	11,027	9,284	11,800	10,077
47,550	47,600	11,043	9,298	11,817	10,091
47,600	47,650	11,060	9,312	11,833	10,105
47,650	47,700	11,076	9,326	11,850	10,119
47,700	47,750	11,093	9,340	11,866	10,133
47,750	47,800	11,109	9,354	11,883	10,147
47,800	47,850	11,126	9,368	11,899	10,161
47,850	47,900	11,142	9,382	11,916	10,175
47,900	47,950	11,159	9,396	11,932	10,189
47,950	48,000	11,175	9,410	11,949	10,203
48,000					
48,000	48,050	11,192	9,424	11,965	10,217
48,050	48,100	11,208	9,438	11,982	10,231
48,100	48,150	11,225	9,452	11,998	10,245
48,150	48,200	11,241	9,466	12,015	10,259
48,200	48,250	11,258	9,480	12,031	10,273
48,250	48,300	11,274	9,494	12,048	10,287
48,300	48,350	11,291	9,508	12,064	10,301
48,350	48,400	11,307	9,522	12,081	10,315
48,400	48,450	11,324	9,536	12,097	10,329
48,450	48,500	11,340	9,550	12,114	10,343
48,500	48,550	11,357	9,564	12,130	10,357
48,550	48,600	11,373	9,578	12,147	10,371
48,600	48,650	11,390	9,592	12,163	10,385
48,650	48,700	11,406	9,606	12,180	10,399
48,700	48,750	11,423	9,620	12,196	10,413
48,750	48,800	11,439	9,634	12,213	10,427
48,800	48,850	11,456	9,648	12,229	10,441
48,850	48,900	11,472	9,662	12,246	10,455
48,900	48,950	11,489	9,676	12,262	10,469
48,950	49,000	11,505	9,690	12,279	10,483
49,000					
49,000	49,050	11,522	9,704	12,295	10,497
49,050	49,100	11,538	9,718	12,312	10,511
49,100	49,150	11,555	9,732	12,328	10,525
49,150	49,200	11,571	9,746	12,345	10,539
49,200	49,250	11,588	9,760	12,361	10,553
49,250	49,300	11,604	9,774	12,378	10,567
49,300	49,350	11,621	9,788	12,394	10,581
49,350	49,400	11,637	9,802	12,411	10,595
49,400	49,450	11,654	9,816	12,427	10,609
49,450	49,500	11,670	9,830	12,444	10,623
49,500	49,550	11,687	9,844	12,460	10,637
49,550	49,600	11,703	9,858	12,477	10,651
49,600	49,650	11,720	9,872	12,493	10,665
49,650	49,700	11,736	9,886	12,510	10,679
49,700	49,750	11,753	9,900	12,526	10,693
49,750	49,800	11,769	9,914	12,543	10,707
49,800	49,850	11,786	9,928	12,559	10,721
49,850	49,900	11,802	9,942	12,576	10,735
49,900	49,950	11,819	9,956	12,592	10,749
49,950	50,000	11,835	9,970	12,609	10,763

* This column must also be used by a qualifying widow(er).

50,000 or over—use tax rate schedules

1990 Tax Rate Schedules

Schedule X—Single

If line 5 is:		The tax is:	of the amount over—
Over—	But not over—		
$0	$19,450	........15%	$0
19,450	47,050	**$2,917.50 + 28%**	**19,450**
47,050	97,620	**10,645.50 + 33%**	**47,050**
97,620	....	Use **Worksheet** below to figure your tax.	

Schedule Z— Head of household

If line 5 is:		The tax is:	of the amount over—
Over—	But not over—		
$0	$26,050	........15%	$0
26,050	67,200	**$3,907.50+ 28%**	**26,050**
67,200	134,930	**15,429.50 + 33%**	**67,200**
134,930	....	Use **Worksheet** below to figure your tax.	

Schedule Y-1—Married filing jointly or Qualifying widow(er)

If line 5 is:		The tax is:	of the amount over—
Over—	But not over—		
$0	$32,450	........15%	$0
32,450	78,400	**$4,867.50 + 28%**	**32,450**
78,400	162,770	**17,733.50 + 33%**	**78,400**
162,770	....	Use **Worksheet** below to figure your tax.	

Schedule Y-2— Married filing separately

If line 5 is:		The tax is:	of the amount over—
Over—	But not over—		
$0	$16,225	........15%	$0
16,225	39,200	**$2,433.75 + 28%**	**16,225**
39,200	123,570	**8,866.75 + 33%**	**39,200**
123,570	....	Use **Worksheet** below to figure your tax.	

Worksheet (Keep for your records)

1. If your filing status is:
   - Single, enter $27,333.60
   - Head of household, enter $37,780.40
   - Married filing jointly or Qualifying widow(er), enter $45,575.60
   - Married filing separately, enter $36,708.85 .... 1. _____

2. Enter your taxable income from line 5 of the Form 1040-ES worksheet ...... 2. _____

3. If your filing status is:
   - Single, enter $97,620
   - Head of household, enter $134,930
   - Married filing jointly or Qualifying widow(er), enter $162,770
   - Married filing separately, enter $123,570 ..... 3. _____

4. Subtract line 3 from line 2. Enter the result. (If the result is zero or less, use the schedule above for your filing status to figure your tax. DO NOT use this worksheet.) ...... 4. _____

5. Multiply the amount on line 4 by 28% (.28). Enter the result .... 5. _____

6. Multiply the amount on line 4 by 5% (.05). Enter the result .... 6. _____

7. Multiply $574 by the number of exemptions claimed. (If married filing separately, see **Note** below.) Enter the result .... 7. _____

8. Compare the amounts on lines 6 and 7. Enter the **smaller** of the two amounts here ..... 8. _____

9. **Tax.** Add lines 1, 5, and 8. .... 9. _____

Note: If married filing separately and you did **not** claim an exemption for your spouse, multiply $574 by the number of exemptions claimed. Add $574 to the result and enter the total on line 7 above.

INCOME TAX RATES—ESTATES AND TRUSTS

Tax Year 1990

Taxable Income		The tax is:	Of the amount
Over—	**But not over—**		**over—**
$ 0	$ 5,450	15%	$ 0
5,450	14,150	$ 817.50 + 28%	5,450
14,150	28,320	$3,253.50 + 33%	14,150
28,320	——	28%	0

Tax Year 1989

Taxable Income		The tax is:	Of the amount
Over—	**But not over—**		**over—**
$ 0	$ 5,200	15%	$ 0
5,200	13,500	$ 780 + 28%	5,200
13,500	27,020	3,104 + 33%	13,500
27,020	——	28%	0

INCOME TAX RATES—CORPORATIONS

Tax Years Beginning After 6/30/87**

Taxable Income	Rate
$ 1—$ 50,000	15%
50,001— 75,000	25
over $ 75,000	34
$100,000—$335,000	5*

    * Additional tax, "phases out" the lower marginal brackets
    ** For fiscal year corporations, the proration rules of § 15 apply.

UNIFIED TRANSFER TAX RATES

For Gifts Made and For Deaths after 1983 and before 1993

If the amount with respect to which the tentative tax to be computed is:	The tentative tax is:
Not over $10,000	18 percent of such amount.
Over $10,000 but not over $20,000	$1,800, plus 20 percent of the excess of such amount over $10,000.
Over $20,000 but not over $40,000	$3,800, plus 22 percent of the excess of such amount over $20,000.
Over $40,000 but not over $60,000	$8,200, plus 24 percent of the excess of such amount over $40,000.
Over $60,000 but not over $80,000	$13,000, plus 26 percent of the excess of such amount over $60,000.
Over $80,000 but not over $100,000	$18,200, plus 28 percent of the excess of such amount over $80,000.
Over $100,000 but not over $150,000	$23,800, plus 30 percent of the excess of such amount over $100,000.
Over $150,000 but not over $250,000	$38,800, plus 32 percent of the excess of such amount over $150,000.
Over $250,000 but not over $500,000	$70,800, plus 34 percent of the excess of such amount over $250,000.
Over $500,000 but not over $750,000	$155,800, plus 37 percent of the excess of such amount over $500,000.
Over $750,000 but not over $1,000,000	$248,300, plus 39 percent of the excess of such amount over $750,000.
Over $1,000,000 but not over $1,250,000	$345,800, plus 41 percent of the excess of such amount over $1,000,000.
Over $1,250,000 but not over $1,500,000	$448,300, plus 43 percent of the excess of such amount over $1,250,000.
Over $1,500,000 but not over $2,000,000	$555,800, plus 45 percent of the excess of such amount over $1,500,000.
Over $2,000,000 but not over $2,500,000	$780,800, plus 49 percent of the excess of such amount over $2,000,000.
Over $2,500,000 but not over $3,000,000	$1,025,800, plus 53 percent of the excess of such amount over $2,500,000.
Over $3,000,000*	$1,290,800, plus 55 percent of the excess of such amount over $3,000,000.

* For large taxable transfers (generally in excess of $10 million) there is a phase-out of the graduated rates and the unified tax credit.

TABLE FOR COMPUTATION OF MAXIMUM CREDIT FOR STATE DEATH TAXES

(A) Adjusted Taxable Estate* equal to or more than—	(B) Adjusted Taxable Estate* less than—	(C) Credit on amount in column (A)	(D) Rates of credit on excess over amount in column (A)
			Percent
0	$ 40,000	0	None
$ 40,000	90,000	0	0.8
90,000	140,000	$ 400	1.6
140,000	240,000	1,200	2.4
240,000	440,000	3,600	3.2
440,000	640,000	10,000	4.0
640,000	840,000	18,000	4.8
840,000	1,040,000	27,600	5.6
1,040,000	1,540,000	38,800	6.4
1,540,000	2,040,000	70,800	7.2
2,040,000	2,540,000	106,800	8.0
2,540,000	3,040,000	146,800	8.8
3,040,000	3,540,000	190,800	9.6
3,540,000	4,040,000	238,800	10.4
4,040,000	5,040,000	290,800	11.2
5,040,000	6,040,000	402,800	12.0
6,040,000	7,040,000	522,800	12.8
7,040,000	8,040,000	650,800	13.6
8,040,000	9,040,000	786,800	14.4
9,040,000	10,040,000	930,800	15.2
10,040,000		1,082,800	16.0

*   Adjusted Taxable Estate = Taxable Estate − $60,000

APPENDIX B

Tax Forms

Department of the Treasury - Internal Revenue Service

Form
1040EZ

**Income Tax Return for
Single Filers With No Dependents**   **1989**

OMB No. 1545-0675

**Name &
address**

Use the IRS mailing label. If you don't have one, please print.

L
A
B
E
L

H
E
R
E

Print your name above (first, initial, last)

Home address (number and street). (If you have a P.O. box, see back.)   Apt. no.

City, town or post office, state, and ZIP code

Please print your numbers like this:

Your social security number

Instructions are on the back. Also, see the Form 1040A/
1040EZ booklet, especially the checklist on page 14.

Presidential Election Campaign Fund
Do you want $1 to go to this fund?   *Note: Checking "Yes" will
not change your tax or
reduce your refund.*   ▶

Yes No

Dollars   **Cents**

**Report
your
income**

1 Total wages, salaries, and tips. This should be shown in Box 10
of your W-2 form(s). (Attach your W-2 form(s).)   **1**

Attach
Copy B of
Form(s)
W-2 here.

2 Taxable interest income of $400 or less. If the total is more
than $400, you cannot use Form 1040EZ.   **2**

3 Add line 1 and line 2. This is your **adjusted gross income.**   **3**

4 Can your parents (or someone else) claim you on their return?

☐ **Yes.** Do worksheet on back; enter amount from line E here.

☐ **No.** Enter 5,100. This is the total of your standard
deduction and personal exemption.   **4**

*Note: You
must check
Yes or No.*

5 Subtract line 4 from line 3. If line 4 is larger than line 3,
enter 0. This is your **taxable income.**   **5**

**Figure
your
tax**

6 Enter your Federal income tax withheld from Box 9 of your
W-2 form(s).   **6**

7 **Tax.** Use the amount on **line 5** to look up your tax in the tax
table on pages 41-46 of the Form 1040A/1040EZ booklet. Use
the **single** column in the table. Enter the tax from the table on
this line.   **7**

**Refund
or
amount
you owe**

8 If line 6 is larger than line 7, subtract line 7 from line 6.
This is your **refund.**   **8**

Attach tax
payment here.

9 If line 7 is larger than line 6, subtract line 6 from line 7. This
is the **amount you owe.** Attach check or money order for
the full amount, payable to "Internal Revenue Service."   **9**

**Sign
your
return**

(Keep a copy
of this form
for your
records.)

I have read this return. Under penalties of perjury, I declare
that to the best of my knowledge and belief, the return is true,
correct, and complete.

Your signature   Date

X

For IRS Use Only—Please
do not write in boxes below.

For Privacy Act and Paperwork Reduction Act Notice, see page 3 in the booklet.   Form 1040EZ (1989)

1989   Instructions for Form 1040EZ

Use this form if:
- Your filing status is single.
- You do not claim any dependents.
- You were under 65 and not blind at the end of 1989.
- Your taxable income (line 5) is less than $50,000.
- You had **only** wages, salaries, tips, and taxable scholarships or fellowships, and your taxable interest income was $400 or less. *Caution: If you earned tips (including allocated tips) that are not included in Box 14 of your W-2, you may not be able to use Form 1040EZ. See page 23 in the booklet.*

If you are not sure about your filing status or dependents, see pages 15 through 20 in the booklet.

If you can't use this form, see pages 11 through 13 in the booklet for which form to use.

Completing your return

Please print your numbers inside the boxes. Do not type your numbers. Do not use dollar signs. You may round off cents to whole dollars. To do so, drop amounts under 50 cents and increase amounts that are 50 cents or more. For example, $129.49 becomes $129 and $129.50 becomes $130. If you round off, do so for all amounts. But if you have to add two or more amounts to figure the amount to enter on a line, include cents when adding and round off only the total.

Name & address

Please use the mailing label we sent you. It can help speed your refund. After you complete your return, put the label in the name and address area. Cross out any errors. Print the right information on the label (including apartment number). **If you don't have a label,** print your name, address, and social security number. If your post office does not deliver mail to your home and you have a P.O. box, show your P.O. box number instead of your home address.

Presidential campaign fund

Congress set up this fund to help pay for Presidential election costs. If you want $1 of your tax to go to this fund, check the "Yes" box. If you check "Yes," your tax or refund will not change.

Report your income

Line 1. If you don't get your W-2 by February 15, contact your local IRS office. You must still report your wages, salaries, and tips even if you don't get a W-2 from your employer. Students, if you received a scholarship or fellowship, see page 23 in the booklet.

Line 2. Banks, savings and loans, credit unions, etc., should send you a Form 1099-INT showing the amount of taxable interest paid to you. You must report all your taxable interest even if you don't get a Form 1099-INT. If you had tax-exempt interest, such as on municipal bonds, write "TEI" in the space to the left of line 2. After "TEI," show the amount of your tax-exempt interest. **Do not** add tax-exempt interest in the total on line 2.

Line 4. If you checked "Yes" because someone can claim you as a dependent, fill in this worksheet to figure the amount to enter on line 4.

	A. Enter the amount from line 1 on front.	**A.** _____
	B. Minimum amount.	**B.** _____ 500.00
Standard deduction worksheet for dependents who checked "Yes" on line 4	**C. Compare** the amounts on lines A and B above. Enter the LARGER of the two amounts here.	**C.** _____
	D. Maximum amount.	**D.** _____ 3,100.00
	E. Compare the amounts on lines C and D above. Enter the SMALLER of the two amounts here and on line 4 on front.	**E.** _____

If you checked "No" because no one can claim you as a dependent, enter 5,100 on line 4. This is the total of your standard deduction (3,100) and personal exemption (2,000).

Figure your tax

Line 6. If you received a Form 1099-INT showing income tax withheld (backup withholding), include the amount in the total on line 6. To the left of line 6, write "Form 1099." If you had two or more employers and had total wages of over $48,000, see page 35 in the booklet.

If you want IRS to figure your tax, skip lines 7 through 9. Then sign and date your return. If you paid too much tax, we will send you a refund. If you didn't pay enough tax, we will send you a bill. We won't charge you interest or a late payment penalty if you pay within 30 days of the notice date or by April 16, 1990, whichever is later. If you want to figure your own tax, complete the rest of your return.

Amount you owe

Line 9. If you owe tax, attach your check or money order for the full amount. Write your social security number, daytime phone number, and "1989 Form 1040EZ" on your payment.

Sign your return

You must sign and date your return. If you pay someone to prepare your return, that person must sign it and show other information. See page 40 in the booklet.

Mailing your return

Mail your return by **April 16, 1990.** Use the envelope that came with your booklet. If you don't have that envelope, see page 49 in the booklet for the address.

Form
1040A

Department of the Treasury—Internal Revenue Service
U.S. Individual
Income Tax Return   **1989**

OMB No. 1545-0085

Step 1
Label

Use IRS
label.
Otherwise,
please print
or type.

L A B E L   H E R E

| Your first name and initial | Last name | Your social security no. |

If a joint return, spouse's first name and initial   Last name

Spouse's social security no.

Home address (number and street). (If you have a P.O. box, see page 15 of the instructions.)   Apt. no.

City, town or post office, state and ZIP code. (If you have a foreign address, see page 15.)

**For Privacy Act
and Paperwork
Reduction Act
Notice, see page 3.**

Presidential Election Campaign Fund

Do you want $1 to go to this fund?. . . . .   ☐ Yes   ☐ No
If joint return, does your spouse want $1 to go to this fund?   ☐ Yes   ☐ No

Note: *Checking "Yes" will
not change your tax or
reduce your refund.*

Step 2
**Check your
filing status**

(Check only one.)

1 ☐ Single (See if you can use Form 1040EZ.)
2 ☐ Married filing joint return (even if only one had income)
3 ☐ Married filing separate return. Enter spouse's social security number above
and spouse's full name here. _____
4 ☐ Head of household (with qualifying person). (See page 16.) If the qualifying person is your child
but not your dependent, enter this child's name here. _____
5 ☐ Qualifying widow(er) with dependent child (year spouse died ▶ 19 ____). (See page 17.)

Step 3
**Figure your
exemptions**

(See page 17 of
instructions.)

If more than 7
dependents,
see page 20.

Attach Copy B of
Form(s) W-2 here.

6a ☐ **Yourself**   If someone (such as your parent) can claim you as a dependent on his or her tax
return, do not check box 6a. But be sure to check the box on line 15b on page 2.
6b ☐ **Spouse**

No. of boxes
checked on
6a and 6b ____

c Dependents: 1. Name (first, initial, and last name)	2. Check if under age 2	3. If age 2 or older, dependent's social security number	4. Relationship	5. No. of months lived in your home in 1989

No. of your
children on 6c
who:

● lived with
you

● didn't live
with you due
to divorce or
separation
(see page 20)

No. of **other**
dependents
listed on 6c

d If your child didn't live with you but is claimed as your dependent
under a pre-1985 agreement, check here . . . . ▶ ☐
e Total number of exemptions claimed.

Add numbers
entered on
lines above ☐

Step 4
**Figure your
total income**

Attach check or
money order here.

7 Wages, salaries, tips, etc. This should be shown in Box 10 of your W-2
form(s). (Attach Form(s) W-2.)   **7**

8a **Taxable** interest income (see page 24). (If over $400, also complete
and attach Schedule 1, Part II.)   **8a**

b **Tax-exempt** interest income (see page 24).
(DO NOT include on line 8a.)   **8b**

9 Dividends. (If over $400, also complete and attach Schedule 1, Part III.)   **9**

10 Unemployment compensation (insurance) from Form(s) 1099-G.   **10**

11 Add lines 7, 8a, 9, and 10. Enter the total. This is your **total income.**   ▶ **11**

Step 5
**Figure your
adjusted
gross
income**

12a Your IRA deduction from applicable worksheet.
Rules for IRAs begin on page 25.   **12a**
b Spouse's IRA deduction from applicable worksheet.
Rules for IRAs begin on page 25.   **12b**
c Add lines 12a and 12b. Enter the total. These are your **total
adjustments.**   **12c**
13 Subtract line 12c from line 11. Enter the result. This is your **adjusted
gross income.** (If this line is less than $19,340 and a child lived with
you, see "Earned Income Credit" (line 25b) on page 37 of instructions.)   ▶ **13**

1989   Form 1040A

Step 6

14	Enter the amount from line 13.	14

Figure your standard deduction,

15a Check if: ☐ **You** were 65 or older ☐ Blind } **Enter number of**
                 ☐ **Spouse** was 65 or older ☐ Blind } **boxes checked** ▶15a ☐

  b If someone (such as your parent) can claim you as a dependent,
     check here . . . . ▶15b ☐

  c If you are married filing separately and your spouse files Form
     1040 and itemizes deductions, see page 29 and check here . . . . ▶15c ☐

16 Enter your standard deduction. See page 30 for the chart (or worksheet)
     that applies to you. Be sure to enter your standard deduction here.   16

exemption amount, and

17 Subtract line 16 from line 14. Enter the result. (If line 16 is more than
     line 14, enter -0-.)   17

18 Multiply $2,000 by the total number of exemptions claimed on line 6e.   18

taxable income

19 Subtract line 18 from line 17. Enter the result. (If line 18 is more than line 17,
     enter -0-.) This is your **taxable income**.   ▶ 19

If You Want IRS To Figure Your Tax, See Page 31 of the Instructions.

Step 7

Figure your tax, credits, supplemental Medicare premium, and payments (including advance EIC payments)

Caution: If you are under age 14 and have more than $1,000 of investment
     income, check here . . . . ▶ ☐
     Also see page 31 to see if you have to use Form 8615 to figure your tax.

20 Find the tax on the amount on line 19. Check if from:
     ☐ Tax Table (pages 41–46) or ☐ Form 8615   20

21 Credit for child and dependent care expenses. Complete and
     attach Schedule 1, Part I.   21

22 Subtract line 21 from line 20. Enter the result. (If line 21 is more than
     line 20, enter -0-.)   22

23 **Supplemental Medicare premium.** See page 35. Complete
     and attach Schedule 2 (Form 1040A).   23

24 Add lines 22 and 23. Enter the total. This is your **total tax** and any
     supplemental Medicare premium.   ▶ 24

25a Total Federal income tax withheld—from Box 9
     of your W-2 form(s). (If any is from Form(s)
     1099, check here ▶ ☐ .)   25a

  b **Earned income credit,** from the worksheet
     on page 38 of the instructions. Also see page 37.   25b

26 Add lines 25a and 25b. Enter the total. These are your **total payments.** ▶ 26

Step 8

Figure your refund or amount you owe

27 If line 26 is more than line 24, subtract line 24 from line 26. Enter the result.
     This is your **refund.**   27

28 If line 24 is more than line 26, subtract line 26 from line 24. Enter the result.
     This is the **amount you owe.** Attach check or money order for full amount
     payable to "Internal Revenue Service." Write your social security number,
     daytime phone number, and "1989 Form 1040A" on it.   28

Step 9

Sign your return

(Keep a copy of this return for your records.)

Under penalties of perjury, I declare that I have examined this return and accompanying schedules and statements, and to the best of my knowledge and belief, they are true, correct, and complete. Declaration of preparer (other than the taxpayer) is based on all information of which the preparer has any knowledge.

Your signature	Date	Your occupation
X		

Spouse's signature (if joint return, both must sign)	Date	Spouse's occupation
X		

Paid preparer's use only

Preparer's signature	Date	Preparer's social security no.
X		

Firm's name (or yours if self-employed)		Employer identification no.

Address and ZIP code		Check if self-employed ☐

1989   Schedule 1 (Form 1040A)   OMB No. 1545-0085

Name(s) shown on Form 1040A   Your social security number

You MUST complete and attach Schedule 1 to Form 1040A only if you:

- Claim the credit for child and dependent care expenses (complete **Part I**)
- Received employer-provided dependent care benefits (complete **Part I**)
- Have over $400 of taxable interest income (complete **Part II**)
- Have over $400 of dividend income (complete **Part III**)

Part I

Child and dependent care expenses (see page 32 of the instructions)

- If you are claiming the child and dependent care credit, complete lines 1 through 12 below. But if you received employer-provided dependent care benefits, first complete lines 13 through 20 on the back.

*Note: If you paid cash wages of $50 or more in a calendar quarter to an individual for services performed in your home, you must file an employment tax return. Get **Form 942** for details.*

- If you are not claiming the credit but you received employer-provided dependent care benefits, only complete lines 1 and 2, below, and lines 13 through 20 on the back.

1 Persons or organizations who provided the care. You MUST complete lines 1 and 2. (See page 33.)

a. Name	b. Address (number, street, city, state, and ZIP code)	c. Identification number (SSN or EIN)	d. Amount paid (see instructions)

(If you need more space, attach schedule.)

2 Add the amounts in column d of line 1 and enter the total.   2

3 Enter the number of qualifying persons who were cared for in 1989. You must have shared the same home with the qualifying person(s). (See the instructions for the definition of a qualifying person.)   3

Note: See the instructions to find out which expenses qualify.

4 Enter the amount of **qualified** expenses you incurred and actually paid in 1989. See the instructions for the amount to enter. DO NOT ENTER MORE THAN $2,400 ($4,800 if you paid for the care of two or more qualifying persons).   4

5 Enter the **excluded benefits,** if any, from line 19 on the back.   5

6 Subtract line 5 from line 4. Enter the result. If line 5 is equal to or more than line 4, STOP HERE; you cannot claim the credit.   6

7 You **must** enter your **earned income.** (See page 34 of the instructions for the definition of earned income.)   7

8 If you are married filing a joint return, you **must** enter your spouse's earned income. (If spouse was a full-time student or disabled, see the instructions for the amount to enter.)   8

9 If you are married filing a joint return, compare the amounts on lines 7 and 8. Enter the **smaller** of the two amounts here.   9

10 • If you are married filing a joint return, compare the amounts on lines 6 and 9. Enter the **smaller** of the two amounts here.

• All others, compare the amounts on lines 6 and 7. Enter the **smaller** of the two amounts here.   10

11 Enter the decimal amount from the table below that applies to the amount on Form 1040A, line 14.

If line 14 is:		Decimal amount is:	If line 14 is:		Decimal amount is:
Over—	But not over—		Over—	But not over—	
$0	10,000	.30	$20,000	22,000	.24
10,000	12,000	.29	22,000	24,000	.23
12,000	14,000	.28	24,000	26,000	.22
14,000	16,000	.27	26,000	28,000	.21
16,000	18,000	.26	28,000		.20
18,000	20,000	.25			

11   ×

12 Multiply the amount on line 10 by the decimal amount on line 11. Enter the result here and on Form 1040A, line 21.   12 =

1989	**Schedule 1 (Form 1040A)**	OMB No. 1545-0085

Name(s) shown on Form 1040A. (Do not complete if shown on other side.) | Your social security number

Part I
(continued)

Complete lines 13 through 20 only if you received employer-provided dependent care benefits. Be sure to also complete lines 1 and 2 of Part I.

13　Enter the total amount of employer-provided dependent care benefits you received for 1989. (This amount should be separately shown on your W-2 form(s) and labeled as "DCB.") DO NOT include amounts that were reported to you as wages in Box 10 of Form(s) W-2.　13

14　Enter the total amount of **qualified** expenses incurred in 1989 for the care of a qualifying person. (See page 34 of the instructions.)　14

15　Compare the amounts on lines 13 and 14. Enter the **smaller** of the two amounts here.　15

16　You **must** enter your **earned income.** (See page 34 of the instructions for the definition of earned income.)　16

17　If you were married at the end of 1989, you **must** enter your spouse's earned income. (If your spouse was a full-time student or disabled, see page 34 of the instructions for the amount to enter.)　17

18　● If you were married at the end of 1989, compare the amounts on lines 16 and 17 and enter the **smaller** of the two amounts here.
　　● If you were unmarried, enter the amount from line 16 here.　18

Note: *If you are also claiming the child and dependent care credit, first fill in Form 1040A through line 20. Then complete lines 3–12 of Part I.*

19　**Excluded benefits.** Enter here the **smallest** of the following:
　　● The amount from line 15, or
　　● The amount from line 18, or
　　● $5,000 ($2,500 if married filing a separate return).　19

20　**Taxable benefits.** Subtract line 19 from line 13. Enter the result. (If zero or less, enter -0-.) Include this amount in the total on Form 1040A, line 7. In the space to the left of line 7, write "DCB."　20

Part II

Interest Income (see page 24 of the instructions)

Complete this part and attach Schedule 1 to Form 1040A if you received over $400 in taxable interest.

Note: *If you received a Form 1099-INT or Form 1099-OID from a brokerage firm, enter the firm's name and the total interest shown on that form.*

1　List name of payer		Amount
	1	

2　Add amounts on line 1. Enter the total here and on Form 1040A, line 8a.　2

Part III

Dividend Income (see page 24 of the instructions)

Complete this part and attach Schedule 1 to Form 1040A if you received over $400 in dividends.

Note: *If you received a Form 1099-DIV from a brokerage firm, enter the firm's name and the total dividends shown on that form.*

1　List name of payer		Amount
	1	

2　Add amounts on line 1. Enter the total here and on Form 1040A, line 9.　2

Form **1040** Department of the Treasury—Internal Revenue Service
U.S. Individual Income Tax Return 19**89**

For the year Jan.–Dec. 31, 1989, or other tax year beginning _____ , 1989, ending _____ , 19___   OMB No. 1545-0074

Label

Use IRS label.
Otherwise,
please print
or type.

Your first name and initial   Last name   Your social security number

If a joint return, spouse's first name and initial   Last name   Spouse's social security number

Home address (number and street). (If a P.O. box, see page 7 of Instructions.)   Apt. no.

City, town or post office, state and ZIP code. (If a foreign address, see page 7.)

For Privacy Act and Paperwork Reduction Act Notice, see Instructions.

Presidential Election Campaign

▶ Do you want $1 to go to this fund? . . . .   Yes ☐   No ☐
If joint return, does your spouse want $1 to go to this fund? .   Yes ☐   No ☐

Note: *Checking "Yes" will not change your tax or reduce your refund.*

Filing Status

Check only one box.

1 ☐ Single
2 ☐ Married filing joint return (even if only one had income)
3 ☐ Married filing separate return. Enter spouse's social security no. above and full name here. _____
4 ☐ Head of household (with qualifying person). (See page 7 of Instructions.) If the qualifying person is your child but not your dependent, enter child's name here. _____
5 ☐ Qualifying widow(er) with dependent child (year spouse died ▶ 19___). (See page 7 of Instructions.)

Exemptions

(See Instructions on page 8.)

If more than 6 dependents, see Instructions on page 8.

6a ☐ **Yourself** If someone (such as your parent) can claim you as a dependent on his or her tax return, do not check box 6a. But be sure to check the box on line 33b on page 2 . .

b ☐ **Spouse** . . . .

No. of boxes checked on 6a and 6b _____

No. of your children on 6c who:
● lived with you _____
● didn't live with you due to divorce or separation (see page 9) _____

No. of other dependents on 6c _____

Add numbers entered on lines above ▶ ☐

c **Dependents:** (1) Name (first, initial, and last name)	(2) Check if under age 2	(3) If age 2 or older, dependent's social security number	(4) Relationship	(5) No. of months lived in your home in 1989
		: :		
		: :		
		: :		
		: :		
		: :		

d If your child didn't live with you but is claimed as your dependent under a pre-1985 agreement, check here ▶ ☐
e Total number of exemptions claimed . . . .

Income

Please attach Copy B of your Forms W-2, W-2G, and W-2P here.

If you do not have a W-2, see page 6 of Instructions.

Please attach check or money order here.

7 Wages, salaries, tips, etc. *(attach Form(s) W-2)* . . . . | 7 |
8a **Taxable** interest income *(also attach Schedule B if over $400)* . . . | 8a |
   b **Tax-exempt** interest income (see page 10). DON'T include on line 8a | 8b |
9 Dividend income *(also attach Schedule B if over $400)* . . . . . . | 9 |
10 Taxable refunds of state and local income taxes, if any, from worksheet on page 11 of Instructions . . | 10 |
11 Alimony received . . . . | 11 |
12 Business income or (loss) *(attach Schedule C)* . . . . | 12 |
13 Capital gain or (loss) *(attach Schedule D)* . . . . | 13 |
14 Capital gain distributions not reported on line 13 (see page 11) . . . | 14 |
15 Other gains or (losses) *(attach Form 4797)* . . . . | 15 |
16a Total IRA distributions . . | 16a | 16b Taxable amount (see page 11) | 16b |
17a Total pensions and annuities | 17a | 17b Taxable amount (see page 12) | 17b |
18 Rents, royalties, partnerships, estates, trusts, etc. *(attach Schedule E)* . . . . | 18 |
19 Farm income or (loss) *(attach Schedule F)* . . . . | 19 |
20 Unemployment compensation (insurance) (see page 13) . . . . . | 20 |
21a Social security benefits. | 21a | 21b Taxable amount (see page 13) | 21b |
22 Other income (list type and amount—see page 13) _____ | 22 |
23 Add the amounts shown in the far right column for lines 7 through 22. This is your **total income** ▶ | 23 |

Adjustments to Income

(See Instructions on page 14.)

24 Your IRA deduction, from applicable worksheet on page 14 or 15 | 24 |
25 Spouse's IRA deduction, from applicable worksheet on page 14 or 15 | 25 |
26 Self-employed health insurance deduction, from worksheet on page 15 | 26 |
27 Keogh retirement plan and self-employed SEP deduction . . | 27 |
28 Penalty on early withdrawal of savings . . . . | 28 |
29 Alimony paid. **a** Recipient's last name _____ and **b** social security number . . | 29 |
30 Add lines 24 through 29. These are your **total adjustments** . . . . ▶ | 30 |

Adjusted Gross Income

31 Subtract line 30 from line 23. This is your **adjusted gross income**. *If this line is less than $19,340 and a child lived with you, see "Earned Income Credit" (line 58) on page 20 of the Instructions. If you want IRS to figure your tax, see page 16 of the Instructions* . . . ▶ | 31 |

Form 1040 (1989)   Page **2**

Tax Compu-tation	**32** Amount from line 31 (adjusted gross income)	**32**	
	33a Check if: ☐ **You** were 65 or older ☐ Blind; ☐ **Spouse** was 65 or older ☐ Blind.		
	Add the number of boxes checked and enter the total here . . . . ▶ **33a**		
	b If someone (such as your parent) can claim you as a dependent, check here . . ▶ **33b** ☐		
	c If you are married filing a separate return and your spouse itemizes deductions, or you are a dual-status alien, see page 16 and check here . . . . ▶ **33c** ☐		
	34 Enter the larger of: { • Your **standard deduction** (from page 17 of the Instructions), **OR** • Your **itemized deductions** (from Schedule A, line 26). If you itemize, attach Schedule A and check here . ▶ ☐ }	**34**	
	35 Subtract line 34 from line 32. Enter the result here	**35**	
	36 Multiply $2,000 by the total number of exemptions claimed on line 6e	**36**	
	37 **Taxable income.** Subtract line 36 from line 35. Enter the result (if less than zero, enter zero) . .	**37**	
	Caution: If under age 14 and you have more than $1,000 of investment income, check here ▶ ☐ and see page 17 to see if you have to use Form 8615 to figure your tax.		
	38 Enter tax. Check if from: **a** ☐ Tax Table, **b** ☐ Tax Rate Schedules, or **c** ☐ Form 8615. (If any is from Form(s) 8814, enter that amount here ▶ **d** _____ .)	**38**	
	39 Additional taxes (see page 18). Check if from: **a** ☐ Form 4970 **b** ☐ Form 4972	**39**	
	40 Add lines 38 and 39. Enter the total . . . . ▶	**40**	
Credits (See Instructions on page 18.)	**41** Credit for child and dependent care expenses *(attach Form 2441)* **41**		
	42 Credit for the elderly or the disabled *(attach Schedule R)* . . . **42**		
	43 Foreign tax credit *(attach Form 1116)* **43**		
	44 General business credit. Check if from: **a** ☐ Form 3800 or **b** ☐ Form (specify) _____ . . **44**		
	45 Credit for prior year minimum tax *(attach Form 8801)* **45**		
	46 Add lines 41 through 45. Enter the total . .	**46**	
	47 Subtract line 46 from line 40. Enter the result (if less than zero, enter zero) . . . . ▶	**47**	
Other Taxes (Including Advance EIC Payments)	**48** Self-employment tax *(attach Schedule SE)*	**48**	
	49 Alternative minimum tax *(attach Form 6251)*	**49**	
	50 Recapture taxes (see page 18). Check if from: **a** ☐ Form 4255 **b** ☐ Form 8611 . .	**50**	
	51 Social security tax on tip income not reported to employer *(attach Form 4137)* . .	**51**	
	52 Tax on an IRA or a qualified retirement plan *(attach Form 5329)*	**52**	
	53 Add lines 47 through 52. Enter the total . . . . ▶	**53**	
Medicare Premium	**54** Supplemental Medicare premium *(attach Form 8808)*	**54**	
	55 Add lines 53 and 54. This is your **total tax** and any supplemental Medicare premium . . . . ▶	**55**	
Payments Attach Forms W-2, W-2G, and W-2P to front.	**56** Federal income tax withheld (if any is from Form(s) 1099, check ▶ ☐) **56**		
	57 1989 estimated tax payments and amount applied from 1988 return **57**		
	58 Earned income credit (see page 20) **58**		
	59 Amount paid with Form 4868 (extension request) **59**		
	60 Excess social security tax and RRTA tax withheld (see page 20) **60**		
	61 Credit for Federal tax on fuels *(attach Form 4136)* **61**		
	62 Regulated investment company credit *(attach Form 2439)* . . **62**		
	63 Add lines 56 through 62. These are your **total payments** . . . . ▶	**63**	
Refund or Amount You Owe	**64** If line 63 is larger than line 55, enter amount **OVERPAID** . . . . ▶	**64**	
	65 Amount of line 64 to be **REFUNDED TO YOU** . . . . ▶	**65**	
	66 Amount of line 64 to be **APPLIED TO YOUR 1990 ESTIMATED TAX** ▶ **66**		
	67 If line 55 is larger than line 63, enter **AMOUNT YOU OWE.** Attach check or money order for full amount payable to "Internal Revenue Service." Write your social security number, daytime phone number, and "1989 Form 1040" on it	**67**	
	68 Penalty for underpayment of estimated tax (see page 21) . . . **68**		

Sign Here
(Keep a copy of this return for your records.)

Under penalties of perjury, I declare that I have examined this return and accompanying schedules and statements, and to the best of my knowledge and belief, they are true, correct, and complete. Declaration of preparer (other than taxpayer) is based on all information of which preparer has any knowledge.

▶ Your signature	Date	Your occupation
▶ Spouse's signature (if joint return, BOTH must sign)	Date	Spouse's occupation

Paid Preparer's Use Only

Preparer's signature ▶	Date	Check if self-employed ☐	Preparer's social security no.
Firm's name (or yours if self-employed) and address ▶		E.I. No. ZIP code	

SCHEDULES A&B
(Form 1040)

Department of the Treasury
Internal Revenue Service

Schedule A—Itemized Deductions

(Schedule B is on back)

▶ Attach to Form 1040. ▶ See Instructions for Schedules A and B (Form 1040).

OMB No. 1545-0074

1989

Attachment Sequence No. **07**

Name(s) shown on Form 1040

Your social security number

Medical and Dental Expenses (Do not include expenses reimbursed or paid by others.) (See Instructions on page 23.)	**1a** Prescription medicines and drugs, insulin, doctors, dentists, nurses, hospitals, medical insurance premiums you paid, etc . .	**1a**	
	b Other. (List—include hearing aids, dentures, eyeglasses, transportation and lodging, etc.) ▶		
		1b	
	2 Add the amounts on lines 1a and 1b. Enter the total here . . .	**2**	
	3 Multiply the amount on Form 1040, line 32, by 7.5% (.075) . .	**3**	
	4 Subtract line 3 from line 2. If zero or less, enter -0-. **Total** medical and dental . . ▶	**4**	
Taxes You Paid (See Instructions on page 24.)	**5** State and local income taxes	**5**	
	6 Real estate taxes	**6**	
	7 Other taxes. (List—include personal property taxes.) ▶		
		7	
	8 Add the amounts on lines 5 through 7. Enter the total here. **Total** taxes . . ▶	**8**	
Interest You Paid (See Instructions on page 24.)	**9a** Deductible home mortgage interest (from Form 1098) that you paid to financial institutions. Report deductible points on line 10.	**9a**	
	b Other deductible home mortgage interest. (If paid to an individual, show that person's name and address.) ▶		
		9b	
	10 Deductible points. (See Instructions for special rules.)	**10**	
	11 Deductible investment interest. (See page 25.)	**11**	
	12a Personal interest you paid. (See page 25.) . [**12a** [		
	b Multiply the amount on line 12a by 20% (.20). Enter the result .	**12b**	
	13 Add the amounts on lines 9a through 11, and 12b. Enter the total here. **Total** interest ▶	**13**	
Gifts to Charity (See Instructions on page 25.)	**14** Contributions by cash or check. (If you gave $3,000 or more to any one organization, show to whom you gave and how much you gave.) ▶	**14**	
	15 Other than cash or check. (You must attach Form 8283 if over $500.)	**15**	
	16 Carryover from prior year	**16**	
	17 Add the amounts on lines 14 through 16. Enter the total here. **Total** contributions . ▶	**17**	
Casualty and Theft Losses	**18** Casualty or theft loss(es) (attach Form 4684). (See page 26 of the Instructions.) . . . . ▶	**18**	
Moving Expenses	**19** Moving expenses (attach Form 3903 or 3903F). (See page 26 of the Instructions.) . . . . ▶	**19**	
Job Expenses and Most Other Miscellaneous Deductions (See page 26 for expenses to deduct here.)	**20** Unreimbursed employee expenses—job travel, union dues, job education, etc. (You MUST attach Form 2106 in some cases. See Instructions.) ▶	**20**	
	21 Other expenses (investment, tax preparation, safe deposit box, etc.). List type and amount ▶		
		21	
	22 Add the amounts on lines 20 and 21. Enter the total. . . .	**22**	
	23 Multiply the amount on Form 1040, line 32, by 2% (.02). Enter the result here	**23**	
	24 Subtract line 23 from line 22. Enter the result. If zero or less, enter -0- . . . . . ▶	**24**	
Other Miscellaneous Deductions	**25** Other (from list on page 26 of Instructions). List type and amount ▶ . . . . ▶	**25**	
Total Itemized Deductions	**26** Add the amounts on lines 4, 8, 13, 17, 18, 19, 24, and 25. Enter the total here. Then enter on Form 1040, line 34, the LARGER of this total or your standard deduction from page 17 of the Instructions . . . . ▶	**26**	

For Paperwork Reduction Act Notice, see Form 1040 Instructions.

Schedule A (Form 1040) 1989

Schedules A&B (Form 1040) 1989

OMB No. 1545-0074 · Page **2**

Name(s) shown on Form 1040. (Do not enter name and social security number if shown on other side.) | **Your social security number**

Schedule B—Interest and Dividend Income

Attachment Sequence No. 08

Part I Interest Income

(See Instructions on pages 10 and 27.)

Note: If you received a Form 1099-INT or Form 1099-OID from a brokerage firm, list the firm's name as the payer and enter the total interest shown on that form.

If you received more than $400 in taxable interest income, you must complete Parts I and III. List ALL interest received in Part I. If you received, as a nominee, interest that actually belongs to another person, or you received or paid accrued interest on securities transferred between interest payment dates, see page 27.

Interest Income		Amount
1 Interest income from seller-financed mortgages. (See Instructions and list name of payer.) ▶	1	
2 Other interest income. (List name of payer.) ▶	2	
3 Add the amounts on lines 1 and 2. Enter the total here and on Form 1040, line 8a. ▶	3	

Part II Dividend Income

(See Instructions on pages 10 and 27.)

Note: If you received a Form 1099-DIV from a brokerage firm, list the firm's name as the payer and enter the total dividends shown on that form.

If you received more than $400 in gross dividends and/or other distributions on stock, you must complete Parts II and III. If you received, as a nominee, dividends that actually belong to another person, see page 27.

Dividend Income		Amount
4 Dividend income. (List name of payer—include on this line capital gain distributions, nontaxable distributions, etc.) ▶	4	
5 Add the amounts on line 4. Enter the total here	5	
6 Capital gain distributions. Enter here and on Schedule D*	6	
7 Nontaxable distributions. (See the Instructions for Form 1040, line 9.)	7	
8 Add the amounts on lines 6 and 7. Enter the total here	8	
9 Subtract line 8 from line 5. Enter the result here and on Form 1040, line 9 ▶	9	

*If you received capital gain distributions but do not need Schedule D to report any other gains or losses, see the Instructions for Form 1040, lines 13 and 14.

Part III Foreign Accounts and Foreign Trusts

(See Instructions on page 27.)

If you received more than $400 of interest or dividends, OR if you had a foreign account or were a grantor of, or a transferor to, a foreign trust, you must answer both questions in Part III.

	Yes	No
10a At any time during 1989, did you have an interest in or a signature or other authority over a financial account in a foreign country (such as a bank account, securities account, or other financial account)? (See page 27 of the Instructions for exceptions and filing requirements for Form TD F 90-22.1.)		
b If "Yes," enter the name of the foreign country ▶		
11 Were you the grantor of, or transferor to, a foreign trust that existed during 1989, whether or not you have any beneficial interest in it? If "Yes," you may have to file Form 3520, 3520-A, or 926.		

For Paperwork Reduction Act Notice, see Form 1040 Instructions. | Schedule B (Form 1040) 1989

SCHEDULE C
(Form 1040)

Department of the Treasury
Internal Revenue Service

Profit or Loss From Business
(Sole Proprietorship)
Partnerships, Joint Ventures, Etc., Must File Form 1065.

▶ Attach to Form 1040 or Form 1041.   ▶ See Instructions for Schedule C (Form 1040).

OMB No. 1545-0074

1989

Attachment
Sequence No. **09**

Name of proprietor	Social security number (SSN)

A Principal business or profession, including product or service (see Instructions)

B Principal business code
(from page 2) ▶

C Business name and address ▶ ....

D Employer ID number (Not SSN)

E Method(s) used to value closing inventory: **(1)** ☐ Cost   **(2)** ☐ Lower of cost or market   **(3)** ☐ Other (attach explanation)   **(4)** ☐ Does not apply (if checked, skip line G)

F Accounting method: **(1)** ☐ Cash   **(2)** ☐ Accrual   **(3)** ☐ Other (specify) ▶ ....

		Yes	No
G	Was there any change in determining quantities, costs, or valuations between opening and closing inventory? (If "Yes," attach explanation.)		
H	Are you deducting expenses for business use of your home? (If "Yes," see Instructions for limitations.)		
I	Did you "materially participate" in the operation of this business during 1989? (If "No," see Instructions for limitations on losses.)		

J If this schedule includes a loss, credit, deduction, income, or other tax benefit relating to a tax shelter required to be registered, check here.   ▶ ☐
If you checked this box, you MUST attach **Form 8271.**

Part I   Income

1	Gross receipts or sales	**1**	
2	Returns and allowances	**2**	
3	Subtract line 2 from line 1. Enter the result here	**3**	
4	Cost of goods sold and/or operations (from line 39 on page 2)	**4**	
5	Subtract line 4 from line 3 and enter the **gross profit** here	**5**	
6	Other income, including Federal and state gasoline or fuel tax credit or refund (see Instructions)	**6**	
7	Add lines 5 and 6. This is your **gross income** . . . . ▶	**7**	

Part II   Expenses

8	Advertising	**8**	**22** Repairs	**22**	
9	Bad debts from sales or services (see Instructions)	**9**	**23** Supplies (not included in Part III)	**23**	
10	Car and truck expenses . . .	**10**	**24** Taxes	**24**	
11	Commissions	**11**	**25** Travel, meals, and entertainment:		
12	Depletion	**12**	**a** Travel	**25a**	
13	Depreciation and section 179 deduction from **Form 4562** (not included in Part III)	**13**	**b** Meals and entertainment .		
14	Employee benefit programs (other than on line 20)	**14**	**c** Enter 20% of line 25b subject to limitations (see Instructions) .		
15	Freight (not included in Part III)	**15**	**d** Subtract line 25c from line 25b	**25d**	
16	Insurance (other than health) .	**16**	**26** Utilities (see Instructions) . .	**26**	
17	Interest:		**27** Wages (less jobs credit) . . .	**27**	
a	Mortgage (paid to banks, etc.) .	**17a**	**28** Other expenses (list type and amount):		
b	Other	**17b**	....		
18	Legal and professional services .	**18**	....		
19	Office expense	**19**	....		
20	Pension and profit-sharing plans .	**20**	....		
21	Rent or lease:		....		
a	Machinery and equipment . .	**21a**	....		
b	Other business property . . .	**21b**		**28**	

29	Add amounts in columns for lines 8 through 28. These are your **total expenses** . . . . ▶	**29**	
30	**Net profit or (loss).** Subtract line 29 from line 7. If a profit, enter here and on Form 1040, line 12, and on Schedule SE, line 2. If a loss, you MUST go on to line 31. (Fiduciaries, see Instructions.)	**30**	

31 If you have a loss, you MUST check the box that describes your investment in this activity (see Instructions) . . . . .   **31a** ☐ All investment is at risk.
If you checked 31a, enter the loss on Form 1040, line 12, and Schedule SE, line 2.   **31b** ☐ Some investment is not at risk.
If you checked 31b, you MUST attach **Form 6198.**

For Paperwork Reduction Act Notice, see Form 1040 Instructions.   Schedule C (Form 1040) 1989

Schedule C (Form 1040) 1989   Page **2**

Part III Cost of Goods Sold and/or Operations (See Instructions.)

32	Inventory at beginning of year. (If different from last year's closing inventory, attach explanation.)	32	
33	Purchases less cost of items withdrawn for personal use	33	
34	Cost of labor. (Do not include salary paid to yourself.)	34	
35	Materials and supplies	35	
36	Other costs	36	
37	Add lines 32 through 36	37	
38	Inventory at end of year	38	
39	**Cost of goods sold and/or operations.** Subtract line 38 from line 37. Enter the result here and on page 1, line 4	39	

Part IV Principal Business or Professional Activity Codes (*Caution: Codes have been revised. Check your code carefully.*)

Locate the major business category that best describes your activity (for example, Retail Trade, Services, etc.). Within the major category, select the activity code that most closely identifies the business or profession that is the principal source of your sales or receipts. **Enter this 4-digit code on page 1, line B.** (**Note:** *If your principal source of income is from farming activities, you should file* **Schedule F** *(Form 1040), Farm Income and Expenses.*)

Construction

Code
0018 Operative builders (for own account)

General contractors
0034 Residential building
0059 Nonresidential building
0075 Highway and street construction
3889 Other heavy construction (pipe laying, bridge construction, etc.)

Building trade contractors, including repairs
0232 Plumbing, heating, air conditioning
0257 Painting and paper hanging
0273 Electrical work
0299 Masonry, dry wall, stone, tile
0414 Carpentering and flooring
0430 Roofing, siding, and sheet metal
0455 Concrete work
0885 Other building trade contractors (excavation, glazing, etc.)

Manufacturing, Including Printing and Publishing

0638 Food products and beverages
0653 Textile mill products
0679 Apparel and other textile products
0695 Leather, footware, handbags, etc.
0810 Furniture and fixtures
0836 Lumber and other wood products
0851 Printing and publishing
0877 Paper and allied products
1032 Stone, clay, and glass products
1057 Primary metal industries
1073 Fabricated metal products
1099 Machinery and machine shops
1115 Electric and electronic equipment
1883 Other manufacturing industries

Mining and Mineral Extraction

1511 Metal mining
1537 Coal mining
1552 Oil and gas
1719 Quarrying and nonmetallic mining

Agricultural Services, Forestry, Fishing

1933 Crop services
1958 Veterinary services, including pets
1974 Livestock breeding
1990 Other animal services
2113 Farm labor and management services
2212 Horticulture and landscaping
2238 Forestry, except logging
0836 Logging
2246 Commercial fishing
2469 Hunting and trapping

Wholesale Trade—Selling Goods to Other Businesses, Etc.

Durable goods, including machinery, equipment, wood, metals, etc.
2618 Selling for your own account
2634 Agent or broker for other firms—more than 50% of gross sales on commission

Nondurable goods, including food, fiber, chemicals, etc.
2659 Selling for your own account

2675 Agent or broker for other firms—more than 50% of gross sales on commission

Retail Trade—Selling Goods to Individuals and Households

3012 Selling door-to-door, by telephone or party plan, or from mobile unit
3038 Catalog or mail order
3053 Vending machine selling

Selling From Showroom, Store, or Other Fixed Location

Food, beverages, and drugs
3079 Eating places (meals or snacks)
3086 Catering services
3095 Drinking places (alcoholic beverages)
3210 Grocery stores (general line)
0612 Bakeries selling at retail
3236 Other food stores (meat, produce, candy, etc.)
3251 Liquor stores
3277 Drug stores

Automotive and service stations
3319 New car dealers (franchised)
3335 Used car dealers
3517 Other automotive dealers (motorcycles, recreational vehicles, etc.)
3533 Tires, accessories, and parts
3558 Gasoline service stations

General merchandise, apparel, and furniture
3715 Variety stores
3731 Other general merchandise stores
3756 Shoe stores
3772 Men's and boys' clothing stores
3913 Women's ready-to-wear stores
3921 Women's accessory and specialty stores and furriers
3939 Family clothing stores
3954 Other apparel and accessory stores
3970 Furniture stores
3996 TV, audio, and electronics
3988 Computer and software stores
4119 Household appliance stores
4317 Other home furnishing stores (china, floor coverings, etc.)
4333 Music and record stores

Building, hardware, and garden supply
4416 Building materials dealers
4432 Paint, glass, and wallpaper stores
4457 Hardware stores
4473 Nurseries and garden supply stores

Other retail stores
4614 Used merchandise and antique stores (except motor vehicle parts)
4630 Gift, novelty, and souvenir shops
4655 Florists
4671 Jewelry stores
4697 Sporting goods and bicycle shops
4812 Boat dealers
4838 Hobby, toy, and game shops
4853 Camera and photo supply stores
4879 Optical goods stores
4895 Luggage and leather goods stores
5017 Book stores, excluding newsstands
5033 Stationery stores
5058 Fabric and needlework stores
5074 Mobile home dealers
5090 Fuel dealers (except gasoline)
5884 Other retail stores

Finance, Insurance, Real Estate, and Related Services

5520 Real estate agents or brokers
5579 Real estate property managers
5710 Subdividers and developers, except cemeteries
5538 Operators and lessors of buildings, including residential
5553 Operators and lessors of other real property
5702 Insurance agents or brokers
5744 Other insurance services
6064 Security brokers and dealers
6080 Commodity contracts brokers and dealers, and security and commodity exchanges
6130 Investment advisors and services
6148 Credit institutions and mortgage bankers
6155 Title abstract offices
5777 Other finance and real estate

Transportation, Communications, Public Utilities, and Related Services

6114 Taxicabs
6312 Bus and limousine transportation
6361 Other highway passenger transportation
6338 Trucking (except trash collection)
6395 Courier or package delivery services
6510 Trash collection without own dump
6536 Public warehousing
6551 Water transportation
6619 Air transportation
6635 Travel agents and tour operators
6650 Other transportation services
6676 Communication services
6692 Utilities, including dumps, snowplowing, road cleaning, etc.

Services (Personal, Professional, and Business Services)

Hotels and other lodging places
7096 Hotels, motels, and tourist homes
7211 Rooming and boarding houses
7237 Camps and camping parks

Laundry and cleaning services
7419 Coin-operated laundries and dry cleaning
7435 Other laundry, dry cleaning, and garment services
7450 Carpet and upholstery cleaning
7476 Janitorial and related services (building, house, and window cleaning)

Business and/or personal services
7617 Legal services (or lawyer)
7633 Income tax preparation
7658 Accounting and bookkeeping
7518 Engineering services
7682 Architectural services
7708 Surveying services
7245 Management services
7260 Public relations
7286 Consulting services
7716 Advertising, except direct mail
7732 Employment agencies and personnel supply
7799 Consumer credit reporting and collection services

7856 Mailing, reproduction, commercial art and photography, and stenographic services
7872 Computer programming, processing, data preparation, and related services
7922 Computer repair, maintenance, and leasing
7773 Equipment rental and leasing (except computer or automotive)
7914 Investigative and protective services
7880 Other business services

Personal services
8110 Beauty shops (or beautician)
8318 Barber shop (or barber)
8334 Photographic portrait studios
8532 Funeral services and crematories
8714 Child day care
8730 Teaching or tutoring
8755 Counseling (except health practitioners)
8771 Ministers and chaplains
6882 Other personal services

Automotive services
8813 Automotive rental or leasing, without driver
8839 Parking, except valet
8953 Automotive repairs, general and specialized
8896 Other automotive services (wash, towing, etc.)

Miscellaneous repair, except computers
9019 TV and audio equipment repair
9035 Other electrical equipment repair
9050 Reupholstery and furniture repair
2881 Other equipment repair

Medical and health services
9217 Offices and clinics of medical doctors (MDs)
9233 Offices and clinics of dentists
9258 Osteopathic physicians and surgeons
9241 Podiatrists
9274 Chiropractors
9290 Optometrists
9415 Registered and practical nurses
9431 Other health practitioners
9456 Medical and dental laboratories
9472 Nursing and personal care facilities
9886 Other health services

Amusement and recreational services
8557 Physical fitness facilities
9597 Motion picture and video production
9688 Motion picture and tape distribution and allied services
9613 Videotape rental
9639 Motion picture theaters
9670 Bowling centers
9696 Professional sports and racing, including promoters and managers
9811 Theatrical performers, musicians, agents, producers, and related services
9837 Other amusement and recreational services

8888 Unable to classify

| SCHEDULE D
(Form 1040)

Department of the Treasury
Internal Revenue Service | **Capital Gains and Losses**
(And Reconciliation of Forms 1099-B)
▶ Attach to Form 1040.   ▶ See Instructions for Schedule D (Form 1040).
▶ For more space to list transactions for lines 2a and 9a, get Schedule D-1 (Form 1040). | OMB No. 1545-0074
1989
Attachment
Sequence No. **12A** |

Name(s) shown on Form 1040 | Your social security number

1 Report here the total sales of stocks, bonds, etc., reported for 1989 to you on Form(s) 1099-B or on an equivalent substitute statement(s). If this amount differs from the total of lines 2c and 9c, column (d), attach a statement explaining the difference. See the Instructions for line 1 for examples . . . . . | **1** |

Part I   Short-Term Capital Gains and Losses—Assets Held One Year or Less

(a) Description of property (Example, 100 shares 7% preferred of "Z" Co.)	(b) Date acquired (Mo., day, yr.)	(c) Date sold (Mo., day, yr.)	(d) Sales price (see Instructions)	(e) Cost or other basis (see Instructions)	(f) LOSS If (e) is more than (d), subtract (d) from (e)	(g) GAIN If (d) is more than (e), subtract (e) from (d)
2a Stocks, Bonds, and Other Securities (Include all Form 1099-B transactions. See Instructions.)						
2b Amounts from Schedule D-1, line 2b (attach Schedule D-1) .						
2c Total (add column (d) of lines 2a and 2b). ▶ **2c**						
2d Other Transactions (Include Real Estate **Transactions From Forms 1099-S.)**						

3 Short-term gain from sale or exchange of your home from Form 2119, line 8a or 14 .	**3**		
4 Short-term gain from installment sales from Form 6252, line 22 or 30	**4**		
5 Net short-term gain or (loss) from partnerships, S corporations, and fiduciaries. .	**5**		
6 Short-term capital loss carryover	**6**		
7 Add all of the transactions on lines 2a, 2b, and 2d and lines 3 through 6 in columns (f) and (g) . .	**7** (	)	
8 Net short-term gain or (loss), combine columns (f) and (g) of line 7		**8**	

Part II   Long-Term Capital Gains and Losses—Assets Held More Than One Year

9a Stocks, Bonds, and Other Securities (Include all Form 1099-B transactions. See Instructions.)						
9b Amounts from Schedule D-1, line 9b (attach Schedule D-1) .						
9c Total (add column (d) of lines 9a and 9b). ▶ **9c**						
9d Other Transactions (Include Real Estate **Transactions From Forms 1099-S.)**						

10 Long-term gain from sale or exchange of your home from Form 2119, line 8a, 10, or 14 .	**10**		
11 Long-term gain from installment sales from Form 6252, line 22 or 30	**11**		
12 Net long-term gain or (loss) from partnerships, S corporations, and fiduciaries . .	**12**		
13 Capital gain distributions	**13**		
14 Enter gain from Form 4797, line 7 or 9	**14**		
15 Long-term capital loss carryover	**15**		
16 Add all of the transactions on lines 9a, 9b, and 9d and lines 10 through 15 in columns (f) and (g)	**16** (	)	
17 Net long-term gain or (loss), combine columns (f) and (g) of line 16		**17**	

For Paperwork Reduction Act Notice, see Form 1040 Instructions.   Schedule D (Form 1040) 1989

Schedule D (Form 1040) 1989   Attachment Sequence No. **12A**   Page **2**

Name(s) shown on Form 1040. (Do not enter name and social security number if shown on other side.)	Your social security number

Part III   Summary of Parts I and II

18 Combine lines 8 and 17, and enter the net gain or (loss) here. If result is a gain, **stop here** and also enter the gain on Form 1040, line 13. If the result is a (loss), go on to line 19	**18**	
19 If line 18 is a (loss), enter here and as a (loss) on Form 1040, line 13, the **smaller** of:		
a The (loss) on line 18; **or**		
b ($3,000) or, if married filing a separate return, ($1,500)	**19** (	)
Note: *When figuring whether l9a or 19b is **smaller,** treat both numbers as if they are positive.*		
Go on to Part IV if the loss on line 18 is more than $3,000 ($1,500, if married filing a separate return), OR if taxable income on Form 1040, line 37, is zero.		

Part IV   Figure Your Capital Loss Carryovers From 1989 to 1990

Section A.—Figure Your Carryover Limit

20 Enter taxable income or loss from Form 1040, line 37. **(If Form 1040, line 37, is zero, see the Instructions for the amount to enter.)**	**20**	
Note: *For lines 21 through 36, treat all amounts as* positive.		
21 Enter the loss shown on line 19	**21**	
22 Enter the amount shown on Form 1040, line 36	**22**	
23 Combine lines 20, 21, and 22. If zero or less, enter zero	**23**	
24 Enter the **smaller** of line 21 or line 23	**24**	

Section B.—Figure Your Short-Term Capital Loss Carryover
(Complete this section only if there is a loss shown on line 8 and line 19. Otherwise, go on to Section C.)

25 Enter the loss shown on line 8		**25**	
26 Enter the gain, if any, shown on line 17	**26**		
27 Enter the amount shown on line 24	**27**		
28 Add lines 26 and 27.		**28**	
29 Subtract line 28 from line 25. If zero or less, enter zero. This is your **short-term capital loss carryover from 1989 to 1990**.		**29**	

Section C.—Figure Your Long-Term Capital Loss Carryover
(Complete this section only if there is a loss shown on line 17 and line 19.)

30 Enter the loss shown on line 17		**30**	
31 Enter the gain, if any, shown on line 8		**31**	
32 Enter the amount shown on line 24	**32**		
33 Enter the amount, if any, shown on line 25	**33**		
34 Subtract line 33 from line 32. If zero or less, enter zero		**34**	
35 Add lines 31 and 34.		**35**	
36 Subtract line 35 from line 30. If zero or less, enter zero. This is your **long-term capital loss carryover from 1989 to 1990**		**36**	

Part V   Complete This Part Only If You Elect Out of the Installment Method and Report a Note or Other Obligation at Less Than Full Face Value

37 Check here if you elect out of the installment method . . . . ▶ ☐	
38 Enter the face amount of the note or other obligation . . . . ▶	
39 Enter the percentage of valuation of the note or other obligation . . . . . ▶	

Part VI   Reconcile Forms 1099-B for Bartering Transactions

(Complete this part if you received one or more Form(s) 1099-B or an equivalent substitute statement(s) reporting bartering income.)

Amount of bartering income from Form 1099-B or equivalent statement reported on form or schedule

40 Form 1040, line 22	**40**	
41 Schedule C (Form 1040)	**41**	
42 Schedule D (Form 1040)	**42**	
43 Schedule E (Form 1040)	**43**	
44 Schedule F (Form 1040)	**44**	
45 Other form (identify) (if not taxable, indicate reason—attach additional sheets if necessary) ▶		
....		
....	**45**	
46 Total (add lines 40 through 45)	**46**	

Note: *The amount on line 46 should be the same as the total bartering income on all Forms 1099-B and equivalent statements received.*

SCHEDULE E (Form 1040) Department of the Treasury Internal Revenue Service	**Supplemental Income and Loss** (From rents, royalties, partnerships, estates, trusts, REMICs, etc.) ▶ Attach to Form 1040 or Form 1041. ▶ See Instructions for Schedule E (Form 1040).	OMB No. 1545-0074 **1989** Attachment Sequence No. **13**

Name(s) shown on return | Your social security number

| **Part I** | **Income or Loss From Rentals and Royalties** | **Caution:** *Your rental loss may be limited. See Instructions.* |

1 Show the kind and location of **rental property:**

A ....

B ....

C ....

2 For each rental property listed on line 1, did you or your family use it for personal purposes for more than the greater of 14 days or 10% of the total days rented at fair rental value during the tax year?

	Yes	No
A		
B		
C		

3 For each **rental real estate property** listed on line 1, did you actively participate in its operation during the tax year? (See Instructions.)

	Yes	No
A		
B		
C		

Rental and Royalty Income:		**Properties**			**D Totals**
		A	**B**	**C**	(Add columns A, B, and C)
4 Rents received	4				4
5 Royalties received	5				5
Rental and Royalty Expenses:					
6 Advertising	6				
7 Auto and travel	7				
8 Cleaning and maintenance	8				
9 Commissions	9				
10 Insurance	10				
11 Legal and other professional fees	11				
12 Mortgage interest paid to banks, etc. (see Instructions)	12				12
13 Other interest	13				
14 Repairs	14				
15 Supplies	15				
16 Taxes	16				
17 Utilities (see Instructions)	17				
18 Wages and salaries	18				
19 Other (list) ▶	19				
20 Add lines 6 through 19	20				20
21 Depreciation expense or depletion (see Instructions)	21				21
22 Total expenses. Add lines 20 and 21	22				
23 Income or (loss) from rental or royalty properties. Subtract line 22 from line 4 (rents) or line 5 (royalties). If the result is a (loss), see Instructions to find out if you must file **Form 6198**	23				
24 Deductible rental loss. **Caution:** *Your rental loss on line 23 may be limited. See Instructions to find out if you must file Form 8582*	24	(	)(	)(	)

25 **Income.** Add rental and royalty income from line 23. Enter the total income here . . . . | 25 |

26 **Losses.** Add royalty losses from line 23 and rental losses from line 24. Enter the total losses here . . . | 26 | (|) |

27 Combine amounts on lines 25 and 26. Enter the net income or (loss) here . . . . | 27 |

28 Net farm rental income or (loss) from Form 4835. (Also complete line 43 on page 2.) . . . . | 28 |

29 Total rental and royalty income or (loss). Combine amounts on lines 27 and 28. Enter the result here. If Parts II, III, and IV on page 2 do not apply to you, enter the amount from line 29 on Form 1040, line 18. Otherwise, include the amount from line 29 in the total on line 42 on page 2 . . . . | 29 |

For Paperwork Reduction Act Notice, see Form 1040 Instructions.   Schedule E (Form 1040) 1989

Schedule E (Form 1040) 1989 — Attachment Sequence No. **13** — Page **2**

Name(s) shown on return. (Do not enter name and social security number if shown on other side.)	Your social security number

Note: *If you report amounts from farming or fishing on Schedule E, you must include your gross income from those activities on line 43 below.*

Part II   Income or Loss From Partnerships and S Corporations

If you report a loss from an at-risk activity, you MUST check either column **(e)** or **(f)** to describe your investment in the activity. See Instructions. If you check column **(f)**, you must attach **Form 6198.**

30	(a) Name	(b) Enter **P** for partnership; **S** for S corporation	(c) Check if foreign partnership	(d) Employer identification number	Investment At Risk? (e) All is at risk	(f) Some is not at risk
A						
B						
C						
D						
E						

	Passive Income and Loss		Nonpassive Income and Loss		
	(g) Passive loss allowed from Form 8582	(h) Passive income from Schedule K–1	(i) Nonpassive loss from Schedule K–1	(j) Section 179 deduction (see Instructions for limits)	(k) Nonpassive income from Schedule K–1
A					
B					
C					
D					
E					
31a Totals					
b Totals					

32	Add amounts in columns (h) and (k) of line 31a. Enter the total income here	32	
33	Add amounts in columns (g), (i), and (j) of line 31b. Enter the total here	33	( )
34	Total partnership and S corporation income or (loss). Combine amounts on lines 32 and 33. Enter the result here and include in the total on line 42 below	34	

Part III   Income or Loss From Estates and Trusts

35	(a) Name	(b) Employer identification number
A		
B		
C		

	Passive Income and Loss		Nonpassive Income and Loss	
	(c) Passive deduction or loss allowed from Form 8582	(d) Passive income from Schedule K–1	(e) Deduction or loss from Schedule K–1	(f) Other income from Schedule K–1
A				
B				
C				
36a Totals				
b Totals				

37	Add amounts in columns (d) and (f) of line 36a. Enter the total income here	37	
38	Add amounts in columns (c) and (e) of line 36b. Enter the total here	38	( )
39	Total estate and trust income or (loss). Combine amounts on lines 37 and 38. Enter the result here and include in the total on line 42 below	39	

Part IV   Income or Loss From Real Estate Mortgage Investment Conduits (REMICs)—Residual Holder

40	(a) Name	(b) Employer identification number	(c) Excess inclusion from Schedules Q, line 2c (see Instructions)	(d) Taxable income (net loss) from Schedules Q, line 1b	(e) Income from Schedules Q, line 3b

41	Combine amounts in columns (d) and (e) only. Enter the result here and include in the total on line 42 below	41	

Part V   Summary of Parts I Through IV

42	TOTAL income or (loss). Combine amounts on lines 29, 34, 39, and 41. Enter the result here and on Form 1040, line 18 ▶	42	

Part VI   Reconciliation of Farming and Fishing Income

43	Farmers and fishermen: Enter your **gross** farming and fishing income reported in Parts I, II, and III (see Instructions)	43	

Schedule R
(Form 1040)

Department of the Treasury
Internal Revenue Service

Credit for the Elderly or the Disabled

▶ For Paperwork Reduction Act Notice, see Form 1040 Instructions.
▶ Attach to Form 1040.   ▶ See separate Instructions for Schedule R.

OMB No. 1545-0074

1989

Attachment
Sequence No. **17**

Name(s) shown on Form 1040 | Your social security number

You may be able to use Schedule R to reduce your tax if by the end of 1989:

● You were 65 or older, **OR**

● You were under 65, you retired on **permanent and total** disability, and you received taxable disability income.

Even if one of the situations described above applies to you, you must meet other tests to be able to take the credit on Schedule R. See the separate Schedule R Instructions for details.

Note: *In most cases IRS can figure this credit for you. See page 16 of the Form 1040 Instructions.*

Part I **Check the Box That Applies to Your Filing Status and Age** (Check only one box)

If your filing status is:	And by the end of 1989:		Check box:
Single*	1 You were 65 or older.	**1**	☐
	2 You were under 65 and you retired on permanent and total disability	**2**	☐
	* Includes Head of household and Qualifying widow(er) with dependent child		
Married filing a joint return	3 Both spouses were 65 or older	**3**	☐
	4 Both spouses were under 65, but only one spouse retired on permanent and total disability	**4**	☐
	5 Both spouses were under 65, and both retired on permanent and total disability	**5**	☐
	6 One spouse was 65 or older, and the other spouse was under 65 and retired on permanent and total disability	**6**	☐
	7 One spouse was 65 or older, and the other spouse was under 65 and **NOT** retired on permanent and total disability	**7**	☐
Married filing a separate return	8 You were 65 or older, and you did not live with your spouse at any time in 1989.	**8**	☐
	9 You were under 65, you retired on permanent and total disability, and you did not live with your spouse at any time in 1989	**9**	☐

Note: *If you checked the box on line 1, 3, 7, or 8, skip Part II and complete Part III on the back. All others, complete Parts II and III.*

Part II **Statement of Permanent and Total Disability** (Complete **only** if you checked the box on line 2, 4, 5, 6, or 9 above)

IF: 1 You filed a physician's statement for this disability for 1983 or an earlier year, or you filed a statement for tax years after 1983 and your physician checked Box B on the statement, **AND**

2 Due to your continued disabled condition you were unable to engage in any substantial gainful activity in 1989, check this box. ▶ ☐

If you checked this box, you do not have to file another statement for 1989. If you did not check this box, have your physician complete the following statement:

Physician's Statement

I certify that _____

Name of disabled person

was permanently and totally disabled on January 1, 1976, or January 1, 1977, **OR** was permanently and totally disabled on the date he or she retired. If retired after December 31, 1976, enter the date retired. ▶ _____

Physician: Sign your name on **either** line A or B below and check the box to the right of your signature.

A The disability has lasted, or can be expected to last, continuously for at least a year . . . . _____   **A** ☐

Physician's signature   Date

B There is no reasonable probability that the disabled condition will ever improve . . . . _____   **B** ☐

Physician's signature   Date

Physician's name | Physician's address

Instructions for Statement

Taxpayer

If you retired after December 31, 1976, enter the date you retired in the space provided.

Physician

A person is permanently and totally disabled when—

● He or she cannot engage in any substantial gainful activity because of a physical or mental condition; and

● A physician determines that the disability:

1. has lasted, or can be expected to last, continuously for at least a year; or

2. can be expected to lead to death.

(Continued on back)

Schedule R (Form 1040) 1989

Part III **Figure the Amount of Your Credit**

10   Enter: $5,000 if you checked the box on line 1, 2, 4, or 7 in Part I, **OR**
         $7,500 if you checked the box on line 3, 5, or 6 in Part I, **OR**   } **10**
         $3,750 if you checked the box on line 8 or 9 in Part I.

   Caution: *If you checked the box on line 2, 4, 5, 6, or 9 in Part I, you **MUST** complete line 11 below. Otherwise, skip line 11 and enter the amount from line 10 on line 12.*

11   Enter on line 11 your taxable disability income (and also your spouse's if you checked the box on line 5 in Part I) that you reported on Form 1040. However, if you checked the box on line 6 in Part I, enter on line 11 the taxable disability income of the spouse who was under age 65 **PLUS** $5,000. (For more details on what to include, see the Instructions.) **11**

12   If you completed line 11 above, compare the amounts on lines 10 and 11, and enter the **smaller** of the two amounts here. Otherwise, enter the amount from line 10 . . . .   **12**

13   Enter the following pensions, annuities, or disability income that you (and your spouse if you file a joint return) received in 1989 (see Instructions):

   a   Nontaxable part of social security benefits; and
         Nontaxable part of railroad retirement benefits treated as   } **13a**
         social security.

   b   Nontaxable veterans' pensions; and
         Any other pension, annuity, or disability benefit that is   } **13b**
         excluded from income under any other provision of law.

   c   Add lines 13a and 13b. (Even though these income items are not taxable, they **must** be included to figure your credit.) If you did not receive any of the types of nontaxable income listed on line 13a or 13b, enter -0- on line 13c **13c**

14   Enter the amount from Form 1040, line 32.   **14**

15   Enter: $7,500 if you checked the box on   }
             line 1 or 2 in Part I, **OR**

         $10,000 if you checked the box on   **15**
         line 3, 4, 5, 6, or 7 in Part I, **OR**

         $5,000 if you checked the box
         on line 8 or 9 in Part I.

16   Subtract line 15 from line 14. Enter the result. If line 15 is more than line 14, enter -0- **16**

17   Divide the amount on line 16 by 2. Enter the result **17**

18   Add lines 13c and 17. Enter the total **18**

19   Subtract line 18 from line 12. Enter the result. If the result is zero or less, stop here; you **cannot** take the credit. Otherwise, go on to line 21 . . . .   **19**

20   Decimal amount used to figure the credit. . . . .   **20**   × .15

21   Multiply the amount on line 19 by the decimal amount (.15) on line 20. Enter the result here and on Form 1040, line 42. **Caution:** *If you file Schedule C, D, E, or F (Form 1040), your credit may be limited. See the instructions for line 21 for the amount of credit you can claim* **21**

SCHEDULE SE (Form 1040) Department of the Treasury Internal Revenue Service	**Social Security Self-Employment Tax** ▶ See Instructions for Schedule SE (Form 1040). ▶ Attach to Form 1040.	OMB No. 1545-0074 19**89** Attachment Sequence No. **18**

Name of person with **self-employment** income (as shown on social security card)	Social security number of person with **self-employment** income ▶	

Who Must File Schedule SE

You must file Schedule SE if:

- Your net earnings from self-employment were $400 or more (or you had wages of $100 or more from an electing church or church-controlled organization); AND
- Your wages (subject to social security or railroad retirement tax) were less than $48,000.

Exception. If your only self-employment income was from earnings as a minister, member of a religious order, or Christian Science practitioner, AND you filed **Form 4361** and received IRS approval not to be taxed on those earnings, DO NOT file Schedule SE. Instead, write "Exempt–Form 4361" on Form 1040, line 48.

For more information about Schedule SE, see the Instructions.

Note: *Most people can use the short Schedule SE on this page. But, you may have to use the longer Schedule SE that is on the back.*

Who MUST Use the Long Schedule SE (Section B)

You must use Section B if ANY of the following applies:

- You choose the "optional method" to figure your self-employment tax (see Section B, Part II);
- You are a minister, member of a religious order, or Christian Science practitioner and you received IRS approval (from **Form 4361**) not to be taxed on your earnings from these sources, but you owe self-employment tax on other earnings;
- You were an employee of a **church or church-controlled** organization that chose by law not to pay employer social security taxes;
- You had tip income that is subject to social security tax, but you did not report those tips to your employer; OR
- You were a government employee with wages subject ONLY to the 1.45% Medicare part of the social security tax.

Section A—Short Schedule SE
(Read above to see if you must use the long Schedule SE on the back (Section B).)

1	Net farm profit or (loss) from Schedule F (Form 1040), line 36, and farm partnerships, Schedule K-1 (Form 1065), line 14a	**1**	
2	Net profit or (loss) from Schedule C (Form 1040), line 30, and Schedule K-1 (Form 1065), line 14a (other than farming). See the Instructions for other income to report	**2**	
3	Add lines 1 and 2. Enter the total. If the total is less than $400, **do not** file this schedule; you **do not** owe self-employment tax . . . . ▶	**3**	
4	The largest amount of combined wages and self-employment earnings subject to social security or railroad retirement tax (tier 1) for 1989 is	**4**	$48,000 | 00
5	Total social security wages and tips (from Form(s) W-2) and railroad retirement compensation (tier 1) . . .	**5**	
6	Subtract line 5 from line 4. Enter the result. If the result is zero or less, stop here; you **do not** owe self-employment tax . . . . ▶	**6**	
7	Enter the **smaller** of line 3 or line 6	**7**	
8	Rate of tax	**8**	×.1302
9	**Self-employment tax.** If line 7 is $48,000, enter $6,249.60. Otherwise, multiply the amount on line 7 by the decimal amount on line 8 and enter the result. Also enter this amount on Form 1040, line 48 . .	**9**	

For Paperwork Reduction Act Notice, see Form 1040 Instructions.   Schedule SE (Form 1040) 1989

Schedule SE (Form 1040) 1989 | Attachment Sequence No. **18** | Page **2**

| Name of person with **self-employment** income (as shown on social security card) | Social security number of person with **self-employment** income ▶ | : : |

Section B—Long Schedule SE

(Before completing, see if you can use the short Schedule SE on the other side (Section A).)

A If you are a minister, member of a religious order, or Christian Science practitioner, AND you filed **Form 4361**, but you had $400 or more of **other** earnings subject to self-employment tax, continue with Part I and check here . . . . ▶ ☐

B If your only earnings subject to self-employment tax were wages from an electing church or church-controlled organization that is exempt from employer social security taxes and you are not a minister or a member of a religious order, skip lines 1–3b. Enter zero on line 3c and go to line 5a.

Part I   Figure Social Security Self-Employment Tax

1 Net farm profit or (loss) from Schedule F (Form 1040), line 36, and farm partnerships, Schedule K-1 (Form 1065), line 14a . . .	**1**		
2 Net profit or (loss) from Schedule C (Form 1040), line 30, and Schedule K-1 (Form 1065), line 14a (other than farming). See Instructions for other income to report. (Employees of an electing church or church-controlled organization **do not** enter your Form W-2 wages on this line. See the Instructions.) . .	**2**		
3a Enter the amount from line 1 (**or,** if you elected the farm optional method, from line 11 below)	**3a**		
b Enter the amount from line 2 (**or,** if you elected the nonfarm optional method, from line 13 below) . .	**3b**		
c Add lines 3a and 3b. Enter the total. If the total is less than $400, **do not** file this schedule; you **do not** owe self-employment tax. (**Exception:** *If you were an employee of an electing church or church-controlled organization and the total of lines 3a and 3b is less than $400, enter zero and complete the rest of this schedule.*)	**3c**		
4 The largest amount of combined wages and self-employment earnings subject to social security or railroad retirement tax (tier 1) for 1989 is	**4**	$48,000	00
5a Total social security wages and tips (from Form(s) W-2) and railroad retirement compensation (tier 1). **Note:** *Government employees whose wages were subject only to the 1.45% Medicare tax and employees of certain church or church-controlled organizations should **not** include those wages on this line. See Instructions*	**5a**		
b Unreported tips subject to social security tax (from Form 4137, line 9) or to railroad retirement tax (tier 1)	**5b**		
c Add lines 5a and 5b. Enter the total	**5c**		
6a Subtract line 5c from line 4. Enter the result. If the result is zero or less, enter zero and stop here; you **do not** owe self-employment tax . . . . ▶	**6a**		
b Enter your Medicare qualified government wages. See the Instructions to see if you must use the worksheet in those instructions to figure your self-employment tax . **6b**			
c Enter your Form W-2 wages of $100 or more from an electing church or church-controlled organization **6c**			
d Add lines 3c and 6c. Enter the total . . . . ▶	**6d**		
7 Enter the **smaller** of line 6a or line 6d . . .	**7**		
8 Rate of tax	**8**	× .1302	
9 **Self-employment tax.** If line 7 is $48,000, enter $6,249.60. Otherwise, multiply the amount on line 7 by the decimal amount on line 8 and enter the result. Also enter this amount on Form 1040, line 48 . .	**9**		

Part II   Optional Method To Figure Net Earnings (See "Who Can File Schedule SE" in the Instructions.)

See Instructions for limitations. Generally, you may use this part **only** if:

A Your **gross** farm income[1] was not more than $2,400; **or**

B Your **gross** farm income[1] was more than $2,400 and your **net** farm profits[2] were **less** than $1,600; **or**

C Your **net** nonfarm profits[3] were less than $1,600 and also **less** than two-thirds (⅔) of your **gross** nonfarm income.[4]

Note: *If line 2 above is two-thirds (⅔) or more of your gross nonfarm income[4], or if line 2 is $1,600 or more, you may **not** use the optional method.*
[1]From Schedule F (Form 1040), line 11, and Schedule K-1 (Form 1065), line 14b.   [3]From Schedule C (Form 1040), line 30, and Schedule K-1 (Form 1065), line 14a.
[2]From Schedule F (Form 1040), line 36, and Schedule K-1 (Form 1065), line 14a.   [4]From Schedule C (Form 1040), line 7, and Schedule K-1 (Form 1065), line 14c.

10 Maximum income for optional methods	**10**	$1,600	00
11 **Farm Optional Method**—If you meet test **A** or **B** above, enter the **smaller** of: two-thirds (⅔) of gross farm income from Schedule F (Form 1040), line 11, and farm partnerships, Schedule K-1 (Form 1065), line 14b; **or** $1,600. Also enter this amount on line 3a above	**11**		
12 Subtract line 11 from line 10. Enter the result	**12**		
13 **Nonfarm Optional Method**—If you meet test **C** above, enter the **smallest** of: two-thirds (⅔) of gross nonfarm income from Schedule C (Form 1040), line 7, and Schedule K-1 (Form 1065), line 14c; **or** $1,600; **or,** if you elected the farm optional method, the amount on line 12. Also enter this amount on line 3b above	**13**		

For Paperwork Reduction Act Notice, see Form 1040 Instructions.   Schedule SE (Form 1040) 1989

Form **1041**

Department of the Treasury—Internal Revenue Service

U.S. Fiduciary Income Tax Return   19**89**

IRS Use Only

For the calendar year 1989 or fiscal year   beginning _____ , 1989, and ending _____ , 19___   OMB No. 1545-0092

Check applicable boxes:

☐ Decedent's estate
☐ Simple trust
☐ Complex trust
☐ Grantor type trust
☐ Bankruptcy estate
☐ Family estate trust
☐ Pooled income fund
☐ Initial return
☐ Amended return
☐ Final return

Name of estate or trust (grantor type trust, see instructions)

Name and title of fiduciary

Address of fiduciary (number and street or P.O. Box)

City, state, and ZIP code

Number of Schedules K-1 attached (see instructions) . . . ▶

Employer identification number

Date entity created

Nonexempt charitable and split-interest trusts, check applicable boxes (see instructions):

☐ Described in section 4947(a)(1)
☐ Not a private foundation
☐ Described in section 4947(a)(2)

Income

1	Dividends	1
2	Interest income	2
3	Income (or losses) from partnerships, other estates, or other trusts (see instructions)	3
4	Net rental and royalty income (or loss) (attach Schedule E (Form 1040))	4
5	Net business and farm income (or loss) (attach Schedules C and F (Form 1040))	5
6	Capital gain (or loss) (attach Schedule D (Form 1041))	6
7	Ordinary gain (or loss) (attach Form 4797)	7
8	Other income (state nature of income)	8
9	**Total** income (add lines 1 through 8) ▶	9

Deductions

10	Interest	10	
11	Taxes	11	
12	Fiduciary fees	12	
13	Charitable deduction (from Schedule A, line 6)	13	
14	Attorney, accountant, and return preparer fees	14	
15a	Other deductions NOT subject to the 2% floor (attach schedule).	15a	
b	Allowable miscellaneous itemized deductions subject to the 2% floor	15b	
c	Add lines 15a and 15b	15c	
16	**Total** (add lines 10 through 15c)		16
17	Adjusted total income (or loss) (subtract line 16 from line 9). Enter here and on Schedule B, line 1. ▶		17
18	Income distribution deduction (from Schedule B, line 17) (see instructions) (attach Schedules K-1 (Form 1041))		18
19	Estate tax deduction (including certain generation-skipping transfer taxes) (attach computation)		19
20	Exemption		20
21	**Total** deductions (add lines 18 through 20) ▶		21

Tax and Payments

22	Taxable income of fiduciary (subtract line 21 from line 17)	22
23	**Total** tax (from Schedule G, line 7) ▶	23
24a	Payments: 1989 estimated tax payments and amount applied from 1988 return	24a
b	Treated as credited to beneficiaries	24b
c	Subtract line 24b from line 24a	24c
d	Tax paid with extension of time to file: ☐ Form 2758 ☐ Form 8736 ☐ Form 8800	24d
e	Federal income tax withheld	24e
	Credits: **f** Form 2439 _____; **g** Form 4136 _____; **h** Other _____; Total ▶	24i
25	**Total** payments (add lines 24c through 24e, and 24i) ▶	25
26	If line 23 is larger than line 25, enter **TAX DUE**	26
27	If line 25 is larger than line 23, enter **OVERPAYMENT**	27
28	Amount of line 27 to be: **a Credited to 1990 estimated tax** ▶ _____; **b Refunded** ▶	28
29	**Penalty** for underpayment of estimated tax (see instructions)	29

Please Sign Here

Under penalties of perjury, I declare that I have examined this return, including accompanying schedules and statements, and to the best of my knowledge and belief, it is true, correct, and complete. Declaration of preparer (other than fiduciary) is based on all information of which preparer has any knowledge.

▶ _____   _____   ▶ _____
Signature of fiduciary or officer representing fiduciary   Date   EIN of fiduciary (see instructions)

Paid Preparer's Use Only

Preparer's signature ▶	Date	Check if self-employed ▶ ☐	Preparer's social security no.
Firm's name (or yours if self-employed) and address ▶		E.I. No. ▶	
		ZIP code ▶	

For Paperwork Reduction Act Notice, see page 1 of the separate Instructions.

Form **1041** (1989)

Form 1041 (1989)   Page **2**

Schedule A   Charitable Deduction—Do not complete for a simple trust or a pooled income fund.
(Write the name and address of each charitable organization to whom your contributions total $3,000 or more on an attached sheet.)

1	Amounts paid or permanently set aside for charitable purposes from current year's gross income . . .	1
2	Tax-exempt interest allocable to charitable distribution (see instructions)	2
3	Subtract line 2 from line 1	3
4	Enter the net short-term capital gain and the net long-term capital gain of the current tax year allocable to corpus paid or permanently set aside for charitable purposes (see instructions)	4
5	Amounts paid or permanently set aside for charitable purposes from gross income of a prior year (see instructions)	5
6	Total (add lines 3 through 5). Enter here and on page 1, line 13	6

Schedule B   Income Distribution Deduction (see instructions)

1	Adjusted total income (from page 1, line 17) (see instructions)	1
2	Adjusted tax-exempt interest (see instructions) . . . . · .	2
3	Net gain shown on Schedule D (Form 1041), line 17, column (a). (If net loss, enter zero.) . . .	3
4	Enter amount from Schedule A, line 4	4
5	Long-term capital gain included on Schedule A, line 1	5
6	Short-term capital gain included on Schedule A, line 1	6
7	If the amount on page 1, line 6, is a capital loss, enter here as a positive figure	7
8	If the amount on page 1, line 6, is a capital gain, enter here as a negative figure	8
9	Distributable net income (combine lines 1 through 8)	9
10	Amount of income for the tax year determined under the governing instrument (accounting income) |10|	
11	Amount of income required to be distributed currently (see instructions)	11
12	Other amounts paid, credited, or otherwise required to be distributed (see instructions)	12
13	Total distributions (add lines 11 and 12). (If greater than line 10, see instructions.)	13
14	Enter the total amount of tax-exempt income included on line 13	14
15	Tentative income distribution deduction (subtract line 14 from line 13)	15
16	Tentative income distribution deduction (subtract line 2 from line 9)	16
17	Income distribution deduction. Enter the smaller of line 15 or line 16 here and on page 1, line 18 . .	17

Schedule G   Tax Computation (see instructions)

1	Tax: **a** Tax rate schedule ....; **b** Other taxes ....; . . . . Total ▶	1c
2a	Foreign tax credit (attach Form 1116)	2a	
b	Credit for fuel produced from a nonconventional source.	2b	
c	General business credit. Check if from:	
	☐ Form 3800 or ☐ Form (specify) ▶	2c	
d	Credit for prior year minimum tax (attach Form 8801)	2d	
3	**Total** credits (add lines 2a through 2d) . . . . ▶	3
4	Subtract line 3 from line 1c	4
5	Recapture taxes. Check if from: ☐ Form 4255 ☐ Form 8611	5
6	Alternative minimum tax (attach Form 8656)	6
7	**Total** tax (add lines 4 through 6). Enter here and on page 1, line 23 . . . . ▶	7

Other Information (see instructions)

		Yes	No
1	If the fiduciary's name or address has changed, enter the old information ▶		
2	Did the estate or trust receive tax-exempt income? (If "Yes," attach a computation of the allocation of expenses.) . . . Enter the amount of tax-exempt interest income and exempt-interest dividends ▶ $		
3	Did the estate or trust have any passive activity losses? (If "Yes," enter these losses on **Form 8582**, Passive Activity Loss Limitations, to figure the allowable loss.)		
4	Did the estate or trust receive all or any part of the earnings (salary, wages, and other compensation) of any individual by reason of a contract assignment or similar arrangement?		
5	At any time during the tax year, did the estate or trust have an interest in or a signature or other authority over a financial account in a foreign country (such as a bank account, securities account, or other financial account)? (See the instructions for exceptions and filing requirements for Form TD F 90-22.1.) . . . . If "Yes," enter the name of the foreign country ▶		
6	Was the estate or trust the grantor of, or transferor to, a foreign trust which existed during the current tax year, whether or not the estate or trust has any beneficial interest in it? (If "Yes," you may have to file Form 3520, 3520-A, or 926.)		
7	Check this box if this entity has filed or is required to file **Form 8264**, Application for Registration of a Tax Shelter . ▶ ☐		
8	Check this box if this entity is a complex trust making the section 663(b) election . . . . ▶ ☐		
9	Check this box to make a section 643(e)(3) election (attach Schedule D (Form 1041)) . . . . ▶ ☐		
10	Check this box if the decedent's estate has been open for more than 2 years . . . . ▶ ☐		
11	Check this box if the trust is a participant in a Common Trust Fund that was required to adopt a calendar year . . ▶ ☐		

SCHEDULE K-1 (Form 1041)	**Beneficiary's Share of Income, Deductions, Credits, Etc.—1989**	OMB No. 1545-0092
Department of the Treasury Internal Revenue Service	for the calendar year 1989, or fiscal year beginning ...., 1989, ending ...., 19 ..... **Complete a separate Schedule K-1 for each beneficiary.**	1989

Name of estate or trust

Beneficiary's identifying number ▶	Estate's or trust's employer identification number ▶
Beneficiary's name, address, and ZIP code	Fiduciary's name, address, and ZIP code

Reminder: *If you received a short year 1987 Schedule K-1 that was from a trust required to adopt a calendar year, be sure to include one-fourth of those amounts reported as income, in addition to the items reported on this Schedule K-1, on the appropriate lines of your 1989 Form 1040 and related schedules.*

	(a) Allocable share item	(b) Amount	(c) Calendar year 1989 Form 1040 filers enter the amounts in column (b) on:
1	Interest		Schedule B, Part I, line 2
2	Dividends		Schedule B, Part II, line 4
3a	Net short-term capital gain		Schedule D, line 5, column (g)
b	Net long-term capital gain		Schedule D, line 12, column (g)
4a	Other taxable income: (itemize)		Schedule E, Part III
	(1) Rental, rental real estate, and business income from activities acquired before 10/23/86		
	(2) Rental, rental real estate, and business income from activities acquired after 10/22/86		
	(3) Other income		
b	Depreciation, including cost recovery (itemize):		
	(1) Attributable to line 4a(1)		
	(2) Attributable to line 4a(2)		
	(3) Attributable to line 4a(3)		
c	Depletion (itemize):		
	(1) Attributable to line 4a(1)		
	(2) Attributable to line 4a(2)		
	(3) Attributable to line 4a(3)		
d	Amortization (itemize):		
	(1) Attributable to line 4a(1)		
	(2) Attributable to line 4a(2)		
	(3) Attributable to line 4a(3)		
5	Income for minimum tax purposes		
6	Income for regular tax purposes (add lines 1 through 4a)		
7	Adjustment for minimum tax purposes (subtract line 6 from line 5)		Form 6251, line 4t
8	Estate tax deduction (including certain generation-skipping transfer taxes) (attach computation)		Schedule A, line 25
9	Excess deductions on termination (attach computation)		Schedule A, line 21
10	Foreign taxes (list on a separate sheet)		Form 1116 or Schedule A (Form 1040), line 7
11	Tax preference items (itemize):		
a	Accelerated depreciation		(Include on the applicable
b	Depletion		line of Form 6251)
c	Amortization		
12	Other (itemize):		
a	Trust payments of estimated taxes credited to you		Form 1040, line 57
b	Tax-exempt interest		Form 1040, line 8b
c	Short-term capital loss carryover		Schedule D, line 6, column (f)
d	Long-term capital loss carryover		Schedule D, line 15, column (f)
e	....		(Include on the applicable line
f	....		of appropriate tax form)
g			

For Paperwork Reduction Act Notice, see page 1 of the Instructions for Form 1041.   **Schedule K-1 (Form 1041) 1989**

	OMB No. 1545-0099

Form 1065

Department of the Treasury
Internal Revenue Service

U.S. Partnership Return of Income

▶ **See separate instructions.**

For calendar year 1989, or fiscal year beginning _____ , 1989, and ending _____ , 19 __

1989

A Principal business activity	**Use IRS label. Other-wise, please print or type.**	**Name**
B Principal product or service		**Number and street (or P.O. box number if mail is not delivered to street address)**
C Business code number		**City or town, state, and ZIP code**

D Employer identification number

E Date business started

F Total assets (see Specific Instructions)
$

G Check applicable boxes: **(1)** ☐ Initial return   **(2)** ☐ Final return   **(3)** ☐ Change in address   **(4)** ☐ Amended return

H Enter number of partners in this partnership . . . . ▶ _____

I Check this box if this is a limited partnership . . . . ▶ ☐

J Check this box if any partners in the partnership are also partnerships . . . . ▶ ☐

K Check this box if this partnership is a partner in another partnership . . . . ▶ ☐

See page 4, items L through T, for Additional Information Required.

Designation of Tax Matters Partner (See instructions.)

Enter below the general partner designated as the tax matters partner (TMP) for the tax year of this return:

Name of designated TMP ▶ _____

Identifying number of TMP ▶ _____

Address of designated TMP ▶ _____

Caution: *Include **only** trade or business income and expenses on lines 1a–21 below. See the instructions for more information.*

Income

1a Gross receipts or sales	**1a**	75 000			
b Less returns and allowances	**1b**		**1c**	75 000	
2 Cost of goods sold and/or operations (Schedule A, line 7)	**2**			
3 Gross profit (subtract line 2 from line 1c)	**3**	75 000		
4 Ordinary income (loss) from other partnerships and fiduciaries (attach schedule)	**4**			
5 Net farm profit (loss) (attach Schedule F (Form 1040))	**5**			
6 Net gain (loss) (Form 4797, Part II, line 18)	**6**			
7 Other income (loss)	**7**			
8 **Total** income (loss) (combine lines 3 through 7)	**8**	75 000		

Deductions (see instructions for limitations)

9a Salaries and wages (other than to partners)	**9a**	42 000			
b Less jobs credit	**9b**		**9c**	42 000	
10 Guaranteed payments to partners			**10**	12 000	
11 Rent			**11**	24 000	
12 Interest (see instructions)			**12**		
13 Taxes			**13**	4 600	
14 Bad debts			**14**		
15 Repairs			**15**		
16a Depreciation (attach Form 4562) (see instructions)	**16a**			
b Less depreciation reported on Schedule A and elsewhere on return .	**16b**		**16c**		
17 Depletion (**Do not deduct oil and gas depletion.**)			**17**		
18a Retirement plans, etc.			**18a**		
b Employee benefit programs			**18b**		
19 Other deductions (attach schedule)			**19**		
20 **Total** deductions (add lines 9c through 19)			**20**		
21 Ordinary income (loss) from trade or business activities (subtract line 20 from line 8)			**21**		

Please Sign Here

Under penalties of perjury, I declare that I have examined this return, including accompanying schedules and statements, and to the best of my knowledge and belief, it is true, correct, and complete. Declaration of preparer (other than general partner) is based on all information of which preparer has any knowledge.

▶ _____ Signature of general partner   ▶ _____ Date

Paid Preparer's Use Only

Preparer's signature ▶	Date	Check if self-employed ▶ ☐	Preparer's social security no.
Firm's name (or yours if self-employed) and address ▶		E.I. No. ▶	
		ZIP code ▶	

For Paperwork Reduction Act Notice, see page 1 of separate instructions.

Form **1065** (1989)

Form 1065 (1989)   Page **2**

Schedule A   Cost of Goods Sold and/or Operations

1 Inventory at beginning of year	**1**	
2 Purchases less cost of items withdrawn for personal use	**2**	
3 Cost of labor	**3**	
4a Additional section 263A costs (see instructions—attach schedule)	**4a**	
b Other costs (attach schedule)	**4b**	
5 Total (add lines 1 through 4b)	**5**	
6 Inventory at end of year	**6**	
7 Cost of goods sold (subtract line 6 from line 5). Enter here and on page 1, line 2	**7**	

8a Check all methods used for valuing closing inventory:

    (i) ☐ Cost

    (ii) ☐ Lower of cost or market as described in Regulations section 1.471-4

    (iii) ☐ Writedown of "subnormal" goods as described in Regulations section 1.471-2(c)

    (iv) ☐ Other (specify method used and attach explanation) ▶ _____

  b Check if the LIFO inventory method was adopted this tax year for any goods (if checked, attach Form 970) . . . . ▶ ☐

  c Do the rules of section 263A (with respect to property produced or acquired for resale) apply to the partnership? . . ☐ **Yes** ☐ **No**

  d Was there any change in determining quantities, cost, or valuations between opening and closing inventory? . . . ☐ **Yes** ☐ **No**
If "Yes," attach explanation.

Schedule H   Income (Loss) From Rental Real Estate Activities

1 In the space provided below, show the kind and location of each rental property. Attach a schedule if more space is needed.

    Property A _____

    Property B _____

    Property C _____

Rental Real Estate Income		Properties			Totals (add columns A, B, C, and amounts from any attached schedules)	
		A	**B**	**C**		
2 Gross income	**2**				**2**	
Rental Real Estate Expenses						
3 Advertising	**3**					
4 Auto and travel	**4**					
5 Cleaning and maintenance . .	**5**					
6 Commissions	**6**					
7 Insurance	**7**					
8 Legal and other professional fees	**8**					
9 Interest	**9**					
10 Repairs	**10**					
11 Taxes	**11**					
12 Utilities	**12**					
13 Wages and salaries	**13**					
14 Depreciation from Form 4562 .	**14**					
15 Other (list) ▶ _____ _____ _____	**15**					
16 Total expenses. Add lines 3 through 15	**16**				**16**	
17 Net income (loss) from rental real estate activities. Subtract line 16 from line 2. Enter net income (loss) from the total column on Schedule K, line 2 .	**17**				**17**	

Form 1065 (1989)   Page **3**

Schedule K	Partners' Shares of Income, Credits, Deductions, Etc.		
	(a) Distributive share items		**(b) Total amount**

		(a) Distributive share items		(b) Total amount
Income (Loss)	**1**	Ordinary income (loss) from trade or business activities (page 1, line 21)	**1**	
	2	Net income (loss) from rental real estate activities (Schedule H, line 17)	**2**	
	3a	Gross income from other rental activities **3a**		
	b	Less expenses (attach schedule) **3b**		
	c	Net income (loss) from other rental activities	**3c**	
	4	Portfolio income (loss) (see instructions):		
	a	Interest income.	**4a**	
	b	Dividend income	**4b**	
	c	Royalty income	**4c**	
	d	Net short-term capital gain (loss) (Schedule D, line 4)	**4d**	
	e	Net long-term capital gain (loss) (Schedule D, line 9)	**4e**	
	f	Other portfolio income (loss) (attach schedule)	**4f**	
	5	Guaranteed payments to partners	**5**	
	6	Net gain (loss) under section 1231 (other than due to casualty or theft) (see instructions) .	**6**	
	7	Other income (loss) (attach schedule)	**7**	
Deductions	**8**	Charitable contributions (attach list)	**8**	
	9	Section 179 expense deduction (attach Form 4562)	**9**	
	10	Deductions related to portfolio income (do not include investment interest expense) . . .	**10**	
	11	Other deductions (attach schedule)	**11**	
Credits	**12a**	Credit for income tax withheld	**12a**	
	b	Low-income housing credit: (1) Partnerships to which section 42(j)(5) applies	**12b(1)**	
		(2) Other than on line 12b(1).	**12b(2)**	
	c	Qualified rehabilitation expenditures related to rental real estate activities (attach schedule)	**12c**	
	d	Credits (other than credits shown on lines 12b and 12c) related to rental real estate activities (attach schedule)	**12d**	
	e	Credits related to other rental activities (see instructions) (attach schedule)	**12e**	
	13	Other credits and expenditures (attach schedule)	**13**	
Self-Employ-ment	**14a**	Net earnings (loss) from self-employment	**14a**	
	b	Gross farming or fishing income	**14b**	
	c	Gross nonfarm income	**14c**	
Adjustments and Tax Preference Items	**15a**	Accelerated depreciation of real property placed in service before 1987	**15a**	
	b	Accelerated depreciation of leased personal property placed in service before 1987 . . .	**15b**	
	c	Depreciation adjustment on property placed in service after 1986	**15c**	
	d	Depletion (other than oil and gas)	**15d**	
	e	(1) Gross income from oil, gas, and geothermal properties	**15e(1)**	
		(2) Deductions allocable to oil, gas, and geothermal properties	**15e(2)**	
	f	Other adjustments and tax preference items (attach schedule)	**15f**	
Invest-ment Interest	**16a**	Interest expense on investment debts	**16a**	
	b	(1) Investment income included on lines 4a through 4f above	**16b(1)**	
		(2) Investment expenses included on line 10 above	**16b(2)**	
Foreign Taxes	**17a**	Type of income _____		
	b	Foreign country or U.S. possession _____		
	c	Total gross income from sources outside the U.S. (attach schedule)	**17c**	
	d	Total applicable deductions and losses (attach schedule)	**17d**	
	e	Total foreign taxes (check one): ▶ ☐ Paid ☐ Accrued	**17e**	
	f	Reduction in taxes available for credit (attach schedule)	**17f**	
	g	Other foreign tax information (attach schedule)	**17g**	
Other	**18a**	Total expenditures to which a section 59(e) election may apply (attach schedule) . . .	**18a**	
	b	Attach schedule for other items and amounts not reported above (see instructions) . . .		
Analysis	**19a**	Total distributive income/payment items (combine lines 1 through 7 above)	**19a**	
	b	Analysis by type of partner:		

		(a) Corporate	(b) Individual		(c) Partnership	(d) Exempt organization	(e) Nominee/Other
			i. Active	ii. Passive			
	1. General partners						
	2. Limited partners						

Form 1065 (1989)   Page **4**

Schedule L   Balance Sheets

(See the instructions for Question N on page 8 of the Instructions before completing Schedules L and M.)

Assets	Beginning of tax year		End of tax year	
	(a)	(b)	(c)	(d)
1 Cash				
2 Trade notes and accounts receivable				
a Less allowance for bad debts				
3 Inventories				
4a U.S. government obligations				
b Tax-exempt securities				
5 Other current assets (attach schedule) . . .				
6 Mortgage and real estate loans				
7 Other investments (attach schedule) . . .				
8a Buildings and other depreciable assets . . .				
b Less accumulated depreciation				
9a Depletable assets				
b Less accumulated depletion				
10 Land (net of any amortization)				
11a Intangible assets (amortizable only)				
b Less accumulated amortization				
12 Other assets (attach schedule)				
13 **Total** assets				
Liabilities and Capital				
14 Accounts payable				
15 Mortgages, notes, bonds payable in less than 1 year				
16 Other current liabilities (attach schedule)				
17 All nonrecourse loans				
18 Mortgages, notes, bonds payable in 1 year or more				
19 Other liabilities (attach schedule)				
20 Partners' capital accounts				
21 **Total** liabilities and capital				

Schedule M   Reconciliation of Partners' Capital Accounts

(Show reconciliation of each partner's capital account on Schedule K-1 (Form 1065), Item K.)

(a) Partners' capital accounts at beginning of year	(b) Capital contributed during year	(c) Income (loss) from lines 1, 2, 3c, and 4 of Sch. K	(d) Income not included in column (c), plus nontaxable income	(e) Losses not included in column (c), plus unallowable deductions	(f) Withdrawals and distributions	(g) Partners' capital accounts at end of year (combine columns (a) through (f))
			( )	( )		

Additional Information Required (continued from page 1)

	Yes	No
L Check accounting method: (1) ☐ Cash (2) ☐ Accrual (3) ☐ Other		
M Check this box if this is a partnership subject to the consolidated partnership audit procedures of sections 6221 through 6233 (see instructions) . . . . ▶ ☐		
N Does the partnership meet **all** the requirements shown in the Instructions for **Question N**?		
O Was there a distribution of property or a transfer (for example, by sale or death) of a partnership interest during the tax year?		
If "Yes," see the instructions concerning an election to adjust the basis of the partnership's assets under section 754.		
P Does the partnership have any foreign partners?		
Q At any time during the tax year, did the partnership have an interest in or a signature or other authority over a financial account in a foreign country (such as a bank account, securities account, or other financial account)? (See the instructions for exceptions and filing requirements for form TD F 90-22.1.)		
If "Yes," write the name of the foreign country. ▶ _____		
R Was the partnership the grantor of, or transferor to, a foreign trust which existed during the current tax year, whether or not the partnership or any partner has any beneficial interest in it? If "Yes," you may have to file Forms 3520, 3520-A, or 926		
S Check this box if the partnership has filed or is required to file **Form 8264,** Application for Registration of a Tax Shelter ▶ ☐		
T Check this box if the partnership is a publicly traded partnership as defined in section 469(k)(2) . . . . ▶ ☐		

SCHEDULE K-1 (Form 1065) Department of the Treasury Internal Revenue Service	**Partner's Share of Income, Credits, Deductions, Etc.** ▶ **See separate instructions.** For calendar year 1989 or fiscal year beginning _____, 1989, and ending _____, 19	OMB No. 1545-0099 **1989**

Partner's identifying number ▶	Partnership's identifying number ▶
Partner's name, address, and ZIP code	Partnership's name, address, and ZIP code

A Is this partner a general partner? . . . ☐ Yes ☐ No

B Partner's share of liabilities:

Nonrecourse . . . . $ _____

Other . . . . $ _____

C What type of entity is this partner? ▶ _____

D Is this partner a ☐ domestic or a ☐ foreign partner?

     (i) Before decrease   (ii) End of
     or termination   year

E Enter partner's percentage of:

Profit sharing . . . . _____% _____%

Loss sharing . . . . _____% _____%

Ownership of capital . . . _____% _____%

F IRS Center where partnership filed return ▶ _____

G(1) Tax shelter registration number ▶ _____

  (2) Type of tax shelter ▶ _____

H(1) Did the partner's ownership interest in the partnership change after Oct. 22, 1986? . . . . ☐ Yes ☐ No

If "Yes," attach statement. (See Form 1065 Instructions.)

  (2) Did the partnership start or acquire a new activity after Oct. 22, 1986? . . . . ☐ Yes ☐ No

If "Yes," attach statement. (See Form 1065 Instructions.)

I Check here if this partnership is a publicly traded partnership as defined in section 469(k)(2) . . . . ☐

J Check here if this is an amended Schedule K-1 . . . . ☐

K Reconciliation of partner's capital account:

(a) Capital account at beginning of year	(b) Capital contributed during year	(c) Income (loss) from lines 1, 2, 3, and 4 below	(d) Income not included in column (c), plus nontaxable income	(e) Losses not included in column (c), plus unallowable deductions	(f) Withdrawals and distributions	(g) Capital account at end of year (combine columns (a) through (f))
				( ) ( )		

Reminder: *If you received a 1987 Schedule K-1 that was for a short year and you chose to report the 1987 amounts over a 4-year period, be sure to include one-fourth of the short year amounts, in addition to the items reported on this Schedule K-1, on the appropriate lines of your 1989 Form 1040 and related schedules.*

Caution: *Refer to Partner's Instructions for Schedule K-1 (Form 1065) before entering information from this schedule on your tax return.*

	(a) Distributive share item		(b) Amount	(c) 1040 filers enter the amount in column (b) on:
Income (Loss)	1	Ordinary income (loss) from trade or business activities . . .	1	} (See Partner's Instructions for Schedule K-1 (Form 1065))
	2	Net income (loss) from rental real estate activities	2	
	3	Net income (loss) from other rental activities	3	
	4	Portfolio income (loss):		
	a	Interest	4a	Sch. B, Part I, line 2
	b	Dividends	4b	Sch. B, Part II, line 4
	c	Royalties	4c	Sch. E, Part I, line 5
	d	Net short-term capital gain (loss)	4d	Sch. D, line 5, col. (f) or (g)
	e	Net long-term capital gain (loss)	4e	Sch. D, line 12, col. (f) or (g)
	f	Other portfolio income (loss) (attach schedule)	4f	(Enter on applicable lines of your return)
	5	Guaranteed payments to partner.	5	} (See Partner's Instructions for Schedule K-1 (Form 1065))
	6	Net gain (loss) under section 1231 (other than due to casualty or theft)	6	
	7	Other income (loss) (attach schedule)	7	(Enter on applicable lines of your return)
Deductions	8	Charitable contributions	8	Sch. A, line 14 or 15
	9	Expense deduction for recovery property (section 179) (attach schedule) . .	9	} (See Partner's Instructions for Schedule K-1 (Form 1065))
	10	Deductions related to portfolio income	10	
	11	Other deductions (attach schedule).	11	
Credits	12a	Credit for income tax withheld	12a	See Partner's Instructions for Schedule K-1 (Form 1065)
	b	Low-income housing credit: (1) Partnerships to which section 42(j)(5) applies	b(1)	} Form 8586, line 5
		(2) Other than on line 12b(1)	b(2)	
	c	Qualified rehabilitation expenditures related to rental real estate activities (attach schedule)	12c	} (See Partner's Instructions for Schedule K-1 (Form 1065))
	d	Credits (other than credits shown on lines 12b and 12c) related to rental real estate activities (attach schedule)	12d	
	e	Credits related to rental activities other than rental real estate (see instructions) (attach schedule)	12e	
	13	Other credits and expenditures (attach schedule)	13	

For Paperwork Reduction Act Notice, see Form 1065 Instructions.   **Schedule K-1 (Form 1065) 1989**

Schedule K-1 (Form 1065) (1989)   Page **2**

		(a) Distributive share item		(b) Amount	(c) 1040 filers enter the amount in column (b) on:
Self-em- ployment	**14a**	Net earnings (loss) from self-employment	**14a**		Sch. SE, Section A or B
	b	Gross farming or fishing income	**14b**		} (See Partner's Instructions for Schedule K-1 (Form 1065))
	c	Gross nonfarm income	**14c**		
Adjustments and Tax Preference Items	**15a**	Accelerated depreciation of real property placed in service before 1987	**15a**		
	b	Accelerated depreciation of leased personal property placed in service before 1987	**15b**		(See Form 6251 Instructions and Partner's Instructions for Schedule K-1 (Form 1065))
	c	Depreciation adjustment on property placed in service after 1986	**15c**		
	d	Depletion (other than oil and gas)	**15d**		
	e	(1) Gross income from oil, gas, and geothermal properties . .	**e(1)**		
		(2) Deductions allocable to oil, gas, and geothermal properties .	**e(2)**		
	f	Other adjustments and tax preference items (attach schedule) .	**15f**		
Investment Interest	**16a**	Interest expense on investment debts	**16a**		Form 4952, line 1
	b	(1) Investment income included on Schedule K-1, lines 4a through 4f	**b(1)**		} (See Partner's Instructions for Schedule K-1 (Form 1065))
		(2) Investment expenses included on Schedule K-1, line 10 . .	**b(2)**		
Foreign Taxes	**17a**	Type of income _____			Form 1116, Check boxes
	b	Name of foreign country or U.S. possession _____			Form 1116, Part I
	c	Total gross income from sources outside the U.S. (attach schedule)	**17c**		Form 1116, Part I
	d	Total applicable deductions and losses (attach schedule) . . .	**17d**		Form 1116, Part I
	e	Total foreign taxes (check one): ▶ ☐ Paid ☐ Accrued . .	**17e**		Form 1116, Part II
	f	Reduction in taxes available for credit (attach schedule) . . .	**17f**		Form 1116, Part III
	g	Other foreign tax information (attach schedule)	**17g**		See Form 1116 Instructions
Other	**18a**	Total expenditures to which a section 59(e) election (relating to the optional 10-year writeoff of certain tax preference items) may apply (attach schedule).			(See Partner's Instructions for Schedule K-1 (Form 1065))
	b	Other items and amounts not reported on lines 1 through 17g, 19, and 20 that are required to be reported separately to you			
Recapture of Tax Credits	**19a**	Low-income housing credit: Partnerships to which section 42(j)(5) applies	**19a**		} Form 8611, line 8
	b	Low-income housing credit recapture other than on line 19a . .	**19b**		

		Investment Tax Credit Property:	**A**	**B**	**C**	
Recapture of Tax Credits	**20**					
	a	Description of property (State whether recovery or nonrecovery property. If recovery property, state whether regular percentage method or section 48(q) election used.) .				Form 4255, top
	b	Date placed in service .				Form 4255, line 2
	c	Cost or other basis . . .				Form 4255, line 3
	d	Class of recovery property or original estimated useful life .				Form 4255, line 4
	e	Date item ceased to be investment credit property				Form 4255, line 8

Other Information Provided by Partnership:

_____

_____

_____

_____

_____

_____

Form 1120-A

Department of the Treasury
Internal Revenue Service

U.S. Corporation Short-Form Income Tax Return

Instructions are separate. See them to make sure you qualify to file Form 1120-A.
For calendar year 1989 or tax year beginning _____, 1989, ending _____, 19 ____

OMB No. 1545-0890

1989

A Check this box if corp. is a personal service corp. (as defined in Temp. Regs. sec. 1.441-4T— see instructions) ▶ ☐

Use IRS label. Otherwise, please print or type.

Name

Number and street (or P.O. box number if mail is not delivered to street address)

City or town, state, and ZIP code

B Employer identification number

C Date incorporated

D Total assets (see Specific Instructions)

$

E Check applicable boxes: **(1)** ☐ Initial return   **(2)** ☐ Change in address
F Check method of accounting: **(1)** ☐ Cash **(2)** ☐ Accrual **(3)** ☐ Other (specify) . . ▶

Income

1a	Gross receipts or sales _____ **b** Less returns and allowances _____	**c** Balance ▶	**1c**
2	Cost of goods sold and/or operations (see instructions)		**2**
3	Gross profit (line 1c less line 2)		**3**
4	Domestic corporation dividends subject to the 70% deduction		**4**
5	Interest		**5**
6	Gross rents		**6**
7	Gross royalties		**7**
8	Capital gain net income (attach Schedule D (Form 1120))		**8**
9	Net gain or (loss) from Form 4797, Part II, line 18 (attach Form 4797)		**9**
10	Other income (see instructions)		**10**
11	**Total** income—Add lines 3 through 10 . . . . ▶		**11**

Deductions (See Instructions for limitations on deductions.)

12	Compensation of officers (see instructions)		**12**
13a	Salaries and wages _____ **b** Less jobs credit _____	**c** Balance ▶	**13c**
14	Repairs		**14**
15	Bad debts		**15**
16	Rents		**16**
17	Taxes		**17**
18	Interest		**18**
19	Contributions **(see instructions for 10% limitation)** . . .		**19**
20	Depreciation (attach Form 4562) . . . . **20** _____		
21	Less depreciation claimed elsewhere on return . . **21a** _____		**21b**
22	Other deductions (attach schedule)		**22**
23	**Total** deductions—Add lines 12 through 22 . . . . . . ▶		**23**
24	Taxable income before net operating loss deduction and special deductions (line 11 less line 23) . .		**24**
25	**Less: a** Net operating loss deduction (see instructions) . . . . . **25a** _____		
	b Special deductions (see instructions) . . . . **25b** _____		**25c**

Tax and Payments

26	Taxable income—Line 24 less line 25c		**26**
27	**Total tax** (Part I, line 7)		**27**
28	**Payments:**		
a	1988 overpayment credited to 1989 . **28a** _____		
b	1989 estimated tax payments . . **28b** _____		
c	Less 1989 refund applied for on Form 4466 **28c** (_____) Bal ▶	**28d**	
e	Tax deposited with Form 7004	**28e**	
f	Credit from regulated investment companies (attach Form 2439)	**28f**	
g	Credit for Federal tax on fuels (attach Form 4136)	**28g**	
h	Total payments—Add lines 28d through 28g		**28h**
29	Enter any **penalty** for underpayment of estimated tax—Check ▶ ☐ if Form 2220 is attached . . .		**29**
30	**Tax due**—If the total of lines 27 and 29 is larger than line 28h, enter amount owed . . .		**30**
31	**Overpayment**—If line 28h is larger than the total of lines 27 and 29, enter amount overpaid .		**31**
32	Enter amount of line 31 you want: **Credited to 1990 estimated tax** ▶ _____ **Refunded** ▶		**32**

Please Sign Here

Under penalties of perjury, I declare that I have examined this return, including accompanying schedules and statements, and to the best of my knowledge and belief, it is true, correct, and complete. Declaration of preparer (other than taxpayer) is based on all information of which preparer has any knowledge.

▶ _____   _____   ▶ _____
  Signature of officer   Date   Title

Paid Preparer's Use Only

Preparer's signature ▶	Date	Check if self-employed ▶ ☐	Preparer's social security number
Firm's name (or yours if self-employed) and address ▶		E.I. No. ▶	
		ZIP code ▶	

For Paperwork Reduction Act Notice, see page 1 of the instructions.

Form **1120-A** (1989)

Form 1120-A (1989)   Page **2**

Part I   Tax Computation

1	Income tax (see instructions to figure the tax). Check this box if the corp. is a qualified personal service corp. (see instructions). ▶ ☐	**1**
2a	General business credit. Check if from: ☐ Form 3800 ☐ Form 3468 ☐ Form 5884 ☐ Form 6478 ☐ Form 6765 ☐ Form 8586 **2a**	
b	Credit for prior year minimum tax (attach Form 8801) **2b**	
3	Total credits—Add lines 2a and 2b	**3**
4	Line 1 less line 3	**4**
5	Recapture taxes. Check if from: ☐ Form 4255 ☐ Form 8611	**5**
6	Alternative minimum tax (attach Form 4626)	**6**
7	Total tax—Add lines 4 through 6. Enter here and on line 27, page 1.	**7**

Additional Information (See instruction F.)

G   Refer to the list in the instructions and state the principal:

    (1) Business activity code no. ▶ _____

    (2) Business activity ▶ _____

    (3) Product or service ▶ _____

H   Did any individual, partnership, estate, or trust at the end of the tax year own, directly or indirectly, 50% or more of the corporation's voting stock? (For rules of attribution, see section 267(c).)   Yes ☐   No ☐

If "Yes," attach schedule showing name, address, and identifying number.

I   Enter the amount of tax-exempt interest received or accrued during the tax year . . . . ▶ |$ |

J (1) If an amount for cost of goods sold and/or operations is entered on line 2, page 1, complete (a) through (c):

    (a) Purchases (see instructions) . .

    (b) Additional sec. 263A costs (see instructions —attach schedule) .

    (c) Other costs (attach schedule) . .

(2) Do the rules of section 263A (with respect to property produced or acquired for resale) apply to the corporation? . . . Yes ☐   No ☐

K At any time during the tax year, did you have an interest in or a signature or other authority over a financial account in a foreign country (such as a bank account, securities account, or other financial account)? (See instruction F for filing requirements for form TD F 90-22.1.) . . . . Yes ☐   No ☐

If "Yes," enter the name of the foreign country ▶ _____

L Enter amount of cash distributions and the book value of property (other than cash) distributions made in this tax year ▶ |$ |

Part II   Balance Sheets

		(a) Beginning of tax year		(b) End of tax year	
Assets	1 Cash				
	2a Trade notes and accounts receivable				
	b Less allowance for bad debts	(	)	(	)
	3 Inventories				
	4 U.S. government obligations . . . . , .				
	5 Tax-exempt securities (see instructions)				
	6 Other current assets (attach schedule)				
	7 Loans to stockholders . . .				
	8 Mortgage and real estate loans				
	9a Depreciable, depletable, and intangible assets				
	b Less accumulated depreciation, depletion, and amortization . .	(	)	(	)
	10 Land (net of any amortization)				
	11 Other assets (attach schedule)				
	12 Total assets				
Liabilities and Stockholders' Equity	13 Accounts payable.				
	14 Other current liabilities (attach schedule)				
	15 Loans from stockholders . . .				
	16 Mortgages, notes, bonds payable.				
	17 Other liabilities (attach schedule)				
	18 Capital stock (preferred and common stock)				
	19 Paid-in or capital surplus				
	20 Retained earnings				
	21 Less cost of treasury stock	(	)	(	)
	22 Total liabilities and stockholders' equity				

Part III   Reconciliation of Income per Books With Income per Return (Must be completed by all filers)

1 Net income per books		**5** Income recorded on books this year not included on this return (itemize) _____	
2 Federal income tax			
3 Income subject to tax not recorded on books this year (itemize) _____		**6** Deductions on this return not charged against book income this year (itemize) _____	
4 Expenses recorded on books this year not deducted on this return (itemize)		**7** Income (line 24, page 1). Enter the sum of lines 1 through 4 less the sum of lines 5 and 6	

Form 1120

Department of the Treasury
Internal Revenue Service

U.S. Corporation Income Tax Return

For calendar year 1989 or tax year beginning _____, 1989, ending _____, 19 ____

▶ Instructions are separate. See page 1 for Paperwork Reduction Act Notice.

OMB No. 1545-0123

1989

Check if a—
A Consolidated return ☐
B Personal holding co. ☐
C Personal service corp.(as defined in Temp. Regs. sec. 1.441-4T—see instructions) ☐

Use IRS label. Otherwise, please print or type.

Name

Number and street (or P.O. box number if mail is not delivered to street address)

City or town, state, and ZIP code

D Employer identification number

E Date incorporated

F Total assets (see Specific Instructions)

G Check applicable boxes: (1) ☐ Initial return (2) ☐ Final return (3) ☐ Change in address

$

Income

1a	Gross receipts or sales _____ b Less returns and allowances _____ c Bal ▶	1c	
2	Cost of goods sold and/or operations (Schedule A, line 7)	2	
3	Gross profit (line 1c less line 2)	3	
4	Dividends (Schedule C, line 19)	4	
5	Interest	5	
6	Gross rents	6	
7	Gross royalties	7	
8	Capital gain net income (attach Schedule D (Form 1120))	8	
9	Net gain or (loss) from Form 4797, Part II, line 18 (attach Form 4797) . .	9	
10	Other income (see instructions—attach schedule)	10	
11	**Total** income—Add lines 3 through 10 . . . . ▶	11	

Deductions

(See instructions for limitations on deductions.)

12	Compensation of officers (Schedule E, line 4)	12	
13a	Salaries and wages _____ b Less jobs credit _____ c Balance ▶	13c	
14	Repairs	14	
15	Bad debts	15	
16	Rents	16	
17	Taxes	17	
18	Interest	18	
19	Contributions (**see instructions for 10% limitation**)	19	
20	Depreciation (attach Form 4562) 20		
21	Less depreciation claimed on Schedule A and elsewhere on return . . 21a	21b	
22	Depletion	22	
23	Advertising	23	
24	Pension, profit-sharing, etc., plans	24	
25	Employee benefit programs	25	
26	Other deductions (attach schedule)	26	
27	**Total** deductions—Add lines 12 through 26 . . . . ▶	27	
28	Taxable income before net operating loss deduction and special deductions (line 11 less line 27) .	28	
29	**Less: a** Net operating loss deduction (see instructions) 29a		
	b Special deductions (Schedule C, line 20) 29b	29c	

Tax and Payments

30	Taxable income—Line 28 less line 29c	30	
31	**Total tax** (Schedule J, line 10)	31	
32	**Payments: a** 1988 overpayment credited to 1989 32a		
	b 1989 estimated tax payments . . . 32b		
	c Less 1989 refund applied for on Form 4466 32c ( ) d Bal ▶ 32d		
	e Tax deposited with Form 7004 32e		
	f Credit from regulated investment companies (attach Form 2439) . . 32f		
	g Credit for Federal tax on fuels (attach Form 4136) 32g	32h	
33	Enter any **penalty** for underpayment of estimated tax—Check ▶ ☐ if Form 2220 is attached .	33	
34	**Tax due**—If the total of lines 31 and 33 is larger than line 32h, enter amount owed	34	
35	**Overpayment**—If line 32h is larger than the total of lines 31 and 33, enter amount overpaid . .	35	
36	Enter amount of line 35 you want: **Credited to 1990 estimated tax** ▶ ____ **Refunded** ▶	36	

Please Sign Here

Under penalties of perjury, I declare that I have examined this return, including accompanying schedules and statements, and to the best of my knowledge and belief, it is true, correct, and complete. Declaration of preparer (other than taxpayer) is based on all information of which preparer has any knowledge.

▶ Signature of officer _____ Date _____ ▶ Title _____

Paid Preparer's Use Only

Preparer's signature ▶	Date	Check if self-employed ☐	Preparer's social security number
Firm's name (or yours if self-employed) and address ▶		E.I. No. ▶	
		ZIP code ▶	

Form 1120 (1989)   Page **2**

Schedule A   Cost of Goods Sold and/or Operations (See instructions for line 2, page 1.)

1 Inventory at beginning of year	**1**	
2 Purchases	**2**	
3 Cost of labor	**3**	
4a Additional section 263A costs (see instructions—attach schedule)	**4a**	
b Other costs (attach schedule)	**4b**	
5 Total—Add lines 1 through 4b	**5**	
6 Inventory at end of year	**6**	
7 Cost of goods sold and/or operations—Line 5 less line 6. Enter here and on line 2, page 1 . . .	**7**	

8a Check all methods used for valuing closing inventory:

    (i) ☐ Cost   *(ii)* ☐ Lower of cost or market as described in Regulations section 1.471-4 (see instructions)

    (iii) ☐ Writedown of "subnormal" goods as described in Regulations section 1.471-2(c) (see instructions)

    (iv) ☐ Other (Specify method used and attach explanation.) ▶ _____

    b Check if the LIFO inventory method was adopted this tax year for any goods (if checked, attach Form 970) . . . . . ☐

    c If the LIFO inventory method was used for this tax year, enter percentage (or amounts) of closing inventory computed under LIFO . . . . | **8c** |

    d Do the rules of section 263A (with respect to property produced or acquired for resale) apply to the corporation? . . ☐ Yes   ☐ No

    e Was there any change in determining quantities, cost, or valuations between opening and closing inventory? If "Yes," attach explanation . . . . ☐ Yes   ☐ No

Schedule C   Dividends and Special Deductions (See instructions.)

	(a) Dividends received	(b) %	(c) Special deductions: (a) × (b)
1 Dividends from less-than-20%-owned domestic corporations that are subject to the 70% deduction (other than debt-financed stock)		70	
2 Dividends from 20%-or-more-owned domestic corporations that are subject to the 80% deduction (other than debt-financed stock)		80 *see instructions*	
3 Dividends on debt-financed stock of domestic and foreign corporations (section 246A)			
4 Dividends on certain preferred stock of less-than-20%-owned public utilities		41.176	
5 Dividends on certain preferred stock of 20%-or-more-owned public utilities		47.059	
6 Dividends from less-than-20%-owned foreign corporations and certain FSCs that are subject to the 70% deduction		70	
7 Dividends from 20%-or-more-owned foreign corporations and certain FSCs that are subject to the 80% deduction		80	
8 Dividends from wholly owned foreign subsidiaries subject to the 100% deduction (section 245(b))		100	
9 Total—Add lines 1 through 8. See instructions for limitation			
10 Dividends from domestic corporations received by a small business investment company operating under the Small Business Investment Act of 1958		100	
11 Dividends from certain FSCs that are subject to the 100% deduction (section 245(c)(1))		100	
12 Dividends from affiliated group members subject to the 100% deduction (section 243(a)(3))		100	
13 Other dividends from foreign corporations not included on lines 3, 6, 7, 8, or 11			
14 Income from controlled foreign corporations under subpart F (attach Forms 5471)			
15 Foreign dividend gross-up (section 78)			
16 IC-DISC and former DISC dividends not included on lines 1, 2, or 3 (section 246(d))			
17 Other dividends			
18 Deduction for dividends paid on certain preferred stock of public utilities (see instructions)			
19 Total dividends—Add lines 1 through 17. Enter here and on line 4, page 1. ▶			
20 Total deductions—Add lines 9, 10, 11, 12, and 18. Enter here and on line 29b, page 1 . . . . ▶			

Schedule E   Compensation of Officers (See instructions for line 12, page 1.)

Complete Schedule E only if total receipts (line 1a, plus lines 4 through 10, of page 1, Form 1120) are $500,000 or more.

(a) Name of officer	(b) Social security number	(c) Percent of time devoted to business	Percent of corporation stock owned		(f) Amount of compensation
			(d) Common	(e) Preferred	
1		%	%	%	
		%	%	%	
		%	%	%	
		%	%	%	
		%	%	%	

2 Total compensation of officers . . . .

3 Less: Compensation of officers claimed on Schedule A and elsewhere on return . . . . (   )

4 Compensation of officers deducted on line 12, page 1 . . . .

Form 1120 (1989)   Page **3**

Schedule J	Tax Computation

1 Check if you are a member of a controlled group (see sections 1561 and 1563) . . . . . . ▶ ☐

2 If the box on line 1 is checked:

  a Enter your share of the $50,000 and $25,000 taxable income bracket amounts (in that order):

    (i) ⎿$_____⏌   *(ii)* ⎿$_____⏌

  b Enter your share of the additional 5% tax (not to exceed $11,750) ▶   ⎿$_____⏌

3 Income tax (see instructions to figure the tax). Check this box if the corporation is a qualified personal service corporation (see instructions). ▶ ☐ **3**

4a Foreign tax credit (attach Form 1118)	**4a**	
b Possessions tax credit (attach Form 5735)	**4b**	
c Orphan drug credit (attach Form 6765)	**4c**	
d Credit for fuel produced from a nonconventional source (see instructions)	**4d**	
e General business credit. Enter here and check which forms are attached: ☐ Form 3800 ☐ Form 3468 ☐ Form 5884 ☐ Form 6478 ☐ Form 6765 ☐ Form 8586	**4e**	
f Credit for prior year minimum tax (attach Form 8801)	**4f**	

5 Total—Add lines 4a through 4f **5**

6 Line 3 less line 5 . . . . **6**

7 Personal holding company tax (attach Schedule PH (Form 1120)) **7**

8 Recapture taxes. Check if from: ☐ Form 4255 ☐ Form 8611 . . . . **8**

9a Alternative minimum tax (attach Form 4626) **9a**

  b Environmental tax (attach Form 4626) **9b**

10 Total tax—Add lines 6 through 9b. Enter here and on line 31, page 1 . . . . **10**

Additional Information (See instruction F.)   Yes | No

H Refer to the list in the instructions and state the principal:

  (1) Business activity code no. ▶ _____

  (2) Business activity ▶ _____

  (3) Product or service ▶ _____

I (1) Did the corporation at the end of the tax year own, directly or indirectly, 50% or more of the voting stock of a domestic corporation? (For rules of attribution, see section 267(c).) . .

  If "Yes," attach a schedule showing: (a) name, address, and identifying number; (b) percentage owned; and (c) taxable income or (loss) before NOL and special deductions of such corporation for the tax year ending with or within your tax year.

  (2) Did any individual, partnership, corporation, estate, or trust at the end of the tax year own, directly or indirectly, 50% or more of the corporation's voting stock? (For rules of attribution, see section 267(c).) If "Yes," complete (a) through (c) . . . .

    (a) Attach a schedule showing name, address, and identifying number.

    (b) Enter percentage owned ▶ _____

    (c) Was the owner of such voting stock a person other than a U.S. person? (See instructions.) **Note:** *If "Yes," the corporation may have to file Form 5472.* . . . . . .

    If "Yes," enter owner's country ▶ _____

J Was the corporation a U.S. shareholder of any controlled foreign corporation? (See sections 951 and 957.) . . . .

  If "Yes," attach Form 5471 for each such corporation.

K At any time during the tax year, did the corporation have an interest in or a signature or other authority over a financial account in a foreign country (such as a bank account, securities account, or other financial account)? . . . .

  (See instruction F and filing requirements for form TD F 90-22.1.)

  If "Yes," enter name of foreign country ▶ _____

L Was the corporation the grantor of, or transferor to, a foreign trust that existed during the current tax year, whether or not the corporation has any beneficial interest in it? . . . .

  If "Yes," the corporation may have to file Forms 3520, 3520-A, or 926.

M During this tax year, did the corporation pay dividends (other than stock dividends and distributions in exchange for stock) in excess of the corporation's current and accumulated earnings and profits? (See sections 301 and 316.)

  If "Yes," file Form 5452. If this is a consolidated return, answer here for parent corporation and on **Form 851**, Affiliations Schedule, for each subsidiary.

N During this tax year, did the corporation maintain any part of its accounting/tax records on a computerized system? . . . . .

O Check method of accounting:

  (1) ☐ Cash

  (2) ☐ Accrual

  (3) ☐ Other (specify) ▶ _____

P Check this box if the corporation issued publicly offered debt instruments with original issue discount . . . . . . ☐

  If so, the corporation may have to file Form 8281.

Q Enter the amount of tax-exempt interest received or accrued during the tax year ▶ ⎿$_____⏌

R Enter the number of shareholders at the end of the tax year if there were 35 or fewer shareholders ▶

Form 1120 (1989)   Page **4**

Schedule L	**Balance Sheets**	Beginning of tax year		End of tax year	
	Assets	(a)	(b)	(c)	(d)
1	Cash				
2a	Trade notes and accounts receivable . . .				
b	Less allowance for bad debts				
3	Inventories				
4	U.S. government obligations				
5	Tax-exempt securities (see instructions) .				
6	Other current assets (attach schedule) . .				
7	Loans to stockholders				
8	Mortgage and real estate loans				
9	Other investments (attach schedule) . . .				
10a	Buildings and other depreciable assets . .				
b	Less accumulated depreciation . . .				
11a	Depletable assets				
b	Less accumulated depletion . . .				
12	Land (net of any amortization)				
13a	Intangible assets (amortizable only) . . .				
b	Less accumulated amortization . . .				
14	Other assets (attach schedule)				
15	Total assets				
	Liabilities and Stockholders' Equity				
16	Accounts payable				
17	Mortgages, notes, bonds payable in less than 1 year				
18	Other current liabilities (attach schedule) .				
19	Loans from stockholders				
20	Mortgages, notes, bonds payable in 1 year or more				
21	Other liabilities (attach schedule)				
22	Capital stock: **a** Preferred stock				
	b Common stock				
23	Paid-in or capital surplus.				
24	Retained earnings—Appropriated (attach schedule)				
25	Retained earnings—Unappropriated. . .				
26	Less cost of treasury stock		( )		( )
27	Total liabilities and stockholders' equity . .				

Schedule M-1	**Reconciliation of Income per Books With Income per Return** (You are not required to complete this schedule if the total assets on line 15, column (d), of Schedule L are less than $25,000.)

1 Net income per books		7 Income recorded on books this year not included on this return (itemize):
2 Federal income tax		**a** Tax-exempt interest $ _ _ _ _ _ _ _ _ _ _
3 Excess of capital losses over capital gains . .		_ _
4 Income subject to tax not recorded on books this year (itemize): _ _ _ _ _ _ _ _ _ _ _ _		_ _
_ _		8 Deductions on this return not charged against book income this year (itemize):
5 Expenses recorded on books this year not deducted on this return (itemize):		**a** Depreciation . . . $ _ _ _ _ _ _ _ _ _
a Depreciation . . . $ _ _ _ _ _ _ _ _ _ _ _		**b** Contributions carryover $ _ _ _ _ _ _ _ _ _
b Contributions carryover $ _ _ _ _ _ _ _ _ _		_ _
c Travel and entertainment . $ _ _ _ _ _ _ _		_ _
_ _		_ _
_ _		9 Total of lines 7 and 8 . . . . . .
6 Total of lines 1 through 5		10 Income (line 28, page 1)—line 6 less line 9 .

Schedule M-2	**Analysis of Unappropriated Retained Earnings per Books (line 25, Schedule L)** (You are not required to complete this schedule if the total assets on line 15, column (d), of Schedule L are less than $25,000.)

1 Balance at beginning of year		5 Distributions: **a** Cash . . . . .
2 Net income per books		**b** Stock . . . . .
3 Other increases (itemize): _ _ _ _ _ _ _ _ _		**c** Property . . . .
_ _		6 Other decreases (itemize): _ _ _ _ _ _ _ _ _
_ _		_ _
_ _		7 Total of lines 5 and 6 . . . .
4 Total of lines 1, 2, and 3		8 Balance at end of year (line 4 less line 7)

Form 1120S

Department of the Treasury
Internal Revenue Service

U.S. Income Tax Return for an S Corporation

For the calendar year 1989, or tax year beginning _____, 1989, ending _____, 19 ____

▶ **For Paperwork Reduction Act Notice, see page 1 of separate instructions.**

OMB No. 1545-0130

1989

A Date of election as an S corporation	Use IRS label. Other- wise, please print or type.	**Name**
		Number and street (P.O. box number if mail is not delivered to street address)
B Business code no. (see Specific Instructions)		**City or town, state, and ZIP code**

C Employer identification number

D Date incorporated

E Total assets (see Specific Instructions)
$

F Check applicable boxes: (1) ☐ Initial return (2) ☐ Final return (3) ☐ Change in address (4) ☐ Amended return

G Check this box if this is an S corporation subject to the consolidated audit procedures of sections 6241 through 6245 (see instructions before checking this box) . . ▶ ☐

H Enter number of shareholders in the corporation at end of the tax year . . . . ▶

Caution: Include **only** trade or business income and expenses on lines 1a through 21. See the instructions for more information.

Income

1a Gross receipts or sales ⎿_____⎸ **b** Less returns and allowances ⎿_____⎸ **c** Bal ▶	**1c**	
2 Cost of goods sold and/or operations (Schedule A, line 7)	**2**	
3 Gross profit (subtract line 2 from line 1c)	**3**	
4 Net gain (or loss) from Form 4797, line 18 (see instructions)	**4**	
5 Other income (see instructions—attach schedule)	**5**	
6 **Total** income (loss)—Combine lines 3, 4, and 5 and enter here . . . . ▶	**6**	

Deductions (See instructions for limitations.)

7 Compensation of officers	**7**	
8a Salaries and wages ⎿_____⎸ **b** Less jobs credit ⎿_____⎸ **c** Bal ▶	**8c**	
9 Repairs	**9**	
10 Bad debts (see instructions)	**10**	
11 Rents	**11**	
12 Taxes	**12**	
13 Interest (see instructions)	**13**	
14a Depreciation (attach Form 4562) (see instructions) . . . . . **14a** ⎿_____⎸		
b Depreciation reported on Schedule A and elsewhere on return . . **14b** ⎿_____⎸		
c Subtract line 14b from line 14a	**14c**	
15 Depletion (**Do not deduct oil and gas depletion.** See instructions.) . .	**15**	
16 Advertising	**16**	
17 Pension, profit-sharing, etc. plans	**17**	
18 Employee benefit programs	**18**	
19 Other deductions (attach schedule)	**19**	
20 **Total** deductions—Add lines 7 through 19 and enter here . . . . ▶	**20**	
21 Ordinary income (loss) from trade or business activities—Subtract line 20 from line 6 . .	**21**	

Tax and Payments

22 Tax:		
a Excess net passive income tax (attach schedule) . . . . . **22a** ⎿_____⎸		
b Tax from Schedule D (Form 1120S) . . . . **22b** ⎿_____⎸		
c Add lines 22a and 22b (see instructions for additional taxes)	**22c**	
23 Payments:		
a Tax deposited with Form 7004 . . . . **23a** ⎿_____⎸		
b Credit for Federal tax on fuels (attach Form 4136) . . . . **23b** ⎿_____⎸		
c Add lines 23a and 23b	**23c**	
24 Tax due—If line 22c is larger than line 23c, enter amount owed. See instructions for Paying the Tax . . . . ▶	**24**	
25 **Overpayment**—If line 23c is larger than line 22c, enter amount overpaid . . . . ▶	**25**	

Please Sign Here

Under penalties of perjury, I declare that I have examined this return, including accompanying schedules and statements, and to the best of my knowledge and belief, it is true, correct, and complete. Declaration of preparer (other than taxpayer) is based on all information of which preparer has any knowledge.

▶ _____   _____   ▶ _____
Signature of officer   Date   Title

Paid Preparer's Use Only

Preparer's signature ▶		Date	Check if self-employed ▶ ☐	Preparer's social security number
Firm's name (or yours if self-employed) and address ▶			E.I. No. ▶
			ZIP code ▶

Form **1120S** (1989)

Schedule A **Cost of Goods Sold and/or Operations** (See instructions for Schedule A.)

1 Inventory at beginning of year	**1**	
2 Purchases	**2**	
3 Cost of labor	**3**	
4a Additional section 263A costs (attach schedule) (see instructions)	**4a**	
b Other costs (attach schedule)	**4b**	
5 Total—Add lines 1 through 4b	**5**	
6 Inventory at end of year	**6**	
7 Cost of goods sold and/or operations—Subtract line 6 from line 5. Enter here and on line 2, page 1	**7**	

8a Check all methods used for valuing closing inventory:
   (i) ☐ Cost
   (ii) ☐ Lower of cost or market as described in Regulations section 1.471-4
   (iii) ☐ Writedown of "subnormal" goods as described in Regulations section 1.471-2(c)
   (iv) ☐ Other (specify method used and attach explanation) ▶ _____

   b Check this box if the LIFO inventory method was adopted this tax year for any goods (if checked, attach Form 970) . . . ▶☐

   c If the LIFO inventory method was used for this tax year, enter percentage (or amounts) of closing inventory computed under LIFO . . . | **8c** |

   d Do the rules of section 263A (with respect to property produced or acquired for resale) apply to the corporation? . . . ☐ Yes ☐ No
   e Was there any change in determining quantities, cost, or valuations between opening and closing inventory? . . . . ☐ Yes ☐ No
   If "Yes," attach explanation.

Additional Information Required (continued from page 1)

	Yes	No
I Did you at the end of the tax year own, directly or indirectly, 50% or more of the voting stock of a domestic corporation? For rules of attribution, see section 267(c). If "Yes," attach a schedule showing: (1) name, address, and employer identification number; and (2) percentage owned.		
J Refer to the listing of business activity codes at the end of the Instructions for Form 1120S and state your principal:		
(1) Business activity ▶ _____ (2) Product or service ▶ _____		
K Were you a member of a controlled group subject to the provisions of section 1561?		
L At any time during the tax year, did you have an interest in or a signature or other authority over a financial account in a foreign country (such as a bank account, securities account, or other financial account)? (See instructions for exceptions and filing requirements for form TD F 90-22.1.)		
If "Yes," enter the name of the foreign country ▶ _____		
M Were you the grantor of, or transferor to, a foreign trust which existed during the current tax year, whether or not you have any beneficial interest in it? If "Yes," you may have to file Form 3520, 3520-A, or 926		
N During this tax year did you maintain any part of your accounting/tax records on a computerized system?		
O Check method of accounting: **(1)** ☐ Cash **(2)** ☐ Accrual **(3)** ☐ Other (specify) ▶ _____		
P Check this box if the S corporation has filed or is required to file **Form 8264,** Application for Registration of a Tax Shelter . . . . ▶☐		
Q Check this box if the corporation issued publicly offered debt instruments with original issue discount . . . . . ▶☐		
If so, the corporation may have to file **Form 8281,** Information Return for Publicly Offered Original Issue Discount Instruments.		
R If the corporation: (1) filed its election to be an S corporation after December 31, 1986, (2) was a C corporation prior to making the election, and (3) at the beginning of the tax year had net unrealized built-in gain as defined in section 1374(d)(1), enter the net unrealized built-in gain (see instructions) ▶		

Designation of Tax Matters Person (See instructions.)

Enter below the shareholder designated as the tax matters person (TMP) for the tax year of this return:

Name of
designated TMP ▶ _____   Identifying
number of TMP ▶ _____

Address of
designated TMP ▶ _____

Form 1120S (1989)   Page **3**

Schedule K	Shareholders' Shares of Income, Credits, Deductions, Etc. (See Instructions.)

(a) Pro rata share items		(b) Total amount	

Income (Loss) and Deductions

1	Ordinary income (loss) from trade or business activities (page 1, line 21)	**1**	
2a	Gross income from rental real estate activities **2a**		
b	Less expenses (attach schedule). **2b**		
c	Net income (loss) from rental real estate activities	**2c**	
3a	Gross income from other rental activities **3a**		
b	Less expenses (attach schedule) **3b**		
c	Net income (loss) from other rental activities	**3c**	
4	Portfolio income (loss):		
a	Interest income	**4a**	
b	Dividend income	**4b**	
c	Royalty income	**4c**	
d	Net short-term capital gain (loss) (Schedule D (Form 1120S))	**4d**	
e	Net long-term capital gain (loss) (Schedule D (Form 1120S))	**4e**	
f	Other portfolio income (loss) (attach schedule)	**4f**	
5	Net gain (loss) under section 1231 (other than due to casualty or theft) (see instructions) . . .	**5**	
6	Other income (loss) (attach schedule)	**6**	
7	Charitable contributions (attach list)	**7**	
8	Section 179 expense deduction (attach Form 4562)	**8**	
9	Expenses related to portfolio income (loss) (attach schedule) (see instructions)	**9**	
10	Other deductions (attach schedule)	**10**	

Credits

11a	Credit for alcohol used as a fuel (attach Form 6478)	**11a**	
b	Low-income housing credit: **(1)** From partnerships to which section 42(j)(5) applies	**11b(1)**	
	(2) Other than on line 11b(1)	**11b(2)**	
c	Qualified rehabilitation expenditures related to rental real estate activities (attach schedule) . . .	**11c**	
d	Credits (other than credits shown on lines 11b and 11c) related to rental real estate activities (attach schedule) . . .	**11d**	
e	Credits related to other rental activities (see instructions) (attach schedule)	**11e**	
12	Other credits and expenditures (attach schedule)	**12**	

Investment Interest

13a	Interest expense on investment debts	**13a**	
b	**(1)** Investment income included on lines 4a through 4f above	**13b(1)**	
	(2) Investment expenses included on line 9 above	**13b(2)**	

Adjustments and Tax Preference Items

14a	Accelerated depreciation of real property placed in service before 1987	**14a**	
b	Accelerated depreciation of leased personal property placed in service before 1987	**14b**	
c	Depreciation adjustment on property placed in service after 1986	**14c**	
d	Depletion (other than oil and gas)	**14d**	
e	**(1)** Gross income from oil, gas, or geothermal properties	**14e(1)**	
	(2) Deductions allocable to oil, gas, or geothermal properties	**14e(2)**	
f	Other adjustments and tax preference items (attach schedule)	**14f**	

Foreign Taxes

15a	Type of income		
b	Name of foreign country or U.S. possession		
c	Total gross income from sources outside the U.S. (attach schedule)	**15c**	
d	Total applicable deductions and losses (attach schedule)	**15d**	
e	Total foreign taxes (check one): ▶ ☐ Paid ☐ Accrued	**15e**	
f	Reduction in taxes available for credit (attach schedule)	**15f**	
g	Other foreign tax information (attach schedule)	**15g**	

Other Items

16	Total property distributions (including cash) other than dividends reported on line 18 below . . .	**16**	
17	Other items and amounts not included on lines 1 through 16 above, that are required to be reported separately to shareholders (attach schedule).		
18	Total dividend distributions paid from accumulated earnings and profits contained in other retained earnings (line 27, Schedule L)	**18**	

Form 1120S (1989)   Page **4**

Schedule L	Balance Sheets	Beginning of tax year		End of tax year	
	Assets	(a)	(b)	(c)	(d)
1	Cash				
2	Trade notes and accounts receivable . . .				
a	Less allowance for bad debts				
3	Inventories				
4	U.S. government obligations				
5	Tax-exempt securities				
6	Other current assets (attach schedule). . .				
7	Loans to shareholders				
8	Mortgage and real estate loans				
9	Other investments (attach schedule) . . .				
10	Buildings and other depreciable assets . . .				
a	Less accumulated depreciation				
11	Depletable assets				
a	Less accumulated depletion				
12	Land (net of any amortization)				
13	Intangible assets (amortizable only)				
a	Less accumulated amortization				
14	Other assets (attach schedule)				
15	Total assets				
	Liabilities and Shareholders' Equity				
16	Accounts payable				
17	Mortgages, notes, bonds payable in less than 1 year				
18	Other current liabilities (attach schedule) . .				
19	Loans from shareholders				
20	Mortgages, notes, bonds payable in 1 year or more				
21	Other liabilities (attach schedule)				
22	Capital stock				
23	Paid-in or capital surplus				
24	Accumulated adjustments account				
25	Other adjustments account				
26	Shareholders' undistributed taxable income previously taxed				
27	Other retained earnings (see instructions). .				
	Check this box if the corporation has subchapter C earnings and profits at the close of the tax year ▶ ☐ (see instructions)				
28	Total retained earnings per books—Combine amounts on lines 24 through 27, columns (a) and (c) (see instructions) .				
29	Less cost of treasury stock.	(	)	(	)
30	Total liabilities and shareholders' equity . .				

Schedule M	Analysis of Accumulated Adjustments Account, Other Adjustments Account, and Shareholders' Undistributed Taxable Income Previously Taxed (If Schedule L, column (c), amounts for lines 24, 25, or 26 are not the same as corresponding amounts on line 9 of Schedule M, attach a schedule explaining any differences. See instructions.)

		Accumulated adjustments account	Other adjustments account	Shareholders' undistributed taxable income previously taxed
1	Balance at beginning of year			
2	Ordinary income from page 1, line 21 . . .			
3	Other additions			
4	Total of lines 1, 2, and 3			
5	Distributions other than dividend distributions			
6	Loss from page 1, line 21			
7	Other reductions			
8	Add lines 5, 6, and 7			
9	Balance at end of tax year—subtract line 8 from line 4			

SCHEDULE K-1	**Shareholder's Share of Income, Credits, Deductions, Etc.**	OMB No. 1545-0130

SCHEDULE K-1
(Form 1120S)
Department of the Treasury
Internal Revenue Service

Shareholder's Share of Income, Credits, Deductions, Etc.
▶ **See separate instructions.**
For calendar year 1989 or tax year
beginning _____, 1989, and ending _____, 19 ___

OMB No. 1545-0130

1989

Shareholder's identifying number ▶	Corporation's identifying number ▶
Shareholder's name, address, and ZIP code	Corporation's name, address, and ZIP code

A Shareholder's percentage of stock ownership for tax year (see Instructions for Schedule K-1) . . . . ▶ _____ %

B Internal Revenue Service Center where corporation filed its return ▶

C (1) Tax shelter registration number (see Instructions for Schedule K-1) . . . . ▶ _____
(2) Type of tax shelter ▶

D If the shareholder acquired corporate stock after 10/22/86, check here ▶ ☐ and enter the shareholder's weighted percentage increase in stock ownership for 1989 (see Instructions for Schedule K-1) . . . . ▶ _____ %

E If any activity for which income or loss is reported on line 1, 2, or 3, was started or acquired by the corporation after 10/22/86, check here ▶ ☐ and enter the date of start up or acquisition in the date space on line 1, 2, or 3 **below.**

Reminder: *If you received a 1987 Schedule K-1 that was for a short year and you chose to report the 1987 amounts over a 4-year period, be sure to include one-fourth of the short year amounts, in addition to the items reported on this Schedule K-1, on the appropriate lines of your 1989 Form 1040 and related schedules.*

Caution: *Refer to Shareholder's Instructions for Schedule K-1 before entering information from Schedule K-1 on your tax return.*

	(a) Pro rata share items		(b) Amount	(c) Form 1040 filers enter the amount in column (b) on:
Income (Loss) and Deductions	**1** Ordinary income (loss) from trade or business activities. If applicable, enter date asked for in item E . . . . . ▶ _____	**1**		See Shareholder's Instructions for Schedule K-1 (Form 1120S).
	2 Net income (loss) from rental real estate activities. If applicable, enter date asked for in item E . . . . . ▶ _____	**2**		
	3 Net income (loss) from other rental activities. If applicable, enter date asked for in item E . . . . . ▶ _____	**3**		
	4 Portfolio income (loss):			
	a Interest	**4a**		Sch. B, Part I, line 2
	b Dividends	**4b**		Sch. B, Part II, line 4
	c Royalties	**4c**		Sch. E, Part I, line 5
	d Net short-term capital gain (loss)	**4d**		Sch. D, line 5, col. (f) or (g)
	e Net long-term capital gain (loss)	**4e**		Sch. D, line 12, col. (f) or (g)
	f Other portfolio income (loss) *(attach schedule)*	**4f**		(Enter on applicable line of your return.)
	5 Net gain (loss) under section 1231 (other than due to casualty or theft)	**5**		See Shareholder's Instructions for Schedule K-1 (Form 1120S).
	6 Other income (loss) *(attach schedule)*	**6**		(Enter on applicable line of your return.)
	7 Charitable contributions	**7**		Sch. A, line 14 or 15
	8 Section 179 expense deduction *(attach schedule)*	**8**		See Shareholder's Instructions for Schedule K-1 (Form 1120S).
	9 Expenses related to portfolio income (loss) *(attach schedule)* . .	**9**		
	10 Other deductions *(attach schedule)*	**10**		
Credits	**11a** Credit for alcohol used as fuel	**11a**		Form 6478, line 10
	b Low-income housing credit: **(1)** From Partnerships to which section 42(j)(5) applies	**b(1)**		Form 8586, line 5
	(2) Other than on line 11b(1)	**b(2)**		
	c Qualified rehabilitation expenditures related to rental real estate activities *(attach schedule)*	**11c**		See Shareholder's Instructions for Schedule K-1 (Form 1120S).
	d Credits (other than credits shown on lines 11b and 11c) related to rental real estate activities *(attach schedule)*	**11d**		
	e Credits related to other rental activities (see instructions) *(attach schedule)*	**11e**		
	12 Other credits and expenditures *(attach schedule)*	**12**		
Investment Interest	**13a** Interest expense on investment debts	**13a**		Form 4952, line 1
	b (1) Investment income included on lines 4a through 4f above	**b(1)**		See Shareholder's Instructions for Schedule K-1 (Form 1120S).
	(2) Investment expenses included on line 9 above	**b(2)**		

For Paperwork Reduction Act Notice, see Form 1120S Instructions.   **Schedule K-1 (Form 1120S) 1989**

Schedule K-1 (Form 1120S) (1989)   Page **2**

	(a) Pro rata share items		(b) Amount	(c) Form 1040 filers enter the amount in column (b) on:
Adjustments and Tax Preference Items	**14a** Accelerated depreciation of real property placed in service before 1987	**14a**		
	b Accelerated depreciation of leased personal property placed in service before 1987.	**14b**		See Shareholder's Instructions for Schedule K-1 (Form 1120S) and Form 6251 Instructions.
	c Depreciation adjustment on property placed in service after 1986 .	**14c**		
	d Depletion (other than oil and gas)	**14d**		
	e (1) Gross income from oil, gas, or geothermal properties . . .	**e(1)**		
	(2) Deductions allocable to oil, gas, or geothermal properties . .	**e(2)**		
	f Other adjustments and tax preference items *(attach schedule)* . .	**14f**		
Foreign Taxes	**15a** Type of income ▶			Form 1116, Check boxes
	b Name of foreign country or U.S. possession ▶			Form 1116, Part I
	c Total gross income from sources outside the U.S. *(attach schedule)*	**15c**		Form 1116, Part I
	d Total applicable deductions and losses *(attach schedule)*. . . .	**15d**		Form 1116, Part I
	e Total foreign taxes (check one): ▶ ☐ Paid ☐ Accrued . .	**15e**		Form 1116, Part II
	f Reduction in taxes available for credit *(attach schedule)*	**15f**		Form 1116, Part III
	g Other foreign tax information *(attach schedule)*.	**15g**		See Form 1116 Instructions
Other Items	**16** Property distributions (including cash) other than dividend distributions reported to you on Form 1099-DIV.	**16**		See Shareholder's Instructions for Schedule K-1 (Form 1120S).
	17 Amount of loan repayments for "Loans from Shareholders". . .	**17**		
	18 Low-income housing credit: **a** Partnerships to which section 42(j)(5) applies	**18a**		} Form 8611, line 8
	b Other than on line 18a.	**18b**		

		A	B	C	
Recapture of Tax Credits	**19** Investment Credit Properties:				
	a Description of property (State whether recovery or non-recovery property. If recovery property, state whether regular percentage method or section 48(q) election is used.)				Form 4255, top
	b Date placed in service .				Form 4255, line 2
	c Cost or other basis . .				Form 4255, line 3
	d Class of recovery property or original estimated useful life .				Form 4255, line 4
	e Date item ceased to be investment credit property				Form 4255, line 8

Supplemental Schedules	**20** Supplemental information that is required to be reported separately to each shareholder (attach additional schedules if more space is needed):
	....
	....
	....
	....
	....
	....
	....
	....
	....
	....
	....

Form **2106**	**Employee Business Expenses**	OMB No. 1545-0139
Department of the Treasury Internal Revenue Service	▶ **See separate Instructions.** ▶ **Attach to Form 1040.**	**1989** Attachment Sequence No. **54**

Your name	Social security number	Occupation in which expenses were incurred
	: :	

Part I   **Employee Business Expenses**

STEP 1 Enter Your Expenses		Column A Other Than Meals and Entertainment		Column B Meals and Entertainment	
1 Vehicle expense from line 28 or line 34	1			/////	
2 Parking fees, tolls, and local transportation, including train, bus, etc. . .	2			/////	
3 Travel expense while away from home overnight, including lodging, airplane, car rental, etc. **Do not** include meals and entertainment . . .	3			/////	
4 Business expenses not included on lines 1 through 3. **Do not** include meals and entertainment	4			/////	
5 Meals and entertainment expenses. (See the separate Instructions.) . .	5	/////			
6 Add lines 1 through 5 and enter the **total expenses** here	6			/////	

Note: *If you were not reimbursed for any expenses in Step 1, skip lines 7–9 and enter the amount from line 6 on line 10.*

STEP 2   Enter Amounts Your Employer Gave You For Expenses Listed In STEP 1
        (See the separate Instructions for lines 7 and 8.)

7 Enter amounts your employer gave you that were **not** reported to you on Form W-2 (See Instructions.).	7			/////	
8 Enter the amount your employer gave you for expenses listed in Step 1 that were **separately identified** on Form W-2 as employee business expenses. (Do **not** include any amounts that were reported to you as wages in Box 10 of Form W-2.) (See Instructions.)	8			/////	
9 Add the amounts on lines 7 and 8. Enter the total here	9			/////	

STEP 3   Figure Expenses To Deduct on Schedule A (Form 1040)

10 Subtract line 9 from line 6	10			/////	
Note: *If **both columns** of line 10 are zero, **stop here**. If Column A is less than zero, report the amount as income. See the separate Instructions for how to report.*		/////		/////	
11 Enter 20% (.20) of line 10, Column B	11	/////			
12 Subtract line 11 from line 10	12			/////	
13 Add the amounts on line 12 of both columns and enter the total here. **Also enter the total on Schedule A (Form 1040), line 20.** (Qualified performing artists and handicapped employees, see the separate Instructions for special rules on where to enter the total.) . . . . ▶	13				

For Paperwork Reduction Act Notice, see Instructions   Form **2106** (1989)

Form 2106 (1989)   Page **2**

| Part II | Vehicle Expenses (Use either your actual expenses (Section C) or the standard mileage rate (Section B).) (Rural mail carriers, see page 1 of the separate Instructions.) |

Section A.—General Information		(a) Vehicle 1	(b) Vehicle 2
14 Enter the date vehicle was placed in service	14	/ /	/ /
15 Total mileage vehicle was used during 1989	15	miles	miles
16 Miles included on line 15 that vehicle was used for business	16	miles	miles
17 Percent of business use (divide line 16 by line 15)	17	%	%
18 Average daily round trip commuting distance	18	miles	miles
19 Miles included on line 15 that vehicle was used for commuting	19	miles	miles
20 Other personal mileage (add lines 16 and 19 and subtract the total from line 15).	20	miles	miles

21 Do you (or your spouse) have another vehicle available for personal purposes? . . . . ☐ Yes ☐ No

22 If your employer provided you with a vehicle, is personal use during off duty hours permitted? . . ☐ Yes ☐ No ☐ Not applicable

23a Do you have evidence to support your deduction? ☐ Yes ☐ No. **23b** If "Yes," is the evidence written? ☐ Yes ☐ No

Section B.—Standard Mileage Rate (Do not use this section unless you own the vehicle.)

24 Enter the smaller of line 16 or 15,000 miles (Rural mail carriers, see the separate Instructions.) . .	24	miles
25 Subtract line 24 from line 16	25	miles
26 Multiply line 24 by 25½¢ (.255) (See the separate Instructions if vehicle is fully depreciated.) . . .	26	
27 Multiply line 25 by 11¢ (.11)	27	
28 Add lines 26 and 27. Enter total here and on line 1	28	

Section C.—Actual Expenses		(a) Vehicle 1	(b) Vehicle 2
29 Gasoline, oil, repairs, vehicle insurance, etc.	29		
30 Vehicle rentals.	30		
31 Add lines 29 and 30	31		
32 Multiply line 31 by the percentage on line 17	32		
33 Depreciation from lines 36 and 37, column (f) (See separate Instructions.)	33		
34 Add lines 32 and 33. Enter total here and on line 1	34		
35 Value of employer-provided vehicle multiplied by the percentage on line 17 (See Instructions.)	35		

Section D.—Depreciation of Vehicles (You can only claim depreciation for a vehicle you own. There is a limit on the amount of depreciation and Section 179 deduction you can claim. See the separate instructions for the limit. If line 17 above is 50 percent or less, you cannot claim the Section 179 deduction and you must figure depreciation using the straight line method over 5 years.)

	Cost or other basis (a)	Basis for depreciation (Business use only—see separate Instructions) (b)	Method of figuring depreciation (c)	Depreciation deduction (d)	Section 179 deduction (e)	Total column (d) + column (e) (enter on line 33) (f)
36 Vehicle 1						
37 Vehicle 2						

Form **2119** Department of the Treasury Internal Revenue Service	**Sale of Your Home** ▶ See Separate Instructions. ▶ Attach to Form 1040 for year of sale.	OMB No. 1545–0072 **1989** Attachment Sequence No. **22**

Please Type or Print	Your first name and initial (If joint, also give spouse's name and initial.) Last name	Your social security number
	Present home address (no., street, and apt. no., or rural route) (or P.O. box no. if mail is not delivered to street address)	Spouse's social security number
	City, town or post office, state, and ZIP code	

Part I   Facts About You and Your Home

1a Date former main home was sold ▶

b Enter the face amount of any mortgage, note (for example, second trust), or other financial instrument on which you will receive periodic payments of principal or interest from this sale. (See Instructions for line 1b.)▶ $

		Yes	No
2a	Have you bought or built a new main home?		
b	Are any rooms in either main home rented out or used for business for which a deduction is allowed? . . . . (If "Yes," see Instructions.)		
3a	Were you 55 or older on date of sale?		
b	Was your spouse 55 or older on date of sale? . . . . **If you answered "No" to 3a and 3b, do not complete 3c through 3f or Part III.**		
c	Did the person who answered "Yes" to 3a or 3b own and use the property sold as a main home for a total of at least 3 years (except for short absences) of the 5-year period before the sale?		
d	**If you answered "Yes" to 3c, do you choose to take the one-time exclusion of the gain on the sale?**		
e	At time of sale, who owned the home ? ☐ you ☐ your spouse ☐ both of you		
f	Social security number of spouse, at time of sale, if different from above ▶ (Enter "None" if you were not married at time of sale.)		

Part II   Figure Your Gain (Do not include amounts that you deduct as moving expenses.)

4	Selling price of home. (Do not include personal property items.)	**4**	
5	Expense of sale. (Include sales commissions, advertising, legal, etc.)	**5**	
6	Subtract line 5 from line 4. This is the amount realized	**6**	
7	Basis of home sold. (See Instructions.)	**7**	
8a	Subtract line 7 from line 6 (gain on sale). If zero or less, enter zero and do not complete the rest of the form. Enter the gain from this line on Schedule D, line 3 or 10,* unless you bought another main home or checked "Yes" to 3d. Then continue with this form	**8a**	
b	If you haven't replaced your home, do you plan to do so within the replacement period? . . . . ☐ Yes ☐ No (If "Yes," see Instructions under When and Where To File.)		

Part III   If Age 55 or Older, Figure Your One-Time Exclusion   (Complete this part only if you checked "Yes" to 3d.)

9	Enter the **smaller** of line 8a or $125,000 ($62,500, if married filing separate return) (See Instructions.)	**9**	
10	Subtract line 9 from line 8a (gain). If zero, do not complete rest of form. Enter the gain from this line on Schedule D, line 10,* unless you bought another main home. Then continue with this form . . .	**10**	

Part IV   Figure Gain To Be Postponed and Adjusted Basis of New Home   (Complete this part if you bought another main home.)

11	Fixing-up expenses. (See Instructions for time limits.)	**11**	
12	Subtract line 11 from line 6 (adjusted sales price)	**12**	
13a	Cost of new home	**13a**	
b	Enter the date you moved into your new main home ▶ ------------------		
14	Subtract line 13a plus line 9 (if applicable) from line 12. If result is zero or less, enter zero. Do not enter more than line 8a or line 10 (if applicable). This is the gain taxable this year. Enter the gain from this line on Schedule D, line 3 or 10*.	**14**	
15	Subtract line 14 from line 8a. **However**, if you completed Part III, subtract line 14 from line 10. (This is the gain to be postponed.)	**15**	
16	Subtract line 15 from line 13 (adjusted basis of new main home)	**16**	

*Caution: If you completed Form 6252 for the home in 1a, do not enter your taxable gain from Form 2119 on Schedule D.

Please Sign Here	Under penalties of perjury, I declare that I have examined this form, including attachments, and to the best of my knowledge and belief, it is true, correct, and complete.
	Your signature _____ Date _____ Spouse's Signature _____ Date _____
	(If joint return, both must sign.) (Sign and date only if not attached to your tax return.)

For Paperwork Reduction Act Notice, see separate Instructions.   Form **2119** (1989)

19**89** 🏛️ Department of the Treasury
Internal Revenue Service

Instructions for Form 2119
Sale of Your Home

(Section references are to the Internal Revenue Code.)

Paperwork Reduction Act Notice.—We ask for this information to carry out the Internal Revenue laws of the United States. We need it to ensure that taxpayers are complying with these laws and to allow us to figure and collect the right amount of tax. You are required to give us this information.

The time needed to complete and file this form will vary depending on individual circumstances. The estimated average time is:

Recordkeeping	46 min.
Learning about the law or the form	10 min.
Preparing the form	42 min.
Copying, assembling, and sending the form to IRS	20 min.

If you have comments concerning the accuracy of these time estimates or suggestions for making this form more simple, we would be happy to hear from you. You can write to the **Internal Revenue Service,** Washington, DC 20224, Attention: IRS Reports Clearance Officer, T:FP; or the **Office of Management and Budget,** Paperwork Reduction Project (1545-0072), Washington, DC 20503.

Who Must File.—You must use Form 2119 to report the sale of your main home even if you had a loss. If you had a gain, use this form to postpone paying tax on it. If you were age 55 or older on the date you sold your home and certain other conditions are met, you can choose to exclude all or part of the gain from your income. See the instructions for Part III.

If you sold your home on the installment method, complete **Form 6252,** Installment Sale Income, and Form 2119.

Get **Pub. 523,** Tax Information on Selling Your Home, for more information.

If your home is damaged by fire, storm, or other casualty, see **Form 4684,** Casualties and Thefts, and its separate Instructions and **Pub. 547,** Nonbusiness Disasters, Casualties, and Thefts.

If your home is condemned for public use, you can choose to postpone gain under the rules for a condemnation, or you can choose to treat the transaction as a sale of your home. For details, get Pub. 523 and **Pub. 549,** Condemnations and Business Casualties and Thefts.

Main Home.—You file Form 2119 only for the sale of your main home. It can be a house, a houseboat, housetrailer, cooperative apartment, condominium, etc. If you have more than one home, your main home is the one you live in most of the time.

Replacement Period for Postponing Gain.—Generally, if you buy or build, and move into another main home within the replacement period, you must postpone paying tax on all or part of the gain. (See instructions for Part IV.) The replacement period is 48 months. It runs from 2 years before to 2 years after you sell your former home.

If at the time or after you sell your former main home, you are on active duty in the U.S. Armed Forces for more than 90 days, or if you live and work outside the U.S., you have a longer replacement period.

When and Where To File.—File Form 2119 with your tax return for the year of sale even if you did not replace your home.

If you plan to replace the home, but have not done so by the time you file your return, complete lines 1 and 2 and Part II only. Do not enter on Schedule D the gain from line 8a of Form 2119. See the following instructions for filing a second Form 2119.

If you had a gain on the sale and did not replace your home by the time you file your tax return, you may have to file a second Form 2119 at a later date. The following tells when another Form 2119 is required and how to file it.

● File a second Form 2119 if, after you file your return, you replace your home within the replacement period.

If the new home costs at least as much as the adjusted sales price of the old home (line 12), no tax is due. But, you must still file the form. Send it to the place you would file your next tax return based on the address where you live. You must enter your name, address, signature, and the date, since the form will not be attached to your return.

If the new home costs less than the adjusted sales price of the old home (line 12), part of your gain will have to be included in income for the year of sale. In this case, amend your tax return for the year of sale using **Form 1040X,** Amended U.S. Individual Income Tax Return. Fill out and attach Form 2119 to Form 1040X, along with Schedule D (Form 1040) showing the gain. Interest will be charged on any additional tax due.

● If, when you filed your return, you had planned to replace your home within the replacement period, but later you did not do so, your entire gain is taxable for the year of sale. Amend your tax return for that year using Form 1040X. Fill out and attach Form 2119 to Form 1040X, along with Schedule D (Form 1040) showing the gain.

● If, when you filed your return, you paid taxes on the gain because you had not planned to replace your residence, but you later did replace it within the replacement period, you can claim a refund for part or all of those taxes. Claim the refund by filing Form 1040X for the year of sale. Attach Form 2119.

Part III—One-Time Exclusion for People Age 55 or Older.—Generally, you can choose to exclude from your income up to $125,000 ($62,500 if married filing a separate return) of the gain from the sale of your main home. (See the instructions for line 9.) You make this choice by answering "Yes" to question 3d in Part I, and by filling in Part III. But, you must meet **all** of the following tests:

1. You or your spouse were age 55 or older on the date of sale.

2. You or your spouse have never excluded gain on the sale of a home after July 26, 1978.

3. The spouse who was age 55 or older owned and lived in the home for periods adding up to at least 3 years within the 5 years ending on the date of sale.

As long as you meet the above tests, you can choose the exclusion for the sale of any main home you wish.

For purposes of test 3, if you were physically or mentally unable to care for yourself, count as time living in your main home any time during the 5-year period that you lived in a facility such as a nursing home. The facility must be one that is licensed by a state or political subdivision to care for people in your condition. For this rule to apply you must have owned and used your residence as your main home for a total of at least one year during the 5-year period.

The gain you exclude is never taxed. But, if the gain is more than the amount you are allowed to exclude, the excess is either included in your income in the year of sale, or it is postponed as explained in Part IV. Generally, you can make or revoke the choice within 3 years from the due date

(including extensions) of your tax return for the year of sale. Use Form 1040X with Form 2119 attached to amend your return.

Married Taxpayers. If you and your spouse own the property jointly and file a joint return, only one of you must meet the age, ownership, and use tests to be able to make the choice. If you do not own the property jointly, the spouse who owns the property must meet these tests.

If you are married at the time of sale, both you and your spouse must agree to exclude the gain. If you do not file a joint return with that spouse, your spouse must agree to exclude the gain by signing a statement saying, "I agree to the Part III election." The statement and signature may be made on a separate piece of paper or in the bottom margin of Form 2119.

If you sell a home while you are married, and one spouse already made an election prior to the marriage, neither of you can exclude gain on the sale.

The choice to exclude gain does not apply separately to you and your spouse. If you choose to exclude gain during marriage and later divorce, neither of you can make the choice again.

Part IV—Postponing Gain.—If you buy or build, and move into another main home within the replacement period, you must usually postpone paying tax on all or part of the gain. If your new home costs at least as much as the adjusted sales price (line 12) of your old home, you must postpone paying tax on the entire gain. If it costs less, in most cases you must postpone paying tax on part of the gain.

If one spouse dies after the old home is sold and before the new home is purchased, the gain from the sale of the old home is postponed if the above requirements are met **and:**

1. The spouses were married on the date of death, **and**

2. The surviving spouse uses the new home as his or her main home.

This rule applies regardless of whether the title of the old home is in one spouse's name or held jointly. Get **Pub. 523** for more information.

If you sell your new home in a later year and do not replace it, the gain on which you postponed the tax will be taxed then. If you do replace it, you must continue to postpone paying tax on the gain. If you bought more than one main home during the replacement period, only the last one you bought qualifies as your new home for postponing the tax.

During the replacement period, any sale after the first one does not qualify for postponing tax, unless you sold the home because of a job change and you qualify for a moving expense deduction. Get **Pub. 521,** Moving Expenses, for details.

Applying Separate Gain to Basis of New Home.—If the old home was owned by only one spouse, but you and your spouse own the new home jointly, you and your spouse may elect to divide the gain and the adjusted basis. If you owned the old home jointly, and you own new homes separately, you may elect to divide the gain to be postponed. In both situations. you both must:

1. Use the old and new homes as your main homes; and

2. Sign a statement that says, "We agree to reduce the basis of the new home(s) by the gain from selling the old home." This statement can be made in the bottom margin of Form 2119 or on an attached sheet. If both of you do not sign, you must figure gain to be taxed in the regular way without allocation.

Line-by-Line Instructions

You may not take double benefits. For example, you cannot use the moving expenses that are part of your moving expense deduction on **Form 3903,** Moving Expenses, to lower the amount of gain on the sale of your old home or to add to the cost of your new home.

Line 1b.—If you report the sale of your home on Form 6252, using the installment method, fill out Form 2119 first. Do not enter the taxable gain from line 8a of Form 2119 on Schedule D (Form 1040).

Line 2b.—If you rent out any rooms, or use part of your home for business for which you take a deduction on your tax return, check "Yes." Report the part of the gain that applies to such use on **Form 4797,** Sales of Business Property, and subtract it from line 8a or line 10 of Form 2119. You cannot postpone tax or take the exclusion on the part of the gain that is reported on Form 4797.

Line 4—Selling Price of Home.—Enter the amount of money you received, plus the amount of all notes, mortgages, or other debts that are part of the sale, and the fair market value of any other property you received.

Note: *Report interest received on a note as income for the tax year in which you received it.*

Line 5—Expense of Sale.—Enter your expense of sale, such as commissions, advertising expenses, attorney and legal fees, you paid in selling the old home. Loan charges, such as points charged the seller, are selling expenses. Do not include fixing-up expenses. Put them on line 11 below.

Line 7—Basis of Home Sold.—Include the original cost of the home, commissions, and other expenses you paid when you bought the home, plus the cost of improvements. Subtract any depreciation, casualty losses, or energy credits you took on your tax return(s), and the postponed gain on the sale or exchange of a previous home. Get **Pub. 551,** Basis of Assets, for details.

If you acquired your home other than by purchase, such as by gift, inheritance, or trade, see Pub. 523 and Pub. 551 to figure the basis.

Line 9—One-Time Exclusions.—Enter the smaller of the gain on line 8a or $125,000 ($62,500 if you are married filing a separate return). However, see Pub. 523 if either of the following is true:

● Before you and your spouse were married, either of you sold a home and was age 55 or older at the time of that sale.

● You are now single but sold a home while you were married, and at the time of sale, you or your spouse was age 55 or older.

Line 11—Fixing-Up Expenses.—These are expenses for decorating and repairing to help sell your old home. Include on line 11 only expenses for work performed within 90 days before the contract to sell was signed **and** that you paid for within 30 days after the sale. Do not include capital expenses for permanent improvements or replacements. These are added to the basis of the property sold.

Line 13—Cost of New Home.—The cost of your new home includes one or more of the following:

(a) cash payments;

(b) the amount of any mortgage or other debt on the new home;

(c) commissions and other purchase expenses you paid that were not deducted as moving expenses;

(d) construction costs made within 2 years before and 2 years after the sale of the old home (when you build your own home, do not include the value of your own labor); and

(e) if you buy rather than build your new home, all capital expenses made within 2 years before and 2 years after the sale of the old home.

Name and Signature.—Enter your name and social security number. You do not need to enter your address or to sign and date Form 2119 if you attach it to your Form 1040 or Form 1040X. But, you must enter your address, sign, and date it if you send it in by itself. If this Form 2119 is for you and your spouse, you both must sign it.

Form **2441**	**Child and Dependent Care Expenses**	OMB No. 1545-0068
Department of the Treasury Internal Revenue Service	▶ **Attach to Form 1040.** ▶ **See separate Instructions.**	19**89** Attachment Sequence No. **23**

Name(s) shown on Form 1040	Your social security number

- If you are claiming the child and dependent care credit, complete Parts I and II below. But if you received employer-provided dependent care benefits, first complete Part III on the back.
- If you are not claiming the credit but you received employer-provided dependent care benefits, only complete Part I, below, and Part III on the back.

Part I   **Persons or Organizations Who Provided the Care—You must complete this part.** (See the Instructions. If you need more space, attach a statement.)

1 **(a)** Name	**(b)** Address (number, street, city, state, and ZIP code)	**(c)** Identification number (SSN or EIN)	**(d)** Amount paid (see Instructions)

2   Add the amounts in column (d) of line 1 and enter the total . . . . | **2** | |

*Note: If you paid cash wages of $50 or more in a calendar quarter to an individual for services performed in your home, you must file an employment tax return. Get **Form 942** for details.*

Part II   **Credit for Child and Dependent Care Expenses**

3   Enter the number of qualifying persons who were cared for in 1989. (See the Instructions for the definition of qualifying persons.) **Caution: To qualify, the person(s) must have shared the same home with you in 1989** . . . . ▶ | **3** | |

4   Enter the amount of **qualified** expenses you incurred and actually paid in 1989. Also see the Instructions if you received employer-provided dependent care benefits. See **What Are Qualified Expenses?** in the Instructions. **Do not enter more than** $2,400 ($4,800 if you paid for the care of two or more qualifying persons) . . . . | **4** | |

5   Enter the **excluded benefits,** if any, from line 21 on page 2 . . . . | **5** | |

6   Subtract line 5 from line 4 and enter the result. If the result is zero or less, stop here; you **cannot** claim the credit . . . . | **6** | |

7   You **must** enter your **earned income.** (See the Instructions for the definition of earned income.) . . | **7** | |

8   If you are married filing a joint return, you **must** enter your spouse's earned income. (If your spouse was a full-time student or disabled, see the Instructions for the amount to enter.) . . . . | **8** | |

9   If you are married filing a joint return, compare the amounts on lines 7 and 8. Enter the **smaller** of the two amounts here . . . . | **9** | |

10   • If you are married filing a joint return, compare the amounts on lines 6 and 9. Enter the **smaller** of the two amounts here.
     • All others, compare the amounts on lines 6 and 7. Enter the **smaller** of the two amounts here. | **10** | |

11   Enter the decimal amount from the table below that applies to the adjusted gross income on Form 1040, line 32 . . . . | **11** | ✕ |

If line 32 is:		Decimal amount is:	If line 32 is:		Decimal amount is:
Over—	But not over—		Over—	But not over—	
$0—10,000		.30	$20,000—22,000		.24
10,000—12,000		.29	22,000—24,000		.23
12,000—14,000		.28	24,000—26,000		.22
14,000—16,000		.27	26,000—28,000		.21
16,000—18,000		.26	28,000		.20
18,000—20,000		.25			

12   Multiply the amount on line 10 by the decimal amount on line 11, and enter the result . . . . . | **12** | |

13   Multiply any child and dependent care expenses for 1988 that you paid in 1989 by the percentage that applies to the adjusted gross income on your 1988 Form 1040, line 32, or Form 1040A, line 14. Enter the result. (You must complete Part I and attach a statement. See the Instructions.) . . . . | **13** | |

14   Add the amounts on lines 12 and 13. See the Instructions for the amount of credit you can claim . . | **14** | |

For Paperwork Reduction Act Notice, see separate Instructions.   Form **2441** (1989)

Form 2441 (1989)   Page **2**

Part III	Employer-Provided Dependent Care Benefits			

Caution: Be sure to also complete Part I on page 1.

15	Enter the total amount of employer-provided dependent care benefits you received for 1989. (This amount should be separately shown on your W-2 forms and labeled as "DCB.") Do **not** include amounts that were reported to you as wages in Box 10 of Form(s) W-2	**15**		
16	Enter the total amount of **qualified** expenses incurred in 1989 for the care of a qualifying person (see the Instructions)	**16**		
17	Compare the amounts on lines 15 and 16. Enter the **smaller** of the two amounts here	**17**		
18	You **must** enter your **earned income.** (See the Instructions for lines 7 and 8 for the definition of earned income.)	**18**		
19	If you were married at the end of 1989, you **must** enter your spouse's earned income. (If your spouse was a full-time student or disabled, see the Instructions for lines 7 and 8 for the amount to enter.) . .	**19**		
20	• If you were married at the end of 1989, compare the amounts on lines 18 and 19 and enter the **smaller** of the two amounts here. • If you were unmarried, enter the amount from line 18 here.	**20**		
21	**Excluded benefits.** Enter here the **smallest** of the following: • The amount from line 17, or • The amount from line 20, or • $5,000 ($2,500 if married filing a separate return).	**21**		
22	**Taxable benefits.** Subtract line 21 from line 15. Enter the result, but not less than zero. Also include this amount in the total on Form 1040, line 7. On the dotted line next to line 7, write "DCB" . . .	**22**		

Note: *If you are also claiming the child and dependent care credit, fill in Form 1040 through line 40. Then complete Part II of this form. Be sure to include any amount shown on line 22 above when figuring your earned income in Part II.*

Form 3903

Department of the Treasury
Internal Revenue Service

Moving Expenses

▶ **Attach to Form 1040.**

▶ **See separate Instructions.**

OMB No. 1545-0062

1989

Attachment
Sequence No. **62**

Name(s) shown on Form 1040

Your social security number

1	Enter the number of miles from your **old** home to your **new** workplace	**1**
2	Enter the number of miles from your **old** home to your **old** workplace	**2**
3	Subtract line **2** from line **1**. Enter the result (but not less than zero) . . . . ▶	**3**

If line **3** is 35 or more miles, complete the rest of this form. If line **3** is less than 35 miles, you may not take a deduction for moving expenses. This rule does not apply to members of the armed forces.

Part I   Moving Expenses

Section A.—Transportation of Household Goods

4 Transportation and storage for household goods and personal effects **4**

Section B.—Expenses of Moving From Old To New Home

5 Travel and lodging **not** including meals **5**

6 Total meals **6**

7 Multiply line 6 by 80% (.80) **7**

8 Add lines 5 and 7 . . . .   **8**

Section C.—Pre-move Househunting Expenses

9 Travel and lodging **not** including meals **9**

10 Total meals **10**

11 Multiply line 10 by 80% (.80) **11**

12 Add lines 9 and 11. . . . .   **12**

Section D.—Temporary Quarters (for any 30 days in a row after getting your job)

13 Lodging expenses **not** including meals **13**

14 Total meals **14**

15 Multiply line 14 by 80% (.80) **15**

16 Add lines 13 and 15 . . . .   **16**

Section E.—Qualified Real Estate Expenses

17 Expenses of (check one): **a** ☐ selling or exchanging your old home; or
                    b ☐ if renting, settling an unexpired lease **17**

18 Expenses of (check one): **a** ☐ buying your new home, or
                    b ☐ if renting, getting a new lease **18**

Part II   Dollar Limitations

19 Add lines 12 and 16 . . . .   **19**

20 Enter the **smaller** of line 19 or $1,500 ($750 if married filing a separate return, and at the end of 1989 you lived with your spouse who also started work during 1989) **20**

21 Add lines 17, 18, and 20 . . . .   **21**

22 Enter the **smaller** of line 21 or $3,000 ($1,500 if married filing a separate return, and at the end of 1989 you lived with your spouse who also started work during 1989) **22**

23 Add lines 4, 8, and 22. This is your moving expense deduction. **Enter here and on Schedule A (Form 1040), line 19.** (Note: *Any payments your employer made for any part of your move (including the value of any services furnished in kind) should be included on Form W-2. Report that amount on **Form 1040, line 7.** See **Reimbursements** in the Instructions.*) . . . . ▶   **23**

For Paperwork Reduction Act Notice, see separate Instructions.

Form **3903** (1989)

Form **4562**	**Depreciation and Amortization**	OMB No. 1545-0172
Department of the Treasury Internal Revenue Service	▶ See separate instructions. ▶ Attach this form to your return.	**1989** Attachment Sequence No. **67**

Name(s) as shown on return	Identifying number

Business or activity to which this form relates

Part I **Depreciation** *(Use Part III for automobiles, certain other vehicles, computers, and property used for entertainment, recreation, or amusement.)*

Section A.—Election To Expense Depreciable Assets (Section 179)

1 Maximum dollar limitation	**1**		$10,000
2 Total cost of section 179 property placed in service during the tax year (see instructions)	**2**		
3 Threshold cost of section 179 property before reduction in limitation	**3**		$200,000
4 Reduction in limitation (Subtract line 3 from line 2, but do not enter less than -0-.)	**4**		
5 Dollar limitation for tax year (Subtract line 4 from line 1, but do not enter less than -0-.)	**5**		

(a) Description of property	(b) Date placed in service	(c) Cost	(d) Elected cost
6			

7 Listed property—Enter amount from line 28	**7**	
8 Tentative deduction (Enter the lesser of: (a) line 6 plus line 7; or (b) line 5.)	**8**	
9 Taxable income limitation (Enter the lesser of :(a) Taxable income; or (b) line 5) (see instructions) . .	**9**	
10 Carryover of disallowed deduction from 1988 (see instructions)	**10**	
11 Section 179 expense deduction (Enter the lesser of: (a) line 8 plus line 10; or (b) line 9.)	**11**	
12 Carryover of disallowed deduction to 1990 (Add lines 8 and 10, less line 11.) . . ▶ **12**		

Section B.—MACRS Depreciation

(a) Classification of property	(b) Date placed in service	(c) Basis for depreciation (Business use only—see instructions)	(d) Recovery period	(e) Convention	(f) Method	(g) Depreciation deduction
13 General Depreciation System (GDS) (see instructions): *For assets placed in service ONLY during tax year beginning in 1989*						
a 3-year property						
b 5-year property						
c 7-year property						
d 10-year property						
e 15-year property						
f 20-year property						
g Residential rental property			27.5 yrs.	MM	S/L	
			27.5 yrs.	MM	S/L	
h Nonresidential real property			31.5 yrs.	MM	S/L	
			31.5 yrs.	MM	S/L	
14 Alternative Depreciation System (ADS) (see instructions): *For assets placed in service ONLY during tax year beginning in 1989*						
a Class life					S/L	
b 12-year			12 yrs.		S/L	
c 40-year			40 yrs.	MM	S/L	

15 Listed property—Enter amount from line 27	**15**	
16 GDS and ADS deductions for assets placed in service before 1989 (see instructions)	**16**	

Section C.—ACRS and/or Other Depreciation

17 Property subject to section 168(f)(1) election (see instructions)	**17**	
18 ACRS and/or other depreciation (see instructions)	**18**	

Section D.—Summary

19 Total (Add deductions on line 11 and lines 13 through 18.) Enter here and on the appropriate line of your return (Partnerships and S corporations—see instructions.)	**19**	
20 For assets shown above and placed in service during the current year, enter the portion of the basis attributable to section 263A costs (see instructions). . . . . ▶ **20**		

For Paperwork Reduction Act Notice, see page 1 of the separate instructions.   Form **4562** (1989)

Form 4562 (1989)   Page **2**

Part II   **Amortization**

(a) Description of property	(b) Date amortization begins	(c) Cost or other basis	(d) Code section	(e) Amortization period or percentage	(f) Amortization for this year
21 Amortization for property placed in service **only** during tax year beginning in 1989			/////	/////	/////

22 Amortization for property placed in service before 1989	**22**	
23 Total. Enter here and on "Other Deductions" or "Other Expenses" line of your return	**23**	

Part III   **Listed Property.—Automobiles, Certain Other Vehicles, Computers, and Property Used for Entertainment, Recreation, or Amusement**

If you are using the standard mileage rate or deducting vehicle lease expense, complete columns (a) through (d) of Section A, all of Section B, and Section C if applicable.

Section A.—Depreciation   (Caution: *See instructions for limitations for automobiles.*)

24a Do you have evidence to support the business use claimed? ☐ **Yes** ☐ **No**   **24b** If "Yes," is the evidence written? ☐ **Yes** ☐ **No**

(a) Type of property (list vehicles first)	(b) Date placed in service	(c) Business use percentage (%)	(d) Cost or other basis (see instructions for leased property)	(e) Basis for depreciation — business use only	(f) Recovery period	(g) Method	(h) Depreciation deduction	(i) Elected section 179 cost
25 *Property used more than 50% in a trade or business:*								
26 *Property used 50% or less in a trade or business:*								
						S/L		/////
						S/L		/////
						S/L		/////

27 Total (Enter here and on line 15, page 1.)	**27**	/////
28 Total (Enter here and on line 7, page 1.)	**28**	

Section B.—Information Regarding Use of Vehicles—*If you deduct expenses for vehicles:*
- *Always complete this section for vehicles used by a sole proprietor, partner, or other "more than 5% owner," or related person.*
- *If you provided vehicles to your employees, first answer the questions in Section C to see if you meet an exception to completing this section for those vehicles.*

	(a) Vehicle 1		(b) Vehicle 2		(c) Vehicle 3		(d) Vehicle 4		(e) Vehicle 5		(f) Vehicle 6	
29 Total business miles driven during the year (DO NOT include commuting miles) . .												
30 Total commuting miles driven during the year												
31 Total other personal (noncommuting) miles driven												
32 Total miles driven during the year (Add lines 29 through 31)												
	Yes	No	Yes	No	Yes	No	Yes	No	Yes	No	Yes	No
33 Was the vehicle available for personal use during off-duty hours?												
34 Was the vehicle used primarily by a more than 5% owner or related person? . . .												
35 Is another vehicle available for personal use?												

Section C.—Questions for Employers Who Provide Vehicles for Use by Their Employees
(Answer these questions to determine if you meet an exception to completing Section B. Note: Section B must always be completed for vehicles used by sole proprietors, partners, or other more than 5% owners or related persons.)

	Yes	No
36 Do you maintain a written policy statement that prohibits all personal use of vehicles, including commuting, by your employees?		
37 Do you maintain a written policy statement that prohibits personal use of vehicles, except commuting, by your employees? (See instructions for vehicles used by corporate officers, directors, or 1% or more owners.)		
38 Do you treat all use of vehicles by employees as personal use?		
39 Do you provide more than five vehicles to your employees and retain the information received from your employees concerning the use of the vehicles?.		
40 Do you meet the requirements concerning qualified automobile demonstration use (see instructions)?		/////

Note: *If your answer to 36, 37, 38, 39, or 40 is "Yes," you need not complete Section B for the covered vehicles.*

Form **4626**	**Alternative Minimum Tax—Corporations**	OMB No. 1545-0175
Department of the Treasury Internal Revenue Service	**(including environmental tax)** ▶ **See separate instructions.** ▶ **Attach to your tax return.**	**1989**

Name as shown on tax return	Employer identification number

1	Taxable income or (loss) before net operating loss deduction	**1**	
2	**Adjustments:**		
a	Depreciation of tangible property placed in service after 1986	**2a**	
b	Amortization of certified pollution control facilities placed in service after 1986 . . .	**2b**	
c	Amortization of mining exploration and development costs paid or incurred after 1986	**2c**	
d	Amortization of circulation expenditures paid or incurred after 1986 (personal holding companies only)	**2d**	
e	Basis adjustments in determining gain or loss from sale or exchange of property . . .	**2e**	
f	Long-term contracts entered into after February 28, 1986	**2f**	
g	Installment sales of certain property	**2g**	
h	Merchant marine capital construction funds	**2h**	
i	Section 833(b) deduction (Blue Cross, Blue Shield, and similar type organizations only)	**2i**	
j	Tax shelter farm activities (personal service corporations only)	**2j**	
k	Passive activities (closely held corporations and personal service corporations only) .	**2k**	
l	Certain loss limitations	**2l**	
m	Other	**2m**	
n	Combine lines 2a through 2m		**2n**	
3	**Tax preference items:**		
a	Depletion	**3a**	
b	Tax-exempt interest from private activity bonds issued after August 7, 1986	**3b**	
c	Appreciated property charitable deduction	**3c**	
d	Add lines 3a through 3c		**3d**	
e	Intangible drilling costs	**3e**	
f	Reserves for losses on bad debts of financial institutions	**3f**	
g	Accelerated depreciation of real property placed in service before 1987	**3g**	
h	Accelerated depreciation of leased personal property placed in service before 1987 (personal holding companies only)	**3h**	
i	Amortization of certified pollution control facilities placed in service before 1987 . .	**3i**	
j	Add lines 3e through 3i		**3j**	
4	Combine lines 1, 2n, 3d, and 3j		**4**	
5	**Excess book income adjustment:**		
a	Enter your adjusted net book income	**5a**	
b	Subtract line 4 from line 5a (even if one or both of these figures is a negative number). (Enter zero if the result is zero or less)	**5b**	
c	Multiply line 5b by 50%		**5c**	
6	Combine lines 4 and 5c. If zero or less, stop here (you are not subject to the alternative minimum tax) . . .	**6**	
7	Alternative tax net operating loss deduction. (Do not enter more than 90% of line 6.)	**7**	
8	Alternative minimum taxable income (subtract line 7 from line 6)	**8**	
9	**Exemption phase-out computation:**		
a	Tentative exemption amount. Enter $40,000 (members of a controlled group, see instructions)	**9a**	
b	Enter $150,000 (members of a controlled group, see instructions)	**9b**	
c	Subtract line 9b from line 8. If zero or less, enter zero	**9c**	
d	Multiply line 9c by 25%	**9d**	
e	Exemption. Subtract line 9d from line 9a. If zero or less, enter zero		**9e**	
10	Subtract line 9e from line 8. If zero or less, enter zero		**10**	
11	Multiply line 10 by 20%		**11**	
12	Alternative minimum tax foreign tax credit		**12**	
13	Tentative minimum tax (subtract line 12 from line 11)		**13**	
14	General business credit allowed against alternative minimum tax (see instructions) . . .		**14**	
15	Regular tax liability before all credits except the foreign tax credit and possessions tax credit		**15**	
16	**Alternative minimum tax**—Add lines 14 and 15 and subtract the total from line 13. If the result is greater than zero, enter on line 9a, Schedule J, Form 1120, or on the comparable line of other income tax returns .		**16**	
17	**Environmental tax**—Subtract $2,000,000 from line 6 (computed without regard to your environmental tax deduction), and multiply the result, if any, by 0.12% (.0012). Enter on line 9b, Schedule J, Form 1120, or on the comparable line of other income tax returns (members of a controlled group, see instructions) . . .		**17**	

For Paperwork Reduction Act Notice, see separate instructions.   Form **4626** (1989)

Form **4684**	**Casualties and Thefts**	OMB No. 1545-0177

Form **4684**

Department of the Treasury
Internal Revenue Service

► See separate Instructions.
► To be filed with Form 1040, 1041, 1065, 1120, etc.
Use a separate Form 4684 for each different casualty or theft.

19**89**

Attachment Sequence No. **26**

Name(s) shown on tax return

Identifying number

SECTION A.—Personal Use Property *(Casualties and thefts to property **not** used in a trade or business or for income-producing purposes.)*

1 Description of Properties (Show kind, location, and date of purchase for each.)

Property A ....
Property B ....
Property C ....
Property D ....

	Properties (Use a separate column for each property lost or damaged from one casualty or theft.)			
	A	B	C	D
2 Cost or other basis of each property				
3 Insurance or other reimbursement (whether or not you submit a claim). See Instructions				
Note: *If line 2 is **more** than line 3, skip line 4.*				
4 Gain from casualty or theft. If line 3 is **more** than line 2, enter the difference here and skip lines 5 through 13				
5 Fair market value before casualty or theft . .				
6 Fair market value after casualty or theft . . .				
7 Subtract line 6 from line 5				
8 Enter the **smaller** of line 2 or line 7				
9 Subtract line 3 from line 8				

10 Casualty or theft loss. Add amounts from line 9 for all columns . . . .

11 Enter the amount from line 10 or $100, whichever is **smaller**. . . . .

12 Subtract line 11 from line 10 . . . .

Caution: *Use only one Form 4684 for lines 13 through 18.*

13 Add the line 12 amounts from all Forms 4684, Section A . . . .

14 Add the line 4 amounts from all Forms 4684, Section A . . . .

15 If line 14 is **more** than line 13, enter the difference here and on Schedule D. Do not complete the rest of the form. (See Instructions.) Otherwise, enter zero and complete lines 16 through 18. If line 14 is **equal** to line 13, do not complete the rest of the form . . . .

16 If line 13 is **more** than line 14, enter the difference . . . .

17 Enter 10% of your adjusted gross income (Form 1040, line 31). Estates and trusts, see Instructions . . . . .

18 Subtract line 17 from line 16. If zero or less, enter zero. Enter on Schedule A (Form 1040), line 18. Estates and trusts, enter on the "other deductions" line of your tax return . . . .

For Paperwork Reduction Act Notice, see page 1 of separate Instructions.

Form **4684** (1989)

Form 4684 (1989)   **26**   Page **2**

Name(s) shown on tax return (Do not enter name and identifying number if shown on other side.) | Identifying number

SECTION B.—Business and Income-Producing Property *(Note: If from a passive activity, see Instructions.)*
(Casualties and thefts to property used in a trade or business or for income-producing purposes.)

Part I   Casualty or Theft Gain or Loss (Use a separate Part I for each different casualty or theft.)

1   Description of Properties (Show kind, location, and date of purchase for each.)
    Property A ....
    Property B ....
    Property C ....
    Property D ....

	Properties (Use a separate column for each property lost or damaged from one casualty or theft.)			
	A	B	C	D
2 Cost or adjusted basis of each property				
3 Insurance or other reimbursement (whether or not you submit a claim). See Instructions				
Note: *If line 2 is **more** than line 3, skip line 4.*				
4 Gain from casualty or theft. If line 3 is **more** than line 2, enter the difference here and on line 11 or 16, column (c). However, see Instructions for line 15. Also, skip lines 5 through 10				
5 Fair market value **before** casualty or theft . . .				
6 Fair market value **after** casualty or theft . . .				
7 Subtract line 6 from line 5				
8 Enter the **smaller** of line 2 or line 7				
Note: *If the property was totally destroyed by casualty, or lost from theft, enter on line 8, in each column, the amount from line 2.*				
9 Subtract line 3 from line 8				

10   Casualty or theft loss. Add amounts from line 9 for all columns. Enter here and on line 11 **or** 16 . . . .

Part II   Summary of Gains and Losses (From separate Parts I)

(a) Identify casualty or theft	(b) Losses from casualties or thefts		(c) Gains from casualties or thefts includible in income
	(i) Trade, business, rental or royalty property	(ii) Income-producing property	
Casualty or Theft of Property Held One Year or Less			
11			
12 Totals. Add amounts on line 11 for each column			

13   Combine line 12, columns (b)(i) and (c). Enter the net gain or (loss) here and on Form 4797, Part II, line 14. (If Form 4797 is not otherwise required, see Instructions.) . . . .

14   Enter the amount from line 12, column (b)(ii) here and on Schedule A (Form 1040), line 21. Partnerships, S corporations, estates and trusts, see Instructions . . . .

Casualty or Theft of Property Held More Than One Year			
15 Casualty or theft gains from Form 4797, Part III, line 32			
16			
17 Total losses. Add amounts on line 16, columns (b)(i) and (b)(ii) . . .			/////////

18   Total gains. Add lines 15 and 16, column (c) . . . .

19   Add amounts on line 17, columns (b)(i) and (b)(ii) . . . .

    Partnerships, enter the amount from line 20 or line 21 on your Schedule K-1, line 7. S corporations, enter the amount from line 20 on your Schedule K-1, line 6.

20   If the loss on line 19 is **more** than the gain on line 18:

    a   Combine line 17, column (b)(i) and line 18. Enter the net gain or (loss) here and on Form 4797, Part II, line 14. (If Form 4797 is not otherwise required, see Instructions.) . . . .

    b   Enter the amount from line 17, column (b)(ii) here and on Schedule A (Form 1040), line 21. Estates and trusts, enter on the "other deductions" line of your tax return . . . .

21   If the loss on line 19 is **equal** to or **smaller** than the gain on line 18, combine these lines and enter here and on Form 4797, Part I, line 3 . . . .

Form **4797**

Department of the Treasury
Internal Revenue Service

Sales of Business Property

(Also, Involuntary Conversions and Recapture Amounts Under
Sections 179 and 280F)

▶ **Attach to your tax return. See separate Instructions.**

OMB No. 1545-0184

19**89**

Attachment
Sequence No. **27**

Name(s) shown on return	Identifying number

Part I **Sales or Exchanges of Property Used in a Trade or Business and Involuntary Conversions From Other Than Casualty and Theft—Property Held More Than 1 Year**

1 Enter here the gross proceeds from the sale or exchange of real estate reported to you for 1989 on Form(s) 1099-S (or an equivalent statement) that you will be including on lines 2 or 10 (column d), or on line 20. (Form 1099-S is a Statement for Recipients of Proceeds From Real Estate Transactions.) **1**

(a) Description of property	**(b)** Date acquired (mo., day, yr.)	**(c)** Date sold (mo., day, yr.)	**(d)** Gross sales price	**(e)** Depreciation allowed (or allowable) since acquisition	**(f)** Cost or other basis, plus improvements and expense of sale	**(g)** LOSS ((f) minus the sum of (d) and (e))	**(h)** GAIN ((d) plus (e) minus (f))
2							

3 Gain; if any, from Form 4684, Section B, line 21 . . . .

4 Section 1231 gain from installment sales from Form 6252, line 22 or 30 . . . .

5 Gain, if any, from line 32, from other than casualty and theft . . . .

6 Add lines 2 through 5 in columns (g) and (h) . . . . ( )

7 Combine columns (g) and (h) of line 6. Enter gain or (loss) here, and on the appropriate line as follows (partnerships see the Instructions for line references):

If line 7 is zero or a loss, enter the amount on line 11 below and skip lines 8 and 9. (S corporations enter the loss on Schedule K (Form 1120S), line 5.) If line 7 is a gain and you did not have any prior year section 1231 losses, or they were recaptured in an earlier year, enter the gain as a long-term capital gain on Schedule D and skip lines 8, 9, and 12 below.

8 Nonrecaptured net section 1231 losses from prior years (see Instructions) . . . .

9 Subtract line 8 from line 7. If zero or less, enter zero . . . .

If line 9 is zero, enter the amount from line 7 on line 12 below. If line 9 is more than zero, enter the amount from line 8 on line 12 below, and enter the amount from line 9 as a long-term capital gain on Schedule D. See Line-by-Line Instructions for line 9.

Part II **Ordinary Gains and Losses**

(a) Description of property	**(b)** Date acquired (mo., day, yr.)	**(c)** Date sold (mo., day, yr.)	**(d)** Gross sales price	**(e)** Depreciation allowed (or allowable) since acquisition	**(f)** Cost or other basis, plus improvements and expense of sale	**(g)** LOSS ((f) minus the sum of (d) and (e))	**(h)** GAIN ((d) plus (e) minus (f))
10 Ordinary gains and losses not included on lines 11 through 16 (include property held 1 year or less):							

11 Loss, if any, from line 7 . . . .

12 Gain, if any, from line 7, or amount from line 8 if applicable . . . .

13 Gain, if any, from line 31 . . . .

14 Net gain or (loss) from Form 4684, Section B, lines 13 and 20a . . . .

15 Ordinary gain from installment sales from Form 6252, line(s) 21 and/or 29 . . . .

16 Recapture of section 179 deduction for partners and S corporation shareholders from property dispositions by partnerships and S corporations (see Instructions) . . . .

17 Add lines 10 through 16 in columns (g) and (h) . . . . ( )

18 Combine columns (g) and (h) of line 17. Enter gain or (loss) here, and on the appropriate line as follows: . . . .
 a For all except individual returns: Enter the gain or (loss) from line 18 on the return being filed.
 b For individual returns:
  (1) If the loss on line 11 includes a loss from Form 4684, Section B, Part II, column (b)(ii), enter that part of the loss here and on line 21 of Schedule A (Form 1040). Identify as from "Form 4797, line 18b(1)" . . . .
  (2) Redetermine the gain or (loss) on line 18, excluding the loss (if any) on line 18b(1). Enter here and on Form 1040, line 15

For Paperwork Reduction Act Notice, see page 1 of separate Instructions.

Form **4797** (1989)

Form 4797 (1989)   Page **2**

Part III	**Gain From Disposition of Property Under Sections 1245, 1250, 1252, 1254, and 1255**		

19	Description of sections 1245, 1250, 1252, 1254, and 1255 property:	Date acquired (mo., day, yr.)	Date sold (mo., day, yr.)
A			
B			
C			
D			

Relate lines 19A through 19D to these columns ▶	Property A	Property B	Property C	Property D
20 Gross sales price				
21 Cost or other basis plus expense of sale				
22 Depreciation (or depletion) allowed (or allowable)				
23 Adjusted basis, subtract line 22 from line 21				
24 Total gain, subtract line 23 from line 20				
25 If section 1245 property:				
a Depreciation allowed (or allowable) (see Instructions)				
b Enter the **smaller** of line 24 or 25a				
26 If section 1250 property: If straight line depreciation was used, enter zero on line 26g unless you are a corporation subject to section 291.				
a Additional depreciation after 12/31/75				
b Applicable percentage multiplied by the **smaller** of line 24 or line 26a (see Instructions)				
c Subtract line 26a from line 24. If line 24 is not more than line 26a, skip lines 26d and 26e				
d Additional depreciation after 12/31/69 and before 1/1/76				
e Applicable percentage multiplied by the **smaller** of line 26c or 26d (see Instructions)				
f Section 291 amount (for corporations only)				
g Add lines 26b, 26e, and 26f				
27 If section 1252 property: Skip this section if you did not dispose of farmland or if you are a partnership.				
a Soil, water, and land clearing expenses				
b Line 27a multiplied by applicable percentage (see Instructions)				
c Enter the **smaller** of line 24 or 27b				
28 If section 1254 property:				
a Intangible drilling and development costs, expenditures for development of mines and other natural deposits, and mining exploration costs (see Instructions)				
b Enter the **smaller** of line 24 or 28a				
29 If section 1255 property:				
a Applicable percentage of payments excluded from income under section 126 (see Instructions)				
b Enter the **smaller** of line 24 or 29a				

Summary of Part III Gains (Complete property columns A through D, through line 29b before going to line 30.)

30 Total gains for all properties (add columns A through D, line 24)	
31 Add columns A through D, lines 25b, 26g, 27c, 28b, and 29b. Enter here and on line 13. (see the Instructions for Part IV if this is an installment sale)	
32 Subtract line 31 from line 30. Enter the portion from casualty and theft on Form 4684, Section B, line 15. Enter the portion from other than casualty and theft on Form 4797, line 5	

Part IV	**Complete This Part Only if You Elect Out of the Installment Method and Report a Note or Other Obligation at Less Than Full Face Value**

33 Check here if you elect out of the installment method ▶ ☐	
34 Enter the face amount of the note or other obligation ▶	
35 Enter the percentage of valuation of the note or other obligation ▶	

Part V	**Computation of Recapture Amounts Under Sections 179 and 280F When Business Use Drops to 50% or Less** (See Instructions for Part V.)

	(a) Section 179	**(b) Section 280F**
36 Section 179 expense deduction or section 280F recovery deductions		
37 Depreciation or recovery deductions (see Instructions)		
38 Recapture amount (subtract line 37 from line 36) (see Instructions for where to report)		

Form **6251**

Department of the Treasury
Internal Revenue Service

Alternative Minimum Tax—Individuals

▶ See separate Instructions.
▶ Attach to Form 1040 or Form 1040NR. Estates and trusts, use Form 8656.

OMB No. 1545-0227

1989

Attachment Sequence No. **32**

Name(s) shown on Form 1040

Your social security number

1 Taxable income from Form 1040, line 37 (can be less than zero)	**1**	
2 Net operating loss deduction, if any, from Form 1040, line 22. (Enter as a positive amount.)	**2**	
3 Add lines 1 and 2	**3**	
4 **Adjustments:** (See Instructions before completing.)		
a Standard deduction, if applicable, from Form 1040, line 34	**4a**	
b Personal exemption amount from Form 1040, line 36	**4b**	
c Medical and dental expense	**4c**	
d Miscellaneous itemized deductions from Schedule A (Form 1040), line 24 .	**4d**	
e Taxes from Schedule A (Form 1040), line 8	**4e**	
f Refund of taxes	**4f** ( )	
g Personal interest from Schedule A (Form 1040), line 12b	**4g**	
h Other interest adjustments	**4h**	
i Combine lines 4a through 4h	**4i**	
j Depreciation of property placed in service after 1986	**4j**	
k Circulation and research and experimental expenditures paid or incurred after 1986	**4k**	
l Mining exploration and development costs paid or incurred after 1986 . . .	**4l**	
m Long-term contracts entered into after 2/28/86	**4m**	
n Pollution control facilities placed in service after 1986	**4n**	
o Installment sales of certain property	**4o**	
p Adjusted gain or loss	**4p**	
q Certain loss limitations	**4q**	
r Tax shelter farm loss	**4r**	
s Passive activity loss	**4s**	
t Beneficiaries of estates and trusts	**4t**	
u Combine lines 4j through 4t	**4u**	
5 **Tax preference items:** (See Instructions before completing.)		
a Appreciated property charitable deduction	**5a**	
b Tax-exempt interest from private activity bonds issued after 8/7/86 . . .	**5b**	
c Depletion	**5c**	
d Add lines 5a through 5c	**5d**	
e Accelerated depreciation of real property placed in service before 1987 . .	**5e**	
f Accelerated depreciation of leased personal property placed in service before 1987	**5f**	
g Amortization of certified pollution control facilities placed in service before 1987	**5g**	
h Intangible drilling costs	**5h**	
i Add lines 5e through 5h	**5i**	
6 Combine lines 3, 4i, 4u, 5d, and 5i	**6**	
7 Alternative tax net operating loss deduction. (Do not enter more than 90% of line 6.) See Instructions. .	**7**	
8 Alternative minimum taxable income (subtract line 7 from line 6). If married filing a separate return, see Instructions.	**8**	
9 Enter: $40,000 ($20,000 if married filing separately; $30,000 if single or head of household) . . .	**9**	
10 Enter: $150,000 ($75,000 if married filing separately; $112,500 if single or head of household) . . .	**10**	
11 Subtract line 10 from line 8. If the result is -0- or less, enter -0- here and on line 12 and go to line 13 . .	**11**	
12 Multiply line 11 by 25% (.25)	**12**	
13 Subtract line 12 from line 9. If the result is -0- or less, enter -0-. If completing this form for a child under age 14, see the Instructions for the amount to enter on this line	**13**	
14 Subtract line 13 from line 8. If the result is -0- or less, enter -0- here and on line 19	**14**	
15 Multiply line 14 by 21% (.21)	**15**	
16 Alternative minimum tax foreign tax credit. See Instructions	**16**	
17 Tentative minimum tax (subtract line 16 from line 15)	**17**	
18 Enter your tax from Form 1040, **line 38**, minus any foreign tax credit on Form 1040, line 43. If an amount is entered on line 39 of **Form 1040**, see Instructions	**18**	
19 **Alternative minimum tax** (subtract line 18 from line 17). Enter on Form 1040, line 49. If the result is -0- or less, enter -0-. If completing this **form** for a child under age 14, see the Instructions for the amount to enter .	**19**	

For Paperwork Reduction Act Notice, see separate Instructions.

Form **6251** (1989)

Form **8582**	**Passive Activity Loss Limitations**	OMB No. 1545-1008
Department of the Treasury Internal Revenue Service	▶ See separate Instructions. ▶ Attach to Form 1040 or Form 1041.	**1989** Attachment Sequence No. **88**

Name(s) shown on return	Identifying number

Part I **Computation of 1989 Passive Activity Loss**

Caution: See the Instructions for Worksheets 1 and 2 on pages 6 and 7 before completing Part I.

Rental Real Estate Activities With Active Participation (For the definition of active participation see **Active Participation in a Rental Real Estate Activity** in the Instructions.)

Activities acquired before 10-23-86 (Pre-enactment):

1a Activities with net income (from Worksheet 1, Part 1, column (a)) **1a**
1b Activities with net loss (from Worksheet 1, Part 1, column (b)) **1b**
1c Combine lines 1a and 1b **1c**

Activities acquired after 10-22-86 (Post-enactment):

1d Activities with net income (from Worksheet 1, Part 2, column (a)) **1d**
1e Activities with net loss (from Worksheet 1, Part 2, column (b)) **1e**
1f Combine lines 1d and 1e **1f**
1g Net income or (loss). Combine lines 1c and 1f. **1g**
1h Prior year unallowed losses (from Worksheet 1, Parts 1 and 2, column (c)) **1h**
1i Combine lines 1g and 1h **1i**

All Other Passive Activities

Activities acquired before 10-23-86 (Pre-enactment):

2a Activities with net income (from Worksheet 2, Part 1, column (a)) **2a**
2b Activities with net loss (from Worksheet 2, Part 1, column (b)) **2b**
2c Combine lines 2a and 2b **2c**

Activities acquired after 10-22-86 (Post-enactment):

2d Activities with net income (from Worksheet 2, Part 2, column (a)) **2d**
2e Activities with net loss (from Worksheet 2, Part 2, column (b)) **2e**
2f Combine lines 2d and 2e **2f**
2g Net income or (loss). Combine lines 2c and 2f **2g**
2h Prior year unallowed losses (from Worksheet 2, Parts 1 and 2, column (c)) **2h**
2i Combine lines 2g and 2h **2i**

3 Combine lines 1i and 2i. If the result is net income or -0-, see the Instructions for line 3. If this line and line 1c or line 1i are losses, go to line 4. Otherwise, enter -0- on lines 8 and 9 and go to line 10 **3**

Part II **Computation of the Special Allowance for Rental Real Estate With Active Participation**

Note: Treat all numbers entered in Parts II and III as positive amounts. (See Instructions on page 7 for examples.)

4 Enter the **smaller** of the loss on line 1i or the loss on line 3. If line 1i is -0- or net income, enter -0- and complete lines 5 through 9 **4**
5 Enter $150,000. If married filing separately, see the Instructions **5**
6 Enter modified adjusted gross income, but not less than -0- (see Instructions) **6**

Note: If line 6 is equal to or greater than line 5, skip line 7, enter -0-on lines 8 and 9, and then go to line 10. Otherwise, go to line 7.

7 Subtract line 6 from line 5 **7**
8 Multiply line 7 by 50% (.5). **Do not** enter more than $25,000. If married filing separately, see Instructions **8**
9 Enter the **smaller** of line 4 or line 8 **9**

Part III **Computation of Passive Activity Loss Allowed**

10 Combine lines 1c and 2c. If the result is net income or -0-, skip to line 16. (See Instructions.) **10**
11 If line 1c shows income, has no entry, or shows -0-, enter -0-. Otherwise, enter the **smaller** of line 1c or line 8 **11**
12 Subtract line 11 from line 10. If line 11 is equal to or greater than line 10, enter -0-. **12**
13 Subtract line 9 from line 3 **13**
14 Enter the **smaller** of line 12 or line 13 **14**
15 Multiply line 14 by 20% (.2) and enter the result **15**
16 Enter the amount from line 9 **16**
17 **Passive activity loss allowed for 1989.** Add lines 15 and 16 **17**
18 Add the income, if any, on lines 1a, 1d, 2a, and 2d and enter the total **18**
19 **Total losses allowed from all passive activities for 1989.** Add lines 17 and 18. See the Instructions to find out how to report the losses on your tax return **19**

For Paperwork Reduction Act Notice, see separate Instructions.   Form **8582** (1989)

Form 8615

Department of the Treasury
Internal Revenue Service

Computation of Tax for Children Under Age 14 Who Have Investment Income of More Than $1,000

▶ See instructions below and on back.
▶ Attach ONLY to the Child's Form 1040, Form 1040A, or Form 1040NR.

OMB No. 1545-0998

1989

Attachment
Sequence No. **33**

General Instructions

Purpose of Form. For children under age 14, investment income (such as taxable interest and dividends) over $1,000 is taxed at the parent's rate if the parent's rate is higher than the child's rate.

Do not use this form if the child's investment income is $1,000 or less. Instead, figure the tax in the normal manner on the child's income tax return. For example, if the child had $900 of taxable interest income and $200 of wages, Form 8615 is not required to be completed and the child's tax should be figured on Form 1040A using the Tax Table.

If the child's investment income is more than $1,000, use this form to see if any of the child's investment income is taxed at the parent's rate and, if so, to figure the

child's tax. For example, if the child had $1,100 of taxable interest income and $200 of wages, complete Form 8615 and attach it to the child's Form 1040A.

Investment Income. As used on this form, "investment income" includes all taxable income other than earned income as defined on page 2. It includes income such as taxable interest, dividends, capital gains, rents, royalties, etc. It also includes pension and annuity income and income (other than earned income) received as the beneficiary of a trust.

Who Must File. Generally, Form 8615 must be filed for any child who was under age 14 on January 1, 1990, and who had more than $1,000 of investment income. If neither parent was alive on December 31,

1989, do not use Form 8615. Instead, figure the child's tax based on his or her own rate.

Note: *Beginning in 1989, the parent may be able to elect to report the child's investment income on his or her return. If the parent makes this election, the child will not have to file a return or Form 8615. For more details, see the instructions for Form 1040 or Form 1040A, or get **Form 8814**, Parent's Election To Report Child's Interest and Dividends.*

Additional Information. For more information about the tax on investment income of children, please get **Pub. 929**, Tax Rules for Children and Dependents.

(Instructions continue on back.)

Child's name shown on return

Child's social security number

Parent's name (first, initial, and last). (**Caution:** See instructions on back before completing.)

Parent's social security number

Parent's filing status (check one): ☐ Single, ☐ Married filing jointly, ☐ Married filing separately, ☐ Head of household, or ☐ Qualifying widow(er)

Enter number of exemptions claimed on parent's return ▶ . . . . ☐

	Step 1	Figure child's net investment income		
1	Enter the child's investment income, such as taxable interest and dividend income (see the instructions). (If this amount is $1,000 or less, stop here; do not file this form.)	**1**		
2	If the child DID NOT itemize deductions on Schedule A (Form 1040 or Form 1040NR), enter $1,000. If the child ITEMIZED deductions, see the instructions	**2**		
3	Subtract the amount on line 2 from the amount on line 1. Enter the result. (If zero or less, stop here; do not complete the rest of this form but ATTACH it to the child's return.) . . .	**3**		
4	Enter the child's **taxable** income (from Form 1040, line 37; Form 1040A, line 19; or Form 1040NR, line 35)	**4**		
5	Compare the amounts on lines 3 and 4. Enter the **smaller** of the two amounts here . . . . . . ▶	**5**		

	Step 2	Figure tentative tax based on the tax rate of the parent listed above		
6	Enter the parent's **taxable** income (from Form 1040, line 37; Form 1040A, line 19; Form 1040EZ, line 5; or Form 1040NR, line 35). But if the parent transferred property to a trust, see the instructions . . .	**6**		
7	Enter the total, if any, of the net investment income from Forms 8615, line 5, of ALL OTHER children of the parent. (Do not include the amount on line 5 above.)	**7**		
8	Add the amounts on lines 5, 6, and 7. Enter the total	**8**		
9	Tax on the amount on line 8 based on the **parent's** filing status	**9**		
10	Enter the parent's tax (from Form 1040, line 38; Form 1040A, line 20; Form 1040EZ, line 7; or Form 1040NR, line 36)	**10**		
11	Subtract the amount on line 10 from the amount on line 9. Enter the result. (If no amount is entered on line 7, enter the amount from line 11 on line 13; skip lines 12a and 12b.)	**11**		
12a	Add the amounts on lines 5 and 7. Enter the total	**12a**		
b	Divide the amount on line 5 by the amount on line 12a. Enter the result as a decimal (rounded to two places)	**12b**	× .	
13	Multiply the amount on line 11 by the decimal amount on line 12b. Enter the result . . . . . . ▶	**13**		

	Step 3	Figure child's tax		
	Note: *If the amounts on lines 4 and 5 are the same, skip to line 16.*			
14	Subtract the amount on line 5 from the amount on line 4. Enter the result · ·	**14**		
15	Tax on the amount on line 14 based on the **child's** filing status	**15**		
16	Add the amounts on lines 13 and 15. Enter the total	**16**		
17	Tax on the amount on line 4 based on the **child's** filing status	**17**		
18	Compare the amounts on lines 16 and 17. Enter the **larger** of the two amounts here and on Form 1040, line 38; Form 1040A, line 20; or Form 1040NR, line 36. Be sure to check the box for "Form 8615" . ▶	**18**		

For Paperwork Reduction Act Notice, see back of form.

Form **8615** (1989)

Paperwork Reduction Act Notice. We ask for this information to carry out the Internal Revenue laws of the United States. We need it to ensure that taxpayers are complying with these laws and to allow us to figure and collect the right amount of tax. You are required to give us this information.

The time needed to complete and file this form will vary depending on individual circumstances. The estimated average time is:

Recordkeeping . . . . . 13 minutes

Learning about the law or the form . . . . 11 minutes

Preparing the form . . . 37 minutes

Copying, assembling, and sending the form to IRS . . . 17 minutes

If you have comments concerning the accuracy of these time estimates or suggestions for making this form more simple, we would be happy to hear from you. You can write to either IRS or the Office of Management and Budget at the addresses listed in the instructions of the tax return with which this form is filed.

Line-by-Line Instructions

We have provided specific instructions for most of the lines on the form. Those lines that do not appear in these instructions are self-explanatory.

Parent's Name and Social Security Number. If the child's parents were married to each other and filed a joint return, enter the name and social security number of the parent who is listed first on the joint return. For example, if the father's name is listed first on the return and his social security number is entered in the block labeled "Your social security number," enter his name and social security number in the spaces provided on Form 8615.

If the parents were married but filed separate returns, enter the name and social security number of the parent who had the **higher** taxable income. If you do not know which parent had the higher taxable income, see Pub. 929.

If the parents were unmarried, treated as unmarried for Federal income tax purposes, or separated either by a divorce or separate maintenance decree, enter the name and social security number of the parent who had custody of the child for most of the year (the custodial parent). **Exception.** If the custodial parent remarried and filed a joint return with his or her spouse, enter the name and social security number of the person who is listed first on the joint return, even if that person is not the child's parent. If the custodial parent and his or her spouse filed separate returns, enter the name and social security number of the person with the **higher** taxable income, even if that person is not the child's parent.

Incomplete Information for Parent. If a parent or guardian of a child cannot obtain the necessary information to complete Form 8615 before the due date of the child's return, reasonable estimates of the parent's taxable income or filing status and the net investment income of the parent's other children may be made. The appropriate line of Form 8615 must be marked "Estimated." For more information, see Pub. 929.

Line 1. If the child had no earned income (defined below), enter the child's adjusted gross income (from Form 1040, line 32; Form 1040A, line 14; or Form 1040NR, line 31).

If the child had earned income, use the following worksheet to figure the amount to enter on line 1. However, if any of the following applies, use the worksheet in Pub. 929 instead of the one below to figure the amount to enter on Form 8615, line 1:

● The child files **Form 2555,** Foreign Earned Income.

● The child had a net loss from self-employment.

● The child claims a net operating loss deduction.

Worksheet (keep for your records)

1. Enter the amount from the child's Form 1040, line 23; Form 1040A, line 11; or Form 1040NR, line 23, whichever applies . . _____

2. Enter the child's earned income (defined below) plus any deduction the child claims on Form 1040, line 28, or Form 1040NR, line 27, whichever applies . . _____

3. Subtract the amount on line 2 from the amount on line 1. Enter the result here and on Form 8615, line 1 . . . . _____

Earned income includes wages, tips, and other payments received for personal services performed. Generally, earned income is the total of the amounts reported on Form 1040, lines 7, 12, and 19; Form 1040A, line 7; or Form 1040NR, lines 8, 13, and 20.

Line 2. If the child itemized deductions on **Schedule A** (Form 1040 or Form 1040NR), enter on line 2 the **greater** of:

● $500 plus the portion of the amount on Schedule A (Form 1040), line 26 (or Schedule A (Form 1040NR), line 10), that is directly connected with the production of the investment income on Form 8615, line 1; OR

● $1,000.

Line 6. Enter the taxable income shown on the tax return of the parent identified at the top of Form 8615. If the parent's taxable income is less than zero, enter zero on line 6.

If the parent filed a joint return, enter the total taxable income shown on that return even if the parent's spouse is not the child's parent.

Caution: *If the parent transferred property to a trust which sold or exchanged the property during the year at a gain, include any gain that was taxed to the trust under Internal Revenue Code section 644 in the amount entered on line 6. Write "Section 644" and the amount on the dotted line next to line 6. Also, see the **Caution** below line 10.*

Line 7. If the individual identified as the parent on this Form 8615 is also identified as the parent on any other Form 8615, add the amounts, if any, from line 5 on each of the other Forms 8615 and enter the total on line 7.

Lines 9, 15, and 17. Figure the tax using the Tax Table or Tax Rate Schedules, whichever applies.

Line 10. Enter the tax shown on the tax return of the parent identified at the top of Form 8615. If the parent filed a joint return, enter the tax shown on that return even if the parent's spouse is not the child's parent.

Caution: *If line 6 includes any gain taxed to a trust under Internal Revenue Code section 644, add the tax imposed under section 644(a)(2)(A) to the tax shown on the parent's return. Enter the total on line 10 instead of entering the tax from the parent's return. Write "Section 644" on the dotted line next to line 10.*

Line 18. Compare the amounts on lines 16 and 17 and enter the **larger** of the two amounts on line 18. Be sure to check the box for "Form 8615" on the appropriate line of the child's tax return even if the amount on line 17 is the larger of the two amounts.

Amended Return. If after the child's return is filed, the parent's taxable income is changed or the net investment income of any of the parent's other children is changed, the child's tax must be refigured using the adjusted amounts. If the child's tax is changed as a result of the adjustment(s), file **Form 1040X,** Amended U.S. Individual Income Tax Return, to correct the child's tax.

Alternative Minimum Tax. A child whose tax is figured on Form 8615 may be subject to the alternative minimum tax. Get **Form 6251,** Alternative Minimum Tax–Individuals, to see if the child owes this tax.

APPENDIX C

Glossary of Tax Terms

The words and phrases appearing below have been defined to reflect their conventional use in the field of taxation. Such definitions may therefore be incomplete for other purposes.

A

Accelerated cost recovery system. A method whereby the cost of a fixed asset generates deductions for tax purposes. Instituted by the Economic Recovery Tax Act of 1981, the system places assets into one of various recovery periods and prescribes the applicable percentage of cost that can be deducted each year. In this regard, it largely resolves the controversy that had arisen with prior depreciation procedures in determining estimated useful life and in predicting salvage value. § 168.

Accelerated depreciation. Various methods of depreciation that yield larger deductions in the earlier years of the life of an asset than the straight-line method. Examples include the double-declining-balance and the sum-of-the-years' digits methods of depreciation. §§ 167(b)(2) and (3).

Accounting method. The method under which income and expenses are determined for tax purposes. Important accounting methods include the cash basis and the accrual basis. Special methods are available for the reporting of gain on installment sales, recognition of income on construction projects (the completed contract and percentage of completion methods), and the valuation of inventories (last-in, first-out and first-in, first-out). §§ 446–474. See also *accrual basis, cash basis, completed contract method, percentage of completion method,* etc.

Accounting period. The period of time, usually a year, used by a taxpayer for the determination of tax liability. Unless a fiscal year is chosen, taxpayers must determine and pay their income tax liability by using the calendar year (January 1 through December 31) as the period of measurement. An example of a fiscal year is July 1 through June 30. A change in accounting periods (e.g., from a calendar year to a fiscal year) generally requires the consent of the IRS. Some new taxpayers such as a newly formed corporation, are free to select either an initial calendar or fiscal year without the consent of the IRS. §§ 441–443. See also *annual accounting period concept.*

Accrual basis. A method of accounting that reflects expenses incurred and income earned for any one tax year. In contrast to the cash basis of accounting, expenses need not be paid to be deductible, nor need income be received to be taxable. Unearned income (e.g., prepaid interest and rent) generally is taxed in the year of receipt regardless of the method of accounting used by the taxpayer. § 446(c)(2). See also *accounting method, cash basis,* and *unearned income.*

Accumulated adjustments account. An account that comprises an S corporation's post-1982 income, loss, and deductions for the tax year (including nontaxable income and nondeductible losses and expenses). After the year-end income and expense adjustments are made, the account is reduced by distributions made during the tax year.

Accumulated earnings credit. A reduction allowed in arriving at accumulated taxable income in determining the accumulated earnings tax. See also *accumulated earnings tax* and *accumulated taxable income.*

Accumulated earnings tax. A special tax imposed on corporations that accumulate (rather than distribute) their earnings beyond the reasonable needs of the business. The accumulated earnings tax and related interest is imposed on accumulated taxable income in addition to the corporate income tax. §§ 531–537.

Accumulated taxable income. The base upon which the accumulated earnings tax is imposed. Generally, it is the taxable income of the corporation as adjusted for certain items (e.g., the Federal income tax, excess charitable contributions, the dividends-received deduction) less the dividends paid deduction and the accumulated earnings credit. § 535.

Accumulating trusts. See *discretionary trusts.*

Acquiescence. Agreement by the IRS on the results reached in most of the Regular decisions of the U.S. Tax Court; sometimes abbreviated *acq.* or *A.* See also *nonacquiescence.*

Acquisition.   See *corporate acquisition.*

ACRS.   See *accelerated cost recovery system.*

Ad valorem tax.   A tax imposed on the value of property. The most common ad valorem tax is that imposed by states, counties and cities on real estate. Ad valorem taxes can, however, be imposed on personal property, as well. See also *personalty.*

Adjusted basis.   The cost or other basis of property reduced by depreciation allowed or allowable and increased by capital improvements. Other special adjustments are provided in § 1016 and the Regulations thereunder. See also *basis.*

Adjusted gross estate.   The gross estate of a decedent reduced by § 2053 expenses (e.g., administration, funeral) and § 2054 losses (e.g., casualty). The determination of the adjusted gross estate is necessary in testing for the extension of time for installment payment of estate taxes under § 6166. See also *gross estate.*

Adjusted gross income.   A tax determination peculiar to individual taxpayers. Generally, it represents the gross income of an individual, less business expenses and less any appropriate capital gain or loss adjustment. See also *gross income.*

Adjusted ordinary gross income.   A determination peculiar to the personal holding company tax imposed by § 541. In ascertaining whether a corporation is a personal holding company, personal holding company income divided by adjusted ordinary gross income must equal 60 percent or more. Adjusted ordinary gross income is the corporation's gross income less capital gains, § 1231 gains, and certain expenses. § 543(b)(2). See also *personal holding company income.*

Adjusted taxable estate.   The taxable estate reduced by $60,000. The adjusted taxable estate is utilized in applying § 2011 for determining the limit on the credit for state death taxes paid that will be allowed against the Federal estate tax. See also *taxable estate.*

Administration.   The supervision and winding up of an estate. The administration of an estate runs from the date of an individual's death until all assets have been distributed and liabilities paid.

Administrator.   A person appointed by the court to administer (manage or take charge of) the assets and liabilities of a decedent (the deceased). Such person may be a male (administrator) or a female (administratrix). See also *executor.*

AFTR.   Published by Prentice-Hall, *American Federal Tax Reports* contain all of the Federal tax decisions issued by the U.S. District Courts, U.S. Claims Court, U.S. Court of Appeals, and the U.S. Supreme Court.

AFTR2d.   The second series of the *American Federal Tax Reports,* dealing with 1954 and 1986 Code case law.

Alimony.   Alimony deductions result from the payment of a legal obligation arising from the termination of a marital relationship. Designated alimony payments generally are included in the gross income of the recipient and are deductible *for* AGI by the payor.

Allocable share of income.   Certain entities receive conduit treatment under the Federal income tax law. This means the earned income or loss is not taxed to the entity, but such amounts are allocated to the owners or beneficiaries thereof, regardless of the magnitude or timing of corresponding distributions. The portion of the entity's income that is taxed to the owner or beneficiary is the allocable share of the entity's income or loss for the period. Such allocations are determined by (1) the partnership agreement relative to the partners, (2) a weighted-average stock ownership computation relative to shareholders of an S corporation, and (3) the controlling will or trust instrument relative to the beneficiaries of an estate or trust.

Allocation.   The assignment of income for various tax purposes. A multistate corporation's nonbusiness income usually is allocated to the state where the nonbusiness assets are located; it is not apportioned with the rest of the entity's income. The income and expense items of an estate or trust are allocated between income and corpus components. Specific items of income, expense, gain, loss, and credit can be allocated to specific partners or shareholders in an S corporation, if a substantial economic nontax purpose for the allocation is established. See also *apportionment* and *substantial economic effect.*

Alternate valuation date.   Property passing from a person by death may be valued for death tax purposes as of the date of death or the alternate valuation date. The alternate valuation date is six months from the date of death or the date the property is disposed of by the estate, whichever comes first. The use of the alternate valuation date requires an affirmative election on the part of the executor or administrator of the estate. The election of the alternate valuation date is not available unless it decreases the amount of the gross estate *and* reduces the estate tax liability.

Alternative minimum tax (AMT).   Simply stated, the AMT is a fixed percentage of alternative minimum taxable income (AMTI). AMTI generally starts with the taxpayer's adjusted gross income (for individuals) or taxable income (for other taxpayers). To this amount, the taxpayer (1) adds designated preference items (e.g., the appreciation on charitable contribution property), (2) makes other specified adjustments (e.g., to reflect a longer, straight-line cost recovery deduction), (3) subtracts certain AMT itemized deductions for individuals (e.g., interest incurred on housing but not taxes paid), and (4) subtracts an exemption amount (e.g., $40,000 on an individual joint return). The taxpayer must pay the greater of the resulting AMT (reduced by only the foreign tax credit and a reduced investment credit) or the regular income tax (reduced by all allowable tax credits).

Amortization.   The tax deduction for the cost or other basis of an intangible asset over the asset's estimated useful life. Examples of amortizable intangibles include patents, copyrights, and leasehold interests. The intangible goodwill cannot be amortized for income tax purposes because it possesses no estimated useful life. As to tangible assets, see *depreciation.* As to natural resources, see *depletion.* See also *estimated useful life* and *goodwill.*

Amount realized.   The amount received by a taxpayer upon the sale or exchange of property. The measure of the amount realized is the sum of the cash and the fair market value of any property or services received by the taxpayer, plus any related debt assumed by the buyer. Determining the amount realized is the starting point for arriving at realized gain or loss. § 1001(b). See also *realized gain or loss* and *recognized gain or loss.*

Annual accounting period concept.   In determining a taxpayer's income tax liability, only those transactions taking place during a specified tax year are taken into consideration. For reporting and payment purposes, therefore, the tax life of taxpayers is divided into equal annual accounting periods. See also *accounting period* and *mitigation of the annual accounting period concept.*

Annual exclusion.   In computing the taxable gifts for any one year, each donor may exclude the first $10,000 of a gift to each donee. Usually, the annual exclusion is not available for gifts of future interests. § 2503(b). See also *election to split gifts* and *future interest.*

Annuitant.   The party entitled to receive payments from an annuity contract. See also *annuity.*

Annuity.   A fixed sum of money payable to a person at specified times for a specified period of time or for life. If the party making the payment (i.e., the obligor) is regularly engaged in this type of business (e.g., an insurance company), the arrangement is classified as a commercial annuity. A private annuity involves an obligor that is not regularly engaged in selling annuities (e.g., a charity or family member).

Anticipatory assignment of income.   See *assignment of income.*

Appellate court.   For Federal tax purposes, appellate courts include the Courts of Appeals and the Supreme Court. If the party losing in the trial (or lower) court is dissatisfied with the result, the dispute may be carried to the appropriate appellate court. See also *Court of Appeals* and *trial court.*

Apportionment.   The assignment of the business income of a multistate corporation to specific states for income taxation. Usually, the apportionment procedure accounts for the property, payroll, and sales activity levels of the various states, and a proportionate assignment of the entity's total income is made thereby, using a three-factor apportionment formula. These activities indicate the commercial domicile of the corporation, relative to that income. Some states exclude nonbusiness income from the apportionment procedure; they *allocate* nonbusiness income to the states where the nonbusiness assets are located. See also *domicile, nonbusiness income, payroll factor, property factor,* and *sales factor.*

Arm's length.   The standard under which unrelated parties would carry out a particular transaction. Suppose, for example, X Corporation sells property to its sole shareholder for $10,000. In determining whether $10,000 is an arm's length price, one would ascertain the amount for which the corporation could have sold the property to a disinterested third party.

Articles of incorporation.   The legal document specifying a corporation's name, period of existence, purpose and powers, authorized number of shares, classes of stock, and other conditions for operation. These articles are filed by the organizers of the corporation with the state of incorporation. If the articles are satisfactory and other conditions of the law are satisfied, the state will issue a charter recognizing the organization's status as a corporation.

Assessment.   The process whereby the IRS imposes an additional tax liability. If, for example, the IRS audits a taxpayer's income tax return and finds gross income understated or deductions overstated, it will assess a deficiency in the amount of the tax that should have been paid in light of the adjustments made. See also *deficiency.*

Assignment of income.   A procedure whereby a taxpayer attempts to avoid the recognition of income by assigning to another the property that generates the income. Such a procedure will not avoid the recognition of income by the taxpayer making the assignment if it can be said that the income was earned at the point of the transfer. In this case, usually referred to as an anticipatory assignment of income, the income will be taxed to the person who earns it.

Association.   An organization treated as a corporation for Federal tax purposes even though it may not qualify as such under applicable state law. What is designated as a trust or a partnership, for example, may be classified as an association if it clearly possesses corporate attributes. Corporate attributes include centralized management, continuity of life, free transferability of interests, and limited liability. § 7701(a) (3).

At-risk amount.   The taxpayer has an amount at risk in a business or investment venture to the extent that it has subjected personal assets to the risks of the business. Typically, the taxpayer's at-risk amount includes (1) the amount of money or other property that the investor contributed to the venture for the investment, (2) the amount of any of the entity's liabilities for which the taxpayer personally is liable and that relate to the investment, and (3) an allocable share of nonrecourse debts incurred by the venture from third parties in arm's length transactions, with respect to real estate investments.

At-risk limitation.   Generally, a taxpayer can deduct losses relative to a trade or business, S corporation, partnership, or investment asset only to the extent of the at-risk amount.

Attribution.   Under certain circumstances, the tax law applies attribution rules to assign to one taxpayer the ownership interest of another taxpayer. If, for example, the stock of X Corporation is held 60 percent by M and 40 percent by S, M may be deemed to own 100 percent of X Corporation if M and S are mother and son. In such a case, the stock owned by S is attributed to M. Stated differently, M has a 60 percent direct and a 40 percent indirect interest in X Corporation. It can also be said that M is the constructive owner of S's interest.

Audit.   Inspection and verification of a taxpayer's return or other transactions possessing tax consequences. See also *correspondence audit, field audit,* and *office audit.*

B

Bailout.   Various procedures whereby the owners of an entity can obtain the entity's profits with favorable tax consequences. With corporations, for example, the bailout of corporate profits without dividend consequences might be the desired objective. The alternative of distributing the profits to the shareholders as dividends generally is less attractive since dividend payments are not deductible. See also *preferred stock bailout.*

Bargain sale or purchase.   A sale of property for less than fair market value. The difference between the sale or purchase price and the fair market value of the property may have tax consequences. If, for example, a corporation sells property worth $1,000 to one of its shareholders for $700, the $300 difference probably represents a constructive dividend to the shareholder. Suppose, instead, the shareholder sells the property (worth $1,000) to his or her corporation for $700. The $300 difference probably represents a contribution by the shareholder to the corporation's capital. Bargain sales and purchases among members of the same family may lead to gift tax consequences. See also *constructive dividends.*

Basis.   The acquisition cost assigned to an asset for income tax purposes. For assets acquired by purchase, basis would be cost (§ 1012). Special rules govern the basis of property received by virtue of another's death (§ 1014) or by gift (§ 1015), the basis of stock received on a transfer of property to a controlled corporation (§ 358), the basis of the property transferred to the corporation (§ 362), and the basis of property received upon the liquidation of a corporation (§§ 334 and 338). See also *adjusted basis.*

Beneficiary.   A party who will benefit from a transfer of property or other arrangement. Examples include the beneficiary of a trust, the beneficiary of a life insurance policy, and the beneficiary of an estate.

Bequest.   A transfer by will of personal property. To bequeath is to leave such property by will. See also *devise* and *personal property.*

Blockage rule.   A factor to be considered in valuing a large block of stock. Application of this rule generally justifies a discount in the fair market value since the disposition of a large amount of stock at any one time may depress the value of such shares in the market place.

Bona fide.   In good faith, or real. In tax law, this term is often used in connection with a business purpose for carrying out a transaction. Thus, was there a bona fide business purpose for a shareholder's transfer of a liability to a controlled corporation? § 357(b)(1)(B). See also *business purpose.*

Book value.   The net amount of an asset after reduction by a related reserve. The book value of machinery, for example, is the amount of the machinery less the reserve for depreciation.

Boot.   Cash or property of a type not included in the definition of a nontaxable exchange. The receipt of boot will cause an otherwise nontaxable transfer to become taxable, to the extent of the lesser of the fair market value of such boot or the realized gain on the transfer. For example, see transfers to controlled corporations under § 351(b) and like-kind exchanges under § 1031(b). See also *like-kind exchange* and *realized gain or loss.*

Brother-sister corporations.   More than one corporation owned by the same shareholders. If, for example, C and D each own one-half of the stock in X Corporation and Y Corporation, X and Y are brother-sister corporations.

B.T.A.   The Board of Tax Appeals was a trial court that considered Federal tax matters. This Court is now designated as the U.S. Tax Court.

Built-in gains tax.   A penalty tax designed to discourage a shift of the incidence of taxation on unrealized gains from a C corporation to its shareholders, via an S election. Under this provision, any recognized gain during the first 10 years of S status generates a corporate-level tax on a base not to exceed the aggregate untaxed built-in gains brought into the S corporation upon its election from C corporation taxable years.

Burden of proof.   The requirement in a lawsuit to show the weight of evidence and thereby gain a favorable decision. Except in cases of tax fraud, the burden of proof in a tax case generally is on the taxpayer. See also *fraud.*

Business bad debts.   A tax deduction allowed for obligations obtained in connection with a trade or business that have become either partially or completely worthless. In contrast with nonbusiness bad debts, business bad debts are deductible as business expenses. § 166. See also *nonbusiness bad debts.*

Business purpose.   A justifiable business reason for carrying out a transaction. It has long been established that mere tax avoidance is not an acceptable business purpose. The presence of a business purpose is crucial in the area of corporate reorganizations and certain liquidations. See also *bona fide.*

Buy and sell agreement.   An arrangement, particularly appropriate in the case of a closely held corporation or a partnership, whereby the surviving owners (shareholders or partners) or the entity agrees to purchase the interest of a withdrawing owner. The buy and sell agreement provides for an orderly disposition of an interest in a business and may aid in setting the value of such interest for death tax purposes. See also *cross-purchase buy and sell agreement* and *entity buy and sell agreement.*

C

Calendar year.   See *accounting period.*

Capital asset.   Broadly speaking, all assets are capital except those specifically excluded by the Code. Major categories of noncapital assets include property held for resale in the normal course of business (inventory), trade accounts and notes receivable, and depreciable property and real estate used in a trade or business (§ 1231 assets). § 1221. See also *capital gain* and *capital loss.*

Capital contribution.   Various means by which a shareholder makes additional funds available to the corporation (placed at the risk of the business) without the receipt of additional stock. Such contributions are added to the basis of the shareholder's existing stock investment and do not generate income to the corporation. § 118.

Capital expenditure.   An expenditure that should be added to the basis of the property improved. For income tax purposes, this generally precludes a full deduction for the expenditure in the year paid or incurred. Any cost recovery in the form of a tax deduction would come in the form of depreciation, depletion, or amortization. § 263.

Capital gain.   The gain from the sale or exchange of a capital asset. See also *capital asset.*

Capital loss.   The loss from the sale or exchange of a capital asset. See also *capital asset.*

Capital stock tax.   A state-level tax, usually imposed on out-of-state corporations for the privilege of doing business in the state. The tax may be based on the entity's apportionable income or payroll, or on its apportioned net worth as of a specified date.

Cash basis.   A method of accounting that reflects deductions as paid and income as received in any one tax year. However, deductions for prepaid expenses that benefit more than one tax year (e.g., prepaid rent and prepaid interest) usually must be spread over the period benefited rather than deducted in the year paid. § 446(c) (1). See also *constructive receipt of income.*

Cash surrender value.   The amount of money that an insurance policy would yield if cashed in with the insurance company that issued the policy.

CCH.   Commerce Clearing House (CCH) is the publisher of a tax service and of Federal tax decisions (USTC series).

C corporation.   A regular corporation governed by Subchapter C of the Code. Distinguished from S corporations, which fall under Subchapter S of the Code.

Centralized management.   A concentration of authority among certain persons who may make independent business decisions on behalf of the entity without the need for continuing approval by the owners of the entity. It is a characteristic of a corporation since day-to-day business operations are handled by appointed officers and not by the shareholders. Reg. § 301.7701–2(c). See also *association.*

Cert. den.   By denying the Writ of Certiorari, the U.S. Supreme Court refuses to accept an appeal from a U.S. Court of Appeals. The denial of certiorari does not, however, mean that the U.S. Supreme Court agrees with the result reached by the lower court. See also *certiorari.*

Certiorari.   Appeal from a U.S. Court of Appeals to the U.S. Supreme Court is by Writ of Certiorari. The Supreme Court need not accept the appeal and usually does not (*cert. den.*), unless a conflict exists among the lower courts that must be resolved or a constitutional issue is involved. See also *cert. den.*

Cf.   Compare.

Civil fraud.   See *fraud.*

Claims Court.   A trial court (court of original jurisdiction) that decides litigation involving Federal tax matters. Previously known as the U.S. Court of Claims, appeal from the U.S. Claims Court is to the Court of Appeals for the Federal Circuit.

Clifford trust.   A grantor trust whereby the grantor (creator) of the trust retains the right to possess again the property transferred in trust (a reversionary interest is retained) upon the occurrence of an event (e.g., the death of the beneficiary) or the expiration of a period of time. Unless the requirements of § 673 are satisfied, the income from the property placed in trust will continue to be taxed to the grantor. See also *grantor trust* and *reversionary interest.*

Closely held corporation.   A corporation, the stock ownership of which is not widely dispersed. Rather, a few shareholders are in control of corporate policy and are in a position to benefit personally from such policy.

Collapsing.   To disregard a transaction or one of a series of steps leading to a result. See also *step-transaction approach, substance vs. form concept,* and *telescoping.*

Common law state.   See *community property.*

Community property.   The states with community property systems are Louisiana, Texas, New Mexico, Arizona, California, Washington, Idaho, Nevada, and Wisconsin. The rest of the states are common law property jurisdictions. The difference between common law and community property systems centers around the property rights possessed by married persons. In a common law system, each spouse owns whatever he or she earns. Under a community property system, one-half of the earnings of each spouse is considered owned by the other spouse. Assume, for example, H and W are husband and wife and their only income is the $50,000 annual salary H receives. If they live in New York (a common law state), the $50,000 salary belongs to H. If, however, they live in Texas (a community property state), the $50,000 salary is owned one-half each by H and W. See also *separate property.*

Completed contract method.   A method of reporting gain or loss on certain long-term contracts. Under this method of accounting, gross income and expenses are recognized in the tax year in which the contract is completed. Reg. § 1.451–3. See also *percentage of completion method.*

Complex trusts.   Complex trusts are those that are not simple trusts. Such trusts may have charitable beneficiaries, accumulate income, and distribute corpus. §§ 661–663. See also *simple trusts.*

Concur.   To agree with the result reached by another, but not necessarily with the reasoning or the logic used in reaching such a result. For example, Judge R agrees with Judges S and T (all being members of the same court) that the income is taxable but for a different reason. Judge R would issue a concurring opinion to the majority opinion issued by Judges S and T.

Condemnation.   The taking of property by a public authority. The taking is by legal action, and the owner of the property is compensated by the public authority.

Conduit concept.   An approach the tax law assumes in the tax treatment of certain entities and their owners. The approach permits specified tax characteristics to pass through the entity without losing their identity. Under the conduit concept, for example, long-term capital losses realized by a partnership are passed through as such to the individual partners. Varying forms of the conduit concept are applicable for partnerships, trusts, estates, and S corporations.

Consent dividends.   For purposes of avoiding or reducing the penalty tax on the unreasonable accumulation of earnings or the personal holding company tax, a corporation may declare a consent dividend. In a consent dividend, no cash or property is distributed to the shareholders, although the corporation obtains a dividends paid deduction. The consent dividend is taxed to the shareholders and increases the basis in their stock investment. § 565.

Consolidated returns.   A procedure whereby certain affiliated corporations may file a single return, combine the tax transactions of each corporation, and arrive at a single income tax liability for the group. The election to file a consolidated return is usually binding on future years. See §§ 1501–1505 and the Regulations thereunder.

Consolidation.   The combination of two or more corporations into a newly created corporation. Thus, A Corporation and B Corporation combine to form C Corporation. A consolidation may qualify as a nontaxable reorganization if certain conditions are satisfied. §§ 354 and 368(a)(1)(A).

Constructive dividends.   A taxable benefit derived by a shareholder from the shareholder's corporation, although such benefit was not designated as a dividend. Examples include unreasonable compensation, excessive rent payments, bargain purchases of corporate property, and shareholder use of corporate property. Constructive dividends generally are a problem limited to closely held corporations. See also *bargain sale or purchase, closely held corporation,* and *unreasonable compensation.*

Constructive ownership.   See *attribution.*

Constructive receipt of income.   If income is unqualifiedly available although not physically in the taxpayer's possession, it is subject to the income tax. An example would be accrued interest on a savings account. Under the constructive receipt of income concept, such interest is taxed to a depositor in the year available, rather than the year actually withdrawn. The fact that the depositor uses the cash basis of accounting for tax purposes is irrelevant. See Reg. § 1.451–2. See also *cash basis.*

Continuity of life or existence.   The death or other withdrawal of an owner of an entity does not terminate the existence of such entity. This is a characteristic of a corporation since the death or withdrawal of a shareholder does not affect the corporation's existence. Reg. § 301.7701–2(b). See also *association.*

Contributions to the capital of a corporation. See *capital contribution.*

Contributory qualified pension or profit sharing plan.   A plan funded with both employer and employee contributions. Since the employee's contributions to the plan are subject to income tax, a later distribution of such contributions to the employee generally are tax-free. See also *qualified pension or profit sharing plan.*

Controlled foreign corporation.   Any foreign corporation in which more than 50 percent of the total combined voting power of all classes of stock entitled to vote or the total value of the stock of the corporation is owned by "U.S. shareholders" on any day during the taxable year of the foreign corporation. For purposes of this definition, a U.S. shareholder is any U.S. person who owns, or is considered as owning, 10 percent or more of the total combined voting power of all classes of voting stock of the foreign corporation. Stock owned directly, indirectly, and constructively is used in this measure.

Controlled group.   A controlled group of corporations is required to share the lower-level corporate tax rates and various other tax benefits among the members of the group. A controlled group may be either a brother-sister or a parent-subsidiary group.

Corporate acquisition.   The takeover of one corporation by another if both parties retain their legal existence after the transaction. An acquisition can be effected via a stock purchase or through a tax-free exchange of stock. See also *corporate reorganization* and *merger.*

Corporate liquidation.   Occurs when a corporation distributes its net assets to its shareholders and ceases its legal existence. Generally, a shareholder recognizes capital gain or loss upon such liquidation of the entity regardless of the corporation's balance in its earnings and profits account. However, the distributing corporation recognizes gain and loss on assets that it distributes to shareholders in kind.

Corporate reorganization.   Occurs, among other instances, when one corporation acquires another in a merger or acquisition, a single corporation divides into two or more entities, a corporation makes a substantial change in its capital structure, or a corporation undertakes a change in its legal name or domicile. The exchange of stock and other securities in a corporate reorganization can be effected favorably for tax purposes if certain statutory requirements are followed strictly. Such tax consequences include the nonrecognition of any gain that is realized by the shareholders except to the extent of boot received. See also *corporate acquisition* and *merger.*

Corpus.   The body or principal of a trust. Suppose, for example, G transfers an apartment building into a trust, income payable to W for life, remainder to S upon W's death. Corpus of the trust is the apartment building.

Correspondence audit.   An audit conducted by the IRS by mail. Typically, the IRS writes to the taxpayer requesting the verification of a particular

deduction or exemption. The completion of a special form or the remittance of copies of records or other support is all that is requested of the taxpayer. See also *audit, field audit,* and *office audit.*

Court of Appeals. Any of 13 Federal courts that consider tax matters appealed from the U.S. Tax Court, a U.S. District Court, or the U.S. Claims Court. Appeal from a U.S. Court of Appeals is to the U.S. Supreme Court by Writ of Certiorari. See also *appellate court* and *trial court.*

Credit for prior transfers. The death tax credit for prior transfers applies when property is taxed in the estates of different decedents within a 10-year period. The credit is determined using a decreasing statutory percentage, with the magnitude of the credit decreasing as the length of time between the multiple deaths increases.

Criminal fraud. See *fraud.*

Cross-purchase buy and sell agreement. Under this type of arrangement, the surviving owners of the business agree to buy out the withdrawing owner. Assume, for example, R and S are equal shareholders in T Corporation. Under a cross-purchase buy and sell agreement, R and S would contract to purchase the other's interest should that person decide to withdraw from the business. See also *buy and sell agreement* and *entity buy and sell agreement.*

Current earnings and profits. A corporate distribution is deemed to be first from the entity's current earnings and profits and then from accumulated earnings and profits. Shareholders recognize dividend income to the extent of the earnings and profits of the corporation. A dividend results to the extent of current earnings and profits even if there is a larger negative balance in accumulated earnings and profits.

Current use valuation. See *special use value.*

Curtesy. A husband's right under state law to all or part of his wife's property upon her death. See also *dower.*

D

Death benefit. A payment made by an employer to the beneficiary or beneficiaries of a deceased employee on account of the death of the employee. Under certain conditions, the first $5,000 of such payment is exempt from the income tax. § 101(b)(1).

Death tax. A tax imposed on property transferred by the death of the owner. See also *credit for prior transfers, estate tax,* and *inheritance tax.*

Decedent. An individual who has died.

Deduction. The Federal income tax is not imposed upon gross income. Rather, it is imposed upon net income. Congressionally identified deductions are subtracted from gross income to arrive at the tax base taxable income.

Deductions in respect of a decedent. Deductions accrued to the point of death but not recognizable on the final income tax return of a decedent because of

the method of accounting used. Such items are allowed as deductions on the estate tax return and on the income tax return of the estate (Form 1041) or the heir (Form 1040). An example of a deduction in respect of a decedent is interest expense accrued up to the date of death by a cash basis debtor.

Deferred compensation. Compensation that will be taxed when received and not when earned. An example is contributions by an employer to a qualified pension or profit sharing plan on behalf of an employee. Such contributions will not be taxed to the employee until they are distributed (e.g., upon retirement). See also *qualified pension or profit sharing plan.*

Deficiency. Additional tax liability owed by a taxpayer and assessed by the IRS. See also *assessment* and *statutory notice of deficiency.*

Deficiency dividends. Once the IRS has established a corporation's liability for the personal holding company tax in a prior year, the tax may be reduced or avoided by the issuance of a deficiency dividend under § 547. The deficiency dividend procedure is not available in cases where the deficiency was due to fraud with intent to evade tax or to a willful failure to file the appropriate tax return [§ 547(g)]. Nor does the deficiency dividend procedure avoid the usual penalties and interest applicable for failure to file a return or pay a tax.

Deficit. A negative balance in the earnings and profits account.

Delaware subsidiary holding company. An entity established to optimize the state income tax liabilities of a multistate corporation. A subsidiary is formed and domiciled with nexus in Delaware or some other state that exempts portfolio income from the state tax base. The subsidiary then holds and manages all of the corporation's nonbusiness assets.

Demand loan. A loan payable upon request by the creditor, rather than on a specific date.

Depletion. The process by which the cost or other basis of a natural resource (e.g., an oil or gas interest) is recovered upon extraction and sale of the resource. The two ways to determine the depletion allowance are the cost and percentage (or statutory) methods. Under the cost method, each unit of production sold is assigned a portion of the cost or other basis of the interest. This is determined by dividing the cost or other basis by the total units expected to be recovered. Under the percentage (or statutory) method, the tax law provides a special percentage factor for different type of minerals and other natural resources. This percentage is multiplied by the gross income from the interest to arrive at the depletion allowance. §§ 613 and 613A.

Depreciation. The deduction for the cost or other basis of a tangible asset over the asset's estimated useful life. As to intangible assets, see *amortization.* As to natural resources, see *depletion.* See also *estimated useful life.*

Depreciation recapture. Upon the disposition of depreciable property used in a trade or business, gain or loss is measured by the difference between the

consideration received (the amount realized) and the adjusted basis of the property. Such gain recognized could be § 1231 gain and qualify for long-term capital gain treatment. The recapture provisions of the Code (e.g., §§ 1245 and 1250) may operate to convert some or all of the previous § 1231 gain into ordinary income. The justification for depreciation recapture is that it prevents a taxpayer from converting a dollar of ordinary deduction (in the form of depreciation) into deferred tax-favored income (§ 1231 or long-term capital gain). The depreciation recapture rules do not apply when the property is disposed of at a loss or via a gift. See also *Section 1231 gains and losses.*

Determination letter.   Upon the request of a taxpayer, an IRS District Director will comment on the tax status of a completed transaction. Determination letters are frequently used to clarify employee status, determine whether a retirement or profit sharing plan qualifies under the Code, and determine the tax-exempt status of certain nonprofit organizations.

Devise.   A transfer by will of real estate. See also *bequest.*

Disclaimer.   The rejection, refusal, or renunciation of a claim, power, or property. Section 2518 sets forth the conditions required to avoid gift tax consequences as the result of a disclaimer.

Discretionary trusts.   Trusts under which the trustee or another party has the right to accumulate (rather than distribute) the income for each year. Depending on the terms of the trust instrument, such income may be accumulated for future distributions to the income beneficiaries or added to corpus for the benefit of the remainderperson. See also *corpus* and *income beneficiary.*

Disproportionate.   Not pro rata or ratable. Suppose, for example, X Corporation has two shareholders, C and D, each of whom owns 50 percent of its stock. If X Corporation distributes a cash dividend of $2,000 to C and only $1,000 to D, the distribution is disproportionate. The distribution would have been proportionate if C and D had received $1,500 each.

Disregard of corporate entity.   To treat a corporation as if it did not exist for tax purposes. In such event, each shareholder would account for an allocable share of all corporate transactions possessing tax consequences. See also *entity.*

Dissent.   To disagree with the majority. If, for example, Judge B disagrees with the result reached by Judges C and D (all of whom are members of the same court), Judge B could issue a dissenting opinion.

Distributable net income (DNI).   The measure that determines the nature and amount of the distributions from estates and trusts that the beneficiaries thereof must include in income. DNI also limits the amount that estates and trusts can claim as a deduction for such distributions. § 643(a).

Distributions in kind.   A transfer of property "as is." If, for example, a corporation distributes land to its shareholders, a distribution in kind has taken place. A sale of land followed by a distribution of the cash proceeds would not be a distribution in kind of the land.

District Court.   A Federal District Court is a trial court for purposes of litigating Federal tax matters. It is the only trial court for which a jury trial can be obtained. See also *trial court.*

Dividend.   A nondeductible distribution to the shareholders of a corporation. A dividend constitutes gross income to the recipient if it is from the current or accumulated earnings and profits of the corporation.

Dividends received deduction.   A deduction allowed a corporate shareholder for dividends received from a domestic corporation. The deduction usually is 70 percent of the dividends received, but it could be 80 or 100 percent depending upon the ownership percentage held by the payee corporation. §§ 243–246.

Dock sale.   A purchaser uses its owned or rented vehicles to take possession of the product at the seller's shipping dock. In most states, the sale is apportioned to the operating state of the purchaser, rather than the seller. See also *apportionment* and *sales factor.*

Domestic corporation.   A corporation created or organized in the United States or under the law of the United States or any state or territory. § 7701(a)(4). Only dividends received from domestic corporations qualify for the dividends received deduction (§ 243). See also *foreign corporation.*

Domicile.   A person's legal home.

Donee.   The recipient of a gift.

Donor.   The maker of a gift.

Double-weighted apportionment formula.   A means by which the total taxable income of a multistate corporation is assigned to a specific state. Usually, the payroll, property, and sales factors are equally treated, and the weighted average of these factors is used in the apportionment procedure. In some states, however, the sales factor may receive a double weight, or it may be the only factor considered. These latter formulas place a greater tax burden on the income of out-of-state corporations. See also *apportionment, payroll factor, property factor, sales factor,* and *UDITPA.*

Dower.   A wife's right to all or part of her deceased husband's property, unique to common law states as opposed to community property jurisdictions. See also *curtesy.*

E

Earned income.   Income from personal services. Distinguished from passive, portfolio, and other unearned income. See § 911 and the Regulations thereunder.

Earnings and profits.   Measures the economic capacity of a corporation to make a distribution to shareholders that is not a return of capital. Such a distribution will result in dividend income to the shareholders to the extent of the corporation's current and accumulated earnings and profits.

Election to split gifts.   A special election for Federal gift tax purposes whereby husband and wife can treat a gift by one of them to a third party as being made one-half by each. If, for example, H (the husband)

makes a gift of $20,000 to S, W (the wife) may elect to treat $10,000 of the gift as coming from her. The major advantage of the election is that it enables the parties to take advantage of the nonowner spouse's (W in this case) annual exclusion and unified credit. § 2513. See also *annual exclusion.*

Employee stock ownership plan (ESOP). A type of qualified profit sharing plan that invests in securities of the employer. In a noncontributory ESOP, the employer usually contributes its shares to a trust and receives a deduction for the fair market value of such stock. Generally, the employee recognizes no income until the stock is sold after its distribution to him or her upon retirement or other separation from service. See also *qualified pension or profit sharing plan.*

En banc. The case was considered by the whole court. Typically, for example, only one of the judges of the U.S. Tax Court will hear and decide on a tax controversy. However, when the issues involved are unusually novel or of wide impact, the case will be heard and decided by the full Court sitting *en banc.*

Encumbrance. A liability, such as a mortgage. If the liability relates to a particular asset, the asset is encumbered.

Entity. An organization or being that possesses separate existence for tax purposes. Examples are corporations, partnerships, estates, and trusts. See also *disregard of corporate entity.*

Entity accounting income. Entity accounting income is not identical to the taxable income of a trust or estate, nor is it determined in the same manner as the entity's financial accounting income would be. The trust document or will determines whether certain income, expenses, gains, or losses are allocated to the corpus of the entity or to the entity's income beneficiaries. Only those items that are allocated to the income beneficiaries are included in entity accounting income.

Entity buy and sell agreement. A buy and sell agreement whereby the entity is to purchase the withdrawing owner's interest. When the entity is a corporation, the agreement generally involves a stock redemption on the part of the withdrawing shareholder. See also *buy and sell agreement* and *cross-purchase buy and sell agreement.*

Escrow. Money or other property placed with a third party as security for an existing or proposed obligation. C, for example, agrees to purchase D's stock in X Corporation but needs time to raise the necessary funds. The stock is placed by D with E (the escrow agent), with instructions to deliver it to C when the purchase price is paid.

Estate. An entity that locates, collects, distributes, and discharges the assets and liabilities of a decedent.

Estate tax. A tax imposed on the right to transfer property by death. Thus, an estate tax is levied on the decedent's estate and not on the heir receiving the property. See also *death tax* and *inheritance tax.*

Estimated useful life. The period over which an asset will be used by the taxpayer. Assets such as goodwill do not have an estimated useful life. The estimated useful life of an asset is essential to measuring the annual tax deduction for depreciation and amortization.

Estoppel. The process of being stopped from proving something (even if true) in court due to prior inconsistent action. It is usually invoked as a matter of fairness to prevent one party (either the taxpayer or the IRS) from taking advantage of a prior error.

Excise tax. A tax on the manufacture, sale, or use of goods or on the carrying on of an occupation or activity, or a tax on the transfer of property. Thus, the Federal estate and gift taxes are, theoretically, excise taxes.

Executor. A person designated by a will to administer (manage or take charge of) the assets and liabilities of a decedent. Such party may be a male (executor), female (executrix), or a trust company (executor). See also *administrator.*

Exemption. An amount by which the tax base is reduced for all qualifying taxpayers. Individuals can receive personal and dependency exemptions, and taxpayers apply an exemption in computing their alternative minimum taxable income. Often, the exemption amount is phased out as the tax base becomes sizable.

Exemption equivalent. The maximum value of assets that could be transferred to another party without incurring any Federal gift or death tax because of the application of the unified tax credit.

Exempt organization. An organization that is either partially or completely exempt from Federal income taxation. § 501.

F

Fair market value. The amount at which property would change hands between a willing buyer and a willing seller, neither being under any compulsion to buy or to sell and both having reasonable knowledge of the relevant facts. Reg. § 20.2031–1(b).

Federal Register. The first place that the rules and regulations of U.S. administrative agencies (e.g., the U.S. Treasury Department) are published.

F.2d. An abbreviation for the Second Series of the *Federal Reporter,* the official series in which decisions of the U.S. Claims Court and of the U.S. Court of Appeals are published.

F.Supp. The abbreviation for *Federal Supplement,* the official series in which the reported decisions of the U.S. Federal District Courts are published.

Feeder organization. An entity that carries on a trade or business for the benefit of an exempt organization. However, such a relationship does not result in the feeder organization itself being tax-exempt. § 502.

Fiduciary. A person who manages money or property for another and who must exercise a standard of care in such management activity imposed by law or contract. A trustee, for example, possesses a fiduciary responsibility to the beneficiaries of the trust to follow the terms of the trust and the requirements of applicable state law. A breach of fiduciary responsibility would make the trustee liable to the beneficiaries for any damage caused by such breach.

Field audit.   An audit conducted by the IRS on the business premises of the taxpayer or in the office of the tax practitioner representing the taxpayer. See also *audit, correspondence audit,* and *office audit.*

FIRPTA.   Under the Foreign Investment in Real Property Tax Act, gains or losses realized by nonresident aliens and non-U.S. corporations on the disposition of U.S. real estate create U.S.-source income and are subject to U.S. income tax.

First-in, first-out (FIFO).   An accounting method for determining the cost of inventories. Under this method, the inventory on hand is deemed to be the sum of the cost of the most recently acquired units. See also *last-in, first-out (LIFO).*

Fiscal year.   See *accounting period.*

Flat tax.   In its pure form, a flat tax would eliminate all exclusions, deductions, and credits and impose a one-rate tax on gross income.

Foreign corporation.   A corporation that is not organized under the laws of one of the states or territories of the United States. § 7701(a)(5). See also *domestic corporation.*

Foreign currency transaction.   An exchange that could generate a foreign currency gain or loss for a U.S. taxpayer. For instance, if A contracts to purchase foreign goods, payable in a currency other than U.S. dollars, at a specified date in the future, any change in the exchange rate between the dollar and that currency will generate a foreign currency gain or loss upon completion of the contract. This gain or loss is treated as separate from the underlying transaction; it may create ordinary or capital gain or loss.

Foreign personal holding company (FPHC).   A foreign corporation in which (1) 60 percent or more of the gross income for the taxable year is FPHC income and (2) more than 50 percent of the total combined voting power or the total value of the stock is owned, directly or indirectly, by five or fewer individuals who are U.S. persons (the U.S. group) at any time during the taxable year. The 60 percent of gross income test drops to 50 percent or more after the 60 percent requirement has been met for one tax year, until the foreign corporation does not meet the 50 percent test for three consecutive years or the stock ownership requirement is not met for an entire tax year.

Foreign sales corporation.   An entity qualifying for a partial exemption of its gross export receipts from U.S. tax. Most FSC's must maintain a presence in a foreign country. In addition, an FSC cannot issue preferred stock, nor can it have more than 25 shareholders.

Foreign tax credit or deduction.   A U.S. citizen or resident who incurs or pays income taxes to a foreign country on income subject to U.S. tax may be able to claim some of these taxes as a deduction or a credit against the U.S. income tax. §§ 27 and 901–905.

Form 706.   The U.S. Estate Tax Return. In certain cases, this form must be filed for a decedent who was a resident or citizen of the United States.

Form 709.   The U.S. Gift Tax Return.

Form 709–A.   The U.S. Short Form Gift Tax Return.

Form 870.   The signing of Form 870 (Waiver of Restriction on Assessment and Collection of Deficiency in Tax and Acceptance of Overassessments) by a taxpayer permits the IRS to assess a proposed deficiency without issuing a statutory notice of deficiency (90-day letter). This means the taxpayer must pay the deficiency and cannot file a petition to the U.S. Tax Court. § 6213(d).

Form 872.   The signing of this form by a taxpayer extends the period during which the IRS can make an assessment or collection of a tax. In other words, Form 872 extends the applicable statute of limitations. § 6501(c)(4).

Form 1041.   The U.S. Fiduciary Income Tax Return, required to be filed by estates and trusts. See Appendix B for a specimen form.

Form 1065.   The U.S. Partnership Return of Income. See Appendix B for a specimen form.

Form 1120.   The U.S. Corporation Income Tax Return. See Appendix B for a specimen form.

Form 1120–A.   The U.S. Short-Form Corporation Income Tax Return. See Appendix B for a specimen form.

Form 1120S.   The U.S. Small Business Corporation Income Tax Return, required to be filed by S corporations. See Appendix B for a specimen form.

Fraud.   Tax fraud falls into two categories: civil and criminal. Under civil fraud, the IRS may impose as a penalty an amount equal to 75 percent of the underpayment [§ 6653(b)]. Fines and/or imprisonment are prescribed for conviction of various types of criminal tax fraud (§§ 7201–7207). Both civil and criminal fraud require a specific intent on the part of the taxpayer to evade the tax; mere negligence is not enough. Criminal fraud requires the additional element of willfulness (i.e., done deliberately and with evil purpose). In practice, it becomes difficult to distinguish between the degree of intent necessary to support criminal, rather than civil, fraud. In either situation, the IRS has the burden of proving fraud. See also *burden of proof.*

Free transferability of interests.   The capability of the owner of an entity to transfer his or her ownership interest to another without the consent of the other owners. It is a characteristic of a corporation since a shareholder usually can freely transfer the stock to others without the approval of the existing shareholders. Reg. § 301.7701–2(e). See also *association.*

Fringe benefits.   Compensation or other benefits received by an employee that are not in the form of cash. Some fringe benefits (e.g., accident and health plans, group term life insurance) may be excluded from the employee's gross income and thus are not subject to the Federal income tax.

Future interest.   An interest that will come into being at some future point in time. It is distinguished from a present interest, which is already in existence. Assume, for example, that D transfers securities to a newly created trust. Under the terms of the trust instru-

ment, income from the securities is to be paid each year to W for her life, with the securities passing to S upon W's death. W has a present interest in the trust since she is currently entitled to receive the income from the securities. S has a future interest since he must wait for W's death to benefit from the trust. The annual exclusion of $10,000 is not allowed for a gift of a future interest. § 2503(b). See also *annual exclusion* and *election to split gifts.*

G

General partner. A partner who is fully liable in an individual capacity for the debts of the partnership to third parties. A general partner's liability is not limited to the investment in the partnership. See also *limited partner.*

General power of appointment. See *power of appointment.*

Gift. A transfer of property for less than adequate consideration. Gifts usually occur in a personal setting (such as between members of the same family). They are excluded from the income tax base but may be subject to a transfer tax.

Gift splitting. See *election to split gifts.*

Gift tax. A tax imposed on the transfer of property by gift. Such tax is imposed upon the donor of a gift and is based on the fair market value of the property on the date of the gift.

Gifts within three years of death. Some taxable gifts automatically are included in the gross estate of the donor if death occurs within three years of the gift. § 2035.

Goodwill. The reputation and built-up business of a company. For accounting purposes, goodwill has no basis unless it is purchased. In the purchase of a business, goodwill generally is the difference between the purchase price and the value of the assets acquired. The intangible asset goodwill cannot be amortized for tax purposes. Reg. § 1.167(a)–3. See also *amortization.*

Grantor. A transferor of property. The creator of a trust is usually designated as the grantor of the trust.

Grantor trust. A trust under which the grantor retains control over the income or corpus (or both) to such an extent that such grantor will be treated as the owner of the property and its income for income tax purposes. The result is to make the income from a grantor trust taxable to the grantor and not to the beneficiary who receives it. §§ 671–677. See also *Clifford trust* and *reversionary interest.*

Gross estate. The property owned or previously transferred by a decedent that is subject to the Federal death tax. Distinguished from the probate estate, which is property actually subject to administration by the administrator or executor of an estate. §§ 2031–2046. See also *adjusted gross estate* and *taxable estate.*

Gross income. Income subject to the Federal income tax. Gross income does not include all economic income. That is, certain exclusions are allowed (e.g., interest on municipal bonds). For a manufactur-

ing or merchandising business, gross income usually means gross profit (gross sales or gross receipts less cost of goods sold). § 61 and Reg. § 1.61–3(a). See also *adjusted gross income* and *taxable income.*

Gross up. To add back to the value of the property or income received the amount of the tax that has been paid. For gifts made within three years of death, any gift tax paid on the transfer is added to the gross estate. § 2035.

Group term life insurance. Life insurance coverage permitted by an employer for a group of employees. Such insurance is renewable on a year-to-year basis, and typically no cash surrender value is built up. The premiums paid by the employer on such insurance are not taxed to the employees on coverage of up to $50,000 per person. § 79 and Reg. § 1.79–1(b).

Guaranteed payments. Payments made by a partnership to a partner for services rendered or for the use of capital to the extent that such payments are determined without regard to the income of the partnership. Such payments are treated as though they were made to a nonpartner and thus are usually deductible by the entity.

Guardianship. A legal arrangement under which one person (a guardian) has the legal right and duty to care for another (the ward) and his or her property. A guardianship is established because of the ward's inability to legally act on his or her own behalf (e.g., because of minority [he or she is not of age] or mental or physical incapacity).

H

Head of household. An unmarried individual who maintains a household for another and satisfies certain conditions set forth in § 2(b). Such status enables the taxpayer to use a set of income tax rates that are lower than those applicable to other unmarried individuals but higher than those applicable to surviving spouses and married persons filing a joint return.

Heir. A person who inherits property from a decedent.

Hobby. An activity not engaged in for profit. The Code restricts the amount of losses that an individual can deduct with respect to hobby activities so that such transactions cannot be used to offset income from other sources. § 183.

Holding period. The period of time during which property has been held for income tax purposes. The holding period is significant in determining whether gain or loss from the sale or exchange of a capital asset is long term or short term. § 1223.

H.R. 10 plans. See *Keogh plans.*

Hot assets. This term refers to unrealized receivables and substantially appreciated inventory under § 751. When hot assets are present, the sale of a partnership interest or the disproportionate distribution of such assets can cause ordinary income to be recognized.

I

Imputed interest.   For certain long-term sales of property, the IRS can convert some of the gain from the sale into interest income if the contract does not provide for a minimum rate of interest to be paid by the purchaser. The application of this procedure has the effect of forcing the seller to recognize less long-term capital gain and more ordinary income (interest income). § 483 and the Regulations thereunder.

Incident of ownership.   An element of ownership or degree of control over a life insurance policy. The retention by an insured of an incident of ownership in a life insurance policy will cause the policy proceeds to be included in the insured's gross estate upon death. § 2042(2) and Reg. § 20.2042–1(c). See also *gross estate* and *insured.*

Includible gain.   Section 644 inposes a special tax on trusts that sell or exchange property at a gain within two years after the date of its transfer in trust by the transferor. The provision applies only if the fair market value of the property at the time of the initial transfer exceeds the adjusted basis of the property immediately after the transfer. The tax imposed by § 644 is the amount of additional tax the transferor would pay (including any minimum tax) had the gain been included in the transferor's gross income for the tax year of the sale. However, the tax applies only to an amount known as *includible gain.* This is the lesser of the following: the gain recognized by the trust on the sale or exchange of any property, or the excess of the fair market value of such property at the time of the initial transfer in trust by the transferor over the adjusted basis of such property immediately after the transfer.

Income beneficiary.   The party entitled to income from property. In a typical trust situation, A is to receive the income for life with corpus or principal passing to B upon A's death. In this case, A is the income beneficiary of the trust.

Income in respect of a decedent.   Income earned by a decedent at the time of death but not reportable on the final income tax return because of the method of accounting that appropriately is utilized. Such income is included in the gross estate and will be taxed to the eventual recipient (either the estate or heirs). The recipient will, however, be allowed an income tax deduction for the estate tax attributable to the income. § 691.

Income shifting.   Occurs when an individual tranfers some of his or her gross income to a taxpayer who is subject to a lower tax rate, thereby reducing the total income tax liability of the group. Income shifting produces a successful assignment of income. It can be accomplished by transferring income-producing property to the lower-bracket taxpayer or to an effective trust for his or her benefit, or by transferring ownership interests in a family partnership or in a closely held corporation.

Incomplete transfer.   A transfer made by a decedent during lifetime that, because of certain control or enjoyment retained by the transferor, is not considered complete for Federal estate tax purposes. Thus, some or all of the fair market value of the property transferred is included in the transferor's gross estate. §§ 2036–2038. See also *gross estate* and *revocable transfer.*

Individual retirement account (IRA).   Individuals with earned income are permitted to set aside up to 100 percent of such income per year (not to exceed $2,000) for a retirement account. The amount so set aside can be deducted by the taxpayer and is subject to income tax only upon withdrawal. The Code limits the amount of this contribution that can be deducted *for* AGI depending upon (1) whether the taxpayer or spouse is an active participant in an employer-provided qualified retirement plan and (2) the magnitude of the taxpayer's AGI before the IRA contribution is considered. § 219. See also *simplified employee pensions.*

Inheritance tax.   A tax imposed on the right to receive property from a decedent. Thus, theoretically, an inheritance tax is imposed on the heir. The Federal estate tax is imposed on the estate. See also *death tax* and *estate tax.*

In kind.   See *distributions in kind.*

Installment method.   A method of accounting enabling a taxpayer to spread the recognition of gain on the sale of property over the collection period. Under this procedure, the seller computes the gross profit percentage from the sale (the gain divided by the selling price) and applies it to each payment received, to arrive at the gain to be recognized. § 453.

Insured.   A person whose life is the subject of an insurance policy. Upon the death of the insured, the life insurance policy matures and the proceeds become payable to the designated beneficiary. See also *life insurance.*

Intangible asset.   Property that is a "right" rather than a physical object. Examples are patents, stocks and bonds, goodwill, trademarks, franchises, and copyrights. See also *amortization* and *tangible property.*

Inter vivos transfer.   A transfer of property during the life of the owner. Distinguished from testamentary transfers, wherein the property passes at death.

Interest-free loans.   Bona fide loans that carry no interest (or a below-market rate). If made in a nonbusiness setting, the imputed interest element is treated as a gift from the lender to the borrower. If made by a corporation to a shareholder, a constructive dividend could result. In either event, the lender may have interest income to recognize. § 7872.

Internal Revenue Code.   The collected statutes that govern the taxation of income, property transfers, and other transactions in the United States and the enforcement of such provisions. Enacted by Congress, the Code is amended frequently, but it has not been reorganized since 1954. Because of the extensive revisions to the statutes that occurred with respect to the Tax Reform Act of 1986, Title 26 of the U.S. Code is now known as the Internal Revenue Code of 1986.

Interpolated terminal reserve.   The measure used in valuing insurance policies for gift and estate tax purposes when the policies are not paid up at the time of their transfer. Reg. § 20.2031–8(a)(3), Ex. (3).

Intestate.   No will exists at the time of death. Under such circumstances, state law prescribes who

will receive the decedent's property. The laws of intestate succession generally favor the surviving spouse, children, and grandchildren, and then parents and grandparents and brothers and sisters.

Investment income.   Consisting of virtually the same elements as portfolio income, a measure by which to justify a deduction for interest on investment indebtedness. See also *investment indebtedness* and *portfolio income.*

Investment indebtedness.   Debt incurred to carry or incur investments by the taxpayer in assets that will produce portfolio income. Limitations are placed upon interest deductions that are incurred with respect to such debt (generally to the corresponding amount of investment income).

Investment tax credit.   A special tax credit equal to 6 or 10 percent of the qualified investment in tangible personal property used in a trade or business. Expired as of the end of 1985.

Investment tax credit recapture.   When property is disposed of or ceases to be used in the trade or business of the taxpayer, some of the investment tax credit claimed on such property may be recaptured as additional tax liability. § 47(a). See also *investment tax credit* and *Section 38 property.*

Involuntary conversion.   The loss or destruction of property through theft, casualty, or condemnation. Any gain realized on an involuntary conversion can, at the taxpayer's election, be deferred for Federal income tax purposes if the owner reinvests the proceeds within a prescribed period of time in property that is similar or related in service or use. § 1033.

IRA.   See *individual retirement account.*

Itemized deductions.   Personal and employee expenditures allowed by the Code as deductions from adjusted gross income. Examples include certain medical expenses, interest on home mortgages, and charitable contributions. Itemized deductions are reported on Schedule A of Form 1040.

J

Jeopardy assessment.   If the collection of a tax appears in question, the IRS may assess and collect the tax immediately without the usual formalities. The IRS can terminate a taxpayer's taxable year before the usual date if it feels that the collection of the tax may be in peril because the taxpayer plans to leave the country. §§ 6851 and 6861–6864.

Joint and several liability.   Permits the IRS to collect a tax from one or all of several taxpayers. A husband and wife who file a joint income tax return usually are collectively or individually liable for the full amount of the tax liability. § 6013(d) (3).

Joint tenancy.   The undivided ownership of property by two or more persons with the right of survivorship. Right of survivorship gives the surviving owner full ownership of the property. Suppose, for example, B and C are joint owners of a tract of land. Upon B's death, C becomes the sole owner of the property. As to the death tax consequences upon the death of a joint

tenant, see § 2040. See also *tenancy by the entirety* and *tenancy in common.*

Joint venture.   A one-time grouping of two or more persons in a business undertaking. Unlike a partnership, a joint venture does not entail a continuing relationship among the parties. A joint venture is treated like a partnership for Federal income tax purposes. § 7701(a)(2).

K

Keogh plans.   A designation for retirement plans available to self-employed taxpayers. They are also referred to as H.R. 10 plans. Under such plans a taxpayer may deduct each year up to either 20 percent of net earnings from self-employment or $30,000, whichever is less.

L

Lapse.   The expiration of a right either by the death of the holder or upon the expiration of a period of time. Thus, a power of appointment lapses upon the death of the holder if such holder has not exercised the power during life or at death (through a will).

Last-in, first-out (LIFO).   An accounting method for valuing inventories for tax purposes. Under this method, it is assumed that the inventory on hand is valued at the cost of the earliest acquired units. § 472. See also *first-in, first-out (FIFO).*

Layperson.   Nonmember of a specified profession.

Leaseback.   The transferor of property later leases it back. In a sale-leaseback situation, for example, R sells property to S and subsequently leases such property from S. Thus, R becomes the lessee and S the lessor.

Legacy.   A transfer of cash or other property by will.

Legal age.   The age at which a person may enter into binding contracts or commit other legal acts. In most states, a minor reaches legal age or majority (comes of age) at age 18.

Legal representative.   A person who oversees the legal affairs of another; for example, the executor or administrator of an estate or a court appointed guardian of a minor or incompetent person.

Legatee.   The recipient of property under a will and transferred by the death of the owner.

Lessee.   One who rents property from another. In the case of real estate, the lessee is also known as the tenant.

Lessor.   One who rents property to another. In the case of real estate, the lessor is also known as the landlord.

LEXIS.   An on-line database system, produced by Mead Data Services, by which the tax researcher can obtain access to the Internal Revenue Code, Regulations, administrative rulings, and court case opinions.

Life estate.   A legal arrangement under which the beneficiary (the life tenant) is entitled to the income from the property for his or her life. Upon the death of the life tenant, the property is transferred to the holder of the remainder interest. See also *income beneficiary* and *remainder interest.*

Life insurance.   A contract between the holder of a policy and an insurance company (the carrier) under which the company agrees, in return for premium payments, to pay a specified sum (the face value or maturity value of the policy) to the designated beneficiary upon the death of the insured. See also *insured.*

Lifetime exemption.   See *specific exemption.*

Like-kind exchange.   An exchange of property held for productive use in a trade or business or for investment (except inventory and stocks and bonds) for other investment or trade or business property. Unless non-like-kind property (boot) is received, the exchange is nontaxable. § 1031. See also *boot.*

Limited liability.   The liability of an entity and its owners to third parties is limited to the investment in the entity. This is a characteristic of a corporation since shareholders generally are not responsible for the debts of the corporation and, at most, may lose the amount paid in for the stock issued. Reg. § 301.7701–2(d). See also *association.*

Limited partner.   A partner whose liability to third-party creditors of the partnership is limited to the amount invested by such partner in the partnership. See also *general partner* and *limited partnership.*

Limited partnership.   A partnership in which some of the partners are limited partners. At least one of the partners in a limited partnership must be a general partner. See also *general partner* and *limited partner.*

Liquidating distribution.   A distribution by a partnership or corporation that is in complete liquidation of the entity's trade or business activities. Typically, such distributions generate capital gain or loss to the investors without regard, for instance, to the earnings and profits of the corporation or to the partnership's basis in the distributed property. They can, however, lead to recognized gain or loss at the corporate level.

Liquidation.   See *corporate liquidation.*

Lobbying expenditure.   An expenditure made for the purpose of influencing legislation. Such payments can result in the loss of the exempt status of, and the imposition of Federal income tax on, an exempt organization.

Long-term capital gain deduction.   Before 1987, noncorporate taxpayers were allowed a deduction *for* AGI to the extent of 60 percent of the net long-term capital gains that they recognized during the year.

Long-term capital gain or loss.   Results from the sale or other taxable exchange of a capital asset that had been held by the seller for more than one year or from other transactions involving statutorily designated assets, including § 1231 property and patents.

Lump-sum distribution.   Payment of the entire amount due at one time rather than in installments. Such distributions often occur from qualified pension or profit sharing plans upon the retirement or death of a covered employee.

M

Majority.   See *legal age.*

Malpractice.   Professional misconduct; an unreasonable lack of skill.

Marital deduction.   A deduction allowed against the taxable estate or taxable gifts upon the transfer of property from one spouse to another.

Market value.   See *fair market value.*

Merger.   The absorption of one corporation by another under which the corporation being absorbed loses its legal identity. X Corporation is merged into B Corporation, and the shareholders of X Corporation receive stock in B Corporation in exchange for their stock in X Corporation. After the merger, X Corporation ceases to exist as a separate legal entity. If a merger meets certain conditions, it is nontaxable to the parties involved. § 368(a) (1)(A). See also *corporate acquisition* and *corporate reorganization.*

Minimum tax.   See *alternative minimum tax.*

Minority.   See *legal age.*

Mitigation.   To make less severe. See also *mitigation of the annual accounting period concept* and *mitigation of the statute of limitations.*

Mitigation of the annual accounting period concept.   Various tax provisions that provide relief from the effect of the finality of the annual accounting period concept. For example, the net operating loss carryover provisions allow the taxpayer to apply the negative taxable income of one year against a corresponding positive amount in another tax accounting period. See also *annual accounting period concept.*

Mitigation of the statute of limitations.   A series of tax provisions that prevents either the IRS or a taxpayer from obtaining a double benefit from the application of the statute of limitations. It would be unfair, for example, to permit a taxpayer to depreciate an asset previously expensed, but which should have been capitalized, if the statute of limitations prevents the IRS from adjusting the tax liability for the year the asset was purchased. §§ 1311–1315. See also *statute of limitations.*

Mortgagee.   The party who holds the mortgage; the creditor.

Mortgagor.   The party who mortgages the property; the debtor.

Most suitable use value.   For gift and estate tax purposes, property that is transferred normally is valued in accordance with its most suitable or optimal use. Thus, if a farm is worth more as a potential shopping center, the value as a shopping center will control, even though the transferee (the donee or heir) continues to use the property as a farm. For an exception to this rule

concerning the valuation of certain kinds of real estate transferred by death, see *special use value.*

Multistate corporation.   A corporation that has operations in more than one of the states of the United States. Issues arise relative to the assignment of appropriate amounts of the entity's taxable income to the states in which it has a presence. See also *allocation, apportionment, nexus,* and *UDITPA.*

Multistate Tax Commission.   A regulatory body of the states that develops operating rules and regulations for the implementation of UDITPA and other provisions that assign the total taxable income of a multistate corporation to specific states. See also *allocation, apportionment,* and *UDITPA.*

Multi-tiered partnerships.   See *tiered partnerships.*

N

Necessary.   Appropriate and helpful in furthering the taxpayer's business or income-producing activity. §§ 162(a) and 212. See also *ordinary.*

Negligence.   Failure to exercise the reasonable or ordinary degree of care of a prudent person in a situation that results in harm or damage to another. Code § 6653(a) imposes a penalty on taxpayers who show negligence or intentional disregard of rules and Regulations with respect to the underpayment of certain taxes.

Net operating loss.   To mitigate the effect of the annual accounting period concept, § 172 allows taxpayers to use an excess loss of one year as a deduction for certain past or future years. In this regard, a carryback period of 3 years and a carryforward period of 15 years currently is allowed. See also *mitigation of the annual accounting period concept.*

Net worth method.   An approach used by the IRS to reconstruct the income of a taxpayer who fails to maintain adequate records. Under this method, the gross income for the year is estimated as the increase in net worth of the taxpayer (assets in excess of liabilities) with appropriate adjustment for nontaxable receipts and nondeductible expenditures. The net worth method often is used when tax fraud is suspected.

Nexus.   A multistate corporation's taxable income can be apportioned to a specific state only if the entity has established a sufficient presence, or nexus, with that state. State law, which often follows UDITPA, specifies various activities that lead to such nexus in various states. See also *apportionment* and *UDITPA.*

Ninety-day letter.   See *statutory notice of deficiency.*

Nonacquiescence.   Disagreement by the IRS on the result reached by the U.S. Tax Court in a Regular Decision. Sometimes abbreviated *non-acq.* or *NA.* See also *acquiescence.*

Nonbusiness bad debts.   A bad debt loss incurred not in connection with a creditor's trade or business. Such loss is classified as a short-term capital loss and will be allowed only in the year the debt becomes entirely worthless. In addition to family loans, many investor losses fall into the classification of nonbusiness bad debts. § 166(d). See also *business bad debts.*

Nonbusiness income.   Income generated from investment assets or from the taxable disposition thereof. In some states, the nonbusiness income of a multistate corporation is held out of the apportionment procedure and allocated to the state in which the nonbusiness asset is located. See also *allocation* and *apportionment.*

Noncontributory qualified pension or profit sharing plan.   A plan funded entirely by the employer with no contributions being made by the covered employees. See also *qualified pension or profit sharing plans.*

Nonliquidating distribution.   A payment made by a partnership or corporation to the entity's owner is a nonliquidating distribution when the entity's legal existence does not cease thereafter. If the payor is a corporation, such a distribution can result in dividend income to the shareholders. If the payor is a partnership, the partner usually assigns a basis in the distributed property that is equal to the lesser of the partner's basis in the partnership interest or the basis of the distributed asset to the partnership. In this regard, the partner first assigns basis to any cash that he or she receives in the distribution. The partner's remaining basis, if any, is assigned to the noncash assets according to their relative bases to the partnership.

Nonrecourse debt.   Debt secured by the property that it is used to purchase. The purchaser of the property is not personally liable for the debt upon default. Rather, the creditor's recourse is to repossess the related property. Nonrecourse debt generally does not increase the purchaser's at-risk amount.

Nonresident alien.   An individual who is not a citizen or resident of the United States. Citizenship is determined under the immigration and naturalization laws of the United States. Residency is determined under § 7701(b) of the Internal Revenue Code.

Nonseparately stated income.   The net income of an S corporation that is combined and allocated to the shareholders. Other items, such as capital gains and charitable contributions, that could be treated differently on the individual tax returns of the shareholders are not included in this amount but are allocated to the shareholders separately.

O

Obligee.   The party to whom someone else is obligated under a contract. Thus, if C loans money to D, C is the obligee and D is the obligor under the loan.

Obligor.   See *obligee.*

Office audit.   An audit conducted by the IRS in the agent's office. See also *audit, correspondence audit,* and *field audit.*

On all fours.   A judicial decision exactly in point with another as to result, facts, or both.

Optimal use value.   Synonym for most suitable use value.

Ordinary.   Common and accepted in the general industry or type of activity in which the taxpayer is engaged. It comprises one of the tests for the deductibility of expenses incurred or paid in connection with a trade or business; for the production or collection of income; for the management, conservation, or maintenance of property held for the production of income; or in connection with the determination, collection, or refund of any tax. §§ 162(a) and 212. See also *necessary.*

Ordinary and necessary.   See *necessary* and *ordinary.*

Ordinary gross income.   A concept peculiar to personal holding companies and defined in § 543(b)(1). See also *adjusted ordinary gross income.*

P

Partner.   See *general partner* and *limited partner.*

Partnership.   For income tax purposes, a partnership includes a syndicate, group, pool, or joint venture, as well as ordinary partnerships. In an ordinary partnership, two or more parties combine capital and/or services to carry on a business for profit as co-owners. § 7701(a)(2). See also *limited partnership* and *tiered partnerships.*

Passive investment income.   Passive investment income means gross receipts from royalties, certain rents, dividends, interest, annuities, and gains from the sale or exchange of stock and securities. With certain exceptions, if the passive investment income of an S corporation exceeds 25 percent of the corporation's gross receipts for three consecutive years, S status is lost.

Passive foreign investment company (PFIC). A non-U.S. corporation that generates a substantial magnitude of personal holding company income. Upon receipt of an excess distribution from the entity or the sale of its shares, its U.S. shareholders are taxable on their pro rata shares of the tax that has been deferred with respect to the corporation's taxable income, plus an applicable interest charge.

Passive loss.   Any loss from (1) activities in which the taxpayer does not materially participate, (2) rental activities, or (3) tax shelter activities. Net passive losses cannot be used to offset income from nonpassive sources. Rather, they are suspended until the taxpayer either generates net passive income (and a deduction of such losses is allowed) or disposes of the underlying property (at which time the loss deductions are allowed in full). Landlords who actively participate in the rental activities can deduct up to $25,000 of passive losses annually. However, this amount is phased out when the landlord's AGI exceeds $100,000. Passive loss limitations are phased in beginning in 1987. See also *portfolio income.*

Payroll factor.   The proportion of a multistate corporation's total payroll that is traceable to a specific state. Used in determining the taxable income that is to be apportioned to that state. See also *apportionment.*

Pecuniary bequest.   A bequest of money to an heir by a decedent. See also *bequest.*

Percentage depletion.   See *depletion.*

Percentage of completion method.   A method of reporting gain or loss on certain long-term contracts. Under this method of accounting, the gross contract price is included in income as the contract is completed. Reg. § 1.451–3. See also *completed contract method.*

Personal and household effects.   Items owned by a decedent at the time of death. Examples include clothing, furniture, sporting goods, jewelry, stamp and coin collections, silverware, china, crystal, cooking utensils, books, cars, televisions, radios, stereo equipment, etc.

Personal holding company.   A corporation that satisfies the requirements of § 542. Qualification as a personal holding company means a penalty tax will be imposed on the corporation's undistributed personal holding company income for the year.

Personal holding company income.   Income as defined by § 543. Such income includes interest, dividends, certain rents and royalties, income from the use of corporate property by certain shareholders, income from certain personal service contracts, and distributions from estates and trusts. Such income is relevant in determining whether a corporation is a personal holding company and is therefore subject to the penalty tax on personal holding companies. See also *adjusted ordinary gross income.*

Personal property.   Generally, all property other than real estate. It is sometimes designated as personalty when real estate is termed realty. Personal property can also refer to property not used in a taxpayer's trade or business or held for the production or collection of income. When used in this sense, personal property could include both realty (e.g., a personal residence) and personalty (e.g., personal effects such as clothing and furniture). See also *bequest.*

Personalty.   Personalty is all property that is not attached to real estate (realty) and is movable. Examples of personalty are machinery, automobiles, clothing, household furnishings, inventory, and personal effects. See also *ad valorem tax* and *realty.*

P-H.   Prentice-Hall is the publisher of a tax service and of Federal tax decisions (AFTR and AFTR2d series).

PHINet.   An on-line database system, produced by Prentice-Hall Information Services, by which the tax researcher can obtain access to the Internal Revenue Code, Regulations, administrative rulings, and court case opinions.

Portfolio income.   Income from interest, dividends, rentals, royalties, capital gains, or other investment sources. Net passive losses cannot be used to offset net portfolio income. See also *passive loss* and *investment income.*

Power of appointment.   A legal right granted to someone by will or other document that gives the holder the power to dispose of property or the income from property. When the holder may appoint the prop-

erty to his or her own benefit, the power usually is designated as a general power of appointment. If the holder cannot benefit himself or herself but may only appoint to certain other persons, the power is a special power of appointment. For example, assume G places $500,000 worth of securities in trust granting D the right to determine each year how the trustee is to divide the income between A and B. Under these circumstances, D has a special power of appointment. If D had the further right to appoint the income to himself, he or she probably possesses a general power of appointment. For the estate tax and gift tax effects of powers of appointment, see §§ 2041 and 2514. See also *testamentary power of appointment.*

Preferred stock bailout.   A process wherein the issuance, sale, and later redemption of a preferred stock dividend was used by a shareholder to obtain long-term capital gains without any loss of voting control over the corporation. In effect, therefore, the shareholder was able to bail out corporate profits without suffering the consequences of dividend income treatment. This procedure led to the enactment by Congress of § 306, which, if applicable, converts the prior long-term capital gain on the sale of the stock to ordinary income. Under these circumstances, the amount of ordinary income is limited to the shareholder's portion of the corporation's earnings and profits existing when the preferred stock was issued as a stock dividend. See also *bailout.*

Present interest.   See *future interest.*

Presumption.   An inference in favor of a particular fact. If, for example, the IRS issues a notice of deficiency against a taxpayer, a presumption of correctness attaches to the assessment. Thus, the taxpayer has the burden of proof of showing that he or she does not owe the tax listed in the deficiency notice. See also *rebuttable presumption.*

Previously taxed income (PTI).   Before the Subchapter S Revision Act of 1982, the undistributed taxable income of an S corporation was taxed to the shareholders as of the last day of the corporation's tax year and usually could be withdrawn by the shareholders without tax consequences at some later point in time. The role of PTI has been taken over by the accumulated adjustments account. See also *accumulated adjustments account.*

Principal.   Property as opposed to income. The term is often used as a synonym for the corpus of a trust. If, for example, G places real estate in trust with income payable to A for life and the remainder to B upon A's death, the real estate is the principal, or corpus, of the trust.

Private foundation.   An exempt organization that is subject to additional statutory restrictions on its activities and on contributions thereto. Excise taxes may be levied on certain prohibited transactions, and the Code places more stringent restrictions on the deductibility of contributions to private foundations. § 509.

Pro se.   The taxpayer represents himself or herself before the court, without the benefit of counsel.

Probate.   The legal process wherein the estate of a decedent is administered. Generally, the probate process involves collecting a decedent's assets, liquidating liabilities, paying necessary taxes, and distributing property to heirs.

Probate court.   The usual designation for the state or local court that supervises the administration (probate) of a decedent's estate.

Probate estate.   The property of a decedent that is subject to administration by the executor or administrator of an estate. See also *administration.*

Property factor.   The proportion of a multistate corporation's total property that is traceable to a specific state. Used in determining the taxable income that is to be apportioned to that state. See also *apportionment.*

Property tax.   An *ad valorem* tax, usually levied by a city or county government, on the value of real or personal property that the taxpayer owns on a specified date. Most states exclude intangible property and assets owned by exempt organizations from the tax base, and some exclude inventory, pollution control or manufacturing equipment, and other items to provide relocation or retention incentives to the taxpayer.

Prop.Reg.   An abbreviation for Proposed Regulation. A Regulation may first be issued in proposed form to give interested parties the opportunity for comment. When and if a Proposed Regulation is finalized, it is designated as a Regulation (abbreviated Reg.).

Pro rata.   Proportionately. Assume, for example, a corporation has 10 shareholders, each of whom owns 10 percent of the stock. A pro rata dividend distribution of $1,000 would mean that each shareholder would receive $100.

PTI.   See *previously taxed income.*

Public Law 86-272.   A Congressional limit on the ability of the state to force a multistate corporation to assign income to that state. Under P.L. 86-272, where orders for tangible personal property are both filled and delivered outside of the state, the entity must establish more than the mere solicitation of such orders before any income can be apportioned to the state. See also *apportionment.*

Public policy limitation.   A concept developed by the courts precluding an income tax deduction for certain expenses related to activities deemed to be contrary to the public welfare. In this connection, Congress has incorporated into the Code specific disallowance provisions covering such items as illegal bribes, kickbacks, and fines and penalties. §§ 162(c) and (f).

Q

Qualified pension or profit sharing plan.   An employer-sponsored plan that meets the requirements of § 401. If these requirements are met, none of the employer's contributions to the plan will be taxed to the employee until distributed to him or her (§ 402). The employer will be allowed a deduction in the year the contributions are made (§ 404). See also *contributory qualified pension or profit sharing plan, deferred*

compensation, and *noncontributory pension or profit sharing plan.*

Qualified terminable interest property (QTIP). Generally, the marital deduction (for gift and estate tax purposes) is not available if the interest transferred will terminate upon the death of the transferee spouse and pass to someone else. Thus, if H places property in trust, life estate to W, and remainder to their children upon W's death, this is a terminable interest that will not provide H (or H's estate) with a marital deduction. If, however, the transfer in trust is treated as qualified terminable interest property (the QTIP election is made), the terminable interest restriction is waived and the marital deduction becomes available. In exchange for this deduction, the surviving spouse's gross estate must include the value of the QTIP election assets, even though he or she has no control over the ultimate disposition of the asset. Terminable interest property qualifies for this election if the donee (or heir) is the only beneficiary of the asset during his or her lifetime and receives income distributions relative to the property at least annually. As to gifts, the donor spouse is the one who makes the QTIP election. As to property transferred by death, the executor of the estate of the deceased spouse has the right to make the election. §§ 2056(b)(7) and 2523(f).

R

RAR.   A Revenue agent's report, which reflects any adjustments made by the agent as a result of an audit of the taxpayer. The RAR is mailed to the taxpayer along with the 30-day letter, which outlines the appellate procedures available to the taxpayer.

Realized gain or loss.   The difference between the amount realized upon the sale or other disposition of property and the adjusted basis of such property. § 1001. See also *adjusted basis, amount realized, basis,* and *recognized gain or loss.*

Realty.   Real estate. See also *personalty.*

Reasonable needs of the business.   The usual justification for avoiding the penalty tax on unreasonable accumulation of earnings. In determining the amount of taxable income subject to this tax (accumulated taxable income), § 535 allows a deduction for "such part of earnings and profits for the taxable year as are retained for the reasonable needs of the business." § 537.

Rebuttable presumption.   A presumption that can be overturned upon the showing of sufficient proof. See also *presumption.*

Recapture.   To recover the tax benefit of a deduction or a credit previously taken. See also *depreciation recapture* and *investment tax credit recapture.*

Recapture potential.   A measure with respect to property that, if disposed of in a taxable transaction, would result in the recapture of depreciation (§§ 1245 or 1250), deferred LIFO gain, or deferred installment method gain.

Recognized gain or loss.   The portion of realized gain or loss subject to income taxation. See also *realized gain or loss.*

Regulations.   The U.S. Treasury Department Regulations (abbreviated Reg.) represent the position of the IRS as to how the Internal Revenue Code is to be interpreted. Their purpose is to provide taxpayers and IRS personnel with rules of general and specific application to the various provisions of the tax law. Regulations are published in the *Federal Register* and in all tax services.

Related parties.   Various Code Sections define related parties and often include a variety of persons within this (usually detrimental) category. Generally, related parties are accorded different tax treatment from that which applies to other taxpayers who would enter into similar transactions. For instance, realized losses that are generated between related parties are not recognized in the year of the loss. However, these deferred losses can be used to offset recognized gains that occur upon the subsequent sale of the asset to a nonrelated party. Other uses of a related-party definition include the conversion of gain upon the sale of a depreciable asset into all ordinary income (§ 1239) and the identification of constructive ownership of stock relative to corporate distributions, redemptions, liquidations, reorganizations, and compensation.

Remainder interest.   The property that passes to a beneficiary after the expiration of an intervening income interest. If, for example, G places real estate in trust with income to A for life and remainder to B upon A's death, B has a remainder interest. See also *life estate* and *reversionary interest.*

Remand.   To send back. An appellate court may remand a case to a lower court, usually for additional fact finding. In other words, the appellate court is not in a position to decide the appeal based on the facts determined by the lower court. Remanding is abbreviated "rem'g."

Reorganization.   See *corporate reorganization.*

Return of capital.   When a taxpayer reacquires financial resources that he or she previously had invested in an entity or venture, the return of his or her capital investment itself does not increase gross income for the recovery year. A return of capital may occur with respect to an annuity or insurance contract, the sale or exchange of any asset, or a distribution from a partnership or corporation.

Revenue neutral.   A change in the tax system that results in the same amount of revenue. Revenue neutral, however, does not mean that any one taxpayer will pay the same amount of tax as was previously the case. Thus, as a result of a tax law change, corporations could pay more taxes, but the excess revenue will be offset by lesser taxes on individuals.

Revenue Procedure.   A matter of procedural importance to both taxpayers and the IRS concerning the administration of the tax laws is issued as a Revenue Procedure (abbreviated Rev.Proc.). A Revenue Procedure is first published in an Internal Revenue Bulletin (I.R.B.) and later transferred to the appropriate Cumulative Bulletin (C.B.). Both the Internal Revenue Bulletins and the Cumulative Bulletins are published by the U.S. Government Printing Office.

Revenue Ruling.   A Revenue Ruling (abbreviated Rev.Rul.) is issued by the National Office of the IRS to express an official interpretation of the tax law as applied to specific transactions. Unlike a Regulation, it is more limited in application. A Revenue Ruling is first published in an Internal Revenue Bulletin (I.R.B.) and later transferred to the appropriate Cumulative Bulletin (C.B.). Both the Internal Revenue Bulletins and the Cumulative Bulletins are published by the U.S. Government Printing Office.

Reversed (Rev'd.).   An indication that a decision of one court has been reversed by a higher court in the same case.

Reversing (Rev'g.).   An indication that the decision of a higher court is reversing the result reached by a lower court in the same case.

Reversionary interest.   The property that reverts to the grantor after the expiration of an intervening income interest. Assume, for example, G places real estate in trust with income to A for 11 years, and upon the expiration of this term, the property returns to G. Under these circumstances, G holds a reversionary interest in the property. A reversionary interest is the same as a remainder interest, except that, in the latter case, the property passes to someone other than the original owner (e.g., the grantor of a trust) upon the expiration of the intervening interest. See also *Clifford trust*, *grantor trust*, and *remainder interest*.

Revocable transfer.   A transfer of property whereby the transferor retains the right to recover the property. The creation of a revocable trust is an example of a revocable transfer. § 2038. See also *incomplete transfer*.

Rev.Proc.   Abbreviation for an IRS Revenue Procedure. See *Revenue Procedure*.

Rev.Rul.   Abbreviation for an IRS Revenue Ruling. See *Revenue Ruling*.

Right of survivorship.   See *joint tenancy*.

S

Sales factor.   The proportion of a multistate corporation's total sales that is traceable to a specific state. Used in determining the taxable income that is to be apportioned to that state. See also *apportionment*.

Sales tax.   A state- or local-level tax on the retail sale of specified property. Generally, the purchaser pays the tax, but the seller collects it, as an agent for the government. Various taxing jurisdictions allow exemptions for purchases of specific items, including certain food, services, and manufacturing equipment. If the purchaser and seller are in different states, a *use tax* usually applies.

Schedule PH.   A tax form required to be filed by corporations that are personal holding companies. The form must be filed in addition to Form 1120 (U.S. Corporation Income Tax Return).

S corporation.   The designation for a small business corporation. See also *Subchapter S*.

Section 38 property.   Property that qualified for the investment tax credit. Generally, this included all tangible property (other than real estate) used in a trade or business. § 48.

Section 306 stock.   Preferred stock issued as a nontaxable stock dividend that, if sold or redeemed, would result in ordinary income recognition. § 306(c). See also *preferred stock bailout*.

Section 306 taint.   The ordinary income that would result upon the sale or other taxable disposition of § 306 stock.

Section 1231 assets.   Depreciable assets and real estate used in a trade or business and held for the appropriate holding period. Under certain circumstances, the classification also includes timber, coal, domestic iron ore, livestock (held for draft, breeding, dairy, or sporting purposes), and unharvested crops. § 1231(b). See also *Section 1231 gains and losses*.

Section 1231 gains and losses.   If the combined gains and losses from the taxable dispositions of § 1231 assets plus the net gain from business involuntary conversions (of both § 1231 assets and long-term capital assets) is a gain, such gains and losses are treated as long-term capital gains and losses. In arriving at § 1231 gains, however, the depreciation recapture provisions (e.g., §§ 1245 and 1250) are first applied to produce ordinary income. If the net result of the combination is a loss, such gains and losses from § 1231 assets are treated as ordinary gains and losses. § 1231(a). See also *depreciation recapture* and *Section 1231 assets*.

Section 1244 stock.   Stock issued under § 1244 by qualifying small business corporations. If § 1244 stock becomes worthless, the shareholders may claim an ordinary loss rather than the usual capital loss, within statutory limitations.

Section 1245 recapture.   Upon a taxable disposition of § 1245 property, all depreciation claimed on such property is recaptured as ordinary income (but not to exceed recognized gain from the disposition).

Section 1250 recapture.   Upon a taxable disposition of § 1250 property, some of the depreciation or cost recovery claimed on the property may be recaptured as ordinary income.

Separate property.   In a community property jurisdiction, separate property is that property that belongs entirely to one of the spouses. Generally, it is property acquired before marriage or acquired after marriage by gift or inheritance. See also *community property*.

Sham.   A transaction without substance that will be disregarded for tax purposes.

Short-term capital gain or loss.   Results from the sale or other taxable exchange of a capital asset that had been held by the seller for one year or less or from other transactions involving statutorily designated assets, including nonbusiness bad debts.

Simple trusts.   Simple trusts are those that are not complex trusts. Such trusts may not have a chari-

table beneficiary, accumulate income, or distribute corpus. See also *complex trusts.*

Simplified employee pensions.   An employer may make contributions to an employee's individual retirement account (IRA) in amounts not exceeding the lesser of 15 percent of compensation or $30,000 per individual. § 219(b)(2). See also *individual retirement account.*

Small business corporation.   A corporation that satisfies the definition of § 1361(b), § 1244(c)(2), or both. Satisfaction of § 1361(b) permits an S election, and satisfaction of § 1244 enables the shareholders of the corporation to claim an ordinary loss on the worthlessness of stock.

Special power of appointment.   See *power of appointment.*

Special use value.   An option that permits the executor of an estate to value, for death tax purposes, real estate used in a farming activity or in connection with a closely held business at its current use value rather than at its most suitable or optimal use value. Under this option, a farm is valued for farming purposes even though, for example, the property might have a higher potential value as a shopping center. For the executor of an estate to elect special use valuation, the conditions of § 2032A must be satisfied. See also *most suitable use value.*

Specific bequest.   A bequest of ascertainable property or cash to an heir of a decedent. Thus, if D's will passes his personal residence to W and grants $10,000 in cash to S, both W and S receive specific bequests.

Specific exemption.   For transfers made before 1977, each donor was allowed a lifetime exemption from the gift tax for $30,000. The exemption could be used to offset any taxable gifts made.

Specific legatee.   The recipient of designated property under a will and transferred by the death of the owner.

Spin-off.   A type of reorganization wherein, for example, A Corporation transfers some assets to B Corporation in exchange for enough B stock to represent control. A Corporation then distributes the B stock to its shareholders.

Split-off.   A type of reorganization wherein, for example, A Corporation transfers some assets to B Corporation in exchange for enough B stock to represent control. A Corporation then distributes the B stock to its shareholders in exchange for some of their A stock.

Split-up.   A type of reorganization wherein, for example, A Corporation transfers some assets to B Corporation and the remainder to Z Corporation in return for which it receives enough B and Z stock to represent control of each corporation. The B and Z stock is then distributed by A Corporation to its shareholders in return for all of their A stock. The result of the split-up is that A Corporation is liquidated, and its shareholders now have control of B and Z Corporations.

Sprinkling trust.   When a trustee has the discretion to either distribute or accumulate the entity accounting income of the trust and to distribute it among the trust's income beneficiaries in varying magnitudes, a sprinkling trust exists. The trustee can "sprinkle" the income of the trust.

Standard deduction.   A minimum amount allowed to individual taxpayers as a deduction *from* AGI to minimize recordkeeping responsibilities. An additional standard deduction amount is allowed to taxpayers who are either blind or age 65 or older. A limited standard deduction is allowed to a taxpayer who is claimed as a dependent on another's tax return.

Statute of limitations.   Provisions of the law that specify the maximum period of time in which action may be taken on a past event. Code §§ 6501–6504 contain the limitation periods applicable to the IRS for additional assessments, and §§ 6511–6515 relate to refund claims by taxpayers.

Statutory depletion.   See *depletion.*

Statutory notice of deficiency.   Commonly referred to as the 90-day letter, this notice is sent to a taxpayer upon request, upon the expiration of the 30-day letter, or upon exhaustion by the taxpayer of his or her administrative remedies before the IRS. The notice gives the taxpayer 90 days in which to file a petition with the U.S. Tax Court. If such a petition is not filed, the IRS will issue a demand for payment of the assessed deficiency. §§ 6211–6216. See also *deficiency* and *thirty-day letter.*

Step-down in basis.   A reduction in the income tax basis of property.

Step-transaction approach.   Disregarding one or more transactions to arrive at the final result. Assume, for example, that the shareholders of A Corporation liquidate the corporation and thereby receive cash and operating assets. Immediately after the liquidation, the shareholders transfer the operating assets to newly formed B Corporation. Under these circumstances, the IRS may contend that the liquidation of A Corporation be disregarded (thereby depriving the shareholders of capital gain treatment). What may really have happened is a reorganization of A Corporation with a distribution of boot (ordinary income) to A's shareholders. If this is so, there will be a carryover of basis in the assets transferred from A Corporation to B Corporation.

Step-up in basis.   An increase in the income tax basis of property. The classic step-up in basis occurs when a decedent dies owning appreciated property. Since the estate or heir acquires a basis in the property equal to the property's fair market value on the date of death (or alternate valuation date if available and elected), any appreciation is not subject to the income tax. Thus, a step-up in basis is the result, with no income tax consequences.

Stock attribution.   See *attribution.*

Stock redemption.   Occurs when a corporation buys back its own stock from a specified shareholder. Typically, the corporation recognizes any realized gain or loss on the noncash assets that it uses to effect a redemption, and the shareholder obtains a capital gain or loss upon receipt of the purchase price.

Subchapter S.   Sections 1361–1379 of the Internal Revenue Code. An elective provision permitting certain small business corporations (§ 1361) and their shareholders (§ 1362) to elect to be treated for income tax purposes in accordance with the operating rules of §§ 1363–1379. Of major significance is the fact that S corporations usually avoid the corporate income tax and corporate losses can be claimed by the shareholders.

Substance vs. form concept.   A standard used when one must ascertain the true reality of what has occurred. Suppose, for example, a father sells stock to his daughter for $1,000. If the stock is really worth $50,000 at the time of the transfer, the substance of the transaction is probably a gift to her of $49,000.

Substantial economic effect.   Partnerships are allowed to allocate items of income, expense, gain, loss, and credit in any manner that is authorized in the partnership agreement, provided that such allocation has an economic effect aside from the corresponding tax results. The necessary substantial economic effect is present, for instance, if the post-contribution appreciation in the value of an asset that was contributed to the partnership by a partner were allocated to that partner for cost recovery purposes.

Surviving spouse.   When a husband or wife predeceases the other spouse, the survivor is known as a surviving spouse. Under certain conditions, a surviving spouse may be entitled to use the income tax rates in § 1(a) (those applicable to married persons filing a joint return) for the two years after the year of death of his or her spouse.

Survivorship.   See *joint tenancy.*

T

Tangible property.   All property that has form or substance and is not intangible. See also *intangible asset.*

Tax benefit rule.   A rule that limits the recognition of income from the recovery of an expense or loss properly deducted in a prior tax year to the amount of the deduction that generated a tax saving. Assume, for example, that last year T (an individual) had medical expenses of $3,000 and adjusted gross income of $30,000. Because of the 7.5 percent limitation, T was able to deduct only $750 of these expenses [$3,000 − (7.5% × $30,000)]. If, in this year, T is reimbursed by his insurance company for $900 of these expenses, the tax benefit rule limits the amount of income from the reimbursement to $750 (the amount previously deducted with a tax saving).

Tax Court.   The U.S. Tax Court is one of three trial courts of original jurisdiction that decide litigation involving Federal income, death, or gift taxes. It is the only trial court where the taxpayer must not first pay the deficiency assessed by the IRS. The Tax Court will not have jurisdiction over a case unless the statutory notice of deficiency (90-day letter) has been issued by the IRS and the taxpayer files the petition for hearing within the time prescribed.

Tax on unearned income of a child under age 14.   Passive income, such as interest and dividends, that is recognized by such a child is taxed *to him or her* at the rates that would have applied had the income been incurred by the child's parents, generally to the extent that such income exceeds $1,000. The additional tax is assessed regardless of the source of the income or the income's underlying property. If the child's parents are divorced, the custodial parent's rates are used. The parents' rates reflect any applicable alternative minimum tax and the phase-outs of lower tax brackets and other deductions.

Tax preference items.   Those items that may result in the imposition of the alternative minimum tax. §§ 55–58. See also *alternative minimum tax.*

Tax year.   See *accounting period.*

Taxable estate.   Defined in § 2051, the taxable estate is the gross estate of a decedent reduced by the deductions allowed by §§ 2053–2057 (e.g., administration expenses, marital, charitable, and ESOP deductions). The taxable estate is the amount that is subject to the unified transfer tax at death. See also *adjusted taxable estate* and *gross estate.*

Taxable gift.   Defined in § 2503, a taxable gift is the amount of the gift that is subject to the unified transfer tax. Thus, a taxable gift has been adjusted by the annual exclusion and other appropriate deductions (e.g., marital and charitable).

Taxable income.   The tax base with respect to the prevailing Federal income tax. Taxable income is defined by the Internal Revenue Code, Treasury Regulations, and pertinent court cases. Currently, taxable income includes gross income from all sources except those specifically excluded by the statute. In addition, taxable income is reduced for certain allowable deductions. Deductions for business taxpayers must be related to a trade or business. Individuals also can deduct certain personal expenses in determining their taxable incomes. See also *gross income.*

Tax-free exchange.   Transfers of property specifically exempted from income tax consequences by the tax law. Examples are a transfer of property to a controlled corporation under § 351(a) and a like-kind exchange under § 1031(a).

T.C.   An abbreviation for the U.S. Tax Court used to cite a Regular Decision of the U.S. Tax Court.

T.C. Memo.   An abbreviation used to refer to a Memorandum Decision of the U.S. Tax Court.

Telescoping.   To look through one or more transactions to arrive at the final result. It is also designated as the *step-transaction approach* or the *substance vs. form concept* (see these terms).

Tenancy by the entirety.   Essentially, a joint tenancy between husband and wife. See also *joint tenancy* and *tenancy in common.*

Tenancy in common.   A form of ownership whereby each tenant (owner) holds an undivided interest in property. Unlike a joint tenancy or a tenancy by the entirety, the interest of a tenant in common does not terminate upon that individual's death (there is no right of survivorship). Assume, for example, B and C acquire real estate as equal tenants in common, each having

furnished one-half of the purchase price. Upon B's death, his one-half interest in the property passes to his estate or heirs, not to C. For a comparison of results, see also *joint tenancy* and *tenancy by the entirety*.

Terminable interest.   An interest in property that terminates upon the death of the holder or upon the occurrence of some other specified event. The transfer of a terminable interest by one spouse to the other may not qualify for the marital deduction. §§ 2056(b) and 2523(b). See also *marital deduction.*

Testamentary disposition.   The passing of property to another upon the death of the owner.

Testamentary power of appointment.   A power of appointment that can be exercised only through the will (upon the death) of the holder. See also *power of appointment.*

Thin capitalization.   When debt owed by a corporation to the shareholders becomes too large in relation to the corporation's capital structure (i.e., stock and shareholder equity), the IRS may contend that the corporation is thinly capitalized. In effect, this means that some or all of the debt will be reclassified as equity. The immediate result is to disallow any interest deduction to the corporation on the reclassified debt. To the extent of the corporation's earnings and profits, interest payments and loan repayments are treated as dividends to the shareholders.

Thirty-day letter.   A letter that accompanies a revenue agent's report issued as a result of an IRS audit of a taxpayer (or the rejection of a taxpayer's claim for refund). The letter outlines the taxpayer's appeal procedure before the IRS. If the taxpayer does not request any such procedures within the 30-day period, the IRS will issue a statutory notice of deficiency (the 90-day letter). See also *statutory notice of deficiency.*

Three-factor apportionment formula.   A means by which the total taxable income of a multistate corporation is assigned to a specific state. Usually, the payroll, property, and sales factors are treated equally, and the weighted average of these factors is used in the apportionment procedure. In some states, however, the sales factor may receive a double weight, or it may be the only factor considered. These latter formulas place greater tax burden on the income of out-of-state corporations. See also *apportionment, payroll factor, property factor, sales factor,* and *UDITPA.*

Throwback rule.   If there is no income tax in the state to which a sale would otherwise be assigned for apportionment purposes, the sale essentially is exempt from state income tax, even though the seller is domiciled in a state that levies an income tax. Nonetheless, if the seller's state has adopted a throwback rule, the sale is attributed to the *seller's* state, and the transaction is subjected to a state-level tax. See also *apportionment* and *sales factor.*

Tiered partnerships.   An ownership arrangement wherein one partnership (the parent or first tier) is a partner in one or more partnerships (the subsidiary/subsidiaries or second tier). Frequently, the first tier is a holding partnership, and the second tier is an operating partnership.

Trade or business.   Any business or professional activity conducted by a taxpayer. The mere ownership of rental or other investment assets does not constitute a trade or business. Generally, a trade or business generates relatively little passive investment income.

Transfer tax.   A tax imposed upon the transfer of property. See also *unified transfer tax.*

Transferee liability.   Under certain conditions, if the IRS is unable to collect taxes owed by a transferor of property, it may pursue its claim against the transferee of such property. The transferee's liability for taxes is limited to the extent of the value of the assets transferred. For example, the IRS can force a donee to pay the gift tax when such tax cannot be paid by the donor making the transfer. §§ 6901–6905.

Treasury Regulations.   See *Regulations.*

Trial court.   The court of original jurisdiction; the first court to consider litigation. In Federal tax controversies, trial courts include U.S. District Courts, the U.S. Tax Court, and the U.S. Claims Court. See also *appellate court, Claims Court, District Court,* and *Tax Court.*

Trust.   A legal entity created by a grantor for the benefit of designated beneficiaries under the laws of the state and the valid trust instrument. The trustee holds a fiduciary responsibility to manage the trust's corpus assets and income for the economic benefit of all of the beneficiaries.

Trustee.   An individual or corporation that takes the fiduciary responsibilities under a trust agreement.

U

UDITPA.   The Uniform Division of Income for Tax Purposes Act has been adopted in some form by many of the states. The Act develops criteria by which the total taxable income of a multistate corporation can be assigned to specific states. See also *allocation, apportionment, Multistate Tax Commission,* and *nexus.*

Undistributed personal holding company income.   The penalty tax on personal holding companies is imposed on the corporation's undistributed personal holding company income for the year. The adjustments necessary to convert taxable income to undistributed personal holding company income are set forth in § 545.

Unearned income.   Income received but not yet earned. Normally, such income is taxed when received, even for accrual basis taxpayers.

Unified tax credit.   A credit allowed against any unified transfer tax. §§ 2010 and 2505.

Unified transfer tax.   A set of tax rates applicable to transfers by gift and death made after 1976. § 2001(c).

Uniform Gift to Minors Act.   A means of transferring property (usually stocks and bonds) to a minor. The designated custodian of the property has the legal right to act on behalf of the minor without requiring a guardianship. Generally, the custodian possesses the right to change investments (e.g., sell one type of stock

and buy another), apply the income from the custodial property to the minor's support, and even terminate the custodianship. In this regard, however, the custodian is acting in a fiduciary capacity on behalf of the minor. The custodian could not, for example, appropriate the property for his or her own use, because it belongs to the minor. During the period of the custodianship, the income from the property is taxed to the minor. The custodianship terminates when the minor reaches legal age. See also *guardianship* and *legal age.*

Unitary state.   A state that has adopted the unitary theory in its apportionment of the total taxable income of a multistate corporation to the state.

Unitary theory.   Under the unitary theory, the sales, property, and payroll of related corporations are combined for *nexus* and *apportionment* purposes, and the worldwide income of the unitary entity is apportioned to the state. Subsidiaries and other affiliated corporations that are found to be part of the corporation's unitary business (because they are subject to overlapping ownership, operation, or management) are included in the apportionment procedure. This approach can be limited if a *water's edge election* is in effect.

Unrealized receivables.   Amounts earned by a cash basis taxpayer but not yet received. Because of the method of accounting used by the taxpayer, such amounts have no income tax basis. When unrealized receivables are distributed to a partner, they generally convert a transaction from nontaxable to taxable, or they convert otherwise capital gain to ordinary income.

Unreasonable compensation.   A deduction is allowed for "reasonable" salaries or other compensation for personal services actually rendered. To the extent compensation is "excessive" ("unreasonable"), no deduction is allowed. The problem of unreasonable compensation usually is limited to closely held corporations, where the motivation is to pay out profits in some form that is deductible to the corporation. Deductible compensation therefore becomes an attractive substitute for nondeductible dividends when the shareholders also are employed by the corporation.

Unrelated business income.   Income recognized by an exempt organization that is generated from activities not related to the exempt purpose of the entity. For instance, the pharmacy located in a hospital often generates unrelated business income. § 511.

Unrelated business income tax.   Levied on the unrelated business taxable income of an exempt organization.

Use tax.   A sales tax that is collectible by the seller where the purchaser is domiciled in a different state.

U.S.-owned foreign corporation.   A foreign corporation in which 50 percent or more of the total combined voting power or total value of the stock of the corporation is held directly or indirectly by U.S. persons. A U.S. corporation is treated as a U.S.-owned foreign corporation if dividend or interest income paid by such corporation is classified as foreign source under § 861.

U.S. real property interest.   Any direct interest in real property situated in the United States and any interest in a domestic corporation (other than solely as a creditor) unless the taxpayer can establish that a domestic corporation was not a U.S. real property holding corporation during the shorter of the period after June 18, 1980, during which the taxpayer held an interest in such corporation, or for the five-year period ending on the date of disposition of such interest (the base period).

USSC.   An abbreviation for the U.S. Supreme Court.

U.S. Tax Court.   See *Tax Court.*

USTC.   Published by Commerce Clearing House, *U.S. Tax Cases* contain all of the Federal tax decisions issued by the U.S. District Courts, U.S. Claims Court, U.S. Courts of Appeals, and the U.S. Supreme Court.

V

Value.   See *fair market value.*

Vested.   Absolute and complete. If, for example, a person holds a vested interest in property, such interest cannot be taken away or otherwise defeated.

Voting trust.   A trust that holds the voting rights to stock in a corporation. It is a useful device when a majority of the shareholders in a corporation cannot agree on corporate policy.

W

Wash sale.   A loss from the sale of stock or securities that is disallowed because the taxpayer has, within 30 days before or after the sale, acquired stock or securities substantially identical to those sold. § 1091.

Water's edge election.   A limitation on the worldwide scope of the unitary theory. If a corporate water's edge election is in effect, the state can consider only the activities that occur within the boundaries of the United States in the apportionment procedure. See also *apportionment* and *unitary theory.*

WESTLAW.   An on-line database system, produced by West Publishing Company, by which the tax researcher can obtain access to the Internal Revenue Code, Regulations, administrative rulings, and court case opinions.

Writ of Certiorari.   See *certiorari.*

APPENDIX D

Table of Code Sections Cited

[See Title 26 U.S.C.A.]

Comprehensive Tax Return Problems

Problem 1–Individual

1. Ronald M. and Susan J. Bradford, both age 45, are married and file a joint income tax return. Ronald is employed as an engineer, and Susan is a self-employed attorney. They have three dependent children: John, age 12; Paul, age 14; and George, age 17. Since June 15, 1986, Susan's nephew, Eric Jones, has lived with them. Eric, whose parents were killed in an automobile accident, is 19 years old and is a full-time student at Purdue University. Eric works part-time and earned $2,400 during the year. Ronald and Susan provided over half of Eric's support for the year. The Bradfords live at 1864 Southern Avenue, Lafayette, IN 47902. Ronald's Social Security number is 233–45–6789 and Susan's is 345–67–8910. Other relevant Social Security Numbers are as follows: Eric, 265–33–1982; John, 459–86–8554; Paul, 431–96–8134; and, George, 455–94–6765.

2. From January 1 to May 20, Ronald earned $30,000 from Research Corporation, Mobile, Alabama. Research Corporation withheld Federal income tax of $5,183.16, state income tax of $900, and $2,253 of FICA (Social Security tax). Ronald received a better offer from Hi-Tech Corporation of Lafayette, Indiana, and began working for Hi-Tech on June 1, earning $49,000 in his new job. Hi-Tech withheld Federal income tax of $9,543, state income tax of $1,470, and $3,604.80 of FICA (Social Security). On December 20, Ronald received a year-end bonus of $1,000 from Hi-Tech. This amount was included on his W–2 Form, which also reported his salary of $49,000 and moving expense reimbursement of $3,000 (see item 10), for a total of $53,000.

3. Susan was employed until May 31, 1989 as a staff attorney by Brown and Company, a law firm in Mobile, Alabama. During that time she earned $25,000. Her employer withheld $4,745 of Federal income tax, $750 of state income tax, and $1,877.50 of FICA (Social Security) tax.

4. Ronald and Susan received the following interest income during 1989:

First National Bank	$ 350
Second National Bank	1,300
Lafayette Savings & Loan	865

5. The Bradfords received the following dividend income during 1989:

Abner Corporation	$780
Bailey Corporation	430
Crown Corporation	600

On December 10, they gave 100 shares of Edwards Corporation stock to their oldest son, George. The stock's basis was $5,000, and its fair market value was $8,000. On December 15, Edwards Corporation declared a dividend of $10 per share. The dividend was payable December 30 to shareholders of record as of December 20.

6. Upon moving to Lafayette, Susan was unable to find suitable employment with a law firm. As a result, she established her own practice, beginning July 1, 1989. Her office is located at 234 Lahr Street, Lafayette, IN 47902 and she practices under the name of "S.J. Bradford, Attorney." Her employer identification number is 12-3456789. She elected to use the cash basis of accounting. The following items relate to her practice during 1989:

Gross receipts from clients	$65,000
Expenses	
Advertising	1,200
Bank service charges	68
Dues and publications	550
Insurance	4,500
Interest	1,370
Legal and professional services	900
Office rent	7,300
Office supplies	925
Utilities and phone	820
Secretary's wages	6,400
Payroll taxes	660
Contributions to employee pension plans	960
Miscellaneous expenses	375

Susan used her personal automobile for business purposes, accumulating a total of 5,000 business miles from July 1 to December 31. She acquired the following equipment for use in her business (with all assets being placed in service on July 1):

Office furniture	$8,000
Microcomputer	4,200
Printer	1,500

Susan elected to expense the maximum allowable portion of the cost of the office furniture under the provisions of § 179. She elected to compute her cost recovery allowance on all of the assets using the MACRS percentage method.

On November 15, a client who owed Susan $1,000 for services rendered was declared bankrupt. Susan feels there is no chance for any collection of the account.

7. The Bradfords were involved in several property transactions during the year:

a. On March 5, they acquired 100 shares of Simpson Corporation common stock for $162 a share. The company experienced financial difficulties

and did not pay the regular semiannual dividend in June. As a result, Ronald and Susan decided to sell the stock before matters got worse. On November 23 they sold the stock for $50 a share.

b. On May 6, 1968, Susan inherited a vacation home in Florida from her Uncle Marvin. Marvin's adjusted basis for the property was $38,000. The fair market value at the date of Marvin's death was $52,000 (the value elected by the executor of Marvin's estate). Because the Bradfords felt they would not be able to return to Florida frequently enough to justify keeping the home, they sold it on August 12 for $157,000.

c. When they decided to move from Mobile to Lafayette, they sold their Alabama residence. The selling price of the home was $200,000, and the broker charged a five-percent sales commission. The Bradfords incurred fixing-up expenses of $2,000 on the residence, which they had owned since October 4, 1975. Their basis in the residence was $110,000. In Lafayette, they acquired a new residence for $166,000. The closing date on the sale of their Mobile residence was May 30. They moved into the new Lafayette residence on June 1.

d. On November 29, Susan sold a one-acre lot in Mobile to her sister Sarah. Susan's basis in the lot was $15,000. She sold the lot for $10,000. Susan had purchased the lot on April 17, 1978.

8. The Bradfords own a rental house located at 512 Walker Street, Huntsville, AL 35899. The rental unit was occupied during the entire year, producing rental income of $14,000. To avoid managerial duties with regard to the property, the Bradfords paid a commission, of $1,400 to a property management company. The only other expenditures related to the property were $2,000 for real property taxes and $800 for real estate insurance on the property. The property was acquired on March 2, 1981, at a cost of $100,000, of which $10,000 was allocated to the lot. The rental house is being depreciated over a 15-year period using the statutory ACRS percentage rate.

9. On January 2, 1986 Ronald loaned $3,000 to his friend, David Smith, who signed a note agreeing to repay the loan on June 30, 1988. David declared bankruptcy in October, 1989 and Ronald was unable to collect on the loan.

10. The Bradford family incurred the following expenses in moving from Mobile to Lafayette:

Cost of moving household goods	$3,600
Travel, meals ($200) and lodging	600
House-hunting expenses (including meals of $100)	1,100
Temporary living expenses including meals of $200 (5 days)	800
Cost of fitting drapes in new house	900

Hi-Tech Corporation reimbursed Ronald for $3,000 of the moving expenses. The reimbursement was included on Ronald's W–2 Form (refer to item 2).

11. Ronald attended an engineering convention in Boston in October, incurring the following unreimbursed expenses:

Airfare	$560
Taxi fares	35
Meals and lodging	300

12. Susan contributed $4,000 to her Keogh plan. The contribution was made in December 1989.

13. The Bradfords had the following expenditures during the year:

Prescription medicines and drugs	$ 980
Medical insurance premiums	1,540
Doctor and hospital bills	2,450
Real estate taxes on residence	6,540
Home mortgage interest	8,630
Credit card interest on consumer purchases	948
Cash contributions	
Community church	2,200
United Way	1,500
Professional dues and subscriptions	1,300
Tax return preparation fee	500

14. On August 1, the Bradfords acquired a rundown garage apartment for $15,000 (not including land). Their plan was to have the apartment restored to good condition and hold it as rental property. On October 5, the electrician they had hired to rewire the apartment accidentally left his soldering iron on while he was away for lunch. When he returned, fire had destroyed the apartment. Unfortunately, the Bradfords had not insured the building. Between August 1 and October 5, they had spent $1,700 on repairs on the apartment.

15. The Bradfords paid $500 each month for household and child care expenses. They filed the appropriate employment tax returns. Their employer identification number is 22–3344556. Relevant information regarding the providers of child care are as follows: Mary Tyler, 111 Main St., Mobile, AL 35761; Social Security number 461–66–5201; $2,500 (amount paid). Ann Weaver, 407 Elm Avenue, Lafayette, IN 47902; Social Security number 359–46–3211; $3,500 (amount paid).

16. The Bradfords made timely estimated Federal income tax payments of $36,000 during the year.

17. Ronald and Susan both desire that $1 be directed to the Presidential Election Campaign Fund.

Requirements
You are to complete the Bradfords' Federal income tax return for 1989. If they have a refund due, they would like to receive the entire amount, and not have it credited against tax for next year.

Problem 2–Individual

1. Paul J. and Judy L. Vance are married and file a joint return. Paul is 54 years of age, and Judy is 51. Paul is self-employed as a dentist, and Judy is a college professor. Paul's Social Security number is 333–45–6666, and Judy's is 566–77–8888. The Vances live at 621 Franklin Avenue, Cincinnati, OH 45211. They have a son, Vince (Social Security number 576–18–7928), age 23, who lives at home. Vince is a law student at the University of Cincinnati

and worked part-time during the year, earning $1,500, which he spent for his own support. In addition, he received a $2,000 scholarship from the University of Cincinnati. Paul and Judy provided $2,000 toward Vince's support. They also provided over half the support of their daughter, Joan (Social Security number 575–92–4321), age 19, who is a full-time student at Edgecliff College. Joan worked part-time during the year, earning $1,200. She filed a joint return with her husband, Patrick, who earned $8,000 during the year.

2. Paul's mother, Vera (Social Security number 421–81–6945), age 87, lives with the Vances. Vera received $900 in Social Security benefits and $950 of interest during the year, all of which she used for her own support. Paul and his brother George each incurred out-of-pocket costs of $900 for Vera's support. In addition, Paul provided lodging for Vera during the entire year. Paul has determined that the fair rental value of the lodging is $1,200. George is willing to do whatever is necessary to enable Paul to claim Vera as a dependent.

3. Judy is a lecturer at Xavier University in Cincinnati, where she earned $30,000. The University withheld Federal income tax of $3,720, state income tax of $600, Cincinnati city income tax of $300, and $2,253 of FICA (Social Security tax).

4. The Vances received $1,200 of interest from State Savings Bank on a joint account. They received interest of $1,000 on City of Cincinnati bonds they bought in January with the proceeds of a loan from Third National Bank of Cincinnati. They paid interest of $1,200 on the loan. Paul received a dividend of $540 on General Bicycle Corporation stock he owns. Judy received a dividend of $390 on Acme Clothing Corporation stock she owns. Paul and Judy received a dividend of $865 on jointly owned stock in Maple Company.

5. Paul practices under the name "Paul J. Vance, DDS." His business is located at 645 West Avenue, Cincinnati, OH 45211, and his employer identification number is 01–2222222. Paul's gross billings during the year were $170,000. Accounts receivable were $3,600 at the beginning of the year and $4,200 at the end of the year. The end-of-year balance does not include a $700 account from a customer who declared bankruptcy on November 9. The $700 was billed in July for work done during May and June. Paul uses the cash method of accounting for his business. Paul's business expenses are as follows:

Advertising	$ 1,200
Professional dues	490
Professional journals	360
Contributions to employee benefit plans	2,000
Malpractice insurance	3,200
Fine for overbilling State of Ohio for work performed on welfare patient	5,000
Insurance on office contents	720
Interest on money borrowed to refurbish office	900
Accounting services	1,800
Miscellaneous office expense	388
Office rent	6,000
Dental supplies	7,672

Utilities and telephone	3,360
Wages	30,000
Payroll taxes	2,400

Included in the $30,000 of wages is $8,000 paid to a new receptionist Paul hired on March 1. The receptionist is handicapped and was certified as a member of a targeted group for purposes of the jobs credit.

In June, Paul decided to refurbish his office. This project was completed and the assets placed in service on July 1. Paul's expenditures included $8,000 for new office furniture, $6,000 for new dental equipment, and $2,000 for a new word processor. Paul elected to compute his cost recovery allowance using the MACRS percentage method.

6. Judy's mother, Sarah, died on July 2, 1974, leaving Judy her entire estate. Included in the estate was Sarah's residence (address 325 Oak Street, Cincinnati, OH 45211). Sarah's basis in the residence was $30,000. Fair market value of the residence on July 2, 1974, was $50,000. The property was distributed to Judy on September 9, 1974. The Vances have held the property as rental property and have managed it themselves. From March 1, 1975, until April 30 of 1989 the house was rented to the same tenant. The tenant was transferred to a branch office in California and moved out at the end of April. Since they did not want to bother finding a new tenant, Paul and Judy decided to sell the house, which they did on June 2. They received $140,000 for the house, less a six-percent commission charged by the broker. They had depreciated the house using the straight-line method of depreciation with an estimated useful life of 20 years and an estimated salvage value of zero. In computing depreciation, they had allocated a value of $5,000 to the lot on which the house is located. The Vances collected rent of $1,100 a month during the four months the house was occupied during the year. They incurred the following related expenses during this period:

Property insurance	$200
Property taxes (paid by buyer of the property but allocated to the Vances)	550
Maintenance	220

7. The Vances sold 1,000 shares of Capp Corporation stock they had received as a wedding present on June 25, 1960. The stock was worth $95 per share in January. By September 3, its value had dropped to $81 per share, and the Vances sold the stock on that date. They had been given the stock by Paul's father, who had paid $1 per share for it in 1950. Its value at the date of gift was $4.50 per share. No gift tax was paid on the gift.

8. During the year Paul purchased numerous state lottery tickets (cost of $400). One ticket won $10,000, which Paul received.

9. Judy is required by her employer to visit several high schools in the Cincinnati area to evaluate Xavier University students who are doing their practice teaching. However, she is not reimbursed for the expenses she incurs in doing this. During the year, she drove her personal automobile 6,800 miles in fulfilling this obligation.

10. Paul and Judy have given you a file containing the following receipts for expenditures during the year:

Medicines and drugs	$ 376
Doctor and hospital bills	1,148
Medical insurance premiums	1,320
Penalty for underpayment of last year's state income tax	362
Real estate taxes on personal residence	4,762
Interest on home mortgage (paid to Home State Savings & Loan)	8,250
Interest on credit cards (consumer purchases)	595
Cash contribution to St. Matthew's church	3,080
Payroll deductions for Judy's contributions to the United Way	150
Professional dues (Judy)	325
Professional subscriptions (Judy)	245
Fee for preparation of 1988 tax return	500

11. The Vances made timely estimated Federal income tax payments of $82,000 during the year. They made estimated state income tax payments of $1,400 and estimated city income tax payments of $700.

12. The Vances do not desire that $1 be directed to the Presidential Election Campaign Fund.

Requirements

You are to prepare Paul and Judy Vance's Federal income tax return for 1989.

Problem 3–Corporation

Novelco Corporation was formed in October 1, 1976, by Jim and Anne Adams to manufacture and assemble novelty items (mainly key chains, ballpoint pens, and campaign buttons). These items usually are customized with the client's name (and/or logo) for distribution as promotional material. Pertinent information regarding Novelco is summarized as follows:

- The business address is 5210 Union Street, Leesville, IL 60930.
- Employer identification number is 71–0395674; the principal business activity code is 3998.
- Jim and Anne Adams, brother and sister, each own one-half of the outstanding common stock, and no other class of stock is authorized. Every three years, they rotate the positions of president and vice president. Currently, Anne is the president and Jim the vice president. Both are full-time employees, and the corporation has no other officers. Each receives a salary of $60,000. Jim's Social Security number is 581–00–0836; Anne's is 581–00–2604.
- The corporation uses the accrual method of acounting and reports on a calendar year basis. The specific chargeoff method is used in handling bad debt losses, and inventories are determined under the lower of cost or market method with full absorption of cost. For book and tax purposes, the straight-line method of depreciation is used.

- During 1989 the corporation distributed a cash dividend of $50,000. Because a customer was injured on the business premises and has threatened legal action for personal damages, a reserve for contingencies is to be established in the amount of $40,000.
- In November 1989, the corporation received a refund of $24,000 from the IRS due to overpayment on its 1988 estimated income tax liability.

Selected portions of Novelco's profit and loss statement reflect the following debits and credits:

Account	Debit	Credit
Gross sales		$2,500,000
Sales returns and allowances	$ 20,000	
Cost of goods sold	1,450,000	
Dividends received from stock investments in less than 20% owned U.S. corporations		30,000
Interest income		
Certificates of deposit	$12,000	
State bonds	14,000	26,000
Premiums on term life insurance (the policies are owned by the corporation and cover Jim and Ann Adams; the corporation is the designated beneficiary	14,000	
Compensation of officers	120,000	
Salaries and wages—indirect	70,000	
Repairs	4,000	
Bad debts	5,000	
Rental expense	12,000	
Taxes (state, local, payroll—indirect)	23,000	
Interest expense		
Loan to purchase state bonds	$ 2,000	
Other business loans and mortgages	27,000	29,000
Charitable contributions	31,000	
Depreciation—indirect	5,000	
Advertising in trade journals	10,000	
Other expenses (e.g., office expenses, sales commissions, legal and accounting fees)	60,000	
Long-term loss from the sale of stock held as an investment—no carryback was available	4,000	
Information regarding the cost of goods sold:		
Beginning inventory (1–1–89)		$ 120,000
Ending inventory (12–31–89)		160,000
Purchases (including subcontracted parts and raw materials)		900,000
Cost of labor–direct		450,000
Other costs (e.g., utilities, small tools, depreciation–direct [$14,000])		140,000

Net income per books (before any income tax accrual) is $699,000.
A comparative balance sheet for Novelco reveals the following information:

Assets	January 1, 1989	December 31, 1989
Cash	$ 28,682	$ 53,122
Trade notes and accounts receivable	125,000	140,000
Inventories	120,000	160,000
Federal and state government bonds	140,000	140,000
Other current assets	18,000	24,000
Other investments	108,000	240,000
Buildings and other depreciable assets	304,000	304,000
Accumulated depreciation	(105,000)	(124,000)
Land	115,000	165,000
Other assets	17,000	24,000
Total assets	$ 870,682	$1,126,122

Liabilities and Equity		
Accounts payable	$ 24,000	$ 12,000
Other current liabilities	11,000	6,000
Mortgages	168,000	——
Capital stock	200,000	200,000
Retained earnings (appropriated and unappropriated)	467,682	908,122
Total liabilities and equity	$ 870,682	$1,126,122

During 1989, Novelco made estimated tax payments to the IRS of $240,000. Prepare a Form 1120 for Novelco for tax year 1989.

Problem 4—S Corporation

Jay Mitchell (243–58–8695) and Stan Marshall (221–51–8695) are 70% and 30% owners of Dana, Inc. (73–8264911), a service company located in Dime Box, Texas. The company's S corporation election was made on January 15, 1989. The following information was taken from the income statement for 1989:

Tax-exempt interest	$ 1,000
Gross rents	5,000
Gross royalties	10,000
Service income	110,000
Salaries and wages	55,000
Repairs	2,000
Officers' compensation	15,000
Bad debts	5,000
Rent expense	5,000
Taxes	5,000
Expenses relating to tax-exempt income	500
Charitable contributions	2,000
Payroll penalties	1,500
Advertising expenses	5,000
Other deductions	10,000

A partially completed comparative balance sheet appears as follows:

	Beginning of the Year	End of the Year
Cash	$6,000	$ 6,500
Accounts receivable	2,000	4,000
Loan to Jay Mitchell	–0–	2,000
Total	$8,000	$12,500
Accounts payable	$2,000	$ 1,800
Other current liabilities	–0–	1,200
Capital stock	6,000	6,000
Retained earnings	–0–	?
Previously taxed income	–0–	?
Accumulated adjustments account	–0–	?
Other adjustments account	–0–	?
Total liabilities/shareholders' equity	$8,000	$12,500

The corporation distributed $16,500 to the two shareholders during the year. From the available information, prepare Form 1120S and Schedule K–1 for Jay Mitchell. If any information is missing, make realistic assumptions.

Problem 5–Partnership

James R. Wesley (297–19–9261), Rita B. Healthy (284–74–7832), Susan C. Yourez (257–62–3544), and Frank T. Bizzano (219–75–3822) are equal partners in WHYB, a small business management advisory partnership. The partnership uses the cash basis and calendar year and began operations on January 1 two years before the start of the current year. Since that time, it has experienced a 30% growth rate each year. Its current address is 2937 Skyline Speedway, Bloomington, IN 47401. During the current year, each partner withdrew $40,000. The following information was taken from the partnership's income statement for the current year.

Receipts	
Fees collected	$75,000
Tax-exempt interest	1,600
Payments	
Advertising	5,000
Contribution to Boy Scouts	800
Employee salaries	42,000
Equipment rental	6,000
Office rent	24,000
Salary, James R. Wesley	12,000
Taxes	4,600
Utilities	3,700
Insurance premiums	2,200

a. Prepare Form 1065 and Schedule K for WHYB Partnership, leaving blank any items where insufficient information has been provided.

b. Prepare Schedule K–1 for James R. Wesley.

Problem 6–Fiduciary

Prepare the 1989 Fiduciary income Tax Return (Form 1041) for the Kathryn Anne Thomas Trust. In addition, determine the amount and character of the income and expense items that each beneficary must report for 1989 and prepare a Schedule K–1 for Harold Thomas.

The 1989 activities of the trust include the following:

Office building rental income	$600,000
Rental expenses	
Management	85,000
Utilities and maintenance	375,000
Taxes and insurance	115,000
Straight-line cost recovery	200,000
Taxable interest income	100,000
Tax-exempt interest income	50,000
Net long-term capital gains	265,000
Fiduciary's fees	120,000

Under the terms of the trust instrument, depreciation, net capital gains and losses, and one-third of the fiduciary's fees are allocable to corpus. The trustee is required to distribute $30,000 to Harold every year. In 1989, the trustee distributed $60,000 to Harold and $35,000 to Patricia Thomas. No other distributions were made.

The trustee, Wisconsin State National Bank, is located at 3100 East Wisconsin Avenue, Milwaukee, WI 53201. Its employer identification number is 84–7602487.

Harold lives at 9880 East North Avenue, Shorewood, WI 53211. His identification number is 498–01–8058.

Patricia lives at 6772 East Oklahoma Avenue, St. Francis, WI 53204. Her identification number is 499–02–6531.

Subject Index

A

AAA. *See* Accumulated adjustments account
Abandoned spouse rule, 2–28, 2–29 to 2–30
Accelerated cost recovery system (ACRS)
  antichurning rules, 8–18 to 8–19
  asset depreciation range, 8–7, 8–11, 8–24
  auto expense computation, 9–13 to 9–15, 9–36
  business and personal use of automobiles and other listed property, 8–19 to 8–23
  controlled corporations, 16–28
  corporations, 16–19, 17–3 to 17–4
  cost recovery tables for property other than realty, 8–30, 8–31, 8–38, 8–39
  cost recovery tables for real property, 8–32 to 8–37, 8–39
  description of, 8–7 to 8–8
  earnings and profits, 17–3 to 17–4
  election to expense assets, 8–16 to 8–18
  eligible property, 8–8
  half-year convention, 8–9, 8–11, 8–13, 8–15
  investment tax credit, 8–9 to 8–10, 8–19, 11–4 to 11–5
  limits on deductibility, 8–17 to 8–22
  modified, 14–6 to 14–7
  personalty, 8–8 to 8–13, 8–19 to 8–22, 8–24
  realty, 8–13 to 8–15, 8–25, 13–29, 13–31 to 13–34
  recapture, 13–28 to 13–36, 16–6, 16–9 to 16–10, 16–28
  reconcilation of taxable and net income, 16–19 to 16–20
  recovery periods and methods, 8–8 to 8–15, 8–24
  recovery periods under alternative depreciation system, 8–23 to 8–25
  related-party transactions, 8–18 to 8–19
  straight-line depreciation, 8–5, 8–8, 8–11, 8–13, 8–14, 8–15 to 8–16
  tax planning, 8–27 to 8–29
  See also Alternative minimum taxable income
Accelerated depreciation. *See* Accelerated cost recovery system
Accident and health benefits, 1–19, 4–3, 4–10 to 4–11, 4–15, 4–26
  See also Employee fringe benefits
Accounting income, 3–3 to 3–4
  entity, 26–6 to 26–8

Accounting methods
  accounts and notes receivable, 13–3, 13–4
  alternative minimum tax, 14–11 to 14–12, 14–24
  bad debts, 72
  change of method, –3-6, 15–12 to 15–13, 15–23
  charitable contributions, 10–20
  claim of right doctrine, 3–7
  clear reflection of income concept, 1–23, 3–6, 3–11, 5–7, 15–9, 15–12
  constructive receipt of income, 3–6 to 3–7, 3–8 to 3–9, 3–31, 15–9
  corporations, 3–6, 5–8, 15–10, 15–29, 16–7, 17–3, 17–4
  correcting errors, 15–13
  deductibility of taxes, 10–8 to 10–9, 10–11
  deferral of advance payments, 3–11 to 3–12, 3–31
  deferral of income, 3–7, 3–10, 3–11 to 3–12, 3–29 to 3–31
  determination by IRS, 3–6, 15–9
  election to expense assets under ACRS, 8–16 to 8–18
  estates, 26–5
  exceptions applicable to accrual basis taxpayers, 3–10 to 3–12
  exceptions applicable to cash basis taxpayers, 3–8 to 3–10
  farming, 5–8, 15–10, 15–29
  gross income, 3–4, 3–6 to 3–12, 3–31
  hybrid method, 15–8, 15–12
  imputed interest, 15–18 to 15–20, 15–29
  incorrect method, 15–13, 15–15
  interest expense, 10–17
  inventories, 3–5, 15–9, 15–10, 15–13, 15–29
  long-term contracts, 3–6, 14–11 to 14–12, 15–24 to 15–28, 17–4
  partnerships, 5–8, 15–10, 15–29
  permissible methods, 3–6, 15–8 to 15–9
  personal service corporations, 15–10, 16–7
  prepaid expenses, 15–9
  prepaid income, 3–10 to 3–11, 3–31
  recovery periods, 8–8 to 8–15
  reporting interest income, 15–19 to 15–20
  research and experimental expenditures, 7–15 to 7–17
  reserves for estimated expenses, 5–9
  S corporations, 16–7, 20–28
  special methods, 15–15 to 15–28

B

C

G

J